PSYCHOLOGICAL PROCESSES THAT AFFECT CRITICAL THINKING

Psychological research has helped to clarify how people think critically—and why, often, they do not. Here are a few of the topics relevant to critical thinking that are discussed in this book, and the chapters in which they appear.

FACTORS THAT ENHANCE CRITICAL THINKING

- Scientific methods and reasoning (Chapter 2)
- Conditions promoting independent action and nonconformity (Chapter 8)
- Conditions promoting individuation (Chapter 8)
- Inductive, deductive, and dialectical reasoning (Chapter 9)
- Reflective judgment (Chapter 9)
- Creative problem solving (Chapter 9)
- Algorithms, heuristics (Chapter 9)
- Intelligence (Chapter 9)
- Metacognition (Chapter 9)
- Improving memory (Chapter 10)
- Reducing negative emotions (Chapter 11)
- Cognitive development (Chapter 13)
- Role of appraisals and rethinking in coping with stress and illness (Chapter 11)
- Attributions that affect feelings and behaviour (Chapters 8, 11, 12)
- Wisdom derived from life experiences (Chapter 13)
- Cognitive therapy (Chapter 16)

BARRIERS TO CRITICAL THINKING

- Pseudoscientific thinking (Chapters 1 and 2)
- Conformity (Chapter 8)
- Deindividuation (Chapter 8)
- Diffusion of responsibility (Chapter 8)
- Entrapment (Chapter 8)
- Groupthink (Chapter 8)
- Coercive persuasion (Chapter 8)
- Prejudice and ethnocentrism (Chapter 8)
- Stereotypes (Chapter 8)
- Self-serving bias (Chapter 8)
- Mindlessness (Chapter 9)
- Cognitive biases (e.g., confirmation and hindsight biases) (Chapter 9)
- Cognitive dissonance (Chapter 9)
- Mental sets (Chapter 9)
- Nonreflective judgment (Chapter 9)
- Fallibility of memory (Chapter 10)
- Emotional reasoning (Chapter 11)
- Defence mechanisms (Chapter 14)
- Vulnerability to the "Barnum Effect" (Chapter 14)
- Cognitive distortions in mood disorders (Chapters 11, 15)

PSYCHOLOGY

PSYCHOLOGY

FOURTH
CANADIAN
EDITION

CAROLE WADE
DOMINICAN UNIVERSITY OF CALIFORNIA

CAROL TAVRIS

DEBORAH SAUCIER
UNIVERSITY OF ONTARIO INSTITUTE OF TECHNOLOGY

LORIN ELIAS
UNIVERSITY OF SASKATCHEWAN

PEARSON

Toronto

Vice-President, Editorial Director: Gary Bennett
Editor-in-Chief: Michelle Sartor
Acquisitions Editor: Matthew Christian
Sponsoring Editor: Carolin Sweig
Marketing Manager: Lisa Gillis
Senior Developmental Editor: Patti Altridge
Project Manager: Lesley Deugo
Production Editor: Lila Campbell
Copy Editor: Alison Kooistra
Proofreader: Karen Alliston
Composition: Cenveo Publisher Services
Photo Research: Tara Smith and MRM Associates
Permissions Research: MRM Associates
Manufacturing Coordinator: Susan Johnson
Art Director: Julia Hall
Cover and Interior Designer: Miguel Acevedo

10 9 8 7 6 5 4 3 2 1 [QG]

Library and Archives Canada Cataloguing in Publication
   Psychology / Carole Wade ... [et al.].—4th Canadian ed.

Includes index.
ISBN 978-0-205-02927-3

   1. Psychology—Textbooks. I. Wade, Carole

BF121.P82 2013   150   C2011-905159-1

ISBN 978-0-205-02927-3

Brief Contents

Contents

From the Authors

Every time we revise this textbook, our enthusiasm for psychology is reignited. These are especially exciting times for psychology teachers and students, because the field is bubbling over with many new ideas, possibilities, and controversies inspired by the biomedical revolution in science and society. Biological findings have led to an integration of specialties within psychology as well as collaboration with scholars from other fields: Neuroscientists and behavioural geneticists are working with social psychologists, behaviourists, cognitive theorists, developmental psychologists, economists, and others to better understand human behaviour.

It is unwise, however, to jump on any bandwagon uncritically, without thinking about the direction in which it's headed. When we first wrote this book, psychology was undergoing a different revolution: Researchers were coming to understand the scientific and social importance of making psychology the study of all human beings, not just, as the joke had it at the time, the study of young, white, male . . . rats. For us, integrating the burgeoning new research on gender and culture was an invigorating challenge. It was important (and fun!) to show students that "culture" is not merely a thin veneer on human behaviour, but a factor that shapes our behaviour profoundly in every domain—from how often people think it is appropriate to bathe, to the conditions that make people angry enough to kill for the sake of their honour, to whether a person wants to stand out in a group or fit in. Nonetheless, from the beginning we maintained a commitment to thinking critically about this research. We rejected the common practice of equating "mainstreaming culture and gender" with simply throwing in a gender or cultural difference wherever one existed, without assessing its significance and explaining its likely causes.

Likewise, we believe it is crucial to assess the biomedical revolution thoughtfully and critically, rather than simply to report new findings. PET scans and fMRIs are amazing tools, but like all tools, they can be misused to distort or exaggerate. Evolutionary psychology is extremely interesting, but some people are inclined to apply it unskeptically to any behaviour or attribute of interest ("There must be an evolutionarily adaptive reason for baldness, pimples, and collecting ceramic sheep"). The excitement about biological research in general often creates a kind of pop-reductionism, in which many people come to think that biology explains nearly everything.

For these reasons, we believe that the original goal of our book—the goal of integrating critical and scientific thinking into the warp and woof of our writing is more important now than ever. The public in general, and students in particular, need to learn about the astonishing new developments in neuroscience, but they also need to learn to think intelligently about them. Not all of these developments are as dramatic or applicable as they are often made to appear in the popular press. Not all of the findings that are reported are based on good science, no matter how fancy the tools that produce them.

A textbook, in short, is not a laundry list of items, and its writers are not simply reporters. For us, the primary job of an introductory textbook in psychology is to help students learn to think like a psychologist, and to understand why scientific and critical thinking is so important to the decisions they make in their own lives.

GUIDING PRINCIPLES AND FEATURES

1. Thinking Critically about Critical Thinking

In a textbook, true critical thinking cannot be reduced to a set of rhetorical questions, a short boxed feature, or a formula for analyzing studies; it is a process that must be woven seamlessly into the narrative. The primary way we "do" critical and creative thinking is by applying a three-pronged approach: We *define* it, we *model* it, and we give students a chance to *practise* it.

The first step is to define what critical thinking is and what it is not. Chapter 1 introduces **Eight Guidelines to Critical Thinking,** which we draw on throughout the text as we evaluate research and popular ideas. These guidelines are also listed and described briefly on the inside front cover of the book.

The second step is to model these guidelines in our evaluations of research and popular ideas. Many, though by no means all, of our **critical-thinking discussions** in the text itself are signaled by a "mental gears" symbol shown in the margin, along with "signposts" containing provocative questions. We have explicitly identified the relevant guideline in each signpost so that students can see more easily how the guidelines are actually applied. *The questions in the signposts are not, in themselves, illustrations of critical thinking.* Rather, they serve as pointers to critical analyses in the text and invite the reader into the discussion.

The Meaning of Heritability

Suppose you want to measure flute-playing ability in a large group of music students, so you have some independent raters assign each student a score from 1 to 20. When you plot the scores, you find that some people are what you might call melodically disadvantaged and should forget about a musical career, others are flute geniuses, and the rest fall somewhere in between. What causes the variation in this group of students? Why are some so musically talented and others so inept? Are these differences primarily genetic, or are they the result of experience and motivation?

To answer such questions, behavioural geneticists compute a statistic called **heritability**, which gives an estimate of the *proportion of the total variance in a trait that is attributable to genetic variation within a group*. Because the heritability of a trait is expressed as a proportion (such as 0.60, or 60/100), the maximum value it can have is 1.00 (equivalent to "100% of the variance"). Height is highly heritable; that is, within a group of equally well-nourished individuals, most of the variation among them will be accounted for by their genetic differences. In contrast, table manners have low heritability because most variation among individuals is accounted for by differences in upbringing. Our guess is that flute-playing ability—and musical ability in general—falls somewhere in the middle. Differences in the ability to correctly perceive musical pitch and melody appear to be highly heritable; some people, it seems, really are born with a "tin ear" (Drayna et al., 2001). Nonetheless, musical training can enhance normal musical ability, and lack of musical training can keep a person with normal ability from tuning in to the nuances of music.

Many people hold completely mistaken ideas about heritability. But as genetic findings pour in, the public will need to understand this concept more than ever. You cannot understand the nature–nurture issue without understanding the following

Thinking Critically

Define Your Terms

What does it mean to say that some trait is highly heritable? If you want to improve your flute playing and someone tells you that musical ability is heritable, should you stop practising?

Thinking · **Critically**   Ask Questions: Define Your Terms

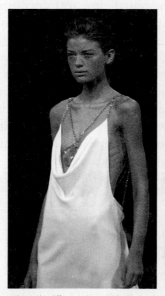

What is the difference between being slender and being too thin? Does the fashion model on the left look good to you or does she look emaciated? Likewise, what is the difference between being "pleasantly plump" and being too fat? Nikki Blonsky, the exuberant star of the movie *Hairspray*, is overweight but physically fit. Does she look good to you or does she look too fat?

i blogs, YouTube, Facebook, and Twitter, and are constant topics for entertainment magazines and talk shows.

Female ballet dancers and actors, jockeys of both sexes, some other athletes, and course models are under enormous professional pressure to be thin. (In 2006, many

Some of the **critical-thinking signposts** include a provocative photograph that we believe will stimulate thought. It's one thing to ask students to think critically about, say, the line that divides fashionable slimness from unhealthy gauntness, but quite another when they see a photo of an emaciated fashion model next to the healthy, but heavier, singer Nikki Blonsky.

quick QUIZ

✔ **Quick Review** on **MyPsychLab**

Find out whether you are an educated consumer of quizzes.

1. Which of the following is the most important predictor of successful therapy? (a) how long it lasts, (b) the insight it provides the client, (c) the bond between therapist and client, (d) whether the therapist and client are matched according to gender

2. In general, which type of psychotherapy is most effective for anxiety and depression?

3. What kind of psychologist is trained to help people cope with chronic illness or disability or recover from injury?

4. What are four possible sources of harm in psychotherapy?

5. Ferdie is spending too much time playing softball and not enough time studying, so he signs up for "sportaholic therapy (ST)." The therapist tells him the cure for his "addiction" is to quit softball cold turkey and tap his temples three times whenever he feels the urge to play. After a few months, Ferdie announces that ST isn't helping and he's going to stop coming. The therapist gives him testimonials of other clients who swear by ST, explaining that Ferdie's doubts are actually a sign that the therapy is working. What is the major scientific flaw in this argument? (Bonus: What kind of therapy might help Ferdie manage his time better?)

Answers:

1. c 2. cognitive-behavior 3. rehabilitation psychologist 4. the use of empirically unsupported techniques, inappropriate or coercive influence, the therapist's prejudice or biased treatment, and unethical behavior 5. The therapist has violated the principle of falsifiability (see Chapter 2). If Ferdie is helped by the treatment, that shows it works; if he is not helped, that still shows it works and Ferdie is simply denying its benefits. Also, Ferdie is not hearing testimonials from people who have dropped out of ST and were not helped by it. (Bonus: A good behavioral time-management program might help, so Ferdie can play softball and get other things done, too.)

The third step is to give the student opportunities to practise what we've preached. Throughout each chapter are periodic **Quick Quizzes** that encourage students to check their progress, and to go back and review if necessary. These quizzes do more than just test for memorization of definitions; they tell students whether they comprehend the issues. Many of them include critical-thinking items. These items invite the student to reflect on the implications of findings and consider how psychological principles might illuminate real-life issues.

2. Exploring New Research in Biology and Neuroscience

For examples of how we cover biological research, see our discussions of:

- Genetics and personality (pp. 554–558)
- Epigenetics (pp. 102–103)
- Stem cells and the production of new neurons (pp. 115–117)
- Schizophrenia (pp. 614–618)
- Sexual desire and behaviour (pp. 466–469)
- Weight and body shape (pp. 450–454)

Findings from the Human Genome Project, studies of behavioural genetics, discoveries about the brain, technologies such as PET scans and fMRI, and the proliferation of medications for psychological disorders—all have had a profound influence on our understanding of human behaviour and on interventions to help people with chronic problems. This work cannot be confined to a single chapter. Accordingly, we report new findings from the biological front wherever they are relevant throughout the book: in discussions of neurogenesis in the brain, memory, emotion, stress, child development, aging, mental illness, personality, and many other topics.

To further emphasize the integration of biology with other areas of research in understanding human problems, many chapters also have a feature called **Biology and . . .**: While we caution students about the dangers of ignoring biological research, we also caution them about the dangers of reducing complex behaviours solely to biology by overgeneralizing from limited data, failing to consider other explanations, and oversimplifying solutions. Our goal is to provide students with a structure for interpreting research they will hear or read about in the future.

BIOLOGY and Classical Conditioning

Pavlov and Peanut Butter

A century ago, when Ivan Pavlov taught dogs to salivate to the sound of a bell, he focused on the observable associations between unconditioned and conditioned stimuli and responses. Although he was interested in the biological basis of classical conditioning, techniques for studying that topic were limited. Today, sophisticated technology has changed that. We'll give you a taste of the research being done, and in our first example, one taste involves peanut butter.

In an imaginative study, British researchers trained 13 hungry volunteers to associate abstract computer images with the pleasant smell of peanut butter or vanilla (Gottfried, O'Doherty, & Dolan, 2003). The volunteers had to say which side of the screen an image appeared on, and soon they were reacting faster to the images associated with the pleasant food odours than to other images. Using functional MRI, the researchers discovered that when the participants saw the images—which presumably had now become conditioned stimuli for pleasure or appetite—their brains showed surges of activity in two areas known to be involved in motivation and emotion, the amygdala and a specific area of the prefrontal cortex (see Chapter 4).

You're stuffed after a good meal, yet you suddenly find room for dessert. Why?

3. Mainstreaming Culture and Gender

For examples of how we treat gender issues, see our discussions of:

- Sex differences in the brain (pp. 140–142)
- Gender and emotion (pp. 423–425)
- Gender and heroism (pp. 294–295)
- Gender and transgender identity (pp. 515–521)
- Evolutionary theories of sexual behaviour (pp. 87–89)
- Weight and eating disorders in women and men (pp. 456–460)

At the time of our first edition, some considered our goal of incorporating research on gender and culture into introductory psychology to be quite radical, either a sop to political correctness or a fluffy and superficial fad. Today, the issue is no longer whether to include these topics, but how best to do it. From the beginning, our own answer has been to include studies of gender and culture in the main body of the text, wherever they are relevant to the larger discussion, rather than relegating these studies to an intellectual silo of separate chapters or boxed features.

Over the years, most psychologists have come to appreciate the influence of culture on all aspects of life, from nonverbal behaviour to the deepest attitudes about how the world should be. We raise empirical findings about culture and ethnicity as topics warrant throughout the book. In addition, Chapter 8 highlights the sociocultural perspective in psychology and includes extended discussions of ethnocentrism, prejudice, and cross-cultural relations. However, the scientific study of cultural diversity is not synonymous with the popular movement called multiculturalism. The study of culture, in our view, should increase students' understanding of what culture means, how and why ethnic and national groups differ, and why no group is inherently better, kinder, or more moral than another. Thus we try to apply critical thinking to our own coverage of culture, avoiding the twin temptations of ethnocentrism and stereotyping.

For examples of how we treat culture, see our discussions of:

- Cultural influences on personality (pp. 563–569)
- Ethnic identity and acculturation (pp. 296–297)
- Ethnocentrism (pp. 297–299)
- Culture and the diagnosis of mental disorder (pp. 585–586)
- Addiction rates and drug abuse (pp. 605–607)
- Attitudes toward achievement (pp. 346–348)

CULTURE and *the Cortex*

Can Culture Shape the Brain?

Earlier we saw that experiences at different times of a person's life can affect the structure of the brain and the strength of synaptic connections. Culture, of course, provides many of those experiences, but neuropsychologists and other brain researchers are just starting to study how it may affect the way specific areas in the cortical lobes are organized or activated.

Consider bilingualism. Do bilingual people use different parts of their brains for their two languages? Evidence on this question has been mixed, but there have been some intriguing findings. One team of surgeons found that the retrieval of semantic information by bilinguals may indeed depend on which language they are speaking. While using electrical stimulation to map the brains of bilingual patients undergoing brain surgery, the surgeons asked the patients (who were awake) to name pictured objects in both of their languages. From the pattern of errors made during the electrical stimulation, the researchers could tell which brain areas were being used in the object-naming task. Sites specific to a patient's first language were widely distributed, but those associated with a second language were confined to the back part of the temporal and parietal lobes (Lucas, McKhann, & Ojemann, 2004). This type of information, if it is verified by future research, will be important for brain surgeons to know!

In this edition, an occasional feature (comparable to **BIOLOGY and . . .**) called **CULTURE and . . .** highlights this theme: for example, **CULTURE and . . .** "Thinking," "Psychotherapy," "the Ideal Body," "Mental Disorder," "Intelligence Testing," "Control," and "Mental Illness."

4. Facing the Controversies

Psychology has always been full of lively, sometimes angry, debates, and we feel that students should not be sheltered from them. They are what makes psychology so interesting! In this book we candidly address controversies in the field of psychology, try to show why they are occurring, and suggest the kinds of questions that might lead to useful answers in each case.

For examples of our treatment of controversies in psychology, see our discussions of:

- The contributions and limitations of evolutionary psychology (pp. 89–92)
- Parental influence on children's personalities (pp. 560–561)
- Medication for psychological disorders (pp. 629–631)
- The "scientist-practitioner" gap (pp. 645–648)

5. Applications and Active Learning: Getting Involved

Throughout this book, we have kept in mind one of the soundest findings about learning: It requires the active encoding of material. Several pedagogical features in particular encourage students to become actively involved in what they are reading.

Get Involved exercises in each chapter make active learning entertaining. They consist of quick demonstrations, mini-studies, or ways to help students relate course material to their own lives. Instructors may want to assign some of these exercises to the entire class and then discuss the results and what they might mean.

Get INVOLVED!   RECALLING RUDOLPH'S FRIENDS

You can try this test of recall if you are familiar with the poem that begins "'Twas the night before Christmas" or the song "Rudolph the Red-Nosed Reindeer." Rudolph had eight reindeer friends; name as many of them as you can. After you have done your best, turn to the Get Involved exercise on page 374 for a recognition test on the same information.

Taking Psychology with You, a feature that concludes each chapter, illustrates the practical implications of psychological research for individuals, groups, institutions, and society. This feature, now with a special focus on "Thinking Critically in Everyday Life," tackles topics of personal interest and relevance to many students.

Taking Psychology with YOU

Thinking Critically in Everyday Life

Psychology Can Help You Get Better Grades

How can you use psychology to improve your grades? Do you remember at the beginning of the chapter where we discussed what psychology is and how it is concerned with behaviour and mental processes? Well, part of psychology studies memory strategies that can help you understand course material, absorb it thoroughly as you study, and successfully retrieve it when you need it. Ideally, these strategies will help you with taking tests and with applying this material during everyday life. So what are you waiting for? Go make psychology work for you!

Read, Recite, Review

Reading is not enough. The types of encoding we discuss in more detail in Chapter 10 (memory), such as *elaborate encoding* and *deep processing*, are useful because they force you to be an active rather than a passive learner. Many students believe that the best way to study for an exam is to read and reread a textbook passage until they think that they've "got it." This passive strategy feels intuitively right, but it is actually much less effective than actively rehearsing and recalling the material. In the *read-recite-review strategy*, you read the passage, close the book, hide your notes, write down (or say out loud) everything you can recall, and then review what you've read to see if you understood and remember the information. In a series of experiments, researchers compared this strategy with simply rereading and taking notes. Participants took free recall tests on the material, answered multiple-choice questions, and took short-answer tests right after studying and again a week later. The active read-recite-review strategy was the hands-down winner (McDaniel, Howard, & Einstein, 2009).

Retrieval Practice

Most students define "learning" as the ability to retrieve the correct answer to a question from memory. But then what? Once retrieved, say for an exam, does that answer stay put or vanish quickly like steam on a bathroom mirror? Cognitive psychologists have found that *retrieval practice* is necessary if a memory is going to undergo consolidation and therefore remain available for a long time—even after your course is over. In a series of experiments in which students learned words in foreign languages, once a student had learned a word it was (a) repeatedly studied but dropped from further testing, (b) repeatedly tested but dropped from further studying, or (c) dropped from studying and testing. To the surprise of the students themselves, who were completely unable to predict how they would do on the tests, studying after learning had no effect on their subsequent ability to recall the foreign words. But repeated testing (i.e., practice in repeatedly retrieving the words from memory) had a large, significant benefit (Karpicke & Roediger, 2008). So when your professors (and your textbook authors) want to keep quizzing you, why, it's only for your own good. . . .

Mnemonics

In addition to using elaborative rehearsal, deep processing, strategies such as read-recite-review, and retrieval practice, people who want to give their powers of memory a boost sometimes use mnemonics [neh-MON-iks], formal strategies and tricks for encoding, storing, and retaining information. (Mnemosyne, pronounced neh-MOZ-eh-nee, was the ancient Greek goddess of memory. Can you remember her?) Some mnemonics take the form of easily memorized rhymes (e.g., "Thirty days hath September/April, June, and November..."). Others use formulas (e.g., "Please never, never, never question our mother's singing and baking" for the names of the provinces from east to west). Still others use visual images or word associations. The best mnemonics force you to encode material actively and thoroughly. They may also reduce the amount of information by chunking it, which is why, in ads, many companies use words for their phone numbers instead of unmemorable numbers ("1-888-GOT-JUNK").

Apply Your Learning

Add meaning to the material you are learning by applying it to your own experiences. The more meaningful the material, the more likely it is to link up with information already in long-term memory. Meaningfulness also reduces the number of chunks of information you have to learn. Common ways of adding meaning include making up a story about the material, thinking of examples, and forming visual images. If you are trying to remember a difficult concept in a chapter, you might make the concept meaningful by thinking of an example from your own life.

YOU are about to learn…

- why insanity is not the same thing as having a mental disorder.
- how mental disorders differ from normal problems.
- why the standard professional guide to the diagnosis of mental disorders is controversial.
- why popular "projective" tests like the Rorschach Inkblot Test are not reliable.

You Are About to Learn . . . consists of a set of learning objectives that cover each major section within a chapter. Other pedagogical features designed to help students study and learn better include **review tables**; a **running glossary** that defines boldfaced technical terms on the pages where they occur for handy reference and study; a **cumulative glossary** at the back of the book; a list of **key terms** at the end of each chapter that includes page numbers so that students can find the sections where the terms are covered; **chapter outlines**; and **chapter summaries** in paragraph form to help students review.

Watch, Simulate, Explore, Listen, and Research…

Throughout the printed text, you will find the following icons that link you to related content on MyPsychLab. In the Pearson eText, these icons are hyperlinked directly to the online resources.

Watch See video clips of observational scenarios and role plays. If you are a visual learner, this is for you!

Simulate Engage in practical experiments and observe the outcomes of other simulations that put concepts into action and bring the text to life.

Explore Dive into a deeper understanding of critical concepts by exploring a variety of interesting and challenging activities.

Listen Connect to chapter content by listening to podcasts and audio clips that help you envision scenarios and illuminate key concepts.

Research Discover more about the scientists and researchers within the world of psychology.

New to This Edition

In this fourth Canadian edition of *Psychology*, we have retained the text's basic approach and pedagogy. We have made no changes just for the sake of making changes. Many of the book's features have been tested by time and student reaction; students and instructors like them. However, we have made **three** organizational changes that we think students and instructors will welcome.

1. We have combined the chapter on emotion with the former chapter on stress and health; the new chapter (Chapter 11) is "Emotion, Stress, and Health." As a result, this edition has 16 chapters rather than 17, a number that many instructors and students find more manageable.
2. Each of the concluding discussions in "Taking Psychology with You" is now focused on "thinking critically in everyday life"—how students can take not only the content of each chapter into their lives but also principles of thinking critically about issues that the chapter raises.
3. We now have a feature embedded in many chapters—"Culture and . . ." —that is parallel to the popular "Biology and . . ." feature.

In every chapter, we have also updated the research to reflect progress and cutting-edge discoveries. Here are a few highlights from the new material in this book:

- Chapter 1 (What Is Psychology?) includes valuable study advice with the **read-recite-review strategy** located in the "Thinking Critically in Everyday Life: Psychology Can Help You Get Better Grades" section.

- Chapter 3 (Genes, Evolution, and Environment) now covers **noncoding DNA**, the genetic dissimilarities of "identical" twins, and the exciting new field of **epigenetics**.

- Chapter 4 (The Brain: Source of Mind and Self) includes research on teaching monkeys to use brain waves to control a robotic arm; using electric stimulation to restore awareness in patients who are in a minimally conscious state; using brain activity to identify which pictures a person is looking at; the production of induced pluripotent stem cells; and drugs to enhance cognitive function and potentially delete traumatic memories, as an introduction to **neuroethics**.

- Chapter 6 (Sensation and Perception) now reports fascinating new Swedish research on the ultimate illusion—body swapping—and a discussion of a leading explanation of **phantom limb pain**, along with an exciting new way to treat it, using just a simple, inexpensive mirror.

- Chapter 10 (Memory) includes new research on working memory and its importance for staying on task; on the role of the hippocampus not only in memory formation but also recall; and on the impact of too much arousal on memory (a field study in the Horror Labyrinth of the London Dungeon).

- Chapter 16 (Approaches to Treatment and Therapy) has an expanded discussion of medications for emotional disorders; a critical assessment of new drugs and the increasing use of prescription "cocktails"; and problems due to conflicts of interest, placebo effects, and publication bias in drug research. It also includes new material on deep brain stimulation and TMS; the use of virtual-reality treatments for Iraq War veterans; and the next generation of cognitive-behaviour therapy, which focuses on mindfulness and acceptance.

Student Supplements

MyPsychLab *(www.mypsychlab.com)*
The moment you know. Educators know it. Students know it. It's that inspired moment when something that was difficult to understand suddenly makes perfect sense. Our MyLab products have been designed and refined with a single purpose in mind—to help educators create that moment of understanding with their students.

MyPsychLab delivers **proven results** in helping individual students succeed. It provides **engaging experiences** that personalize, stimulate, and measure learning for each student. And, it comes from a **trusted partner** with educational expertise and an eye on the future.

MyPsychLab can be used by itself or linked to any learning management system. To learn more about how MyPsychLab combines proven learning applications with powerful assessment, visit **www.mypsychlab.com**.

Included in MyPsychLab, the new **Pearson Psychology Experiments Tool** presents a suite of data-generating study demonstrations, self-inventories, and surveys that allow students to experience firsthand some of the main concepts covered in their Psychology textbook. Each item in the Experiments Tool generates anonymous data from introductory psychology students around the world that instructors can download and use in lecture or as homework assignments. The Experiments Tool provides opportunities for students to actively participate in doing psychology and for instructors to analyze, interpret, and discuss the results.

Student Study Guide (ISBN 978-0-205-24750-9) for *Psychology,* Fourth Canadian Edition. The fourth Canadian edition study guide contains material to help reinforce students' understanding of the concepts covered in the text. Each chapter provides an overview to introduce students to the chapter; learning-objective exercises to test students' understanding of the main themes; and multiple-choice pre- and post-tests for gauging students' progress. Contact a Pearson Canada sales representative for a package ISBN of the text and study guide.

CourseSmart for Students CourseSmart goes beyond traditional expectations—providing instant, online access to the textbooks and course materials you need at an average savings of 60%. With instant access from any computer and the ability to search your text, you'll find the content you need quickly, no matter where you are. And with online tools like highlighting and note-taking, you can save time and study efficiently. See all the benefits at **www.coursesmart.com/students**.

Video Resources for Students and Instructors

The MyPsychLab Video Series Comprehensive, current, and cutting-edge videos exclusively from Pearson. This new video series offers instructors and students the most current and cutting-edge introductory psychology video content available anywhere. These exclusive videos take the viewer into today's research laboratories, inside the body and brain through breathtaking animations, and out into the street for real-world applications. Guided by the Design, Development and Review team, a diverse group of introductory psychology professors, this comprehensive new series features 17 half-hour episodes organized around the major topics of the introductory psychology course syllabus. The MyPsychLab video series was designed with flexibility in mind. Each half-hour episode in the MyPsychLab video series is made up of several five-minute clips which can be viewed separately or together:

- *The Big Picture* introduces the topic of the episode and draws in the viewer.
- *The Basics* uses the power of video to present foundational topics, especially those that students find difficult to understand.
- *Special Topics* dives deeper into high-interest and often cutting-edge topics, showing research in action.
- *Thinking Like a Psychologist* models critical thinking and explores research methods.
- *In the Real World* focuses on applications of psychological research.
- *What's In It for Me?* These clips show students the relevance of psychological research to their lives.

Students can access the videos anytime within MyPsychLab, and each clip is accompanied by enriching self-assessment quizzes. Instructors can access the videos for classroom presentation in MyPsychLab or on DVD.

Supplements For Instructors

Instructor supplements are available for download from a password-protected section of Pearson Canada's online catalogue (vig.pearsoned.ca). Navigate to your book's catalogue page to view a list of those supplements that are available. See your local sales representative for details and access.

For your convenience, these resources are also available on the **Instructor's Resource CD-ROM** (978-0-205-25791-1). The CD-ROM includes the following instructor supplements:

The Instructor's Resource Manual includes lecture launchers/discussion topics, in-class activities, out-of-class activities, handouts, transparency masters, descriptions of MyLab assets, Pearson video listings and descriptions, external video listings and descriptions, and web resources.

Test Item File This peer-reviewed test bank contains almost 6000 questions, including multiple-choice, true–false, matching, short-answer, and essay items. Included in the test bank are

- explanations of the answers for all multiple-choice and true–false items.
- the key points to include in a good answer for all items requiring written answers (short-answer, essay, and integrative essay questions).
- a *Total Assessment Guide* for each chapter. This table shows at a glance what kinds of questions are available. For each topic area, the table lists questions by question type and by level of understanding (factual, conceptual, or applied).
- two 10-item *Quick Quizzes* for each chapter (one for the Appendix). These quizzes are ready for use; all you need to do is copy them. The answer key for each quiz, containing page references and explanations, can be copied and given to students as a learning aid when you return the quiz. (Note that the items in these quizzes, though similar, do not duplicate any items in the Test Item File itself.)

MyTest for *Psychology*, Fourth Canadian Edition, from Pearson Canada is a powerful assessment generation program that helps instructors easily create and print quizzes, tests, and exams, as well as homework or practice handouts. Questions and tests can all be authored online, allowing instructors ultimate flexibility and the ability to efficiently manage assessments at any time, from anywhere.

PowerPoint Presentations cover the key concepts and figures in each chapter.

Image Library provides electronic versions of the figures and tables that appear in the text.

peerScholar Firmly grounded in published research, peerScholar is a powerful online pedagogical tool that helps develop your students' critical and creative thinking skills. peerScholar facilitates this through the process of creation, evaluation, and reflection. Working in stages, students begin by submitting a written assignment. peerScholar then circulates their work for others to review, a process that can be anonymous or not depending on your preference. Students receive peer feedback and evaluations immediately, reinforcing their learning and driving the development of higher-order thinking skills. Students can then re-submit revised work, again depending on your preference. Contact your Pearson representative to learn more about peerScholar and the research behind it.

CourseSmart goes beyond traditional expectations, providing instant, online access to the textbooks and course materials you need at a lower cost for students. And even as students save money, you can save time and hassle with a digital eTextbook that allows you to search for the most relevant content at the very moment you need it. Whether it's evaluating textbooks or creating lecture notes to help students with difficult concepts, CourseSmart can make life a little easier. See how when you visit **www.coursesmart.com/instructors.**

Technology Specialists. Pearson's Technology Specialists work with faculty and campus course designers to ensure that Pearson technology products, assessment tools, and online course materials are tailored to meet your specific needs. This highly qualified team is dedicated to helping schools take full advantage of a wide range of educational resources, by assisting in the integration of a variety of instructional materials and media formats. Your local Pearson Canada sales representative can provide you with more details on this service program.

Pearson Custom Library For enrollments of at least 25 students, you can create your own textbook by choosing the chapters that best suit your own course needs. *To begin building your custom text, visit www.pearsoncustomlibrary.com.* You may also work with a dedicated Pearson Custom editor to create your ideal text—publishing your own original content or mixing and matching Pearson content. *Contact your local Pearson representative to get started.*

Supplementary Texts

Contact your Pearson Canada representative to package any of the following supplementary texts with *Psychology*, Fourth Canadian Edition. A package ISBN is required for your bookstore order.

Current Directions in Introductory Psychology, Second Edition (ISBN 0-13-714350-8): The second edition of this reader includes more than 20 articles selected for undergraduates from *Current Directions in Psychological Science*. These timely, cutting-edge articles allow instructors to show students how psychologists go about their research and how they apply it to real-world problems.

Forty Studies That Changed Psychology, Sixth Edition (ISBN 0-13-603599-X) by Roger Hock (Mendocino College): Presenting the seminal research studies that have shaped modern psychological study, this brief supplement provides an overview of the environment that gave rise to each study, its experimental design, its findings, and its impact on current thinking in the discipline.

The Psychology Major: Careers and Strategies for Success, Fourth Edition (ISBN 0-205-68468-8) by Eric Landrum (Idaho State University) and Stephen Davis (Emporia State University): This paperback provides valuable information about career options available to psychology majors, tips for improving academic performance, and a guide to the APA style of reporting research.

Authors' Acknowledgments

Acknowledgments

Many people contributed to this project, which has evolved through four editions now. Our thanks go out to the following individuals:

Jennifer Burkitt
Greg Christie
Farhad Dastur
Chai Duncan
John Elias
Lana Elias
Mileva Elias ☺
Noam Elias ☺
Isabelle Gauthier

Peter Hall
Ben Heppner*
Duane Janzen
Bryan Kolb
Ky Pruesse
Mia Saucier ☺
Rob Sutherland
Matt Tata
Regan Patrick

Thanks also to the many reviewers from across Canada for their comments and suggestions on the fourth Canadian edition manuscript.

Wayne Avery, Vancouver Community College
Rachel Baker, Cape Breton University
Darren Hannesson, Vancouver Island University
Antonia Henderson, Langara College
Gieselle Kolaric, Thompson Rivers University

Jason Leboe, University of Manitoba
Lynn McCaw, Vancouver Island University
Stuart McKelvie, Bishop's University
Sarah Murray, Kwantlen Polytechnic University
Susana Phillips, Kwantlen Polytechnic University
Lisa Sinclair, University of Winnipeg

Additionally, we would also like to thank the many talented people at Pearson Canada, including

Vice-President, Editorial Director: Gary Bennett
Editor-in-Chief: Michelle Sartor
Acquisitions Editor: Matthew Christian
Sponsoring Editor: Carolin Sweig
Senior Developmental Editor: Patti Altridge
Duncan MacKinnon, senior sales and editorial representative and psychology specialist
Marketing Manager: Lisa Gillis
Project Manager: Lesley Deugo
Copy Editor: Alision Kooistra
Proofreader: Karen Alliston

Deborah Saucier
Lorin Elias

2011

About the Authors

CAROLE WADE earned her PhD in cognitive psychology at Stanford University. She began her academic career at the University of New Mexico, where she taught courses in psycholinguistics and developed the first course at the university on the psychology of gender. She was professor of psychology for ten years at San Diego Mesa College, then taught at College of Marin and Dominican University of California. In addition to this text, she and Carol Tavris have written *Invitation to Psychology; Psychology in Perspective;* and *The Longest War: Sex Differences in Perspective.* Dr. Wade has a long-standing interest in making psychology accessible to students and the general public. In particular, she has focused her efforts on the teaching and promotion of critical-thinking skills, diversity issues, and the enhancement of undergraduate education in psychology. She chaired the APA Board of Educational Affairs's Task Force on Diversity Issues at the Precollege and Undergraduate Levels of Education in Psychology, as well as the APA's Public Information Committee; has been a G. Stanley Hall lecturer at the APA convention; and served on the steering committee for the National Institute on the Teaching of Psychology. Dr. Wade is a Fellow of the American Psychological Association and a charter member of the Association for Psychological Science. When she isn't busy with her professional activities, she can be found riding the trails of northern California on her Morgan horse, McGregor, or one of his Arabian stable mates, Condé or Ricochet.

CAROL TAVRIS earned her PhD in the interdisciplinary program in social psychology at the University of Michigan, and as a writer and lecturer she has sought to educate the public about the importance of critical and scientific thinking in psychology. In addition to this text, she and Carole Wade have written *Invitation to Psychology; Psychology in Perspective;* and *The Longest War: Sex Differences in Perspective.* Dr. Tavris is also coauthor, with Elliot Aronson, of *Mistakes Were Made (But Not by Me): Why We Justify Foolish Beliefs, Bad Decisions, and Hurtful Acts;* and author of *The Mismeasure of Woman* and *Anger: The Misunderstood Emotion.* She has written on psychological topics for a wide variety of magazines, journals, edited books, and newspapers. Many of her book reviews and opinion essays for the *Los Angeles Times, The New York Times Book Review, The TLS, Scientific American,* and other publications have been collected in *Psychobabble and Biobunk: Using Psychology to Think Critically About Issues in the News.* Dr. Tavris lectures widely on topics involving science vs. pseudoscience in psychology and psychiatry, on writing about science for the public, and many other subjects of contemporary interest. She has taught in the psychology department at UCLA and at the Human Relations Center of the New School for Social Research in New York. She is a Fellow of the American Psychological Association and a charter Fellow of the Association for Psychological Science; and a member of the editorial board of the APS journal *Psychological Science in the Public Interest.* When she is not writing or lecturing, she can be found walking the trails of the Hollywood Hills with her border collie, Sophie.

DEBORAH SAUCIER earned her PhD in psychology at the University of Western Ontario. She earned her BSc and MSc degrees in psychology from the University of Victoria. Currently, she is the Dean of Science at the University of Ontario Institute of Technology. Dr. Saucier researches how individual differences in spatial cognition are related to steroid hormones in human and non-human animals. She receives research funding from the Natural Sciences and Engineering Research Council, and her research has been published in *Nature, Behavioural Neuroscience, Journal of Neuroscience, Brain and Cognition, Laterality,* and *Cognitive Brain Research.* When Dr. Saucier is not busy discussing issues like bedtime with her daughter, Mia, she tries to get on top of her gardening and quilting, although she is often out playing with Mia and her soft-coated wheaten terriers (Khali and Zoe) and accident-prone black cat (Pixie).

LORIN ELIAS earned his PhD in behavioural neuroscience at the University of Waterloo. He was then appointed as an assistant professor in the Department of Psychology at the University of Saskatchewan, the same institution where he completed his BA (Honours) degree in psychology. He now serves the Department of Psychology at the University of Saskatchewan as a full professor. Dr. Elias is an active and award-winning teacher and researcher. He has won several teaching excellence awards and teaches a variety of courses in cognitive neuroscience and evolutionary psychology at both the undergraduate and graduate levels while maintaining an active research program. His federally funded research program has mainly focused on the functional differences between the left and right hemispheres of the brain. However, he has also investigated a number of unusual perceptual phenomena, including a condition called synesthesia. Dr. Elias's research has been published in a number of academic journals, including *Neuropsychologia*, *Brain and Cognition*, *Laterality*, *Neurosurgery*, *Cognitive Brain Research*, and *Behavioural Neuroscience*. When Dr. Elias is not busy writing, teaching, doing research, or performing other professional duties, he can be found riding his "steel horse" (a Honda Bros motorcycle) on one of the few smooth and twisty roads to be found in Saskatchewan.

Lorin Elias and Deborah Saucier also co-authored *Neuropsychology: Clinical and Experimental Foundations*, for Pearson Allyn & Bacon, published in 2006.

PSYCHOLOGY

1 WHAT IS PSYCHOLOGY?

ASK QUESTIONS . . . be willing to WONDER

- How does "pop psych" on the internet and TV differ from the psychology in this book?

- If you want to think critically, must you always be critical?

- If you call yourself a psychotherapist, will you be breaking the law?

- What's the difference between a psychologist, a clinical psychologist, and a psychiatrist?

Would you like to unlock the secret of happiness? Manage your stress? Fall in love? Get over love? Improve your study habits? Stop procrastinating? Get rich? Lose weight? Stop worrying?

If you are like most people, you probably answered "You bet" to at least some of these questions. If so, the internet is full of advice for you. Some advice comes from experts who know what they're talking about; some comes from bloggers who know as much about psychology as they do about astrophysics; some comes from psychotherapists who will send you a diagnosis and treatment program based solely on what you write in an email. And hundreds of Internet companies offer "natural" herbal remedies for anxiety, nervousness, sexual problems, and depression, or prescription drugs at impossibly low prices. A better life may seem to be just a click away.

Perhaps you would prefer a book? There's *Why Your Life Sucks: And What You Can Do About It; Idea Mapping: How to Access Your Hidden Brain Power, Learn Faster, Remember More, and Achieve Success in Business;* and *How to Make Anyone Fall in Love with You* (and then you will undoubtedly want the sequel, *How to Make Someone Love You Forever! In 90 Minutes or Less*). If you like things laid out in easy-to-follow lists, you can buy *Ten Secrets for Success and Inner Peace,* and if 10 is too many, you can try *Getting Unstuck: 8 Simple Steps to Solving Any Problem.*

How in the world are you supposed to separate out useful information in this sea of opinions, marketing ploys, and downright rubbish? Fortunately for you, you are taking an introductory psychology course, and by the time you finish it you will have some good answers.

Before you head for the bookstore, however, we want to tell you that the psychology you are about to study—*real* psychology—bears little relation to the popular psychology ("pop psych") seen on television or found in these and thousands of similar books on the Web. It is more complex, more informative, and, we think, far more helpful because it is based on scientific research and **empirical evidence**—evidence gathered by careful observation, experimentation, and measurement.

The psychology you will be studying also addresses a far broader range of issues than does popular psychology. When people think of psychology, they usually think of mental and emotional disorders, personal problems, and psychotherapy. But psychologists take as their subject the entire spectrum of brave and cowardly, intelligent and foolish, beautiful and brutish things that people do. They want to know how ordinary human beings—and other animals, too—learn, remember, solve problems, perceive, feel, and get along (or fail to get along) with others. They are therefore as likely to study commonplace experiences—rearing children, gossiping, remembering a shopping list, daydreaming, making love, and making a living—as exceptional ones.

Psychologists use scientific methods to study many puzzles of human behaviour. Why do people lose their inhibitions when they dress up in funny outfits? Why do people strive to become champion athletes in spite of physical disabilities? And what would motivate terrorists to kill themselves and thousands of innocent people?

◀●▶ Simulate
Psychology Experiments Survey: What Do You Know About Psychology?

empirical   Relying on or derived from observation, experimentation, or measurement.

psychology   The discipline concerned with behaviour and mental processes and how they are affected by an organism's physical state, mental state, and external environment; the term is often represented by ψ, the Greek letter psi (usually pronounced "sigh").

psychobabble   Pseudoscience and quackery covered by a veneer of psychological and scientific-sounding language.

Psychology can be defined generally as *the discipline concerned with behaviour and mental processes and how they are affected by an organism's physical state, mental state, and external environment.* This definition, however, is a little like defining a car as a vehicle for transporting people from one place to another, without explaining how a car differs from a train or a bus, how a Ford differs from a Ferrari, or how a catalytic converter works. To get a clear picture of what psychology is, you are going to need to know more about its methods, its findings, and its ways of interpreting information. We will begin by looking more closely at what psychology is *not*.

▨ YOU are about to learn . . .

◆ how "psychobabble" differs from serious psychology.
◆ what's wrong with psychologists' nonscientific competitors, such as astrologers and psychics.

PSYCHOLOGY, PSEUDOSCIENCE, AND POPULAR OPINION

In recent decades, the public's appetite for psychological information has created a huge market for "**psychobabble**": pseudoscience and quackery covered by a veneer of psychological and scientific-sounding language. Pseudoscience promises easy fixes to life's problems and challenges, such as resolving your unhappiness as an adult by "reliving" the supposed trauma of your birth, or becoming more creative on the job by "reprogramming" your brain. Some forms of psychobabble play on the modern consumer's love of technology. All sorts of electrical gizmos have been marketed with the promise that they will get both halves of your brain working at their peak: the Graham Potentializer, the Tranquilite, the Floatarium, the Transcutaneous Electro-Neural Stimulator, the Brain SuperCharger, and the Whole Brain Wave Form Synchro-Energizer. (We are not making these up.) And today you can find all sorts of psychobabble on the internet, where promoters promise that a higher IQ or a perfect love life or a better personality is just a click away.

Because so many pop-psych ideas have filtered into public consciousness, the media, education, and even the law, we all need to distinguish between psychobabble and serious psychology, and between unsupported *popular opinion* and findings based on *research evidence*. Are unhappy memories "repressed" and then accurately recalled years later, as if they had been tape-recorded? Do most women suffer from emotional symptoms of premenstrual syndrome (PMS)? Do policies of abstinence from alcohol reduce rates of alcoholism? Do abused children inevitably become abusive parents, caught in a "cycle of abuse"? If you play Beethoven's symphonies to your infant, will your baby become smarter? Many people would answer "yes" to these questions, but empirical evidence has shown that these and many other widely held ideas about human behaviour are, in fact, wrong.

One purpose of an introductory course like the one you are taking is to correct misconceptions—by teaching you how psychologists study them and showing you how their research might confirm or dispel ideas that many of us take for granted. Two researchers, Annette Kujawski Taylor and Patricia Kowalski (2004), wondered how many students come into their first psych course with a bunch of mistaken ideas in their heads and whether a semester of learning helps dislodge those ideas.

To answer these questions, they gave 90 introductory students a "Psychological Information" questionnaire on the first day of class. The test consisted of 36 true-or-false items—for example, "Under hypnosis you can perform feats that are otherwise impossible," "Too much sugar causes hyperactivity in children," "At any point in time, we use only 10% of our brains," and "Listening to Mozart will enhance your thinking and creativity." The students also rated their confidence in each of their responses on a scale of one (not at all confident) to 10 (very confident). All the items were on topics that the course was scheduled to cover, and all of them were false. As a group, the students failed the test miserably: Their accuracy was only 38.5%, which is actually worse than chance, and they had more confidence in their wrong answers than their correct ones! Moreover, students with high grade-point averages did no better than those with low ones. So much for common sense.

During the last week of class, the same students took another test, one that included all of the earlier items plus 12 new true items that were randomly mixed in but not scored. This time, we're happy to say, the students' overall accuracy was much better: 66.3%. The researchers attributed this change in part to the fact that instruction had explicitly focused on the scientific evidence refuting such beliefs. (As you will see, we take the same approach in this book.) Yet even at the end of the course, more than a third of the students' responses were wrong, meaning that there was still plenty of room left for improvement. The researchers then dug deeper into the evidence, analyzing the students' confidence ratings. They found that by the end of the semester, the students had gained confidence in their correct beliefs and lost confidence in those beliefs that were still incorrect, suggesting that they were beginning to be unsure about their misconceptions, were in the process of questioning them, and perhaps were on the way to giving them up. If so, they were learning one of the most important

The marriage of old-fashioned pseudoscience and modern technology has produced gizmos like the "Synchro-Energizer," which supposedly alters consciousness, boosts intelligence, and enhances sexual functioning, all by simply bombarding you with lights and sounds of different frequencies and intensities.

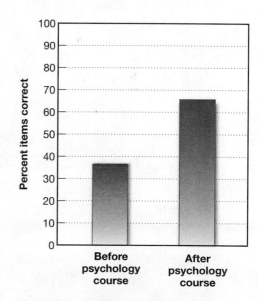

FIGURE 1.1 Psychology: It's Not Just "Common Sense"

On the first day of class, students in an introductory psychology course actually did worse than chance on a true–false psychological information questionnaire. But by the end of the semester, after they had learned to examine the scientific evidence for their beliefs, their performance had greatly improved.

Nonscientific approaches to psychological problems, such as astrology and psychic readings, promise easy answers and quick solutions—even for pets! But can they deliver?

◉ **Watch**
Carlos

lessons in science: Uncertainty about untested assumptions and beliefs can be a good thing.

Throughout this book and your introductory course, you, too, will repeatedly find that popular opinion and "common sense" are not always reliable guides to human behaviour. The kind of research you will be learning about won't always provide the answers you might have wished for, and sometimes it will be unable to provide final answers. Our goal, however, is to show you why the scientific investigation of even our most cherished beliefs can lead to answers that are far more sensible than "common sense."

Common sense, information in the media, and personal experience are not the only sources of misunderstandings about human behaviour. Psychology has many nonscientific competitors: palm reading, graphology, fortune-telling, numerology, and the most popular, astrology. Like psychologists, promoters of these competing systems try to explain people's problems and predict their behaviour. If you are having romantic problems, an astrologer may advise you to choose an Aries instead of an Aquarius as your next love, and a "past-lives channeller" may say it's because you were jilted in a former life. Belief in these unscientific approaches is widespread, even in scientifically advanced countries; between one-third and one-half of Americans and Canadians believe in astrology, and 17% of Americans have sought out a fortune teller or psychic for advice (De Robertis & Delaney, 2000; National Science Board, 2000).

Yet whenever the claims of psychics and astrologers are put to the test, those claims turn out to be so vague as to be meaningless ("Spirituality will increase next year")—or just plain wrong (Park, 2000; Radford, 2005; Shermer, 1997). In 2008, one well-known Canadian psychic, who calls herself the "psychic to the stars," predicted that George Clooney would marry and have a child, Sean Penn would be wounded in the Middle East, and John Edwards would win the U.S. presidency after Hillary Clinton dropped out of the race. Obviously, she was wrong on all counts. Moreover, contrary to what you might think from watching TV shows like *Medium*, no psychic has ever found a missing child, identified a serial killer, or helped police solve any other crime solely by using "psychic powers." The "help" given by psychics merely adds to the heartbreak the victim's family feels. In 2004, when 11-year-old Carlie Brucia was abducted, her family's hopes were raised by a psychic's report that Carlie was alive. In fact, the child had been raped and murdered.

So why does belief in psychobabble persist? For one thing, it gives people a sense of control and predictability in a confusing world; indeed, our brains are probably wired to look for patterns in events, even when no patterns exist (Hood, 2009). Psychobabble also confirms our existing beliefs and prejudices, whereas scientific psychology often challenges them. You do not have to be a psychologist to know that people do not always take kindly to having their beliefs challenged. You rarely hear someone cheerfully say, "Oh, thank you for explaining to me why my irrational beliefs are mistaken!" The person is more likely to say, "Oh, buzz off, and take your stupid ideas with you."

Psychological findings do not have to be surprising or counterintuitive, however, to be important. Like scientists in other fields, psychological researchers strive not only to discover new phenomena and correct mistaken ideas but also to deepen our understanding of an already familiar world—by identifying the varieties of love, the origins of violence, or the reasons that a great song can lift our hearts.

YOU are about to learn . . .

- what it means to think critically.
- why not all opinions are created equal.
- eight guidelines for evaluating psychological claims.

THINKING CRITICALLY AND CREATIVELY ABOUT PSYCHOLOGY

In this book, you will gain practice in distinguishing scientific psychology from pseudoscience by thinking critically. Critical thinking is the ability and willingness to assess claims and make objective judgments on the basis of well-supported reasons and evidence, rather than emotion or anecdote. Critical thinkers are able to look for flaws in arguments and to resist claims that have no support. They realize that criticizing an argument is not the same as criticizing the person making it, and they are willing to engage in vigorous debate about the validity of an idea. Critical thinking, however, is not merely negative thinking. It includes the ability to be creative and constructive—the ability to come up with alternative explanations for events, think of implications of research findings, and apply new knowledge to social and personal problems. Critical thinking is indispensable in ordinary life. Without it, people cannot formulate a rational argument or see through misleading ads that play on their emotions. They may have trouble assessing a political proposal or candidate, deciding whether or when to have children, or making medical decisions.

Most people know that you have to exercise the body to keep it in shape, but they may not realize that clear thinking also requires effort and practice. All around us we can see examples of flabby thinking. Sometimes people justify their mental laziness by proudly telling you they are open-minded. It's good to be open-minded, many scientists have observed, but not so open that your brains fall out! Open-mindedness does not mean that all opinions are created equal and that everybody's beliefs are as good as anyone else's (Hare, 2009).

On matters of personal preference, all opinions are created equal: If you prefer the look of a Ford Taurus to the look of a Honda Accord, no one can argue with you. But if you say, "The Ford is a better car than a Honda," you have uttered more than mere opinion. Now you have to support your belief with evidence of the car's reliability, track record, and safety (Ruggiero, 2004). And if you say, "Fords are the best in the world and Hondas do not exist; they are a conspiracy of the Japanese government," you forfeit the right to have your opinion taken seriously. Your opinion, if it ignores reality, is *not* equal to any other.

Critical thinking is not only indispensable in ordinary life; it is also fundamental to all science, including psychological science. By exercising critical thinking, you will be able to distinguish serious psychology from the psychobabble that clutters the internet, the

critical thinking The ability and willingness to assess claims and make objective judgments on the basis of well-supported reasons and evidence, rather than emotion or anecdote.

◀○ **Simulate**
Distinguishing Independent and Dependent Variables

✳ **Explore**
How to Be a Critical Thinker

Coin Toss

Urban Legend

TEACH BOTH THEORIES... LET THE KIDS DECIDE.

CHEMISTRY / ALCHEMY / PHRENOLOGY / NEUROLOGY / MAGIC / $E = MC^2$ / PHYSICS / ASTROLOGY / ASTRONOMY

We often hear that all viewpoints should be taught to students in the name of "fairness" and "open-mindedness," but not all viewpoints, theories, and opinions are equally valid or supported by the evidence.

media, and bookstores. (In the study of introductory students' misconceptions described earlier, students who did well on a critical-thinking test showed the greatest improvement over the semester.) Critical thinking requires logical skills, but other kinds of skills and dispositions are also important (Anderson, 2005; Halpern, 2002; Levy, 1997; Paul, 1984; Ruggiero, 2004). Here are eight essential critical-thinking guidelines that we will be emphasizing throughout this book.

 Ask Questions; Be Willing to Wonder. What is the one kind of question that most exasperates parents of young children? "Why is the sky blue, Mommy?" "Why doesn't the plane fall?" "Why don't pigs have wings?" Unfortunately, as children grow up, they tend to stop asking "why" questions. (Why do you think this is?)

"The trigger mechanism for creative thinking is the disposition to be curious, to wonder, to inquire," observed Vincent Ruggiero (1988). "Asking 'What's wrong here?' and/or 'Why is this the way it is, and how did it come to be that way?' leads to

Thinking Critically and Creatively
about Psychological Issues

These eight critical-thinking guidelines will help you evaluate psychological findings, claims in the media, and problems that you encounter in your own life.

ASK QUESTIONS; BE WILLING TO WONDER
When faced with a life-threatening disease like cancer, why do some people (like Terry Fox) risk their lives to help their fellow human beings, while others focus all their attention on their own well-being? Social psychologists explore these and many other questions, as we will see in Chapter 8.

DEFINE YOUR TERMS
People refer to intelligence all the time, but what is it exactly? Does the artistic genius of Emily Carr count as intelligence? Is intelligence captured by an IQ score, or does it also include wisdom and practical "smarts"? We will consider some answers in Chapter 9.

the identification of problems and challenges." We hope that you will not approach psychology as received wisdom but will ask many questions about the theories and findings presented in this book. Be on the lookout, too, for questions about human behaviour that have not yet been asked, or have been asked but not answered—the way a psychological scientist would. In 2005, the editors of *Science*, one of the world's foremost science journals, celebrated the publication's 125th anniversary by identifying 125 scientific puzzles that scientists hope to solve at least partially over the next few decades, and among them were several psychological ones (Kennedy & Norman, 2005). What is the biological basis of consciousness? How are memories stored and retrieved? Why do we sleep and dream? Why are there critical periods for language learning? What causes schizophrenia? What is the biological basis of addiction? Psychological scientists are not discouraged by the fact that questions like these have not yet been answered; they see them as an exciting challenge.

EXAMINE THE EVIDENCE

When demonstrating "levitation" and other supposedly magical phenomena, illusionists exploit people's tendency to trust the evidence of their own eyes even when such evidence is misleading, as discussed in Chapter 6.

ANALYZE ASSUMPTIONS AND BIASES

People often assume that drug effects are purely biological, and many Canadians and Americans also share a cultural bias that all psychoactive drugs are inevitably harmful. The Rastafarian church, however, regards marijuana as a "wisdom weed." Will these young Jamaican members react to the drug in the same way as someone who buys it on the street and smokes it alone or at a party? We will find out in Chapters 5 and 15.

Define Your Terms. Once you have raised a general question, the next step is to frame it in clear and concrete terms. "What makes people happy?" is a fine question for midnight reveries, but it will not lead to answers until you have defined what you mean by "happy." Do you mean being in a state of euphoria most of the time? Do you mean feeling pleasantly contented with life? Do you mean being free of serious problems or pain?

Vague or poorly defined terms in a question can lead to misleading or incomplete answers. For example, have you ever wondered how common it is for schoolchildren to be bullied? The answer depends on how you define "bullying." If you mean "ever mistreated in any way by another child," then nearly every child has been bullied. If you mean "subjected to repeated verbal harassment and taunting," the numbers are lower. And if you mean "physically attacked and threatened," the numbers are lower still. The definition makes all the difference (Best, 2001).

DON'T OVERSIMPLIFY

When you're feeling angry, is it better to "let it out" (as this man is certainly doing here!) or "keep it bottled up"? Either answer oversimplifies. Depending on the circumstances, sometimes it is helpful to express your feelings, but sometimes venting your anger makes everything worse, as we discuss in Chapter 11.

AVOID EMOTIONAL REASONING

Intense feelings about controversial issues such as gay marriage can keep us from considering other viewpoints. The resolution of differences requires that we move beyond emotional reasoning and instead weigh point and counterpoint, as discussed in Chapter 9.

Examine the Evidence. Have you ever heard someone in the heat of an argument exclaim, "I just know it's true, no matter what you say" or "That's my opinion; nothing's going to change it"? Have you ever made such statements yourself? Accepting a conclusion without evidence, or expecting others to do so, is a sure sign of lazy thinking. A critical thinker asks, "What evidence supports or refutes this argument and its opposition? How reliable is the evidence?"

Or have you ever received some dire warning or funny "true" story emailed by a friend, and then forwarded it on to your entire address book, only to learn later that it was a hoax or an urban legend? A critical thinker would ask, "Is this story something I'd better check out on Snopes.com before I tell 90 000 of my closest friends?"

Sometimes, of course, checking the reliability of the evidence for a claim is not practical. In those cases, critical thinkers consider whether the evidence came from a reliable source (Lipps, 2004). Reliable authorities exercise critical thinking themselves.

TOLERATE UNCERTAINTY

Many parents, because they naturally want their children to turn out well, have trouble accepting uncertainty about how to raise them. For example, should they let their baby sleep with them, or will that make the baby too dependent and clingy? In Chapter 14, we will look at why there is often no single right answer to what parents "should" do.

CONSIDER OTHER INTERPRETATIONS

Hypnosis has traditionally been considered a "trance state," in which people involuntarily do things they ordinarily couldn't or wouldn't do. But might there be another interpretation of the surprising things that hypnotized people often do? We'll look at competing explanations in Chapter 5.

They have education or experience in the field in which they claim expertise. They don't pressure people to agree with them. They are trusted by other experts in the field. They share their evidence openly. In psychology, they draw on research conducted according to certain rules and procedures, which you will be learning about in the next chapter.

Analyze Assumptions and Biases. *Assumptions* are beliefs that are taken for granted. Critical thinkers try to identify and evaluate the unspoken assumptions on which claims and arguments may rest—in the books they read, the political speeches they hear, and the advertisements that bombard them every day. The assumption might be "All Toronto Maple Leafs fans are idiots," or "You need the product we are selling," or "People have free will, and are entirely responsible for any crimes they commit" (or, conversely, "People's behaviour is a result of their biology or upbringing, so they aren't responsible for anything they do"). Everyone, of course, makes assumptions about how the world works; we could not function otherwise. But if we do not make explicit our own assumptions and those of other people, our ability to judge an argument's merits can be impaired.

When an assumption or belief keeps us from considering the evidence fairly, or causes us to ignore the evidence completely, it becomes a *bias.* Often a bias remains hidden until someone challenges our belief and we get defensive and angry. For instance, most of us, psychologists included, believe that parents are the most important influence in shaping a child's personality. Could anything be more obvious? Isn't that what parenting books, therapists, and magazine articles have been telling us for years? In her book *The Nurture Assumption*, Judith Rich Harris (1998) dared to question that assumption. Genes and peers, she argued, are more important influences on a child's personality and behaviour than how the parents raise the child. Because this idea challenged a widespread bias, it immediately provoked a storm of disbelief, outrage, and scorn. Some critics focused on Harris's lack of credentials instead of her facts or her logic (although she had authored a successful developmental psychology text, she does not have a PhD), and many attacked the book without even bothering to read it. That is the nature of a bias: It creates intellectual blinders. (In Chapter 14 we will look more closely at Harris's argument—in as unbiased a manner as possible.)

Avoid Emotional Reasoning. Emotion has a place in critical thinking. Passionate commitment to a view motivates people to think boldly, to defend unpopular ideas, and to seek evidence for creative new theories. But when "gut feelings" replace clear thinking, the results can be dangerous. "Persecutions and wars and lynchings," observed Edward de Bono (1985), "are all a result of gut feeling."

All of us are apt to feel threatened and get defensive whenever our most cherished beliefs are challenged. We value these beliefs highly, in part because they offer explanations for phenomena that might otherwise seem puzzling or frightening—for example, the existence of death and suffering—and because they simplify a complicated world (Preston & Epley, 2005). Because our feelings feel so *right*, so natural, we may not realize that people who hold an opposing viewpoint feel just as strongly as we do. But they usually do, which means that emotional conviction alone cannot settle arguments. You probably hold strong feelings about many topics of psychological interest, such as drug use, the causes of crime, racism, the origins of intelligence, gender differences, and homosexuality. As you read this book, you may find yourself quarrelling with findings that you dislike. Disagreement is fine; it means that you are reading actively and are engaged with the material. All we ask is that you think about why you are disagreeing: Is it because the evidence is unpersuasive or because the results make you feel anxious or annoyed?

Don't Oversimplify. A critical thinker looks beyond the obvious, resists easy generalizations, and rejects either–or thinking. For instance, is it better to feel you have control over everything that happens to you, or to accept with tranquility whatever life serves up? Either position oversimplifies. As we will see in Chapter 11, a sense of control has many important benefits, but sometimes it is best to "go with the flow."

One common form of oversimplification is *argument by anecdote*—generalizing to everyone from a personal experience or a few examples: One crime committed by a paroled ex-convict means that parole should be abolished; one friend who hates her school means that everybody who goes there hates it. Anecdotes are often the source of stereotyping as well: One dishonest welfare mother means they are all dishonest; one encounter with an unconventional Vancouverite means they are all flaky. Critical thinkers want more evidence than one or two stories before drawing such sweeping conclusions.

Consider Other Interpretations. A critical thinker creatively generates as many reasonable explanations of the topic at hand as possible before settling on the most likely one. Suppose a newsmagazine reports that chronically depressed people are more likely than other people to develop cancer. Before concluding that depression causes cancer, you would need to consider some other possibilities. Perhaps depressed people are more likely to smoke and drink excessively, and it is those unhealthy habits that increase their cancer risk. Or perhaps, in studies of depression and cancer, early, undetected cancers were responsible for patients' feelings of depression. Alternative explanations such as these must be ruled out by further investigation before we can conclude that depression is a direct cause of cancer. (It's not, by the way.)

Once several explanations of a phenomenon have been generated, a critical thinker chooses the one that accounts for the most evidence while making the fewest unverified assumptions—a principle known as **Occam's Razor**, after the fourteenth-century philosopher who first formulated it. Thus, if a fortune teller reads your palm and predicts that soon you will fall in love on a blind date, travel to Zanzibar, and have twins, then one of two things must be true (Steiner, 1989):

◆ The fortune teller can actually sort out the infinite number of interactions among people, animals, events, objects, and circumstances that could affect your life, and can know the outcome for sure. Moreover, this fortune teller is able to alter all the known laws of physics and defy the hundreds of studies showing that no one, under proper procedures for validating psychic predictions, has been able to predict the future for any given individual.

OR

◆ The fortune teller is faking it.

A critical thinker would prefer the second alternative because it requires fewer assumptions and has the most supporting evidence.

Tolerate Uncertainty. Ultimately, learning to think critically teaches us one of the hardest lessons of life: how to live with uncertainty. Sometimes there is little or no evidence available to examine. Sometimes

Occam's Razor The principle of choosing the solution that accounts for the most evidence while making the fewest unverified assumptions.

"I still don't have all the answers, but I'm beginning to ask the right questions."

the evidence permits only tentative conclusions. Sometimes the evidence seems strong enough to permit conclusions . . . until, exasperatingly, new evidence throws our beliefs into disarray. Critical thinkers are willing to accept this state of uncertainty. They are not afraid to say, "I don't know" or "I'm not sure." This admission is not an evasion but a spur to further creative inquiry. Critical thinkers know that the more important the question, the less likely it is to have a single simple answer.

The need to accept a certain amount of uncertainty does not mean that we must abandon all beliefs and convictions. That would be impossible, in any case: We all need values and principles to guide our actions. As Vincent Ruggiero (1988) writes, "It is not the embracing of an idea that causes problems—it is the refusal to relax that embrace when good sense dictates doing so. It is enough to form convictions with care and carry them lightly, being willing to reconsider them whenever new evidence calls them into question."

Critical thinking is a process, not a once-and-for-all accomplishment. No one ever becomes a perfect critical thinker, entirely unaffected by emotional reasoning and wishful thinking. We are all less open-minded than we think; it is always easier to poke holes in another person's argument than to critically examine our own position. Yet we think the journey is well worth the mental effort, because the ability to think critically will help you in countless ways, from saving you money to improving your relationships.

As you read this book, keep in mind the eight guidelines we have described, which are summarized for you in Review 1.1 (on p. 15). Practice in critical thinking really can help students understand psychological concepts better. That is why we have given you many opportunities to apply these guidelines to psychological theories and to the personal and social issues that affect us all. Look for questions in the margin, accompanied by a little head with working "gears," which will draw your attention to a discussion where one of the guidelines is especially relevant. In Quick Quizzes and with some photos, the icon will identify questions that give you practice in applying the guidelines yourself. (However, critical thinking is important throughout every chapter, not just where the icon appears.) At the end of each chapter, a feature called "Taking Psychology with You" will help you apply critical thinking to a topic in the chapter and take its message home with you.

quickQUIZ

✓●—Quick Review on MyPsychLab

Amelia and Harold are arguing about the death penalty. "Look, I just feel strongly that it's barbaric, ineffective, and wrong," says Harold. "You're nuts," says Amelia. "I believe in an eye for an eye, and besides, I'm absolutely sure it's a deterrent to further crime." Which lapses of critical thinking might Amelia and Harold be committing?

Answers:

Here are some problems in their style of argument; feel free to think of others.
(1) They are reasoning emotionally ("I feel strongly about this, so I'm right and you're wrong").
(2) They have not examined evidence that supports or contradicts their arguments. What do studies show about the link between the death penalty and crime? Is the death penalty applied fairly to rich and poor, men and women, nonwhites and whites? How often are innocent people executed?
(3) They have not examined the assumptions and biases they bring to the discussion.
(4) They may not be clearly defining the problem about which they are arguing. What is the purpose of the death penalty, for example? Is it to deter criminals, to satisfy the public desire for revenge, or to keep criminals from being paroled and returned to the streets?

REView 1.1

Guidelines to Thinking Critically About Psychological Issues

	Guideline	Example
	Ask questions; be willing to wonder	"Can I recall events from my childhood accurately?"
	Define your terms	"By 'childhood,' I mean ages 3 to 12; by 'events,' I mean things that happened to me personally, like a trip to the zoo or a stay in the hospital; by 'accurately,' I mean the event basically happened the way I think it did."
	Examine the evidence	"I feel I recall my fifth birthday party perfectly, but studies show that people often reconstruct past events inaccurately."
	Analyze assumptions and biases	"I've always assumed that memory is like a tape recorder—perfectly accurate for every moment of my life—but maybe this is just a bias, because it's so reassuring."
	Avoid emotional reasoning	"I really want to believe this memory is true, but that doesn't mean it is."
	Don't oversimplify	"Some of my childhood memories could be accurate, others mistaken, and some partly right and partly wrong."
	Consider other interpretations	"Some 'memories' could be based on what my parents told me later, not on my own recall."
	Tolerate uncertainty	"I may never know for sure whether some of my childhood memories are real or accurate."

NOTE: You will be reading a lot more about the reliability of memory in Chapter 10.

 YOU are about to learn . . .

- the lesson of phrenology for modern psychology.
- how and when psychology became a formal discipline.
- three early schools of psychology.

PSYCHOLOGY'S PAST: FROM THE ARMCHAIR TO THE LABORATORY

Now that you know what psychology is and what it isn't, and why studying it requires critical thinking, let us see how psychology developed into a modern science.

Until the nineteenth century, psychology was not a formal discipline. Of course, most of the great thinkers of history, from Aristotle to Zoroaster, raised questions

On this phrenological "map," notice the tiny space allocated to self-esteem and the large one devoted to cautiousness!

that today would be called psychological. They wanted to know how people take in information through their senses, use information to solve problems, and become motivated to act in brave or villainous ways. They wondered about the elusive nature of emotion, and whether it controls us or is something we can control. Like today's psychologists, they wanted to *describe, predict, understand,* and *modify* behaviour in order to add to human knowledge and increase human happiness. But unlike modern psychologists, scholars of the past did not rely heavily on empirical evidence. Often, their observations were based simply on anecdotes or descriptions of individual cases.

This does not mean that the forerunners of modern psychology were always wrong. On the contrary, they often had insights and made observations that were verified by later work. Hippocrates (c. 460 BCE–377 BCE), the Greek physician known as the founder of modern medicine, observed patients with head injuries and inferred that the brain must be the ultimate source of "our pleasures, joys, laughter, and jests as well as our sorrows, pains, griefs, and tears." And so it is. In the first century AD, the Stoic philosophers observed that people do not become angry or sad or anxious because of actual events, but because of their *explanations* of those events. And so they do. In the seventeenth century, the English philosopher John Locke (1632–1704) argued that the mind works by associating ideas arising from experience, and this notion continues to influence many psychologists today.

But without empirical methods, the forerunners of psychology also committed terrible blunders. A good example comes from the early 1800s, when the theory of **phrenology** (Greek for "study of the mind") became wildly popular in Europe and North America. Inspired by the writings and lectures of Austrian physician Franz Joseph Gall (1758–1828), phrenologists argued that different brain areas accounted for specific character and personality traits, such as "stinginess" and "religiosity." Moreover, they said such traits could be "read" from bumps on the skull. Thieves, for example, supposedly had large bumps above the ears. When phrenologists examined people with "stealing bumps" who were *not* thieves, they explained away this counter-evidence by saying that other bumps on the skull represented positive traits that must be holding the person's thieving impulses in check.

In North America, all sorts of people eagerly sought the services of phrenologists. Parents used them to make decisions about child rearing; schools used them to decide which teachers to hire; young people used them when choosing a career or a mate; and businesses used them to find out which employees were likely to be loyal and honest (Benjamin, 1998). Some phrenologists offered classes or self-study programs for people who wanted to overcome their deficiencies—the forerunners of today's many self-improvement programs and seminars. Enthusiasm for phrenology did not disappear until well into the twentieth century, even though phrenology was a classic pseudoscience—sheer nonsense.

The Birth of Modern Psychology

phrenology   The now discredited theory that different brain areas account for specific character and personality traits, which can be "read" from bumps on the skull.

At about the time that phrenology was peaking in popularity, several pioneering men and women in Europe and North America were starting to study psychological issues using scientific methods. In 1879, the first psychological laboratory was officially established in Leipzig, Germany, by Wilhelm Wundt [VIL-helm Voont]. Wundt (1832–1920) was trained in medicine and philosophy and wrote many volumes on psychology, physiology, natural history, ethics, and logic. But he is especially revered by psychologists because he was the first person to announce (in 1873) that he intended to make psychology a science and because his laboratory was the first to have its results published in a scholarly journal. Although it started out as just a few rooms in an old building, the Leipzig laboratory soon became the place to go for anyone who wanted to become a psychologist. Many of North America's first psychologists got their training there. One of Wundt's students, Mark Baldwin, was appointed at the University of Toronto in 1889 (despite very public and vocal criticism from other academics), and he helped found "modern" psychology in Canada.

Researchers in Wundt's laboratory did not study the entire gamut of topics that modern psychologists do. Most concentrated on sensation, perception, reaction times, imagery, and attention, and avoided learning, personality, and abnormal behaviour. One of Wundt's favourite research methods was to train volunteers to carefully observe, analyze, and describe their own sensations, mental images, and emotional reactions. This was not as easy as it sounds. Wundt's volunteers had to make 10 000 practice observations before they were allowed to participate in an actual study. Once trained, they might take as long as 20 minutes to report what their inner experiences had been during the 1.5-second experiment. The goal was to break behaviour down into its most basic elements, much as a chemist might break down water into hydrogen plus oxygen.

Although Wundt hoped that this introspective method would produce reliable, verifiable results, most psychologists eventually rejected it as too subjective. But Wundt is still usually credited with formally initiating the movement to make psychology a science.

Wilhelm Wundt (1832–1920).

◆ Research
Wilhelm Wundt

Three Early Psychologies

During the early decades of psychology's existence as a formal discipline, three schools of psychological thought became popular. One soon faded, another disappeared as a separate school but continued to influence the field, and the third remains alive today, despite passionate debate about whether it belongs in scientific psychology at all.

STRUCTURALISM. In North America, Wundt's ideas were popularized in somewhat modified form by one of his students, E. B. Titchener (1867–1927), who gave Wundt's approach the name structuralism. Like Wundt, structuralists hoped to analyze sensations, images, and feelings into basic elements. For example, a person might be asked to listen to a metronome clicking and to report exactly what he or she heard. Most people said they perceived a pattern (such as *CLICK click click CLICK click click*), even though the clicks of a metronome are actually all the same. Or a person might be

structuralism   An early psychological approach that emphasized the analysis of immediate experience into basic elements.

asked to break down all the different components of taste when biting into an orange (sweet, tart, wet, and so on).

Despite an intensive program of research, however, structuralism soon went the way of the dinosaur. After you have discovered the building blocks of a particular sensation or image and how they link up, what then? Years after structuralism's demise, Wolfgang Köhler (1959) recalled how he and his colleagues had responded to it as students: "What had disturbed us was . . . the implication that human life, apparently so colourful and so intensely dynamic, is actually a frightful bore."

The structuralists' reliance on introspection by volunteers also got them into trouble. Despite their training, introspectors often produced conflicting reports. When asked what image came to mind when they heard the word *triangle*, most respondents said they imagined a visual image of a form with three sides and three corners, but one person might report a flashing red form with equal angles, whereas another reported a revolving colourless form with one angle larger than the other two. Some people even claimed they could think about a triangle without forming any visual image at all (Boring, 1953). It was hard, therefore, to know what mental attributes of a triangle were basic.

FUNCTIONALISM. Another early approach to scientific psychology, called functionalism, emphasized the function or purpose of behaviour, as opposed to its analysis and description. One of functionalism's leaders was William James (1842–1910), an American philosopher, physician, and psychologist who argued that searching for building blocks of experience, as Wundt and Titchener tried to do, was a waste of time. The brain and the mind are constantly changing, he noted. Permanent ideas—of triangles or anything else—do not appear periodically before the "footlights of consciousness." Attempting to grasp the nature of the mind through introspection, wrote James (1890/1950), is "like seizing a spinning top to catch its motion, or trying to turn up the gas quickly enough to see how the darkness looks."

Whereas the structuralists asked *what* happens when an organism does something, the functionalists asked *how* and *why*. They were inspired in part by the evolutionary theories of British naturalist Charles Darwin (1809–1882). Darwin had argued that a biologist's job is not merely to describe, say, the puffed-out chest of a pigeon or the drab markings of a lizard, but also to figure out how these attributes enhance survival. Do they help the animal attract a mate or hide from its enemies? Similarly, the functionalists wanted to know how specific behaviours and mental processes help a person or animal adapt to the environment, so they looked for underlying causes and practical consequences of these behaviours and processes. Unlike the structuralists, they felt free to pick and choose among many methods, and they broadened the field of psychology to include the study of children, animals, religious experiences, and what James called the "stream of consciousness"—a term still used because it so beautifully describes the way thoughts flow like a river, tumbling over each other in waves, sometimes placid, sometimes turbulent.

As a school of psychology, functionalism, like structuralism, was short-lived. It lacked the kind of precise theory or program of research that wins recruits, and it endorsed the study of consciousness just as that concept was about to fall out of favour. Yet the functionalists' emphasis on the causes and consequences of behaviour was to set the course for psychological science.

PSYCHOANALYSIS. The nineteenth century also saw the development of various psychological therapies. In North America, for example, the wildly popular "Mind Cure" movement lasted from 1830 to 1900; "mind cures" were efforts to correct the "false ideas" that were said to make people anxious, depressed, and unhappy

William James (1842–1910).

◈ Research
Charles Darwin

William James

functionalism An early psychological approach that emphasized the function or purpose of behaviour and consciousness.

(Caplan, 1998; Moskowitz, 2001). The Mind Cure movement was the forerunner of modern cognitive therapies (see Chapter 16).

However, the form of therapy that would have the greatest impact worldwide for much of the twentieth century had its roots in Vienna, Austria. While researchers in Europe and North America were working in their laboratories, struggling to establish psychology as a science, Sigmund Freud (1856–1939), an obscure neurologist, was in his office, listening to his patients' reports of depression, nervousness, and obsessive habits. Freud became convinced that many of his patients' symptoms had mental, not physical, causes. Their distress, he concluded, was due to conflicts and emotional traumas that had occurred in early childhood and that were too threatening to be remembered consciously, such as forbidden sexual feelings for a parent.

Freud argued that conscious awareness is merely the tip of a mental iceberg. Beneath the visible tip, he said, lies the unconscious part of the mind, containing unrevealed wishes, passions, guilty secrets, unspeakable yearnings, and conflicts between desire and duty. Many of these urges and thoughts are sexual or aggressive in nature. We are not aware of them as we go blithely about our daily business, yet they make themselves known—in dreams, slips of the tongue, apparent accidents, and even jokes. Freud (1905a) wrote, "No mortal can keep a secret. If the lips are silent, he chatters with his fingertips; betrayal oozes out of him at every pore."

Freud's ideas were not an overnight sensation; his first book, *The Interpretation of Dreams* (1900/1953), managed to sell only 600 copies in the eight years following its publication. Eventually, however, his ideas evolved into a broad theory of personality and a method of psychotherapy, both of which became known as **psychoanalysis**. Most Freudian concepts were, and still are, rejected by most empirically oriented psychologists, as we will see. But they had a profound influence on the philosophy, literature, and art of the twentieth century, and Freud's name is now as much a household word as Einstein's.

From these early beginnings in philosophy, natural science, and medicine, psychology has grown into a complex discipline encompassing many specialties, perspectives, and methods. Today the field is like a large, sprawling family. The members of this family share common great-grandparents, but some of the cousins have formed alliances, some are quarrelling, and a few are barely speaking to one another.

Sigmund Freud (1856–1939).

◆ **Research**
Sigmund Freud

✳ **Explore**
Timeline of Important Dates in Psychology

psychoanalysis A theory of personality and a method of psychotherapy, originally formulated by Sigmund Freud, that emphasizes unconscious motives and conflicts.

 Make sure psychology's past is still present in your memory by choosing the correct response from each pair of terms in parentheses.

1. Psychology has been a science for more than (2000/135) years.
2. The forerunners of modern psychology depended heavily on (casual observation/ empirical methods).
3. Credit for founding modern psychology is generally given to (William James/ Wilhelm Wundt).
4. Early psychologists who emphasized how behaviour helps an organism adapt to its environment were known as (structuralists/functionalists).
5. The idea that emotional problems spring from unconscious conflicts originated with (the Mind Cure movement/psychoanalysis).

Answers:

1. 135 2. casual observation 3. Wilhelm Wundt 4. functionalists 5. psychoanalysis

quickQUIZ

✓ **Quick Review** on **MyPsychLab**

Donald O. Hebb (1904–1985) argued that all behaviour is the result of physical changes within the nervous system.

YOU are about to learn . . .

◆ the five major perspectives in psychology.
◆ why the psychodynamic perspective is the "thumb on the hand of psychology."
◆ how humanism and feminism have influenced psychology.

PSYCHOLOGY'S PRESENT: BEHAVIOUR, BODY, MIND, AND CULTURE

If you had a noisy, rude, surly neighbour, and you asked a group of psychologists to explain why this person was so miserable, they might give you different answers. Depending on their theoretical perspective, they might cite your neighbour's biological makeup, his belligerent attitude toward the world, the way he was brought up, an environment that encourages his nasty temper, or the influence of his unconscious motives. Modern psychologists tend to examine human behaviour through several lenses.

The Major Psychological Perspectives

The five lenses that predominate in psychology today are the *biological, learning, cognitive, sociocultural,* and *psychodynamic* perspectives. These approaches reflect different questions about human behaviour, different assumptions about how the mind works, and, most important, different ways of explaining why people do what they do.

1 **The biological perspective** focuses on how bodily events affect behaviour, feelings, and thoughts. Researchers such as McGill University's Donald O. Hebb argue that all behavioural and mental phenomena arise as the result of physical activity within the brain (Hebb, 1949). Electrical impulses shoot along the intricate pathways of the nervous system. Hormones course through the bloodstream, telling internal organs to slow down or speed up. Chemical substances flow across the tiny gaps that separate one microscopic brain cell from another. Biological psychologists study how these physical events interact with events in the external environment to produce perceptions, memories, and behaviour.

Researchers in this perspective study how biology affects learning and performance, perceptions of reality, the experience of emotion, and vulnerability to emotional disorder. They study how the mind and body interact in illness and health. They investigate the contributions of genes and other biological factors in the development of abilities and personality traits. And a popular specialty, evolutionary psychology, follows in the tradition of functionalism by focusing on how genetically influenced behaviour that was functional or adaptive during our evolutionary past may be reflected in many of our present behaviours, mental processes, and traits (see Chapter 3). The message of the biological approach is that we cannot really know ourselves if we do not know our bodies.

2 **The learning perspective** is concerned with how the environment and experience affect a person's (or a nonhuman animal's) actions. Within this perspective, *behaviourists* focus on the environmental rewards and punishers that maintain or discourage specific behaviours. Behaviourists do not invoke the mind or mental

biological perspective A psychological approach that emphasizes bodily events and changes associated with actions, feelings, and thoughts.

evolutionary psychology A field of psychology emphasizing evolutionary mechanisms that may help explain human commonalities in cognition, development, emotion, social practices, and other areas of behaviour.

learning perspective A psychological approach that emphasizes how the environment and experience affect a person's or animal's actions; it includes behaviourism and social-cognitive learning theories.

states to explain behaviour. They prefer to stick to what they can observe and measure directly: acts and events taking place in the environment. For example, do you have trouble sticking to a schedule? A behaviourist would analyze the environmental distractions that could help account for this common problem. **Behaviourism** was the dominant school of scientific psychology in North America for nearly half a century, through to the 1960s. *Social-cognitive learning theorists*, on the other hand, combine elements of behaviourism with research on thoughts, values, expectations, and intentions. They believe that people learn not only by adapting their behaviour to the environment, but also by imitating others and by thinking about the events happening around them.

As we will see in other chapters, the learning perspective has many practical applications. Historically, the behaviourists' insistence on precision and objectivity has done much to advance psychology as a science, and learning research in general has given psychology some of its most reliable findings.

3 **The cognitive perspective** emphasizes what goes on in people's heads—how people reason, remember, understand language, solve problems, explain experiences, acquire moral standards, and form beliefs. (The word *cognitive* comes from the Latin for "to know.") A "cognitive revolution" in psychology during the 1970s brought this perspective to the forefront. One of its most important contributions has been to show how people's thoughts and explanations affect their actions, feelings, and choices. Using clever methods to infer mental processes from observable behaviour, cognitive researchers have been able to study phenomena that were once only the stuff of speculation, such as emotions, motivations, and insight. They are designing computer programs that model how humans perform complex tasks, discovering what goes on in the mind of an infant, and identifying types of intelligence not measured by conventional IQ tests. The cognitive approach is one of the strongest forces in psychology, and it has inspired an explosion of research on the intricate workings of the mind.

4 **The sociocultural perspective** focuses on social and cultural forces outside the individual, forces that shape every aspect of behaviour, from how we kiss to what and where we eat. Most of us underestimate the impact of other people, the social context, and cultural rules on nearly everything we do. We are like fish that are unaware they live in water, so obvious is water in their lives. Sociocultural psychologists study the water—the social and cultural environment that people "swim" in every day.

Within this perspective, *social psychologists* focus on social rules and roles, how groups affect attitudes and behaviour, why people obey authority, and how each of us is affected by other people—spouses, lovers, friends, bosses, parents, and strangers. *Cultural psychologists* examine how cultural rules and values—both explicit and unspoken—affect people's development, behaviour, and feelings. They might study how culture influences people's willingness to help a stranger in distress, or how it influences what people do when they are angry. Because human beings are social animals who are profoundly affected by their different cultural worlds, the sociocultural perspective has made psychology a more representative and rigorous discipline.

Ask Questions; Be Willing to Wonder

What makes us who we are? Psychologists often approach this question differently, depending on whether they take a biological, learning, cognitive, sociocultural, or psychodynamic perspective. Today, however, many researchers are asking a better question: How do the many kinds of influences on us combine and interact to make us who we are?

behaviourism   An approach to psychology that emphasizes the study of observable behaviour and the role of the environment as a determinant of behaviour.

cognitive perspective   A psychological approach that emphasizes mental processes in perception, memory, language, problem solving, and other areas of behaviour.

sociocultural perspective
A psychological approach that emphasizes social and cultural influences on behaviour.

psychodynamic perspective
A psychological approach that emphasizes unconscious dynamics within the individual, such as inner forces, conflicts, or the movement of instinctual energy.

5　The psychodynamic perspective deals with unconscious dynamics within the individual, such as inner forces, conflicts, or instinctual energy. Its origins are in Freud's theory of psychoanalysis, but many other psychodynamic theories now exist. Psychodynamic psychologists try to dig below the surface of a person's behaviour to get to its unconscious roots; they think of themselves as archeologists of the mind.

Psychodynamic psychology is the thumb on the hand of psychology—connected to the other fingers, but also set apart from them because it differs radically from the other approaches in its language, methods, and standards of acceptable evidence. Although some psychological scientists are doing empirical studies of psychodynamic concepts, many others believe that psychodynamic approaches belong in philosophy or literature rather than in academic psychology. You are unlikely to find psychoanalysis mentioned much in mainstream journals of psychological science (Robins, Gosling, & Craik, 1999). Outside empirical psychology, however, many psychotherapists, novelists, and lay people are attracted to the psychodynamic emphasis on such grand psychological issues as relations between the sexes, the power of sexuality, and the universal fear of death. Later in this book, we will candidly discuss the many controversies surrounding psychodynamic ideas.

Review 1.2 summarizes these five perspectives and shows you how they might be applied to a concrete issue: the problem of violence. See if you can apply these perspectives to another issue of your choosing.

Other Influential Movements in Psychology

Throughout psychology's history, various movements and intellectual trends have emerged that do not fit neatly into any of the major perspectives. In the 1960s, proponents of humanist psychology rejected the two dominant psychological approaches of the time: psychoanalysis and behaviourism. Humanists regarded psychoanalysis, with its emphasis on dangerous sexual and aggressive impulses, as too pessimistic a view of human nature, one that overlooked human resilience and the capacity for joy. And humanists regarded behaviourism, with its emphasis on observable acts, as too mechanical and "mindless" a view of human nature, one that ignored what really matters to most people—their uniquely human hopes and aspirations. In the humanists' view, human behaviour is not completely determined by either unconscious conflicts or the environment. People are capable of free will and therefore have the ability to make more of themselves than either psychoanalysts or behaviourists would predict. The goal of humanist psychology was, and still is, to help people express themselves creatively and achieve their full potential.

Although humanism is no longer a dominant movement in psychology, it has had considerable influence both inside and outside the field. Many psychologists across all perspectives embrace some humanist ideas, although most regard humanism as a philosophy of life rather than a systematic approach to psychology. Further, many topics raised by the humanists, such as creativity, joy, humour, and courage, are now being studied by scientific psychologists from many fields. For example, a contemporary research specialty known as *positive psychology* focuses on the qualities that enable people to be happy, optimistic, and resilient in times of stress (Gable & Haidt, 2005; Seligman & Csikszentmihaly, 2000). And humanism has had a direct influence on psychotherapy and the human potential and self-help movements.

humanist psychology　A psychological approach that emphasizes personal growth and the achievement of human potential, rather than the scientific understanding and assessment of behaviour.

feminist psychology　A psychological approach that analyzes the influence of social inequities on gender relations and on the behaviour of the two sexes.

REViEW 1.2

Five Major Psychological Perspectives

	Perspective	Major Topics of Study	Sample Finding on Violence
	Biological	The nervous system, hormones, brain chemistry, heredity, evolutionary influences	Brain damage caused by birth complications or child abuse might incline some people toward violence.
	Learning	Environment and experience	
	Behavioural	Environmental determinants of observable behaviour	Violence increases when it pays off.
	Social-Cognitive	Environmental influences, observation and imitation, beliefs and values	Violent role models can influence some children to behave aggressively.
	Cognitive	Thinking, memory, language, problem solving, perceptions	Violent people are often quick to perceive provocation and insult.
	Sociocultural	Social and cultural contexts	
	Social Psychology	Social rules and roles, groups, relationships	People are often more aggressive in a crowd than they would be on their own.
	Cultural Psychology	Cultural norms, values, expectations	Cultures based on herding rather than agriculture tend to train boys to be aggressive.
	Psychodynamic	Unconscious thoughts, desires, conflicts	A man who murders prostitutes may have unconscious conflicts about his mother and about sexuality.

Another important movement, which emerged in the early 1970s, was feminist psychology. As women began to enter psychology in greater numbers, they documented evidence of a pervasive bias in the research methods used and in the very questions that researchers had been asking (Bem, 1993; Crawford & Marecek, 1989; Hare-Mustin & Marecek, 1990). They noted that many studies used only men as participants—and usually only young, white, middle-class men, at that—and they showed why it was often inappropriate to generalize to everyone else from such a narrow research base. They spurred the growth of research on topics that had long been ignored in psychology, including menstruation, motherhood, the dynamics of power and sexuality in relationships, definitions of masculinity and femininity, gender roles, and sexist attitudes. They critically examined the male bias in psychotherapy, starting with Freud's own case studies (Hare-Mustin, 1991). And they analyzed the social consequences of

Anxiety is a common problem. To test your understanding of the five major perspectives in psychology, match each possible explanation of anxiety with a perspective listed beside the explanations.

1. Anxious people often think about the future in distorted ways.
2. Anxiety is due to forbidden, unconscious desires.
3. Anxiety symptoms often bring hidden rewards, such as being excused from exams.
4. Excessive anxiety can be caused by a chemical imbalance.
5. A national emphasis on competition and success promotes anxiety about failure.

a. learning
b. psychodynamic
c. sociocultural
d. biological
e. cognitive

Answers:

1.e 2.b 3.a 4.d 5.c

psychological findings, showing how research has often been used to justify the lower status of women and other disadvantaged groups.

Feminist psychology greatly advanced efforts to make psychology the study of all human beings, and other groups have made similar contributions. In 1976, black psychologist Robert Guthrie, in *Even the Rat Was White*, wrote a searing and influential indictment of racism in psychological research. Since the 1970s, African-American, Latino, and Asian psychologists, gay and lesbian psychologists, and psychologists with disabilities have hugely expanded the theoretical and empirical vistas of psychology, as we will see throughout this book.

 YOU are about to learn . . .

◆ why you can't assume that all therapists are psychologists, or that all psychologists are therapists.
◆ the three major areas of psychologists' professional activities.
◆ the difference between a clinical psychologist and a psychiatrist.

WHAT PSYCHOLOGISTS DO

Now you know the main viewpoints that guide psychologists in their work. But what do psychologists actually do with their time between breakfast and dinner?

To most people, the word *psychologist* conjures up an image of a therapist listening intently while a client, perhaps stretched out on a couch, pours forth his or her troubles. Many psychologists do in fact fit this image (though chairs are more common than couches these days). Many others, however, do not. The professional activities of psychologists generally fall into three broad categories: (1) teaching and doing research in colleges and universities; (2) providing health or mental-health services, often referred to as **psychological practice**; and (3) conducting research or applying its findings in nonacademic settings such as business, sports, government, law, and the military (see Review 1.3 on p. 25). Some psychologists

✳ **Explore**
Psychologists at Work

psychological practice Providing health or mental-health services.

REViEW 1.3

What Is a Psychologist?

Not all psychologists do clinical work. Many do research, teach, work in business, or consult. The professional activities of psychologists with doctorates fall into three general categories.

Academic/Research Psychologists	Clinical Psychologists	Psychologists in Industry, Law, or Other Settings
Specialize in areas of pure or applied research, such as:	Do psychotherapy and sometimes research; may work in any of these settings:	Do research or serve as consultants to institutions on, for example:
Human development	Private practice	Sports
Psychometrics (testing)	Mental-health clinics	Consumer issues
Health	General hospitals	Advertising
Education	Mental hospitals	Organizational problems
Industrial/organizational psychology	Research laboratories	Environmental issues
Physiological psychology	Colleges and universities	Public policy
Sensation and perception		Opinion polls
Design and use of technology		Military training
		Animal behaviour
		Legal issues

move flexibly across these areas. A researcher might also provide counselling services in a mental-health setting, such as a clinic or a hospital; a university professor might teach, do research, and serve as a consultant in legal cases.

Psychological Research

Most psychologists who do research have doctoral degrees (PhDs, or EdDs, doctorates in education). Some, seeking knowledge for its own sake, work in **basic psychology**, doing "pure" research. Others, concerned with the practical uses of knowledge, work in **applied psychology**. The two approaches are complementary: Applied psychology has direct relevance to human problems, but without basic psychology there would be little knowledge to apply. A psychologist doing basic research might ask "How does peer pressure influence people's attitudes and behaviour?" An applied psychologist might ask "How can knowledge about peer pressure be used to reduce binge drinking in college and university?"

Research psychology is the aspect of psychology least recognized or understood by the public. Ludy Benjamin (2003), bemoaning the fact that psychology has never had a United States postage stamp commemorating the discipline or its founders (unlike dozens of other fields, including poultry farming and truck driving), notes that the public "has minimal understanding of psychology as a science and even less appreciation for what psychological scientists do" or how psychological research contributes to human welfare.

basic psychology   The study of psychological issues in order to seek knowledge for its own sake rather than for its practical application.

applied psychology   The study of psychological issues that have direct practical significance; also, the application of psychological findings.

We hope that by the time you finish this book, you will have a greater appreciation for what research psychologists do and how their work contributes to human welfare. Here are just a few of the major nonclinical specialties in psychology:

◆ *Experimental psychologists* conduct laboratory studies of learning, motivation, emotion, sensation and perception, physiology, and cognition. Do not be misled by the term *experimental*, though; other psychologists also do experiments.

◆ *Educational psychologists* study psychological principles that explain learning and search for ways to improve educational systems. Their interests range from the application of findings on memory and thinking to the use of rewards to encourage achievement.

◆ *Developmental psychologists* study how people change and grow over time—physically, mentally, and socially. In the past, their focus was mainly on childhood but many now study adolescence, young adulthood, the middle years, or old age.

◆ *Industrial/organizational psychologists* study behaviour in the workplace. They are concerned with group decision making, employee morale, work motivation, productivity, job stress, personnel selection, marketing strategies, equipment design, and many other issues.

◆ *Psychometric psychologists* design and evaluate tests of mental abilities, aptitudes, interests, and personality. Nearly all of us have had firsthand experience with one or more of these tests in school or at work.

Psychological Practice

Psychological practitioners—whose goal is to understand and improve people's physical and mental health—work in mental hospitals, general hospitals, clinics, schools, counselling centres, and private practice. Since the late 1970s, the proportion of psychologists who are practitioners has steadily increased; practitioners now account for more than half of all psychologists in Canada (Lefton, Boyes, & Ogden, 2000).

Some practitioners are *counselling psychologists*, who generally help people deal with problems of everyday life, such as test anxiety, family conflicts, or low job motivation. Others are *school psychologists*, who work with parents, teachers, and students to enhance students' performance and resolve emotional difficulties. The majority, however, are *clinical psychologists*, who diagnose, treat, and study mental or emotional problems. Clinical psychologists are trained to do psychotherapy with severely disturbed people, as well as with those who are simply troubled or unhappy or who want to learn to handle their problems better.

In most provinces, psychological services can be provided by individuals with master's degrees in psychology. However, most clinical psychologists have a PhD, some have an EdD, and a smaller but growing number have a PsyD (doctorate in psychology, pronounced "sy-dee"). Clinical psychologists typically do four or five years of graduate work in psychology, plus at least a one-year internship under the direction of a practising psychologist. Clinical programs leading to a PhD or EdD are usually designed to prepare a person both as a scientist and as a clinical practitioner; they require completion of a dissertation, a major scholarly project (usually involving research) that contributes to knowledge in the field. Currently, no programs lead to a PsyD in Canada. However, this type of program is growing in popularity in the United States. It tends to focus on professional practice and does not usually require a research dissertation, although it typically requires the student to complete a major study, literature review, or other scholarly project. Although PsyD degrees are not yet common in Canada, they are recognized by most professional regulatory bodies, and many individuals with PsyD degrees currently practise clinical psychology in Canada. Following the Canadian Psychological Association's (CPA) report supporting the development of PsyD training programs in Canada (Robinson, 1988), Memorial University became the first in this country to offer a PsyD.

People often confuse the term *clinical psychologist* with three other terms: *psychotherapist*, *psychoanalyst*, and *psychiatrist*. But these terms mean different things:

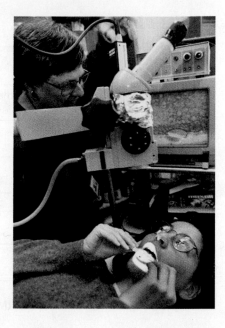

- ◆ A **psychotherapist** is simply anyone who does any kind of psychotherapy. The term is not legally regulated; in fact, people can say that they are "therapists" of one sort or another without having any training at all.

- ◆ A **psychoanalyst** is a person who practises one particular form of therapy: psychoanalysis. To call yourself a psychoanalyst, you must obtain specialized training at a psychoanalytic institute and undergo extensive psychoanalysis yourself. At one time, admission to a psychoanalytic institute required an MD or a PhD, but this is no longer true; clinical social workers with master's degrees, and even interested lay people, are now often admitted.

- ◆ A **psychiatrist** is a medical doctor (MD) who has completed a three-year residency in psychiatry to learn how to diagnose and treat mental disorders under the supervision of more experienced physicians. Like some clinical psychologists, some psychiatrists do research on mental problems instead of, or in addition to, working with patients. In private practice, psychiatrists may treat any kind of emotional disorder; in hospitals, they treat the most severe disorders, such as major depression and schizophrenia. Although psychiatrists and clinical psychologists often do similar work, psychiatrists, because of their medical training, are more likely to focus on possible biological causes of mental disorders and often

treat these problems with medication. They can write prescriptions, but they may also have some training in current psychological theories and methods (Luhrmann, 2000).

Other mental-health professionals include licensed clinical social workers (LCSWs) and marriage, family, and child counsellors (MFCCs). These professionals ordinarily treat general problems in adjustment and family conflicts rather than severe mental disturbance, although their work may also bring them into contact with people who have serious problems—violent delinquents, people with drug addictions, sex offenders, or individuals involved in domestic violence or child abuse. Licensing requirements vary from region to region, but usually include a master's degree in psychology or social work and one or two years of supervised experience. (For a summary of the types of psychotherapists and the training they receive, see Review 1.4.) As if this weren't complicated enough, there are thousands of counsellors who specialize in treating all kinds of problems, from sexual abuse to alcoholism; there is, however, no uniform set of standards regulating their training. Some may have nothing more than a brief "certification" course.

Some psychologists are researchers, others are practitioners, and some are both. At the top, psychological scientist Linda Bartoshuk uses technology to study how the anatomy of the tongue influences the way we experience different tastes. At the bottom, a clinical psychologist helps a couple in therapy.

psychotherapist Unregulated person who does any kind of psychotherapy.

psychoanalyst A person who practises psychoanalysis, and who has obtained specialized training at a psychoanalytic institute and undergone extensive psychoanalysis personally.

psychiatrist A medical doctor (MD) who has completed a three-year residency in psychiatry to learn how to diagnose and treat mental disorders under the supervision of more experienced physicians.

REVieW 1.4

Types of Psychotherapists

Just as not all psychologists are psychotherapists, not all psychotherapists are clinical psychologists. Here are the major terms used to refer to mental-health professionals:

Psychotherapist	A person who does psychotherapy; may have anything from no degree to an advanced professional degree; the term is unregulated.
Clinical psychologist	Diagnoses, treats, and/or studies mental and emotional problems, both mild and severe; has a PhD, an EdD, or a PsyD.
Psychoanalyst	Practises psychoanalysis; has specific training in this approach after an advanced degree (usually, but not always, an MD or a PhD); may treat any kind of emotional disorder or pathology.
Psychiatrist	Does work similar to that of a clinical psychologist, but is likely to take a more biological approach; has a medical degree (MD) with a specialty in psychiatry.
Licensed clinical social worker (LCSW); marriage, family, and child counsellor (MFCC)	Typically treats common individual and family problems, but may also deal with more serious problems such as addiction or abuse. Licensing requirements vary, but generally has at least an MA in psychology or social work.

Many research psychologists, and some practitioners, are worried about the increase in the number of counsellors and psychotherapists who are unschooled in research methods and the empirical findings of psychology, and who use unvalidated therapy techniques (Beutler, 2000; Lilienfeld, Lynn, & Lohr, 2003). Critics trace this development in part to the rise of freestanding professional schools, which are not affiliated with any university. Some of these schools offer a quality education, but others do not. Although the verbal Graduate Record Exam scores of applicants have been falling for several decades, acceptance rates in doctoral psychology programs have skyrocketed since the 1970s and 1980s—and the biggest rise has been in clinical programs, from the 4–6% range in the 1970s to 21% in 2003 (Norcross, Kohout, & Wicherski, 2005). In a review of the evidence on graduate training in clinical psychology, Donald Peterson (2003) found that the poorer-quality programs are turning out more and more ill-prepared graduates. "To deny an increased likelihood of incompetent practice by insufficiently talented, poorly trained psychologists," Peterson writes, "defies all reason."

Many practitioners, on the other hand, argue that psychotherapy is an art and that training in research methods is largely irrelevant to the work they do with clients. In Chapter 16, we will return to the important issue of the widening gap in training and attitudes between scientists and many therapists. These differences contributed to the formation of the Association for Psychological Science (APS). The widening gap between scientists and

ScienceCartoonsPlus.com

Because not all therapists are well educated about psychological findings, consumers should ask about a potential therapist's training and credentials.

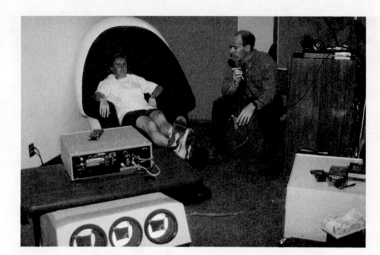 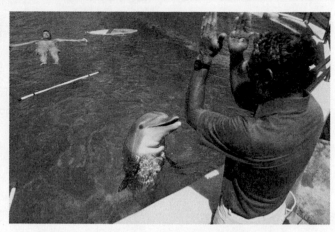

Psychologists work in all sorts of settings, from classrooms to courtrooms. On the left, sports psychologist Sean McCain helps an Olympic athlete relax and rehearse mentally what she would do physically during an actual athletic event. On the right, Louis Herman studies a dolphin's ability to understand an artificial language consisting of hand signals. In response to the gestural sequence "person" and "over," the dolphin will leap over the person in the pool.

practitioners, along with increased demands by insurers for evidence that psychotherapy is demonstrably effective, has motivated several prominent clinical psychologists to call for evidence-based treatment and collaboration between researchers and clinicians, in hopes of bridging the gap and improving patient care (Kazdin, 2008).

Regulation of Psychological Research, Training, and Practice in Canada

In 1939, the Canadian Psychological Association (CPA) was formed. At that time, its main purpose was to ensure that psychology in Canada could contribute effectively to the war effort. Since then, its mandate has broadened considerably. It now serves to help advance psychological research, promote and regulate psychological education, and support the practice of psychology in Canada. The CPA promotes research by publishing several scholarly journals (such as *Canadian Psychology* and the *Canadian Journal of Experimental Psychology*) and sponsoring conferences to promote the exchange of scientific information. Its regulation of psychological education is accomplished in part through its accreditation of clinical psychology graduate programs across the country.

Despite its role in regulating education in psychology, the CPA is not a professional regulatory body for psychological researchers or practitioners. As you will see in the following chapter, the ethical and other guidelines that must be followed by research psychologists are determined by other regulatory bodies. Individuals who wish to offer psychological services in Canada need not seek membership with the CPA, nor do they need to be doctoral graduates of a CPA-accredited program. Instead, Canada's 1982 *Constitution Act* stipulates that regulation of psychological practice is a responsibility of the province, and each province has its own legislation and sanctioned body to regulate psychological services. A few provinces (such as Ontario, Manitoba, and British Columbia) require that individuals who call themselves "psychologists" possess a doctoral degree in psychology. People with master's degrees can still register with the provincial regulatory body and provide psychological services, but they are referred to as "psychological associates," according to the provincial regulations.

quickQUIZ

✔• Quick Review on **MyPsychLab**

Can you match the specialties on the left with their defining credentials and approaches on the right?

1. psychotherapist
2. psychiatrist
3. clinical psychologist
4. research psychologist
5. psychoanalyst

a. Is trained in a therapeutic approach started by Freud
b. Has a PhD, PsyD, or EdD, and does research on, or psychotherapy for, mental-health problems
c. May have any credential, or none
d. Has an advanced degree (usually a PhD) and does applied or basic research
e. Has an MD; tends to take a medical approach to mental-health problems

Answers:

1. c 2. e 3. b 4. d 5. a

Psychology in the Community

During the second half of the twentieth century, psychology expanded rapidly in terms of scholars, publications, and specialties, and today the field is experiencing a "knowledge explosion" (Adair & Vohra, 2003). Psychology's largest professional organization, the American Psychological Association (APA), has 53 divisions. Some represent major fields such as developmental psychology or physiological psychology. Others represent specific research or professional interests, such as the psychology of women, the psychology of men, ethnic minority issues, sports, the arts, environmental concerns, gay and lesbian issues, peace, psychology and the law, and health.

As psychology has grown, psychologists have found ways to contribute to their communities in about as many fields as you can think of. They consult with companies to improve worker satisfaction and productivity. They establish programs to improve race relations and reduce ethnic tensions. They advise commissions on how pollution and noise affect mental health. They do rehabilitation training for people who are physically or mentally disabled. They assist the police in emergencies involving hostages or disturbed persons. They educate judges and juries about eyewitness testimony. They conduct public-opinion surveys. They run suicide-prevention hotlines. They advise zoos on the care and training of animals. They help coaches improve the athletic performance of their teams. And on and on. Is it any wonder that people are a little fuzzy about what a psychologist is?

BIOLOGY, CULTURE, and *Psychology*

Beyond the Borders

The differences we have described among psychological perspectives and specialties have produced many passionate arguments. Not all psychologists, however, feel they must swear allegiance to one approach or another. Indeed, there is a growing trend in psychology to cross the borders that have traditionally divided one specialty from another. This trend has been fuelled by two developments. One is a revolution in our understanding of biology's influence on behaviour. Neuropsychologists are now studying the workings of the brain and its influence on emotions and behaviour. Cognitive psychologists are looking at the neurological aspects of thinking, decision making, and problem solving. Social psychologists have taken an interest in the brain and have even developed a new specialty called "social neuroscience." Clinical scientists are examining the separate and combined effects of medication and psychotherapy in the treatment of psychological disorders. Behavioural geneticists are documenting the contributions of genetics to everything from the origins of personality to the origins of mental illness. Indeed, researchers who study almost any important phenomenon—aggression, anger, love, sexuality, child development, aging, prejudice, war—often now do so by combining psychological findings and biological ones. We will be covering much of the new biological research throughout this book, and, in most chapters, the heading "Biology and . . ." will alert you to discussions of some exciting, cutting-edge findings that have resulted from these efforts.

The second major development is that psychologists are increasingly looking outward to culture as well as inward to biology. They are documenting the many ways in which culture and ethnicity shape and influence much of what we do. Developmental psychologists are looking at culture's impact on mental, social, and linguistic development. Cognitive psychologists are studying cultural influences on achievement, problem solving, and test performance. Social psychologists are examining how a culture's norms and history affect rates of aggression and cooperation. Clinical researchers are exploring how the cultural backgrounds of therapists and clients affect the bond between them and the ultimate success of psychotherapy. Psychologists studying sensation are discovering how culture affects which tastes and smells delight or disgust us. Accordingly, throughout this book you will find a heading called "Culture and . . . ," which will alert you to some of the most exciting results from research incorporating culture.

The modern field of psychology is like a giant mosaic made up of many fragments, yielding a rich, multicoloured psychological portrait. Psychologists may argue about which part of the portrait is most important, but they also have much in common. All psychological scientists, whatever their specialty, believe in the importance of gathering empirical evidence instead of relying on hunches. And one thing will always unite psychologists: a fascination with the unending mysteries of human behaviour and the human mind. If you too have wondered what makes people tick; if you love a mystery and want to know not only who did it but also why they did it; if you are willing to reconsider what you think you think . . . then you are in the right course. We invite you now to step into the world of psychology, the discipline that dares to explore the most complex topic on earth: *you*.

✳ Explore
Diversity in Psychological Inquiry

Race and Ethnicity in Psychological Inquiry

Are you ready to have some light shed on the mysteries of human behaviour? Then keep reading!

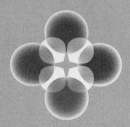

Psychology Can Help You Get Better Grades

How can you use psychology to improve your grades? Do you remember at the beginning of the chapter where we discussed what psychology is and how it is concerned with behaviour and mental processes? Well, part of psychology studies memory strategies that can help you understand course material, absorb it thoroughly as you study, and successfully retrieve it when you need it. Ideally, these strategies will help you with taking tests and with applying this material during everyday life. So what are you waiting for? Go make psychology work for you!

Read, Recite, Review

Reading is not enough. The types of encoding we discuss in more detail in Chapter 10 (memory), such as *elaborate encoding* and *deep processing,* are useful because they force you to be an active rather than a passive learner. Many students believe that the best way to study for an exam is to read and reread a textbook passage until they think that they've "got it." This passive strategy feels intuitively right, but it is actually much less effective than actively rehearsing and recalling the material. In the *read-recite-review strategy,* you read the passage, close the book, hide your notes, write down (or say out loud) everything you can recall, and then review what you've read to see if you understood and remember the information. In a series of experiments, researchers compared this strategy with simply rereading and taking notes. Participants took free recall tests on the material, answered multiple-choice questions, and took short-answer tests right after studying and again a week later. The active read-recite-review strategy was the hands-down winner (McDaniel, Howard, & Einstein, 2009).

Retrieval Practice

Most students define "learning" as the ability to retrieve the correct answer to a question from memory. But then what? Once retrieved, say, for an exam, does that answer stay put or vanish quickly like steam on a bathroom mirror? Cognitive psychologists have found that *retrieval practice* is necessary if a memory is going to undergo consolidation and therefore remain available for a long time—even after your course is over. In a series of experiments in which students learned words in foreign languages, once a student had learned a word it was (a) repeatedly studied but dropped from further testing, (b) repeatedly tested but dropped from further studying, or (c) dropped from studying and testing. To the surprise of the students themselves, who were completely unable to predict how they would do on the tests, studying after learning had no effect on their subsequent ability to recall the foreign words. But repeated testing (i.e., practice in repeatedly retrieving the words from memory) had a large, significant benefit (Karpicke & Roediger, 2008). So when your professors (and your textbook authors) want to keep quizzing you, why, it's only for your own good. . . .

Mnemonics

In addition to using elaborative rehearsal, deep processing, strategies such as read-recite-review, and retrieval practice, people who want to give their powers of memory a boost sometimes use mnemonics [neh-MON-iks], formal strategies and tricks for encoding, storing, and retaining information. (Mnemosyne, pronounced neh-MOZ-eh-nee, was the ancient Greek goddess of memory. Can you remember her?) Some mnemonics take the form of easily memorized rhymes (e.g., "Thirty days hath September/April, June, and November..."). Others use formulas (e.g., "Please never, never, never question our mother's singing and baking" for the names of the provinces from east to west). Still others use visual images or word associations. The best mnemonics force you to encode material actively and thoroughly. They may also reduce the amount of information by chunking it, which is why, in ads, many companies use words for their phone numbers instead of unmemorable numbers ("1-888-GOT-JUNK").

Apply Your Learning

Add meaning to the material you are learning by applying it to your own experiences. The more meaningful the material, the more likely it is to link up with information already in long-term memory. Meaningfulness also reduces the number of chunks of information you have to learn. Common ways of adding meaning include making up a story about the material, thinking of examples, and forming visual images. If you are trying to remember a difficult concept in a chapter, you might make the concept meaningful by thinking of an example from your own life.

Avoid Cramming

We recommend that you take your time when studying. Leisurely learning, spread out over several sessions, usually produces better results than harried cramming (although reviewing material just before a test can be helpful). In terms of hours spent, "distributed" (spaced) learning sessions are more efficient than "massed" ones. In other words, three separate one-hour study sessions may result in more retention than one session of three hours. Remember, only moderate amounts of stress may help memory; thus, keeping study time distributed may reduce stress associated with studying to a moderate level.

Also take time off from studying. If possible, minimize interference by using study breaks for rest or recreation. Sleep is the ultimate way to reduce interference. In a classic study, students who slept for eight hours after learning lists of nonsense syllables retained them better than students who went about their usual business (Jenkins & Dallenbach, 1924). Sleep is not always possible, of course, but periodic mental relaxation usually is.

Whatever strategies you use, you will find that active learning produces more comprehension and better retention than does passive reading or listening. The mind does not gobble up information automatically; you must make the material digestible. Even then, you should not expect to remember everything you read or hear. Nor should you want to. Piling up facts without distinguishing the important from the trivial is just confusing.

Popular books and podcasts that promise a "perfect," "photographic" memory, or "instant recall" of everything you learn, fly in the face of what psychologists know about how the mind operates. Our advice: Forget them. The fastest route to a good memory is to follow the principles suggested by the findings in this section.

SUMMARY

PSYCHOLOGY, PSEUDOSCIENCE, AND POPULAR OPINION

◆ *Psychology* is the discipline concerned with behaviour and mental processes and how they are affected by an organism's external and internal environment. Psychology's methods and reliance on *empirical evidence* distinguish it from pseudoscience and "psychobabble." An introductory psychology course can correct many misconceptions about human behaviour.

◆ Psychologists have many pseudoscientific competitors, such as astrologers and psychics. But when put to the test, the claims and predictions of these competitors turn out to be meaningless or just plain wrong. Psychobabble is appealing because it confirms our beliefs and prejudices; in contrast, psychology often challenges them, although it also seeks to extend our understanding of familiar facts.

THINKING CRITICALLY AND CREATIVELY ABOUT PSYCHOLOGY

◆ One benefit of studying psychology is the development of *critical-thinking* skills and attitudes. Critical thinking helps people evaluate competing findings on psychological issues that are personally and socially important.

◆ The critical thinker asks questions, defines terms clearly, examines the evidence, analyzes assumptions and biases, avoids emotional reasoning, avoids oversimplification, considers alternative interpretations, and tolerates uncertainty. Critical thinking is an evolving process rather than a once-and-for-all accomplishment.

PSYCHOLOGY'S PAST: FROM THE ARMCHAIR TO THE LABORATORY

◆ Psychology's forerunners made some valid observations and had useful insights, but without rigorous empirical methods they also made serious errors in the description and explanation of behaviour, as in the case of *phrenology*.

◆ The official founder of scientific psychology was Wilhelm Wundt, who formally established the first psychological laboratory in 1879, in Leipzig, Germany. His work led to *structuralism*, the first of many approaches to the field. Structuralism emphasized the analysis of immediate experience into basic elements. It was soon abandoned, in part because of its reliance on *introspection*.

◆ Another early approach, *functionalism*, was inspired in part by the evolutionary theories of Charles Darwin; it emphasized the purpose of behaviour. One of its leading proponents was William James. Functionalism, too, did not last long as a distinct school of psychology, but it greatly affected the course of psychological science.

◆ Psychology as a method of psychotherapy has roots in Sigmund Freud's theory of *psychoanalysis*, which emphasizes unconscious causes of mental and emotional problems.

PSYCHOLOGY'S PRESENT: BEHAVIOUR, BODY, MIND, AND CULTURE

◆ Several points of view predominate today in psychology. The *biological perspective* emphasizes bodily events associated with actions, thoughts, and feelings, and also genetic contributions to behaviour. Within this perspective, a popular new specialty, *evolutionary psychology*, is following in the footsteps of functionalism. The *learning perspective* emphasizes how the environment and a person's history affect behaviour; within this perspective, *behaviourists* reject mentalistic explanations, and *social-cognitive learning theorists* combine elements of behaviourism with the study of thoughts, values, and intentions. The *cognitive perspective* emphasizes mental processes in perception, problem solving, belief formation, and other human activities. The *sociocultural perspective* explores how social contexts and cultural rules affect an individual's beliefs and behaviour. And the *psychodynamic perspective*, which originated with Freud's theory of psychoanalysis, emphasizes unconscious motives, conflicts, and desires; it differs greatly from the other approaches in its methods and standards of evidence.

◆ Not all approaches to psychology fit neatly into one of the five major perspectives. For example, two important movements, *humanist psychology* and *feminist psychology*, have influenced the questions researchers ask, the methods they use, and their awareness of biases in the field. A contemporary research specialty called *positive psychology* follows in the tradition of humanism by focusing on the positive aspects of human behaviour.

WHAT PSYCHOLOGISTS DO

◆ Psychologists do research and teach in colleges and universities; provide mental-health services (*psychological practice*); and conduct research and apply findings in a wide variety of nonacademic settings. *Applied psychology* is concerned with the practical uses of psychological knowledge. *Basic psychology* is concerned with knowledge for its own sake. Among the many psychological specialties are experimental, educational, developmental, industrial and organizational, psychometric, counselling, school, and clinical psychology.

◆ *Psychotherapist* is an unregulated term for anyone who does therapy, including persons who have no credentials or training at all. Licensed therapists differ according to their training and approach. *Clinical psychologists* have a PhD, an EdD, or a PsyD; *psychiatrists* have an MD; *psychoanalysts* are trained in psychoanalytic institutes; and licensed clinical social workers, counsellors with various specialties, and marriage, family, and child counsellors may have a variety of postgraduate degrees. Many psychologists are concerned about an increase in poorly trained psychotherapists who lack credentials or a firm understanding of research methods and findings.

BIOLOGY, CULTURE, AND PSYCHOLOGY: BEYOND THE BORDERS

◆ Many, if not most, psychologists draw on more than one school of psychology. Indeed, there is a growing trend in psychology to cross the borders that have traditionally divided one specialty from another, a trend encouraged by increased interest in biological and cultural influences on behaviour.

◆ Although psychologists differ in their perspectives and goals, psychological scientists, whatever their specialty, generally agree on which methods of study are acceptable, and all psychologists are united by their fascination with the mysteries of behaviour.

MyPsychLab

Visit **www.mypsychlab.com** to help you get the best grade!
Test your knowledge and grasp difficult concepts through

• Custom study plans: See where you are strong and where you go wrong

• Interactive simulations

• Video and audio clips

KEY TERMS

Use this list to check your understanding of terms and people in this chapter. If you have trouble with a term, you can find it on the page listed.

empirical   *3*

psychology   *4*

psychobabble   *4*

critical thinking   *7*

Occam's Razor   *13*

phrenology   *16*

structuralism   *17*

functionalism   *18*

psychoanalysis   *19*

biological perspective   *20*

evolutionary psychology   *20*

learning perspective   *20*

behaviourism   *21*

cognitive perspective   *21*

sociocultural perspective   *21*

psychodynamic perspective   *21*

humanist psychology   *22*

feminist psychology   *22*

psychological practice   *24*

basic psychology   *25*

applied psychology   *25*

psychotherapist   *27*

psychoanalyst   *27*

psychiatrist   *27*

2 HOW PSYCHOLOGISTS DO RESEARCH

ASK QUESTIONS . . . be willing to WONDER

- If you want to be a psychologist so that you can help people, why in the world do you need to study statistics and research methods?

- If you hear that TV watching is linked to hyperactivity, can you say which causes which?

- How could you find out whether driving while talking on a cellphone is dangerous?

- Why do psychologists study animals—the nonhuman kind?

Suppose that you are the parent of a nine-year-old boy who has been diagnosed as autistic. Your child lives in his own private world, cut off from normal social interaction. He does not speak, and he rarely looks you in the eye. Sometimes he spends hours rocking back and forth, and occasionally, in frustration, he does self-destructive things, like poking pencils in his ears. He has never been able to function in a public-school classroom.

You are ecstatic, then, when you hear about a new technique called "facilitated communication (FC)," which promises to release your child from his mental prison. According to proponents of this technique, when autistic children are placed in front of a keyboard and an adult "facilitator" gently places a hand over the child's hand or forearm, children who have never used words are suddenly able to peck out complete sentences, answer questions, and divulge their thoughts. One child reportedly typed, "I amn not a utistivc on thje typ" (I am not autistic on the typewriter). Some children, through their facilitators, have supposedly even mastered high-school-level subjects or have written poetry of astonishing beauty. The fee is steep, but it certainly seems worth it.

Or is it?

The situation we have described is not hypothetical; thousands of hopeful parents have been drawn to the promise of facilitated communication. Psychological scientists, however, have been more cautious. Before accepting claims and testimonials about any program or therapy, they put those claims and testimonials to the test. In the case of FC, they have done experiments involving hundreds of autistic children and their facilitators (e.g., Mostert, 2001; Romanczyk et al., 2003). Their techniques have been simple: They show the child a picture to identify but show the facilitator a different picture or no picture at all; or they keep the facilitator from hearing the questions being put to the child. Under these conditions, the child types only what the facilitator sees or hears, not what the child does.

This research shows that what happens in facilitated communication is exactly what happens when a medium guides a person's hand over a Ouija board to help the person receive "messages" from a "spirit": The person doing the "facilitating" unconsciously nudges the other person's hand in the desired direction, remaining unaware of having influenced the responses produced (Probst, 2005; Wegner, Fuller, & Sparrow, 2003). In other words, FC is really *facilitator* communication. This finding is vitally important, because if parents waste their time and money on a treatment that doesn't work, they may never get genuine help for their children, and they will suffer when their false hopes are finally shattered by reality.

This is why research methods matter so much to psychologists: These methods allow researchers to separate reliable information from unfounded beliefs, sort out conflicting views, and correct false ideas that may cause people harm. Some students would rather not

Thinking Critically   Examine the Evidence

Facilitator sees this picture.   Betsy sees this picture and Betsy types "HAT."

Using FC, Betsy Wheaton, a child with autism, appeared to type that her family had sexually abused her; she was removed from her home. But when researcher Howard Shane tested her by showing pictures of different objects separately to Betsy and her facilitator, Betsy typed only what the facilitator saw. If Betsy saw a cup but the facilitator saw a hat (left), Betsy typed "hat" (right). Because of this evidence, FC was stopped and Betsy was reunited with her family.

study research methods; "Let's just cut straight to the findings," they say. But these methods are the tools of the psychological scientist's trade, and understanding them is crucial for everyone who reads or hears about a new program or an "exciting finding" that is said to be based on psychological research. Knowing the difference between claims based on good research and those based on sloppy research or anecdotes can help you make wiser psychological and medical decisions, can prevent you from spending money on worthless programs, and sometimes can even save lives.

YOU are about to learn . . .

- ◆ the characteristics of an ideal scientist.
- ◆ the nature of a scientific theory.
- ◆ the secret of a good scientific definition.
- ◆ the risk scientists take when testing their ideas.
- ◆ why secrecy is a big "no-no" in science.

WHAT MAKES PSYCHOLOGICAL RESEARCH SCIENTIFIC?

When we say that psychologists are scientists, we do not mean they work with complicated gadgets and machines (although some do). The scientific enterprise has more to do with attitudes and procedures than with gear. Here are a few key characteristics of the ideal scientist:

1 **Precision.** Scientists sometimes launch an investigation simply because of a hunch they have about some behaviour. Often, however, they start out with a general **theory,** an organized system of assumptions and principles that purports to explain certain phenomena and how they are related. Many people misunderstand what scientists mean by a theory. A scientific theory is not just someone's personal opinion, as in "It's only a theory." Many scientific theories are tentative, pending more research, but others, such as the theory of gravity and the theory of evolution, are accepted by nearly all scientists.

From a hunch or theory, the psychological scientist derives a **hypothesis,** a statement that attempts to describe or explain a given behaviour. Initially, this statement may be quite general, as in, say, "Misery loves company." But before any research can be done, the hypothesis must be made more precise. For example, "Misery loves company" might be rephrased as "People who are anxious about a threatening situation tend to seek out others facing the same threat."

A hypothesis, in turn, leads to predictions about what will happen in a particular situation. In a prediction, terms such as *anxiety* or *threatening situation* are given **operational definitions,** which specify how the phenomena in question are to be observed and measured. "Anxiety" might be defined operationally as a score on an anxiety questionnaire and "threatening situation" as the threat of an electric shock. The prediction might be, "If you raise people's anxiety scores by telling them they are going to receive electric shocks, and then give them the choice of waiting alone or with others who are in the same situation, they will be more likely to choose to wait with others than they would be if they were not anxious." The prediction can then be tested using systematic methods.

2 **Skepticism.** Scientists do not accept ideas on faith or authority; their motto is "Show me!" Some of the greatest scientific advances have been made by those who dared to doubt what everyone else assumed to be true: that the sun revolves around the Earth or that madness is a sign of demonic possession. Skepticism means treating conclusions, both new and old, with caution. Caution, however, must be balanced by openness to new ideas and evidence. Otherwise, the scientist may wind up as shortsighted as the famous physicist Lord Kelvin, who at the end of the nineteenth century reputedly confidently declared that radio had no future, X rays were a hoax, and "heavier-than-air flying machines" were impossible.

3 **Reliance on empirical evidence.** Unlike plays and poems, scientific theories and hypotheses are not judged by how pleasing or entertaining they are. An idea may initially generate excitement because it is plausible or imaginative, but eventually it must be backed by empirical evidence. A collection of anecdotes or an appeal to authority will not do, nor will the intuitive appeal of the idea or its popularity. As Nobel Prize–winning scientist Peter Medawar (1979) once wrote, "The intensity of the conviction that a hypothesis is true has no bearing on whether it is true or not."

4 **Willingness to make "risky predictions."** A related principle is that a scientist must state an idea in such a way that it can be *refuted* or disproven by counterevidence. This important rule, known as the **principle of falsifiability,** does not mean that the idea *will* be disproven, only that it *could* be if contrary evidence were to be discovered. In other words, a scientist must risk disconfirmation by predicting not only what will happen but also what will *not* happen. In the "misery loves company" study, the hypothesis would be supported if most anxious people sought each other out, but would be disconfirmed if most anxious people went off alone to sulk and

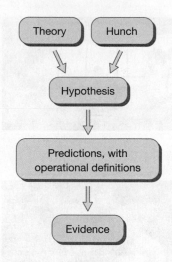

Theory → Hunch → Hypothesis → Predictions, with operational definitions → Evidence

theory An organized system of assumptions and principles that purports to explain a specified set of phenomena and their interrelations.

hypothesis A statement that attempts to predict or to account for a set of phenomena; scientific hypotheses specify relations among events or variables and are empirically tested.

operational definition A precise definition of a term in a hypothesis, which specifies the operations for observing and measuring the process or phenomenon being defined.

principle of falsifiability The principle that a scientific theory must make predictions that are specific enough to expose the theory to the possibility of disconfirmation; that is, the theory must predict not only what will happen but also what will *not* happen.

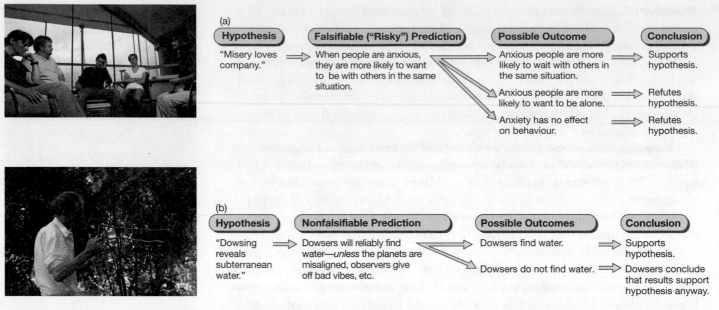

FIGURE 2.1 The Principle of Falsifiability

The scientific method requires researchers to expose their ideas to the possibility of counterevidence, as in row (a). In contrast, people claiming psychic powers, such as dowsers (who say they can find underground water with a "dowsing rod" that bends when water is present), typically interpret all possible outcomes as support for their assertions, as in row (b). Their claims are therefore untestable.

worry, or if anxiety had no effect on their behaviour (see Figure 2.1). A willingness to risk disconfirmation forces the scientist to take negative evidence seriously and to abandon mistaken hypotheses.

The principle of falsifiability is often violated in everyday life, because all of us are vulnerable to the **confirmation bias**: the tendency to look for and accept evidence that supports our pet theories and assumptions and to ignore or reject evidence that contradicts our beliefs. For example, if an RCMP officer is convinced of a suspect's guilt, he or she may interpret anything the suspect says, even claims of innocence, as confirming evidence that the suspect is guilty ("Of course he says he's innocent; he's a liar"). But what if the suspect *is* innocent? The principle of falsifiability compels scientists—and the rest of us—to resist the confirmation bias and to consider counterevidence.

5   **Openness.** Science depends on the free flow of ideas and full disclosure of the procedures used in a study. Secrecy is a big "no-no"; scientists must be willing to tell others where they got their ideas, how they tested them, and what the results were. They must do this clearly and in detail so that other scientists can repeat, or *replicate*, their studies and verify—or challenge—the findings. Replication is an essential part of the scientific process because sometimes what seems to be a fabulous phenomenon turns out to be only a fluke.

If you think about it, you will see that these principles of good science correspond to the critical-thinking guidelines described in Chapter 1. Formulating a prediction with operational definitions corresponds to "define your terms." Openness to new ideas encourages scientists to "ask questions" and "consider other interpretations." Reliance on empirical evidence helps scientists avoid oversimplification. The principle of falsifiability forces scientists to "analyze assumptions and biases" in a fair-minded

✱ **Explore**
Confirmation Bias

confirmation bias   The tendency to look for or pay attention only to information that confirms one's own belief.

Can you identify which rule of science was violated in each of the following cases?

1. For years, writer Norman Cousins told how he had cured himself of a rare, life-threatening disease through a combination of humour and vitamins. In a best-selling book, he recommended the same approach to others.

2. Benjamin Rush, an eighteenth-century physician, believed that yellow fever should be treated by bloodletting. Many of his patients died, but Rush did not lose faith in his approach. He simply attributed each recovery to his treatment and each death to the severity of the disease (Stanovich, 2006).

Answers:

1. Cousins offered only a personal account and did not gather empirical evidence from scientific studies or consider cases of sick people who were not helped by humour and vitamins. 2. Rush violated the principle of falsifiability: He interpreted a patient's survival as support for his treatment and explained away each death by saying that the person had been too ill for the treatment to work. Thus, no possible counterevidence could refute the theory (which, by the way, was dead wrong—the "treatment" was actually as dangerous as the disease).

fashion. And until their results have been replicated and verified, scientists must "tolerate uncertainty."

Do psychologists and other scientists always live up to these lofty standards? Not always. Being only human, they may put too much trust in their personal experiences, be biased by a conflict of interest when they are funded by private industry, or permit ambition to interfere with openness. Like everyone else, they may find it hard to admit that the evidence does not support their hypothesis; it is far easier to be skeptical about someone else's ideas than about your own (Tavris & Aronson, 2007).

Commitment to one's theories is not in itself a bad thing. Passion is the fuel of progress. It motivates researchers to think boldly and do the exhaustive testing that is often required to support an idea. But passion can cloud perceptions, and in a few sad cases has even led to fraud and deception. That is why science is a communal activity. Scientists are expected to submit their results to professional journals, which send the findings to experts in the field for evaluation before deciding whether to publish them. This process, called *peer review*, ensures that the work lives up to accepted scientific standards. Peer review and scientific publication are supposed to precede announcements to the public through press releases, internet postings, or popular books. The research community acts as a jury, scrutinizing and sifting the evidence, judging its integrity, approving some viewpoints and relegating others to the scientific scrap heap.

The peer-review process is not perfect, but it does give science a built-in system of checks and balances. Individuals are not necessarily objective, honest, or rational, but science forces them to subject their findings to scrutiny and to justify their claims.

YOU are about to learn . . .

◆ how participants are selected for psychological studies, and why it matters.

◆ the methods psychologists use to describe behaviour.

◆ the advantages and disadvantages of each descriptive method.

DESCRIPTIVE STUDIES: ESTABLISHING THE FACTS

Psychologists gather evidence to support their hypotheses by using different methods, depending on the kinds of questions they want to answer. These methods are not mutually exclusive, however. Just as a police detective may rely on DNA samples, fingerprints, and interviews of suspects to figure out "who done it," psychological sleuths often draw on different techniques at different stages of an investigation.

No matter the method, one of the first challenges facing any researcher is to select the participants for the study. Ideally, the researcher would prefer to get a representative sample, a group of participants that accurately represents the larger population that the researcher is interested in. Suppose you wanted to learn about drug use among third-year university students. Questioning or observing every third-year student in the country would obviously not be practical; instead, you would need to recruit a sample. You could use special selection procedures to ensure that this sample contained the same proportion of women, men, immigrants, indigenous peoples, francophones, and so on as in the general population of third-year university students. Even then, a sample drawn just from your own school or town might not produce results applicable to the entire country or even your province.

A sample's size is less critical than its representativeness. A small but representative sample may yield accurate results, whereas a large study that fails to use proper sampling methods may yield questionable results. But in practice, those who study human behaviour must often settle for a sample of people who happen to be available—a "convenience" sample—and more often than not, this means undergraduates. Psychologist Peter Killeen noted, with tongue only partly in cheek, that students are "cheaper than white rats, and they're more similar to the population to which we hope to generalize. And they seldom bite" (quoted in Jaffe, 2005).

Typically, undergraduates are younger than the general population. They are also more likely to be female and to have better cognitive skills. Does that matter? One researcher decided to find out by analyzing statistical reviews of social-science studies that had used student and adult nonstudent samples in the same research (Peterson, 2001). These studies cumulatively represented about 350 000 participants. It turned out that 81% of the conclusions based on university students were the same as those based on nonstudents. But of course this means that 19% of the conclusions were different; and in fact, they went in *opposite* directions. This finding does not mean we should throw out all results based solely on students. Many psychological processes, such as basic perceptual or memory processes, are likely to be the same in students as in anyone else; after all, students are not a separate species, no matter what they (or their professors) may sometimes think! When considering other topics, however, we may need to be cautious about drawing conclusions until the research can be replicated with nonstudents.

We turn now to the specific methods used most commonly in psychological research. As you read about these methods, you may want to list their advantages and disadvantages in order to remember them better. Then check your list against the one in Review 2.1 on page 56. We will begin with descriptive methods, which allow researchers to describe and predict behaviour but not necessarily to choose one explanation over competing ones.

representative sample   A group of individuals, selected from a population for study, which matches the population on important characteristics such as age and sex.

descriptive methods   Methods that yield descriptions of behaviour but not necessarily causal explanations.

case study   A detailed description of a particular individual being studied or treated.

Case Studies

A case study (or *case history*) is a detailed description of a particular individual based on careful observation or formal psychological testing. It may include information about a person's childhood, dreams, fantasies, experiences, and relationships—anything that will provide insight into the person's behaviour. Case studies are most commonly used by clinicians, although academic researchers use them as well, especially when they are just beginning to study a topic or when practical or ethical considerations prevent them from gathering information in other ways.

Suppose you want to know whether the first few years of life are critical for acquiring a first language. Can children who have missed out on hearing speech (or, in the case of deaf children, seeing signs) catch up later on? Obviously, psychologists cannot answer this question by isolating children and seeing what happens. So instead they have studied unusual cases of language deprivation.

One such case involved a 13-year-old girl who had been cruelly locked up in a small room since the age of 18 months, strapped for hours to a potty chair. Her mother, a battered wife, barely cared for her, and no one in the family spoke a word to her. If she made the slightest sound, her severely disturbed father beat her. When she was finally rescued, "Genie," as researchers called her, did not know how to chew or stand erect and was not toilet trained. She spat on anything that was handy, including other people, and her only sounds were high-pitched whimpers. Eventually, she was able to learn some rules of social conduct, and she began to understand short sentences and to use words to convey her needs, describe her moods, and even lie. But even after many years, Genie's grammar and pronunciation remained abnormal. She never learned to use pronouns correctly, ask questions, produce proper negative sentences, or use the little word endings that communicate tense, number, and possession (Curtiss, 1977, 1982; Rymer, 1993). This sad case, along with similar ones, suggests that a critical period exists for language development, with the likelihood of fully mastering a first language declining steadily after early childhood and falling off drastically at puberty (Pinker, 1994).

Case studies illustrate psychological principles in a way that abstract generalizations and cold statistics never can, and they produce a more detailed picture of an individual than other methods do. In biological research, cases of patients with brain damage have yielded important clues to how the brain is organized (see Chapter 4). But in most instances, case studies have serious drawbacks. Information is often missing or hard to interpret; for example, no one knows what Genie's language development was like before she was locked up or whether she was born with mental deficits. The observer who writes up the case may have certain biases that influence which facts get noticed or overlooked. The person who is the focus of the study may have selective or inaccurate memories, making any conclusions unreliable. Most important, because that person may be unrepresentative of the group the researcher is interested in, this method has only limited usefulness for deriving general principles of behaviour. For all these reasons, case studies are usually only sources, rather than tests, of hypotheses.

Be wary, then, of the compelling cases reported in the media by individuals ("I was a multiple personality") or by therapists ("I cured someone who had a multiple personality"). Often these stories are only "arguing by anecdote," and they are not a basis for drawing firm conclusions about anything.

This picture, drawn by Genie, a young girl who endured years of isolation and mistreatment, shows one of her favourite pastimes: listening to researcher Susan Curtiss playing the piano. Genie's drawings were used along with other case material to study her mental and social development.

Thinking Critically

Don't Oversimplify

Case studies are often enormously compelling, which is why talk shows love them. But often they are merely anecdotes. What are the dangers in using case studies to draw general conclusions about human nature?

Observational Studies

In observational studies, the researcher observes, measures, and records behaviour, taking care to avoid intruding on the people (or animals) being observed. Unlike case studies, observational studies usually involve many participants. Often an observational study is the first step in a program of research; it is helpful to have a good description of behaviour before you try to explain it.

observational study   A study in which the researcher carefully and systematically observes and records behaviour without interfering with the behaviour; it may involve either naturalistic or laboratory observation.

Get INVOLVED!

A STUDY OF PERSONAL SPACE

Try a little naturalistic observation of your own. Go to a public place where people voluntarily seat themselves near others, such as a movie theatre or a cafeteria with large tables. If you choose a setting where many people enter at once, you might recruit some friends to help you; you can divide the area into sections and give each observer one section to observe. As individuals and groups sit down, note how many seats they leave between themselves and the next person. On average, how far do people tend to sit from strangers? Once you have your results, see how many possible explanations you can come up with.

The primary purpose of *naturalistic observation* is to find out how people or animals act in their normal social environments. Psychologists use naturalistic observation wherever people happen to be—at home, on playgrounds or streets, in schoolrooms, or in offices. In one study, a social psychologist and his students ventured into a common human habitat: bars. They wanted to know whether people in bars drink more when they are in groups than when they are alone. They visited all 32 pubs in a mid-sized city, ordered beers, and recorded on napkins and pieces of newspaper how much the other patrons imbibed. They found that drinkers in groups consumed more than individuals who were alone. Those in groups did not drink any faster; they just lingered in the bar longer (Sommer, 1977).

The students who did this study did not rely on their impressions or memories of how much people drank. In observational studies, researchers count, rate, or measure behaviour systematically, to guard against noticing only what they expect or want to see, and they keep careful records so that others can check their observations. Observers must also take pains to avoid being obvious about what they are doing so that those who are being observed will behave naturally. If the students who studied drinking habits had marched into those bars with camcorders and announced their intentions to the customers, the results might have been quite different.

Psychologists using laboratory observation have gathered valuable information about brain and muscle activity during sleep. Psychologists using naturalistic observation have studied how people in crowded places modify their gaze and body position to preserve a sense of privacy.

Sometimes psychologists prefer to make observations in a laboratory setting. In *laboratory observation*, researchers have more control of the situation. They can use sophisticated equipment, determine the number of people who will be observed, maintain a clear line of vision, and so forth. Say you wanted to know how infants of different ages respond when left with a stranger. You might have parents and their infants come to your laboratory, observe them playing together for a while, then have a stranger enter the room and, a few minutes later, have the parent leave. You could record signs of distress in the children, interactions with the stranger, and other behaviour. If you did this, you would find that very young infants carry on cheerfully with whatever they are doing when the parent leaves. However, by the age of about eight months, many children will burst into tears or show other signs of what child psychologists call "separation anxiety."

One shortcoming of laboratory observation is that the presence of researchers and special equipment may cause people to behave differently than they would in their usual surroundings. Further, whether they are in natural or laboratory settings, observational studies, like other descriptive methods, are more useful for describing behaviour than for explaining it. For example, the barroom results we described do not necessarily mean that being in a group makes people drink a lot. People may join a group because they are already interested in drinking and find it more comfortable to hang around the bar if they are with others. Similarly, if we observe infants protesting whenever a parent leaves the room, is it because they have become attached to their parents and want them nearby, or have they simply learned from experience that crying brings an adult with a cookie and a cuddle? Observational studies alone cannot answer such questions.

Tests

Psychological tests, sometimes called *assessment instruments*, are procedures for measuring and evaluating personality traits, emotions, aptitudes, interests, abilities, and values. Typically, tests require people to answer a series of written or oral questions. The answers may then be totalled to yield a single numerical score, or a set of scores. *Objective tests*, also called *inventories*, measure beliefs, feelings, or behaviours of which an individual is aware; *projective tests* are designed to tap unconscious feelings or motives (see Chapter 15).

At one time or another, you no doubt have taken a personality test, an achievement test, or a vocational-aptitude test. Hundreds of psychological tests are used in industry, education, the military, and the helping professions, and many tests are also used in research. Some tests are given to individuals, others to large groups. These measures help clarify differences among people, as well as differences in the reactions of the same person on different occasions or at different stages of life. Tests may be used to promote self-understanding, to evaluate psychological treatments, or, in scientific research, to draw generalizations about human behaviour. Well-constructed psychological tests are a great improvement over simple self-evaluation, because many people have a distorted view of their own abilities and traits.

One test of a good test is whether it is standardized—whether uniform procedures exist for giving and scoring the test. It would hardly be fair to give some people detailed instructions and plenty of time and others only vague instructions and limited time. Those who administer the test must know exactly how to explain the tasks involved, how much time to allow, and what materials to use. Scoring is usually done by referring to norms, or established standards of performance. The usual procedure for developing norms is to give the test to a large group of people who resemble those for whom the test is intended. Norms determine which scores can be considered high, low, or average.

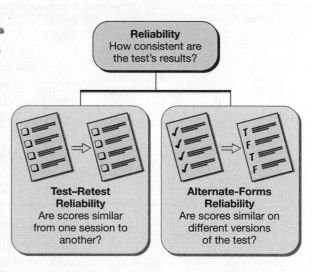

Reliability
How consistent are the test's results?

Test–Retest Reliability
Are scores similar from one session to another?

Alternate-Forms Reliability
Are scores similar on different versions of the test?

psychological tests Procedures used to measure and evaluate personality traits, emotional states, aptitudes, interests, abilities, and values.

standardize In test construction, to develop uniform procedures for giving and scoring a test.

norms In test construction, established standards of performance.

Test construction presents many challenges. For one thing, the test must be reliable—that is, it must produce the same results from one time and place to the next or from one scorer to another. A vocational-interest test is not reliable if it says that Greg would make a wonderful engineer but a poor journalist, but then gives different results when Greg retakes the test a week later. Psychologists can measure *test-retest reliability* by giving the test twice to the same group of people and comparing the two sets of scores statistically. If the test is reliable, individuals' scores will be similar from one session to another. This method has a drawback, however: People tend to do better the second time they take a test, after they have become familiar with it. A solution is to compute *alternate-forms reliability* by giving different versions of the same test to the same group on two separate occasions. The items on the two forms are similar in format but are not identical in content. Performance cannot improve because of familiarity with the items, although people may still do somewhat better the second time around because they have learned the procedures expected of them.

To be useful, a test must also be **valid**, which means that it must measure what it sets out to measure. A creativity test is not valid if what it actually measures is verbal sophistication. If the items broadly represent the trait in question, the test is said to have *content validity*. If you were testing, say, employees' job satisfaction, and your test tapped a broad array of relevant beliefs and behaviours (e.g., "Do you feel you have reached a dead end at work?" "Are you bored with your assignments?"), it would have content validity. If the test asked only how workers felt about their salary level, it would lack content validity and would be of little use; after all, highly paid people are not always satisfied with their jobs, and people who earn low wages are not always dissatisfied.

Most tests are also judged on *criterion validity*, the ability to predict independent measures, or criteria, of the trait in question. The criterion for a scholastic aptitude test might be grades; the criterion for a test of shyness might be behaviour in social situations. To find out whether your job-satisfaction test had criterion validity, you might return a year later to see whether it correctly predicted absenteeism, resignations, or requests for job transfers.

Teachers, parents, and employers do not always stop to question a test's validity, especially when the results are summarized in a single, precise-sounding number, such as an IQ score of 115 or a job applicant's ranking of 5. Among psychologists and educators, however, controversy exists about the validity and usefulness of even some widely used tests, including tests like the Test of English as a Foreign Language (TOEFL) or standardized IQ tests. In Canada and 80 other countries, if you are a non-native English speaker, admission to university can depend primarily on your score on the TOEFL. Given the marginal relation between scores on the TOEFL and academic performance for undergraduates (Simner, 1998), the Canadian Psychological Association (CPA) suggested that the TOEFL should not be used as an admission tool for universities but rather as a test of English proficiency. Indeed, as we will see in Chapter 3, not everyone has access to the opportunities that lead to strong test scores and strong real-world performance. And as we will see in Chapter 9, motivation, study skills, self-discipline, practical "smarts," and other traits not measured by specific tests are major influences on success in school and on the job.

Criticisms and reevaluations of psychological tests keep psychological assessment honest and scientifically rigorous. In contrast, the pop-psych tests found in magazines, in newspapers, and on the internet usually have not been evaluated for either validity

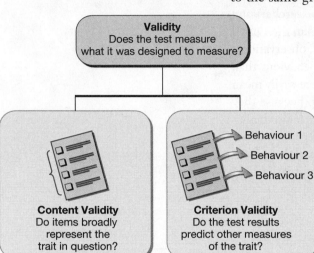

Validity
Does the test measure
what it was designed to measure?

Content Validity
Do items broadly
represent the
trait in question?

Behaviour 1
Behaviour 2
Behaviour 3

Criterion Validity
Do the test results
predict other measures
of the trait?

reliability   In test construction, the consistency of scores derived from a test, from one time and place to another.

validity   The ability of a test to measure what it was designed to measure.

or reliability. These questionnaires have inviting headlines, such as "Which Breed of Dog Do You Most Resemble?" or "The Seven Types of Lover," but they are merely lists of questions that someone thought sounded good.

Surveys

Whereas psychological tests usually generate information about people indirectly, surveys are questionnaires and interviews that gather information by asking people *directly* about their experiences, attitudes, or opinions. Most of us are familiar with national opinion surveys, such as those conducted by Ipsos, Harris/Decima, or Statistics Canada (**www.statscan.ca**). Surveys have been done on hundreds of topics, from consumer preferences to sexual preferences.

Surveys produce bushels of data, but they are not easy to do well. Sampling problems are often an issue. For example, when a talk-radio host invites people to send comments about a political matter, the results are not likely to generalize to the population as a whole, even if thousands of people respond. Why? As a group, people who like Rex Murphy are likely quite different from those who are fans of Jian Ghomeshi. Popular polls and surveys also frequently suffer from a **volunteer bias**: People who are willing to volunteer their opinions may differ from those who remain silent. When you read about a survey (or any other kind of study), always ask who participated. A nonrepresentative sample does not necessarily mean that a survey is worthless or uninteresting, but it does mean that the results may not hold true for other groups.

Yet another problem with surveys is that people sometimes lie, especially when the survey is about a touchy or embarrassing topic. ("What? Me do that disgusting/illegal/dishonest thing? Never!") For example, in studies comparing self-reports of illicit drug use with urinalysis results from the same individuals, between 30 and 70% of those who test positive for cocaine or opiates deny having used drugs recently (Tourangeau & Yan, 2007). The likelihood of lying is reduced when respondents are guaranteed anonymity and allowed to respond in private. Researchers can also check for lying by asking the same question several times with different wording to see whether the answers are consistent. But not all surveys use these techniques, and even when respondents are trying to be truthful, they may misinterpret the survey questions, hold inaccurate perceptions of their own behaviour, or misremember the past.

When you hear about the results of a survey or opinion poll, you also need to consider which questions were (and were not) asked and how the questions were phrased. These aspects of a survey's design may reflect assumptions about the topic or encourage certain responses—as political pollsters well know. Many years ago, the famed sex researcher Alfred Kinsey, in his pioneering surveys of sexual habits (Kinsey, Pomeroy, & Martin, 1948; Kinsey et al., 1953), made it his practice always to ask, *"How many times have you* (masturbated, had nonmarital sex, etc.)?" rather than *"Have you ever* (masturbated, had nonmarital sex, etc.)?" The first way of phrasing the question tended to elicit more truthful responses than the second because it removed the respondent's self-consciousness about having done any of these things. The second way of phrasing the question would have permitted embarrassed respondents to reply with a simple but dishonest "No."

Technology can help researchers overcome some of the problems inherent in doing surveys. Because many people feel more anonymous

surveys Questionnaires and interviews that ask people directly about their experiences, attitudes, or opinions.

volunteer bias A shortcoming of findings derived from a sample of volunteers instead of a representative sample; the volunteers may differ from those who did not volunteer.

Thinking Critically

Analyze Assumptions

A magazine has just published a survey of its female readers; the survey is called "Would you be unfaithful?" It reports that "87% of all women report that they would cheat in the right circumstance." Is the assumption that the sample represents all married Canadian women justified? What would be a more accurate title for the survey?

"Are you (a) contented, (b) happy, (c) very happy, (d) wildly happy, (e) deliriously happy?"

when they "talk" to a computer than when they fill out a paper-and-pencil questionnaire, computerized questionnaires can reduce lying (Turner et al., 1998). Participants are usually volunteers and are not randomly selected, but because web-based samples are often huge, consisting of hundreds of thousands of respondents, they are more diverse than traditional samples in terms of gender, socioeconomic status, geographic region, and age. In these respects they tend to be more representative of the general population than traditional samples are (Gosling et al., 2004). Even when people from a particular group make up only a small proportion of the respondents, in absolute numbers they may be numerous enough to provide useful information about that group. For example, whereas a typical sample of 1000 representative Canadians might include only a handful of Buddhists, a huge internet sample might draw hundreds.

Internet surveys also carry certain risks, however. It is hard for researchers to know whether participants understand the instructions and the questions and are taking them seriously. Also, many tests and surveys on the web have never been validated, which is why drawing conclusions from them about your personality or mental adjustment could be dangerous to your mental health! Always check the credentials of those designing the test or survey and be sure it is not just something someone made up at his or her computer in the middle of the night.

---

quickQUIZ

✓●⌐**Quick Review** on **MyPsychLab**

How would you describe your understanding of descriptive methods?

A. Which descriptive method would be most appropriate for studying each of the following topics? (All of them, by the way, have been investigated by psychologists.)

1. Ways in which the games of boys differ from those of girls
2. Changes in attitudes toward nuclear disarmament after a television movie about nuclear holocaust
3. The math skills of children in Canada versus Japan
4. Physiological changes that occur when people watch violent movies
5. The development of a male infant who was reared as a female after his penis was accidentally burned off during a routine surgery

a. case study
b. naturalistic observation
c. laboratory observation
d. survey
e. test

B. Professor Flummox gives her new test of aptitude for studying psychology to her psychology students at the start of the year. At the end of the year, she finds that those who did well on the test averaged only a C in the course. The test lacks _____.

C. Over a period of 55 years, a British woman sniffed large amounts of cocaine, which she obtained legally under British regulations for the treatment of addicts. Yet she appeared to show no negative effects (Brown & Middlefell, 1989). What does this case tell us about the dangers or safety of cocaine?

Answers:

A. 1. b 2. d 3. e 4. c 5. a B. Validity (more specifically, criterion validity) C. Not much. Snorting cocaine may be relatively harmless for some people, such as this woman, but extremely harmful for others. Also, the cocaine she received may have been less potent than cocaine purchased on the street. Critical thinking requires that we resist generalizing from a single case.

YOU are about to learn . . .

◆ what it means to say that two things, such as grades and TV watching, are "negatively" correlated.

◆ whether a positive correlation between TV watching and hyperactivity means that too much TV makes kids hyperactive.

CORRELATIONAL STUDIES: LOOKING FOR RELATIONS

In descriptive research, psychologists often want to know whether two or more phenomena are related and, if so, how strongly. For example, are students' grade-point averages related to the number of hours they spend watching television, playing video games, or texting? To find out, a psychologist would do a **correlational study.**

Measuring Correlations

The word **correlation** is often used as a synonym for "relation." Technically, however, a correlation is a numerical measure of the *strength* of the relation between two things. The "things" may be events, scores, or anything else that can be recorded and tallied. In psychological studies, such things are called **variables** because they can vary in quantifiable ways. Height, weight, age, income, IQ scores, number of smiles in a given time period—anything that can be measured, rated, or scored can serve as a variable.

A **positive correlation** means that high values of one variable are associated with high values of the other and that low values of one variable are associated with low values of the other. Height and weight are positively correlated; so are IQ scores and school grades. Rarely is a correlation perfect, however. Some tall people weigh less than some short ones; some people with average IQs are academic superstars and some with high IQs get poor grades. Figure 2.2a shows a positive correlation between men's educational level and their annual income. Each dot represents a man; you can find each man's educational level by drawing a horizontal line from his dot to the vertical axis. You can find his income by drawing a vertical line from his dot to the horizontal axis.

A **negative correlation** means that high values of one variable are associated with *low* values of the other. Figure 2.2b shows a negative correlation between average income and the incidence of dental disease for groups of 100 families. Each dot represents one group. As you can see, in general the higher the income, the fewer the dental problems. Here's another example: In general, the older adults are, the fewer kilometres they can run. How about hours spent watching TV and grade-point averages? You guessed it; they're negatively correlated: Spending lots of hours in front of the television is associated with lower grades (Potter, 1987; Ridley-Johnson, Cooper, & Chance, 1983). See whether you can think of other variables that are negatively correlated. Remember that a negative correlation tells you that the *more* of one thing, the *less* of another. If no relation exists between two variables, we say that they are *uncorrelated* or that there is a *zero correlation* (see Figure 2.2c). For example, shoe size and IQ scores are uncorrelated.

The statistic used to express a correlation is called the **coefficient of correlation.** This number conveys both the size of the correlation and its direction. A perfect positive correlation has a coefficient of +1.00, and a perfect negative correlation has a coefficient of –1.00. Suppose you weighed 10 people and listed them from lightest to

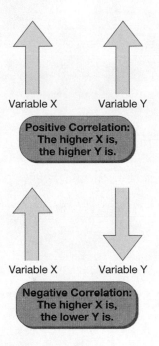

Variable X   **Variable Y**

Positive Correlation: The higher X is, the higher Y is.

Variable X   **Variable Y**

Negative Correlation: The higher X is, the lower Y is.

correlational study A descriptive study that looks for a consistent relation between two phenomena.

correlation A measure of how strongly two variables are related to one another.

variables Characteristics of behaviour or experience that can be measured or described by a numeric scale.

positive correlation An association between increases in one variable and increases in another—or between decreases in one and in another.

negative correlation An association between increases in one variable and decreases in another.

coefficient of correlation A measure of correlation that ranges in value from –1.00 to +1.00.

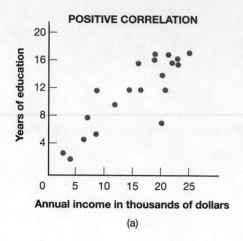

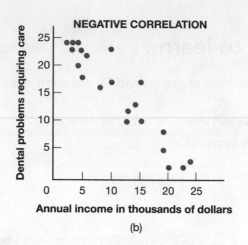

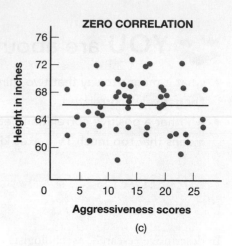

FIGURE 2.2 Correlations

Graph (a) shows a positive correlation: In general, income rises with education. Graph (b) shows a negative correlation: In general, the higher people's incomes, the fewer dental problems they have. Graph (c) shows a zero correlation between height and aggressiveness.

heaviest, then measured their heights and listed them from shortest to tallest. If the names on the two lists were in exactly the same order, the correlation between weight and height would be +1.00. If the correlation between two variables is +0.80, it means that they are strongly related. If the correlation is −0.80, the relation is just as strong, but it is negative. When there is no association between two variables, the coefficient is zero or close to zero.

Cautions about Correlations

Correlational findings are common in psychology and often make the news. But beware; many supposed "correlations" reported in the media or on the internet are based on rumour and anecdote, and turn out to be small or meaningless. Some are merely *illusory correlations*, apparent associations between two things that are not really related. For example, for several years, claims of an association between autism and vaccination for childhood diseases have alarmed many parents. The supposed culprit is thimerosal, a preservative used in vaccines such as the one for H1N1. However, no convincing evidence exists that thimerosal is involved in autism. After this preservative was removed from most vaccines, the incidence of autism did not decline, as it would have if thimerosal were to blame. And study after study has failed to find any connection whatsoever (Offit, 2008). As just one example, in a study of all children born in Denmark between 1991 and 1998 (over half a million children), the incidence of autism in vaccinated children was actually a bit *lower* than in unvaccinated children (Madsen et al., 2002). Finally, in early 2010, *The Lancet*, the journal that had published the original report on the correlation, retracted the report, citing numerous problems with the research. Thus, the apparent link between vaccination and autism is almost certainly a coincidence, arising from the fact that symptoms of childhood autism are often first recognized at about the same time that children are vaccinated.

You can see why an understanding of correlations matters. Unfortunately, despite the retraction and the studies that failed to find a connection, some parents continue to avoid vaccinating their children. For many preventable diseases such as measles or whooping cough, fewer than 65% of Canadian children are fully immunized (Public Health Agency of Canada, 2006). At the same time, failure to immunize often results in resurgence of these diseases, which can be lethal in children whose parents have refused to have them vaccinated (Health Canada, 2009).

✱ Explore
Correlations Do Not Show Causation

Thinking Critically   Consider Other Interpretations

The number of hours toddlers spend watching TV is correlated with their risk of being hyperactive at age 7. Does that mean TV watching causes hyperactivity problems? Are there other possible explanations for this finding?

Even when correlations are meaningful, they can still be hard to interpret, because *a correlation does not establish causation.* It is often easy to assume that if variable A predicts variable B, A must be causing B—that is, making B happen—but that is not necessarily so. A positive correlation has been found between the number of hours that children watch television between ages 1 and 3 and their risk of hyperactivity (impulsivity, attention problems, difficulty concentrating) by age 7 (Christakis et al., 2004). Does this mean that watching TV *causes* hyperactivity? Maybe so, but it is also possible

◉ Watch
Toddlers and TV

Baby TV

---

quickQUIZ

✓ **Quick Review** on **MyPsychLab**

Are you clear about correlations?

A. Identify each of the following as a positive or negative correlation.
1. The higher a male monkey's level of the hormone testosterone, the more aggressive he is likely to be.
2. The older people are, the less frequently they tend to have sexual intercourse.
3. The hotter the weather, the more crimes against persons (such as muggings) tend to occur.

B. Now see whether you can generate two or three possible explanations for each of the preceding findings.

Answers:

A. 1. positive 2. negative 3. positive B. 1. The hormone may cause aggressiveness; acting aggressively may stimulate hormone production, or some third factor, such as age or dominance, may influence aggressiveness and hormone production independently. 2. Older people may have less interest in sex than younger people, have less energy or more physical ailments, or simply lack partners. 3. Hot temperatures may make people edgy and cause them to commit crimes; potential victims may be more plentiful in warm weather because more people go outside; criminals may find it more comfortable to be out committing their crimes in warm weather than in cold. (Our explanations for these correlations are not the only ones possible.)

that children with a disposition to become hyperactive are more attracted to television than those disposed to be calm. Or perhaps the harried parents of distractible children are more likely than other parents to rely on TV as a babysitter. It's also possible that neither variable causes the other directly: Perhaps parents who allow their young kids to watch a lot of TV have attention problems themselves and therefore create a home environment that fosters hyperactivity and inattentiveness. Likewise, the negative correlation between TV watching and grades mentioned earlier might exist because heavy TV watchers have less time to study, because they have some personality trait that causes an attraction to TV *and* an aversion to studying, because they use TV as an escape when their grades are low . . . you get the idea.

The moral of the story: When two variables are associated, one variable may or may not be causing the other.

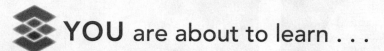 **YOU** are about to learn . . .

- ◆ why psychologists rely so heavily on experiments.
- ◆ what control groups control for.
- ◆ who is "blind" in single- and double-blind experiments, and what they are not supposed to "see."
- ◆ some special challenges in doing cross-cultural research.

EXPERIMENTS: HUNTING FOR CAUSES

Researchers gain plenty of illuminating information from descriptive studies, but when they want to track down the causes of behaviour, they rely heavily on the *experimental method*. An experiment allows the researcher to control and manipulate the situation being studied. Instead of being a passive recorder of behaviour, the researcher actively does something that he or she believes will affect people's behaviour and then observes what happens. These procedures allow the experimenter to draw conclusions about cause and effect—about what causes what.

Experimental Variables

Imagine that you are a psychologist whose research interest is multitasking. Almost everyone multitasks these days, and you would like to know whether that's a good thing or a bad thing. Specifically, you would like to know whether using a handheld cellphone while driving is dangerous or not—an important question because most people have done so. Motor vehicle statistics show that talking on a cellphone while driving is associated with an increase in accidents, but maybe that's just for people who are risk takers or lousy drivers to begin with. To pin down cause and effect, you decide to do an experiment.

In a laboratory, you ask participants to "drive" using a computerized driving simulator equipped with an automatic transmission, steering wheel, gas pedal, and brake pedal. The object, you tell them, is to maximize the distance covered by driving on a busy highway while avoiding collisions with other cars. Some of the participants talk on the cellphone while driving; others just drive. You are going to compare how many collisions the two groups have. The basic design of this experiment is illustrated in Figure 2.3, which you may want to refer to as you read the next few pages.

◀⊙ Simulate
Psychology Experiments Tool:
Implicit Association Test

⊙ Watch
Classic video footage of Konrad Lorenz on controlling an experiment

experiment   A controlled test of a hypothesis in which the researcher manipulates one variable to discover its effect on another.

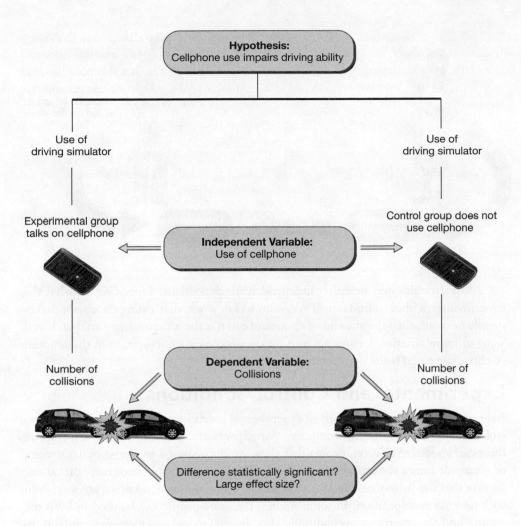

FIGURE 2.3 Do Cellphone Use and Driving Mix?
The text describes this experimental design to test the hypothesis that talking on a cellphone while driving impairs driving skills and leads to accidents.

The aspect of an experimental situation manipulated or varied by the researcher is known as the **independent variable**. The reaction of the participants—the behaviour that the researcher tries to predict—is the **dependent variable**. Every experiment has at least one independent and one dependent variable. In our example, the independent variable is cellphone use (use versus nonuse). The dependent variable is the number of collisions.

Ideally, everything in the experimental situation except the independent variable is held constant—that is, kept the same for all participants. You would not have some people use a stick shift and others an automatic, unless transmission type were an independent variable. Similarly, you would not have some people go through the experiment alone and others perform in front of an audience. Holding everything but the independent variable constant ensures that whatever happens is due to the researcher's manipulation and nothing else. It allows you to rule out other interpretations.

Understandably, students often have trouble keeping independent and dependent variables straight. You might think of it this way: The dependent variable—the outcome of the study—*depends* on the independent variable. When psychologists set up an experiment, they think, "If I do X, the people in my study will do Y." The "X" represents the independent variable; the "Y" represents the dependent variable, as illustrated:

independent variable A variable that an experimenter manipulates.

dependent variable A variable that an experimenter predicts will be affected by manipulations of the independent variable.

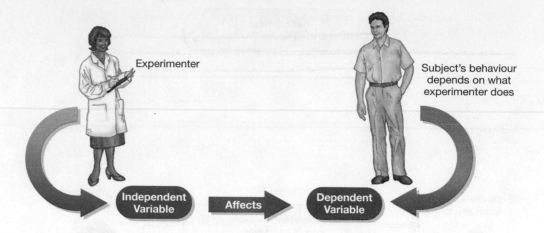

Experimenter

Subject's behaviour depends on what experimenter does

Independent Variable → Affects → Dependent Variable

Most variables may be either independent or dependent, depending on what the experimenter wishes to find out. If you want to know whether eating chocolate makes people nervous, then the amount of chocolate eaten is the independent variable. If you want to know whether feeling nervous makes people eat chocolate, then the amount of chocolate eaten is the dependent variable.

Experimental and Control Conditions

Experiments usually require both an experimental condition and a comparison, or control condition. In the control condition, participants are treated exactly as they are in the experimental condition, except that they are not exposed to the same treatment, or manipulation of the independent variable. Without a control condition, you cannot be sure that the behaviour you are interested in would not have occurred anyway, even without your manipulation. In some studies, the same people can be used in both the control and the experimental conditions; they are said to serve as their own controls. In other studies, individuals are assigned to either an *experimental group* or a *control group*.

In our cellphone study, we could have drivers serve as their own controls by having them drive once while using a cellphone and once without a phone. But for this illustration, we will use two different groups. Participants who talk on the phone while driving make up the experimental group, and those who just drive along silently make up the control group. We want these two groups to be roughly the same in terms of average driving skill. It would not do to start out with a bunch of new drivers in the experimental group and a bunch of experienced drivers in the control group. We also probably want the two groups to be similar in age, education, driving history, and other characteristics so that none of these variables will affect our results. One way to accomplish this is to use random assignment of people to one group or another—for example, by randomly assigning them numbers and putting those with even numbers in one group and those with odd numbers in another. If we have enough participants in our study, individual characteristics that could possibly affect the results are likely to be roughly balanced in the two groups, so we can safely ignore them.

Sometimes researchers use several experimental or control groups. In our cellphone study, we might want to examine the effects of short versus long phone conversations, or conversations on different topics—say, work, personal matters, and *very* personal matters. In that case, we would have more than one experimental group to compare with the control group. In our hypothetical example, though, we'll just have one experimental group, and everyone in it will drive for 15 minutes while talking on the cellphone.

control condition In an experiment, a comparison condition in which participants are not exposed to the same treatment as in the experimental condition.

random assignment A procedure for assigning people to experimental and control groups in which each individual has the same probability as any other of being assigned to a given group.

This description does not cover all the procedures used by psychological researchers. For example, in some kinds of studies, people in the control group get a **placebo**—a fake treatment or sugar pill that looks, tastes, or smells like the real treatment or medication, but is phony. If the placebo produces the same result as the real thing, the reason must be the participants' expectations rather than the treatment itself. Placebos are critical in testing new drugs, because of the optimism that a potential "miracle cure" often brings with it. Medical placebos usually take the form of pills or injections that contain no active ingredients.

Control groups, by the way, are also crucial in many nonexperimental studies. For example, some psychotherapists have published books arguing that girls develop problems with self-esteem and confidence as soon as they hit adolescence. But unless the writers have also tested or surveyed a comparable group of teenage boys, there is no way of knowing whether low self-esteem is a problem unique to girls or is just as typical for boys (see Chapter 13).

Experimenter Effects

Because their expectations can influence the results of a study, participants should not know whether they are in an experimental or a control group. When this is so (as it usually is), the experiment is said to be a **single-blind study**. But participants are not the only ones who bring expectations to the laboratory; so do researchers. And researchers' expectations, biases, and hopes for a particular result may cause them to inadvertently influence the participants' responses through facial expressions, posture, tone of voice, or some other cue.

Many years ago, Robert Rosenthal (1966) demonstrated how powerful such **experimenter effects** can be. He had students teach rats to run a maze. Half of the students were told that their rats had been bred to be "maze bright," and half were told that their rats had been bred to be "maze dull." In reality, there were no genetic differences between the two groups of rats, yet the supposedly brainy rats actually did learn the maze more quickly, apparently because of the way the students were handling and treating them. If an experimenter's expectations can affect a rodent's behaviour, reasoned Rosenthal, surely they can affect a human being's behaviour, and he went on to demonstrate this point in many other studies (Rosenthal, 1994). Even an experimenter's friendly smile or cold demeanour can affect people's responses.

Thinking Critically

Consider Other Interpretations

You have developed a new form of therapy that you believe cures anxiety. Sixty-three percent of the people who go through your program improve. What else, besides your therapy, could account for this result? Why shouldn't you rush out to open an anxiety clinic?

placebo An inactive substance or fake treatment used as a control in an experiment or given by a medical practitioner to a patient.

single-blind study An experiment in which participants do not know whether they are in an experimental or a control group.

experimenter effects Unintended changes in study participants' behaviour due to cues inadvertently given by the experimenter.

THE POWER OF A SMILE

Get INVOLVED!

Prove to yourself how easy it is for experimenters to affect the behaviour of a study's participants by giving off nonverbal cues. As you walk around campus, quickly glance at individuals approaching you and either smile or maintain a neutral expression; then observe the other person's expression. Try to keep the duration of your glance the same whether you smile or not. You might record the results as you collect them instead of relying on your memory. Chances are that people you smile at will smile back, whereas those you approach with a neutral expression will do the same. What does this tell you about the importance of doing double-blind studies?

Experimenter   Participant

Single-blind Study
Experimenter knows who is in which group; participants do not.

Experimenter   Participant

Double-blind Study
Neither experimenter nor participants know who is in which group.

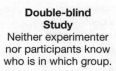

double-blind study   An experiment in which neither the people being studied nor the individuals running the study know who is in the control group and who is in the experimental group until after the results are tallied.

field research   Descriptive or experimental research conducted in a natural setting outside the laboratory.

One solution to the problem of experimenter effects is to do a **double-blind study**. In such a study, the person running the experiment, the one having actual contact with the participants, also does not know who is in which group until the data have been gathered. Double-blind procedures are essential in drug research. Different doses of a drug (and whether it is the active drug or a placebo) are coded in some way, and the person administering the drug is kept in the dark about the code's meaning until after the experiment. To run our cellphone study in a double-blind fashion, we could use a simulator that automatically records collisions and have the experimenter give instructions through an intercom so that he or she will not know which group a participant is in until after the results are tallied.

Because experiments allow conclusions about cause and effect, and because they permit researchers to distinguish real effects from placebo effects, they have long been the method of choice in psychology. However, like all methods, the experiment has its limitations. Just as in other kinds of studies, the participants are typically university students and may not always be representative of the larger population. Moreover, in an experiment, the researcher designs and sets up what is often a rather artificial situation and the participants try to do as they are told. In their desire to cooperate or to present themselves in a positive light, they may act in ways that they ordinarily would not (Kihlstrom, 1995). For this reason, many psychologists have called for more **field research**, the careful study of behaviour in natural contexts such as schools and the workplace (Cialdini, 2009). For example, have you ever wondered if women are more "talkative" than men, as the stereotype suggests? A field study of people in their everyday lives would be the best way to answer this question. Indeed, such a study has been done: The participants wore an unobtrusive recording device as they went about their normal lives, and the researchers found no gender differences at all (Mehl et al., 2007).

Every research method has both its strengths and its weaknesses. Did you make a list of each method's advantages and disadvantages, as we suggested earlier? If so, compare it now with the one in Review 2.1.

REVIEW 2.1

Research Methods in Psychology: Their Advantages and Disadvantages

Method	Advantages	Disadvantages
Case study	Good source of hypotheses. Provides in-depth information on individuals. Unusual cases can shed light on situations or problems that are unethical or impractical to study in other ways.	Vital information may be missing, making the case hard to interpret. The person's memories may be selective or inaccurate. The individual may not be representative or typical.
Naturalistic observation	Allows description of behaviour as it occurs in the natural environment. Often useful in first stages of a research program.	Allows researcher little or no control of the situation. Observations may be biased. Does not allow firm conclusions about cause and effect.

Laboratory observation	Allows more control than naturalistic observation. Allows use of sophisticated equipment.	Allows researcher only limited control of the situation. Observations may be biased. Does not allow firm conclusions about cause and effect. Behaviour may differ from behaviour in the natural environment.
Test	Yields information on personality traits, emotional states, aptitudes, and abilities.	Difficult to construct tests that are reliable and valid.
Survey	Provides a large amount of information on large numbers of people.	If sample is nonrepresentative or biased, it may be impossible to generalize from the results. Responses may be inaccurate or untrue.
Correlational study	Shows whether two or more variables are related. Allows general predictions.	Usually does not permit identification of cause and effect.
Experiment	Allows researcher to control the situation. Permits researcher to identify cause and effect and to distinguish placebo effects from treatment effects.	Situation is artificial, and results may not generalize well to the real world. Sometimes difficult to avoid experimenter effects.

CULTURE and *Research*

Special Challenges

Doing good research is demanding enough, but the challenges are multiplied when psychologists venture into societies other than their own to learn which attitudes, behaviours, and traits are universal and which are specific to particular groups. Here are three major concerns that arise in cross-cultural research:

1   **Methods and sampling.** Right off the bat, researchers must worry about how one language translates into another. Speakers of English know that "Mary had a little lamb" means she owned one, not that she gave birth to it, ate it, or had an affair with it—but that's not clear from the words alone! Further, sometimes the term for a concept or emotional experience that is central in one culture (say, the Chinese concept of "filial piety," honouring your ancestors) may have no exact linguistic equivalent in another. In doing cross-cultural research, scientists must also be sure that their

samples are similar in all important ways except for ethnicity or nationality. Otherwise, what seems like a cultural difference may really be a difference in education, crowding, or some other noncultural factor.

2 **Stereotyping.** When researchers describe average differences across societies, they may be tempted to oversimplify their findings, which can lead to stereotyping. Of course, cultural rules, on average, do make Nigerians different from Australians and Cambodians different from Italians. Yet within every society, individuals vary according to their temperaments, beliefs, and learning histories. The challenge is to understand average cultural differences without implying that everyone in Culture A is as different from everyone in Culture B as chocolate is from cheese (see Chapter 14).

3 **Reification.** To *reify* means to regard an intangible process, such as a feeling, as if it were a literal object. For example, when people say, "I have a lot of anger buried in me," they are treating anger as if it were a thing that sits inside them like a kidney, when in fact it is a cluster of mental and physical reactions that come and go. In cultural psychology, reification—treating "culture" as a thing instead of a collection of beliefs and traditions—can lead to circular reasoning, as in "Country A attacks its neighbours because it has a warlike culture, and we know it is a warlike culture because it attacks its neighbours." This is like telling a man with a leg injury that he can't walk because he's lame (Lonner & Malpass, 1994). Cultural psychologists must therefore work to identify not only the average differences in traits and behaviours across cultures but also the underlying mechanisms that account for them—*why* Country A is "warlike," and why it changed from being peaceful (Heine & Norenzayan, 2006; Matsumoto & Yoo, 2006).

quickQUIZ

✓• **Quick Review** on **MyPsychLab**

Quizzes are a part of all student cultures, so you can't escape this one.

A. Name the independent and dependent variables in studies designed to answer the following questions:
1. Whether sleeping after learning a poem improves memory for the poem
2. Whether the presence of other people affects a person's willingness to help someone in distress
3. Whether listening to heavy metal makes people aggressive

B. Identify three special challenges in doing cross-cultural research.

C. On a TV show, Dr. Blitznik announces a fabulous new program: Chocolate Immersion Therapy (CIT). "People who spend one day a week doing nothing but eating chocolate are soon cured of eating disorders, depression, and poor study habits," claims Dr. Blitznik. What should you find out about CIT before signing up?

Answers:

A. 1. Opportunity to sleep after learning is the independent variable; memory for the poem is the dependent variable. 2. The presence of other people is the independent variable; willingness to help others is the dependent variable. 3. Exposure to heavy metal is the independent variable; aggressive behaviour is the dependent variable. B. Problems in methodology (e.g., translation problems) and sampling; stereotyping; reification of culture when explaining results. C. Some questions to ask: Is there research showing that people who went through CIT did better than those in a control group who did not have the therapy or who had a different therapy—say, Broccoli Immersion Therapy? If so, how many people were studied? How were they selected, and how were they assigned to the therapy and no-therapy groups? Did the person running the experiment know who was getting CIT and who was not? How long did the "cures" last? Has the research been peer reviewed? Has it been replicated?

Doing good cross-cultural research is therefore difficult, requiring the right methods and the ability to interpret them critically. But the results are essential for a deeper, more accurate understanding of human behaviour in all its rich variety.

 ## YOU are about to learn . . .

◆ why averages can be misleading.

◆ how psychologists can tell whether a finding is impressive or trivial.

◆ why some findings are significant statistically yet unimportant in practical terms.

◆ how psychologists can combine results from many studies of a question to get a better overall answer.

EVALUATING THE FINDINGS

If you are a psychologist who has just done an observational study, a survey, or an experiment, your work has just begun. Once you have some results in hand, you must do three things with them: (1) describe them, (2) assess how reliable and meaningful they are, and (3) figure out how to explain them.

Descriptive Statistics: Finding Out What's So

Let's say that 30 people in the cellphone experiment talked on the phone and 30 did not. We have recorded the number of collisions for each person on the driving simulator. Now we have 60 numbers. What can we do with them?

The first step is to summarize the data. The world does not want to hear how many collisions each person had. It wants to know what happened in the cellphone group as a whole, compared to what happened in the control group. To provide this information, we need numbers that sum up our data. Such numbers, known as descriptive statistics, are often depicted in graphs and charts.

A good way to summarize the data is to compute group averages. The most commonly used type of average is the arithmetic mean. (For two other types, see the Appendix.) The mean is calculated by adding up all the individual scores and dividing the result by the number of scores. We can compute a mean for the cellphone group by adding up the 30 collision scores and dividing the sum by 30. Then we can do the same for the control group. Now our 60 numbers have been boiled down to 2. For the sake of our example, let's assume that the cellphone group had an average of 10 collisions, whereas the control group's average was only 7.

descriptive statistics Statistical procedures that organize and summarize research data.

arithmetic mean An average that is calculated by adding up a set of quantities and dividing the sum by the total number of quantities in the set.

◀◉ Simulate
Doing Simple Statiste

Most people assume that "on average" means "typically"—but sometimes it doesn't! Averages can be misleading if you don't know the extent to which events deviated from the statistical mean and how they were distributed.

FIGURE 2.4 Same Mean, Different Meaning

In both distributions of scores, the mean is 5, but in (a) the scores are clustered around the mean, whereas in (b) they are widely dispersed, so the standard deviations for the distributions will be quite different. In which distribution is the mean more "typical" of all scores?

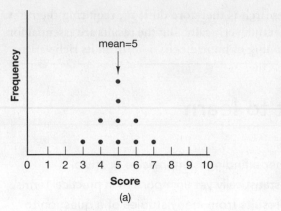

(a)

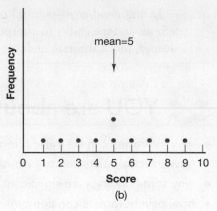

(b)

We must be careful, however, about how we interpret these averages. It is possible that no one in our cellphone group actually had 10 collisions. Perhaps half the people in the group were dangerous drivers and had 15 collisions, whereas the others were more cautious and had only 5. Perhaps almost all the participants in the group had 9, 10, or 11 collisions. Perhaps the number of accidents ranged from 0 to 15. The mean does not tell us about such variability in the participants' responses. For that, we need other descriptive statistics. For example, the **standard deviation** tells us how clustered or spread out the individual scores are around the mean; the more spread out they are, the less "typical" the mean is. (See Figure 2.4 and, for more details, the Appendix.) Unfortunately, when research is reported in the news, you usually hear only about the mean.

Inferential Statistics: Asking "So What?"

At this point in our study, we have one group with an average of 10 collisions and another with an average of 7. Should we break out the champagne? Hold a press conference? Call our mothers?

Better hold off. Perhaps if one group had an average of 15 collisions and the other an average of 1, we could get excited. But rarely does a psychological study hit you between the eyes with a sensationally clear result. In most cases, there is some possibility that the difference between the two groups was due simply to chance. Despite all our precautions, perhaps the people in the cellphone group just happened to be a little more accident-prone, and their collisions had nothing to do with talking on the phone.

To find out how meaningful the data are, psychologists use **inferential statistics**. These statistics do not merely describe or summarize the data; they permit a researcher to draw *inferences* (conclusions based on evidence) about how meaningful the findings are. Like descriptive statistics, inferential statistics involve the application of mathematical formulas to the data. (Again, see the Appendix for details.)

Historically, the most commonly used inferential statistics have been **significance tests**, which tell researchers how likely a result was to have occurred by chance. In our cellphone study, a significance test will tell us how likely it is that the difference between the experimental group and the control group occurred by chance. It is not possible to rule out chance entirely, but if the likelihood that a result occurred by chance is quite low, we can say that the result is *statistically significant*. This means that there is a high probability that the difference is real.

By convention, psychologists consider a result to be significant if it would be expected to occur by chance 5 or fewer times in 100 repetitions of the study. Another way of saying this is that the result is significant at the .05 ("point oh five") level. If the difference could be expected to occur by chance in 6 out of 100 studies, we would have

standard deviation A commonly used measure of variability that indicates the average difference between scores in a distribution and their mean.

inferential statistics Statistical procedures that allow researchers to draw inferences about how statistically meaningful a study's results are.

significance tests Statistical tests that show how likely it is that a study's results occurred merely by chance.

to say that the results failed to support the hypothesis—that the difference we obtained might well have occurred merely by chance—although we might still want to do further research to be sure. You can see that psychologists refuse to be impressed by just any old result.

Statistically significant results allow psychologists to make general predictions about human behaviour. These predictions are usually stated as probabilities ("On average, we can expect 60% of all students to do X, Y, or Z"). However, they usually do not tell us with any certainty what a particular individual will do in a particular situation. Probabilistic results are typical in all the sciences, not just psychology. Medical research, for example, can tell us that the odds are high that someone who smokes will get lung cancer, but because many variables interact to produce any particular case of cancer, research cannot tell us for sure whether Aunt Bessie, who smokes two packs a day, will come down with the disease.

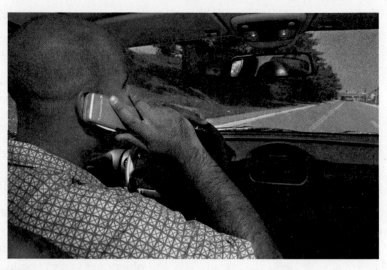

In a real study of cellphone use while driving, a participant "drives" in a high-tech driving simulator.

By the way, many studies similar to our hypothetical one have confirmed the dangers of talking on a cellphone while driving. In one study, cellphone users, whether their phones were handheld or hands-free, were as impaired in their driving ability as intoxicated drivers were (Ishigami & Klein, 2009; Strayer, Drews, & Crouch, 2006). Because of such research, some provinces have made it illegal to drive while using a handheld cellphone. Others are considering making any cellphone use by a driver illegal. We will revisit this topic, and the general issue of multitasking, in Chapter 9.

Interpreting the Findings

The last step in any study is to figure out what the findings mean. Trying to understand behaviour from uninterpreted findings is like trying to become fluent in Swedish by reading a Swedish–English dictionary. Just as you need the grammar of Swedish to tell you how the words fit together, the psychologist needs hypotheses and theories to explain how the facts that emerge from research fit together.

CHOOSING THE BEST EXPLANATION. Sometimes it is hard to choose between competing explanations of a finding. Does cellphone use disrupt driving by impairing coordination, by increasing a driver's vulnerability to distraction, by interfering with the processing of information, or by some combination of these or other factors? Several explanations may fit the results equally well, which means that more research will be needed to determine the best one.

Sometimes the best interpretation of a finding does not emerge until a hypothesis has been tested in different ways. Although the methods we have described tend to be appropriate for different questions (see Review 2.2 on p. 63), sometimes one method can be used to confirm, disconfirm, or extend the results obtained with another. If the findings of studies using various methods converge, there is greater reason to be confident about them. If they conflict, researchers must modify their hypotheses or do more research.

Here is an example. When psychologists compare the mental-test scores of young people and old people, they usually find that younger people outscore older ones. This type of research, in which groups are compared at a given time, is called cross-sectional.

Cross-sectional Study

Different groups compared at one time:

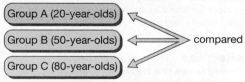

cross-sectional study   A study in which people (or animals) of different ages are compared at a given time.

But **longitudinal studies** can also be used to investigate mental abilities across the life span. In a longitudinal study, the same people are followed over a period of time and are reassessed at regular intervals:

Longitudinal Study
Same group compared at different times:

Group A at age 20 ⟶ Group A at age 50 ⟶ Group A at age 80

In contrast to cross-sectional studies, longitudinal studies find that as people age, they sometimes perform as well as they ever did on certain mental tests. A *general* decline in ability may not occur until people reach their 70s or 80s (see Chapter 13). Why do results from the two types of studies conflict? Probably because cross-sectional studies measure generational differences; younger generations tend to outperform older ones in part because they are better educated or are more familiar with the tests used. Without longitudinal studies, we might falsely conclude that all types of mental ability inevitably decline with advancing age.

JUDGING THE RESULT'S IMPORTANCE. Sometimes psychologists agree on the reliability and meaning of a finding but not on its ultimate relevance for theory or practice. Part of the problem is statistical. Traditional tests of significance continue to be used in the overwhelming majority of psychological studies, which is why we have described them here, but these tests have important drawbacks (Cumming et al., 2007; Erceg-Hurn & Mirosevich, 2008). A result may be statistically significant yet be small and of little consequence in everyday life because the independent variable does not explain most of the variation in people's behaviour. On the other hand, a result may not quite reach statistical significance yet be worth following up on. Because of these and other problems, many psychology journals now encourage or require the use of statistical procedures that reveal the **effect size**—that is, how powerful the independent variable really is (how much of the variation in the data the variable accounts for). If the independent variable explains 5% of the variation, it's not very powerful, even if the result is statistically significant; if it explains 40%, it's pretty impressive.

One popular statistical technique, called **meta-analysis**, combines and analyzes data from many studies on a particular topic instead of assessing each study's results separately. A single result based on a small sample may be just a coincidence; in fact, significance levels can vary considerably from one replication of a study to another (Cumming, 2008). Meta-analysis comes to the rescue, revealing how much of the variation in scores across *all* the studies in the analysis can be explained by a particular variable.

Further, studies often conflict with each other, and meta-analysis can provide us with a clearer picture. For instance, one meta-analysis of nearly 50 years of research found that gender does account for a good deal of the variance in performance on certain spatial-visual tasks, such as the ability to mentally rotate objects, with males doing better on average (Voyer, Voyer, & Bryden, 1995). In contrast, other meta-analyses have shown that gender accounts for very little of the variance in performance on tests of verbal and math ability, usually only 1 to 5% (Hyde, 2005, 2007). Thus, gender effects may depend on the task studied.

Techniques such as meta-analysis are useful because rarely does one study prove anything, in psychology or any other field. That is why you should be suspicious of headlines that announce a sudden major scientific breakthrough based on a single study. Breakthroughs do occur, but they are rare.

longitudinal study A study in which people (or animals) are followed and periodically reassessed over a period of time.

effect size The amount of variance among scores in a study accounted for by the independent variable.

meta-analysis A procedure for combining and analyzing data from many studies; it determines how much of the variance in scores across all studies can be explained by a particular variable.

REView 2.2

Psychological Research Methods Contrasted

Psychologists may use different methods to answer different questions about a topic. This table shows some ways in which the methods described in this chapter can be used to study different questions about aggression. Sometimes, however, two or more methods can be used to investigate the same question, and findings based on one method may extend, support, or disconfirm findings based on another.

Method	Purpose	Example
Case study	To understand the development of aggressive behaviour in a particular individual; to formulate research hypotheses about the origins of aggressiveness	Developmental history of a serial killer
Naturalistic observation	To describe the nature of aggressive acts in early childhood	Observation of hitting, kicking, etc., during free-play periods in a preschool
Laboratory observation	To find out whether aggressiveness in pairs of same-sex and different-sex children differs in frequency or intensity	Observation through a one-way window of same-sex and different-sex pairs of pre-schoolers; pairs must negotiate who gets to play with an attractive toy that has been promised to each child
Test	To compare the personality traits of aggressive and nonaggressive persons	Administration of personality tests to violent and nonviolent prisoners
Survey	To find out how common domestic violence is in the general population	Questionnaire asking anonymous respondents (in a sample representative of the population) about the occurrence of slapping, hitting, etc., in their homes
Correlational study	To examine the relation between aggressiveness and television viewing	Administration to university students of a paper-and-pencil test of aggressiveness and a questionnaire on number of hours spent watching TV weekly; computation of coefficient of correlation
Experiment	To find out whether high air temperatures elicit aggressive behaviour	Arrangement for individuals to "shock" a "learner" (actually a confederate of the experimenter) while seated in a room heated to either 22°C or 29°C

quickQUIZ

✔•─Quick Review on MyPsychLab

Major scientific breakthrough! Self–tests help!

A. Check your understanding of the descriptive–inferential distinction by placing a check in the appropriate column for each phrase:

	Descriptive statistics	Inferential statistics
1. Summarize the data	_____	_____
2. Give likelihood of data occurring by chance	_____	_____
3. Include the mean	_____	_____
4. Give measure of statistical significance	_____	_____
5. Tell you whether to call your mother about your results	_____	_____

B. If a researcher studies the same group over many years, the study is said to be _____.

C. On the internet, you read about a "Fantastic Scientific Breakthrough in Treating Shyness." Why should you be cautious about this announcement?

Answers:

A. 1. descriptive 2. inferential 3. descriptive 4. inferential 5.inferential B. longitudinal C. Scientific progress usually proceeds gradually, not all at once. And besides, anyone can post a claim on the internet, so you will want to ask, "What's the original source of this claim?"

◆◉ YOU are about to learn . . .

◆ why psychologists sometimes lie to people taking part in their studies.

◆ why psychologists study nonhuman animals.

KEEPING THE ENTERPRISE ETHICAL

←◉ Simulate
Ethics in Psychological Research

Because rigorous research methods are the very heart of science, psychologists spend considerable time discussing and debating their procedures for collecting and evaluating data. And they are also concerned about the ethical principles governing research and practice. In all institutions that receive federal funding, a review committee must approve all studies and make sure they conform to federal regulations (The Tri-Council Policy Statement, TCPS2). In addition, the Canadian Psychological Association (CPA) has a code of ethics that all members must follow. In general, both of these codes advocate that research follow these eight major principles (Canadian Institutes of Health Research, Natural Sciences and Engineering Research Council of Canada, and Social Sciences and Humanities Research Council of Canada, 2010): (1) respect for human dignity; (2) respect for free and informed consent; (3) respect for vulnerable persons, such as children; (4) respect for privacy and confidentiality; (5) respect for justice and inclusiveness; (6) balancing harms and benefits; (7) minimizing harm; and (8) maximizing benefit. In practice, these principles mean that, before participating in an experiment, individuals must know what to expect during the session and must voluntarily choose to take part (that is, they must give "informed consent").

The Ethics of Studying Human Beings

The TCPS and CPA codes call on psychological scientists to respect the dignity and welfare of human participants. People must participate voluntarily and must know enough about the study to make an intelligent decision about participating, a doctrine known as **informed consent**. Researchers must also protect participants from physical and mental harm, and if any risk exists, they must warn the participants in advance and give them an opportunity to withdraw at any time.

The policy of informed consent sometimes clashes with an experimenter's need to disguise the true purpose of the study. In such cases, if the purpose were revealed in advance, the results would be ruined because the participants would not behave naturally. In social psychology especially, a study's design sometimes calls for an elaborate deception. For example, a confederate of the researcher might pretend to be having a seizure. The researcher can then find out whether bystanders—the uninformed participants—will respond to a person needing help. If the participants knew that the confederate was only acting, obviously they would not bother to intervene or call for assistance.

Sometimes people have been misled about procedures that are intentionally designed to make them uncomfortable, angry, guilty, ashamed, or anxious so that researchers can learn what people do when they feel this way. In studies of embarrassment and anger, people have been made to look clumsy in front of others, have been called insulting names, or have been told they were incompetent. In studies of dishonesty, participants have been entrapped into cheating and have then been confronted with evidence of their guilt. Today, the TCPS and the CPA's ethical guidelines require researchers to show that any deceptive procedures are justified by a study's potential value, to consider alternative procedures, and to thoroughly debrief participants about the true purpose and methods of the study afterward. When people are debriefed and told why deception was necessary, they are rarely resentful and say that they are willing to take part in further studies (Bröder, 1998). But the issues raised by deception will always be with us, and both the Tri-Council and the CPA frequently reevaluate their ethical codes to deal with deception.

In addition, participants have the right to expect that their responses will be confidential unless they explicitly consent to public disclosure. This requirement can present researchers with a dilemma because psychologists often investigate sensitive issues, such as illegal drug use. Because of the need for confidentiality, responses must be anonymous. Confidentiality is also an issue in psychological practice. In Canada, unlike in the United States, communications between the psychologist and the client are not privileged. A court can compel a psychologist to reveal the content of discussions with a client. Further, Canadian law requires that certain types of information must be reported (for example, child abuse), regardless of any potential harm that may come to the client. Many of these conflicts can be avoided by ensuring that a potential participant or client understands the limits of confidentiality before he or she begins to disclose potentially sensitive information.

👁 **Watch**
Before Informed
Consent: Robert Guthrie

The Ethics of Studying Animals

Ethical issues also arise in animal research. Animals have always been used in psychological studies and still play a crucial role. Although sometimes they are not harmed (as in research on mating in hamsters, which is fun for the hamsters), sometimes they are (as in research on epilepsy where they must be given seizures). Some studies require an animal's death, as when rats brought up in deprived or enriched environments are

informed consent The doctrine that anyone who participates in human research must do so voluntarily and must know enough about the study to make an intelligent decision about whether to take part.

Psychologists sometimes use animals to study learning, memory, emotion, and social behaviour. On the left, John Boitano and Kathryn Scavo observe a swimming rat as it learns the location of platforms in a pool of dark water. On the right, Frans de Waal stands in front of a group of chimpanzees socializing in an outdoor play area.

sacrificed so that their brains can be examined for any effects. Psychologists study animals for many reasons:

♦ *To conduct basic research on a particular species.* For example, researchers have learned a great deal about the unusually lusty and cooperative lives of bonobo apes.

♦ *To discover practical applications.* For example, behavioural studies have shown farmers how to reduce crop destruction by birds and deer without resorting to their traditional method—shooting the animals.

♦ *To study issues that cannot be studied experimentally with human beings because of practical or ethical considerations.* For example, research on monkeys has demonstrated the effects of maternal deprivation on emotional development, and the effects of later experience in overcoming early deprivation.

♦ *To clarify theoretical questions.* For example, we might not attribute the longer lifespans of women solely to lifestyle factors and health practices if we discover that a male–female difference exists in other mammals as well.

♦ *To improve human welfare.* For example, animal studies have helped researchers develop ways to reduce chronic pain and rehabilitate human and animal patients with neurological disorders—to name only a few benefits.

◉ Watch
Studying Squid

Animal Rights Terrorists

Animal research, however, has provoked angry disputes. Many animal-rights proponents want to eliminate all research using animals, and some activists have severely damaged research laboratories (sometimes causing the deaths of the lab animals they have "freed"), or have threatened or carried out acts of violence against researchers and their families. On the other side, some defenders of animal research do not acknowledge that confinement in laboratories can be psychologically and physically harmful for some species, and that abuses have occurred. This conflict has motivated psychologists to find ways to improve the treatment of research animals. In Canada, animal research is governed by the Canadian Council on Animal Care (CCAC) and by CPA's ethical code covering the humane treatment of animals. Both codes are comprehensive, and cover everything from the housing and care of research animals to encouraging researchers to develop alternative procedures that take advantage of new technology. The difficult task for scientists is to balance the many benefits of animal research with an acknowledgment of past abuses and a compassionate attitude toward species other than our own.

Now that you have finished the first two chapters of this book, you are ready to explore more deeply what psychologists have learned about human psychology. The methods of psychological science, as we will see repeatedly in the remainder of the book, have overturned some deeply entrenched assumptions about the way people think, feel, act, and adapt to events in their lives, and have yielded information that greatly improves the well-being of humans. These methods illuminate our human errors and biases and enable us to seek knowledge with an open mind. Biologist Thomas Huxley put it well: The essence of science, he said, is "to sit down before the fact as a little child, be prepared to give up every preconceived notion, follow humbly wherever and to whatever abyss nature leads, or you shall learn nothing."

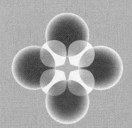

Taking Psychology with YOU

Thinking Critically in Everyday Life

Lying with Statistics

We have seen that statistical procedures are indispensable tools for assessing research. But in the real world, statistics can be manipulated, misrepresented, and even made up by people hoping to promote a particular political or social agenda. That is why an essential part of critical and scientific thinking is learning not only how to use statistics correctly but also how to identify their misuse.

A primary reason for the misuse of statistics is "innumeracy" (mathematical illiteracy). For instance, it has been argued that each year, between 62 500 and 80 000 Canadians have used a gun for self-defence (e.g., Mauser & Buckner, 1997). Why haven't we heard these astounding numbers on the news? Well, because the numbers come from a study (Mauser, 1995) in which 1505 Canadians were surveyed and 2.1% (31 people) responded that in the last five years they had used a gun to protect themselves against a person or an animal. This percentage was then multiplied by the population of Canada to obtain the larger figure (note the difference between 31 and 80 000 Canadians), which assumes that the sample was representative and that everyone in Canada has equal access to firearms!

We don't want you to distrust all statistics. Statistics don't lie; people do—or, more likely, they misinterpret what the numbers mean. When statistics are used correctly, they neither confuse nor mislead. On the contrary, they can expose unwarranted conclusions, promote clarity and precision, and protect us from our biases and blind spots. You need to be careful, though. Here are a few things you can do when you hear that "2 million people do this" or "one out of four people are that":

Ask how the number was computed. Suppose someone on your campus gives a talk about a hot social issue and cites some big number to show how serious and widespread the problem is. You should ask how the number was calculated. Was it based on government data, such as the census? Did it come from just one small study or from a meta-analysis of many studies? Or is it pure conjecture?

Ask about base rates and absolute numbers. If we tell you that the relative risk of getting ulcers is increased by 300% in university students who eat a bagel every morning (relax, it isn't!), that sounds pretty scary, but it does not tell you much. You would need to know how many students get ulcers in the first place, and then how many bagel-eating students get ulcers. If the "300% increased risk" is a jump from 100 students in every thousand to 300 in every thousand, then you might reasonably be concerned. If the number shifts from one in every thousand to three in every thousand, that is still a 300% increase, but the risk is very small and could even be a random fluke. Many health findings are presented in alarming percentage terms, as an increased risk of this or that, when the actual, absolute numbers are quite trivial (Bluming & Tavris, 2009; Gigerenzer et al., 2008).

Check to see how terms were defined. For example, if we hear that "one out of every four women" will be raped at some point in her life, we need to ask: How was rape defined? If women are asked if they have ever experienced any act of unwanted sex, the percentages are higher than if they are asked specifically whether they have been forced or coerced into intercourse against their will.

Always look for the control group. In a magazine article, women claimed that taking Viagra had improved their sex lives dramatically. But in a controlled study of 583 women, 43% of those taking a placebo pill said *their* sex lives had also improved—a percentage no different from the one in the Viagra group (Basson et al., 2002). If an experiment does not have a control group, especially if it is a study of a medication, treatment, or self-improvement program, then, as they say in New York, "Fuhgeddaboudit."

Be cautious about correlations. We said this before, but we'll say it again: With correlational findings, you usually can't be sure what's causing what. For example, longitudinal research on the effects of daycare on young children has found a correlation between time spent in daycare and aggressiveness, with the effect lasting through grade 6 (Belsky et al., 2007). This news has led to many "We told you so's" from people who believe that daycare is harmful to children and many outright rejections of the findings from people who believe that daycare is neutral or beneficial. Both sides have missed the boat: Not only is the correlation weak, but it also does not establish causation. The children could not be randomly assigned to daycare and home care groups; the parents chose the type of care. Thus we can't be sure whether (a) being in preschool increases aggressiveness or (b) aggressive children are more likely to be enrolled in preschool or (c) children who spend more time at home with their mothers simply have fewer playmates around to be aggressive *with!*

The statistics that most people like best are usually the ones that support their own opinions and prejudices. Unfortunately, bad statistics, repeated again and again, can infiltrate popular culture, spread like a virus on the internet, and become difficult to eradicate. The information in this chapter will get you started on telling the difference between numbers that are helpful and those that mislead or deceive. In future chapters, we will give you other information to help you think critically and scientifically about popular claims and findings that make the news.

SUMMARY

WHAT MAKES PSYCHOLOGICAL RESEARCH SCIENTIFIC?

◆ Research methods provide a way for psychologists to separate well-supported conclusions from unfounded belief. An understanding of these methods can also help people think critically about psychological issues and become astute consumers of psychological findings and programs.

◆ The ideal scientist states hypotheses and predictions precisely, is skeptical of claims that rest solely on faith or authority, relies on empirical evidence, resists the *confirmation bias* and complies with the *principle of falsifiability*, and is open about methods and results so that findings can be *replicated*. The public nature of science and the *peer review* process give science a built-in system of checks and balances.

DESCRIPTIVE STUDIES: ESTABLISHING THE FACTS

◆ In any study, the researcher would ideally like to use a representative sample, one that is similar in composition to the larger population the researcher wishes to describe. But in practice, researchers must often use "convenience" samples, which typically means university undergraduates. In the study of many topics, the consequences are minimal, but in other cases, conclusions about "people in general" must be interpreted with caution.

◆ *Descriptive methods* allow psychologists to describe and predict behaviour but not necessarily to choose one explanation over others. Such methods include case studies, observational studies, psychological tests, and surveys, as well as correlational studies.

◆ *Case studies* are detailed descriptions of individuals. They are often used by clinicians and can also be valuable in exploring new research topics and addressing questions that would otherwise be difficult to study. But because the person under study may not be representative of people in general, case studies are typically sources rather than tests of hypotheses.

◆ In *observational studies*, the researcher systematically observes and records behaviour without interfering in any way with the behaviour. *Naturalistic observation* is used to find out how animals and people behave in their natural environments. *Laboratory observation* allows more control and the use of special equipment; behaviour in the laboratory, however, may differ in certain ways from behaviour in natural contexts.

◆ *Psychological tests* are used to measure and evaluate personality traits, emotional states, aptitudes, interests, abilities,

and values. A good test is one that has been *standardized*, is scored using established *norms*, and is both *reliable* and *valid*. Critics have questioned the reliability and validity of even some widely used tests.

◆ *Surveys* are questionnaires or interviews that ask people directly about their experiences, attitudes, and opinions. Unrepresentative samples and *volunteer bias* can influence the generalizability of survey results. Findings can also be affected by the fact that respondents sometimes lie, misremember information, or misinterpret the questions. Technology and use of the internet can help psychologists minimize some of these problems, but they also introduce some new methodological challenges. People should be cautious about tests they take on the internet because not all of them meet scientific standards.

CORRELATIONAL STUDIES: LOOKING FOR RELATIONS

◆ In descriptive research, studies that look for relations between phenomena are known as *correlational*. A *correlation* is a measure of the strength of a positive or negative relation between two variables and is expressed by the *coefficient of correlation*. Many correlations reported in the media or on the internet are based on rumour and anecdote and are not supported by data. Even when a correlation is real, it does not necessarily demonstrate a causal relation between the variables.

EXPERIMENTS: HUNTING FOR CAUSES

◆ *Experiments* allow researchers to control the situation being studied, manipulate an *independent variable*, and assess the effects of the manipulation on a *dependent variable*. Experimental studies usually require a comparison or *control condition* and often involve *random assignment* of participants to experimental and control groups. In some studies, those in the control group receive a *placebo*, or fake treatment. *Single-blind* and *double-blind* procedures can be used to prevent the expectations of the participants or the experimenter from affecting the results.

◆ Because experiments allow conclusions about cause and effect, they have long been the method of choice in psychology. However, like laboratory observations, experiments create a special situation that may call forth behaviour not typical in other environments. Many psychologists, therefore, have called for more *field research*.

EVALUATING THE FINDINGS

◆ Psychologists use *descriptive statistics*, such as the *arithmetic mean* and the *standard deviation*, to summarize data. They use *inferential statistics* to find out how impressive the data are. *Significance tests* tell the researchers how likely it is that the results of a study occurred merely by chance. The results are said to be *statistically significant* if this likelihood is very low. Statistically significant results allow psychologists to make predictions about human behaviour, but, as in all sciences, probabilistic results do not tell us with any certainty what a particular individual will do in a situation.

◆ Choosing among competing interpretations of a finding can be difficult, and care must be taken to avoid going beyond the facts. Sometimes the best interpretation does not emerge until a hypothesis has been tested in more than one way—for example, by using both *cross-sectional* and *longitudinal* methods.

◆ Statistical significance does not always imply real-world importance because the amount of variation in the data accounted for by the independent variable—the *effect size*—may be small. Conversely, a result that does not quite reach significance may be potentially useful. Therefore, many psychologists are now turning to other inferential measures. The technique of *meta-analysis*, for example, reveals how much of the variation in scores across many different studies can be explained by a particular variable.

KEEPING THE ENTERPRISE ETHICAL

◆ The Tri-Council Policy Statement and the CPA's ethical code require researchers to obtain the *informed consent* of anyone who is participating in a study or experiment, protect them from harm, and warn them in advance of any risks. Many studies require deceptive procedures. Concern about the morality of such procedures has led to guidelines to protect participants.

◆ Psychologists study animals in order to gain knowledge about particular species, discover practical applications of psychological principles, study issues that cannot be studied with human beings for practical or ethical reasons, clarify theoretical questions, and improve human and animal welfare. Debate over the use of animals in research has led to more comprehensive regulations governing their treatment and care.

TAKING PSYCHOLOGY WITH YOU

◆ Statistics help scientists understand the complexities of behaviour, but statistics can also be misrepresented and misused.

MyPsychLab

Visit **www.mypsychlab.com** to help you get the best grade!
Test your knowledge and grasp difficult concepts through

• Custom study plans: See where you are strong and where you go wrong
• Interactive simulations
• Video and audio clips

KEY TERMS

theory 39	case study 42	surveys 47
hypothesis 39	observational studies 43	volunteer bias 47
operational definition 39	psychological tests 45	correlational study 49
principle of falsifiability 39	standardize 45	correlation 49
confirmation bias 40	norms 45	variables 49
representative sample 42	reliability 46	positive correlation 49
descriptive methods 42	validity 46	negative correlation 49

coefficient of correlation *49*

experiment *52*

independent variable *53*

dependent variable *53*

control condition *54*

random assignment *54*

placebo *55*

single-blind study *55*

experimenter effects *55*

double-blind study *56*

field research *56*

descriptive statistics *59*

arithmetic mean *59*

standard deviation *60*

inferential statistics *60*

significance tests *60*

cross-sectional study *61*

longitudinal study *62*

effect size *62*

meta-analysis *62*

informed consent *65*

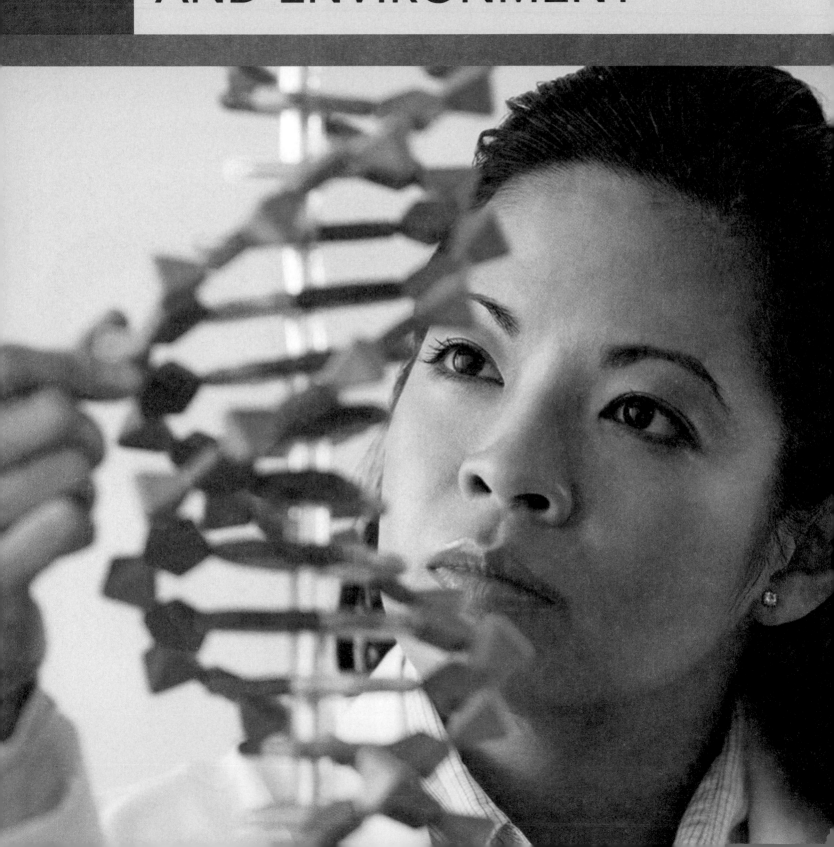

3 GENES, EVOLUTION, AND ENVIRONMENT

ASK QUESTIONS . . . be willing to WONDER

- If a trait is "genetic," is it inevitable?

- Why do kittens, monkeys, toddlers, and grownups all love to play and "monkey around"?

- Why do babies learn a first language so quickly, when adults usually struggle with a second one?

- Has evolution made men, but not women, naturally promiscuous?

Think of all the ways in which human beings are alike. Everywhere, no matter what their backgrounds or where they live, people love, work, argue, dance, sing, complain, and gossip. They rear families, celebrate marriages, and mourn losses. They reminisce about the past and plan for the future. They help their friends and fight their enemies. They smile with amusement, frown with displeasure, and glare in anger. *Where do all these commonalities come from?*

Think of all the ways in which human beings differ. Some are extroverts, always ready to make new friends or speak up in a crowd; others are shy and introverted, preferring the safe and familiar. Some are ambitious and enterprising; others are placid, content with the way things are. Some take to academics like a cat to catnip; others struggle in school but have plenty of street smarts and practical know-how. Some are overwhelmed by even petty problems; others remain calm and resilient in the face of severe difficulties. *Where do all these differences come from?*

For many years, psychologists addressing these questions tended to fall into two camps. On one side were the *nativists*, who emphasized genes and inborn characteristics, or *nature*; on the other side were the *empiricists*, who focused on learning and experience, or *nurture*. Edward L. Thorndike (1903), one of the leading psychologists of the early 1900s, staked out the first position when he claimed that "in the actual race of life . . . the chief determining factor is heredity." But in words that became famous, his contemporary, behaviourist John B. Watson (1925), insisted that experience could write virtually any message on the *tabula rasa*, the blank slate, of human nature: "Give me a dozen healthy infants, well-formed, and my own specified world to bring them up in and I'll guarantee to take any one at random and train him to become any type of specialist I might select—doctor, lawyer, artist, merchant-chief and yes, even beggar-man and thief, regardless of his talents, penchants, tendencies, abilities, vocations, and race of his ancestors."

In this chapter, we examine the contributions of both nature and nurture in shaping our human commonalities and our individual differences. We will focus largely on findings from two related areas: evolutionary psychology and behavioural genetics. Researchers in **evolutionary psychology** emphasize the evolutionary mechanisms that might help explain commonalities in language learning, attention, perception, memory, sexual behaviour, emotion, reasoning, and many other aspects of human psychology. Researchers in **behavioural genetics** attempt to tease apart the relative contributions of heredity and environment to explain individual differences in personality, mental ability, and other characteristics.

The long and short of it: Human beings are both similar and different.

evolutionary psychology A field of psychology emphasizing evolutionary mechanisms that may help explain human commonalities in cognition, development, emotion, social practices, and other areas of behaviour.

behavioural genetics An interdisciplinary field of study concerned with the genetic bases of individual differences in behaviour and personality.

genes The functional units of heredity; they are composed of DNA and specify the structure of proteins.

chromosomes Within every cell, rod-shaped structures that carry the genes.

DNA (deoxyribonucleic acid) The chromosomal molecule that transfers genetic characteristics by way of coded instructions for the structure of proteins.

genome The full set of genes in each cell of an organism (with the exception of sperm and egg cells).

The long and short of it: Human beings are both similar and different. Keep in mind, however, that virtually no one argues in terms of nature *versus* nurture anymore. Scientists today understand that heredity and environment constantly interact to produce our psychological traits and even most of our physical ones. This interaction works in two directions. First, genes affect the kinds of experiences we have: A teenager with a genetic aptitude for schoolwork may be more likely than other kids to join a spelling-bee team and get books and science kits as birthday presents. These experiences reward and encourage the development of academic skills. Conversely, although most people don't realize it, experience also affects our genes: Stress, diet, emotional events, and hormonal changes can all influence which genes are active or inactive at any given time over a person's lifetime (Fraga et al., 2005; Mischel, 2009). The study of this type of stable change in gene expression (that does not involve changes in the underlying DNA structure) is called *epigenetics*. Try, then, as you read this chapter, to resist the temptation to think of nature and nurture in either–or terms.

 YOU are about to learn . . .

◆ what the chemical code in our genes encodes for.

◆ what a complete map of the human genes reveals—and does not reveal.

UNLOCKING THE SECRETS OF GENES

Let's begin by looking at what genes are and how they operate. **Genes**, the basic units of heredity, are located on **chromosomes**, rod-shaped structures found in the centre (nucleus) of every cell of the body. Each sperm cell and each egg cell (ovum) contains 23 chromosomes, so when a sperm and egg unite at conception, the fertilized egg and all the body cells that eventually develop from it (except for sperm cells and ova) contain 46 chromosomes, arranged in 23 pairs.

Chromosomes consist of threadlike strands of **DNA (deoxyribonucleic acid)** molecules, and genes consist of small segments of this DNA. Each human chromosome contains thousands of genes, each with a fixed location. Collectively, all the genes together—the best estimates put the number at around 25 000—are referred to as the human **genome.** Most of these genes are found in other animals as well, but others are uniquely human, setting us apart from chimpanzees, wasps, and mice. Many genes contribute directly to a particular trait, but others work indirectly by switching other genes on or off throughout a person's life. Everyone inherits many genes in the same form as everyone else; other genes vary, contributing to our individuality.

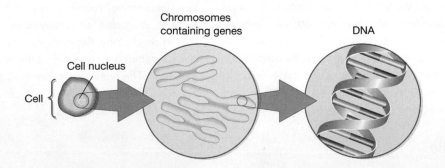

Cell

Cell nucleus

Chromosomes containing genes

DNA

Within each gene, four basic chemical elements of DNA—the bases adenine, thymine, cytosine, and guanine, identified by the letters A, T, C, and G—are arranged in a particular order: for example, ACGTCTCTATA. . . . This sequence may contain thousands or even tens of thousands of "letters," which together constitute a code for the synthesis of one of the many proteins that affect virtually every aspect of the body, from its structure to the chemicals that keep it running. But this is a simplification. Many genes can make more than one protein, depending on when and where different "coding" segments of DNA on the gene are activated. Thus our measly 25 000 or so genes—barely more than a common worm has—are able to produce hundreds of thousands of different proteins (Pennisi, 2005).

Identifying even a single gene is a daunting task; biologist Joseph Levine and geneticist David Suzuki (1993) once compared it to searching for someone when all you know is that the person lives somewhere on earth. However, new technologies now allow scientists to survey hundreds of thousands of "letters" at once instead of looking for one gene at a time. Using powerful computer programs, scientists can compare the genes of people who share a particular disease or trait with those of people who do not have it. A catalogue has been developed that describes millions of patterns of human genetic variation so that researchers can study the consequences of those variations. One method, which has been used to search for the genes associated with many physical and mental conditions, involves doing *linkage studies*. These studies take advantage of the tendency of genes lying close together on a chromosome to be inherited together across generations. The researchers start out by looking for a **genetic marker,** a DNA segment that varies considerably among individuals and whose location on the chromosome is already known. They then look for patterns of inheritance of these markers in large families in which a condition—say, depression or impulsive violence—is common. If a marker tends to exist only in family members who have the condition, then it can be used as a genetic landmark: The gene involved in the condition is apt to be located nearby on the chromosome, so the researchers have some idea where to search for it. The linkage method was used, for example, to locate the gene responsible for Huntington's disease, a fatal neurological disorder that affects motor control, intellectual functioning, and memory (Huntington's Disease Collaborative Research Group, 1993). Although in this instance only one gene was involved, the search took a decade of painstaking work.

In 2000, after years of heated competition, an international collaboration of researchers called the Human Genome Project and a private company, Celera Genomics, both announced that they had completed a rough draft of a map of the entire human genome, and since then the map has been greatly refined. Using high-tech methods, researchers have identified the sequence of nearly all 3 billion units of DNA (those A's, C's, T's, and G's) and have been able to determine the boundaries between genes and how the genes are arranged on the chromosomes (see Figure 3.1). This project has been costly and time-consuming, but it reflects the view among many scientists that the twenty-first century will be the century of the gene.

Even when researchers locate a gene, however, they do not automatically know its role in physical or psychological functioning. Usually, locating a gene is just the first tiny step in understanding what it does and how it works. Also, be wary of media reports implying that some gene is the *only* one involved in a complex psychological ability or trait, such as autism or shyness. It seems that nearly every year brings another report about some gene that supposedly explains a human trait. A few years back, newspapers even announced the discovery of a "worry gene." Don't worry about it! Most human traits, even such seemingly straightforward ones as height and eye

✱ Explore
Building Blocks of Genetics

◉ Watch
How the Human Genome Map Affects You

Junk DNA

genetic marker   A segment of DNA that varies among individuals, has a known location on a chromosome, and can function as a genetic landmark for a gene involved in a physical or mental condition.

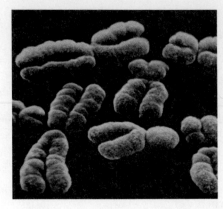

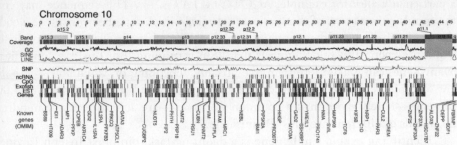

FIGURE 3.1 Mapping Human Genes.
Genes are located on chromosomes, some of which are shown on the left, magnified almost 55 000 times. On the right, a small portion of the map for chromosome 10 shows 52 genes identified by the Human Genome Project, including some that have been linked to prostate cancer, leukemia, and obesity.

✳ Explore
Dominant and Recessive Traits

colour, are influenced by more than one gene pair. Psychological traits are especially likely to depend on multiple genes, with each one accounting for just a small part of the variance among people. Conversely, any single gene is apt to influence many different behaviours. So at this point, all announcements of a "gene for this" or a "gene for that" should be viewed with extreme caution.

quickQUIZ

✔ **Quick Review** on **MyPsychLab**

The Human Genome Project has not discovered any quiz-taking genes.

1. What does it mean to say that the gene–environment interaction works in both directions?
2. The basic unit of heredity is called a (a) gene, (b) chromosome, (c) genome, (d) DNA molecule.
3. What does the code within a gene encode for?
4. *True or false*: Most human genetic traits depend on a single gene.

Answers:

1. Genes affect the environments we experience, and environmental factors affect the activity of genes over a person's lifetime.   2. a   3. the synthesis of a particular protein   4. False

 YOU are about to learn . . .

♦ the meaning of evolution.
♦ one reason that some traits become more common during evolution and others become less common.
♦ why some evolutionary psychologists assume the existence of innate "mental modules" in the human mind.
♦ some innate human characteristics.

THE GENETICS OF SIMILARITY

What accounts for the similarities among all human beings everywhere in the world, such as the universal capacity for language or loyalty to a family or clan? Evolutionary psychologists believe the answer lies partly in genetic dispositions that developed during the evolutionary history of our species. As British geneticist Steve Jones (1994) writes, "Each gene is a message from our forebears and together they contain the whole story of human evolution."

Evolution and Natural Selection

To read the messages from the past that are locked in our genes, we must first understand the nature of evolution itself. **Evolution** is basically a change in gene frequencies within a population, a change that typically takes place over many generations. As particular genes become more common or less common in the population, so do the characteristics they influence. These developments account for changes within a species, and when the changes are large enough they can result in the formation of new species.

Why do gene frequencies in a population change? Why don't they remain static from one generation to another? One reason is that during the division of the cells that produce sperm and eggs, if an error occurs in the copying of the original DNA sequence, genes can spontaneously change, or undergo **mutation**. In addition, during the formation of a sperm or an egg, small segments of genetic material cross over (exchange places) from one member of a chromosome pair to another, before the final cell division. As genes spontaneously mutate and recombine during the production of sperm and eggs, new genetic variations—and therefore potential new traits—keep arising.

But that is only part of the story. According to the principle of **natural selection,** first formulated in general terms by the British naturalist Charles Darwin in *On the Origin of Species* (1859/1964), the fate of these genetic variations depends on the environment. Darwin did not actually know about genes, as their discovery had not yet been widely publicized, but he realized that a species' characteristics must somehow be transmitted biologically from one generation to the next.

The fundamental idea behind natural selection is this: If, in a particular environment, individuals with a genetically influenced trait tend to be more successful than other individuals in finding food, surviving the elements, and fending off enemies—and therefore better at staying alive long enough to produce offspring—their genes will become more and more common in the population. Their genes will have been "selected" by reproductive success, and over many generations these genes may even spread throughout the species. In contrast, individuals whose traits are not as adaptive in the struggle for survival will not be as "reproductively fit": They will tend to die before reproducing, and therefore their genes, and the traits influenced by those genes, will become less and less common and eventually may even disappear.

Scientists debate how gradually or abruptly evolutionary changes occur and whether competition for survival is always the primary mechanism of change, but they agree on the basic importance of evolution. Over the past century and a half, Darwin's ideas have been resoundingly supported by findings in anthropology, botany, and molecular genetics (Coyne, 2009). Scientists have watched evolutionary developments occurring before their very eyes in organisms that change rapidly, such as microbes, insects,

"Heard the one about the three orangutans who went into a bar?" Evolutionary psychologists are interested in the origins of many human behaviours, such as smiling and laughter, which are universal among primates and are part of our shared evolutionary heritage.

◆ **Research**
Charles Darwin

Darwin's image can be found on countless T-shirts, bumper stickers, and mugs. His theory of evolution forms the basis of modern biology and has had a growing influence in psychology.

evolution   A change in gene frequencies within a population over many generations; a mechanism by which genetically influenced characteristics of a population may change.

mutation   Changes in genes, sometimes due to an error in the copying of the original DNA sequence during the division of the cells that produce sperm and eggs.

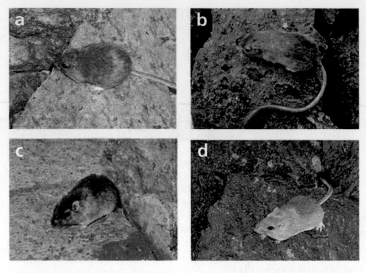

Natural selection allows animals to survive by adapting to the environment. In the deserts of Arizona, most rock pocket mice are sandy-coloured and are well camouflaged against the beige rocks they scamper over (a). Their colouring therefore protects them against owls and other predators. But in areas where ancient lava flows have left large deposits of black rock, the same species has evolved to be dark-coated and thus equally well disguised (b). You can see how vulnerable these mice are when their coats do *not* blend with the colour of the rocks (c and d). Researchers have identified the gene involved in the evolution of dark coloration in these mice (Nachman, Hoekstra, & D'Agostino, 2003).

natural selection The evolutionary process in which individuals with genetically influenced traits that are adaptive in a particular environment tend to survive and to reproduce in greater numbers than do other individuals; as a result, their traits become more common in the population.

and various plants. They have also observed rapid evolutionary changes due to human activity. For example, the horns of bighorn rams have been getting smaller because of trophy hunting, which removes animals with larger horns from the breeding population (Coltman et al., 2003).

However, this "survival of the fittest" account of evolution cannot explain all the physical and behavioural traits that reflect a gene's success (that is, increase or decrease within a population). For example, why does a peacock (but not the female of the same species, the peahen) have such an incredibly large and colourful tail? Certainly not to avoid being spotted by predators! Darwin himself was puzzled by some of the physical traits he observed in nature and eventually became dissatisfied with natural selection as the only cause (or agent) of evolution. In Darwin's second book on evolution, *The Descent of Man* (1874), he proposed another type of selection: *sexual selection*. In natural selection, nature determines which genes survive and reproduce, and which genes disappear from the planet. In sexual selection, the members of either the other sex or the same sex, with which one is competing, determine a gene's fate. Two types of sexual selection exist:

- *Intersexual selection.* In this type, a member of one sex chooses a mate from the other sex on the basis of certain characteristics. For males, the choice appears to be most influenced by physical factors such as attractiveness and youth. For females, the choice is similarly influenced by physical factors, such as height and muscularity, but the resources that the male has access to also come into play. We will explore the tactics of intersexual selection later in this chapter.

- *Intrasexual selection.* In this type, members of the same sex compete for a partner of the other sex. Males might compete with each other by becoming more muscular or acquiring and displaying resources (such as wealth), whereas females might compete by enhancing their appearance and youthful look through such techniques as hair colouring or using makeup.

A renewed interest in sexual selection over the past 20 years has led to numerous "culturally driven" behaviours being reexamined from an evolutionary framework. In his book *The Mating Mind: How Sexual Choice Shaped the Evolution of Human Nature*, Geoffrey Miller hypothesizes that a number of behaviours, such as artistic innovation, music, and humour, are the result of sexually selected psychological traits dating back to the Pleistocene epoch (Miller, 2000). In order to excel in these areas, one requires considerable intelligence and creativity. These are also traits that are indicative of high genetic quality when viewed in the context of mate selection. In fact, the trait "artistic intelligence" ranked third out of nine (behind kindness and being socially exciting) in a comprehensive survey of preferred partner traits for both males and females (Buss & Barnes, 1986). Thus, an exceptional musician, imaginative painter, or witty comedian may attain higher reproductive success than a physically comparable counterpart owing to enhanced creative intelligence.

TRAITS AND PREFERENCES. Evolutionary biologists often start with an observation about some characteristic and then try to account for it in evolutionary terms. For example, why do male peacocks have such fabulous and flamboyant feathers while females look so drab and dull? Those long plumes certainly did not help the males avoid predators! The evolutionary answer is that during the history of the species, males who put on a flashy display (evidence that they had "good genes" and could afford to carry around the extra plumage) were better able to attract females. In contrast, a female peacock did not have to put on such a display to attract competing males. Instead, all she had to do was hang around and pick the best potential mate: the guy with the best genes and fanciest feathers. She didn't even have to dress up!

Evolutionary psychologists work in the same way as biologists, but some take a slightly different tack: They start by asking what sorts of challenges human beings might have faced in their prehistoric past—say, having to decide which foods were safe to eat, or needing to size up a stranger's intentions quickly. Then they draw inferences about the behavioural tendencies that might have been selected because they helped our forebears solve these survival problems and enhanced their reproductive fitness. (They make no assumption about whether the behaviour is adaptive or intelligent in the *present* environment.) Finally, they do research to see if those tendencies actually exist throughout the world.

For example, our ancestors' need to avoid eating poisonous or rancid food might have led eventually to an innate dislike for bitter tastes and rotten smells; those individuals who happened to be born with such dislikes would have stood a better chance of surviving long enough to reproduce. Similarly, it made good survival sense for our ancestors to develop an innate capacity for language and an ability to recognize faces and emotional expressions. But they would not have had much need for an innate ability to read or drive, inasmuch as books and cars had not yet been invented (Pinker, 1994).

MENTAL MODULES. For many evolutionary psychologists, a guiding assumption is that the human mind is not a general-purpose computer waiting to be programmed. Instead, they say, it developed as a collection of specialized and independent **mental modules** to handle specific survival problems, such as the need to locate food or find a mate (Buss, 1995, 1999; Cosmides, Tooby, & Barkow, 1992; Marcus, 2004; Mealey, 1996; Pinker, 2002). A particular module may involve several dispersed but interconnected areas of the brain, just as a computer file can be fragmented on a hard drive (Pinker, 1997). Critics worry that the idea of mental modules is no improvement over instinct theory, the once-popular notion in psychology that virtually every human activity and capacity, from cleanliness to cruelty, is innate. Frans de Waal (2002), an evolutionary theorist who believes that someday all psychology departments will have a picture of Darwin hanging on the wall, has accused some of his colleagues who argue for mental modules of mistakenly assuming that if a trait exists and has a genetic component, then it must be adaptive and must correspond to a module. This assumption, he points out, is incorrect: Male pattern baldness and pimples, for example, are not particularly adaptive! Many evolved and inherited traits are merely by-products of other traits (for example, your bellybutton is a by-product of being a placental mammal), and some can even be costly; the problems that many people have with aching backs are no doubt an unfortunate consequence of our evolved ability to walk on two feet. To understand our evolutionary legacy, de Waal argues, we must consider not just individual traits in isolation but also the whole package of traits that characterizes the species. This is as true for psychological traits as for physical ones.

Those who subscribe to the modules approach respond that evidence from psychology and other disciplines can distinguish behaviour that has a biological origin from behaviour that does not. As Steven Pinker (1994) explains, if a mental module for some behaviour exists, then neuroscientists should eventually discover the brain circuits or subsystems associated with it. Further, he adds, "When children solve problems for which they have mental modules, they should look like geniuses, knowing things they have not been taught; when they solve problems that their minds are not equipped for, it should be a long hard slog."

Watch
Genetic Time Clock

mental modules A collection of specialized and independent sections of the brain, developed to handle specific survival problems, such as the need to locate food or find a mate.

Thinking Critically

Don't Oversimplify

Many people oversimplify evolutionary theory by concluding that if a trait exists, it must have aided survival by serving some beneficial purpose. Not so! Baldness, for example, may be beautiful, but it is not necessarily adaptive.

The debate over modules will undoubtedly continue. But whether or not modules are the best way to describe traits that appear to be inherited, you should be careful to avoid the common error of assuming that if some behaviour or trait exists, it must be adaptive.

Innate Human Characteristics

Because of the way our species evolved, many abilities, tendencies, and characteristics are either present at birth in all human beings or develop rapidly as a child matures. These traits include not just the obvious ones, such as the ability to stand on two legs or to grasp objects with the forefinger and thumb, but also less obvious ones. Here are just a few examples:

1 **Infant reflexes.** Babies are born with a number of reflexes—simple, automatic responses to specific stimuli. For example, all infants will suck something put to their lips; by aiding nursing, this reflex enhances their chances of survival.

2 **An interest in novelty.** Novelty is intriguing to human beings and many other species. If a rat has had its dinner, it will prefer to explore an unfamiliar wing of a maze rather than the familiar wing where food is. Human babies reveal a surprising interest in looking at and listening to unfamiliar things—which, of course, includes most of the world. A baby will even stop nursing momentarily upon seeing someone new.

3 **A desire to explore and manipulate objects.** All birds and mammals have this innate inclination. Primates, especially, like to "monkey" with things, taking them apart and scrutinizing the pieces, apparently for the sheer pleasure of it (Harlow, Harlow, & Meyer, 1950). Human babies shake rattles, bang pots, and grasp whatever is put into their tiny hands. For human beings, the natural impulse to handle interesting objects can be overwhelming, which may be one reason why the command "Don't touch" is so often ignored by children, museum-goers, and shoppers.

4 **An impulse to play and fool around.** Think of kittens, puppies, lion cubs, panda cubs, and young primates who will play with and pounce on each other all day until hunger or naptime calls. Play and exploration may be biologically adaptive because they help members of a species find food and other necessities of life and learn to cope with their environments. Indeed, the young of many species enjoy *practice play*, behaviour that will be used for serious purposes when they are adults (Vandenberg, 1985). A kitten, for example, will stalk and attack a ball of yarn. In human beings, play teaches children how to get along with others and gives them a chance to practise their motor and linguistic skills (Pellegrini & Galda, 1993).

5 **Basic cognitive skills.** Many evolutionary psychologists believe that people are born with abilities that make it easy to learn to interpret the expressions and gestures of others, identify faces, figure out what others are thinking or feeling, distinguish plants from animals, distinguish living from nonliving things, and acquire language (Geary & Huffman, 2002). Young infants have even been credited

All primates, including human beings, are innately disposed to explore the environment, manipulate objects, play, and "monkey around."

with a rudimentary understanding of number (Izard et al., 2009). Of course, tiny infants cannot count. By the age of only one week, however, they will spend more time looking at a new set of three items after getting used to a set of two items, or vice versa, which means that they can recognize the difference. By seven months, most infants prefer to look at videotapes in which the number of adults mouthing a word (two or three adults) matches the number of voices saying the word in synchrony with the images (Jordan & Brannon, 2006). By 18 months, infants know that four is more than three, which is more than two, which is more than one—suggesting that the brain is designed to understand "more than" and "less than" relations for small numbers. Evolutionary psychologists believe that these and other fundamental cognitive skills evolved because they were useful to our ancestors and aided their survival.

Although most archaeological evidence suggests that humans have spent the vast majority of their time on earth as hunter–gatherers on the African savannah (Orians & Heerwagen, 1992), the natural and sexual selection pressures that existed in this environment were quite different from the pressures we face today. For example, on the savannah, vitamins would have been hard to come by. One of the best sources would have been fruits, which were some of the sweetest foods available. Therefore, individuals preferring (and seeking) sweet foods would have been more likely to survive and reproduce. Since our ancestors were the ones who preferred sweets, so do we. However, we now often satisfy that preference with candy, not fruit. A behaviour that *was* adaptive is now maladaptive. Roger Bingham was probably thinking of such ancestral carry-overs when he wrote, "We live in the space age with a brain from the stone age."

In other chapters, we will consider the adaptive and evolutionary aspects of sensory and perceptual abilities (Chapter 6), learning (Chapter 7), ethnocentrism (Chapter 8), cognitive biases (Chapter 9), memory (Chapter 10), emotions and emotional expressions (Chapter 11), stress reactions (Chapter 11), the tendency to gain weight when food is plentiful (Chapter 12), and attachment (Chapter 13). For now, let us look more closely at two areas that are of particular interest to evolutionary psychologists and that are also the source of much controversy: the development of language and the nature of mating practices around the world.

quickQUIZ

✔•[Quick Review on **MyPsychLab**

How evolved is your understanding of evolutionary psychology?

1. What two processes during the formation of sperm and eggs help explain genetic changes within a population?
2. Which is the best statement of the principle of natural selection? (a) Over time, the environment naturally selects some traits over others. (b) Genetic variations become more common over time if they affect traits that are adaptive in a particular environment. (c) A species constantly improves as parents pass along their best traits to their offspring.
3. Many evolutionary psychologists believe that the human mind evolved as (a) a collection of specialized modules to handle specific survival problems; (b) a blank slate; (c) a collection of specific instincts for every human activity or capacity.
4. Which of the following is not part of our biological heritage? (a) a sucking reflex at birth; (b) a motive to explore and manipulate objects; (c) a lack of interest in novel objects; (d) a love of play.

Answers:

1.spontaneous genetic mutations and crossover of genetic material between members of a chromosome pair, which occur before the final cell division   2.b   3.a   4.c

 # YOU are about to learn . . .

◆ what language enables us to do that other animals cannot.
◆ the evidence that infants' brains are equipped with an innate facility for acquiring language.
◆ the evidence that learning and environment influence language development.

OUR HUMAN HERITAGE: LANGUAGE

Try to read this sentence aloud:

Kamaunawezakusomamanenohayawewenimtuwamaanasana.

Can you tell where one word begins and another ends? Unless you know Swahili, the syllables of this sentence will sound like gibberish.[1]

Well, to a baby learning its native tongue, *every* sentence must, at first, be gibberish. How, then, does an infant pick out discrete syllables and words from the jumble of sounds in the environment, much less figure out what the words mean and how to combine them? Is there something special about the human brain that allows a baby to discover how language works? Darwin thought so: Language, wrote Darwin (1874), is an instinctive ability unique to human beings. Many modern researchers think he was right.

The Nature of Language

To evaluate Darwin's claim, we must first appreciate that a **language** is not just any old communication system; it is a set of rules for combining elements that are inherently meaningless into utterances that convey meaning. The elements are usually sounds, but they can also be the gestures of American Sign Language (ASL) and other manual languages used by deaf and hearing-impaired people.

language A system that combines meaningless elements such as sounds or gestures to form structured utterances that convey meaning.

[1] *Kama unaweza kusoma maneno haya, wewe ni mtu wa maana sana*, in Swahili, means "If you can read these words, you are a remarkable person."

Thinking Critically

Define Your Terms

People often confuse language with speech. But to a psycholinguist, a language is any communication system that can produce an infinite number of meaningful utterances, whether its elements are gestures or sounds. In North America, many hearing-impaired people use American Sign Language (ASL), and deaf children learn to sign in ASL as easily as hearing children learn to speak.

Some nonhuman animals are able to acquire aspects of language if they get help from their human friends (see Chapter 9). However, we seem to be the only species that acquires language naturally. Other primates use grunts, screeches, and gestures to warn each other of danger, attract attention, express emotions, and even refer to other individuals, but the sounds are not combined to produce original sentences (at least, as far as anyone can tell). Bongo the chimp may make a sound of delight when he encounters food, but he cannot say, "The bananas in the next grove are a lot riper than the ones we ate last week and sure beat our usual diet of termites."

In contrast, language, whether spoken or signed, allows human beings to express and comprehend an infinite number of novel utterances, created on the spot. This ability is critical; except for a few fixed phrases ("How are you?" "Get a life!"), most of the utterances we produce or hear over a lifetime are new. For example, in this book you will find few, if any, sentences that you have read, heard, or spoken before in exactly the same form. Yet you can understand what you are reading, and you can produce new sentences of your own about the material.

◉ **Watch**
Child-Directed Speech

The Innate Capacity for Language

At one time, most psychologists assumed that children acquired language by imitating adults and paying attention when adults corrected their mistakes. Then along came linguist Noam Chomsky (1957, 1980), who argued that language was far too complex to be learned bit by bit, as one might learn a list of world capitals.

Children, says Chomsky, not only must figure out which sounds or gestures form words; they also must take the *surface structure* of a sentence—the way the sentence is actually spoken or signed—and infer an underlying *deep structure*—how the sentence is to be understood. For example, although "Mary kissed John" and "John was kissed by Mary" have different surface structures, any five-year-old knows that the two sentences have essentially the same underlying meaning, in which Mary is the actor and John gets the kiss:

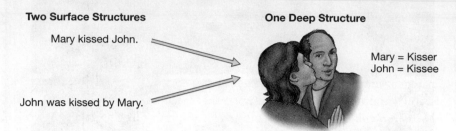

Two Surface Structures

Mary kissed John.

John was kissed by Mary.

One Deep Structure

Mary = Kisser
John = Kissee

Conversely, "Bill heard the trampling of the hikers," a single surface structure, can have two different underlying structures: one in which the hikers are actors doing the trampling and one in which they are the unfortunate objects of the trampling. Your ability to discern two different deep structures tells you that the sentence's meaning is ambiguous:

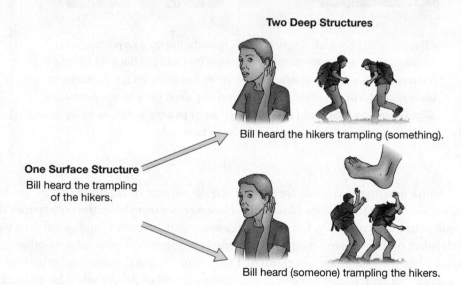

Two Deep Structures

Bill heard the hikers trampling (something).

One Surface Structure
Bill heard the trampling of the hikers.

Bill heard (someone) trampling the hikers.

language acquisition device According to many psycholinguists, an innate mental module that allows young children to develop language if they are exposed to an adequate sampling of conversation.

To transform surface structures into deep ones, says Chomsky, children must apply rules of grammar (*syntax*). These rules govern word order and other linguistic features that determine the role a word plays in a sentence (such as, say, kisser or kissee). Most people, even adults, cannot actually state the grammatical rules of their language ("In English, adjectives usually precede the noun they describe"), yet they are able to apply thousands of such rules without even thinking about it. No native speaker of English would say, "He threw the ball big."

Because no one actually teaches us grammar when we are toddlers, the human brain, Chomsky argues, must contain a **language acquisition device,** an innate mental module that allows young children to develop language if they are exposed to an adequate sampling of conversation; just as a bird is designed to fly, human beings are designed to use language. Another way of saying this is that children are born with a *universal grammar*—that is, their brains are sensitive to the core features common to all languages, such as nouns and verbs, subjects and objects, and negatives. These common features occur even in languages as seemingly different as Mohawk and English, or Okinawan and Bulgarian (Baker, 2001; Cinque, 1999; Pesetsky, 1999).

Over the years, linguists and *psycholinguists* (researchers who study the psychology of language) have gathered much evidence in support of the Chomskyan position:

1   **Children in different cultures go through similar stages of linguistic development.** For example, they will often form their first negatives simply by adding "no" or "not" at the beginning or end of a sentence ("No get dirty"); at a later stage, they will use double negatives ("He don't want no milk"; "Nobody don't like me"), even when their language does not allow such constructions (Klima & Bellugi, 1966; McNeill, 1966).

2   **Children combine words in ways that adults never would.** They reduce a parent's sentence ("Let's go to the store!") to their own two-word version ("Go store!") and make many charming errors that an adult would not ("The alligator goed kerplunk"; "Daddy taked me"; "Hey, Horton heared a Who") (Ervin-Tripp, 1964; Marcus et al., 1992). Such errors, which linguists call **overregularizations,** are not random; they show that the child has grasped a grammatical rule (e.g., add the *t* or *d* sound to make a verb past tense, as in *walked* or *hugged*) and is merely overgeneralizing it (*taked, goed*).

◉ **Watch**
Stimulating Language Development

3   **Adults do not consistently correct their children's syntax, yet children learn to speak or sign correctly anyway.** Learning explanations of language acquisition assume that children are rewarded for saying the right words and are punished for making errors. But parents do not stop to correct every error in their children's speech, so long as they can understand what the child is trying to say (Brown, Cazden, & Bellugi, 1969). Indeed, parents often *reward* children for incorrect statements! The two-year-old who says "Want milk!" is likely to get it; most parents would not wait for a more grammatical (or polite) request.

4   **Children not exposed to adult language might invent a language of their own.** Deaf children who have never learned a standard language, either signed or spoken, have made up their *own* sign languages out of thin air. Across cultures, these languages often show similarities in sentence structure; for example, children in America and Taiwan have produced similar languages, as have children in Spain and Turkey (Goldin-Meadow, 2003). The most astounding case comes from Nicaragua, where a group of deaf children of hearing parents, sent to two special schools, created a homegrown but grammatically complex sign language that is unrelated to Spanish (Senghas & Coppola, 2001; Senghas, Kita, & Özyürek, 2004). Scientists have had a unique opportunity to observe the evolution of this language as it has developed from a few simple signs to a full-blown linguistic system.

These deaf Nicaraguan children have invented their own grammatically complex sign language, one that is unrelated to Spanish or to any conventional gestural language.

5   **Infants as young as seven months can derive simple linguistic rules from a string of sounds.** If babies are repeatedly exposed to artificial "sentences" with an ABA pattern, such as "Ga ti ga" or "Li na li," until they get bored, they will then prefer new sentences with an ABB pattern (such as "Wo fe fe") over new sentences with an ABA pattern (such as "Wo fe wo"). (They indicate this preference by looking longer at a flashing light associated with the novel pattern than one associated with the familiar pattern.) Conversely, when the original sentences have an ABB structure, babies will prefer novel ones with an ABA structure. To many researchers, these responses suggest that babies can discriminate the different types of structures (Marcus et al., 1999). Astonishingly, this ability emerges even before they can understand or produce any words.

overregularizations Non-random errors in grammar that show that the child has grasped a grammatical rule.

computer neural networks
Mathematical models of the brain that "learn" by adjusting the connections among hypothetical neurons in response to incoming data.

✻ Explore
Healthy vs. Unhealthy Behaviour and Brain Functioning

Chomsky's ideas revolutionized thinking about language and human nature, and even the terms they used (language "acquisition" replaced language "learning"). He himself has had little to say about the evolutionary implications of his argument, but others believe that an innate facility for language evolved in human beings because it was extraordinarily beneficial (Pinker, 1994). In particular, it permitted our prehistoric ancestors to convey precise information about time, space, and events (as in "Honey, are you going on the mammoth hunt today?") and allowed them to negotiate alliances that were necessary for survival ("If you share your nuts and berries with us, we'll share our mammoth with you"). According to one theorist, language may also have developed because it provides the human equivalent of the mutual grooming that other primates rely on to forge social bonds (Dunbar, 2004). Just as other primates will clean, stroke, and groom each other for hours as a sign of affection and connection, human friends will sit for hours and chat over coffee. The difference between chimpanzee and human forms of "stroking" is that language allows us to maintain cooperative social relations in ever-larger groups (Dunbar, 2004). It enables us to make requests, provide helpful information, and share thoughts and attitudes across many social contexts (Tomasello, 2008).

Learning and Language

Despite the evidence for Chomsky's view that language is innate, some theorists still give experience a greater role. They argue that instead of inferring grammatical rules, children learn the probability that any given word or syllable will follow another—something that infants as young as eight months are able to do (Saffran, Aslin, & Newport, 1996; Seidenberg, 1997; Seidenberg, MacDonald, & Saffran, 2002). Eventually, children also learn how nonadjacent words co-occur (e.g., *the* and *ducky* in "the yellow ducky") and are able to generalize their knowledge to learn syntactic categories and patterns (Gerken, Wilson, & Lewis, 2005; Lany & Gómez, 2008). In this view, infants are more like statisticians than grammarians.

Although the capacity for language may be innate, parents can foster their children's language development by talking and reading with them.

Using computers, some theorists have been able to design **computer neural networks,** mathematical models of the brain that can "learn" some aspects of language, such as regular and irregular past-tense verbs, without the help of a language acquisition device or preprogrammed rules. Neural networks simply adjust the connections among hypothetical "neurons" in response to incoming data, such as repetitions of a word in its past-tense form. The success of these computer models, say their designers, suggests that children, too, may be able to acquire linguistic features without getting a head start from inborn brain modules (Rodriguez, Wiles, & Elman, 1999; Rumelhart & McClelland, 1987).

Even theorists who emphasize an inborn grammatical capacity acknowledge that in any behaviour as complex as language, nurture must also play a role. Although there are commonalities in language acquisition around the world, there are also some major differences that do not seem explainable by a "universal grammar" (Gopnik, Choi, & Baumberger, 1996; Slobin, 1985, 1991). Furthermore, although most children have the capacity to acquire language from mere exposure to it, parents do help things along. They may not go around correcting their children's speech all day, but they do recast and expand their children's clumsy or ungrammatical sentences ("Monkey climbing!" "Yes, the monkey is climbing the tree") (Bohannon & Stanowicz, 1988). Children, in turn, often imitate those recasts and expansions, suggesting that they are learning from them (Bohannon & Symons, 1988). It is likely, therefore, that language development depends on both biological readiness and social experience.

quickQUIZ

✔•─Quick Review on **MyPsychLab**

Use your human capacity for language to answer these questions.

1. The central distinction between human language and other communication systems is that language (a) allows for the generation of an infinite number of new utterances, (b) is spoken, (c) is learned only after explicit training, (d) expresses meaning directly through surface structures.

2. What five findings support the existence of an innate "universal grammar"?

3. Those who reject Chomsky's ideas believe that instead of figuring out grammatical rules when acquiring language, children learn _____.

Answers:

1. a 2. Children everywhere go through similar stages of linguistic development; children combine words in ways that adults would not; adults do not consistently correct their children's syntax; groups of children not exposed to adult language may make up their own; and even infants only a few months old appear to distinguish different sentence structures. 3. the probability that any given word or syllable will follow another one

YOU are about to learn . . .

◆ how evolutionary psychologists explain male–female differences in courtship and mating.

◆ some problems with evolutionary theories of courtship and mating preferences.

◆ the basic issue that divides evolutionary psychologists and their critics.

OUR HUMAN HERITAGE: COURTSHIP AND MATING

Most psychologists agree that the evolutionary history of our species has made certain kinds of learning either difficult or easy. Most acknowledge that simple behaviours, such as smiling or preferring sweet tastes, resemble instincts, behaviours that are relatively uninfluenced by learning and that occur in all members of the species. And most agree that human beings inherit some of their cognitive, perceptual, emotional, and linguistic capacities. But social scientists disagree heartily about whether biology and evolution can help account for complex social customs, such as warfare, cooperation, and altruism (the willingness to help others). Nowhere is this disagreement more apparent than in debates over the origins of male–female differences in sexual behaviour, so we are going to focus here on that endlessly fascinating topic.

Evolution and Sexual Strategies

In 1975, one of the world's leading experts on ants, Edward O. Wilson, published a book that had a big impact. It was titled *Sociobiology: The New Synthesis*, the "synthesis" being the application of biological principles to the social and sexual customs of both nonhuman animals and human beings. **Sociobiology** became a popular topic for researchers and the public, generating great controversy.

Sociobiologists contend that evolution has bred into each of us a tendency to act in ways that maximize our chances of passing on our genes, and to help our close biological relatives, with whom we share many genes, do the same. In this view, just as

"It's a guy thing."

sociobiology   An interdisciplinary field that emphasizes evolutionary explanations of social behaviour in animals, including human beings.

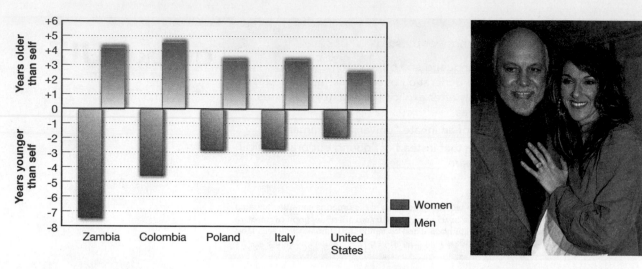

FIGURE 3.2 Preferred Age in a Mate

In most societies, men say they prefer to marry women younger than themselves, whereas women prefer men who are older (Buss, 1995). Evolutionary psychologists attribute these preferences to male concern with a partner's fertility and female concern with a partner's material resources and status. Although people may make comments about age differences when the man is much older than the woman, as in the case of Canadian singer Celine Dion and her much older husband, René Angélil, people are far more apt to make disapproving comments when the woman is much older.

✱ **Explore**
Strategies in Mate Selection

nature has selected physical characteristics that have proven adaptive, so it has selected psychological traits and social customs that aid individuals in propagating their genes. Customs that enhance the odds of such transmission survive in the form of kinship bonds, dominance arrangements, taboos against female adultery, and many other aspects of social life.

In addition, sociobiologists believe that because the males and females of most species have faced different kinds of survival and mating problems, the sexes have evolved to differ profoundly in aggressiveness, dominance, and sexual strategies (Symons, 1979; Trivers, 1972). In many species, they argue, it is adaptive for males to compete with other males for access to young and fertile females, and to try to win and then inseminate as many females as possible. The more females a male mates with, the more genes he can pass along. (The human record in this regard was achieved by a man who fathered 899 children [Daly & Wilson, 1983]. What else he did with his time is unknown.) But according to sociobiologists, females need to shop for the best genetic deal, as it were, because they can conceive and bear only a limited number of offspring. Having such a large biological investment in each pregnancy, females cannot afford to make mistakes. Besides, mating with a lot of different males would produce no more offspring than staying with just one. So females try to attach themselves to dominant males who have resources and status and are likely to have "superior" genes. The result of these two opposite sexual strategies, in this view, is that males generally want sex more often than females do; males are often fickle and promiscuous, whereas females are usually devoted and faithful; males are drawn to sexual novelty and even rape, whereas females want stability and security; males are relatively undiscriminating in their choice of sexual partners, whereas females are cautious and choosy; and males are competitive and concerned about dominance, whereas females are less so.

Evolutionary psychologists generally agree with these conclusions, but whereas sociobiologists often study nonhuman species and argue by analogy, many evolutionary psychologists consider such analogies simplistic and misleading. For example, because male scorpion flies force themselves on females, some sociobiologists have drawn an analogy between this behaviour and human rape and have concluded that human rape must have the same evolutionary origins and reproductive purposes (Thornhill & Palmer, 2000). But this analogy does not bear scrutiny. Human rape has many motives, including, among others, revenge, sadism, and conformity to peer pressure (see Chapter 12). It is often committed by high-status men who could easily find consenting sexual partners. All too frequently its victims are children or the elderly, who do not reproduce. And sadistic rapists often injure or kill their victims, hardly a way to perpetuate one's genes. In general, therefore, evolutionary psychologists rely less on comparisons with other species than sociobiologists do, focusing instead on commonalities in human mating and dating practices around the world. As a result of this difference, evolutionary psychologists also rely on different assumptions than sociobiologists do. Although both groups assume that human bodies and behaviours have been subject to evolutionary selection pressures, Darwin's account of speciation (the origin of new species) is irrelevant to evolutionary psychologists. Instead, the evolutionary psychologists simply assume that—as mentioned previously in this chapter—humans have spent the vast majority of their time on earth living as hunter–gatherers, probably on the African savannah.

Nevertheless, both groups emphasize the evolutionary origins of many human sex differences that appear to be universal, or at least very common. In one massive project, 50 scientists studied 10 000 people in 37 cultures located on six continents and five islands (Buss, 1994; Schmitt, 2003). Around the world, they found, men are more violent and more socially dominant than women are. Men are more interested in the youth and beauty of their sexual partners, presumably because youth is associated with fertility (see Figure 3.2). According to their responses on questionnaires, men are more sexually jealous and possessive, presumably because if a man's mate had sex with other men, he could never be 100% sure that her children were genetically his as well. They are quicker than women to have sex with partners they don't know well and more inclined toward polygamy and promiscuity, presumably so that their sperm will be distributed as widely as possible. Women, in contrast, tend to emphasize the financial resources or prospects of a potential mate, his status, and his willingness to commit to a relationship. On questionnaires, they say they would be more upset by a partner's emotional infidelity than by his sexual infidelity, presumably because abandonment by the partner might leave them without the support and resources needed to raise their offspring. Many studies have reported similar results (e.g., Bailey et al., 1994; Buss, 1996, 2000; Buunk et al., 1996; Daly & Wilson, 1983; Mealey, 2000; Sprecher, Sullivan, & Hatfield, 1994).

Culture and the "Genetic Leash"

Evolutionary views of sex differences have become enormously popular. Many academics and lay people are persuaded that there are indeed evolutionary advantages for males in sowing their seed far and wide and evolutionary advantages for females in finding a man with a good paycheque.

But critics, including some evolutionary theorists, have challenged this conclusion on conceptual and methodological grounds:

1 **Stereotypes versus actual behaviour.** Many critics argue that current evolutionary explanations of infidelity and monogamy are based on simplistic *stereotypes* of gender differences. The actual behaviour of humans and other animals often fails to conform to images of sexually promiscuous males and coy, choosy females (Barash & Lipton, 2001; Birkhead, 2001; Fausto-Sterling, 1997; Hrdy, 1994; Roughgarden, 2004). In many species of birds, fish, and mammals, including human beings, females are sexually ardent and often have many male partners. The female's sexual behaviour does not seem to depend only on the goal of being fertilized by the male: Females have sex when they are not ovulating and even when they are already pregnant. And in many species, from penguins to primates, males do not just mate and run. They stick around, feeding the infants, carrying them, and protecting them from predators (Hrdy, 1988; Snowdon, 1997).

Consider Other Interpretations

Evolutionary theories have been criticized on conceptual and methodological grounds. Do genes hold culture on a tight leash; a long, flexible one; or none at all?

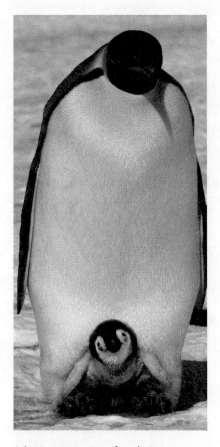

A basic assumption of evolutionary approaches to sexuality is that females across species have a greater involvement in child rearing than males do. But there are many exceptions. Female emperor penguins, for example, take off every winter, leaving behind males like this one to care for the young.

FIGURE 3.3 Attitudes toward Chastity

In many places, men care more about a partner's chastity than women do, as evolutionary psychologists would predict. But culture has a powerful impact on these attitudes, as this graph shows. Notice that in China, both sexes prefer a partner who has not yet had intercourse, whereas in Sweden, chastity is a nonissue. (From Buss, 1995.)

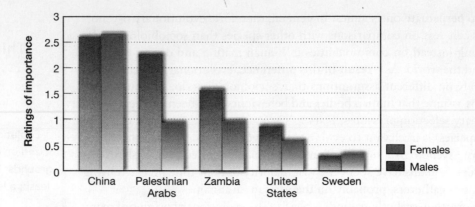

Human sexual behaviour, especially, is amazingly varied and changeable across time and place. Cultures range from those in which women have many children to those in which they have very few, from those in which men are intimately involved in child rearing to those in which they take no part at all, from those in which women may have many lovers to those in which women may be killed for having sex outside of marriage (Hatfield & Rapson, 1996/2005). In many places, the chastity of a potential mate is much more important to men than to women; but in other places, it is important to both sexes—or to neither one (see Figure 3.3). In some places, just as evolutionary theory predicts, a relatively few men—those with the greatest wealth and power—have a far greater number of offspring than other men do; but in many societies, including some polygamous ones, powerful men do not have more children than men who are poor or who are low in status (Brown, Laland, & Mulder, 2009). Sexual attitudes and practices also vary tremendously within a culture, as is immediately apparent to anyone surveying the panorama of sexual attitudes and behaviours within the United States and Canada (Laumann et al., 2004; Levine, 2002).

Much of the data cited by evolutionary psychologists have come from questionnaires and interviews. In this research, when people (often undergraduates) are asked to rank the qualities they most value in a potential mate, sex differences appear, just as evolutionary theory would predict (Kenrick et al., 2001). But when we *examine the evidence* more closely, we find problems. For example, despite their differences, *both* sexes usually rank kindness, intelligence, and understanding over physical qualities or financial status.

2 **Convenience versus representative samples.** In Chapter 2 we saw that "convenience samples" of undergraduates sometimes produce research results that do not apply to nonstudents. This may well be the case in much of the evolutionary research on attitudes toward sex and marriage. In a recent national study, researchers at the U.S. Centers for Disease Control and Prevention (CDC) interviewed more than 12 000 men and women aged 15 to 44 about sex, living together, marriage, divorce, and parenting (Martinez et al., 2006). The agency had conducted similar surveys since 1973 but only with women. This time, the researchers *asked a question* that in retrospect seems obvious: What about men? Thus they were able to draw conclusions about male and female attitudes based on a sample that was far more representative of the general population than those used by most researchers. What they found throws a different light on evolutionary notions of sex differences.

For example, as we've seen, in the evolutionary view, women on the whole value commitment to a relationship more than men do and are more dedicated to parenting. Yet 66% of the men, compared to only 51% of the women, agreed or strongly agreed with the statement "It is better to get married than go through life being single." Further, most women *and* men agreed that "It is more important for a man to spend a lot of time with his family than be successful at his career." Among fathers in their first marriage, 90% were living with their kids and spent considerable time feeding and bathing them, helping them with homework, and taking them to activities. And 94% of both sexes agreed that "The rewards of being a parent are worth it despite the cost and work it takes."

As always, we need to *avoid oversimplification*. Some results did go in the stereotypical direction. More men than women (60% versus 51%) agreed that it was acceptable for unmarried 18-year-olds to have sexual relations "if they have strong affection for each other." Women were also more likely to be married by age 30 than men were. And decades of research have found that men are likely to have more premarital sexual partners than women are. But taken as a whole, the CDC findings suggest that men are just as interested in serious family relationships as women are.

3 **What people say versus what they do.** There is yet another problem in surveys inspired by evolutionary theories. Some critics have *questioned an assumption* underlying those surveys: that people's responses are a good guide to their actual choices and actions. When you ask people which would upset them more, their mate's having sex with someone else or their mate's falling in love with someone else, women are usually likelier than men to say that emotional infidelity would be worse (although there are big variations across cultures). But when one researcher asked people about their *actual* experiences with infidelity, men and women did not differ at all in the degree to which they had focused on the emotional or sexual aspects of their partners' behaviour (C. Harris, 2003). In fact, men, supposedly the more sexually jealous sex, were significantly more likely than women to have tolerated their partners' sexual unfaithfulness, whereas women were more likely to have ended their relationships over it. If you are thinking critically, you may be wondering whether these questionnaire results are any more reliable than those on dating preferences. Good question! The answer is yes. From studies that had people keep diaries of how they spend their time each day, we know that men's behaviour has changed along with their attitudes. Women still do more housework and child care than men do, but since the 1960s, the time men spend on housework has more than doubled, and since the 1980s the time they spend on primary child care has nearly tripled (Bianchi, Robinson, & Milkie, 2006; Wang & Bianchi, 2009).

How large an influence does our Stone Age past have on our current courtship and mating customs?

4 **The Fred Flintstone problem.** Finally, some scientists have questioned evolutionary psychologists' emphasis on the Pleistocene age, which extended from about 2 million to about 11 000 years ago. Recent analysis of the human genome in Africans, East Asians, and Europeans suggests that during the past 10 000 to 15 000 years, natural selection has continued to influence genes associated with taste, smell, digestion, bone structure, skin colour, fertility, and even brain function (Voigt et al., 2006). Some of these changes might have begun when humans abandoned hunting and gathering in favour of agriculture, a switch that made certain genetic dispositions

more adaptive and others less so. David Buller (2005), a philosopher who was captivated by evolutionary psychology until he took a closer look, concludes that "There is no reason to think that contemporary humans are, like Fred and Wilma Flintstone, just Pleistocene hunter–gatherers struggling to survive and reproduce in evolutionarily novel suburban habitats."

Even if the Pleistocene period did strongly influence human mating preferences, those preferences may differ from the ones usually emphasized by evolutionary theory. Our prehistoric ancestors, unlike the undergraduates in many mate-preference studies, did not have 5000 fellow students to choose from. They lived in small bands, and if they were lucky they might get to choose between Urp and Ork, and that's about it; they could not hold out for some gorgeous babe or handsome millionaire down the road. Because there was a small range of potential partners to choose from, there would have been no need for the kinds of sexual strategies described by evolutionary theorists (Hazan & Diamond, 2000). Instead, evolution might have instilled in us a tendency to select a mate based on similarity (the person's genes, background, and age roughly match our own) and proximity (the person is around a lot). Indeed, similarity and proximity are among the strongest predictors today of the mates people actually choose, whatever they may say on questionnaires (see Chapter 12). Debate over these matters can become quite heated because of worries that evolutionary arguments will be used to justify social and political inequalities and even violent behaviour. In the past, evolutionary ideas have been used to promote **social Darwinism,** the notion that the wealthy and successful are more reproductively fit than other people. Such arguments have also led some people to conclude that men, with less investment in child rearing and more interest in status and dominance, are destined to control business and politics. More than 30 years ago, Edward Wilson (1975) certainly thought so. "Even with identical education and equal access to all professions [for both sexes]," he writes, "men are likely to continue to play a disproportionate role in political life, business, and science."

social Darwinism   The notion that the wealthy and successful are more reproductively fit than other people.

quickQUIZ

✓ **Quick Review** on **MyPsychLab**

Males and females alike have evolved to be able to answer these questions.

1. Which of the following would an evolutionary psychologist expect to be more typical of males than of females? (a) promiscuity, (b) choosiness about sexual partners, (c) concern with dominance, (d) interest in young partners, (e) emphasis on physical attractiveness of partners

2. What major issue divides evolutionary theorists and their critics in debates over courtship and mating?

3. A friend of yours, who has read some sociobiology, tells you that men will always be more sexually promiscuous than women because during evolution, the best reproductive strategy for a male primate has been to try to impregnate many females. What kind of evidence would you need in order to evaluate this claim?

Answers:

1.all but b   2.the relative influence of biology and culture   3.You would not want to look just for confirming evidence (recall the principle of falsifiability from Chapter 2). You would want to look also for evidence of female promiscuity and male monogamy among humans and other species and changes in human sexual customs in response to changing social conditions.

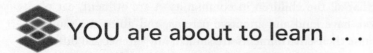

YOU are about to learn . . .

◆ what it means to say that a trait is "heritable."
◆ three important facts about heritability.
◆ how researchers estimate a trait's heritability.

THE GENETICS OF DIFFERENCE

We have been focusing on the origins of human similarities. We turn now to the second great issue in debates about nature and nurture: the origins of the differences among us. We begin with a critical discussion of what it means to say that a trait is "heritable." Then, to illustrate how behavioural geneticists study differences among people that might be influenced by genes, we will examine in detail a single, complex issue: the genetic and environmental contributions to intelligence. In other sections of this book, you will be reading about behavioural–genetic findings on many other topics, including biological rhythms (Chapter 5), taste perception (Chapter 6), weight and body shape (Chapter 12), sexual orientation (Chapter 12), personality and temperament (Chapter 14), addiction (Chapter 15), and mental disorders (Chapter 15).

The Meaning of Heritability

Suppose you want to measure flute-playing ability in a large group of music students, so you have some independent raters assign each student a score from 1 to 20. When you plot the scores, you find that some people are what you might call melodically disadvantaged and should forget about a musical career, others are flute geniuses, and the rest fall somewhere in between. What causes the variation in this group of students? Why are some so musically talented and others so inept? Are these differences primarily genetic, or are they the result of experience and motivation?

To answer such questions, behavioural geneticists compute a statistic called **heritability**, which gives an estimate of the *proportion of the total variance in a trait that is attributable to genetic variation within a group.* Because the heritability of a trait is expressed as a proportion (such as 0.60, or 60/100), the maximum value it can have is 1.00 (equivalent to "100% of the variance"). Height is highly heritable; that is, within a group of equally well-nourished individuals, most of the variation among them will be accounted for by their genetic differences. In contrast, table manners have low heritability because most variation among individuals is accounted for by differences in upbringing. Our guess is that flute-playing ability— and musical ability in general—falls somewhere in the middle. Differences in the ability to correctly perceive musical pitch and melody appear to be highly heritable; some people, it seems, really are born with a "tin ear" (Drayna et al., 2001). Nonetheless, musical training can enhance normal musical ability, and lack of musical training can keep a person with normal ability from tuning in to the nuances of music.

Many people hold completely mistaken ideas about heritability. But as genetic findings pour in, the public will need to understand this concept more than ever. You cannot understand the nature–nurture issue without understanding the following important facts about heritability:

1 **An estimate of heritability applies only to a particular group living in a particular environment.** Heritability may be high in one group and low in

Thinking Critically

Define Your Terms

What does it mean to say that some trait is highly heritable? If you want to improve your flute playing and someone tells you that musical ability is heritable, should you stop practising?

heritability A statistical estimate of the proportion of the total variance in some trait that is attributable to genetic differences among individuals within a group.

another. Suppose that all the children in community A are affluent, eat plenty of high-quality food, have kind and attentive parents, and go to the same top-notch schools. Because their environments are similar, any intellectual differences among them will have to be due largely to their genetic differences. In other words, mental ability in this group will be highly heritable. In contrast, suppose the children in community B are rich, poor, and in between. Some of them have healthy diets; others live on fatty foods and cupcakes. Some attend good schools; others go to inadequate ones. Some have doting parents, and some have unloving and neglectful ones. These children's intellectual differences could be due to their environmental differences and, if that is so, the heritability of intelligence for this group will be low. Indeed, in a study that followed 48 000 American children from birth to age 7, intelligence did depend greatly on socioeconomic status. In impoverished families, 60% of the variance in IQ was accounted for by environmental factors shared by family members, and the contribution of genes was close to zero. In affluent families, the result was nearly exactly the reverse: Heritability was extremely high, and shared environment contributed hardly at all (Turkheimer et al., 2003).

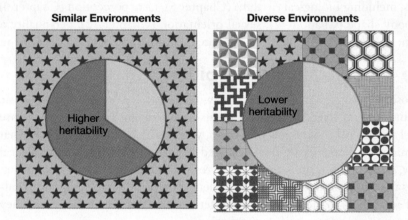

Similar Environments   **Diverse Environments**

Higher heritability   Lower heritability

2   **Heritability estimates do not apply to individuals, only to variations within a group.** You inherited half your genes from your mother and half from your father, but your *combination* of genes has never been seen before and will never be seen again (unless you have an identical twin). You also have a unique history of family relationships, intellectual training, and life experiences. It is impossible to know just how your genes and your personal history have interacted to produce the person you are today. For example, if you are a great flute player, no one can say whether your ability is mainly a result of inherited musical talent, living all your life in a family of devoted flute players, a private obsession that you acquired at age 6 when you saw the opera *The Magic Flute*—or a combination of all three. For one person, genes may make a tremendous difference in some aptitude or disposition; for another, the environment may be far more important. Scientists can study only the extent to which differences among people in general are explained by their genetic differences.

3   **Even highly heritable traits can be modified by the environment.** Although height is highly heritable, malnourished children may not grow to be as tall as they would with sufficient food, and children who eat an extremely nutritious diet may grow to be taller than anyone thought they could. Hair colour is genetically determined, but a trip to a hair stylist can transform you from a brunette to a blonde,

or vice versa. The same principle applies to psychological traits, although biological determinists sometimes fail to realize this. They argue, for example, that because IQ is highly heritable, IQ and school achievement cannot be boosted much (Herrnstein & Murray, 1994; Murray, 2008). But even if the first part of the statement is true, the second part does not necessarily follow, as we will see.

For instance, most of us have five fingers on each hand, something that is specified in our genetic recipe. If we went out and looked for people who didn't have five fingers per hand—say, those who had four fingers—we would probably conclude that genes had nothing to do with the number of fingers people have. We would find that most people with fewer than five fingers on each hand have lost digits as the result of accidents. This does not mean that their genes did not influence the number of fingers they were born with—just that the environment modified this heritable trait (Ridley, 2000).

Computing Heritability

Scientists have no way to estimate the heritability of a trait or behaviour directly, so they must *infer* it by studying people whose degree of genetic similarity is known. You might think that the simplest approach would be to compare biological relatives within families; everyone knows about families that are famous for some talent or trait. But family traits do not tell us much because close relatives usually share environments as well as genes. If Carlo's parents and siblings all love lasagna, that does not mean a taste for lasagna is heritable! The same applies if everyone in Carlo's family has a high IQ, is mentally ill, or is moody.

A better approach is to study adopted children (e.g., Loehlin, Horn, & Willerman, 1996; Plomin & DeFries, 1985). Such children share half their genes with each birth parent, but they grow up in a different environment, apart from their birth parents. On the other hand, they share an environment with their adoptive parents and siblings but not their genes:

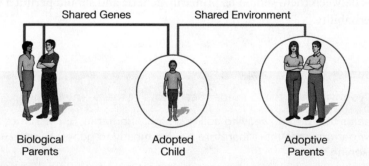

Shared Genes | Shared Environment

Biological Parents | Adopted Child | Adoptive Parents

Researchers can compare correlations between the traits of adopted children and those of their biological and adoptive relatives and can use the results to compute an estimate of heritability.

Another approach is to compare identical twins with fraternal twins. **Identical (monozygotic) twins** develop when a fertilized egg (zygote) divides into two parts that then develop as two separate embryos. Because the twins come from the same fertilized egg, they share all their genes. Some surprising recent work, however, suggests that duplicated or missing blocks of DNA (sets of those A's, C's, G's, and T's that we discussed earlier) can exist in one identical twin but not the other (Bruder et al., 2008). (Identical twins may be slightly different at birth, however, because of differences in the blood supply to the two fetuses or other chance factors.) In contrast, **fraternal (dizygotic) twins** develop when a woman's ovaries release two eggs instead of one and

identical (monozygotic) twins Twins that develop when a fertilized egg divides into two parts that develop into separate embryos.

fraternal (dizygotic) twins Twins that develop from two separate eggs fertilized by different sperm; they are no more alike genetically than are any other pair of siblings.

each egg is fertilized by a different sperm. Fraternal twins are womb mates, but they are no more alike genetically than any other two siblings (they share, on average, only half their genes), and they may be of different sexes:

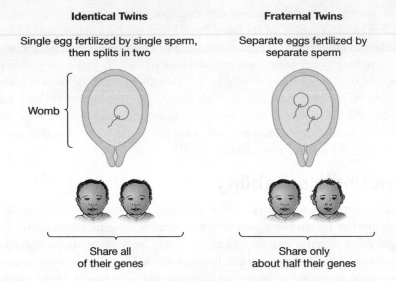

Identical Twins
Single egg fertilized by single sperm, then splits in two

Fraternal Twins
Separate eggs fertilized by separate sperm

Womb

Share all of their genes

Share only about half their genes

Behavioural geneticists can estimate the heritability of a trait by comparing groups of same-sex fraternal twins with groups of identical twins. The assumption is that if identical twins are more alike than fraternal twins, then the increased similarity must be due to genetic influences. Perhaps, however, identical twins are treated differently than fraternal twins. To avoid this problem, investigators have studied identical twins who were separated early in life and reared apart. (Until recently, adoption policies and attitudes toward births out of wedlock permitted such separations to occur.) In theory, separated identical twins share all their genes but not their environments. Any similarities between them should be primarily genetic and should permit a direct estimate of heritability.

quickQUIZ

✓• Quick Review on MyPsychLab

We hope you will treat this quiz identically to all others—by taking it.

1. Diane hears that basket-weaving ability is highly heritable. She assumes that her own low performance must therefore be due mostly to genes. What is wrong with her reasoning?

2. Bertram hears that basket-weaving ability is highly heritable. He concludes that schools should not bother trying to improve the skills of children who lack this talent. What is wrong with his reasoning?

3. Basket-weaving skills seem to run in Andy's family. Why shouldn't Andy conclude that his own talent is genetic?

4. Why do behavioural geneticists find it useful to study twins?

Answers:

1. Heritability applies only to differences among individuals within a group, not to particular individuals. 2. A trait may be highly heritable and still be susceptible to modification. 3. Family members share not just genes but also environments. 4. Identical twins growing up together share an environment, and so do fraternal twins. So if identical twins are more alike than fraternal twins, then the increased similarity is assumed to be genetic. Identical twins reared apart share only their genes, not their environment, so similarities between them should be primarily genetic also.

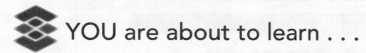

YOU are about to learn . . .

♦ the extent to which intelligence may be heritable.

♦ a common error in the argument that one group is genetically smarter than another.

♦ how the environment nurtures or thwarts mental ability.

OUR HUMAN DIVERSITY: THE CASE OF INTELLIGENCE

Behavioural-genetics research has transformed our understanding of many aspects of behaviour that were once explained solely in psychological terms. Some findings, such as the discovery that certain mental illnesses have a genetic component, have been accepted readily. Other findings, however, have inflamed political passions and upset people. No topic has aroused more controversy than the origins of human intelligence.

Genes and Individual Differences

In heritability studies, the usual measure of intellectual functioning is an **intelligence quotient (IQ)** score. Scores on an IQ test reflect how a child has performed compared with other children of the same age, or how an adult has performed compared with other adults. The average score for each age group is arbitrarily set at 100. The distribution of scores in the population approximates a normal (bell-shaped) curve, where scores near the average (mean) are the most common and very high or very low scores are rare. Two-thirds of all test-takers score between 85 and 115.

Most psychologists believe that IQ tests measure a general quality that affects most aspects of mental ability, but the tests also have many critics. Some argue that intelligence comes in many varieties, more than are captured by a single score. Others argue that IQ tests are culturally biased, tapping mostly those abilities that depend on experiences in a middle-class environment and favouring white people over people of other ethnicities. We discuss the measurement of intelligence and debates surrounding this concept more fully in Chapter 9. For now, keep in mind that most heritability estimates apply only to those mental skills that affect IQ test scores and that these estimates are likely to be more valid for some groups than for others. You cannot use a heritability estimate from one group of people and apply it to another, different group of people.

Despite these important qualifications, it is clear that the kind of intelligence that produces high IQ scores is highly heritable, at least in the middle-class samples usually studied. For children and adolescents, heritability estimates average around 0.40 or 0.50; that is, about half of the variance in IQ scores is explainable by genetic differences (Chipuer, Rovine, & Plomin, 1990; Devlin, Daniels, & Roeder, 1997; Plomin, 1989). For adults, the estimates until late middle age are even higher—in the 0.60 to 0.80 range (Bouchard, 1995; McClearn et al., 1997; McGue et al., 1993). That is, the genetic contribution becomes relatively larger and the environmental one relatively smaller with age. Some psychologists, however, note that most people who adopt children are screened to make sure they have a secure income, are psychologically stable, and so forth. As a result, critics argue, there is not much "variation" in adopted children's environments, which spuriously inflates the variation due to heredity (Nisbett, 2009). In studies of twins, the scores of identical twins are always much more

✳ Explore
Intelligence and IQ Testing

intelligence quotient (IQ)
A measure of intelligence originally computed by dividing a person's mental age by his or her chronological age and multiplying the result by 100; it is now derived from norms provided for standardized intelligence tests.

FIGURE 3.4 Correlations in Siblings' IQ Scores
The IQ scores of identical twins are highly correlated, even when they are reared apart. The figures represented in this graph are based on average correlations across many studies (Bouchard & McGue, 1981).

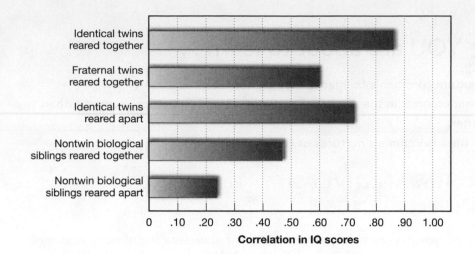

Correlation in IQ scores

✳ **Explore**
Correlations between IQ Scores and Relationship

highly correlated than those of fraternal twins, a difference that reflects the influence of genes. In fact, the scores of identical twins reared *apart* are more highly correlated than those of fraternal twins reared *together*, as you can see in Figure 3.4. In adoption studies, the scores of adopted children are more highly correlated with those of their birth parents than with those of their biologically unrelated adoptive parents; the higher the birth parents' scores, the higher the child's score is likely to be. As adopted children grow into adolescence, the correlation between their IQ scores and those of their biologically unrelated family members diminishes, and in adulthood the correlation falls to *zero* (Bouchard, 1997b; Scarr, 1993; Scarr & Weinberg, 1994). (This does not mean that adoption has no positive effects; adopted children score higher on IQ tests than do birth siblings who were not adopted, probably because adoptees grow up in more enriched environments [van Ijzendoorn et al., 2005].)

The Question of Group Differences

If genes influence individual differences in intelligence, do they also help account for differences between groups, as many people assume? Unfortunately, the history of this issue has been marred by ethnic, class, and gender prejudice. As Stephen Jay Gould (1996) notes, genetic research has often been bent to support the belief that some groups are destined by "the harsh dictates of nature" to be subordinate to others. Because this issue has enormous political and social importance, we are going to examine it closely.

Most of the focus has been on black–white differences in IQ, because black children score, on average, some 10 to 12 points lower than do white children. (We are talking about averages; the distributions of scores for black children and white children overlap considerably.) A few psychologists have proposed a genetic explanation of this difference (Jensen, 1969, 1981; Rushton, 1988). As you can imagine, this topic is not merely academic. Racists have used theories of genetic differences between groups to justify their own hatreds, and politicians have used them to argue for cuts in programs that would benefit blacks, other minorities, and poor children. Some researchers themselves have concluded that there is little point in spending money on programs that try to raise the IQs of low-scoring children, of whatever race (Murray, 2008; Rushton & Jensen, 2005; Herrnstein & Murray, 1994).

Genetic explanations, however, have a fatal flaw: They use heritability estimates based mainly on white samples to estimate the role of heredity in *group* differences,

Thinking Critically

Analyze Assumptions and Biases

Most behavioural-genetics studies show the heritability of intelligence to be high. A popular book argues that heredity must play a similarly large role in average IQ differences between ethnic groups. What's wrong with the assumption behind that reasoning?

◈ **Research**
Arthur Jensen

a procedure that is not valid. This problem sounds pretty technical, but it is really not too difficult to understand, so stay with us.

Consider, first, not people, but tomatoes. (Figure 3.5 will help you visualize the following "thought experiment.") Suppose you have a bag of tomato seeds that vary genetically; all things being equal, some will produce tomatoes that are puny and taste-less, and some will produce tomatoes that are plump and delicious. Now you take a bunch of these seeds in your left hand and another bunch from the same bag in your right hand. Though one seed differs genetically from another, there is no *average* dif-ference between the seeds in your left hand and those in your right. You plant the left hand's seeds in pot A, with some enriched soil that you have doctored with nitrogen and other nutrients, and you plant the right hand's seeds in pot B, with soil from which you have extracted nutrients. You sing to pot A and put it in the sun; you ignore pot B and leave it in a dark corner.

When the tomato plants grow, they will vary *within* each pot in terms of height, the number of tomatoes produced, and the size of the tomatoes, purely because of genetic differences. But there will also be an average difference between the plants in pot A and those in pot B: The plants in pot A will be healthier and bear more tomatoes. This difference *between* pots is owing entirely to the different soils and the care that has been given to them—even though the heritability of the *within*-pot differences is 100% (Lewontin, 1970). The same is true for real plants, by the way; if you take iden-tical, cloned plants and grow them at different elevations, they will develop differently (Lewontin, 2001).

The principle is the same for people as it is for tomatoes. Although intellectual differences *within* groups are at least partly genetic in origin, that does not mean dif-ferences *between* groups are genetic. Blacks and whites do not grow up, on the average, in the same "pots" (environments). Because of a long legacy of racial discrimination and de facto segregation, black children, as well as Latino and other minority chil-dren, often receive far fewer nutrients—literally, in terms of food, and figuratively, in terms of education, encouragement by society, and intellectual opportunities (Nisbett, 2009). Ethnic groups also differ in countless cultural ways that affect their perfor-mance on IQ tests. And negative stereotypes about ethnic groups may cause members of these groups to doubt their own abilities, become anxious and self-conscious, and perform more poorly than they otherwise would on tests (see Chapter 9).

Doing good research on the origins of group differences in IQ is extremely dif-ficult in the United States, where racism affects the lives of even affluent, success-ful black people. However, the few studies that have overcome past methodological problems fail to reveal any genetic differences between blacks and whites in whatever it is that IQ tests measure. One study found that children fathered by black and white American soldiers in Germany after the Second World War and reared in similar German communities by similar families did not differ significantly in IQ (Eyferth, 1961). Another showed that, contrary to what a genetic theory would predict, degree of African ancestry (which can be roughly estimated from skin colour, blood analysis, and genealogy) is not related to measured intelligence (Scarr et al., 1977). And white and black infants do equally well on a test that measures their preference for novel stimuli, a predictor of later IQ scores (Fagan, 1992).

An intelligent reading of the research on intelligence, therefore, does not direct us to conclude that differences among cultural, ethnic, or national groups are per-manent, genetically determined, or signs of any group's innate superiority. On the contrary, the research suggests that we should make sure that all children grow up in the best possible soil, with room for the smartest and the slowest to find a place in the sun.

FIGURE 3.5 The Tomato Plant Experiment

In the hypothetical experiment described in the text, even if the dif-ferences among plants within each pot were due entirely to genetics, the aver-age differences between pots could be environmental. The same general prin-ciple applies to individual and group differences among human beings.

The Environment and Intelligence

By now you may be wondering what kinds of experiences hinder intellectual development and what kinds of environmental "nutrients" promote it. Here are some of the influences associated with reduced mental ability:

◉ Watch
Brain Development and Nutrition

◆ *Poor prenatal care.* If a pregnant woman is malnourished, contracts infections, takes certain drugs, smokes, is exposed to secondhand smoke, or drinks alcohol regularly, her child is at risk of having learning disabilities and a lower IQ.

◆ *Malnutrition.* The average IQ gap between severely malnourished and well-nourished children can be as high as 20 points (Stoch & Smythe, 1963; Winick, Meyer, & Harris, 1975).

◆ *Exposure to toxins.* Lead, especially, can damage the nervous system, even at fairly low levels, producing attention problems, lower IQ scores, and poorer school achievement (Hornung, Lanphear, & Dietrich, 2009; Lanphear et al., 2005; Needleman et al., 1996). Many children in the United States are exposed to dangerous levels of lead from dust, contaminated soil, lead paint, and old lead pipes, and the concentration of lead in black children's blood is 50% higher than in white children's (Lanphear et al., 2002). Air pollution, which people cannot control directly, also appears to be a serious risk factor. A recent longitudinal study of nonsmoking inner-city women found a link between delayed cognitive development in the women's children and the level of pollutants from fossil fuels that the mothers were exposed to during pregnancy. The culprit appears to be a chemical spewed from vehicles and power plants. Even after controlling for other factors, such as lead exposure, the researchers found that by age 3, the children of highly exposed mothers were more than twice as likely as other children to be developmentally delayed (Perera et al., 2006).

◆ *Stressful family circumstances.* Factors that predict reduced intellectual competence include, among others, having a father who does not live with the family, a mother with a history of mental illness, parents with limited work skills, and a history of stressful events, such as domestic violence, early in life (Sameroff et al., 1987). On average, each risk factor reduces a child's IQ score by four points. Children with seven risk factors score more than *30 points lower* than those with no risk factors. And when children live in severely disadvantaged neighbourhoods, their verbal IQs decline over time, even after they have moved to better areas; the drop is comparable to that seen when a child misses a year of school (Sampson, Sharkey, & Raudenbush, 2008).

Severe poverty, exposure to toxic materials, run-down neighbourhoods, and stressful family circumstances can all have a negative impact on children's cognitive development and IQ.

In contrast, a healthy and stimulating environment can raise mental performance (Guralnick, 1997; Nelson, Westhues, & MacLeod, 2003; Ramey & Ramey, 1998). In one longitudinal study called the Abecedarian Project, inner-city children who received lots of mental enrichment at home and in child care or school, starting at infancy, had much better school achievement than did children in a control group (Campbell & Ramey, 1995). In another important study, of abandoned children living in Romanian orphanages, researchers randomly assigned some children to remain in the orphanages and others to move to good foster homes. By age 4, the fostered children scored dramatically higher on IQ tests than did those left behind. Children who moved before age 2 showed the largest gains, almost 15 points on average. A comparison group of children reared in their

The children of migrant workers (left) often spend long hours doing backbreaking field work and may miss out on the educational opportunities and intellectual advantages available to middle-class children (right).

biological homes did even better, with average test scores 10 to 20 points higher than those of the foster children (Nelson et al., 2007). (Since this study was done, Romania has stopped institutionalizing abandoned children younger than two unless they are seriously disabled.)

Although no single activity is going to turn anyone into a genius, certain experiences do appear to contribute to overall intelligence. In general, children's mental abilities improve when their parents talk to them about many topics and describe things accurately and fully, encourage them to think things through, read to them, and expect them to do well. A child's abilities also improve when the child's peers value and strive for intellectual achievement (Harris, 2009). Some kinds of enrichment classes may also help. When Canadian researchers randomly assigned grade 1 students to weekly piano, singing, or drama lessons during the school year, or to a control group that received no extracurricular lessons, those children who learned to play the piano or sing showed an average IQ increase of seven points by the end of the school year—compared to 4.3 points in the other groups. This difference was not large, but it was statistically significant (Schellenberg, 2004). The music lessons might have helped the children pay attention, use their memories, and hone their fine-motor skills, thus contributing to the development of brain areas involved in intelligence.

Perhaps the best evidence for the importance of environmental influences on intelligence is the fact that IQ scores in developed countries have been climbing steadily for at least three generations (Flynn, 1987, 1999) (see Figure 3.6). A similar increase has been documented in Kenya, a developing country: Rural children aged six to eight scored about 11 points higher in 1998 than their peers did in 1984—the fastest rise in a group's average IQ scores ever reported (Daley et al., 2003). Genes cannot possibly have changed enough to account for these findings. Most psychologists attribute the increases to improvements in education, the growth in jobs requiring abstract thought, and better nutrition and health (Neisser, 1998).

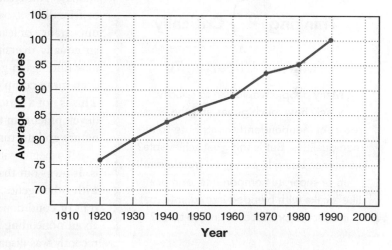

FIGURE 3.6 Climbing IQ Scores

Raw scores on IQ tests have been rising in developed countries for many decades at a rate much too steep to be accounted for by genetic changes. Because test norms are periodically readjusted to set the average score at 100, most people are unaware of the increase. On this graph, average scores are calibrated according to 1989 norms. As you can see, performance was much lower in 1918 than in 1989. (Adapted from Horgan, 1995.)

quickQUIZ

✓•[Quick Review on **MyPsychLab**

Are you thinking intelligently about intelligence?

1. On average, behavioural-genetics studies estimate the heritability of intelligence to be (a) about 0.90, (b) about 0.20, (c) low at all ages, (d) higher for adults than for children.
2. *True or false:* If a trait such as intelligence is highly heritable within a group, then differences between groups must also be due mainly to heredity.
3. The available evidence (does/does not) show that ethnic differences in average IQ scores are due to genetic differences.
4. Name four environmental factors associated with reduced mental ability.

Answers:

1. d   2. false   3. does not   4. poor prenatal care, malnutrition, exposure to toxins, and stressful family circumstances

We see, then, that although heredity may provide the range of a child's intellectual potential—a Homer Simpson can never become an Einstein—many other factors affect where in that range the child will fall.

BEYOND NATURE VERSUS NURTURE

This chapter opened with two questions: What makes us alike as human beings, and why do we differ? Today, a prevalent but greatly oversimplified answer is: It's all genetic. Genes, it's claimed, make men sexually adventurous and women sexually choosy. You either have a gene for smartness, musical ability, math genius, or friendliness, or you don't. In this climate, many people who believe in the importance of learning, opportunities, and experience feel that they must take an equally oversimplified position: Genes, they say, don't matter at all. As new findings in genetics emerge, scientists are finding that this interaction is even more complex than anyone imagined just a few years ago (Barry, 2007). This is not a textbook on genetics, but we think you should know about a few developments in the field that promise to radically alter our understanding of nature and nurture in the coming years.

To begin with, scientists are revisiting the whole notion of what a gene is. It turns out that some individual genes may be fragmented and intertwined with other genes, making the search for genes associated with any particular trait or condition even more difficult. Scientists are also rethinking their ideas about noncoding DNA, the DNA that is found outside of genes and that until recently was disparagingly referred to as "junk DNA." Mutations in this DNA could possibly be associated with common diseases. Messages from noncoding DNA, along with random chemical events in cells, may also affect the "expression" (activity) of certain genes.

As we have seen, however, heredity and environment always interact to produce the unique mixture of qualities that make up a human being. At the start of this chapter, we mentioned that genes switch on or off depending on the experiences a person has and on the activity of other genes. Gene expression also varies because of random biochemical processes within bodily cells, which geneticists call "noise." As a result of these extraordinary developments, a specialty called **epigenetics** has emerged to study changes in gene expression due to mechanisms other than structural changes in the DNA itself. In part because of epigenetic influences, identical twins and even

Thinking { Critically

Tolerate Uncertainty

Many people would like to specify precisely how much genes and the environment independently contribute to human qualities. But is this goal achievable? Is a human being like a jigsaw puzzle made up of separate components, or more like a cake with blended ingredients that interact to produce its unique taste?

◉ **Watch**
Cloned Child

epigenetics   The study of changes in gene expression due to mechanisms other than structural changes in DNA.

cloned, genetically identical animals living in exactly the same environment can differ considerably in appearance and behaviour (Raser & O'Shea, 2005). Yes, you read that right: Even clones can differ (as fans of *Battlestar Galactica* already know). The study of epigenetics is demonstrating that the timing and pattern of genetic activity are critical not only before birth but throughout life (Feinberg, 2008). This means that the genome is not a static blueprint for development but more like a constantly changing network of interlinked influences, including environmental ones. Even more astonishing, work with animals finds that at least some epigenetic changes can be transmitted to the next generation (Champagne, 2009).

Thus we can no more speak of genes, or of the environment, "causing" personality or intelligence in a straightforward way than we can speak of butter, sugar, or flour individually causing the taste of a cake (Lewontin, Rose, & Kamin, 1984). Many people do speak that way, however, out of a desire to make things clearer than they actually are, and sometimes to justify prejudices about ethnicity, gender, or class.

An unstated assumption in many debates about nature and nurture is that the world would be a better place if certain kinds of genes prevailed. This assumption overlooks the fact that nature loves genetic diversity, not similarity. The ability of any species to survive depends on such diversity. If every penguin, porpoise, or person had exactly the same genetic strengths and weaknesses, these species could not survive changes in the environment; a new virus or a change in climate would wipe out the entire group. With diversity, at least some penguins, porpoises, or people have a chance of making it.

Psychological diversity is adaptive, too. Each of us has something valuable to contribute, whether it is artistic talent, academic ability, creativity, social skill, athletic prowess, a sense of humour, mechanical aptitude, practical wisdom, a social conscience, or the energy to get things done. In our complicated, fast-moving world, all these qualities are needed. The challenge, for any society, is to promote the potential of each of its members.

Genes are not destiny. In fact, because of "noise" and other influences on gene expression, even identical twins and cloned animals are not exactly alike. The first cat ever cloned (left) was named CC, for "carbon copy," but she's not really a carbon copy of her genetically identical mother. The two have different coat patterns and different personalities.

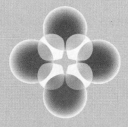

Taking Psychology with YOU

Thinking Critically in Everyday Life

Genetic Testing and You

Imagine that you have been feeling depressed and you go to a clinical psychologist for help.

The psychologist interviews you, gives you a battery of psychological tests, lets you talk about your problems—and then has your blood drawn to check your DNA, to find out if you have a genetic predisposition for depression.

The psychologist has your blood drawn? Right now, this scenario is purely hypothetical, but perhaps not for long. Two leading experts in behavioural genetics, Robert Plomin and John Crabbe (2000), have predicted that in the not-so-distant future, therapists will routinely have their clients' DNA tested to gather information for use in diagnosis and treatment. This is already possible, they note, for Alzheimer's disease: Having a DNA marker for a gene that codes for a particular protein heightens an individual's risk of developing the disease. Would you want to be tested for a gene that increases the risk of developing Alzheimer's? How would you feel about being tested for a gene that increases the risk of an early death? Would you want to know so that you could plan accordingly, or would you rather let the chips fall where they may? Pregnant women and their partners are often tested to determine whether they are carrying genes that are likely to condemn their children to a fatal or painful disease. When the test results are positive, many choose to abort the pregnancies. But what if you could be tested for a gene that increases your future child's risk of developing a mental or emotional disorder, such as schizophrenia or autism? Would you want to have that sort of test, and what would you do with the results? What if the test were for a more common condition, such as a reading disability or obesity? And what if the condition was homosexuality, which is not a disorder at all but which some people fear; or being very short, which in some quarters is a social disadvantage but is hardly a disability? If prenatal genetic testing revealed that your child had a somewhat increased chance of being gay or short, what would you do with that information? Would you consider aborting the fetus?

In coming years, as noninvasive methods of genetic testing such as blood tests are introduced and become widespread, all of us are going to have to think long and hard about such questions. You can use information from this chapter to evaluate the pros and cons of such testing for yourself or a family member. Here are some things to keep in mind:

Genes are not destiny. It is true that some diseases, such as Huntington's, are caused by a single gene. However, as we have seen, most traits are influenced by many genes, by environmental factors, and by biochemical and other events within cells. That is why knowing that you have markers for one or two genes that may contribute to a trait or disorder does not necessarily tell you much in practical terms.

Knowing about a genetic disposition can create a premature diagnosis

or a self-fulfilling prophecy. If parents and school officials know that a child is at risk of developing a learning disorder, they may treat the child as cognitively impaired even though the child has not shown any signs of a problem. If a person is aware of having a genetic predisposition toward depression, he or she may not develop the skills to cope with setbacks, deciding incorrectly that "there's nothing I can do."

Genes do not absolve you of responsibility. Some judges are allowing or even compelling defendants in criminal cases to be genetically tested for mental conditions or behavioural tendencies in order to help determine the extent of their responsibility for the crime or likelihood of repeating it (Hoffmann & Rothenberg, 2005). But "my genes made me do it" is not necessarily a good excuse for bad behaviour. Not only does the environment play a large role in behaviour, but also the flexible human brain allows us to do an end run around many of our genetic tendencies by modifying them, ignoring them, or controlling them. As David Barash (2001), an evolutionary psychologist, put it, a strong case can be made that "we are never so human as when we behave contrary to our natural inclinations, those most in tune with our biological impulses."

Genetic information could be used to discriminate against individuals. Critics of genetic testing worry that insurance companies will refuse coverage to adults and children who are currently healthy but whose DNA reveals them to have some genetic predisposition for developing a physical or psychological disorder later in life. Employers who pay insurance premiums for their workers might be reluctant to hire such individuals. So far, such cases of genetic discrimination have been rare. But some bioethicists and scholars are concerned that current laws may not adequately protect people's right to keep genetic information private.

Knowing your genetic risk does not necessarily tell you what to do about it. If your child has a physical disorder called phenylketonuria (PKU), which prevents the body from assimilating protein and

causes mental retardation, the solution is obvious: Limit the intake of protein. But in the case of behavioural, cognitive, or emotional problems, the answer is usually not so straightforward. Often we simply don't yet know how to treat problems that have a genetic component, or many possible approaches exist and we don't know which one is best.

Genetic testing can be liberating or stigmatizing. Knowing that a condition or trait is "not your fault" may help you live with it or accept the limitations it imposes. For example, knowing that your child's autism is genetic and not caused by bad parenting will keep you from feeling unnecessary guilt. On the other hand, genetic testing can activate prejudices against anyone with less-than-ideal looks or abilities.

In the past, such prejudices led to the discredited social movement called *eugenics*, which aimed to "improve" the species through forced sterilization of low-IQ people. As a result, from the beginning of the twentieth century until the mid-1960s, thousands of mentally ill and developmentally delayed North Americans were sterilized against their will (Bruinius, 2006).

Defenders of genetic testing answer that the goal of prenatal screening is not to improve the human species; it is to relieve the suffering of parents and children, and therefore prospective parents should not feel guilty for taking advantage of this technology (Cowan, 2008). But to some social critics, prenatal testing for run-of-the-mill human qualities reflects a view of children as products to be perfected instead of as individuals to be appreciated for who they are (Sandel, 2007).

If abortion would be an option for you, how serious and how likely would an inherited condition have to be before you would consider aborting a fetus? Would a 10% likelihood be enough, or 50%, or would you require near certainty? Would you want to know, while you are still young, that you carry genes associated with some disorder that usually doesn't strike until middle or old age? How might this information change your life?

SUMMARY

UNLOCKING THE SECRETS OF GENES

◆ In general, *evolutionary psychologists* study our commonalities and *behavioural geneticists* study our differences. Historically, *nativists* have emphasized "nature" and *empiricists* "nurture," but scientists today understand that heredity and environment interact to produce our psychological traits and even most of our physical ones. This interaction works in both directions: Genes affect the environments we choose, and the environment affects the activity of genes over our lifetimes.

◆ *Genes*, the basic units of heredity, are located on *chromosomes*, which consist of strands of *DNA*. Within each gene, a sequence of four elements of DNA constitutes a chemical code that helps determine the synthesis of a particular protein. In turn, proteins affect virtually all the structural and biochemical characteristics of the organism.

◆ Most human traits depend on more than one gene pair, which makes tracking down the genetic contributions to a trait extremely difficult. One method for doing so involves the use of *linkage studies*, which look for patterns of inheritance of the *genetic markers* whose locations on the genes are already known.

◆ Researchers have completed a map of the entire human *genome*. However, this map does not automatically tell us what a particular gene does or how it does so, or how multiple genes interact and influence behaviour.

THE GENETICS OF SIMILARITY

◆ Evolutionary psychologists argue that many fundamental human similarities can be traced to the processes of *evolution*, especially *natural selection*. They draw inferences about the behavioural tendencies that might have been selected because they helped our forebears solve survival problems and enhanced reproductive fitness; they then conduct research to see if such tendencies actually exist throughout the world.

◆ Many evolutionary psychologists believe that the mind is not a general-purpose computer, but instead evolved as a collection of specialized *mental modules* to handle specific survival problems. Among the candidates for such modules are inborn reflexes, an attraction to novelty, a motive to explore and manipulate objects, an impulse to play, and the capacity for certain basic cognitive skills, including a rudimentary understanding of number. However, because some behaviour or trait exists does not necessarily mean that it is adaptive or the product of natural selection.

OUR HUMAN HERITAGE: LANGUAGE

◆ Human beings are the only species that uses language to express and comprehend an infinite number of novel utterances. Noam Chomsky argues that the ability to take the *surface structure* of any utterance and apply rules of syntax to infer its underlying *deep structure* must depend on an innate faculty for language, a *language acquisition device* sensitive to a *universal grammar* (features common to all languages). Many findings support this view: Children from different cultures go through similar stages of language development; children's language is full of *overregularizations* reflecting grammatical rules; adults do not correct their children's syntax consistently; groups of children who have never been exposed to adult language often invent their own; and young infants can derive linguistic rules from strings of sounds. An innate capacity for language might have evolved in humans because it enhanced the chances of survival.

◆ Some scientists, on the other hand, have devised models of language acquisition that do not assume an innate capacity (*computer neural networks*). Some argue that instead of inferring grammatical rules, children learn the statistical probability that any given word or syllable will follow another. Moreover, it seems clear that parental practices, such as recasting a child's incorrect sentence, aid in language acquisition. Biological readiness and experience thus interact in the development of language.

OUR HUMAN HERITAGE: COURTSHIP AND MATING

◆ *Sociobiologists* and evolutionary psychologists argue that males and females have evolved different sexual and courtship strategies in response to survival problems faced in the distant past. In this view, it has been adaptive for males to be promiscuous, to be attracted to young partners, and to want sexual novelty, and for females to be monogamous, to be choosy about partners, and to prefer security to novelty.

◆ Critics argue that evolutionary explanations of infidelity and monogamy are based on simplistic stereotypes of gender differences; that they rely too heavily on answers to questionnaires, which often do not reflect real-life choices; that convenience samples used in questionnaire studies are not necessarily representative of people in general; and that the evolutionary emphasis on the Pleistocene Age may not be warranted. Moreover, our ancestors probably did not have a wide range of partners to choose from; what may have evolved is mate selection based on similarity and proximity. The central issue dividing evolutionary theorists and their critics is the length of the "genetic leash."

THE GENETICS OF DIFFERENCE

◆ Behavioural geneticists often study differences among individuals by using data from studies of adopted children and of *identical* and *fraternal twins*. These data yield an estimate of the *heritability* of traits and abilities—the extent to which differences in a trait or ability within a group of individuals is accounted for by genetic differences.

◆ Heritability estimates do not apply to specific individuals or to differences between groups. They apply only to differences within a particular group living in a particular environment; for example, heritability is higher for children in affluent families than in impoverished ones. Moreover, even highly heritable traits can often be modified by the environment.

OUR HUMAN DIVERSITY: THE CASE OF INTELLIGENCE

◆ Heritability estimates for intelligence (as measured by IQ tests) average about 0.40 to 0.50 for children and adolescents and 0.60 to 0.80 for adults. Identical twins are more similar in IQ test performance than fraternal twins, and adopted children's scores correlate more highly with those of their biological parents than with those of their nonbiological relatives. These results do not mean that genes determine intelligence; the remaining variance in IQ scores must owe largely to environmental influences.

◆ Several studies have reported markers for genes that may influence IQ performance. But each of these genes, if confirmed, is likely to contribute just a tiny piece to the puzzle of genetic variation in intelligence.

◆ It is a mistake to draw conclusions about *group* differences from heritability estimates based on differences *within* a group. The available evidence fails to support genetic explanations of black–white differences in performance on IQ tests.

◆ Environmental factors such as poor prenatal care, malnutrition, exposure to toxins, and stressful family circumstances are associated with lower performance on intelligence tests. Conversely, a healthy and stimulating environment, and certain kinds of enrichment activities, can improve performance. IQ scores have been rising in many countries for several generations, most likely because of improved diet and education and the increase in jobs requiring abstract thought.

BEYOND NATURE VERSUS NURTURE

◆ Neither nature nor nurture can entirely explain people's similarities or differences. New discoveries about the role of noncoding DNA, and findings in the field of epigenetics, show that the interaction between genes and environment is far more complex than anyone once imagined. Genetic and environmental influences blend and become indistinguishable in the development of any individual.

TAKING PSYCHOLOGY WITH YOU

◆ When deciding whether to have genetic testing, critical thinkers will consider the personal and social consequences, such as whether test results can reveal a risk that has practical relevance, could be misused by their employer or insurance company, might stigmatize them if others knew about it, would help them accept and live with a problem, or could create a self-fulfilling prophecy.

MyPsychLab

Visit **www.mypsychlab.com** to help you get the best grade!
Test your knowledge and grasp difficult concepts through

• Custom study plans: See where you are strong and where you go wrong
• Interactive simulations
• Video and audio clips

KEY TERMS

evolutionary psychology 74

behavioural genetics 74

genes 74

chromosomes 74

DNA (deoxyribonucleic acid) 74

genome 74

genetic marker 75

evolution 77

mutation 77

natural selection 78

mental modules 79

language 82

language acquisition device 84

overregularizations 85

computer neural networks 86

sociobiology 87

social Darwinism 92

heritability 93

identical (monozygotic) twins 95

fraternal (dizygotic) twins 95

intelligence quotient (IQ) 97

epigenetics 102

4 THE BRAIN: SOURCE OF MIND AND SELF

ASK QUESTIONS . . . be willing to WONDER

- Can the experiences you have change your brain?

- How can high-tech brain scans mislead as well as inform?

- Are people either "left-brained" or "right-brained"?

- Where in the brain is your "self"?

- Are there "his" and "hers" brains?

AFTER SUFFERING damage to the right side of the brain, a Swiss stroke patient developed a puzzling symptom. Although the left side of his body was weak and he had trouble seeing objects in his left field of vision, what concerned him most was the blandness of the hospital food. The man had become obsessed with fine dining, a phenomenon his neuropsychologist later dubbed "gourmand syndrome." In his diary, the patient wrote, "It is time for. . . a good sausage with hash browns or some spaghetti Bolognese, or risotto and a breaded cutlet, nicely decorated, or a scallop of game in cream sauce with spaetzle." After recovering, he quit his job as a political journalist and became a food columnist (Regard & Landis, 1997).

Julie appears perfectly normal when you first meet her, but it soon becomes apparent that she lives in a bewildering place: the eternal present. Since suffering brain damage when a freight train hit her car, Julie has been unable to recall people and events from either the distant past or a few minutes ago. She cannot remember her daughter, who died in the accident. She knows she has a husband, but he must be reintroduced to her whenever she sees him. She can cook and make a phone call, but when she tries to read, the words from the start of the paragraph vanish by the time she gets to the end. She keeps meticulous notes about her day, but she feels she is faking her way through life (Mason, 2008).

These cases, and thousands like them, teach us that the 1500-gram organ inside our skull provides the bedrock for everything we do and think. When injury or disease affects the brain's functioning, life is inevitably altered physically, emotionally, or mentally. Sometimes the changes are subtle and even benign, as in the case of "gourmand syndrome." All too often they are not.

Nearly every week, discoveries about the brain make headlines, as new research is announced and old puzzles begin to be solved. For example:

◆ Researchers have used electrical stimulation of the brain to restore awareness to a patient who spent several years in a "minimally conscious state" (which leaves the brain more intact than does a "persistent vegetative state," from which there is no recovery). During that time, the man was almost completely unresponsive. But when surgeons inserted fine wires into his brain and connected them to a pacemaker-like device implanted in his chest, he regained knowledge of his environment, recognized his parents, and was able to hold brief conversations (Schiff et al., 2007).

◆ A team of scientists say they have developed a way to determine which photographs of natural images a person is looking at by decoding patterns of activity in visual areas of the person's brain (Kay et al., 2008). Two of the researchers themselves looked at 1750 images while having their brains

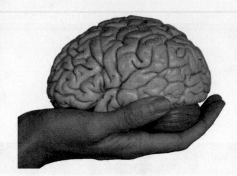
scanned; the team then constructed a mathematical model based on activity shown in the scans. When the two researchers looked at 120 new images, the model correctly predicted which ones they were seeing.

Neuropsychologists and *neuroscientists* study the brain and the rest of the nervous system in hopes of gaining a better understanding of behaviour and of what is possible for this organ. They are concerned with the biological foundations of consciousness, perception, memory, emotion, stress, and mental disorders—of everything, in fact, that human beings feel and do. In this chapter, we will examine the structure of the brain and the rest of the nervous system as background for our later discussions of these and other topics.

At this very moment, your own brain, assisted by other parts of your nervous system, is busily taking in these words. Whether you are excited, curious, or bored, your brain is registering some sort of emotional reaction. As you continue reading, your brain will (we hope) store away much of the information in this chapter. Later on, your brain may enable you to smell a flower, climb the stairs, greet a friend, solve a problem, or chuckle at a joke. But the brain's most startling accomplishment is its knowledge that it is doing all these things. This self-awareness makes brain research different from the study of anything else in the universe. Neuroscientists must use the cells, biochemistry, and circuitry of their own brains to understand the cells, biochemistry, and circuitry of brains in general.

William Shakespeare called the brain "the soul's frail dwelling house." Actually, this miraculous organ is more like the main room in a house filled with many alcoves and passageways—the "house" being the nervous system as a whole. Before we can understand the windows, walls, and furniture of this house, we need to become acquainted with the overall floor plan.

YOU are about to learn . . .

- why you automatically pull your hand away from something hot "without thinking."
- the major parts of the nervous system and their primary functions.

THE NERVOUS SYSTEM: A BASIC BLUEPRINT

The function of a nervous system is to gather and process information, produce responses to stimuli, and coordinate the workings of different cells. Even the lowly jellyfish and the humble earthworm have the beginnings of such a system. In very simple organisms that do little more than move, eat, and eliminate wastes, the "system" may be no more than one or two nerve cells. In human beings, who do such complex things as dance, cook, and take psychology courses, the nervous system contains billions of cells. Scientists divide this intricate network into two main parts: the central nervous system and the peripheral (outlying) nervous system (see Figure 4.1).

The Central Nervous System

central nervous system (CNS) The portion of the nervous system consisting of the brain and spinal cord.

The **central nervous system (CNS)** receives, processes, interprets, and stores incoming sensory information—information about tastes, sounds, smells, colour, pressure on the skin, the state of internal organs, and so forth. It also sends out messages destined for muscles, glands, and internal organs. The CNS is usually conceptualized as having two components: the brain, which we will consider in detail later, and the spinal cord, which is actually an extension of the brain. The spinal cord runs from the base of the brain down the centre of the back, protected by a column of bones (the spinal column), and it acts as a bridge between the brain and the parts of the body below the neck.

The spinal cord produces some behaviours on its own without any help from the brain. These spinal reflexes are automatic, requiring no conscious effort. For example, if you accidentally touch a hot iron, you will immediately pull your hand away, even before your brain has had a chance to register what has happened. Nerve impulses bring a message to the spinal cord (hot!), and the spinal cord immediately sends out a command via other nerves, telling muscles in your arm to contract and to pull your hand away from the iron. (Reflexes above the neck, such as sneezing and blinking, involve the lower part of the brain rather than the spinal cord.)

The neural circuits underlying many spinal reflexes are linked to neural pathways that run up and down the spinal cord, to and from the brain. Because of these connections, reflexes can sometimes be influenced by thoughts and emotions. An example is erection in men, a spinal reflex that can be inhibited by anxiety or distracting thoughts and initiated by erotic thoughts. Some reflexes can be brought under conscious control. If you concentrate, you may be able to keep your knee from jerking when it is tapped, as it normally would. Similarly, most men can learn to voluntarily delay ejaculation, another spinal reflex.

The Peripheral Nervous System

The peripheral nervous system (PNS) handles the central nervous system's input and output. It contains all portions of the nervous system outside the brain and spinal cord, right down to the nerves in the tips of the fingers and toes. If your brain could not collect information about the world by means of a peripheral nervous system, it would be like a radio without a receiver. In the peripheral nervous system, sensory nerves carry messages from special receptors in the skin, muscles, and other internal and external sense organs to the spinal cord, which sends them along to the brain. These nerves put us in touch with both the outside world and the activities of our own bodies. Motor nerves carry orders from the central nervous system to muscles, glands, and internal organs. They enable us to move, and they cause glands to contract and to secrete substances, including chemical messengers called hormones.

Scientists further divide the peripheral nervous system into two parts: the somatic (bodily) nervous system and the autonomic (self-governing) nervous system. The somatic nervous system, sometimes called the skeletal nervous system, consists of nerves that are connected to sensory receptors—cells that enable you to sense the world—and also to the skeletal muscles that permit voluntary action. When you feel a bug on your arm, or when you turn off a light or write your name, your somatic system is active. The autonomic nervous system regulates the functioning of blood vessels, glands, and internal (visceral) organs such as the bladder, stomach, and heart. When you see someone you have a crush on and your heart pounds, your hands get sweaty, and your cheeks feel hot, you can blame your autonomic nervous system.

The autonomic nervous system is itself divided into two parts: the sympathetic nervous system and the parasympathetic nervous system. These two parts work together, but in opposing ways, to adjust the body to changing circumstances (see Figure 4.2). The sympathetic system acts like the accelerator of a car, mobilizing the body for action and an output of energy. It makes you blush, sweat, and breathe more deeply, and it pushes up your heart rate and blood pressure. As we discuss in Chapter 11,

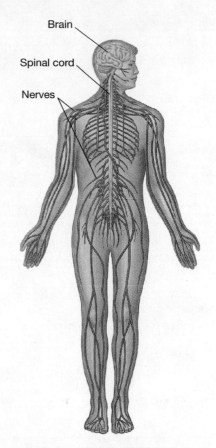

Brain

Spinal cord

Nerves

FIGURE 4.1 The Central and Peripheral Nervous Systems

The central nervous system includes the brain and the spinal cord. The peripheral nervous system consists of 43 pairs of nerves that transmit information to and from the central nervous system. Twelve pairs of cranial nerves in the head enter the brain directly; 31 pairs of spinal nerves enter the spinal cord at the spaces between the vertebrae.

spinal cord A collection of neurons and supportive tissue running from the base of the brain down the centre of the back, protected by a column of bones (the spinal column).

peripheral nervous system (PNS) All portions of the nervous system outside the brain and spinal cord; it includes sensory and motor nerves.

somatic nervous system The subdivision of the peripheral nervous system that connects to sensory receptors and to skeletal muscles; sometimes called the skeletal nervous system.

autonomic nervous system The subdivision of the peripheral nervous system that regulates the internal organs and glands.

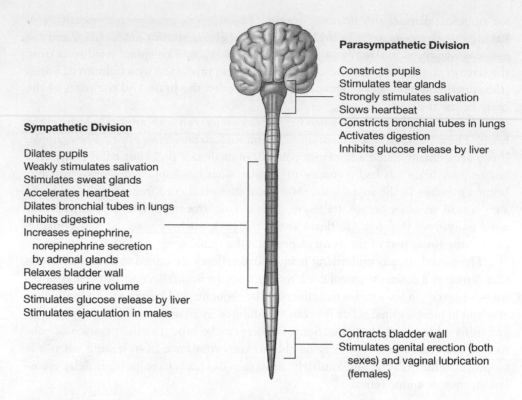

Parasympathetic Division

Constricts pupils
Stimulates tear glands
Strongly stimulates salivation
Slows heartbeat
Constricts bronchial tubes in lungs
Activates digestion
Inhibits glucose release by liver

Sympathetic Division

Dilates pupils
Weakly stimulates salivation
Stimulates sweat glands
Accelerates heartbeat
Dilates bronchial tubes in lungs
Inhibits digestion
Increases epinephrine,
   norepinephrine secretion
   by adrenal glands
Relaxes bladder wall
Decreases urine volume
Stimulates glucose release by liver
Stimulates ejaculation in males

Contracts bladder wall
Stimulates genital erection (both
   sexes) and vaginal lubrication
   (females)

FIGURE 4.2 The Autonomic Nervous System

In general, the sympathetic division of the autonomic nervous system prepares the body to expend energy and the parasympathetic division restores and conserves energy. Sympathetic nerve fibres exit from areas of the spinal cord shown in red in this illustration; parasympathetic fibres exit from the base of the brain and from spinal cord areas shown in green.

◄⊙Simulate
Psychology Experiments Survey: Do You Fly or Fight?

✱Explore
Autonomic Nervous System

sympathetic nervous system The subdivision of the autonomic nervous system that mobilizes bodily resources and increases the output of energy during emotion and stress.

parasympathetic nervous system The subdivision of the autonomic nervous system that operates during relaxed states and that conserves energy.

when you are in a situation that requires you to fight, flee, or cope, the sympathetic nervous system whirls into action. The parasympathetic system is more like a brake: It does not stop the body, of course, but it does tend to slow things down and keep them running smoothly. It enables the body to conserve and store energy. If you have to jump out of the way of a speeding motorcyclist, sympathetic nerves increase your heart rate. Afterward, parasympathetic nerves slow it down again and keep its rhythm regular.

❖ YOU are about to learn . . .

♦ which cells function as the nervous system's "communication specialists," and how they "talk" to each other.

♦ the functions of glial cells, the most numerous cells in the brain.

♦ why researchers are excited about the discovery of stem cells in the brain.

♦ how learning and experience alter the brain's circuits.

♦ what happens when levels of neurotransmitters are too low or too high.

♦ which brain chemicals mimic the effects of morphine by dulling pain and promoting pleasure.

♦ which hormones are of special interest to psychologists, and why.

quick**QUIZ**

✓•☐**Quick Review** on **MyPsychLab**

Pause now to mentally fill in the missing parts of the nervous system "house." Then see whether you can briefly describe what each part of the system does.

```
                    Nervous
                    System
           ┌───────────┴───────────┐
      1.  ?___                 2.  ?___
      Nervous                     Nervous
      System                      System
      ┌────┴────┐            ┌───────┴───────┐
   Brain      3.  ?___    4.  ?___       Autonomic
                           Nervous        Nervous
                           System         System
                                     ┌───────┴───────┐
                                  5.  ?___        6.  ?___
                                  Nervous         Nervous
                                  System          System
```

Answers:

1. central: processes, interprets, and stores information and issues orders to muscles, glands, and organs   2. peripheral: transmits information to and from the CNS   3. spinal cord: serves as a bridge between the brain and the peripheral nervous system, produces reflexes   4. somatic: controls the skeletal muscles   5. sympathetic: mobilizes the body for action, energy output   6. parasympathetic: conserves energy, maintains the body in a quiet state

COMMUNICATION IN THE NERVOUS SYSTEM

The blueprint we just described provides only a general idea of the nervous system's structure. Now let's turn to the details. The nervous system is made up in part of **neurons**, or *nerve cells*. They are the brain's communication specialists, transmitting information to, from, and within the central nervous system. Neurons are held in place by **glia**, or *glial cells* (from the Greek for "glue"), which make up 90% of the brain's cells.

Glial cells are more than just glue, however. They provide the neurons with nutrients, insulate them, protect the brain from toxic agents, and remove cellular debris when neurons die. They also communicate chemically with each other and with neurons; and without them, neurons could not function effectively. One kind of glial cell appears to give neurons the go-ahead to form connections and to start "talking" to each other (He & Sun, 2007; Ullian, Christopherson, & Barres, 2004). And over time, glia help determine which neural connections get stronger or weaker, suggesting that they play a vital role in learning and memory (Bains & Oliet, 2007; Fields, 2004).

It's neurons, though, that are considered the building blocks of the nervous system, though in structure they are more like snowflakes than blocks, exquisitely delicate and differing from one another greatly in size and shape (see Figure 4.3). In the giraffe, a neuron that runs from the spinal cord down the animal's hind leg may be three metres long! In the human brain, neurons are microscopic. No one is sure

Neurons in the outer layers of the brain.

neuron   A cell that conducts electrochemical signals; the basic unit of the nervous system; also called a *nerve cell*.

glia [GLY-uh or GLEE-uh]   Cells that support, nurture, and insulate neurons, remove debris when neurons die, enhance the formation and maintenance of neural connections, and modify neuronal functioning.

FIGURE 4.3 Different Kinds of Neurons

Neurons vary in size and shape, depending on their location and function. More than 200 types of neurons have been identified in mammals.

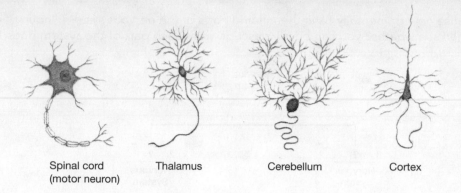

Spinal cord (motor neuron)   Thalamus   Cerebellum   Cortex

how many neurons the human brain contains, but a typical estimate is 100 billion, about the same number as there are stars in our galaxy, and some estimates go much higher.

The Structure of the Neuron

As you can see in Figure 4.4, a neuron has three main parts: *dendrites*, a *cell body*, and an *axon*. The **dendrites** look like the branches of a tree; indeed, the word *dendrite* means "little tree" in Greek. Dendrites act like antennas, receiving messages from as many as 10 000 other nerve cells and transmitting these messages toward the cell body. They also do some preliminary processing of those messages. The **cell body**, which is shaped roughly like a sphere or a pyramid, contains the biochemical machinery for keeping the neuron alive. It also plays the key role in determining whether the neuron should "fire"—transmit a message to other neurons—depending on inputs from other neurons. The **axon** (from the Greek for "axle") transmits messages away from the cell body to other neurons or to muscle or gland cells. Axons commonly divide at the end into branches called *axon terminals*. In adult human beings, axons vary from only a few microns to more than a metre in length. Dendrites and axons give each neuron a double role: As one researcher put it, a neuron is first a catcher, then a batter (Gazzaniga, 1988).

dendrites A neuron's branches that receive information from other neurons and transmit it toward the cell body.

cell body The part of the neuron that keeps it alive and determines whether or not it will fire.

axon A neuron's extending fibre that conducts impulses away from the cell body and transmits them to other neurons.

✳ Explore
The Structure of Neurons

FIGURE 4.4 The Structure of a Neuron

Incoming neural impulses are received by the dendrites of a neuron and are transmitted to the cell body. Outgoing signals pass along the axon to terminal branches.

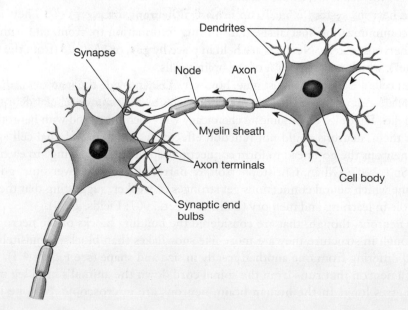

Synapse

Node   Axon

Dendrites

Myelin sheath

Axon terminals

Cell body

Synaptic end bulbs

Many axons, especially the larger ones, are insulated by a surrounding layer of fatty material called the myelin sheath, which in the central nervous system is made up of glial cells. Constrictions in this covering, called nodes, divide it into segments, which make it look a little like a string of link sausages (see Figure 4.4 again). One purpose of the myelin sheath is to prevent signals in adjacent cells from interfering with each other. Another, as we will see shortly, is to speed up the conduction of neural impulses. In individuals with multiple sclerosis, loss of myelin causes erratic nerve signals, leading to loss of sensation, weakness or paralysis, lack of coordination, or vision problems.

In the peripheral nervous system, the fibres of individual neurons (axons and sometimes dendrites) are collected together in bundles called nerves, rather like the lines in a telephone cable. The human body has 43 pairs of peripheral nerves; one nerve from each pair is on the left side of the body and the other is on the right. Most of these nerves enter or leave the spinal cord, but 12 pairs in the head, the cranial nerves, connect directly to the brain. In Chapter 6, we will discuss the cranial nerves involved in smell, hearing, and vision.

Neurons in the News

For most of the twentieth century, scientists assumed that if neurons in the central nervous system were injured or damaged, they could never grow back (regenerate). But then the conventional wisdom got turned upside down. Animal studies showed that severed axons in the spinal cord *can* regrow if you treat them with certain nervous system chemicals (Schnell & Schwab, 1990). Researchers are hopeful that regenerated axons will eventually enable people with spinal cord injuries to use their limbs again.

In the past two decades, scientists have also had to rethink another entrenched assumption: that mammals produce no new CNS cells after infancy. In the early 1990s, Canadian neuroscientists, working with mice, immersed immature cells from the animals' brains in a growth-promoting protein and showed that these cells could give birth to new neurons in a process called neurogenesis. Even more astonishing, the new neurons continued to divide and multiply (Reynolds & Weiss, 1992). Since then, scientists have discovered that the human brain and other body organs also contain such cells, which are now known as stem cells. Stem cells involved in learning and memory seem to divide and mature throughout adulthood. Animal studies find that physical exercise, effortful mental activity, and an enriched environment promote the production and survival of new cells, whereas aging and stress can inhibit their production and nicotine can kill them (Berger, Gage, & Vijayaraghavan, 1998; Kempermann, 2006; Shors, 2009).

Stem-cell research is one of the hottest areas in biology and neuroscience. The reason: Scientists prefer working with cells from aborted fetuses and from embryos that are a few days old, which consist of just a few cells. (Fertility clinics store many such embryos because several "test tube" fertilizations are created for every patient who hopes to become pregnant; eventually, the extra embryos are destroyed.) In Canada, embryonic stem cells (ES) can be obtained only from sources approved by the Assisted Human Reproduction Agency of Canada, a regulatory body for stem-cell research.

myelin sheath   A fatty insulation that may surround the axon of a neuron.

nerve   A bundle of nerve fibres (axons and sometimes dendrites) in the peripheral nervous system.

neurogenesis   The production of new neurons from immature stem cells.

stem cells   Immature cells that renew themselves and have the potential to develop into mature cells; given encouraging environments, stem cells from early embryos can develop into any cell type.

In an area of the brain associated with learning and memory, immature stem cells give rise to new neurons, and physical and mental stimulation promotes the production and survival of these neurons. These mice, who have toys to play with, tunnels to explore, wheels to run on, and other mice to share their cage with, will grow more cells than mice living alone in standard cages.

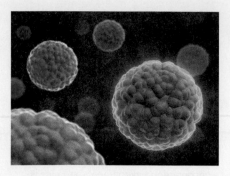

Tiny stem cells like these (magnified 1200 times in this photo) have provoked both excitement and controversy.

ES cells are especially useful because they can differentiate into any type of cell, from neurons to kidney cells, whereas those from adults are more limited and are harder to keep alive. But in recent years, scientists have successfully reprogrammed cells from adult organs, most notably skin cells, to become stem cells (e.g., Takahashi et al., 2007; Yu et al., 2007). Like ES cells, these "induced pluripotent stem (iPS) cells" seem capable of giving rise to all types of cells, although it is still unclear whether they will prove to be equally versatile.

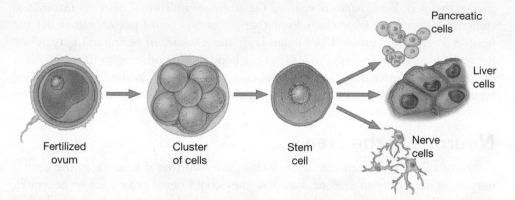

With respect to the brain, scientists have already had some success in animals. For example, in one study, mice with recent spinal cord injuries regained much of their ability to walk normally after being injected with stem cells derived from human fetal brain tissue. Microscopic analysis showed that most of the cells had turned into either neurons or a particular type of glial cell (Cummings et al., 2005). Excitingly, recent research by Rob Sutherland and colleagues has demonstrated that when the rat brain is treated with certain chemicals and exercise, it can regenerate new neurons and also gain improvements in memory (Spanswick, Lehmann, & Sutherland, 2011). Patient-advocacy groups hope that transplanted stem cells will eventually help people recover from diseases of the brain (such as Alzheimer's) and from damage to the spinal cord and other parts of the body.

A long road lies ahead, and many daunting technical hurdles remain to be overcome before stem-cell research yields practical benefits for human patients. Increasing the rate of neurogenesis may alleviate or improve some medical conditions but have negative or no effects on others (Scharfman & Hen, 2007). But we live in exciting times: Each year brings more incredible findings about neurons, findings that only a short time ago would have seemed like science fiction.

How Neurons Communicate

Neurons do not directly touch each other, end to end. Instead, they are separated by a minuscule space called the *synaptic cleft*, where the axon terminal of one neuron nearly touches a dendrite or the cell body of another. The entire site—the axon terminal, the cleft, and the covering membrane of the receiving dendrite or cell body—is called a synapse. Because a neuron's axon may have hundreds or even thousands of terminals, a single neuron may have synaptic connections with a great many others. As a result, the number of synapses in the nervous system runs into the trillions or perhaps even the quadrillions.

Neurons speak to one another, or in some cases to muscles or glands, in an electrical and chemical language. When a nerve cell is stimulated, a change in electrical potential occurs between the inside and the outside of the cell. The physics of this

✱ **Explore**
The Synapse

synapse   The site where transmission of a nerve impulse from one nerve cell to another occurs; it includes the axon terminal, the synaptic cleft, and receptor sites in the membrane of the receiving cell.

process involves the sudden, momentary inflow of positively charged sodium ions across the cell's membrane, followed by the outflow of positively charged potassium ions. The result is a brief change in electrical voltage, called an **action potential**, which produces an electric current, or impulse.

If an axon is unmyelinated, the action potential at each point in the axon gives rise to a new action potential at the next point; thus, the impulse travels down the axon somewhat as fire travels along the fuse of a firecracker. But in myelinated axons, the process is a little different. Because of myelin, sodium and potassium ions cannot cross the cell's membrane except at the breaks (nodes) between the myelin's "sausages." In myelinated axons, the action potential "hops" from one node to the next. (More precisely, positively charged ions flow down the axon at a fast rate, causing regeneration of the action potential at each node.) This arrangement allows the impulse to travel faster than it could if the action potential had to be regenerated at every point along the axon. Nerve impulses travel more slowly in babies than in older children and adults, because when babies are born, the myelin sheaths on their axons are not yet fully developed.

When a neural impulse reaches the axon terminal's buttonlike tip, it must get its message across the synaptic cleft to another cell. At this point, *synaptic vesicles*, tiny sacs in the tip of the axon terminal, open and release a few thousand molecules of a chemical substance called a **neurotransmitter**. Like sailors carrying a message from one island to another, these molecules then diffuse across the synaptic cleft (see Figure 4.5).

action potential A brief change in electrical voltage that occurs between the inside and the outside of an axon when a neuron is stimulated; it serves to produce an electrical impulse.

neurotransmitter A chemical substance that is released by a transmitting neuron at the synapse and that alters the activity of a receiving neuron.

✳ Explore
The Nerve Impulse in Afferent and Efferent Neurons

The Action Potential

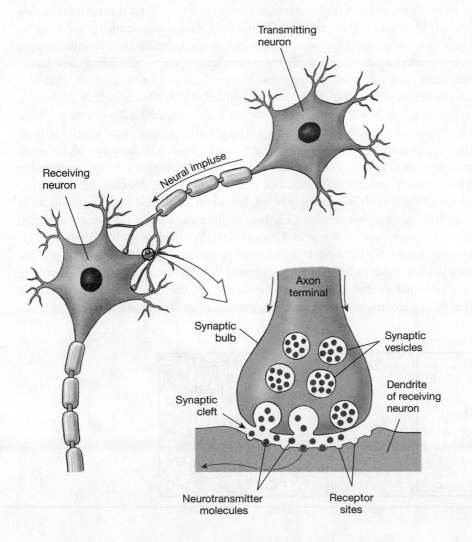

FIGURE 4.5 Neurotransmitter Crossing a Synapse
Neurotransmitter molecules are released into the synaptic cleft between two neurons from vesicles (chambers) in the transmitting neuron's axon terminal. The molecules then bind to receptor sites on the receiving neuron. As a result, the electrical state of the receiving neuron changes and the neuron becomes either more likely to fire an impulse or less so, depending on the type of neurotransmitter.

Transmitting neuron

Receiving neuron

Neural impulse

Axon terminal

Synaptic bulb

Synaptic vesicles

Synaptic cleft

Dendrite of receiving neuron

Neurotransmitter molecules

Receptor sites

When they reach the other side, the neurotransmitter molecules bind briefly with *receptor sites*, special molecules in the membrane of the receiving neuron's dendrites (or sometimes cell body), fitting these sites much as a key fits a lock. Changes occur in the receiving neuron's membrane, and the ultimate effect is either *excitatory* (a voltage shift in a positive direction) or *inhibitory* (a voltage shift in a negative direction), depending on which receptor sites have been activated. If the effect is excitatory, the probability that the receiving neuron will fire increases; if it is inhibitory, the probability decreases. Inhibition in the nervous system is extremely important. Without it, we could not sleep or coordinate our movements. Excitation of the nervous system would be overwhelming, producing convulsions.

What any given neuron does at any given moment depends on the net effect of all the messages being received from other neurons. Only when the cell's voltage reaches a certain threshold will it fire. Thousands of messages, both excitatory and inhibitory, may be coming into the cell, and the receiving neuron must essentially average them. The message that reaches a final destination depends on the rate at which individual neurons are firing, how many are firing, what types of neurons are firing, where the neurons are located, and the degree of synchrony among different neurons. It does *not* depend on how strongly the individual neurons are firing, however, because a neuron always either fires or doesn't. Like the turning on of a light switch, the firing of a neuron is an all-or-none event.

The Plastic Brain

When we are born, most of our synapses have not yet formed, but during infancy new synapses proliferate at a great rate (see Figure 4.6). Axons and dendrites continue to grow, and tiny projections on dendrites, called *spines*, increase in size and number, producing more complex connections among the brain's nerve cells. Just as new learning and stimulating environments promote the production of new neurons, they also produce increases in synaptic complexity (Diamond, 1993; Greenough & Anderson, 1991; Greenough & Black, 1992; Kolb, Gibb, & Robinson, 2003; Rosenzweig, 1984). During childhood, unused synaptic connections are also pruned away as cells or their branches die and are not replaced, leaving behind a more efficient neural network. These changes may help explain why critical or sensitive periods for the development of certain sensory and cognitive abilities occur early in life. During these periods, acquisition of these skills is amazingly rapid, but when the period ends, learning slows and may even become irreversible (Thomas & Johnson, 2008). (We discuss critical periods in language development in Chapter 3 and critical periods in visual development in Chapter 6.) Pruning and increases in synaptic density, however, are not confined to childhood; in fact, they have another developmental phase in adolescence and may continue all through life. For the most part, the brain retains flexibility in adapting to new experiences, an adaptability neuroscientists call *plasticity*.

plasticity The brain's ability to change and adapt in response to experience—for example, by reorganizing or growing new neural connections.

FIGURE 4.6 Getting Connected

Neurons in a newborn's brain are widely spaced, but they immediately begin to form new connections. These drawings show the marked increase in the number of connections from birth to age 15 months.

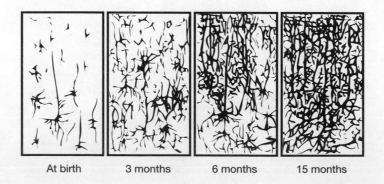

| At birth | 3 months | 6 months | 15 months |

Plasticity is vividly demonstrated in cases of people with brain damage who have experienced remarkable recoveries; for example, individuals who cannot recall simple words after a stroke but are speaking normally within months, or who cannot move an arm after a head injury but regain full use of the limb after physical therapy. Their brains have apparently rewired themselves to adapt to the damage (Liepert et al., 2000).

One research team raised an intriguing question: When people who have been blind from birth or early childhood try to determine where a sound is coming from, what happens in the part of the brain that processes visual information in sighted people? Might regions normally devoted to vision "switch gears" in some blind individuals and begin to process input from other senses instead? Using brain-scan technology called positron-emission tomography (to be described later in this chapter), these researchers examined the brains of people as they localized sounds heard through speakers (Gougoux et al., 2005). Some participants were sighted and others had been blind from early in life. When the participants heard sounds through both ears, activity in the occipital cortex, an area associated with vision, decreased in the sighted persons but *not* in the blind ones. When one ear was plugged, blind participants who did especially well at localizing sounds showed activation in two areas of the occipital cortex; neither sighted people nor blind people with ordinary ability showed such activation. What's more, the degree of activation in these regions was correlated with the blind people's accuracy in the task (see Figure 4.7). The brains of those with the best performance had apparently adapted to blindness by recruiting visual areas to take part in activities involving hearing—a dramatic example of plasticity.

Building on this research, the researchers wondered what would happen if sighted persons were blindfolded, so that they, too, could not see. In a series of studies, they had sighted volunteers wear blindfolds for five days. Before donning the blindfolds, the volunteers' brain scans showed that the visual areas in their brains were quiet during tasks requiring hearing or touch (for example, touching Braille letters). By day 5, however, these areas were lighting up during the tasks. Then, after the blindfolds were removed, the visual centres once again quieted down (Pascual-Leone et al., 2005). The visual areas of the brain apparently possess the computational machinery necessary for processing nonvisual information, but this machinery remains dormant until circumstances require its activation (Amedi et al., 2005). And when people have been blind for most of their lives, new connections may form, permitting lasting structural changes in the brain's wiring.

Thus, the brain is a dynamic organ: Its circuits are continually being modified in response to information, challenges, and changes in the environment. As scientists come to understand this process better, they may be able to apply their knowledge by designing improved rehabilitation programs for people with sensory impairments, developmental disabilities, and brain injuries.

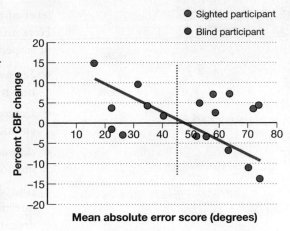

FIGURE 4.7 Adapting to Blindness

In some blind people, brain areas usually associated with vision may become active in tasks requiring hearing. The purple circles to the left of the dotted line represent blind individuals with low error rates in a sound-localization task; those to the right represent blind individuals with high error rates. The graph shows that error rates for blind people—but not sighted ones—were correlated with changes in cerebral blood flow (CBF), and thus neural activity, in a *visual* area of the brain. The more accurate blind people were, the greater the activity in this region.

Chemical Messengers in the Nervous System

The nervous system "house" would remain forever dark and lifeless without chemical couriers such as the *neurotransmitters*. Let's look more closely now at these substances and at two other types of chemical messengers: *endorphins and hormones*.

NEUROTRANSMITTERS: VERSATILE COURIERS. As we have seen, neurotransmitters make it possible for one neuron to excite or inhibit another. Neurotransmitters exist not only in the brain but also in the spinal cord, the peripheral nerves, and certain glands. Through their effects on specific nerve circuits, these substances can affect mood, memory, and well-being. The nature of the effect depends on the

✳ **Explore**
Neuronal Transmission

level of the neurotransmitter, its location, and the type of receptor it binds with. Here are a few of the better-understood neurotransmitters and some of their known or suspected effects:

◆ *Serotonin* affects neurons involved in sleep, appetite, sensory perception, temperature regulation, pain suppression, and mood.

◆ *Dopamine* affects neurons involved in voluntary movement, learning, memory, emotion, pleasure or reward, and, possibly, response to novelty.

◆ *Acetylcholine* affects neurons involved in muscle action, cognitive functioning, memory, and emotion.

◆ *Norepinephrine* affects neurons involved in increased heart rate and the slowing of intestinal activity during stress, and neurons involved in learning, memory, dreaming, waking from sleep, and emotion.

◆ *GABA (gamma-aminobutyric acid)* is the major inhibitory neurotransmitter in the brain.

◆ *Glutamate* is the major excitatory neurotransmitter in the brain; it is released by about 90% of the brain's neurons.

Harmful effects can occur when neurotransmitter levels are too high or too low. Abnormal GABA levels have been implicated in sleep and eating disorders and in convulsive disorders, including epilepsy. People with Alzheimer's disease lose brain cells responsible for producing acetylcholine and other neurotransmitters, and these deficits help account for their devastating memory problems. A loss of cells that produce dopamine is responsible for the tremors and rigidity of Parkinson's disease. In multiple sclerosis, immune cells overproduce glutamate, which damages or kills glial cells that normally make myelin.

We want to warn you, however, that pinning down the relation between neurotransmitter abnormalities and behavioural or physical abnormalities is extremely tricky. Each neurotransmitter plays multiple roles, and the functions of different substances often overlap. Further, it is always possible that something about a disorder leads to abnormal neurotransmitter levels instead of the other way around. For example, although drugs that boost or decrease levels of particular neurotransmitters are sometimes effective in treating certain mental disorders, this fact does not necessarily mean that abnormal neurotransmitter levels *cause* the disorders. After all, aspirin can relieve a headache, but headaches are not caused by a lack of aspirin!

Many of us regularly ingest things that affect our own neurotransmitters. For example, most recreational drugs produce their effects by blocking or enhancing the actions of neurotransmitters. So do some herbal remedies. St. John's wort, which is often taken for depression, prevents the cells that release serotonin from reabsorbing excess molecules that have remained in the synaptic cleft; as a result, serotonin levels rise. Many people do not realize that such remedies, because they affect the nervous system's biochemistry, can interact with other medications and can be harmful in high doses.

Even ordinary foods can influence the availability of neurotransmitters in the brain. For example, *tryptophan*, an amino acid found in protein-rich foods (dairy products, meat, fish, and poultry), is a precursor (building block) of serotonin. Ordinarily, serotonin reduces alertness and promotes relaxation, but the effects of tryptophan are not what you might therefore expect. High-protein foods contain several amino acids that all compete for a ride on molecules headed for brain cells. Because tryptophan occurs in foods in small quantities, it doesn't stand much of a chance if all you eat is protein. It could be compared to a tiny child trying to push aside a crowd of adults for a

◉ **Watch**
ALS Lost Nerve Power

Muhammad Ali and Michael J. Fox both have Parkinson's disease, which involves a loss of dopamine-producing cells. They have used their fame to draw public attention to the disorder.

seat on the subway. Carbohydrates, however, stimulate the production of the hormone insulin, and insulin causes all the other amino acids to be drawn out of the bloodstream while having little effect on tryptophan, increasing the odds that tryptophan will make it to the brain. Paradoxically, then, a high-carbohydrate, no-protein meal is likely to make you relatively calm or lethargic and a high-protein one is likely to promote alertness, all else being equal (Spring, Chiodo, & Bowen, 1987).

Because of these and other complexities affecting the path between the dinner plate and the brain, if you're looking for brain food you are most likely to find it in a well-balanced diet.

ENDORPHINS: THE BRAIN'S NATURAL OPIATES.   Another intriguing group of chemical messengers is known collectively as endogenous opioid peptides, or more popularly as endorphins. Endorphins have effects similar to those of natural opiates; that is, they reduce pain and promote pleasure. They are also thought to play a role in appetite, sexual activity, blood pressure, mood, learning, and memory. Some endorphins function as neurotransmitters, but most act primarily by altering the effects of neurotransmitters—for example, by limiting or prolonging those effects.

Endorphin levels seem to shoot up when an animal or a person is afraid or under stress. This is no accident; by making pain bearable in such situations, endorphins give a species an evolutionary advantage. When an organism is threatened, it needs to do something fast. Pain, however, can interfere with action: A mouse that pauses to lick a wounded paw may become a cat's dinner. But, of course, the body's built-in system of counteracting pain is only partly successful, especially when painful stimulation is prolonged.

"PSST—ENDORPHINS. AND THEY'RE PERFECTLY LEGAL."

In Chapter 12, we will see that a link also exists between endorphins and human attachment. Research with animals suggests that in infancy, contact with the mother stimulates the flow of endorphins, which strengthens the infant's bond with her. Some researchers now think that this "endorphin rush" also occurs in the early stages of passionate love between adults, accounting for the feeling of euphoria that "falling" for someone creates (Diamond, 2004).

HORMONES: LONG-DISTANCE MESSENGERS.   Hormones, which make up the third class of chemical messengers, are produced primarily in endocrine glands. They are released directly into the bloodstream, which carries them to organs and cells that may be far from their point of origin. Hormones have dozens of jobs, from promoting bodily growth to aiding digestion to regulating metabolism. Neurotransmitters and hormones are not always chemically distinct; the two classifications are like social clubs that admit some of the same members. A particular chemical, such as norepinephrine, may belong to more than one classification, depending on where it is located and what function it is performing. Nature has been efficient, giving some substances more than one task.

The following hormones, among others, are of particular interest to psychologists:

1   **Melatonin**, which is secreted by the *pineal gland* deep within the brain, helps to regulate daily biological rhythms and promotes sleep, as we discuss in Chapter 5.

2   **Oxytocin**, which is secreted by another small gland in the brain, the *pituitary gland*, enhances uterine contractions during childbirth and facilitates the ejection of milk during nursing. Psychologists are interested in this hormone because along with another hormone, *vasopressin*, it contributes to relationships in both sexes by promoting attachment and trust (see Chapter 12).

✱ **Explore**
The Endocrine System

endorphins [en-DOR-fins]
Chemical substances in the nervous system that are similar in structure and action to opiates; they are involved in pain reduction, pleasure, and memory and are known technically as *endogenous opioid peptides*.

hormones   Chemical substances, secreted by organs called *glands*, that affect the functioning of other organs.

endocrine glands   Internal organs that produce hormones and release them into the bloodstream.

melatonin A hormone, secreted by the pineal gland, that is involved in the regulation of daily biological rhythms.

oxytocin A hormone, secreted by the pituitary gland, that stimulates uterine contractions during childbirth, facilitates the ejection of milk during nursing, and seems to promote, in both sexes, attachment and trust in relationships.

adrenal hormones Hormones that are produced by the adrenal glands and that are involved in emotion and stress.

sex hormones Hormones that regulate the development and functioning of reproductive organs and that stimulate the development of male and female sexual characteristics; they include androgens, estrogens, and progesterone.

3 **Adrenal hormones**, which are produced by the *adrenal glands* (organs that are perched right above the kidneys), are involved in emotion and stress (see Chapter 11). These hormones also rise in response to other conditions, such as heat, cold, pain, injury, burns, and physical exercise, and in response to some drugs, such as caffeine and nicotine. The outer part of each adrenal gland produces *cortisol*, which increases blood-sugar levels and boosts energy. The inner part produces *epinephrine* (commonly known as adrenaline) and *norepinephrine*. When adrenal hormones are released in your body, activated by the sympathetic nervous system, they increase your arousal level and prepare you for action. Adrenal hormones also enhance memory, as we discuss in Chapter 10.

4 **Sex hormones**, which are secreted by tissue in the gonads (testes in men, ovaries in women) and also by the adrenal glands, include three main types, all occurring in both sexes but in differing amounts and proportions in males and females after puberty. *Androgens* (the most important of which is *testosterone*) are masculinizing hormones produced mainly in the testes but also in the ovaries and the adrenal glands. Androgens set in motion the physical changes males experience at puberty—for example, a deepened voice and facial and chest hair—and cause pubic and underarm hair to develop in both sexes. Testosterone also influences sexual arousal in both sexes. *Estrogens* are feminizing hormones that bring on physical changes in females at puberty, such as breast development and the onset of menstruation, and that influence the course of the menstrual cycle. *Progesterone* contributes to the growth and maintenance of the uterine lining in preparation for a fertilized egg, among other functions. Estrogens and progesterone are produced mainly in the ovaries but also in the testes and the adrenal glands.

Researchers are studying the possible involvement of sex hormones in behaviour not linked to sex or reproduction. For example, some researchers believe that the body's natural estrogen may contribute to learning and memory in both sexes by promoting the formation of synaptic connections in certain areas of the brain and by indirectly increasing the production of acetylcholine (Lee & McEwen, 2001; Maki & Resnick, 2000; Sherwin, 1998a). But the most common belief about the nonsexual effects of sex hormones—that fluctuating levels of estrogen and progesterone make most women "emotional" before menstruation—is far from conclusively supported by research, as we discuss in Chapter 5.

Review 4.1 summarizes the three types of brain chemicals we have described and their effects.

REview 4.1

Nervous-System Chemicals and Their Effects

Type	Function	Effects	Where Produced	Examples
Neurotransmitters	Enable neurons to excite or inhibit each other	Diverse, depending on which circuits are activated or suppressed	Brain, spinal cord, peripheral nerves, certain glands	Serotonin, dopamine, norepinephrine
Endorphins	Usually modulate the effects of neurotransmitters	Reduce pain, promote pleasure; also linked to learning, memory, and other functions	Brain, spinal cord	(Several varieties, not discussed in this text)
Hormones	Affect functioning of target organs and tissues	Dozens, ranging from promotion of digestion to regulation of metabolism	Primarily in endocrine glands	Epinephrine, norepinephrine, estrogens, androgens

Get your glutamate going by taking this quiz.

A. Which word in parentheses better fits each of the following definitions?

1. Basic building blocks of the nervous system (*nerves, neurons*)
2. Cell parts that receive nerve impulses (*axons, dendrites*)
3. Site of communication between neurons (*synapse, myelin sheath*)
4. Opiate-like substance in the brain (*dopamine, endorphin*)
5. Chemicals that make it possible for neurons to communicate (*neurotransmitters, hormones*)
6. Hormone closely associated with emotional excitement (*epinephrine, estrogen*)

B. Imagine that you are depressed, and you hear about a treatment for depression that affects the levels of several neurotransmitters thought to be involved in the disorder. Based on what you have learned, what questions would you want to ask before deciding whether to try the treatment?

Answers:

 # YOU are about to learn . . .

♦ why patterns of electrical activity in the brain are called "brain waves."

♦ how scanning techniques reveal changes in brain activity while people listen to music, solve math problems, or do other activities.

♦ the limitations of brain scans as a way of understanding the brain.

MAPPING THE BRAIN

We come now to the main room of the nervous system "house": the brain. A disembodied brain stored in a formaldehyde-filled container is a putty-coloured, wrinkled glob of tissue. It takes an act of imagination to envision this modest-looking organ writing *Hamlet*, discovering radium, or inventing the paper clip.

In a living person, of course, the brain is encased in a thick protective vault of bone. How, then, can scientists study it? One approach is to study patients who have had a part of the brain damaged or removed because of disease or injury. Another, the *lesion method*, involves damaging or removing sections of brain in animals and then observing the effects.

ELECTRICAL AND MAGNETIC DETECTION.   The brain can also be probed with devices called *electrodes*. Some electrodes are coin-shaped and are simply pasted or taped onto the scalp. They detect the electrical activity of millions of neurons in particular regions of the brain and are widely used in research and medical diagnosis. The electrodes are connected by wires to a machine that translates the electrical energy from the brain into wavy lines on a moving piece of paper or visual patterns on a screen. That is why electrical patterns in the brain are known as "brain waves." Different wave patterns are associated with sleep, relaxation, and mental concentration (see Chapter 5).

Electrodes are used to produce an overall picture of electrical activity in different areas of the brain.

A brain-wave recording is called an **electroencephalogram (EEG)**. A standard EEG is useful but not very precise because it reflects the activities of many cells at once. "Listening" to the brain with an EEG machine is like standing outside a sports stadium: You know when something is happening, but you can't be sure what it is or who is doing it. Fortunately, computer technology can be combined with EEG technology to get a clearer picture of brain activity patterns associated with specific events and mental processes. The computer suppresses all the background "noise," leaving only the pattern of electrical response to the event being studied.

For even more precise information, researchers use *needle electrodes*, very thin wires or hollow glass tubes that can be inserted into the brain, either directly in an exposed brain or through tiny holes in the skull. Only the skull and the membranes covering the brain need to be anesthetized; the brain itself, which processes all sensation and feeling, paradoxically feels nothing when touched. Therefore, a human patient or an animal can be awake and not feel pain during the procedure. Needle electrodes can be used both to record electrical activity from the brain and to stimulate the brain with weak electrical currents. Stimulating a given area often results in a specific sensation or movement. *Microelectrodes* are so fine that they can be inserted into single cells.

A different way of stimulating the brain, **transcranial magnetic stimulation (TMS)**, delivers a large current through a wire coil placed on a person's head. The current produces a magnetic field about 40 000 times greater than Earth's natural magnetic field. This procedure causes neurons under the coil to fire. It can be used to produce motor responses (say, a twitch in the thumb or a knee jerk) and can also be used by researchers to briefly inactivate an area and observe the effects on behaviour—functioning, in effect, as a "virtual" (and temporary) lesion method. The drawback is that when neurons fire, they cause many other neurons to become active too, so it is often hard to tell which neurons are critical for a particular task. Still, TMS has produced some important findings—for example, that a brain area involved in processing visual patterns is also active when a person merely imagines the stimulus (Kosslyn et al., 1999). TMS has also been used to treat depression (see Chapter 16), but interpreting the results can be tricky, as many studies have not employed appropriate controls (Guse, Falkai, & Wobrock, 2010).

SCANNING THE BRAIN. Since the mid-1970s, many other amazing doors to the brain have opened. The **PET scan (positron-emission tomography)** goes beyond anatomy to record biochemical changes in the brain as they are happening. One type of PET scan takes advantage of the fact that nerve cells convert glucose, the body's main fuel, into energy. A researcher can inject a person with a glucose-like substance that contains a harmless radioactive element. This substance accumulates in brain areas that are particularly active and are consuming glucose rapidly. The substance emits radiation, which is detected by a scanning device, and the result is a computer-processed picture of biochemical activity on a display screen, with different colours indicating different activity levels. Other kinds of PET scans measure blood flow or oxygen consumption, which also reflect brain activity.

PET scans, which were originally designed to diagnose abnormalities, have produced evidence that certain brain areas in people with emotional disorders are either unusually quiet or unusually active. But PET technology can also show which parts of the brain are active during ordinary activities and emotions. It lets researchers see which areas are busiest when a person hears a song, recalls a sad memory, works on a math problem, or shifts attention from one task to another. The PET scans in Figure 4.8a show what an average brain looks like when a person is doing various tasks.

electroencephalogram (EEG) A recording of neural activity detected by electrodes.

transcranial magnetic stimulation (TMS) A method of stimulating brain cells, using a powerful magnetic field produced by a wire coil placed on a person's head; it can be used by researchers to temporarily inactivate neural circuits and is also being used therapeutically.

PET scan (positron-emission tomography) A method for analyzing biochemical activity in the brain, using injections of a glucose-like substance containing a radioactive element.

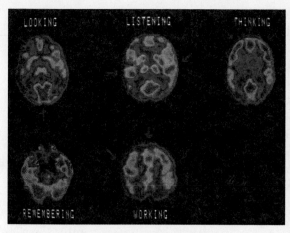 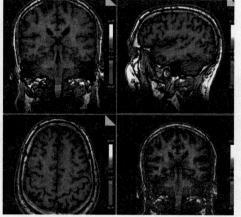

FIGURE 4.8 Scanning the Brain

In the PET scans on the left, arrows and the colour red indicate areas of highest activity, and violet indicates areas of lowest activity as a person does different things. On the right, an fMRI shows the activity (red areas) in the motor cortex of the brain during limb movement.

Another technique, MRI (magnetic resonance imaging), allows the exploration of "inner space" without injecting chemicals. Powerful magnetic fields and radio frequencies are used to produce vibrations in the nuclei of atoms making up body organs. The vibrations are then picked up as signals by special receivers. A computer analyzes the signals, taking into account their strength and duration, and converts them into a high-contrast picture of the organ (see Figure 4.8b). An ultrafast version of MRI, called *functional MRI (fMRI)*, can capture brain changes many times a second as a person performs a task, such as reading a sentence or solving a puzzle. Typically, fMRI relies on how much oxygen is in the blood that flows to specific regions of the brain, as active regions of the brain require more blood flow (and oxygen) than nonactive areas. Today, thousands of facilities across North America are using MRIs for research and assessment.

Review 4.2 summarizes the methods we have discussed, and others are becoming available every year. Researchers are using fMRI scans, in particular, to correlate activity in specific brain areas with everything from racial attitudes to moral reasoning to meditation. Researchers in an applied field called "neuromarketing" are even using them to study which parts of the brain are activated while people watch TV commercials or political ads.

◉ Watch
MKM and Brain Scans

MRI (magnetic resonance imaging) A method for studying body and brain tissue, using magnetic fields and special radio receivers; *functional MRI* (fMRI) is a faster form often used in psychological research.

REViEW 4.2

Windows on the Brain

Method	What Is Learned
Case studies of persons with brain damage	How damage to or loss of neural circuits affects behaviour and cognition
Lesion studies with animals	How damage to or loss of neural circuits affects behaviour
EEGs	Patterns of electrical activity in the brain
Needle electrodes and microelectrodes	More precise information about electrical activity in small groups of neurons or single neurons
Transcranial magnetic stimulation (TMS)	What happens behaviourally when a brain area is temporarily inactivated
PET scans	Visually displayed information about areas that are active or quiet during an activity or response and about changes associated with disorders
MRI	Visually displayed information about brain structures
Functional MRI	Visually displayed information about areas that are active or quiet during an activity or response and about changes associated with disorders

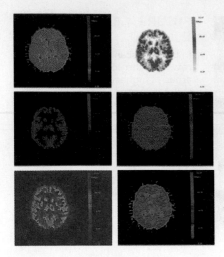

FIGURE 4.9 Colouring
the Brain
By altering the colours used in a PET
scan, researchers can create the
appearance of dramatic brain
differences. These scans are actually
images of the same brain.

CONTROVERSIES AND CAUTIONS. Exciting though these developments and technologies are, we need to understand that technology cannot replace critical thinking (Wade, 2006). As one team of psychologists who are using MRIs to study cognition and emotion wrote, "Just because you're imaging the brain doesn't mean you can stop using your head" (Cacioppo et al., 2003). Because brain-scan images seem so "real" and scientific, many people fail to realize that these images can convey oversimplified and sometimes misleading impressions. By manipulating the colour scales used in PET scans, researchers can either accentuate or minimize contrasts between two brains. Small contrasts can be made to look dramatic, larger ones to look insignificant. An individual's brain can even be made to appear completely different depending on the colours used, as the photographs in Figure 4.9 show (Dumit, 2004). The nature of fMRI studies may sometimes produce highly inflated correlations between brain activity and measures of personality and emotion (Vul et al., 2009). Yet the press usually reports these findings uncritically, giving the impression that neuroscientists know more about the relation between the brain and psychological processes than they really do.

There's another reason for caution about these methods: As of yet, brain scans do not tell us precisely what is happening inside a person's head, either mentally or physiologically. They tell us *where* things happen, but not *why* or *how* they happen—for example, how different circuits connect to produce behaviour. Enthusiasm for technology has produced a mountain of findings, but it has also resulted in some unwarranted conclusions about "brain centres" or "critical circuits" for this or that behaviour. If you know that one part of the brain is activated when you are thinking about your beloved, what exactly do you know about love? Does that part also light up when you are watching a love scene in a movie, looking at a hot-fudge sundae, or thinking about happily riding your horse through the hills?

For these reasons, one neuroscientist has called the search for brain centres and circuits "the new phrenology" (Uttal, 2001). Another drew this analogy (cited in Wheeler, 1998): A researcher scans the brains of gum-chewing volunteers, finds out which parts of their brains are active, and concludes that he or she has found the brain's "gum-chewing centre"!

Even if there were a gum-chewing centre, yours might not be in the same place as someone else's. Each brain is unique, first because a unique genetic package is present in each of us at birth, and second because your unique experiences and sensations are constantly altering your brain's biochemistry and neural networks. Thus, if you are a string musician, the area in your brain associated with music production is likely to be larger than that of nonmusicians; the earlier in life you started to play, the larger it becomes (Jancke, Schlaug, & Steinmetz, 1997). And if you are a cab driver, the area in your hippocampus responsible for visual representations of the environment is likely to be larger than average (Maguire et al., 2000). Variability among brains is one reason that efforts to diagnose mental disorders like depression and attention deficit disorder by examining brain scans have so far been disappointing. Roger Sperry (1982), a brain researcher whom we will meet again in this chapter, said it well: "The individuality inherent in our brain networks makes that of fingerprints or facial features gross and simple by comparison."

Descriptive studies using brain scans, then, are just a first step in understanding brain processes and must be interpreted with great caution. Nonetheless, they provide an exciting look at the brain at work and play, and we will be reporting many findings from PET scan and fMRI research throughout this book. The brain can no longer hide from researchers behind the fortress of the skull. It is now possible to get a clear visual image of our most enigmatic organ without so much as lifting a scalpel.

Thinking **Critically**

Don't Oversimplify

Brain scans provide us with fabulous
windows on the brain. But if a scan
shows that a brain area is active
when you're doodling, does that
mean the area is a "doodling
centre"?

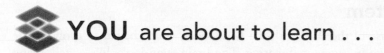 **YOU** are about to learn . . .

- the major parts of the brain and some of their major functions.
- why it is a good thing that the outer covering of the human brain is so wrinkled.
- how a bizarre nineteenth-century accident illuminated the role of the frontal lobes.

A TOUR THROUGH THE BRAIN

Most modern brain theories assume that different brain parts perform different (though greatly overlapping) tasks. This concept, known as **localization of function**, goes back at least to Franz Joseph Gall (1758–1828), the Austrian anatomist who thought that personality traits were reflected in the development of specific areas of the brain (see Chapter 1). Gall's theory of phrenology was completely wrong-headed (so to speak), but his general notion of specialization in the brain had merit.

To learn about what the major brain structures do, let's take an imaginary stroll through the brain. Pretend that you have shrunk to a microscopic size and that you are wending your way through the "soul's frail dwelling house," starting at the lower part, just above the spine. Figure 4.10 shows the major structures we will encounter along our tour; you may want to refer to it as we proceed. Keep in mind that any activity—feeling an emotion, having a thought, performing a task—involves many different structures. Our description, therefore, is a simplification.

localization of function Specialization of particular brain areas for particular functions.

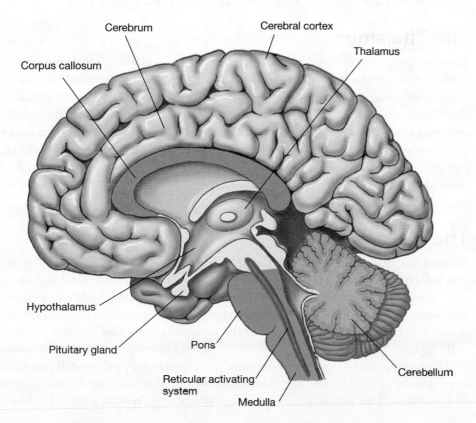

FIGURE 4.10 Major Structures of the Human Brain

This cross-section depicts the brain as if it were split in half. The view is of the inside surface of the right half, and it shows the structures described in the text.

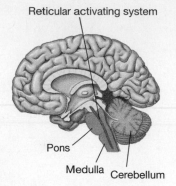

Reticular activating system

Pons

Medulla   Cerebellum

brain stem   The part of the brain at the top of the spinal cord, consisting of the medulla and the pons.

pons   A structure in the brain stem involved in, among other things, sleeping, waking, and dreaming.

medulla [muh-DUL-uh]   A structure in the brain stem responsible for certain automatic functions, such as breathing and heart rate.

reticular activating system (RAS)   A dense network of neurons found in the core of the brain stem; it arouses the cortex and screens incoming information.

cerebellum   A brain structure that regulates movement and balance and is involved in the learning of certain kinds of simple responses.

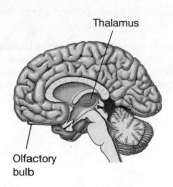

Thalamus

Olfactory bulb

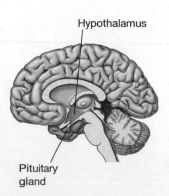

Hypothalamus

Pituitary gland

The Brain Stem

We begin at the base of the skull with the **brain stem**, which began to evolve some 500 million years ago in segmented worms. The brain stem looks like a stalk rising out of the spinal cord. Pathways to and from upper areas of the brain pass through its two main structures: the medulla and the pons. The pons is involved in (among other things) sleeping, waking, and dreaming. The medulla is responsible for bodily functions that do not have to be consciously willed, such as breathing and heart rate. Hanging has long been used as a method of execution because when it breaks the neck, nerve pathways from the medulla are severed, stopping respiration.

Extending upward from the core of the brain stem is the **reticular activating system (RAS)**. This dense network of neurons, which extends above the brain stem into the centre of the brain and has connections with areas that are higher up, screens incoming information and arouses the higher centres when something happens that demands their attention. Without the RAS, we could not be alert or perhaps even conscious.

The Cerebellum

Standing atop the brain stem and looking toward the back part of the brain, we see a structure about the size of a small fist. It is the **cerebellum**, or "lesser brain," which contributes to a sense of balance and coordinates the muscles so that movement is smooth and precise. If your cerebellum were damaged, you would probably become exceedingly clumsy and uncoordinated. You might have trouble using a pencil, threading a needle, or even walking. In addition, this structure is involved in remembering certain simple skills and acquired reflexes (Daum & Schugens, 1996; Krupa, Thompson, & Thompson, 1993). But the cerebellum, which was once considered just a motor centre, is not as "lesser" as its name implies: It plays a part in such complex cognitive tasks as analyzing sensory information, solving problems, and understanding words (Fiez, 1996; Gao et al., 1996; Müller, Courchesne, & Allen, 1998; Timmann et al., 2010).

The Thalamus

Deep in the brain's interior, roughly at its centre, we can see the **thalamus**, the busy traffic officer of the brain. As sensory messages come into the brain, the thalamus directs them to higher areas. For example, the sight of a sunset sends signals that the thalamus directs to a vision area, and the sound of an oboe sends signals that the thalamus sends on to an auditory area. The only sense that completely bypasses the thalamus is the sense of smell, which has its own private switching station, the *olfactory bulb*. The olfactory bulb lies near areas involved in emotion. Perhaps that is why particular odours—the smell of fresh laundry, gardenias, a steak sizzling on the grill—often rekindle vivid memories.

The Hypothalamus and the Pituitary Gland

Beneath the thalamus sits a structure called the **hypothalamus** (*hypo* means "under"). It is involved in drives associated with the survival of both the individual and the species—hunger, thirst, emotion, sex, and reproduction. It regulates body temperature by triggering sweating or shivering, and it controls the complex operations of the autonomic nervous system. It also contains the biological clock that controls the body's daily rhythms (see Chapter 5).

Hanging down from the hypothalamus, connected to it by a short stalk, is a cherry-sized endocrine gland called the **pituitary gland**, mentioned earlier in our discussion of hormones. The pituitary is often called the body's "master gland" because the hormones it secretes affect many other endocrine glands. The master, however, is really only a supervisor. The true boss is the hypothalamus, which sends chemicals to the pituitary that tell it when to "talk" to the other endocrine glands. The pituitary, in turn, sends hormonal messages out to these glands.

Many years ago, in a study that became famous, James Olds and Peter Milner reported finding "pleasure centres" in the hypothalamus (Olds, 1975; Olds & Milner, 1954). Olds and Milner trained rats to press a lever in order to get a buzz of electricity delivered through tiny electrodes to parts of the hypothalamus. Some rats would press the bar thousands of times an hour, for 15 or 20 hours at a time, until they collapsed from exhaustion. When they revived, they went right back to the bar. When forced to make a choice, the pleasure-loving little rodents opted for electrical stimulation over such temptations as water, food, and even an attractive rat of the other sex making provocative gestures (provocative to another rat, anyway).

It certainly did seem as though the brain had "pleasure centres." However, controversy has existed ever since about just how to interpret the rats' responses. Were Olds and Milner's rats really feeling pleasure or merely some kind of craving or compulsion? (When people's brains are stimulated in the same way, they do not report feelings of pleasure or behave like those rats did.) Moreover, today researchers believe that brain stimulation activates complex neural pathways rather than discrete centres.

The hypothalamus, along with the two structures we will come to next, has often been considered part of a loosely interconnected set of structures called the limbic system, shown in Figure 4.11. (*Limbic* comes from the Latin for "border": These structures form a sort of border between the higher and lower parts of the brain.) Some anatomists also include parts of the thalamus in this system. Structures in this region are heavily involved in emotions that we share with other animals, such as rage and fear (MacLean, 1993). The usefulness of speaking of the limbic system as an integrated set of structures is now in dispute, because these structures also have other functions, and because parts of the brain outside of the limbic system are involved in emotion. However, the term *limbic system* is still in wide use among researchers, so we thought you should know it.

The Amygdala

The amygdala (from the ancient Greek word for "almond") is responsible for evaluating sensory information, quickly determining its emotional importance, and contributing to the initial decision to approach or withdraw from a person or situation (see Chapter 11). For example, it instantly assesses danger or threat. The amygdala also plays an important role in mediating anxiety and depression; PET scans find that depressed and anxious patients show increased neural activity in this structure (Davidson et al., 1999; Drevets, 2000). The amygdala is also involved in forming and retrieving emotional memories (see Chapter 10).

The Hippocampus

Another important area traditionally classified as limbic is the hippocampus, whose shape must have reminded someone of a sea horse, for in Latin that is what its name means. This structure compares sensory information with what the brain has learned to expect about the world. When expectations are met, it tells the reticular activating system to "cool it." There's no need for neural alarm bells to go off every time a car goes by, a bird chirps, or you feel your saliva trickling down the back of your throat!

thalamus A brain structure that relays sensory messages to the cerebral cortex.

hypothalamus A brain structure involved in emotions and drives that are vital to survival, such as fear, hunger, thirst, and reproduction; it regulates the autonomic nervous system.

pituitary gland A small endocrine gland at the base of the brain, which releases many hormones and regulates other endocrine glands.

limbic system A group of brain areas involved in emotional reactions and motivated behaviour.

amygdala [uh-MIG-dul-uh] A brain structure involved in the arousal and regulation of emotion and the initial emotional response to sensory information.

hippocampus A brain structure involved in the storage of new information in memory.

✳ **Explore**
The Limbic System

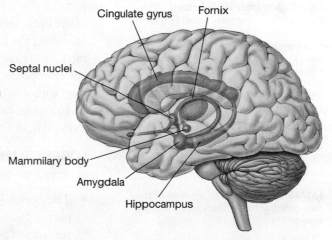

FIGURE 4.11 The Limbic System

Structures of the limbic system play an important role in memory and emotion. The text describes two of these structures, the amygdala and the hippocampus. The hypothalamus is also often included as part of the limbic system.

Cingulate gyrus | Fornix
Septal nuclei
Mammillary body
Amygdala
Hippocampus

The hippocampus has also been called the "gateway to memory." It enables us to form spatial memories so that we can accurately navigate through our environment. And, along with adjacent brain areas, it enables us to form new memories about facts and events—the kind of information you need to identify a flower, tell a story, or recall a vacation trip. The information is then stored in the cerebral cortex, which we will be discussing shortly. For example, when you recall meeting someone yesterday, various aspects of the memory—information about the person's greeting, tone of voice, appearance, and location—are probably stored in different locations in the cortex. But without the hippocampus, the information would never get to these destinations. As we will see in Chapter 10, this structure is also involved in the retrieval of information during recall. We know about the central role the hippocampus plays in memory in part from research on brain-damaged patients with severe memory problems.

The Cerebrum

At this point in our tour, the largest part of the brain still looms above us. It is the cauliflower-like **cerebrum,** where the higher forms of thinking take place. The complexity of the human brain's circuitry far exceeds that of any computer in existence, and much of its most complicated wiring is packed into this structure. Compared to many other creatures, we humans may be ungainly, feeble, and thin-skinned, but our well-developed cerebrum enables us to overcome these limitations and creatively control our environment (and, some would say, to mess it up).

The cerebrum is divided into two separate halves, or **cerebral hemispheres,** connected by a large band of fibres called the **corpus callosum.** In general, the right hemisphere is in charge of the left side of the body and the left hemisphere is in charge of the right side of the body. As we will see shortly, the two hemispheres also have somewhat different tasks and talents, a phenomenon known as **lateralization.**

THE CEREBRAL CORTEX. Working our way right up through the top of the brain, we find that the cerebrum is covered by several thin layers of densely packed cells known collectively as the **cerebral cortex.** Cell bodies in the cortex, as in many other parts of the brain, produce a greyish tissue; hence the term *grey matter*. In other parts of the brain (and in the rest of the nervous system), long, myelin-covered axons prevail, providing the brain's white matter. Although the cortex is only about three millimetres thick, it contains almost three-fourths of all the cells in the human brain. The cortex has many deep crevasses and wrinkles, which enable it to contain its billions of neurons without requiring us to have the heads of giants—heads that would be too big to permit us to be born. In other mammals, which have fewer neurons, the cortex is less crumpled; in rats, it is quite smooth.

LOBES OF THE CORTEX. In each cerebral hemisphere, deep fissures divide the cortex into four distinct regions, or lobes (see Figure 4.12):

◆ The **occipital lobes** (from the Latin for "in back of the head") are at the lower back part of the brain. Among other things, they contain the *visual cortex, where visual signals are processed.* Damage to the visual cortex can cause impaired visual recognition or blindness.

◆ The **parietal lobes** (from the Latin for "pertaining to walls") are at the top of the brain. They contain the *somatosensory cortex, which receives information about pressure, pain, touch, and temperature from all over the body.* The areas of the somatosensory cortex that receive signals from the hands and the face are disproportionately large because these body parts are particularly sensitive. Parts of the parietal lobes are also involved in attention and various mental operations.

cerebrum [suh-REE-brum] The largest brain structure, consisting of the upper part of the brain; divided into two hemispheres, it is in charge of most sensory, motor, and cognitive processes. From the Latin for "brain."

cerebral hemispheres The two halves of the cerebrum.

corpus callosum [CORE-puhs cah-LOW-suhm] The bundle of nerve fibres connecting the two cerebral hemispheres.

lateralization Specialization of the two cerebral hemispheres for particular operations.

cerebral cortex A collection of several thin layers of cells covering the cerebrum; it is largely responsible for higher mental functions. *Cortex* is Latin for "bark" or "rind."

occipital [ahk-SIP-uh-tuhl] lobes Lobes at the lower back part of the brain's cerebral cortex; they contain areas that receive visual information.

◆ The **temporal lobes** (from the Latin for "pertaining to the temples") are at the sides of the brain, just above the ears and behind the temples. They are involved in memory, perception, and emotion, and they contain the *auditory cortex*, which processes sounds. An area of the left temporal lobe known as *Wernicke's area* is involved in language comprehension.

◆ The **frontal lobes**, as their name indicates, are located toward the front of the brain, just under the skull in the area of the forehead. They contain the **motor cortex**, which issues orders to the 600 muscles of the body that produce voluntary movement. In the left frontal lobe, a region known as *Broca's area* handles speech production. During short-term memory tasks, areas in the frontal lobes are especially active. The frontal lobes are also involved in emotion and in the ability to make plans, think creatively, and take initiative.

Because of their different functions, the lobes of the cerebral cortex tend to respond differently when stimulated. If a surgeon applied an electrical current to your somatosensory cortex in the parietal lobes, you might feel a tingling in the skin or a sense of being gently touched. If your visual cortex in the occipital lobes were electrically stimulated, you might report a flash of light or swirls of colour. And, eerily, many areas of your cortex, when stimulated, would produce no obvious response or sensation. These "silent" areas are sometimes called the *association cortex* because they are involved in higher mental processes.

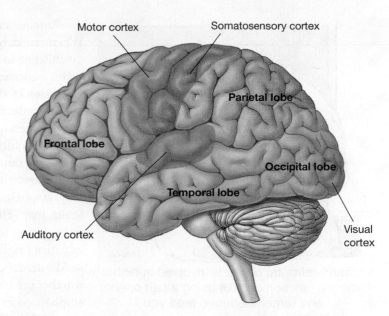

FIGURE 4.12 Lobes of the Cerebral Cortex

Deep fissures divide the cortex of each cerebral hemisphere into four regions.

✳ **Explore**
The Visual Cortex

CULTURE and *the Cortex*

Can Culture Shape the Brain?

Earlier we saw that experiences at different times of a person's life can affect the structure of the brain and the strength of synaptic connections. Culture, of course, provides many of those experiences, but neuropsychologists and other brain researchers are just starting to study how it may affect the way specific areas in the cortical lobes are organized or activated.

Consider bilingualism. Do bilingual people use different parts of their brains for their two languages? Evidence on this question has been mixed, but there have been some intriguing findings. One team of surgeons found that the retrieval of semantic information by bilinguals may indeed depend on which language they are speaking. While using electrical stimulation to map the brains of bilingual patients undergoing brain surgery, the surgeons asked the patients (who were awake) to name pictured objects in both of their languages. From the pattern of errors made during the electrical stimulation, the researchers could tell which brain areas were being used in the object-naming task. Sites specific to a patient's first language were widely distributed, but those associated with a second language were confined to the back part of the temporal and parietal lobes (Lucas, McKhann, & Ojemann, 2004). This type of information, if it is verified by future research, will be important for brain surgeons to know!

parietal [puh-RYE-uh-tuhl] lobes Lobes at the top of the brain's cerebral cortex; they contain areas that receive information on pressure, pain, touch, and temperature.

temporal lobes Lobes at the sides of the brain's cerebral cortex; they contain areas involved in hearing, memory, perception, emotion, and (in the left lobe, typically) language comprehension.

frontal lobes Lobes at the front of the brain's cerebral cortex; they contain areas involved in short-term memory, higher-order thinking, initiative, social judgment, and (in the left lobe, typically) speech production.

DOG TRAINING (ADVANCED)

BOWL   HUMAN BRAIN

"The prefrontal cortex is involved in higher mental functioning, like using a can opener and remembering to feed you."

www.CartoonStock.com

Another cultural factor that may affect brain organization is literacy. When researchers have compared the brains of literate and illiterate people, the illiterate individuals tend to have less white matter in a part of the parietal cortex associated with reading and verbal memory and in several other areas (Petersson et al., 2007). A different kind of literacy—technological literacy—may also affect brain activity. Some scientists speculate that internet searching, text messaging, and social networking may strengthen the neural circuits involved in filtering information and making quick decisions, while possibly weakening others, such as those involved in sustained attention (Small, 2008).

When two cultures value different skills among their members, or when they emphasize different approaches to acquiring certain skills, people's brains may reflect those differences. For example, the patterns of brain activity during mathematical processing are different in native Chinese than in native English speakers (Tang et al., 2006). In addition, brain activation in Westerners and Asians during a simple visual–spatial task depends on whether the task requires a person to attend to the visual context (a strategy emphasized in Asian cultures) or to ignore the visual context (which is encouraged in Western cultures). In both groups, fMRI scans show activation in frontal and parietal regions associated with attentional control to be greater when people are making judgments not typical for their cultural background (Hedden et al., 2008). This makes sense, since those judgments require more attention and effort.

As we will see throughout this book, cultures often have a profound influence on their members' symbols, attitudes, and ways of navigating the world. We should not be surprised if those influences show up in fMRI studies of perception, problem solving, language, and thinking. Many people might be inclined to jump to the conclusion that our brains make us different, overlooking the more likely inference that it's our differences that shape our brains.

● ● ●

THE PREFRONTAL CORTEX. Psychologists are especially interested in the most forward part of the frontal lobes, the *prefrontal cortex.* This area barely exists in mice and rats and takes up only 3.5% of the cerebral cortex in cats and about 7% in dogs, but it accounts for approximately one-third of the entire cortex in human beings. It is the most recently evolved part of our brains, and is associated with such complex abilities as reasoning, decision making, and planning.

Scientists have long known that the frontal lobes, and the prefrontal cortex in particular, must have something to do with personality. The first clue appeared in 1848, when a bizarre accident drove a 2.5-centimetre-thick, 1-metre-long iron rod clear through the head of a young railroad worker named Phineas Gage. As you can see in the photo, the rod (which is still displayed at Harvard University, along with Gage's skull) entered beneath the left eye and exited through the top of the head, destroying much of the prefrontal cortex (H. Damasio et al., 1994). Miraculously, Gage survived this trauma and, by most accounts, he retained the ability to speak, think, and remember. But his friends complained that he was "no longer Gage." In a sort of Jekyll-and-Hyde transformation, he had changed from a mild-mannered, friendly, efficient worker into a foul-mouthed, ill-tempered, undependable lout who could not hold a steady job or stick to a plan. His employers had to let him go, and he was reduced to exhibiting himself as a circus attraction.

There is some controversy about the details of this sad incident, but many other cases of brain injury, whether from stroke or trauma, support the conclusion that most scientists draw from the Gage case: that parts of the frontal lobes are involved in social judgment, rational decision making, and the ability to set goals and to make and carry

◉ Watch
Connie: Head Injury

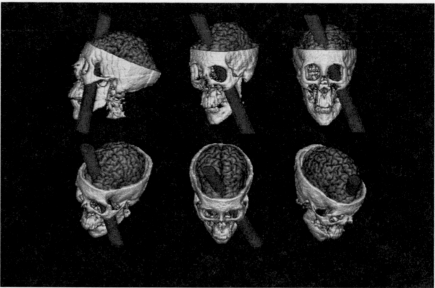

On the left is the only known photo of Phineas Gage, taken after his recovery from an accident in which an iron rod penetrated his skull, altering his behaviour and personality dramatically. The exact location of the brain damage remained controversial for almost a century and a half, until Hanna and Antonio Damasio and their colleagues (1994) used measurements of Gage's skull and MRIs of normal brains to plot possible trajectories of the rod. The reconstruction on the right shows that the damage occurred in an area of the prefrontal cortex associated with emotional processing and rational decision making.

out plans. Like Gage, people with damage in these areas sometimes mismanage their finances, lose their jobs, and abandon their friends. Interestingly, the mental deficits that characterize damage to these areas are accompanied by a flattening out of emotion and feeling, which suggests that normal emotions are necessary for everyday reasoning and the ability to learn from mistakes (Damasio, 1994, 2003).

The frontal lobes also govern the ability to do a series of tasks in the proper sequence and to stop doing them at the proper time. The pioneering Soviet psychologist Alexander Luria (1980) studied many cases in which damage to the frontal lobes disrupted these abilities. One man observed by Luria kept trying to light a match after it was already lit. Another planed a piece of wood in the hospital carpentry shop until it was gone and then went on to plane the workbench!

Review 4.3 summarizes the major parts of the brain that we have discussed and their primary functions.

REVIEW 4.3

Functions Associated with the Major Brain Structures

The functions listed here are just some of those that have been linked with these structures.

Structure	Functions
Brain stem	
Pons	Sleeping, waking, dreaming
Medulla	Automatic functions such as breathing, heart rate
Reticular activating system (RAS) (extends into centre of the brain)	Screening of incoming information, arousal of higher centres, consciousness

(Continued)

REViEW 4.3 (Continued)

Cerebellum	Balance, muscular coordination, memory for simple skills and learned reflexes, possible involvement in more complex mental tasks
Thalamus	Relay of impulses from higher centres to the spinal cord and of incoming sensory information (except for olfactory sensations) to other brain centres
Hypothalamus	Behaviours necessary for survival, such as hunger, thirst, emotion, reproduction; regulation of body temperature; control of autonomic nervous system
Pituitary gland	Under direction of the hypothalamus, secretion of hormones that affect other glands
Amygdala	Initial evaluation of sensory information to determine its importance; mediation of anxiety and depression; formation and retrieval of emotional memories
Hippocampus	Comparison of sensory information with expectations, modulation of the RAS; formation of new memories about facts and events, as well as other aspects of memory
Cerebrum (including cerebral cortex) Occipital lobes Parietal lobes Temporal lobes Frontal lobes	Higher forms of thinking Visual processing Processing of pressure, pain, touch, temperature Memory, perception, emotion, hearing, language comprehension Movement, short-term memory, planning, goal setting, creative thinking, initiative, social judgment, rational decision making, speech production

quickQUIZ

✓ Quick Review on MyPsychLab

Pause to see how your own brain is working by taking this quiz.

Match each description on the left with a term on the right.

1. Filters out irrelevant information
2. Known as the "gateway to memory"
3. Controls the autonomic nervous system; involved in drives associated with survival
4. Consists of two hemispheres
5. Wrinkled outer covering of the brain
6. Site of the motor cortex; associated with planning and taking initiative

a. reticular activating system
b. cerebrum
c. hippocampus
d. cerebral cortex
e. frontal lobes
f. hypothalamus

Answers:

1.a 2.c 3.f 4.b 5.d 6.e

 YOU are about to learn . . .

- what would happen if the two cerebral hemispheres could not communicate with each other.
- why researchers often refer to the left hemisphere as "dominant."
- why "left-brainedness" and "right-brainedness" are exaggerations.

THE TWO HEMISPHERES OF THE BRAIN

We have seen that the cerebrum is divided into two hemispheres that control opposite sides of the body. Although similar in structure, these hemispheres have somewhat separate talents, or areas of specialization.

Split Brains: A House Divided

In a normal brain, the two hemispheres communicate with one another across the corpus callosum, the bundle of fibres that connects them. Whatever happens in one side of the brain is instantly flashed to the other side. What would happen, though, if the two sides were cut off from one another?

In 1953, Ronald E. Myers and Roger W. Sperry took the first step toward answering this question by severing the corpus callosum in cats. They also cut parts of the nerves leading from the eyes to the brain. Normally, each eye transmits messages to both sides of the brain. After this procedure, a cat's left eye sent information only to the left hemisphere and its right eye sent information only to the right hemisphere.

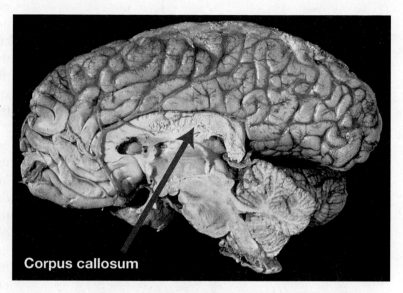

Corpus callosum

A cross-section of a human brain, showing the corpus callosum.

At first, the cats did not seem to be affected much by this drastic operation. But Myers and Sperry showed that something profound had happened. They trained the cats to perform tasks with one eye blindfolded; for example, a cat might have to push a panel with a square on it to get food but ignore a panel with a circle. Then the researchers switched the blindfold to the cat's other eye and tested the animal again. Now the cats behaved as if they had never learned the trick. Apparently, one side of the brain did not know what the other side was doing; it was as if the animals had two minds in one body. Later studies confirmed this result with other species, including monkeys (Sperry, 1964).

In all the animal studies, ordinary behaviour, such as eating and walking, remained normal. In the early 1960s, a team of surgeons decided to try cutting the corpus callosum in patients with debilitating, uncontrollable epilepsy. In severe forms of this disease, disorganized electrical activity spreads from an injured area to other parts of the brain. The surgeons reasoned that cutting the connection between the two halves of the brain might stop the spread of electrical activity from one side to the other. The surgery was done, of course, for the sake of the patients, who were desperate. But there was a bonus for scientists, who would be able to find out what each cerebral hemisphere can do when it is quite literally cut off from the other.

The results of this *split-brain surgery* generally proved successful. Seizures were reduced and sometimes disappeared completely. In their daily lives, split-brain patients did not seem much affected by the fact that the two hemispheres were incommunicado. Their personalities and intelligence remained intact; they could walk, talk, and in general lead normal lives. Apparently, connections in the undivided deeper parts of the brain kept body movements and other functions normal. But in a series of ingenious studies, Sperry and his colleagues (and later other researchers) showed that perception and memory had been affected, just as they had been in the earlier animal research. Sperry won a Nobel Prize for his work.

It was already known that the two hemispheres are not mirror images of each other. In most people, language is largely handled by the left hemisphere; thus, a person who suffers brain damage because of a *stroke*—a blockage in or rupture of a blood

◄⦿Simulate
Psychology Experiments Tool: Hemispheric Specialization

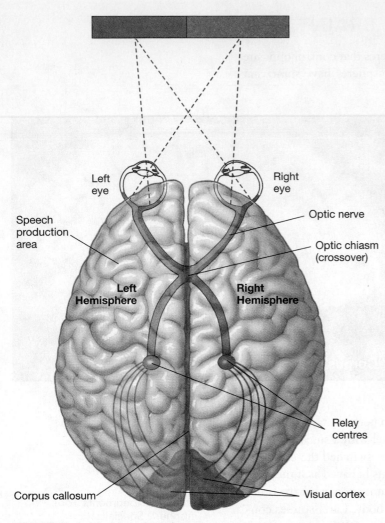

FIGURE 4.13 Visual Pathways

Each cerebral hemisphere receives information from the eyes about the opposite side of the visual field. Thus, if you stare directly at the corner of a room, everything to the left of the juncture is represented in your right hemisphere and vice versa. This is so because half the axons in each optic nerve cross over (at the *optic chiasm*) to the opposite side of the brain. Normally, each hemisphere immediately shares its information with the other one, but in split-brain patients, severing the corpus callosum prevents such communication.

vessel in the brain—is much more likely to have language problems if the damage is in the left side than if it is in the right. Sperry and his colleagues wanted to know how splitting the brain would affect language and other abilities.

To understand this research, you must know how nerves connect the eyes to the brain. (The human patients, unlike Myers and Sperry's cats, did not have these nerves cut.) If you look straight ahead, everything in the left side of the scene before you—the *visual field*—goes to the right half of your brain, and everything in the right side of the scene goes to the left half of your brain. This is true for both eyes (see Figure 4.13).

The procedure was to present information only to one or the other side of the patients' brains. In one early study, the researchers took photographs of different faces, cut them in two, and pasted different halves together (Levy, Trevarthen, & Sperry, 1972). The reconstructed photographs were then presented on slides. The person was told to stare at a dot in the middle of the screen, so that half of the image fell to the left of this point and half to the right. Each image was flashed so quickly that the person had no time to move his or her eyes. When the patients were asked to say what they had seen, they named the person in the right part of the image (which would be the little boy in Figure 4.14). But when they were asked to point with their left hands to the face they had seen, they chose the person in the left side of the image (the moustached man in the figure). Further, they claimed they had noticed nothing unusual about the original photographs! Each side of the brain saw a different half-image and automatically filled in the missing part. Neither side knew what the other side had seen.

Why did the patients name one side of the picture but point to the other? Speech centres are usually in the left hemisphere. When the person responded with speech, it was the left side of the brain doing the talking. When the person pointed with the left hand, which is controlled by the right side of the brain, the right hemisphere was giving its version of what the person had seen.

Get INVOLVED!

TAP, TAP, TAP

Have a right-handed friend tap on a paper with a pencil held in the right hand for one minute. Then have the person do the same with the left hand, using a fresh sheet of paper. Finally, repeat the procedure, having the person talk at the same time as tapping. For most people, talking will decrease the rate of tapping—but more for the right hand than for the left, probably because both activities involve the same hemisphere (the left one), and there is competition between them. (Left-handed people vary more in terms of which hemisphere is dominant for language, so the results for them will be more variable.)

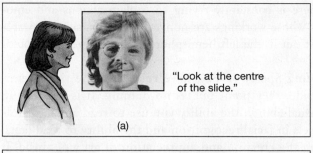

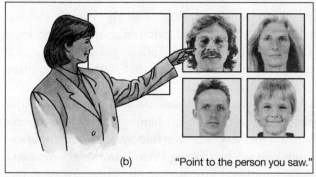

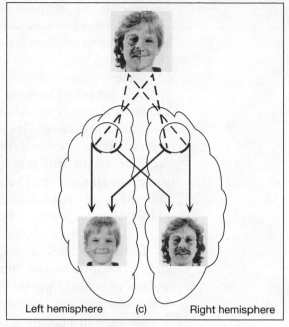

Left hemisphere   (c)   Right hemisphere

FIGURE 4.14 Divided View

Split-brain patients were shown composite photographs (a) and were then asked to pick out the face they had seen from a series of intact photographs (b). They said they had seen the face on the right side of the composite, yet they pointed with their left hands to the face that had been on the left. Because the two cerebral hemispheres could not communicate, the verbal left hemisphere was aware of only the right half of the picture, and the relatively mute right hemisphere was aware of only the left half (c).

In another study, the researchers presented slides of ordinary objects and then suddenly flashed a slide of a nude woman. Both sides of the brain were amused, but because only the left side had speech, the two sides responded differently. When the picture was flashed to one woman's left hemisphere, she laughed and identified it as a nude. When it was flashed to her right hemisphere, she said nothing but began to chuckle. Asked what she was laughing at, she said, "I don't know. . . nothing. . . oh—that funny machine." The right hemisphere could not describe what it had seen, but it reacted emotionally just the same (Gazzaniga, 1967).

The Two Hemispheres: Allies or Opposites?

The split-brain operation is still being performed, and split-brain patients continue to be studied. Research on left–right differences has also been done with people whose brains are intact (Springer & Deutsch, 1998). Electrodes and brain scans have been used to measure activity in the left and right hemispheres while people perform different tasks. The results confirm that nearly all right-handed people and a majority of left-handers process language mainly in the left hemisphere. The left side is also more active during some logical, symbolic, and sequential tasks, such as solving math problems and understanding technical material.

Because of its cognitive talents, many researchers refer to left hemisphere *dominance*. They believe that the left hemisphere usually exerts control over the right hemisphere. Split-brain researcher Michael Gazzaniga (1983) once argued that without help from the left side, the right side's mental skills would probably be "vastly inferior to the cognitive skills of a chimpanzee." He and others also believe that a mental

Simulate
Split-Brain Experiments

Research
Michael Gazzaniga

((•● **Listen**
Handedness

◈ **Research**
Roger Sperry

"module" in the left hemisphere is constantly trying to explain actions and emotions generated by brain parts whose workings are nonverbal and outside of awareness. As one neuropsychologist put it, the left hemisphere is the brain's spin doctor (Broks, 2004).

Other researchers, including Sperry (1982), have rushed to the right hemisphere's defence. The right side, they point out, is no dummy. It is superior in problems requiring spatial–visual ability, the ability you use to read a map or follow a dress pattern, and it excels in facial recognition and the ability to read facial expressions. It is active during the creation and appreciation of art and music. It recognizes nonverbal sounds, such as a dog's barking. The right brain also has some language ability. Typically, it can read a word briefly flashed to it and can understand an experimenter's instructions. In a few split-brain patients, right-brain language ability has been well developed, showing that individual variation exists in brain lateralization.

Some researchers have also credited the right hemisphere with having a cognitive style that is intuitive and holistic, in contrast to the left hemisphere's more rational and analytic mode. Over the years, this idea has been oversold by books and programs that promise to make people more creative by making them more "right-brained." But the right hemisphere is not always a hero: For example, it contains regions that process fear and sadness, emotions that often cause us to withdraw from others (see Chapter 11). Further, the differences between the two hemispheres are relative, not absolute—a matter of degree. In most real-life activities, the two sides cooperate naturally, with each making a valuable contribution. For example, mathematical ability involves not only areas in the left frontal lobe but also areas in both the left and the right parietal lobes. The former are needed to compute exact sums using language ("2 times 5 is 10"), and the latter are needed for using visual or spatial imagery, such as a mental "number line," to estimate quantity or magnitude ("6 is closer to 9 than to 2") (Dehaene et al., 1999).

Be cautious, then, about thinking of the two sides as two "minds." As Sperry (1982) himself noted long ago, "The left–right dichotomy. . . is an idea with which it is very easy to run wild."

quick**QUIZ**

✓—[**Quick Review** on **MyPsychLab**

Use as many parts of your brain as necessary to answer these questions.

1. Bearing in mind that both sides of the brain are involved in most activities, see whether you can identify which of the following is (are) more closely associated with the left hemisphere: (a) enjoying a musical recording, (b) wiggling the left big toe, (c) giving a speech in class, (d) balancing a chequebook, (e) recognizing a long-lost friend.

2. Thousands of people have taken courses and bought tapes that promise to develop the creativity and intuition of their right hemispheres. What characteristics of human thought might explain the eagerness of some people to glorify "right-brainedness" and disparage "left-brainedness" (or vice versa)?

Answers:

1. c, d 2. One possible answer: Human beings like to make sense of the world, and one easy way to do that is to divide humanity into opposing categories. This kind of either–or thinking can lead to the conclusion that fixing up one brain hemisphere (e.g., making "left-brained" types more "right-brained") will make individuals happier and the world a better place. If only it were that simple!

◆ YOU are about to learn . . .

◆ why some brain researchers think a unified "self" is only an illusion.

◆ findings and fallacies about sex differences in the brain.

TWO STUBBORN ISSUES IN BRAIN RESEARCH

If you have mastered the definitions and descriptions in this chapter, you are prepared to follow news of advances in neuroscience. However, many questions remain about how the brain works, and we will end this chapter with two of them.

Where Is the Self?

When you say, "I am feeling unhappy," your amygdala, your serotonin receptors, your endorphins, and all sorts of other brain parts and processes are active, but who, exactly, is the "I" doing the feeling? When you say, "My mind is playing tricks on me," who is the "me" watching your mind play those tricks, and who is it that's being tricked? Isn't the self observing itself a little like a finger pointing at its own tip? Because the brain is the site of self-awareness, people even disagree about what language to use when referring to it. If we say that your brain stores events or registers emotions, we imply a separate "you" that is "using" that brain. But if we leave "you" out of the picture and just say the brain does these things, we risk ignoring the motives, personality traits, and social conditions that powerfully affect what people do—what *you* do.

Most religions resolve the problem by teaching that an immortal self or soul exists entirely apart from the mortal brain, a doctrine known as *dualism*. But modern brain scientists usually consider mind to be a matter of matter. They may have religious convictions about a soul or a spiritual response to the awesome complexity and interconnectedness of nature, but most assume that what we call "mind," "consciousness," "self-awareness," or "subjective experience" can be explained in physical terms as a product of the cerebral cortex.

Our conscious sense of a unified self may even be an illusion. Neurologist Richard Restak (1994) notes that many of our actions and choices occur without any direction by a central, conscious self. Cognitive scientist Daniel Dennett (1991) suggests that the brain or mind consists of independent brain parts that deal with different aspects of thought and perception, constantly conferring with each other and revising their "drafts" of reality. And Michael Gazzaniga proposes that the brain is organized as a loose confederation of independent modules, or mental systems, all working in parallel, with most of these modules operating outside of conscious awareness. One verbal module, an "interpreter" (usually in the left hemisphere), is constantly explaining the actions, moods, and thoughts produced by the other modules (Gazzaniga, 1998; Roser & Gazzaniga, 2004). The result is the sense of a unified self.

The idea that the self is an illusion echoes the teachings of many Eastern spiritual traditions. Buddhism, for example, teaches that the self is not a unified "thing" but rather a collection of thoughts, perceptions, concepts, and feelings that shift and change from moment to moment. To Buddhists, the unity and the permanence of the self are a mirage. Such notions are contrary,

Thinking Critically

Tolerate Uncertainty

We all have a sense of being a conscious "self," and brain research shows that consciousness arises from our brains. But if that is the case, where in the brain is this self located? Can this age-old question be answered?

"THEN IT'S AGREED—YOU CAN'T HAVE A MIND WITHOUT A BRAIN, BUT YOU CAN HAVE A BRAIN WITHOUT A MIND."

ScienceCartoonsPlus.com

⊙ **Watch**
Relaxation

of course, to what most people in the West, including psychologists, have always believed about their "selves."

Whether or not the self is an illusion, we all have a sense of self; otherwise, there would be no need for the words *I* and *me*. Yet even in these days of modern technology, and despite much debate among scientists and philosophers, the neural circuits responsible for our sense of self remain hazy. How is the inner life of the mind, our sense of subjective experience, linked to the physical processes of the brain? Some neuroscientists argue that specific groups of neurons form unique neuronal "coalitions" for seeing red, seeing our grandmother, or feeling joy (Koch, 2004). Others emphasize the transient synchronization of millions of neurons across wide areas of the brain, synchronization that changes from moment to moment (Greenfield & Collins, 2005). But in either case, how does that brain activity *cause* a person's joy on seeing her adored grandmother in a new red hat? We don't know. Nor do we understand why some patients with severe degeneration of the frontal lobes have unimpaired memories and language yet undergo a change in self comparable to Phineas Gage's transformation (Levenson & Miller, 2007). These patients can walk, talk, and function, and yet their families and friends don't know them; they are no longer "themselves."

Psychologists, neuroscientists, cognitive scientists, and philosophers all hope to learn more about how our brains and nervous systems give rise to the self. In the meantime, what do you think about the existence and location of your own "self". . . and who, by the way, is doing the thinking?

Are There "His" and "Hers" Brains?

A second stubborn issue for brain scientists concerns sex differences in the brain. On this issue, either–or thinking is a great temptation. Because of the centuries of prejudice against women and a legacy of biased research on gender differences, some scientists and laypeople do not even want to consider the possibility that the brains of women and men might differ, on average, in some ways. Others go overboard in the opposite direction, convinced that most, if not all, differences between the sexes are in fact "all in the brain." To evaluate this issue intelligently, we need to ask two separate questions: *Do* the brains of males and females differ? And if so, what, if anything, do the differences have to do with men's and women's behaviour, abilities, or ways of solving problems?

Let's consider the first question. Many anatomical and biochemical sex differences have been found in human and animal brains. For example, in a study of nine autopsied brains, researchers found that the women's brains had an average of 11% more cells in areas of the cortex associated with the processing of auditory information; in fact, all the women had more of these cells than did any of the men (Witelson, Glazer, & Kigar, 1994). Brain scans show that parts of the frontal lobes and the limbic system are larger in women, relative to the overall size of their brains, whereas parts of the parietal cortex and the amygdala are larger in men (Goldstein et al., 2001; Gur et al., 2002). Women also have more cortical folds in the frontal and parietal lobes (Luders et al., 2004).

Researchers are also using brain scans to search for average sex differences in brain activity when people work on particular tasks. In one study, 19 men and 19 women were asked to say whether pairs of nonsense words rhymed, a task that required them to process and compare sounds. MRI scans showed that in both sexes an area at the front of the left hemisphere was activated. But in 11 of the women and none of the

Thinking Critically

Avoid Emotional Reasoning

Perhaps no topic in brain research generates as much passion and emotional thinking as that of sex differences in the brain. To think clearly about this issue, we need to distinguish what the empirical evidence shows from what it means for people's everyday lives.

men, the corresponding area in the right hemisphere was also active (Shaywitz et al., 1995). In another MRI study, 10 men and 10 women listened to a John Grisham thriller being read aloud. Men and women alike showed activity in the left temporal lobe, but women also showed some activity in the right temporal lobe, as you can see in Figure 4.15 (Phillips et al., 2001). These findings, along with many others, provide evidence for a sex difference in lateralization: For some types of tasks, especially those involving language, men seem to rely more heavily on one side of the brain whereas women tend to use both sides.

Thus, the answer to our first question is that yes, average sex differences in the brain do exist. But we are still left with our second question: *What do the differences mean for the behaviour or personality traits of men and women in ordinary life?* Some writers have been quick to assume that brain differences explain, among other things, women's allegedly superior intuition, women's love of talking about feelings and men's love of talking about sports, women's greater verbal ability, men's edge in math ability, and why men won't ask for directions when they're lost. There are at least three problems with such conclusions:

1   **Many supposed gender differences (in intuition, abilities, and so forth) are stereotypes.** Remember, the overlap between the sexes is greater than the difference between them. As we saw in Chapter 2, even when gender differences are statistically significant, they are often quite small in practical terms (Hyde, 2005). Some supposed differences, on closer inspection, even disappear. For example, are women more talkative than men, as many pop-psych books about the sexes assert? To test this assumption, psychologists wired up a sample of men and women with voice recorders that tracked their conversations while they went about their daily lives. There was no significant gender difference in the number of words spoken: Both sexes used about 16 000 words per day on average, with large individual differences among the participants (Mehl et al., 2007). Likewise, the difference between boys and girls in math scores is shrinking and in some studies is approaching zero (Hyde & Linn, 2006; Spelke, 2005).

2   **A brain difference does not necessarily produce a difference in behaviour or performance.** In many studies, males and females have shown different patterns of brain activity while they are doing something or while an ability is being tested, but they have not differed in the behaviour or ability in question—which, after all, is presumably the thing to be explained. In the rhyme-judgment task, for example, both sexes did equally well, despite the differences in their MRIs. Another research team used MRI scans to examine the brains of men and women who had equivalent IQ scores. Women's brains had more white-matter areas related to intelligence, whereas men's brains had more grey-matter areas related to intelligence; there were some other differences as well (Haier et al., 2005). The researchers concluded that brains may be organized differently yet produce the same intellectual abilities.

3   **Sex differences in the brain could be the result rather than the cause of behavioural differences.** As we saw earlier in this chapter, culture and

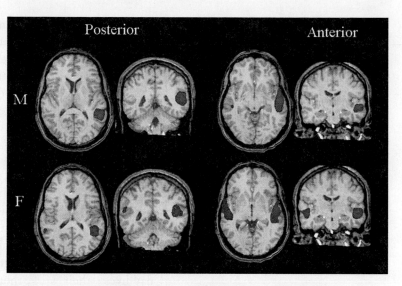

FIGURE 4.15 Gender and the Brain

When women and men listened to a John Grisham thriller read aloud, they showed activity in the left temporal lobe, but women also showed some activity in the right temporal lobe (Phillips et al., 2001). (Because of the orientation of these MRI images, the left hemisphere is seen on the right and vice versa.) Along with other evidence, these results suggest a sex difference in lateralization on tasks involving language.

experience are constantly sculpting the circuitry of the brain, affecting the way brains are organized and how they function. Women and men, of course, often have different experiences in childhood and throughout their lives. Thus, in commenting on the study that had people listen to a John Grisham novel, one of the researchers noted: "We don't know if the [sex difference we found] is because of the way we're raised, or if it's hard-wired in the brain" (quoted in Hotz, 2000).

In sum, the answer to our second question, whether anatomical differences are linked to behaviour, is: It's uncertain. There are tantalizing clues, suggesting that sex differences in the brain influence reactions to acute or chronic stress, the likelihood of suffering depression and attention deficit hyperactivity disorder, memory for emotional events, strategies for navigating around the environment, and other aspects of behaviour (Cahill, 2005; Becker et al., 2008). But we simply do not yet know which of these findings is important for how individuals manage their everyday lives—their work, their relationships, their families. It is important to keep an open mind about new findings on sex differences in the brain, but because the practical significance of these findings (if any) is not yet clear, it is also important not to oversimplify, as one popular book after another keeps doing. The topic of sex differences in the brain is a sexy one, and research in this area can easily be exaggerated and misused.

We think you'll agree that findings about the brain are pretty fascinating. However, these findings should not deflect attention from all the other influences that make us who we are, for better or worse: our relationships, our experiences, our standing in society, our culture. Keep in mind (as well as in your brain!) that analyzing a human being in terms of physiology alone is like analyzing the Taj Mahal solely in terms of the materials that were used to build it. Even if we could monitor every cell and circuit of the brain, we would still need to understand the circumstances, thoughts, and cultural rules that affect whether we are gripped by hatred, consumed by grief, lifted by love, or transported by joy.

◄⊙ **Simulate**
Physiological Bases of
Behavioural Problems

⊙ **Watch**
Memory and Exercise

---

quickQUIZ

✓• Quick Review on MyPsychLab

Men and women alike have brains that can answer these questions.

1. Many brain researchers and cognitive scientists believe that the self is not a unified "thing" but a collection of _____.

2. A new study reports that in a sample of 11 brains, 4 of the 6 women's brains but only 2 of the 5 men's brains had multiple chocolate receptors. (*Note:* We made this up; there's no such thing as a chocolate receptor!) The researchers conclude that their findings explain why so many women are addicted to chocolate. What concerns should a critical thinker have about this study?

Answers:

1. independent modules or mental systems   2. The sample size was very small; have the results been replicated? Were the sex differences more impressive than the similarities? Might eating chocolate affect chocolate receptors rather than the other way around? Most important, was the number of receptors actually related to the amount of chocolate eaten by the brains' owners in real life?

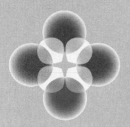

Taking Psychology with YOU

Thinking Critically in Everyday Life

Cosmetic Neurology: Tinkering with the Brain

Should healthy people be permitted, even encouraged, to take "brain boosters" or "neuroenhancers"—drugs that will sharpen concentration and memory? What about a pill that could erase a traumatic memory? If having cosmetic surgery can change parts of your body you don't like, what's wrong with allowing "cosmetic neurology" to tinker with parts of your brain you don't like?

For centuries, people have been seeking ways to stimulate their brains to work more efficiently, with caffeine being an especially popular drug of choice. No one objects to research showing that diet and exercise can improve learning and memory. For example, no one has a problem with the finding that omega-3s, found in some kinds of fish, may help protect against age-related mental decline (Beydoun et al., 2007; van Gelder et al., 2007). But when it comes to medications that increase alertness or appear to enhance memory and other cognitive functions, it's another kettle of fish oil, so to speak. What questions should critical thinkers ask, and what kind of evidence would be needed, to make wise decisions about using such medications? A new interdisciplinary specialty, *neuroethics*, has been formed to address the many legal, ethical, and scientific questions raised by brain research, including those raised by the development of neuroenhancing drugs (Gazzaniga, 2005).

Much of the buzz has focused on Provigil (modafinil), a drug approved for treating narcolepsy and other sleep disorders, and Ritalin and Adderall, approved for attention deficit disorders. Many students, pilots, business people, and jetlagged travellers are taking one

or another of these drugs, either obtaining them illegally from friends or the internet, or getting their own prescriptions. Naturally, most of these users claim the drugs help them, and one review of the literature concluded that Provigil does improve memory and may have other cognitive benefits (Minzenberg & Carter, 2008).

Yet, as is unfortunately true of just about all medications, there is a downside that rarely makes news, especially with new drugs that promise easy fixes for old human problems and have not yet been tested over many years. Adderall, like all amphetamines, can cause nervousness, headaches, sleeplessness, allergic rashes, and loss of appetite, and, as the label says, it has "a high potential for abuse." Provigil, too, is habit-forming. Another memory-enhancing drug being studied targets a type of glutamate receptor in the brain. The drug apparently improves short-term memory nicely—at the price of detracting from long-term memories (Talbot, 2009).

Even when a drug is benign for most of its users, there may be surprising and unexpected consequences. For example, cognitive psychologists have found that the better able people are to focus and concentrate on a task—the reason for taking stimulants in the first place—the less *creative* they often are. Creativity, after all, comes from being able to let our minds roam freely, at leisure. One neurologist therefore worries that the routine use of mind-enhancing drugs among students could create "a generation of very focussed accountants" (quoted in Talbot, 2009).

Some bioethicists and neuroscientists feel that cognitive enhancement is perfectly fine, because it is human nature

for people to try to improve themselves, and society will benefit when people learn faster and remember more. After all, we use eyeglasses to improve vision and hearing aids to improve hearing; why not use pills to improve our memories and other mental skills? One team of scientists has argued that improving brain function with pills is no more objectionable than eating right or getting a good night's sleep. They wrote, "In a world in which human workspans and lifespans are increasing, cognitive enhancement tools. . . will be increasingly useful for improved quality of life and extended work productivity, as well as to stave off normal and pathological age-related cognitive declines" (Greely et al., 2008).

Other scientists and social critics, however, consider cosmetic neurology to be a form of cheating that will give those who can afford the drugs an unfair advantage and increase socioeconomic inequalities. They think the issue is no different from the (prohibited) use of performance-enhancing steroids in athletics. Yes, people wear glasses and hearing aids, but glasses and hearing aids do not have side effects or interact negatively with other treatments. Many neuroethicists also worry that ambitious parents will start giving these medications to their children to try to boost the child's academic performance, despite possible hazards for the child's developing brain. One reporter covering the pros and cons of neuroenhancers concluded, "All this may be leading to the kind of society I'm not sure I want to live in: a society where we're even more overworked and driven by technology than we already are, and where we have to take drugs to keep up" (Talbot, 2009).

How about using drugs not to enhance memory but to erase it—especially memories of sorrowful and traumatic events? By altering the biochemistry of the brain in mice or rats, or using a toxin to kill targeted cells, researchers have been able to wipe out the animals' memories of a learned shock, their ability to recall a learned fear, or their memory of an object previously seen, while leaving other memories intact (Cao et al., 2008; Han et al., 2009; Serrano et al., 2008). If these results eventually apply to human beings, what, again, are the implications?

Some victims of sexual or physical abuse, wartime atrocities, or a sudden horrifying disaster might welcome the chance to be rid of their disturbing memories. But could a "delete" button for the brain be used too often, changing the storehouse of memories that make us who we are? Could memory erasure be misused by unscrupulous governments to eliminate dissent, as George Orwell famously predicted it would in his great novel *1984*? Should we wish to erase memories that evoke embarrassment or guilt, emotions that are unpleasant yet enable us to develop and retain a sense of morality and learn from our mistakes? And would we come to regret the obliteration of a part of our lives, as Jim Carrey's character did in the film *Eternal Sunshine of the Spotless Mind*? Such concerns may be the reason that most people, when asked if they would take a pill to eradicate a painful memory, respond loudly and clearly: No, thanks (Berkowitz et al., 2008).

In contrast, many people might say "Yes, please" to brain-enhancing drugs. But before they do, they will need to think critically—by separating anecdotes from data, real dangers from false alarms, and immediate benefits from long-term risks. What is to be gained from neuroenhancers, and what might be lost?

SUMMARY

◆ Neuropsychologists and other scientists study the brain because it is the bedrock of consciousness, perception, memory, and emotion.

THE NERVOUS SYSTEM: A BASIC BLUEPRINT

◆ The function of the nervous system is to gather and process information, produce responses to stimuli, and coordinate the workings of different cells. Scientists divide it into the *central nervous system* (CNS) and the *peripheral nervous system* (PNS). The CNS, which includes the brain and *spinal cord*, receives, processes, interprets, and stores information and sends out messages destined for muscles, glands, and organs. The PNS transmits information to and from the CNS by way of *sensory* and *motor nerves*.

◆ The peripheral nervous system consists of the *somatic nervous system*, which permits sensation and voluntary actions, and the *autonomic nervous system*, which regulates blood vessels, glands, and internal (visceral) organs. The autonomic system usually functions without conscious control. The autonomic nervous system is further divided into the *sympathetic nervous system*, which mobilizes the body for action, and the *parasympathetic nervous system*, which conserves energy.

COMMUNICATION IN THE NERVOUS SYSTEM

◆ Neurons are the basic units of the nervous system. They are held in place by *glial cells*, which nourish, insulate, and protect them, and enable them to function properly. Each neuron consists of *dendrites*, a *cell body*, and an *axon*. In the peripheral nervous system, axons (and sometimes dendrites) are collected together in bundles called *nerves*. Many axons are insulated by a *myelin sheath* that speeds up the conduction of neural impulses and prevents signals in adjacent cells from interfering with one another.

◆ Research has disproven two old assumptions: that neurons in the human central nervous system cannot be induced to regenerate and that no new neurons form after early infancy. In the laboratory, neurons have been induced to regenerate. And scientists have learned that *stem cells* in brain areas associated with learning and memory continue to divide and mature throughout adulthood, giving rise to new neurons. A stimulating environment seems to enhance this process of *neurogenesis*.

◆ Communication between two neurons occurs at the *synapse*. Many synapses have not yet formed at birth. During development, axons and dendrites continue to grow as a result of both physical maturation and experience with the world, and throughout life, new learning results in new synaptic connections in the brain. Thus, the brain's circuits are not fixed and immutable but are continually changing in response to information, challenges, and changes in the environment, a phenomenon known as *plasticity*. In some people who have been blind from an early age, brain regions usually devoted to vision are activated by sound—a dramatic example of plasticity.

◆ When a wave of electrical voltage (*action potential*) reaches the end of a transmitting axon, *neurotransmitter* molecules are released into the *synaptic cleft*. When these molecules bind to *receptor sites* on the receiving neuron, that neuron becomes either more likely to fire or less so. The message that reaches a final destination depends on how frequently particular neurons are firing, how many are firing, what types are firing, their degree of synchrony, and where they are located.

◆ Neurotransmitters play a critical role in mood, memory, and psychological well-being. Abnormal levels of neurotransmitters have been implicated in several disorders, such as Alzheimer's disease and Parkinson's disease.

◆ *Endorphins*, which act primarily by modifying the action of neurotransmitters, reduce pain and promote pleasure. Endorphin levels seem to shoot up when an animal or person is afraid or is under stress. Endorphins have also been linked to the pleasures of human attachment.

◆ *Hormones*, produced mainly by the *endocrine glands*, affect and are affected by the nervous system. Psychologists are especially interested in *melatonin*, which promotes sleep and helps regulate bodily rhythms; *oxytocin* and *vasopressin*, which play a role in attachment and trust; *adrenal hormones* such as *epinephrine* and *norepinephrine*, which are involved in emotions and stress; and the *sex hormones*, which are involved in the physical changes of puberty, the menstrual cycle (*estrogens* and *progesterone*), sexual arousal (*testosterone*), and some nonreproductive functions—including, some researchers believe, mental functioning.

MAPPING THE BRAIN

◆ Researchers study the brain by observing patients with brain damage; by using the lesion method with animals; and by using such techniques as *electroencephalograms* (EEGs), *transcranial magnetic stimulation* (TMS), *positron-emission tomography* (PET scans), *magnetic resonance imaging* (MRI), and *functional MRI* (fMRI).

◆ Brain scans reveal which parts of the brain are active during different tasks but do not tell us precisely what is happening, either physically or mentally, during the task. They do not reveal discrete "centres" for a particular function, and they must be interpreted cautiously.

A TOUR THROUGH THE BRAIN

◆ All modern brain theories assume *localization of function*, although a particular area may have several functions, and many areas are likely to be involved in any particular activity.

◆ In the lower part of the brain, in the *brain stem*, the *medulla* controls automatic functions such as heartbeat and breathing, and the *pons* is involved in sleeping, waking, and dreaming. The *reticular activating system* (RAS) screens incoming information and is responsible for alertness. The *cerebellum* contributes to balance and muscle coordination and may also play a role in some higher mental operations.

◆ The *thalamus* directs sensory messages to appropriate higher centres. The *hypothalamus* is involved in emotion and in drives associated with survival. It also controls the operations of the autonomic nervous system, and sends out chemicals that tell the *pituitary gland* when to "talk" to other endocrine glands. Along with other structures, the hypothalamus has traditionally been considered part of the *limbic system*, which is involved in emotions that we share with other animals. However, the usefulness of speaking of the limbic system as an integrated set of structures is now in dispute.

◆ The *amygdala* is responsible for evaluating sensory information and quickly determining its emotional importance, and for the initial decision to approach or withdraw from a person or situation. It is also involved in forming and retrieving emotional memories. The *hippocampus* has been called the "gateway to memory" because it plays a critical role in the formation of long-term memories for facts and events. It is also involved in other aspects of memory. Like the hypothalamus, these two structures have traditionally been classified as "limbic."

◆ Much of the brain's circuitry is packed into the *cerebrum*, which is divided into two *hemispheres* and is covered by thin layers of cells known collectively as the *cerebral cortex*. The *occipital*, *parietal*, *temporal*, and *frontal lobes* of the cortex have specialized (but partially overlapping) functions. The *association cortex* appears to be responsible for higher mental processes. The *frontal lobes*, particularly areas in the *prefrontal cortex*, are involved in social judgment, the making and carrying out of plans, and decision making.

THE TWO HEMISPHERES OF THE BRAIN

◆ Studies of *split-brain* patients, whose *corpus callosum* has been cut, show that the two cerebral hemispheres have somewhat different talents. In most people, language is processed mainly in the left hemisphere, which is generally specialized for logical, symbolic, and sequential tasks. The right hemisphere is associated with spatial–visual tasks, facial recognition, and the creation and appreciation of art and music. In most mental activities, however, the two hemispheres cooperate as partners, with each making a valuable contribution.

TWO STUBBORN ISSUES IN BRAIN RESEARCH

◆ One of the oldest questions in the study of the brain is where the "self" resides. Many brain researchers and cognitive scientists believe that a unified self may be something of an illusion. Some argue that the brain operates as a collection of independent modules or mental systems, perhaps with one of them functioning as an "interpreter." But much remains to be learned about the relation between the brain and the mind.

◆ Brain scans and other techniques have revealed some differences in the brains of males and females, and in lateralization during tasks involving language (with females more likely to use both hemispheres). Controversy exists, however, about what such differences mean in real life. Speculation has often focused on behavioural or cognitive differences that are small and insignificant. Biological differences do not necessarily explain behavioural ones, and sex differences in experience could affect brain organization rather than the other way around.

TAKING PSYCHOLOGY WITH YOU

◆ Scholars in the new field of *neuroethics* are addressing the implications of "cosmetic neurology," especially questions raised by the development of drugs that are "neuroenhancers."

MyPsychLab

Visit **www.mypsychlab.com** to help you get the best grade!
Test your knowledge and grasp difficult concepts through

• Custom study plans: See where you are strong and where you go wrong
• Interactive simulations
• Video and audio clips

KEY TERMS

central nervous system (CNS) *110*	cell body *114*	endorphins *121*
spinal cord *111*	axon *114*	hormones *121*
peripheral nervous system (PNS) *111*	myelin sheath *115*	endocrine glands *121*
somatic nervous system *111*	nerve *115*	melatonin *122*
autonomic nervous system *111*	neurogenesis *115*	oxytocin *122*
sympathetic nervous system *112*	stem cells *115*	adrenal hormones *122*
parasympathetic nervous system *112*	synapse *116*	sex hormones *122*
neuron *113*	action potential *117*	electroencephalogram (EEG) *124*
glia *113*	neurotransmitter *117*	transcranial magnetic stimulation
dendrites *114*	plasticity *118*	(TMS) *124*

5 BODY RHYTHMS AND MENTAL STATES

ASK QUESTIONS . . . be willing to WONDER

- If you didn't know what time it was, would your body?

- Why do we need to sleep—and dream?

- Can hypnotized people be made to do things against their will?

- Why can a glass of wine make a person feel happy and excited on one occasion but tired and depressed on another?

In Lewis Carroll's immortal story *Alice's Adventures in Wonderland*, the ordinary rules of everyday life keep dissolving in a sea of logical contradictions. First Alice shrinks to within only a few centimetres of the ground, then she shoots up taller than the treetops. The strange antics of Wonderland's inhabitants make her smile one moment and shed a pool of tears the next. "Dear dear!" muses the harried heroine. "How queer everything is today! . . . I wonder if I've been changed in the night? Let me think: *was* I the same when I got up this morning? I almost think I can remember feeling a little different. But if I'm not the same, the *next* question is, 'Who in the world am I?' Ah, *that's* the great puzzle!"

In a way, we all live in a sort of Wonderland. For a third of our lives, we reside in a realm where the ordinary rules of logic and experience are suspended: the dream world of sleep. Throughout the day, mood, alertness, efficiency, and **consciousness** itself— our awareness of ourselves and the environment—are in perpetual flux, sometimes shifting as dramatically as Alice's height. Sometimes we are hyper-alert and attentive to our own feelings and everything around us;

at other times we daydream, "space out," or go on "automatic pilot."

Starting from the assumption that mental and physical states are as intertwined as sunshine and shadow, psychologists, along with other scientists, are exploring the links between fluctuations in subjective experience and changes in brain activity and hormone levels. They have come to view changing states of consciousness as part of the rhythmic ebb and flow of experience over time. For example, dreaming, traditionally classified as a state of consciousness, is also part of a 90-minute cycle of brain activity.

Examining a person's ongoing rhythmic cycles is like watching a motion picture of consciousness. Studying the person's distinct states of consciousness is more like looking at separate snapshots. In this chapter, we will first run the motion picture, to see how functioning and consciousness vary predictably over time. Then we will zoom in on one specific snapshot—the world of dreams— and examine it in some detail. Finally, we will turn to two techniques that have been used to "retouch" or alter the film: hypnosis and the use of recreational drugs.

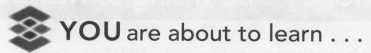

YOU are about to learn . . .

- how biological rhythms affect our physiology and performance.
- why you feel out of sync when you fly across time zones or change shifts at work.
- why some people get the winter blues.
- how culture and learning affect reports of "PMS" and estimates of its incidence.

BIOLOGICAL RHYTHMS: THE TIDES OF EXPERIENCE

Pseudoscientific ideas about biological rhythms have been around for more than a century. At some point, you may have come across an ad on the internet for "biorhythm charts," which supposedly foretell fluctuations in mood, alertness, and physical performance over your entire lifetime—solely on the basis of when you were born. Those who sell these charts claim they can foresee your good days and tell when you will be susceptible to accidents, errors, and illness. Well, save your money. Whenever researchers have taken the trouble to test such claims scientifically—for example, by examining occupational accidents in light of the charts' predictions—they have found the charts completely useless (Hines, 1998).

It *is* true, however, that the human body changes over the course of a day, a week, a year. We all experience dozens of periodic, fairly regular ups and downs in physiological functioning, which is what scientists mean when they speak of **biological rhythms.** A biological clock in our brains governs the waxing and waning of hormone levels, urine volume, blood pressure, and even the responsiveness of brain cells to stimulation. Biological rhythms are typically synchronized with external events, such as changes in clock time, temperature, and daylight—a process called **entrainment.** But many of these rhythms continue to occur even in the absence of external time cues; they are **endogenous,** or generated from within.

Many biological rhythms, called **circadian rhythms,** occur approximately every 24 hours. The best-known circadian rhythm is the sleep–wake cycle, but there are hundreds of others that affect physiology and performance. For example, body temperature fluctuates about one degree centigrade each day, peaking, on average, in the late afternoon and hitting a low point, or trough, in the wee hours of the morning.

Other rhythms occur less often than once a day—say, once a month, or once a season. In the animal world, seasonal rhythms are common. Birds migrate south in the fall, bears hibernate in the winter, and marine animals become active or inactive, depending on bimonthly changes in the tides. In human beings, the female menstrual cycle occurs every 28 days on average. And some rhythms occur more frequently than once a day, many of them on about a 90-minute cycle. These include physiological changes during sleep and (unless social customs intervene) stomach contractions, hormone levels, susceptibility to visual illusions, verbal and spatial performance, brainwave responses during cognitive tasks, alertness, and daydreaming (Escera, Cilveti, & Grau, 1992; Klein & Armitage, 1979; Kripke, 1974; Lavie, 1976).

Biological rhythms influence everything from the effectiveness of medicines taken at different times of the day to alertness and performance on the job. With a better understanding of these internal tempos, we may be able to design our days to take better advantage of our bodies' natural tempos. Let's look more closely at how these cycles operate.

consciousness Awareness of oneself and the environment.

biological rhythm A periodic, more or less regular fluctuation in a biological system; may or may not have psychological implications.

entrainment The synchronization of biological rhythms with external cues, such as fluctuations in daylight.

endogenous Generated from within rather than by external cues.

circadian [sur-CAY-dee-un] rhythm A biological rhythm with a period (from peak to peak or trough to trough) of about 24 hours; from the Latin *circa,* "about," and *dies,* "a day."

Stefania Follini (left) spent four months in a New Mexico cave (above), nine metres underground, as part of an Italian study on biological rhythms. Her only companions were a computer and two friendly mice. In the absence of clocks, natural light, or changes in temperature, she tended to stay awake for 20 to 25 hours and then sleep for 10. Because her days were longer than usual, when she emerged she thought she had been in the cave for only two months.

Circadian Rhythms

Circadian rhythms exist in plants, animals, insects, and human beings. They reflect the adaptation of organisms to the many changes associated with the rotation of Earth on its axis, such as changes in light, air pressure, and temperature.

In most societies, external time cues abound, and people's circadian rhythms become entrained to them, following a strict 24-hour schedule. To identify endogenous rhythms, therefore, scientists must isolate volunteers from sunlight, clocks, environmental sounds, and all other cues to time. Some hardy souls have spent weeks or even months alone in caves and salt mines, linked to the outside world only by a one-way phone line and a cable transmitting physiological measurements to the surface. Nowadays, however, volunteers usually live in specially designed rooms equipped with stereo systems, comfortable furniture, and temperature controls.

When participants in these studies have been allowed to sleep, eat, and work whenever they wished, free of the tyranny of the timepiece, a few have lived a "day" that is much shorter or longer than 24 hours. If allowed to take daytime naps, however, most participants soon settle into a day that averages about 24.3 hours (Moore, 1997). And when people are put on an artificial 28-hour day, in an environment free of all time cues, their body temperature and certain hormone levels follow a cycle that is very close to 24 hours—24.18 hours, to be precise (Czeisler et al., 1999). These rhythms are remarkably similar in length from one person to the next. For many people, alertness, like temperature, peaks in the late afternoon and falls to a low point in the very early morning (Lavie, 2001).

((◦• **Listen**
Brain Time

THE BODY'S CLOCK. Circadian rhythms are controlled by a biological clock, or overall coordinator, located in a tiny teardrop-shaped cluster of cells in the hypothalamus called the **suprachiasmatic nucleus (SCN)**. Neural pathways from special receptors in the back of the eye transmit information to the SCN and allow it to respond to changes in light and dark. The SCN then sends out messages that cause the brain and

suprachiasmatic [soo-pruh-kye-az-MAT-ick] **nucleus (SCN)** An area of the brain containing a biological clock that governs circadian rhythms.

body to adapt to these changes. Other clocks also exist, scattered around the body, and some may operate independently of the SCN, but for most circadian rhythms the SCN is regarded as the master pacemaker.

The SCN regulates fluctuating levels of hormones and neurotransmitters, and they in turn provide feedback that affects the SCN's functioning. For example, during the dark hours, one hormone regulated by the SCN, **melatonin,** is secreted by the pineal gland, deep within the brain. When you go to sleep in a darkened room, your melatonin level rises; when you wake up in the morning to a lightened room, it falls. Melatonin, in turn, appears to help keep the biological clock in phase with the light–dark cycle (Haimov & Lavie, 1996; Lewy et al., 1992).

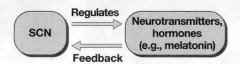

Melatonin therapy has been used to treat insomnia and synchronize the disturbed sleep–wake cycles of blind people who lack light perception and whose melatonin production does not cycle normally (Sack & Lewy, 1997). But efforts to treat the insomnia of sighted people by giving them melatonin have had mixed results. Lots of people are taking over-the-counter melatonin supplements to help them sleep or to reduce jet lag, but it's unlikely that these supplements are very helpful. There are no federal standards to assure their quality, and no one has yet identified which dosages are effective (if any) or studied their long-term safety.

Travel can be exhausting, and jet lag makes it worse.

melatonin A hormone, secreted by the pineal gland, that is involved in the regulation of daily biological (circadian) rhythms.

internal desynchronization A state in which biological rhythms are not in phase (synchronized) with one another.

WHEN THE CLOCK IS OUT OF SYNC. Under normal conditions, the rhythms governed by the SCN are synchronized, just as wristwatches can be synchronized. Their peaks may occur at different times, but they occur in phase with one another; thus, if you know when one rhythm peaks, you can predict fairly well when another will. But when your normal routine changes, your circadian rhythms may be thrown out of phase with one another. Such **internal desynchronization** often occurs when people take airplane flights across several time zones. Sleep and wake patterns usually adjust quickly, but temperature and hormone cycles can take several days to return to normal. The resulting jet lag affects energy level, mental skills, and motor coordination.

Internal desynchronization also occurs when a worker must adjust to a new shift. Efficiency drops, the person feels tired and irritable, accidents become more likely, and sleep disturbances and digestive disorders may occur. For police officers, emergency room personnel, airline pilots, truck drivers, and operators of nuclear power plants, the consequences can be a matter of life and death. In the United States, a National Commission on Sleep Disorders concluded that lack of alertness in night-shift equipment operators might have contributed, along with other factors, to the 1989 *Exxon Valdez* oil spill off the coast of Alaska and to disastrous accidents during the 1980s at the Three Mile Island and Chernobyl nuclear power plants. Even relatively small desynchronizations can have deadly effects. University of British Columbia researcher Stanley Coren (1996) studied the records of all accidental deaths in the United States over a three-year period. He found that the spring shift to daylight saving time (and the minimal sleep loss associated with it) produced a short-term increase in the likelihood of accidental death, but that the fall shift back to standard time had little effect.

Night work itself is not necessarily a problem: With a schedule that always stays the same, even on weekends, people often adapt and do fine. However, many swing- and night-shift assignments are made on a rotating basis, so a worker's circadian rhythms never have a chance to resynchronize. Some scientists hope eventually to help rotating-shift workers resynchronize their rhythms by using melatonin or other techniques to "reset the clock" (Revell & Eastman, 2005), but so far these techniques are not ready for prime time. The best approach at present is to follow circadian principles by switching workers from one shift to another as infrequently as possible.

One reason that a simple cure for desynchronization has so far eluded scientists is that circadian rhythms are not perfectly regular in daily life. They can be affected by illness, stress, fatigue, excitement, exercise, drugs, mealtimes, and ordinary daily experiences. In research with mice, these rhythms were even influenced by diet. Mice usually sleep during the day, but putting them on a high-fat diet altered the activity of genes involved in appetite and metabolism, and the mice began waking up and eating during the day (Kohsaka et al., 2007).

Further, circadian rhythms differ greatly from individual to individual because of genetic differences (Hur, Bouchard, & Lykken, 1998). For example, a variation in a single gene seems to be the reason that some people are early birds, bouncing out of bed at the crack of dawn, while others are night owls who do their best work late at night and can't be pried out of bed until noon (Archer et al., 2003). (Schools are not designed to accommodate night owls.) You may be able to learn about your own personal pulses through careful self-observation, and you may want to try putting that information to use when planning your daily schedule.

Moods and Long-Term Rhythms

According to Ecclesiastes, "To every thing there is a season, and a time for every purpose under the heaven." Modern science agrees: Long-term cycles have been observed in everything from the threshold for tooth pain to conception rates. Folklore holds that our moods follow similar rhythms, particularly in response to seasonal changes and, in women, to menstrual changes. But do they?

DOES THE SEASON AFFECT MOODS?   Clinicians report that some people become depressed during particular seasons, typically winter, when periods of daylight are short—a pattern that has come to be known as *seasonal affective disorder (SAD)*

Get INVOLVED!

MEASURING YOUR ALERTNESS CYCLES

For at least three days, except when you are sleeping, keep an hourly record of your mental alertness level, using this five-point scale: 1 = extremely drowsy or mentally lethargic, 2 = somewhat drowsy or mentally lethargic, 3 = moderately alert, 4 = alert and efficient, 5 = extremely alert and efficient. Does your alertness level appear to follow a circadian rhythm, reaching a high point and a low point once every 24 hours? Or does it follow a shorter rhythm, rising and falling several times during the day? Are your cycles the same on weekends as during the week? Most important, how well does your schedule mesh with your natural fluctuations in alertness?

This woman is receiving light therapy for seasonal affective disorder (SAD). This type of treatment has become popular and appears to be effective. But fewer people actually have SAD than is commonly thought, and the causes remain uncertain.

(N. E. Rosenthal, 2006). During the winter months, SAD patients report feelings of sadness, lethargy, drowsiness, and a craving for carbohydrates. To counteract the presumed effects of sunless days, some physicians and therapists have been treating SAD patients with phototherapy, having them sit in front of bright fluorescent lights at specific times of the day, usually early in the morning. In some cases, they have also begun prescribing antidepressants and other drugs.

Evaluating the actual prevalence of SAD is difficult, however. Information comes mainly from clinical case reports rather than controlled studies, and as we saw in Chapter 2, case studies have serious drawbacks. Many clinicians, extrapolating from patients who believe they suffer from SAD, think the disorder affects as much as 20% of the population. Most scientific surveys indicate that the prevalence of SAD is much lower. Canadian samples (mostly from Ontario) suggest that 2% to 3% of our population suffers from SAD, compared to less than 1% in the United States (Blazer, Kessler, & Swartz, 1998). European samples exhibit rates similar to those in North America, showing a prevalence of 1% to 3%. However, in Asia, the condition appears less common, occurring in 0% to 1% of the population. Across these studies, it appears that SAD is much more common among women than men. Some studies claim that the female-to-male ratio is as high as 4:1, but the results of many studies combined suggest that the ratio is closer to 2:1 (Lam & Levitt, 1999).

As for the effectiveness of light treatments, research on this question too has been flawed. A review of 173 light-treatment studies published between 1975 and 2003 found that only 20 had used an acceptable design and suitable controls (Golden et al., 2005). However, a meta-analysis of the data from those 20 studies did shed some light on the subject, so to speak. When people with SAD were exposed to either a brief period (such as 30 minutes) of bright light after waking or to light that slowly became brighter, simulating the dawn, their symptoms were in fact reduced. Light therapy even helped people with mild to moderate non-seasonal depression (see also Wirz-Justice et al., 2005).

Many researchers believe that the circadian rhythms of SAD patients are out of sync—that, in essence, they have a chronic form of jet lag (Lewy et al., 2006). Some researchers have concluded that SAD patients must have some abnormality in the way they produce or respond to melatonin. For example, in one study, SAD patients produced melatonin for about half an hour longer at night in the winter than in the summer, whereas control subjects showed no such seasonal pattern (Wehr et al., 2001). However, why would light therapy also help some people with *non*seasonal cases of depression? True cases of SAD may in fact have a biological basis, but the evidence to date remains inconclusive. When people get the winter blues, the reason could also be that they hate cold weather, are physically inactive, do not get outside much, or feel lonely during the winter holidays.

DOES THE MENSTRUAL CYCLE AFFECT MOODS?   Controversy has persisted about another long-term rhythm, the female menstrual cycle, which occurs, on average, every 28 days. During the first half of this cycle, an increase in the hormone estrogen causes the lining of the uterus to thicken in preparation for a possible pregnancy. At mid-cycle, the ovaries release a mature egg, or ovum. Afterward, the ovarian sac that contained the egg begins to produce progesterone, which helps prepare the uterine lining to receive the egg. Then, if conception does not occur, estrogen and progesterone levels fall, the uterine lining sloughs off as the menstrual flow, and the cycle begins again. The interesting question for psychologists is whether these physical changes are correlated with emotional or intellectual changes, as folklore and tradition would have us believe.

Most people seem to think so. In the 1970s, a vague cluster of physical and emotional symptoms—including fatigue, headache, irritability, and depression—associated with the days preceding menstruation came to be thought of as an illness and was given a label: *"premenstrual syndrome" ("PMS")* (Parlee, 1994). Since then, most laypeople, doctors, and psychiatrists have assumed, uncritically, that many women "suffer" from PMS or from its supposedly more extreme and debilitating version, "premenstrual dysphoric disorder" ("PMDD"). Since then, several popular books and countless magazine articles have asserted that most women suffer from it. The medical literature, too, assumes a high incidence; when we scanned the abstracts of articles on "PMS" spanning three recent years, we found estimates ranging from 13% to "most women."

What does the evidence actually show? Many women do have *physical* symptoms associated with menstruation, including cramps, breast tenderness, and water retention, although women vary tremendously in this regard. And of course these physical symptoms can make some women grumpy or unhappy, just as pain can make men grumpy or unhappy. But *emotional* symptoms associated with menstruation—notably, irritability and depression—are pretty rare, which is why we put "PMS" in quotation marks. Just as with SAD, more people claim to have symptoms than actually do. In reality, fewer than 5% of all women have such symptoms predictably over their cycles (Brooks-Gunn, 1986; Reid, 1991; Walker, 1994).

"You've been charged with driving under the influence of testosterone."

For both sexes, the hormonal excuse rarely applies.

There are no hormonal excuses for avoiding this quiz.

1. The functioning of the biological clock governing circadian rhythms is affected by the hormone _____.
2. Jet lag occurs because of _____.
3. For most women, the days before menstruation are reliably associated with (a) depression, (b) irritability, (c) elation, (d) creativity, (e) none of these, (f) a and b.

Answers:

quickQUIZ

✓•⬜Quick Review on MyPsychLab

1. melatonin   2. internal desynchronization   3. e

YOU are about to learn . . .

- the stages of sleep.
- what happens when we go too long without enough sleep.
- how sleep disorders disrupt normal sleep.
- the mental benefits of sleep.

THE RHYTHMS OF SLEEP

Perhaps the most perplexing of all our biological rhythms is the one governing sleep and wakefulness. Sleep, after all, puts us at risk: Muscles that are usually ready to respond to danger relax, and one's senses grow dull. As the late British psychologist Christopher Evans (1984) once noted, "The behaviour patterns involved in sleep are glaringly, almost insanely, at odds with common sense." Then, why is sleep such a profound necessity?

The Realms of Sleep

Let's start with some of the changes that occur in the brain during sleep. Until the early 1950s, little was known about these changes. Then a breakthrough occurred in the laboratory of physiologist Nathaniel Kleitman, who at the time was the only person in the world who had spent his entire career studying sleep. Kleitman had given one of his graduate students, Eugene Aserinsky, the tedious task of finding out whether the slow, rolling eye movements that characterize the onset of sleep continue throughout the night. To both men's surprise, eye movements did occur but they were rapid, not slow (Aserinsky & Kleitman, 1955). Using electroencephalography (EEG) to measure the brain's electrical activity (see Chapter 4), these researchers, along with another of Kleitman's students, William Dement, were able to correlate the rapid eye movements with changes in sleepers' brain-wave patterns (Dement, 1992). Adult volunteers were soon spending their nights sleeping in laboratories while scientists measured changes in their brain activity, muscle tension, breathing, and other physiological responses.

As a result of this research, today we know that during sleep, periods of **rapid eye movement (REM) sleep** alternate with periods of fewer eye movements, or *non-REM (NREM) sleep*, in a cycle that recurs every 90 minutes or so. The REM periods last from a few minutes to as long as an hour, averaging about 20 minutes in length. Whenever they begin, the pattern of electrical activity from the sleeper's brain changes to resemble that of alert wakefulness. Non-REM periods are themselves divided into distinct stages, each associated with a particular brain-wave pattern (see Figure 5.1).

When you first climb into bed, close your eyes, and relax, your brain emits bursts of *alpha waves*. On an EEG recording, alpha waves have a regular, slow rhythm and a high amplitude (height). Gradually, these waves slow down even further, and you drift into the Land of Nod, passing through four stages, each deeper than the previous one:

- *Stage 1.* Your brain waves become small and irregular, and you feel yourself drifting on the edge of consciousness, in a state of light sleep. If awakened, you may recall fantasies or a few visual images.

- *Stage 2.* Your brain emits occasional short bursts of rapid, high-peaking waves called *sleep spindles*. Minor noises probably won't disturb you.

- *Stage 3.* In addition to the waves that are characteristic of stage 2, your brain occasionally emits *delta waves*, very slow waves with very high peaks.

rapid eye movement (REM) sleep Sleep periods characterized by eye movement, loss of muscle tone, and dreaming.

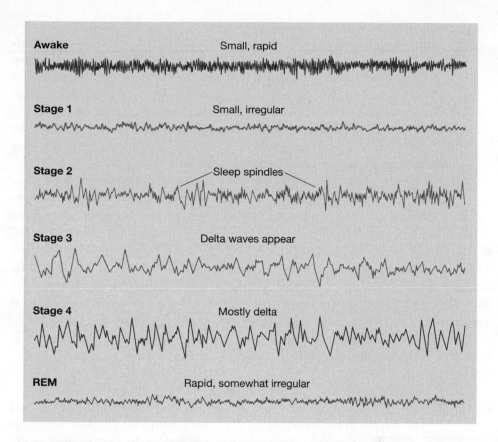

Awake   Small, rapid

Stage 1   Small, irregular

Stage 2   Sleep spindles

Stage 3   Delta waves appear

Stage 4   Mostly delta

REM   Rapid, somewhat irregular

FIGURE 5.1 Brain-Wave Patterns during Wakefulness and Sleep

Most types of brain waves are present throughout sleep, but different ones predominate at different stages.

Your breathing and pulse have slowed down, your muscles are relaxed, and you are hard to rouse.

◆ *Stage 4.* Delta waves have now largely taken over, and you are in deep sleep. It will probably take vigorous shaking or a loud noise to awaken you. Oddly, though, if you walk in your sleep, this is when you are likely to do so. No one yet knows what causes sleepwalking, which occurs more often in children than adults, but it seems to involve unusual patterns of delta-wave brain activity (Bassetti et al., 2000).

This sequence of stages takes about 30 to 45 minutes. Then you move back up the ladder from stage 4 to 3 to 2 to 1. At that point, about 70 to 90 minutes after the onset of sleep, something peculiar happens. Stage 1 does not turn into drowsy wakefulness, as one might expect. Instead, your brain begins to emit long bursts of very rapid, somewhat irregular waves. Your heart rate increases, your blood pressure rises, and your breathing speeds up and becomes more irregular. Small twitches in your face and fingers may occur. In men, the penis becomes somewhat erect as vascular tissue relaxes and blood fills the genital area faster than it exits. In women, the clitoris enlarges and vaginal lubrication increases. At the same time, most skeletal muscles go limp, preventing your aroused brain from producing physical movement. You have entered the realm of REM.

Because cats sleep up to 80% of the time, it is easy to catch them in the various stages of slumber. A cat in non-REM sleep (left) remains upright, but during the REM phase (right), its muscles go limp and it flops onto its side.

Thinking Critically

Consider Other Interpretations

In a state between sleeping and waking, some people have thought they've seen a ghost or a visitor from space in their bedroom—a pretty scary experience. What other explanation is possible?

Because the brain is extremely active while the body is entirely inactive, REM sleep has also been called "paradoxical sleep." It is during these periods that vivid dreams are most likely to occur. People report dreams when they are awakened from non-REM sleep, too; in one study, dream reports occurred 82% of the time when sleepers were awakened during REM sleep, but they also occurred 51% of the time when people were awakened during non-REM sleep (Foulkes, 1962). Non-REM dreams, however, tend to be shorter, less vivid, and more realistic than REM dreams, except in the hour or so before a person wakes up in the morning.

Occasionally, as the sleeper wakes up, a curious phenomenon occurs. The person emerges from REM sleep before the muscle paralysis characteristic of that stage has entirely disappeared, and becomes aware of an inability to move. About 30% of the general population has experienced at least one such episode, and about 5% have had a "waking dream" in this state. Their eyes are open, but what they "see" are dreamlike hallucinations, most often shadowy figures. They may even "see" a ghost or space alien sitting on their beds or hovering in a hallway, a scary image that they would regard as perfectly normal if it were part of a midnight nightmare. Instead of saying "Ah! How interesting! I am having a waking dream!" some people interpret this experience literally and come to believe they have been visited by aliens or are being haunted by ghosts (Clancy, 2005; McNally, 2003).

REM and non-REM sleep continue to alternate throughout the night. As the hours pass, stages 3 and 4 tend to shorten or even disappear and REM periods tend to lengthen and occur closer together (see Figure 5.2). This pattern explains why you are likely to be dreaming when the alarm clock goes off in the morning. But the cycles are far from regular. An individual may bounce directly from stage 4 back to stage 2 or go from REM to stage 2 and then back to REM. Also, the time between REM and non-REM is highly variable, differing from person to person and also within any given individual.

The reasons for REM sleep are still controversial. If you wake people up every time they lapse into REM sleep, nothing dramatic will happen. When finally allowed to sleep normally, however, they will spend a longer time than usual in the REM phase, and it will be hard to rouse them. Electrical brain activity associated with REM may burst through into non-REM sleep and even into wakefulness, as if the person is making up for something he or she had been deprived of.

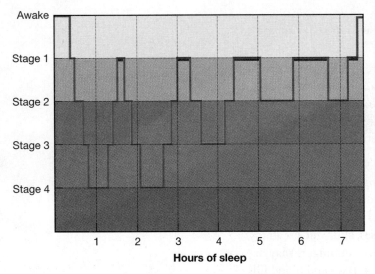

FIGURE 5.2 **A Typical Night's Sleep for a Young Adult**

In this graph, the thin horizontal red bars represent time spent in REM sleep. REM periods tend to lengthen as the night wears on, but stages 3 and 4, which dominate during non-REM sleep early in the night, may disappear as morning approaches (from Kelly, 1981).

Some researchers have proposed that this "something" is connected with dreaming, but that idea has problems. For one thing, in rare cases, brain-damaged patients have lost the capacity to dream, yet they continue to show the normal sleep stages, including REM (Bischof & Bassetti, 2004). Moreover, although all mammals experience REM sleep—the only known exceptions are the bottlenose dolphin and the porpoise—it seems unlikely that rats and anteaters have the cognitive abilities required to construct dreams. Moles, which can hardly move their eyes at all, nonetheless show EEG patterns associated with REM sleep. According to one well-known dream researcher, "no one, but no one, has been able to come up with a convincing explanation for REM sleep" (G. William Domhoff, personal communication).

Whatever your age, sometimes the urge to sleep is irresistible, especially because in fast-paced modern societies, many people—even young children—do not get as much sleep as they need.

Why We Sleep

Generally speaking, sleep appears to provide a time-out period, so that the body can eliminate waste products from muscles, repair cells, conserve or replenish energy stores, strengthen the immune system, or recover abilities lost during the day. When we do not get enough sleep, our bodies operate abnormally. For example, levels of hormones necessary for normal muscle development and proper immune system functioning decline (Leproult, Van Reeth, et al., 1997).

Although most people can still get along reasonably well after a day or two of sleeplessness, sleep deprivation that lasts for four days or longer is quite uncomfortable, and soon becomes unbearable. In animals, forced sleeplessness leads to infections and eventually death, and the same seems to be true for people. In one tragic case, a 51-year-old man abruptly began to lose sleep. After sinking deeper and deeper into an exhausted stupor, he developed a lung infection and died. An autopsy showed that he had lost almost all of the large neurons in two areas of the thalamus that have been linked to sleep and hormonal circadian rhythms (Lugaresi et al., 1986).

THE MENTAL CONSEQUENCES OF SLEEPLESSNESS.   Sleep is also necessary for normal *mental* functioning. Chronic sleep deprivation increases levels of the stress hormone cortisol, which may damage or impair brain cells that are necessary for learning and memory (Leproult, Copinschi, et al., 1997). Also, new brain cells may either fail to develop or may mature abnormally (Guzman-Marin et al., 2005). Perhaps in part because of such damage, after the loss of even a single night's sleep, mental flexibility, attention, and creativity all suffer. After several days of staying awake, people may even begin to have hallucinations and delusions (Dement, 1978).

Of course, sleep deprivation rarely reaches that point, but people frequently suffer milder versions. According to Statistics Canada, 3.3 million Canadians (about 1 out of 7 people over the age of 15) are plagued by chronic insomnia—difficulty falling or staying asleep (Statistics Canada, 2005). Insomnia can result from worry and anxiety, psychological problems, physical problems such as arthritis, and irregular or overly demanding work and study schedules. The result can be grogginess the next day. In a Canadian study of insomnia, Laval University's Charles Morin followed almost 400 insomniacs undergoing treatment for the condition. More than half the group (54%) improved with treatment, but 27% relapsed afterward, indicating that the treatment was only a short-term solution (Morin et al., 2009). For advice on how to get a better night's sleep, see Taking Psychology with You.

The driver of this truck crashed when he apparently fell asleep at the wheel. Thousands of serious and fatal car and truck accidents occur each year because of driver fatigue.

Another cause of daytime sleepiness is sleep apnea, a disorder in which breathing periodically stops for a few moments, causing the person to choke and gasp. Breathing may cease hundreds of times a night, often without the sleeper's realizing it. Sleep apnea is seen most often in older males and overweight people but also occurs in others. It has several causes, from blockage of air passages to failure of the brain to control respiration correctly. Over time, it can cause high blood pressure and irregular heartbeat; it may gradually erode a person's health, and is associated with a shortened life expectancy (Young et al., 2008).

In narcolepsy, another serious disorder, an individual is subject to irresistible and unpredictable daytime attacks of sleepiness lasting from 5 to 30 minutes. When the person lapses into sleep, he or she is likely to fall immediately into the REM stage. Some 27 000 Canadians suffer from this condition, many without knowing it. Narcolepsy seems to be caused by the degeneration of certain neurons in the hypothalamus, possibly owing to an autoimmune malfunction or genetic abnormalities (Lin, Hungs, & Mignot, 2001; Mieda et al., 2004).

Other disorders also disrupt sleep, including some that involve odd or dangerous behaviour. For example, in REM behaviour disorder, the muscle paralysis associated with REM sleep does not occur, and the sleeper (usually a male) becomes physically active, often acting out a dream. If dreaming about football, he may try to "tackle" a piece of furniture; if dreaming about a kitten, he may try to pet it. A person with this disorder is unaware of what he is doing, but his partner is likely to be all too aware!

However, the most common cause of daytime sleepiness is probably the most obvious one—staying up late and therefore not getting enough sleep. Two-thirds of all North Americans get fewer than the recommended seven or eight hours of sleep and students get only about six hours of sleep per night on average. Some people do fine on relatively few hours of sleep, but most adults need more than six hours for optimal performance and many adolescents need ten. When people don't get enough sleep, they are more likely to get into traffic and work accidents. In the United States, the National Transportation Safety Board estimates that drowsiness is involved in 100 000 vehicle accidents a year, causing 1500 road deaths and 71 000 injuries. Sleep deprivation also leads to accidents and errors in the workplace, a concern especially for first-year doctors doing their medical residency. Many countries limit work hours for airline pilots, truck drivers, and nuclear-plant operators, but medical residents still often work 24- to 30-hour shifts (Landrigan et al., 2008).

sleep apnea A disorder in which breathing briefly stops during sleep, causing the person to choke and gasp and momentarily awaken.

narcolepsy A sleep disorder involving sudden and unpredictable daytime attacks of sleepiness or lapses into REM sleep.

REM behaviour disorder A disorder in which the muscle paralysis that normally occurs during REM sleep is absent or incomplete, and the sleeper is able to act out his or her dreams.

Don't doze off as we tell you this, but lack of sleep has also been linked to lower grades (Wolfson & Carskadon, 1998). In one real-world experiment, researchers had elementary and middle-school students go to sleep at their normal time for a week, earlier than usual for a week, and much later than usual for a week. Their teachers, who were blind to which condition a child was in during any given week, reported more academic and attention problems when a child stayed up late (Fallone et al., 2005). And it is not just young children who need their sleep. As sleep researcher James Maas (1998) has noted, many high school and college students drag themselves through the day "like walking zombies . . . moody, lethargic, and unprepared or unable to learn."

Late hours or inadequate sleep won't do anything for your grade-point average. Daytime drowsiness can interfere with reaction time, concentration, and the ability to learn.

THE MENTAL BENEFITS OF SLEEP.   Just as sleepiness can interfere with good mental functioning, so a good night's sleep can promote it—and not just because you are well rested. In a classic study conducted nearly a century ago, students who slept for eight hours after learning lists of nonsense syllables retained them better than students who went about their usual business (Jenkins & Dallenbach, 1924). For years, researchers attributed this result to the lack of new information coming into the brain during sleep, information that could interfere with already-established memories. Today, however, many scientists believe that sleep plays a more active role by contributing to consolidation, in which the synaptic changes associated with recently stored memories become durable and stable, making memory more reliable (Stickgold, 2005) (see Chapter 10). One theory is that during sleep the neural changes involved in a recent memory are reactivated, making those changes in memory more permanent (Rasch et al., 2007).

Improvements in memory have been associated most closely with REM sleep and slow-wave sleep (stages 3 and 4), and with memory for specific motor and perceptual skills. For example, in one study, when people or animals learned a perceptual task and were allowed to get normal REM sleep, their memory for the task was better the next day, even when they had been awakened during non-REM periods. When they were deprived of REM sleep, however, their memories were impaired (Karni et al., 1994). But sleep also seems to strengthen other kinds of memories, including the recollection of events, locations, and facts (Rasch & Born, 2008). Emotional memories, especially, are improved with sleep: When people look at emotionally arousing scenes in the morning or evening and are then tested for their memory of the materials after 12 hours of daytime wakefulness or nighttime sleep, those tested after sleeping recall the emotional scenes more reliably than the neutral ones (Hu, Stylos-Allan, & Walker, 2006). They also do better on negative emotional scenes than other participants do (Payne et al., 2008). (See Figure 5.3.) And when people learn a computerized task—hitting keys when they see a dot in different places on a screen—some of the same brain areas that are active during the task are active later during REM sleep (Maquet et al., 2000).

If sleep enhances memory, perhaps it also enhances problem solving, which relies on information stored in memory. At least one study suggests that it does. German researchers gave volunteers a math test that required them to use two mathematical rules to generate one string of numbers from another and to deduce the final digit in the new sequence as quickly as possible. The volunteers were not told about a hidden shortcut that would enable them to calculate the final digit almost immediately.

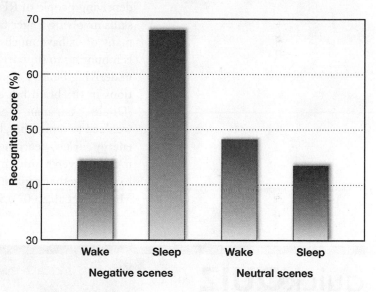

FIGURE 5.3 Sleep and Consolidation in Memory

When college students studied neutral scenes (e.g., an ordinary car) and emotionally negative scenes (e.g., a car totalled in an accident), sleep affected how well they later recognized the objects in the scenes. Students who studied the scenes in the evening and then got a night's sleep before being tested did better at recognizing emotional objects than did those who studied the scenes in the morning and were tested after 12 hours of daytime wakefulness (Payne et al., 2008).

consolidation A process by which the synaptic changes associated with recently stored memories become durable and stable, causing memory to become more reliable.

One group was trained in the evening and then got to snooze for eight hours before returning to the problem. Another group was also trained in the evening but then stayed awake for eight hours before coming back to the problem. A third group was trained in the morning and stayed awake all day, as the individuals normally would, before taking the test. Those people who had the nighttime sleep were nearly three times likelier to discover the hidden shortcut than those in the other two groups (Wagner et al., 2004). On the basis of other research, the scientist who led this study attributed the insight-enhancing effects of sleep to the long-term storage of memories during deep (slow-wave) sleep, which occurs primarily during the first four hours of the night. In a related study, researchers had people solve problems in a word game in the morning and again in the afternoon. Before starting the afternoon session, some participants took naps that included REM sleep. Others merely rested or took naps that included no REM sleep. Only those in the REM-sleep group improved their scores in the afternoon, apparently because they realized at some level that half the answers to the morning's puzzles were also answers to the afternoon's problems (Cai et al., 2009).

Researchers are not unanimous on the role of sleep in learning and memory; some studies have produced negative results (Vertes & Siegel, 2005). In one study, researchers who believe that sleep promotes consolidation found to their surprise that depriving people of REM sleep actually improved memory for motor and perceptual skills involving finger tapping and mirror tracing (Rasch et al., 2009). (Of course, not many of us have much occasion to use these particular skills!) Nonetheless, evidence is mounting to support the importance of sleep in memory and problem solving. The underlying biology appears to involve not only the formation of new synaptic connections in the brain but also the weakening of connections that are no longer needed (Donlea, Ramanan, & Shaw, 2009; Gilestro, Tononi, & Cirelli, 2009). In other words, we sleep to remember, but we also sleep to forget, so that the brain will have space and energy for new learning. Remember that the next time you are tempted to pull an all-nighter. Even a quick nap may help your mental functioning and increase your ability to put together separately learned facts in new ways (Lau, Alger, & Fishbein, 2008; Mednick et al., 2002). Sleep is not a waste of time; it's an excellent use of it.

---

quickQUIZ

✔•Quick Review on MyPsychLab

Wake up and take this quiz!

A. Match each term with the appropriate phrase.

1. REM periods	a. delta waves and talking in one's sleep
2. Alpha	b. irregular brain waves and light sleep
3. Stage 4 sleep	c. person is relaxed but awake
4. Stage 1 sleep	d. active brain but inactive muscles

B. Sleep is necessary for normal (a) physical and mental functioning, (b) mental functioning but not physical functioning, (c) physical functioning but not mental functioning.

C. What happens when people are deprived of REM sleep over a short period?

D. *True or false:* Most people need more than six hours of sleep a night.

E. *True or false:* Only REM sleep has been associated with dreaming and memory consolidation.

Answers:

A. 1. d 2. c 3. a 4. b B. a C. When they fall asleep, they spend more time than usual in the REM phase and they become harder to wake during this phase. D. true E. false

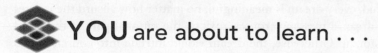 **YOU** are about to learn . . .

◆ Freud's theory that dreams are the "royal road to the unconscious."
◆ how dreams might be related to your current problems and concerns.
◆ how dreams might be related to ordinary daytime thoughts.
◆ how dreams could be caused by meaningless brain-stem signals.

EXPLORING THE DREAM WORLD

Every culture has its theories about dreams. In some cultures, dreams are believed to occur when the spirit leaves the body to wander the world or speak to the gods. In others, dreams are thought to reveal the future. A Chinese Taoist of the third century BCE pondered the possible reality of the dream world. He told of dreaming that he was a butterfly flitting about. "Suddenly I woke up and I was indeed Chuang Tzu. Did Chuang Tzu dream he was a butterfly, or did the butterfly dream he was Chuang Tzu?"

For years, researchers believed that everyone dreams, and, indeed, most people who claim they never have dreams will in fact report them if they are awakened during REM sleep. However, as we noted earlier, there are rare cases of people who apparently do not dream at all. Most of these individuals have suffered some brain injury (Pagel, 2003).

In dreaming, the focus of attention is inward, though occasionally an external event, such as a wailing siren, can influence the dream's content. While a dream is in progress, it may be vivid or vague, terrifying or peaceful. It may also seem to make perfect sense—until you wake up and recall it as illogical, bizarre, and disjointed. Although most of us are unaware of our bodies or where we are while we are dreaming, some people say that they occasionally have **lucid dreams**, in which they know they are dreaming and feel as though they are conscious (LaBerge & Levitan, 1995). A few even claim that they can control the action in these dreams, much as a scriptwriter decides what will happen in a movie, although this ability is probably rare.

One issue that has bothered sleep researchers for years is whether the eye movements of REM sleep correspond to events and actions in a dream. Are the eyes tracking these images? Some researchers believe that in adult dreamers, eye movements do resemble those of waking life, when the eyes and head move in synchrony as the person moves about and shifts his or her gaze (J. H. Herman, 1992). But others think that eye movements are no more related to dream content than are inner-ear muscle contractions, which also occur during REM sleep.

Why do the images in dreams arise at all? Why doesn't the brain just rest, switching off all thoughts and images and launching us into a coma? Why, instead, do we spend our nights taking a chemistry exam, reliving an old love affair, flying through the air, or fleeing from monsters in the fantasy world of our dreams? We will consider four of the leading explanations and then evaluate them.

Dreams as Unconscious Wishes

One of the first psychological theorists to take dreams seriously was Sigmund Freud, the founder of psychoanalysis. After analyzing many of his patients' dreams and some of his own, Freud concluded that our nighttime fantasies provide insight into desires, motives, and conflicts of which we are unaware—a "royal road to the unconscious." In dreams, said Freud (1900/1953), we are able to express our unconscious wishes and desires, which are often sexual or violent in nature.

Simulate
Psychology Experiments Survey: Are Dreams Meaningful?

Listen
Lucid Dreaming

lucid dream A dream in which the dreamer is aware of dreaming.

According to Freud, every dream is meaningful, no matter how absurd the images might seem. But if a dream's message arouses anxiety, the rational part of the mind must disguise and distort it. Otherwise, the dream would intrude into consciousness and waken the dreamer. In dreams, therefore, one person may be represented by another—for example, a father by a brother—or even by several different characters. Similarly, thoughts and objects are translated into symbolic images. A penis may be disguised as a snake, umbrella, or dagger; a vagina as a tunnel or cave; and the human body as a house. Because reality is distorted in such ways, a dream resembles a psychosis, a severe mental disturbance; each night, we must become temporarily delusional so that our anxiety will be kept at bay and our sleep will not be disrupted.

To understand a dream, said Freud, we must distinguish its *manifest content*, the aspects of it that we consciously experience during sleep and may remember upon waking, from its hidden *latent content*, the unconscious wishes and thoughts being expressed symbolically. Freud warned against the simple-minded translation of symbols, however—the kind of interpretation that often turns up in magazines and popular books promising to tell you exactly what your dreams mean. Each dream, said Freud, had to be analyzed in the context of the dreamer's waking life, as well as the person's associations with the dream's contents. Not everything in a dream is symbolic. Sometimes, Freud cautioned, "A cigar is only a cigar."

Dreams as Efforts to Deal with Problems

Another explanation holds that dreams reflect the ongoing *conscious* preoccupations of waking life, such as concerns over relationships, work, sex, or health (Cartwright, 1977; Hall, 1953a, b). In this *problem-focused approach* to dreams, the symbols and metaphors in a dream do not disguise its true meaning; they convey it. For example, psychologist Gayle Delaney told of a woman who dreamed she was swimming underwater. The woman's eight-year-old son was on her back, his head above the water. Her husband was supposed to take a picture of them, but for some reason he wasn't doing so, and she was starting to feel as if she were going to drown. To Delaney, the message was obvious: The woman was "drowning" under the responsibilities of child care, and her husband wasn't "getting the picture" (in Dolnick, 1990).

The problem-focused explanation of dreaming is supported by findings that dreams are more likely to contain material related to a person's current concerns than chance would predict (Domhoff, 1996). For example, among university and college students, who are often worried about grades and tests, test-anxiety dreams are common: The dreamer is unprepared for or unable to finish an exam, or shows up for the wrong exam, or can't find the room where the exam is being given (Halliday, 1993; Van de Castle, 1994). (Sound familiar?) For their part, instructors sometimes dream that they have forgotten their lecture notes at home, or that their notes contain only blank pages and they have nothing to say! Traumatic experiences can also affect people's dreams. In a cross-cultural study in which children kept dream diaries for a week, Palestinian children living in neighbourhoods under threat of violence reported more themes of persecution and violence than did Finnish or Palestinian children living in peaceful environments (Punamaeki & Joustie, 1998).

Some psychologists believe that dreams not only reflect our waking concerns but also provide us with an opportunity to resolve them (Barrett, 2001; Cartwright, 1996). Rosalind Cartwright has been investigating this hypothesis for

Anxiety dreams are common throughout life.

© Betsy Streeter/www.CartoonStock.com

many years. Among people suffering the grief of divorce, she has found, recovery is related to a particular pattern of dreaming: The first dream of the night often comes sooner than it ordinarily would, lasts longer, and is more emotional and storylike. Depressed people's dreams tend to become less negative and more positive as the night wears on, and this pattern, too, predicts recovery (Cartwright et al., 1998). Cartwright concludes that getting through a crisis or a rough period in life takes "time, good friends, good genes, good luck, and a good dream system."

Dreams as Thinking

Like the problem-focused approach, the *cognitive approach* to dreaming emphasizes current concerns, but it makes no claims about problem solving during sleep. In this view, dreaming is simply a modification of the cognitive activity that goes on when we are awake. In dreams, we construct reasonable simulations of the real world, drawing on the same kinds of memories, knowledge, metaphors, and assumptions about the world that we do when we're not sleeping (Antrobus, 1991, 2000; Domhoff, 2003; Foulkes, 1999). Thus the content of our dreams may include thoughts, concepts, and scenarios that are or are not related to our daily problems. We are most likely to dream about our families, friends, studies, jobs, or recreational interests—topics that also occupy our waking thoughts.

In the cognitive view, the brain is doing the same kind of work during dreams that it does when we are awake, which is why parts of the cerebral cortex involved in perceptual and cognitive processing are highly activated during dreaming. The difference is that when we are asleep we are cut off from sensory input and feedback from the world and our bodily movements; the only input to the brain is its own output. Our

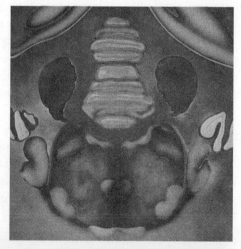
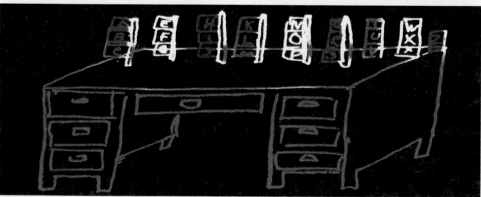

These drawings from dream journals show that the images in dreams can be either abstract or literal. In either case, the dream may reflect a person's concerns, problems, and interests. The two fanciful paintings at the top represent the dreams of a person who worked all day long with brain tissue, which the drawings rather resemble. The desk was sketched in 1939 by a scientist to illustrate his dream about a mechanical device for instantly retrieving quotations—a sort of early desktop computer!

dreaming thoughts therefore tend to be more unfocused and diffuse than our waking ones—unless, of course, we're daydreaming!

This view predicts that if a person could be totally cut off from all external stimulation while awake, mental activity would be much like that during dreaming, with the same hallucinatory quality. In Chapter 6, we will see that this is, in fact, the case. The cognitive approach also predicts that as cognitive abilities and brain connections mature during childhood, dreams should change in nature, and they do. Toddlers may not dream at all, in the sense that adults do. And although young children may experience visual images during sleep, their cognitive limitations keep them from creating true narratives until age 7 or 8 (Foulkes, 1999). Their dreams are infrequent and tend to be bland and static, about everyday things ("I saw a dog; I was sitting"). But as they grow up, their dreams gradually become more and more intricate, dynamic, and storylike.

Dreams as Interpreted Brain Activity

A fourth approach to dreaming, the activation–synthesis theory, draws heavily on physiological research. According to this explanation, first proposed by psychiatrist J. Allan Hobson (1988, 1990), dreams are not "children of an idle brain," as Shakespeare called them. Rather, they are largely the result of neurons firing spontaneously in the lower part of the brain, in the pons, during REM sleep. These neurons control eye movement, gaze, balance, and posture, and they send messages to sensory and motor areas of the cortex responsible during wakefulness for visual processing and voluntary action.

According to the activation–synthesis theory, the signals originating in the pons have no psychological meaning in themselves. But the cortex tries to make sense of them by *synthesizing*, or integrating, them with existing knowledge and memories to produce some sort of coherent interpretation. This is just what the cortex does when signals come from sense organs during ordinary wakefulness. The idea that one part of the brain interprets what has gone on in other parts—whether you are awake or asleep—is consistent with many modern theories of how the brain works (see Chapter 4).

When neurons fire in the part of the brain that handles balance, for instance, the cortex may generate a dream about falling. When signals occur that would ordinarily produce running, the cortex may manufacture a dream about being chased. Because the signals from the pons occur randomly, the cortex's interpretation—the dream—is likely to be incoherent and confusing. And because the cortical neurons that control the initial storage of new memories are turned off during sleep, we typically forget our dreams upon waking unless we write them down or immediately recount them to someone else.

Since Hobson's original formulation, he and his colleagues have added further details and modifications (Hobson, Pace-Schott, & Stickgold, 2000). The brain stem, they say, sets off responses in emotional and visual parts of the brain. At the same time, brain regions that handle logical thought and sensations from the external world shut down. These changes would account for the fact that dreams tend to be emotionally charged, hallucinatory, and illogical.

Wishes, in this view, do not cause dreams; brain mechanisms do. Dream content, says Hobson (2002), may be "as much dross as gold, as much cognitive trash as treasure, and as much informational noise as a signal of something." But that does not mean dreams are *always* meaningless. Hobson (1988) has argued that the brain "is so inexorably bent upon the quest for meaning that it attributes and even creates meaning

**ACTIVATION–SYNTHESIS
THEORY OF DREAMS**

2. Cerebral cortex synthesizes signals, tries to interpret them ("I'm running through the woods")

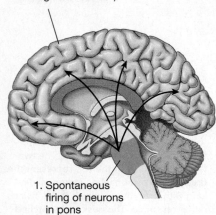

1. Spontaneous firing of neurons in pons

activation–synthesis theory The theory that dreaming results from the cortical synthesis and interpretation of neural signals triggered by activity in the lower part of the brain.

Get INVOLVED!

KEEP A DREAM DIARY

It can be fun to record your dreams. Keep a notebook or a tape recorder by your bedside. As soon as you wake up in the morning (or if you awaken during the night while dreaming), record everything you can about your dreams—even short fragments. After you have collected several dreams, see which theory or theories discussed in this chapter seem to explain them best. Do your dreams contain any recurring themes? Do they provide any clues to your current problems, activities, or concerns? (By the way, if you are curious about other people's dreams, you can find lots of them online at www.dreambank.net.)

when there is little or none to be found in the data it is asked to process." By studying these attributed meanings, you can learn about your unique perceptions, conflicts, and concerns—not by trying to dig below the surface of the dream, as Freud would, but by examining the surface itself. Or you can relax and enjoy the nightly entertainment that dreams provide.

Evaluating Dream Theories

How are we to evaluate these attempts to explain dreaming? All four approaches account for some of the evidence, but each one also has its drawbacks (see Review 5.1).

Most psychologists today accept Freud's notion that dreams are more than incoherent ramblings of the mind and that they can have psychological meaning. But most consider the traditional psychoanalytic interpretations of dreams to be far-fetched. No reliable rules exist for interpreting the supposedly latent content of dreams, and there is no objective way to know whether a particular interpretation is correct. Nor is there any convincing empirical support for most of Freud's claims. Freudian interpretations are common in popular books and newspaper columns, and, of course, on the internet, but they are only the writers' personal hunches.

As for dreaming as a way of solving problems, it seems pretty clear that some dreams are related to current worries and concerns. But skeptics doubt that people can actually solve problems or resolve conflicts while sound asleep (Blagrove, 1996; Squier & Domhoff, 1998). Dreams, they say, merely give expression to our problems. The insights into those problems that people attribute to dreaming could be occurring after they wake up and have a chance to think about what is troubling them.

The activation–synthesis theory has also come in for criticism (Domhoff, 2003). Not all dreams are as disjointed or as bizarre as the theory predicts; in fact, many tell a coherent, if fanciful, story. Moreover, the activation–synthesis approach does not account well for dreaming that goes on outside REM sleep. Some neuropsychologists emphasize different brain mechanisms involved in dreams, and many believe that dreams do reflect a person's goals and desires.

Finally, the cognitive approach to dreams is a fairly new one, so some of its specific claims remain to be tested against neurological and cognitive evidence. At present, however, it is a leading contender because it incorporates many elements of other theories and fits what we currently know about waking cognition and cognitive development.

Thinking Critically

Tolerate Uncertainty

Researchers dream of explaining dreams, and some popular writers say they can tell you what yours mean. But, at present, we can't be sure about the function and meaning of dreams. Do all dreams have hidden meanings? Are all dreams caused by the random firing of brain cells? Is dreaming all that different from our waking thoughts?

REVIEW 5.1

Four Dream Theories Compared

Theory	Purpose of Dreaming	Weaknesses
Psychoanalytic	To express unconscious wishes, thoughts, and conflicts	Interpretations are often far-fetched; there is no reliable way to interpret "latent" meanings
Problem-focused	To express ongoing concerns of waking life and/or resolve current concerns and problems	Some theorists are skeptical about the ability to resolve problems during sleep
Cognitive	Same as in waking life—to express concerns and interests	Some specific claims remain to be tested
Activation–synthesis	None; dreams occur because of random brain-stem signals, though cortical interpretations of those signals may reflect concerns and conflicts	Does not explain coherent, storylike dreams or non-REM dreams

Perhaps it will turn out that different kinds of dreams have different purposes and origins. We all know from experience that some of our dreams seem to be related to daily problems, some are vague and incoherent, and some are anxiety dreams that occur when we are worried or depressed. For the time being, we are going to have to live with the uncertainty about what those fascinating stories and images in our sleeping brains really mean.

quickQUIZ

✓•Quick Review on MyPsychLab

See if you can dream up answers to this question.

In his dreams, Andy is an infant crawling through a dark tunnel looking for something he has lost. Which theory of dreams would be most receptive to each of the following explanations?

1. Andy recently found a valuable watch he had misplaced.
2. While Andy was sleeping, neurons in his pons that would ordinarily stimulate parts of the brain involved in leg-muscle movements were active.
3. Andy has repressed an early sexual attraction to his mother; the tunnel symbolizes her vagina.
4. Andy has broken up with his lover and is working through the emotional loss.

Answers:

1. the cognitive approach (the dreamer is thinking about a recent experience)
2. the activation–synthesis theory   3. psychoanalytic theory   4. the problem-focused approach

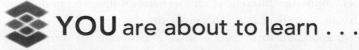 YOU are about to learn . . .

- common misconceptions about what hypnosis can do.
- the legitimate uses of hypnosis in psychology and medicine.
- two ways of explaining what happens during hypnosis.

THE RIDDLE OF HYPNOSIS

For many years, stage hypnotists, "past-lives channellers," and some psychotherapists have been reporting that they can "age regress" hypnotized people to earlier years or even earlier centuries. Some therapists claim that hypnosis helps their patients accurately retrieve long-buried memories, and a few even claim that hypnosis has helped their patients recall alleged abductions by extraterrestrials. What are we to make of all this?

Hypnosis is a procedure in which a practitioner suggests changes in the sensations, perceptions, thoughts, feelings, or behaviour of the participant (Kirsch & Lynn, 1995). The participant, in turn, tries to alter his or her cognitive processes in accordance with the hypnotist's suggestions (Nash & Nadon, 1997). Hypnotic suggestions typically involve performance of an action ("Your arm will slowly rise"), an inability to perform an act ("You will be unable to bend your arm"), or experiencing distorted perception or memory ("You will feel no pain," "You will forget being hypnotized until I give you a signal"). People usually report that their response to a suggestion feels involuntary, as if it happened without their willing it.

To induce hypnosis, the hypnotist typically suggests that the person being hypnotized feels relaxed, is getting sleepy, and feels the eyelids getting heavier and heavier. In a singsong or monotonous voice, the hypnotist assures the participant that he or she is sinking "deeper and deeper." Sometimes the hypnotist has the person concentrate on a colour or a small object, or on certain bodily sensations. People who have been hypnotized report that the focus of attention turns outward, toward the hypnotist's voice. They sometimes compare the experience to being totally absorbed in a good book, play, or favourite piece of music. Almost always the hypnotized person remains fully aware of what is happening and remembers the experience later, unless explicitly instructed to forget it—and even then, the memory can be restored by a prearranged signal.

Because hypnosis has been used for everything from parlour tricks and stage shows to medical and psychological treatments, it is important to understand just what this procedure can and cannot achieve. We will begin with a general look at the major findings on hypnosis; then we will consider two leading explanations of hypnotic effects.

The Nature of Hypnosis

Since the late 1960s, thousands of articles on hypnosis have appeared. Based on controlled laboratory and clinical research studies, most researchers agree on the following points (Kirsch & Lynn, 1995; Nash, 2001; Nash & Nadon, 1997):

1 **Hypnotic responsiveness depends more on the efforts and qualities of the person being hypnotized than on the skill of the hypnotist.** Some people are more responsive to hypnosis than others, but why they are is unknown. Surprisingly, hypnotic susceptibility is unrelated to general personality traits such as gullibility, trust, submissiveness, or conformity (Nash & Nadon, 1997). And it is only weakly related to the ability to become easily absorbed in activities and the world of imagination (Council, Kirsch, & Grant, 1996; Nash & Nadon, 1997).

2 **Hypnotized people cannot be forced to do things against their will.** Like drunkenness, hypnosis can be used to justify letting go of inhibitions ("I know this looks silly but, after all, I'm hypnotized"). Hypnotized individuals may even comply with a suggestion to do something that looks embarrassing or dangerous. But the individual is choosing to turn responsibility over to the hypnotist and to cooperate with the hypnotist's suggestions (Lynn, Rhue, & Weekes,

hypnosis A procedure in which the practitioner suggests changes in the sensations, perceptions, thoughts, feelings, or behaviour of the participant.

Thinking Critically

Analyze Assumptions and Biases

Is it hypnosis that enables the man stretched out between two chairs to hold the weight of the man standing on him, without flinching? This audience assumes so, but the only way to find out whether hypnosis produces unique abilities is to do research with control groups. It turns out that people can do the same thing even when they are not hypnotized.

1990). There is no evidence that hypnotized people will do anything that actually violates their morals or that constitutes a real danger to themselves or others (Laurence & Perry, 1988).

3 **Feats performed while under hypnosis can be performed by motivated people without hypnosis.** Hypnotized subjects sometimes perform what seem like extraordinary mental or physical feats, but most research finds that hypnosis does not actually enable people to do things that would otherwise be impossible. With proper motivation, support, and encouragement, the same people could do the same things even without being hypnotized (Chaves, 1989; Spanos, Stenstrom, & Johnson, 1988).

4 **Hypnosis does not increase the accuracy of memory.** Many people assume that hypnosis can enhance the recall of forgotten experiences, but this is not true. In rare cases, hypnosis has been used successfully to jog the memories of crime victims, but usually the memories of hypnotized witnesses have been completely mistaken. Although hypnosis does sometimes boost the amount of information recalled, it also increases *errors*, perhaps because hypnotized people are more willing than others to guess, or because they mistake vividly imagined possibilities for actual memories (Dinges et al., 1992; Kihlstrom, 1994). The hypnotized person is often completely convinced that his or her "memories" are real, but they are not. Because errors and pseudo memories are so common in hypnotically induced recall, Canadian law does not permit the use of "hypnotically refreshed" testimony in courts of law.

5 **Hypnosis does not produce a literal re-experiencing of long-ago events.** When clinical psychologist Michael Yapko (1994) surveyed 869 family therapists, he was alarmed to discover that more than half believed that "hypnosis can be used to recover memories from as far back as birth." This belief is just dead wrong. When people are regressed to an earlier age, their mental and moral performance remains adult-like (Nash, 1987). Their brain-wave patterns and reflexes do not become childish; they do not reason as children do or show child-size IQs. They may use baby talk or report that they feel four years old again, but the reason is not that they are reliving the experience of being four; they are just willing to play the role.

6 **Hypnotic suggestions have been used effectively for many medical and psychological purposes.** Although hypnosis is not of much use for finding out what happened in the past, it can be useful in treating psychological and medical problems. Its greatest success is in pain management; some people experience dramatic relief of pain resulting from conditions as diverse as burns, cancer, and childbirth; others have learned to cope better emotionally with chronic pain. Hypnotic suggestions have also been used in the treatment of stress, anxiety, obesity, asthma, irritable bowel syndrome, chemotherapy-induced nausea, and even skin disorders (Nash & Barnier, 2007; Patterson & Jensen, 2003).

Theories of Hypnosis

Over the years, people have proposed many explanations of what hypnosis is and how its effects are produced. One early notion, that hypnosis is a "trance state," was eventually rejected by most researchers. Today, two competing theories predominate, with most scientists taking a position somewhere in the middle.

DISSOCIATION THEORIES.   One leading approach was originally proposed by the late Ernest Hilgard (1977, 1986), who argued that hypnosis, like lucid dreaming and even simple distraction, involves dissociation, a split in consciousness in which one part of the mind operates independently of the rest of consciousness. In many hypnotized persons, said Hilgard, while most of the mind is subject to hypnotic suggestion, one part is a *hidden observer*, watching but not participating. Unless given special instructions, the hypnotized person remains unaware of the observer.

In his research, Hilgard attempted to question the hidden observer directly. In one procedure, hypnotized volunteers had to submerge an arm in ice water for several seconds, an experience that is normally excruciating. They were told that they would feel no pain, but that the nonsubmerged hand would be able to signal the level of any hidden pain by pressing a key. In this situation, many people said they felt little or no pain—yet at the same time, the free hand was busily pressing the key. After the session, these people continued to insist that they had been pain-free, unless the hypnotist asked the hidden observer to issue a separate report.

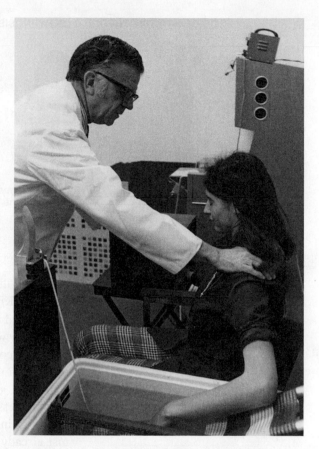

A person whose arm is immersed in ice water ordinarily feels intense pain. But Ernest Hilgard, a pioneer in hypnosis research, found that when hypnotized people are told the pain will be minimal, they report little or no discomfort and seem unperturbed.

DISSOCIATION THEORIES OF HYPNOSIS

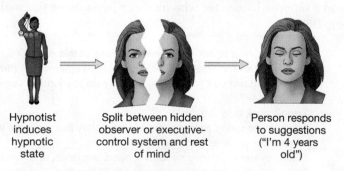

Hypnotist induces hypnotic state

Split between hidden observer or executive-control system and rest of mind

Person responds to suggestions ("I'm 4 years old")

The late Ken Bowers and colleagues at the University of Waterloo advanced a related theory, which runs counter to the theory that hypnosis is a unique dissociated state. Instead, it holds that the control of executive function (probably subserved by the frontal lobes) is weakened during hypnosis, but that this does not result in a unique dissociated state (Woody & Bowers, 1994). The result is an altered state of consciousness similar to that found in patients with frontal lobe disorders. Because the dissociated systems are freed from control by the executive, they are more easily influenced by suggestions from the hypnotist. Like the activation–synthesis theory of dreaming, dissociation theories of hypnosis are consistent with modern brain theories, which hold that one part of the brain operates as a reporter and interpreter of activities carried out unconsciously by other brain parts (see Chapter 4).

THE SOCIOCOGNITIVE APPROACH.   The second major approach to hypnosis, the *sociocognitive explanation of hypnosis*, holds that the effects of hypnosis result from

dissociation A split in consciousness in which one part of the mind operates independently of others.

SOCIOCOGNITIVE THEORIES OF HYPNOSIS

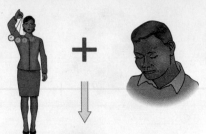

Social influence of hypnotist ("You're going back in time")

+

Person's own cognitions ("I believe in age regression")

Person conforms to suggestions ("I'm 4 years old")

an interaction between the social influence of the hypnotist (the "socio" part) and the abilities, beliefs, and expectations of the subject (the "cognitive" part) (Kirsch, 1997; Sarbin, 1991; Spanos, 1991). The hypnotized person is basically playing a role, one that has analogies in ordinary life, in which we willingly submit to the suggestions of parents, teachers, doctors, therapists, and television commercials. In this view, even the "hidden observer" is simply a reaction to the social demands of the situation and the suggestions of the hypnotist (Kirsch & Lynn, 1998).

The hypnotized person is not merely faking or play-acting, however. A person who has been instructed to fool an observer by faking a hypnotic state will tend to overplay the role and will stop playing it as soon as the observer leaves the room. In contrast, hypnotized participants continue to follow the hypnotic suggestions even when they think they are not being watched (Kirsch et al., 1989; Spanos et al., 1993). Like many social roles, the role of hypnotized person is so engrossing and involving that actions required by the role may occur without the person's conscious intent.

Sociocognitive views explain why some people under hypnosis report spirit possession or "memories" of alien abductions (Clancy, 2005; Spanos, 1996). The individual goes to a therapist looking for an explanation of his or her loneliness, unhappiness, nightmares, puzzling symptoms (such as waking up in the middle of the night in a cold sweat), or the waking dreams we described earlier. If the therapist already believes in alien abduction, he or she may hypnotize the person and then shape the client's story by giving subtle and not-so-subtle hints about what the person should say. Here is an exchange between one therapist who believes in UFO abductions and a supposed abductee who has been hypnotized (quoted in Newman & Baumeister, 1996):

Dr. Fiore:	Now I'm going to ask you a few questions at this point. You will remember everything because you want to remember. When you were being poked everywhere, did they do any kind of vaginal examination?
Sandi:	I don't think they did.
Dr. Fiore:	Now you're going to let yourself know if they put a needle in any part of your body, other than the rectum.
Sandi:	No. They were carrying needles around, big ones, and I was scared for a while they were going to put one in me, but they didn't. [Body tenses.]
Dr. Fiore:	Now just let yourself relax. At the count of three you're going to remember whether they did put one of those big needles in you. If they did, know that you're safe, and it's all over, isn't it? And if they didn't, you're going to remember that too, at the count of three. One . . . two . . . three.
Sandi:	They did.

The sociocognitive view can also explain apparent cases of past-life regression. In a fascinating program of research, Nicholas Spanos and his colleagues directed hypnotized Canadian university students to regress past their own births to previous lives. About a third of the students (who already believed in reincarnation) reported being able to do so. But when they were asked, while supposedly reliving a past life, to name the leader of their country, say whether the country was at peace or at war, or describe the money used in their community, the students could not do it. (One young man, who thought he was Julius Caesar, said the year was 50 AD and he was emperor of Rome. But Caesar died in 44 BCE and was never crowned emperor, and dating years as AD or BC did not begin until several centuries later.) Not knowing anything about the language, dates, customs, and events of their "previous lives" did not deter the students from constructing a story about them, however. They tried to fulfill the requirements of the role by weaving events, places, and persons from their *present* lives into their accounts, and by picking up cues from the experimenters. The researchers concluded that the act of "remembering" another self involves the construction of a fantasy that accords with the rememberer's own beliefs and also the beliefs of others—in this case, those of the authoritative hypnotist (Spanos et al., 1991).

How Can We Study What People Perceive under Hypnosis?

At first glance, hypnotized people seem to perceive the world quite differently from those who are not hypnotized. If a hypnotist suggests that a chicken is present, a hypnotized person will probably report seeing a chicken even though none is there. If a hypnotist instructs a hypnotized person to forget her own name, she is apt to report doing so. But are these reports of hallucinations or changes in memory accurate? Have perception and memory really been altered? Or, as the sociocognitive approach suggests, is the individual simply playing a role, acting as he or she is expected to act?

A series of studies conducted at Carleton University by the late Nicholas Spanos and his colleagues investigated this possibility. In one clever study, the researchers told 45 highly suggestible hypnotized participants that they were going to be presented with a blank sheet of paper. However, when the paper was presented, it was not blank after all; instead, it had the number eight printed on it. After the session was over, the participants were asked to indicate whether the paper had really been blank. In an attempt to pressure the participants into providing "accurate" (as opposed to hypnotically suggested) descriptions, the researchers told them that only "fakers" would claim the page was blank. Fifteen of the 45 participants still claimed that the page was blank—yet when they were given the opportunity to draw what had appeared on the page, 14 of the 15 correctly drew the number eight (Spanos, Flynn, & Gabora, 1989). This suggests that, under hypnosis, suggested "illusions" do not alter perception, but rather they alter the report of what's perceived.

Spanos and his colleagues also conducted a number of experiments on hypnosis and memory. Hypnotists claim that hypnosis can be used not only to enhance memory but also to produce "hypnotic amnesia." Spanos instructed highly hypnotizable people and less hypnotizable "simulators" to forget a list of previously learned words. On a subsequent test of memory, both recognition and recall memory were lower in the "simulators." However, these individuals recognized previously learned lists at levels below chance, indicating that they indeed remembered at least some of the words but had actively avoided indicating so (Spanos, James, & de Groot, 1990). Like the "blank" sheet of paper study, this experiment indicates that at least some of the effects of hypnosis are not really changes in perception or memory. Instead, hypnosis produces changes in people's reports of these events.

Thinking Critically

Consider Other Interpretations

Under hypnosis, Jim describes the chocolate cake at his fourth birthday and Joan remembers a former life as a twelfth-century French peasant. But lemon cake was served at Jim's party and Joan can't speak twelfth-century French. What explanation best accounts for these vivid but incorrect memories?

BIOLOGY *and Hypnosis*

Now You See It . . .

Debates over what hypnosis really is and how it works have intensified as scientists have begun to use technology in the hope of better understanding this mysterious phenomenon. We have known for some time from EEG studies that alpha waves are common when a person is in a relaxed hypnotic state. This is not surprising, because alpha waves are associated with relaxed wakefulness. The invention of brain scans, however, permits a far more detailed and useful picture of what is going on in the brain of a hypnotized person.

One recent brain-scan study showed that hypnosis can reduce conflict between two mental tasks (Raz, Fan, & Posner, 2005). The researchers gave participants the Stroop test, which is often used to study what happens when colour perception conflicts with reading. You look at words denoting colours (*blue, red, green, yellow . . .*), with some letters printed in the corresponding colour (e.g., *red* printed in red) and others in a different colour (e.g., *red* printed in blue). It is a lot harder to identify the colour of the ink a word is printed in when the word's meaning and its colour are different. To see what we mean, try identifying as quickly as you can the colours of the words in the adjacent illustration. It's pretty hard, right?

red
yellow
green
blue
red
blue
yellow
green
blue
red

In the study, hypnotized participants were told that later, after they were no longer hypnotized, they would see words from the Stroop test on a computer screen, but the words would seem like strings of meaningless symbols—like "characters in a foreign language that you do not know." During the test, easily hypnotized people were faster and better at identifying the clashing colours the words were printed in than people who were less easily hypnotized; in fact, the "Stroop effect" virtually disappeared. Apparently, the easily hypnotized people were literally not seeing the colour words; they were seeing gibberish. Moreover, during the task, these people had reduced activity in a brain area that decodes written words and in another area toward the front of the brain that monitors conflicting thoughts. Because of the suggestions made while they had been hypnotized, these individuals apparently were able to pay less attention to the words themselves during the task and thus were able to avoid reading them. They could focus solely on the colour of the ink.

Other research has found changes in various regions of the brain when people are hypnotized and lying in a PET scanner. In one study, highly hypnotizable people, under hypnosis, were able to visually drain colour from a drawing of red, blue, green, and yellow rectangles, or to see colour when the same drawing was presented in grey tones. When they were told to see colour in the grey drawing, their brains showed activation in areas associated with colour perception; when they were told to see grey in the coloured drawing, the same areas showed decreased activation (Kosslyn et al., 2000).

But what do findings like these mean for theories of hypnosis? The fact that hypnosis can affect patterns of activity in the brain has encouraged those who believe that hypnosis is a special state, different from elaborate role-playing or extreme concentration. Others feel that it is far too soon to draw any conclusions from this research about the mechanisms or nature of hypnosis. *Every* experience alters the brain in some way; there is no reason to think that hypnosis is any exception, however it may work. Moreover, recent research finds that suggestion can reduce the Stroop effect in highly suggestible people even *without* hypnosis (Raz et al., 2006).

Further research may tell us whether there is something special about hypnosis or not. But whatever the outcome of this debate, all hypnosis researchers agree on certain things—for example, that hypnosis does not cause memories to become sharper or allow early experiences to be replayed with perfect accuracy. The study of hypnosis is teaching us much about human suggestibility, the power of imagination, and the way we perceive the present and remember the past.

quick**QUIZ**

✔•⎡Quick Review⎤ on **MyPsychLab**

We'd like to plant a suggestion in your mind—that you'd be wise to take this quiz.

A. True or false:
  1. A hypnotized person is usually aware of what is going on and remembers the experience later.
  2. Hypnosis gives us special powers that we do not ordinarily have.
  3. Hypnosis reduces errors in memory.
  4. Hypnotized people play no active part in their behaviour and thoughts.
  5. According to Hilgard, hypnosis is a state of consciousness involving a "hidden observer."
  6. Sociocognitive theorists view hypnosis as mere faking or conscious playacting.
B. Some people believe that hypnotic suggestions can bolster the immune system and help a person fight disease. However, support for this belief has been modest so far, and many studies have had methodological flaws (Miller & Cohen, 2001). One therapist dismissed these concerns by saying that a negative result just means that the hypnotist lacks skill or the right personality. As a critical thinker, can you spot what is wrong with his reasoning? (Think back to the qualities of the ideal scientist, discussed in Chapter 2.)

Answers:

A. 1. true 2. false 3. false 4. false 5. true 6. false B. The therapist's argument violates the principle of falsifiability. If a result is positive, he counts it as evidence. But if a result is negative, he refuses to count it as counterevidence ("Maybe the hypnotist just wasn't good enough"). With this kind of reasoning, there is no way to tell whether the hypothesis is right or wrong.

YOU are about to learn . . .

◆ the major types of psychoactive drugs.
◆ how recreational drugs affect the brain.
◆ how people's prior drug experiences, individual characteristics, expectations, and mental sets influence their reactions to drugs.

CONSCIOUSNESS-ALTERING DRUGS

In Jerusalem, hundreds of Hasidic men celebrate the completion of the annual reading of the holy Torah by dancing for hours in the streets. For them, dancing is not a diversion; it is a path to religious ecstasy. In Saskatchewan, several Dakota–Sioux adults sit naked in the darkness and crushing heat of the sweat lodge; their goal is euphoria, the transcendence of pain, and connection with the Great Spirit of the Universe.

⊙ **Watch**
Kathy: Substance Abuse

All cultures have found ways to alter consciousness. The Mevlevis of Turkey (left), the famous whirling dervishes, spin in an energetic but controlled manner in order to achieve religious rapture. People in many cultures meditate (centre) as a way to quiet the mind and achieve spiritual enlightenment. And in some cultures, psychoactive drugs are used for religious or artistic inspiration, as in the case of the Huichol Indians of western Mexico, shown here (right) collecting Peyote.

In the Amazon jungle, a young man training to be a shaman, a religious leader, takes a whiff of hallucinogenic snuff made from the bark of the virola tree; his goal is to enter a trance and communicate with animals, spirits, and supernatural forces.

These three rituals, although seemingly quite different, are all aimed at release from the confines of ordinary consciousness. Cultures around the world have devised such practices, often as part of their religions. Because attempts to alter mood and consciousness appear to be universal, some writers believe they reflect a human need, one as basic as the need for food and water (Siegel, 1989).

William James (1902/1936), who was fascinated by alterations in consciousness, would have agreed. After inhaling nitrous oxide ("laughing gas"), he wrote, "Our normal waking consciousness, rational consciousness as we call it, is but one special type of consciousness, whilst all about it, parted from it by the filmiest of screens, there lie potential forms of consciousness entirely different." James hoped that psychologists would study these other forms of consciousness, but, for half a century, few did. Then, in the 1960s, attitudes changed. During that decade of social upheaval, millions of people began to seek ways of deliberately producing altered states of consciousness, especially through the use of psychoactive drugs. Researchers became interested in the psychology, as well as the physiology, of such drugs. The "filmy screen" described by James finally began to lift.

Classifying Drugs

A **psychoactive drug** is a substance that alters perception, mood, thinking, memory, or behaviour by changing the body's biochemistry. Around the world and throughout history, people have used psychoactive drugs: tobacco, alcohol, marijuana, opium, cocaine, peyote, mescaline—and, of course, tea and coffee. The reasons for taking such drugs vary: to alter consciousness as part of a religious ritual, for recreation, to decrease physical pain or discomfort, or for psychological escape. But human beings are not the only species that likes to get high on occasion; so do many other animals. Baboons ingest tobacco, elephants love the alcohol in fermented fruit, and reindeer and rabbits seek out intoxicating mushrooms (Siegel, 1989).

In Western societies, a whole pharmacopoeia of recreational drugs exists, and each year seems to see the introduction of new ones, both natural and synthetic. Most of these drugs can be classified as *stimulants*, *depressants*, *opiates*, or *psychedelics*, depending on their effects on the central nervous system and their impact on behaviour and mood (see Review 5.2). Here we describe only their physiological and psychological effects; Chapter 15 covers addiction, and Chapter 16 reviews drugs used in treating mental and emotional disorders.

psychoactive drug   A drug capable of influencing perception, mood, cognition, or behaviour.

REViEW 5.2

Some Psychoactive Drugs and Their Effects

Class of Drug	Type	Common Effects	Some Results of Abuse/Addiction
Amphetamines Methamphetamine	Stimulants	Wakefulness, alertness, raised metabolism, elevated mood	Nervousness, headaches, loss of appetite, high blood pressure, delusions, psychosis, heart damage, convulsions, death
Cocaine	Stimulant	Euphoria, excitation, feelings of energy, suppressed appetite	Excitability, sleeplessness, sweating, paranoia, anxiety, panic, depression, heart damage, heart failure, injury to nose if sniffed
Tobacco (nicotine)	Stimulant	Varies from alertness to calmness, depending on mental set, setting, and prior arousal; decreases appetite for carbohydrates	*Nicotine:* heart disease, high blood pressure, impaired circulation, erectile problems in men, damage throughout the body due to lowering of a key enzyme *Tar:* lung cancer, emphysema, mouth and throat cancer, many other health risks
Caffeine	Stimulant	Wakefulness, alertness, shortened reaction time	Restlessness, insomnia, muscle tension, heartbeat irregularities, high blood pressure
Alcohol (1–2 drinks)	Depressant	Depends on setting and mental set; tends to act like a stimulant because it reduces inhibitions and anxiety	
Alcohol (several/many drinks)	Depressant	Slowed reaction time, tension, depression, reduced ability to store new memories or to retrieve old ones, poor coordination	Blackouts, cirrhosis of the liver, other organ damage, mental and neurological impairment, psychosis, death with very large amounts
Tranquilizers (e.g., Valium); barbiturates (e.g., phenobarbItal)	Depressants	Reduced anxiety and tension, sedation	Increased dosage needed for effects; impaired motor and sensory functions, impaired permanent storage of new information, withdrawal symptoms; possibly convulsions, coma, death (especially when taken with other drugs)
Opium, heroin, morphine, codeine, codeine-based pain relievers	Opiates	Euphoria, relief of pain	Loss of appetite, nausea, constipation, withdrawal symptoms, convulsions, coma, possibly death
LSD, psilocybin, mescaline, *Salvia divinorum*	Psychedelics	Depending on the drug: Exhilaration, visions and hallucinations, insightful experiences	Psychosis, paranoia, panic reactions
Marijuana	Mild psychedelic (classification controversial)	Relaxation, euphoria, increased appetite, reduced ability to store new memories, other effects depending on mental set and setting	Throat and lung irritation, possible lung damage if smoked heavily

1   **Stimulants speed up activity in the central nervous system.** They include, among other drugs, nicotine, caffeine, cocaine, amphetamines ("uppers"), and methamphetamine hydrochloride ("crank," "speed"). In moderate amounts, stimulants produce feelings of excitement, confidence, and well-being or euphoria. In large amounts, they make a person anxious, jittery, and hyper-alert. In very large doses, they may cause convulsions, heart failure, and death.

stimulants Drugs that speed up activity in the central nervous system.

Amphetamines are synthetic drugs taken in pill form, injected, smoked, or inhaled ("snorted"). Methamphetamine is structurally similar to amphetamines and is used in the same ways; it comes in two forms, as a powder ("crank," "speed") or in a purer form, a crystalline solid ("glass," "ice"). Cocaine ("coke") is a natural drug, derived from the leaves of the coca plant. Rural workers in Bolivia and Peru chew coca leaf every day, without apparent ill effects. In North America, the drug is usually inhaled, injected, or smoked in the highly refined form known as crack. These methods give the drug a more immediate, powerful, and dangerous effect than when coca leaf is chewed. Amphetamines, methamphetamine, and cocaine make users feel peppy but do not actually increase energy reserves. Fatigue, irritability, and depression may occur when the effects of these drugs wear off.

2 **Depressants slow activity in the central nervous system.** **Depressants** include alcohol, tranquilizers, barbiturates, and most of the common chemicals that some people inhale ("huffing"). Depressants usually make a person feel calm or drowsy, and they may reduce anxiety, guilt, tension, and inhibitions. In large amounts, they may produce insensitivity to pain and other sensations. Like stimulants, in very large doses they can cause irregular heartbeats, convulsions, and death.

People are often surprised to learn that alcohol is a central nervous system depressant. In small amounts, alcohol has some of the effects of a stimulant because it suppresses activity in parts of the brain that normally inhibit impulsive behaviour, such as loud laughter and clowning around. In the long run, however, it slows down nervous system activity. Like barbiturates and opiates, alcohol can be used as an anesthetic; if you drink enough, you will eventually pass out. Over time, alcohol damages the liver, heart, and brain. Extremely large amounts of alcohol can kill, by inhibiting the nerve cells in the brain areas that control breathing and heartbeat. Every so often the news reports the death of a university student who had large amounts of alcohol "funnelled" into him as part of an initiation or competition. On the other hand, *moderate* social drinking—a drink or two of wine or liquor per day—is associated with a variety of health benefits, especially for adults over age 40. These benefits include reduced risk of heart attack and stroke, and antidiabetic effects (Davies et al., 2002; Mukamal et al., 2003; Reynolds et al., 2003).

3 **Opiates relieve pain.** **Opiates** include opium, derived from the opium poppy; morphine, a derivative of opium; heroin, a derivative of morphine; and synthetic drugs such as methadone. All these drugs mimic the action of endorphins, and most have a powerful effect on the emotions. When injected, they may produce a rush—a sudden feeling of euphoria. They may also decrease anxiety and motivation, although the effects vary.

4 **Psychedelic drugs disrupt normal thought processes, such as the perception of time and space.** Sometimes, **psychedelic drugs** produce hallucinations, especially visual ones. Some psychedelics, such as lysergic acid diethylamide (LSD), are made in the laboratory. Others, such as mescaline (from the peyote cactus), *Salvia divinorum* (a plant native to Mexico), and psilocybin (from certain species of mushrooms), are natural substances. Emotional reactions to psychedelics vary from person to person and from one time to another for any individual. A "trip" may be mildly pleasant or unpleasant, a mystical revelation or a nightmare.

Some commonly used drugs fall outside these four classifications, combine elements of more than one category, or have uncertain effects. For example, athletes

depressants Drugs that slow activity in the central nervous system.

opiates Drugs, derived from the opium poppy, that relieve pain and commonly produce euphoria.

psychedelic drugs Consciousness-altering drugs that produce hallucinations, change thought processes, or disrupt the normal perception of time and space.

An LSD trip can be a ticket to agony or ecstasy. These drawings were done under the influence of the drug as part of a test conducted by the U.S. government in the late 1950s. Twenty minutes after the first dose, before the drug had taken effect, the artist drew the charcoal self-portrait on the left. After 2 hours and 45 minutes, he had become agitated and inarticulate and drew the "portrait" in the centre. Three hours later, as the drug was wearing off ("I can feel my knees again"), he made the crayon drawing on the right, complaining that the "pencil" in his hand was hard to hold.

and bodybuilders often illegally use **anabolic steroids**, synthetic derivatives of testosterone that are taken in pill form or by injection, to increase muscle mass and strength. Perhaps the most famous instance of steroid use by a professional athlete was Ben Johnson's record-setting 100-metre dash at the Seoul Olympics in 1988. Sixty-two hours after winning the race in a blistering 9.79 seconds, Johnson was stripped of his gold medal and Olympic record (although his record stood in the *Guinness Book of World Records*) because examiners found illegal anabolic steroids in his blood. Steroids have been implicated in numerous physical problems in men, including heart and liver disease, decreased testicle size, and erection difficulties (Pope & Katz, 1992).

Marijuana ("pot," "grass," "weed"), which is smoked or, less commonly, eaten in foods such as brownies, is probably the most widely used illicit drug in North America and Europe. Some researchers classify it as a mild psychedelic, but others feel that its chemical makeup and psychological effects place the substance outside the major classifications. The active ingredient in marijuana is tetrahydrocannabinol (THC), which is derived from the hemp plant, *Cannabis sativa*. In some respects, THC appears to be a mild stimulant, increasing heart rate and making tastes, sounds, and colours seem more intense. But users often report reactions ranging from mild euphoria to relaxation or even sleepiness. Although THC has not been shown to be carcinogenic, some researchers believe that very heavy smoking of the drug (which is high in tar) may increase the risk of lung damage (Barsky et al., 1998; Zhu et al., 2000). In moderate doses, marijuana can interfere with the transfer of information to long-term memory, a characteristic it shares with alcohol. In large doses, it can cause hallucinations and a sense of unreality. Sometimes the drug impairs coordination, concentration, visual perception, and reaction times, though it is not clear how long these effects last. On the other hand, studies find that marijuana has some medical benefits, such as relief from pain, as we will see later when we discuss debates about legalizing drugs.

Anabolic steroids helped Ben Johnson complete a record-setting run at the Seoul Olympics in 1988, but they also eventually cost him his gold medal and Olympic record.

anabolic steroids Synthetic derivatives of testosterone that are taken in pill form or by injection, to increase muscle mass and strength.

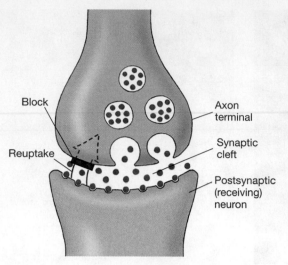

Block

Axon terminal

Reuptake

Synaptic cleft

Postsynaptic (receiving) neuron

FIGURE 5.4 Cocaine's Effect on the Brain

Cocaine blocks the brain's reabsorption ("reuptake") of the neurotransmitters dopamine and norepinephrine, so levels of these substances rise. The result is overstimulation of certain brain circuits and a brief euphoric high. Then, when the drug wears off, a depletion of dopamine may cause the user to "crash" and become sleepy and depressed.

The Physiology of Drug Effects

Psychoactive drugs produce their effects primarily by acting on brain neurotransmitters, the chemical substances that carry messages from one nerve cell to another. A drug may increase or decrease the release of neurotransmitters at the synapse; prevent the reabsorption of excess neurotransmitter molecules by the cells that have released them; block the effects of a neurotransmitter on a receiving nerve cell; or bind to receptors that would ordinarily be triggered by a neurotransmitter (see Chapter 4). Figure 5.4 shows how one drug, cocaine, increases the amount of norepinephrine and dopamine in the brain by blocking the reabsorption of these substances. Cocaine, too, seems to increase the transmission of serotonin (Rocha et al., 1998).

These biochemical changes affect cognitive and emotional functioning. For example, because of alcohol's effect on parts of the brain involved in judgment, drinkers are often unable to gauge their own competence. Just a couple of drinks can affect perception, response time, coordination, and balance, despite the drinker's own impression that his or her performance is unchanged or even improved. Liquor also affects memory, possibly by interfering with the work of serotonin. Information stored before a drinking session remains intact during the session but is retrieved more slowly (Haut et al., 1989). The ability to store new memories for later use also suffers after the consumption of only two or three drinks (Parker, Birnbaum, & Noble, 1976). Consuming small amounts does not seem to affect *sober* mental performance, but even occasional heavy drinking impairs later abstract thought. In other words, a Saturday night binge is potentially more dangerous than a daily drink.

As for other recreational drugs, there is no evidence that *light or moderate* use can damage the human brain enough to affect cognitive functioning, but nearly all researchers agree that heavy or very frequent use is another matter (see Chapter 15). For example, one study found that heavy users of methamphetamine had damage to dopamine cells and performed more poorly than other people on tests of memory, attention, and movement, even though they had not used the drug for at least 11 months (Volkow et al., 2001).

Not all drugs are equally dangerous, however. Controversy exists especially about ecstasy (MDMA), a synthetic drug that has properties of both a hallucinogen and a stimulant and that is said to increase empathy, insight, and energy. Ecstasy has provoked a great deal of hysteria; claims have been made, mostly on the basis of research with animals receiving huge doses, that the drug permanently damages serotonin cells, wipes out memory, and causes tremors like those of Parkinson's disease. But some of the best-known reports of these presumed dangers were based on research having major methodological problems; one influential report even had to be retracted in 2003 by the prestigious journal *Science* after irregularities and errors came to light. An impartial review of ecstasy research concluded that there was no evidence that ecstasy causes lasting damage "with the possible (but as yet unproven) exception of mild memory loss" (Kish, 2003). Heavy use may cause a reduction in serotonin levels, but this change has not been shown to be permanent, and it could be caused by other drugs that most heavy users take (Buchert et al., 2003).

The use of some psychoactive drugs, such as heroin and tranquilizers, can lead to **tolerance**: Over time, more and more of the drug is needed to get the same effect. When habitual heavy users stop taking a drug, they may suffer severe **withdrawal** symptoms, which, depending on the drug, may include nausea, abdominal cramps, sweating, muscle spasms, depression, and sleep problems.

tolerance Increased resistance to a drug's effects accompanying continued use.

withdrawal Physical and psychological symptoms that occur when someone addicted to a drug stops taking it.

The Psychology of Drug Effects

People often assume that the effects of a drug are automatic, the inevitable result of the drug's chemistry ("I couldn't help what I said—the booze made me do it"). But reactions to a psychoactive drug involve more than the drug's chemical properties. They also depend on a person's individual condition, experience with the drug, environmental setting, and mental set.

Thinking **Critically**

Consider Other Interpretations

One person takes a drink and flies into a rage. Another has a drink and "mellows out." What qualities of the user rather than the drug might account for this difference?

1 **Individual factors include body weight, metabolism, initial state of emotional arousal, personality characteristics, and physical tolerance for the drug.** For example, women generally get drunker than men on the same amount of alcohol because women are smaller, on average, and their bodies metabolize alcohol differently (Fuchs et al., 1995). (Female alcoholics also seem to suffer more rapid and severe organ damage than do male alcoholics.) Similarly, many Asians have a genetically determined adverse reaction to even small amounts of alcohol, which can cause severe headaches, facial flushing, and diarrhea (Cloninger, 1990). For individuals, a drug may have one effect after a tiring day and a different one after a rousing quarrel, or the effect may vary with the time of day because of the body's circadian rhythms. And some differences among individuals in their responses to a drug may be due to their personality traits. PET scans show that when people prone to anger and irritability wear nicotine patches, dramatic bursts of activity occur in the brain while they are working on competitive or aggressive tasks. These changes do not occur, however, in more relaxed and cheerful people, or in control subjects wearing fake patches (Fallon et al., 2004).

2 **"Experience with the drug" refers to the number of times a person has taken it.** Trying a drug—a cigarette, an alcoholic drink, a stimulant—for the first time is often a neutral or unpleasant experience. But reactions typically change once a person has become familiar with the drug's effects.

3 **"Environmental setting" refers to the context in which a person takes the drug.** A person might have one glass of wine at home alone and feel sleepy but have three glasses of wine at a party and feel full of energy. Someone might feel happy and high drinking with good friends but fearful and nervous drinking with strangers. In one study of reactions to alcohol, most of the drinkers became depressed, angry, confused, and unfriendly. Then it dawned on the researchers that anyone might become depressed, angry, confused, and unfriendly if asked to drink bourbon at 9:00 A.M. in a bleak hospital room, which was the setting for the experiment (Warren & Raynes, 1972).

The motives for using a drug, expectations about its effects, and the setting in which it is used all contribute to a person's reactions to the drug. For example, drinking alone to drown your sorrows is likely to produce a different reaction than partying with friends.

4 **"Mental set" refers to expectations about the drug's effects, as well as reasons for taking it.** Some people drink to become more sociable, friendly, or seductive; some drink to try to reduce feelings of anxiety or depression; and some drink in order to have an excuse for abusiveness or violence. Addicts use drugs to escape from the real world; people living with chronic pain use the same drugs in order to function in the real world (Portenoy, 1994). As we will see again in Chapter 15, the motives for taking a drug greatly influence its effects.

Sometimes expectations can have a more powerful effect than the chemical properties of the drug itself. In several imaginative studies, researchers compared people who were drinking liquor (vodka and tonic) with those who *thought* they were drinking liquor but were actually getting only tonic and lime juice. (Vodka has a subtle taste, and most people could not tell the real and phony drinks apart.) The experimenters found a "think–drink" effect: Men behaved more belligerently when they thought they were drinking vodka than when they thought they were drinking plain tonic water, *regardless of the actual content of the drinks*. And both sexes reported feeling sexually aroused when they thought they were drinking vodka, whether or not they actually got vodka (Abrams & Wilson, 1983; Marlatt & Rohsenow, 1980).

The culture in which you live in turn shapes the expectations and beliefs about drugs. Many people start their day with a cup of coffee because it increases alertness, but when coffee was first introduced in Europe, people protested. Women said it suppressed their husbands' sexual performance and made men inconsiderate—and maybe it did! In the nineteenth century, North Americans regarded marijuana as a mild sedative with no mind-altering properties. They did not expect it to give them a high, and it didn't; it merely put them to sleep (Weil, 1972/1986). Today, motives for using marijuana have changed, and these changes have no doubt affected how people respond to the drug.

None of this means that alcohol and other drugs are merely placebos; psychoactive drugs, as we have seen, do have physiological effects, many of them extremely potent. But an understanding of the psychological factors involved in drug use may help us think critically about the ongoing national debate about which drugs, if any, should be legal. In "Taking Psychology with You," we discuss some points to consider as you decide what your own position is on this issue.

Attitudes about drugs vary with the times. Cigarette smoking was once promoted as healthy and glamorous. And before it was banned in Canada in 1908, cocaine was widely touted as a cure for everything from toothaches to timidity. It was used in teas, tonics, throat lozenges, and even soft drinks (including, briefly, Coca-Cola, which derived its name from the coca plant).

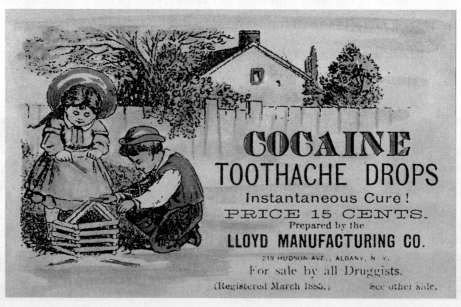

There's no debate about whether or not you should take this quiz.

A. Name the following:
1. Three stimulants used illegally
2. Two drugs that interfere with the formation of new long-term memories
3. Three types of depressant drugs
4. A legal recreational drug that acts as a depressant on the central nervous system
5. Four factors that influence a person's psychological reactions to a drug

B. A bodybuilder who has been taking anabolic steroids says the drugs make him more aggressive. What are some other possible interpretations?

Answers:

A. 1. cocaine, amphetamines, and methamphetamine **2.** marijuana and alcohol **3.** barbiturates, tranquilizers, and alcohol **4.** alcohol **5.** the person's physical condition, previous experience with the drug, environmental setting, and mental set. **B.** The bodybuilder's increased aggressiveness may be due to his expectations (a placebo effect); bodybuilding itself may increase aggressiveness; the culture of the bodybuilding gym may encourage aggressiveness; other influences in his life or other drugs he is taking may be making him more aggressive; or he may only think he is more aggressive and his behaviour may contradict his self-perceptions.

As we have seen in this chapter, changes in consciousness and body rhythms are not only interesting in themselves; they also show us how our expectations and explanations of our own mental and physical states affect what we do and how we feel. Research on SAD and PMS, the purposes of sleep, the meaning of dreams, the nature of hypnosis, and the dangers and benefits of drugs have done much to dispel many popular but mistaken ideas about these topics. And the scientific scrutiny of biological rhythms, dreaming, hypnotic suggestion, and drug-induced states has deepened our understanding of the intimate relationship between body and mind.

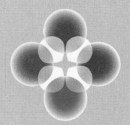

Taking Psychology with YOU

Thinking Critically in Everyday Life

The Drug Debate

Because the consequences of drug *abuse* are so devastating to individuals and to society, people often have trouble thinking critically about drug laws and policies: Which drugs should be legal, which should be illegal, and which should be "decriminalized" (that is, not made legal, but not used as a reason for arresting and jailing their users)? At one extreme, some people cannot accept evidence that their favourite drug—be it coffee, tobacco, alcohol, or marijuana—might have harmful effects. At the other extreme, some cannot accept the evidence that their most hated drug—be it alcohol, morphine, marijuana, or the coca leaf—might not be dangerous in all forms or amounts and might even have some beneficial effects. Both sides often confuse potent drugs with others that have only subtle effects and confuse light or moderate use with heavy or excessive use.

Once a drug is declared illegal, many people assume it is deadly, even though some legal drugs are more dangerous than illegal ones. Addiction to prescription painkillers and sedatives used for recreational rather than medical purposes ("pharming") has risen dramatically among teenagers and adults. Nicotine, which of course is legal, is as addictive as heroin and cocaine, which are illegal. Tobacco use contributes to more than 45 000 deaths a year in

Canada, significantly more deaths than those from all other forms of drug use combined (Health Canada, 1999a). Yet most people have a far more negative view of heroin and cocaine than of nicotine and prescription painkillers.

A study in Vancouver compared death rates from heroin overdose with heroin supply. Because heroin supply cannot be measured directly, it was estimated by the amount of opiate drugs seized in East/Southeast Asia between 1980 and 1999. The number of deaths in British Columbia from heroin overdose during that time was very strongly related to the number of heroin seizures, suggesting that the enforcement services performing the seizures are not effectively preventing the drugs from doing harm.

Emotions run especially high in debates over marijuana. Heavy use has some physical risks, just as heavy use of any drug does. However, a review of studies done between 1975 and 2003 failed to find any compelling evidence that marijuana causes chronic mental or behavioural problems in teenagers or young adults. The researchers observed that cause and effect could just as well work in the other direction; that is, people with problems could be more likely to abuse the drug (Macleod et al., 2004).

Moreover, marijuana has certain medical benefits: It reduces the nausea and vomiting that often accompany chemo-therapy treatment for cancer and treatments for AIDS; it reduces the physical tremors, loss of appetite, and other symptoms caused by multiple sclerosis; it helps reduce the frequency of seizures in some patients with epilepsy; and it alleviates the retinal swelling caused by glaucoma (Grinspoon & Bakalar, 1993; Zimmer & Morgan, 1997). In some studies, it has reduced the frequency of seizures in people who already suffer from them. However, in other studies, cannabinoids have had pro-epileptic effects, making convulsions stronger or more frequent (Corcoran et al., 2005). In Canada, the government amended the *Narcotic Control Regulations* in July 2001, and the *Marihuana Medical Access Regulations* came into force. Unlike the previous, unconditional ban on marijuana, these regulations outline a framework that allows the use of marijuana by people suffering from serious illnesses (such as multiple sclerosis or cancer) wherein the benefits of using marijuana are expected to outweigh the risks associated with the drug's use.

For these reasons, Canada's National Health Service has begun a pilot project that allows pharmacies in British Columbia to sell medicinal marijuana without a prescription. In doing so, Canada became the first country in the world to regulate and sell marijuana to patients. The U.S. government has also taken steps to decriminalize possession of marijuana (which is not the same thing as making possession legal), but this process is ongoing and it currently faces vehement opposition. Canada's Senate Special Committee on Illegal Drugs has actually recommended the legalization of marijuana. Other countries have already taken this step, including Spain, Italy, Portugal, the Netherlands, and Belgium.

Canadian organizations have also taken steps to provide supervised "safe injection sites" to drug addicts in the hope of "harm reduction" from overdoses and the spread of diseases like HIV/AIDS. In September 2003, the first such site in North America opened in downtown Vancouver. To enable it to operate, Health Canada granted the site an exemption under the *Controlled Substances Act*. The site has been very popular, and it currently supervises about 650 injections each day (Wood et al., 2002). The very existence of such sites is still extremely controversial in Canada, and debate rages about their implementation and funding.

Where, given the research findings, do you stand in this debate? Which illegal psychoactive drugs, if any, do you think should be legalized? Can we create mental sets and environmental settings that promote safe recreational use of some drugs, minimize the likelihood of drug abuse, and permit the medicinal use of beneficial drugs? What do you think?

SUMMARY

BIOLOGICAL RHYTHMS: THE TIDES OF EXPERIENCE

◆ *Consciousness* is the awareness of oneself and the environment. Changing states of consciousness are often associated with *biological rhythms*—periodic fluctuations in physiological functioning. These rhythms are typically *entrained* (synchronized) to external cues, but many are also *endogenous*, generated from within even in the absence of time cues. *Circadian* fluctuations occur about once a day; other rhythms occur less frequently or more frequently than that.

◆ When people live in isolation from all time cues, they tend to live a day that is just slightly longer than 24 hours. Circadian rhythms are governed by a biological "clock" in the *suprachiasmatic nucleus (SCN)* of the hypothalamus. The SCN regulates, and in turn is affected by, the hormone *melatonin*, which responds to changes in light and dark and which increases during the dark hours. When a person's normal routine changes, the person may experience *internal desynchronization*, in which the usual circadian rhythms are thrown out of phase with one another.

The result may be fatigue, mental inefficiency, and an increased risk of accidents.

◆ Folklore holds that moods follow long-term biological rhythms. Some people do show a recurrence of depression every winter, in a pattern that has been labelled *seasonal affective disorder (SAD)*, but serious seasonal depression is rare. The causes of SAD are not yet clear, but may involve an abnormality in the secretion of melatonin. Light treatments can be effective.

◆ Another long-term rhythm is the menstrual cycle, during which various hormone levels rise and fall. Well-controlled double-blind studies on "PMS" do not support claims that emotional symptoms are reliably and universally tied to the menstrual cycle. Overall, women and men do not differ in the emotional symptoms they report or in the number of mood swings they experience over the course of a month.

◆ Expectations and learning affect how both sexes interpret bodily and emotional changes. Few people of either sex are likely to undergo dramatic monthly mood swings or personality changes because of hormones.

THE RHYTHMS OF SLEEP

◆ During sleep, periods of *rapid eye movement (REM)* alternate with *non-REM sleep* in approximately a 90-minute rhythm. Non-REM sleep is divided into four stages on the basis of characteristic brain-wave patterns. During REM sleep, the brain is active, and there are other signs of arousal, yet most of the skeletal muscles are limp; vivid dreams are reported most often during REM sleep. Some people have had "waking dreams" when they emerge from REM sleep before the paralysis of that stage has subsided and, occasionally, people have interpreted the resulting hallucinations as real. The purposes of REM are still a matter of controversy.

◆ Sleep is necessary not only for bodily restoration but also for normal mental functioning. Many people get less than the optimal amount of sleep. Some suffer from insomnia, *sleep apnea, narcolepsy,* or *REM behaviour disorder*. Researchers are concerned about the growing number of sleep-deprived people in modern societies.

◆ Sleep may be necessary for the consolidation of memories. Improvements in memory due to sleep have been associated most closely with REM sleep and slow-wave sleep and with memory for specific skills. Sleep also seems to improve insight and problem solving.

EXPLORING THE DREAM WORLD

◆ Dreams are sometimes recalled as illogical and disjointed. Some people say they have *lucid dreams*, in which they know they are dreaming. Researchers disagree about whether the eye movements of REM sleep are related to events and actions in dreams.

◆ The *psychoanalytic theory of dreams* holds that they allow us to gratify forbidden or unrealistic wishes and desires that have been forced into the unconscious part of the mind. In dreams, according to Freud, thoughts and objects are disguised as symbolic images.

◆ The *problem-solving approach to dreams* holds that they express current concerns. They may even help us solve current problems and work through emotional issues, especially during times of crisis. Findings on the dreams of divorced people support this view.

◆ The *cognitive approach to dreams* holds that they are simply a modification of the cognitive activity that goes on when we are awake. The difference is that during sleep we are cut off from sensory input from the world and our bodily movements, so our thoughts tend to be more diffuse and unfocused. This explanation is supported by research on the content of dreams and changes in children's dreams as they mature cognitively.

◆ The *activation–synthesis theory* of dreaming holds that dreams occur when the cortex tries to make sense of, or interpret, spontaneous neural firing initiated in the pons. The resulting synthesis of these signals with existing knowledge and memories results in a dream. In this view, dreams do not disguise unconscious wishes, but they can reveal a person's perceptions, conflicts, and concerns.

◆ All the current theories of dreams have some support, and all have weaknesses. Most psychologists today accept the notion that dreams are more than incoherent ramblings of the mind, but many psychologists quarrel with psychoanalytic interpretations. Some psychologists doubt that people can solve problems during sleep. The activation–synthesis theory does not seem to explain coherent, storylike dreams or non-REM dreams. The cognitive approach is now a leading contender, but some of its specific claims remain to be tested.

THE RIDDLE OF HYPNOSIS

◆ *Hypnosis* is a procedure in which the practitioner suggests changes in a participant's sensations, perceptions, thoughts, feelings, or behaviour, and the participant tries to comply. Although hypnosis has been used successfully for many medical and psychological purposes, it does not produce special abilities. Hypnosis can sometimes improve memory for facts about real events, but it also results in confusion between facts and vividly imagined possibilities. Therefore, "hypnotically refreshed" accounts are often full of errors and pseudo memories.

◆ A leading explanation of hypnosis and its effects is that hypnosis involves *dissociation*, a split in consciousness. In one version of this approach, the split is between a part of consciousness that is hypnotized and a *hidden observer* that watches but does not participate. In another version, the split is between an executive-control system in the brain and other brain systems responsible for thinking and acting. Dissociation theories are consistent with modern models of the brain.

◆ Another leading approach, the *sociocognitive explanation*, regards hypnosis as a product of normal social and cognitive processes. In this view, hypnosis is a form of role-playing in which the hypnotized person uses active cognitive strategies, including imagination, to comply with the hypnotist's suggestions. The role is so engrossing that the person interprets it as real. Sociocognitive processes can account for the apparent age and past-life "regressions" of people under hypnosis and their reports of alien abductions: These individuals are simply playing a role based on fantasy, imagination, and suggestion.

◆ As we saw in Biology and Hypnosis, brain-scan studies are increasing our understanding of what happens in the brain during hypnosis. But it is too soon to draw any conclusions from this research about what hypnosis really is and how it works.

CONSCIOUSNESS-ALTERING DRUGS

◆ In all cultures, people have found ways to produce altered states of consciousness. For example, *psychoactive drugs* alter cognition and emotion by acting on neurotransmitters in the brain. Most psychoactive drugs are classified as *stimulants*, *depressants*, *opiates*, or *psychedelics*, depending on their central nervous system effects and their impact on behaviour and mood. However, some common drugs, such as marijuana, fall outside these categories.

◆ When used frequently and in large amounts, some psychoactive drugs can damage neurons in the brain and impair learning and memory. Their use may lead to *tolerance*, in which increasing dosages are needed for the same effect, and *withdrawal* symptoms if a person tries to quit. But certain drugs, such as alcohol and marijuana, also have some health benefits when used in moderation. And the effects of ecstasy are controversial; much of the research has been flawed, and permanent negative effects so far are unproven.

◆ Reactions to a psychoactive drug are influenced not only by its chemical properties but also by the user's individual condition, prior experience with the drug, environmental setting, and *mental set*—the person's expectations and motives for taking the drug. Expectations can be even more powerful than the drug itself, as shown by the "think–drink" effect. Expectations and beliefs about drugs are in turn affected by a person's culture.

TAKING PSYCHOLOGY WITH YOU

◆ People often find it difficult to distinguish drug use from drug abuse, to differentiate between heavy use and light or moderate use, and to separate issues of a drug's legality or illegality from the drug's potential dangers and benefits.

MyPsychLab

Visit **www.mypsychlab.com** to help you get the best grade!
Test your knowledge and grasp difficult concepts through

• Custom study plans: See where you are strong and where you go wrong

• Interactive simulations

• Video and audio clips

KEY TERMS

consciousness *150*
biological rhythm *150*
entrainment *150*
endogenous *150*
circadian rhythm *150*
suprachiasmatic nucleus (SCN) *151*
melatonin *152*
internal desynchronization *152*
rapid eye movement (REM) sleep *156*

sleep apnea *160*
narcolepsy *160*
REM behaviour disorder *160*
consolidation *161*
lucid dream *163*
activation–synthesis theory *166*
hypnosis *169*
dissociation *171*
psychoactive drug *176*

stimulants *177*
depressants *178*
opiates *178*
psychedelic drugs *178*
anabolic steroids *179*
tolerance *180*
withdrawal *180*

6 SENSATION AND PERCEPTION

ASK QUESTIONS . . . be willing to WONDER

- Why do some people see religious images in a tortilla or a grilled cheese sandwich?

- Why does having a cold make it harder to taste the flavour of food?

- Why does pain sometimes persist long after the reason for it is gone?

- Can subliminal messages affect what you buy and believe?

A university student reports spotting three triangular "UFOs" hovering over the highway during rush hour. An image of Jesus on a garage door draws huge crowds of people who regard the likeness with reverence. A photograph published shortly after September 11, 2001, appears to show a sinister face in smoke billowing from the doomed World Trade Center, which some people interpret as Osama bin Laden's.

We have all heard reports like these. Some of us scoff at them; others take them seriously. Are UFOs, visions of faces in everyday objects, and other strange sightings reported only by people who are silly or gullible, or do smart, savvy people see them too? If such experiences are illusions, then why are they so frequent and so detailed, and why are those who have them so confident that what they saw was real?

In this chapter, we will try to answer these questions by exploring how our senses take in information from the environment and how our brain uses this information to construct a model of the world. We will focus on two closely connected sets of processes that enable us to know what is happening both inside our bodies and in the world beyond our own skins. The first, sensation, is the detection of physical energy emitted or reflected by physical objects. The cells that do the detecting are located in the *sense organs*—the eyes, ears, tongue, nose, skin, and internal body tissues. Sensory processes produce an immediate awareness of sound, colour, form, and other building blocks of consciousness. Without sensation, we would lose touch—literally—with reality. But to make sense of the world impinging on our senses, we also need perception, a set of mental operations that organizes sensory impulses into meaningful patterns. Our sense of vision produces a two-dimensional image on the back of the eye, but we perceive the world in three dimensions. Our sense of hearing brings us the sound of a C, an E, and a G played simultaneously on the piano, but we perceive a C-major chord. Sometimes, a single sensory image produces two alternating perceptions, as illustrated by the examples at the top of page 190.

Sensation and perception are the foundation of learning, thinking, and acting, and findings on these processes can often be put to practical use—for example, in the design of hearing aids and industrial robots and in the training of flight controllers, astronauts, and others who must make crucial decisions based on what they sense and perceive. An understanding of sensation and perception can also help all of us think more critically about our own experiences, because although these processes are usually accurate, sometimes they are not.

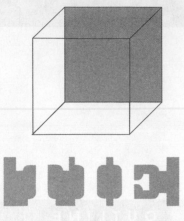

If you stare at the cube, the surface on the outside and front will suddenly be on the inside and back or vice versa, because your brain can interpret the sensory image in two different ways. The other blue-and-white drawing can also be perceived in two ways. Do you see them?

◄◎Simulate
Psychology Experiments Survey: Which Senses Do You Use?

YOU are about to learn . . .

◆ why we experience separate sensations even though they all rely on similar neural signals.

◆ what kind of code in the nervous system helps explain why a pinprick and a kiss feel different.

◆ how psychologists measure the sensitivity of our senses.

◆ the bias that influences whether or not you think you hear the phone ringing when you are in the shower.

◆ what happens when people are deprived of all external sensory stimulation.

◆ why we sometimes fail to see an object that we're looking straight at.

OUR SENSATIONAL SENSES

At some point you probably learned that there are five senses, corresponding to five sense organs: vision (eyes), hearing (ears), taste (tongue), touch (skin), and smell (nose). Actually, there are more than five senses, though scientists disagree about the exact number. The skin, which is the organ of touch or pressure, also senses heat, cold, and pain, not to mention itching and tickling. The ear, which is the organ of hearing, also contains receptors that account for a sense of balance. The skeletal muscles contain receptors responsible for a sense of bodily movement.

All of our senses evolved to help us survive. Even pain, which causes so much human misery, is an indispensable part of our evolutionary heritage, for it alerts us to illness and injury. People who are born with a rare condition that prevents them from feeling the usual hurts and aches of life are susceptible to burns, bruises, and broken bones, and they often die at an early age because they can't take advantage of pain's warning signals.

Sensory experiences contribute immeasurably to our quality of life, even when they are not directly helping us stay alive. They entertain us, amuse us, soothe us, inspire us. If we really pay attention to our senses, said poet William Wordsworth, we can "see into the life of things" and hear "the still, sad music of humanity."

The Riddle of Separate Sensations

Sensation begins with the **sense receptors**, cells located in the sense organs. The receptors for smell, pressure, pain, and temperature are extensions (dendrites) of sensory neurons (see Chapter 4). The receptors for vision, hearing, and taste are specialized cells separated from sensory neurons by synapses.

When the sense receptors detect an appropriate stimulus—light, mechanical pressure, or chemical molecules—they convert the energy of the stimulus into electrical impulses that travel along nerves to the brain. Sense receptors are like military scouts who scan the terrain for signs of activity. These scouts cannot make many decisions on their own. They must transmit what they learn to field officers—sensory neurons in the peripheral nervous system. The field officers in turn must report to generals at a command centre—the cells of the brain. The generals are responsible for analyzing the reports, combining information brought in by different scouts, and deciding what it all means.

The "field officers" in the sensory system—the sensory nerves—all use exactly the same form of communication, a neural impulse. It is as if they must all send their

sensation   The detection of physical energy emitted or reflected by physical objects; it occurs when energy in the external environment or the body stimulates receptors in the sense organs.

perception   The process by which the brain organizes and interprets sensory information.

sense receptors   Specialized cells that convert physical energy in the environment or the body to electrical energy that can be transmitted as nerve impulses to the brain.

messages on a bongo drum and can only go "boom." How, then, are we able to experience so many different kinds of sensations? The answer is that the nervous system encodes the messages. One kind of code, which is *anatomical*, was first described in 1826 by the German physiologist Johannes Müller in his **doctrine of specific nerve energies**. According to this doctrine, different sensory modalities (such as vision and hearing) exist because signals received by the sense organs stimulate different nerve pathways leading to different areas of the brain. Signals from the eye cause impulses to travel along the optic nerve to the visual cortex. Signals from the ear cause impulses to travel along the auditory nerve to the auditory cortex. Light and sound waves produce different sensations because of these anatomical differences.

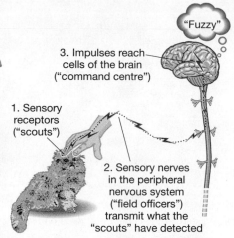

The doctrine of specific nerve energies implies that what we know about the world ultimately reduces to what we know about the state of our own nervous system: We see with the brain, not the eyes, and hear with the brain, not the ears. It follows that if sound waves could stimulate nerves that end in the visual part of the brain, we would "see" sound. In fact, a similar sort of crossover does occur if you close your right eye and press lightly on the right side of the lid: You will "see" a flash of light seemingly coming from the left. The pressure produces an impulse that travels up the optic nerve to the visual area in the right side of the brain, where it is interpreted as coming from the left side of the visual field. By taking advantage of such sensory substitution, researchers hope one day to enable blind people to see by teaching them to interpret impulses from other senses that are then routed to the visual areas of the brain. Canadian neuroscientist Maurice Ptito, for example, is studying the effectiveness of a device that translates images from a camera into a pattern of electronic pulses that is sent to electrodes on the tongue, which in turn sends information about the pattern to areas of the brain that process images (Chabat et al., 2007; Ptito et al., 2005). Using this device, congenitally blind people have learned to make out shapes, and their visual areas, long quiet, have suddenly become active!

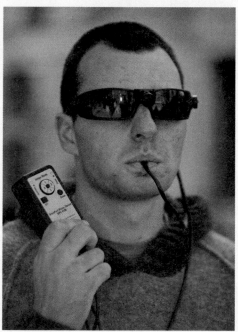

This experimental device, which sends signals from the tongue to visual brain areas, has enabled blind persons to make out some shapes—an example of sensory crossover applied to a real-life problem.

Sensory crossover also occurs in a rare condition called **synesthesia**, in which the stimulation of one sense also consistently evokes a sensation in another. A person with synesthesia may say that the colour purple smells like a rose, the aroma of cinnamon feels like velvet, or the sound of a note on a clarinet tastes like cherries. These are not merely metaphors to a synesthete; the person actually experiences the second sensation. Novelist Vladimir Nabokov said that the letter B made him see burnt sienna and T made him see pistachio green; physicist Richard Feynman saw the N in an equation as "mildly violet-bluish." People who "see" digits or letters in different colours (e.g., the number "2" in red) may have trouble naming the colour of a digit or letter when it is printed in a competing colour (e.g., the number "2" printed in blue) (Smilek et al., 2002).

It is probably more accurate to describe synesthesia as "perceptual crossover" than "sensory crossover." Experiments conducted at the University of Waterloo have demonstrated that it is the meaning of a stimulus that evokes the secondary perception, not simply the sensation of the object (such as a letter or number) alone (Dixon et al., 2000). Therefore, it is the perception of the object that leads to a synesthetic dual perception.

Synesthesia is just starting to be studied with brain-scanning technology. While listening to words, synesthetes demonstrate activation in some brain areas that are associated with visual perception (Elias et al., 2002; Nunn et al., 2002). No one knows yet why the phenomenon occurs, but researchers have offered many theories. For example, one popular theory is that all people display some degree of synesthesia early in development, and most of us (but not synesthetes) lose the dual perceptions as our brains mature and the connections between perceptual areas are "pruned." Synesthesia also clearly runs in

doctrine of specific nerve energies The principle that different sensory modalities exist because signals received by the sense organs stimulate different nerve pathways leading to different areas of the brain.

synesthesia A condition in which stimulation of one sense also evokes another.

families, and it is much more common in females, suggesting a genetic component (Baron-Cohen & Harrison, 1997; Martino & Marks, 2001). In one interesting case, a woman who had recovered from a stroke experienced sounds as a tingling sensation on the left side of her body (Ro et al., 2007). No one is certain yet about the neurological basis of synesthesia, but there are two leading theories. One attributes the condition to a lack of normal disinhibition in signals between different sensory areas of the brain (e.g., Cohen Kadosh et al., 2009). The other attributes it to a greater number of neural connections between different sensory brain areas (e.g., Bargary & Mitchell, 2008; Rouw & Scholte, 2007).

Synesthesia, however, is an anomaly; for most of us, the senses remain separate. Anatomical encoding does not completely solve the riddle of why this is so. For one thing, linking the different skin senses to distinct nerve pathways has proven difficult. The doctrine of specific nerve energies also fails to explain variations of experience *within* a particular sense—the sight of pink versus red, the sound of a piccolo versus the sound of a tuba, or the feel of a pinprick versus the feel of a kiss. An additional kind of code is therefore necessary. This second kind of code has been called *functional*.

Functional codes rely on the fact that sensory receptors and neurons fire, or are inhibited from firing, only in the presence of specific sorts of stimuli. At any particular time, then, some cells in the nervous system are firing and some are not. Information about *which* cells are firing, *how many* cells are firing, the *rate* at which cells are firing, and the *patterning* of each cell's firing forms a functional code. You might think of such a code as the neurological equivalent of Morse code but much more complicated. Functional encoding may occur all along a sensory route, starting in the sense organs and ending in the brain.

Measuring the Senses

Just how sensitive are our senses? The answer comes from the field of *psychophysics*, which is concerned with how the physical properties of stimuli are related to our psychological experience of them. Drawing on principles from both physics and psychology, psychophysicists have studied how the strength or intensity of a stimulus affects the strength of sensation in an observer.

◄◉ Simulate
Methods of Constant Stimuli

ABSOLUTE THRESHOLDS.   One way to find out how sensitive the senses are is to show people a series of signals that vary in intensity and ask them to say which signals they can detect. The smallest amount of energy that a person can detect reliably is known as the **absolute threshold.** The word *absolute* is a bit misleading because people detect borderline signals on some occasions and miss them on others. "Reliable" detection is said to occur when a person can detect a signal 50% of the time.

If you were having your absolute threshold for brightness measured, you might be asked to sit in a dark room and look at a wall or screen. You would then be shown flashes of light, varying in brightness, one flash at a time. Your task would be to say whether you noticed a flash. Some flashes you would never see. Some you would always see. And sometimes you would miss seeing a flash, even though you had noticed one of equal brightness on other trials. Such errors seem to occur in part because of random firing of cells in the nervous system, which produces fluctuating background noise, something like the background noise in a radio transmission.

By studying absolute thresholds, psychologists have found that our senses are very sharp indeed. If you have normal sensory abilities, you can see a candle flame on a clear, dark night from almost 50 kilometres away. You can hear a ticking watch in a perfectly quiet room from more than seven metres away. You can smell a drop of perfume diffused through a three-room apartment, and feel the wing of a bee falling on your cheek from a height of only one centimetre (Galanter, 1962).

absolute threshold   The smallest quantity of physical energy that can be reliably detected by an observer.

Different species sense the world differently. The flower on the left was photographed in normal light. The one on the right, photographed under ultraviolet light, is what a butterfly might see, because butterflies have ultraviolet receptors. The hundreds of tiny bright spots are nectar sources.

Yet despite these impressive sensory skills, our senses are tuned in to only a narrow band of physical energies. For example, we are visually sensitive to only a tiny fraction of the electromagnetic energy that surrounds us; we do not see radio waves, infrared waves, or microwaves (see Figure 6.1). Other species can pick up signals that we cannot. Dogs can detect high-frequency sound waves that are beyond our range, as you know if you have ever called your pooch with a "silent" doggie whistle. Bats and porpoises can hear sounds two octaves beyond our range, and bees can see ultraviolet light, which merely gives human beings a sunburn.

DIFFERENCE THRESHOLDS. Psychologists also study sensory sensitivity by having people compare two stimuli and judge whether they are the same or different. For example, a person might be asked to compare the weight of two blocks, the brightness of two lights, or the saltiness of two liquids. The smallest difference in stimulation that a person can detect reliably (again, half of the time) is called the **difference threshold** or *just noticeable difference (jnd)*. When you compare two stimuli, A and B, the difference threshold will depend on the intensity or size of A. The larger or more intense A is, the greater the change must be before you can detect a difference. If you are comparing the weights of two pebbles, you might be able to detect a difference of only a few grams, but

difference threshold   The smallest difference in stimulation that can be reliably detected by an observer when two stimuli are compared; also called *just noticeable difference (jnd)*.

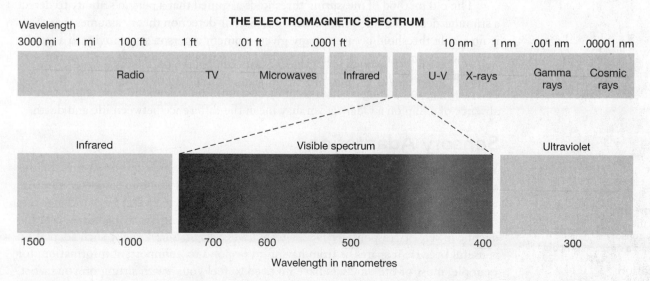

FIGURE 6.1 The Visible Spectrum of Electromagnetic Energy
Our visual system detects only a small fraction of the electromagnetic energy around us.

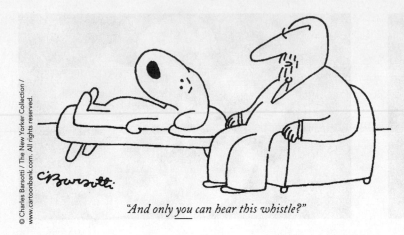

"And only you can hear this whistle?"

you would not be able to detect such a subtle difference if you were comparing two massive boulders.

SIGNAL-DETECTION THEORY. Despite their usefulness, the procedures we have described have a serious limitation. Measurements for any given individual may be affected by the person's general tendency, when uncertain, to respond, "Yes, I noticed a signal (or a difference)" or "No, I didn't notice anything." Some people are habitual yea-sayers, willing to gamble that the signal was really there. Others are habitual naysayers, cautious and conservative. In addition, alertness, motives, and expectations can influence how a person responds on any given occasion. If you are in the shower and you are expecting an important call, you might think you heard the telephone ring when it did not. In laboratory studies, when observers want to impress the experimenter, they may lean toward a positive response.

Fortunately, these problems of response bias are not insurmountable. According to signal-detection theory, an observer's response in a detection task can be divided into a *sensory process*, which depends on the intensity of the stimulus, and a *decision process*, which is influenced by the observer's response bias. Methods are available for separating these two components. For example, the researcher can include some trials in which no stimulus is present and others in which a weak stimulus is present. Under these conditions, four kinds of responses are possible: The person either (1) detects a signal that was present (a "hit"), (2) says the signal was there when it wasn't (a "false alarm"), (3) fails to detect the signal when it was present (a "miss"), or (4) correctly says the signal was absent when it was absent (a "correct rejection").

Yea-sayers will have more hits than naysayers, but they will also have more false alarms because they are too quick to say, "Yup, it was there." Naysayers will have more correct rejections than yea-sayers, but they will also have more misses because they are too quick to say, "Nope, nothing was there." This information can be fed into a mathematical formula that yields separate estimates of a person's response bias and sensory capacity. The individual's true sensitivity to a signal of any particular intensity can then be predicted.

The old method of measuring thresholds assumed that a person's ability to detect a stimulus depended solely on the stimulus. Signal-detection theory assumes that there is no single threshold because at any given moment a person's sensitivity to a stimulus depends on a decision that he or she actively makes. Signal-detection methods have many real-world applications, from screening applicants for jobs that require keen hearing to training air-traffic controllers, whose decisions about the presence or absence of a blip on a radar screen may mean the difference between life and death.

RESPONSES IN SIGNAL DETECTION

Stimulus Is...

	Present	Absent
Person's Response "Present"	Hit	False alarm
"Absent"	Miss	Correct rejection

Sensory Adaptation

Variety, they say, is the spice of life. It is also the essence of sensation, for our senses are designed to respond to change and contrast in the environment. When a stimulus is unchanging or repetitious, sensation often fades or disappears. Receptors or nerve cells higher up in the sensory system get "tired" and fire less frequently. The resulting decline in sensory responsiveness is called **sensory adaptation**. Usually such adaptation is useful because it spares us from having to respond to unimportant information; for example, most of the time you have no need to feel your watch sitting on your wrist. Sometimes, however, adaptation can be hazardous, as when you no longer smell a gas leak that you noticed when you first entered the kitchen.

signal-detection theory
A psychophysical theory that divides the detection of a sensory signal into a sensory process and a decision process.

sensory adaptation
The reduction or disappearance of sensory responsiveness when stimulation is unchanging or repetitious.

NOW YOU SEE IT, NOW YOU DON'T

Sensation depends on change and contrast in the environment. Hold your hand over one eye and stare at the dot in the middle of the circle on the right. You should have no trouble maintaining an image of the circle. However, if you do the same with the circle on the left, the image will fade. The gradual change from light to dark does not provide enough contrast to keep your visual receptors firing at a steady rate. The circle reappears only if you close and reopen your eye or shift your gaze to the X.

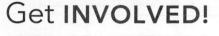
Get INVOLVED!

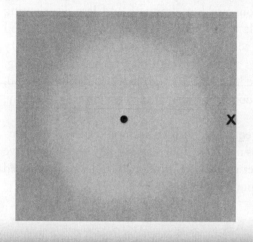
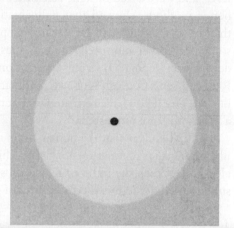

We never completely adapt to extremely intense stimuli—a terrible toothache, the odour of ammonia, the heat of the desert sun. And we rarely adapt completely to visual stimuli, whether they are weak or intense. Eye movements, voluntary and involuntary, cause the location of an object's image on the back of the eye to keep changing, so visual receptors don't have a chance to "fatigue." But in the laboratory, researchers can stabilize the image of a simple pattern, such as a line, at a particular point on the back of a person's eye. They use an ingenious device consisting of a tiny projector mounted on a contact lens. Although the eyeball moves, the image of the object stays focused on the same receptors. In minutes, the image begins to disappear.

What would happen if our senses adapted to *most* incoming stimuli? Would we sense nothing, or would the brain substitute its own images for the sensory experiences no longer available by way of the sense organs? In early studies of sensory deprivation conducted at McGill University, researchers studied this question by isolating male volunteers from all patterned sight and sound. A translucent visor restricted vision, a U-shaped pillow and noise from an air conditioner and fan restricted hearing, and cotton gloves and cardboard cuffs restricted touch. The volunteers took brief breaks to eat and use the bathroom, but otherwise they lay in bed, doing nothing. The results were dramatic. Within a few hours, many of the men felt edgy. Some were so disoriented that

Thinking Critically

Don't Oversimplify

Is sensory deprivation pleasant or unpleasant? The answer isn't "either–or"; it depends on the circumstances and how you interpret your situation. Being isolated against your will can be terrifying, but many people have found meditating alone, away from all sights and sounds, to be calming and pleasant.

sensory deprivation The absence of normal levels of sensory stimulation.

In his films, famed director Alfred Hitchcock always appeared briefly in one of the scenes, but few noticed him even when they were aware he would appear—an instance of inattentional blindness.

selective attention The focusing of attention on selected aspects of the environment and the blocking out of others.

inattentional blindness Failure to consciously perceive something you are looking at because you are not attending to it.

Hard though it is to believe, even a person in a gorilla suit may go unnoticed if people's attention is elsewhere.

they quit the study the first day. Those who stayed longer became confused, restless, and grouchy. Many reported bizarre visions, such as a squadron of squirrels or a procession of marching eyeglasses. It was as though they were having the kinds of "waking dreams" described in Chapter 5. Few were willing to remain in the study for more than two or three days (Heron, 1957).

According to research conducted at the University of British Columbia, the notion that sensory deprivation is unpleasant or even dangerous turned out to be an oversimplification (Suedfeld, 1975). In many of the studies, the experimental procedures themselves probably aroused anxiety: Participants were told about "panic buttons" and were asked to sign "release from legal liability" forms. Later research, using better methods, showed that hallucinations are less dramatic and less disorienting than at first thought. In fact, many people enjoy limited periods of deprivation, and some perceptual and intellectual abilities actually improve. Your response to sensory deprivation depends on your expectations and interpretations of what is happening. Reduced sensation can be scary if you are locked in a room for an indefinite period, but relaxing if you have retreated to that room voluntarily for a little time out—at, say, a luxury spa or a monastery.

Still, it is clear that the human brain requires a minimum amount of sensory stimulation in order to function normally. This need may help explain why people who live alone often keep the radio or television set running continuously and why prolonged solitary confinement is used as a form of punishment or even torture.

Sensing without Perceiving

If too little stimulation can be bad for you, so can too much, because it can lead to fatigue and mental confusion. If you have ever felt exhausted, nervous, and headachy after a day crammed with activities, you know firsthand about sensory overload. When people find themselves in a state of overload, they often cope by blocking out unimportant sights and sounds and focusing only on those they find interesting or useful. Psychologists have called this the "cocktail party phenomenon" because, at a noisy cocktail party, a person typically focuses on just one conversation, ignoring other voices, the clink of ice cubes, music, and bursts of laughter across the room.

Even when overload is not a problem, our capacity for selective attention—the ability to focus on some parts of the environment and block out others—protects us from being overwhelmed by countless sensory signals that are constantly impinging on our sense receptors. Competing sensory messages all enter the nervous system, however, and they get some processing, enabling the person to pick up anything important, such as her own name spoken by someone several metres away.

That's the good news. The bad news is that selective attention, by its very nature, causes us to miss much that is going on around us; as a result, our conscious awareness of the environment is much less complete than most people think. We may even fail to consciously register objects that we're looking straight at, a phenomenon known as inattentional blindness. We look, but we do not see (Mack, 2003). When people are shown a video of a ball-passing game and are asked to count the number of passes, they will often miss something as seemingly obvious as a man in a gorilla suit walking slowly through the ball court and thumping his chest (Simons & Chabris, 1999)!

Selective attention, then, is a mixed blessing. It protects us from overload and allows us to focus on what's important, but it also deprives us of sensory information that we may need. That could be disastrous if you are so focused on listening to a voice on your cellphone while you are driving that you fail to see a pedestrian crossing the street in front of you.

If you are not overloaded, try answering these questions.

1. Even on the clearest night, some stars cannot be seen by the naked eye because they are below the viewer's _____ threshold.

2. If you jump into a cold lake but moments later the water no longer seems so cold, sensory _____ has occurred.

3. If you are immobilized in a hospital bed, with no roommate and no TV or radio, and you feel edgy and disoriented, you may be suffering the effects of _____.

4. During a break from your job as a waiter, you are so engrossed in a book that you fail to notice the clattering of dishes or orders being called out to the cook. This is an example of _____.

5. In real-life detection tasks, is it better to be a "naysayer" or a "yea-sayer"?

Answers:

1. absolute 2. adaptation 3. sensory deprivation 4. selective attention 5. Neither; it depends on the consequences of a "miss" or a "false alarm" and the probability of an event occurring. You might want to be a yea-sayer if you are just out the door, you think you hear the phone ringing, and you are expecting a call about a job interview. You might want to be a naysayer if you are just out the door, you think you hear the phone ringing, and you are on your way to a job interview and don't want to be late.

◆ YOU are about to learn . . .

- how the physical characteristics of light waves correspond to the psychological dimensions of vision.
- the basics of how the eye works, and why the eye is not a camera.
- how we see colours, and why we can describe a colour as bluish green but not as reddish green.
- how we know how far away things are.
- why we see objects as stable even though sensory stimulation from the object is constantly changing.
- why perceptual illusions are valuable to psychologists.

VISION

Vision is the most frequently studied of all the senses, and with good reason. More information about the external world comes to us through our eyes than through any other sense organ. (Perhaps that is why people say "I see what you mean" instead of "I hear what you mean.") Because we evolved to be most active in the daytime, we are equipped to take advantage of the sun's illumination. Animals that are active at night tend to rely more heavily on hearing.

What We See

The stimulus for vision is light; even cats, raccoons, and other creatures famous for their ability to get around in the dark need some light to see. Visible light comes from the sun and other stars and from light bulbs, and it is also reflected off objects. Light

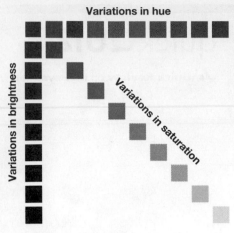

Variations in hue

Variations in brightness

Variations in saturation

travels in the form of waves, and the *physical* characteristics of these waves affect three *psychological* dimensions of our visual world: hue, brightness, and saturation.

1　**Hue,** the dimension of visual experience specified by colour names, is related to the *wavelength* of light—that is, to the distance between the crests of a light wave. Shorter waves tend to be seen as violet and blue, longer ones as orange and red. (We say "tend to" because other factors also affect colour perception, as we will see later.) The sun produces white light, a mixture of all the visible wavelengths. Sometimes, drops of moisture in the air act as a prism: They separate the sun's white light into the colours of the visible spectrum, and we are treated to a rainbow.

2　**Brightness** is the dimension of visual experience related to the amount, or *intensity,* of the light an object emits or reflects. Intensity corresponds to the amplitude (maximum height) of the wave. Generally speaking, the more light an object reflects, the brighter it appears. However, brightness is also affected by wavelength: Yellows appear brighter than reds and blues when physical intensities are actually equal.

3　**Saturation** (colourfulness) is the dimension of visual experience related to the *complexity* of light—that is, to the wideness or narrowness of the range of wavelengths. When light contains only a single wavelength, it is said to be "pure," and the resulting colour is said to be completely saturated. At the other extreme is white light, which lacks any colour and is completely unsaturated. In nature, pure light is extremely rare. Usually, we sense a mixture of wavelengths, and we see colours that are duller and paler than completely saturated ones.

hue　The dimension of visual experience specified by colour names and related to the wavelength of light.

brightness　Lightness or luminance; the dimension of visual experience related to the amount of light emitted from or reflected by an object.

saturation　Vividness or purity of colour; the dimension of visual experience related to the complexity of light waves.

retina　Neural tissue lining the back of the eyeball's interior, which contains the receptors for vision.

An Eye on the World

Light enters the visual system through the eye, a wonderfully complex and delicate structure. As you read this section, examine Figure 6.2. Notice that the front part of the eye is covered by the transparent *cornea.* The cornea protects the eye and bends incoming light rays toward a lens located behind it. A camera lens focuses incoming light by moving closer to or farther from the shutter opening. However, the lens of the eye works by subtly changing its shape, becoming more or less curved to focus light from objects that are close or far away. The amount of light that gets into the eye is controlled by muscles in the *iris,* the part of the eye that gives it colour. The iris surrounds the round opening, or *pupil,* of the eye. When you enter a dim room, the pupil widens, or dilates, to let more light in. When you emerge into bright sunlight, the pupil gets smaller, contracting to allow in less light. You can see these changes by watching your eyes in a mirror as you change the lighting.

The visual receptors are located in the back of the eye, or *retina.* (The retina also contains special cells that communicate information about light and dark to the brain area that regulates biological rhythms, as discussed in Chapter 5.) In a developing embryo, the retina forms from tissue that projects out from the brain, not from tissue destined to form other parts of the eye; thus, the retina is actually an extension of the brain. As Figure 6.3 shows, when the lens of the eye focuses light on the retina, the result is an upside-down image (which can actually be seen with an instrument used by eye specialists). Light from the top of the visual field stimulates light-sensitive receptor cells in the bottom part of the retina, and

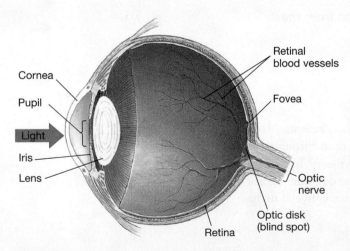

Cornea

Pupil

Light

Iris

Lens

Retinal blood vessels

Fovea

Optic nerve

Optic disk (blind spot)

Retina

FIGURE 6.2 Major Structures of the Eye

Light passes through the pupil and lens and is focused on the retina at the back of the eye. The point of sharpest vision is at the fovea.

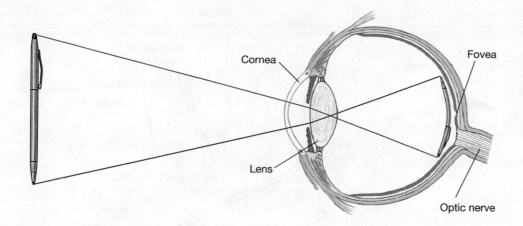

vice versa. The brain interprets this upside-down pattern of stimulation as something that is right side up.

About 120 million to 125 million receptors in the retina are long and narrow and are called rods. Another 7 million or 8 million receptors are cone-shaped and are called, appropriately enough, cones. The centre of the retina, or *fovea*, where vision is sharpest, contains only cones, clustered densely together. From the centre to the periphery, the ratio of rods to cones increases, and the outer edges contain virtually no cones.

Rods are more sensitive to light than cones are. They enable us to see in dim light and at night. (Cats see well in dim light in part because they have a high proportion of rods.) Because rods occupy the outer edges of the retina, they also handle peripheral (side) vision. But rods cannot distinguish different wavelengths of light so they are not sensitive to colour, which is why it is often hard to distinguish colours clearly in dim light. The cones, on the other hand, are differentially sensitive to specific wavelengths of light and allow us to see colours. However, the cones need much more light than rods do to respond, so they don't help us much when we are trying to find a seat in a darkened movie theatre (see Review 6.1).

We have all noticed that it takes some time for our eyes to adjust fully to dim illumination. This process of dark adaptation involves chemical changes in the rods and cones. The cones adapt quickly, within 10 minutes or so, but they never become very sensitive to the dim illumination. The rods adapt more slowly, taking 20 minutes or longer, but are ultimately much more sensitive. After the first phase of adaptation, you can see better but not well; after the second phase, your vision is as good as it will ever get.

Rods and cones are connected by synapses to *bipolar neurons*, which in turn communicate with neurons called ganglion cells (see Figure 6.4). The axons of the ganglion

Explore
Normal Vision–Nearsightedness

Light and the Optic Nerve

Receptive Fields

rods Visual receptors that respond to dim light.

cones Visual receptors involved in colour vision.

dark adaptation A process by which visual receptors become maximally sensitive to dim light.

ganglion cells Neurons in the retina of the eye that gather information from receptor cells (by way of intermediate bipolar cells); their axons make up the optic nerve.

REViEW 6.1

Differences between Rods and Cones

	Rods	Cones
How many?	120–125 million	7–8 million
Where most concentrated?	Periphery of retina	Centre (fovea) of retina
How sensitive?	High sensitivity	Low sensitivity
Sensitive to colour?	No	Yes

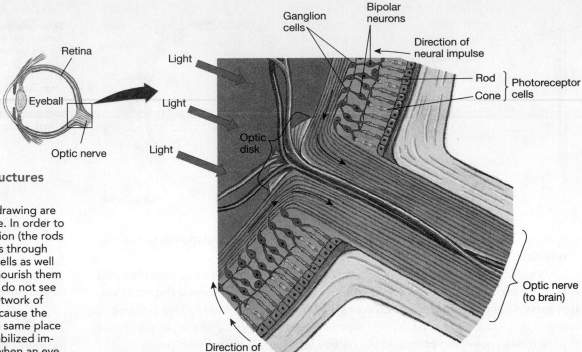

FIGURE 6.4 The Structures of the Retina

For clarity, all cells in this drawing are greatly exaggerated in size. In order to reach the receptors for vision (the rods and cones), light must pass through the ganglion and bipolar cells as well as the blood vessels that nourish them (not shown). Normally, we do not see the shadow cast by this network of cells and blood vessels because the shadow always falls on the same place on the retina, and such stabilized images are not sensed. But when an eye doctor shines a moving light into your eye, the treelike shadow of the blood vessels falls on different regions of the retina and you may see it—a rather eerie experience.

👁 **Watch**
Blind Spot

cells converge to form the *optic nerve*, which carries information out through the back of the eye and on to the brain. Where the optic nerve leaves the eye, at the *optic disk*, there are no rods or cones. The absence of receptors produces a blind spot in the field of vision. Normally, we are unaware of the blind spot because (1) the image projected on the spot is hitting a different, "non-blind" spot in the other eye; (2) our eyes move so fast that we can pick up the complete image; and (3) the brain fills in the gap. You can find your blind spot by doing the Get Involved exercise on this page.

Why the Visual System Is Not a Camera

Although the eye is often compared to a camera, the visual system, unlike a camera, does not passively record the external world. Neurons in the visual system actively build up a picture of the world by detecting its meaningful features.

Get INVOLVED!

FIND YOUR BLIND SPOT

A blind spot exists where the optic nerve leaves the back of your eye. Find the blind spot in your left eye by closing your right eye and looking at the magician. Then slowly move the book toward and away from yourself. The rabbit should disappear when the book is 23 to 30 centimetres from your eye.

Ganglion cells and neurons in the thalamus of the brain respond to simple features in the environment, such as spots of light and dark. But in mammals, special feature detector cells in the visual cortex respond to more complex features. This fact was first demonstrated by David Hubel and Torsten Wiesel (1962, 1968) who painstakingly recorded impulses from individual cells in the brains of cats and monkeys. In 1981, they received a Nobel Prize for their work. Hubel and Wiesel found that different neurons were sensitive to different patterns projected on a screen in front of the animal's eyes. Most cells responded maximally to moving or stationary lines that were oriented in a particular direction and located in a particular part of the visual field. One type of cell might fire most rapidly in response to a horizontal line in the lower right part of the visual field, another to a diagonal line at a specific angle in the upper left part of the visual field. In the real world, such features make up the boundaries and edges of objects.

Since this pioneering work was done, scientists have found that other cells in the visual system have more complex specialties, such as bull's eyes and spirals. Some cells in the right temporal lobe even appear to respond maximally to *face*s (Kanwisher, 2000; Ó Scalaidhe, Wilson & Goldman-Rakic, 1997; Young & Yamane, 1992). Some scientists have concluded that evolution has equipped us with an innate *face module* in the brain. The existence of such a module could help explain why infants show a preference for looking at faces instead of images that scramble the features of a face, and why a person with brain damage may continue to recognize faces even after losing the ability to recognize other objects. In a case described by Morris Moscovitch at the University of Toronto, a patient could recognize a face made up entirely of vegetables, like the one in the painting, but he could not recognize the component vegetables (Moscovitch, Winocur, & Behrmann, 1997).

A facility for deciphering faces makes evolutionary sense because it would have ensured our ancestors' ability to quickly distinguish friend from foe or, in the case of infants, mothers from strangers. However, the existence of face modules remains controversial among neuroscientists. Some think that infants' apparent preference for faces is really a preference for curved lines, or eye contact, or patterns that have more elements in the upper part (e.g., two eyes) than in the lower part (e.g., just a mouth) (Turati, 2004). Moreover, some of the brain cells that supposedly make up the face module respond to other things, too, depending on a person's experiences and interests. In one fascinating study, cells in the presumed face module fired when car buffs examined pictures of classic cars but not when they looked at pictures of exotic birds, whereas the exact opposite was true for birdwatchers (Gauthier et al., 2000). Cars, of course, do not have faces! In another study by the same researchers, cells in the "face module" fired after people were trained to distinguish among cute—but faceless—imaginary creatures called greebles (Gauthier et al., 1999) (see Figure 6.5).

Even if face modules and other specialized modules do exist, the brain cannot possibly contain a special area for every conceivable object. In general, the brain's job is to take fragmentary information about edges, angles, shapes, motion, brightness, texture, and patterns and figure out that a chair is a chair and that it is next to the dining room table. The perception of any given object probably depends on the activation of many cells in far-flung parts of the brain and on the overall pattern and rhythm of their activity (Bower, 1998).

How We See Colours

For 300 years, scientists have been trying to figure out why we see the world in living colour. We now know that different processes explain different stages of colour vision.

Cases of brain damage support the idea that particular systems of brain cells are highly specialized. One man's injury left him unable to identify ordinary objects, which he said often looked like "blobs." However, he had no trouble with faces, even when they were incomplete or upside down. When shown this painting, he could easily see the face, but he could not see the vegetables from which it was composed (Moscovitch, Winocur, & Behrmann, 1997).

feature detector cells Cells in the visual cortex that are sensitive to specific features of the environment.

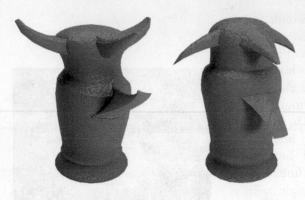

FIGURE 6.5 Greebles
Researchers trained people to recognize hypothetical "greebles" and to identify the creatures' "family" and "sex" according to subtle differences in their features. During the task, "face modules" in the participants' brains were active—yet greebles have no faces. The researchers concluded that face modules may not be responding to faces per se. Instead, they claimed that these brain areas might be specialized for distinguishing between visually similar objects within a given category. Faces happen to be visually similar (most faces contain similar features in similar places), and therefore the neural architecture for distinguishing between complex, visually similar objects might also be used for distinguishing between faces (Gauthier et al., 1999).

◆ Research
Thomas Young and Hermann von Helmholtz

THE TRICHROMATIC THEORY. The trichromatic theory (also known as the *Young-Helmholtz theory*) applies to the first level of processing, which occurs in the retina of the eye. The retina contains three basic types of cones. One type responds maximally to blue (or more precisely, to a range of wavelengths near the short end of the spectrum, which give rise to the experience of blue), another to green, and a third to red. The thousands of colours we see result from the combined activity of these three types of cones.

Total colour blindness is usually due to a genetic variation that causes cones of the retina to be absent or nonfunctional. The visual world then consists of black, white, and shades of grey. Many species of animals are totally colour blind, but the condition is extremely rare in human beings. Most "colour blind" people are actually *colour deficient*. Usually, the person is unable to distinguish red and green; the world is painted in shades of blue, yellow, brown, and grey. In rarer instances, a person may be blind to blue and yellow and may see only reds, greens, and greys. Colour deficiency is found in about 8% of white men, 5% of Asian men, and 3% of indigenous men and black men (Sekuler & Blake, 1994). Because of the way the condition is inherited, it is rare in women.

THE OPPONENT-PROCESS THEORY. The opponent-process theory applies to the second stage of colour processing, which occurs in ganglion cells in the retina and in neurons in the thalamus and visual cortex of the brain. These cells, known as *opponent-process cells*, either respond to short wavelengths but are inhibited from firing by long wavelengths, or vice versa (DeValois & DeValois, 1975). Some opponent-process cells respond in opposite fashion to red and green; that is, they fire in response to one and turn off in response to the other. Others respond in opposite fashion to

Get INVOLVED!

A CHANGE OF HEART

Opponent-process cells that switch on or off in response to green send an opposite message—"red"—when the green is removed, producing a negative afterimage. Stare at the black dot in the middle of this heart for at least 20 seconds. Then shift your gaze to a white piece of paper or a white wall. Do you get a "change of heart"? You may see an image of a red heart with a blue border.

blue and yellow. (A third system responds in opposite fashion to white and black and thus yields information about brightness.) The net result is a colour code that is passed along to the higher visual centres. Because this code treats red and green, and also blue and yellow, as antagonistic, we can describe a colour as bluish green or yellowish green but not as reddish green or yellowish blue. The existence of opponent-process cells in the visual system was first predicted by Ewald Hering (contradicting claims by Helmholtz), although Hering did not specify that these cells would be in the brain instead of the eye.

Opponent-process cells that are *inhibited* by a particular colour produce a burst of firing when the colour is removed, just as they would if the opposing colour were present. Similarly, cells that *fire* in response to a colour stop firing when the colour is removed, just as they would if the opposing colour were present. These facts explain why we are susceptible to seeing a *negative afterimage* when we stare at a particular hue—why we see, for instance, red after staring at green (see the Get Involved exercise above). A sort of neural rebound effect occurs: The cells that switch on or off to signal the presence of "green" send the opposite signal ("red") when the green is removed—and vice versa.

Constructing the Visual World

We do not see a retinal image; that image is merely grist for the mill of the mind, which actively interprets the image and constructs the world from the often fragmentary data of the senses. In the brain, sensory signals that give rise to vision, hearing, taste, smell, and touch are combined from moment to moment to produce a unified model of the world. This is the process of *perception*.

FORM PERCEPTION. To make sense of the world, we must know where one thing ends and another begins. In vision, we must separate the teacher from the lectern; in hearing, we must separate the piano solo from the orchestral accompaniment; in taste, we must separate the marshmallow from the hot chocolate. This process of dividing up the world occurs so rapidly and effortlessly that we take it completely for granted— until we must make out objects in a heavy fog or words in the rapid-fire conversation of someone speaking a foreign language. The *Gestalt psychologists* (Max Wertheimer, Wolfgang Köhler, & Kurt Koffka) started a movement that began in Germany and was influential in the 1920s and 1930s; they were among the first to study how people organize the world visually into meaningful units and patterns. In German, Gestalt means "form" or "configuration." The Gestalt psychologists' motto was "The whole is more than the sum of its parts." They observed that when we perceive something, properties emerge from the configuration as a whole that are not found in any particular component. When you watch a movie, for example, the motion you see is nowhere in the film, which consists of separate static frames projected at 24 frames per second.

One thing the Gestalt psychologists noted was that people always organize the visual field into *figure* and *ground*. The figure stands out from the rest of the environment (see Figure 6.6). Some things stand out as figure by virtue of their intensity or size; it is hard to ignore the blinding flash of a camera or a tidal wave approaching your piece of beach. The lower part of a scene tends to be seen as figure, the upper part as background (Vecera, Vogel, & Woodman, 2002). Unique objects also stand out, such as a banana in a bowl of oranges. Moving objects in an otherwise still environment, such as a shooting star, will usually be seen as figure. Indeed, it is hard to ignore a sudden change of any kind in the environment because our brains are geared to respond to change and contrast. However, selective attention—the ability to concentrate on some stimuli and to filter out others—gives us some control over what we perceive as

trichromatic theory A theory of colour perception that proposes three mechanisms in the visual system, each sensitive to a certain range of wavelengths; their interaction is assumed to produce all the different experiences of hue.

opponent-process theory A theory of colour perception that assumes that the visual system treats pairs of colours as opposing or antagonistic.

✱ **Explore**
Top-Down Processing

◀⊙ **Simulate**
Gestalt Laws of Perception

FIGURE 6.6 Figure and Ground

Which do you notice first in this drawing by M. C. Escher—the fish, geese, or salamanders? It will depend on whether you see the blue, red, or gold sections as figure or ground.

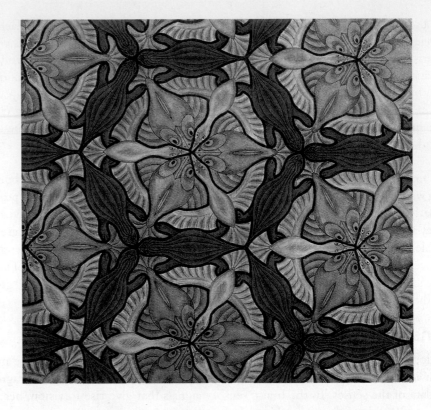

◀⊙ Simulate
Distinguishing Figure-Ground Relationships

Gestalt principles Principles that describe the brain's organization of sensory information into meaningful units and patterns.

figure and ground, and sometimes it blinds us to things we would otherwise interpret as figure, as we saw earlier.

Other **Gestalt principles** describe strategies used by the visual system to group sensory building blocks into perceptual units (Köhler, 1929; Wertheimer, 1923/1958). The Gestalt psychologists believed that these strategies are present from birth or develop automatically early in infancy as a result of maturation. Modern research, however, suggests that at least some of them depend on experience (Quinn & Bhatt, 2005). Here are a few well-known Gestalt principles:

1 **Proximity.** Things that are near each other tend to be grouped together. Thus you perceive the dots on the left as three groups of dots, not as 12 separate, unrelated ones. Similarly, you perceive the pattern on the right as vertical columns of dots, not as horizontal rows:

2 **Closure.** The brain tends to fill in gaps in order to perceive complete forms. This is fortunate because we often need to decipher less-than-perfect images. The following figures are easily perceived as a triangle, a face, and the letter E, even though none of the figures is complete:

if you are looking down f[...]
the ground if you are afra[...]

VISUAL CONSTANCIE[S]
would be a confusing pla[...]
conditions, viewing angl[...]
changing as we move ab[...]
objects themselves. This [...]
the sensory patterns they [...]
The best-studied constan[...]

1 **Shape constancy.** [...]
shape of the retinal i[...]
changes. If you hold [...]

RELATIVE SIZE

The smaller an object'[...]
farther away the obje[...]

RELATIVE CLARITY

Because of particles i[...]
or smog—distant obje[...]
or less detailed.

3 **Similarity.** Things that are alike in some way (for example, in colour, shape, or size) tend to be perceived as belonging together. In the figure on the left, you see the circles as forming an X. In the one on the right, you see horizontal bars rather than vertical columns because the horizontally aligned stars share the same colour:

4 **Continuity.** Lines and patterns tend to be perceived as continuing in time or space. You perceive the figure on the left as a single line partially covered by an oval, rather than as two separate lines touching an oval. In the figure on the right, you see two lines, one curved and one straight, instead of two curved and two straight lines, touching at one focal point:

Since the Gestalt principles were discovered, researchers have identified other cues that help us identify which parts of what we see form objects or scenes. But consumer products are sometimes designed with little thought for these cues, which is why it can be a major challenge to find the pause button on your DVD player's remote control or to change from AM to FM on your car radio (Bjork, 2000; Norman, 1988). Good design requires, among other things, that crucial distinctions be visually obvious. For instance, knobs and switches with different functions should differ in colour, texture, or shape, and they should stand out as figure. How would you use this information to redesign some of the products you use?

DEPTH AND DISTANCE PERCEPTION. Ordinarily we need to know not only *what* something is, but also *where* it is. Touch gives us this information directly, but vision does not, so we must infer an object's location by estimating its distance or depth.

To perform this remarkable feat, we rely in part on **binocular cues—cues that require the use of two eyes**. One such cue is **convergence, the turning of the eyes inward**, which occurs when they focus on a nearby object. The closer the object, the greater the convergence, as you know if you have ever tried to "cross" your eyes by looking at your own nose. As the angle of convergence changes, the corresponding muscular changes provide information to the brain about distance.

The two eyes also receive slightly different retinal images of the same object. You can prove this by holding a finger about 30 centimetres in front of your face and looking at it with only one eye at a time. Its position will appear to shift when you change eyes. Now hold up two fingers, one closer to your nose than the other. Notice that the amount of space between the two fingers appears to change when you switch eyes. The slight difference in lateral (sideways) separation between two objects as seen by the left eye and the right eye is called **retinal disparity**. Because retinal disparity increases as the distance between two objects increases, the brain can use it to infer depth and calculate distance.

Binocular cues help us estimate distances up to about 15 metres. For objects farther away, we use only **monocular cues, cues that do not depend on using both eyes.** One such cue is *interposition*: When an object is interposed between the viewer and a second object, partly blocking the view of the second object, the first object is perceived as being closer. Another monocular cue is *linear perspective:* When two lines

Simulate
Psychology Experiments
Tool: Ambiguous Figures

binocular cues Visual cues to depth or distance requiring two eyes.

convergence The turning inward of the eyes, which occurs when they focus on a nearby object.

retinal disparity The slight difference in lateral separation between two objects as seen by the left eye and the right eye.

monocular cues Visual cues to depth or distance that can be used by one eye alone.

will be round. When you set the Frisbee on a table and back away from it, its image becomes elliptical, yet you continue to identify the Frisbee as round.

2   **Location constancy.** We perceive stationary objects as remaining in the same place even though the retinal image moves about as we move our eyes, heads, and bodies. As you drive along the highway, telephone poles and trees fly by—on your retina. But you know that these objects do not move on their own, and you also know that your body is moving, so you perceive the poles and trees as staying put.

3   **Size constancy.** We see an object as having a constant size even when its retinal image becomes smaller or larger. A friend approaching on the street does not seem to be growing; a car pulling away from the curb does not seem to be shrinking. Size constancy depends in part on familiarity with objects; you know people and cars do not change size from moment to moment. It also depends on the apparent distance of an object. An object that is close produces a larger retinal image than the same object farther away, and the brain takes this into account. For example, when you move your hand toward your face, your brain registers the fact that the hand is getting closer, and you correctly perceive its unchanging size despite the growing size of its retinal image. There is, then, an intimate relationship between perceived size and perceived distance.

4   **Brightness constancy.** We see objects as having a relatively constant brightness even though the amount of light they reflect changes as the overall level of illumination changes. Snow remains white even on a cloudy day. We are not fooled because the brain registers the total illumination in the scene, and we automatically take this information into account.

5   **Colour constancy.** We see an object as maintaining its hue despite the fact that the wavelength of light reaching our eyes from the object may change as the illumination changes. For example, outdoor light is "bluer" than indoor light, and objects outdoors therefore reflect more "blue" light than those indoors. Conversely, indoor light from incandescent lamps is rich in long wavelengths and is therefore "yellower." Yet objects usually look the same colour in both places: An apple looks red whether you look at it in your kitchen or outside on the patio. Part of the explanation involves sensory adaptation, which we discussed earlier. Outdoors, we quickly adapt to short-wavelength (bluish) light, and indoors, we adapt to long-wavelength light. As a result, our visual responses are similar in the two situations. Also, when computing the colour of a particular object, the brain takes into account *all* the wavelengths in the visual field immediately around the object. If an apple is bathed in bluish light, so, usually, is everything around it. The increase in blue light reflected by the apple is cancelled in the visual cortex by the increase in blue light reflected by the apple's surroundings, and so the apple continues to look red. Colour constancy is further aided by our knowledge of the world. We know that apples are usually red and bananas are usually yellow, and the brain uses that knowledge to recalibrate the colours in those objects when the lighting changes (Mitterer & de Ruiter, 2008).

VISUAL ILLUSIONS: WHEN SEEING IS MISLEADING. Perceptual constancies allow us to make sense of the world. Occasionally, however, we can be fooled, and the result is a *perceptual illusion*. For psychologists, illusions are valuable because they are systematic errors that provide us with hints about the perceptual strategies of the mind.

✱ Explore
Five Well-Known Illusions

Monocular

Most cues to depth d
two eyes. Some mono
are shown here.

LIGHT AND SHADO
Both of these attributes
appearance of three di

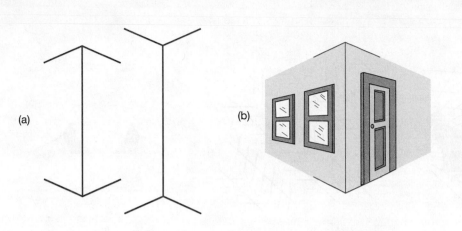

(a)

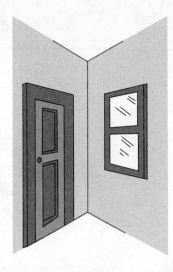

(b)

FIGURE 6.7 The Müller-Lyer Illusion

The two lines in part (a) are exactly the same length. We are probably fooled into perceiving them as different because the brain interprets the one with the outward-facing branches as farther away, as if it were the far corner of a room, and the one with the inward-facing branches as closer, as if it were the near edge of a building (b).

Although illusions can occur in any sensory modality, visual illusions have been the best studied. Visual illusions sometimes occur when the strategies that normally lead to accurate perception are overextended to situations where they don't apply. Compare the lengths of the two vertical lines in Figure 6.7. If you are like most people, you perceive the line on the right as slightly longer than the one on the left. Yet they are exactly the same length. (Go ahead, measure them; everyone does.) This is the Müller-Lyer illusion, named after the German sociologist who first described it in 1889.

One explanation for the Müller-Lyer illusion is that the branches on the lines serve as perspective cues that normally suggest depth (Gregory, 1963). The line on the left is like the near edge of a building; the one on the right is like the far corner of a room (see part [b] of the figure). Although the two lines produce retinal images of the same size, the one with the outward-facing branches suggests greater distance. We are fooled into perceiving it as longer because we automatically apply a rule about the relationship between size and distance that is normally useful: When two objects produce the same-sized retinal image and one is farther away, the farther one is larger. The problem, in this case, is that there is no actual difference in the distance of the two lines, so the rule is inappropriate.

Just as there are size, shape, location, brightness, and colour constancies, so there are size, shape, location, brightness, and colour inconstancies, resulting in illusions. For example, the perceived colour of an object depends on the wavelengths reflected by its immediate surroundings, a fact well known to artists and interior designers. Thus, you never see a good, strong red unless other objects in the surroundings reflect the blue and green part of the spectrum. When two objects that are the same colour have different surroundings, you may mistakenly perceive them as different (see Figure 6.8).

Some illusions are simply a matter of physics. Thus, a chopstick in a half-filled glass of water looks bent because water and air refract light differently. Other illusions occur due to misleading messages from the sense organs, as in sensory adaptation. Still others, like the Müller-Lyer illusion, seem to occur because the brain misinterprets sensory information. Figure 6.9 shows some other startling illusions.

In everyday life, most illusions are harmless and entertaining. Occasionally, however, an illusion interferes with the performance of some task or skill. For example, in baseball, two types of pitches that drive batters batty are the rising fastball, in which the ball seems to jump a few centimetres when it reaches home plate, and the breaking curveball, in which the ball seems to loop toward the batter and then fall at the last

FIGURE 6.8 Psychology: It's Not Just "Common Sense"

The way you perceive a colour depends on the colours around it. In this work by Joseph Albers, the adjacent Xs are actually the same colour, but against different backgrounds they look different.

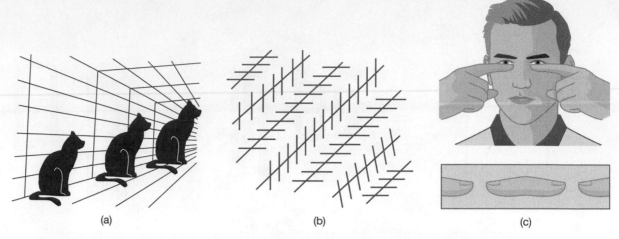

(a)   (b)   (c)

FIGURE 6.9 Fooling the Eye

Although perception is usually accurate, we can be fooled. In part (a) the cats as drawn are all the same size; in part (b) the diagonal lines are all parallel. To see the illusion depicted in part (c), hold your index fingers 13 to 26 centimetres in front of your eyes as shown, then focus straight ahead. Do you see a floating "fingertip frankfurter"? Can you move your fingers to make it shrink or expand?

moment; both of these pitches are physical impossibilities. According to one explanation, such illusions occur when batters wrongly estimate a ball's speed and momentarily shift their gaze to where they think it will cross home plate (Bahill & Karnavas, 1993).

Some illusions can also contribute to industrial and automobile accidents. For example, because large objects often appear to move more slowly than small ones, drivers sometimes underestimate the speed of onrushing trains at railroad crossings and think they can beat the train, with tragic results.

Perhaps the ultimate perceptual illusion occurred when Swedish researchers tricked people into feeling that they were swapping bodies with another person or even a mannequin (Petkova & Ehrsson, 2008). The participants wore virtual-reality goggles connected to a camera on the other person's (or mannequin's) head. This allowed them to see the world from the other body's point of view as an experimenter simultaneously stroked both bodies with a rod. Most people soon had the weird sensation that the other body was actually their own; they even cringed when the other body was poked or threatened. The researchers speculate that some day the body-swapping illusion could be helpful in marital counselling, allowing each partner to literally see things from the other's point of view, or in therapy with people who have distorted body images.

Talk about an illusion! The person on the left is wearing virtual-reality goggles and the mannequin on the right is outfitted with a camera that feeds images to the goggles. As a result, the person quickly comes to feel as though he has swapped bodies with the mannequin.

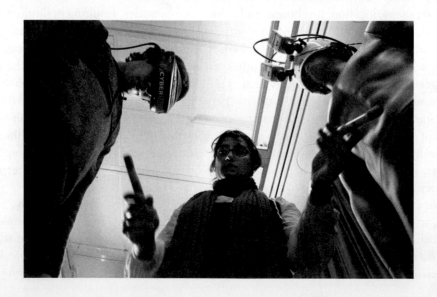

This quiz is no illusion.

1. How can two Gestalt principles help explain why you can make out the Big Dipper on a starry night?
2. *True or false:* Binocular cues help us locate objects that are very far away.
3. Hold one hand about 30 centimetres from your face and the other one about 15 centimetres away. (a) Which hand will cast the smaller retinal image? (b) Why don't you perceive that hand as smaller?
4. From an evolutionary point of view, people are most likely to have a mental module for recognition of (a) flowers, (b) bugs, (c) faces, (d) chocolate, (e) cars.

Answers:

1. Proximity of certain stars encourages you to see them as clustered together to form a pattern; closure allows you to "fill in the gaps" and see the contours of a "dipper." 2. false 3. (a) The hand that is 30 centimetres away will cast a smaller retinal image. (b) Your brain takes the differences in distance into account in estimating size; also, you know how large your hands are. The result is size constancy. 4. c

 ## YOU are about to learn . . .

♦ the basics of how we hear.
♦ why a note played on a flute sounds different from the same note played on an oboe.
♦ how we locate the source of a sound.

HEARING

Like vision, the sense of hearing, or *audition*, provides a vital link with the world around us. Because social relationships rely so heavily on hearing, when people lose their hearing they sometimes come to feel socially isolated. That is why many hearing-impaired people feel strongly about teaching deaf children American Sign Language (ASL) or other gestural systems, which allow them to communicate and forge close relationships with other signers.

What We Hear

The stimulus for sound is a wave of pressure created when an object vibrates (or, sometimes, when compressed air is released, as in a pipe organ). The vibration (or release of air) causes molecules in a transmitting substance to move together and apart. This movement produces variations in pressure that radiate in all directions. The transmitting substance is usually air, but sound waves can also travel through water and solids, as you know if you have ever put your ear to the wall to hear voices in the next room.

As with vision, *physical* characteristics of the stimulus—in this case, a sound wave—are related in a predictable way to *psychological* aspects of our auditory experience.

1   **Loudness** is the psychological dimension of auditory experience related to the intensity of a wave's pressure. Intensity corresponds to the amplitude, or maximum height, of the wave. The more energy a wave contains, the higher its peak.

loudness The dimension of auditory experience related to the intensity of a pressure wave.

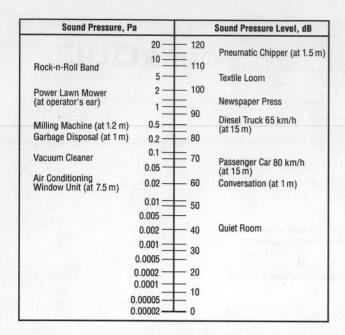

Sound Pressure, Pa		Sound Pressure Level, dB
	20 — 120	Pneumatic Chipper (at 1.5 m)
	10 —	
Rock-n-Roll Band	— 110	
	5 —	Textile Loom
Power Lawn Mower	2 — 100	
(at operator's ear)		Newspaper Press
	1 — 90	
Milling Machine (at 1.2 m)	0.5 —	Diesel Truck 65 km/h
Garbage Disposal (at 1 m)	0.2 — 80	(at 15 m)
Vacuum Cleaner	0.1 — 70	Passenger Car 80 km/h
	0.05 —	(at 15 m)
Air Conditioning	0.02 — 60	Conversation (at 1 m)
Window Unit (at 7.5 m)		
	0.01 — 50	
	0.005 —	
	0.002 — 40	Quiet Room
	0.001 —	
	0.0005 — 30	
	0.0002 — 20	
	0.0001 —	
	0.00005 — 10	
	0.00002 — 0	

FIGURE 6.10 A Comparison of Sound Pressure and Sound Pressure Level

✱ **Explore**
Major Structures of the Ear

Frequency and Amplitude of Sound Waves

pitch   The dimension of auditory experience related to the frequency of a pressure wave; the height or depth of a tone.

timbre   The distinguishing quality of a sound; the dimension of auditory experience related to the complexity of the pressure wave.

Perceived loudness is also affected by how high or low a sound is. If low and high sounds produce waves with equal amplitudes, the low sound may seem quieter.

Sound intensity is measured in units called *decibels* (dB). A decibel is one-tenth of a *bel*, a unit named for Alexander Graham Bell, the inventor of the telephone. The average absolute threshold of hearing in human beings is zero decibels. Decibels are not equally distant, as centimetres on a ruler are. A 60-decibel sound (such as that of a sewing machine) is not 50% louder than a 40-decibel sound (such as that of a whisper); it is 100 times louder because the decibel scale is a logarithmic one. Figure 6.10 shows the intensity in decibels of some common sounds.

2   **Pitch** is the dimension of auditory experience related to the frequency of the sound wave and, to some extent, its intensity. *Frequency* refers to how rapidly the air (or other medium) vibrates—that is, the number of times per second the wave cycles through a peak and a low point. One cycle per second is known as one *hertz* (Hz). The healthy ear of a young person normally detects frequencies in the range of 16 Hz (the lowest note on a pipe organ) to 20 000 Hz (the scraping of a grasshopper's legs).

3   **Timbre** is the distinguishing quality of a sound. It is the dimension of auditory experience related to the *complexity* of the sound wave—to the relative breadth of the range of frequencies that make up the wave. A pure tone consists of only one frequency, but in nature, pure tones are extremely rare. Usually what we hear is a complex wave consisting of several subwaves with different frequencies. A particular combination of frequencies results in a particular timbre. Timbre is what makes a note played on a flute, which produces relatively pure tones, sound different from the same note played on an oboe, which produces very complex sounds.

When many sound-wave frequencies are present but are not in harmony, we hear noise. When all the frequencies of the sound spectrum occur, they produce a hissing sound called *white noise.* Just as white light includes all wavelengths of the visible light spectrum, so white noise includes all frequencies of the audible sound spectrum. People sometimes use white noise machines to mask other sounds when they are trying to sleep.

An Ear on the World

As Figure 6.11 shows, the ear has an outer, a middle, and an inner section. The soft, funnel-shaped outer ear is well designed to collect sound waves, but hearing would still be quite good without it. The essential parts of the ear are hidden from view, inside the head.

A sound wave passes into the outer ear and through a two-centimetre-long canal to strike an oval-shaped membrane called the *eardrum.* The eardrum is so sensitive that it can respond to the movement of a single molecule! A sound wave causes it to vibrate with the same frequency and amplitude as the wave itself. This vibration is passed along to three tiny bones in the middle ear, the smallest bones in the human

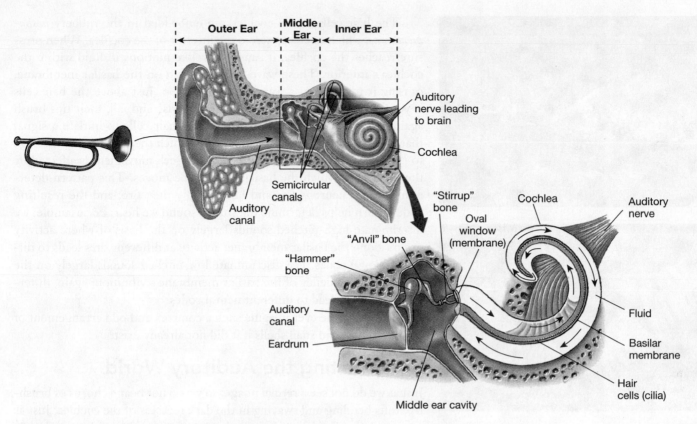

FIGURE 6.11 Major Structures of the Ear

Sound waves collected by the outer ear are channelled down the auditory canal, causing the eardrum to vibrate. These vibrations are then passed along to the tiny bones of the middle ear. Movement of these bones intensifies the force of the vibrations and funnels them to a small membrane separating the middle and inner ear. The receptor cells for hearing (hair cells), located in the organ of Corti within the snail-shaped cochlea, initiate nerve impulses that travel along the auditory nerve to the brain.

body. These bones, known informally as the hammer, the anvil, and the stirrup, move one after the other, which has the effect of intensifying the force of the vibration. The innermost bone, the stirrup, pushes on a membrane that opens into the inner ear.

The actual organ of hearing, the **organ of Corti**, is a chamber inside the **cochlea**, a snail-shaped structure within the inner ear. The organ of Corti plays the same role in hearing that the retina plays in vision. It contains the all-important receptor cells, which in this case look like bristles and are called *hair cells*, or *cilia*. Brief exposure to extremely loud noises, like those from a gunshot or a jet airplane (140 dB), or sustained exposure to more moderate noises, like those from shop tools or truck traffic (90 dB), can damage these fragile cells (see Figure 6.10 again). They flop over, like broken blades of grass, and if the damage reaches a critical point, hearing loss occurs. In modern societies, with their rock concerts, deafening bars, and millions of automobiles, snowmobiles, power saws, leaf blowers, jackhammers, and MP3 players (often played at full blast), such impairment is common, even among teenagers and young adults (Agrawal, Platz, & Niparko, 2008). Unfortunately, damaged hair cells do not regenerate. Scientists are now doing basic research on possible ways to grow new hair cells (Izumikawa et al., 2005; Sage et al., 2005), but these approaches have not yet led to therapies for hearing loss, and damage to these cells in human beings is currently irreversible.

👁 **Watch**
Noise and the Brain

Ear Ringing

Mosquito

organ of Corti [core-tee]
A structure in the cochlea containing hair cells that serve as the receptors for hearing.

cochlea [KOCK-lee-uh] A snail-shaped, fluid-filled organ in the inner ear, containing the structure where the receptors for hearing are located.

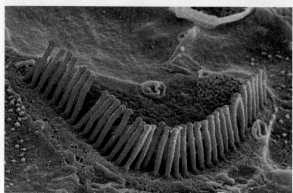

If prolonged, the 120-decibel music at a rock concert can damage or destroy the delicate hair cells of the inner ear and impair the hearing of fans who are sitting or standing close to the speakers. The microphotograph shows minuscule bristles (cilia) projecting from a single hair cell.

This border collie can rotate an ear to pick up sounds coming from different directions. We humans can't do that, and must therefore rely on other cues to locate sounds.

The hair cells of the cochlea are embedded in the rubbery *basilar membrane*, which stretches across the interior of the cochlea. When pressure reaches the cochlea, it causes wavelike motions in fluid within the cochlea's interior. These waves of fluid push on the basilar membrane, causing it to move in a wavelike fashion, too. Just above the hair cells is yet another membrane. As the hair cells rise and fall, their tips brush against it, and they bend. This causes the hair cells to initiate a signal that is passed along to the *auditory nerve*, which then carries the message to the brain. The particular pattern of hair-cell movement is affected by the manner in which the basilar membrane moves. This pattern determines which neurons fire and how rapidly they fire, and the resulting code in turn helps determine the sort of sound we hear. For example, we discriminate high-pitched sounds largely on the basis of where activity occurs along the basilar membrane; activity at different sites leads to different neural codes. We discriminate low-pitched sounds largely on the basis of the frequency of the basilar membrane's vibration; again, different frequencies lead to different neural codes.

Could anyone ever imagine such a complex and odd arrangement of bristles, fluids, and snail shells if it did not already exist?

Constructing the Auditory World

Just as we do not see a retinal image, so we do not hear a chorus of brushlike tufts bending and swaying in the dark recesses of the cochlea. Just as we do not see a jumbled collection of lines and colours, so we do not hear a chaotic collection of disconnected pitches and timbres. Instead, we use our perceptual powers to organize patterns of sound and to construct a meaningful auditory world.

For example, in class, your psychology instructor hopes you will perceive his or her voice as *figure* and the hum of a passing airplane, cheers from the athletic field, or the distant sounds of a construction crew as *ground*. Whether these hopes are realized will depend, of course, on where you choose to direct your attention. Other Gestalt principles also seem to apply to hearing. The *proximity* of notes in a melody tells you which notes go together to form phrases; *continuity* helps you follow a melody on one violin when another violin is playing a different melody; *similarity* in timbre and pitch helps you pick out the soprano voices in a chorus and hear them as a unit; *closure* helps you understand a cellphone caller's words even when interference makes some of the individual sounds unintelligible.

McGill University's Albert Bregman describes the grouping of sounds as the creation of an "auditory scene." Although some sounds are discrete, single events, such as the slam of a door, many are part of an ongoing, perhaps repetitive activity, such as the dripping of a tap. These ongoing sounds are perceived as an "auditory stream," which in turn allows the creation of an auditory scene. The Gestalt principle of common fate states that we perceive stimulus elements as a unit if they move together. Bregman has argued that common fate is the most important principle in hearing because sounds often evolve together across time, sharing a "common fate" across this time (Bregman, 1990; Huron, 1991).

Besides needing to organize sounds, we need to know where they are coming from. We can estimate the *distance* of a sound's source by using loudness as a cue. For example, we know that a train sounds louder when it is 20 metres away than when it is a kilometre off. To locate the *direction* a sound is coming from, we depend in part on the fact that we have two ears. A sound arriving from the right reaches the right ear a fraction of a second sooner than it reaches the left ear, and vice versa. The sound may also provide a bit more energy to the right ear (depending on its frequency) because it has to get around the head to reach the left ear. It is hard to localize sounds that are coming from directly behind you or from directly above your head because such sounds reach both ears at the same time. When you turn or cock your head, you are actively trying to overcome this problem. Many animals do not have to do this because the lucky creatures can move their ears independently of their heads.

quickQUIZ

✓●Quick Review on **MyPsychLab**

How well can you localize the answers to these questions?

1. Which psychological dimensions of hearing correspond to the intensity, frequency, and complexity of the sound wave?

2. Fred has a nasal voice and Ted has a gravelly voice. Which psychological dimension of hearing describes the difference?

3. An extremely loud or sustained noise can permanently damage the _____ of the ear.

4. During a lecture, a classmate draws your attention to a buzzing fluorescent light that you had not previously noticed. What will happen to your perception of figure and ground?

Answers:

1. loudness, pitch, timbre 2. timbre 3. hair cells (cilia) 4. The buzzing sound will become figure and the lecturer's voice will become ground, at least momentarily.

 # YOU are about to learn . . .

♦ the basics of how we taste, smell, and feel.

♦ why saccharin and caffeine taste bitter to some people but not to others.

♦ why you have trouble tasting your food when you have a cold.

♦ why pain is complicated to understand and treat.

♦ how two senses inform us of the movement of our own bodies.

OTHER SENSES

Psychologists have been particularly interested in vision and audition because of the importance of these senses to human survival. However, research on other senses is growing rapidly as awareness of how they contribute to our lives increases and new ways are found to study them.

Taste: Savoury Sensations

Taste, or *gustation*, occurs because chemicals stimulate thousands of receptors in the mouth. These receptors are located primarily on the tongue, but some are also found in the throat, inside the cheeks, and on the roof of the mouth. If you look at your tongue in a mirror, you will notice many tiny bumps; they are called **papillae** (from the Latin for "pimple"), and they come in several forms. In all but one of these forms, the sides of each papilla are lined with **taste buds**, which up close look a little like segmented oranges (see Figure 6.12). Because of genetic differences, human tongues can have as few as 500 or as many as 10 000 taste buds (Miller & Reedy, 1990).

papillae [pa-PILL-ee] Knoblike elevations on the tongue, containing the taste buds (singular: papilla).

taste buds Nests of taste receptor cells.

FIGURE 6.12 Taste Receptors

The illustration on the left shows taste buds lining the sides of a papilla on the tongue's surface. The illustration on the right shows an enlarged view of a single taste bud.

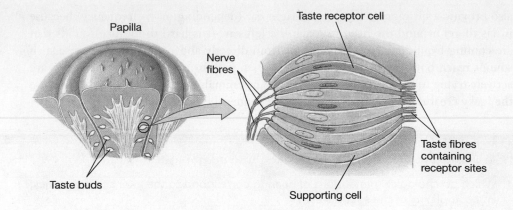

Papilla

Nerve fibres

Taste buds

Taste receptor cell

Taste fibres containing receptor sites

Supporting cell

The taste buds are commonly referred to, mistakenly, as the receptors for taste. The actual receptor cells are *inside* the buds, 15 to 50 to a bud. These cells send tiny fibres out through an opening in the bud; the receptor sites are on these fibres. The receptor cells are replaced by new cells about every 10 days. However, after age 40 or so, the total number of taste buds (and therefore receptors) declines.

Traditionally, researchers have considered four tastes to be basic: *salty*, *sour*, *bitter*, and *sweet*, each produced by a different type of chemical. Today most researchers also include a fifth taste, umami (from the Japanese for "delicious"), which is the taste of monosodium glutamate (MSG) and is found in many protein-rich foods, including meat, shellfish, and seaweed. The basic tastes are part of our evolutionary heritage: Bitterness and sourness help us identify foods that are rancid or poisonous; sweetness helps us identify foods that are healthful or rich in calories; salt is necessary for all body functions; and umami may help us identify protein-rich foods.

The basic tastes can be perceived at any spot on the tongue that has receptors, and differences among the areas are small. Interestingly, the centre of the tongue contains no taste buds, and so it cannot produce any sort of taste sensation. But, as in the case of the eye's blind spot, you will not usually notice the lack of sensation because the brain fills in the gap. When you bite into an egg or a piece of bread or an orange, its unique flavour is composed of some combination of the four or five basic tastes, but the physiological details are still hazy. It has even been difficult to identify the receptors for the basic tastes, although recently researchers have proposed candidates for the receptors that process bitter, sweet, and umami (Chaudhari, Landin, & Roper, 2000; Damak et al., 2003; Huang et al., 1999; Max et al., 2001; Montmayeur et al., 2001; Zhang et al., 2003). Researchers are now hot on the trail of the specific receptors that process each of the basic tastes (Chandrashekar et al., 2006).

Get INVOLVED!

THE SMELL OF TASTE

Demonstrate for yourself that smell enhances the sense of taste. While holding your nose, take a bite of a slice of apple, and then do the same with a slice of raw potato. You may find that you can't taste much difference. If you think you do taste a difference, perhaps your expectations are influencing your response. Try the same thing, but close your eyes this time and have someone else feed you the slices. Can you still tell them apart? It's also fun to do this little test with flavoured jelly beans. They are still apt to taste sweet, but you may be unable to identify the separate flavours.

Everyone knows that people live in different "taste worlds" (Bartoshuk, 1998). Some people love broccoli and others hate it. Some people can eat chili peppers that are burning hot and others cannot tolerate the mildest jalapeño. One reason for these differences is genetic. In the United States, about 25% of people are *supertasters* who find saccharin, caffeine, broccoli, and many other substances unpleasantly bitter. (Women, especially Asian women, are overrepresented in this group.) "Tasters," in contrast, detect less bitterness, and "nontasters" detect none at all. Supertasters also perceive sweet tastes as sweeter and salty tastes as saltier than other people do, and they feel more "burn" from substances such as ginger, pepper, and hot chilies (Bartoshuk et al., 1998; Lucchina et al., 1998). Supertasters have more taste buds than other people, and certain papillae on their tongues are smaller, are more densely packed, and look different from those of nontasters (Reedy et al., 1993).

Other taste preferences are a matter of culture and learning. Many North Americans who enjoy raw oysters, raw smoked salmon, and raw herring are nevertheless put off by other forms of raw seafood that are popular in Japan, such as sea urchin and octopus. And within a given culture, some people will greedily gobble up a dish that makes others turn green. Some of these learned taste preferences seem to begin in the womb or during breastfeeding. A baby whose mother drank carrot juice while pregnant or nursing is likely to be more enthusiastic about eating porridge mixed with carrot juice than porridge mixed with water, whereas babies without this exposure show no such preference (Mennella, Jagnow, & Beauchamp, 2001).

The attractiveness of a food can be affected by its colour, temperature, and texture. As Goldilocks found out, a bowl of cold porridge is not nearly as delicious as one that is properly heated. And any peanut butter fan will tell you that chunky and smooth peanut butters just don't taste the same. Even more important for taste is a food's odour. Much of what we call "flavour" is really the smell of gases released by the foods we put in our mouths. Indeed, subtle flavours such as chocolate and vanilla would have little taste if we could not smell them (see Figure 6.13). Smell's influence on flavour explains why you have trouble tasting your food when you have a stuffy nose. Most people who have chronic trouble detecting tastes have a problem with smell, not taste.

Smell: The Sense of Scents

The great author and educator Helen Keller, who became blind and deaf as a toddler, once called smell "the fallen angel of the senses." Yet our sense of smell, or *olfaction*, although seemingly crude when compared to a bloodhound's, is actually quite good; the human nose can detect aromas that the most sophisticated machines fail to detect. And this sense is also far more useful than most people realize.

The receptors for smell are specialized neurons embedded in a tiny patch of mucous membrane in the upper part of the nasal passage, just beneath the eyes (see Figure 6.14). Millions of receptors in each nasal cavity respond to chemical molecules in the air. When you inhale, you pull these molecules into the nasal cavity, but they can also enter from the mouth, wafting up the throat like smoke up a chimney. These molecules trigger responses in the receptors that combine to yield the yeasty smell of freshly baked bread or the spicy smell of a eucalyptus tree. Signals from the receptors are carried to the brain's olfactory bulb by the *olfactory nerve*, which is made up of the receptors' axons. From the olfactory bulb, they travel to a higher region of the brain.

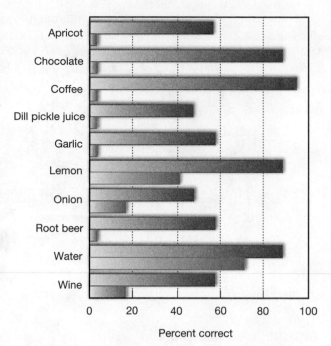

FIGURE 6.13 Taste Test
The turquoise bars show the percentages of people that could identify a substance dropped on the tongue when they were able to smell it. The gold bars show the percentage that could identify the substance when they were prevented from smelling it. (From Mozell et al., 1969.)

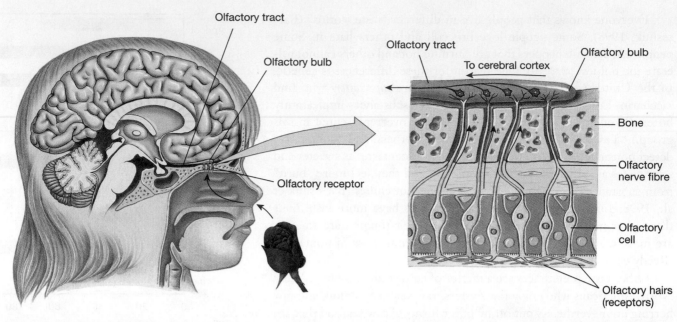

Olfactory tract

Olfactory bulb

Olfactory receptor

Olfactory tract

To cerebral cortex

Olfactory bulb

Bone

Olfactory nerve fibre

Olfactory cell

Olfactory hairs (receptors)

FIGURE 6.14 Receptors for Smell

Airborne chemical molecules (vapours) enter the nose and circulate through the nasal cavity, where the smell receptors are located. The receptors' axons make up the olfactory nerve, which carries signals to the brain. When you sniff, you draw more vapours into the nose and speed their circulation. Vapours can also reach the nasal cavity through the mouth by way of a passageway from the throat.

Smell has not only evolutionary but also cultural significance. These pilgrims in Japan are purifying themselves with holy incense for good luck and health.

Figuring out the neural code for smell has been a real challenge. Of the 10 000 or so smells we detect (rotten, burned, musky, fruity, spicy, flowery, resinous, putrid . . .), none seems to be more basic than any other. Moreover, as many as 1000 kinds of receptors exist, each kind responding to a part of an odour molecule's structure (Axel, 1995; Buck & Axel, 1991). In 2004, Richard Axel and Linda Buck won a Nobel Prize for this discovery. Distinct odours activate unique combinations of receptors, and signals from different types of receptors are combined in individual neurons in the brain. Some neurons seem to respond only to particular mixtures of odours rather than the individual odours in a mixture, which may explain why a mixture of clove and rose may be perceived as carnation rather than as two separate smells (Zou & Buck, 2006).

Although smell is less vital for human survival than for the survival of other animals, it is still important. We sniff out danger by smelling smoke, food spoilage, and gas leaks, so a deficit in the sense of smell is nothing to turn up your nose at. Such a loss can result from infection, disease, injury to the olfactory nerve, or smoking. A person who has smoked two packs a day for 10 years must abstain from cigarettes for 10 more years before the sense of smell returns to normal (Frye, Schwartz, & Doty, 1990).

Odours, of course, have psychological effects on us, which is why we buy perfumes and sniff flowers. Perhaps because olfactory centres in the brain are linked to areas that process memories and emotions, specific smells often evoke vivid, emotionally coloured memories (Herz & Cupchik, 1995; Vroon, 1997). The smell of hot chocolate may trigger fond memories of cozy winter mornings from your childhood; the smell of rubbing alcohol may remind you of an unpleasant trip to the hospital. Odours can also influence people's everyday behaviour, which is why shopping malls and hotels often install aroma diffusers in hopes of putting you in a good mood.

Many dubious, unsupported claims have been made for the powers of particular aromas, but now some serious research is being done. For example, Dutch researchers have found that the citrus scent of an all-purpose cleaner, unobtrusively left in a hidden bucket, can activate the mental concept *cleaning* and can even affect people's "cleaning behaviour" (Holland, Hendriks, & Aarts, 2005). In one of their studies, participants wrote down five activities they were planning to do during the rest of the day. Those who had been exposed to the scent listed a cleaning activity more often than those who had not been exposed to it. In another study, participants did a task and then moved to another room, where they were invited to sit at a table and eat a crumbly biscuit as a hidden video camera recorded their hand movements. People who had been exposed to the cleaning scent while working on the initial task were much more likely to wipe away crumbs from the table than those who had not been exposed! Apparently, activation of the concept *cleaning* made them more likely to clean up after themselves. After each of these studies, the researchers questioned the participants and found that none had been aware of the scent's influence. In fact, most were not even aware of having smelled the scent at all. Clearly, scent can have a nonconscious influence on what we think and do.

Senses of the Skin

The skin's usefulness is more than just skin deep. Besides protecting our innards, our nearly two square metres of skin help us identify objects and establish intimacy with others. By providing a boundary between ourselves and everything else, the skin also gives us a sense of ourselves as distinct from the environment.

The basic skin senses include *touch* (or pressure), *warmth*, *cold*, and *pain*. Within these four types are variations such as itch, tickle, and painful burning. Although certain spots on the skin are especially sensitive to the four basic skin sensations, for many years scientists had difficulty finding distinct receptors for these sensations, except in the case of pressure. But then Swedish researchers found a new kind of nerve fibre that seems responsible for some types of itching (Schmelz et al., 1997). Another team has found that the same fibres that detect pain from a punch in the nose or a burn also seem to detect the kind of pathological itch that is unrelated to histamines and that can't be relieved by antihistamine medications (Johanek et al., 2008). Moreover, scientists recently identified a possible cold receptor (McKemy, Neuhausser, & Julius, 2002; Peier et al., 2002).

Perhaps specialized fibres will also be discovered for other skin sensations. In the meantime, many aspects of touch continue to baffle science—for example, why gently touching adjacent pressure spots in rapid succession produces tickle, why scratching quells (or sometimes worsens!) an itch, and why the simultaneous stimulation of warm and cold spots produces not a lukewarm sensation but the sensation of heat. Decoding the messages of the skin senses will eventually tell us how we are able to distinguish sandpaper from velvet and glue from grease.

The Mystery of Pain

Pain, which is not only a skin sense but also an internal sense, has come under special scrutiny. Pain differs from other senses in an important way: When the stimulus producing it is removed, the sensation may continue—sometimes for years. Chronic pain disrupts lives, puts stress on the body, and causes depression and despair.

THE GATE-CONTROL THEORY OF PAIN. For many years, a leading explanation of pain has been the gate-control theory of pain, which was first proposed by Canadian psychologist Ronald Melzack and British physiologist Patrick Wall (1965). According to this theory, pain impulses must get past a "gate" in the spinal cord. The gate is not an actual structure, but rather a pattern of neural activity that either blocks pain messages coming from the skin, muscles, and internal organs or lets those signals through. Normally, the gate is kept shut, either by impulses coming into the spinal cord from large fibres that respond to pressure and other kinds of stimulation, or by signals coming

Watch
Aromatherapy

Alzheimer's Smell Test

A nurse examines Ashlyn Blocker's feet for injuries. Because of a rare condition, Ashlyn cannot feel pain from scrapes and scratches. Despite the suffering that pain causes, it is useful because it alerts us to injury.

Watch
Brain Pain

gate-control theory of pain
The theory that the experience of pain depends in part on whether pain impulses get past a neurological "gate" in the spinal cord and thus reach the brain.

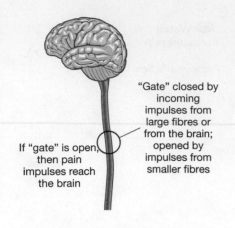

If "gate" is open, then pain impulses reach the brain

"Gate" closed by incoming impulses from large fibres or from the brain; opened by impulses from smaller fibres

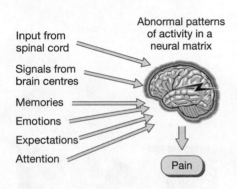

Input from spinal cord

Signals from brain centres

Memories

Emotions

Expectations

Attention

Abnormal patterns of activity in a neural matrix

Pain

phantom pain   The experience of pain in a missing limb or other body part.

kinesthesis [KIN-es-THEE-sís]   The sense of body position and movement of body parts; also called *kinesthesia*.

equilibrium   The sense of balance.

semicircular canals   Sense organs in the inner ear that contribute to equilibrium by responding to rotation of the head.

down from the brain itself. But when body tissue is injured, the large fibres are damaged and smaller fibres open the gate, allowing pain messages to reach the brain unchecked.

Because the gate-control theory emphasizes the role of the brain in controlling the gate, it correctly predicts that thoughts and feelings can influence our reactions to pain. When we dwell on our pain, focusing on it and talking about it constantly instead of acting in spite of it, we often intensify our experience of it (Sullivan, Tripp, & Santor, 1998). Conversely, when we are distracted from our pain, we may not feel it as we usually would—which is why we hear, from time to time, of athletes who are able to finish a performance despite sprained ankles or even broken bones. The gate-control theory also correctly predicts that mild pressure, or other kinds of stimulation, can interfere with severe or protracted pain by closing the spinal gate. When we vigorously rub a banged elbow or apply ice packs, heat, or stimulating ointments to injuries, we are applying this principle.

UPDATING THE GATE-CONTROL THEORY. The gate-control theory has been highly useful, but it does not fully explain the many instances of severe, chronic pain that occur without any sign of injury or disease whatsoever.

In the strange phenomenon of **phantom pain**, for instance, a person continues to feel pain that seemingly comes from an amputated limb or from an organ that has been surgically removed. An amputee may feel the same aching, burning, or sharp pain from sores, calf cramps, throbbing toes, or even ingrown toenails that he or she endured before the surgery. Even when the spinal cord has been completely severed, amputees often continue to report phantom pain from areas below the break. There are no nerve impulses for the spinal-cord gate to block or let through. So why is there pain?

These puzzles led Ronald Melzack (1992, 1993) to revise the gate-control theory. The brain, he says, not only responds to incoming signals from sensory nerves but is also capable of generating pain (and other sensations) entirely on its own. An extensive *matrix* (network) of neurons in the brain gives us a sense of our own bodies and body parts. When this matrix produces abnormal patterns of activity, the result is pain. Such abnormal patterns can occur not only because of input from peripheral nerves, but also as a result of memories, emotions, expectations, or signals from various brain centres. In the case of phantom pain, the abnormal patterns may arise because of a lack of sensory stimulation or because of the person's efforts to move a nonexistent limb. Evidence that brain areas associated with a missing limb continue to function in its absence is consistent with this view (Davis et al., 1998).

At present, however, no general theory completely explains *phantom pain*, or for that matter normal pain, which has turned out to be extremely complicated, both physiologically and psychologically. Different types of pain (from, say, a thorn, a bruise, or a hot iron) involve different chemical changes and different changes in nerve-cell activity at the site of injury or disease, as well as in the spinal cord and brain. These changes may suppress the pain or may amplify it by making neurons hyperexcitable. Further, recent evidence suggests that chronic, pathological pain involves *glia*, the cells that support nerve cells (see Chapter 4). Challenges to the immune system during viral and bacterial infections, and substances released by neurons along the pain pathway after an injury, activate glial cells in the spinal cord. The glia then release inflammatory substances that may worsen the pain and keep it going (Watkins & Maier, 2003). These chemicals can spread to spinal cord areas far from the site where they were released, which may help explain why injured people sometimes report pain in body areas that were not hurt.

A leading explanation of phantom pain is that the brain has reorganized itself: The area in the sensory cortex that formerly corresponded to the missing body part has been "invaded" by neurons from another area, often one corresponding to the face. Higher brain centres then interpret messages from those neurons as coming from the nonexistent body part (Cruz et al., 2005; Ramachandran & Blakeslee, 1998). Even though the missing limb can no longer send signals through touch and internal sensations, memories of these signals remain in the nervous system, including memories of pain, paralysis, and cramping that occurred prior to amputation. The result is an inaccurate "body map" in the brain and pain signals that cannot be shut off.

Vilayanur Ramachandran, the neurologist who first proposed this theory, has developed an extraordinarily simple but effective treatment for phantom-limb pain. Ramachandran wondered whether he could devise an illusion to trick the brain of an amputee with phantom arm pain into perceiving the missing limb as moving and pain-free. He placed a simple mirror upright and perpendicular to the sufferer's body, such that the amputee's intact arm was reflected in the mirror. From the amputee's perspective, the result was an illusion of two functioning arms. The amputee was then instructed to move both arms in synchrony while looking into the mirror. With this technique, which has now been used with many people, the brain is fooled into thinking its owner has two healthy arms or legs, resynchronizes the signals—and phantom pain vanishes (Ramachandran & Altschuler, 2009). Neurologists have been testing this method with Iraq veterans, and are finding it to be more successful than control therapies in which patients just mentally visualize having two intact limbs (Anderson-Barnes et al., 2009; Chan et al., 2007).

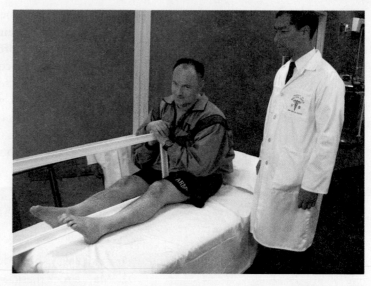

After his right leg was destroyed in an explosion while he was in Iraq, Army Sgt. Nicholas Paupore experienced excruciating phantom limb pain—as though the missing leg were constantly being shocked or stabbed. Even morphine didn't help. Then, as part of a clinical trial, he underwent a simple daily treatment. A mirror was placed at a strategic angle to reflect his intact leg, tricking his brain into registering two healthy legs that he could move freely. The pain almost immediately subsided. A year after therapy, he had only occasional, milder pain, and needed no medication. In some patients, mirror therapy has eliminated phantom pain entirely.

The Environment Within

We usually think of our senses as pipelines to the "outside" world, but two senses keep us informed about the movements of our own bodies. Kinesthesis tells us where our body parts are located and lets us know when they move. This information is provided by pain and pressure receptors located in the muscles, joints, and tendons (tissues that connect muscles to bones). Without kinesthesis, you could not touch your finger to your nose with your eyes shut. In fact, you would have trouble with any voluntary movement. Think of how hard walking is when your leg has "fallen asleep" or how clumsy you are at chewing when a dentist has numbed your jaw with Novocaine.

Equilibrium, or the sense of balance, gives us information about our bodies as a whole. Along with vision and touch, it lets us know whether we are standing upright or on our heads and tells us when we are falling or rotating. Equilibrium relies primarily on three semicircular canals in the inner ear (refer to Figure 6.11 on page 213). These thin tubes are filled with fluid that moves and presses on hairlike receptors whenever the head rotates. The receptors initiate messages that travel through a part of the auditory nerve that is not involved in hearing.

Normally, kinesthesis and equilibrium work together to give us a sense of our own physical reality—something we take utterly for granted but should not. Oliver Sacks (1985) told the heartbreaking story of Christina, a young British woman who suffered irreversible damage to her kinesthetic nerve fibres because of a mysterious inflammation. At first, Christina was as floppy as a rag doll; she could not sit up, walk, or stand.

These performers from Quebec's famed Cirque du Soleil have turned their kinesthetic talents into artistry.

Then, slowly, she learned to do these things, relying on visual cues and sheer willpower. But her movements remained unnatural; she had to grasp a fork with painful force or she would drop it. More important, despite her remaining sensitivity to light touch on the skin, she said she could no longer experience herself as physically embodied: "It's like something's been scooped right out of me," she told Sacks, "right at the centre."

With equilibrium, we come, as it were, to the end of our senses. Every second, millions of sensory signals reach the brain, which combines and integrates them to produce a model of reality from moment to moment. How does it know how to do this? Are our perceptual abilities inborn, or must we learn them? We turn next to this issue.

---

quickQUIZ

✓● Quick Review on MyPsychLab

Can you make sense of the following sensory problems?

A. What explanation of each problem is most likely?

1. April always has trouble tasting foods, especially those with subtle flavours.
2. May, a rock musician, does not hear as well as she used to.
3. June has chronic shoulder pain, though the injury that initially caused it seems to have healed. (Hint: Think about the gate-control theory and its revisions.)

B. After seeing a new pain-relief ointment advertised on TV, you try it and find that it seems to work. What other explanation is possible for the decrease in your pain?

Answers:

A. 1. April may have an impaired sense of smell, possibly due to disease, illness, or cigarette smoking. **2.** Hearing impairment has many causes, but in May's case we might suspect that prolonged exposure to loud music has damaged the hair cells of her cochlea. **3.** Nerve fibres that normally close the pain "gate" might have been damaged, or a matrix of cells in the brain might be producing abnormal activity. **B.** The relief you feel may be due at least in part to a placebo effect, which has decreased activity in the pain matrix of your brain or has led to increased production of endorphins.

 YOU are about to learn . . .

◆ whether babies see the world in the way adults do.

◆ what happens when people who are born blind or deaf have their sight or hearing restored.

◆ how psychological and cultural factors affect perception.

PERCEPTUAL POWERS: ORIGINS AND INFLUENCES

What happens when babies first open their eyes? Do they see the same sights, hear the same sounds, smell the same smells, and taste the same tastes that an adult does? Are their strategies for organizing the world wired into their brains from the beginning? Or is an infant's world, as William James once suggested, only a "blooming, buzzing confusion," waiting to be organized by experience and learning? The truth lies somewhere between these two extremes.

Inborn Abilities

In human beings, most basic sensory abilities, and many perceptual skills, are inborn or develop very early. Infants can distinguish salty from sweet and can discriminate among odours. They can distinguish a human voice from other sounds. They will startle to a loud noise and turn their heads toward its source, showing that they perceive sound as localized in space. Many visual skills are also present at birth or they develop shortly afterward. Human infants can discriminate sizes and colours very early, possibly even right away. They can distinguish contrasts, shadows, and complex patterns after only a few weeks. And depth perception develops very early, during the first few months.

Testing an infant's perception of depth requires considerable ingenuity. One clever procedure that was used for decades was to place infants on a device called a *visual cliff* (Gibson & Walk, 1960). The "cliff" is a pane of glass covering a shallow surface and a deep one (see Figure 6.15). Both surfaces are covered by a checkerboard pattern. The infant is placed on a board in the middle, and the child's mother tries to lure the baby across either the shallow side or the deep side. Babies only six months of age will crawl across the shallow side but will refuse to crawl out over the "cliff." Their hesitation shows that they have depth perception.

Of course, by six months of age, a baby has had quite a bit of experience with the world. But infants younger than six months can also be tested on the visual cliff, even though they cannot yet crawl. At only two months of age, babies show a drop in heart rate when placed on the deep side of the cliff, but no change when they are placed on the shallow side. A slowed heart rate is usually a sign of increased attention. Thus, although these infants may not be frightened the way an older infant would be, it seems they can perceive the difference between the shallow and deep sides of the cliff (Banks & Salapatek, 1984).

Critical Periods

Although many perceptual abilities are inborn, experience also plays a vital role. If an infant misses out on certain experiences during a crucial window of time—a *critical period*—perception will be impaired. Innate abilities will not survive because cells in the nervous system deteriorate, change, or fail to form appropriate neural pathways.

One way to study critical periods is to see what happens when the usual perceptual experiences of early life fail to take place. To do this, researchers usually study animals whose sensory and perceptual systems are similar to our own. For example, like human infants, kittens are born with the visual ability to detect horizontal and vertical lines and other spatial orientations as well; at birth, kittens' brains are equipped with the same kinds of feature detector cells that adult cats have. But if they are deprived of normal visual experience, these cells deteriorate or change and perception suffers (Crair, Gillespie, & Stryker, 1998; Hirsch & Spinelli, 1970).

In one famous study, kittens were exposed to either vertical or horizontal black and white stripes. Special collars kept them from seeing anything else, even their own bodies (see Figure 6.16). After several months, the kittens exposed only to vertical stripes seemed blind to all horizontal contours; they bumped into horizontal obstacles, and they ran to play with a bar that an experimenter held vertically but not to a bar held horizontally. In contrast, those exposed only to horizontal stripes bumped into vertical obstacles and ran to play with horizontal bars but not vertical ones (Blakemore & Cooper, 1970).

Critical periods for sensory development also exist in human beings. When adults who have been blind from infancy have their vision restored, they may see, but often

FIGURE 6.15 A Cliff-Hanger

Infants as young as six months usually hesitate to crawl past the apparent edge of a visual cliff, which suggests that they are able to perceive depth.

⏩ Simulate
The Visual Cliff

FIGURE 6.16 Vision and Early Experience

Cats were reared in darkness for five months after birth, but for several hours each day were put in a special cylinder that permitted them to see only vertical or horizontal lines, and nothing else. Later on, cats who were exposed only to vertical lines had trouble perceiving horizontal ones, and those exposed only to horizontal lines had trouble perceiving vertical ones (Blakemore & Cooper, 1970).

they do not see. Areas in the brain normally devoted to vision may have taken on different functions when these individuals were blind. As a result, their depth perception may be poor, causing them to trip constantly. They cannot always make sense of what they see; to identify objects, they may have to touch or smell them. They may have trouble recognizing faces and emotional expressions. They may even lack size constancy, and may need to remind themselves that people walking away from them are not shrinking in size (Fine et al., 2003)! But if an infant's congenital blindness is corrected early, during a critical period occurring during the first nine months or so, the prognosis is much better (though visual discriminations may never become entirely normal). In one study of infants who underwent corrective surgery when they were between one week and nine months of age, improvement began after as little as one hour of visual experience (Maurer et al., 1999).

Similar findings apply to hearing. When adults who were born deaf, or who lost their hearing before learning to speak, receive cochlear implants (devices that stimulate the auditory nerve and allow auditory signals to travel to the brain), they tend to find sounds confusing. They are unable to learn to speak normally, and often they ask to have the implants removed. But cochlear implants are more successful in children and in adults who became deaf late in life (Rauschecker, 1999). Young children presumably have not yet passed through the critical period for processing sounds, and adults have already had years of auditory experience.

In sum, our perceptual powers are both inborn and dependent on experience. Because neurological connections in infants' brains and sensory systems are not completely formed, their senses are far less acute than an adult's. It takes time and experience before their sensory abilities fully develop. But an infant's world is clearly not the blooming, buzzing confusion that William James took it to be.

Psychological and Cultural Influences

The fact that some perceptual processes appear to be innate does not mean that all people perceive the world in the same way. A camera doesn't care what it "sees." A digital recorder doesn't ponder what it "hears." A robot arm on a factory assembly line holds no opinion about what it "touches." But because we human beings care about what we see, hear, taste, smell, and feel, psychological factors can influence what we perceive and how we perceive it. Here are a few of these factors:

1 **Needs.** When we need something, have an interest in it, or want it, we are especially likely to perceive it. For example, hungry individuals are faster than others at seeing words related to hunger when the words are flashed briefly on a screen (Wispé & Drambarean, 1953).

2 **Beliefs.** What we hold to be true about the world can affect our interpretation of ambiguous sensory signals. For example, if you believe that extraterrestrials occasionally visit Earth, and you see a round object in the sky (where there are few points of reference to help you judge distance), you may see a spaceship. (Impartial investigations of UFO sightings show that they are really weather balloons, rocket launchings, swamp gas, military aircraft, or ordinary celestial bodies, such as planets and meteors.) Images that remind people of a crucified Jesus have been reported on walls, dishes, and plates of spaghetti, causing

● **Watch**
Cochlear Implants

People often see what they want to see. Diana Duyser, a cook at a Florida casino, took a bite out of a grilled cheese sandwich and believed she saw the image of the Virgin Mary in what remained of it. She preserved the sandwich in plastic for 10 years and then decided to sell it. An online casino bought it on eBay for $28,000, even with a bite of it missing!

great excitement among those who believe that divine messages can be found on everyday objects—until other explanations emerge. Do you remember that image of Jesus on the garage door, in our opening story? It turned out to be caused by two streetlights that merged the shadows of a bush and a "For Sale" sign in the yard.

3 Emotions. Emotions can also influence our interpretation of sensory information. A small child afraid of the dark may see a ghost instead of a robe hanging on the door, or a monster instead of a beloved doll. Pain, in particular, is affected by emotion. Soldiers who are seriously wounded often deny being in much pain, even though they are alert and are not in shock. Their relief at being alive may offset the anxiety and fear that contribute so much to pain (although distraction and the body's own pain-fighting mechanisms may also be involved). Conversely, negative emotions such as anger, fear, sadness, or depression can prolong and intensify a person's pain (Fernandez & Turk, 1992; Fields, 1991). Interestingly, when people perceive their pain as resulting from another person's malicious intent (e.g., they think the other person intentionally stepped on their toe), they feel the hurt more than they would if they thought it was simply due to a clumsy accident (Gray & Wegner, 2008).

4 Expectations. Previous experiences often affect how we perceive the world (Lachman, 1996). The tendency to perceive what you expect is called a **perceptual set**. Perceptaul sets can come in handy; they help us fill in words in sentences, for example, when we haven't really heard every one. But perceptual sets can also cause misperceptions. In Center Harbor, Maine, local legend has it that veteran newscaster Walter Cronkite was sailing into port one day when he heard a small crowd on shore shouting "Hello, Walter . . . hello, Walter." Pleased, he waved and took a bow. Only when he ran aground did he realize what they had really been shouting: "Shallow water . . . shallow water." (By the way, this paragraph has a misspelled word. Did you notice it? If not, it was probably because you expected all the words in this book to be spelled correctly.)

CULTURE and *Perception*

Of Carpenters and Context

Our needs, beliefs, emotions, and expectations are all affected, in turn, by the culture we live in. Different cultures give people practice with different environments. In a classic study done in the 1960s, researchers found that members of some African tribes were much less likely to be fooled by the Müller-Lyer illusion and other geometric illusions than were Westerners. In the West, the researchers observed, people live in a "carpentered" world, full of rectangular structures. Westerners are also used to interpreting two-dimensional photographs and perspective drawings as representations of a three-dimensional world. Therefore, they interpret the kinds of angles used in the Müller-Lyer illusion as right angles extended in space, a habit that increases susceptibility to the illusion. The rural Africans in the study, living in a less carpentered environment and in round huts, seemed more likely to take the lines in the figures literally, as two-dimensional, which could explain why they were less susceptible to the illusion (Segall, Campbell, & Herskovits, 1966; Segall et al., 1999).

Culture also affects perception by shaping our stereotypes, directing our attention, and telling us what to notice or ignore. Westerners, for example, tend to focus

perceptual set A habitual way of perceiving, based on expectations.

mostly on the figure when viewing a scene and much less on the ground. East Asians, in contrast, tend to pay attention to the overall context and the relationship between figure and ground. When Japanese people and Americans were shown underwater scenes containing brightly coloured fish that were larger and moving faster than other objects in the scene, they reported the same numbers of details about the fish, but the Japanese reported more details about everything else in the background (Masuda & Nisbett, 2001). One of the researchers, Richard Nisbett, commented, "If it ain't moving, it doesn't exist for an American" (quoted in Shea, 2001).

Thinking Critically

Consider Other Interpretations

These photos of a U.S. school (left) and a Japanese school (right) were among a large number of randomly selected photos of schools, hotels, and post offices taken in the two countries. Japanese scenes tend to be more ambiguous and complex than American scenes, which may help explain why the Japanese attend more closely to context than Americans do (Miyamoto, Nisbett, & Masuda, 2006).

Why should the Japanese pay more attention to context than Americans? One possibility is that a greater concern with the social world directs the attention of the Japanese to contexts of all types. Another possibility is that in Japanese environments, specific objects really do stand out less than in comparable American environments, so living in Japan tends to direct a person's attention to the whole visual field. Indeed, when researchers randomly sampled pictures of hotels, elementary schools, and post offices from small, medium, and large cities in Japan and the United States, they found that the Japanese scenes were more ambiguous and contained more elements than comparable American scenes—just the kind of scenes that encourage attention to context (Miyamoto, Nisbett, & Masuda, 2006).

As you can see . . . well, what you see partly depends on the culture you live in! When travellers visit another culture and are surprised to find that its members "see things differently," they may be literally correct.

YOU are about to learn . . .

◆ that perception is often unconscious.
◆ whether "subliminal perception" tapes will help you lose weight or reduce your stress.

PUZZLES OF PERCEPTION

We come, finally, to two intriguing questions about perception that have captured the public's imagination for years. First, can we ever perceive what is happening in the world when it is below our usual sensory threshold? Second, can we pick up signals from the world or from other people without using our usual sensory channels at all?

Subliminal Perception: How Persuasive?

As we saw earlier in our discussion of selective attention, even when people are oblivious to speech sounds, they are processing and recognizing those sounds at some level. But such sounds and sights are above people's absolute thresholds. Is it also possible to perceive and respond to messages that are below the absolute threshold—too quiet to be consciously heard or too brief or dim to be consciously seen? Perhaps you have seen ads for products that will supposedly help you learn another language or raise your self-esteem (or, our favourite, learn to love housework) by taking advantage of such "subliminal perception." What are the facts?

PERCEIVING WITHOUT AWARENESS. First, a simple visual stimulus can indeed affect your behaviour even when you are unaware that you saw it. For example, people sometimes correctly "sense" a change in a scene (say, in the colour or location of an object) even though the change was shown too quickly to be consciously recognized and identified (Rensink, 2004). And people subliminally exposed to a face will tend to prefer that face over one they did not "see" in this way (Bornstein, Leone, & Galley, 1987).

In many studies, researchers have used a method called **priming**, in which a person is exposed to information (subliminally or explicitly) and is later tested to see whether the information affects performance on another task (see Chapter 10). Researchers have found that when words flashed subliminally are related to some personality trait,

priming A method used to measure unconscious cognitive processes, in which a person is exposed to information and is later tested to see whether the information affects behaviour or performance on another task or in another situation.

such as honesty, people are more likely later to judge someone they read about as having that trait. They have been "primed" to evaluate the person that way (Bargh, 1999).

Several investigators at the University of Waterloo have demonstrated interesting effects while presenting stimuli without participants' being aware of it. Jim Cheesman and Phil Merikle have found that presentations of colour words shown without participant awareness still influence the subsequent naming speed of a colour patch (Cheesman & Merikle, 1986). Also at Waterloo, Erin Strahan and her advisers demonstrated that thirsty people who have been primed by thirst-related words are likely to drink more of a sweet beverage than thirsty people who are not primed, and they also find ads for a thirst-quenching drink more persuasive (Strahan, Spencer, & Zanna, 2002). Findings such as these show that people often know more than they think they know. In fact, nonconscious processing appears to occur not only in perception but also in memory, thinking, and decision making, as we will see in Chapters 9 and 10. However, even in the laboratory, where researchers have considerable control, subliminal perception can be hard to demonstrate and replicate. The strongest evidence comes from studies using simple stimuli (faces or single words such as *bread*) rather than complex stimuli such as sentences ("Eat whole-wheat bread, not white bread").

PERCEPTION VERSUS PERSUASION. If subliminal priming can affect judgments and preferences, can it be used to manipulate people's attitudes and behaviour? Subliminal persuasion techniques were a hot topic back in the 1950s, when an advertising executive claimed to have increased popcorn and Coke sales at a theatre by secretly flashing the words EAT POPCORN and DRINK COKE on the movie screen. The claim turned out to be a hoax, devised to save the man's struggling advertising company. Ever since, scientists have been skeptical, and most attempts to demonstrate subliminal persuasion have been disappointing.

However, this has not deterred people who market subliminal tapes that promise to help you lose weight, stop smoking, relieve stress, read faster, boost your motivation, lower your cholesterol, stop biting your nails, overcome jet lag, or stop taking drugs, all without any effort on your part. If only those claims were true! But in study after study, placebo tapes—tapes that do not contain the messages that participants think they do—are just as "effective" as subliminal tapes (Eich & Hyman, 1992; Merikle & Skanes, 1992; Moore, 1992, 1995). In one typical experiment, people listened to tapes labelled "memory" or "self-esteem," but some heard tapes that were incorrectly labelled. About half showed improvement in the area specified by the label whether it was correct or not; the improvement was due to expectations alone (Greenwald et al., 1991).

Three Canadian psychologists from the University of Waterloo have suggested that previous efforts at subliminal persuasion left out an important ingredient: the person's motivation. Instead of trying to influence people directly by using a subliminal message such as "Drink Coke," these researchers used subliminal messages—the words *thirst* and *dry*—to make participants feel thirsty and prime them to drink. Later, when given a chance to drink, the primed participants did in fact drink more than control participants did, but only if they had been moderately thirsty to begin with (Strahan, Spencer, & Zanna, 2002).

Does this mean that advertisers can seduce us into buying soft drinks or voting for political candidates by slipping subliminal slogans and images into television and

((•● Listen
Subliminal Messages

magazine ads? The priming research has renewed the debate. However, given the many studies that have found no evidence of subliminal persuasion and the subtlety of the effects that do occur (you have to be somewhat thirsty already to be primed to want to drink), we think there's little cause for worry about subliminal manipulation. If advertisers want you to buy something, they will probably do better to spend their money on above-threshold messages. And if you want to improve yourself or your life, you'll have to do it the old-fashioned way: by working at it consciously.

Please remain conscious to answer this question.

A study appears to find evidence of "sleep learning"—the ability to perceive and retain material played on an audio recording while a person sleeps. What would you want to know about this research before deciding to record this chapter and play it by your bedside all night instead of studying it in the usual way?

quickQUIZ

✔️ **Quick Review** on **MyPsychLab**

Answers:

Was there a control group that listened to, say, a musical selection or white noise? How complicated was the material that was allegedly learned: a few key words, whole sentences, a whole lecture by Professor Arbuckle? Were the results large enough to have any practical applications? How did the researchers determine that the participants really were asleep? (When brain-wave measures are used to verify that volunteers are actually sleeping, no "sleep learning" takes place.)

As we have seen throughout this chapter, we do not register the world "out there" passively; we mentally construct it. All of us, even those of us who are not usually gullible, have needs and beliefs that can fool us into seeing things we *want* to see. All of us occasionally read meanings into sensory experiences that are not inherent in the experience itself; who has not seen nonexistent water on a hot highway, or felt a nonexistent insect on the skin after merely thinking about bugs?

The great Greek philosopher Plato once said that "knowledge is nothing but perception," but he was wrong. Simple perception is *not* always the best path to knowledge. Because our sense organs evolved for particular purposes, our sensory windows on the world are partly shuttered. But we can use reason, ingenuity, and scientific inquiry to pry those shutters open. Ordinary perception tells us that the sun circles the Earth, but the great astronomer Copernicus was able to figure out nearly five centuries ago that the opposite is true. Ordinary perception will never let us see ultraviolet and infrared rays directly, but we know they are there, and we can measure them. If research can enable us to overturn the everyday evidence of our senses, who knows what surprises science has in store for us?

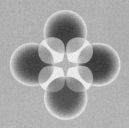

Extrasensory Perception: Reality or Illusion?

Eyes, ears, mouth, nose, skin—we rely on these organs for our experience of the external world. Some people, however, claim they can send and receive messages about the world without relying on the usual sensory channels, by using extrasensory perception (ESP). Reported ESP experiences involve things like telepathy, the direct communication of messages from one mind to another without the usual sensory signals, and precognition, the perception of an event that has not yet happened. Most ESP claims challenge everything we currently know to be true about the way the world and the universe operate. A lot of people are ready to accept these claims. Should they?

Evidence or Coincidence? Much of the supposed evidence for extrasensory perception comes from anecdotal accounts. But people are not always reliable reporters of their own experiences. They often embellish and exaggerate, or they recall only part of what happened. They also tend to forget incidents that don't fit their beliefs, such as "premonitions" of events that fail to occur. Many ESP experiences could merely be unusual coincidences that are memorable because they are dramatic. What passes for telepathy or precognition could also be based on what a person knows or deduces through ordinary means. If Joanne's father has had two heart attacks, her premonition that her father will die shortly (followed, in fact, by her father's death) may not be so impressive.

The scientific way to establish a phenomenon is to produce it under controlled conditions. Extrasensory perception has been studied extensively by researchers in the field of *parapsychology*. But ESP studies have often been poorly designed, with inadequate precautions against fraud and improper statistical analysis. After an exhaustive review, the National Research Council concluded that there was "no scientific justification . . . for the existence of parapsychological phenomena" (Druckman & Swets, 1988). Other investigators have presented rational explanations for the apparent perception of various "psychic" phenomena. For example, at Laurentian University, Michael Persinger and his colleagues presented evidence that these perceptions are related to signs of temporal lobe epilepsy in otherwise neurologically normal individuals (Persinger & Makarec, 1987). People who report having "psychic" experiences also tend to show some signs of epilepsy!

The history of research on psychic phenomena has been one of initial enthusiasm because of apparently positive results (Bem & Honorton, 1994; Dalton et al., 1996), followed by disappointment when results cannot be replicated (Milton & Wiseman, 1999, 2001). The thousands of studies done since the 1940s have failed to make a convincing case for ESP. One researcher who tried for 30 years to establish the reality of psychic phenomena finally gave up in defeat. "I found no psychic phenomena," she wrote, "only wishful thinking, self-deception, experimental error, and even an occasional fraud. I became a sceptic" (Blackmore, 2001).

The issue has not gone away, however. Many people really, really want to believe that ESP exists. James Randi, a famous magician who is dedicated to educating the public about psychic deception, has for years offered a million dollars to anyone who can demonstrate ESP or other paranormal powers under close observation. Many have taken up the challenge; no one has succeeded. We think Randi's money is safe.

Lessons from a Magician. Despite the lack of evidence for ESP, many people say they believe in it. Perhaps you yourself have had an experience that seemed to involve ESP, or perhaps you have seen a convincing demonstration by someone else. Surely you can trust the evidence of your own eyes. Or can you? We will answer this question with a true story, one that contains an important lesson about why it's a good idea to think critically regarding ESP.

During the 1970s, Andrew Weil (who is now known for his efforts to promote alternative medicine) set out to investigate the claims of a self-proclaimed psychic named Uri Geller (Weil, 1974a, b). Weil, who believed in telepathy, felt that ESP might be explained by principles of modern physics, and he was receptive to Geller's claims. When he met Geller at a private gathering, he was not disappointed. Geller correctly identified a cross and a Star of David sealed inside separate envelopes. He made a stopped watch start running and made a ring sag into an oval shape, apparently without touching them. He also made keys change shape. Weil came away a convert. What he had seen with his own eyes seemed impossible to deny . . . until he went to visit the Amazing Randi.

To Weil's astonishment, Randi was able to duplicate much of what Geller had done. He, too, could bend keys and guess the contents of sealed envelopes. But Randi's feats were tricks, and he was willing to show Weil exactly how they were done. Weil suddenly experienced "a sense of how strongly the mind can impose its own interpretations on perceptions; how it can see what it expects to see, but not see the unexpected."

Weil was dis-illusioned—literally. Even when he knew what to look for in a trick, he could not catch the Amazing Randi doing it. Weil learned that our sense impressions of reality are not the same as reality. Our eyes, our ears, and especially our brains can play tricks on us.

SUMMARY

◆ *Sensation* is the detection and direct experience of physical energy as a result of environmental or internal events. *Perception* is the process by which sensory impulses are organized and interpreted.

OUR SENSATIONAL SENSES

◆ Sensation begins with the *sense receptors*, which convert the energy of a stimulus into electrical impulses that travel along nerves to the brain. Separate sensations can be accounted for by *anatomical codes* (as set forth by the *doctrine of specific nerve energies*) and *functional codes* in the nervous system. In *sensory substitution*, sensory crossover from one modality to another occurs and, in *synesthesia*, sensation in one modality evokes a sensation in another modality, but these experiences are rare.

◆ Psychologists specializing in *psychophysics* have studied sensory sensitivity by measuring *absolute* and *difference thresholds*. *Signal-detection theory*, however, holds that responses in a detection task consist of both a sensory process and a decision process and will vary with the person's motivation, alertness, and expectations.

◆ Our senses are designed to respond to change and contrast in the environment. When stimulation is unchanging, *sensory adaptation* occurs. Too little stimulation can cause *sensory deprivation*, and too much stimulation can cause *sensory overload*. *Selective attention* prevents overload and allows us to focus on what is important, but it also deprives us of sensory information we may need, as in *inattentional blindness*.

VISION

◆ Vision is affected by the wavelength, frequency, and complexity of light, which produce the psychological dimensions of visual experience—*hue*, *brightness*, and *saturation*. The visual receptors, *rods* and *cones*, are located in the *retina* of the eye. They send signals (via other cells) to the *ganglion cells* and ultimately to the *optic nerve*, which carries visual information to the brain. Rods are responsible for vision in dim light; cones are responsible for colour vision. *Dark adaptation* occurs in two stages.

◆ Specific aspects of the visual world, such as lines at various orientations, are detected by *feature-detector cells* in the visual areas of the brain. Some of these cells respond maximally to complex patterns. A heated debate is now going on about the existence of specialized "face modules" in the brain. In general, however, the brain takes in fragmentary information about lines, angles, shapes, motion, brightness, texture, and other features of what we see and comes up with a unified view of the world.

◆ The *trichromatic* and *opponent-process* theories of colour vision apply to different stages of processing. In the first stage, three types of cones in the retina respond selectively to different wavelengths of light. In the second, *opponent-process cells* in the retina and the thalamus respond in opposite fashion to short and long wavelengths of light.

◆ Perception involves the active construction of a model of the world from moment to moment. The *Gestalt principles* (for example, *figure and ground*, *proximity*, *closure*, *similarity*, and *continuity*) describe visual strategies used by the brain to perceive forms.

◆ We localize objects in visual space by using both *binocular* and *monocular* cues to depth. Binocular cues include *convergence* and *retinal disparity*. Monocular cues include, among others, *interposition* and *linear perspective*. *Perceptual constancies* allow us to perceive objects as stable despite changes in the sensory patterns they produce. *Perceptual illusions* occur when sensory cues are misleading or when we misinterpret cues.

HEARING

◆ Hearing (*audition*) is affected by the intensity, frequency, and complexity of pressure waves in the air or other transmitting substance, corresponding to the experience of *loudness*, *pitch*, and *timbre* of the sound. The receptors for hearing are *hair cells (cilia)* embedded in the *basilar membrane*, in the interior of the *cochlea* (in the *organ of Corti*). These receptors pass signals along the *auditory nerve*. The sounds we hear are determined by patterns of hair-cell movement, which produce different neural codes. When we localize sounds, we use as cues subtle differences in how pressure waves reach each of our ears.

OTHER SENSES

◆ Taste (*gustation*) is a chemical sense. Elevations on the tongue, called *papillae*, contain many *taste buds*, which in turn contain the taste receptors. The basic tastes include salty, sour, bitter, sweet, and umami. Responses to a particular taste depend in part on genetic differences among individuals; for example, some people are "supertasters."

Taste preferences are also affected by culture and learning, and by the texture, temperature, and smell of food.

◆ Smell (*olfaction*) is also a chemical sense. No basic odours have been identified, and up to 1000 different receptor types exist. But researchers have discovered that distinct odours activate unique combinations of receptor types, and they have started to identify those combinations. Odours also have psychological effects and can affect behaviour even when people are unaware of their influence. Cultural and individual differences also affect people's responses to particular odours.

◆ The skin senses include touch (pressure), warmth, cold, pain, and variations such as itch and tickle. Except in the case of pressure, it has been difficult to identify specialized receptors for these senses, but researchers have reported a receptor for one kind of itching and a possible receptor for cold.

◆ Pain is both a skin sense and an internal sense. According to the *gate-control theory*, the experience of pain depends on whether neural impulses get past a "gate" in the spinal cord and reach the brain. According to a revised version of this theory, a matrix of neurons in the brain can generate pain even in the absence of signals from sensory neurons, which may help explain the puzzling phenomenon of *phantom pain*. No one theory, however, completely explains perception of pain, which involves the release of many chemicals all along the pain pathways, and also the involvement of *glial cells*.

◆ *Kinesthesis* tells us where our body parts are located, and *equilibrium* tells us the orientation of the body as a whole. Together, these two senses provide us with a feeling of physical embodiment.

PERCEPTUAL POWERS: ORIGINS AND INFLUENCES

◆ Many fundamental perceptual skills are inborn or are acquired shortly after birth. By using the *visual cliff*, for example, psychologists have learned that babies have depth perception by the age of 6 months and possibly even earlier. However, without certain experiences during *critical periods* early in life, cells in the nervous system deteriorate, change, or fail to form appropriate neural pathways, and perception is impaired. This is why efforts to correct congenital blindness or deafness are most successful when they take place early in life.

◆ Psychological influences on perception include needs, beliefs, emotions, and expectations (which produce *perceptual sets*). These influences are determined by culture, which gives people practice with certain kinds of experiences and affects what they attend to.

PUZZLES OF PERCEPTION

◆ In the laboratory, studies using *priming* show that simple visual subliminal messages can influence certain behaviours, judgments, and motivational states, such as thirst. However, no evidence indicates that "subliminal-perception" tapes or other commercial subliminal techniques can alter complex behaviours.

TAKING PSYCHOLOGY WITH YOU

◆ Years of research have failed to produce convincing evidence for extrasensory perception (ESP). What so-called psychics do is no different from what all good magicians do: capitalize on people's beliefs and expectations.

MyPsychLab

Visit **www.mypsychlab.com** to help you get the best grade!
Test your knowledge and grasp difficult concepts through

• Custom study plans: See where you are strong and where you go wrong
• Interactive simulations
• Video and audio clips

KEY TERMS

sensation *190*
perception *190*
sense receptors *190*
doctrine of specific nerve energies *191*
synesthesia *191*
absolute threshold *192*
difference threshold *193*
signal-detection theory *194*
sensory adaptation *194*
sensory deprivation *195*
selective attention *197*
inattentional blindness *197*
hue *198*
brightness *198*
saturation *198*

retina *198*
rods *199*
cones *199*
dark adaptation *199*
ganglion cells *199*
feature detector cells *201*
trichromatic theory *203*
opponent-process theory *203*
Gestalt principles *204*
binocular cues *205*
convergence *205*
retinal disparity *205*
monocular cues *205*
perceptual constancy *207*
loudness *211*

pitch *212*
timbre *212*
organ of Corti *213*
cochlea *213*
papillae *215*
taste buds *215*
gate-control theory of pain *219*
phantom pain *220*
kinesthesis *220*
equilibrium *220*
semicircular canals *220*
perceptual set *225*
priming *227*

7 LEARNING AND CONDITIONING

ASK QUESTIONS . . . be willing to WONDER

- Why are so many people scared to death of snakes and spiders?
- Why do efforts to crack down on wrongdoers often fail?
- Is there anything wrong with paying kids to get good grades?
- Why does playing violent video games make some people aggressive and others not?

It's January 1, a brand-new year. The sins and lapses of the old year are behind you; the slate is clean and you're ready for a fresh start. Optimistically, you sit down to record your New Year's resolutions: to eat fewer fatty foods, study harder, get more exercise, manage your spending . . . (you can fill in the rest). How likely are you to achieve these goals? Within weeks, days, or even hours, many people find themselves reverting to their old habits ("Well, maybe just one *small* chocolate bar"). They may decide that trying to mend their ways is pointless because they lack the willpower to do it. In this chapter, however, we will see that in fact, these factors often have little to do with the ability to change your ways.

People do not want to fix just their own behaviour, of course; they are forever trying to fix other people's behaviour as well. We imprison criminals, spank children, give the finger to a driver who cuts us off, and impose zero tolerance policies for the slightest infraction of a rule. On the positive side, we give children gold stars for good work, give their parents bumper stickers that praise their children's successes, give bonuses to employees, and give out trophies for top performance.

Do any of these efforts get the results we hope for? Well, yes and no. Once you understand the laws of **learning**, you will realize that behaviour, whether it's your own or other people's, *can* change for the better—and you will also understand why often it does not.

Research on learning has been heavily influenced by **behaviourism**, the school of psychology that accounts for behaviour in terms of observable acts and events, without reference to mental entities such as "mind" or "will" (see Chapter 1). Behaviourists focus on **conditioning**, which involves associations between environmental stimuli and responses. They have shown that two types of conditioning, *classical conditioning* and *operant conditioning*, can explain a great deal of behaviour both in animals and in people. But other approaches, including *social-cognitive learning theories*, hold that omitting mental processes from explanations of human learning is like omitting passion from descriptions of sex: You may explain the form, but you miss its essence. To social-cognitive theorists, learning includes not only changes in behaviour but also changes in thoughts, expectations, and knowledge, which in turn influence behaviour in a reciprocal, or two-way, process.

learning A relatively permanent change in behaviour (or behavioural potential) due to experience.

behaviourism An approach to psychology that emphasizes the study of observable behaviour and the role of the environment as a determinant of behaviour.

conditioning A basic kind of learning that involves associations between environmental stimuli and the organism's responses.

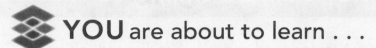
YOU are about to learn . . .

◆ how classical conditioning explains why a dog might salivate when it sees a light bulb or hears a buzzer.

◆ four important features of classical conditioning.

◆ what is actually learned in classical conditioning.

CLASSICAL CONDITIONING

At the turn of the twentieth century, the great Russian physiologist Ivan Pavlov (1849–1936) was studying salivation in dogs as part of his Nobel prize–winning research program on digestion. One of his procedures was to make a surgical opening in a dog's cheek and insert a tube that conducted saliva away from the animal's salivary gland so that the saliva could be measured. To stimulate the reflexive flow of saliva, Pavlov placed meat powder or other food in the dog's mouth (see Figure 7.1).

Pavlov was a truly dedicated scientific observer. Many years later, as he lay dying, he even dictated his sensations for posterity! And he instilled in his students the same passion for detail. During his salivation studies, one of the assistants noticed something that most people would have overlooked or dismissed as trivial. After a dog had been brought to the laboratory a few times, it would start to salivate *before* the food was placed in its mouth. The sight or smell of the food, the dish in which the food was kept, and even the sight of the person who delivered the food were enough to start the dog's mouth watering. These new salivary responses were clearly not inborn, so they must have been acquired through experience.

At first, Pavlov treated the dog's drooling as just an annoying secretion. But he quickly realized that his assistant had stumbled onto an important phenomenon, one that Pavlov came to believe was the basis of most learning in human beings and other animals (Pavlov, 1927). He called that phenomenon a "conditional" reflex because it depended on environmental conditions. Later, an error in the translation of his writings transformed "conditional" into "conditioned," the word most commonly used today.

Pavlov soon dropped what he had been doing and turned to the study of conditioned reflexes, to which he devoted the last three decades of his life. Why were his dogs salivating to things other than food?

FIGURE 7.1 **Pavlov's Method**
The photo shows Ivan Pavlov (with the white beard), flanked by his students and a canine subject. The drawing depicts an apparatus similar to the one he used; saliva from a dog's cheek flowed down a tube and was measured by the movement of a needle on a revolving drum.

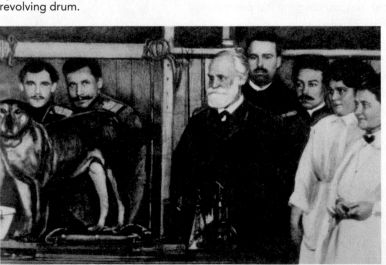

New Reflexes from Old

Pavlov initially speculated about what his dogs might be thinking and feeling when they drooled before getting their food. Was the doggy equivalent of "Oh boy, dinner!" going through their minds? He soon decided, however, that such speculation was pointless. Instead, he focused on analyzing the environment in which the conditioned reflex arose.

The original salivary reflex, according to Pavlov, consisted of an **unconditioned stimulus (US)**, food in the dog's mouth, and an **unconditioned response (UR)**, salivation. By an unconditioned stimulus, Pavlov meant an event or thing that elicits a response automatically or reflexively. By an unconditioned response, he meant the response that is automatically produced:

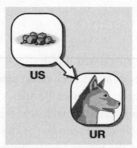

Learning occurs, said Pavlov, when a neutral stimulus (one that does not yet produce a particular response, such as salivation) is regularly paired with an unconditioned stimulus:

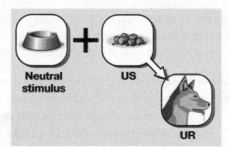

The neutral stimulus then becomes a **conditioned stimulus (CS)**, which elicits a learned or **conditioned response (CR)** that is usually similar or related to the original, unlearned one. In Pavlov's laboratory, the sight of the food dish, which had not previously elicited salivation, became a CS for salivation:

The procedure by which a neutral stimulus becomes a conditioned stimulus became known as **classical conditioning**, also called *Pavlovian* or *respondent* conditioning. Pavlov and his students went on to show that all sorts of things can become conditioned

unconditioned stimulus (US)
The classical-conditioning term for a stimulus that elicits a reflexive response in the absence of learning.

unconditioned response (UR)
The classical-conditioning term for a reflexive response elicited by a stimulus in the absence of learning.

conditioned stimulus (CS)
The classical-conditioning term for an initially neutral stimulus that comes to elicit a conditioned response after being associated with an unconditioned stimulus.

conditioned response (CR)
The classical-conditioning term for a response that is elicited by a conditioned stimulus; it occurs after the conditioned stimulus is associated with an unconditioned stimulus.

classical conditioning The process by which a previously neutral stimulus acquires the capacity to elicit a response through association with a stimulus that already elicits a similar or related response. Also called *Pavlovian* or *respondent* conditioning.

FIGURE 7.2 Acquisition and Extinction of a Salivary Response

A neutral stimulus that is consistently followed by an unconditioned stimulus for salivation will become a conditioned stimulus for salivation (left). But when this conditioned stimulus is then repeatedly presented without the unconditioned stimulus, the conditioned salivary response will weaken and eventually disappear (right); it has been extinguished.

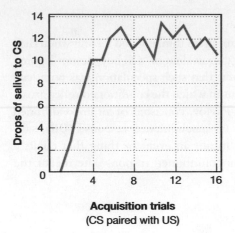

Acquisition trials
(CS paired with US)

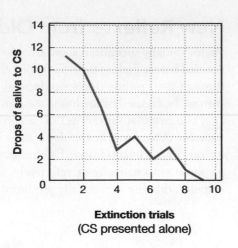

Extinction trials
(CS presented alone)

✱ **Explore**
Three Stages of Classical Conditioning

✱ **Explore**
Process of Extinction and Spontaneous Recovery

extinction   The weakening and eventual disappearance of a learned response; in classical conditioning, it occurs when the conditioned stimulus is no longer paired with the unconditioned stimulus.

spontaneous recovery
The reappearance of a learned response after its apparent extinction.

higher-order conditioning
In classical conditioning, a procedure in which a neutral stimulus becomes a conditioned stimulus through association with an already established conditioned stimulus.

stimuli for salivation if they are paired with food: the ticking of a metronome and other sounds, a touch on the leg, or even a pinprick or an electric shock. And since Pavlov's day, many automatic, involuntary responses besides salivation have been classically conditioned—for example, heartbeat, stomach secretions, blood pressure, reflexive movements, blinking, and muscle contractions. In the laboratory, the optimal interval between the presentation of the neutral stimulus and the presentation of the US depends on the kind of response involved, although it is often quite short, sometimes less than a second.

Principles of Classical Conditioning

Classical conditioning occurs in all species, from amoebas to *Homo sapiens*. Let us look more closely at some important features of this process: extinction, higher-order conditioning, and stimulus generalization and discrimination.

EXTINCTION.   Conditioned responses do not necessarily last forever. If, after conditioning, the conditioned stimulus is repeatedly presented without the unconditioned stimulus, the conditioned response eventually disappears and **extinction** is said to have occurred (see Figure 7.2). Suppose that you train your dog Deke to salivate to the sound of a bell, but then you ring the bell every five minutes and do *not* follow it with food. Deke will salivate less and less to the bell and will soon stop salivating altogether; salivation will have been extinguished. Extinction is not the same as unlearning or forgetting, however. If you come back the next day and ring the bell, Deke may salivate again for a few trials, although the response will probably be weaker. The reappearance of the response, called **spontaneous recovery**, explains why completely eliminating a conditioned response often requires more than one extinction session.

HIGHER-ORDER CONDITIONING.   Sometimes a neutral stimulus can become a conditioned stimulus by being paired with an already established CS, a procedure known as **higher-order conditioning**. Say Deke has learned to salivate to the sight of his food dish. Now you flash a bright light before presenting the dish. With repeated pairings of the light and the dish, Deke may learn to salivate to the light. The procedure for higher-order conditioning is illustrated in Figure 7.3.

Higher-order conditioning may explain why some words trigger emotional responses in us—why they can inflame us to anger or evoke warm, sentimental feelings. When words are paired with objects or other words that already elicit some emotional response, they too may come to elicit that response (Staats & Staats, 1957). For example, a child may learn a positive response to the word *birthday* because of its association

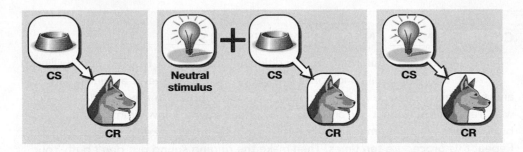

FIGURE 7.3 Higher-Order Conditioning

In this illustration of higher-order conditioning, the food dish is a previously conditioned stimulus for salivation (left). When the light, a neutral stimulus, is paired with the dish (centre), the light also becomes a conditioned stimulus for salivation (right).

with gifts and attention. Conversely, the child may learn a negative response to ethnic or national labels if the labels are paired with words that the child has already learned are disagreeable, such as *dumb* or *dirty*. Higher-order conditioning, in other words, may contribute to the formation of prejudices.

✳ Explore
Higher-Order Conditioning
Process of Stimulus

Generalization and Stimulus Distinction in Classical Conditioning

STIMULUS GENERALIZATION AND DISCRIMINATION. After a stimulus becomes a conditioned stimulus for some response, other, similar stimuli may produce a similar reaction—a phenomenon known as **stimulus generalization**. For example, if you condition your patient pooch Deke to salivate to middle C on the piano, Deke may also salivate to D, which is one tone above C, even though you did not pair D with food. Stimulus generalization is described nicely by an old English proverb: "He who hath been bitten by a snake fears a rope."

The mirror image of stimulus generalization is **stimulus discrimination**, in which *different* responses are made to stimuli that resemble the conditioned stimulus in some way. Suppose that you have conditioned Deke to salivate to middle C on the piano by repeatedly pairing the sound with food. Now you play middle C on a guitar, *without* following it by food (but you continue to follow C on the piano by food). Eventually, Deke will learn to salivate to a C on the piano and not to salivate to the same note on the guitar; that is, he will discriminate between the two sounds. If you kept at this long enough, you could train Deke to be a pretty discriminating drooler!

stimulus generalization After conditioning, the tendency to respond to a stimulus that resembles one involved in the original conditioning; in classical conditioning, it occurs when a stimulus that resembles the CS elicits the CR.

stimulus discrimination The tendency to respond differently to two or more similar stimuli; in classical conditioning, it occurs when a stimulus similar to the CS fails to evoke the CR.

What Is Actually Learned in Classical Conditioning?

For classical conditioning to be most effective, the stimulus to be conditioned should *precede* the unconditioned stimulus rather than follow it or occur simultaneously with it. This makes sense because in classical conditioning, the conditioned stimulus becomes a *signal* for the unconditioned stimulus. Classical conditioning is in fact an evolutionary adaptation, one that enables the organism to anticipate and prepare for a biologically important event that is about to happen. In Pavlov's studies, for instance, a bell, buzzer, or other stimulus was a signal that meat was coming, and the dog's salivation was preparation for digesting food. Today, therefore, many psychologists contend that what an animal or person actually learns in classical conditioning is not merely an association between two paired stimuli that occur close together in time, but rather *information* conveyed by one stimulus about another: for example, "If a tone sounds, food is likely to follow."

This view is supported by the research of Robert Rescorla (1988), who showed, in a series of imaginative studies, that the mere pairing of an unconditioned stimulus and a neutral stimulus is not enough to produce learning. To become a conditioned stimulus, the neutral stimulus must reliably signal, or *predict*, the unconditioned stimulus. If food occurs just as often *without* a preceding tone as with it, the tone is unlikely to become a

Get INVOLVED!

CONDITIONING AN EYE-BLINK RESPONSE

Try out your behavioural skills by conditioning an eye-blink response in a willing friend, using classical-conditioning procedures. You will need a drinking straw and something to make a ringing sound; a spoon tapped on a water glass works well. Tell your friend that you are going to use the straw to blow air in his or her eye, but do not say why. Immediately before each puff of air, make the ringing sound. Repeat this procedure ten times. Then make the ringing sound but *don't* puff. Your friend will probably blink anyway, and may continue to do so for one or two more repetitions of the sound before the response extinguishes. Can you identify the US, the UR, the CS, and the CR in this exercise?

conditioned stimulus for salivation, because the tone does not provide any information about the probability of getting food. Think of it this way: If every phone call you got brought bad news that made your heart race, your heart might soon start pounding every time the phone rang—a conditioned response. Ordinarily, though, upsetting calls occur randomly among a far greater number of routine ones. The ringtone may sometimes be paired with a racing heart, but it doesn't always signal disaster, so no conditioned heart-rate response occurs.

Rescorla concluded that "Pavlovian conditioning is not a stupid process by which the organism willy-nilly forms associations between any two stimuli that happen to co-occur. Rather, the organism is better seen as an information seeker using logical and perceptual relations among events, along with its own preconceptions, to form a sophisticated representation of its world." Not all learning theorists agree; an orthodox behaviourist would say that it is silly to talk about the preconceptions of a rat. The important point, however, is that concepts such as "information seeking," "preconceptions," and "representations of the world" open the door to a more cognitive view of classical conditioning.

quickQUIZ

✓• Quick Review on **MyPsychLab**

Classical-conditioning terms can be hard to learn, so make sure to take this quiz before going on.

A. Name the unconditioned stimulus, unconditioned response, conditioned stimulus, and conditioned response in these two situations.

1. Five-year-old Samantha is watching a storm from her window. A huge bolt of lightning is followed by a tremendous thunderclap, and Samantha jumps at the noise. This happens several more times. There is a brief lull and then another lightning bolt. Samantha jumps in response to the bolt.

2. Gregory's mouth waters whenever he eats anything with lemon in it. One day, while reading an ad that shows a big glass of lemonade, Gregory finds that his mouth has started to water.

B. In the view of many learning theorists, pairing a neutral and unconditioned stimulus is not enough to produce classical conditioning; the neutral stimulus must _____ the unconditioned stimulus.

Answers:

A. 1. US = the thunderclap; UR = jumping elicited by the noise; CS = the sight of the lightning; CR = jumping elicited by the lightning   2. US = the taste of lemon; UR = salivation elicited by the taste of lemon; CS = the picture of a glass of lemonade; CR = salivation elicited by the picture   B. signal or predict

YOU are about to learn . . .

◆ why advertisers often include pleasant music and gorgeous scenery in ads for their products.

◆ how classical conditioning might explain your irrational fear of heights or mice.

◆ how you might be conditioned to like certain tastes and odours and be turned off by others.

◆ how sitting in a doctor's office can make you feel sick and placebos can make you feel better.

◆ how technology is helping researchers study the biological basis of classical conditioning.

CLASSICAL CONDITIONING IN REAL LIFE

If a dog can learn to salivate to the ringing of a bell, so can you. In fact, you have probably learned to salivate to the sound of a lunch bell, the phrase *hot fudge sundae*, and "mouth-watering" pictures of food. But classical conditioning affects us every day in many other ways.

One of the first psychologists to recognize the real-life implications of Pavlovian theory was John B. Watson, who founded behaviourism in North America and enthusiastically promoted Pavlov's ideas. Watson believed that the whole rich array of human emotion and behaviour could be accounted for by conditioning principles. For example, he thought that you learned to love another person when that person was paired with stroking and cuddling. Most psychologists (and nonpsychologists, too) think Watson was wrong about love, which is a lot more complicated than he thought (see Chapter 12). But he was right about the power of classical conditioning to affect our emotions, preferences, and tastes.

John B. Watson (1878–1958).

Learning to Like

Classical conditioning plays a big role in our emotional responses to objects, people, symbols, events, and places. It can explain why sentimental feelings sweep over us when we see a school mascot, a national flag, or the logo of the Olympic games. These objects have been associated in the past with positive feelings:

US (stirring music)

UR (positive emotion)

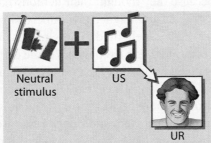

Neutral stimulus + US

UR

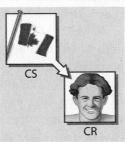

CS

CR

Many advertising techniques take advantage of classical conditioning's role in emotional responses. In one study, students at the University of British Columbia

Why do most people fear snakes, and why do some even develop a snake phobia?

looked at slides of either a beige pen or a blue pen. During the presentation, half of the students heard the theme song from a recent popular movie, and half heard a selection of traditional music from India. (The experimenter made the reasonable assumption that the theme music would be more appealing to the students in the study.) Later the students were allowed to choose one of the pens. Almost three-fourths of those who heard the theme music chose a pen that was the same colour as the one they had seen in the slides. An equal number of those who heard the Indian music chose a pen that *differed* in colour from the one they had seen (Gorn, 1982).

In classical-conditioning terms, the music in this study was an unconditioned stimulus for internal responses associated with pleasure or displeasure, and the pens became conditioned stimuli for similar responses. You can see why advertisers often pair their products with music, attractive people, or other appealing sounds and images.

Learning to Fear

Positive emotions are not the only ones that can be classically conditioned; so can dislikes and fears. A person can learn to fear just about anything if it is paired with something that elicits pain, surprise, or embarrassment. Human beings, however, are biologically primed or "prepared" to acquire some kinds of fears more readily than others. It is far easier to establish a conditioned fear of spiders, snakes, and heights than of butterflies, flowers, and toasters. The former can be dangerous to your health, so in the process of evolution, human beings acquired a tendency to learn quickly to be wary of them and to retain this fear (LoBue & DeLoache, 2008; Öhman & Mineka, 2001). Some theorists believe that evolution has also instilled in humans a readiness to learn to fear unfamiliar members of ethnic groups other than their own, and that this tendency too resists extinction, and may contribute to the emotional underpinnings of prejudice (Navarrete et al., 2009; Olsson et al., 2005).

When fear of an object or situation becomes irrational and interferes with normal activities, it qualifies as a *phobia* (see Chapter 15). To demonstrate how a phobia might be learned, John Watson and Rosalie Rayner (1920/2000) deliberately established a rat phobia in an 11-month-old boy named Albert. Their goal was to demonstrate how an inborn reaction of fear could transfer to a wide range of stimuli; today we call this stimulus generalization. They also wanted to demonstrate that adult emotional responses, such as specific fears, could originate in early childhood. The research procedures used by Watson and Rayner had some flaws, and for ethical reasons, no psychologist today would attempt to do such a thing to a child. Nevertheless, the study's main conclusion, that fears can be conditioned, is still well accepted.

"Little Albert" was a placid child who rarely cried. (Watson and Rayner deliberately chose such a child because they thought their demonstration would do him relatively little harm.) When Watson and Rayner gave Albert a live, furry rat to play with, he showed no fear; in fact, he was delighted. The same was true when they showed him a variety of other objects, including a rabbit and some cotton wool. However, like most children, Albert was innately afraid of loud noises. When the researchers made a loud noise behind his head by striking a steel bar with a hammer, he would jump and fall sideways onto the mattress where he was sitting. The noise made by the hammer was an unconditioned stimulus for the unconditioned response of fear.

Having established that Albert liked rats, Watson and Rayner set about teaching him to fear them. Again they offered him a rat, but this time, as he reached for it, one of the researchers struck the steel bar. Startled, Albert fell onto the mattress. A week later, the researchers repeated this procedure several times. Albert began to whimper and tremble. Finally, they held out the rat to him without making the noise. Albert fell over, cried, and crawled away so quickly that he almost reached the edge of the table he was sitting on before an adult caught him; the rat had become a conditioned stimulus for fear:

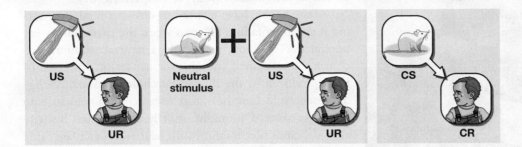

Tests done a few days later showed that Albert's fear had generalized to other hairy or furry objects, including a white rabbit, cotton wool, a Santa Claus mask, and even John Watson's hair.

Unfortunately, Watson and Rayner lost access to Little Albert, so we do not know how long the child's fears lasted. Further, because the study ended early, Watson and Rayner had no opportunity to reverse the conditioning. However, Watson and Mary Cover Jones did reverse another child's conditioned fear—one that was, as Watson put it, "home-grown" rather than psychologist-induced (Jones, 1924). A three-year-old named Peter was deathly afraid of rabbits. Watson and Jones eliminated his fear with a method called **counterconditioning**, in which a conditioned stimulus is paired with some other stimulus that elicits a response incompatible with the unwanted response. In this case, the rabbit (the CS) was paired with a snack of milk and crackers, and the snack produced pleasant feelings that were incompatible with the conditioned response of fear. At first, the researchers kept the rabbit some distance from Peter, so that his fear would remain at a low level. Otherwise, Peter might have learned to fear milk and crackers! Then gradually, over several days, they brought the rabbit closer and closer. Eventually Peter learned to like rabbits:

✳ **Explore**
Classical Conditioning of Little Albert

◉ **Watch**
Little Albert

  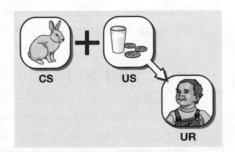 

Peter was even able to sit with the rabbit in his lap, playing with it with one hand while he ate with the other. A variation of this procedure, called *systematic desensitization*, was later devised for treating phobias in adults (see Chapter 16).

Accounting for Taste

Classical conditioning can also explain learned reactions to many foods and odours. In the laboratory, researchers have taught animals to dislike foods or odours by pairing them with drugs that cause nausea or other unpleasant symptoms. One research team trained slugs to associate the smell of carrots, which slugs normally like, with a bitter-tasting chemical they detest. Soon the slugs were avoiding the smell of carrots.

counterconditioning In classical conditioning, the process of pairing a conditioned stimulus with a stimulus that elicits a response that is incompatible with an unwanted conditioned response.

Whether we say "yuck" or "yum" to a food may depend on a past experience involving classical conditioning. This Inuit family is eating mattak, the raw fatty skin of a beluga whale, which is considered a delicacy by this culture. You may not respond as positively to this treat.

✱ **Explore**
Taste Aversion

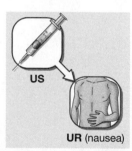

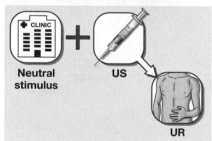

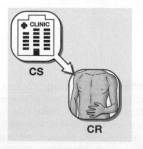

The researchers then demonstrated higher-order conditioning by pairing the smell of carrots with the smell of potato. Sure enough, the slugs began to avoid the smell of potato as well (Sahley, Rudy, & Gelperin, 1981).

Many people have learned to dislike a food after eating it and then falling ill, even when the two events were unrelated. The food, previously a neutral stimulus, becomes a conditioned stimulus for nausea or other symptoms produced by the illness. Psychologist Martin Seligman once told how he himself was conditioned to hate béarnaise sauce. One night, shortly after he and his wife ate a delicious filet mignon with béarnaise sauce, he came down with the flu. Naturally, he felt wretched. His misery had nothing to do with the béarnaise sauce, of course, yet the next time he tried it, he found to his annoyance that he disliked the taste (Seligman & Hager, 1972).

Notice that unlike conditioning in the laboratory, Seligman's aversion to the sauce occurred after only one pairing of the sauce with illness and with a considerable delay between the conditioned and unconditioned stimuli. Moreover, Seligman's wife did not become a conditioned stimulus for nausea, and neither did his dinner plate or the waiter, even though they had also been paired with illness. Why? In earlier work with rats, John Garcia and Robert Koelling (1966) had provided the answer: the existence of a greater biological readiness to associate sickness with taste than with sights or sounds (the "Garcia effect"). Like the tendency to acquire certain fears, this biological tendency probably evolved because it enhanced survival: Eating bad food is more likely to be followed by illness and death than are particular sights or sounds.

Psychologists have taken advantage of this phenomenon to develop humane ways of discouraging predators from preying on livestock, using conditioned taste aversions instead of traps and poisons. In one classic study, researchers laced sheep meat with a nausea-inducing chemical; coyotes and wolves fell for the bait, and as a result they developed a conditioned aversion to sheep (Gustavson et al., 1974). Similar techniques have been used to deter other predators—for example, to deter raccoons from killing chickens, and ravens and crows from eating crane eggs (Garcia & Gustavson, 1997).

Reacting to Medical Treatments

Because of classical conditioning, medical treatments can create unexpected misery or relief from symptoms for reasons that are entirely unrelated to the treatment itself. For example, unpleasant reactions to a treatment can generalize to a wide range of other stimuli. This is a particular problem for cancer patients. The nausea and vomiting resulting from chemotherapy often generalize to the place where the therapy takes place, the waiting room, the sound of a nurse's voice, or the smell of rubbing alcohol. The drug treatment is an unconditioned stimulus for nausea and vomiting, and through association, the other previously neutral stimuli become conditioned stimuli for these responses. Even *mental images* of the sights and smells of the clinic can become conditioned stimuli for nausea (Dadds et al., 1997; Redd et al., 1993).

Some cancer patients also acquire a classically conditioned anxiety response to anything associated with their chemotherapy. In one study, patients who drank lemon-lime Kool-Aid before their therapy sessions developed an anxiety response to the drink—an example of higher-order conditioning. They continued to feel anxious even when the drink was offered in their homes rather than at the clinic (Jacobsen et al., 1995).

On the other hand, patients may have *reduced* pain and anxiety when they receive *placebos,* pills and injections that have no active ingredients or treatments that have no direct physical effect on the problem. Placebos can be amazingly powerful, especially when they take the form of an injection, a large pill, or a pill with a brand name (Benedetti & Levi-Montalcini, 2001). Why do placebos work? Biological psychologists have shown that placebos can actually affect the brain in much the same way as real treatments do (see Chapter 6). Cognitive psychologists emphasize the role of expectations (at least in humans); expectations of getting better may reduce anxiety and thus boost the immune system, or perhaps they encourage us to cope better with our symptoms. In contrast, behaviourists argue that the doctor's white coat, the doctor's office, and pills or injections all become conditioned stimuli for relief from symptoms because these stimuli have been associated in the past with *real* drugs (Ader, 2000). The real drugs are the unconditioned stimuli, and the relief they bring is the unconditioned response. Placebos acquire the ability to elicit similar reactions, thereby becoming conditioned stimuli.

The expectancy explanation of placebo effects and the classical-conditioning explanation are not mutually exclusive (Kirsch, 2004; Stewart-Williams & Podd, 2004). As we saw earlier, many researchers now accept the view that classical conditioning itself involves the expectation that the conditioned stimulus will be followed by the unconditioned stimulus. Thus, at least some classically conditioned placebo effects may involve the patient's expectations. In fact, the patient's previous conditioning history may be what created those expectations to begin with.

BIOLOGY *and* Classical Conditioning

Pavlov and Peanut Butter

A century ago, when Ivan Pavlov taught dogs to salivate to the sound of a bell, he focused on the observable associations between unconditioned and conditioned stimuli and responses. Although he was interested in the biological basis of classical conditioning, techniques for studying that topic were limited. Today, sophisticated technology has changed that. We'll give you a taste of the research being done, and in our first example, one taste involves peanut butter.

In an imaginative study, British researchers trained 13 hungry volunteers to associate abstract computer images with the pleasant smell of peanut butter or vanilla (Gottfried, O'Doherty, & Dolan, 2003). The volunteers had to say which side of the screen an image appeared on, and soon they were reacting faster to the images associated with the pleasant food odours than to other images. Using functional MRI, the researchers discovered that when the participants saw the images—which presumably had now become conditioned stimuli for pleasure or appetite—their brains showed surges of activity in two areas known to be involved in motivation and emotion, the amygdala and a specific area of the prefrontal cortex (see Chapter 4).

You're stuffed after a good meal, yet you suddenly find room for dessert. Why?

FIGURE 7.4 A Drug for Extinction

A fear of heights is a common phobia. Studies have used virtual-reality images in therapy with people suffering from a phobia for heights. Participants had to "look down" to the bottom of a building while peering over a catwalk. Those who received a drug that facilitates extinction improved significantly more than did those who got a placebo.

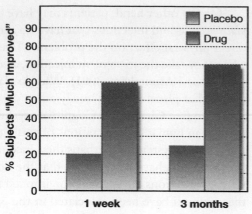

Then the participants got to eat either vanilla ice cream or peanut butter sandwiches until they were full. Afterward, the images associated with the food a person had just eaten no longer produced such quick reactions and no longer evoked the same brain activity. The images associated with the other food, however, continued to produce the same reaction times and brain responses. These results may explain why feeling full is not an all-or-none phenomenon—why we can have our fill of one food, yet still be tempted by another: The stimuli associated with the second food continue to fire up our motivational brain centres. This helps to ensure that we eat a variety of foods and get a variety of nutrients. The results also explain the "dessert tray phenomenon": At a restaurant, just when you think you can't eat another bite, the server brings over some desserts and suddenly you have room for that luscious-looking piece of cheesecake after all.

Researchers are also exploring the biological basis of fear conditioning and fear extinction. The acquisition of a conditioned fear appears to involve a receptor in the amygdala for the neurotransmitter glutamate. Giving rats a drug that blocks this receptor prevents extinction of a conditioned fear, whereas giving a drug that enhances the receptor's activity speeds up extinction (Walker et al., 2002). Inspired by these results, researchers set out to learn whether the receptor-enhancing drug (which is safe in humans) could help people with a phobic fear of heights (Davis et al., 2005). Using a double-blind procedure, they gave the drug to 15 such people and a placebo to 15 others. The participants then underwent two therapy sessions in which they donned virtual-reality goggles and "rode" a glass elevator to progressively higher floors in a virtual hotel—an incredibly scary thing to do if you're terrified of heights. They could also "walk" out on a bridge and look down on a fountain in the hotel lobby. During each session, and again at one-week and three-month follow-up sessions, the participants rated their discomfort at each "floor." Combining the therapy with the drug reduced symptoms far more than combining it with the placebo, as you can see in Figure 7.4. Further, in their everyday lives, people who got the drug were less likely than the controls to avoid heights.

Finally, DNA analysis has been used to investigate how genetic differences might explain why some people are more likely than others to become anxious and fearful. In a study done in Sweden, researchers conditioned university students to startle in response to pictures of faces. Only those students who had a particular gene associated with reactivity in the amygdala acquired the conditioned startle response. Moreover, those students who carried a gene associated with impaired cognitive control in the prefrontal cortex showed resistance to extinction of the response (Lonsdorf et al., 2009).

Such research helps us understand the biological mechanisms that underlie our innate and conditioned fears, and the principles of behaviourism that can help us control and even overcome them (see Chapter 16).

We hope you have not acquired a classically conditioned fear of quizzes.
See whether you can supply the correct term to describe the outcome in each of these situations.

1. After a child learns to fear spiders, he also responds with fear to ants, beetles, and other crawling bugs.

2. A toddler is afraid of the bath, so her father puts just a little water in the tub and gives the child a lollipop to suck on while she is being washed. Soon the little girl loses her fear of the bath.

3. A factory worker's mouth waters whenever a noontime bell signals the beginning of his lunch break. One day, the bell goes haywire and rings every half hour. By the end of the day, the worker has stopped salivating to the bell.

4. Work on how certain brain areas respond to conditioned stimuli associated with food shows that (a) brain activity decreases after a person fills up on the food but remains high for other foods; (b) the brain responds equally to desired and disliked foods; (c) brain mechanisms ensure that we eat the same basic set of foods all the time; (d) taste preferences cannot be classically conditioned.

Answers:

1. stimulus generalization   2. counterconditioning   3. extinction   4. a

---

🔷 YOU are about to learn . . .

◆ how the consequences of your actions affect your future behaviour.

◆ what praising a child and quitting your nagging have in common.

OPERANT CONDITIONING

At the end of the nineteenth century, in the first known scientific study of anger, G. Stanley Hall (1899) asked people to describe angry episodes they had experienced or observed. One person told of a three-year-old girl who broke out in seemingly uncontrollable sobs when she was kept home from a ride. In the middle of her outburst, the child suddenly stopped and asked her nanny in a perfectly calm voice if her father was in. Told no, and realizing that he was not around to put a stop to her tantrum, she immediately resumed her sobbing.

Children, of course, cry for many valid reasons—pain, discomfort, fear, illness, fatigue—and these cries deserve an adult's sympathy and attention. The child in Hall's study, however, was crying because she had learned from prior experience that an outburst of sobbing would pay off by bringing her attention and possibly the ride she wanted. Her tantrum illustrates one of the most basic laws of learning: *Behaviour becomes more likely or less likely depending on its consequences.*

This principle is at the heart of **operant conditioning** (also called *instrumental conditioning*), the second type of conditioning studied by behaviourists. In classical conditioning, it does not matter whether an animal's or person's behaviour has consequences. In Pavlov's procedure, for example, the dog learned an association between two events that were not under its control (e.g., a tone and the delivery of food) and the animal got food whether or not it salivated. But in operant conditioning, the

the neighborhood Jerry Van Amerongen

An instantaneous learning experience.

© Creators Syndicate Inc. By permission of Jerry Van Amerongen and Creators Syndicate, Inc.

operant conditioning The process by which a response becomes more likely to occur or less so, depending on its consequences.

organism's response (the little girl's sobbing, for example) *operates* or produces effects on the environment. These effects, in turn, influence whether the response will occur again.

Classical conditioning and operant conditioning also tend to differ in the types of responses they involve. In classical conditioning, the response is typically reflexive, an automatic reaction to something happening in the environment, such as the sight of food or the sound of a bell. Generally, responses in operant conditioning are complex and are not reflexive—for instance, riding a bicycle, writing a letter, climbing a mountain . . . or throwing a tantrum.

The Birth of Radical Behaviourism

Operant conditioning has been studied since the start of the twentieth century, although it was not called that until later. Edward Thorndike (1898), then a young doctoral candidate, set the stage by observing cats as they tried to escape from a complex "puzzle box" to reach a scrap of fish located just outside the box. At first, the cat would scratch, bite, or swat at parts of the box in an unorganized way. Then, after a few minutes, it would chance on the successful response (loosening a bolt, pulling a string, or hitting a button) and rush out to get the reward. Placed in the box again, the cat now took a little less time to escape, and after several trials, the animal immediately made the correct response. According to Thorndike, this response had been "stamped in" by the satisfying result of getting the food. In contrast, annoying or unsatisfying results "stamped out" behaviour. Behaviour, said Thorndike, is controlled by its consequences.

This general principle was elaborated and extended to more complex forms of behaviour by B. F. (Burrhus Frederic) Skinner (1904–1990). Skinner called his approach "radical behaviourism" to distinguish it from the behaviourism of John Watson, who emphasized classical conditioning. Skinner argued that to understand behaviour we should focus on the external causes of an action and the action's consequences. He avoided terms that Thorndike used, such as "satisfying" and "annoying," which reflect assumptions about what an organism feels and wants. To explain behaviour, he said, we should look outside the individual, not inside.

The Consequences of Behaviour

In Skinner's analysis, which has inspired an immense body of research, a response ("operant") can be influenced by two types of consequences:

1 **Reinforcement strengthens the response or makes it more likely to recur.**
   When your dog begs for food at the table, and you give her the lamb chop off your plate, her begging is likely to increase:

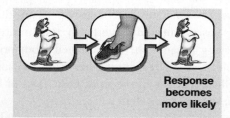

**Response
becomes
more likely**

Reinforcers are roughly equivalent to rewards, and many psychologists use *reward* and *reinforcer* as approximate synonyms. However, strict behaviourists avoid the word *reward* because it implies that something has been earned that results in happiness or satisfaction. To a behaviourist, a stimulus is a reinforcer if it strengthens the preceding behaviour, whether or not the organism experiences

reinforcement The process by which a stimulus or event strengthens or increases the probability of the response that it follows.

pleasure or a positive emotion. Conversely, no matter how pleasurable a reward is, it is not a reinforcer if it does not increase the likelihood of a response. It's great to get a cheque, but if you get paid regardless of the effort you put into your work, the money will not reinforce "hard-work behaviour."

2 **Punishment weakens the response or makes it less likely to recur.** Any aversive (unpleasant) stimulus or event may be a *punisher*. If your dog begs for a lamb chop off your plate, and you lightly swat her nose and shout "No," her begging is likely to decrease—as long as you don't feel guilty and then give her the lamb chop anyway:

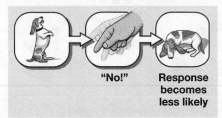

"No!"   Response becomes less likely

Parents, employers, and governments resort to reinforcers and punishers all the time—to get kids to behave well, employees to work hard, and constituents to pay taxes—but they do not always use them effectively. For example, they may wait too long to deliver the reinforcer or punisher. In general, the sooner a consequence follows a response, the greater its effect; you are likely to respond more reliably when you do not have to wait ages for your paycheque, a smile, or a compliment. When there is a delay, other responses occur in the interval, and the connection between the desired or undesired response and the consequence may not be made.

PRIMARY AND SECONDARY REINFORCERS AND PUNISHERS. Food, water, light stroking of the skin, and a comfortable air temperature are naturally reinforcing because they satisfy biological needs. They are therefore known as **primary reinforcers**. Similarly, pain and extreme heat or cold are inherently punishing and are therefore known as **primary punishers**. Primary reinforcers and punishers can be powerful, but they have some drawbacks, both in real life and in research. For one thing, a primary reinforcer may be ineffective if an animal or person is not in a deprived state; a glass of water is not much of a reward if you just drank three glasses. Also, for obvious ethical reasons, psychologists cannot go around using primary punishers (say, by hitting the people in their study) or taking away primary reinforcers (say, by starving their volunteers).

Fortunately, behaviour can be controlled just as effectively by **secondary reinforcers** and **secondary punishers**, which are learned. Money, praise, applause, good grades, awards, and gold stars are common secondary reinforcers. Criticism, demerits, scolding, fines, and bad grades are common secondary punishers. Most behaviourists believe that secondary reinforcers and punishers acquire their ability to influence behaviour by being paired with primary reinforcers and punishers. (If that reminds you of classical conditioning, reinforce your excellent thinking with a pat on the head! Indeed, secondary reinforcers and punishers are often called *conditioned* reinforcers and punishers.) As a secondary reinforcer, money has considerable power over most people's behaviour because it can be exchanged for primary reinforcers such as food and shelter. It is also associated with other secondary reinforcers, such as praise and respect.

POSITIVE AND NEGATIVE REINFORCERS AND PUNISHERS. In our example of the begging dog, something pleasant (getting the lamb chop) followed the dog's begging response, so the response increased. Similarly, if you get a good grade after

punishment The process by which a stimulus or event weakens or reduces the probability of the response that it follows.

primary reinforcer A stimulus that is inherently reinforcing, typically satisfying a physiological need; an example is food.

primary punisher A stimulus that is inherently punishing; an example is electric shock.

secondary reinforcer A stimulus that has acquired reinforcing properties through association with other reinforcers.

secondary punisher A stimulus that has acquired punishing properties through association with other punishers.

studying, your efforts to study are likely to continue or increase. This kind of process, in which a pleasant consequence makes a response more likely, is known as **positive reinforcement**. But there is another type of reinforcement, **negative reinforcement**, which involves the *removal* of something *unpleasant*. Negative reinforcement occurs when you *escape* from something aversive or *avoid* it by preventing it from ever occurring. For example, if someone nags you to study but stops nagging when you comply, your studying is likely to increase because you will then avoid the nagging:

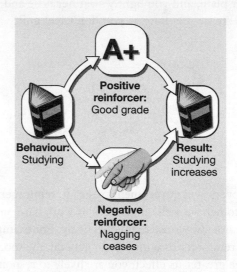

Likewise, negative reinforcement occurs when taking a pill eliminates your pain or when you take a certain route across campus to avoid a rude person.

The positive–negative distinction can also be applied to punishment: Something unpleasant may occur following some behaviour (positive punishment), or something *pleasant* may be *removed* (negative punishment). For example, if your friends tease you for being an egghead (positive punishment) or if studying makes you lose time with your friends (negative punishment), you may stop studying:

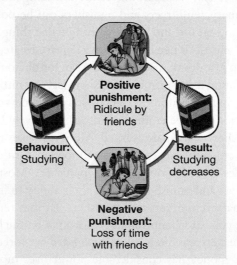

positive reinforcement
A reinforcement procedure in which a response is followed by the presentation of, or increase in intensity of, a reinforcing stimulus; as a result, the response becomes stronger or more likely to occur.

negative reinforcement
A reinforcement procedure in which a response is followed by the removal, delay, or decrease in intensity of an unpleasant stimulus; as a result, the response becomes stronger or more likely to occur.

The distinction between positive and negative reinforcement and punishment has been a source of confusion for generations of students. You will master these terms more quickly if you understand that "positive" and "negative" have nothing to do with "good" or "bad." They refer to whether something is given or taken away. In the case of reinforcement, think of a positive reinforcer as something that is added or obtained (imagine a plus sign) and a negative reinforcer as avoidance of, or escape from, something unpleasant (imagine a minus sign). *In either case, a response becomes more likely.* Do you recall what happened when Little Albert learned to fear rats through a process of classical conditioning? After he acquired this fear, crawling away was negatively reinforced by escape from the now-fearsome rodent. The negative reinforcement that results from escaping or avoiding something unpleasant explains why so many fears are long-lasting. When you avoid a feared object or situation, you also cut off all opportunities to extinguish your fear.

Understandably, people often confuse negative reinforcement with positive punishment, because both involve an unpleasant stimulus. With punishment, you are subjected to the unpleasant stimulus; with negative reinforcement, you escape from it or avoid it. To keep these terms straight, remember that punishment, whether positive or negative, *decreases* the likelihood of a response; and reinforcement, whether positive or negative, *increases* it. In real life, punishment and negative reinforcement often go hand in hand. If you use a chain collar to teach your dog to heel, a brief tug on the collar punishes the act of walking; release of the collar negatively reinforces the act of standing by your side.

You can positively reinforce your studying of this material by taking a short break. As you master the material, a decrease in your anxiety will negatively reinforce studying. But we hope you won't punish your efforts by telling yourself "I'll never get it" or "It's too hard"!

((•• Listen
Punishment and Reinforcement

quickQUIZ

✓• Quick Review on **MyPsychLab**

What kind of consequence will follow if you can't answer these questions?

1. A child nags her father for a cookie; he keeps refusing. Finally, unable to stand the nagging any longer, he hands over the cookie. For him, the ending of the child's pleading is a _____. For the child, the cookie is a _____.

2. An able-bodied driver is careful not to park in a handicapped space anymore after paying a large fine for doing so. The loss of money is a _____.

3. Identify which of the following are commonly used as secondary reinforcers: quarters spilling from a slot machine, a winner's blue ribbon, a piece of candy, an A on an exam, frequent-flyer miles.

4. During late afternoon "happy hours," bars and restaurants sell drinks at a reduced price and appetizers are often free. What undesirable behaviour may be rewarded by this practice?

Answers:

1. negative reinforcer; positive reinforcer 2. punisher—or more precisely, a negative punisher (because something desirable was taken away) 3. All but the candy are secondary reinforcers. 4. One possible answer: The reduced prices, free appetizers, and cheerful atmosphere all reinforce heavy alcohol consumption just before rush hour, thus possibly contributing to binge drinking and drunk driving.

 YOU are about to learn . . .

♦ four important features of operant conditioning.

♦ why it's not always a good idea to reinforce a response every time it occurs.

♦ how operant principles help explain superstitious behaviour.

♦ what it means to "shape" behaviour.

♦ some biological limits on operant conditioning.

FIGURE 7.5 The Skinner Box

When a rat in a Skinner box presses a bar, a food pellet or drop of water is automatically released. The photo shows Skinner at work on one of the boxes.

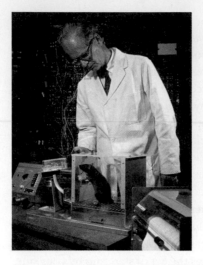

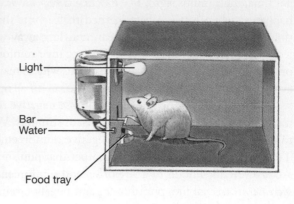

"Oh, not bad. The light comes on, I press the bar, they write me a cheque. How about you?"

PRINCIPLES OF OPERANT CONDITIONING

Thousands of operant-conditioning studies have been done, many using animals. A favourite experimental tool is the *Skinner box*, a cage equipped with a device that delivers a reinforcer, usually food, when an animal makes a desired response, or a punisher, such as a brief shock, when the animal makes an undesired response (see Figure 7.5). Today, computers record responses and chart the rate of responding and cumulative responses across time.

Early in his career, Skinner (1938) used the Skinner box for a classic demonstration of operant conditioning. A rat that had previously learned to eat from the pellet-releasing device was placed in the box. The animal proceeded to scurry about the box, sniffing here and there, and randomly touching parts of the floor and walls. Quite by accident, it happened to press a lever mounted on one wall, and immediately a pellet of tasty rat food fell into the food dish. The rat continued its movements and again happened to press the bar, causing another pellet to fall into the dish. With additional repetitions of bar-pressing followed by food, the animal began to behave less randomly and to press the bar more consistently. Eventually, Skinner had the rat pressing the bar as fast as it could.

EXTINCTION.   In operant conditioning, as in classical, **extinction** is a procedure that causes a previously learned response to stop. In operant conditioning, extinction takes place when the reinforcer that maintained the response is withheld or is no longer available. At first, there may be a spurt of responding, but then the responses gradually taper off and eventually cease. Suppose you put a coin in a vending machine and get nothing back. You may throw in another coin, or perhaps even two, but then you will probably stop trying. The next day, you may put in yet another coin, an example of *spontaneous recovery*. Eventually, however, you will give up on that machine. Your response will have been extinguished.

STIMULUS GENERALIZATION AND DISCRIMINATION.   In operant conditioning, as in classical, **stimulus generalization** may occur. That is, responses may generalize to stimuli that were not present during the original learning situation but resemble the original stimuli in some way. For example, a pigeon that has been trained to peck at a picture of a circle may also peck at a slightly oval figure. But if you wanted to train the bird to discriminate between the two shapes, you would present both the circle and the oval, giving reinforcers whenever the bird pecked at the circle and withholding reinforcers when it pecked at the oval. Eventually, **stimulus discrimination** would

extinction   The weakening and eventual disappearance of a learned response; in operant conditioning, it occurs when a response is no longer followed by a reinforcer.

stimulus generalization   In operant conditioning, the tendency for a response that has been reinforced (or punished) in the presence of one stimulus to occur (or be suppressed) in the presence of other similar stimuli.

stimulus discrimination   In operant conditioning, the tendency of a response to occur in the presence of one stimulus but not in the presence of other, similar stimuli that differ from it on some dimension.

occur. Pigeons, in fact, have learned to make some extraordinary discriminations. They even learned to discriminate between two paintings by different artists, such as Vincent Van Gogh and Marc Chagall (Watanabe, 2001). And then, when presented with a new pair of paintings by those same two artists, they were able to tell the difference between them!

Sometimes an animal or person learns to respond to a stimulus only when some other stimulus, called a **discriminative stimulus**, is present. The discriminative stimulus signals whether a response, if made, will pay off. In a Skinner box containing a pigeon, a light may serve as a discriminative stimulus for pecking at a circle. When the light is on, pecking brings a reward; when it is off, pecking is futile. Human behaviour is controlled by many discriminative stimuli, both verbal ("Store hours are 9 to 5") and nonverbal (traffic lights, doorbells, the ring of your cellphone, other people's facial expressions). Learning to respond correctly when such stimuli are present allows us to get through the day efficiently and to get along with others.

LEARNING ON SCHEDULE. When a response is first acquired, learning is usually most rapid if the response is reinforced each time it occurs; this procedure is called **continuous reinforcement**. However, once a response has become reliable, it will be more resistant to extinction if it is rewarded on an **intermittent (partial) schedule of reinforcement,** which involves reinforcing only some responses, not all of them. Skinner (1956) happened on this fact when he ran short of food pellets for his rats and was forced to deliver reinforcers less often. (Not all scientific discoveries are planned.) On intermittent schedules, a reinforcer is delivered only after a certain number of responses occur or after a certain amount of time has passed since a response was last reinforced; these patterns affect the rate, form, and timing of behaviour. (The details are beyond the scope of this book.)

Intermittent reinforcement helps explain why people often get attached to "lucky" hats, charms, and rituals. A batter pulls his earlobe, gets a home run, and from then on always pulls his earlobe before each pitch. A student takes an exam with a purple pen and gets an A, and from then on will not take an exam without a purple pen. Such rituals persist because sometimes they are followed purely coincidentally by a reinforcer—a home run, a good grade—and so they become resistant to extinction.

Skinner (1948) once demonstrated this phenomenon by creating eight "superstitious" pigeons in his laboratory. He rigged the pigeons' cages so that food was delivered every 15 seconds, even if the birds didn't lift a feather. Pigeons are often in motion, so when the food came, each animal was likely to be doing something. That something was then reinforced by delivery of the food. The behaviour, of course, was reinforced entirely by chance, but it still became more likely to occur and thus to be reinforced again. Within a short time, six of the pigeons were practising some sort of consistent ritual: turning in counter clockwise circles, bobbing their heads up and down, or swinging their heads to and fro. None of these activities had the least effect on the delivery of the reinforcer; the birds were behaving "superstitiously," as if they thought their movements were responsible for bringing the food.

Now listen up, because here comes one of the most useful things to know about operant conditioning: If you want a response to persist after it has been learned, you should reinforce it *intermittently*, not continuously. If you are giving Harry, your hamster, a treat every time he pushes a ball with his nose, and then you suddenly stop the reinforcement, Harry will soon stop pushing that ball. Because the change in reinforcement is large, from continuous to none at all, Harry will easily discern the change. But if you have been reinforcing Harry's behaviour only every so often, the

Thinking Critically

Consider Other Interpretations

People cling to superstitious rituals because they think they work. Could this "effectiveness" be an illusion, explainable in terms of operant principles?

⊙Watch
Pigeon Ping Pong

discriminative stimulus A stimulus that signals when a particular response is likely to be followed by a certain type of consequence.

continuous reinforcement A reinforcement schedule in which a particular response is always reinforced.

intermittent (partial) schedule of reinforcement A reinforcement schedule in which a particular response is sometimes but not always reinforced.

shaping An operant-conditioning procedure in which successive approximations of a desired response are reinforced.

successive approximations In the operant-conditioning procedure of shaping, behaviours that are ordered in terms of increasing similarity or closeness to the desired response.

✳ **Explore**
The Shaping Process

Dolphins at Sea World

Behavioural techniques such as shaping have many useful applications. Monkeys have been trained to assist their paralyzed owners by opening doors, helping with feeding, and turning the pages of books. Guide dogs help blind people navigate city streets.

change will not be so dramatic, and your hungry hamster will keep responding for quite a while. Pigeons, rats, and people on intermittent schedules of reinforcement have responded in the laboratory thousands of times without reinforcement before throwing in the towel, especially when the timing of the reinforcer varies. Animals will sometimes work so hard for an unpredictable, infrequent bit of food that the energy they expend is greater than that gained from the reward; theoretically, they could actually work themselves to death.

It follows that if you want to get rid of a response, whether it's your own or someone else's, you should be careful *not* to reinforce it intermittently. If you are going to extinguish undesirable behaviour by ignoring it—a child's tantrums, a friend's midnight phone calls, a parent's unwanted advice—you must be absolutely consistent in withholding reinforcement (your attention). Otherwise, the other person will learn that if he or she keeps up the screaming, calling, or advice-giving long enough, it will eventually be rewarded. From a behavioural point of view, one of the most common errors people make is to reward intermittently the very responses that they would like to eliminate.

SHAPING.   For a response to be reinforced, it must first occur. But suppose you want to train Harry the hamster to pick up a marble or a child to use a knife and fork properly. Such behaviours, and most others in everyday life, have almost no probability of appearing spontaneously. You could grow old and grey waiting for them to occur so that you could reinforce them. The operant solution is a procedure called **shaping**.

In shaping, you start by reinforcing a tendency in the right direction, and then you gradually require responses that are more and more similar to the final desired response. The responses that you reinforce on the way to the final one are called **successive approximations**. In the case of Harry and the marble, you might deliver a food pellet if the hamster merely turned toward the marble. Once this response was established, you might then reward the hamster for taking a step toward the marble. After that, you could reward him for approaching the marble, then for touching the marble, then for putting both paws on the marble, and finally for holding it. With the achievement of each approximation, the next one would become more likely, making it available for reinforcement.

Using shaping and other techniques, Skinner was able to train pigeons to play Ping-Pong with their beaks and to "bowl" in a miniature alley, complete with a wooden ball and tiny bowling pins. (Skinner had a great sense of humour.) Animal trainers routinely use shaping to teach animals to act as the "eyes" of the blind and to act as the

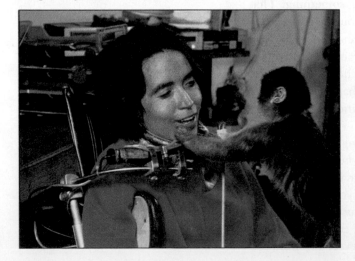
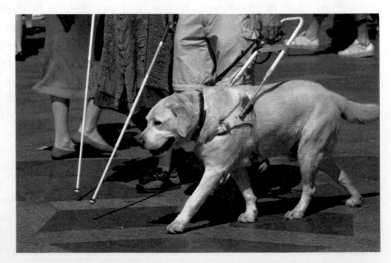

"limbs" of people with spinal cord injuries; these talented companions learn to turn on light switches, open refrigerator doors, and reach for boxes on shelves.

BIOLOGICAL LIMITS ON LEARNING. All principles of operant conditioning, like those of classical conditioning, are limited by an animal's genetic dispositions and physical characteristics; if you try to teach a fish to dance the samba, you're going to get pretty frustrated (and wear out the fish). Operant-conditioning procedures always work best when they capitalize on inborn tendencies.

Years ago, two psychologists who became animal trainers, Keller and Marian Breland (1961), learned what happens when you ignore biological constraints on learning. They found that their animals were having trouble learning tasks that should have been easy. One animal, a pig, was supposed to drop large wooden coins in a box. Instead, the animal would drop the coin, push at it with its snout, throw it in the air, and push at it some more. This odd behaviour actually delayed delivery of the reinforcer (food, which is *very* reinforcing to a pig), so it was hard to explain in terms of operant principles. The Brelands finally realized that the pig's rooting instinct—using its snout to uncover and dig up edible roots—was keeping it from learning the task. They called such a reversion to instinctive behaviour **instinctive drift**.

In human beings, too, operant learning is affected by genetics, biology, and the evolutionary history of our species. As we saw in Chapter 3, human children are biologically disposed to learn language without much effort, and they may be disposed to learn some arithmetic operations as well. Further, temperaments and other inborn dispositions may affect how a person responds to reinforcers and punishments. It will be easier to shape belly-dancing behaviour if a person is temperamentally disposed to be outgoing and extroverted than if the person is by nature shy.

Skinner: The Man and the Myth

Because of his groundbreaking work on operant conditioning, B. F. Skinner is one of the best known psychologists. He is also one of the most misunderstood. For example, many people (even some psychologists) think that Skinner denied the existence of human consciousness and the value of studying it. In reality, Skinner (1972, 1990) maintained that private internal events—what we call perceptions, emotions,

instinctive drift During operant learning, the tendency for an organism to revert to instinctive behaviour.

Get INVOLVED!

SHAPE UP!

Would you like to improve your study habits? Start exercising? Learn to play a musical instrument? Here are a few guidelines for shaping your own behaviour: (1) Set goals that are achievable and specific, for example, "jog ten minutes and increase the time by five minutes each day" instead of "get in shape." (2) Track your progress on a graph or in a diary; evidence of progress serves as a secondary reinforcer. (3) Avoid punishing yourself with self-defeating thoughts such as "I'll never be a good student" or "I'm a food addict." (4) Reinforce small improvements (successive approximations) instead of expecting perfection. By the way, a reinforcer does not have to be a thing; it can be something you like to do, like watching a movie.

Above all, be patient. Like Rome, new habits are not built in a day. You can find information on shaping behaviour—yours or anyone else's—in books such as *Don't Shoot the Dog: The New Art of Teaching and Training*, by Karen Pryor (1999), and *Behaviour Modification: What It Is and How to Do It*, by Garry Martin and Joseph Pear (2007).

👁 **Watch** B. F. Skinner Biography

and thoughts—are as real as any others, and we can study them by examining our own sensory responses, the verbal reports of others, and the conditions under which such events occur. But he insisted that thoughts and feelings cannot *explain* behaviour. These components of consciousness, he said, are themselves simply behaviours that occur because of reinforcement and punishment.

Skinner aroused strong passions in both his supporters and his detractors. Perhaps the issue that most provoked and angered people was his insistence that free will is an illusion. In contrast to humanist and some religious doctrines that human beings have the power to shape their own destinies, his philosophy promoted the *determinist view* that our actions are determined by our environments and our genetic heritage.

Because Skinner thought the environment should be manipulated to alter behaviour, some critics have portrayed him as cold-blooded. One famous controversy regarding Skinner occurred when he invented an enclosed "living space," the Air Crib, for his younger daughter, Deborah, when she was an infant. This "baby box," as it came to be known, had temperature and humidity controls to eliminate the usual discomforts suffered by babies: heat, cold, wetness, and confinement by blankets and clothing. Skinner believed that to reduce a baby's cries of discomfort and make infant care easier for the parents, you should fix the environment. But people imagined, incorrectly, that the Skinners were leaving their child in the baby box all the time without cuddling and holding her, and rumours circulated for years (and still do

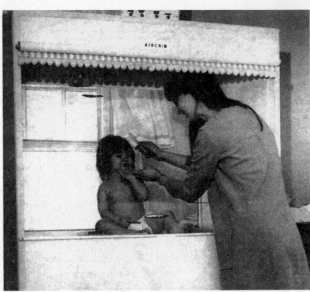

B. F. Skinner invented the Air Crib to provide a more comfortable, less restrictive infant bed than the traditional crib with its bars and blankets. The baby in this Air Crib is Skinner's granddaughter Lisa, with her mother, Julie.

from time to time) that she had sued her father, gone insane, or killed herself. Actually, both of Skinner's daughters were cuddled and doted on, loved their parents deeply, and turned out to be successful, perfectly well-adjusted adults.

Skinner, a kind and mild-mannered man, felt that it would be unethical *not* to try to improve human behaviour by applying behavioural principles. And he practised what he preached, proposing many ways to improve society and reduce human suffering. At the height of public criticism of Skinner, the American Humanist Association recognized his efforts on behalf of humanity by honouring him with its Humanist of the Year Award.

quickQUIZ

✓ **Quick Review** on MyPsychLab

We hope you won't think we're cold or inhumane if we say "You'd better take this quiz."

In each of the following situations, choose the best alternative and give your reason for choosing it.

1. You want your two-year-old to ask for water with a word instead of a grunt. Should you give him water when he says "wa-wa" or wait until his pronunciation improves?

2. Your roommate keeps interrupting your studying even though you have asked her to stop. Should you ignore her completely or occasionally respond for the sake of good manners?

3. Your father, who rarely calls you, has finally left a voice-mail message. Should you reply quickly, or wait awhile so he will know how it feels to be ignored?

Answers:

1. You should reinforce "wa-wa," an approximation of water, because complex behaviours need to be shaped. 2. From a behavioural view, you should ignore her completely because intermittent reinforcement (attention) could cause her interruptions to persist. 3. If you want to encourage communication, you should reply quickly because immediate reinforcement is more effective than delayed reinforcement.

YOU are about to learn . . .

◆ when punishment works in real life and why it often does not.

◆ some effective alternatives to punishment.

◆ how reinforcement can be misused.

◆ why paying children for good grades sometimes backfires.

OPERANT CONDITIONING IN REAL LIFE

Operant principles can clear up many mysteries about why people behave as they do. They can also explain why people have trouble changing when they want to, in spite of all the motivational seminars they attend or resolutions they make. If life remains full of the same old reinforcers, punishers, and discriminative stimuli (a grumpy boss, an unresponsive roommate, a refrigerator stocked with high-fat goodies), any new responses that have been acquired may fail to generalize.

To help people change unwanted, dangerous, or self-defeating habits, behaviourists have carried operant principles out of the laboratory and into the wider world of the classroom, athletic field, prison, mental hospital, nursing home, rehabilitation ward, child-care centre, factory, and office. The use of operant techniques in such real-world settings is called **behaviour modification** (also known as *applied behaviour analysis*).

You don't have to be a psychologist to apply behavioural principles. On the left, a police officer in Calgary reinforces law-abiding behaviour by checking a baby seat at an event featuring free food. On the right, a mother reinforces her autistic son's learning by applauding.

Behaviour modification has had some enormous successes (Kazdin, 2001; Martin & Pear, 2007). Behaviourists have taught parents how to toilet train their children in only a few sessions. They have trained disturbed and intellectually impaired adults to communicate, dress themselves, mingle socially with others, and earn a living. They have taught brain-damaged patients to control inappropriate behaviour, focus their attention, and improve their language abilities. They have helped autistic children improve their social and language skills. And they have helped ordinary folk get rid of unwanted habits, such as smoking and nail biting, or acquire desired ones, such as practising the piano or studying.

In one such example, the Société de l'assurance automobile du Québec (SAAQ) tried to increase seat-belt use throughout the province with the use of radio, TV, and print commercials. However, the police also used behavioural techniques. The police reinforced good behaviour by handing out scratch-and-win tickets to individuals who were wearing seat belts. (Those who were not wearing seat belts received tickets of the other kind.) The rate of seat-belt use in the province dramatically increased, from 40% to 67% to over 93%—the highest rate in Canada (Transport Canada, 1998)! Similar programs have been adopted all over Canada and are now used to reinforce the wearing of bicycle helmets and the use of child safety seats.

behaviour modification The application of operant-conditioning techniques to teach new responses or to reduce or eliminate maladaptive or problematic behaviour; also called applied behaviour analysis.

The response to wrongdoing is often punishment. People assume that fines, long prison terms, yelling, and spanking are good ways to get rid of undesirable behaviour. What does the evidence show?

Yet when nonpsychologists try to apply the principles of conditioning to commonplace problems without thoroughly understanding those principles, their efforts sometimes miss the mark, as we are about to see.

The Pros and Cons of Punishment

In a novel called *Walden Two* (1948/1976), Skinner imagined a utopia in which reinforcers were used so wisely that undesirable behaviour was rare. Unfortunately, we do not live in a utopia; bad habits and antisocial acts abound.

Punishment might seem to be an obvious solution. Although most Western countries have banned the physical punishment of schoolchildren at school, the laws in Canada permit the use of force for correction (for example, spanking) by teachers and parents as long as it is reasonable (although there is great debate over what is reasonable). Some suggest that spanking or slapping is reasonable punishment, while others suggest that this is child abuse. Even the research about spanking is contentious! For instance, some researchers suggest that spanking may lead to physical abuse (for example, Gershoff, 2002), whereas others have taken the position that the research on spanking is, at best, inconclusive (for example, Baumrind, Larzelere, & Cowan, 2002). And, of course, in their relationships people punish one another frequently by yelling, scolding, and sulking. Does all this punishment work?

WHEN PUNISHMENT WORKS. Sometimes punishment is unquestionably effective. For example, punishment can deter some young criminals from repeating their offences. A study of the criminal records of all Danish men born between 1944 and 1947 (nearly 29 000 men) examined repeat arrests (recidivism) through age 26 (Brennan & Mednick, 1994). After any given arrest, punishment reduced rates of subsequent arrests for both minor and serious crimes, though recidivism still remained fairly high. Contrary to the researchers' expectations, however, the severity of punishment made no difference: Fines and probation were about as effective as jail time. What mattered most was the *consistency* of the punishment: When lawbreakers sometimes get away with their crimes, their behaviour is intermittently reinforced and therefore becomes resistant to extinction.

A similar example involves speeding tickets, which are intended to be a punishment. However, some parts of Canada use photo radar, an automated system that mails speeding tickets to speeders. Although photo radar is successful at reducing speeding (for example, Chen, Meckle, & Wilson, 2002), it does not eliminate speeding. In fact, although accidents decreased by 7% in areas with photo radar, the average speed of vehicles decreased by only 3%. Why isn't photo radar more effective? The answer may have something to do with the nature of punishment: When police officers supervise the speed traps, your punishment is immediate; when photo radar devices catch you, you wait for several weeks to receive the ticket. Further, theory predicts that people will slow down on roads they know to be monitored and speed on roads they know are not monitored.

WHEN PUNISHMENT FAILS. What about punishment that occurs every day in families, schools, and workplaces? Laboratory and field studies find that it, too, often fails, for several reasons:

1 **People often administer punishment inappropriately or mindlessly.** They shout things they don't mean, or apply punishment so broadly that it covers all sorts of irrelevant behaviours. In short, they misunderstand the proper application of punishment. One student recounted that his parents used to punish their children before leaving them alone for the evening because of all the naughty things they were going to do. Naturally, the children did not bother to behave.

Thinking Critically

Ask Questions

As we all know, people often do things they're not supposed to. Have you ever wondered why so many people ignore warnings and threats of punishment?

2 **The recipient of harsh or frequent punishment often responds with anxiety, fear, or rage.** Through a process of classical conditioning, these emotional side effects may then generalize to the entire situation in which the punishment occurs—the place, the person delivering the punishment, and the circumstances. These negative emotional reactions can create more problems than the punishment solves. A teenager who has been severely punished may strike back or run away. And extreme punishment—physical abuse—is a risk factor, especially in children, for the development of depression, low self-esteem, violent behaviour, and many other problems (Gershoff, 2002; Widom, DuMont, & Czaja, 2007).

3 **The effectiveness of punishment is often temporary, depending heavily on the presence of the punishing person or circumstances.** All of us can probably remember some transgressions of childhood that we never dared commit when our parents were around, but which we promptly resumed as soon as they were gone. All we learned was not to get caught.

4 **Most misbehaviour is hard to punish immediately. Punishment, like reward, works best if it quickly follows a response.** But outside the laboratory, rapid punishment is often hard to achieve, and during the delay, the behaviour may be reinforced many times. For example, if you punish your dog when you get home for getting into the garbage, the punishment will not do any good because you are too late: Your pet's misbehaviour has already been reinforced by all those delicious "treats."

5 **Punishment conveys little information.** It may tell the recipient what *not* to do, but it does not communicate what the person (or animal) *should* do. Spanking a toddler for messing in her pants will not teach her to use the potty chair, and scolding a student for learning slowly will not teach him to learn more quickly.

6   **An action intended to punish may instead be reinforcing because it brings attention.** Indeed, in some cases, angry attention may be just what the offender is after. If a mother yells at a child who is throwing a tantrum, the very act of yelling may give him what he wants: a reaction from her. In the schoolroom, teachers who scold children in front of other students, thus putting them in the limelight, may unwittingly reward the very misbehaviour they are trying to eliminate.

Because of these drawbacks, most psychologists believe that punishment, especially severe punishment, is a poor way to eliminate unwanted behaviour. In special cases, for example when mentally disabled children are in immediate danger of seriously injuring themselves or a school bully is about to beat up a classmate, temporary physical restraint may be necessary. But even in these cases, alternatives are often available. School programs have successfully reduced school violence by teaching kids problem-solving skills, emotional control, and conflict resolution, and by rewarding good behaviour (Hahn et al., 2008; Wilson & Lipsey, 2007). And in some cases, the best way to discourage a behaviour—a child's nagging for a cookie before dinner, a roommate's interruptions when you're studying—is to extinguish it by ignoring it.

Of course, ignoring a behaviour requires patience and is not always feasible. A dog owner who ignores Fido's backyard barking may soon hear "barking" of another sort from the neighbours. A parent whose child is a video-game addict cannot ignore the behaviour because playing video games is rewarding to the child. One solution: Combine extinction of undesirable acts with reinforcement of alternative ones. The parent of a video-game addict might ignore the child's pleas for "just one more game" and at the same time praise the child for doing something else that is incompatible with video-game playing, such as reading or playing basketball.

Finally, when punishment must be applied, these guidelines should be kept in mind: (1) It should not involve physical abuse; instead, parents can use time-outs and loss of privileges (negative punishers); (2) it should be consistent; (3) it should be accompanied by information about the kind of behaviour that would be appropriate; and (4) it should be followed, whenever possible, by the reinforcement of desirable behaviour.

The Problems with Reward

So far, we have been praising the virtues of reinforcement. But like punishers, rewards do not always work as expected. Let's look at two complications that arise when people try to use them.

MISUSE OF REWARDS. Suppose you are a grade 4 teacher, and a student has just turned in a paper full of grammatical and punctuation errors. This child has little self-confidence and is easily discouraged. What should you do? Many people think you should give the paper a high mark anyway, to bolster the child's self-esteem. Teachers everywhere are handing out lavish praise, happy-face stickers, and high grades in hopes that students' performance will improve as they learn to "feel good about

Thinking ⚙ Critically

Consider Other Interpretations

Many harried parents habitually resort to physical punishment without being aware of its many negative consequences for themselves and their children. Based on your reading of this chapter, what alternatives does this parent have?

themselves." Scientifically speaking, however, there are two things wrong with this approach. First, study after study finds that high self-esteem does not improve academic performance (Baumeister et al., 2003). Second, genuine self-esteem emerges from effort, persistence, and the gradual acquisition of skills. It is nurtured by a teacher's honest appreciation of the content of a student's work combined with constructive feedback on how to correct mistakes or fix weaknesses (Damon, 1995).

One obvious result of the misuse of rewards in schools has been grade inflation at all levels of education. In many schools, C's, which once meant average or satisfactory, are nearly extinct. One study found that a third of university students expected B's just for showing up for class, and 40 percent felt they were entitled to a B merely for doing the required reading (Greenberger et al., 2008). We have talked to students who feel that hard work should even be enough for an A. If you yourself have benefited from grade inflation, you may feel it's a good thing—but remember that critical thinking requires us to separate feelings from facts! The problem is that rewards, including grades, serve as effective reinforcers only when they are tied to the behaviour one is trying to increase, not when they are dispensed indiscriminately. Getting a good grade for "showing-up-in-class behaviour" reinforces going to class, but it does not necessarily reinforce learning much once you are there. (Would you want to be treated by a doctor, be represented by a lawyer, or have your taxes done by an accountant who got through school just by showing up for class?)

WHY REWARDS CAN BACKFIRE.   Most of our examples of operant conditioning have involved **extrinsic reinforcers**, which come from an outside source and are not inherently related to the activity being reinforced. Money, praise, gold stars, applause, hugs, and thumbs-up signs are all extrinsic reinforcers. But people (and probably some other animals, too) also work for **intrinsic reinforcers**, such as enjoyment of the task and the satisfaction of accomplishment. As psychologists have applied operant conditioning in real-world settings, they have found that extrinsic reinforcement sometimes becomes too much of a good thing: If you focus on it exclusively, it can kill the pleasure of doing something for its own sake.

Consider what happened in a classic study of how praise affects children's intrinsic motivation (Lepper, Greene, & Nisbett, 1973). Researchers gave nursery-school children the chance to draw with felt-tipped pens during free play and recorded how long each child spontaneously played with the pens. The children clearly enjoyed this activity. Then the researchers told some of the children that if they would draw with felt-tipped pens they would get a prize, a "Good Player Award" complete with gold seal and red ribbon. After drawing for six minutes, each child got the award as promised. Other children did not expect an award and were not given one. A week later, the researchers again observed the children's free play. Those children who had expected and received an award spent much less time with the pens than they had before the start of the experiment. In contrast, children who had neither expected nor received an award continued to show as much interest in playing with the pens as they had initially, as you can see in Figure 7.6. Similar results have occurred in other studies when children have been offered a reward for doing something they already enjoy.

Why should extrinsic rewards undermine the pleasure of doing something for its own sake? The researchers who did the felt-tipped-pen study suggested that when we are paid for an activity, we interpret it as work. We see our actions as the result of external factors instead of our own interests, skills, and efforts. It is as if we say to ourselves, "Since I'm being paid, it must be something I wouldn't do if I didn't have

←⊙ Simulate
Learning

Thinking 🗲 Critically

Don't Oversimplify

Because reinforcers increase desirable behaviour, some teachers give out high grades whether students deserve them or not. Does this practice improve the students' performance or self-esteem? What do these rewards actually reinforce?

extrinsic reinforcers   Reinforcers that are not inherently related to the activity being reinforced.

intrinsic reinforcers   Reinforcers that are inherently related to the activity being reinforced.

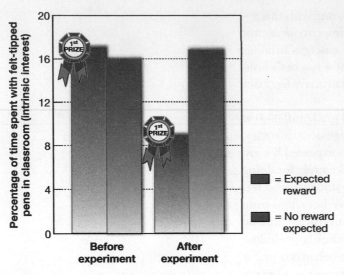

FIGURE 7.6 Turning Work into Play

Extrinsic rewards can sometimes reduce the intrinsic pleasure of an activity. When preschoolers were promised a prize for drawing with felt-tipped pens, the behaviour temporarily increased. But after they got their prizes, they spent less time with the pens than they had before the study began.

to." Then, when the reward is withdrawn, we refuse to "work" any longer. Another possibility is that we tend to regard extrinsic rewards as controlling, so they make us feel pressured and reduce our sense of autonomy and choice ("I guess I have to do what I'm told to do—but *only* what I'm told to do") (Deci et al., 1999). A third, more behavioural explanation is that extrinsic reinforcement sometimes raises the rate of responding above some optimal, enjoyable level—for example, by causing the children in the felt-tipped-pen study to play with the pens longer than they would have on their own. Then the activity really does become work.

Findings on extrinsic versus intrinsic reinforcements have wide-ranging implications. For example, economists have shown that financial rewards can undermine ethical and moral norms like honesty, hard work, and fairness toward others, and can decrease people's willingness to contribute to the common good (e.g., by paying taxes and giving to charity). In other words, an emphasis solely on money encourages selfishness (Bowles, 2008).

We must be careful, however, not to oversimplify this issue. The effects of extrinsic rewards depend on many factors, including a person's initial motivation, the context in which rewards are achieved, and in the case of praise, the sincerity of the praiser (Henderlong & Lepper, 2002). If you get praise, money, a high grade, or a trophy for doing a task *well*, for achieving a certain level of performance, or for improving your performance rather than for just doing the task, your intrinsic motivation is not likely to decline; in fact, it may increase (Cameron, Banko, & Pierce, 2001; Pierce et al., 2003). Such rewards are apt to make you feel competent rather

Get INVOLVED!

WHAT'S REINFORCING YOUR BEHAVIOUR?

For each activity you do, indicate whether the reinforcers controlling your behaviour are primarily extrinsic or intrinsic.

Activity	Reinforcers mostly extrinsic	Reinforcers mostly intrinsic	Reinforcers about equally extrinsic and intrinsic
Studying	_____	_____	_____
Housework	_____	_____	_____
Worship	_____	_____	_____
Grooming	_____	_____	_____
Job	_____	_____	_____
Dating	_____	_____	_____
Attending class	_____	_____	_____
Reading unrelated to school	_____	_____	_____
Sports	_____	_____	_____
Cooking	_____	_____	_____

Is there an area of your life in which you would like intrinsic reinforcement to play a larger role? What can you do to make that happen?

than controlled. And if you have always been crazy about reading or about playing the banjo, you will keep reading or playing even when you do not happen to be getting a grade or applause for doing so. In such cases, you will probably attribute your continued involvement in the activity to your own intrinsic interests and motivation rather than to the reward.

So, what is the take-home message about extrinsic rewards? First, they are often useful or necessary: Few people would trudge off to work every morning if they never got paid; and in the classroom, teachers may need to offer incentives to unmotivated students. But extrinsic rewards should be used carefully and should not be overdone, so that intrinsic pleasure in an activity can blossom. Educators, employers, and policy makers can avoid the trap of either–or thinking by recognizing that most people do their best when they get tangible rewards for real achievement *and* when they have interesting, challenging, and varied kinds of work to do.

quickQUIZ

✓ Quick Review on MyPsychLab

Is the art of mastering quizzes intrinsically reinforcing yet?

A. According to behavioural principles, what is happening here?

1. An adolescent whose parents have hit him for minor transgressions since he was small runs away from home.

2. A young woman whose parents paid her to clean her room while she was growing up is a slob when she moves to her own apartment.

3. Two parents scold their young daughter every time they catch her sucking her thumb. The thumb sucking continues anyway.

B. Public school systems are rewarding students for perfect attendance by giving them money, shopping sprees, laptops, and video games. What are the pros and cons of such practices?

C. In some Canadian provinces, doctors are paid for each visit by a patient or for each service performed, regardless of the length of the visit. In contrast, some other provincial health ministries allow doctors to receive a fixed amount per patient for an entire year. Given what you know about operant conditioning, what are the advantages and disadvantages of each system?

Answers:

A. 1. The physical punishment was painful, and through a process of classical conditioning, the situation in which it occurred also became unpleasant. Because escape from an unpleasant stimulus is negatively reinforcing, the boy ran away. **2.** Extrinsic reinforcers are no longer available, and room-cleaning behaviour has been extinguished. Also, extrinsic rewards may have displaced the intrinsic satisfaction of having a tidy room. **3.** Punishment has failed, possibly because it rewards thumb sucking with attention or because thumb sucking still brings the child pleasure whenever the parents are not around. **B.** The rewards may improve attendance (they have in some schools), and students who attend more regularly may become more interested in their studies and do better in school. But extrinsic rewards can also decrease intrinsic motivation, and when they are withdrawn (e.g., when the student goes to another school), attendance may plummet ("If there's no reward, why should I attend?"). Further, students may come to expect bigger bigger rewards, upping the ante. In some schools, especially those that have de-emphasized penalties for poor attendance, the rewards have backfired and attendance has actually fallen. (Bonus question: Can you now apply these points to parents who pay their children for everything from brushing their teeth to behaving themselves in a restaurant?) **C.** In the fee-for-service system, the doctor is rewarded by having a greater number of tests performed and for having short visits (she can then see more patients in a day). However, this system also rewards doctors for unnecessary tests and patient visits, contributing to the explosion in health care costs. In the fixed-amount system, the doctor receives the same reward for clients who require little attention as she would for seeing a client that requires a lot of attention. As such, this system does not reward the doctor for performing unnecessary tests (although this system does reward doctors who do not accept seriously ill clients, who presumably would require extensive treatment and take up much of their time).

⬡ YOU are about to learn . . .

◆ how you can learn something without any obvious reinforcement.

◆ why two people can learn different lessons from exactly the same experience.

◆ how we often learn not by doing but by watching.

LEARNING AND THE MIND

◀◉ **Simulate**
Psychology Experiments Tool:
Learning

For half a century, most learning theories held that learning could be explained by specifying the behavioural "ABCs": *antecedents* (events preceding behaviour), *behaviours*, and *consequences*. Behaviourists liked to compare the mind to an engineer's hypothetical "black box," a device whose workings must be inferred because they cannot be observed directly. To them, the box contained irrelevant wiring; it was enough to know that pushing a button on the box would produce a predictable response. But even as early as the 1930s, a few behaviourists could not resist peeking into that black box.

Latent Learning

Behaviourist Edward Tolman (1938) committed virtual heresy at the time by noting that his rats, when pausing at turning points in a maze, seemed to be *deciding* which way to go. Moreover, the animals sometimes seemed to be learning even without any reinforcement. What, he wondered, was going on in their little rat brains that might account for this puzzle?

Because of latent learning, when these children are older they will already know a lot about "supermarket behaviour"— like how to navigate the aisles, find the shortest line at the cashier stand, unload groceries from the cart, and maybe even choose the best carrots.

latent learning A form of learning that is not immediately expressed in an overt response; it occurs without obvious reinforcement.

In a classic experiment, Tolman and C. H. Honzik (1930) placed three groups of rats in mazes and observed their behaviour daily for more than two weeks. The rats in Group 1 always found food at the end of the maze and quickly learned to find it without going down blind alleys. The rats in Group 2 never found food and, as you would expect, they followed no particular route. Group 3 was the interesting group. These rats found no food for ten days and seemed to wander aimlessly, but on the eleventh day they received food, and then they quickly learned to run to the end of the maze. By the following day, they were doing as well as Group 1, which had been rewarded from the beginning (see Figure 7.7).

Group 3 had demonstrated **latent learning**, learning that is not immediately expressed in performance. A great deal of human learning also remains latent until circumstances allow or require it to be expressed. A driver gets out of a traffic jam and finds her way to Fourth and Kumquat streets using a route she has never used before (without GPS!). A little boy observes a parent setting the table or tightening a screw but does not act on this learning for years; then he finds he knows how to do these things.

Latent learning raises questions about what, exactly, is learned during operant learning. In the Tolman and Honzik study, the rats that did not get any food until the eleventh day seemed to have acquired a mental representation of the maze. They had been learning the whole time; they simply had no reason to act on that learning until they began to find food. Similarly, the driver taking a new route can do so because she already knows how the city is laid out. What seems to be acquired in latent learning,

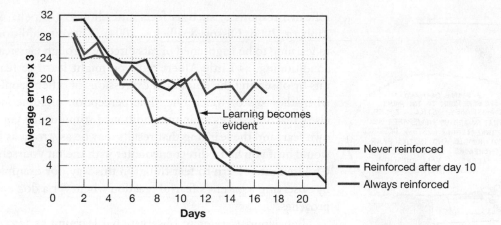

FIGURE 7.7 Latent Learning

In a classic experiment, rats that always found food in a maze made fewer and fewer errors in reaching the food (green curve). In contrast, rats that received no food showed little improvement (blue curve). But rats that got no food for ten days and then found food on the eleventh day showed rapid improvement from then on (red curve). This result suggests that learning involves cognitive changes that can occur in the absence of reinforcement and that may not be acted on until a reinforcer becomes available (Tolman & Honzik, 1930).

therefore, is not a specific response, but *knowledge* about responses and their consequences. We learn how the world is organized, which paths lead to which places, and which actions can produce which payoffs. This knowledge permits us to be creative and flexible in reaching our goals.

Social-Cognitive Learning Theories

During the 1960s and 1970s, many learning theorists concluded that human behaviour could not be understood without taking into account the human capacity for higher-level cognitive processes. They agreed with behaviourists that human beings, along with the rat and the rabbit, are subject to the laws of operant and classical conditioning. But they added that human beings, unlike the rat or the rabbit, are full of attitudes, beliefs, and expectations that affect the way they acquire information, make decisions, reason, and solve problems. Today, this view has become very influential.

We will use the term **social-cognitive theory** for all theories that combine behavioural principles with cognitive ones to explain behaviour (Bandura, 1986; Mischel, 1973; Mischel & Shoda, 1995). These theories share an emphasis on the importance of beliefs, perceptions, and observations of other people's behaviour in determining what we learn, what we do at any given moment, and the personality traits we develop (see Chapter 14). To a social-cognitive theorist, differences in beliefs and perceptions help explain why two people who live through the same event may come away with entirely different lessons from it (Bandura, 2001). All siblings know this. One sibling may regard being grounded by their father as evidence of his all-around meanness, whereas another may see the same behaviour as evidence of his care and concern for his children. For these siblings, being grounded is likely to affect their behaviour differently.

LEARNING BY OBSERVING. Late one night, a friend living in a rural area was awakened by a loud clattering noise. A raccoon had knocked over a "raccoon-proof" garbage can and seemed to be demonstrating to an assembly of other raccoons how to open it: If you jump up and down on the can's side, the lid will pop off. According to our friend, the observing raccoons learned from this episode how to open stubborn garbage cans, and the observing humans learned how smart raccoons can be. In short, they all benefited from **observational learning**, learning by watching what others do and what happens to them for doing it.

The behaviour the raccoons learned through observation was an operant one, but observational learning also plays an important role in the acquisition of automatic,

◀●Simulate
Latent Learning

◀●Simulate
Psychology Experiments Survey:
What Learning Techniques Do You Use?

social-cognitive theories Theories that emphasize how behaviour is learned and maintained through observation and imitation of others, positive consequences, and cognitive processes such as plans, expectations, and beliefs.

observational learning A process in which an individual learns new responses by observing the behaviour of another (a model) rather than through direct experience; sometimes called vicarious conditioning.

Social-cognitive theorists emphasize the influence of thoughts and perceptions on behaviour (at least in humans).

✳ **Explore**
Bandura's Study on Observational Learning

Observation is how line dancers learn their steps.

reflexive responses, such as fears and phobias (Mineka & Zinbarg, 2006; Olsson & Phelps, 2004). Thus, in addition to learning to be frightened of rats directly through classical conditioning, as Little Albert did, you might learn to fear rats by observing the emotional expressions of other people when they see or touch one. The perception of someone else's reaction serves as an unconditioned stimulus for your own fear, and the learning that results may be as strong as it would be if you had a direct encounter with the rat yourself. Children often learn to fear things in this way, for example by observing a parent's fearful reaction whenever a dog approaches.

Behaviourists refer to observational learning as *vicarious conditioning*, and believe it can be explained in stimulus–response terms. But social-cognitive theorists believe that in human beings observational learning cannot be fully understood without taking into account the thought processes of the learner (Meltzoff & Gopnik, 1993). They emphasize the knowledge that results when a person sees a *model*—another person—behaving in certain ways and experiencing the consequences (Bandura, 1977).

None of us would last long without observational learning. Learning would be both inefficient and dangerous. We would have to learn to avoid oncoming cars by walking into traffic and suffering the consequences, or learn to swim by jumping into a deep pool and flailing around. But observational learning has its dark side as well: People often imitate antisocial or unethical actions (they observe a friend cheating and decide they can get away with it too) or self-defeating and harmful ones (they watch a film star smoking and take up the habit in an effort to look just as cool).

Many years ago, Albert Bandura and his colleagues showed just how important observational learning is for children who are learning the rules of social behaviour (Bandura, Ross, & Ross, 1963). The researchers had nursery-school children watch a short film of two men, Rocky and Johnny, playing with toys. (Apparently the children did not think this behaviour was the least bit odd.) In the film, Johnny refuses to share his toys, and Rocky responds by hitting him. Rocky's aggressive actions are rewarded because he winds up with all the toys. Poor Johnny sits dejectedly in the corner, while Rocky marches off with a bag full of loot and a hobbyhorse under his arm.

After viewing the film, each child was left alone for 20 minutes in a playroom full of toys, including some of the items shown in the film. Watching through a one-way mirror, the researchers found that the children were much more aggressive in their play than a control group that had not seen the film. Some children imitated Rocky almost exactly. At the end of the session, one little girl even asked the experimenter for a bag!

Of course, people also imitate positive activities they observe. Matt Groening, the creator of the cartoon show *The Simpsons*, decided it would be funny if the Simpsons' eight-year-old daughter Lisa played the baritone sax. Sure enough, across the country little girls began imitating her. Cynthia Sikes, a saxophone teacher in New York, told *The New York Times* that "when the show started, I got an influx of girls coming up to me saying, 'I want to play the saxophone because Lisa Simpson plays the saxophone.'"

Now in his eighties, Albert Bandura continues his research, focusing on how social-cognitive research can be translated into changes in behaviour associated with healthy living (Bandura, 2004). Bandura notes that popular soap operas that model contraception, AIDs prevention, and education for women have all resulted in changes for the better when compared to regions that do not broadcast these programs.

Findings on latent learning, observational learning, and the role of cognition in learning can help us evaluate arguments in the passionate debate about the effects of media violence. Children and teenagers throughout the world see countless acts of violence on television, in films, and in video games. Does all this blood-and-guts mayhem affect them? Do you think it has affected *you*? In "Taking Psychology with You," we offer evidence that bears on these questions and suggest ways of resolving them without oversimplifying the issues.

Although the behavioural and social-cognitive approaches to learning differ in emphasis, they share a fundamental optimism about the possibilities of change for individuals and societies. In the learning view, we do not have to sit around hoping that people will magically have a change of heart and stop harming themselves or others. Instead, we can focus on changing the reinforcers, role models, and media images that affect people's attitudes and actions.

Skinner himself never wavered in his determination to apply learning principles to fashion better, healthier environments for everyone. In 1990, just a week before his death, ailing and frail, he addressed an overflow crowd at the annual meeting of the American Psychological Association, making the case one last time for the approach he was convinced could create a better society. When you see the world as the learning theorist views it, Skinner was saying, you see the folly of human behaviour, but you also see the possibility of improving it.

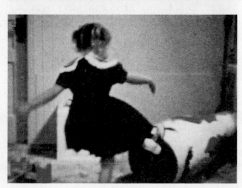

In studies by Albert Bandura and his colleagues, children watched films of an adult kicking, punching, and hammering on a big rubber doll (top). Later, the children imitated the adult's behaviour, some of them almost exactly.

◉ Watch
Bandura's Bobo Doll Experiment

quickQUIZ

✓●—[Quick Review on **MyPsychLab**]

Does your perception of quizzes make you eager to answer them?

1. A friend asks you to meet her at a new restaurant across town. You have never been to this specific address, but you find your way there anyway because you have experienced _____ learning.

2. To a social-cognitive theorist, the fact that we can learn without being reinforced for any obvious responses shows that we do not learn specific responses but rather _____.

3. After watching her teenage sister put on lipstick, a little girl takes a lipstick and applies it to her own lips. She has acquired this behaviour through a process of _____.

✳ Explore
Media Violence and Societal Aggression

Answers:

1. latent   2. knowledge about responses and their consequences   3. observational learning

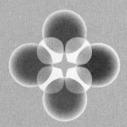

Taking Psychology with YOU

Thinking Critically in Everyday Life

Does Media Violence Make You Violent?

In a $5 billion lawsuit against video-game manufacturers, the families of victims who had been shot at a high school by two fellow students claimed that the tragedy would never have happened had the killers not played video games that were full of violence and bloodshed. When another gunman went on a murderous rampage at a university, several commentators immediately assumed that video games must have spurred him to kill. How should we evaluate such claims? Does violence depicted in films, on TV, and in video games lead to violent crime?

First, examine the evidence. In this chapter, you read about Albert Bandura's finding that children imitate antisocial behaviour. Since that research was done, hundreds of studies of children, teenagers, and adults have corroborated his results, convincing many psychologists that observing aggression

does increase aggression. Meta-analysis shows that the greater the exposure to violence in movies and on television, the stronger the likelihood of a person's behaving aggressively, even after researchers control for social class, intelligence, and other factors (e.g., Anderson & Bushman, 2001). Moreover, when grade-school children cut back on time spent watching TV or playing video games, which are often violent in nature, the children's aggressiveness declines (Robinson et al., 2001). A review by a group of prominent scientists concluded that "research on violent television and films, video games, and music reveals unequivocal evidence that media violence increases the likelihood of aggressive and violent behaviour," both in the short term and long term (Anderson et al., 2003).

Next, consider other interpretations. Nonetheless, some psychologists and social critics believe that the

relation is not strong enough to worry about (e.g., Freedman, 2002; Ferguson, 2009). Indeed, two meta-analyses of the research on video games found little support for the idea that violent games cause most players to become more aggressive (Ferguson, 2007; Sherry, 2001). There's also the pesky issue of cause and effect: Individuals who are already aggressive tend to be drawn to violent images. And children and teens watch many different programs and movies and have many models to observe besides those they see in the media, including parents and peers. For every teenager who is obsessed with playing God of War III and who entertains grim fantasies of blowing up the world, dozens more think the game is just plain fun and then go off to do their homework. Interestingly, although the number of violent video games increased throughout the 1990s, overall rates of teenage violence actually declined.

Finally, don't oversimplify. In the social-cognitive view, both conclusions about the relation of media violence to violent behaviour have merit. Repeated acts of aggression in the media do model behaviour and responses to conflict that a few people may imitate, just as media ads influence what many people buy and what many people think the ideal male or female body should look like. Video games that directly reward violence—for example, by awarding points or moving the player to the next level after a "kill"—increase feelings of hostility, aggressive thinking, and aggressive behaviour (Carnagey & Anderson, 2005). Violent media may also desensitize people to the pain or distress of others. In a field study, people who had just seen a violent movie took longer to come to the aid of a woman struggling to pick up her crutches than did people who had seen a nonviolent movie or people still waiting to see one of the two movies (Bushman & Anderson, 2009).

However, perceptions and interpretations of events, personality dispositions such as aggressiveness and sociability, and the social context in which the violence is viewed can all affect how a person responds (Feshbach & Tanguey, 2008). One person may learn from seeing people being blown away in a film that violence is cool and masculine; another may decide that the violent images are ugly and stupid; a third may conclude that they don't mean anything at all, that they are just part of the story.

What should be done, if anything, about media violence? Even if only a small percentage of viewers learn to be aggressive from observing all that violence, the social consequences can be serious, because the total audiences for TV, movies, and video games are immense (Bushman & Anderson, 2001). But censorship, which some people think is the answer, brings its own set of problems, quite apart from constitutional issues of free speech: Should we ban *Hamlet*? Bloody graphic comics? *Iron Man II*? Films that truthfully depict the realities of war, murder, and torture?

Consider, too, that it's not just video games and other visual media that can increase aggression. In two studies, students read a violent passage from the Bible, with two sentences inserted in which God sanctions the violence. Later, in what they thought was a different study, they played a competitive reaction-time game with a partner. In the game, they were more willing to blast their competitor with a loud noise than were students who had been told the violent passage was from an ancient scroll or students who had read a passage that did not mention God (Bushman et al., 2007). Participants who believed in God were most affected by the passage in which God condones the violence, but many nonbelievers were affected too. Although the general message of the scriptures is one of peace and reconciliation, the Bible is also full of violence, some of it sanctioned by God. Yet few people would be willing to ban the Bible or censure its violent parts.

As you can see, determining a fair and equitable policy regarding media violence will not be easy. It will demand good evidence—and good thinking.

SUMMARY

◆ Research on learning has been heavily influenced by behaviourism, which accounts for behaviour in terms of observable events without reference to mental entities such as "mind" or "will." Behaviourists have focused on two types of conditioning: classical and operant.

CLASSICAL CONDITIONING

◆ Classical conditioning was first studied by Russian physiologist Ivan Pavlov. In this type of learning, when a neutral stimulus is paired with an unconditioned stimulus (US) that elicits some reflexive unconditioned response (UR), the neutral stimulus comes to elicit a similar or related response. The neutral stimulus then becomes a conditioned stimulus (CS), and the response it elicits is a conditioned response (CR). Nearly any kind of involuntary response can become a CR.

◆ In extinction, the conditioned stimulus is repeatedly presented without the unconditioned stimulus, and the conditioned response eventually disappears, although later it may reappear (spontaneous recovery). In higher-order conditioning, a neutral stimulus becomes a conditioned stimulus by being paired with an already established conditioned stimulus. In stimulus generalization, after a stimulus becomes a conditioned stimulus for some response, other similar stimuli may produce the same reaction. In stimulus discrimination, different responses are made to stimuli that resemble the conditioned stimulus in some way.

◆ Many theorists believe that what an animal or person learns in classical conditioning is not just an association between the unconditioned and conditioned stimulus, but also information conveyed by one stimulus about another. Indeed, classical conditioning appears to be an evolutionary adaptation that allows an organism to prepare for a biologically important event. Considerable evidence exists to show that a neutral stimulus does not become a CS unless it reliably signals or predicts the US.

CLASSICAL CONDITIONING IN REAL LIFE

◆ Classical conditioning helps account for positive emotional responses to particular objects and events, fears and phobias, reactions to particular foods and odours, and reactions to medical treatments and placebos. John Watson showed how fears may be learned and then may be unlearned through a process of counterconditioning. Because of evolutionary adaptations, human beings (and many other species) are biologically primed to acquire some classically conditioned responses easily, such as conditioned taste aversions and certain fears.

◆ As we saw in "Biology and Classical Conditioning," work on classical conditioning is now integrating findings on motivation, learning, and biology. For example, brain changes occur in response to conditioned stimuli for appetite or pleasure, and those changes may affect people's motivation to eat even when they are already full. Using a drug to enhance the activity of a certain receptor in the amygdala speeds up the extinction of a phobia (fear of heights) during virtual-reality treatments. And genetic differences contribute to individual differences in susceptibility to conditioned fears.

OPERANT CONDITIONING

◆ In operant conditioning, behaviour becomes more likely to occur or less so depending on its consequences. Responses in operant conditioning are generally not reflexive and are more complex than in classical conditioning. Research in this area is closely associated with B. F. Skinner, who called his approach "radical behaviourism."

◆ In the Skinnerian analysis, reinforcement strengthens or increases the probability of a response and punishment weakens or decreases the probability of a response. Immediate consequences usually have a greater effect on a response than do delayed consequences.

◆ Reinforcers are called primary when they are naturally reinforcing because they satisfy a biological need. They are called secondary when they have acquired their ability to strengthen a response through association with other reinforcers. A similar distinction is made for punishers.

◆ Reinforcement and punishment may be either positive or negative, depending on whether the consequence involves a stimulus that is presented or one that is removed or avoided. In positive reinforcement, something pleasant follows a response; in negative reinforcement, something unpleasant is removed. In positive punishment, something unpleasant follows the response; in negative punishment, something pleasant is removed.

◆ Using the Skinner box and similar devices, behaviourists have shown that extinction, stimulus generalization, and stimulus discrimination occur in operant conditioning as well as in classical conditioning. A discriminative stimulus signals that a response is likely to be followed by a certain type of consequence.

◆ *Continuous reinforcement* leads to the most rapid learning. However, intermittent (partial) reinforcement makes a response resistant to extinction (and, therefore, helps account for the persistence of superstitious rituals). One of the most common errors people make is to reward intermittently the responses they would like to eliminate.

◆ *Shaping* is used to train behaviours with a low probability of occurring spontaneously. Reinforcers are given for successive approximations to the desired response until the desired response is achieved.

◆ Biology places limits on what an animal or person can learn through operant conditioning, or how easily it is learned. For example, animals sometimes have trouble learning a task because of *instinctive drift*.

OPERANT CONDITIONING IN REAL LIFE

◆ *Behaviour modification*, the application of operant-conditioning principles, has been used successfully in many settings, but when used inappropriately, reinforcement and punishment both have their pitfalls.

◆ Punishment, when used properly, can discourage undesirable behaviour, including criminal behaviour. But it is frequently misused and can have unintended consequences. It is often administered inappropriately because of the emotion of the moment; it may produce rage and fear; its effects are often only temporary; it is hard to administer immediately; it conveys little information about the kind of behaviour that is desired; and it may provide attention that is rewarding. Extinction of undesirable behaviour, combined with reinforcement of desired behaviour, is generally preferable to the use of punishment.

◆ Reinforcers can also be misused. Rewards that are given out indiscriminately, as in efforts to raise children's self-esteem, do not reinforce desirable behaviour. And an exclusive reliance on extrinsic reinforcement can sometimes undermine the power of intrinsic reinforcement. But money and praise do not usually interfere with intrinsic pleasure when a person is rewarded for succeeding or making progress rather than for merely participating in an activity, or when a person is already highly interested in the activity.

LEARNING AND THE MIND

◆ Even during behaviourism's heyday, some researchers were probing the "black box" of the mind. In the 1930s, Edward Tolman studied latent learning, in which no obvious reinforcer is present during learning and a response is not expressed until later on, when reinforcement does become available. What appears to be acquired in latent learning is not a specific response but rather knowledge about responses and their consequences.

◆ The 1960s and 1970s saw the increased influence of social-cognitive theories of learning, which focus on observational learning and the role played by beliefs, interpretations of events, and other cognitions in determining behaviour. Social-cognitive theorists argue that in observational learning, as in latent learning, what is acquired is knowledge rather than a specific response. Because people differ in their perceptions and beliefs, they may learn different lessons from the same event or situation. Perceptions, personality traits, and social context can all influence how people respond.

TAKING PSYCHOLOGY WITH YOU

◆ Because people differ in their perceptions and beliefs, some people become more aggressive after exposure to violent images in the media, but most people do not. Social-learning research shows that personality traits and the social context influence how people respond to what they see and the lessons they take from any experience.

MyPsychLab

Visit **www.mypsychlab.com** to help you get the best grade!
Test your knowledge and grasp difficult concepts through

• Custom study plans: See where you are strong and where you go wrong

• Interactive simulations

• Video and audio clips

KEY TERMS

learning 236
behaviourism 236
conditioning 236
unconditioned stimulus (US) 237
unconditioned response (UR) 237
conditioned stimulus (CS) 237
conditioned response (CR) 237
classical conditioning 237
extinction (in classical conditioning) 238
spontaneous recovery 238
higher-order conditioning 238
stimulus generalization (in classical conditioning) 239
stimulus discrimination (in classical conditioning) 239

counterconditioning 243
operant conditioning 247
reinforcement 248
punishment 249
primary reinforcer 249
primary punishers 249
secondary reinforcer 249
secondary punisher 249
positive reinforcement 250
negative reinforcement 250
extinction (in operant conditioning) 252
stimulus generalization (in operant conditioning) 252
stimulus discrimination (in operant conditioning) 252

discriminative stimulus 253
continuous reinforcement 253
intermittent (partial) schedule of reinforcement 253
shaping 254
successive approximations 254
instinctive drift 255
behaviour modification (applied behaviour analysis) 257
extrinsic reinforcers 261
intrinsic reinforcers 261
latent learning 264
social-cognitive theories 265
observational learning 265

8 BEHAVIOUR IN SOCIAL AND CULTURAL CONTEXT

ASK QUESTIONS . . . be willing to WONDER

- Why do ordinary people sometimes do unspeakably evil things?

- When people argue about political or social issues, how come so few ever change their views?

- What enables some people to choose conscience over conformity?

- What causes prejudice? What reduces it?

When Mohamed Atta was in graduate school in Germany, studying urban planning, his friends saw him as a good man who, like many students, was troubled by the social injustice he observed in the world. Atta was especially disturbed by the gap between rich and poor, although he himself came from a well-to-do family; his father was a lawyer and two sisters became university professors. "I knew Mohamed as a guy searching for justice," his German friend Volker Hauth told the *Los Angeles Times* (Reza, Williams, & Dahlburg, 2001). "Atta was very religious," said another friend. "He was very full of idealism and he was a humanist." In 2000, Atta left Germany for good. On September 11, 2001, he led the 19 hijackers who attacked the World Trade Center and the Pentagon, killing almost 3000 people.

In 1994 in Rwanda, members of the Hutu tribe shot or hacked to death nearly one million people from the minority Tutsi, a rival tribe. At one point, thousands of Tutsi took refuge in a Benedictine convent, believing the nuns there would shelter them. Instead, the mother superior, Sister Gertrude, and another nun, Sister Maria Kisito—both of them Hutu—reported the Tutsi refugees to the Hutu militia. More than 7000 Tutsi were killed in the ensuing massacre. When the two nuns were brought to trial in Belgium, where they fled after the war, Sister Gertrude told the court she did it because "we were all going to perish." But observers testified that when 500 Tutsi fled to the convent's garage, the two nuns brought the militiamen gasoline. The garage was set afire, and anyone trying to escape the flames was hacked to death. The two women were sentenced to 15- and 12-year terms for crimes against humanity.

In 1961, Adolf Eichmann, who had been a high-ranking officer of the Nazi elite, was sentenced to death for his part in the deportation and killing of millions of Jews during World War II. He was proud of his efficiency at his work and his ability to resist feeling pity for his victims. But when the Israelis captured him, he insisted that he was not anti-Semitic. Shortly before his execution, Eichmann said, "I am not the monster I am made out to be. I am the victim of a fallacy" (Brown, 1986).

The fallacy to which Eichmann referred was the widespread belief that a person who does monstrous deeds must be a monster. Mohamed Atta, Sisters Gertrude and Maria Kisito, and Adolf Eichmann all committed terrible deeds. Were they all deranged? Or evil? There does seem to be so much evil and cruelty in the world, and yet so much kindness, sacrifice, and heroism too. How can we even begin to explain either side of human nature?

Thinking Critically   Ask Questions

Mohamed Atta, Rwandan Hutu nuns Sister Gertrude and Sister Maria Kisito at their trial in Brussels, and Adolf Eichmann at his trial in Israel. All of these people committed crimes that horrified the world. Were they "monsters"?

The fields of *social psychology* and *cultural psychology* approach this question by examining the powerful influence of the social and cultural environment on the actions of individuals and groups. In this chapter, we will focus on the foundations of social psychology, basic principles that can help us understand why people who are not "crazy" or "monstrous" nonetheless do unspeakably evil things, and, conversely, why otherwise ordinary people may reach heights of heroism when the occasion demands. We will look at the influence of roles and attitudes, how people's behaviour is affected by the groups and situations they are in, and the conditions under which people conform or dissent. Finally, we will consider some of the social and cultural reasons for prejudice and conflict between groups.

YOU are about to learn . . .

◆ how social roles and cultural norms regulate behaviour without our being aware of it.

◆ the power of roles and situations to make people behave in ways they never would have predicted for themselves.

◆ how people can be entrapped into violating their moral principles.

ROLES AND RULES

"We are all fragile creatures entwined in a cobweb of social constraints," social psychologist Stanley Milgram once said. The constraints he referred to are social **norms**, rules about how we are supposed to act, enforced by threats of punishment if we violate them and promises of reward if we follow them. Norms are the conventions of everyday life that make interactions with other people predictable and orderly; like a cobweb, they are often as invisible as they are strong. Every society has norms for just about everything in human experience: for conducting courtships, for raising children, for making decisions, for behaviour in public places. Some norms are enshrined in law, such as "A person may not beat up another person, except in self-defence." Some are unspoken cultural

norms (social) Rules that regulate social life, including explicit laws and implicit cultural conventions.

understandings, such as "A man may beat up another man who insults his masculinity." And some are tiny, unspoken regulations that people learn to follow unconsciously, such as "You may not sing at the top of your lungs on a public bus."

When people observe that "everyone else" seems to be violating a social norm, they are more likely to do so too—and this is the mechanism by which entire neighbourhoods can deteriorate. In six natural field experiments conducted in the Netherlands, researchers found that passersby were more likely to litter, to park illegally, and even to steal a five-euro bill from a mailbox if the sidewalks were dirty and unswept, if graffiti marked the walls, or if strangers were setting off illegal fireworks (Keizer, Lindenberg, & Steg, 2008). Conversely, people's behaviour will become more constructive if they think that's the norm. When hotels put notices in guest bathrooms that "the majority of guests in this room reuse their towels" (in contrast to simply requesting the guest to do the same because it's good for the environment), more than half agree to participate in the reuse program (Goldstein, Cialdini, & Griskevicius, 2008).

In every society, people also fill a variety of social **roles**, positions that are regulated by norms about how people in those positions should behave. Gender roles define the proper behaviour for a man and a woman. Occupational roles determine the correct behaviour for a manager and an employee, or a professor and a student. Family roles set tasks for parent and child. Certain aspects of every role must be carried out or there will be penalties—emotional, financial, or professional. As a student, for instance, you know just what you have to do to pass your psychology course (or you should by now!). How do you know what a role requirement is? You know when you violate it, intentionally or unintentionally, because you will probably feel awfully uncomfortable, or other people will try to make you feel that way.

The requirements of a social role are in turn shaped by the culture you live in. **Culture** can be defined as a program of shared rules that govern the behaviour of people in a community or society, and a set of values, beliefs, and customs shared by most members of that community and passed from one generation to another (Lonner, 1995). You learn most of your culture's rules and values the way you learn your culture's language: without thinking about it.

For example, cultures differ in their rules for *conversational distance:* how close people normally stand to one another when they are speaking (Hall, 1959, 1976). In general, Arabs like to stand close enough to feel your breath, touch your arm, and see your eyes—a distance that makes many Canadians and northern Europeans uneasy, unless they are talking intimately with a lover. The English and the Swedes stand farthest

Many roles in modern life require us to give up our individuality. If one of these members of the British Coldstream Guards suddenly broke into a dance, his career would be brief—and the dazzling effect of the parade would be ruined. But when does adherence to a role go too far?

role A given social position that is governed by a set of norms for proper behaviour.

culture A program of shared rules that govern the behaviour of people in a community or society, and a set of values, beliefs, and customs shared by most members of that community.

DARE TO BE DIFFERENT

Get INVOLVED!

Either alone or with a friend, try a mild form of norm violation (nothing alarming, obscene, dangerous, or offensive). For example, stand backward in line at the grocery store or cafeteria; sit right next to a stranger in the library or at a movie, even when other seats are available; sing or hum loudly for a couple of minutes in a public place; or stand "too close" to a friend in conversation. Notice the reactions of onlookers, as well as your own feelings, while you violate this norm. If you do this exercise with someone else, one of you can be the "violator" and the other can write down the responses of others; then switch places. Was it easy to do this exercise? Why or why not?

Arabs stand much closer in conversation than Westerners do, close enough to feel one another's breath and "read" one another's eyes. Most Westerners would feel "crowded" standing so close, even when talking to a friend.

◉ Watch
Personal Space

◈ Research
Stanley Milgram

◉ Watch
Classic Footage of Milgram's Obedience Study

FIGURE 8.1 The Milgram Obedience Experiment
On the left is Milgram's original shock machine; in 1963, it looked pretty ominous. On the right, the "learner" is being strapped into his chair by the experimenter and the "teacher."

apart when they converse; southern Europeans stand closer; and Latin Americans and Arabs stand the closest (Keating, 1994; Sommer, 1969). Even avatars on *Second Life* obey the rules of the player's culture: For example, just as in the physical world, female avatars stand closer to one another when they're talking and make more eye contact than male pairs do, and avatars tend to reduce eye contact as they get closer, if that is the rule in the player's culture (Yee et al., 2007).

If you are talking to someone who has different cultural rules for distance from yours, you are likely to feel very uncomfortable without knowing why. You may feel that the person is crowding you or being strangely cool and distant.

Naturally, people bring their own personalities and interests to the roles they play. Just as two actors will play the same part differently although they are reading from the same script, you will have your own reading of how to play the role of student, friend, parent, or employee. Nonetheless, the requirements of a social role are strong, so strong that they may even cause you to behave in ways that shatter your fundamental sense of the kind of person you are. We turn now to two classic studies that illuminate the power of social roles in our lives.

The Obedience Study

In the early 1960s, Stanley Milgram (1963, 1974) designed a study that would become world-famous. Milgram wanted to know how many people would obey an authority figure when directly ordered to violate their ethical standards. Participants in the study thought they were part of an experiment on the effects of punishment on learning. Each was assigned, apparently at random, to the role of "teacher." Another person, introduced as a fellow volunteer, was the "learner." Whenever the learner, seated in an adjoining room, made an error in reciting a list of word pairs he was supposed to have memorized, the teacher had to give him an electric shock by depressing a lever on a machine (see Figure 8.1). With each error, the voltage (marked from 0 to 450) was to be increased by another 15 volts. The shock levels on the machine were labelled from SLIGHT SHOCK to DANGER—SEVERE SHOCK and, finally, ominously, XXX. In reality, the learners were confederates of Milgram and did not receive any shocks, but none of the teachers ever realized this during the study. The actor-victims played their parts convincingly: As the study continued, they shouted in pain and pleaded to be released, all according to a prearranged script.

Before doing this study, Milgram asked a number of psychiatrists, students, and middle-class adults how many people they thought would "go all the way" to XXX on orders from the researcher. The psychiatrists predicted that most people would refuse to go beyond 150 volts, when the learner first demanded to be freed, and that only one person in a thousand, someone who was disturbed and sadistic, would administer the highest voltage. The nonprofessionals agreed with this prediction, and all of them said that they personally would disobey early in the procedure.

That is not, however, the way the results turned out. Every single person administered some shock to the learner, and about two-thirds of the participants, of all ages and from all walks of life, obeyed to the fullest extent. Many protested to the experimenter, but they backed down when he calmly asserted, "The experiment requires that you continue." They obeyed no matter how much the victim shouted for them to stop and no matter how painful the shocks seemed to be. They obeyed even when they themselves were anguished about the pain they believed they were causing. As Milgram (1974) noted, participants would "sweat, tremble, stutter, bite their lips, groan, and dig their fingernails into their flesh"—but still they obeyed.

Over the decades, more than 3000 people of many different ethnicities have gone through replications of the Milgram study. Most of them, men and women equally, inflicted what they thought were dangerous amounts of shock to another person. Recently, the Milgram experiment was replicated and the results were remarkably similar (Burger, 2009). What was particularly interesting was that although the current replication used conditions that should have made it easier for participants to disobey, the rates of obedience were not different from the original study. Researchers in other countries have also found high percentages of obedience, ranging to more than 90% in Spain and the Netherlands (Meeus & Raaijmakers, 1995; Smith & Bond, 1994).

Milgram and his team subsequently set up several variations of the study to determine the circumstances under which people might disobey the experimenter. They found that virtually nothing the victim did or said changed the likelihood of compliance, even when the victim said he had a heart condition, screamed in agony, or stopped responding entirely, as if he had collapsed. However, people *were* more likely to disobey under certain conditions:

- **When the experimenter left the room,** many people subverted authority by giving low levels of shock but reporting that they had followed orders.

- **When the victim was right there in the room,** and the teacher had to administer the shock directly to the victim's body, many people refused to go on.

- **When two experimenters issued conflicting demands,** with one telling participants to continue and another saying to stop at once, no one kept inflicting shock.

- **When the person ordering them to continue was an ordinary man,** apparently another volunteer instead of the authoritative experimenter, many participants disobeyed.

- **When the participant worked with peers who refused to go further,** he or she often gained the courage to disobey.

Obedience, Milgram concluded, was more a function of the *situation* than of the personalities of the participants. "The key to [their] behaviour," Milgram (1974) summarized, "lies not in pent-up anger or aggression but in the nature of their relationship to authority. They have given themselves to the authority; they see themselves as instruments for the execution of his wishes; once so defined, they are unable to break free."

The Milgram study has had numerous critics. Some consider it unethical because people were kept in the dark about what was really happening until the session was over (of course, telling them in advance would have invalidated the study) and because many suffered emotional pain (Milgram countered that they would not have felt pain if they had simply disobeyed instructions). Some psychologists have questioned Milgram's conclusion that personality traits are virtually irrelevant to whether or not people obey

Thinking Critically

Ask Questions

Jot down your best guess in answering these three questions: (1) What percentage of people are sadistic? (2) If told by an authority to harm an innocent person, what percentage of people would do it? (3) If you were instructed to harm an innocent person, would you do it or would you refuse?

In Milgram's study, when the "teacher" had to administer shock directly to the learner, most subjects refused, but this one continued to obey.

⊙ **Watch**
Milgram's Obedience Study

an authority. Certain traits, they note, especially hostility, narcissism, and rigidity, do increase obedience and a willingness to inflict pain on others (Blass, 2000; Twenge, 2009). Others have objected to the parallel Milgram drew between the behaviour of the study's participants and the brutality of the Nazis and others who have committed acts of barbarism in the name of duty (Darley, 1995). The people in Milgram's study typically obeyed only when the experimenter was hovering right there, and many of them felt enormous discomfort and conflict. In contrast, most Nazis acted without direct supervision by authorities, without external pressure, and without feelings of anguish. Nevertheless, this compelling study has had a tremendous influence on public awareness of the dangers of uncritical obedience. As John Darley (1995) observed, "Milgram shows us the beginning of a path by means of which ordinary people, in the grip of social forces, become the origins of atrocities in the real world."

The Prison Study

◈ Research
Philip Zimbardo

Another famous demonstration of the power of roles is known as the Stanford prison study. Its designers, Philip Zimbardo and Craig Haney, wanted to know what would happen if ordinary university students were randomly assigned to the roles of prisoners and guards (Haney, Banks, & Zimbardo, 1973). And so they set up a serious-looking "prison" in the basement of a Stanford building, complete with individual cells, different uniforms for prisoners and guards, and nightsticks for the guards. The students agreed to live there for two weeks.

Within a short time, most of the prisoners became distressed and helpless. They developed emotional symptoms and physical ailments. Some became apathetic; others

Why did the guards at Abu Ghraib abuse and humiliate their prisoners? Were those guards just "bad apples"? Social psychologists think the answer lies in the roles they were assigned; the implicit permission, if not direct orders, given by their leaders; and the group norms of their peers.

became rebellious. One panicked and broke down. The guards, however, began to enjoy their new power. Some tried to be nice, helping the prisoners and doing little favours for them. Some were "tough but fair," holding strictly to "the rules." But about a third became punitive and harsh, even when the prisoners were not resisting in any way. One guard became unusually sadistic, smacking his nightstick into his palm as he vowed to "get" the prisoners and instructing two of them to simulate sexual acts (they refused). The researchers, who had not expected such a speedy and alarming transformation of ordinary students, ended this study after only six days.

Generations of students and the general public have seen emotionally charged clips from videos of the study made at the time. To the researchers, the results demonstrated how roles affect behaviour: The guards' aggression, they said, was entirely a result of wearing a guard's uniform and having the power conferred by a guard's authority (Haney & Zimbardo, 1998). Some social psychologists, however, have argued that the prison study is really another example of obedience to authority and of how willingly some people obey instructions—in this case, from Zimbardo himself (Haslam & Reicher, 2003). Consider the briefing that Zimbardo provided to the guards at the beginning of the study:

> You can create in the prisoners feelings of boredom, a sense of fear to some degree, you can create a notion of arbitrariness that their life is totally controlled by us, by the system, you, me, and they'll have no privacy. . . . We're going to take away their individuality in various ways. In general what all this leads to is a sense of powerlessness. That is, in this situation we'll have all the power and they'll have none. (*The Stanford Prison Study* video, quoted in Haslam & Reicher, 2003)

These are pretty powerful suggestions to the guards about how they would be permitted to behave, and they convey Zimbardo's personal encouragement ("*we'll* have all the power"), so perhaps it is not surprising that some took Zimbardo at his word and behaved quite brutally. The one sadistic guard later said he was just trying to play the role of the "worst S.O.B. guard" he'd seen in the movies. Even the investigators themselves noted at the time that the data were "subject to possible errors due to selective sampling. The video and audio recordings tended to be focussed upon the more interesting, dramatic events which occurred" (Haney et al., 1973).

Despite these flaws, the Stanford prison study remains a useful cautionary tale. In real prisons and jails, officers and guards do have the kind of power that was given to these students, and they too may be given instructions that encourage them to treat prisoners harshly. Thus the prison study provides a good example of how the social situation affects behaviour, causing some people to behave in ways that seem out of character.

Why People Obey

Of course, obedience to authority or to the norms of a situation is not always harmful or bad. A certain amount of routine compliance with rules is necessary in any group, and obedience to authority has many benefits for individuals and society. A nation could not operate if all its citizens ignored traffic signals, cheated on their taxes, dumped garbage wherever they chose, or assaulted each other. An organization could not function if its members came to work only when they felt like it. But obedience also has a darker aspect. Throughout history, the plea "I was only following orders" has been offered to excuse actions carried out under orders that were foolish, destructive, or illegal. The writer C. P. Snow once observed that "more hideous crimes have been committed in the name of obedience than in the name of rebellion."

Most people follow orders because of the obvious consequences of disobedience: They can be suspended from school, fired from their jobs, or arrested. But they may also obey because they hope to gain advantages or promotions from the authority, or because they expect to learn from the authority's greater knowledge or experience. They obey because they respect the authority's legitimacy. And, most of all, they obey because they do not want to rock the boat, appear to doubt the experts, or be rude, fearing that they will be disliked or rejected for doing so (Collins & Brief, 1995). But what about all those obedient people in Milgram's study who felt they were doing wrong and who wished they were free, but who could not untangle themselves from the "cobweb of social constraints"? How do people become morally disengaged from the consequences of their actions?

One answer is **entrapment**, a process in which individuals escalate their commitment to a course of action in order to justify their investment in it (Brockner & Rubin, 1985). The first stages of entrapment pose no difficult choices, but one step leads to another, and before you realize it you have become committed to a course of action that poses problems (Tavris & Aronson, 2007). In Milgram's study, once participants had given a 15-volt shock, they committed themselves to the experiment. The next level was "only" 30 volts. Because each increment was small, before they knew it most people were administering what they believed were dangerously strong shocks. At that point, it was difficult to explain a sudden decision to quit, especially after reaching 150 volts, the point at which the "learner" made his first verbal protests.

Whichever decision a person makes, to obey an authority or protest, he or she will feel an urgency to justify the choice made (Tavris & Aronson, 2007). Those who obey, for example, usually hand over responsibility to the authority, thereby absolving themselves of accountability for their own actions (Kelman & Hamilton, 1989; Modigliani & Rochat, 1995). In Milgram's study, many who administered the highest

⊙ Watch
The Power of the Situation: Zimbardo

Stanford Prison Experiment

Slot machines rely on the principle of entrapment, which is why casinos make millions and most players don't. A person vows to spend only a few dollars but, after losing them, says, "Well, maybe another couple of tries" or "I've spent so much, now I really have to win something to get back what I've lost."

entrapment   A gradual process in which individuals escalate their commitment to a course of action to justify their investment of time, money, or effort.

levels of shock adopted the attitude "It's his problem; I'm just following orders." In contrast, individuals who refused to give high levels of shock took responsibility for their actions. "One of the things I think is very cowardly," said a 32-year-old engineer, "is to try to shove the responsibility onto someone else. See, if I now turned around and said, 'It's your fault . . . it's not mine,' I would call that cowardly" (Milgram, 1974).

A chilling study of entrapment was conducted with 25 men who had served in the Greek military police during the authoritarian regime that ended in 1974 (Haritos-Fatouros, 1988). A psychologist interviewed the men, identifying the steps used in training them to use torture in questioning prisoners. First the men were ordered to stand guard outside the interrogation and torture cells. Then they stood guard inside the detention rooms, where they observed the torture of prisoners. Then they "helped" beat up prisoners. Once they had obediently followed these orders and became actively involved, the torturers found their actions easier to carry out. Similar procedures have been used to train military and police interrogators to use torture on political opponents and terrorist suspects in places as diverse as Chicago, England, Israel, and Brazil (Conroy, 2000; Huggins, Haritos-Fatouros, & Zimbardo, 2003; Mayer, 2009).

From their standpoint, torturers justify their actions because they see themselves as "good guys" who are just "doing their jobs" (Tavris & Aronson, 2007). This is a difficult concept for people who divide the world into "good guys" versus "bad guys" and cannot imagine that good guys might do cruel things. Yet in everyday life, as in the Milgram study, people often set out on a path that is morally ambiguous, only to find that they have travelled a long way toward violating their own principles. From Greece's torturers to the African nuns, and from Milgram's well-meaning volunteers to all of us in our everyday lives, people face the difficult task of drawing a line beyond which they will not go. For many, the demands of the role and the social pressures of the situation defeat the inner voice of conscience.

quickQUIZ

✓•Quick Review on MyPsychLab

Step into your role of student to answer these questions.

1. About what proportion of the people in Milgram's obedience study administered the highest level of shock? (a) two-thirds, (b) one-half, (c) one-third, (d) one-tenth
2. Which of the following actions by the "learner" reduced the likelihood of being shocked by the "teacher" in Milgram's study? (a) protesting noisily, (b) screaming in pain, (c) complaining of having a heart ailment, (d) nothing he did made a difference
3. A friend of yours, who is moving, asks you to bring over a few boxes. Since you are there anyway, he asks you to fill them with books. Before you know it, you have packed up his kitchen, living room, and bedroom. What social-psychological process is at work here?

Answers:

1. a 2. d 3. entrapment

 YOU are about to learn . . .

♦ two general ways that people explain their own or other people's behaviour—and why it matters.
♦ three self-serving biases in how people think about themselves and the world.

◆ why most people will believe outright lies and nonsensical statements if they are repeated often enough.

◆ whether certain fundamental political and religious attitudes have a genetic component.

SOCIAL INFLUENCES ON BELIEFS AND BEHAVIOUR

Social psychologists are interested not only in what people do in social situations, but also in what is going on in their heads while they are doing it. Researchers in the area of **social cognition** examine how people's perceptions of themselves and others affect their relationships and also how the social environment influences their perceptions, beliefs, and values. Current approaches draw on evolutionary theory, neuroimaging studies, surveys, and experiments to identify universal themes in how human beings perceive and feel about one another. In this section, we will consider two important topics in social cognition: attributions and attitudes.

Attributions

People read detective stories to find out *who* did the dirty deed, but in real life we also want to know *why* people do things. Was it because of a terrible childhood, a mental illness, possession by a demon, or what? According to **attribution theory**, the explanations we make of our behaviour and the behaviour of others generally fall into two categories. When we make a *situational attribution*, we are identifying the cause of an action as something in the situation or environment: "Joe stole the money because his family is starving." When we make a *dispositional attribution*, we are identifying the cause of an action as something in the person, such as a trait or a motive: "Joe stole the money because he is a born thief."

When people are trying to explain someone else's behaviour, they tend to overestimate personality traits and underestimate the influence of the situation (Forgas, 1998; Nisbett & Ross, 1980). In terms of attribution theory, they tend to ignore situational attributions in favour of dispositional ones. This tendency has been called the **fundamental attribution error** (Jones, 1990):

✳ **Explore**
Internal and External Attributions

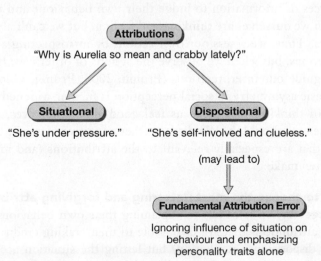

social cognition   An area in social psychology concerned with social influences on thought, memory, perception, and beliefs.

attribution theory   The theory that people are motivated to explain their own and other people's behaviour by attributing causes of that behaviour to a situation or a disposition.

fundamental attribution error   The tendency, in explaining other people's behaviour, to overestimate personality factors and underestimate the influence of the situation.

Were the hundreds of people who obeyed Milgram's experimenters sadistic by nature? Were the student guards in the prison study cruel and the prisoners cowardly

Calvin and Hobbes　　by Bill Watterson

Children learn the value of self-serving attributions at an early age.

✳ Explore
Fundamental Attribution Error

by temperament? Those who think so are committing the fundamental attribution error. The impulse to explain other people's behaviour in terms of their personalities is so strong that we do it even when we know that the other person was *required* to behave in a certain way (Yzerbyt et al., 2001).

The fundamental attribution error is especially prevalent in Western nations, where middle-class people tend to believe that individuals are responsible for their own actions and dislike the idea that the situation has much influence over them. They think that *they* would have refused the experimenter's cruel orders and *they* would have treated fellow-students-temporarily-called-prisoners fairly. In contrast, in countries such as India, where everyone is embedded in caste and family networks, and in Japan, China, Korea, and Hong Kong, where people are more group oriented than in the West, people are more likely to be aware of situational constraints on behaviour (Balcetis, Dunning, & Miller, 2008; Choi et al., 2003). Thus, if someone is behaving oddly, makes a mistake, or commits an ethical lapse, a person from India or China, unlike a Westerner, is more likely to make a situational attribution of the person's behaviour ("He's under pressure") than a dispositional one ("He's incompetent").

A primary reason for the fundamental attribution error is that people rely on different sources of information to judge their own behaviour and that of others. We know what we ourselves are thinking and feeling, but we can't always know the same of others. Thus, we assess our own actions by introspecting about our feelings and intentions, but when we observe the actions of others, we have only their behaviour to guide our interpretations (Pronin, 2008; Pronin, Gilovich, & Ross, 2004). This basic asymmetry in social perception is further widened by *self-serving biases*, habits of thinking that make us feel good about ourselves, even (perhaps especially) when we shouldn't. We discuss other cognitive biases in Chapter 9, but here are two that are especially relevant to the attributions (and misattributions) that people often make:

1　**The bias to choose the most flattering and forgiving attributions of our own lapses.** When it comes to explaining their own behaviour, people tend to choose attributions that are favourable to them, taking credit for their good actions (a dispositional attribution) but letting the situation account for their failures, embarrassing mistakes, or harmful actions (Mezulis et al., 2004). For instance, most North Americans, when angry, will say, "I am furious for good reason; this situation is intolerable." They are less likely to say, "I am furious because I am an ill-tempered grinch." On the other hand, if they do something admirable, such as donating to charity, they are likely to attribute their motives to a personal disposition ("I'm so generous") instead of the situation ("That guy on the phone pressured me into it").

Research performed at the University of British Columbia suggests that culture may affect whether or not we adopt another type of bias: the *group-serving bias*. This term describes our tendency to view the groups to which we belong, or the individuals in these groups, favourably (Heine & Lehman, 1997). In this study, European-Canadian, Asian-Canadian, and Japanese students were asked to evaluate their university and a member of their family. The researchers observed that the Japanese students consistently evaluated their family member and their university less positively than did the Canadians (regardless of their ethnicity). Thus, the Japanese participants (members of a more collectivist society) did not engage in group-serving biases, at either individual or group levels, whereas the Canadian participants (members of a more individualist society) exhibited group-serving biases at all levels of groups to which they belonged. Thus, some group-serving biases result from the degree to which one's culture is collectivist or individualist.

2   **The bias to believe that the world is fair.** According to the **just-world hypothesis**, attributions are also affected by the need to believe that justice usually prevails, that good people are rewarded and bad guys punished (Lerner, 1980; Hafer & Begue, 2005). When this belief is thrown into doubt, we are motivated to restore it (Aguiar et al., 2008). Unfortunately, one common way of restoring the belief in a just world is to call upon a dispositional attribution called *blaming the victim*: Maybe that person wasn't so good after all; he or she must have done *something* to deserve what happened or to provoke it. Blaming the victim is virtually universal when people are ordered to harm others or find themselves entrapped into harming others (Bandura, 1999). In the Milgram study, some "teachers" made comments such as "[The learner] was so stupid and stubborn he deserved to get shocked" (Milgram, 1974). In an innovative series of experiments, Carolyn Hafer of Brock University has found that people who strongly believe that the world is just are more likely to blame the victim than are those who have weaker beliefs in a just world (Hafer, 2000a, 2000b). When their belief in a just world is threatened, such individuals then seek to maintain their belief by finding some reason why the victims deserved what they got (Hafer & Begue, 2005).

Of course, sometimes dispositional (personality) attributions *do* explain a person's behaviour. The point to remember is that the attributions you make can have huge consequences. For example, happy couples usually attribute their partners' occasional thoughtless lapses to something in the situation ("Poor guy is under a lot of stress") and their partners' loving actions to a stable, internal disposition ("He has the sweetest nature"). But unhappy couples do just the reverse. They attribute lapses to their partners' personalities ("He is totally selfish") and good behaviour to the situation ("Yeah, he gave me a present, but only because his mother told him to") (Karney & Bradbury, 2000). You can see why the attributions you make about your partner, your parents, and your friends will affect how you get along with them—and how long you will put up with their failings.

just-world hypothesis The notion that the world is fair and that justice is served, that bad people are punished and good people rewarded.

quickQUIZ

✓•Quick Review on MyPsychLab

To what do you attribute your success in answering these questions?

1. What kind of attribution is being made in each case, situational or dispositional? (a) A man says, "My wife has sure become a grouchy person." (b) The same man says, "I'm grouchy because I had a bad day at the office." (c) A woman reads about high unemployment in poor communities and says, "Well, if those people weren't so lazy, they would find work."

2. What principles of attribution theory are suggested by the items in the preceding question?

Answers:

1. a. dispositional b. situational c. dispositional   2. Item a illustrates the fundamental attribution error; b, the bias to choose a flattering or forgiving explanation of our own lapses; and c, blaming the victim, possibly because of the just-world hypothesis.

Attitudes

✱ **Explore**
Cognitive Dissonance and Attitude Change

People hold attitudes about all sorts of things—politics, food, children, movies, sports heroes, you name it. An *attitude* is a belief about people, groups, ideas, or activities. Some attitudes are *explicit:* We are aware of them, they shape our conscious decisions and actions, and they can be measured on self-report questionnaires. Others are *implicit:* We are unaware of them, they may influence our behaviour in ways we do not recognize, and they are measured in indirect ways (Stanley, Phelps, & Banaji, 2008).

Some of your attitudes change when you have new experiences, and on occasion they change because you rationally decide you were wrong about something. But attitudes also change because of the psychological need for consistency and the mind's normal biases in processing information. In Chapter 9, we discuss **cognitive dissonance**, the uncomfortable feeling that occurs when two attitudes, or an attitude and a behaviour, are in conflict (are dissonant). To resolve this dissonance, most people will change one of their attitudes. For example, if a politician or celebrity you admire does something stupid, immoral, or illegal, you can restore consistency either by lowering your opinion of the person or by deciding that the person's behaviour wasn't so stupid or immoral after all. Usually—and unfortunately for critical thinking—people restore cognitive consistency by dismissing evidence that might otherwise throw their fundamental beliefs into question (Aronson, 2008).

◄◉ **Simulate**
Cognitive Dissonance

cognitive dissonance A state of tension that occurs when a person simultaneously holds two cognitions that are psychologically inconsistent or when a person's belief is incongruent with his or her behaviour.

familiarity effect The tendency of people to feel more positive toward a person, item, product, or other stimulus the more familiar they are with it.

validity effect The tendency of people to believe that a statement is true or valid simply because it has been repeated many times.

SHIFTING OPINIONS AND BEDROCK BELIEFS. All around you, every day, advertisers, politicians, and friends are trying to influence your attitudes. One weapon they use is the drip, drip, drip of a repeated idea. Repeated exposure even to a nonsense syllable such as *zug* is enough to make a person feel more positive toward it (Zajonc, 1968). The **familiarity effect**, the tendency to hold positive attitudes toward familiar people or things, has been demonstrated across cultures, across species, and across states of awareness, from alert to preoccupied. It works even for stimuli you aren't aware of seeing (Monahan, Murphy, & Zajonc, 2000). A related phenomenon is the **validity effect**, the tendency to believe that something is true simply because it has been repeated many times. Repeat something often enough, even the basest lie, and eventually the public will believe it. Hitler's propaganda minister, Joseph Goebbels, called this technique the "Big Lie."

In a series of experiments, Hal Arkes and his associates demonstrated how the validity effect operates (Arkes, 1993; Arkes, Boehm, & Xu, 1991). In a typical study, people read a list of statements, such as "Mercury has a higher boiling point than copper" or

"Over 400 Hollywood films were produced in 1948." They had to rate each statement for its validity, on a scale of 1 (definitely false) to 7 (definitely true). A week or two later, they again rated the validity of some of these statements and also rated others that they had not seen previously. The result: Mere repetition increased the perception that the familiar statements were true. The same effect also occurred for other kinds of statements, including unverifiable opinions (e.g., "At least 75% of all politicians are basically dishonest"), opinions that subjects initially felt were true, and even opinions they initially felt were false. "Note that no attempt has been made to persuade," said Arkes (1993). "No supporting arguments are offered. We just have subjects rate the statements. Mere repetition seems to increase rated validity. This is scary."

On most everyday topics, such as movies and sports, people's attitudes range from casual to committed. If your best friend is neutral about baseball whereas you are an insanely devoted fan, your friendship will probably survive. But when the subject is one involving beliefs that give meaning and purpose to a person's life—most notably, politics and religion—it's another ball game, so to speak. Wars have been fought, and are being fought as you read this, over people's most passionate convictions. Perhaps the attitude that causes the most controversy and bitterness around the world is the one toward religious diversity: accepting or intolerant. Some people of all religions accept a world of differing religious views and practices; they believe that church and state should be separate. But for many fundamentalists (in any religion), religion and politics are inseparable; they believe that one religion should prevail (Jost et al., 2003). You can see, then, why these irreconcilable attitudes cause continuing conflict, and are sometimes used to justify terrorism and war. Why are people so different in these views?

The more familiar things are, the more we tend to like them. The President's Choice brand, which was first introduced in 1984, relies on the familiarity effect to promote everything from decadent chocolate chip cookies to banking services.

BIOLOGY *and Beliefs*

Do Genes Influence Attitudes?

Where do your attitudes come from? Many attitudes result from learning and experience, of course. But research from behavioural genetics has found that some core attitudes stem from personality traits that are heritable. That is, the variation among people in these attitudes is due in part to their genetic differences (Paunonen, 2003; see Chapters 3 and 14). Two such traits are "openness to experience" and "conscientiousness." We would expect people who are open to new experiences to hold positive attitudes toward novelty and change in general—say, in religion, art, music, and social and political events in the larger culture. We would expect people who prefer the familiar and conventional, and who are conscientious about order and obligations, to be drawn to conservative politics, religious denominations, and philosophies. And that is what research finds. For example, in a study of Protestant Christians, fundamentalist Christians scored much lower than liberal Christians on the dimension of openness to experience (Streyffeler & McNally, 1998). Conversely, conservatives score higher than liberals on conscientiousness (Jost, 2006).

Religious *affiliation* is not heritable. Most people choose a religious group because of their parents, ethnicity, culture, and social class, and many people in North America switch their religious affiliation at least once in their lives. But, as studies of twins reared apart have found, *religiosity*—a person's depth of religious feeling and adherence to a religion's rules—does have a genetic component. When religiosity combines with conservatism and authoritarianism (an unquestioning trust in authority), the

When people hold attitudes that are central to their religious and political philosophies, they often fail to realize that the other side feels just as strongly.

result is a deeply ingrained acceptance of tradition and dislike of those who question it (Olson et al., 2001; Saucier, 2000).

Likewise, political affiliation is not heritable; it is largely related to your upbringing and to the friends you make in early adulthood, the key years for deciding which party you want to join. Nor do the casual political opinions held by many swing voters or people who are politically disengaged have a genetic component. But political conservatism has high heritability: 0.65 in men and 0.45 in women (Bouchard, 2004). Various political positions on emotionally hot topics that are associated with conservative or liberal views are also partly heritable. A team of researchers investigated this possibility by drawing on two large samples of more than 8000 sets of twins who had been surveyed about their personality traits, religious beliefs, and political attitudes (Alford, Funk, & Hibbing, 2005). The researchers compared the opinions of fraternal twins (who share, on average, 50% of their genes) with those of identical twins (who share virtually all of their genes). They calculated how often the identical twins agreed on each issue, subtracted the rate at which fraternal twins agreed, and ended up with a rough measure of heritability. As you can see in Figure 8.2, the attitudes showing the highest heritability were those toward school prayer and property taxes; attitudes showing the lowest influence of genes included those toward nuclear power, divorce, modern art, and abortion.

As a result of such evidence, some psychological scientists maintain that ideological belief systems may have evolved in human societies to be organized along a left–right dimension, consisting of two core sets of attitudes: (1) whether a person advocates social change or supports the system as it is, and (2) whether a person thinks inequality is a result of human policies and can be overcome, or is inevitable and should be accepted as part of the natural order (Graham, Haidt, & Nosek, 2009). Liberals tend to prefer the values of progress, rebelliousness, chaos, flexibility, feminism, and equality, whereas conservatives tend to prefer tradition, conformity, order, stability, traditional values, and hierarchy. Those two dimensions underlie a host of specific attitudes. For instance,

FIGURE 8.2 **The Genetics of Belief**

A study of thousands of identical and fraternal twins identified the approximate genetic contribution to the variation in attitudes about diverse topics. Heritability was greatest for school prayer and property tax, and lowest for divorce, modern art, and abortion. But notice that in almost all cases, a person's unique life experiences (the "nonshared environment") were far more influential than genes, especially on attitudes toward topics as unrelated as the draft, censorship, and segregation (Alford, Funk, & Hibbing, 2005).

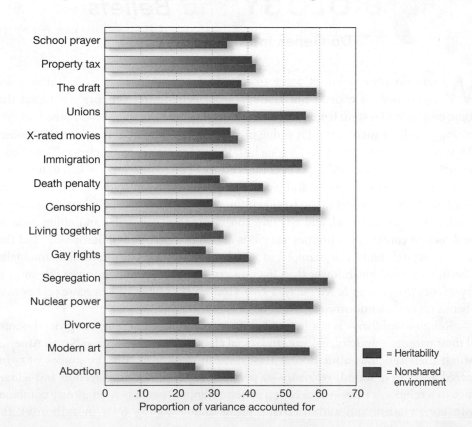

liberal undergraduates are more likely than conservative ones to have favourable attitudes toward atheists, poetry, Asian food, jazz, street people, tattoos, foreign films, erotica, big cities, recreational drugs, and foreign travel—all examples of "openness to experience" rather than preference for the familiar (Jost, Nosek, & Gosling, 2008).

You can see why liberals and conservatives argue so emotionally over issues such as gun control and gay marriage: They are not just arguing about the specific issue, but about each side's underlying assumptions and values that emerge from their personality traits. Evolutionary psychologists point out that both sets of attitudes would have had adaptive benefits over the centuries: Conservatism would have promoted stability, tradition, and order, whereas liberalism would have promoted flexibility and change (Graham, Haidt, & Nosek, 2009).

These findings are provocative, but it is important not to oversimplify them—say, by incorrectly assuming that everyone's political opinions are hardwired and unaffected by events. In fact, the factor that accounts for even more of the variation in political attitudes than heritability is individual life experiences, or what behavioural geneticists call the *nonshared environment* (Alford, Funk, & Hibbing, 2005; see Chapter 14). What do you think might be the personality dispositions that underlie your own ideological commitments? What might be the experiences you have had, because of your family, gender, ethnicity, social class, or unique history, that have shaped your own political views?

Persuasion or "Brainwashing"?

Let's now see how the social-psychological factors discussed thus far might help explain the tragic and disturbing phenomenon of cult suicides. Between 1994 and 1997, more than 70 members of the Order of the Solar Temple either committed mass suicide or engaged in murder–suicide, including more than 30 men, women, and children in Quebec. Cult leaders Luc Jouret and Joseph di Mambro persuaded their followers that if they committed suicide, they would be reborn on the star Sirius and avoid the imminent destruction of Earth. Neither of these leaders ever said to new recruits, "If you follow me, you will eventually give up your marriages, homes, children, and your lives"; but by the end, that is just what all of them did. Are these people mentally ill? Have they been "brainwashed"?

"Brainwashing" implies that a person has had a sudden change of mind without being aware of what is happening; it sounds mysterious and strange. On the contrary, the methods of persuasion are neither mysterious nor unusual (Bloom, 2005; Moghaddam, 2005), but rather involve coercive persuasion—that is, they are designed to suppress an individual's ability to reason, think critically, and make choices in his or her own best interests. Although some people may be more emotionally vulnerable than others to these methods, most of the people who become involved are not distinguishable from the general population. Studies of religious, political, and psychological sects and of terrorist cells have identified some of the key processes of coercive persuasion (Bloom, 2005; Moghaddam, 2005; Ofshe & Watters, 1994; Singer, 2003; Zimbardo & Leippe, 1991):

Sports teams also engage in ritualistic behaviour that use the tactics of coercive persuasion. How many hockey players (or fans for that matter) do you think would be willing to shave off a playoff beard during a winning streak?

◆ **The person is subjected to entrapment.** At first, the new recruit to the cause agrees only to do small things, but gradually the demands increase to spend more time, more money, more sacrifice. Ultimately, people take extreme measures because, over time, they have become entrapped in closed groups led by strong or charismatic leaders (Moghaddam, 2005).

◆ **The person's problems are explained by one simple attribution,** which is repeatedly emphasized.

◆ **The person is offered a new identity and is promised salvation.** There are as many simplistic explanations as there are groups that offer them. Are you afraid or unhappy? It all stems from the pain of being born. Are you struggling financially? It's your fault for not fervently wanting to be rich. Members may also be taught to simplify their problems by blaming a single enemy: Americans, the government, nonbelievers. . . .

◆ **The person's access to disconfirming (dissonant) information is severely controlled.** As soon as a person is a committed believer, the group or leader limits the person's choices, denigrates critical thinking, and suppresses private doubts. Recruits may be physically isolated from the outside world and thus from antidotes to the leader's ideas. They are separated from their families, are indoctrinated, and eventually become emotionally bonded to the group and the leader (Atran, 2003).

Not all instances of coercive persuasion are perceived as negative in our culture. For instance, many of the rituals associated with organized sports also use tactics of coercive persuasion. That is, the lifestyle required of top athletes in our country often involves hazing and team cohabitation, frequently resulting in little time to socialize with non-team members. Furthermore, many athletes will take coercive persuasion to the next level and will deliberately harm themselves. That is, they will take steroids, engage in unsafe needle-sharing practices, and continue to compete while injured because they do not want to succumb to weakness.

A key step in increasing resistance to coercive persuasion, therefore, is to dispel people's illusion of invulnerability to these tactics. Another is to teach people how to articulate and defend their own positions and think critically. These skills prepare people to resist propaganda and make them less vulnerable to manipulation by others (Tormala & Petty, 2002).

quickQUIZ

✓ **Quick Review** on **MyPsychLab**

Now, how can we persuade you to take this quiz without brainwashing you?

1. To win an election, a political party spends $3 million to make sure that the party name is seen and heard frequently and to repeat unverified charges that the opposing party members are unscrupulous. What psychological processes are at play here?

2. Which of the following has a significant heritable component? (a) religious affiliation, (b) political affiliation, (c) attitudes that favour stability and order versus those favouring equality and change, (d) attitudes toward modern art, (e) political conservatism

3. A friend urges you to join a "life-renewal" group called "The Feeling Life." Your friend has been spending increasing amounts of time with her fellow Feelies, and has already contributed more than $2,000 to their cause. You have some doubts about them. What questions would you want to have answered before joining up?

Answers:

1. The familiarity effect and the validity effect. 2. c, e 3. A few things to consider: Is there an autocratic leader who suppresses dissent and criticism while rationalizing this practice as a benefit for members? ("Doubt and disbelief are signs that your feeling side is being repressed.") Have long-standing members given up their friends, families, interests, and ambitions for this group? Does the leader offer simple but unrealistic promises to repair your life and all your troubles? Are members required to make sacrifices by donating large amounts of time and money?

YOU are about to learn . . .

◆ why people in groups often go along with the majority even when the majority is dead wrong.

◆ how "groupthink" can lead to bad, even catastrophic, decisions.

◆ how crowds can create "bystander apathy" and unpredictable violence.

◆ the conditions that increase the likelihood that some people will dissent from the majority opinion, take risks to help others, or blow the whistle on wrongdoers.

INDIVIDUALS IN GROUPS

The need to belong may be the most powerful of all human motivations (Baumeister et al., 2007). This makes good evolutionary sense because, like apes, bees, and elephants, human beings could never have survived without being included and accepted by their tribe. Human beings are so powerfully connected to one another, and so dependent on human companionship, that most people feel and remember the *social* pain of being rejected, humiliated, or excluded more intensely than actual *physical* pain they have endured (Chen et al., 2008; Williams, 2009). The need for social connection also explains why sending a prisoner to solitary confinement is internationally considered a form of torture: Its psychological consequences are even more devastating than physical abuse (Gawande, 2009).

Accordingly, the most powerful weapon that groups have to ensure their members' cooperation, and to weed out unproductive or disruptive members, is ostracism—rejection or permanent banishment. Social rejection impedes the ability to empathize, think critically, and solve problems. It can lead to mental disorders, eating disorders, and attempted suicide. No wonder that when people are rejected by a group they care about, some try to mend the rift, change their behaviour, and get back in the group's good graces, and others respond with rage and violence (Baumeister et al., 2007).

Of course, we all belong to many different groups, which vary in their importance to us. But the point to underscore is that as soon as we join a bunch of other people, we act differently than we would on our own. This change occurs regardless of whether the group has convened to solve problems and make decisions, has gathered to have a party, consists of anonymous bystanders or members of an internet chat room, or is a crowd of spectators or celebrants.

CAN YOU DISCONNECT?

To see for yourself how "social" you are, try this simple experiment: Turn off your cellphone and your laptop. Off! You may use your laptop to take notes in class, but no fair texting while you do. Now, how long can you go without checking email, IMs, tweets, Facebook, or the web to see what's happening? Keep track of your feelings on a (written!) notepad as time passes. Are you feeling anxious? Nervous? How long can you remain "cut off" before you start to feel isolated from your friends and family?

Get INVOLVED!

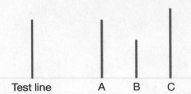

Test line   A   B   C

◈ Research
Solomon Asch

◉ Watch
That's So Rude

Sometimes people like to conform in order to feel part of the group . . . and sometimes they like to assert their individuality.

Conformity

The first thing people in groups do is conform, taking action or adopting attitudes as a result of real or imagined group pressure. Suppose you are required to appear at a psychology laboratory for an experiment on perception. You join seven other students seated in a room. You are shown a 25-centimetre line and asked which of three other lines is identical to it. The correct answer, line A, is obvious, so you are amused when the first person in the group chooses line B. "Bad eyesight," you say to yourself. "He's off by 10 centimetres!" The second person also chooses line B. "What a dope," you think. But by the time the fifth person has chosen line B, you are beginning to doubt yourself. The sixth and seventh students also choose line B, and now you are worried about *your* eyesight. The experimenter looks at you. "Your turn," he says. Do you follow the evidence of your own eyes or the collective judgment of the group?

This was the design for a series of famous studies of conformity conducted by Solomon Asch (1952, 1965). The seven "nearsighted" students were actually Asch's confederates. Asch wanted to know what people would do when a group unanimously contradicted an obvious fact. He found that when people made the line comparisons on their own, they were almost always accurate. But in the group, only 20% of the students remained completely independent on every trial, and often they apologized for not agreeing with the others. One-third conformed to the group's incorrect decision more than half the time, and the rest conformed at least some of the time. Whether they conformed or not, the students often felt uncertain of their decision. As one participant later said, "I felt disturbed, puzzled, separated, like an outcast from the rest." Asch's experiment has been replicated many times and in many countries over the years (Bond & Smith, 1996).

Like obedience, conformity has positive aspects. Society runs more smoothly when people know how to behave in a given situation and when they share the same attitudes and manners. Conformity in dress, preferences, and ideas confers a sense of being in sync with friends and colleagues. Moreover, people often intuitively understand that sometimes the group knows more than they do. In fact, a reliance on group judgment begins in very early childhood, suggesting its adaptive function for the species. In two experiments with three- and four-year-old children, researchers found that when children were given a choice between relying on information provided by a three-adult majority or a single adult about the name of an unfamiliar object, they sided with the majority (Corriveau, Fusaro, & Harris, 2009).

But also like obedience, conformity has negative consequences, notably its power to suppress critical thinking and
creativity. In a group, many people will deny their private
beliefs, agree with silly notions, and even repudiate their own
values.

Groupthink

Close, friendly groups usually work well together. But they
face the problem of getting the best ideas and efforts from their
members while avoiding an extreme form of conformity called
groupthink, the tendency to think alike and suppress dissent.
According to Irving Janis (1982, 1989), groupthink occurs
when a group's need for total agreement overwhelms its need
to make the wisest decision. The symptoms of groupthink
include the following:

"All those in favor say 'Aye.'"
"Aye." *"Aye."* *"Aye."* *"Aye."* *"Aye."*

◆ **An illusion of invulnerability.** The group believes it can
do no wrong and is 100% correct in its decisions.

◆ **Self-censorship.** Dissenters decide to keep quiet rather than make trouble, offend
their friends, or risk being ridiculed.

◆ **Pressure on dissenters to conform.** The leader teases or humiliates dissenters
or otherwise pressures them to go along.

◆ **An illusion of unanimity.** By discouraging dissent and failing to consider
alternative courses of action, leaders and group members create an illusion of
consensus; they may even explicitly order suspected dissenters to keep quiet.

Throughout history, groupthink has led to disastrous decisions in military and
civilian life. In 1986, NASA officials insulated themselves from the dissenting objec-
tions of engineers who warned them that the space shuttle *Challenger* was unsafe; NASA
launched it anyway, and it exploded shortly after takeoff. Tragically, NASA did not
learn immediately from this disaster. When an expert panel warned in 2002 that the
space shuttles still had many safety problems, NASA removed five of the panel's nine
members and two of its consultants. Early in 2003, the *Columbia* exploded upon re-
entry, killing its entire crew. Although most of us have not had to make these kinds of
decisions, we have all likely been in situations where we have gone along with a group,
stifling our own private reservations.

Fortunately, groupthink can be minimized if the leader rewards the expression of
doubt and dissent, protects and encourages minority views, asks group members to generate as many alternative solutions to a problem as they can think of, and has everyone try to think of the risks and disadvantages of the preferred decision. Resistance to
groupthink can also be fostered by creating a group identity that encourages members
to think of themselves as open-minded problem solvers rather than invulnerable know-
it-alls (Turner, Pratkanis, & Samuels, 2003). Leaders who encourage group members
to identify strongly with the collective enterprise are also more likely to hear dissenting opinions, because members will be less willing to support a decision they regard as
harmful to the group's goal (Packer, 2009).

Not all leaders want to run their groups this way, of course. For many people in
positions of power, from prime ministers to company executives, the temptation is great
to surround themselves with others who agree with what they want to do, and to demote
or fire those who disagree on the grounds that they are being "disloyal." Perhaps a key
quality of great leaders is that they are able to rise above this temptation.

groupthink The tendency for all
members of a group to think alike for
the sake of harmony and to suppress
disagreement.

diffusion of responsibility
In groups, the tendency of members to avoid taking action because they assume that others will.

deindividuation In groups or crowds, the loss of awareness of one's own individuality.

◄❚▶ Simulate
Helping a Stranger

👁 Watch
Private Battles in Public Places

Vancouverites disappointed with the loss of the seventh game of the Stanley Cup set police cars on fire, looted businesses, and smashed windows of buildings in the downtown.

The Wisdom and Madness of Crowds

On the TV show "Who Wants to Be a Millionaire?" contestants are given the chance to ask the audience how it would answer a question. This gimmick comes straight from a phenomenon known as the "wisdom of crowds": the fact that a crowd's judgment is often more accurate than that of its individual members (Surowiecki, 2004; Vul & Pashler, 2008). Just as neurons interconnect in networks that create thoughts and actions beyond the scope of any individual neuron, so a crowd creates a social network whose "behaviour" is more than individual members may intend or even be aware of (Goldstone, Roberts, & Gureckis, 2008). But crowds can create havoc, too. They can spread gossip, rumours, misinformation, and panic as fast as the flu. They can turn from joyful and peaceful to violent and destructive in a flash.

DIFFUSION OF RESPONSIBILITY. Suppose you were in trouble on a city street or in another public place—say, being mugged or having a sudden appendicitis attack. Do you think you would be more likely to get help if (a) one other person was passing by, (b) several other people were in the area, or (c) dozens of people were in the area? Most people would choose the third answer, but that is not how human beings operate. On the contrary, the more people there are around you, the *less* likely it is that one of them will come to your aid. Why?

The answer has to do with a group process called the **diffusion of responsibility**, in which responsibility for an outcome is diffused, or spread, among many people, reducing each individual's personal sense of accountability. One result is *bystander apathy*: In crowds, when someone is in trouble, individuals often fail to take action or call for help because they assume that someone else will do so (Darley & Latané, 1968). When the "crowd" consists of online observers, it's even easier to pass the buck. Abraham Biggs Jr., age 19, had been posting to an online discussion board for two years. One day he announced his intention to commit suicide with an overdose of drugs, adding a link to a live video feed from his bedroom. None of the watchers called the police for more than 10 hours, and Biggs died. In contrast, people are more likely to come to a stranger's aid if they are the only ones around to help, because responsibility cannot be diffused.

DEINDIVIDUATION. The most extreme instances of the diffusion of responsibility occur in large, anonymous mobs or crowds. The crowds may consist of cheerful sports spectators or angry rioters. Either way, people often lose awareness of their individuality and seem to hand themselves over to the mood and actions of the crowd, a state called **deindividuation** (Festinger, Pepitone, & Newcomb, 1952). You are more likely to feel deindividuated in a large city, where no one recognizes you, than in a small town, where it is hard to hide. (You are also more likely to feel deindividuated in large classes, where you might—mistakenly!—think you are invisible to the teacher, than in small ones.) Sometimes organizations actively promote the deindividuation of their members in order to enhance conformity and allegiance to the group. This is an important function of uniforms or masks, which eliminate each member's distinctive identity.

Deindividuation has long been considered a prime reason for mob violence. According to this explanation, because deindividuated people in crowds "forget themselves" and do not feel accountable for their actions, they are more likely to violate social norms and laws than they would be on their own: breaking store windows, looting, getting into fights, or rioting at a sports event. But deindividuation does not always make people more combative. Sometimes it makes them more friendly; think of all the chatty, anonymous people on buses and planes who reveal things to their seatmates they would never tell anyone they knew.

What really seems to be happening when people are in large crowds or anonymous situations is not that they become mindless or uninhibited. Rather, they become more likely to conform to the norms of the *specific situation* (Postmes & Spears, 1998). Students who go on wild sprees during spring break may be violating the local laws and norms not because their aggressiveness has been released but because they are conforming to the "Let's party!" norms of their fellow students. Crowd norms can also foster helpfulness, as they often do in the aftermath of disasters, when strangers come out to help victims and rescuers, leaving food, clothes, and tributes.

ANONYMITY AND RESPONSIBILITY. Deindividuation has important legal as well as psychological implications. Should individuals in a crowd be held accountable for their harmful "deindividuated" behaviour? In South Africa, years ago, six black residents of an impoverished township were accused of murdering an 18-year-old black woman who was having an affair with a hated black police officer. The woman was "necklaced" (a tire was placed around her neck and set afire) during a community protest against the police. The crowd danced and sang as she burned to ashes.

The six men were convicted of murder, but their sentence was commuted to 20 months of prison when a British social psychologist, Andrew Colman (1991), testified that deindividuation should reduce the moral blameworthiness of their behaviour. The young men were swept up in the mindless behaviour of the crowd, he argued, and hence were not fully responsible for their actions. Do you agree? An African social scientist, Pumla Gobodo-Madikizela (1994), did not. She interviewed some of the men accused of the necklacing and found they had not been mindless after all. Some were tremendously upset, were well aware of their actions, had debated the woman's guilt, thought about running away, and consciously tried to rationalize their behaviour. Moreover, she argued, we must remember that in every crowd, some people do not go along; they remain mindful of their own values.

And so, should the deindividuation excuse, like the "I was only following orders" excuse, exonerate a person of responsibility for looting, rape, or murder? If so, to what degree? What do you think?

Thinking Critically

Examine the Evidence

How mindless are "mindless" crowds? Should deindividuation be a legitimate excuse for people who loot, rape, or commit murder because the mob is doing it?

On your own, take responsibility for identifying which phenomenon is illustrated in each of the following situations.

1. The prime minister's closest advisers are afraid to disagree with his views on energy policy.
2. You are at a costume party wearing a silly gorilla suit. When you see a chance to play a practical joke on the host, you do it.
3. Walking down a busy street, you see that fire has broken out in a store window. "Someone must have already called the fire department," you say.

Answers:

1. groupthink 2. deindividuation 3. bystander apathy brought on by diffusion of responsibility

quickQUIZ

✓•Quick Review on MyPsychLab

Altruism and Dissent

◄⊙ Simulate
Psychology Experiments Survey:
Could You Be a Hero?

We have seen how roles, norms, and pressures to obey authority and conform to one's group can cause people to behave in ways they might not otherwise. Yet throughout history men and women have disobeyed orders they believed to be wrong and have gone against prevailing cultural beliefs; their actions have sometimes changed the course of history. For instance, until 1929, the government of Canada defined a person entitled to vote in this country as "A male person, including an Indian, excluding a Mongolian or Chinese. . . . No woman, idiot, lunatic or criminal shall vote." Pioneers such as Nellie McClung, Mary Irene Parlby, Emily Murphy, Henrietta Louise Edwards, and Louise McKinney fought for the right of Canadian women to become persons, a legal status that would grant them the right to vote, hold political office, and take a more active role in society. Similarly, indigenous peoples' leaders, such as Phil Fontaine, are working to ensure self-determination, which would result in autonomous communities within Canada, rather than dependence on Aboriginal Affairs and Northern Development Canada. In trying to ensure these rights for indigenous peoples, protesters have clashed with police and occupied lands in dispute.

When we think of heroes, we tend to think of men like the courageous firefighters who work so hard to rescue others after a disaster strikes. But heroism comes in many forms. When Linda Keen, the former head of the Nuclear Safety Commission, recommended that the Chalk River nuclear reactor be shut down so that critical safety upgrades could be performed, she paid a steep price professionally—she was fired. Recently, people throughout the world have called for the prosecution and even the death of Julian Assange, the spokesperson and editor in chief for WikiLeaks, a website devoted to whistle-blowing.

When people think of heroes, they usually think of those who rescue a child, risk gunfire to bring a fellow soldier to safety, or stand up to a bully. This is the kind of heroism traditionally associated with men, who in general have greater physical strength than women. Indeed, a study of Canadian awards that have been given since 1904 to individuals who risked or lost their lives to save others found that only 9% have gone to women, although when people are asked to name heroes they personally know, they name women and men equally (Rankin & Eagly, 2008). The reason is that many acts of selfless risk-taking do not require physical strength. During the Holocaust, women in France, Poland, and the Netherlands were as likely as men to risk their lives to save Jews. Women are more likely than men to donate an organ such as a kidney to save another person's life, and women are more likely to volunteer to serve in dangerous postings around the world in Médecins Sans Frontières (Becker & Eagly, 2004).

Sadly, the costs of dissent, courage, and honesty are often high; remember that most groups do not welcome deviance, nonconformity, and disagreement. Most whistle-blowers, far from being rewarded for their bravery, are punished for it. Studies of whistle-blowers find that half to two-thirds lose their jobs and have to leave their professions entirely. Many lose their homes and families (Alford, 2001).

Nonconformity, protest, and *altruism*, the willingness to take selfless or dangerous action on behalf of others, are in part a matter of personal convictions and conscience. However, just as there are situational reasons for obedience and conformity, so there are external influences on a person's decision to state an unpopular opinion, choose conscience over conformity, or help a stranger in trouble. Here are some of the situational factors involved in deciding to behave courageously:

1 **You perceive the need for intervention or help.** It may seem obvious, but before you can take independent action, you must realize that such action is necessary. Sometimes people willfully blind themselves to wrongdoing to justify their own inaction ("I'm just minding my business"; "I have no idea what they're doing over there at that concentration camp"). But blindness to the need for action also occurs when a situation imposes too many demands on people's attention, as it often does for residents of densely populated cities.

2 **Cultural norms encourage you to take action.** Would you spontaneously tell a passerby that he or she had dropped a pen? Offer to help a person with an injured leg who had dropped an armful of magazines? In a study of strangers' helpfulness to one another across 23 North American cities and 22 cities in other countries, cultural norms were more important than population density in predicting levels of helpfulness. Pedestrians in busy Copenhagen and Vienna, for example, were kinder to strangers than were passersby in busy New York City or Kuala Lumpur, Malaysia (Levine, 2003; Levine, Norenzayan, & Philbrick, 2001). Some cultures place a higher value on helping strangers than other cultures do. Community-oriented Hindus in India believe that people are obligated to help anyone who needs it (parent, friend, or stranger), even if the need is minor. In contrast, individualistic Canadians do not feel as obligated to help friends and strangers or even parents who have minor needs (Miller, Bersoff, & Harwood, 1990).

◉ **Watch**
Wealthy Giving Back

3 **You have an ally.** In Asch's conformity experiment, the presence of one other person who gave the correct answer was enough to overcome agreement with the majority. In Milgram's experiment, the presence of someone who disobeyed the experimenter's instruction to shock the learner sharply increased the number of people who also disobeyed. One dissenting member of a group may be viewed as a troublemaker, but two or three are a coalition. An ally reassures a person of the rightness of the protest, and their combined efforts may eventually persuade the majority (Wood et al., 1994).

4 **You become entrapped.** Once having taken the initial step of getting involved, most people will increase their commitment. In one study, nearly 9000 U.S. federal employees were asked whether they had observed wrongdoing at work, whether they had told anyone about it, and what happened if they had told. Nearly half of the sample had observed some serious cases of wrongdoing, such as stealing federal funds, accepting bribes, or creating a situation that was dangerous to public safety. Of that half, 72% had done nothing at all, but the other 28% reported the problem to their immediate supervisors. Once they had taken that step, a majority of the whistle-blowers eventually took the matter to higher authorities (Graham, 1986).

As you can see, certain social and cultural factors make altruism, disobedience, and dissent more likely to occur, just as other external factors suppress them.

quickQUIZ

✓ Quick Review on MyPsychLab

We hope you won't disobey our order to answer this question.

Imagine that you are chief executive officer of a new electric-car company. You want your employees to feel free to offer their suggestions and criticisms to improve productivity and satisfaction. You also want them to inform managers if they find any evidence that the cars are unsafe, even if that means delaying production. What concepts from this chapter could you use in setting company policy?

Answers:

Some possibilities: You could encourage, or even require, dissenting views; avoid deindividuation by rewarding innovative suggestions and implementing the best ones; stimulate employees' commitment to the task (building a car that will help solve the world's pollution problem); and establish a written policy to protect whistle-blowers. What else can you think of?

YOU are about to learn . . .

- ◆ how people in a multicultural society balance ethnic identity and acculturation.
- ◆ what causes ethnocentric, "us–them" thinking and how to decrease it.
- ◆ how stereotypes benefit us and how they distort reality.

US VERSUS THEM: GROUP IDENTITY

Each of us develops a personal identity that is based on our particular traits and unique life history. But we also develop **social identities** based on the groups we belong to, including our national, religious, political, and occupational groups (Brewer & Gardner, 1996; Tajfel & Turner, 1986).

Ethnic Identity

In multicultural societies such as Canada's, different social identities sometimes collide. In particular, people often face the dilemma of balancing an **ethnic identity**, a close identification with a religious or ethnic group, and **acculturation**, identification with the dominant culture (Phinney, 1996). The hallmarks of having an ethnic identity are that you identify with the group, feel proud to be a member, feel emotionally attached to the group, and behave in ways that conform to the group's rules, values,

social identity The part of a person's self-concept that is based on his or her identification with a nation, religious or political group, occupation, or other social affiliation.

ethnic identity A person's identification with a racial or ethnic group.

acculturation The process by which members of minority groups come to identify with and feel part of the mainstream culture.

Get INVOLVED!

HOW ACCULTURATED ARE YOU?

Do you have an ethnic identity? If you are a member of an ethnic minority within your country, city, or school, how acculturated do you feel? Do you feel at ease in more than one culture, or only in your own? Does your comfort level depend on the situation you're in? Now ask five friends, relatives, or acquaintances, ideally from different ethnic groups, how they would answer these questions. If you feel that you do not have an ethnic heritage other than a national identity, why is that? Would your parents and grandparents feel the same as you do?

Ethnic identities are changing these days, as bicultural North Americans blend aspects of mainstream culture with their own traditions. But many people still like to celebrate the traditions of their ethnic heritage, as illustrated in these photos of Japanese-Canadian college students reviving taiko, traditional Japanese drumming; Ukrainian-Canadian teens wearing national dress; and African-Canadian children lighting Kwanzaa candles.

and norms. Many individuals pick and choose among the values, food, traditions, and customs of the mainstream culture, while also keeping aspects of their heritage that are important to their self-identity.

In these multiethnic times, many people do not want to be pigeonholed into one ethnic category. In 2006, almost 42% of Canadians reported having multiple ethnic origins on the census. Compare this to the almost 19% of Canadians who answered this way on the 1996 census (the first time that this category was available), and we can see that our views of ethnicity are changing. Thus, for many Canadians, ethnicity does not reflect where they were born—especially when we consider that most of the census respondents reporting multiple ethnicities were born in Canada. It is also interesting to note that one-third of all census respondents listed their ethnicity as Canadian, an ethnicity that many Canadians find challenging to define (Statistics Canada, 2008b)! Some observers think that young people are becoming less likely to define themselves by their ethnic identity than by their youth identity—a hip-hopper, a gleek, a pop-culture fan, and so forth. Do you agree? In your world, are traditional ethnic identities breaking down, or are they as strong as ever?

ethnocentrism The belief that one's own ethnic group, nation, or religion is superior to all others.

Ethnocentrism

Social identities give us a sense of place and position in the world. Without them, most of us would feel like loose marbles rolling around in an unconnected universe. It feels good to be part of an "us." But does that mean we must automatically feel superior to "them"?

Ethnocentrism is the belief that your own culture, nation, or religion is superior to all others. Ethnocentrism is universal, probably because it aids survival by increasing people's attachment to their own group and their willingness to work on its behalf. It is even embedded in some languages: The Chinese word for China means "the centre of the world" (consigning the other 5 billion people to the suburbs?) and the Navajo, the Kiowa, and the Inuit call themselves simply "The People."

"It is not enough that we succeed. Cats must also fail."

As bumper stickers and lapel pins show, everyone, but everyone, is ethnocentric!

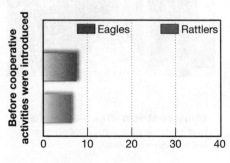
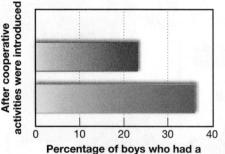

Percentage of boys who had a best friend in the out-group

FIGURE 8.3 The Experiment at Robbers Cave

In this study, competitive games fostered hostility between the Rattlers and the Eagles. Few boys had a best friend from the other group (upper graph). But after the teams had to cooperate to solve various problems, the percentage who made friends across "enemy lines" shot up (lower graph) (Sherif et al., 1961).

👁**Watch**
Nappy Hair Controversy

Ethnocentrism rests on a fundamental social identity: us. As soon as people have created a category called "us," however, they invariably perceive everybody else as "not-us." This in-group solidarity can be manufactured in a minute in the laboratory, as Henri Tajfel and his colleagues (1971) demonstrated in an experiment with British schoolboys. Tajfel showed the boys slides with varying numbers of dots on them and asked the boys to guess how many dots there were. The boys were arbitrarily told that they were "overestimators" or "underestimators" and were then asked to work on another task. In this phase, they had a chance to give points to other boys identified as overestimators or underestimators. Although each boy worked alone in his cubicle, almost every single one assigned far more points to boys he thought were like him, an overestimator or an underestimator. As the boys emerged from their rooms, they were asked, "Which were you?" The answers received either cheers or boos from the others.

Us–them social identities are strengthened when two groups compete with each other. Years ago, Muzafer Sherif and his colleagues used a natural setting, a Boy Scout camp called Robbers Cave, to demonstrate the effects of competition on hostility and conflict between groups (Sherif, 1958; Sherif et al., 1961). Sherif randomly assigned 11- and 12-year-old boys to two groups, the Eagles and the Rattlers. To build a sense of in-group identity and team spirit, he had each group work together on projects such as making a rope bridge and building a diving board. Sherif then put the Eagles and Rattlers in competition for prizes. During fierce games of football, baseball, and tug-of-war, the boys whipped up a competitive fever that soon spilled off the playing fields. They began to raid each other's cabins, call each other names, and start fistfights. No one dared to have a friend from the rival group. Before long, the Eagles and the Rattlers were as hostile toward each other as any two gangs fighting for turf. Their hostility continued even when they were just sitting around together watching movies.

Then Sherif decided to try to undo the hostility he had created and make peace between the Eagles and Rattlers. He and his associates set up a series of predicaments in which both groups needed to work together to reach a desired goal—for example, pooling their resources to get a movie they all wanted to see or pulling a staff truck up a hill on a camping trip. This policy of *interdependence in reaching mutual goals* was highly successful in reducing the boys' "ethnocentrism," competitiveness, and hostility; the boys eventually made friends with their former enemies (see Figure 8.3). Interdependence has a similar effect in adult groups (Gaertner et al., 1990). The reason, it seems, is that cooperation causes people to think of themselves as members of one big group instead of two opposed groups, us and them.

Interestingly, when deciding to help another, your brain responds differently to helping people perceived as "other" compared to those perceived as like "us." In one study, researchers brought together the fans of two different soccer teams and studied their reactions to watching other people receive a painful shock. The participants of the study were allowed to get a shock themselves to reduce the severity of the shock for the other person, an indirect measure of empathy. The researchers found that not only were people more likely to help a fan of their own team and less likely to help a fan of an opposing team, but that neural activity differed depending on whom the participants were helping. When participants helped people who were like them, the anterior insula was active; when participants did not help people who were fans of the opposing team, the nucleus accumbens was active. The anterior insula is a part of the brain associated with empathy, while the nucleus accumbens is a part of the brain associated with reward. These differences in brain activity suggest that when we decide to help others, whether we perceive them as like us or not will affect whether we help them and how empathetic we are to their suffering (Hein et al., 2010). Remember, these differences were elicited just by receiving information about which team the other person cheered for, not the large kinds of differences that often result in intergroup conflicts.

Stereotypes

Think of all the ways that your friends and family members differ: Jeff is stodgy, Ruth is bossy, Farah is outgoing. But if you have never met a person from Turkey or Tibet, you are likely to stereotype Turks and Tibetans. A **stereotype** is a summary impression of a group of people in which all members of the group are viewed as sharing a common trait or traits. There are stereotypes of people who drive Hummers or Hondas, of engineering students and art students.

◉ Watch
Stereotypes

Thinking Critically

Analyze Assumptions and Biases

What is this woman's occupation? Among non-Muslims in the West, the assumption is that Muslim women who wear the full-length black niqab must be repressed sexually as well as politically. But the answer shatters the stereotype. Wedad Lootah, a Muslim living in Dubai, United Arab Emirates, is a marriage counsellor, a sexual activist, and the author of a best-selling Arabic book, *Top Secret: Sexual Guidance for Married Couples*. She wrote it, she says, because of a 52-year-old client who had many children but had never experienced sexual pleasure with her husband. "Finally, she discovered orgasm!" Ms. Lootah reported. "Imagine, all that time she did not know."

stereotype   A summary impression of a group, in which a person believes that all members of the group share a common trait or traits (positive, negative, or neutral).

Stereotypes aren't necessarily bad, and they are sometimes accurate (Jussim et al., 2009). They are, as some psychologists have called them, useful tools in the mental toolbox—energy-saving devices that allow us to make efficient decisions (Macrae & Bodenhausen, 2000). They help us quickly process new information and retrieve memories. They allow us to organize experience, make sense of differences among individuals and groups, and predict how people will behave. In fact, the brain automatically registers and encodes the basic categories of gender, ethnicity, and age, suggesting that there is a neurological basis for the cognitive efficiency of stereotyping (Ito & Urland, 2003).

👁 **Watch**
Arab Cabbies

However, although stereotypes reflect real differences among people, they also distort that reality in three ways (Judd et al., 1995). First, *they exaggerate differences between groups*, making the stereotyped group seem odd, unfamiliar, or dangerous, not like "us." Second, *they produce selective perception*; people tend to see only the evidence that fits the stereotype and reject any perceptions that do not fit. Third, *they underestimate differences within the stereotyped group*, creating the impression that all members of that group are the same.

Cultural values affect how people evaluate the actions of another group and whether a stereotype becomes positive or negative. Chinese students in Hong Kong, where communalism and respect for elders are valued, think that a student who comes late to class or argues with a parent about grades is being selfish and disrespectful of adults. But Australian students, who value individualism, think that the same behaviour is perfectly appropriate (Forgas & Bond, 1985). You can see how the Chinese might form negative stereotypes of "disrespectful" Australians, and how the Australians might form negative stereotypes of the "spineless" Chinese. And it is a small step from negative stereotypes to prejudice.

---

quickQUIZ

✔ **Quick Review** on **MyPsychLab**

Do you have a positive or a negative stereotype of quizzes?

1. Chris, a Cree university student, finds himself caught between two philosophies on his campus. One holds that indigenous peoples should move toward full integration into mainstream culture. The other holds that indigenous peoples should immerse themselves in the history, values, and contributions of their cultures. The first group values _____, whereas the second emphasizes _____.
2. John knows and likes the Asian minority in his town, but he privately believes that English culture is superior to all others. His belief is evidence of his _____.
3. What strategy does the Robbers Cave study suggest for reducing "us–them" thinking and hostility between groups?
4. What are three ways in which stereotypes can distort reality?

Answers:

1. acculturation, ethnic identity   2. ethnocentrism   3. interdependence in reaching mutual goals   4. They exaggerate differences between groups; they produce selective perception; and they underestimate differences within the stereotyped group.

✦ **YOU** are about to learn . . .

- four major causes and functions of prejudice.
- four indirect ways of measuring prejudice.
- four conditions necessary for reducing prejudice and conflict.

GROUP CONFLICT AND PREJUDICE

A **prejudice** consists of a negative stereotype and a strong, unreasonable dislike or hatred of a group. A central feature of a prejudice is that it remains immune to evidence. In his classic book *The Nature of Prejudice*, Gordon Allport (1954/1979) described the responses characteristic of a prejudiced person when confronted with evidence contradicting his or her beliefs:

Mr. X:	The trouble with Jews is that they only take care of their own group.
Mr. Y:	But the record of the Community Chest campaign shows that they give more generously, in proportion to their numbers, to the general charities of the community, than do non-Jews.
Mr. X:	That shows they are always trying to buy favour and intrude into Christian affairs. They think of nothing but money; that is why there are so many Jewish bankers.
Mr. Y:	But a recent study shows that the percentage of Jews in the banking business is negligible, far smaller than the percentage of non-Jews.
Mr. X:	That's just it; they don't go in for respectable business; they are only in the movie business or run night clubs.

Notice that Mr. X doesn't even try to respond to Mr. Y's evidence; he just moves along to another reason for his dislike of Jewish people. That is the slippery nature of prejudice in general and toward Jews in particular. Indeed, many of the stereotypes underlying anti-Semitism are mutually contradictory and constantly shift across generations and nations. Jews were attacked for being Communists in Nazi Germany and Argentina, and for being greedy capitalists in the Communist Soviet Union. They have been criticized for being too secular and for being too mystical, for being weak and ineffectual and for being powerful enough to dominate the world. Although anti-Semitism declined in the 50 years after World War II, it has been on the rise again around the world (Cohen et al., 2009).

The Origins of Prejudice

Prejudice provides the fuel for ethnocentrism. Its targets change, but it persists everywhere in some form because it has so many sources and functions: psychological, social, economic, and cultural.

prejudice A strong, unreasonable dislike or hatred of a group, based on a negative stereotype.

Displacement at work.

👁 Watch
Prejudice

1   **Psychological causes.** Prejudice often serves to ward off feelings of doubt, fear, and insecurity. As research from many nations has confirmed, it is a tonic for low self-esteem: People puff up their own feelings of low self-worth by disliking or hating groups they see as inferior (Islam & Hewstone, 1993; Stephan et al., 1994). Prejudice also allows people to use the target group as a scapegoat ("Those people are the source of all my troubles"), to displace anger and cope with feelings of powerlessness. Immediately after 9/11, some North Americans took out their anger on fellow Americans who happened to be Arab, Sikh, Pakistani, Hindu, or Afghan.

According to *terror management theory*, prejudice may also help people defend against the existential terror of death (Pyszczynski, Rothschild, & Abdollahi, 2008). People in every culture hold political or religious worldviews that provide them with a sense of meaning, purpose, and hope of immortality (either through an afterlife or through a connection to something greater than themselves). If that worldview helps

The Many Targets
of Prejudice

Prejudice has a long and universal history. Why do new prejudices keep emerging, others fade away, and some old ones persist?

Canadians have a long history of persecuting those who were not white and anglophone, including the Japanese, Chinese, Ukrainians, Hutterites, francophones, and Southeast Asians. Prejudices toward indigenous people, women, and homosexuals have long been part of Canadian history. Other prejudices emerge with changing historical events. In the aftermath of 9/11, hostility mounted toward Middle Easterners and Muslims.

alleviate the fear of their own individual mortality, they will be deeply threatened by the mere existence of others who disdain their way of seeing things. According to the theory, many people manage that threat by denigrating opposing groups, attempting to convert them, or, if the threat they pose is perceived as strong enough, trying to exterminate them. More than 350 experiments in 17 countries have supported the hypotheses derived from terror management theory (Greenberg, Solomon, & Arndt, 2008). For example, reminders of death increase people's anxiety, which in turn increases their punitiveness toward others who violate cultural norms, their reverence for cultural symbols of their nation or religion, and their prejudice and hostility toward people who hold different worldviews (Cohen et al., 2009).

2 **Social causes.** Not all prejudices, however, have deep-seated psychological roots. Some are acquired through pressure to conform to the views of friends, relatives,

or associates; if you don't agree with a group's prejudices toward another group, you may be gently or abruptly asked to leave the group. Some are passed along mindlessly from one generation to another, as when parents communicate to their children, "We don't associate with people like that."

3   **Economic causes.** Prejudice makes official forms of discrimination seem legitimate, by justifying the majority group's dominance, status, or greater wealth. Wherever a majority group systematically discriminates against a minority to preserve its power—whites, blacks, Muslims, Hindus, Japanese, Hutu, Christians, Jews, you name it—they will claim that their actions are legitimate because the minority is so obviously inferior and incompetent (Islam & Hewstone, 1993; Jost, Nosek, & Gosling, 2008; Morton et al., 2009; Sidanius, Pratto, & Bobo, 1996).

You can see how prejudice rises and falls with changing economic conditions by observing what happens when two groups are in direct competition for jobs, or when people are worried about their incomes: Prejudice between them increases. Consider the rise and fall of attitudes toward Chinese immigrants in North America in the nineteenth century, as reported in newspapers of the time (Aronson, 2008). When the Chinese were working in the gold mines and potentially taking jobs from white labourers, the white-run newspapers described them as depraved, vicious, and bloodthirsty. Just a decade later, when the Chinese began working on the transcontinental railroad—doing difficult and dangerous jobs that few white

Avoid Emotional Reasoning

In times of war, most people fall victim to emotional reasoning about the enemy. They start thinking of "them" as aggressors who are less than human, often as "vermin," dogs, or pigs. In 2003, students at a Muslim school in Montreal arrived to find that their school had been vandalized, with the words "Death to Arabs" spray-painted on the outside.

men wanted—prejudice against them declined. Whites described them as hard-working, industrious, and law-abiding. Then, after the railroad was finished and the Chinese had to compete for scarce jobs, white attitudes changed again. Whites now thought the Chinese were "criminal," "crafty," "conniving," and "stupid." (The newspapers did not report the attitudes of the Chinese.)

The oldest prejudice in the world may be sexism, and it, too, serves to legitimize existing inequities in power. In research with 15 000 men and women in 19 nations, psychologists found that *hostile sexism*, which reflects active dislike of women, is different from *benevolent sexism*, which puts women on a pedestal. The latter type of sexism is affectionate but patronizing, conveying the attitude that women are so wonderful, good, kind, and moral that they should stay at home, away from the rough-and-tumble (and power and income) of public life (Glick et al., 2000; Glick, 2006). Because benevolent sexism lacks a tone of hostility to women, it doesn't seem like a prejudice to many people, and many women find it alluring to think they are better than men. But both forms of sexism—whether someone thinks women are too good for equality or not good enough—legitimize discrimination against women (Christopher & Wojda, 2008).

Perhaps you are thinking: "Hey, what about men? There are plenty of prejudices against men, too—that they are sexual predators, emotionally heartless, domineering, and arrogant." In fact, according to a 16-nation study of attitudes toward men, many people do believe that men are aggressive and predatory, and overall just not as warm and wonderful as women (Glick et al., 2004). This attitude seems hostile to men, the researchers found, but it also reflects and supports gender inequality by characterizing men as being designed for leadership and dominance.

4 **Cultural and national causes.** Finally, prejudice bonds people to their own ethnic or national group and its ways; by disliking "them," we feel closer to our own group. That feeling, in turn, justifies whatever we do to "them" to preserve our customs and national policies. In fact, although many people assume that prejudice causes war, the reverse is far more often the case: War causes prejudice. When two nations declare war, when one country decides to invade another, or when a weak leader displaces the country's economic problems onto a minority scapegoat, the citizenry's prejudice against that enemy or scapegoat will be inflamed. Of course, sometimes anger at an enemy is justified, but war usually turns legitimate anger into blind prejudice: Those people are not only the enemy; they are less than human and deserve to be exterminated (Keen, 1986; Staub, 1999). That is why enemies are so often described as vermin, rats, mad dogs, heathens, baby killers, or monsters—anything but human beings like us.

PROBING YOUR PREJUDICES

Get **INVOLVED!**

Are you prejudiced? No? Is there any group of people you tend to dislike because of their gender, ethnicity, sexual orientation, nationality, religion, physical appearance, or political views? Write down your deepest thoughts and feelings about this group. Take as long as you want, and do not censor yourself or say what you think you ought to say. Now reread what you have written. Which of the sources of prejudice discussed in the text might be contributing to your views? Do you feel that your attitudes toward the group are legitimate, or are you uncomfortable about having them?

Review 8.1 summarizes the causes of prejudice.

REView 8.1

Sources of Prejudice

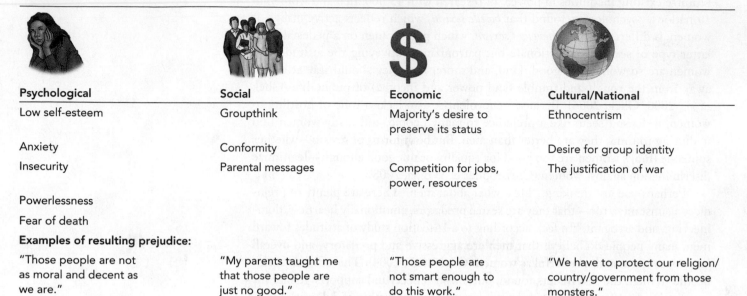

Psychological	Social	Economic	Cultural/National
Low self-esteem	Groupthink	Majority's desire to preserve its status	Ethnocentrism
Anxiety	Conformity		Desire for group identity
Insecurity	Parental messages	Competition for jobs, power, resources	The justification of war
Powerlessness			
Fear of death			

Examples of resulting prejudice:

"Those people are not as moral and decent as we are."	"My parents taught me that those people are just no good."	"Those people are not smart enough to do this work."	"We have to protect our religion/ country/government from those monsters."

Defining and Measuring Prejudice

The good news is that on surveys in Canada, prejudice of all kinds has been dropping sharply. The numbers of people who admit to believing that blacks are inferior to whites, women inferior to men, and gays inferior to straights have plummeted in the last 20 years (Dovidio, 2001; Plant & Devine, 1998; Weaver, 2008).

Yet, as Gordon Allport (1954/1979) observed so long ago, "defeated intellectually, prejudice lingers emotionally." Attitudes may change and discriminatory behaviour may be outlawed, but deep-seated negative feelings and bigotry may nonetheless persist in subtle ways (Dovidio & Gaertner, 2008). And, as we just saw, such feelings may lie dormant during good times, only to be easily aroused during bad times.

That is why prejudice is like a weasel—hard to grasp and hold on to. Another problem is that not all prejudiced people are prejudiced in the same way or to the same extent. Suppose that Raymond wishes to be tolerant and open-minded, but he grew up in a small homogeneous community and feels uncomfortable with members of other cultural and religious groups. Should we put Raymond in the same category as Rupert, an outspoken bigot who actively detests all ethnic groups other than his own? Do good intentions count? What if Raymond knows nothing about Muslims and mindlessly blurts out a remark that reveals his ignorance? Is that prejudice or thoughtlessness? And what about people who say they are not prejudiced but then make sexist or racist remarks? When Mel Gibson was arrested for drunk driving and spewed forth anti-Semitic insults to the arresting officer, should the public have accepted his claim that he isn't "really" prejudiced against Jewish people?

Some social psychologists, while welcoming the evidence that *explicit*, conscious prejudices have declined, have used various measures to see whether *implicit*, unconscious negative feelings between groups have also diminished. They maintain that implicit attitudes, being automatic and unintentional, reflect lingering negative feelings that keep prejudice alive below the surface. They have developed several ways of measuring these feelings (Olson, 2009).

Watch
Unconscious Stereotyping

1 **Measures of social distance.** *Social distance* is a possible behavioural expression of prejudice, a reluctance to get "too close" to another group. Does a straight man stand farther away from a gay man than from another heterosexual? Does a non-disabled woman move away from a woman in a wheelchair? How close will you let "those people" into your social life—work with them, live near them, marry them? A review of decades of representative surveys of North Americans found that while overt prejudice among all of these groups has dropped, most people within each ethnic group are still strongly opposed to virtually all the other ethnic groups living in their neighbourhoods or marrying into their families (Weaver, 2008). But does this fact reflect prejudice or merely a comfort with and preference for one's own ethnicity?

2 **Measures of what people do when they are stressed or angry.** Many people are willing to control their negative feelings under normal conditions, but as soon as they are angry, drunk, or frustrated (as Mel Gibson was), or get a jolt to their self-esteem, their unexpressed prejudice often reveals itself. In one of the first experiments to demonstrate this phenomenon, white students were asked to administer a shock to black or white confederates of the experimenter in what the students believed was a study of biofeedback. In the experimental condition, participants overheard the biofeedback "victim" (who actually received no shock) saying derogatory things about them. In the control condition, participants overheard no such nasty remarks. Then all the participants had another opportunity to shock the victims; their degree of aggression was defined as the amount of shock they administered. At first, white students actually showed *less* aggression toward blacks than toward whites. But as soon as the white students were angered by overhearing derogatory remarks about themselves, they showed *more* aggression toward blacks than toward whites (Rogers & Prentice-Dunn, 1981). The same pattern appears in studies of how English-speaking Canadians behave toward French-speaking Canadians (Meindl & Lerner, 1985), straights toward gays, non-Jewish students toward Jews (Fein & Spencer, 1997), and men toward women (Maass et al., 2003).

3 **Measures of brain activity.** Another method relies on fMRI and PET scans to determine which parts of the brain are involved in forming stereotypes, holding prejudiced beliefs, and feeling disgust, anger, or anxiety about another ethnic group (Cacioppo et al., 2003; Harris & Fiske, 2006; Stanley, Phelps, & Banaji, 2008). In one study, when blacks and whites saw pictures of each other, activity in the amygdala (the brain structure associated with fear and other negative emotions) was elevated. But it was not elevated when people saw pictures of members of their own group (Hart et al., 2000). However, the fact that parts of the

Thinking Critically

Define Your Terms

What does it mean to be "prejudiced"? Is prejudice blatant hostility, or does it also include vague discomfort with another group, a patronizing attitude of superiority, or unconscious feelings of dislike? Does ignorance about an unfamiliar culture count as prejudice?

BLACK FACES

WHITE FACES

GOOD WORDS
love joy triumph
terrific peace
champion honest

BAD WORDS
maggot poison
hatred agony devil
failure detest filth

Typical stimuli used in the IAT.

brain are activated under some conditions does not mean a person is "prejudiced." In a similar experiment, when participants were registering the faces as individuals or as part of a simple visual test rather than as members of the category "blacks," there was no increased activation in the amygdala. The brain may be designed to register differences, it appears, but any negative associations with those differences depend on context and learning (Wheeler & Fiske, 2005).

4   **Measures of implicit attitudes.** A final, controversial method of assessing prejudice is the *Implicit Association Test (IAT)*, which measures the speed of people's positive and negative associations to a target group (Greenwald, McGhee, & Schwartz, 1998; Greenwald et al., 2009). Its proponents have argued that if, for example, white students take longer to respond to black faces associated with positive words (e.g., *triumph, honest*) than to black faces associated with negative words (e.g., *devil, failure*), it must mean that white students have an unconscious prejudice toward blacks. More than 3 million people have taken the test online, and it has also been given to students, business managers, and many other groups to identify their alleged prejudices toward blacks, Asians, women, old people, and other categories (Nosek, Greenwald, & Banaji, 2007).

We say "alleged" prejudices because other social psychologists believe that whatever the test measures, it is not a stable prejudice (De Houwer et al., 2009). Two researchers got an IAT effect by matching target faces with nonsense words and neutral words that had no evaluative connotations at all. They concluded that the IAT does not measure emotional evaluations of the target but rather the *salience* of the word associated with it—how much it stands out. (Negative words attract more attention in general.) When the researchers corrected for these factors, the presumed unconscious prejudice faded away (Rothermund & Wentura, 2004). Moreover, as we saw earlier, people find familiar names, products, and even nonsense syllables to be more pleasant than unfamiliar ones. Some investigators argue that the IAT may simply be measuring, say, white subjects' unfamiliarity with people of different ethnicities and the greater salience of their own ethnicities to them, rather than a true prejudice (Kinoshita & Peek-O'Leary, 2005).

As you can see, defining and measuring prejudice are not easy tasks, and it's important not to oversimplify. To understand prejudice, we must distinguish explicit attitudes from unconscious ones, active hostility from simple discomfort, what people say from what they feel, and what people feel from how they actually behave.

Reducing Conflict and Prejudice

The findings that emerge from the study of prejudice show us that efforts to reduce prejudice by appealing to moral or intellectual arguments are not enough. They must also touch people's deeper insecurities, fears, or negative associations with a group. Of course, given the many sources and functions of prejudice, no one method will work in all circumstances or for all prejudices. But just as social psychologists investigate the situations that increase prejudice and animosity between groups, they have also examined the situations that might reduce them. Here are four of them (Dovidio, Gaertner, & Validzic, 1998; Pettigrew & Tropp, 2006):

((•● Listen
Prejudice

1   **Both sides must have equal legal status, economic opportunities, and power.** This requirement is the spur behind efforts to change laws that permit discrimination. Women would never have gotten the right to vote, attend university, or do "men's work" without persistent challenges to the laws that permitted gender

discrimination. But changing the law is not enough if two groups remain in competition for jobs or if one group retains power and dominance over the other.

You have probably heard that women who work full-time generally earn less in wages than their male counterparts (Desmarais & Curtis, 2001). Research conducted by Serge Desmarais, a social psychologist at the University of Guelph, suggests that men and women often differ not only in the actual pay they receive, but also in their beliefs about the amount of pay they should receive for their work. Desmarais found that when students are allowed to pay themselves for tasks they complete as part of psychology experiments, women participants actually pay themselves less than the men do (Desmarais & Curtis, 1997).

2   **Authorities and community institutions must provide moral, legal, and economic support for both sides.** Society must establish norms of equality and support them in the actions of its officials—teachers, employers, the judicial system, government officials, and the police. Where segregation is official government policy or an unofficial but established practice, conflict and prejudice will not only continue but also seem normal and justified.

3   **Both sides must have opportunities to work and socialize together, formally and informally.** According to the *contact hypothesis*, prejudice declines when people have the chance to get used to another group's rules, food, customs, and attitudes, thereby discovering their shared interests and shared humanity and learning that "those people" aren't, in fact, "all alike." The contact hypothesis has been supported by many studies in the laboratory and in the real world: young people's attitudes toward the elderly; healthy people's attitudes toward the mentally ill; nondisabled children's attitudes toward the disabled; and straight people's prejudices toward gay men and lesbians (Herek & Capitanio, 1996; Pettigrew & Tropp, 2006; Wilner, Walkley, & Cook, 1955).

Multiethnic university campuses are a living laboratory for testing the contact hypothesis. White students who have roommates, friends, and romantic relationships across ethnic lines tend to become less prejudiced and find commonalities (van Laar, Levin, & Sidanius, 2008). Cross-group friendships benefit minorities and reduce their prejudices, too. Minority students who join ethnic student organizations tend to develop, over time, not only an even stronger ethnic identity, but also an increased sense of ethnic victimization. Over time, minority students often come to feel they have less in common with other ethnic groups (Sidanius et al., 2004). But a longitudinal study of minority students at a predominantly white university found that friendships with whites increased their feelings of belonging and reduced their feelings of dissatisfaction with the school. This was especially true for students who had been feeling insecure and sensitive about being rejected as members of a minority (Mendoza-Denton & Page-Gould, 2008). (See Figure 8.4.)

4   **Both sides must cooperate, working together for a common goal.** While contact reduces prejudice, it is also true that prejudice reduces contact. And when groups don't like each other, forced contact just makes each side resentful and even

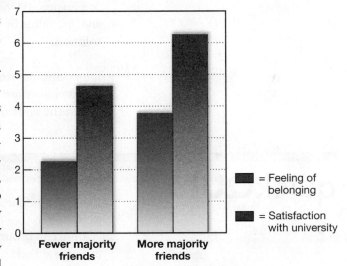

FIGURE 8.4 **The Impact of Cross-Ethnic Friendships on Minority Students' Well-Being**

Cross-ethnic friendships benefit both parties. In a longitudinal study of minority students at a predominantly white university, many minority students at first felt left out of school life and thus dissatisfied with their educational experience. But the more white friends they made, the higher their sense of belonging (purple bar) and satisfaction with the university (green bar). This finding was particularly significant for minority students who had initially been the most sensitive to rejection and who had felt the most anxious and insecure about being in a largely white school.

Tensions between groups often subside when people work together on a common goal. When classrooms are structured so that students of different ethnic groups must cooperate in order to do well on a lesson (left), prejudice decreases. On the right, volunteers from Habitat for Humanity build a new home for low-income people.

more prejudiced, as a longitudinal field survey of students in Germany, Belgium, and England found (Binder et al., 2009). At many multiethnic high schools, ethnic groups form cliques and gangs, fighting one another and defending their own ways.

To reduce the intergroup tension and competition that exist in many schools, Elliot Aronson and his colleagues developed the "jigsaw" method of building cooperation. Students from different ethnic groups work together on a task that is broken up like a jigsaw puzzle; each person needs to cooperate with the others to put the assignment together. Students in such classes, from elementary school through university, tend to do better, like their classmates better, and become less stereotyped and prejudiced in their thinking than students in traditional classrooms (Aronson, 2000; Slavin & Cooper, 1999). Cooperation and interdependence often reduce us–them thinking and prejudice by creating an encompassing social identity—the Eagles and Rattlers solution.

Each of these four approaches to creating greater harmony between groups is important, but none is sufficient on its own. Perhaps one reason that group conflicts and prejudice are so persistent is that all four conditions for reducing them are rarely met at the same time.

quickQUIZ

✔ **Quick Review** on **MyPsychLab**

Try to overcome your prejudice against quizzes by taking this one.

1. What are four ways of measuring implicit or unconscious prejudice?

2. What are four important conditions required for reducing prejudice and conflict between groups?

3. Surveys find that large percentages of individuals from visible minority groups hold negative stereotypes of one another and resent other minorities almost as much as they resent whites. What are some reasons that people who have themselves been victims of stereotyping and prejudice would hold the same attitudes toward others?

Answers:

1. Measures of social distance; of how aggressively people behave toward a target person when they are angry or stressed; of physiological changes in the brain; and of unconscious negative associations with a target group.   2. Both sides must have equal status and power; have the moral, legal, and economic support of authorities; have opportunities to socialize formally and informally; and cooperate for a common goal.   3. Their own ethnocentrism; anxiety, low self-esteem, or feelings of threat; conformity with relatives and friends who share their prejudices; parental lessons; and economic competition for jobs and resources.

YOU are about to learn . . .

◆ how social psychologists explain the persistence of evil.

◆ what "the banality of evil" tells us about human behaviour.

THE QUESTION OF HUMAN NATURE

Throughout this chapter, we have seen that human nature contains the potential for unspeakable acts of cruelty and inspiring acts of goodness. The greatest and most difficult lesson from the study of social psychology echoes the philosopher Erich Fromm's observation: "Even the most sadistic and destructive man is human, as human as the saint." Most people believe that some cultures and individuals are inherently evil and therefore not fully human; if we can just get rid of them, everything will be fine. But from the standpoint of social and cultural psychology, all human beings, like all cultures, contain the potential for both good and evil.

That is why virtually no nation has bloodless hands. The Nazis systematically exterminated millions of Jews, Gypsies, homosexuals, disabled people, and anyone not of the "pure" Aryan "race." But they were not unique. Canadians slaughtered indigenous peoples in North America, Turks slaughtered Armenians, the Khmer Rouge slaughtered millions of fellow Cambodians, the Spanish conquistadors slaughtered indigenous peoples in Mexico and South America, Idi Amin waged a reign of terror against his own people in Uganda, the Japanese slaughtered Koreans and Chinese, despotic political regimes in Argentina and Chile killed thousands of dissidents and rebels, and in the former Yugoslavia, Bosnian Serbs massacred Bosnian Muslims in the name of "ethnic cleansing."

It's easy to conclude that outbreaks of violence like these are a result of inner aggressive drives, the sheer villainy of the perpetrators, or age-old tribal hatreds. But in the social-psychological view, they result from the all-too-normal processes we have discussed in this chapter, including mindless obedience to authority, conformity, groupthink, deindividuation, stereotyping, ethnocentrism, and prejudice. These processes are especially likely to be activated when a government feels weakened and

Thinking Critically

Don't Oversimplify

Many people like to divide individuals and nations into those that are good and those that are evil. What is wrong with thinking this way?

These paintings done during wartime poignantly illustrate one child's effort to portray the horror of war and another's dream of peace. Can we learn to design a world in which conflicts and group differences, though inevitable, need not lead to violence?

vulnerable. By generating an outside enemy, rulers create us–them thinking to impose order and cohesion among their citizens and to create a scapegoat for the country's economic problems (Smith, 1998). The good news is that when circumstances within a nation change, societies can also change from being warlike to being peaceful. Sweden was once one of the most warlike nations on earth, but today it is among the most pacifistic and egalitarian. Less than two decades after Rwanda's Hutu committed genocide against the Tutsi, the country today is one of the safest and most well-functioning African nations (Gourevitch, 2009).

The philosopher Hannah Arendt (1963), who covered the trial of Adolf Eichmann, used the phrase "the banality of evil" to describe how it was possible for Eichmann and other ordinary people in Nazi Germany to commit the monstrous acts they did. (*Banal* means "commonplace" or "unoriginal.") The compelling evidence for the banality of evil is difficult for many people to accept. Of course, some people do stand out as being unusually heroic or unusually sadistic. But as we have seen, good people can do terribly disturbing things when their roles encourage or require them to do so, when the situation takes over and they do not stop to think critically.

The research discussed in this chapter suggests that ethnocentrism and prejudice are part of our human heritage, awaiting the conditions that will awaken them. But it can also help us formulate ways of living in a diverse world. By identifying the conditions that create the banality of evil, perhaps we can create other conditions that foster the "banality of virtue"—everyday acts of kindness, selflessness, and generosity.

◉ Watch
Random Acts of Kindness

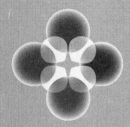

Taking Psychology with YOU

Thinking Critically in Everyday Life

Dealing with Cultural Differences

A French salesman worked for a company that was bought by Canadians. When the new Canadian manager ordered him to step up his sales within the next three months, the employee quit in a huff, taking his customers with him. Why? In France, it takes years to develop customers; in family-owned businesses, relationships with customers may span generations. The Canadian manager wanted instant results, as Canadians often do, but the French salesman knew this was impossible and quit. The Canadian view was "He wasn't up to the job; he's lazy and disloyal, so he stole my customers." The French view was

"There is no point in explaining anything to a person who is so stupid as to think you can acquire loyal customers in three months" (Hall & Hall, 1987).

Both men were committing the fundamental attribution error: assuming that the other person's behaviour was due to personality rather than the situation, in this case a situation governed by cultural rules. Many corporations now realize that such rules are not trivial and that success in a global economy depends on understanding them. But you don't have to go to another country to encounter cultural differences; they are likely to exist in your own hometown.

If you find yourself getting angry over something a person from another culture is doing or not doing, use the skills of critical thinking to find out whether your expectations and perceptions of that person's behaviour are appropriate. Take the time to examine your assumptions and biases, consider other explanations of the person's actions, and avoid emotional reasoning. For example, people who shake hands as a gesture of friendship and courtesy are likely to feel insulted if a person from a non-hand-shaking culture refuses to do the same, unless they have asked themselves the question, "Does everyone have the custom of shaking hands the way I do?"

Similarly, people from Middle Eastern and Latin American cultures are used to bargaining for what they buy; Canadians and northern Europeans are used to having a fixed price. People who do not know how to bargain, therefore, are likely to find bargaining an exercise in frustration because they will not know whether they got taken or got a great deal. In contrast, people from bargaining cultures will feel just as exasperated if a seller offers a flat price. "Where's the fun in this?" they'll say. "The whole human transaction of shopping is gone!"

Learning another culture's rule or custom is hard enough, but it is much more difficult to comprehend cultural differences that are deeply embedded in its language. For example, in Iran the social principle of *taarof* describes the practice of deliberate insincerity, such as giving false praise and making promises you have no intention of keeping. Iranians know that they are supposed to tell you what you want to hear to avoid conflict or to offer hope for a compromise. To

Iranians, these practices are a part of good manners; they are not offended by them. But Canadians and members of other English-speaking cultures are used to "straight talking," to saying directly and succinctly what they want. Therefore they find *taarof* hard to learn, let alone to practise. As an Iranian social scientist told the *New York Times* (Slackman, 2006), "Speech has a different function than it does in the West"—in the West, "yes" generally means yes; in Iran, "yes" can mean yes, but it often means maybe or no. "This creates a rich, poetic linguistic culture," he said. "It creates a multidimensional culture where people are adept at picking up on nuances. On the other hand, it makes for bad political discourse. In political discourse people don't know what to trust."

You can see why critical thinking can help people avoid the tendency to stereotype and to see cultural differences in communication solely in hostile, negative ways. "Why are the Iranians lying to me?" a Canadian might ask. The answer

is that they are not "lying" in Iranian terms; they are speaking in a way that is completely natural for them, according to their cultural rules for communication.

To learn the unspoken rules of a culture, you must look, listen, and observe. What is the pace of life like? Do people regard brash individuality and loud speech as admirable or embarrassing? When customers enter a shop, do they greet and chat with the shopkeeper or ignore the person as they browse? Are people expected to be direct in their speech or evasive? Sociocultural research enhances critical thinking by teaching us to appreciate the many cultural rules that govern people's behaviour, values, attitudes, and ways of doing business. Before you write off someone from a culture different from your own as being rude, foolish, stubborn, or devious, consider other interpretations of that person's behaviour—just as you would want that person to consider other, more forgiving, interpretations of yours.

SUMMARY

◆ Social psychologists study how social roles, attitudes, relationships, and groups influence individuals; cultural psychologists study the influence of culture on human behaviour. Many cultural rules, such as those governing correct conversational distance, are unspoken but nonetheless powerful.

ROLES AND RULES

◆ The environment influences people in countless subtle ways; observing that others have broken rules or laws increases the likelihood that a passerby will do the same. Two classic studies illustrate the power of *norms* and *roles* to affect individual actions. In Milgram's obedience study, most people in the role of "teacher" inflicted what they thought was extreme shock on another person because of the authority of the experimenter. In the Stanford prison study, university students tended to behave in accordance with the role of "prisoner" or "guard" that they had been assigned.

◆ Obedience to authority contributes to the smooth running of society, but obedience can also lead to actions that are deadly, foolish, or illegal. People obey orders because they can be punished if they do not, out of respect for authority, and to gain advantages. Even when they would rather not obey, they may do so because they have been *entrapped*, justifying each step and decision they make, and handing over responsibility for any harmful actions they commit to the authority.

SOCIAL INFLUENCES ON BELIEFS AND BEHAVIOUR

◆ Researchers in the area of *social cognition* study how people's perceptions affect their relationships and how the social environment affects their beliefs and perceptions. According to *attribution theory*, people are motivated to search for causes to which they can attribute their own and other people's behaviour. Their attributions may be *situational* or *dispositional*. The *fundamental attribution error* occurs when people overestimate personality traits as a cause of behaviour and underestimate the influence of the situation. A primary reason for the fundamental attribution error is that people rely on introspection to judge their own behaviour but only have observation to judge the behaviour of others. Attributions are further influenced by three *self-serving biases:* the bias to choose the most flattering and forgiving explanations of our own behaviour; the bias that we are better, smarter, and kinder than others; and the bias that the world is fair (the *just-world hypothesis*).

◆ People hold many *attitudes* about people, things, and ideas. Attitudes may be *explicit* (conscious) or *implicit* (unconscious). Attitudes may change through experience, through conscious decision, or as an effort to reduce *cognitive dissonance*. One powerful way to influence attitudes is by taking advantage of the *familiarity effect* and the *validity effect:* Simply exposing people repeatedly to a name or product makes them like it more, and repeating a statement over and over again makes it seem more believable.

◆ As discussed in "Biology and Beliefs," many attitudes are acquired through learning and social influence, but some are associated with personality traits that have a genetic component and are deeply ingrained. Religious and political affiliations are not heritable, but religiosity and certain political attitudes do have relatively high heritability. Ideological belief systems may have evolved to be organized along a left–right dimension, consisting of two central sets of attitudes: whether a person advocates or opposes social change, and whether a person thinks inequality is a result of human policies and can be overcome or is inevitable and should be accepted as part of the natural order. Attitudes are also profoundly affected by the *nonshared environment*, an individual's unique life experiences.

INDIVIDUALS IN GROUPS

◆ The need to belong is so powerful that the pain of social rejection and exclusion is greater and more memorable than physical pain, which is why groups use the weapon of ostracism or rejection to enforce conformity.

◆ In groups, individuals often behave differently than they would on their own. Conformity permits the smooth running of society and allows people to feel in harmony with others like them. But as the Asch experiment showed, most people will conform to the judgments of others even when the others are plain wrong.

◆ Close-knit groups are vulnerable to *groupthink*, the tendency of group members to think alike, censor themselves, actively suppress disagreement, and feel that their decisions

are invulnerable. Groupthink often produces faulty decisions because group members fail to seek disconfirming evidence for their ideas. However, groups can be structured to counteract groupthink.

◆ Sometimes a group's collective judgment is better than that of its individual members—the "wisdom of crowds." But crowds can also spread panic, rumour, and misinformation. *Diffusion of responsibility* in a group can lead to inaction on the part of individuals, as in *bystander apathy*. The diffusion of responsibility is likely to occur under conditions that promote *deindividuation*, the loss of awareness of one's individuality. Deindividuation increases when people feel anonymous, as in a large group or crowd or when they are wearing masks or uniforms. In some situations, crowd norms lead deindividuated people to behave aggressively, but in others, crowd norms foster helpfulness.

◆ The willingness to speak up for an unpopular opinion, blow the whistle on illegal practices, or help a stranger in trouble and perform other acts of *altruism* is partly a matter of personal belief and conscience. But several situational factors are also important: The person perceives that help is needed; cultural norms support taking action; the person has an ally; and the person becomes entrapped in a commitment to help or dissent.

US VERSUS THEM: GROUP IDENTITY

◆ People develop *social identities* based on their ethnicity, including nationality, religion, occupation, and other social memberships. In culturally diverse societies, many people face the problem of balancing their *ethnic identity* with *acculturation* into the larger society.

◆ *Ethnocentrism*, the belief that one's own ethnic group or religion is superior to all others, promotes "us–them" thinking. One effective strategy for reducing us–them thinking and hostility between groups is *interdependence*, having both sides work together to reach a common goal.

◆ *Stereotypes* help people rapidly process new information, organize experience, and predict how others will behave. But they distort reality by exaggerating differences between groups, underestimating the differences within groups, and producing selective perception.

GROUP CONFLICT AND PREJUDICE

◆ A *prejudice* is an unreasonable negative feeling toward a category of people. Psychologically, prejudice wards off feelings of anxiety and doubt, bolsters self-esteem when a person feels threatened (by providing a scapegoat), and, according to *terror management theory*, protects against the fear of death. Prejudice also has social causes: People acquire prejudices mindlessly, through conformity and parental lessons. Prejudice also serves to justify a majority group's economic interests and dominance. Finally, prejudice serves the cultural and national purpose of bonding people to their social groups and nations, and in extreme cases justifying war. For example, although *hostile sexism* is different from *benevolent sexism*, both legitimize gender discrimination. During times of economic insecurity and competition for jobs, prejudice rises.

◆ Psychologists disagree on whether racism and other prejudices are declining or have merely taken new forms. Some are trying to measure prejudice indirectly, by measuring *social distance*; seeing whether people are more likely to behave aggressively toward a target when they are stressed or angry; observing changes in the brain; or assessing unconscious positive or negative associations with a group, as with the *Implicit Association Test* (IAT). However, the IAT has many critics who claim it is not capturing true prejudice.

◆ Efforts to reduce prejudice need to target both the explicit and implicit attitudes people have. Four conditions help to reduce two groups' mutual prejudices and conflicts: Both sides must have equal legal status, economic standing, and power; both sides must have the legal, moral, and economic support of authorities and cultural institutions; both sides must have opportunities to work and socialize together informally and formally (the *contact hypothesis*); and both sides must work together for a common goal.

THE QUESTION OF HUMAN NATURE

◆ Although many people believe that only bad or evil people do bad deeds, the principles of social and cultural psychology show that under certain conditions, good people can often be induced to do bad things too. Everyone is influenced to one degree or another by the social processes of obedience, entrapment, conformity, persuasion, bystander apathy, groupthink, deindividuation, ethnocentrism, stereotyping, and prejudice.

TAKING PSYCHOLOGY WITH YOU

◆ Sociocultural research enhances critical thinking by identifying the cultural rules that govern people's behaviour, values, communication, and ways of doing business. Understanding these rules can help people examine their assumptions about people in other cultures, and avoid the tendency to jump to conclusions and reason emotionally about group differences.

MyPsychLab

Visit **www.mypsychlab.com** to help you get the best grade!
Test your knowledge and grasp difficult concepts through
- Custom study plans: See where you are strong and where you go wrong
- Interactive simulations
- Video and audio clips

KEY TERMS

norms (social) *274*	just-world hypothesis *283*	social identity *296*
role *275*	cognitive dissonance *284*	ethnic identity *296*
culture *275*	familiarity effect *284*	acculturation *296*
entrapment *279*	validity effect *284*	ethnocentrism *297*
social cognition *281*	groupthink *291*	stereotype *299*
attribution theory *281*	diffusion of responsibility *292*	prejudice *301*
fundamental attribution error *281*	deindividuation *292*	

9 THINKING AND INTELLIGENCE

ASK QUESTIONS . . . be willing to WONDER

- Is all of our thinking conscious?

- Why is it often so hard for people to reason rationally?

- Does a high IQ guarantee success in school and in life?

- Can animals think—and if so, what do they think about?

Each day, in the course of ordinary living, we all make decisions, draw up plans, draw inferences, construct explanations, and organize and reorganize the contents of our mental world. Descartes' famous declaration "I think, therefore I am" could just as well have been reversed: "I am, therefore I think." Our powers of thought and intelligence have inspired humans to immodestly call ourselves *Homo sapiens*, Latin for wise or rational man.

But just how "*sapiens*" are we, really? As children, we all learn how clocks arbitrarily divide time into hours, minutes, and seconds. Yet each spring, when daylight savings time begins, some people fret about tampering with "normal time." One woman complained to her local newspaper that the "extra hour of sunlight" was burning up her front lawn! In Nottingham, England, the mayor decided to distribute flyers to visitors telling them that Robin Hood and his pals never actually lived in nearby Sherwood Forest, inasmuch as they were not real persons; tourism plummeted. In Berlin, Germany, a radio station decided to find out how easily people could be manipulated on the internet by posting an obviously fake video on YouTube, purportedly showing the recently deceased Michael Jackson emerging from a coroner's van—alive. In a single day, the video got 880 000 hits, and the rumour that Jackson was alive and well quickly spread around the globe.

We could go on.

Of course, our cognitive abilities are also pretty impressive. Think for a moment about what thinking does for you. It frees you from the confines of the immediate present: You can think about a trip taken three years ago, a party next Saturday, or the First World War. It carries you beyond the boundaries of reality: You can imagine unicorns and utopias, Martians and magic. You can make plans far into the future and judge the probability of events, both good and bad. Because you think, you do not need to grope your way blindly through your problems but can apply knowledge and reasoning to solve them intelligently and creatively.

Yes, the human mind, which has managed to come up with poetry and penicillin, is a miraculous thing. But the human mind has also managed to come up with traffic jams, junk mail, and war. To better understand why the same species that figured out how to get to the moon is also capable of breathtaking bumbling here on Earth, we will examine in this chapter how people reason, solve problems, and grow in intelligence, as well as some sources of their mental shortcomings.

YOU are about to learn . . .

- the basic elements of thought.
- whether the language you speak affects the way you think.
- how subconscious thinking, nonconscious thinking, and mindlessness help us—and can also cause trouble.

THOUGHT: USING WHAT WE KNOW

Many cognitive psychologists liken the human mind to an information processor, analogous to a computer but far more complex. Information-processing approaches capture the fact that the brain does not passively record information but actively alters and organizes it. When we take action, we physically manipulate the environment; when we think, we *mentally* manipulate internal representations of objects, activities, and situations.

The Elements of Cognition

One type of mental representation is the **concept**, a mental category that groups objects, relations, activities, abstractions, or qualities having common properties. The instances of a concept are seen as roughly similar. For example, *golden retriever*, *cocker spaniel*, and *border collie* are instances of the concept *dog*; and *anger*, *joy*, and *sadness* are instances of the concept *emotion*. Concepts simplify and summarize information about the world so that it is manageable and so that we can make decisions quickly and efficiently. You may never have seen a *basenji* or eaten *escargots*, but if you know that the first is an instance of *dog* and the second an instance of *food*, you will know, roughly, how to respond (unless you do not like to eat snails, which is what escargots are).

Basic concepts have a moderate number of instances and are easier to acquire than those having either few or many instances (Rosch, 1973). What is the object pictured in the margin? You will probably call it an apple. The concept *apple* is more basic than *fruit*, which includes many more instances and is more abstract. It is also more basic than *McIntosh apple*, which is quite specific. Similarly, *book* is more basic than either *printed matter* or *novel*. Children seem to learn basic-level concepts earlier than others, and adults use them more often than others, because basic concepts convey an optimal amount of information in most situations.

The qualities associated with a concept do not necessarily all apply to every instance: Some apples are not red; some dogs do not bark; some birds do not fly. But all the instances of a concept do share a family resemblance. When we need to decide whether something belongs to a concept, we are likely to compare it to a **prototype**, a representative example of the concept (Rosch, 1973). For instance, which dog is doggier, a golden retriever or a chihuahua? Which fruit is more fruitlike, an apple or a pineapple? Which activity is more representative of sports, football or weight lifting? Most people within a culture can easily tell you which instances of a concept are most representative, or prototypical.

The words used to express concepts may influence or shape how we think about them. Many decades ago, Benjamin Lee Whorf, an insurance inspector by profession and a linguist and anthropologist by inclination, proposed that language moulds cognition and perception. For example, said Whorf (1956), because English has only one word for snow and Inuktitut has many (for powdered snow, slushy snow, falling snow. . .), the Inuit notice differences in snow that English speakers do not. He also argued that grammar—the way words are formed and arranged to convey tense and other concepts—affects how we think about the world.

What is this?

concept A mental category that groups objects, relations, activities, abstractions, or qualities having common properties.

basic concepts Concepts that have a moderate number of instances and that are easier to acquire than those having few or many instances.

prototype An especially representative example of a concept.

Some instances of a concept are more representative or prototypical than others. For example, Justin Bieber is an unmarried man and is thus technically a bachelor, but since he is so young (he was born in 1994), few people would use the word "bachelor" to describe him. Would you call the Pope a bachelor? What about Ryan Gosling, who is unmarried?

Whorf's theory was popular for a while and then fell from favour; English speakers can see all Inuit kinds of snow, after all, and they have plenty of adjectives to describe the different varieties. But today Whorf's ideas are once again getting attention. Some researchers are finding that vocabulary and grammar do affect how we perceive the location of objects, think about time, attend to shapes and colours, and remember events (Boroditsky, 2003; Gentner & Goldin-Meadow, 2003). For example, a language spoken by a group in Papua New Guinea refers to blue and green with one word, but distinct shades of green with two separate words. On perceptual discrimination tasks, Papua New Guineans who speak this language handle green contrasts better than blue–green ones, whereas the reverse holds true for English speakers (Roberson, Davies, & Davidoff, 2000). Similar results for the way language affects colour perception have been obtained in studies comparing English with certain African languages (Özgen, 2004).

Here's another example: In many languages, speakers must specify whether an object is linguistically masculine or feminine. (In French and Spanish, for example, *la clé*, the key, is feminine but *le pont*, the bridge, is masculine.) It seems that labelling a concept as masculine or feminine affects the attributes that native speakers ascribe to it. A study of German and Spanish speakers revealed that a German speaker will describe a key (masculine in German) as hard, heavy, jagged, serrated, and useful, whereas a Spanish speaker is more likely to describe a key (feminine) as golden, intricate, little, lovely, and shiny. German speakers will describe a bridge (feminine in German) as beautiful, elegant, fragile, peaceful, and slender, whereas Spanish speakers are more likely to describe a bridge (masculine) as big, dangerous, strong, sturdy, and towering (Boroditsky, Schmidt, & Phillips, 2003).

Concepts are the building blocks of thought, but they would be of limited use if we merely stacked them up mentally. We must also represent their relations to one another. One way we accomplish this may be by storing and using **propositions**, units of meaning that are made up of concepts and that express a unitary idea. A proposition can express nearly any sort of knowledge ("Donna raises poodles") or belief ("Poodles are smart"). Propositions, in turn, are linked together in complicated networks of knowledge, associations, beliefs, and expectations. These networks, which psychologists call

Language may influence our concepts and perceptions of the world. How do you divide up these hues? People who speak a language that has only one word for blue and green, but separate words for shades of green, handle green contrasts better than the blue–green distinction. English speakers do just the opposite.

proposition A unit of meaning that is made up of concepts and expresses a single idea.

cognitive schemas, serve as mental models of aspects of the world. For example, gender schemas represent a person's beliefs and expectations about what it means to be male or female (see Chapter 13). People also have schemas about cultures, occupations, animals, geographical locations, and many other features of the social and natural environment.

Mental images—especially visual images, pictures in the mind's eye—are also important in thinking and in the construction of cognitive schemas. Although no one can directly see another person's visual images, psychologists are able to study them indirectly. One method is to measure how long it takes people to rotate an image in their imaginations, scan from one point to another in an image, or read off some detail from an image. The results suggest that visual images are much like images on a computer screen: We can manipulate them; they occur in a mental space of a fixed size; and small ones contain less detail than larger ones (Kosslyn, 1980; Shepard & Metzler, 1971). Most people also report auditory images (for instance, a song, slogan, or poem you can hear in your "mind's ear"), and many report images in other sensory modalities as well—touch, taste, smell, or pain. Some even report kinesthetic images, imagined feelings in the muscles and joints.

Here, then, is a visual summary of the elements of cognition:

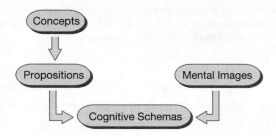

How Conscious Is Thought?

When we think about thinking, we usually have in mind those mental activities that are carried out in a deliberate way with a conscious goal in mind, such as solving a problem, drawing up plans, or making calculated decisions. However, not all mental processing is conscious.

SUBCONSCIOUS THINKING.   Some cognitive processes lie outside of awareness but can be brought into consciousness with a little effort when necessary. These **subconscious processes** allow us to handle more information and to perform more complex tasks than if we depended entirely on conscious, deliberate thought. Many automatic routines are performed "without thinking," though they might once have required careful, conscious attention: knitting, typing, driving a car, decoding the letters in a word in order to read it.

Because of the capacity for automatic processing, people can eat lunch while reading a book or drive a car while listening to music. In such cases, one of the tasks has become automatic and does not require much executive control from the brain's prefrontal cortex. But in daily life, multitasking is usually inefficient. In fact, far from saving time, toggling between two or more tasks increases the time required to complete them; stress goes up, errors increase, reaction times lengthen, and memory suffers (Lien, Ruthruff, & Johnston, 2006). This is *especially* true for people who consider themselves to be accomplished multitaskers and who are heavy users of electronic information. In a series of experiments designed to test the supposed skills of such multitaskers, their performance on each of the tasks they were trying to perform was impaired by interference from the other tasks (Ophir, Nass, & Wagner, 2009). "The shocking discovery of this

cognitive schema   An integrated mental network of knowledge, beliefs, and expectations concerning a particular topic or aspect of the world.

mental image   A mental representation that mirrors or resembles the thing it represents; mental images occur in many and perhaps all sensory modalities.

subconscious processes   Mental processes occurring outside of conscious awareness but accessible to consciousness when necessary.

research," said one of the investigators, is that high multitask-ers "are lousy at everything that's necessary for multitasking. They're suckers for irrelevancy. Everything distracts them."

Multitasking can even be hazardous to your health. As we saw in Chapter 2, cellphone use greatly impairs a person's ability to drive, even when the phone is hands-free. A driver's attention is diverted far more by a phone conversation than by listening to music on the car radio (Strayer & Drews, 2007). Other distrac-tions are equally dangerous. A government study caught drivers on camera checking their stocks, fussing with MP3 players, drink-ing beer, reading emails, applying makeup, flossing their teeth, and putting in contact lenses—all while hurtling down the high-way at high speeds (Klauer et al., 2006). And, of course, there's also texting: In 2008, a commuter train's engineer violated com-pany policy by texting while on the job, and never saw an oncoming freight train. The resulting collision killed 25 people, including the engineer himself.

Some well-learned skills do not require much conscious thought and can be performed while doing other things, but multitasking can also get you into serious trouble. It's definitely not a good idea to talk on your cellphone and drive at the same time. Indeed, in British Columbia and Ontario, it is against the law.

Even when multitasking doesn't put you at risk of an accident, it can be a bad idea. When you do two things at once, brain activity devoted to each task decreases. And while you are switching between tasks, your prefrontal cortex, which prioritizes tasks and enables higher-order thinking, becomes relatively inactive (Jiang, Saxe, & Kanwisher, 2004; Just et al., 2001). That's why we hope you are not trying to learn these facts while you're also watching TV and texting your friends!

NONCONSCIOUS THINKING.   Other kinds of thought processes, **nonconscious processes**, remain outside of awareness. Unlike subconscious thinking, which can enter consciousness with some effort, effort does not bring nonconscious thinking into awareness. For example, you have no doubt had the odd experience of having a solution to a problem pop into mind *after* you have given up trying to find one. With sudden insight, you see how to solve an equation, assemble a cabinet, or finish a puzzle without quite knowing how you managed to find the solution. Similarly, people will often say they rely on intuition—hunches and gut feelings—rather than conscious reasoning to make judgments and decisions.

Insight and intuition probably involve several stages of mental processing (Bowers et al., 1990). First, clues in the problem automatically activate certain memories or knowledge. You begin to see a pattern or structure in the problem, although you cannot yet say what it is; possible solutions percolate in your mind. This nonconscious pro-cessing guides you toward a hunch or a hypothesis. Eventually, your thinking becomes conscious, and you become aware of a probable solution. At this stage, you may feel that a sudden revelation has popped into your mind from nowhere ("Aha, now I see!"), but considerable nonconscious mental work has already occurred. Scientists are now working on establishing links between changes in the brain and the steps involved in insightful problem solving (Bower, 2008; Sheth, Sandkühler, & Bhattacharya, 2009).

Sometimes people solve problems or learn new skills without experiencing the conscious stage at all. For example, some people discover the best strategy for win-ning a card game without ever being able to consciously identify what they are doing (Bechara et al., 1997). Psychologists call this phenomenon **implicit learning**: You learn a rule or an adaptive behaviour, either with or without a conscious inten-tion to do so; but you don't know how you learned it, and you can't state, either to yourself or to others, exactly what it is you have learned (Frensch & Rünger, 2003; Lieberman, 2000). Many of our abilities, from speaking our native language prop-erly to walking up a flight of stairs, are the result of implicit learning.

⊙ **Watch**
The Multitasking Myth

nonconscious processes   Mental processes occurring outside of and not available to conscious awareness.

implicit learning   Learning that oc-curs when you acquire knowledge about something without being aware of how you did so and without being able to state exactly what it is you have learned.

MINDLESSNESS.   Even when our thinking is conscious, often we are not thinking very *hard*. We may act, speak, and make decisions out of habit, without stopping to analyze what we are doing or why we are doing it. This sort of *mindlessness*— mental inflexibility, inertia, and obliviousness to the present context—keeps people from recognizing when a change in a situation requires a change in behaviour (Langer, 1997).

In a classic study of mindlessness, a researcher approached people as they were about to use a photocopier and made one of three requests: "Excuse me, may I use the Xerox machine?" "Excuse me, may I use the Xerox machine, because I have to make copies?" or "Excuse me, may I use the Xerox machine, because I'm in a rush?" Normally, people will let someone go before them only if the person has a legitimate reason, as in the third request. In this study, however, people also complied when the reason sounded like an authentic explanation but was actually meaningless ("because I have to make copies"). They heard the form of the request but they did not hear its content, and they mindlessly stepped aside (Langer, Blank, & Chanowitz, 1978).

Jerome Kagan (1989) has argued that fully conscious awareness is needed only when we must make a deliberate choice, when events happen that cannot be handled automatically, and when unexpected moods and feelings arise. He likened consciousness to firefighters who are quietly playing cards at the station house until an alarm goes off, calling them into action. Some researchers go further, arguing that for certain kinds of complex decisions, such as choosing which car or house to buy, "gut feelings" and unconscious impressions sometimes lead to better choices and more satisfaction than conscious deliberation does (Dijksterhuis et al., 2006). But this idea is still controversial, and in any case, most of us would probably benefit if our mental firefighters paid a little more attention to their jobs. Multitasking, mindlessness, and operating on automatic pilot have their place; life would be impossible if we had to think carefully about every little thing we do, see, or hear. But they can also lead to errors and mishaps, ranging from the trivial (misplacing your keys) to the serious (walking into traffic because you're daydreaming). Cognitive psychologists have, therefore, devoted a great deal of study to mindful, conscious thought and the capacity to reason.

quick**QUIZ**

✓•⌐**Quick Review** on **MyPsychLab**

Stay mindful while taking this quiz.

1. Which concept is most basic: *furniture, chair,* or *high chair*?
2. Which example of the concept *chair* is prototypical: *high chair, rocking chair,* or *dining room chair*?
3. What two findings in the previous section support Whorf's theory that language affects perception and cognition?
4. In addition to concepts and images, _____, which express a unitary idea, have been suggested as a basic form of mental representation.
5. Peter's mental representation of *Thanksgiving* includes associations (e.g., with turkeys), attitudes ("It's a time to be with relatives"), and expectations ("I'm going to gain weight from all that food"). They are all part of his _____ for the holiday.
6. Zelda discovers that she has called her boyfriend's number instead of her mother's, as she intended. Her error can be attributed to _____.

Answers:

sents. 4. propositions 5. cognitive schema 6. mindlessness
and the linguistic gender of a word can affect how people's descriptions of the concept it repre-
3. Colour terms can affect how people respond to colours on visual discrimination tasks,
1. chair 2. A plain, straight-backed dining room chair will be prototypical for most people.

YOU are about to learn . . .

◆ why algorithms and logic can't solve all our problems.

◆ the difference between deductive and inductive reasoning.

◆ the importance of heuristics and dialectical reasoning in solving real-life problems.

◆ how cognitive development affects the ways in which people reason and justify their views.

REASONING RATIONALLY

Reasoning is purposeful mental activity that involves operating on information in order to reach conclusions. Unlike impulsive or nonconscious responding, reasoning requires us to draw specific inferences from observations, facts, or assumptions.

Formal Reasoning: Algorithms and Logic

In *formal reasoning problems*—the kind you might find, say, on an intelligence test or an entrance exam for medical or graduate school—the information needed for drawing a conclusion or reaching a solution is specified clearly, and there is a single right (or best) answer. Established methods usually exist for solving the problem, and you usually know when it has been solved (Galotti, 1989).

In some formal problems and well-defined tasks, all you have to do is apply an **algorithm**, a set of procedures guaranteed to produce a solution even if you do not really know how it works. To solve a problem in long division, you apply a series of operations that you learned in elementary school. To make a cake, you apply an algorithm called a recipe.

For other formal problems, the rules of formal logic are crucial tools to have in your mental toolbox. One such tool is **deductive reasoning**, in which a conclusion *necessarily* follows from a set of observations or propositions (*premises*):

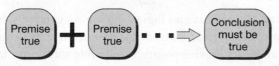

DEDUCTIVE REASONING

Premise true **+** Premise true ‧‧‧⇨ Conclusion must be true

For example, if the premises "All human beings are mortal" and "I am a human being" are true, then the conclusion "I am mortal" must also be true.

We all use deductive reasoning all the time, although many of our premises are implicit rather than explicitly spelled out: "I never have to work on Saturday. Today is Saturday. Therefore, I don't have to work today." But the ability to apply deductive reasoning to abstract problems that are divorced from everyday life does not come as naturally; it depends to some degree on experience, culture, and schooling (Segall et al., 1999). And even in everyday life, almost everyone has trouble thinking deductively in some situations, especially when reasoning about an emotional

reasoning The drawing of conclusions or inferences from observations, facts, or assumptions.

algorithm A problem-solving strategy guaranteed to produce a solution even if the user does not know how it works.

deductive reasoning A form of reasoning in which a conclusion follows necessarily from certain premises; if the premises are true, the conclusion must be true.

⊙ **Watch**
Deductive Reasoning

topic (Blanchette & Richards, 2004). For example, many people mentally reverse a premise, and this error can have serious consequences, as one of our students recognized when he worried about the effects of confusing "All rapists are men" with "All men are rapists."

Another important form of logical thinking is **inductive reasoning**, in which a conclusion *probably* follows from certain premises but could conceivably be false:

INDUCTIVE REASONING

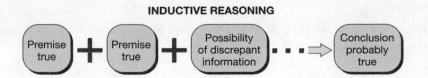

People often think of inductive reasoning as the drawing of general conclusions from specific observations, as when you generalize from past experience: "I had three good meals at Joe's Restaurant; they sure have great food." But an inductive argument can also have premises that are general statements (Copi & Burgess-Jackson, 1992). If your premises are that all cows are mammals and have lungs, all whales are mammals and have lungs, and all humans are mammals and have lungs, you might reasonably conclude that probably all mammals have lungs. Inductive arguments can also have specific conclusions: If your premises are that most people with season tickets to the concert love music, and that Jeannine has season tickets to the concert, you might conclude that Jeannine probably loves music.

Science depends heavily on inductive reasoning because scientists make careful observations and then draw conclusions that they think are probably true. But in inductive reasoning, no matter how much supporting evidence you gather, it is always possible that new information will turn up to show you are wrong. The three meals you ate at Joe's Restaurant may not be typical; perhaps everything else on the menu is awful. Jeannine could have bought those concert tickets not because she loves music but because she wanted to impress a friend. In science, too, new information may show that previous conclusions were faulty and must therefore be revised or modified.

Informal Reasoning: Heuristics and Dialectical Thinking

Useful as they are, algorithms and logical reasoning cannot solve all, or even most, of life's problems. In *informal reasoning problems*, there is often no clearly correct solution. Many approaches, viewpoints, or possible solutions may compete, and you may have to decide which one is most reasonable. Further, the information at your disposal may be incomplete, or people may disagree on what the premises should be. Your position on the controversial issue of abortion, for example, will depend on your premises about when meaningful human life begins, what rights an embryo has, and what rights a woman has to control her own body. People on opposing sides of this issue even disagree on how the premises should be phrased, because they have different emotional reactions to terms such as "rights," "meaningful life," and "control over one's body."

Formal and informal problems usually call for different approaches. Whereas formal problems can often be solved with an algorithm, informal problems often

inductive reasoning A form of reasoning in which the premises provide support for a conclusion, but it is still possible for the conclusion to be false.

call for a **heuristic**, a rule of thumb that suggests a course of action without guaranteeing an optimal solution. Anyone who has ever played chess or a card game is familiar with heuristics (e.g., "Get rid of high cards first"). In these games, working out all the possible sequences of moves would be impossible. Heuristics are also useful to an investor trying to predict the stock market, a doctor trying to determine the best treatment for a patient, and a factory owner trying to boost production: All may be faced with incomplete information on which to base a decision and may therefore resort to rules of thumb that have proven effective in the past.

In thinking about real-life problems, a person must also be able to use **dialectical reasoning**, the process of comparing and evaluating opposing points of view in order to resolve differences. Philosopher Richard Paul (1984) once described dialectical reasoning as movement "up and back between contradictory lines of reasoning, using each to critically cross-examine the other":

Whether you are a chess grand master, pondering your next move in a match against a computer, or just an ordinary person solving ordinary problems, you need to use *heuristics*, rules of thumb that help you decide on a strategy.

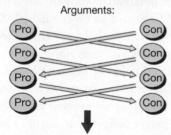

DIALECTICAL REASONING

Arguments:

Most reasonable conclusion based on evidence and logic

◀◉ **Simulate**
Heuristics

heuristic A rule of thumb that suggests a course of action or guides problem solving but does not guarantee an optimal solution.

dialectical reasoning A process in which opposing facts or ideas are weighed and compared, with a view to determining the best solution or resolving differences.

Dialectical reasoning is what juries are supposed to do to arrive at a verdict: consider arguments for and against the defendant's guilt, point and counterpoint. It is also what voters are supposed to do when thinking about whether the government should raise or lower taxes, or about the best way to improve public education.

PRACTISE YOUR DIALECTICAL REASONING

Choose a controversial topic, such as whether marijuana should be legalized or the death penalty should be reinstated. First list all the arguments you can to support your own position. Then list all the arguments you can on the other side of the issue. You do not have to agree with these arguments; just list them. Do you feel a mental block or emotional discomfort while doing this? Can you imagine how opponents of your position would answer your arguments? Having strong opinions is fine; you should have an informed opinion on matters of public interest. But does that opinion get in the way of even imagining a contrary point of view or of altering your view if the evidence warrants a change?

Get INVOLVED!

Reflective Judgment

Many adults clearly have trouble thinking dialectically; they take one position, and that's that. When do people develop the ability to think critically—to question assumptions, evaluate and integrate evidence, consider alternative interpretations, and reach conclusions that can be defended as most reasonable?

To find out, Patricia King and Karen Kitchener (1994, 2002, 2004) provided adolescents and adults, representing a wide variety of backgrounds, with statements describing opposing viewpoints on various topics. Each person then had to answer these questions: What do you think about these statements? How did you come to hold that point of view? On what do you base your position? Can you ever know for sure that your position is correct? Why do you suppose disagreement exists about this issue? From the responses of thousands of participants, gathered over more than a quarter of a century, King and Kitchener identified seven cognitive stages on the road to what they call *reflective judgment* (and we have called critical thinking). At each stage, people make different assumptions about how things are known and use different ways of justifying or defending their beliefs.

In general, people in two *prereflective stages* tend to assume that a correct answer always exists and that it can be obtained directly through the senses ("I know what I've seen") or from authorities ("They said so on the news"; "That's what I was brought up to believe"). If authorities do not yet have the truth, prereflective thinkers tend to reach conclusions on the basis of what "feels right" at the moment. They do not distinguish between knowledge and belief or between belief and evidence, and they see no reason to justify a belief. One respondent at this stage, when asked about evolution, said: "Well, some people believe that we evolved from apes and that's the way they want to believe. But I would never believe that way and nobody could talk me out of the way I believe because I believe the way that it's told in the Bible."

During three *quasi-reflective stages*, people recognize that some things cannot be known with absolute certainty, and they realize that judgments should be supported by reasons, yet they pay attention only to evidence that fits what they already believe. They seem to think that because knowledge is uncertain, any judgment about the evidence is purely subjective. Quasi-reflective thinkers will defend a position by saying, "We all have a right to our own opinion," as if all opinions are created equal. One undergraduate at this stage, when asked whether one opinion on the safety of food additives was right and others were wrong, answered: "No. I think it just depends on how you feel personally because people make their decisions based upon how they feel and what research they've seen. So what one person thinks is right, another person might think is wrong. . . . If I feel that chemicals cause cancer and you feel that food is unsafe without it, your opinion might be right to you and my opinion is right to me."

In the last two stages, a person becomes capable of reflective judgment. He or she understands that although some things can never be known with certainty, some judgments are more valid than others because of their coherence, their fit with the available evidence, their usefulness, and so on. People at these *reflective stages* are willing to consider evidence from a variety of sources and to reason dialectically. This interview with a graduate student illustrates reflective thinking:

Interviewer: Can you ever say you know for sure that your point of view on chemical additives is correct?

Student: No, I don't think so. . . . [But] I think that we can usually be reasonably certain, given the information we have now, and considering our methodologies. . . . It might be that the research wasn't conducted rigorously enough. In other words, we might have flaws in our data or sample, things like that.

Interviewer: How then would you identify the "better opinion"?

Student: One that takes as many factors as possible into consideration. I mean one that uses the higher percentage of the data that we have, and perhaps that uses the methodology that has been most reliable.

Interviewer: And how do you come to a conclusion about what the evidence suggests?

Student: I think you have to take a look at the different opinions and studies that are offered by different groups. Maybe some studies offered by the chemical industry, some studies by the government, some private studies. . . . You have to try to interpret people's motives and that makes it a more complex soup to try to strain out.

Sometimes a person's reasoning varies across two or three adjacent stages, depending on what kind of problem or issue the person is thinking about (King & Kitchener, 2004). But most people show no evidence of reflective judgment until their middle or late twenties, if ever. Still, there's reason for hope: When students get support for thinking reflectively and have opportunities to practise it in their courses, their thinking tends to become more complex, sophisticated, and well-grounded (Kitchener et al., 1993). As one writer noted, the gradual development of thinking skills among university students represents an abandonment of "ignorant certainty" in favour of "intelligent confusion" (Kroll, 1992). It may not seem so, but this is a big step forward! You can see why, in this book, we emphasize thinking about and evaluating psychological findings, and not just memorizing them.

One reason that Auguste Rodin's *The Thinker* became world famous and has been much imitated is that it captures so perfectly the experience of thinking reflectively.

Reflect on the answers to these questions.

quickQUIZ

✓•[Quick Review on MyPsychLab

1. Most of the holiday gifts Mervin bought this year cost more than they did last year, so he concludes that inflation is increasing. Is he using inductive, deductive, or dialectical reasoning?

2. Yvonne is arguing with Henrietta about whether real estate is a better investment than stocks. "You can't convince me," says Yvonne. "I just know I'm right." Yvonne needs training in _____ reasoning.

3. Seymour thinks the media have a liberal political bias, and Sophie thinks they are too conservative. "Well," says Seymour, "I have my truth and you have yours. It's purely subjective." Which of King and Kitchener's stages of thinking describes Seymour's statement?

4. What kind of evidence might resolve the issue that Seymour and Sophie are arguing about?

Answers:

1. inductive 2. dialectical 3. quasi-reflective 4. Researchers might have raters watch a random sample of TV news shows and measure the time devoted to conservative and liberal viewpoints. Or raters could read a random sample of newspaper editorials from across the country and evaluate them as liberal or conservative in outlook. Perhaps you can think of other strategies. Be careful: Ratings can be affected by what people want or expect to perceive.

YOU are about to learn . . .

♦ how biases in reasoning impair the ability to think rationally and critically.

♦ why people worry more about rare but vivid disasters than about dangers that are far more likely.

◆ how the way a decision is framed affects the choices people make.

◆ why people often value fairness above rational self-interest.

◆ how the need to justify the expenditure of time, money, and effort affects how people think about a group they joined or a product they bought.

Thinking Critically

Analyze Assumptions and Biases

Most people assume they make decisions and judgments logically and rationally. But are human beings biased to be biased?

BARRIERS TO REASONING RATIONALLY

Although most people have the capacity to think logically, reason dialectically, and make judgments reflectively, it is abundantly clear that they do not always do so. One obstacle is the need to be right; if your self-esteem depends on winning arguments, you will find it hard to listen with an open mind to competing views. Other obstacles include limited information and a lack of time to reflect carefully. But human thought processes are also tripped up by many predictable, systematic biases and errors. Psychologists have studied dozens of these cognitive pitfalls (Kahneman, 2003). Here we describe just a few.

Exaggerating the Improbable (and Minimizing the Probable)

One common bias is the inclination to exaggerate the probability of rare events. This bias helps to explain why so many people enter lotteries and buy disaster insurance, and why some irrational fears persist. As we discuss in Chapter 7, evolution has equipped us to fear certain natural dangers, such as snakes. However, in modern life, many of these dangers are no longer much of a threat; the risk of a renegade rattler sinking its fangs into you in Victoria or Toronto is pretty low (it is, however, higher in Lethbridge)! Yet the fear lingers on, so we overestimate the danger. Evolution has also given us brains that are terrific at responding to an immediate threat or to acts that provoke outrage even though they pose no threat to the survival of the species (for instance, inequity; Brosnan, 2011). Unfortunately, our brains were not designed to become alarmed by serious *future* threats that do not seem to pose much danger right now, such as global warming (Gilbert, 2006b).

When judging probabilities, people are strongly influenced by the **affect heuristic**: the tendency to consult their emotions (affect) instead of judging probabilities objectively (Slovic & Peters, 2006; Slovic et al., 2002). Emotions can often help us make decisions by narrowing our options or by allowing us to act quickly in an uncertain or dangerous situation. But emotions can also mislead us by preventing us from accurately assessing risk. One unusual field study looked at how people in France responded to the "mad cow" crisis that occurred a few years ago. (Mad cow disease affects the brain and can be contracted by eating meat from contaminated cows.) Whenever many newspaper articles reported the dangers of "mad cow disease," beef consumption fell during the following month. But when news articles, reporting the same dangers, used the technical names of the disease—Creutzfeldt-Jakob disease and bovine spongiform encephalopathy (BSE)—beef consumption stayed the same (Sinaceur, Heath, & Cole, 2005). The more alarming labels caused people to reason emotionally and to overestimate the danger. (During the entire period of the supposed crisis, only six people in France were diagnosed with the disease.) Canada has also had cases of BSE, and although there were anecdotal reports of paradoxical increases in beef consumption, it appears that, as was the case in France, there was a similar negative relation between beef consumption and reports about "mad cow disease" in the media (Peng, McCann-Hiltz, & Goddard, 2004).

Our judgments about risks are also influenced by the **availability heuristic**, the tendency to judge the probability of an event by how easy it is to think of examples or instances of it (Tversky & Kahneman, 1973). The availability heuristic often works hand

affect heuristic The tendency to consult one's emotions instead of estimating probabilities objectively.

availability heuristic The tendency to judge the probability of a type of event by how easy it is to think of examples or instances.

in hand with the affect heuristic. For example, catastrophes and shocking accidents evoke a strong emotional reaction in us, and thus stand out in our minds. They are more available mentally than other kinds of negative events. (An image of a "mad cow"—that sweet, placid creature running amok!—is highly "available.") This is why people overestimate the frequency of deaths from tornadoes and underestimate the frequency of deaths from asthma, which occur dozens of times more often but do not make headlines. It is why news accounts of avalanches make people fear skiing, even though other aspects of skiing are more dangerous—like skiing without a helmet.

Avoiding Loss

In general, people try to avoid or minimize risks and losses when they make decisions. That strategy is rational enough, but people's perceptions of risk are subject to the **framing effect**: the tendency for choices to differ depending on how the choice is presented. When a choice is framed in terms of the risk of losing something, people will respond more cautiously than when the very *same* choice is framed in terms of gain. They will choose a ticket that has a 1% chance of winning a raffle but reject one that has a 99% chance of losing. Or they will rate a condom as effective when they are told it has a 95% success rate in protecting against the AIDS virus, but not when they are told it has a 5% failure rate—which of course is exactly the same thing (Linville, Fischer, & Fischhoff, 1992).

Suppose you had to choose between two health programs to combat a disease expected to kill 600 people. Which would you prefer: a program that will definitely save 200 people, or one with a one-third probability of saving all 600 people and a two-thirds probability of saving none? (Problem 1 in Figure 9.1 illustrates this choice.) When asked this question, most people, including physicians, say they would prefer the first program. In other words,

Because of the affect and availability heuristics, many of us overestimate the chances of suffering a shark attack. Shark attacks are extremely rare, but they are terrifying and easy to visualize.

framing effect The tendency for people's choices to be affected by how a choice is presented, or framed; for example, whether it is worded in terms of potential losses or gains.

FIGURE 9.1 *A Matter of Wording*

The decisions we make can depend on how the alternatives are framed. When asked to choose between the two programs in Problem 1, which are described in terms of lives saved, most people choose the first program. When asked to choose between the programs in Problem 2, which are described in terms of lives lost, most people choose the second program. Yet the alternatives in the two problems are actually identical.

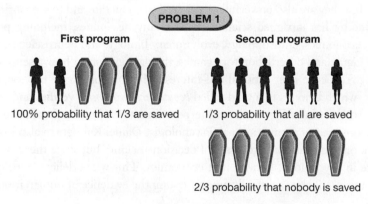

PROBLEM 1

First program — 100% probability that 1/3 are saved

Second program — 1/3 probability that all are saved — 2/3 probability that nobody is saved

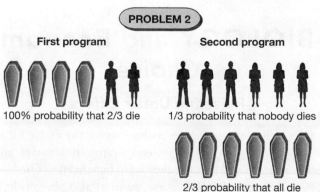

PROBLEM 2

First program — 100% probability that 2/3 die

Second program — 1/3 probability that nobody dies — 2/3 probability that all die

they reject the riskier though potentially more rewarding solution in favour of a sure gain. However, people will take a risk if they see it as a way to *avoid loss*. Suppose now that you have to choose between a program in which 400 people will definitely die and a program in which there is a one-third probability of nobody dying and a two-thirds probability that all 600 will die. If you think about it, you will see that the alternatives are exactly the same as in the first problem; they are merely worded differently (see Problem 2 in Figure 9.1). Yet this time most people choose the second solution. They reject risk when they think of the outcome in terms of lives saved, but they accept risk when they think of the outcome in terms of lives lost (Kahneman, 2002; Tversky & Kahneman, 1981).

Few of us will have to face a decision involving hundreds of lives, but we may have to choose between different medical treatments for ourselves or a relative. Our decision may be affected by whether the doctor frames the choice in terms of chances of surviving or chances of dying.

The Fairness Bias

Interestingly, in certain circumstances we do not try to avoid loss altogether, because we are subject to a *fairness bias*. Imagine that you are playing a two-person game called the *Ultimatum Game*, in which your partner gets $20 and must decide how much to share with you. You can choose to accept your partner's offer, in which case you both get to keep your respective portions, or you can reject the offer, in which case neither of you gets a penny. How low an offer would you accept?

If you think about it, you'll see that it makes sense to accept any amount at all, no matter how paltry, because then at least you will get *something*. But that is not how people respond when playing the Ultimatum Game. If the offer is too low, they are likely to reject it. In industrial societies, offers of 50% are typical and offers below 20–30% are commonly rejected, even when the absolute sums are large. In other societies, the amounts offered and accepted may be higher or lower, but there is always some amount that people consider unfair and refuse to accept (Henrich et al., 2001). People may be competitive and love to win, but they are also powerfully motivated to cooperate and to see fairness prevail.

This finding has intrigued scientists from many disciplines, including psychology, philosophy, economics, anthropology, evolutionary biology, and neuroscience. Using the Ultimatum Game and other laboratory games, they are exploring how a sense of fairness often takes precedence over rational self-interest when people make economic choices. Their work, which belongs to a field called *behavioural economics*, verifies and extends the pioneering work of Nobel Prize–winner Herbert Simon (1955), who first showed that economic decisions are not always rational. Psychologist Daniel Kahneman also won a Nobel for his work on the irrational processes of decision-making, but since there is (as yet) no Nobel Prize in psychology, he won it in economics. This was a delicious irony, because most economists still have a difficult time accepting the evidence of human irrationality.

BIOLOGY and *Economic Choice*

Rejecting Unfair Offers

Why does a desire for fair play sometimes outweigh the desire for economic gain? Evolutionary theorists believe that cooperative tendencies and a desire for fairness and reciprocity evolved because they were beneficial to our forebears (Fehr & Fischbacher, 2003; Trivers, 2004). Of course, cultures also play a role, by establishing rules of cooperation and fairness to ensure peace and harmony among their members, and they enforce these rules by rewarding those who abide by them and punishing cheaters. But the idea that the Golden Rule has a basis in biology has gained support from research with nonhuman primates.

In one study, capuchin monkeys received a token that they could then exchange for a slice of cucumber. The monkeys regarded this exchange as a pretty good deal—until they saw a neighbouring monkey exchanging tokens for an even better reward, a grape. At that point, they began to refuse to exchange their tokens, even though they were then left with no reward at all (Brosnan & de Waal, 2003). Sometimes they even threw the cucumber slice on the ground in apparent disgust!

Some behavioural economists have drawn on the methods of neuroscience, using MRI scans to examine brain activity when people play variations of the Ultimatum Game (Camerer, 2003; Sanfey, Rilling, & Aronson, 2003). While a person is deciding whether to accept a low offer, two brain areas are active: a part of the prefrontal cortex linked to rational problem solving and an area called the anterior insula, which is associated with pain, disgust, and other unpleasant feelings. According to economist Colin Camerer (quoted in D'Antonio, 2004), "Basically the brain toggles between 'Yes, money is good' and 'Ugh, this guy is treating me like crap.'" People with greater activation of the prefrontal cortex are likely to accept low offers; those with greater activation of the anterior insula are likely to refuse. In fact, Camerer estimates that researchers can predict the outcome 70% of the time simply by looking at participants' brain scans.

Now, if only the apparently innate desire for fairness didn't lead human beings to inflict suffering so often on those whom they perceive as being unfair, and if only their ability to cooperate didn't lead so often to cooperation in waging war.

In this drawing, made from a video, the monkey on the right watches as the one on the left exchanges a token for a reward. Later, the observing monkey may refuse a lesser reward.

The Hindsight Bias

Would you have predicted the results of the last election? Would you have predicted the most recent Polaris Music Prize winner for best new album? When people learn the outcome of an event or the answer to a question, they are often sure that they "knew it all along." Armed with the wisdom of hindsight, they see the outcome that actually occurred as inevitable, and they overestimate their ability to have predicted what happened beforehand (Fischhoff, 1975; Hawkins & Hastie, 1990). This **hindsight bias** shows up all the time in evaluating relationships ("I always knew their marriage wouldn't last"), medical judgments ("I could have told you that mole was cancerous"), and military opinions ("The generals should have known that the other side would attack").

The hindsight bias can be adaptive. When we try to make sense of the past, we focus on explaining just one outcome, the one that actually occurred, because explaining outcomes that did not occur can be a waste of time. Then, in light of current knowledge, we reconstruct and misremember our previous judgment (Hoffrage, Hertwig, & Gigerenzer, 2000). But as Scott Hawkins and Reid Hastie (1990) wrote, "Hindsight biases represent the dark side of successful learning and judgment." They are the dark side because when we are sure that we knew something all along, we are also less willing to find out what we need to know in order to make accurate predictions in the future. In medical conferences, for example, when doctors are told what the post-mortem findings were for a patient who died, they tend to think the case was easier to diagnose than it actually was ("I would have known it was a brain tumour"), and so they learn less from the case than they should (Dawson et al., 1988).

Perhaps you feel that we are not telling you anything new because you have always known about the hindsight bias. But then, you may just have a hindsight bias about the hindsight bias.

hindsight bias The tendency to overestimate one's ability to have predicted an event once the outcome is known; the "I knew it all along" phenomenon.

The Confirmation Bias

When people want to make the most accurate judgment possible, they usually try to consider all the relevant information. But as we saw in Chapter 2, when they are thinking about an issue they already feel strongly about, they often succumb to the **confirmation bias**, paying attention only to evidence that confirms their belief and finding fault with evidence or arguments that point in a different direction (Edwards & Smith, 1996; Kunda, 1990; Nickerson, 1998). You rarely hear someone say, "Oh, thank you for explaining to me why my lifelong philosophy of childrearing (or politics, or investing) is wrong. I'm so grateful for the facts!" The person usually says, "Oh, buzz off, and take your cockamamie ideas with you."

Once you start looking for it, you will see the confirmation bias everywhere. Politicians brag about economic reports that confirm their party's position and dismiss counterevidence as biased or unimportant. Police officers who are convinced of a suspect's guilt take anything the suspect says or does as evidence that confirms it, including the suspect's claims of innocence (Davis, 2010). The confirmation bias also affects jury members. Instead of considering and weighing possible verdicts against the evidence, many people quickly construct a story about what happened and then consider only the evidence that supports their version of events. These same people are the most confident in their decisions and most likely to vote for an extreme verdict (Kuhn, Weinstock, & Flaton, 1994). We bet you can see the confirmation bias in your

confirmation bias The tendency to look for or pay attention to only information that confirms one's own belief.

Get INVOLVED!

CONFIRMING THE CONFIRMATION BIAS

Suppose someone deals out four cards, each with a letter on one side and a number on the other. You can see only one side of each card:

Your task is to find out whether the following rule is true: "If a card has a vowel on one side, then it has an even number on the other side." Which two cards do you need to turn over to find out?

The vast majority of people say they would turn over the E and the 6, but they are wrong. You do need to turn over the E (a vowel), because if the number on the other side is even, it confirms the rule, and if it is odd, the rule is false. However, the card with the 6 tells you nothing. The rule does *not* say that a card with an even number must always have a vowel on the other side. Therefore, it doesn't matter whether the 6 has a vowel or a consonant on the other side. The card you do need to turn over is the 7, because if it has a vowel on the other side, that fact disconfirms the rule.

People do poorly on this problem because they are biased to look for confirming evidence and to ignore the possibility of disconfirming evidence. Don't feel too bad if you missed it. Most judges, lawyers, and people with PhDs do, too.

CONNECT THE DOTS

Copy this figure, and try to connect the dots by using no more than four straight lines without lifting your pencil or pen. A line must pass through each point. Can you do it?

Most people have difficulty with this problem because they have a mental set to interpret the arrangement of dots as a square. They then assume that they can't extend a line beyond the apparent boundaries of the square. Now that you know this, you might try again if you haven't yet solved the puzzle. Some solutions are given at the end of this chapter.

own reactions to what you are learning in psychology. In thinking critically, most of us apply a double standard; we think most critically about results we dislike. That is why the scientific method can be so difficult: It forces us to consider evidence that disconfirms our beliefs.

Mental Sets

Another barrier to rational thinking is the development of a **mental set**, a tendency to try to solve new problems by using the same heuristics, strategies, and rules that worked in the past on similar problems. Mental sets make human learning and problem solving efficient; because of them, we do not have to keep reinventing the wheel. But mental sets are not helpful when a problem calls for fresh insights and methods. They cause us to cling rigidly to the same old assumptions and approaches, blinding us to better or more rapid solutions.

One general mental set is the tendency to find patterns in events. This tendency is adaptive because it helps us understand and exert some control over what happens in our lives. But it also leads us to see meaningful patterns even when they do not exist. For example, many people with arthritis think that their symptoms follow a pattern dictated by the weather. They suffer more, they say, when the barometric pressure changes or when the weather is damp or humid. Yet when researchers followed 18 arthritis patients for 15 months, no association whatsoever emerged between weather conditions and the patients' self-reported pain levels, their ability to function in daily life, or a doctor's evaluation of their joint tenderness (Redelmeier & Tversky, 1996). Of course, because of the confirmation bias, the patients refused to believe the results.

mental set   A tendency to solve problems using procedures that worked before on similar problems.

The Need for Cognitive Consistency

Mental sets and the confirmation bias cause us to avoid evidence that contradicts our beliefs. But what happens when disconfirming evidence finally smacks us in the face, and we cannot ignore or discount it any longer? For example, as the twentieth century rolled to an end, predictions of the end of the world escalated. Similar doomsday predictions have been made throughout history and continue to be made today. When these predictions fail, how come we never hear believers say, "Boy, what a fool I was"?

Thinking Critically

Ask Questions

Time and again, doomsday predictions fail. Why don't people who wrongly predict a devastating earthquake or the end of the world feel embarrassed when their forecasts flop?

cognitive dissonance A state of tension that occurs when a person holds two cognitions that are psychologically inconsistent, or when a person's belief is incongruent with his or her behaviour.

postdecision dissonance In the theory of cognitive dissonance, tension that occurs when you believe you may have made a bad decision.

According to the theory of **cognitive dissonance**, people will resolve such conflicts in predictable, though not always obvious, ways (Festinger, 1957). *Dissonance*, the opposite of consistency (*consonance*), is a state of tension that occurs when you hold either two cognitions (beliefs, thoughts, attitudes) that are psychologically inconsistent with one another, or a belief that is incongruent with your behaviour. This tension is uncomfortable, so you will be motivated to reduce it. You may do this by rejecting or modifying one of those inconsistent beliefs, changing your behaviour, denying the evidence, or rationalizing:

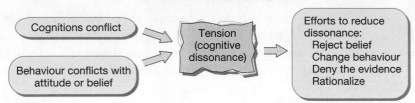

COGNITIVE DISSONANCE

Many years ago, in a famous field study, Leon Festinger and two associates explored people's reactions to failed prophecies by infiltrating a group of people who thought the world would end on December 21 (Festinger, Riecken, & Schachter, 1956). The group's leader, whom the researchers called Marian Keech, promised that the faithful would be picked up by a flying saucer and whisked to safety at midnight on December 20. Many of her followers quit their jobs and spent all their savings, waiting for the end to come. What would they do or say, Festinger and his colleagues wondered, to reduce the dissonance between "The world is still muddling along on the 21st" and "I predicted the end of the world and sold off all my worldly possessions"?

The researchers predicted that believers who had made no public commitment to the prophecy, who awaited the end of the world by themselves at home, would simply lose their faith. However, those who had acted on their conviction by selling their property and waiting with Keech for the spaceship would be in a state of dissonance. They would have to *increase* their religious belief to avoid the intolerable realization that they had behaved foolishly and others knew it. That is just what happened. At 4:45 A.M., long past the appointed hour of the saucer's arrival, the leader had a new vision. The world had been spared, she said, because of the impressive faith of her little band.

Cognitive-dissonance theory predicts that in more ordinary situations, too, people will resist or rationalize information that conflicts with their existing ideas, just as the people in the arthritis study did. For example, cigarette smokers are often in a state of dissonance, because smoking is dissonant with the fact that smoking causes illness. Smokers may try to reduce the dissonance by trying to quit, by rejecting evidence that smoking is bad, by persuading themselves that they will quit later on, by emphasizing the benefits of smoking ("A cigarette helps me relax"), or by deciding that they don't want a long life, anyhow ("It will be shorter but sweeter").

You are particularly likely to reduce dissonance under three conditions (Aronson, 2008):

1 **When you need to justify a choice or decision that you freely made.** All car dealers know about buyer's remorse: The second that people buy a car, they worry that they made the wrong decision or spent too much, a phenomenon called **postdecision dissonance.** You may try to resolve this dissonance by deciding that the car you chose (or the toaster, or house, or spouse) is really, truly the best in the

world. *Before* people make a decision, they can be open-minded, seeking information on the pros and cons of the choice at hand. *After* they make that choice, however, the confirmation bias will kick in, so that they will now notice all the good things about their decision and overlook or ignore evidence that they might have been wrong.

2   **When you need to justify behaviour that conflicts with your view of yourself.** If you consider yourself to be honest, cheating will put you in a state of dissonance. To avoid feeling like a hypocrite, you will try to reduce the dissonance by justifying your behaviour ("Everyone else does it"; "It's just this once"; "I had to do it to get into med school and learn to save lives"). Or if you see yourself as a kind person and you harm someone, you may reduce your dissonance by blaming the person you have victimized or by finding other self-justifying excuses.

3   **When you need to justify the effort put into a decision or choice.** The harder you work to reach a goal, or the more you suffer for it, the more you will try to convince yourself that you value the goal, even if the goal itself is not so great after all (Aronson & Mills, 1959). This explains why hazing, whether in social clubs, on athletic teams, or in the military, turns new recruits into loyal members (see Figure 9.2). You might think that people would hate the group that caused them pain and embarrassment. But the cognition "I went through a lot of awful stuff to join this group" is dissonant with the cognition "only to find I hate the group." Therefore, people must decide either that the hazing was not so bad or that they really like the group. This mental reevaluation is called the **justification of effort**, and it is one of the most popular methods of reducing dissonance.

Some people are secure enough to own up to their mistakes instead of justifying them, and individuals and cultures vary in the kinds of experiences that cause them to

justification of effort   The tendency of individuals to increase their liking for something that they have worked hard or suffered to attain; a common form of dissonance reduction.

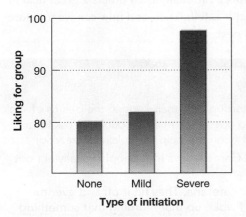

FIGURE 9.2   The Justification of Effort

The more effort you put into reaching a goal, the more highly you are likely to value it. As you can see in the graph on the left, after people listened to a boring group discussion, those who had first gone through a severe initiation to join the group rated it most highly (Aronson & Mills, 1959). In the photo on the right, new recruits at Canadian Forces Base Wainwright are forced to crawl through mud until they are covered from head to toe. They will probably become devoted to the military.

feel dissonance. However, the need for cognitive consistency in those beliefs that are most central to our sense of self and our values is universal (Tavris & Aronson, 2007).

Overcoming Our Cognitive Biases

Sometimes our mental biases are a good thing. For example, cognitive dissonance reduction helps us preserve our self-confidence and avoid sleepless nights second-guessing ourselves, and having a sense of fairness keeps us from behaving like self-centred louts. From this point of view, such biases are not so irrational after all. But our mental biases can also get us into trouble. The confirmation bias, the justification of effort, and a need to reduce postdecision dissonance permit people to stay stuck with decisions that eventually prove to be self-defeating, harmful, or incorrect. Physicians may stick with outdated methods, crown prosecutors may overlook evidence that a criminal suspect might be innocent, and managers may refuse to consider better business practices.

To make matters worse, most people have a "bias blind spot": They acknowledge that *other* people have biases that distort reality, but they think that they themselves are free of bias and see the world as it really is (Pronin, Gilovich, & Ross, 2004; Ross, 2010). This blind spot is itself a bias, and it is a dangerous one because it can prevent individuals, nations, ethnic groups, and religious groups from resolving conflicts with others. Each side thinks that its own proposals for ending a conflict, or its own analyses of political events, are reasonable and fair but the other side's are "biased."

Fortunately, the situation is not entirely hopeless. For one thing, people are not equally irrational in all situations. When they are doing things in which they have some expertise or are making decisions that have serious personal consequences, their cognitive biases often diminish (Smith & Kida, 1991). Further, once we understand a bias, we may, with some effort, be able to reduce or eliminate it, especially if we make an active, mindful effort to do so and take time to think carefully (Kida, 2006).

Some people, of course, seem to think more rationally than others a great deal of the time; we call them "intelligent." Just what is intelligence, and how can we measure and improve it? We take up these questions next.

quickQUIZ

✓• Quick Review on MyPsychLab

In hindsight, will you say this quiz was easy?

1. In 2001, an unknown person sent anthrax through the mail, causing the deaths of five people. Many people became afraid to open their mail, although the risk for any given individual was extremely small. What heuristics help to explain this reaction?

2. *True or false:* Research on the Ultimatum Game shows that people usually act out of rational self-interest.

3. Stu meets a young woman at the student cafeteria. They hit it off and eventually get married. Says Stu, "I knew when I woke up that morning that something special was about to happen." What cognitive bias is affecting his thinking, charmingly romantic though it is?

4. In a classic experiment on cognitive dissonance, students did some boring, repetitive tasks and then had to tell another student, who was waiting to participate in the study, that the work was interesting and fun (Festinger & Carlsmith, 1959). Half the students were offered $20 for telling this lie and the others only $1. Based on what you have learned about cognitive dissonance reduction, which students do you think decided later that the tasks had been fun after all? Why?

Answers:

1. the affect and availability heuristics 2. false 3. the hindsight bias 4. The students who got only $1 were more likely to say that the task had been fun. They were in a state of dissonance because "The task was as dull as dishwater" is dissonant with "I said I enjoyed it—and for a mere dollar, at that." Those who got $20 could rationalize that the large sum (which really was large in the 1950s) justified the lie.

YOU are about to learn . . .

◆ both sides of the debate about whether a single thing called "intelligence" actually exists.

◆ how the original purpose of intelligence testing changed when IQ tests came to North America.

◆ the difficulties of designing intelligence tests that are free of cultural influence.

MEASURING INTELLIGENCE: THE PSYCHOMETRIC APPROACH

Intelligent people disagree on just what intelligence is. Some equate it with the ability to reason abstractly, others with the ability to learn and profit from experience in daily life. Some emphasize the ability to think rationally, others the ability to act purposefully. These qualities are all probably part of what most people mean by **intelligence**, but theorists weigh them differently.

The traditional approach to intelligence, the **psychometric** approach, focuses on how well people perform on standardized aptitude tests, which are designed to measure the ability to acquire skills and knowledge. A typical intelligence test asks you to do several things: provide a specific bit of information, notice similarities between objects, solve arithmetic problems, define words, fill in the missing parts of incomplete pictures, arrange pictures in a logical order, arrange blocks to resemble a design, assemble puzzles, use a coding scheme, or judge what behaviour would be appropriate in a particular situation. Researchers use a statistical method called **factor analysis** to try to identify which basic abilities underlie performance on the various items. This procedure identifies clusters of correlated items that seem to be measuring some common ability, or factor.

Most psychometric psychologists believe that a general ability, or **g factor**, underlies the various abilities and talents measured by intelligence tests (Gottfredson, 2002; Jensen, 1998; Lubinski, 2004; Spearman, 1927; Wechsler, 1955). They can marshal a century of research to support their view (Lubinski, 2004). Tests of g do a good job of predicting not only academic achievement but also the cognitive complexity of people's work, occupational success, and eminence in many fields (Kuncel, Hezlett, & Ones, 2004; Schmidt & Hunter, 2004; Simonton & Song, 2009). But, as we will see, others dispute the existence of a global quality called "intelligence," observing that a person can excel in some kinds of reasoning and problem solving yet do poorly in others (Gould, 1994; Guilford, 1988). This disagreement over how to define intelligence has generated enormous debate among psychologists and has led some writers to argue, only half-jokingly, that intelligence is "whatever intelligence tests measure."

Although intelligence is something that psychologists find rather difficult to define, they have no problem asking students such as yourself what they think intelligence is! Researchers at the University of British Columbia (Paulhus et al., 2002) conducted a series of studies that examined who was considered by students to be *the* exemplar of intelligence. Students nominated a single person who exemplified intelligence. Before reading on—whom would you nominate? Interestingly, several people topped the lists in all 16 years. These individuals included thinkers (such as Einstein),

A psychologist gives a student an intelligence test.

◈ **Research**
Arthur Jensen

Charles Spearman

intelligence An inferred characteristic of an individual, usually defined as the ability to profit from experience, acquire knowledge, think abstractly, act purposefully, or adapt to changes in the environment.

psychometrics The measurement of mental abilities, traits, and processes.

factor analysis A statistical method for analyzing the intercorrelations among various measures or test scores; clusters of measures or scores that are highly correlated are assumed to measure the same underlying trait, ability, or aptitude (factor).

g factor A general intellectual ability assumed by many theorists to underlie specific mental abilities and talents.

◄⊙**Simulate**
Psychology Experiments Survey:
What Is Intelligence?

political leaders (including current and former prime ministers and other world leaders), artists (such as Picasso), inventors (such as Thomas Edison and Bill Gates), and writers (such as Shakespeare). Paulhus and colleagues found that although most of these people were well known, they were not simply famous individuals, as very few popular movie stars or athletes appeared on the lists. Thus, when people are deciding whether an individual is intelligent, individuals compare the features of well-known individuals with their notions of what trait constitutes intelligence. Interestingly, people were more likely to think a person was intelligent if that person was similar to themselves (Paulhus & Landholt, 2000). That is, science majors were more likely to think that Einstein was the exemplar of intelligence, whereas English majors were more likely to identify Shakespeare.

The Invention of IQ Tests

The first widely used intelligence test was devised in 1904, when the French Ministry of Education asked psychologist Alfred Binet (1857–1911) to find a way to identify children who were slow learners so that they could be given remedial work. The ministry was reluctant to let teachers identify such children because the teachers might have prejudices about poor children or might assume that shy or disruptive children were mentally impaired. The government wanted a more objective approach.

◆⊙**Research**
Alfred Binet

BINET'S BRAINSTORM.   Wrestling with the problem, Binet had a great insight: In the classroom, the responses of "dull" children resembled those of ordinary children of younger ages. Bright children, on the other hand, responded like children of older ages. The thing to measure, then, was a child's **mental age (MA)**, or level of intellectual development relative to that of other children. Then instruction could be tailored to the child's capabilities.

The test devised by Binet and his colleague, Théodore Simon, measured memory, vocabulary, and perceptual discrimination. Items ranged from those that most young children could do easily to those that only older children could handle, as determined by the testing of large numbers of children. A scoring system developed later by others used a formula in which a child's mental age was divided by the child's chronological age to yield an **intelligence quotient**, or **IQ** (a quotient is the result of division). Thus a child of 8 who performed like the average 10-year-old would have a mental age of 10 and an IQ of 125 (10 divided by 8, times 100). All average children, regardless of age, would have an IQ of 100 because mental age and chronological age would be the same.

However, this method of figuring IQ had serious flaws. At one age, scores might cluster tightly around the average, whereas at another age they might be more dispersed. As a result, the score necessary to be in the top 10% or 20% or 30% of your age group varied, depending on your age. Also, the IQ formula did not make sense for adults; a 50-year-old who scores like a 30-year-old does not have low intelligence! Today, therefore, intelligence tests are scored differently. The average is usually set arbitrarily at 100, and tests are constructed so that about two-thirds of all people score between 85 and 115. Individual scores are computed from tables based on established norms. These scores are still informally referred to as IQs, and they still reflect how a person compares with other people, either children of a particular age or adults in general. At all ages, the distribution of scores approximates a normal (bell-shaped) curve, with scores near the average (mean) more common than high or low scores (see Figure 9.3).

◄⊙**Simulate**
The Normal Curve

mental age (MA)   A measure of mental development expressed in terms of the average mental ability at a given age.

intelligence quotient (IQ)   A measure of intelligence originally computed by dividing a person's mental age by his or her chronological age and multiplying by 100; it is now derived from norms provided for standardized intelligence tests.

THE IQ TEST COMES TO NORTH AMERICA.   Stanford psychologist Lewis Terman revised Binet's test and established norms for North American children. His version, the *Stanford–Binet Intelligence Scale*, was first published in 1916 and has been updated several times since. The test asks a person to perform a variety of tasks: for example, to fill in missing words in sentences, answer questions requiring general knowledge, predict how a folded paper will look when unfolded, measure a quantity of water using two containers of different sizes, and distinguish between concepts that are similar but not exactly the same (such as, say, *vigour* and *energy*). The older the test-taker is, the more the test requires in the way of verbal comprehension and fluency, spatial ability, and reasoning.

Two decades later, David Wechsler designed another test expressly for adults, which became the *Wechsler Adult Intelligence Scale (WAIS)*; it was followed by the *Wechsler Intelligence Scale for Children (WISC)*. Although the Wechsler tests produced a general IQ score, they also provided specific scores for different kinds of ability. Verbal items tested vocabulary, arithmetic abilities, immediate memory span, ability to recognize similarities (e.g., "How are books and movies alike?"), and general knowledge and comprehension (e.g., "Who was Louis Riel?" "Why do people who want a divorce have to go to court?"). Performance items tested nonverbal skills, such as the ability to recreate a block design within a specified time limit and to identify a part missing from a picture. The current versions of the Wechsler tests have more subtests and, in addition to an overall IQ score, they yield separate scores for verbal comprehension, perceptual reasoning, processing speed, and working memory (the ability to hold information in mind so that it can be used for a task). (See Figure 9.4 for some sample items.)

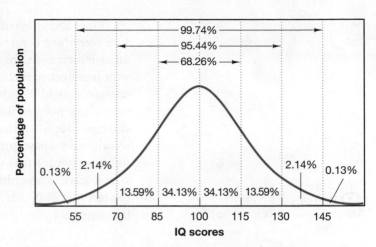

FIGURE 9.3 Expected Distribution of IQ Scores

In a large population, IQ scores tend to be distributed on a normal (bell-shaped) curve. On most tests, about 68% of all people will score between 85 and 115; about 95% will score between 70 and 130; and about 99.7% will score between 55 and 145. In any actual sample, however, the distribution will depart somewhat from the theoretical ideal.

◈ **Research**
Lewis Terman

David Wechsler

FIGURE 9.4 Performance Tasks on the Wechsler Tests

Nonverbal items such as these are particularly useful for measuring the abilities of those who have poor hearing, are not fluent in the tester's language, have limited education, or resist doing classroom-type problems. A large gap between a person's verbal score and performance on nonverbal tasks such as these sometimes indicates a specific learning problem. (Object assembly, digit symbol, and picture completion are adapted from Cronbach, 1990.)

Picture arrangement
(Arrange the panels to make a meaningful story)

Object assembly
(Put together a jigsaw puzzle)

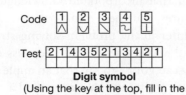

Digit symbol
(Using the key at the top, fill in the appropriate symbol beneath each number)

Picture completion
(Supply the missing feature)

Block design
(Copy the design shown, using another set of blocks)

Binet had emphasized that his test merely *sampled* intelligence and did not measure everything covered by that term. A test score, he said, could be useful, along with other information, for predicting school performance, but it should not be confused with intelligence itself. The tests were designed to be given individually, so that the test-giver could tell when a child was ill or nervous, had poor vision, or was unmotivated. The purpose was to identify children with learning problems, not to rank all children. But when intelligence testing was brought from France to North America, its original purpose got lost at sea. In North America, IQ tests became widely used not to bring slow learners up to the average, but to categorize people in school and in the armed services according to their presumed "natural ability." The testers overlooked the fact that in North America, with its many ethnic groups, people did not all share the same background and experience (Gould, 1996).

◉ Watch
Are Intelligence Tests Valid?

✳ Explore
Correlations between IQ Scores of
Persons of Varying Relationships

CULTURE and *Intelligence Testing*

Can IQ Tests Ever Be Culturally Fair?

Intelligence tests developed between World War I and the 1960s for use in schools favoured city children over rural ones, middle-class children over poor ones, and white children over nonwhite children. One item, for example, asked whether the Emperor Concerto was written by Beethoven, Mozart, Bach, Brahms, or Mahler. (The answer is Beethoven.) Critics complained that the tests did not measure the kinds of knowledge and skills that indicate intelligent behaviour in a minority neighbourhood or in the Far North. They feared that because teachers thought IQ scores revealed the limits of a child's potential, low-scoring children would not get the educational attention or encouragement they needed.

Sometimes, despite your best intentions, you may have only limited success trying to reduce cultural bias. For instance, to illustrate this problem, Darou (1992) uses the following intelligence-test item: "Saw is to whine as snake is to _____". Because the item deals with tools and animals, it seems fairly culturally neutral. However, when Darou tested the item, he rapidly found out that indigenous peoples of the Far North had limited experience with snakes and that they had more experience with chain saws or hand saws, neither of which make the mechanical "whining" sound of table saws. As such, Darou quickly learned that despite his best intentions, this test item was biased.

Test-makers responded by trying to construct tests that were unaffected by culture or that incorporated knowledge and skills common to many different cultures. But these efforts were disappointing. One reason was that cultures differ in the problem-solving strategies they emphasize (Serpell, 1994). In the West, white, middle-class children typically learn to classify things by category—to say that an apple and a peach are similar because they are both fruits, and that a saw and a rake are similar because they are both tools. But children who are not trained in middle-class ways of sorting things may classify objects according to their sensory qualities or functions. For example, they may say that an apple and a peach are similar because they taste good. We think that's a charming and innovative answer, but it is one that test-givers have interpreted as less intelligent (Miller-Jones, 1989).

Thinking ⚙ Critically

Consider Other Interpretations

When tests find IQ differences between groups of children from different cultures, many people assume that the children who score lower are inherently less intelligent. What other explanations are possible?

It is not the case that middle-class urban children always excel on intelligence tests. For instance, using a pictorial test of intelligence, researchers at McGill University found that Inuit children from northern Quebec consistently scored higher than predicted by the U.S. norms (Wright, Taylor, & Ruggiero, 1996). The intelligence test they used in this study required participants to pick a patterned piece to fit into a hole cut from a larger pattern. It appears that individuals with intensive hunting and navigating experience tend to excel on tests that measure spatial or pattern discrimination and/or pattern reproduction, like the one used in the study above (Morton, Allen, & Williams, 1994).

Testing experts also discovered that cultural values and experiences affect many things besides responses to specific test items. These include a person's general attitude toward exams, comfort in the settings required for testing, motivation, rapport with the test-giver, competitiveness, comfort in solving problems independently rather than with others, and familiarity with the conventions for taking tests (Anastasi & Urbina, 1997; López, 1995; Sternberg, 2004).

Moreover, people's performance on IQ and other mental-ability tests may depend on their own expectations about how they will do, and those expectations are affected by cultural stereotypes. Stereotypes that portray women or members of certain ethnic, age, or socioeconomic groups as unintelligent can actually depress the performance of people in those groups. You might think that a woman would say, "So sexists think women are dumb at math? I'll show them!" or that an indigenous person would say, "So racists believe that I'm not as smart as whites? Just give me that exam." But often that is not what happens.

On the contrary, such individuals commonly feel a burden of doubt about their abilities that Claude Steele (1992, 1997) has labelled **stereotype threat**. The threat occurs when people believe that if they do not do well, they will confirm the stereotypes about their group. Negative thoughts intrude and disrupt their concentration ("I hate this test," "I'm no good at math") (Cadinu et al., 2005). The resulting anxiety may then worsen their performance or kill their motivation to even try to do well.

stereotype threat A burden of doubt a person feels about his or her performance, due to negative stereotypes about his or her group's abilities.

STEREOTYPE THREAT

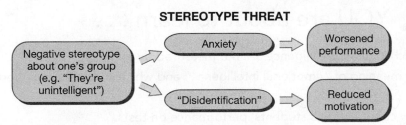

More than 300 studies have shown that stereotype threat can affect the test performance of many different minorities, low-income people, women, and elderly people, all of whom perform better when they are not feeling self-conscious about themselves as members of negatively stereotyped groups (e.g., Aronson, 2010; Brown & Josephs, 1999; Inzlicht & Ben-Zeev, 2000; Levy, 1996; Quinn & Spencer, 2001; Steele & Aronson, 1995). Anything that increases the salience of group stereotypes can increase stereotype threat and affect performance, including taking the test in a setting where you are the only member from your group, or being asked to state your ethnicity before taking the test. The media and even some scholars have sometimes misinterpreted these results to mean that stereotype threat is the *only* reason for group differences in test performance, which it is not (Sackett, Hardison, & Cullen, 2004). It can be, however, an important contributing factor.

Whether or not you feel "stereotype threat" depends on what category you are identifying with at the time. Asian women do worse on math tests when they see themselves as "women" (stereotype = poor at math) rather than as "Asians" (stereotype = good at math) (Shih, Pittinsky, & Ambady, 1999).

What can be done to reduce stereotype threat? One possibility is simply to tell people about it. When students taking introductory statistics were given a difficult test, with no mention of stereotype threat, women did worse than men. But when students were informed about stereotype threat, the sex difference disappeared (Johns, Schmader, & Martens, 2005). (See how psychology can help people?)

This simple approach is unlikely to eliminate all group differences in test scores, however. And that fact points to a dilemma at the heart of intelligence and mental-ability testing. Intelligence and other mental-ability tests put some groups of people at a disadvantage, yet they also measure skills and knowledge useful in the classroom. How can psychologists and educators recognize and accept cultural differences and, at the same time, promote the mastery of the skills, knowledge, and attitudes that can help people succeed in school and in the larger society?

---

quickQUIZ

✔•☐Quick Review on **MyPsychLab**

What's your Quiz Quotient (QQ)?

1. What was Binet's great insight?
2. *True or false:* IQ tests designed to avoid cultural bias frequently fail to eliminate such biases.
3. Hilda, who is 68, is about to take an IQ test, but she is worried because she knows that older people are often assumed to have diminished mental abilities. Hilda is being affected by _____.

Answers:

1. Mental age does not necessarily correspond to chronological age. 2. true 3. stereotype threat

 # YOU are about to learn . . .

- which kinds of intelligence are not measured by standard IQ tests.
- the meaning of "emotional intelligence" and why it might be as important as IQ.
- how culture affects students' performance on tests.

DISSECTING INTELLIGENCE: THE COGNITIVE APPROACH

Critics of standard intelligence tests point out that such tests tell us little about *how* a person goes about answering questions and solving problems. Nor do the tests explain why people with low scores often behave intelligently in real life, making smart consumer decisions, winning at the racetrack, and making wise choices in their relationships instead of repeating the same dumb patterns. Some researchers, therefore, have rejected the psychometric approach in favour of a *cognitive approach*, which assumes that there are many kinds of intelligence and emphasizes the strategies people use when thinking about a problem and arriving at a solution.

The Triarchic Theory

One well-known cognitive theory is Robert Sternberg's **triarchic theory of intelligence** (1988) (*triarchic* means "three-part"). Sternberg (2004) defines intelligence as "the skills and knowledge needed for success in life, according to one's own definition of success, within one's sociocultural context." He distinguishes three aspects of intelligence:

1   **Componential intelligence** refers to the information-processing strategies you draw on when you are thinking intelligently about a problem. These mental "components" include recognizing and defining the problem, selecting a strategy for solving it, mastering and carrying out the strategy, and evaluating the result. Such components are required in every culture but are applied to different kinds of problems. One culture may emphasize the use of these components to solve abstract problems, whereas another may emphasize using the same components to maintain smooth relations.

Some of the operations in componential intelligence require not only analytic skills but also **metacognition**, the knowledge or awareness of your own cognitive processes and the ability to monitor and control those processes. Students who are weak in metacognition fail to notice when a passage in a textbook is difficult, and they do not always realize that they haven't understood what they've been reading. As a result, they spend too little time on difficult material and too much time on material they already know. They are overconfident about their comprehension and memory, and are surprised when they do poorly on exams (Dunlosky & Lipko, 2007). In contrast, students who are strong in metacognition check their comprehension by restating what they have read, testing themselves, backtracking when necessary, and questioning what they are reading. When time is limited, they tackle fairly easy material (where the payoff will be great), and then move on to more difficult material; as a result, they learn better (Metcalfe, 2009).

It works in the other direction, too: The kind of intelligence that enhances academic performance can also help you develop metacognitive skills. Students with poor academic skills typically fail to realize how little they know; they think they're doing fine (Dunning, 2005). The very weaknesses that keep them from doing well on tests or in their courses also keep them from realizing their weaknesses. In one study, students in a psychology course estimated how well they had just done on an exam relative to other students. As you can see in Figure 9.5,

triarchic [try-ARE-kick] theory of intelligence   A theory of intelligence that emphasizes information-processing strategies, the ability to creatively transfer skills to new situations, and the practical application of intelligence.

metacognition   The knowledge or awareness of one's own cognitive processes, and the ability to monitor and control those processes.

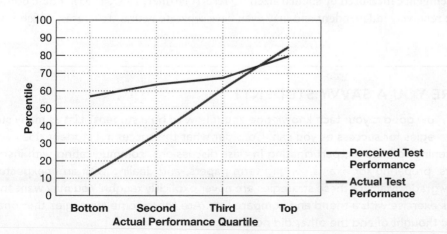

FIGURE 9.5   Ignorance Is Bliss
In school and in other settings, people who perform poorly often have poor metacognitive skills and therefore fail to recognize their own lack of competence. As you can see, the lower that students scored on an exam, the greater the gap between how they thought they had done and how they actually had done (Dunning et al., 2003).

those who had performed in the bottom quartile greatly overestimated their own performance (Dunning et al., 2003). In contrast, people with strong academic skills tend to be more realistic. Often they even underestimate slightly how their performance compares with the performance of others.

2 **Experiential or creative intelligence** refers to your creativity in transferring skills to new situations. People with experiential intelligence cope well with novelty and learn quickly to make new tasks automatic. Those who are lacking in this area perform well only under a narrow set of circumstances. For example, a student may do well in school, where assignments have specific due dates and feedback is immediate, but be less successful after graduation if her job requires her to set her own deadlines and her employer doesn't tell her how she is doing.

3 **Contextual or practical intelligence** refers to the practical application of intelligence, which requires you to take into account the different contexts in which you find yourself. If you are strong in contextual intelligence, you know when to adapt to the environment (you are in a dangerous neighbourhood, so you become more vigilant). You know when to change environments (you had planned to be a teacher but discover that you dislike working with kids, so you switch to accounting). And you know when to fix the situation (your marriage is rocky, so you and your spouse go for counselling).

Contextual knowledge allows you to acquire **tacit knowledge**—practical, action-oriented strategies for achieving your goals that are usually not formally taught or even verbalized but instead must be inferred by observing others. University professors, business managers, and salespeople who have tacit knowledge and practical intelligence tend to be better than others at their jobs. Among students, tacit knowledge about how to be a good student actually predicts academic success as well as many other measures (Sternberg et al., 2000).

Domains of Intelligence

Other psychologists, too, are expanding the definitions of intelligence. As we saw, they point out that someone who excels in one area, or domain, is not necessarily intelligent in all others. Some argue that certain domains, such as musical intelligence, kinesthetic intelligence (the grace and physical self-awareness of athletes and dancers), and the capacity for insight into oneself and others, are as important as the kind of intelligence measured by standardized IQ tests (Gardner, 1983, 1995). These domains are relatively independent and may even have separate neural structures, which is why

"You're wise, but you lack tree smarts."

⬥ Research
Howard Gardner

tacit knowledge Strategies for success that are not explicitly taught but that instead must be inferred.

Get **INVOLVED!**

ARE YOU A SAVVY STUDENT?

How good is your tacit knowledge about how to be a student? List as many strategies for success as you can. Consider what the successful student does when listening to lectures, participating in class discussions, communicating with instructors, preparing for exams, writing term papers, and dealing with an unexpectedly low grade. Many of these strategies are never explicitly taught. You may want to do this exercise with a friend and compare lists. Are there some strategies that one of you thought of and the other did not?

people with brain damage often lose one kind of intelligence without losing their competence in the others.

One of the most important kinds of non-intellectual "smarts" may be **emotional intelligence**, the ability to identify your own and other people's emotions accurately, express your emotions clearly, and manage emotions in yourself and others (Mayer & Salovey, 1997; Salovey & Grewal, 2005). People with high emotional intelligence, popularly known as "EQ," use their emotions to motivate themselves, to spur creative thinking, and to deal empathically with others. People who are lacking in emotional intelligence are often unable to identify their own emotions; they may insist that they are not depressed when a relationship ends, for example, but meanwhile they start drinking too much, become extremely irritable, and stop going out with friends. They may express emotions inappropriately, perhaps by acting violently or impulsively when they are angry or worried. They often misread nonverbal signals from others; they will give a long-winded account of all their problems even when the listener is obviously bored.

People with emotional intelligence are skilled at reading nonverbal emotional cues. Which of these children do you think feels the most confident and relaxed, which one is shyest, and which feels most anxious? What cues are you using to answer?

Simulate
Gardner's Theory of Intelligence

Studies of brain-damaged adults suggest a biological basis for emotional intelligence. Neuroscientist Antonio Damasio (1994) has studied patients with prefrontal-lobe damage that makes them incapable of experiencing strong feelings. Although they score in the normal range on conventional mental tests, these patients persistently make "dumb," irrational decisions in their lives because they cannot assign values to different options based on their own emotional reactions and cannot read emotional cues from others. As we discuss again in Chapter 11, feeling and thinking are not always incompatible, as many people assume; in fact, one often requires the other.

So just what is the relation between brain and intelligence? Unfortunately, the answer is far from clear. For instance, a relatively simple way to investigate the relation between brain and intelligence is to look at the size of the brain and determine whether it is related to performance on intelligence tests. Researchers at the University of Western Ontario (Wickett, Vernon, & Lee, 2000) found that brain volume is significantly correlated with IQ. And researchers at the University of Victoria and the University of British Columbia found that there is a relation between the size of the part of the brain required for integration of information from the two hemispheres and IQ (Strauss, Wada, & Hunter, 1994). That is, they found that as the size of the corpus callosum increased, so did intelligence. However, they caution that their relation may actually reflect the processing required by the types of questions on the intelligence test, rather than being directly related to intelligence.

Thinking Critically about Intelligence(s)

Not everyone is enthusiastic about the proliferation of new "intelligences." Some argue that emotional intelligence is not a special cognitive ability but a collection of ordinary personality traits, such as empathy and extroversion (Matthews, Zeidner, & Roberts, 2003). Others maintain that abilities such as musical or kinesthetic intelligence are better thought of as talents, or else the very concept of intelligence loses all meaning. What is to prevent someone from adding "farming intelligence" or "financial intelligence" to the list?

Nonetheless, broadening the notion of intelligence has been useful for several reasons. It has forced us to think more critically about what we mean by intelligence and to consider how different abilities help us function in our everyday lives. It has

emotional intelligence The ability to identify your own and other people's emotions accurately, express your emotions clearly, and regulate emotions in yourself and others.

Thinking Critically Define Your Terms

Theorists who argue for an expanded definition of intelligence would say that the Dixie Chicks have musical intelligence, a surveyor has spatial intelligence, and a compassionate friend has emotional intelligence. Should the definition be broadened in this way? Or are these abilities better defined as talents?

⊙ Watch
Piano Lessons and Development

generated research on tests that provide ongoing feedback to the test-taker so that the person can learn from the experience and improve his or her performance (Sternberg, 2004). The cognitive approach has also led to a focus on teaching children strategies for improving their abilities in reading, writing, doing homework, and taking tests.

For example, children have been taught to manage their time so that they don't procrastinate and to study differently for multiple-choice exams than for essay exams (Sternberg et al., 1995). Most important, new approaches to intelligence encourage us to overcome the mental set of assuming that the only kind of ability necessary for a successful life is the kind captured by IQ tests.

For a summary of the differences between the psychometric and cognitive approaches, see Review 9.1.

Motivation, Hard Work, and Intellectual Success

Even with a high IQ, emotional intelligence, and practical know-how, you still might get nowhere at all. Talent, unlike cream, does not inevitably rise to the top; success also depends on drive and determination.

⊙ Watch
Mainstreaming Children with Special Needs

Consider a finding from one of the longest-running psychological studies ever conducted. In 1921, researchers began following more than 1500 children with IQ scores in the top 1% of the distribution. These boys and girls were nicknamed Termites after Lewis Terman, who originally directed the research. The Termites started out bright, physically healthy, sociable, and well adjusted. As they entered adulthood, most became successful in the traditional ways of the times: men in careers and women as homemakers (Sears & Barbee, 1977; Terman & Oden, 1959). However, some gifted men failed to live up to their early promise, dropping out of school or drifting into low-level work. When the researchers compared the 100 most successful men in the

REVieW 9.1

The Psychometric and Cognitive Approaches to Intelligence, Compared

	Psychometric	Cognitive
Main focus	How well people perform on standardized tests	Strategies people use when solving problems
What intelligence is	A general intellectual ability captured by IQ scores; or a range of specific verbal and nonverbal abilities	Many different skills and talents in addition to intellectual ones
Deals with emotional intelligence?	No	Yes
Deals with practical intelligence?	No	Yes
Uses well-validated standardized tests?	Yes	Varies with the skill being tested

Terman study with the 100 least successful, they found that the successful men were ambitious, were socially active, had many interests, and had been encouraged by their parents. The least successful drifted casually through life. There was no average difference in IQ between the two groups.

Once you are motivated to succeed intellectually, you need self-discipline to reach your goals. In a longitudinal study of an ethnically diverse neighbourhood school, grade 8 students were assigned a self-discipline score based on the students' self-reports, parents' reports, teachers' reports, and questionnaires (Duckworth & Seligman, 2005). They also included a behavioural measure of self-discipline, the teenagers' ability to delay gratification. (The teens had to choose between taking an envelope containing a dollar and returning it in exchange for getting two dollars a week later.) Self-discipline counted for more than twice as much of the variance in the students' final grades and achievement-test scores as IQ did (see also Chapter 13). As you can see in Figure 9.6, when the researchers divided the students into five groups (quintiles) based on their IQ scores, correlations between self-discipline and academic performance were much stronger than those between IQ and academic performance.

Self-discipline and motivation to work hard at intellectual tasks depend, in turn, on your attitudes about intelligence and achievement, which are strongly influenced by cultural values. For many years, Harold Stevenson and his colleagues studied attitudes toward achievement in Asia and the United States, comparing large samples of grade-school children, parents, and teachers in Minneapolis, Chicago, Sendai (Japan), Taipei (Taiwan), and Beijing (Stevenson, Chen, & Lee, 1993; Stevenson & Stigler, 1992). Their results have much to teach us about the cultivation of intellect.

In 1980, the Asian children far outperformed the North American children on a broad battery of mathematical and reading tests. On computations and word problems, there was virtually no overlap between schools, with the lowest-scoring Beijing schools doing better than the highest-scoring North American schools. (A similar gap occurred in reading scores.) By 1990, the gulf between the Asian and North American children had grown even greater. Only 4% of the Chinese children and 10% of the Japanese children had math scores as low as those of the *average* North American child. These differences could not be accounted for by educational resources: The Chinese

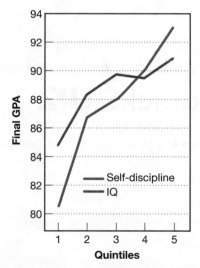

FIGURE 9.6 Grades, IQ, and Self-discipline

When researchers divided grade 8 students into five groups (quintiles) based on their IQ scores and then followed them for a year to test their academic achievement, they found that self-discipline was a stronger predictor of success than IQ was (Duckworth & Seligman, 2005).

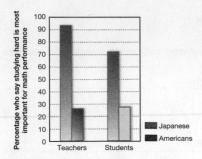

FIGURE 9.7 What's the Secret of Math Success?

Japanese schoolteachers and students are much more likely than their North American counterparts to believe that the secret to doing well in math is working hard. North Americans tend to think that you either have mathematical intelligence or you don't.

had worse facilities and larger classes than the North Americans, and on average, the Chinese parents were poorer and less educated than the North American parents. Nor did it have anything to do with intellectual abilities in general; the North American children were just as knowledgeable and capable as the Asian children on tests of general information.

But the Asian and North American children were worlds apart in their attitudes, expectations, and efforts:

◆ **Beliefs about intelligence.** North American parents, teachers, and children were far more likely than Asians to believe that mathematical ability is innate (see Figure 9.7). North Americans tended to think that if you have this ability you don't have to work hard, and if you don't have it, there's no point in trying.

◆ **Standards.** North American parents had far lower standards for their children's performance; they were satisfied with scores barely above average on a 100-point test. In contrast, Chinese and Japanese parents were happy only with very high scores.

◆ **Values.** North American students did not value education as much as Asian students did, and they were more complacent about mediocre work. When asked what they would wish for if a wizard could give them anything they wanted, more than 60% of the Chinese grade 5 students named something related to their education. Can you guess what the North American children wanted? A majority said money or possessions.

When it comes to intellect, then, it's not just what you've got that counts, but what you do with it. Complacency, fatalism, low standards, and a desire for immediate gratification can prevent people from recognizing what they don't know and reduce their efforts to learn.

quickQUIZ

✓ **Quick Review** on **MyPsychLab**

We hope you're not feeling complacent about your quiz performance.

1. What goals do cognitive theories of intelligence have that psychometric theories do not?
2. Logan understands the material in his statistics class, but on tests he spends the entire period on the most difficult problems and never even gets to the problems he can solve easily. According to the triarchic theory of intelligence, which aspect of intelligence does he need to improve?
3. Tracy does not have an unusually high IQ, but at work she is quickly promoted because she knows how to set priorities, communicate with management, and make others feel valued. Tracy has _____ knowledge about how to succeed on the job.
4. In a study of grade 8 students, _____ was more strongly correlated with school performance than _____ was.
5. What is wrong with defining intelligence as "whatever intelligence tests measure"?

Answers:

1. to understand people's strategies for solving problems and use this information to improve mental performance 2. componential intelligence (specifically, metacognition) 3. tacit 4. self-discipline; IQ 5. This definition implies that a low score must be entirely the scorer's fault rather than the fault of the test. But the test-taker may be intelligent in ways that the test fails to measure, and the test may be measuring traits other than intelligence.

YOU are about to learn . . .

- ◆ whether animals can think.
- ◆ whether some animal species can master aspects of human language.

ANIMAL MINDS

A green heron swipes some bread from a picnicker's table and scatters the crumbs on a nearby stream. When a minnow rises to the bait, the heron strikes, swallowing its prey before you can say "dinnertime." A sea otter, floating calmly on its back, bangs a mussel shell against a stone that is resting on its stomach. When the shell cracks apart, the otter devours the tasty morsel inside, tucks the stone under its flipper, and dives for another shell, which it will open in the same way. Incidents such as these and scores of others have convinced some biologists, psychologists, and ethologists that we are not the only animals with cognitive abilities—that "dumb beasts" are not so dumb after all. But how smart are they?

How smart is this otter?

Animal Intelligence

In the 1920s, Wolfgang Köhler (1925) put chimpanzees in situations in which some tempting bananas were just out of reach and watched to see what the apes would do. Most did nothing, but a few turned out to be quite clever. If the bananas were outside the cage, the chimp might pull them in with a stick. If they were hanging overhead, and there were boxes in the cage, the chimp might pile up the boxes and climb on top of them to reach the fruit. Often the solution came after the chimp had been sitting quietly for a while. It appeared as though the animal had been thinking about the problem and was struck by a sudden insight.

Learning theorists felt that this seemingly impressive behaviour could be accounted for perfectly well by the standard principles of operant learning, without resorting to mental explanations (see Chapter 7). Because of their influence, for years any scientist

In an early study of animal intelligence, Sultan, a talented chimpanzee studied by Wolfgang Köhler, was able to figure out how to reach a cluster of bananas by stacking some boxes and climbing on top of them.

who claimed that animals could think was likely to be ignored or laughed at. Today, however, the study of animal intelligence is booming, especially in the interdisciplinary field of **cognitive ethology**. (Ethology is the study of animal behaviour, especially in natural environments.) Cognitive ethologists argue that some animals can anticipate future events, make plans, and coordinate their activities with those of their comrades (Griffin, 2001).

When we think about animal cognition, we must be careful, because even complex behaviour that appears to be purposeful can be genetically prewired and automatic (Wynne, 2004). The assassin bug of South America catches termites by gluing nest material on its back as camouflage, but it is hard to imagine how the bug's tiny dab of brain tissue could enable it to plan this strategy consciously. Yet explanations of animal behaviour that leave out any sort of consciousness at all and that attribute animals' actions entirely to instinct do not seem to account for some of the amazing things that animals can do. Like the otter that uses a stone to crack mussel shells, many animals use objects in the natural environment as rudimentary tools, and in some nonhuman primates the behaviour is learned.

For example, chimpanzee mothers occasionally show their young how to use stones to open hard nuts (Boesch, 1991). Orangutans in one particular Sumatran swamp have learned to use sticks as tools, held in their mouths, to pry insects from holes in tree trunks and to get seeds out of cracks in a bulblike fruit, whereas nearby groups of orangutans use only brute force to get to the delicacies (van Schaik, 2006). Even some nonprimates may have the capacity to learn to use tools, although the evidence remains controversial among ethologists. Female bottlenose dolphins off the coast of Australia attach sea sponges to their beaks while hunting for food, which protects them from sharp coral and stinging stonefish, and they seem to have acquired this unusual skill from their mothers (Krützen et al., 2005). Is this yet another case of mothers telling their daughters what to wear?

In the laboratory, nonhuman primates have accomplished even more surprising things. For example, dozens of studies have found that chimpanzees have a rudimentary sense of number. In one study, chimpanzees compared two pairs of food wells containing chocolate chips. One pair might contain, say, five chips and three chips, the other four chips and three chips. Allowed to choose which pair they wanted, the chimps almost always chose the one with the higher combined total, showing some sort of summing ability (Rumbaugh, Savage-Rumbaugh, & Pate, 1988). Chimpanzees can even remember over a period of 20 minutes which of two containers holds more bananas (e.g., five versus eight, or six versus ten), after watching the bananas being placed one at a time into the containers. In fact, they do as well as young children on this task (Beran & Beran, 2004).

One of the most controversial questions about animal cognition is whether any animals besides human beings have a **theory of mind**: a system of beliefs about the way one's own mind and the minds of others work, and an understanding of how thoughts and feelings affect behaviour. A theory of mind enables you to draw conclusions about the intentions, feelings, and beliefs of others; empathize with others ("What would I experience if I were in the other person's position?"); deceive others; recognize when someone else is lying; recognize yourself in a mirror; and know when others can or cannot see you. In human beings, a theory of mind starts to develop in the second year and is clearly present by about age 3 or 4 (see Chapter 13).

Some researchers believe that the great apes (chimpanzees, gorillas, and orangutans), dolphins, and elephants have certain abilities that reflect a theory of mind

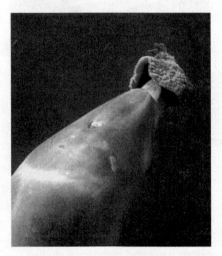

Dodger, a two-year-old dolphin In Shark Bay, Australia, carries a sea sponge on her sensitive beak as protection against stinging creatures and sharp coral. Dolphin "sponge moms" apparently teach the behaviour to their daughters.

cognitive ethology The study of cognitive processes in nonhuman animals.

theory of mind   A system of beliefs about the way one's own mind and the minds of others work, and of how individuals are affected by their beliefs and feelings.

(de Waal, 2001; Plotnik, de Waal, & Reiss, 2006; Suddendorf & Whiten, 2001). In addition, chimpanzees console other chimps who are in distress, use deceptive tactics when competing for food, and point to draw attention to objects, suggesting that they are able to grasp what is going on in another chimp's mind. In the wild, when one male African chimp makes an exaggerated scratching movement on part of its body during social grooming—say, on the forehead—a comrade will then groom the indicated spot, even if he was already grooming some other spot (Pika & Mitani, 2006). Chimps and even monkeys may also be capable of some metacognition. When they are tested on a new task, they will sometimes avoid difficult trials in which they are likely to be wrong. And they will press an icon on a touch screen to request "hints" provided by their human observers when they are unsure of the correct response, even when seeking a hint means getting a lesser reward for a correct answer (Kornell, 2009). These findings suggest that the animals know what they know and don't know.

Animals and Language

A primary ingredient of human cognition is *language*, the ability to combine elements that are themselves meaningless into an infinite number of utterances that convey meaning. Language is often regarded as the last bastion of human uniqueness, a result of evolutionary forces that produced our species (see Chapter 3). Do animals have anything comparable? Many people have wished they could ask their pet what it's like to be a dog, or a cat, or a horse. If only animals could speak!

To qualify as a language, a communication system must meet certain criteria. It must use combinations of sounds, gestures, or symbols that are *meaningful*, not random. It must permit *displacement*, communication about objects and events that are not present here and now but rather are displaced in time or space. And it must have a grammar (syntax) that permits *productivity*, the ability to produce and comprehend an infinite number of new utterances. By these criteria, no nonhuman species has its own language. Animals do communicate, of course, using gestures, body postures, facial expressions, vocalizations, and odours. Some of these signals have highly specific meanings. For example, vervet monkeys seem to have separate calls to warn about leopards versus eagles versus snakes (Cheney & Seyfarth, 1985). But vervets cannot combine these sounds to produce entirely novel utterances, as in "Look out, Harry, that eagle-eyed leopard is a real snake-in-the-grass."

Perhaps, however, some animals could acquire language if they got a little help from their human friends. Since the 1960s, many researchers have provided such help. Because the vocal tract of an ape does not permit speech, most researchers have used innovative approaches that rely on gestures or visual symbols. In one project, chimpanzees learned to use as words geometric plastic shapes arranged on a magnetic board (Premack & Premack, 1983). In another, they learned to punch symbols on a keyboard monitored by a computer (Rumbaugh, 1977). In yet another, they learned hundreds of signs in American Sign Language (ASL) (Fouts & Rigby, 1977; Gardner & Gardner, 1969).

Animals in these studies learned to follow instructions, answer questions, and make requests. They even seemed to use their newfound skills to apologize for being disobedient, scold their trainers, and talk to themselves. Koko, a lowland gorilla, reportedly used signs to say that she felt happy or sad, to refer to past and future events, to mourn for her dead pet kitten, and to lie when she did

Kanzi, a bonobo who answers questions and makes requests by punching symbols on a specially designed computer keyboard, also understands short English sentences. Kanzi is shown here with researcher Sue Savage-Rumbaugh.

Alex was a remarkably clever bird. His abilities have raised intriguing questions about the intelligence of animals and their capacity for specific aspects of language.

something naughty (Patterson & Linden, 1981). Most important, the animals combined individual signs or symbols into longer utterances that they had never seen before.

Unfortunately, in their desire to talk to the animals and their affection for their primate friends, some early researchers overinterpreted the animals' utterances, reading all sorts of meanings and intentions into a single sign or symbol, ignoring scrambled word order ("banana eat me") and unwittingly giving nonverbal cues that might enable the apes to respond correctly. But over the past few decades, as researchers have improved their techniques, they have discovered that with careful training, chimps can indeed acquire some aspects of language, including the ability to use symbols to refer to objects. Some animals have also used signs spontaneously to converse with each other, suggesting that they are not merely imitating or trying to get a reward (Van Cantfort & Rimpau, 1982). Bonobos (a type of ape) are especially adept at language. One bonobo named Kanzi has learned to understand English words, short sentences, and keyboard symbols without formal training (Savage-Rumbaugh & Lewin, 1994; Savage-Rumbaugh, Shanker, & Taylor, 1998). Kanzi responds correctly to commands such as "Put the key in the refrigerator" and "Go get the ball that is outdoors," even when he has never heard the words combined in that particular way before. He picked up language as children do—by observing others using it and through normal social interaction. He has also learned, with training, to manipulate keyboard symbols to request favourite foods or activities (games, TV, visits to friends) and to announce his intentions.

Research on animal language and comprehension of symbols is altering our understanding of animal cognition, and not only of primates. Louis Herman and his colleagues taught dolphins to respond to requests made in two artificial languages, one consisting of computer-generated whistles and another of hand and arm gestures (Herman, Kuczaj, & Holder, 1993; Herman & Morrel-Samuels, 1996). To interpret a request correctly, the dolphins had to take into account both the meaning of the individual symbols in a string of whistles or gestures and the order of the symbols (syntax). For example, they had to understand the difference between "To left Frisbee, right surfboard take" and "To right surfboard, left Frisbee take."

And some psychologists are calling border collies "the new chimps," ever since researchers in Germany reported that a border collie named Rico had a vocabulary of more than 200 words (Kaminski, Call, & Fisher, 2004). When Rico's owner asked him to retrieve an object from another room, Rico could pick the correct object 37 times out of 40. Even more impressive, Rico, like a human child, could learn a new word in just one trial, something chimpanzees cannot do. If given the name of a new object, he could usually infer that his owner wanted him to select that object from among more familiar ones and would often remember the new label weeks later. Similar results have since been reported for another border collie named Betsy (Morell, 2008).

Most amazingly, we now know that birds are not as bird-brained as once assumed. Irene Pepperberg (2000, 2002, 2008) has been working since the late 1970s with African grey parrots. Her favourite, named Alex, could count, classify, and compare objects by vocalizing English words. When he was shown up to six items and was asked how many there were, he responded with spoken (squawked?) English phrases, such as "two cork(s)" or "four key(s)." He even responded correctly to questions about items specified on two or three dimensions, as in "How many blue key(s)?" or "What matter [material] is orange and three-cornered?" Alex also made requests ("Want pasta") and answered simple questions about objects ("What colour [is this]?" "Which is bigger?"). When presented with a blue cork and a blue key and asked "What's the same?" he would correctly respond "colour." He actually scored slightly better with new objects than with familiar ones, suggesting that he was not merely "parroting" a set of stock phrases. He could sum two small sets of objects, such as nuts or jelly beans, for amounts up to six (Pepperberg, 2006).

Alex was also able to say remarkably appropriate things in informal interactions. He would tell Pepperberg, "I love you," "I'm sorry," and, when she was feeling stressed out, "Calm down." One day, sitting on his perch as Pepperberg's accountant was working at a desk, Alex asked the accountant: "Wanna nut?" "No," said the accountant. "Want some water?" "No," she said. "A banana?" "No." After making several other suggestions, Alex finally said, "What *do* you want?" (quoted in Talbot, 2008). To the sorrow of thousands of his admirers all over the world, Alex died in 2007. Pepperberg is continuing her work with other African greys.

Watch
Birds and Language

Thinking about the Thinking of Animals

These results on animal language and cognition are impressive, but scientists are still divided over just what the animals in these studies are doing. Do they have true language? Are they thinking, in human terms? How intelligent are they? Are Kanzi, Rico, and Alex unusual, or are they typical of their species? In their efforts to correct the centuries-old *under*estimation of animal cognition, are modern researchers now reading too much into their data and *over*estimating animals' abilities?

On one side are those who worry about *anthropomorphism*, the tendency to falsely attribute human qualities to nonhuman beings (Wynne, 2004). They like to tell the story of Clever Hans, a "wonder horse" at the turn of the last century who was said to possess mathematical and other abilities (Spitz, 1997). For example, Clever Hans would answer math problems by stamping his hoof the appropriate number of times. But a little careful experimentation by psychologist Oskar Pfungst (1911/1965) revealed that when Clever Hans was prevented from seeing his questioners, his powers left him. It seems that questioners were staring at the horse's feet and leaning forward expectantly after stating the problem, then lifting their eyes and relaxing as soon as he completed the right number of taps. Clever Hans was indeed clever, but not at math or other human skills. He was merely responding to nonverbal signals that people were inadvertently providing. (Perhaps he had a high EQ.)

On the other side are those who warn against *anthropodenial*—the tendency to think, mistakenly, that human beings have nothing in common with other animals, who are, after all, our evolutionary cousins (de Waal, 2001; Fouts, 1997). The need to see our own species as unique, they say, may keep us from recognizing that other species, too, have cognitive abilities, even if not as sophisticated as our own. Those who take this position point out that most modern researchers have gone to great lengths to avoid the Clever Hans problem.

Thinking Critically

Consider Other Interpretations

This old photo shows Clever Hans in action. His story has taught researchers to beware of anthropomorphism when they interpret findings on animal cognition.

quickQUIZ

✓•—Quick Review on MyPsychLab

Your pet beagle may be incredibly smart, but she probably can't help you answer these questions.

1. Which of the following abilities have primates demonstrated, either in the natural environment or the laboratory? (a) the use of objects as simple tools; (b) the summing of quantities; (c) the use of symbols to make requests; (d) an understanding of short English sentences

2. A honeybee performs a little dance that communicates to other bees the direction and distance of food. Because the bee can "talk" about something that is located elsewhere, its communication system shows _____. But because the bee can create only utterances that are genetically wired into its repertoire, its communication system lacks _____.

3. Barnaby thinks his pet snake Curly is harbouring angry thoughts about him because Curly has been standoffish and won't curl around his neck anymore. What error is Barnaby making?

Answers:

1. all of them 2. displacement, productivity 3. anthropomorphism

We human beings are used to thinking of ourselves as the smartest species around because of our astounding ability to adapt to change, find novel solutions to problems, endlessly invent new gizmos, and use language to create everything from puns to poetry. Yet, as this chapter has shown, we are not always as wise in our thinking as we might think. We can, however, boast of one crowning accomplishment: We are the only species that tries to understand its own misunderstandings and improve itself (Gazzaniga, 2008). We want to know what we don't know; we are motivated to overcome our mental shortcomings. This uniquely human capacity for self-examination is probably the best reason to remain optimistic about our cognitive abilities.

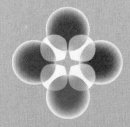

Taking Psychology with YOU

Thinking Critically in Everyday Life

Becoming More Creative

Throughout this book, we have been emphasizing the importance of asking questions, thinking of explanations other than just the most obvious ones, and examining assumptions and biases.

All of these critical-thinking guidelines involve creativity as much as they do reasoning.

Take a few moments to answer these items based on the Remote Associates Test, a test of the mental

flexibility necessary for creativity. Your task is to come up with a fourth word that is associated with each item in a set of three words (Mednick, 1962). For example, an appropriate answer for the set *news—clip—wall* is *paper*. Got the idea? Now try these (the answers are given at the end of this chapter):

1. piggy—green—lash
2. surprise—political—favour
3. mark—shelf—telephone
4. stick—maker—tennis
5. cream—cottage—cloth

Creative thinking requires you to associate elements of a problem in new ways by finding unexpected connections among them. People who are uncreative rely on *convergent thinking*, following a particular set of steps that they think will converge on one correct solution. Then, once they have solved a problem, they tend to develop a mental set and approach future problems the same way. Creative people, in contrast, exercise *divergent thinking*; instead of stubbornly sticking to one tried-and-true path, they explore side alleys and generate several possible solutions. They come up with new hypotheses, imagine other interpretations, and look for connections that are not immediately obvious. For artists and novelists, of course, creativity is a job requirement, but it also takes creativity to invent a tool, put together a recipe from leftovers, find ways to distribute unsold food to the needy, decorate your room. . . .

Creative people do not necessarily have high IQs. Personality characteristics seem more important, especially these three (Helson, Roberts, & Agronick, 1995; McCrae, 1987; Schank, 1988):

Nonconformity. Creative individuals are not overly concerned about what others think of them. They are willing to risk ridicule by proposing ideas that may initially appear foolish or off the mark. Geneticist Barbara McClintock's research was ignored or belittled by many for nearly 30 years. But she was sure she could show how genes move around and produce sudden changes in heredity. In 1983, when McClintock won the Nobel Prize, the judges called her work the second greatest genetic discovery of our time, after the discovery of the structure of DNA.

Curiosity. Creative people are open to new experiences; they notice when reality contradicts expectations, and they are curious about the reason. For example, Wilhelm Roentgen, a German physicist, was studying cathode rays when he noticed a strange glow on one of his screens. Other people had seen the glow, but they ignored it because it didn't jibe with their understanding of cathode rays. Roentgen studied the glow, found it to be a new kind of radiation, and thus discovered X rays.

Persistence. After that imaginary light bulb goes on over your head, you still have to work hard to make the illumination last. Or, as Thomas Edison, who invented the real light bulb, reportedly put it, "Genius is one percent inspiration and ninety-nine percent perspiration." No invention or work of art springs forth full-blown from a person's head. There are many false starts and painful revisions along the way.

If you are thinking critically (and creatively!), you may wonder whether these personal qualities are enough. Do you recall the "Termites" who were the most successful? They were smart, but they also got plenty of encouragement for their efforts. Likewise, some individuals may be more creative than others, but there are also *circumstances* that foster creative accomplishment. Creativity flourishes when schools and employers encourage intrinsic motivation and not just extrinsic rewards such as gold stars and money (see Chapter 7 and Chapter 12). Intrinsic motives include a sense of accomplishment, intellectual fulfillment, the satisfaction of curiosity, and the sheer love of the activity.

Creativity also increases when people have control over how to perform a task or solve a problem, are evaluated unobtrusively instead of being constantly observed and judged, and work independently (Amabile, 1983; Amabile & Khaire, 2008). Organizations encourage creativity when they let people take risks, give them plenty of time to think about problems, and welcome innovation.

In sum, if you hope to become more creative, there are two things you can do. One is to cultivate qualities in yourself: your skills, curiosity, intrinsic motivation, and self-discipline. The other is to seek out the kinds of situations that will permit you to express your abilities and experiment with new ideas.

←⊙**Simulate**
Psychology Experiments Survey: What Is Creativity?

SUMMARY

THOUGHT: USING WHAT WE KNOW

◆ Thinking is the mental manipulation of information. Our mental representations simplify and summarize information from the environment.

◆ A *concept* is a mental category that groups objects, relations, activities, abstractions, or qualities that share certain properties. *Basic concepts* have a moderate number of instances and are easier to acquire than concepts with few or many instances. *Prototypical* instances of a concept are more representative than others. The language we use to express concepts may influence how we perceive and think about the world.

◆ *Propositions* are made up of concepts and express a unitary idea. They may be linked together to form *cognitive schemas*, which serve as mental models of aspects of the world. *Mental images* also play a role in thinking.

◆ Not all mental processing is conscious. *Subconscious processes* lie outside of awareness but can be brought into consciousness when necessary. They allow us to perform two or more actions at once when one action is highly automatic. But multitasking is usually inefficient, introduces errors, and can even be dangerous—for example if done while driving. *Nonconscious processes* remain outside of awareness but nonetheless affect behaviour; they are involved in intuition and insight, and in *implicit learning*. Conscious processing may be carried out in a *mindless* fashion if we overlook changes in context that call for a change in behaviour.

REASONING RATIONALLY

◆ *Reasoning* is purposeful mental activity that involves drawing inferences and conclusions from observations, facts, or assumptions (premises). *Formal reasoning problems* can often be solved by applying an *algorithm* or by using logical processes, such as *deductive* and *inductive* reasoning. *Informal reasoning problems* often have no clearly correct solution. Disagreement may exist about basic premises, information may be incomplete, and many viewpoints may compete. Such problems often call for the application of *heuristics*, or may require *dialectical thinking* about opposing points of view.

◆ Studies of *reflective judgment* show that many people have trouble thinking dialectically. People in the *prereflective* stages do not distinguish between knowledge and belief or between belief and evidence. Those in the

quasi-reflective stages think that because knowledge is sometimes uncertain, any judgment about the evidence is purely subjective. Those who think *reflectively* understand that although some things cannot be known with certainty, some judgments are more valid than others, depending on their coherence, fit with the evidence, and so on. Higher education moves people gradually closer to reflective judgment.

BARRIERS TO REASONING RATIONALLY

◆ The ability to reason clearly and rationally is affected by many cognitive biases. People tend to exaggerate the likelihood of improbable events in part because of the *affect* and *availability heuristics*. They are swayed in their choices by the desire to *avoid loss* and by the *framing effect*—how the choice is presented. They forgo economic gain because of a *fairness bias*, which, as discussed in "Biology and Economic Choice," appears to have evolutionary roots and is being studied using brain scans. They often overestimate their ability to have made accurate predictions (the *hindsight bias*), attend mostly to evidence that supports what they want to believe (the *confirmation bias*), and are mentally rigid, forming *mental sets* and seeing patterns where none exist.

◆ The theory of *cognitive dissonance* holds that people are motivated to reduce the tension that exists when two cognitions, or a cognition and a behaviour, conflict. They can reduce dissonance by rejecting or changing a belief, changing their behaviour, or rationalizing. Dissonance is most uncomfortable, and people are most likely to try to reduce it, after a decision has been made (*postdecision dissonance*); when their actions violate their concept of themselves as honest and kind; and when they have put hard work into an activity (*the justification of effort*).

MEASURING INTELLIGENCE: THE PSYCHOMETRIC APPROACH

◆ Intelligence is hard to define. The *psychometric approach* focuses on how well people perform on standardized aptitude tests. Most psychometric psychologists believe that a general ability, a *g factor*, underlies this performance. Others, however, argue that a person can do well in some kinds of reasoning or problem solving but not in others.

◆ *The intelligence quotient*, or *IQ*, represents how well a person has done on an intelligence test compared to other people. Alfred Binet designed the first widely used intelligence test to identify children who could benefit from remedial work. But in North America, people assumed that intelligence tests revealed natural ability and used the tests to categorize people in school and in the armed services.

◆ IQ tests have been criticized for being biased in favour of white, middle-class people. However, as discussed in "Culture and Intelligence Testing," efforts to construct tests that are free of cultural influence have been disappointing. Culture affects nearly everything to do with taking a test, from attitudes to problem-solving strategies. Negative stereotypes about a person's ethnicity, gender, or age may cause the person to feel *stereotype threat*, which can lead to anxiety that interferes with test performance.

DISSECTING INTELLIGENCE: THE COGNITIVE APPROACH

◆ In contrast to the psychometric approach, *cognitive approaches* to intelligence emphasize several kinds of intelligence and the strategies people use to solve problems. Sternberg's *triarchic theory of intelligence* proposes three aspects of intelligence: *componential* (including *metacognition*), *experiential* or *creative*, and *contextual* or *practical*. Contextual intelligence allows you to acquire *tacit knowledge*, practical strategies that are important for success but are not explicitly taught.

◆ Some psychologists argue that there are other "intelligences" besides those usually considered, such as musical intelligence; kinesthetic intelligence; the capacity for insight into yourself and others; and *emotional intelligence*, the ability to identify your own and other people's emotions accurately, express emotions clearly, and regulate emotions in yourself and others.

◆ Intellectual achievement also depends on motivation, hard work, and self-discipline. Cross-cultural work shows that beliefs about the origins of mental abilities, parental standards, and attitudes toward education can also help account for differences in academic performance.

ANIMAL MINDS

◆ Some researchers, especially those in *cognitive ethology*, argue that nonhuman animals have greater cognitive abilities than has previously been thought. Some animals can use objects as simple tools. Chimpanzees have shown evidence of a simple understanding of number. Some researchers believe that the great apes, dolphins, and elephants have aspects of a *theory of mind*, an understanding of how their own minds and the minds of others work. In some apes and monkeys, these aspects may include some metacognition.

◆ In projects using visual symbol systems or American Sign Language (ASL), primates have acquired linguistic skills. Some animals (even nonprimates such as dolphins and African grey parrots) seem able to use simple grammatical ordering rules to convey or comprehend meaning. However, scientists are divided about how to interpret the findings on animal cognition, with some worrying about *anthropomorphism* and others about *anthropodenial*.

TAKING PSYCHOLOGY WITH YOU

◆ Creativity is part of critical thinking. Creative people rely on *divergent* rather than *convergent* thinking when solving problems. They tend to be nonconformist, curious, and persistent, but certain circumstances also foster creative accomplishment.

Some solutions to the nine-dot problem in the Get Involved exercise on page 333 (from Adams, 1986):

(a)

(b)

Cut the puzzle apart, tape it together
in a different format, and use
one line.

(c)

(d)

1 line 0 Folds

Roll up the puzzle
and draw a spiral
through the dots.

(e)

Lay the paper on the
surface of the Earth.
Circumnavigate the
globe twice + a few
inches, displacing a little
each time so as to pass
through the next row
on each circuit as you
"Go West, young man."

(f)

~ 2 Lines* 0 Folds
*Statistical

Draw dots as large as
possible. Wad paper into
a ball. Stab with pencil.
Open up and see if you
did it. If not, try again.
"Nobody loses: play
until you win."

(g)

May 30, 1974
5 FDR   Navasa
Roosevelt Rds. Ha
Celba, PR 00635
Dear Prof. James L. Adams,
    My dad and I were
doing Puzzles from "Conceptual
Blockbusting." We were mostly
working on the dot ones,
like ⋮⋮⋮ My dad said a
man found a way to do it
with one line. I tried and
did it. Not with folding,
but I used a fat line. I
does'nt say you can't use
a fat line. Like this →
P.S.
acctually you
need a very   Sincerely,
fat writing   Becky Buechel
apparatice.   age:10

(h)

Answers to the creativity test on page 335:
back, party, book, match, cheese

KEY TERMS

concept 318
basic concepts 318
prototype 318
proposition 319
cognitive schema 320
mental image 320
subconscious processes 320
nonconscious processes 321
implicit learning 321
reasoning 323
algorithm 323
deductive reasoning 323
inductive reasoning 324
heuristic 325

dialectical reasoning 325
affect heuristic 328
availability heuristic 328
framing effect 329
hindsight bias 331
confirmation bias 332
mental set 333
cognitive dissonance 334
postdecision dissonance 334
justification of effort 335
intelligence 337
psychometric approach to intelligence 337
factor analysis 337

g factor 337
mental age (MA) 338
intelligence quotient (IQ) 338
stereotype threat 341
triarchic theory of intelligence 343
metacognition 343
tacit knowledge 344
emotional intelligence 345
cognitive ethology 350
theory of mind 350

ASK QUESTIONS . . . be willing to WONDER

- Is everything that ever happened to us stored in the brain?

- What strategies can help us remember better?

- Why can't we remember events from our first two years?

- Do people repress traumatic memories?

In 1982, Thomas Sophonow was arrested for the murder of Barbara Stoppel, a waitress in a doughnut shop in Winnipeg. In 1983 and 1985 he was convicted of murder, largely due to the eyewitness testimony of four individuals who identified him as the killer. However, the courts overturned his conviction in 1986 due to problems with the trial. With a fourth trial looming, in 1986 the Supreme Court of Canada ordered him acquitted. What happened? Given that four eyewitnesses came forward, did a guilty man get away with murder because of some legal technicality? Often, individuals (like Thomas Sophonow) are sent to prison based on the strength of eyewitness testimony. But is an eyewitness's account always reliable? In the absence of corroborating evidence, should a witness's confidence in her memory be sufficient for establishing guilt? A lot is at stake when answering these questions: justice for the victims and avoiding false convictions.

The Sophonow case did not end in 1986. At the conclusion of this chapter we will tell you what ultimately happened.

This chapter will raise some fascinating but troubling questions about memory: When should we trust our memories, and when should we be cautious about doing so? We all forget things that did happen, of course; do we also "remember" things that never happened? Are memory malfunctions the exception to the rule or are they commonplace? And if memory is not always reliable, how can any of us hope to know the story of our own lives? How can we hope to understand the past?

Thinking Critically · Ask Questions

Thomas Sophonow was twice convicted of murdering Barbara Stoppel, based largely on eyewitness testimony. In thinking about this case, a critical thinker would ask: How accurate is eyewitness testimony, even when the witness is the victim? How trustworthy are our memories, even of traumatic events? Psychologists have learned some startling answers, as this chapter will show.

YOU are about to learn . . .

- why memory does not work like a camera—and how it does work.
- why errors can creep into our memories of even surprising or shocking events.
- why having a strong emotional reaction to a remembered event does not mean that the memory is accurate.

RECONSTRUCTING THE PAST

Memory refers to the capacity to retain and retrieve information, and also to the structures that account for this capacity. Human beings are capable of astonishing feats of memory. Most of us can easily remember the words to the national anthem, how to use a bank machine, the most embarrassing experience we ever had, zillions of details about our favourite sports or films, and hundreds of thousands of other bits of information. Memory confers competence; without it, we would be as helpless as newborns, unable to carry out even the most trivial of our daily tasks. Memory also endows us with a sense of personal identity; each of us is the sum of our recollections, which is why we feel so threatened when others challenge our memories. Individuals and cultures alike rely on a remembered history for a sense of coherence and meaning; memory gives us our past and guides our future.

Imagine what life would be like if you could never form any new memories. That does in fact happen in older people who are suffering from dementia, and sometimes it

◄◉Simulate
Psychology Experiments Survey: What Do You Remember?

◉ Watch
Memory Hazards

also occurs in younger people who have brain injuries or diseases. The case of one man, Henry Molaison, whom researchers called H. M. until his death in 2008 at age 82, is probably the most intensely studied in the annals of medicine (Corkin, 1984; Corkin et al., 1997; Hilts, 1995; Milner, 1970; Ogden & Corkin, 1991). In 1953, when H. M. was 27, surgeons removed most of his hippocampus, along with part of the amygdala. The operation was a last-ditch effort to relieve H. M.'s severe and life-threatening epilepsy, which was causing unrelenting, uncontrollable seizures. The operation did achieve its goal: Afterward, the young man's seizures were milder and could be managed with medication. However, McGill's Brenda Milner observed that his memory had been affected profoundly. Although he continued to recall most events that had occurred before the operation, he could no longer remember new experiences for much longer than 15 minutes; facts, songs, stories, and faces all vanished like water down the drain. He would read the same magazine over and over without realizing it. He could not recall the day of the week, the year, or even his last meal.

H. M. loved to do crossword puzzles and play bingo, skills acquired before the operation. But although he remained cheerful, he knew he had memory problems. He would occasionally recall an unusually emotional event, such as the assassination of someone named Kennedy, and he sometimes remembered that both of his parents were dead. But according to Suzanne Corkin, who studied H. M. extensively, these "islands of remembering" were the exceptions in a vast sea of forgetfulness. This good-natured man never knew the scientists who studied him for decades. He always thought he was much younger than he really was, and he was unable to recognize a photograph of his own face; he was stuck in a time warp from the past. We will meet H. M. again at several points in this chapter.

The Manufacture of Memory

In ancient times, philosophers compared memory to a soft wax tablet that would preserve anything that chanced to make an imprint on it. Then, with the advent of the printing press, they began to think of memory as a gigantic library, storing specific events and facts for later retrieval. Today, many people compare memory to a tape recorder or video camera, automatically recording every moment of their lives. In fact, in one of the largest surveys of its kind, 1500 people were surveyed over the telephone and more than 60% agreed that memory was like a video camera with the ability to accurately review memories at a later date (Simons & Chabris, 2011).

Popular and appealing though this belief about memory is, it is utterly wrong. Not everything that happens to us or impinges on our senses is tucked away for later use. Memory is selective. If it were not, our minds would be cluttered with mental junk: the temperature at noon on Thursday, the price of turnips two years ago, a phone number needed only once. Moreover, recovering a memory is not at all like replaying a tape of an event. It is more like watching a few unconnected frames and then figuring out what the rest of the scene must have been like.

One of the first scientists to make this point was the British psychologist Sir Frederic Bartlett (1932). Bartlett asked people to read lengthy, unfamiliar stories from other cultures and then tell the stories back to him. As the volunteers tried to recall the stories, they made interesting errors: They often eliminated or changed details that did not make sense to them, and they added other details to make the story coherent, sometimes even adding a moral. Memory, Bartlett concluded, must therefore be largely a *reconstructive* process. We may reproduce some kinds of simple information

Watch
Alvin: Dementia

Alvin: Living with Dementia

If these happy children remember this birthday party later in life, their constructions may include information picked up from family photographs, videos, and stories. And they will probably be unable to distinguish their actual memories from information they got elsewhere.

Simulate
How Good Is Your Memory for Stories?

Research
Sir Frederick Bartlett

source misattribution The inability to distinguish an actual memory of an event from information you learned about the event elsewhere.

by rote, said Bartlett, but when we remember complex information, we typically alter it in ways that help us make sense of the material, based on what we already know or think we know. Since Bartlett's time, hundreds of studies have found this to be true for everything from stories to conversations to personal experiences.

In reconstructing their memories, people often draw on many sources. Suppose that someone asks you to describe one of your early birthday parties. You may have some direct recollection of the event, but you may also incorporate information from family stories, photographs, or home videos, and even from accounts of other people's birthdays and re-enactments of birthdays on television. You take all these bits and pieces and build one integrated account. Later, you may not be able to distinguish your actual memory from information you got elsewhere—a phenomenon known as **source misattribution**, or sometimes *source confusion* (Johnson, Hashtroudi, & Lindsay, 1993; Mitchell & Johnson, 2009).

A dramatic instance of reconstruction once occurred with H. M. (Ogden & Corkin, 1991). After eating a chocolate Valentine's Day heart, H. M. stuck the shiny red wrapping in his shirt pocket. Two hours later, while searching for his handkerchief, he pulled out the paper and looked at it in puzzlement. When a researcher asked why he had the paper in his pocket, he replied, "Well, it could have been wrapped around a big chocolate heart. It must be Valentine's Day!" But a short time later, when she asked him to take out the paper again and say why he had it in his pocket, he replied, "Well, it might have been wrapped around a big chocolate rabbit. It must be Easter!" Sadly, H. M. *had* to reconstruct the past; his damaged brain could not recall it in any other way. But those of us with normal memory abilities also reconstruct, far more often than we realize.

Of course, some shocking or tragic events—such as earthquakes or accidents—do hold a special place in memory, especially when we have experienced them personally.

Do you remember where you were when Canada won the gold medal in hockey? Many Canadians probably have a "flashbulb" memory of the moment when Sidney Crosby scored the goal in overtime. But even flashbulb memories are not always complete or accurate, and distortions often creep in over time.

So do some unusual, exhilaratingly happy events, such as learning that you just won a lottery. Years ago, Roger Brown and James Kulik (1977) labelled these vivid recollections of emotional events *flashbulb memories* because that term captures the surprise, illumination, and seemingly photographic detail that characterize them.

Some flashbulb memories have lasted for years, even decades. For example, in a Danish study, older people who had lived through the Nazi occupation of their country in World War II often had an accurate memory of verifiable wartime events, such as the time of day that the radio had announced liberation and what the weather had been like at the time (Berntsen & Thomsen, 2005). Yet even flashbulb memories are not always complete or accurate. People typically remember the *gist* of a startling, emotional event they experienced or witnessed, but when researchers question them about their memories over time, errors creep into the details, and after a few years, some people even forget the gist (Neisser & Harsch, 1992).

On September 12, 2001, just one day after the attacks on the World Trade Center and the Pentagon, researchers asked 54 undergraduates when they had first heard the news of the attacks, who had told them the news, and what they had been doing at the time. The students were also asked to report details about a mundane event from the days immediately before the attacks, so that the researchers could compare ordinary memories with flashbulb ones. The students were then retested at various intervals, up to eight months later. Over time, the vividness of the flashbulb memories and the students' confidence in these memories remained higher than for the everyday memories. Their confidence, however, was misplaced. The details reported by the students became less and less consistent (and equally inconsistent) for *both* types of memories (Talarico & Rubin, 2003).

Even with flashbulb memories, then, facts tend to get mixed with a little fiction. Remembering is an active process, one that involves not only dredging up stored information but also putting two and two together to reconstruct the past. Sometimes, unfortunately, we put two and two together and get five.

◄◉ Simulate
Creating False Memories

The Conditions of Confabulation

Because memory is reconstructive, it is subject to **confabulation**—confusing an event that happened to someone else with one that happened to you, or coming to believe that you remember something that never really happened. Such confabulations are especially likely under certain circumstances (Garry et al., 1996; Hyman & Pentland, 1996; Mitchell & Johnson, 2009):

1 **You have thought, heard, or told others about the imagined event many times.** Suppose that at family gatherings you keep hearing about the time that Uncle Gord scared everyone at a New Year's party by pounding a hammer into the wall with such force that the wall collapsed. The story is so colourful that you can practically see Uncle Gord in your mind's eye. The more you think about this event, the more likely you are to believe that you were actually there, even if you were sound asleep in another house. This process has been called *imagination inflation*, because your own active imagination inflates your belief that the event really occurred (Garry & Polaschek, 2000). Even merely explaining how a hypothetical childhood experience *could* have happened inflates people's confidence that it really did. Explaining an event makes it seem more familiar and thus real (Sharman, Manning, & Garry, 2005).

2 **The image of the event contains lots of details that make it feel real.** Ordinarily, we can distinguish an imagined event from a real one by the

confabulation Confusion of an event that happened to someone else with one that happened to you, or a belief that you remember something when it never actually happened.

In the 1980s, Whitley Strieber published the best-seller *Communion*, in which he claimed to have had encounters with some sort of nonhuman beings, possibly aliens from outer space. An art director designed this striking image for the cover. Ever since, many people have assumed that this is what an extraterrestrial must look like, and some have imported the image into their own confabulated memories of alien abduction.

amount of detail we recall; real events tend to produce more details. But the longer you think about an imagined event, the more details you are likely to add—what Gord was wearing, the fact that he'd had too much to drink, the crumbling plaster, people standing around in party hats—and these details may in turn persuade you that the event really happened and that you have a direct memory of it.

3 **The event is easy to imagine.** If imagining an event takes little effort (as does visualizing a man pounding a wall with a hammer), then we tend to think that our memory is real. In contrast, when we must make an effort to form an image of an experience—for example, of being in a place we have never seen or doing something that is utterly foreign to us—our cognitive efforts serve as a cue that the event did not really take place, or that we were not there when it did.

As a result of confabulation, you may end up with a memory that feels emotionally, vividly real to you and yet is completely false. Inaccuracies in memory can occur when you first form a memory (perhaps because your attention is divided or you are distracted) or when you later retrieve the memory (when you might confuse associated thoughts, wishes, and imagined ideas with what really happened) (Mitchell & Johnson, 2009). This means that your feelings about an event, no matter how strong they are, do not guarantee that the event really happened.

Consider again our Gord story, which happens to be true. A woman we know believed for years that she had been present as an 11-year-old child when her uncle destroyed the wall. Because the story was so vivid and upsetting to her, she felt angry at him for what she thought was his mean and violent behaviour, and she assumed that she must have been angry at the time as well. Then, as an adult, she learned that she was not at the party at all but had merely heard about it repeatedly over the years. Moreover, Gord had not pounded the wall in anger, but as a joke, to inform the assembled guests that he and his wife were about to remodel their home. Nevertheless, our friend's family has had a hard time convincing her that her "memory" of this event is entirely wrong, and they are not sure she believes them yet.

As the Gord story illustrates, and as laboratory research verifies, false memories can be as stable over time as true ones (Roediger & McDermott, 1995). There's just no getting around it: Memory is reconstructive.

---

quick**QUIZ**

✓•⎯**Quick Review** on **MyPsychLab**

Can you reconstruct what you have read so far in order to answer these questions?

1. Memory is like (a) a wax tablet, (b) a giant file cabinet, (c) a video camera, (d) none of these.
2. *True or false:* Because they are so vivid, flashbulb memories remain perfectly accurate over time.
3. Which of the following confabulated "memories" might a person be most inclined to accept as having really happened to them, and why? (a) getting lost in a shopping centre at the age of five, (b) taking a class in astrophysics, (c) visiting a monastery in Tibet as a child, (d) being bullied by another kid in grade 4.

Answers:

1. d 2. false 3. a and d, because they are common events that are easy to imagine and that contain a lot of vivid details. It would be harder to induce someone to believe that he or she had studied astrophysics or visited Tibet because these are rare events that take an effort to imagine.

YOU are about to learn . . .

◆ how memories of an event can be affected by the way someone is questioned about it.
◆ why children's memories and testimony about sexual abuse cannot always be trusted.

MEMORY AND THE POWER OF SUGGESTION

The reconstructive nature of memory helps the mind work efficiently. Instead of cramming our brains with infinite details, we can store the essentials of an experience and then use our knowledge of the world to figure out the specifics when we need them. But precisely because memory is reconstructive, it is also vulnerable to suggestion—to ideas implanted in our minds after the event, which then become associated with it. This fact raises thorny problems in legal cases that involve eyewitness testimony or people's memories of what happened, when, and to whom.

The Eyewitness on Trial

Without the accounts of eyewitnesses, many guilty people would go free. Lineups and photo arrays don't necessarily help, because witnesses may simply identify the person who looks most like the perpetrator of the crime (Wells & Olson, 2003). As a result, some convictions based on eyewitness testimony turn out to be tragic mistakes.

Eyewitnesses are especially likely to make mistaken identifications when the suspect's ethnicity differs from their own. Because of unfamiliarity with other ethnic groups, the eyewitness may focus solely on the ethnicity of the person they see committing a crime ("He's Asian"; "She's white"; "He's a Sikh") and ignore the distinctive features that would later make identification more accurate (Levin, 2000; Meissner & Brigham, 2001).

In a program of research spanning over three decades, Elizabeth Loftus and her colleagues have shown that memories are also influenced by the way in which questions are put to the eyewitness and by suggestive comments made during an interrogation or interview. In one classic study, the researchers showed how even subtle changes in the wording of questions can lead a witness to give different answers. Participants first viewed short films depicting car collisions. Afterward, the researchers asked some of them, "About how fast were the cars going when they hit each other?" Other viewers were asked the same question, but with the verb changed to *smashed, collided, bumped,* or *contacted.* Estimates of how fast the cars were going

Analyze Assumptions and Biases

On TV crime shows, witnesses often identify a criminal from a lineup or a group of photos. But these methods can mislead witnesses, who may wrongly identify a person simply because he or she resembles the actual culprit more closely than do the other people standing there or in the photos. Based on psychological findings, many law enforcement agencies are now using better methods, such as having witnesses look at photos of suspects one at a time without being able to go back to an earlier one.

varied, depending on which word was used. *Smashed* produced the highest average speed estimates (40.8 mph, 65.3 km/h), followed by *collided* (39.3 mph, 62.9 km/h), *bumped* (38.1 mph, 61.0 km/h), *hit* (34.0 mph, 54.4 km/h), and *contacted* (31.8 mph, 50.9 km/h) (Loftus & Palmer, 1974).

In a similar study, the researchers asked some participants, "Did you see a broken headlight?" but asked others "Did you see the broken headlight?" (Loftus & Zanni, 1975). The question with *the* presupposes a broken headlight and merely asks whether the witness saw it, whereas the question with *a* makes no such presupposition. People who received questions with *the* were far more likely to report having seen something that had not really appeared in the film than were those who received questions with *a*. If a tiny word like *the* can lead people to "remember" what they never saw, you can imagine how the leading questions of police detectives and lawyers might influence a witness's recall.

Misleading information from other sources can also profoundly alter what witnesses report. Consider what happened when students were shown the face of a young man who had straight hair, then heard a description of the face supposedly written by another witness—a description that wrongly said the man had light, curly hair (see Figure 10.1). When the students reconstructed the face using a kit of facial features, a third of their reconstructions contained the misleading detail, whereas only 5% contained it when curly hair was not mentioned (Loftus & Greene, 1980).

Leading questions, suggestive comments, and misleading information affect people's memories not only for events they have witnessed but also for their own experiences. Researchers have successfully used these techniques to induce people to believe they are recalling complicated events from early in life that never actually happened, such as getting lost in a shopping mall, being hospitalized for a high fever, being harassed by a bully, getting in trouble for playing a prank on a grade 1 teacher, or spilling punch all over the mother of the bride at a wedding (Hyman & Pentland,

FIGURE 10.1 The Influence of Misleading Information
In a study described in the text, students saw the face of a young man with straight hair and then had to reconstruct it from memory. On the left is one student's reconstruction in the absence of misleading information about the man's hair. On the right is another person's reconstruction of the same face after exposure to misleading information that mentioned curly hair (Loftus & Greene, 1980).

1996; Lindsay et al., 2004; Loftus & Pickrell, 1995; Mazzoni et al., 1999). When people were shown a phony Disneyland ad featuring Bugs Bunny, about 16% later recalled having met a Bugs character at Disneyland (Braun, Ellis, & Loftus, 2002). In later studies, the percentages were even higher. Some people even claimed to remember shaking hands with the character, hugging him, or seeing him in a parade. But these memories were impossible, because Bugs Bunny is a Warner Bros. creation and would definitely be *rabbit non grata* at Disneyland!

Children's Testimony

The power of suggestion can affect anyone, but many people are especially concerned about its impact on children who are being questioned regarding possible sexual or physical abuse. How can adults find out whether a young child has been sexually molested without influencing or tainting what the child says? The answer is crucial. Throughout the 1980s and 1990s, accusations of child abuse in daycare centres across North America skyrocketed. One widely publicized case of child abuse associated with an unlicensed daycare centre occurred in Martensville, Saskatchewan, in 1992. The RCMP arrested nine people, including the owners of the service as well as several police officers, and charged them with more than 100 counts of sexual and physical abuse. In no case had parents actually seen such mistreatment and none of the children had complained to their parents, although one parent had noticed a diaper rash on her child—prompting the investigation. During the investigation, the children at the centre were repeatedly questioned by a police officer about the abuse. The officer used suggestive techniques to obtain testimony of abuse. Rumours of child mutilation, satanic cults, and other ritualistic abuse spread rapidly through the community. Were these people really guilty of unspeakably horrible acts, or had the children somehow been persuaded to make up fanciful stories?

Thanks largely to important research by psychological scientists, the hysteria eventually subsided and people were able to assess more clearly what had gone wrong in the interviewing of the children in these cases. Today we know that although most children *do* recollect accurately much of what they have observed or experienced, many children will say that something happened when it did not. Like adults, they can be influenced by leading questions and suggestions from the person interviewing them (Ceci & Bruck, 1995). The question, therefore, is not "Can children's memories be trusted?" but "Under what conditions are children apt to be suggestible, and to report that something happened to them when in fact it did not?"

The answer, from many experimental studies, is that a child is more likely to give a false report when the interviewer strongly believes that the child has been molested and then uses suggestive techniques to get the child to reveal molestation (Bruck, 2003). Interviewers who are biased in this way seek only confirming evidence and ignore discrepant evidence and other explanations for a child's behaviour. They reject a child's denial of having been molested and assume the child is "in denial." They use techniques that encourage imagination inflation ("Let's pretend it happened!") and that

Thinking Critically

Don't Oversimplify

Some people claim that children's memories of sexual abuse are always accurate; others claim that children can't distinguish fantasy from reality. How can we avoid either–or thinking on this emotional issue? Is the question "Are children's memories accurate?" even the right one to ask?

Children's testimony is often crucial in child sexual abuse cases. Under what conditions do children make reliable or unreliable witnesses?

blur reality and fantasy in the child's mind. They pressure or encourage the child to describe terrible events, badger the child with repeated questions, tell the child that "everyone else" said the events happened, or use bribes and threats (Poole & Lamb, 1998).

A team of researchers analyzed the actual transcripts of interrogations of children in the first highly publicized sexual abuse case, the McMartin preschool case (which ended in a hung jury). Then they applied the same suggestive techniques in an experiment with preschool children (Garven et al., 1998). A young man visited children at their preschool, read them a story, and handed out treats. The man did nothing aggressive, inappropriate, or surprising. A week later, an experimenter questioned the children individually about the man's visit. She asked children in one group leading questions ("Did he bump the teacher? Did he throw a crayon at a kid who was talking?" "Did he tell you a secret and tell you not to tell?"). She asked a second group the same questions but also applied influence techniques used by interrogators in the McMartin and other daycare cases: for example, telling the children what "other kids" had supposedly said, expressing disappointment if answers were negative, and praising the children for making allegations.

In the first group, children said "Yes, it happened" to about 17% of the false allegations about the man's visit. And in the second group, they said "yes" to the false allegations suggested to them a whopping 58% of the time. As you can see in Figure 10.2, the three-year-olds in this group, on average, said "yes" to over 80% of the false allegations, and the four- to six-year-olds said "yes" to over half of the allegations. Note that the interviews in this study lasted only 5 to 10 minutes, whereas in actual investigations, interviewers often question children repeatedly over many weeks or months.

Many people believe that children cannot be induced to make up experiences that are truly traumatic, but psychologists have shown that this assumption, too, is wrong.

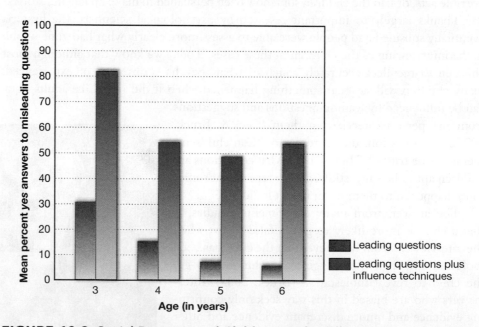

FIGURE 10.2 Social Pressure and Children's False Allegations

When researchers asked three-year-olds leading questions about events that had not occurred—such as whether a previous visitor to their classroom had committed aggressive acts—nearly 30% said that yes, he had. This percentage declined among older children. But when the researchers used influence techniques taken from actual child-abuse investigations, most of the children of all ages agreed with the false allegation (Garven et al., 1998).

When schoolchildren were asked for their recollections of an actual sniper incident at their school, many of those who had been absent from school that day reported memories of hearing shots, seeing someone lying on the ground, and other details they could not possibly have experienced directly. Apparently, they had been influenced by the accounts of the children who had been there (Pynoos & Nader, 1989). Indeed, rumour and hearsay play a big role in promoting false beliefs and memories in children, just as they do in adults (Principe et al., 2006).

As a result of such findings, psychologists have been able to develop ways of interviewing children that reduce the chances of false reporting. For example, if the interviewer says, "Tell me the reason you came to talk to me today," and nothing more, most actual victims will disclose what happened to them (Bruck, 2003). The interviewer must not assume that the child was molested, must avoid leading or suggestive questions, and must understand that children do not speak the way adults do. Young children often drift from topic to topic, and their words may not be the words adults use (Poole & Lamb, 1998). One little girl being interviewed thought her "private parts" were her elbows!

In sum, children, like adults, can be accurate in what they report and, also like adults, they can distort, forget, fantasize, and be misled. As research shows, their memory processes are only human.

---

quickQUIZ

✓ Quick Review on MyPsychLab

Now see how accurate your own memory processes are.

1. *True or false:* Mistaken identifications are more likely when a suspect's ethnicity differs from that of the eyewitness, even when the witness feels certain about being accurate.

2. Research suggests that the best way to encourage truthful testimony by children is to (a) reassure them that their friends have had the same experience, (b) reward them for saying that something happened, (c) scold them if you believe they are lying, (d) avoid leading questions.

3. Some time ago, hundreds of people in psychotherapy began claiming that they could recall long-buried memories of having taken part in satanic rituals involving animal and human torture and sacrifice. Yet the RCMP was unable to confirm any of these reports. Based on what you have learned so far, how might you explain such "memories"?

Answers:

1. true 2. d 3. Therapists who uncritically assumed that satanic cults were widespread may have asked leading questions and otherwise influenced their patients. Patients who were susceptible to their therapists' interpretations may have then confabulated and "remembered" experiences that did not happen, borrowing details from fictionalized accounts or from other troubling experiences in their lives. The result was source misattribution and the patients' mistaken conviction that their memories were real.

 YOU are about to learn . . .

◆ why multiple-choice test items are generally easier than short-answer or essay questions.

◆ whether you can know something without knowing that you know it.

◆ why the computer is often used as a metaphor for the mind.

IN PURSUIT OF MEMORY

Now that we have seen how memory *doesn't* work—namely, like an infallible recording of everything that happens to you—we turn to studies of how it *does* work.

Measuring Memory

◄◉ Simulate
Memory Experiment

Conscious, intentional recollection of an event or an item of information is called **explicit memory**. It is usually measured using one of two methods. The first method tests for **recall**, the ability to retrieve and reproduce information encountered earlier. Essay and fill-in-the-blank exams require recall. The second method tests for **recognition**, the ability to identify information you have previously observed, read, or heard about. The information is given to you, and all you have to do is say whether it is old or new, or perhaps correct or incorrect, or pick it out of a set of alternatives. The task, in other words, is to compare the information you are given with the information stored in your memory. True–false and multiple-choice tests call for recognition.

◄◉ Simulate
Recall and Recongnition

Recognition tests can be tricky, especially when false items closely resemble correct ones. Under most circumstances, however, recognition is easier than recall. Recognition for visual images is particularly impressive. If you show people 2500 slides of faces and places, and later you ask them to identify which ones they saw out of a larger set, they will be able to identify more than 90% of the original slides accurately (Haber, 1970).

The superiority of recognition over recall was once demonstrated in a study of people's memories of their high-school classmates (Bahrick, Bahrick, & Wittlinger, 1975). The participants, aged 17 to 74, first wrote down the names of as many classmates as they could remember. Recall was poor; even when prompted with yearbook pictures, the youngest people failed to name almost a third of their classmates, and the oldest failed to name most of them. Recognition, however, was far better. When asked to look at a series of cards, each of which contained a set of five photographs, and to say which picture in each set showed a former classmate, recent graduates were right 90% of the time—and so were people who had graduated 35 years earlier. The ability to recognize names was nearly as impressive.

Sometimes, information encountered in the past affects our thoughts and actions even though we do not consciously or intentionally remember it, a phenomenon known as **implicit memory** (Schacter, Chiu, & Ochsner, 1993). To get at this subtle sort of memory, researchers must rely on indirect methods instead of the direct ones

explicit memory Conscious, intentional recollection of an event or of an item of information.

recall The ability to retrieve and reproduce from memory previously encountered material.

recognition The ability to identify previously encountered material.

implicit memory Unconscious retention in memory, as evidenced by the effect of a previous experience or previously encountered information on current thoughts or actions.

Get INVOLVED!

RECALLING RUDOLPH'S FRIENDS

You can try this test of recall if you are familiar with the poem that begins "'Twas the night before Christmas" or the song "Rudolph the Red-Nosed Reindeer." Rudolph had eight reindeer friends; name as many of them as you can. After you have done your best, turn to the Get Involved exercise on page 374 for a recognition test on the same information.

used to measure explicit memory. One common method, **priming**, which we introduced in Chapter 6 in our discussion of subliminal perception, asks you to read or listen to some information and then tests you later to see whether the information affects your performance on another type of task.

Suppose that you had to read a list of words, some of which began with the letters *def* (such as *define, defend,* or *deform*). Later you might be asked to complete word stems (such as *def-*) with the first word that came to mind. Even if you could not recognize or recall the original words very well, you would be more likely to complete the word fragments with words from the list than you would be if you had not seen the list. In this procedure, the original words "prime" certain responses on the word-completion task (that is, make them more available), showing that people can retain more knowledge about the past than they realize. They know more than they know that they know (Richardson-Klavehn & Bjork, 1988; Roediger, 1990). And they know it for a very long time. One study primed people with black-and-white picture fragments (rather than word fragments) for only one to three seconds, asking them to name the object the fragments were part of. When they were tested *17 years later*, they were again shown the same fragments and a set they had never seen. Their identification rate for the formerly primed objects was significantly higher, even when people couldn't remember having been in the original study (Mitchell, 2006).

PRIMING

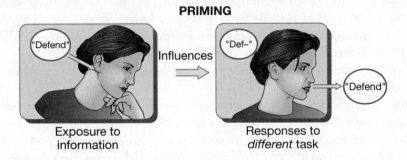

Exposure to information → Influences → Responses to *different* task

Another way to measure implicit memory, the **relearning method**, or *savings method*, was devised by Hermann Ebbinghaus (1885/1913) in the nineteenth century. The relearning method requires you to relearn information or a task that you learned earlier. If you master it more quickly the second time around, you must be remembering something from the first experience.

◆ **Research**
Hermann Ebbinghaus

Models of Memory

Although people usually refer to memory as a single faculty, as in "I must be losing my memory" or "He has a memory like an elephant's," the term *memory* actually covers a complex collection of abilities and processes. If a video camera is not an accurate metaphor for capturing these diverse components of memory, what metaphor would be better?

Many cognitive psychologists liken the mind to an information processor, along the lines of a computer, though more complex. They have constructed *information-processing models* of cognitive processes, liberally borrowing computer-programming terms such as *input, output, accessing,* and *information retrieval*. When you type something on your computer's keyboard, a software program encodes the information into an electronic language, stores it on a hard drive, and retrieves it when you need to use it. Similarly, in information-processing models of memory, we *encode* information (convert it to a form that the brain can process and use), *store*

priming A method for measuring implicit memory in which a person reads or listens to information and is later tested to see whether the information affects performance on another type of task.

relearning method A method for measuring retention that compares the time required to relearn material with the time used in the initial learning of the material.

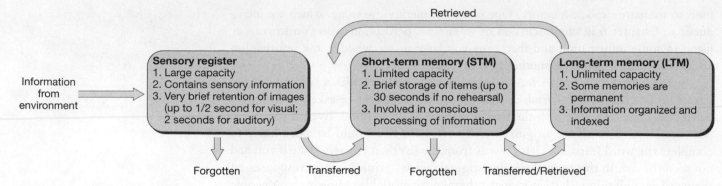

FIGURE 10.3 Three Memory Systems

In the three-box model of memory, information that does not transfer out of the sensory register or short-term memory is assumed to be forgotten forever. Once in long-term memory, information can be retrieved for use in analyzing incoming sensory information or performing mental operations in short-term memory.

the information (retain it over time), and *retrieve* the information (recover it for use). In storage, the information may be represented as concepts, propositions, images, or *cognitive schemas*, mental networks of knowledge, beliefs, and expectations concerning particular topics or aspects of the world. (If you can't retrieve these terms, see Chapter 9.)

In most information-processing models, storage takes place in three interacting memory systems. A *sensory register* retains incoming sensory information for a second or two, until it can be processed further. *Short-term memory (STM)* holds a limited amount of information for a brief period of time, perhaps up to 30 seconds or so, unless a conscious effort is made to keep it there longer. *Long-term memory (LTM)* accounts for longer storage, from a few minutes to decades (Atkinson & Shiffrin, 1968, 1971). Information can pass from the sensory register to short-term memory and in either direction between short-term and long-term memory, as illustrated in Figure 10.3.

This model, which is known informally as the *three-box model of memory*, has dominated research on memory since the late 1960s. The problem is that the human brain does not operate like your average computer. Most computers process instructions and data sequentially, one item after another, and so the three-box model has emphasized sequential operations. In contrast, the brain performs many operations simultaneously, in parallel. It recognizes patterns all at once rather than as a sequence of information bits, and it perceives new information, produces speech, and searches

Get INVOLVED!   RECOGNIZING RUDOLPH'S FRIENDS

If you took the recall test in the Get Involved exercise on page 372, now try a recognition test. From the following list, see whether you can identify the correct names of Rudolph the Red-Nosed Reindeer's eight reindeer friends. The answers are at the end of this chapter—but no fair peeking!

Blitzen	Dander	Dancer	Masher
Cupid	Dasher	Prancer	Comet
Kumquat	Donder	Flasher	Pixie
Bouncer	Blintzes	Trixie	Vixen

Which was easier, recall or recognition? Can you speculate on the reason?

memory all at the same time. It can do these things because millions of neurons are active at once, and each neuron communicates with thousands of others, which in turn communicate with millions more.

Because of these differences between human beings and machines, some cognitive scientists prefer a **parallel distributed processing (PDP)** or *connectionist* model. Instead of representing information as flowing from one system to another, a PDP model represents the contents of memory as connections among a huge number of interacting processing units, distributed in a vast network and all operating in parallel—just like the neurons of the brain (McClelland, 1994; Rumelhart, McClelland, & the PDP Research Group, 1986). As information enters the system, the ability of these units to excite or inhibit each other is constantly adjusted to reflect new knowledge.

In this chapter, we emphasize the three-box model, but keep in mind that the computer metaphor that inspired it could one day be as outdated as the metaphor of memory as a camera.

parallel distributed processing (PDP) model A model of memory in which knowledge is represented as connections among thousands of interacting processing units, distributed in a vast network, and all operating in parallel. Also called a *connectionist model*.

quickQUIZ

✓•Quick Review on MyPsychLab

How well have you encoded and stored what you just learned?

1. Alberta solved a crossword puzzle a few days ago. She no longer recalls the words in the puzzle, but while playing a game of Scrabble, she unconsciously tends to form words that were in the puzzle, showing that she has _____ memories of some of the words.

2. The three basic memory processes are _____, storage, and _____.

3. Do the preceding two questions ask for recall, recognition, or relearning? (And what about *this* question?)

4. One objection to traditional information-processing theories of memory is that, unlike most computers, the brain performs many independent operations _____.

Answers:

1. implicit 2. encoding, retrieval 3. The first two questions both measure recall; the third question measures recognition. 4. simultaneously, or in parallel

 YOU are about to learn . . .

♦ how the three "boxes" in the three-box model of memory operate.

♦ why short-term memory is like a leaky bucket.

♦ why a word can feel like it's "on the tip of your tongue" and what errors you are likely to make when you finally recall it.

♦ the difference between "knowing how" and "knowing that."

THE THREE-BOX MODEL OF MEMORY

The information model of three separate memory systems—sensory, short-term, and long-term—remains a leading approach because it offers a convenient way to organize the major findings on memory, does a good job of accounting for these findings, and

If the visual sensory register did not clear quickly, multiple images might interfere with the accurate perception and encoding of memory.

sensory register A memory system that momentarily preserves extremely accurate images of sensory information.

short-term memory (STM) In the three-box model of memory, a limited-capacity memory system involved in the retention of information for brief periods; it is also used to hold information retrieved from long-term memory for temporary use.

is consistent with the biological facts about memory. Let us now peer into each of the "boxes."

The Sensory Register: Fleeting Impressions

In the three-box model, all incoming sensory information must make a brief stop in the **sensory register**, the entryway of memory. The sensory register includes a number of separate memory subsystems, as many as there are senses. Visual images remain in a visual subsystem for a maximum of half a second. Auditory images remain in an auditory subsystem for a slightly longer time, by most estimates up to two seconds or so.

The sensory register acts as a holding bin, retaining information in a highly accurate form until we can select items for attention from the stream of stimuli bombarding our senses. It gives us a brief time to decide whether information is extraneous or important; not everything detected by our senses warrants our attention. And the identification of a stimulus on the basis of information already contained in long-term memory occurs during the transfer of information from the sensory register to short-term memory.

Information that does not quickly go on to short-term memory vanishes forever, like a message written in disappearing ink. That is why people who see an array of 12 letters for just a fraction of a second can report only four or five of them; by the time they answer, their sensory memories are already fading (Sperling, 1960). The fleeting nature of incoming sensations is actually beneficial; it prevents multiple sensory images—"double exposures"—that might interfere with the accurate perception and encoding of information.

Short-Term Memory: Memory's Scratch Pad

Like the sensory register, **short-term memory (STM)** retains information only temporarily—for up to about 30 seconds by many estimates, although some researchers think that the maximum interval may extend to a few minutes for certain tasks. In short-term memory, the material is no longer an exact sensory image but is an encoding of one, such as a word or a phrase. This material either transfers into long-term memory or decays and is lost forever.

Get INVOLVED!

YOUR SENSORY REGISTER AT WORK

In a dark room or closet, swing a flashlight rapidly in a circle. You will see an unbroken circle of light instead of a series of separate points. The reason: The successive images remain briefly in the sensory register.

Individuals with brain injury, such as H. M., demonstrate the importance of transferring new information from short-term memory into long-term memory. H. M. was able to store information on a short-term basis; he could hold a conversation and his behaviour appeared normal when you first met him. Yet, for the most part, he could not retain explicit information about new facts and events for longer than a few minutes. His terrible memory deficits involved a problem in transferring explicit memories from short-term storage into long-term storage. With a great deal of repetition and drill, patients like H. M. can learn some new visual information, retain it in long-term memory, and recall it normally (McKee & Squire, 1992). But usually information does not get into long-term memory in the first place.

THE LEAKY BUCKET.   People such as H. M. fall at the extreme end on a continuum of forgetfulness, but even those of us with normal memories know from personal experience how frustratingly brief short-term retention can be. We look up a telephone number, are distracted for a moment, and find that the number has vanished from our minds. We meet someone at a meeting and two minutes later find ourselves groping unsuccessfully for the person's name. Is it any wonder that short-term memory has been called a "leaky bucket"?

According to most memory models, if the bucket did not leak it would quickly overflow, because at any given moment, short-term memory can hold only so many items. Years ago, George Miller (1956) estimated its capacity to be "the magical number seven plus or minus two." Five-digit zip codes and seven-digit telephone numbers fall conveniently in this range; 16-digit credit card numbers do not. Some researchers have questioned whether Miller's magical number is so magical after all; estimates of STM's capacity have ranged from two items to 20, with one estimate putting the "magical number" at four (Cowan, 2001; Cowan et al., 2008). Everyone agrees, however, that the number of items that short-term memory can handle at any one time is small.

If this is so, then how do we remember the beginning of a spoken sentence until the speaker reaches the end? After all, most sentences are longer than just a few words. According to most information-processing models of memory, we overcome this problem by grouping small bits of information into larger units, or **chunks**. The real capacity of STM, it turns out, is not a few bits of information but a few chunks (Cowan & Chen, 2009). A chunk may be a word, a phrase, a sentence, or even a visual image, and it depends on previous experience. For most Canadians, the acronym *CBC* is one chunk, not three, and the date *1867* is one chunk, not four. In contrast, the number *8761* is four chunks and *CCB* is three—unless your address is 8761 or your initials are CCB. To take a visual example: If you are unfamiliar with football and look at a field full of players, you probably won't be able to remember their positions when you look away. But if you are a fan of the game, you may see a single chunk of information—say, a wishbone formation—and be able to retain it.

But even chunking cannot keep short-term memory from eventually filling up. Information that is needed for longer periods must therefore be transferred to long-term memory. Items that are particularly meaningful or that have an emotional impact may transfer quickly. But items that require more processing will be displaced with new information, and will thus be lost, unless we do something to keep it in STM for a while, as we will discuss shortly.

chunk   A meaningful unit of information; it may be composed of smaller units.

↤⊕ **Simulate**
Psychology Experiments Tool: Digit Span

These card players are having a great time giving their working memories a workout.

WORKING MEMORY.   In the original three-box model, short-term memory functioned basically as a buffer for holding and rehearsing information until it could be transferred to long-term memory. Since then, many psychologists have concluded that a more complex model is needed, one in which STM also functions more actively as a **working memory** that is intimately involved in thought and intelligence (Baddeley, 1992, 2007; Engle, 2002). In this view, besides retaining new information for brief periods while we are learning it, working memory holds and operates on information that has been retrieved from long-term memory for temporary use, including verbal and visual information. It provides the mental equivalent of a scratch pad while we solve particular problems and carry out particular tasks. And it includes active "executive" processes that control the manipulation of information and interpret it appropriately depending on the task at hand. For example, when you do an arithmetic problem, your working memory contains the numbers and the instructions for doing the necessary operations, and it also carries out those operations and retains the intermediate results from each step.

To accomplish a complex cognitive task, working memory also draws on processes that control attention and enable us to avoid distraction so that information will remain accessible and easily retrieved (Unsworth & Engle, 2007). People who do well on tests of working memory tend to do well in reading comprehension, following directions, taking notes, playing bridge, learning new words, and many other real-life tasks. When they are engrossed in challenging activities that require their concentration and effort, they stay on task longer, and their minds are less likely to wander (Kane et al., 2007).

The ability to bring information from long-term memory into short-term memory or to use working memory is not disrupted in patients like H. M. Not only can they converse but they can also do arithmetic, relate events that predate their injury, and do anything else that requires retrieval of information from long-term into short-term memory. Their problem is with the flow of information in the other direction, from short-term to long-term memory.

Long-Term Memory: Final Destination

The third box in the three-box model of memory is **long-term memory (LTM)**. The capacity of long-term memory seems to have no practical limits. The vast amount of information stored there enables us to learn, get around in the environment, and build a sense of identity and a personal history.

ORGANIZATION IN LONG-TERM MEMORY.   Because long-term memory contains so much information, it must be organized in some way so that we can find the particular items we are looking for. One way to organize words (or the concepts they represent) is by the *semantic categories* to which they belong. *Chair*, for example, belongs to the category *furniture*. In a study done many years ago, people had to memorize 60 words that came from four semantic categories: animals, vegetables, names, and professions. The words were presented in random order, but when people were allowed to recall the items in any order they wished, they tended to recall them in clusters corresponding to the four categories (Bousfield, 1953). This finding has been replicated many times.

Evidence on the storage of information by semantic category also comes from cases of people with brain damage. In one such case, a patient called M. D. appeared to have made a complete recovery after suffering several strokes, with one odd exception: He had trouble remembering the names of fruits and vegetables. M. D. could easily name a picture of an abacus or a sphinx, but he drew a blank when he saw a

working memory   In many models of memory, a cognitively complex form of short-term memory that involves active mental processes that control retrieval of information from long-term memory and interpret that information appropriately for a given task.

long-term memory (LTM)   In the three-box model of memory, the memory system involved in the long-term storage of information.

picture of an orange or a carrot. He could sort pictures of animals, vehicles, and other objects into their appropriate categories, but did poorly with pictures of fruits and vegetables. On the other hand, when M. D. was *given* the names of fruits and vegetables, he immediately pointed to the corresponding pictures (Hart, Berndt, & Caramazza, 1985). Apparently, M. D. still had information about fruits and vegetables, but his brain lesion prevented him from using their names to get to the information when he needed it, unless the names were provided by someone else. This evidence suggests that information in memory about a particular concept (such as *orange*) is linked in some way to information about the concept's semantic category (such as *fruit*).

Indeed, many models of long-term memory represent its contents as a vast network of interrelated concepts and propositions (Anderson, 1990; Collins & Loftus, 1975). In these models, a small part of a conceptual network for *animals* might look something like the one in Figure 10.4. The way people use these networks, however, depends on experience and education. For example, in rural Liberia, the more schooling children have, the more likely they are to use semantic categories in recalling lists of objects (Cole & Scribner, 1974). This makes sense, because in school, children

Culture affects the encoding, storage, and retrieval of information in long-term memory. Navajo healers, who use stylized, symbolic sand paintings in their rituals, must commit to memory dozens of intricate visual designs, because no exact copies are made and the painting is destroyed after each ceremony.

FIGURE 10.4 Part of a Conceptual Grid in Long-Term Memory

Many models of memory represent the contents of long-term semantic memory as an immense network or grid of concepts and the relations among them. This illustration shows part of a hypothetical grid for *animals*.

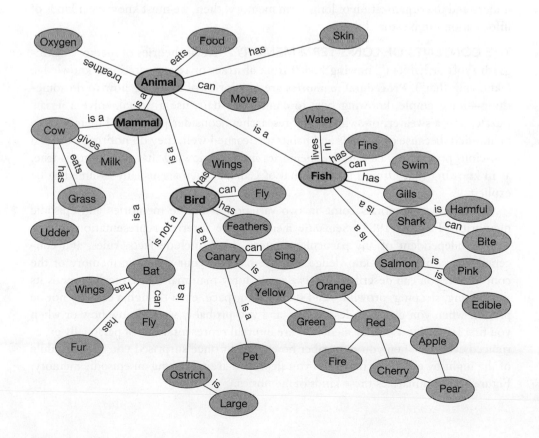

must memorize a lot of information in a short time, and semantic grouping can help. Unschooled children, having less need to memorize lists, do not cluster items and do not remember them as well. But this does not mean that unschooled children have poor memories. When the task is one that is meaningful to them, such as recalling objects that were in a story or a village scene, they remember extremely well (Mistry & Rogoff, 1994).

We organize information in long-term memory not only by semantic groupings but also in terms of the way words sound or look. Have you ever tried to recall some word that was on the "tip of your tongue"? Nearly everyone experiences such *tip-of-the-tongue (TOT) states*, especially when trying to recall the names of acquaintances or famous persons, the names of objects and places, or the titles of movies or books (Burke et al., 1991). TOT states tend to increase as we age (Shafto et al., 2007) and TOT states are even reported by users of sign language, who call them tip-of-the-finger states (Thompson, Emmorey, & Gollan, 2005).

When a word is on the tip of the tongue, people tend to come up with words that are similar in meaning to the right one before they finally recall it. But verbal information in long-term memory also seems to be indexed by sound and form, and it is retrievable on that basis. Incorrect guesses often have the correct number of syllables, the correct stress pattern, the correct first letter, or the correct prefix or suffix (R. Brown & McNeill, 1966). For example, for the target word *sampan* (an Asian boat), a person might say "Siam" or "sarong." Interestingly, emotionally arousing questions increase the frequency of TOT states, suggesting a role for emotion in accessing semantic groupings (Schwartz Bennett, 2010).

Information in long-term memory may also be organized by its familiarity, relevance, or association with other information. The method used in any given instance probably depends on the nature of the memory; you would no doubt store information about the major cities of Europe differently from information about your first date. To understand the organization of long-term memory, then, we must know what kinds of information can be stored there.

THE CONTENTS OF LONG-TERM MEMORY.   Most theories of memory distinguish skills or habits ("knowing how") from abstract or representational knowledge ("knowing that"). **Procedural memories** are memories of knowing how to do something—for example, knowing how to comb your hair, use a pencil, solve a jigsaw puzzle, knit a sweater, or swim. Many researchers consider procedural memories to be implicit, because once skills and habits are learned well, they do not require much conscious processing. **Declarative memories** involve knowing that something is true, as in knowing that Ottawa is the capital of Canada; they are usually assumed to be explicit.

Declarative memories come in two varieties: semantic memories and episodic memories (Tulving, 1985). **Semantic memories** are internal representations of the world, independent of any particular context. They include facts, rules, and concepts—items of general knowledge. On the basis of your semantic memory of the concept *cat*, you can describe a cat as a small, furry mammal that typically spends its time eating, sleeping, prowling, and staring into space, even though a cat may not be present when you give this description, and you probably won't know how or when you first learned it. **Episodic memories** are internal representations of personally experienced events. When you remember how your cat once surprised you in the middle of the night by pouncing on you as you slept, you are retrieving an episodic memory. Figure 10.5 summarizes these kinds of memories.

procedural memories   Memories for the performance of actions or skills ("knowing how").

declarative memories   Memories of facts, rules, concepts, and events ("knowing that"); they include semantic and episodic memories.

semantic memories   Memories of general knowledge, including facts, rules, concepts, and propositions.

episodic memories   Memories of personally experienced events and the contexts in which they occurred.

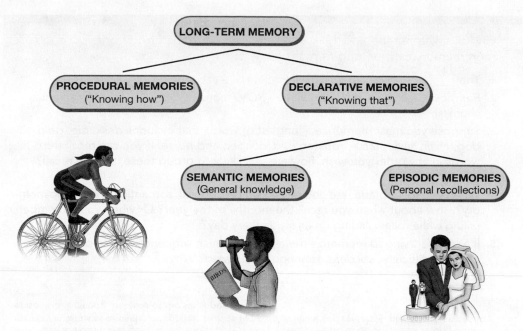

FIGURE 10.5 Types of Long-Term Memories

This diagram summarizes the distinctions among long-term memories. Can you come up with other examples of each memory type?

FROM SHORT-TERM TO LONG-TERM MEMORY: A PUZZLE.

The three-box model of memory is often invoked to explain an interesting phenomenon called the **serial-position effect**. If you are shown a list of items and are then asked immediately to recall them, your retention of any particular item will depend on its position in the list (Bhatarah, Ward, & Tan, 2008; Johnson & Miles, 2009). Recall will be best for items at the beginning of the list (the *primacy effect*) and at the end of the list (the *recency effect*). When retention of all the items is plotted, the result will be a U-shaped curve, as shown in Figure 10.6. A serial-position effect occurs when you are introduced to a lot of people at a party and find you can recall the names of the first few people you met and the last few, but almost no one in between.

According to the three-box model, the first few items on a list are remembered well because short-term memory is relatively empty when they enter, so these items do not have to compete with others to make it into long-term memory. They get thoroughly processed, so they remain memorable. The last few items are remembered for a different reason: At the time of recall, they are still sitting in short-term memory. The items in the middle of a list are not so well retained because by the time they get into short-term memory, it is already crowded. As a result, many of these items drop out of short-term memory before they can be stored in long-term memory. This explanation is supported by a functional MRI study in which recognition memory for words early in a list activated areas in the hippocampus associated with retrieval from long-term memory, but recognition for words that came near the end of the list did not (Talmi et al., 2005). But there is a problem: The recency effect sometimes occurs even after a considerable delay, when the items at the end of a list can no longer be in short-term memory (Davelaar et al., 2004). The serial-position curve, therefore, remains something of a puzzle.

serial-position effect The tendency for recall of the first and last items on a list to surpass recall of items in the middle of the list.

◀⊙Simulate
Psychology Experiments Tool: Serial-Position Effect

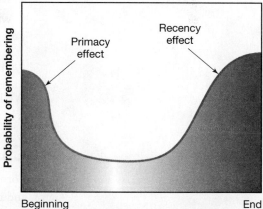

FIGURE 10.6 The Serial-Position Effect

When people try to recall a list of similar items immediately after learning it, they tend to remember the first and last items best and the ones in the middle worst.

quickQUIZ

✓• Quick Review on MyPsychLab

Find out whether the findings just discussed have transferred from your short-term memory to your long-term memory.

1. The _____ holds images for a fraction of a second.
2. For most Canadians, the abbreviation *RCMP* consists of _____ informational chunk(s).
3. Suppose you must memorize a long list of words that includes *desk, pig, gold, dog, chair, silver, table, rooster, bed, copper,* and *horse.* If you can recall the words in any order you wish, how are you likely to group these items in recall? Why?
4. When you roller-blade, are you relying on procedural, semantic, or episodic memory? How about when you recall the months of the year? Or when you remember falling while roller-blading on an icy January day?
5. If a child is trying to memorize the alphabet, which sequence should present the greatest difficulty: *abcdefg, klmnopq,* or *tuvwxyz*? Why?

Answers:

1. sensory register 2. one 3. Desk, chair, table, and bed will probably form one cluster; pig, dog, rooster, and horse a second; and gold, silver, and copper a third. Concepts tend to be organized in long-term memory in terms of semantic categories, such as furniture, animals, and metals. 4. procedural; semantic; episodic 5. klmnopq, because of the serial-position effect.

YOU are about to learn . . .

♦ changes that occur in the brain when you store a short-term versus a long-term memory.
♦ where in the brain memories for facts and events are stored.
♦ which hormones can improve memory.

THE BIOLOGY OF MEMORY

We have been discussing memory solely in terms of information processing, but what is happening in the brain while all of that processing is going on?

Changes in Neurons and Synapses

Forming a memory involves chemical and structural changes at the level of synapses, and these changes differ for short-term memory and long-term memory.

In short-term memory, changes within neurons temporarily alter their ability to release neurotransmitters, the chemicals that carry messages from one cell to another (see Chapter 4). Evidence comes from studies with sea snails, sea slugs, and other organisms that have small numbers of easily identifiable neurons (Kandel, 2001; Kandel & Schwartz, 1982). These primitive animals can be taught simple conditioned responses, such as withdrawing or not withdrawing parts of their bodies in response to a light touch. When the animal retains the skill for only the short term, the neuron or neurons involved temporarily show an increase or decrease in readiness to release neurotransmitter molecules into a synapse.

In contrast, long-term memory involves lasting structural changes in the brain. To mimic what they think may happen during the formation of a long-term memory, researchers apply brief, high-frequency electrical stimulation to groups of neurons in the brains of animals or to brain cells in a laboratory culture. In various areas, especially the hippocampus, this stimulation increases the strength of synaptic responsiveness, a phenomenon known as **long-term potentiation** (Bliss & Collingridge, 1993; Whitlock et al., 2006). In other words, certain receiving neurons become more responsive to transmitting neurons, so those synaptic pathways become more excitable. This idea is far from new, as a Canadian researcher at McGill University, D. O. Hebb, suggested such a thing in 1949 in his book *The Organization of Behaviour*. Hebb suggested that changes in neural activity occur due to a process similar to classical conditioning. It was this theory that prompted the original discoverers of long-term potentiation, Bliss and Lomo (1973), to look for the phenomenon.

Most (though not all) researchers believe that long-term potentiation underlies many and perhaps all forms of learning and memory. The neurotransmitter glutamate seems to play a key role in this process, though the exact biochemical and molecular changes involved are still being debated. However, a number of researchers have criticized the research on long-term potentiation and learning, noting that the drugs rats are given to block glutamate's activity also result in severe motor side effects (Cain et al., 1996; Saucier et al., 1996). This can be particularly problematic when rats are expected to perform motor responses to indicate that they remember (this wouldn't be a problem if we could ask the rats what they remembered). One commonly used task is the water maze (Morris et al., 1982; Sutherland, Whishaw, & Regehr, 1982), in which rats must swim to a hidden platform to escape from the water. When rats are given drugs to block long-term potentiation, they often do bizarre things, such as failing to stay on the platform once they find it or sinking to the bottom of the pool (Cain et al., 1996; Cain, Saucier, & Boon, 1997; Saucier et al., 1996). It is then difficult to untangle the effects that these drugs have on learning from their undesired side effects.

However, in a series of studies, researchers have done just that. Saucier and Cain (1995) have demonstrated that if the rat is given experience with swimming in the maze prior to receiving these drugs, the rat can learn the location of the escape from the maze fairly well—even when its brain cannot produce long-term potentiation. Does this result mean that long-term potentiation is not learning? No. As we discussed in Chapter 2, it is rare that a single experiment disproves a theory. Instead, researchers have incorporated these results into the theory that explains the data (Bannerman, 2009).

Whatever the mechanism, the ultimate result is that the receiving neurons become more receptive to the next signal that comes along. It is a little like increasing the diameter of a funnel's neck to permit more flow through the funnel. In addition, during long-term potentiation, dendrites grow and branch out, and certain types of synapses increase in number (Greenough, 1984). At the same time, in another process, some neurons become *less* responsive than they were previously (Bolshakov & Siegelbaum, 1994).

Most of these changes take time, which probably explains why long-term memories remain vulnerable to disruption for a short while after they are stored (Sutherland, Sparks, & Lehmann, 2010). The neural and synaptic changes that occur when memories are formed are distributed through the brain and involve areas of the brain that appear to learn best when experiences are repeated again and again. Memories become more permanent by the brain repeating the experience by replaying the

long-term potentiation A long-lasting increase in the strength of synaptic responsiveness, thought to be a biological mechanism of long-term memory.

neural activity for hours after its occurrence (Euston, Tatsuno, & McNaughton, 2007). In Chapter 5, we discuss the possible role of sleep in the replay of neural activity and its role in storing new information.

Locating Memories

Scientists have used microelectrodes, brain-scan technology, and other techniques to identify the brain structures responsible for the formation and storage of specific types of memories. The amygdala is involved in the formation and retrieval of memories of fearful and other emotional events (Buchanan, 2007; see Chapter 11). Indeed, enhanced activation of the amygdala is associated with the vividness of flashbulb memories and may be a key mechanism in the production of flashbulb memories (Sharot et al., 2007). Areas in the frontal lobes of the brain are especially active during short-term and working-memory tasks (Goldman-Rakic, 1996; Mitchell & Johnson, 2009). The prefrontal cortex and areas adjacent to the hippocampus in the temporal lobe are also important for the efficient encoding of pictures and words.

But it is the hippocampus that has the starring role in many aspects of memory. It is critical to the formation of long-term declarative memories ("knowing that"); as we have seen in the case of H. M., damage to this structure can cause amnesia for new facts and events. And studies of rats and human beings suggest that the hippocampus is also critical in recalling past experiences (Pastalkova et al., 2008; Corkin, 2002). Surprisingly to many researchers, Suzanne Corkin (2002) reported that H. M. also had severe difficulties recalling past experiences, with impairments in recalling detailed memories of his mother or father or in the events that made up any part of his life before the surgery. This observation flies in the face of the very popular theory of memory consolidation, which suggests that, like concrete, memories take a long time to form, but once formed they become independent of the hippocampus (Squire, 2007). It is because of research that suggests that the hippocampus plays a key role in the formation of new memories and in the recall of episodic memories, no matter how old they are (Steinvorth, Levine, & Corkin, 2005; Sutherland, Sparks, & Lehmann, 2010) that we are now developing a new theory of how memories are formed, stored, and maintained. As we noted above, it appears that the hippocampus replays the neural events that occurred during learning, and that this repetition (often during sleep) is how memories are formed (Euston, Tatsuno, & McNaughton, 2007).

A team of researchers has identified how neurons in the hippocampus may become involved in specific memories. They implanted electrodes into the brains of 13 people about to undergo surgery for severe epilepsy. (This is standard procedure because it enables doctors to pinpoint the location of the brain activity causing the seizures.) As the patients were being prepped, they watched a series of 5- to 10-second film clips of popular shows such as *Seinfeld* or *The Simpsons*, or of animals and landmarks. The researchers recorded which neurons in the hippocampus were firing as the patients watched; for each patient, particular neurons might become highly active during particular videos and respond only weakly to others. After a few minutes, the patients were asked to recall what they had seen. They remembered almost all of the clips, and as they recalled each one, the very neurons that had been active when they first saw it were reignited (Gelbard-Sagiv et al., 2008).

The formation and retention of procedural memories (memory for skills and habits) seem to involve other brain structures and pathways. For example, in work with rabbits, Richard Thompson (1983, 1986) showed that one kind of procedural memory—a simple, classically conditioned response to a stimulus, such as an eye blink in response to a tone—depends on activity in the cerebellum. Human patients with damage in the cerebellum are incapable of this type of conditioning (Daum & Schugens, 1996).

The formation of declarative and procedural memories in different brain areas could explain a curious finding about patients like H. M. Despite their inability to form new declarative memories, with sufficient practice such patients can acquire new procedural memories that enable them to solve a puzzle, read mirror-reversed words, or play tennis—even though they do not recall the training sessions in which they learned these skills. Apparently, the parts of the brain involved in acquiring new procedural memories have remained intact. Patients such as H. M. also retain some implicit memory for verbal material, as measured by priming tasks. Some psychologists conclude that there must therefore be separate systems in the brain for implicit and explicit tasks. As Figure 10.7 shows, this view has been bolstered by brain scans, which reveal differences in the location of brain activity when ordinary subjects perform explicit versus implicit memory tasks (Reber, Stark, & Squire, 1998; Squire et al., 1992).

The brain circuits that take part in the *formation* and *retrieval* of long-term memories, however, are not the same as those involved in long-term *storage* of those memories. Although the hippocampus is vital for formation and retrieval, the ultimate destinations of declarative memories seem to lie in parts of the cerebral cortex (Maviel et al., 2004). In fact, memories may be stored in the same cortical areas that were involved in the original perception of the information: When people remember pictures, visual parts of the brain become active. And when people remember sounds, auditory areas become active, just as they did when the information was first perceived (Nyberg et al., 2000; Thompson & Kosslyn, 2000).

The typical "memory" is a complex cluster of information. When you recall meeting a man yesterday, you remember his greeting, his tone of voice, how he looked, and where he was. Even a single concept, such as *shovel*, includes a lot of information (about its length, what it's made of, what it's used for . . .). These different pieces of information are probably processed separately and stored at different locations that are distributed across wide areas of the brain, with all the sites participating in the representation of the event or concept as a whole. The hippocampus may somehow bind together the diverse aspects of a memory at the time it is formed, so that even though these aspects are stored in different cortical sites, the memory can later be retrieved as one coherent entity (Squire & Zola-Morgan, 1991).

Review 10.1 shows the structures that we have discussed and summarizes some of the memory-related functions associated with them. But we have given you just a few small nibbles from the smorgasbord of findings now available. Neuroscientists hope that someday they will be able to describe the entire stream of events in the brain that occur from the moment you say to yourself "I must remember this" to the moment you actually do remember . . . or find that you can't.

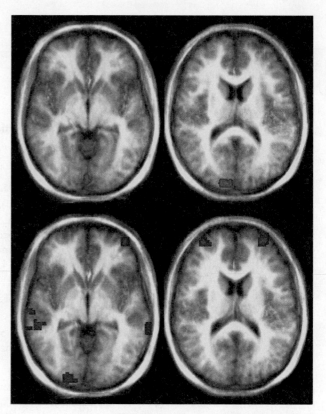

FIGURE 10.7 Brain Activity in Explicit and Implicit Memory

As these composite functional MRI scans show, patterns of brain activity differ depending on the type of memory task involved. When people had an explicit memory for dot patterns they had seen earlier, areas in the visual cortex, temporal lobes, and frontal lobes (indicated by orange in the lower photos) were more active. When people's implicit memories were activated, areas in the visual cortex (blue in the upper photos) were relatively inactive (Reber, Stark, & Squire, 1998).

REVieW 10.1

Some Brain Areas Involved in Memory

No simple summary of brain areas associated with memory can do this complex topic justice. Here are just a few of the areas and functions that have been studied.

Brain Area	Associated Memory Function
Amygdala	Formation and retrieval of emotional memories
Frontal lobes	Short-term memory and working-memory tasks
Prefrontal cortex, parts of temporal lobes	Efficient encoding of words, pictures
Hippocampus	Formation of long-term declarative memories; aids in the retrieval of specific memories; may bind together diverse elements of a memory so that it can be retrieved later as a coherent entity
Cerebellum	Formation and retention of simple classically conditioned responses
Cerebral cortex	Storage of long-term memories, possibly in areas involved in the original perception of the information

BIOLOGY and "Baby Brain"

Does Pregnancy Affect Memory?

In 2002, a group of researchers in England reported that the brains of pregnant women decreased in size as pregnancy progressed (Oatridge et al., 2002). Thankfully, this decrease wasn't permanent (the brains slowly went back to normal after giving birth). Many people thought that this change in brain size was potentially *the* explanation for "baby brain," the putative memory impairments that many pregnant women report (Crawley, Grant, & Hinshaw, 2008). Before we investigate whether or not brain size is related to memory, we need to remember to be critical: What do we know about whether or not pregnant women have poorer memories?

Most of the research on "baby brain" has been performed on rats, although the results may surprise you. Many researchers have found that pregnancy improves memory in a number of different tasks, including spatial memory and working memory (Galea et al., 2000; Pawluski, Walker, & Galea, 2006). These improvements in memory are long-lasting, remaining for months after the rats give birth (Darnaudery et al., 2007). Thus, in the rat, pregnancy appears to improve memory, with greater improvements occurring if rats have more than one pregnancy.

However, there are a number of reports that pregnant women have impaired verbal memory (de Groot et al., 2003); this may extend as long as three months after giving birth (Glynn, 2010). Similar deficits occur with prospective memory, the type of memory you use when you need to remember to do something (Rendell & Henry, 2008). A recent meta-analysis of the effects of pregnancy on memory suggested that real memory deficits occurred, although only for the most difficult tasks (Henry & Rendell, 2007). Why would pregnancy improve memory in rats and impair memory in women?

There are a number of potential reasons, including societal beliefs about how pregnancy hormones affect memory that then may negatively influence self-perception (Crawley, Grant, & Hinshaw, 2008). Further, the control groups used in the human studies might be biased; that is, the women in the control groups were not currently pregnant but many of them had been, a factor that in rats improved memory. Thus, the "deficit" may actually reflect comparisons to women with better-than-average memories. Indeed, when women are studied before they become pregnant, only small differences in memory ability are observed and then only during late pregnancy (Christensen, Leach, & Mackinnon, 2010). Finally, differences between rat research and human research may reflect the differences in tasks that humans are asked to do, most of which do not relate to the survival and care of infants. Indeed, when pregnant women were asked to identify threatening facial expressions, they did better than non-pregnant women (Pearson, Lightmana, & Evans, 2009). Thus, "baby brain" really may be all in our heads. That is, although pregnancy may result in a smaller brain, there is limited evidence that this has any effect on memory.

Hormones, Emotion, and Memory

Have you ever smelled fresh cookies and recalled a tender scene from your childhood? Do you have a vivid memory of seeing a particularly horrifying horror movie? Emotional memories such as these are often especially intense, and the explanation resides partly in our hormones.

Hormones released by the adrenal glands during stress and emotional arousal, including epinephrine (adrenaline) and norepinephrine, can enhance memory. If you give people a drug that prevents their adrenal glands from producing these hormones, they will remember less about emotional stories they heard than a control group will (Cahill et al., 1994). Conversely, if you give animals norepinephrine right after learning, their memories will improve. The link between emotional arousal and memory makes evolutionary sense: Arousal tells the brain that an event or piece of information is important enough to encode and store for future use.

However, extreme arousal is not necessarily a good thing. When animals or people are given very high doses of stress hormones, their memories for learned tasks sometimes suffer instead of improving; a moderate dose may be optimal (Andreano & Cahill, 2006). Two psychologists demonstrated the perils of high stress and anxiety in a real-life setting: the Horror Labyrinth of the London Dungeon (Valentine & Mesout, 2009). The labyrinth is a maze of disorienting mirrored walls set in Gothic vaults. As visitors walk through it, they hear strange noises and screams, and various alarming things suddenly appear, including a "scary person"—an actor dressed in a dark robe, wearing makeup to appear scarred and bleeding. Volunteers wore a wireless heart-rate monitor as they walked through the labyrinth, so that their stress and anxiety levels could be recorded. The higher their stress and anxiety, the less able they were to accurately describe the "scary person" later, and the fewer correct identifications they made of him in a lineup. Such effects on memory do not matter much at an amusement attraction, but they can have serious consequences when crime victims, police officers, and combat soldiers must recall details of a highly stressful experience, such as a shootout or the identity of an enemy interrogator (Morgan et al., 2007).

👁 **Watch**
Estrogen and Memory

Fuel for your memory?

Assuming adrenal hormones do not become *too* high, how might these hormones enhance storage of information in the brain? One possibility is that norepinephrine affects glutamate receptors on the surfaces of nerve cells, increasing the strength of incoming signals (Hu et al., 2007; McGaugh, 1990). Another is that adrenal hormones cause the level of glucose (a sugar) to rise in the bloodstream, and from there the glucose can readily enter the brain. Once in the brain, glucose may enhance memory either directly or by altering the effects of neurotransmitters. If so, increasing the amount of glucose available to the brain should enhance memory. Indeed, this "sweet memories" effect does occur both in aged rats and mice and in human beings. In one encouraging study, healthy older people fasted overnight, drank a glass of lemonade sweetened with either glucose or saccharin, and then took two memory tests. The saccharin-laced drink had no effect on their performance, but lemonade with glucose greatly boosted their ability to recall a taped passage 5 or 40 minutes after hearing it (Manning, Hall, & Gold, 1990).

Before you reach for a candy bar, you should know that the fat in most sugary treats blunts the positive effects of glucose. Moreover, the effective dose of glucose is narrow; too much can impair cognitive functioning instead of helping it. The "sweet memories" effect also depends on your metabolism, what you have eaten that day, and the level of glucose in your brain before you ingest it. In this area, as in others in the biology of memory, we have much to learn. No one knows yet exactly how the brain stores information, how different memory circuits link up with one another, or how a student is able to locate and retrieve information at the drop of a multiple-choice item.

quick**QUIZ**

✓•[Quick Review] on **MyPsychLab**

We hope your memory circuits will link up to help you answer this quiz.

1. Is long-term potentiation associated with (a) increased responsiveness of certain receiving neurons to transmitting neurons, (b) a decrease in receptors on certain receiving neurons, or (c) reaching your true potential?
2. The cerebellum has been associated with _____ memories; the hippocampus has been associated with _____ memories.
3. *True or false:* Hormone research suggests that if you want to remember well, you should be as relaxed as possible while learning.
4. After reading about glucose and memory, should you immediately start gulping down lemonade? Why or why not?

Answers:

1. a 2. procedural, declarative 3. false 4. You should not pig out on sugar yet. You do not know what amount might be effective for you, given your metabolism, brain levels of glucose, and dietary habits. And you need to consider the health risks of consuming sugary foods with lots of calories and little nutritional value.

 YOU are about to learn . . .

◆ how memory can be improved, and why rote methods are not the best strategy.
◆ why memory tricks, although fun, are not always useful.

HOW WE REMEMBER

Once we understand the basics of how memory works, we can use that knowledge to encode and store information so that it sticks in our minds and will be there when we need it. What are the best strategies to use?

Effective Encoding

Our memories, as we have seen, are not exact replicas of experience. Sensory information is summarized and encoded as words or images almost as soon as it is detected. When you hear a lecture you may hang on every word (we hope you do), but you do not memorize those words verbatim. You extract the main points and encode them.

To remember information well, you have to encode it accurately in the first place. With some kinds of information, accurate encoding takes place automatically, without effort. Think about where you usually sit in your psychology class. When were you last there? You can probably provide this information easily, even though you never made a deliberate effort to encode it. But many kinds of information require *effortful encoding*: the plot of a novel, the procedures for assembling a cabinet, the arguments for and against a proposed law. To retain such information, you might have to select the main points, label concepts, or associate the information with personal experiences or with material you already know. Experienced students know that most of the information in a university course requires effortful encoding, otherwise known as studying. The mind does not gobble up information automatically; you must make the material digestible.

Rehearsal

An important technique for keeping information in short-term memory and increasing the chances of long-term retention is *rehearsal*, the review or practice of material while you are learning it. When people are prevented from rehearsing, the contents of their short-term memories quickly fade (Peterson & Peterson, 1959). You are taking advantage of rehearsal when you look up a phone number and then repeat it over and over to keep it in short-term memory until you no longer need it. And when you can't remember a phone number because you have always used speed dial to call it, you are learning what happens when you *don't* rehearse!

✳ Explore
Maintaining Long-Term Memory

PAY ATTENTION!

It seems obvious, but often we fail to remember because we never encoded the information in the first place. For example, which of these pennies is the real one? (The answer is given at the end of this chapter.) Even though Canadians have seen zillions of pennies, most people have trouble recognizing the real one because they have never attended to and encoded the details of a penny's design (Nickerson & Adams, 1979). We are not advising you to do so, unless you happen to be a coin collector or a counterfeiting expert. Just keep in mind that when you do have something to remember, you need to encode it well.

Get INVOLVED!

When actors learn a script, they do not rely on maintenance rehearsal alone. They also use elaborative rehearsal and deep processing, analyzing the meaning of their lines and associating their lines with imagined information about the character they are playing.

maintenance rehearsal   Rote repetition of material in order to maintain its availability in memory.

elaborative rehearsal   Association of new information with already stored knowledge and analysis of the new information to make it memorable.

deep processing   In the encoding of information, the processing of meaning rather than simply the physical or sensory features of a stimulus.

HOW TO REMEMBER BETTER

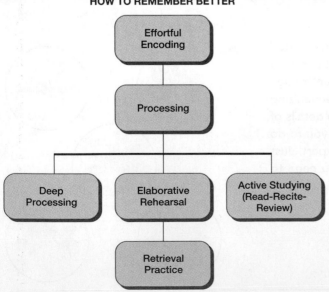

A poignant demonstration of the power of rehearsal once occurred during a session with H. M. (Ogden & Corkin, 1991). The experimenter gave H. M. five digits to repeat and remember, but then she was unexpectedly called away. When she returned after more than an hour, H. M. was able to repeat the five digits correctly. He had been rehearsing them the entire time.

Short-term memory holds many kinds of information, including visual information and abstract meanings. But most people, or at least most hearing people, seem to favour speech for encoding and rehearsing the contents of short-term memory. The speech may be spoken aloud or to oneself. When people make errors on short-term memory tests that use letters or words, they often confuse items that sound the same or similar, such as *d* and *t*, or *bear* and *bare*. These errors suggest that they have been rehearsing verbally.

Some strategies for rehearsing are more effective than others. **Maintenance rehearsal** involves merely the rote repetition of the material. This kind of rehearsal is fine for keeping information in STM, but it will not always lead to long-term retention. A better strategy if you want to remember for the long haul is **elaborative rehearsal**, also called *elaboration of encoding* (Cermak & Craik, 1979; Craik & Tulving, 1975). Elaboration involves associating new items of information with material that has already been stored or with other new facts. It can also involve analyzing the physical, sensory, or semantic features of an item.

Suppose, for example, that you are studying the hypothalamus, first discussed in Chapter 4. Simply memorizing the definition of the hypothalamus is unlikely to help much. But if you can elaborate the concept of the hypothalamus, you are more likely to remember it. For example, knowing that *hypo* means "under" tells you its location, under the thalamus. Knowing that it is part of the limbic system should clue you in to the fact that it is involved in survival drives and emotion. Many students try to pare down what they are learning to the bare essentials, but in fact, knowing more details about something makes it more memorable; that is what elaboration means.

A related strategy for prolonging retention is **deep processing**, or the processing of meaning (Craik & Lockhart, 1972). If you process only the physical or sensory features of a stimulus, such as how the word *hypothalamus* is spelled and how it sounds, your processing will be shallow even if it is elaborated. If you recognize patterns and assign labels to objects or events ("The *hypo*thalamus is *below* the thalamus"), your processing will be somewhat deeper. If you fully analyze the meaning of what you are trying to remember (for example, by encoding the functions and importance of the hypothalamus), your processing will be deeper yet. *Shallow processing* is sometimes useful; when you memorize a poem, for instance, you will want to pay attention to (and elaborately encode) the sounds of the words and the patterns of rhythm in the poem and not just the poem's meaning. Usually, though, deep processing is more effective. That is why, if you try to memorize information that has little or no meaning for you, the information may not stick.

Often, though, we are asked to learn how to group items into categories, such as how to classify songbirds according to their families. You could choose one family (for example, Paridae) and study all the tits, chickadees, and titmice that fall into that family until you know them perfectly (*massed practice*). However, there are thousands of species of songbirds. Learning how to categorize these birds according to their families could take forever. Studies conducted by the Jacoby Lab have demonstrated that a better way to learn is to choose one example from each family and study it (*spaced practice*) alongside examples from numerous other families (Wahlheim et al., in press). The idea is that spaced practice highlights differences among categories, and increases study time and attention. Thus, when you have to learn a large number of concepts, variation may be the key. When you combine spaced practice with what you learned in Chapter 1 about read-recite-review and other strategies for studying, we have no doubt that you will excel at learning the material in this chapter.

"YOU SIMPLY ASSOCIATE EACH NUMBER WITH A WORD, SUCH AS 'TABLE' AND 3,476,029."

S. Harris / www.CartoonStock.com

Perhaps Mnemosyne—the personification of memory in Greek mythology and the origin of the word "mnemonics"—will help you answer this question.

Camille is furious with her history professor. "I read the chapter three times, but I still failed the exam," she fumes. "The test must have been unfair." What's wrong with Camille's reasoning, and what are some other possible explanations for her poor performance, based on principles of critical thinking and what you have learned so far about memory?

Answers:

Camille is reasoning emotionally and is not examining the assumptions underlying her explanation. Perhaps she relied on automatic rather than effortful encoding, used maintenance instead of elaborative rehearsal, and used shallow instead of deep processing when she studied. Perhaps she didn't try to actively retrieve and recall the material while studying. She may also have tried to encode everything instead of being selective.

 YOU are about to learn . . .

♦ the problem with remembering everything.

♦ the major reasons we forget even when we'd rather not.

♦ why most researchers are skeptical about claims of repressed and "recovered" memories.

WHY WE FORGET

Have you ever, in the heat of some deliriously happy moment, said to yourself, "I'll never forget this, never, *never*, NEVER"? Do you find that you can more clearly remember saying those words than the deliriously happy moment itself? Sometimes you encode an event, you rehearse it, you analyze its meaning, you tuck it away in long-term storage, and still you forget it. Is it any wonder that most of us have wished, at one time or another, for a "photographic memory"?

Actually, having a perfect memory is not the blessing that you might suppose. The Russian psychologist Alexander Luria (1968) once told of a journalist, S., who could reproduce giant grids of numbers both forward and backward, even after the passage of 15 years. To accomplish his astonishing feats, he used *mnemonics*

◉ Watch
Mnemonics

(recall from Chapter 1 that mnemonics are tricks or rhymes that allow you to recall information), especially the formation of visual images. But you should not envy him, for he had a serious problem: He could not forget even when he wanted to. Along with the diamonds of experience, he kept dredging up the pebbles. Images he had formed to aid his memory kept creeping into consciousness, distracting him and interfering with his ability to concentrate. At times he even had trouble holding a conversation because the other person's words would set off a jumble of associations. Eventually, S. took to supporting himself by travelling from place to place, demonstrating his mnemonic abilities for audiences.

Or consider two modern cases. Brad Williams and Jill Price both have extraordinary memories and have offered to have their abilities studied by scientists. When given any date going back for decades, they are able to say instantly what they were doing, what day of the week it was, and whether anything of great importance happened on that date. Mention November 7, 1991, to Williams, and he says (correctly), "Let's see; that would be around when Magic Johnson announced he had HIV. Yes, a Thursday. There was a big snowstorm here the week before." Neither Williams nor Price uses mnemonics or can say where their accurate memories come from. Although Williams and his family regard his abilities as a source of amusement, Price describes her nonstop recollections as a mixed blessing (Parker, Cahill, & McGaugh, 2006). The phenomenon of constant, uncontrollable recall, she wrote, is "totally exhausting. Some have called it a gift, but I call it a burden. I run my entire life through my head every day and it drives me crazy!!!"

Paradoxically, then, forgetting is adaptive: We need to forget some things if we wish to remember efficiently. Piling up facts without distinguishing the important from the trivial is just confusing. Nonetheless, most of us forget more than we want to and would like to know why.

In the early days of psychology, in an effort to measure pure memory loss independent of personal experience, Hermann Ebbinghaus (1885/1913) memorized long lists of nonsense syllables, such as *bok*, *waf*, and *ged*, and then tested his retention over a period of several weeks. Most of his forgetting occurred soon after the initial learning and then levelled off (see Figure 10.8a). Ebbinghaus's method of studying memory was adopted by generations of psychologists, but it did not tell them much about the kinds of memories that people care about most.

FIGURE 10.8 Two Kinds of Forgetting Curves

Hermann Ebbinghaus, who tested his own memory for nonsense syllables, found that his forgetting was rapid at first and then tapered off (a). In contrast, when Marigold Linton tested her own memory for personal events over a period of several years, her retention was excellent at first, but then it fell off at a gradual but steady rate (b).

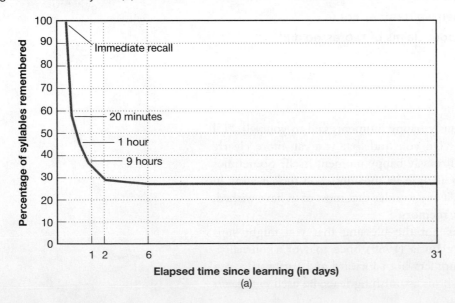

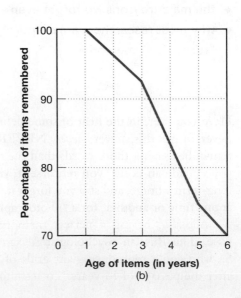

A century later, Marigold Linton decided to find out how people forget real events rather than nonsense syllables. Like Ebbinghaus, she used herself as a subject, but she charted the curve of forgetting over years rather than days. Every day for 12 years she recorded on a four-by-six–inch card two or more things that had happened to her that day. Eventually, she accumulated a catalogue of thousands of discrete events, both trivial ("I have dinner at the Canton Kitchen: delicious lobster dish") and significant ("I land at Orly Airport in Paris"). Once a month, she took a random sampling of all the cards accumulated to that point, noted whether she could remember the events on them, and tried to date the events. Linton (1978) expected the kind of rapid forgetting reported by Ebbinghaus. Instead, as you can see in Figure 10.8b, she found that long-term forgetting was slower and proceeded at a much more constant pace, as details gradually dropped out of her memories.

Of course, some memories, especially those that mark important transitions, are more memorable than others. But why did Marigold Linton, like the rest of us, forget so many details? Psychologists have proposed five mechanisms to account for forgetting: decay, replacement of old memories by new ones, interference, cue-dependent forgetting, and psychological amnesia brought on by repression.

Motor skills, which are stored as procedural memories, can last a lifetime; they never decay.

Decay

One commonsense view, the **decay theory**, holds that memories simply fade with time if they are not accessed now and then. We have already seen that decay occurs in sensory memory and that it occurs in short-term memory as well unless we keep rehearsing the material. However, the mere passage of time does not account so well for forgetting in long-term memory. People commonly forget things that happened only yesterday while remembering events from many years ago. Indeed, some memories, both procedural and declarative, can last a lifetime. If you learned to swim as a child, you will still know how to swim at age 30, even if you have not been in a pool or lake for 22 years. We are also happy to report that some school lessons have great staying power. In one study, people did well on a Spanish test some 50 years after taking Spanish in high school, even though most had hardly used Spanish at all in the intervening years (Bahrick, 1984). Decay alone cannot entirely explain lapses in long-term memory.

decay theory The theory that information in memory eventually disappears if it is not accessed; it applies better to short-term than to long-term memory.

FIGURE 10.9 The Stop-Sign Study

When people who saw a car with a yield sign (left) were later asked if they had seen "the stop sign" (a misleading question), many said they had. Similarly, when those shown a stop sign were asked if they had seen "the yield sign," many said yes. These false memories persisted even after the participants were told about the misleading questions, suggesting that misleading information had erased their original mental representations of the signs (Loftus, Miller, & Burns, 1978).

Replacement

Another theory holds that new information entering memory can wipe out old information, just as recording over a videotape will obliterate the original material. In a study supporting this view, researchers showed people slides of a traffic accident and used leading questions to get them to think that they had seen a stop sign when they had really seen a yield sign, or vice versa (see Figure 10.9). People in

✳ Explore
Encoding, Storage, and Retrieval
in Memory

a control group who were not misled in this way were able to identify the sign they had actually seen. Later, all the participants were told the purpose of the study and were asked to guess whether they had been misled. Almost all of those who had been misled continued to insist that they had *really*, *truly* seen the sign whose existence had been planted in their minds (Loftus, Miller, & Burns, 1978). The researchers interpreted this finding to mean that the subjects had not just been trying to please them and that people's original perceptions had in fact been erased by the misleading information.

Interference

A third theory holds that forgetting occurs because similar items of information interfere with one another in either storage or retrieval; the information may get into memory and stay there, but it becomes confused with other information. Such interference, which occurs in both short- and long-term memory, is especially common when you have to recall isolated facts such as names, addresses, passwords, and area codes.

Suppose you are at a party and you meet someone named Julie. A little later you meet someone named Judy. You go on to talk to other people, and after an hour, you again bump into Julie, but by mistake you call her Judy. The second name has interfered with the first. This type of interference, in which new information interferes with the ability to remember old information, is called **retroactive interference**:

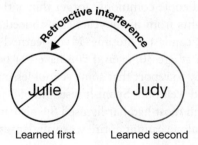

Retroactive interference is illustrated by the story of an absentminded professor of ichthyology (the study of fish) who complained that whenever he learned the name of a new student, he forgot the name of a fish. But whereas with replacement, the new memory erases the old and makes it irretrievable, in retroactive interference the loss of the old memory is sometimes just temporary. With a little concentration, that professor could probably recall his new students and his old fish.

Interference also works in the opposite direction. Old information (such as the foreign language you learned in high school) may interfere with the ability to remember current information (such as the new language you are trying to learn now). This type of interference is called **proactive interference**:

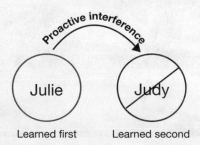

retroactive interference Forgetting that occurs when recently learned material interferes with the ability to remember similar material stored previously.

proactive interference Forgetting that occurs when previously stored material interferes with the ability to remember similar, more recently learned material.

Over a period of weeks, months, and years, proactive interference may cause more forgetting than retroactive interference does, because we have stored up so much information that can potentially interfere with anything new.

Cue-Dependent Forgetting

Often, when we need to remember, we rely on *retrieval cues*, items of information that can help us find the specific information we're looking for. For example, if you are trying to remember the last name of an actor you saw in an old film, it might help to know the actor's first name or another movie the actor starred in.

When we lack retrieval cues, we may feel as if we are lost in the mind's library. In long-term memory, this type of memory failure, called **cue-dependent forgetting**, may be the most common type of all. Willem Wagenaar (1986), who, like Marigold Linton, recorded critical details about events in his life, found that within a year he had forgotten 20% of those details; after five years, he had forgotten 60%. Yet when he gathered cues from witnesses about 10 events that he thought he had forgotten, he was able to recall something about all 10, which suggests that some of his forgetting was cue dependent.

Charlie Chaplin's film *City Lights* provides a classic illustration of state-dependent memory. After Charlie saves a drunken millionaire's life, the two spend the rest of the evening carousing. But the next day, after sobering up, the millionaire fails to recognize Charlie and gives him the cold shoulder. Then, once again, the millionaire gets drunk, and once again greets Charlie as a pal. (Note: Your memory will be best if you are sober during both encoding and recall!)

Cues that were present when you learned a new fact or had an experience are apt to be especially useful later as retrieval aids. That may explain why remembering is often easier when you are in the same physical environment as you were when an event occurred: Cues in the present context match those from the past. Ordinarily, this overlap helps us remember the past more accurately. But it may also help account for the eerie phenomenon of *déjà vu*, the fleeting sense of having been in *exactly* the same situation that you are in now (*déjà vu* means "already seen" in French). Some element in the present situation, familiar from some other context that you cannot identify—even a dream, a novel, or a movie—may make the entire situation seem so familiar that it feels like it happened before (Brown, 2004). In other words, déjà vu may be a kind of mistaken recognition memory. Similar feelings of familiarity can actually be produced in the laboratory. When something about newly presented words, shapes, or photographs resembles elements of stimuli seen previously, people report that the new words, shapes, or photographs are familiar even though they can't recall the original ones (Cleary, 2008).

In everyday forgetting, your mental or physical state may act as a retrieval cue, evoking a **state-dependent memory**. For example, if you were afraid or angry at the time of an event, you may remember that event best when you are once again in the same emotional state (Lang et al., 2001). Your memories can also be biased by whether or not your current mood is consistent with the emotional nature of the material you are trying to remember, a phenomenon known as **mood-congruent memory** (Bower & Forgas, 2000; Buchanan, 2007; Fiedler et al., 2001). You are more likely to remember happy events, and forget or ignore unhappy ones, when you are feeling happy than when you are feeling sad. Likewise, you are apt to remember unhappy events better and remember more of them when you are feeling unhappy,

cue-dependent forgetting The inability to retrieve information stored in memory because of insufficient cues for recall.

state-dependent memory The tendency to remember something when the rememberer is in the same physical or mental state as during the original learning or experience.

mood-congruent memory The tendency to remember experiences that are consistent with one's current mood and overlook or forget experiences that are not.

amnesia The partial or complete loss of memory for important personal information.

repression In psychoanalytic theory, the selective, involuntary pushing of threatening or upsetting information into the unconscious.

which in turn creates a vicious cycle. The more unhappy memories you recall, the more depressed you feel, and the more depressed you feel, the more unhappy memories you recall . . . so you stay stuck in your depression and make it even worse (Joormann & Gotlib, 2007; Wenzel, 2005).

The Repression Controversy

A final theory of forgetting is concerned with **amnesia**, the loss of memory for important personal information. Amnesia most commonly results from organic conditions such as brain disease or head injury, and is often temporary. However, for some individuals brain injury or disease results in profound and long-lasting memory deficits. Researchers at Baycrest Medical Centre in Toronto have relied on implicit memory to teach these individuals to use smartphones to compensate for their impaired explicit memory. Recent studies have demonstrated that, for both the affected individuals and their families, smartphones are effective prostheses that help them remember important events in their lives (Svoboda et al., 2010; Svoboda & Richards, 2009).

In *psychogenic amnesia*, however, the causes of forgetting are psychological, such as a need to escape feelings of embarrassment, guilt, shame, disappointment, or emotional shock. Psychogenic amnesia begins immediately after the precipitating event, involves massive memory loss including loss of personal identity, and usually ends suddenly, after just a few weeks. Despite its frequent portrayal in films and novels, in real life it is quite rare (McNally, 2003).

Psychologists generally accept the notion of psychogenic amnesia. *Traumatic amnesia*, however, is far more controversial. Traumatic amnesia allegedly involves the burying of specific traumatic events for a long period of time, often for many years. When the memory returns, it is supposedly immune to the usual processes of distortion and confabulation, and is recalled with perfect accuracy. The notion of traumatic amnesia originated with the psychoanalytic theory of Sigmund Freud, who argued that the mind defends itself from unwelcome and upsetting memories through the mechanism of **repression**, the involuntary pushing of threatening or upsetting information into the unconscious (see Chapter 14).

Most memory researchers reject the argument that a special unconscious mechanism called "repression" is necessary to explain either psychogenic or traumatic amnesia (Rofé, 2008). Richard McNally (2003) reviewed the experimental and clinical evidence and concluded, "The notion that the mind protects itself by repressing or dissociating memories of trauma, rendering them inaccessible to awareness, is a piece of psychiatric folklore devoid of convincing empirical support." The problem for most people who have suffered disturbing experiences is not that they cannot remember, but rather that they cannot forget: The memories keep intruding. There is no case on record of anyone who has repressed the memory of being in a concentration camp, being in combat, or being the victim of an earthquake or a terrorist attack, although details of even these horrible experiences are subject to distortion and fading over time, as are all memories.

Further, repression is hard to distinguish from normal forgetting. People who seem to forget disturbing experiences could be intentionally keeping themselves from retrieving their painful memories by distracting themselves whenever a memory is reactivated. Or they may be focusing consciously on positive memories instead. Perhaps, understandably, they are not rehearsing unhappy memories, so those memories fade with time. Perhaps they are simply avoiding the retrieval cues that would evoke the memories. But a reluctance to think about an upsetting experience is not the same as an *inability* to remember it (McNally, 2003).

The debate over traumatic amnesia and repression erupted into the public arena in the 1990s, when claims of recovered memories of sexual abuse began to appear. Many women and some men came to believe, during psychotherapy, that they could recall long-buried memories of having been sexually victimized for many years, and in bizarre ways. For therapists who accepted the notion of repression, such claims were entirely believable (Brown, Scheflin, & Whitfield, 1999; Herman, 1992). But most researchers today believe that almost all of these memories were false, having been evoked by therapists who were unaware of the research we described earlier on the power of suggestion and the dangers of confabulation (Lindsay & Read, 1994; McNally, 2003; Schacter, 2001). By asking leading questions, and by encouraging clients to construct vivid images of abuse, revisit those images frequently, and focus on emotional aspects of the images, such therapists unwittingly set up the very conditions that encourage confabulation and false memories.

Thinking Critically

Consider Other Interpretations

How should critical thinkers evaluate someone's claim that they repressed memories of bizarre, traumatic experiences that went on for years, and only remembered what happened decades later, in therapy? What other explanations can account for these apparent memories?

Since the 1990s, accusations have steadily declined and many accusers have reconciled with their families (McHugh et al., 2004). Yet the concept of repression lingers on. Many of its original proponents have turned to the term "dissociation" to account for memory failures in traumatized individuals (see Chapter 15), the idea being that upsetting memories are split off (dissociated) from everyday consciousness. But a review of the research has found no good evidence that early trauma causes such dissociation (Giesbrecht et al., 2008).

Of course, it is obviously possible for someone to forget a single unhappy or deeply unpleasant experience and not recall it for years, just as going back to your elementary school might trigger a memory of the time that you did something embarrassing in front of your whole class. How then should we respond to an individual's claim to have recovered memories of years of traumatic experiences that were previously "repressed"? How can we distinguish true memories from false ones?

Clearly, a person's recollections are likely to be trustworthy if there is corroborating evidence available, such as medical records, police or school reports, or the accounts of other people who had been present at the time. But in the absence of supporting evidence, we may have to tolerate uncertainty, because a person might have a detailed, emotionally rich "memory" that feels completely real but that has been unintentionally confabulated (Bernstein & Loftus, 2009). In such cases, it is important to consider the content of the recovered memory and how it was recovered.

Thus, given what we know about memory, we should be skeptical if the person says that he or she has memories from the first year or two of life; as we will see in the next section, this is not possible, physiologically or cognitively. We should be skeptical if, over time, the person's memories become more and more implausible; for instance, the person says that sexual abuse continued day and night for 15 years without ever being remembered and without anyone else in the household ever noticing anything amiss. We should also be skeptical if a person suddenly recovers a traumatic memory as a result of therapy or after hearing about supposed cases of recovered memory in the news or reading about one in a best-selling autobiography. And we should hear alarm bells go off if a therapist used suggestive techniques, such as hypnosis, dream analysis, "age regression," guided imagery, and leading questions, to "recover" the memories. These techniques are all known to increase confabulation (see Chapter 16).

quickQUIZ

✓• Quick Review on MyPsychLab

If you have not repressed what you just read, try these questions.

1. When reading the novel *Even Cowgirls Get the Blues* years ago, Wilma became a fan of the author, Tom Robbins. Later, she developed a crush on actor/director Tim Robbins, but every time she tried to recall his name, she called him "Tom." Why?

2. When a man at his twentieth high-school reunion sees his old friends, he recalls incidents he thought were long forgotten. Why?

3. What mechanisms other than repression could account for a person's psychogenic amnesia?

Answers:

1. proactive interference 2. The sight of his friends provides retrieval cues for the incidents. 3. The person could be intentionally avoiding the memory by using distraction or focusing on positive experiences; failure to rehearse the memory may be causing it to fade; or the person may be avoiding retrieval cues that would evoke the memory.

YOU are about to learn . . .

◆ why the first few years of life are a mental blank.

◆ why human beings have been called the "storytelling animal."

AUTOBIOGRAPHICAL MEMORIES

For most of us, our memories about our own experiences are by far the most fascinating. We use them to entertain ("Did I ever tell you about the time. . . ?"). We analyze them to learn more about who we are. We modify and embellish them to impress others, and some people even publish them.

Childhood Amnesia: The Missing Years

A curious aspect of autobiographical memory is that most adults cannot recall any events from earlier than the third or fourth year of life. A few people apparently can vaguely recall momentous experiences that occurred when they were as young as two years old, such as the birth of a sibling, but not earlier ones (Fivush & Nelson, 2004; Usher & Neisser, 1993). As adults, we cannot remember being fed in infancy, taking our first steps, or uttering our first halting sentences. We are victims of **childhood amnesia** (sometimes called *infantile amnesia*).

There is something disturbing about childhood amnesia—so disturbing that some people adamantly deny it, claiming to remember events from the second or even the first year of life. But like other false memories, these are merely reconstructions based on photographs, family stories, and imagination. The "remembered" event may not have even taken place. Swiss psychologist Jean Piaget (1952) once reported a memory of nearly being kidnapped at the age of two. Piaget remembered sitting in his pram, watching his nurse as she bravely defended him from the kidnapper. He remembered the scratches she received on her face. He remembered a police officer with a short cloak and white baton who finally chased the kidnapper away. But when Piaget was 15, his nurse wrote to his parents confessing that she had

childhood (infantile) amnesia The inability to remember events and experiences that occurred during the first two or three years of life.

Thinking Critically

Avoid Emotional Reasoning

Many people get upset at the idea that their earliest experiences are lost to memory and angrily insist that memories from the first two years must be accurate. How can research help us think clearly about this issue?

made up the entire story. Piaget noted, "I therefore must have heard, as a child, the account of this story. . . and projected it into the past in the form of a visual memory, which was a memory of a memory, but false."

Of course, we all retain procedural memories from the toddler stage, when we first learned to use a fork, drink from a cup, and pull a wagon. We also retain semantic memories acquired early in life: the rules of counting, the names of people and things, knowledge about objects in the world, words and meanings. Moreover, toddlers who are only one to two years old often reveal nonverbally that they remember past experiences (for example, by imitating something they saw earlier); and some four-year-olds can remember experiences that occurred before age two and a half (Bauer, 2002; McDonough & Mandler, 1994; Tustin & Hayne, 2006). What young children do not do well is encode and retain their early episodic memories—memories of particular events—and carry them into later childhood or adulthood. They can't start doing this consistently until about age four and a half (Fivush & Nelson, 2004).

Freud thought that childhood amnesia was a special case of repression, but memory researchers today think that repression has nothing to do with it, and they point to better explanations:

1 **Brain development.** Parts of the brain involved in the formation or storage of events, and other areas involved in working memory and decision making, are not well developed until a few years after birth, especially the prefontal cortex (McKee & Squire, 1993; Newcombe et al., 2000). In addition, the brains of infants and toddlers are busily attending to all the new experiences of life, but this very fact makes it difficult for them to focus on just one event and shut out everything else that's going on—the kind of focus necessary for encoding and remembering (Gopnik, 2009).

2 **Cognitive development.** Before you can carry memories about yourself with you into adulthood, you have to have a self to remember. The emergence of a self-concept usually does not take place before age 2 (Howe, Courage, & Peterson, 1994). In addition, the cognitive schemas used by preschoolers are very different from those used by older children and adults. Only after acquiring language and starting school do children form schemas that contain the information and cues necessary for recalling earlier experiences (Howe, 2000). Young children's limited vocabularies and language skills also prevent them from narrating some aspects of an experience to themselves or others. Later, after their linguistic abilities have matured, they still cannot use those abilities to recall earlier, preverbal memories, because those memories were not encoded linguistically (Simcock & Hayne, 2002).

3 **Social development.** Preschoolers have not yet mastered the social conventions for reporting events, nor have they learned what is important to others. As a result, they focus on the routine aspects of an experience rather than the distinctive ones that will provide retrieval cues later, and they encode their experiences far less elaborately than adults do. Instead, they tend to rely on adults' questions to provide retrieval cues ("Where did we go for breakfast?" "Who did you go trick-or-treating with?"). This dependency on adults may prevent them from building up a stable core of remembered material that will be available when they are older (Fivush & Hamond, 1991).

Nonetheless, our first memories, even when they are not accurate, may provide useful insights into our personalities, current concerns, ambitions, and attitudes toward life. What are *your* first memories—or, at least, what do you think they are? What might they tell you about yourself?

This infant, whose leg is attached by a string to a colourful mobile, will learn within minutes to make the mobile move by kicking it. She may still remember the trick a week later, an example of procedural memory (Rovee-Collier, 1993). However, when she is older she will not remember the experience itself; she will fall victim to childhood amnesia.

Memory and Narrative: The Stories of Our Lives

The communications researcher George Gerbner once observed that human beings are unique because we are the only animal that tells stories—and lives by the stories we tell. This view of human beings as the "storytelling animal" has had a huge impact in cognitive psychology. The *narratives* we compose to simplify and make sense of our lives have a profound influence on our plans, memories, love affairs, hatreds, ambitions, and dreams.

Thus we say, "I have no academic motivation because I flunked grade 3." We say, "Let me tell you the story of how we fell in love." We say, "When you hear what happened, you'll understand why I felt entitled to take such cold-hearted revenge." These stories are not necessarily fictions; rather, they are attempts to organize and give meaning to the events of our lives. But because these narratives rely heavily on memory, and because memories are reconstructed and are constantly shifting in response to current needs, beliefs, and experiences, our autobiographies are also, to some degree, works of interpretation and imagination. Adult memories thus reveal as much about the present as they do about the past.

When you construct a narrative about an incident in your life, you have many choices about how to do it. The spin you put on a story depends on who the audience is; you are apt to put in, leave out, understate, and embellish different things depending on whether you are telling about an event in your life to a therapist, your boss, or friends on Facebook. Your story is also influenced by your purpose in relating it: for example, to convey facts, entertain, or elicit sympathy. As a result of these influences, distortions are apt to creep in, even when you think you are being accurate. And once those distortions are part of the story, they are likely to become part of your memory of the events themselves (Marsh & Tversky, 2004).

Your culture also affects how you encode and tell your story. North American undergraduates live in a culture that emphasizes individuality, personal feelings, and self-expression. Their earliest childhood memories reflect that fact: They tend to report lengthy, emotionally elaborate memories of events, memories that focus on—who else?—themselves. In contrast, Chinese students, who live in a culture that emphasizes group harmony, social roles, and personal humility, tend to report early memories of family or neighbourhood activities, conflicts with friends or relatives that were resolved, and emotionally neutral events (Wang, 2008).

Once you have formulated a story's central theme ("My father never approved of us"; "My partner was always competitive with me"), that theme may then serve as a cognitive schema that guides what you remember and what you forget (Mather, Shafir, & Johnson, 2000). For example, teenagers who have strong and secure attachments to their mothers remember previous quarrels with their moms as being less intense and conflicted than they reported at the time, whereas teenagers who have more ambivalent and insecure attachments remember such quarrels as being worse than they were (Feeney & Cassidy, 2003). A story's theme may also influence our judgments of events and people in the present. If you have a fight with your partner, the central theme in your story about the fight might be negative ("He was a jerk") or neutral ("It was a mutual misunderstanding"). This theme may bias you to blame or forgive your partner long after you have forgotten what the conflict was all about or who said what (McGregor & Holmes, 1999). You can see that the spin you give a story is critical, so be careful about the stories you tell!

"And here I am at two years of age. Remember? Mom? Pop? No? Or how about this one. My first day of school. Anyone?"

quick**QUIZ**

✔ Quick Review on **MyPsychLab**

You can't blame childhood amnesia if you have forgotten the answers to these questions.

1. A friend of yours claims to remember her birth, her first tooth, and her first birthday party. She is most likely to be (a) lying, (b) confabulating, (c) repressing, (d) revealing wishful thinking, (e) accurately remembering.
2. Give three explanations for childhood amnesia (be specific).
3. Why are the themes in our life stories so important?

Answers:

1. b, d 2. the immaturity of certain brain structures, making it difficult for very young children to focus attention, encode, and remember; cognitive factors such as immature cognitive schemas, lack of linguistic skills, and lack of a self-concept; lack of knowledge of social conventions for encoding and reporting events 3. They guide what we remember and forget about our personal pasts, and affect our judgments of events and people.

By now, if you have been reading this chapter actively, you should be able to recall the many factors that can trip you up when you call upon your memory to add a plot twist to your life story, to remember a fact, or to idly daydream about a past event: confabulation, source misattribution, poor encoding and rehearsal strategies, interference, inadequate retrieval cues, suggestibility, and biases. By now, therefore, you should not be surprised that memory can be as fickle as it can be accurate. As cognitive psychologists have shown repeatedly, we are not merely actors in our personal life dramas; we also write the scripts.

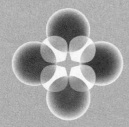

Taking Psychology with YOU

Thinking Critically in Everyday Life

Memory and Myth

Psychological research is having a significant impact on people's ability to think critically about memory. Most notably, awareness of the fallibility of memory is growing among police, interrogators, prosecutors, and judges. At the start of this chapter, we promised to tell you what happened in the case of Thomas Sophonow, who was convicted of the murder of Barbara Stoppel on the strength of eyewitness testimony.

In 2000, the Winnipeg police announced that DNA evidence obtained from the crime scene did not match that of Thomas Sophonow and that they had a new suspect in the murder. In 2001, the Province of Manitoba struck an inquiry into the Sophonow case and found that the investigators had made many critical errors, including in how they questioned eyewitnesses. Thomas Sophonow was awarded $2.6 million in compensation for his wrongful imprisonment.

The case of Thomas Sophonow, though, is far from unique. In Canada alone, there have been similar high-profile cases: Guy Paul Morin, David Milgaard, Steven Truscott, and Donald Marshall Jr., to name a few. When psychological scientists examined 40 cases in which wrongful conviction had been established beyond a doubt, they found that 90% of those cases had involved a false identification by one or more eyewitnesses (Wells et al., 1998).

Of course, not all eyewitness testimony is erroneous. But the potential for errors in identification shows how important it is to gather evidence carefully, ensure adequate legal representation for defendants, conduct police interviews using proper procedures, reduce pressure on witnesses, and obtain a DNA analysis whenever possible.

Inspired by the Innocence Project at the Cardozo School of Law in New York City, grassroots organizations of lawyers and students have been successfully challenging questionable convictions in both the United States and Canada. Since the early 1990s, these efforts have led to the exoneration of some 250 innocent people, some of whom had been condemned to death (see individual cases at www.innocence.org). In 2006, a documentary film, *After Innocence*, chronicled seven cases of wrongful imprisonment; the men involved are still struggling to get their convictions expunged from their records.

How would you feel if your testimony resulted in the conviction of an innocent person? Would you be able to admit your mistake, or would you, as most people do, cling more stubbornly than ever to the accuracy of your memory? Clearly, eyewitnesses can and do make mistakes; ethnic differences can increase these mistakes; even memories of shocking or traumatic experiences are vulnerable to distortion and influence by others; and our confidence in our memories is not a reliable guide to their accuracy. Remember, many eyewitnesses are very confident, and the relation between confidence in memories and the accuracy of these memories is very poor.

Human memory has both tremendous strengths and tremendous weaknesses. Because our deepest sense of ourselves relies on our memories, this is a difficult truth to accept. It is so much easier to give in to emotional reasoning ("I just feel that my memory is absolutely, 100% true!") and not consider other explanations ("Could my brother's account of that family quarrel be more accurate than mine?"). But if we can do so, we will be able to respect the great power of memory and at the same time retain humility about our capacity for error, confabulation, and self-deception.

SUMMARY

RECONSTRUCTING THE PAST

◆ Unlike a tape recorder or video camera, human memory is highly selective and is reconstructive: People add, delete, and change elements in ways that help them make sense of information and events. They often experience *source misattribution*, the inability to distinguish information stored during an event from information added later. Even vivid *flashbulb memories* tend to become less accurate or complete over time.

◆ Because memory is reconstructive, it is subject to *confabulation*, the confusion of imagined events with actual ones. Confabulation is especially likely when the image of the event contains many details; the event is easy to imagine; or people have thought, heard, or told others about the imagined event many times and thus experience *imagination inflation*. Confabulated memories can feel vividly real yet be false.

MEMORY AND THE POWER OF SUGGESTION

◆ The reconstructive nature of memory makes memory vulnerable to suggestion. Eyewitness testimony is especially vulnerable to error when the suspect's ethnicity differs from that of the witness, when leading questions are put to witnesses, or when the witnesses are given misleading information.

◆ Like adults, children often remember the essential aspects of an event accurately. However, like adults, they can also be suggestible, especially when responding to biased interviewing by adults—for example, when they are asked questions that blur the line between fantasy and reality, are asked leading questions, are told what "other kids" had supposedly said, and are praised for making false allegations.

IN PURSUIT OF MEMORY

◆ The ability to remember depends in part on the type of performance called for. In tests of *explicit memory* (conscious recollection), *recognition* is usually better than *recall*. In tests of *implicit memory*, which is measured by indirect methods such as *priming* and the *relearning method*, past experiences may affect current thoughts or actions even when these experiences are not consciously remembered.

◆ In *information-processing models*, memory involves the *encoding*, *storage*, and retrieval of information. In the *three-box model*, there are three interacting systems: the sensory register, short-term memory, and long-term memory. Some cognitive scientists prefer a *parallel distributed processing*

(PDP) or *connectionist model*, which represents knowledge as connections among numerous interacting processing units, distributed in a vast network and all operating in parallel. But the three-box model continues to offer a convenient way to organize the major findings on memory.

THE THREE-BOX MODEL OF MEMORY

◆ In the *three-box model*, incoming sensory information makes a brief stop in the sensory register, which momentarily retains it in the form of sensory images.

◆ *Short-term memory (STM)* retains new information for up to 30 seconds by most estimates (unless rehearsal takes place). The capacity of STM is extremely limited but can be extended if information is organized into larger units by *chunking*. Early models of STM portrayed it mainly as a storage and rehearsal buffer, but many models now envision it also as a working memory, which includes the mental processes that control the retrieval of information from long-term memory and that interpret that information appropriately depending on the task being performed. *Working memory* permits us to control attention, resist distraction, and therefore maintain information in an active, accessible state.

◆ *Long-term memory (LTM)* contains an enormous amount of information that must be organized to make it manageable. Words (or the concepts they represent) are often organized by *semantic categories*. Many models of LTM represent its contents as a network of interrelated concepts. The way people use these networks depends on experience and education. Research on *tip-of-the-tongue (TOT) states* shows that words are also indexed in terms of sound and form.

◆ *Procedural memories* ("knowing how") are memories for how to perform specific actions; *declarative memories* ("knowing that") are memories for abstract or representational knowledge. Declarative memories include *semantic memories* (general knowledge) and *episodic memories* (memories for personally experienced events).

◆ The three-box model is often invoked to explain the *serial-position effect* in memory, but although it can explain the *primacy effect*, it cannot explain why a *recency effect* sometimes occurs after a considerable delay.

THE BIOLOGY OF MEMORY

◆ Short-term memory involves temporary changes within neurons that alter their ability to release neurotransmitters, whereas long-term memory involves lasting structural changes in neurons and synapses. *Long-term potentiation*, an increase in the strength of synaptic responsiveness, seems to be an important mechanism of long-term memory.

◆ The amygdala is involved in the formation and retrieval of emotional memories. Areas of the frontal lobes are especially active during short-term and working memory tasks. The prefrontal cortex and parts of the temporal lobes are involved in the efficient encoding of words and pictures. The hippocampus plays a critical role in the formation and retrieval of long-term declarative memories. Other areas, such as the cerebellum, are crucial for the formation of procedural memories. Studies of patients with amnesia suggest that different brain systems are active during explicit and implicit memory tasks. The long-term storage of declarative memories possibly takes place in cortical areas that were active during the original perception of the information or event. The various components of a memory are probably stored at different sites, with all of these sites participating in the representation of the event as a whole.

◆ Hormones released by the adrenal glands during stress or emotional arousal, including epinephrine and norepinephrine, enhance memory. These adrenal hormones cause the level of glucose to rise in the bloodstream, and glucose may enhance memory directly or by altering the effects of neurotransmitters. But very high hormone levels can interfere with the retention of information; a moderate level is optimal for learning new tasks.

HOW WE REMEMBER

◆ To remember material well, we must encode it accurately in the first place. Some kinds of information, such as material in a university course, require *effortful*, as opposed to *automatic*, encoding. Rehearsal of information keeps it in short-term memory and increases the chances of long-term retention. *Elaborative rehearsal* is more likely to result in transfer to long-term memory than is *maintenance rehearsal*, and *deep processing* is usually a more effective retention strategy than *shallow processing*.

WHY WE FORGET

◆ Forgetting can occur for several reasons. Information in sensory and short-term memory appears to *decay* if it does not receive further processing. New information may erase and replace old information in long-term memory. *Proactive and retroactive interference* may take place. *Cue-dependent forgetting* may occur when *retrieval cues* are inadequate. The most effective retrieval cues are those that were present at the time of the initial experience. A person's mental or physical state may also act as a retrieval cue, evoking a *state-dependent memory*. We tend to remember best those events that are congruent with our current mood (*mood-congruent memory*).

◆ *Amnesia*, the forgetting of important personal information, usually occurs because of disease or injury to the brain. *Psychogenic amnesia*, which involves a loss of personal identity and has psychological causes, is rare. *Traumatic amnesia*, which allegedly involves the forgetting of specific traumatic events for long periods of time, is highly controversial, as is *repression*, the psychodynamic explanation of traumatic amnesia. Because these concepts lack good empirical support, psychological scientists are skeptical about their validity and about the accuracy of "recovered memories." Critics argue that many therapists, unaware of the power of suggestion and the dangers of confabulation, have encouraged false memories of victimization.

AUTOBIOGRAPHICAL MEMORIES

◆ Most people cannot recall any events from earlier than the third or fourth year of life. The reasons for such *childhood amnesia* include the immaturity of certain brain structures, making it difficult for very young children to focus attention, encode, and remember; cognitive factors such as immature cognitive schemas, lack of linguistic skills, and lack of a self-concept; and lack of knowledge of social conventions for encoding and reporting events.

◆ A person's narrative "life story" organizes the events of his or her life and gives them meaning.

TAKING PSYCHOLOGY WITH YOU

◆ DNA evidence has exonerated many people who were falsely convicted of rape and murder, making the public and the criminal-justice system more aware of the limitations of eyewitness testimony and the fallibility of memory.

MyPsychLab

Visit **www.mypsychlab.com** to help you get the best grade!
Test your knowledge and grasp difficult concepts through

• **Custom study plans:** See where you are strong and where you go wrong

• **Interactive simulations**

• **Video and audio clips**

KEY TERMS

source misattribution 364
confabulation 365
explicit memory 372
recall 372
recognition 372
implicit memory 372
priming 373
relearning method 373
parallel distributed processing
  (PDP) model 375
sensory register 376

short-term memory (STM) 376
chunks 377
working memory 378
long-term memory (LTM) 378
procedural memories 380
declarative memories 380
semantic memories 380
episodic memories 380
serial-position effect 381
long-term potentiation 383
maintenance rehearsal 390

elaborative rehearsal 390
deep processing 390
decay theory 393
retroactive interference 394
proactive interference 394
cue-dependent forgetting 395
state-dependent memory 395
mood-congruent memory 395
amnesia 396
repression 396
childhood (infantile) amnesia 398

Answers to the Get Involved exercises on pages 372 and 374:
Rudolph's eight friends were Dasher, Dancer, Prancer, Vixen, Comet, Cupid, Donder, and Blitzen.

Answer to the Get Involved exercise on page 389:
The real penny is the left one in the bottom row.

11 EMOTION, STRESS, AND HEALTH

ASK QUESTIONS . . . be willing to WONDER

- Do people everywhere in the world feel the same emotions?

- Do we have any control over our emotions or do they just "come out of nowhere"?

- Does stress increase your chances of getting sick?

- When life hands you a lemon of a problem, how can you make lemonade?

Clara Harris, age 45, a dentist, former beauty queen, and mother of twin boys, was sentenced to 20 years in prison and a $10,000 fine for the first-degree murder of her husband. The jury ruled that the defendant had acted with "sudden passion" when she ran over him repeatedly with her Mercedes-Benz in the parking lot of the hotel where they had been married 11 years before. Clara Harris testified that she had become frightened, angry, and humiliated when she learned that her husband was having an affair. When he told her she was "too big," but that his mistress had a "perfect body," Dr. Harris said she joined a fitness club, went to the hairdresser every day, and made plans to have liposuction and breast-enlargement surgery. Later, suspecting that her husband had not broken off his affair, she hired a private detective to follow him. Learning that he and his mistress were at the hotel, she confronted them in the hotel parking lot. Running him over "happened in a fraction of a second," she said. "I didn't have time to think."

Almost everyone can understand Clara Harris's feelings. Most of us will, at some time, taste the bitterness of rejection and feel the excruciating pangs of embarrassment and humiliation. Fortunately, most people do not act on their furious impulses, or at least they act on them in nonviolent ways. Why do people sometimes give in to their emotions, apparently losing control of them, whereas others are able to keep rage and other unpleasant feelings from turning into violent or self-destructive actions?

In this chapter, we will explore this question and others, as we examine the physiology and psychology of emotions and stress. Prolonged negative emotions such as anger can certainly be stressful, and stress can certainly produce negative emotions. Both of these processes, however, are shaped by how we interpret the events that happen to us, by the demands of the situation we are in, and by the rules of our culture.

YOU are about to learn . . .

◆ which facial expressions of emotion most people recognize the world over.

◆ which parts of the brain are involved with different aspects of emotion.

◆ how mirror neurons generate empathy, mood contagion, and synchrony.

◆ which two hormones provide the energy and excitement of emotion.

◆ how thoughts create emotions—and why an infant can't feel shame or guilt.

THE NATURE OF EMOTION

People often curse their emotions, wishing to be freed from anger, jealousy, shame, guilt, and grief. Yet imagine a life without emotions. You would be unmoved by the magic of music. You would never care about losing someone you love, not only because you would not know sadness but also because you would not know love. You would never laugh because nothing would strike you as funny. And you would be a social isolate because you would not be able to know what other people were feeling.

Emotions evolved to help people meet the challenges of life: They bind people together, motivate them to achieve their goals, and help them make decisions and plans (Nesse & Ellsworth, 2009). When you are faced with a decision between two appealing and justifiable career alternatives, for example, your sense of which one "feels right" emotionally may help you make the better choice. Disgust evolved as a mechanism that protects infants and adults from eating tainted or poisonous food (Oaten, Stevenson, & Case, 2009). Even embarrassment and blushing, so painful to the individual, serve an important function: appeasing others when you feel you have made a fool of yourself, broken a moral rule, or violated a social norm (Dijk, de Jong, & Peters, 2009; Keltner & Anderson, 2000). And the positive emotions of joy, love, laughter, and playfulness do not appear to be simply selfish feelings of pleasure; their adaptive function may be to help increase mental flexibility and resilience, build bonds with others, stimulate creativity, and reduce stress, as we will see later in this chapter (Baas, De Dreu, & Nijstad, 2008; Kok, Catalino, & Frederickson, 2008).

In defining **emotion**, psychologists focus on three major components: *physiological* changes in the face, brain, and body; *cognitive* processes such as interpretations of events; and *cultural* influences that shape the experience and expression of emotion. If we compare human emotions to a tree, the biological capacity for emotion is the trunk and root system; thoughts and explanations create the many branches; and culture is the gardener that shapes the tree and prunes it, cutting off some limbs and cultivating others. Let's begin with the trunk.

Thinking ⚙ Critically

Don't Oversimplify

Many people wish they could be free of sadness, anger, jealousy, and other feelings that make them miserable. But what would our lives be like without emotions, even the troubling ones?

emotion A state of arousal involving facial and bodily changes, brain activation, cognitive appraisals, subjective feelings, and tendencies toward action.

primary emotions Emotions that are considered to be universal and biologically based.

Emotion and the Body

Research on the physiological aspects of emotion suggests that people everywhere are born with certain basic or **primary emotions**, which include fear, anger, sadness, joy, surprise, disgust, and contempt (Izard, 2007). These emotions have distinctive physiological patterns and corresponding facial expressions, and the situations that evoke them are the same all over the world: Everywhere, sadness follows perception of loss, fear follows perception of threat and bodily harm, anger follows perception of insult or injustice, and so forth (Scherer, 1997). In contrast, **secondary emotions** include all the variations and blends of emotion that vary from one culture to another or that depend on cognitive complexity.

Neuroscientists and other researchers are studying the biological aspects of emotions: facial expressions, brain regions and circuits, and the autonomic nervous system.

THE FACE OF EMOTION. The most obvious place to look for emotion is on the face, where emotions are often visibly expressed. Charles Darwin (1872/1965) argued that human facial expressions—the smile, the frown, the grimace, the glare—are as innate as the wing flutter of a frightened bird, the purr of a contented cat, and the snarl of a threatened wolf. Such expressions evolved, he said, because they allowed our ancestors to tell at a glance the difference between a friendly stranger and a hostile one.

Modern psychologists have supported Darwin's ideas about the evolutionary functions of emotion (Hess & Thibault, 2009). Paul Ekman and his colleagues have gathered abundant evidence for the universality of seven basic facial expressions of emotion, which correspond to the list of emotions usually identified as primary: anger, happiness, fear, surprise, disgust, sadness, and contempt (Ekman, 2003; Ekman et al., 1987). In every culture they have studied—in Brazil, Canada, Chile, Estonia, Germany, Greece, Hong Kong, Italy, Japan, New Guinea, Scotland, Sumatra, Turkey, and the United States—a large majority of people recognize the emotional expressions portrayed by those in other cultures (see Figure 11.1). Even most members of isolated tribes who have never watched a movie or read *People* magazine, such as

secondary emotions Emotions that are specific to certain cultures.

◄⊙ Simulate
Emotion and Motivation

◆ Research
Charles Darwin

FIGURE 11.1 Some Universal Expressions
Can you tell what feelings are being conveyed here? Most people around the world can readily identify expressions of surprise, disgust, happiness, sadness, anger, fear, and contempt—no matter what the age, culture, sex, or historical era of the person conveying the emotion. Some researchers think that pride might also be a universal emotion. Can you find the face of pride in this group?

👁 **Watch**
Show Your Pride

the Foré of New Guinea or the Minangkabau of West Sumatra, can recognize the emotions expressed in pictures of people who are entirely foreign to them, and we can recognize theirs. Lately, some researchers have argued that pride is also a basic human emotion; its adaptive function is to motivate people to achieve and excel, and thereby to increase their attractiveness to others and to their groups (Williams & DeSteno, 2009), as well as to signal status (Shariff & Tracy, 2009). Children as young as four years old, and people from an isolated cultural group in Africa, can reliably identify facial and bodily expressions of pride. Blind people who have just won an athletic competition will spontaneously throw their arms in the air in a V-for-victory symbol of triumph, though they have never seen anyone do it (Tracy & Robins, 2007, 2008).

Ekman and his associates developed a special coding system to analyze and identify each of the nearly 80 muscles of the face, as well as the combinations of muscles associated with various emotions (Ekman, 2003). When people try to hide their feelings and put on an emotion, they generally use different groups of muscles than they do for authentic ones. For example, when people try to pretend that they feel sad, only 15% manage to get the eyebrows, eyelids, and forehead wrinkle exactly right, mimicking the way true grief is expressed spontaneously. Authentic smiles last only two seconds; false smiles may last 10 seconds or more (Ekman, Friesen, & O'Sullivan, 1988).

THE FUNCTIONS OF FACIAL EXPRESSIONS.   Interestingly, facial expressions not only reflect our internal feelings; they also *influence* them. In the process of **facial feedback**, the facial muscles send messages to the brain about the basic emotion being expressed: A smile tells us that we're happy, a frown that we're angry or perplexed (Izard, 1990). When people are told to smile and look pleased or happy, their positive feelings increase; when they are told to look angry, displeased, or disgusted, positive feelings decrease (Kleinke, Peterson, & Rutledge, 1998). If you put on an angry face, your heart rate will rise faster than if you put on a happy face (Levenson, Ekman, & Friesen, 1990). The next time you are feeling sad or afraid, try purposely smiling, even if no one is around. Keep smiling. Does facial feedback work for you?

As Darwin suggested, facial expressions also probably evolved to help us communicate our emotional states to others and provoke a response from them—"Come help me!" "Get away!" (Fridlund, 1994). This signalling function begins in infancy. A baby's expressions of misery, angry frustration, or disgust are apparent to most parents, who respond by soothing an uncomfortable baby, feeding a grumpy one, or removing unappealing food from a disgusted one (Izard, 1994b; Stenberg & Campos, 1990). And an infant's smile of joy usually melts the heart of the weariest parent, provoking a happy cuddle. Babies seem primed to respond to adults' expressions, too. Tiny newborns will suck longer on a pacifier if it produces a happy face than if it produces a face with a neutral or negative expression (Walker-Andrews, 1997). (If you become a parent, remember this.)

Starting at the end of their first year, babies begin to alter their own behaviour in reaction to their parents' facial expressions of emotion, and this ability, too, has survival value. Do you recall the visual-cliff studies described in Chapter 6? These studies were originally designed to test for depth perception, which emerges early in infancy. But in one experiment, one-year-old babies were put on a more ambiguous visual cliff that did not drop off sharply and thus did not automatically evoke fear, as the original cliff did. In this case, the babies' behaviour depended on their mothers' expressions: 74% crossed the cliff when their mothers put on a happy, reassuring expression, but not a single infant crossed when the mother showed an expression of fear (Sorce et al.,

facial feedback   The process by which the facial muscles send messages to the brain about the basic emotion being expressed.

Facial expressions do not always convey the emotion being felt. A poised, social smile like Michaëlle Jean's (left) may have nothing to do with true feelings of happiness. And true feelings of happiness may not be obvious at all. Although Clara Hughes (right) was rejoicing after completing the women's 5000 metres speed skating race in the Vancouver 2010 Winter Olympics, she looks as if she could be angry or in pain.

1985). If you have ever watched a toddler take a tumble and then look at his or her parent before deciding whether to cry or to forget it, you will understand the influence of parental facial expressions. And you can see why they have had such survival value for babies: An infant needs to be able to read the parent's facial signals of alarm or safety because young children do not yet have the experience necessary for judging danger.

But there are cultural and social limits to the universal readability of facial expressions. For one thing, people are better at identifying emotions expressed by others in their own ethnic, national, or regional group than they are at recognizing the emotions of foreigners (Elfenbein & Ambady, 2003). Second, within a culture, facial expressions can have different meanings depending on the situation; a smile can mean "I'm happy!" or "I don't want to make you angry while I tell you this." Likewise, people will interpret identical facial expressions—even of basic emotions such as disgust, sadness, and anger—in very different ways, depending on what else they are observing in the social context. Thus, almost everyone recognizes the facial expression of disgust, if that's all they see. But when they see a picture of the same disgusted expression on a man with his arm raised as if to strike, they will say the expression is anger (Aviezer et al., 2008).

Finally, of course, facial expressions are only part of the emotional picture. People can feel sad, anxious, or angry without letting it show—and, conversely, they can use facial expressions to lie about their feelings. In Shakespeare's play *Henry VI*, the villain who will become the evil King Richard III says:

> *Why, I can smile, and murder while I smile;*
> *And cry content to that which grieves my heart;*
> *And wet my cheeks with artificial tears,*
> *And frame my face to all occasions.*

EMOTION AND THE BRAIN. Various parts of the brain are involved in the different components of emotional experience: recognizing another person's emotion, feeling a specific emotion, expressing an emotion, and acting on an emotion. For example, people who have a stroke that affects brain areas involved in the experience of disgust are often unable to feel disgusted. One young man with stroke damage in these regions had little or no emotional response to images and ideas that would be disgusting to most people, such as feces-shaped chocolate (Calder et al., 2000). Are you making a disgusted expression as you read that? He couldn't.

Most emotions motivate a response of some sort: to embrace or approach the person who instills joy in you, attack a person who makes you angry, withdraw from a food that disgusts you, or flee from a person or situation that frightens you. The

◉ Watch
How to Be Happy

◄◉ Simulate
Recognizing Facial Expressions of Emotions

prefrontal regions of the brain are involved in these impulses to approach or withdraw. Regions of the *right* prefrontal region are specialized for the impulse to withdraw or escape (as in disgust and fear). Regions of the *left* prefrontal cortex are specialized for the motivation to approach others (as in happiness, a positive emotion, and anger, a negative one) (Carver & Harmon-Jones, 2009; Harmon-Jones, Peterson, & Harris, 2009). People who have greater-than-average activation of the left areas, compared with the right, have more positive feelings, a quicker ability to recover from negative emotions, and a greater ability to suppress negative emotions (Urry et al., 2004). People with damage to this area often lose the capacity for joy.

Parts of the prefrontal cortex are also involved in the *regulation* of emotion, helping us modify and control our feelings, keeping us on an even keel, and responding appropriately to others (Jackson et al., 2003). A degenerative disease that destroys cells in parts of the frontal lobes causes not only a loss of cells, say researchers, but a "loss of self." It blunts the sufferer's ability to respond to the emotions of others, understand why they and others feel as they do, and adjust their own emotional responses appropriately: A loving mother becomes indifferent to her child's injury; a businessman does embarrassing things and doesn't notice the reaction of others (Levenson & Miller, 2007).

The amygdala, a small structure in the brain's limbic system, plays a key role in emotion, especially anger and fear. The amygdala is responsible for evaluating sensory information, determining its emotional importance, and making the initial decision to approach or withdraw from a person or situation (Adolphs, 2001; LeDoux, 1996). The amygdala instantly assesses danger or threat, which is a good thing, because otherwise you could be standing in the street asking, "Is it wise to cross now, while that very large truck is coming toward me?" The amygdala's initial response may then be overridden by a more accurate appraisal from the cortex. This is why you jump with fear when you suddenly feel a hand on your back in a dark alley, and why your fear evaporates when the cortex registers that the hand belongs to a friend whose

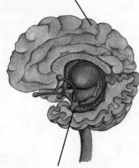

2. The cerebral cortex generates a more complete picture; it can override signals sent by the amygdala ("It's only Mike in a down coat").

1. The amygdala scrutinizes information for its emotional importance ("It's a bear! Be afraid! Run!").

Get INVOLVED!

TURN ON YOUR RIGHT HEMISPHERE

These faces have expressions of happiness on one side and sadness on the other. Look at the nose of each face: Which face looks happier? Which face looks sadder?

(a)

(b)

You are likely to see face b as the happier one and face a as the sadder one. The reason is that in most people the left side of a picture is processed by the right side of the brain, where recognition of emotional expression primarily occurs (Oatley & Jenkins, 1996).

lousy idea of humour is to scare you in a dark alley. If either the amygdala or critical areas of the cortex are damaged, abnormalities result in the ability to process fear. For example, people with damage in the amygdala often have difficulty recognizing fear in others, and people with damage in the cortex may have difficulty turning off their own fear responses (see Chapter 15).

MIRROR, MIRROR, IN THE BRAIN: NEURONS FOR IMITATION AND EMPATHY.   Some years ago, a team of Italian neuroscientists made an accidental, astonishing discovery. They had implanted wires in the brains of macaque monkeys, in regions involved in planning and carrying out movement. Every time a monkey moved and grasped an object, the cells fired and the monitor registered a sound. One day, a graduate student heard the monitor go off when the monkey was simply observing him eating an ice-cream cone. The neuroscientists looked more closely, and found that certain neurons in the monkeys' brains were firing not only when the monkeys were picking up peanuts and eating them but also when the monkeys were merely observing their human caretakers doing exactly the same thing (Ferrari, Rozzi, & Fogassi, 2005). These neurons responded only to very specific actions: A neuron that fired when a monkey grasped a peanut would also fire when the scientist grasped a peanut but not when the scientist grasped something else. The scientists called these cells **mirror neurons**. Incredibly, human mirror neurons do not simply recognize another person's action; they respond only when the action is *intentional* rather than accidental (Iacoboni, 2008; Iacoboni et al., 2005).

Mirror neurons are clearly at work in this conversation.

In human beings, mirror neurons enable us to identify with what others are feeling, understand other people's intentions, and imitate their actions and gestures (Fogassi & Ferrari, 2007; Molnar-Szakacs et al., 2005). For example, when you see another person in pain, one reason you feel a jolt of empathy is that mirror neurons involved in pain are firing. When you watch a spider crawl up someone's leg, one reason you have a creepy sensation is that your mirror neurons are firing—the same ones that would fire if the spider were crawling up your own leg. When you see another person's facial expression, your own facial muscles will often subtly mimic it, activating a similar emotional state (Dimberg, Thunberg, & Elmehed, 2000). When you have an emotional response to music, mirror neurons are involved (Chapin et al., 2010). Mirror neurons thus appear to be the underlying mechanism for human empathy, nonverbal rapport, and *mood contagion*, the spreading of an emotion from one person to another. Have you ever been in a cheerful mood, had lunch with a depressed friend, and come away feeling vaguely depressed yourself? Have you ever stopped to have a chat with a friend who was nervous about an upcoming exam and ended up feeling edgy yourself? That's mood contagion at work.

When two people feel rapport with one another's emotions, nonverbal signals, and posture, however, the more synchronized their gestures become, the more cooperatively they will behave with each other, and the more cheerful they will feel (Wiltermuth & Heath, 2009). This phenomenon may be the reason that synchronized human activities—marches, bands, dancing—are socially and emotionally beneficial. And it means that our friends and neighbours may have more power over our moods than we realize. For example, in a prospective study that followed nearly 5000 people for 20 years, people who were in a "happy network"—whose partners, siblings, and

mirror neurons   Brain cells that fire when a person or animal observes others carrying out an action; they are involved in empathy, imitation, and reading emotions.

Talk about "mirror neurons"! These volunteers, videotaped in a study of conversational synchrony, are obviously in sync with one another, even though they have just met. The degree to which two people's gestures and expressions are synchronized reflects the rapport they feel with one another. Such synchrony can also create a contagion of moods (Grahe & Bernieri, 1999).

👁**Watch**
Relationships and Love

neighbours living nearby became happier over time—were more likely to become happier themselves (Fowler & Christakis, 2008). The researchers concluded that happiness, like health, is a "collective phenomenon."

THE ENERGY OF EMOTION. Once the brain areas associated with emotion are activated, the next stage of the emotional relay is the release of hormones to enable you to respond quickly. When you are under stress or feeling an intense emotion, the sympathetic division of the autonomic nervous system spurs the adrenal glands to send out *epinephrine* and *norepinephrine* (see Chapter 4). These chemical messengers produce arousal and alertness. The pupils dilate, widening to allow in more light; the heart beats faster; blood pressure increases; breathing speeds up; and blood sugar rises. These changes provide the body with the energy needed to take action, whether you are happy and want to get close to someone you love, or are scared and want to escape a person who is frightening you (Löw et al., 2008).

Epinephrine in particular provides the energy of an emotion, that familiar tingle of excitement. At high levels, it can create the sensation of being "seized" or "flooded" by an emotion that is out of your control. In a sense, you *are* out of control, because you cannot consciously alter your heart rate and blood pressure. However, you can learn to control your actions when you are under the sway of an emotion—even intense anger, as we discuss later in "Taking Psychology with You." As arousal subsides, anger may pale into annoyance, ecstasy into contentment, fear into suspicion, past emotional whirlwinds into calm breezes.

Although epinephrine and norepinephrine are released during many emotional states, emotions also differ from one another physiologically: Fear, disgust, anger, sadness, surprise, and happiness are associated with different patterns of brain activity and autonomic nervous system activity, as measured by heart rate, electrical conductivity of the skin, and finger temperature (Damasio et al., 2000; Levenson, 1992). These distinctive patterns may explain why people all over the world use similar terms to describe the primary emotions, saying they feel "hot and bothered" when they are angry or "cold and clammy" when they are afraid. These metaphors capture what is going on in their bodies.

In sum, the physiology of emotion involves characteristic facial expressions; activity in specific parts of the brain, notably the amygdala, specialized parts of the prefrontal cortex, and mirror neurons; and sympathetic nervous system activity that prepares the body for action (see Review 11.1).

REVIEW 11.1

Emotion and the Body

Facial Expressions	Reflect internal feelings, influence internal feelings (facial feedback), communicate feelings, signal intentions, affect behaviour and feelings of others (mood contagion), conceal or pretend an emotion (lie).
The Brain	Specific areas are involved in specific emotions (e.g., disgust) and in different aspects of emotion (e.g., recognizing facial expressions in others, expressing an emotion oneself).
Amygdala	Determines emotional importance of incoming sensory information; is responsible for the initial decision to approach or withdraw; is involved in learning, recognizing, and expressing fear.
Cortex	Appraises the significance of emotional information from the amygdala. The left prefrontal cortex is associated with "approach" emotions (e.g., happiness, anger), the right prefrontal cortex with "withdrawal" emotions (e.g., fear, sadness).
Mirror Neurons	Found in various parts of the brain, these cells fire in imitation of the actions or emotions of another person, creating empathy for another's feelings or pain and generating mood contagion.
Autonomic Nervous System	Activates the hormones epinephrine and norepinephrine, which produce energy and alertness. Certain emotions are associated with distinctive patterns of autonomic nervous system activity (e.g., making people feel "hot" when they are angry, "cold" when they are afraid).

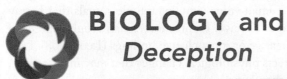

BIOLOGY and *Deception*

Can Lies Be Detected in the Brain and Body?

On the TV crime drama *Lie to Me*, whenever the bad guys lie during an interrogation, a psychologist ("the world's leading detection expert") says he can tell immediately that they are lying. What a great skill! Lots of people want to be able to nab a liar: governments, employers, police, and partners. The problem is that justice depends not only on finding out "who done it" but also on protecting those who didn't do anything. The challenge for social scientists and for law enforcement is to better identify liars without falsely accusing truth-tellers.

Unfortunately, the fictional psychologist on *Lie to Me* is lying about his ability to detect lies. Even the consultant to the program, Paul Ekman, who has been studying facial expressions for decades, admits that the show often sacrifices psychological science for the sake of entertainment. For example, the show promotes the idea that some people have a "natural" ability to detect the lies of others. But even highly educated and trained individuals have only about a 54% chance of detecting a lie (Bond & DePaulo, 2008). (For the rest of us, the success rate is 50%, no better than flipping a coin.) People may speak hesitantly in telling a story, seem stressed in their speech, or avoid looking the interrogator in the eye for many reasons (DePaulo et al., 2003; Leo, 2008). They may be frightened, not know what answers are expected, have nervous mannerisms, or come from a culture that regards direct eye contact as confrontational or rude.

For centuries, people have tried to determine when a person is lying by detecting physiological responses that cannot be controlled consciously.

Watch
Lie Spy

Thinking Critically

Analyze Assumptions and Biases

Many people assume that because physiological changes, such as an elevated heart rate, are involved in emotional states, physiological measurements can tell us whether someone is afraid, guilty, or lying. Is this assumption valid? What evidence does it overlook?

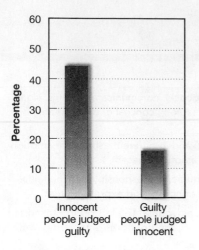

FIGURE 11.2   Misjudging the Innocent

This graph shows the average percentages across three studies of incorrect classifications by lie detectors. Nearly half of the innocent people were classified as guilty, and a significant number of guilty people were classified as innocent. The suspect's guilt or innocence had been independently confirmed by other means, such as by confessions of other suspects (Iacono & Lykken, 1997).

This is the idea behind the *polygraph machine* ("lie detector"), which was invented in 1915 by a Harvard professor named William Marston. The polygraph is based on the assumption that a lie generates emotional arousal. A person who is guilty and fearful of being found out will therefore have increased activity in the autonomic nervous system while responding to incriminating questions: a faster heart rate, increased respiration rate, and increased electrical conductance of the skin.

Law-enforcement officers are still enthusiastic about the polygraph, but most psychological scientists regard polygraph tests as invalid because no physiological patterns of autonomic arousal are specific to lying (Leo, 2008; Lykken, 1998). Machines cannot tell whether you are feeling guilty, angry, nervous, amused, or revved up from an exciting day. Innocent people may be tense and nervous about the whole procedure. They may react to the word *bank*, not because they robbed a bank but because they recently bounced a cheque; in either case, the machine will record a lie. The reverse mistake is also common: People who are motivated to escape detection can often beat the machine by tensing muscles or thinking about an exciting experience during neutral questions.

The polygraph will correctly catch many liars and guilty people. The main problem is that it also falsely identifies many innocent people as having lied (Saxe, 1994). (See Figure 11.2.) For this reason, in 1987 the Supreme Court of Canada decided that the results of polygraph tests would no longer be admissible as evidence in Canadian courts.

Because of the unreliability of the polygraph, researchers are trying to find other ways of measuring physiological signs of lying. The Computer Voice Stress Analyzer is based on the assumption that the human voice contains telltale signals that betray a speaker's emotional state and intent to deceive. Its promoters claim high degrees of accuracy, but research has yielded negative or inconclusive findings (Leo, 2008). Like the polygraph, the voice analyzer detects physiological changes that may indicate fear, anger, or other signs of stress rather than lying.

The *Guilty Knowledge Test* uses a series of multiple-choice questions, each offering one relevant answer about the crime under investigation and several neutral answers, chosen so that an innocent suspect will not be able to discriminate the neutral choices from the relevant one (Lykken, 1998). If a suspect's physiological responses to the relevant answer are consistently larger than to the neutral alternatives, the investigator infers that the suspect is guilty (Ben-Shakhar & Elaad, 2003). This method has a much better track record of identifying the guilty without falsely accusing the innocent, but it too has limitations: The investigator must have enough information about the crime to be able to ask questions that only the guilty person knows and remembers.

The hottest new effort at lie detection is brain imaging. Some researchers are trying to find "brain fingerprints" by using fMRIs of brain activity to see whether they can infer that a person possesses guilty knowledge of a crime and is lying about it. Two companies are already advertising that they can predict with better than 90% certainty if someone is telling the truth. Don't buy it. Areas of the brain that light up on an MRI when people are allegedly lying are also those involved with many other cognitive functions, including memory, self-awareness, and self-monitoring (Greely & Illes, 2007). And because of the normal variability among people in their autonomic and brain reactivity, innocent but highly reactive people are still likely to be mislabelled guilty by these tests (Stix, 2008).

To date, all of this work has produced unreliable results because it rests on a faulty assumption: that there are inevitable, universally identifiable biological signs that reveal with high accuracy when a person is lying. We're telling the truth!

We hope that a little surge of hormonal energy will help you answer these questions.

1. Three-year-old Mia sees her dad dressed as a gorilla and runs away in fear. What brain structure is probably involved in her emotional reaction?

2. Ana Maria is watching an old Laurel and Hardy film, which makes her chuckle and makes her want to see more funny movies. Which side of her prefrontal cortex is likely to be most active?

3. Casey is watching *Horrible Hatchet Homicides in the Haunted House*. What cells in his brain are making him wince when the hero is being attacked?

4. Casey is watching *Horrible Hatchet Homicides in the Haunted House II*. What hormones are causing his heart to pound and his palms to sweat when the murderer is stalking an unsuspecting victim?

Answers:

1. the amygdala 2. the left 3. mirror neurons 4. epinephrine and norepinephrine

Emotion and the Mind

Two friends of ours returned from a mountain-climbing trip to Nepal. One said, "I was ecstatic! The crystal-clear skies, the millions of stars, the friendly people, the majestic mountains, the harmony of the universe!" The other said, "I was miserable! The bedbugs and fleas, the lack of toilets, the yak-butter tea, the awful food, the unforgiving mountains!" Same trip, two different emotional reactions to it. Why?

In the first century CE, the Stoic philosophers suggested an answer: People do not become angry or sad or ecstatic because of actual events, but because of their explanations of those events. Modern psychologists have verified the Stoics' ideas experimentally.

Many years ago, Stanley Schachter and Jerome Singer (1962) argued that the experience of emotion depends both on physiological arousal and on how you interpret and explain that arousal. In their classic experiment, participants were told that they were being given a vitamin but were actually given either epinephrine or saline. Participants who were told that the vitamin could have side effects consistent with epinephrine (for example, increased heart rate) interpreted their change in physical state as being due to the injection and not due to an emotional state. However, some participants were not told of the possible side effects of epinephrine. When these participants were paired with confederates who acted emotionally, they tended to interpret the changes in their heart rate as reflecting emotional states. Thus, Schachter and Singer suggest that although your body may be churning away in high gear, when you can explain and label those changes, you will not feel a true emotion. This idea spurred other investigators to study how emotions are created or influenced by beliefs, perceptions of the situation, expectations, and *attributions*—the explanations people make of their own and other people's behaviour (see Chapter 8) (Fairholme et al., 2009; Lindquist & Barrett, 2008). Human beings, after all, are the only species that can say, "The more I thought about it, the madder I got." In fact, we often do think ourselves into an emotional state, and sometimes we can think ourselves out of it.

One classic test of Schachter and Singer's theory was conducted at the University of British Columbia by Dutton and Aron (1974). These researchers

◈ **Research**
Stanley Schachter

◉ **Watch**
Emotion Regulation: James Coan

Get INVOLVED!

EXAMINING YOUR EMOTIONS AFTER AN EXAM

After your next psychology test, write down the reasons you think you got the grade you did. Do you attribute the grade to your own efforts or perhaps a lack of effort? If you did not do as well as you hoped, do you blame yourself or do you blame your instructor for being too hard or "unfair"? If you did do well, do you take credit for your good grade, or do you think your success was just a lucky fluke? How are these explanations related to your feelings about your grade?

When male hikers met a female research assistant on a scary suspension bridge, they found her more attractive than did males who met the same female on a lower, more stable bridge, just as the Schachter-Singer theory would predict.

◀◉ **Simulate**
Psychology Experiments Survey: How Do You Deal with Your Emotions?

used a rather unorthodox methodology to manipulate arousal in their male participants—they employed a very high suspension bridge over the Capilano Gorge in North Vancouver. The male hikers participating in the experiment met an attractive female research assistant in one of two conditions. Some met her while crossing the suspension (scary) bridge, whereas others met her while standing on a lower and more stable bridge. Following this meeting, the male hikers were asked to rate the attractiveness of the female research assistant. Those males who met her on the scary bridge rated her as more attractive. In a clever twist, the researchers also had the female research assistant leave her phone number with all the participants. Just as the attractiveness ratings would suggest, the males who met her on the scary bridge were more likely to actually call her for a date later on. Therefore, the feelings of arousal that the male hikers experienced on the scary bridge were misinterpreted as *attraction*. If she had not been present, these feelings of arousal probably would have been interpreted as *fear*.

Psychologists have studied the role of cognitions in all kinds of emotions, from joy to sadness. For example, imagine that you get an A on your psychology midterm; how will you feel? Or perhaps you get a D on that midterm; how will you feel then? Most people assume that success brings happiness and failure brings unhappiness, but the emotions you feel will depend more on how you explain your grade than on what you actually get. Do you attribute your grade to your own efforts (or lack of them) or to the teacher, fate, or luck? In a series of experiments, students who believed they did well because of their own efforts tended to feel proud, competent, and satisfied. Those who believed they did well because of a lucky fluke tended to feel gratitude, surprise, or guilt ("I don't deserve this"). Those who believed their failures were their own fault tended to feel regretful, guilty, or resigned. And those who blamed others tended to feel angry (Weiner, 1986).

Here is a more surprising example of how thoughts affect emotions. Of two Olympic finalists, one who wins a second-place silver medal and one who wins a third-place bronze medal, who will feel happier? Won't it be the silver medallist? Nope. In a study of athletes' reactions to placing second and third at national and international competitions, the bronze medallists were happier than the silver medallists (Medvec, Madey, & Gilovich, 1995). Apparently, the athletes were comparing their performance to what might have been. The second-place winners, comparing themselves to the gold medallists, were unhappy that they didn't get the gold. But the third-place winners, comparing themselves to those who did worse than they, were happy that they earned a medal at all!

Cognitions and physiology are inextricably linked in the experience of emotion. Thoughts affect emotions, and emotional states influence thoughts (Fairholme et al., 2009). For example, blaming others for your woes can make you feel angry, but once

Thinking ⚙ Critically

Analyze Assumptions and Biases

Most people assume that second-place winners feel happier about their performance than third-place winners do. Yet when psychologists questioned this assumption, they found that the opposite is true. Certainly, Olympic moguls bronze medallist Shannon Bahrke (right) is happier than silver medallist Jennifer Heil of Canada (left). (Hannah Kearney of the USA, centre, won the gold.)

you are angry you may be more inclined to think the worst of other people's motives. The complicated mix of emotions that people feel when they have "disappointing wins" (outcomes that were not as good as they had expected) or "relieving losses" (bad outcomes that could have been worse) shows how powerfully thoughts affect emotional responses.

Some emotions require only minimal, simple cognitions or are primitive feelings that occur beneath awareness (Ruys & Stapel, 2008). A conditioned sentimental response to a patriotic symbol or a warm, fuzzy feeling toward a familiar souvenir involves simple, nonconscious reactions (Izard, 1994a; Murphy, Monahan, & Zajonc, 1995). An infant's primitive emotions do not have much mental sophistication: "Hey, I'm mad because no one is feeding me!" As a child's cerebral cortex matures, however, cognitions become more complex, and so do emotions: "Hey, I'm mad because this situation is entirely unfair!" Some emotions depend completely on the maturation of higher cognitive capacities. Shame and guilt, for example, do not occur until a child is two or three years old. These *self*-conscious emotions require the emergence of a sense of self and the ability to perceive that you have behaved badly or let down another person (Baumeister, Stillwell, & Heatherton, 1994; Tangney et al., 1996).

Children need to be old enough to have a sense of self before they can feel the moral emotions of shame, guilt, or remorse.

quickQUIZ

✓●[Quick Review on **MyPsychLab**]

How are your thoughts affecting your feelings about this quiz?

1. Dara and Dinah both get a B on their psychology midterm, but while Dara is ecstatic and proud, Dinah is furious. What expectations and attributions are probably affecting their emotional reactions?

2. At a party, you see a stranger flirting with your date. You are flooded with jealousy. What cognitions might be causing this emotion? *Be specific.* What alternative thoughts might reduce your jealous feelings?

Answers:

1. Dara was probably expecting a lower grade and is attributing her B to her own efforts; Dinah was probably expecting a higher grade and is attributing her B to the instructor's unfairness, bad luck, or other external reasons. 2. Possible thoughts causing jealousy are "My date finds other people more attractive," "That person is trying to steal my date," or "My date's behaviour is humiliating me." But you could be thinking, "It's a compliment to me that other people find my date attractive" or "It pleases me that my date is getting such deserved attention."

 YOU are about to learn . . .

◆ why people from different cultures disagree on what makes them angry, jealous, or disgusted.

◆ why some psychologists question whether there are primary and secondary emotions.

◆ how cultural rules affect the way people display or suppress their emotions.

◆ why people often do "emotion work" to convey emotions they do not feel.

◆ whether women are really "more emotional" than men.

Today, almost all theories of emotion hold that attributions, beliefs, and the meanings people give to events are essential to the creation of most emotions. But where do these attributions, beliefs, and meanings come from? When people decide that it is shameful for a man to dance on a table with a lampshade on his head, or for a woman to walk down a street with her arms and legs uncovered, where do their ideas about shame originate? If you are a person who loudly curses others when you are angry, where did you learn that cursing is acceptable? To answer these questions, we turn to the third major aspect of emotional experience: the role of culture.

EMOTION AND CULTURE

A young wife leaves her house one morning to draw water from the local well as her husband watches from the porch. On her way back from the well, a male stranger stops her and asks for some water. She gives him a cupful and then invites him home to dinner. He accepts. The husband, wife, and guest have a pleasant meal together. In a gesture of hospitality, the husband invites the guest to spend the night with his wife. The guest accepts. In the morning, the husband leaves early to bring home breakfast. When he returns, he finds his wife again in bed with the visitor.

At what point in this story will the husband feel angry? The answer depends on his culture (Hupka, 1981, 1991). A North American husband would feel rather angry at a wife who had an extramarital affair, and a wife would feel rather angry at being offered to a guest as if she were a lamb chop. But a Pawnee husband of the nineteenth century would be enraged at any man who dared ask his wife for water. An Ammassalik Inuit husband finds it perfectly honourable to offer his wife to a stranger, but only once; he would be angry to find his wife and the guest having a second encounter. And a century ago, a Toda husband in India would not be angry at all because the Todas allowed both husband and wife to take lovers. Both spouses might feel angry, though, if one of them had a *sneaky* affair, without announcing it publicly.

In most cultures, people feel angry in response to insult and the violation of social rules, but as this story shows, they often disagree about what an insult is or what the correct rule should be. In this section, we will explore how culture influences the emotions we feel and the ways in which we express them.

How Culture Shapes Emotions

Are some emotions specific to particular cultures and not found elsewhere? What does it mean that some languages have words for subtle emotional states that other languages lack? The Germans have *schadenfreude*, a feeling of joy at another's misfortune. The Japanese speak of *hagaii*, helpless anguish tinged with frustration. And Tahitians have *mehameha*, a trembling sensation that Tahitians feel when ordinary categories of perception are suspended—at twilight, in the brush, watching fires glow without heat. In the West, an event that cannot be identified is usually greeted with fear, yet *mehameha* does not describe what Westerners call fear or terror (Levy, 1984).

Do these interesting linguistic differences mean that Germans are actually more likely than others to feel *schadenfreude*, the Japanese to feel *hagaii*, and the Tahitians to feel *mehameha*? Or are they just more willing to give these subtle emotions a single name? Many psychologists would say that all human beings are capable of feeling the primary, hardwired emotions, the ones that have distinctive physiological hallmarks in the brain, face, and nervous system. But individuals might indeed differ in their abilities to experience secondary emotions, including variations such as *schadenfreude*, *hagaii*, or *mehameha*.

The difference between primary emotions and more complex cultural variations is reflected in language all over the world. In Chapter 9, we noted that a *prototype* is a typical representative of a class of things. People everywhere consider the primary emotions to be prototypical examples of the concept *emotion*: For example, most people will say that *anger* and *sadness* are more representative of an emotion than *irritability* and *nostalgia* are. Prototypical emotions are reflected in the emotion words that young children learn first: *happy*, *sad*, *mad*, and *scared*. As children develop, they begin to draw emotional distinctions that are less prototypical and more specific to their language and culture, such as *ecstatic*, *depressed*, *hostile*, or *anxious* (Hupka, Lenton, & Hutchison, 1999; Russell & Fehr, 1994; Shaver, Wu, & Schwartz, 1992). In this way, they come to experience the nuances of emotional feeling that their cultures emphasize.

Other psychologists, however, don't think much of the primary–secondary distinction because, for them, there is *no* aspect of any emotion that is not influenced by culture or context or that even clearly separates one emotion from another (Barrett, 2006; Elfenbein & Ambady, 2003). Anger may be universal, but the way it is experienced will vary from culture to culture—whether it feels good or bad, useful or destructive. Culture even affects which emotions are defined as basic or primary. Anger is regarded as a primary emotion by Western psychologists, but in Asian cultures, shame

Thinking Critically

Ask Questions

What does it mean if one language has a term for an emotion that another language lacks, like *schadenfreude* or *hagaii*? Are people whose languages include these words actually more likely to feel the emotion, or just to have a term that describes it?

Thinking Critically

Ask Questions

Anger is considered a primary emotion in Western societies. But in some cultures, such as the Inuit, anger is not tolerated because it threatens the community's need for closeness. Inuit mothers like this one often calmly ignore an angry baby, conveying the message that complaining is not welcome. What emotions would be "primary" among the Inuit?
Does culture shape the basic experience of emotion or only the forms it takes?

and loss of face are more central emotions (Kitayama & Markus, 1994). And on the tiny Micronesian atoll of Ifaluk, everyone would say that *fago* is the most fundamental emotion. *Fago*, translated as "compassion/love/sadness," reflects the sad feeling one has when a loved one is absent or in need, and the pleasurable sense of compassion in being able to care and help (Lutz, 1988).

Everyone agrees, nonetheless, that cultures determine much of what people feel emotional *about*. For example, disgust is universal, but the content of what produces disgust changes as an infant matures, and it varies across cultures (Rozin, Lowery, & Ebert, 1994). People in some cultures learn to become disgusted by bugs (which other people find beautiful or tasty), unfamiliar sexual practices, dirt, death, contamination by a handshake with a stranger, or particular foods (e.g., meat if they are vegetarian; or pork if they are Muslims or Orthodox Jews).

Communicating Emotions

Suppose that someone who was dear to you died. Would you cry, and if so, would you do it alone or in public? Your answer will depend in part on your culture's **display rules** for emotion (Ekman et al., 1987; Gross, 1998). In some cultures, grief is expressed by weeping; in others, by tearless resignation; and in still others by dance, drink, and song. Once you feel an emotion, how you express it is rarely a matter of "I say what I feel." You may be obliged to disguise what you feel. You may wish you could feel what you say.

Around the world, the cultural rules for expressing emotions differ. The display rule for a formal Japanese wedding portrait is "no direct expressions of emotion," but not every member of this family has learned that rule yet.

Even the smile, which seems a straightforward signal of friendliness, has many meanings and uses that are not universal. North Americans smile more frequently than Germans, not because we are inherently friendlier but because Germans differ in their notions of when a smile is appropriate. After a business meeting, North Americans often complain that the Germans were cold and aloof, and the Germans often complain that North Americans were excessively cheerful, hiding their real feelings under the mask of a smile (Hall & Hall, 1990). The Japanese smile even more than North Americans do, to disguise embarrassment, anger, or other negative emotions whose public display is considered rude and incorrect.

Display rules also govern *body language*, nonverbal signals of body movement, posture, gesture, and gaze (Birdwhistell, 1970). Many aspects of body language are specific to particular languages and cultures, which makes even the simplest gesture subject to misunderstanding and offence. The sign of the University of Texas football team, the Longhorns, is to extend the index finger and the pinkie. In Italy and other parts of Europe, that gesture means you're saying a man's wife has been unfaithful to him—a serious insult.

Display rules tell us not only what to do when we are feeling an emotion, but also how and when to show an emotion we do not feel. Most people are expected to demonstrate sadness at funerals, happiness at weddings, and affection toward relatives. What if we don't actually feel sad, happy, or affectionate? Acting out an emotion we do not really feel because we believe it is socially appropriate is called **emotion work**. It is part of our efforts to regulate our emotions when we are with others (Gross, 1998). Sometimes emotion work is a job requirement. Flight attendants, waiters, and customer-service representatives must put on a happy face to convey cheerfulness, even if they are privately angry about a rude or drunken customer. Bill collectors must put on a stern face to convey threat, even if they feel sorry for the person they are collecting money from (Hochschild, 2003).

Gender and Emotion

"Women are too emotional," men often complain. "Men are too uptight," women often reply. This is a familiar gender stereotype. But what does "too emotional" mean? We need to define our terms and examine our assumptions. And we need to consider the larger culture in which men and women live, which shapes the rules and norms that govern how the sexes are supposed to behave.

Although women are more likely than men to suffer from clinical depression (see Chapter 15), there is little evidence that one sex feels any of the everyday emotions more often than the other, whether the emotion is anger, worry, embarrassment, anxiety, love, or grief (Archer, 2004; Deffenbacher et al., 2003; Fischer et al., 1993; C. Harris, 2003; Kring & Gordon, 1998; Shields, 2005). The major difference between the sexes has less to do with whether they feel emotions than with how and when their emotions are expressed, and how they are perceived by others.

For example, in Western cultures, both sexes unconsciously associate "angry" with male and "happy" with female. When researchers showed students a series of computer-generated, fairly sex-neutral faces with a range of angry to happy expressions, the students consistently rated the angry faces as being masculine and the happy faces as feminine (Becker et al., 2007). This stereotyped link between gender and emotion

Arms and hands communicate interest, emphasis, and emotion, just as words do.

◉**Watch**
Hand Gesturing Study

display rules Social and cultural rules that regulate when, how, and where a person may express (or suppress) emotions.

emotion work Expression of an emotion, often because of a role requirement, that a person does not really feel.

Thinking Critically

Define Your Terms

People say that women are the emotional sex, but they often fail to define their terms. What, for example, does *emotional* mean? Does it refer to how quickly or intensely people react, the kinds of thoughts that provoke them, or how emotions are expressed?

may explain why a man who expresses anger in a professional context is considered high status, but a professional woman who does exactly the same thing loses status. She's considered to be an angry person, someone "out of control" (Brescoll & Uhlmann, 2008). Powerful women thus often face a dilemma: express anger when a subordinate or adversary has done something illegal or incompetent (and risk being thought "overemotional") or behave calmly (and risk being seen as "cold and unemotional").

Conversely, women who don't smile when others expect them to are often disliked, even if they are actually smiling as often as men would. This may be why North American women, on average, smile more than men do, gaze at their listeners more, have more emotionally expressive faces, use more expressive hand and body movements, and touch others more (DePaulo, 1992; Kring & Gordon, 1998). Women smile more than men to pacify others, convey deference to someone of higher status, or smooth over conflicts (Hess, Adams, & Kleck, 2005; Shields, 2005).

Women also talk about their emotions more than men do. They are far more likely to cry and to acknowledge emotions that reveal vulnerability and weakness, such as "hurt feelings," fear, sadness, loneliness, shame, and guilt (Grossman & Wood, 1993; Timmers, Fischer, & Manstead, 1998). In contrast, most North American men express only one emotion more freely than women: anger toward strangers, especially other men. Otherwise, men are expected to control and mask negative feelings. When they are worried or afraid, they are more likely than women to use vague terms, saying that they feel moody, frustrated, or on edge (Fehr et al., 1999).

However, the influence of a particular situation often overrides gender rules (LaFrance, Hecht, & Paluck, 2003). You won't find many gender differences in emotional expressiveness at a football game or the Stanley Cup final! Another important situational constraint on emotional expression is the status of the participants (Snodgrass, 1992). A man is as likely as a woman to control his temper when the target of the anger is someone with higher status or power; few people will readily sound off at a professor, police officer, or employer. And the sexes do similar emotion work when the situation or job requires it. A male flight attendant has to smile as much with passengers as a female attendant does, and a female RCMP agent has to be as emotionally strong and controlled as a male agent.

Both sexes feel emotionally attached to friends, but often they express their affections differently. From childhood on, girls tend to prefer "face-to-face" friendships based on shared feelings; boys tend to prefer "side-by-side" friendships based on shared activities.

Even where gender differences exist, they are not universal. Italian, French, Spanish, and Middle Eastern men and women can have entire conversations using highly expressive hand gestures and facial expressions. In contrast, in Asian cultures, both sexes are taught to control emotional expression (Matsumoto, 1996; Mesquita & Frijda, 1992). Israeli and Italian men are more likely than women to mask feelings of sadness, but British, Spanish, Swiss, and German men are *less* likely than their female counterparts to inhibit this emotion (Wallbott, Ricci-Bitti, & Bänninger-Huber, 1986).

In sum, the answer to "Which sex is more emotional?" is this: sometimes men, sometimes women, and sometimes neither, depending on the circumstances and the cultural context.

---

quickQUIZ

✔●─ **Quick Review** on **MyPsychLab**

Please do not display anger if you miss a question.

1. In Western theories of emotion, anger would be called a _____ emotion, whereas *fago* would be called a _____ emotion.

2. Maureen is working in a fast-food restaurant and is becoming irritated with a customer who isn't ordering fast enough. She is supposed to be pleasant to all customers, but instead she snaps, "Hey, whaddaya want to order, slowpoke?" To keep her job and her temper, Maureen needs practice in _____.

3. In a class discussion, a student says something that embarrasses a student from another culture. The second student smiles to disguise his discomfort; the first student, thinking he is not being taken seriously, gets angry. This misunderstanding reflects the students' different _____ for the expression of embarrassment and anger.

4. *True or false:* Throughout the world, women are more emotionally expressive than men.

Answers:

1. primary, secondary 2. emotion work 3. display rules 4. false

---

 YOU are about to learn . . .

♦ how your body responds to physical, emotional, and environmental stressors.

♦ why being "stressed out" increases the risk of illness in some people but not others.

♦ how psychological factors affect the immune system.

♦ when having a sense of control over events is beneficial and when it is not.

THE NATURE OF STRESS

The emotion "tree," as we have seen, can take many shapes, depending on physiology, cognitive processes, and cultural rules. These same three factors can help us understand those difficult situations in which negative emotions become chronically stressful, and in which chronic stress can create negative emotions.

◄● Simulate
Psychology Experiments Survey:
Will This Survey Stress You Out?

When people say they are "under stress," they mean all sorts of things: that they are having recurring conflicts with a parent, are feeling frustrated and angry about their lives, are fighting with a partner, are overwhelmed with caring for a sick child, can't keep up with work obligations, or just lost a job. Are these stressors linked to illness—to migraines, stomachaches, flu, or more life-threatening diseases such as cancer? And do they affect everyone in the same way?

Stress and the Body

◈ **Research**
Hans Selye

The modern era of stress research began in 1956, when Canadian endocrinologist Hans Selye published *The Stress of Life*. Environmental stressors such as heat, cold, toxins, and danger, Selye wrote, disrupt the body's equilibrium. The body then mobilizes its resources to fight off these stressors and restore normal functioning. Selye described the body's response to stressors of all kinds as a **general adaptation syndrome**, a set of physiological reactions that occur in three phases:

1 **The alarm phase,** in which the body mobilizes the sympathetic nervous system to meet the immediate threat. The threat could be anything from taking a test you haven't studied for to running from a rabid dog. As we saw earlier, the release of adrenal hormones epinephrine and norepinephrine occurs with any intense emotion. It boosts energy, tenses muscles, reduces sensitivity to pain, shuts down digestion (so that blood will flow more efficiently to the brain, muscles, and skin), and increases blood pressure. Decades before Selye, psychologist Walter Cannon (1929) described these changes as the "fight or flight" response, a phrase still in use.

Stress hormones elevated

Blood flow increases

Heart rate speeds up

Digestion slows

Muscles tense

2 **The resistance phase,** in which your body attempts to resist or cope with a stressor that cannot be avoided. During this phase, the physiological responses of the alarm phase continue, but these very responses make the body more vulnerable to other stressors. For example, when your body has mobilized to deal with a heat wave or pain from a broken leg, you may find you are more easily annoyed by minor frustrations. In most cases, the body will eventually adapt to the stressor and return to normal.

3 **The exhaustion phase,** in which persistent stress depletes the body of energy, thereby increasing vulnerability to physical problems and illness. The same reactions that allow the body to respond effectively in the alarm and resistance phases are unhealthy as long-range responses. Tense muscles can cause headache and neck pain. Increased blood pressure can become chronic hypertension. If normal digestive processes are interrupted or shut down for too long, digestive disorders may result.

general adaptation syndrome According to Hans Selye, a series of physiological reactions to stress occurring in three phases: alarm, resistance, and exhaustion.

Selye did not believe that people should aim for a stress-free life. Some stress, he said, is positive and productive, even if it also requires the body to produce short-term energy: competing in an athletic event, falling in love, working hard on a project you enjoy. And some negative stress is simply unavoidable; it's called life.

CURRENT APPROACHES. One of Selye's most important observations was that the very biological changes that are adaptive in the short run, because they permit the body to respond quickly to danger, can become hazardous in the long run (McEwen, 1998, 2007). Modern researchers are learning exactly how this happens.

When you are under stress, your brain's hypothalamus sends messages to the endocrine glands along two major pathways. One, as Selye observed, activates the sympathetic division of the autonomic nervous system for "fight or flight," producing the release of epinephrine and norepinephrine from the inner part (medulla) of the adrenal glands. In addition, the hypothalamus initiates activity along the **HPA axis** (HPA stands for hypothalamus–pituitary–adrenal cortex): The hypothalamus releases chemical messengers that communicate with the pituitary gland, which in turn sends messages to the outer part (cortex) of the adrenal glands. The adrenal cortex secretes *cortisol* and other hormones that elevate blood sugar and protect the body's tissues from inflammation in case of injury (see Figure 11.3).

One result of HPA axis activation is increased energy, which is crucial for short-term responses to stress (Kemeny, 2003). But if cortisol and other stress hormones stay high too long, they can lead to hypertension, immune disorders, other physical ailments, and possibly emotional problems. Elevated levels of stress hormones also motivate animals (and presumably humans, too) to seek out rich comfort foods and store the extra calories as abdominal fat.

An understanding of the cumulative effects of external sources of stress may partially explain why people at the lower rungs of the socioeconomic ladder have worse health and higher mortality rates for almost every disease and medical condition than do those at the top regardless of ethnicity, gender, or where in Canada they live (Adler & Snibbe, 2003; Health Canada, 2008). Poverty disproportionately

HPA (hypothalamus–pituitary–adrenal cortex) axis A system activated to energize the body to respond to stressors. The hypothalamus sends chemical messengers to the pituitary, which in turn prompts the adrenal cortex to produce cortisol and other hormones.

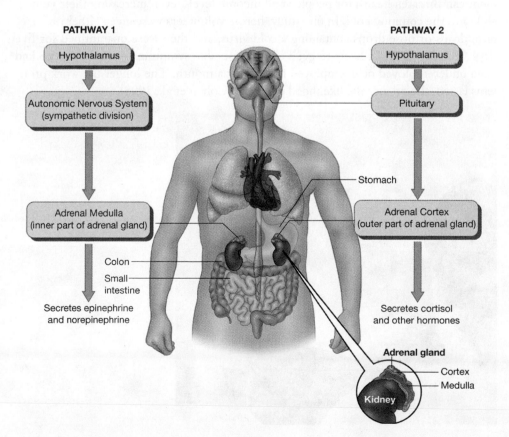

FIGURE 11.3 The Brain and Body under Stress

When a person is in danger or under stress, the hypothalamus sends messages to the endocrine glands along two major pathways. In one, the hypothalamus activates the sympathetic division of the autonomic nervous system, which stimulates the adrenal medulla to produce epinephrine and norepinephrine. The result is the many bodily changes associated with "fight or flight." In the other pathway, messages travel along the HPA axis to the adrenal cortex, which produces cortisol and other hormones. The result is increased energy and protection from tissue inflammation in case of injury.

affects single-parent families (especially those headed by women), families on social assistance, and urban families of Canada's indigenous peoples (Anand et al., 2001; McIntyre, Connor, & Warren, 2000). Further, children may be most vulnerable to the chronic stress associated with poverty.

Although the health risks associated with poverty in Canada cannot be easily attributed to health care access, in practice, poor Canadians may be less likely to go to the doctor when they are ill or to fill prescriptions to treat their illnesses (Williamson & Fast, 1998). Obviously this may be because many poor Canadians may not have money to buy medications or to pay for transportation to the doctor (Williamson & Fast, 1998). However, research conducted at McGill University has found that poor Canadians are also more likely to have high-fat diets, to consume inadequate quantities of vitamins and minerals, and to be obese—factors that are associated with numerous health risks (e.g., Johnson-Down et al., 1997). As well, impoverished Canadians may experience higher levels of discrimination and the environmental stress of living in areas with higher crime rates, fewer community services, run-down housing, and greater exposure to hazards such as chemical contamination (Health Canada, 2008; Taylor, Repetti, & Seeman, 1997; Wandersman & Nation, 1998). In fact, some researchers suggest that poverty can be thought of as a series of accumulated stressors and that living within an impoverished community only intensifies these stressors (Kupersmidt et al., 1995; McLoyd, 1998). These effects snowball for children, with accumulated negative effects on their physical health, mental health, and cognitive abilities (such as memory) extending to adolescence and adulthood (Evans & Kim, 2007; Evans & Schamberg, 2009). In 2007, one in 10 children (defined as individuals under the age of 18) in Canada lived in poverty (Vanier Institute of the Family, 2010).

Because work is central in most people's lives, the effects of persistent unemployment can threaten health for people at all income levels, even increasing their vulnerability to the common cold. In one study, heroic volunteers were given either ordinary nose drops or nose drops containing a cold virus, and then were quarantined for five days. The people most likely to get a cold's miserable symptoms were those who had been underemployed or unemployed for at least a month. The longer the work problems lasted, the greater the likelihood of illness (Cohen et al., 1998).

Chronic stress lasting a month or more boosts the risk of catching a cold. The risk is increased among people undergoing problems with their friends or loved ones; it is highest among people who are out of work (Cohen et al., 1998).

Nonetheless, the physiological changes caused by stress do not occur to the same extent in everyone. People's responses to stress vary according to their learning history, gender, preexisting medical conditions, and genetic predisposition for high blood pressure, heart disease, obesity, diabetes, or other health problems (McEwen, 2000, 2007; Røysamb et al., 2003; Taylor, Klein, et al., 2000). This is why some people respond to the same stressor with much greater increases in blood pressure, heart rate, and hormone levels than other individuals do, and their physical changes take longer to return to normal. These hyperresponsive individuals may be the ones most at risk for eventual illness.

THE IMMUNE SYSTEM: PNI. Researchers in the growing field of *health psychology* (and its medical relative, *behavioural medicine*) investigate all aspects of how mind and body affect each other to preserve wellness or cause illness. Some health psychologists have teamed up with other researchers to develop an interdisciplinary specialty with the cumbersome name **psychoneuroimmunology**, or **PNI** for short. The "psycho" part stands for psychological processes such as emotions and perceptions; "neuro" for the nervous and endocrine systems; and "immunology" for the immune system, which enables the body to fight disease and infection.

PNI researchers are especially interested in the white blood cells of the immune system, which are designed to recognize foreign or harmful substances (*antigens*), such as flu viruses, bacteria, and tumour cells, and then destroy or deactivate them. The immune system deploys different kinds of white blood cells as weapons, depending on the nature of the enemy. For example, natural killer cells are important in tumour detection and rejection, and are involved in protection against the spread of cancer cells and viruses. Helper T cells enhance and regulate the immune response; they are the primary target of the HIV virus that causes AIDS. Chemicals produced by the immune cells are sent to the brain, and the brain in turn sends chemical signals to stimulate or restrain the immune system. Anything that disrupts this communication loop, whether drugs, surgery, or chronic stress, can weaken or suppress the immune system (Segerstrom & Miller, 2004).

Some PNI researchers have gotten right down to the level of cell damage to see how stress can lead to illness, aging, and even premature death. At the end of every chromosome is a protein complex called a *telomere* that, in essence, tells the cell how long it has to live. Every time a cell divides, enzymes whittle away a tiny piece of the telomere; when it is reduced to almost nothing, the cell stops dividing and dies. Chronic stress, especially if it begins in childhood, appears to shorten the telomeres (Epel, 2009). One team of researchers compared two groups of healthy women between the ages of 20 and 50: 19 who had healthy children and 39 who were the primary caregivers of a child chronically ill with a serious disease, such as cerebral palsy. Of course, the mothers of the sick children felt that they were under stress, but they also had significantly greater cell damage than did the mothers of healthy children. In fact, the cells of the highly stressed women looked like those of women at least 10 years older, and their telomeres were much shorter (Epel et al., 2004). But don't despair— researchers have recently found that meditation practice not only reduces stress and stress-induced immune responses, but also increases enzymes that repair telomeres (Epel et al., 2009; Jacobs et al., 2011; Lin, Epel, & Blackburn, 2009).

psychoneuroimmunology (PNI) The study of the relationships among psychology, the nervous and endocrine systems, and the immune system.

👁 **Watch**
Stress and Wellness

The immune system consists of fighter cells that look more fantastical than any alien creature Hollywood could design. This one is about to engulf and destroy a cigarette-shaped parasite that causes a tropical disease.

Consider Other Interpretations

Most people think stress is something "out there" that just happens to them. However, there is another way of looking at stress—as something in you, something that depends on your thoughts and emotions. For example, do you see your work as an endless set of assignments you will never complete or as challenging tasks to master? The answer will affect how stressed you are.

Stress and the Mind

Before you try to persuade your instructors that the stress of constant studying is bad for your health, consider this mystery: The large majority of individuals who are living with stressors, even serious ones such as loss of a job or the death of a loved one, do not get sick (Bonanno, 2004; Taylor, Repetti, & Seeman, 1997). What protects them?

OPTIMISM AND PESSIMISM. When something bad happens to you, what is your first reaction? Do you tell yourself that you will somehow come through it okay, or do you gloomily mutter, "More proof that if something can go wrong for me, it will"? In a fundamental way, optimism—the general expectation that things will go well in spite of occasional setbacks—makes life possible. If people are in a jam but believe things will get better eventually, they will keep striving to make that prediction come true. Even despondent fans of the Toronto Maple Leafs, who have not won the Stanley Cup since 1967, maintain a lunatic optimism that "there's always next year."

In general, optimism is better for your health and well-being than pessimism is (Carver & Scheier, 2002; Geers, Wellman, & Lassiter, 2009). This does not mean that an optimistic outlook will always prolong the life of a person who already has a serious illness: A team of Australian researchers who followed 179 patients with lung cancer over a period of eight years found that optimism made no difference in who lived or in how long they lived (Schofield et al., 2004). But optimism does seem to produce good health and even prolong life in people without life-threatening illnesses, whereas the "catastrophizing" style of pessimists is associated with untimely death (Maruta et al., 2000; Peterson et al., 1998).

One reason is that optimists simply take better care of themselves. They do not deny their problems or avoid facing bad news; rather, they regard the problems and bad news as difficulties they can overcome. They are more likely than pessimists to be active problem solvers, get support from friends, and seek information that can help them (Brissette, Scheier, & Carver, 2002; Chang, 1998; Geers, Wellman, & Lassiter, 2009). They keep their senses of humour, plan for the future, and reinterpret the situation in a positive light. Pessimists, in contrast, often do self-destructive things: They drink too much, smoke, fail to wear a seat belt, drive too fast, and refuse to take medication for illness (Peterson et al., 1998).

Pessimists naturally accuse optimists of being unrealistic, and often that is true! Yet health and well-being may depend on having some "positive illusions" about yourself, your abilities, and your circumstances (Taylor, Kemeny, et al., 2000). Positive illusions have both psychological benefits and physiological ones. Optimism is directly associated with better immune function, such as a rise in the natural killer cells that fight infection (Räikkönen et al., 1999; Segerstrom, 2007). And people who see themselves in "self-enhancing" ways—thinking, for example, that they are smarter and healthier than average—also show immunological benefits. They have lower physiological activation in the face of chronic difficulties, thereby reducing the wear and tear on their body's regulatory systems (Taylor, Lerner, et al., 2003).

Can pessimists be cured of their gloomy outlook? Optimists think so! One way is by teaching pessimists to follow the oldest advice in the world: to count their blessings instead of their burdens. Even among people with serious illnesses, such as a neuromuscular disease, a focus on the positive aspects of life increases well-being and reduces the number of physical symptoms they report (Emmons & McCullough, 2003).

THE SENSE OF CONTROL. Optimism is related to another important cognitive ingredient in health: having an internal locus of control. **Locus of control** refers to your general expectation about whether you can control the things that happen to you (Rotter, 1990). People who have an *internal locus of control* ("internals") tend to believe that they are responsible for what happens to them. Those who have an *external locus of control* ("externals") tend to believe that their lives are controlled by luck, fate, or other people. Having an internal locus of control is associated with good health, academic achievement, political activism, and emotional well-being (Lang & Heckhausen, 2001; Strickland, 1989).

PESSIMISM CLUB
TODAY IS THE LAST DAY to KEEP REPEATING THE SAME STUPID MISTAKES

OPTIMISM CLUB
TODAY IS THE FIRST DAY OF THE REST OF YOUR LIFE.

SCHWADRon

© Harley Schwadron / www.CartoonStock.com

Most people can tolerate all kinds of stressors if they feel able to predict or control them. Consider crowding. Mice get really nasty when they're crowded, but many people love crowds, voluntarily getting squashed in New York's Times Square on New Year's Eve or at a rock concert. Human beings show signs of stress not when they are actually crowded but when they *feel* crowded (Evans, Lepore, & Allen, 2000). Cortisol is elevated when people feel that they are being judged negatively by others or have no control over the task at hand (Dickerson & Kemeny, 2004; Miller, Chen, & Zhou, 2007). People who have the greatest control over their work pace and activities, such as executives and managers, have fewer illnesses and stress symptoms than do employees who have little control, who feel trapped doing repetitive tasks, and who have a low chance of promotion (Karasek & Theorell, 1990). The greatest threat to health and well-being occurs when people feel caught in a situation they cannot escape, one that goes on without a foreseeable end.

👁 **Watch**
Locus

Feeling in control affects the immune system, which may be why it helps to speed up recovery from surgery and some diseases (E. Skinner, 1996). People who have an internal locus of control are better able than externals to resist infection by cold viruses and even the health-impairing effects of poverty and discrimination (Cohen, Tyrrell, & Smith, 1993; Krieger & Sidney, 1996; Lachman & Weaver, 1998). As with optimism, feeling in control also makes people more likely to take action to improve their health when necessary. For example, in studies of patients recovering from heart attacks, those who believed the heart attack occurred because they smoked, didn't exercise, or had a stressful job were more likely to change their bad habits and recover quickly. In contrast, those who thought their illness was due to bad luck or fate—factors outside their control—were less likely to generate plans for recovery and more likely to resume their old unhealthy habits (Affleck et al., 1987; Ewart, 1995).

Overall, a sense of control is a good thing, but critical thinkers might want to ask: Control over what? It is surely not beneficial for people to believe they can control absolutely every aspect of their lives; some things, such as death, taxes, or being a random victim of a crime, are out of anyone's control. Health and well-being are not enhanced by self-blame ("Whatever goes wrong with my health is my fault") or the belief that

locus of control A general expectation about whether the results of your actions are under your own control (internal locus) or beyond your control (external locus).

Thinking Critically Examine the Evidence

Who has more stress: corporate managers in highly competitive jobs or assembly-line workers in routine and predictable jobs? People who are bossed suffer more from job stress than their bosses do, especially if the employees cannot control many aspects of their work (Karasek & Theorell, 1990).

all disease can be prevented by doing the right thing ("If I take vitamins and hold the right positive attitude, I'll never get sick").

CULTURE and *Control*

What Can We Change, and What Must We Accept?

Eastern and Western cultures tend to hold different attitudes toward the ability and desirability of controlling one's own life. In general, Western cultures celebrate **primary control**, in which people try to influence events by exerting direct control over them: If you are in a bad situation, you change it, fix it, or fight it. The Eastern approach emphasizes **secondary control**, in which people try to accommodate to a bad situation by changing their own aspirations or desires: If you have a problem, you live with it or act in spite of it (Rothbaum, Weisz, & Snyder, 1982).

A Japanese psychologist once offered some examples of Japanese proverbs that teach the benefits of yielding to the inevitable (Azuma, 1984): *To lose is to win* (giving in, to protect the harmony of a relationship, demonstrates the superior trait of generosity); *willow trees do not get broken by piled-up snow* (no matter how many problems pile up in your life, flexibility will help you survive them); and *the true tolerance is to tolerate the intolerable* (some "intolerable" situations are facts of life that no amount of protest will change). You can imagine how long "To lose is to win" would survive on the football field, or how long most Canadian (even Saskatchewan Roughrider) fans would be prepared to tolerate the intolerable! Yet an important part of coping, for any of us, is learning to accept limited resources, irrevocable losses, and circumstances over which we have little or no direct influence—all aspects of secondary control (E. Skinner, 2007).

People who are ill or under stress can reap the benefits of both Western and Eastern forms of control by avoiding either–or thinking: for example, by taking responsibility for future actions while not blaming themselves unduly for past ones.

primary control An effort to modify reality by changing other people, the situation, or events; a "fighting back" philosophy.

secondary control An effort to accept reality by changing your own attitudes, goals, or emotions; a "learn to live with it" philosophy.

Among first-year students who are doing poorly in their classes, future success depends on maintaining enough primary control to keep working hard and learning to study better, *and* on the ability to come to terms with the fact that success is not going to drop into their laps without effort (Hall et al., 2006). Among women who are recovering from sexual assault or coping with cancer, adjustment is related to a woman's belief that she is not to blame for being raped or for getting sick but that she *is* in charge of taking care of herself from now on (Frazier, 2003; Taylor, Lichtman, & Wood, 1984). "I felt that I had lost control of my body somehow," said one cancer survivor, "and the way for me to get back some control was to find out as much as I could." This way of thinking allows people to avoid guilt and self-blame while retaining a belief that they can take steps to get better.

Many problems require us to decide what we can change and to accept what we cannot; perhaps the secret of healthy control lies in knowing the difference.

---

quickQUIZ

✓• Quick Review on MyPsychLab

We hope these questions are not sources of stress for you.

1. Steve is unexpectedly called on in class to discuss a question. He hasn't the faintest idea of the answer, and he feels his heart pound and his palms sweat. According to Selye, Steve is in the _____ phase of his stress response.

2. Maria has worked as a file clerk for 17 years in a job that is closely supervised and boring. Her boss must make many rapid-fire decisions every day and is always complaining of the pressures of responsibility. Which of them probably has the more stressful job? (a) Maria, (b) the boss, (c) both equally, (d) neither job is stressful (*Bonus:* Why?)

3. Erin usually takes credit for doing well on her work assignments and blames her failures on lack of effort. Andi attributes her successes to luck and blames her failures on the fact that she is an indecisive Gemini. Erin has an _____ locus of control whereas Andi has an _____ locus.

4. Adapting to the reality that you have a chronic medical condition is an example of (primary/secondary) control; joining a protest to make a local company clean up its hazardous wastes is an example of (primary/secondary) control.

5. On television, a self-described health expert explains that "no one gets sick if they don't want to be sick," because we can all control our bodies. As a critical thinker, how should you assess this claim?

Answers:

1. alarm 2. a, because Maria has less control than her boss does over every aspect of her work 3. internal, external 4. secondary, primary 5. First, you would want to define your terms: What does "control" mean, and what kind of control is the supposed expert referring to? People can control some things, such as how much they exercise and whether they smoke, and they can control some aspects of treatment once they become ill, but they cannot control everything that happens to them. Second, you would examine the assumption that control is always a good thing; the belief that we have total control over our lives could lead to depression and unwarranted self-blame when illness strikes.

❖ YOU are about to learn . . .

♦ which emotion may be most hazardous to your heart.

♦ whether chronic depression leads to physical illness.

♦ why confession is often as healthy for the body as it is for the soul.

STRESS AND EMOTION

⊙ **Watch**
Puppy Love

Perhaps you have heard people say things like "She was so depressed, it's no wonder she got sick" or "He's always so angry, he's going to give himself a heart attack one day." Are negative emotions, especially anger and depression, hazardous to your health?

First, we can eliminate the popular belief that there is a "cancer-prone" personality. (This notion was initially promoted by the tobacco industry to draw attention away from smoking as a leading cause of cancer.) Research has thoroughly discredited this belief; studies of thousands of people around the world, from Japan to Finland, have found no link between personality traits and risk of cancer (Nakaya et al., 2003).

Second, we need to separate the effects of negative emotions on healthy people from the effects of such emotions on people who are ill. Once a person already has a virus or medical condition or is living in a chronically stressful situation, negative emotions such as anxiety and helplessness can indeed increase the risk of illness and affect the speed of recovery (Kiecolt-Glaser et al., 1998). People who become depressed after a heart attack are significantly more likely to die from cardiac causes in the succeeding year, even controlling for severity of the disease and other risk factors (Frasure-Smith et al., 1999). But can anger and depression be causes of illness on their own?

Hostility and Depression: Do They Hurt?

One of the first modern efforts to link emotions and illness occurred in the 1970s, with research on the "Type A" personality, a set of qualities thought to be associated with heart disease: ambitiousness, impatience, anger, working hard, and having high standards for oneself. Later work ruled out all of these factors except one: The toxic ingredient in the Type A personality turned out to be hostility (Myrtek, 2007).

By "hostility" we do not mean the irritability or anger that everyone feels on occasion, but *cynical* or *antagonistic hostility*, which characterizes people who are mistrustful of others and always ready to provoke mean, furious arguments. In a classic study of male physicians who had been interviewed as medical students 25 years earlier, those who were chronically angry and resentful were five times as likely as nonhostile men to get heart disease, even when other risk factors such as smoking and a poor diet were taken into account (Ewart & Kolodner, 1994; Williams, Barefoot, & Shekelle, 1985) (see Figure 11.4). These findings have been replicated in other

FIGURE 11.4 Hostility and Heart Disease

Anger is more hazardous to health than a heavy workload. Men who had the highest hostility scores as young medical students were the most likely to have coronary heart disease 25 years later (Williams, Barefoot, & Shekelle, 1985).

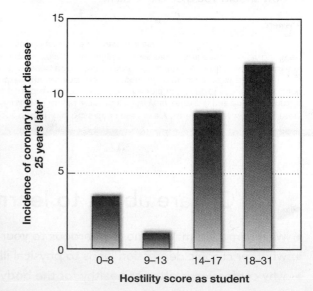

large-scale studies, with people of differing ethnicities, and with women as well as men (Krantz et al., 2006; Williams et al., 2000). Proneness to anger is a significant risk factor all on its own for impairments of the immune system, elevated blood pressure, heart disease, and even slower healing of wounds (Chida & Hamer, 2008; Gouin et al., 2008; Suinn, 2001).

Clinical depression, too, is linked to at least a doubled risk of later heart attack and cardiovascular disease (Frasure-Smith & Lespérance, 2005; Schulz et al., 2000). But what accounts for that link? One prospective study of more than 1000 men found that the answer was exercise: The depressed men who had further episodes were less physically active than men who exercised regularly (Whooley et al., 2008). But another large prospective study found no differences in physical activity between depressed and nondepressed older adults. Instead, they found that depressed people were more likely to accumulate fat in the belly and midriff (perhaps because of the elevated cortisol that often occurs with depression), where it is more likely to increase the risk of diabetes and cardiovascular disease (Vogelzangs et al., 2008). Either way, you can see that the reason depression might lead to heart disease over time is not depression itself, but more likely the lethargy and overeating that depression can produce in some of its sufferers.

For some time, researchers thought that depression might also lead to cancer, but now it looks as though cancer can cause depression, and not just because the diagnosis is "depressing." Cancerous tumours, as well as the immune system that is fighting them, produce high levels of a chemical that can cause the emotional and behavioural symptoms of depression. A study of rats, which after all are not aware of having cancer, found that the animals would float passively in water instead of swimming for safety, and show other signs of anxiety and apathy (Pyter et al., 2009). It also appears that the tumour itself acts as a stressor that can result in changes in the brain that are associated with depression (Xiu, Lin, & Wei, 2010).

Positive Emotions: Do They Help?

Just as negative emotions can be unhealthful, positive emotions seem to be healthful. Consider the findings from a study of 180 Catholic nuns. Researchers examined autobiographies composed by the nuns when they were about 22 years old to see whether the quality of their writing predicted the onset of Alzheimer's disease later in life. (It did.) When other researchers scored the writings for their emotional content, they found a strong association between the frequency of positive emotions described— such as happiness, love, hope, gratitude, contentment, amusement—and longevity six decades later (Danner, Snowdon, & Friesen, 2001). The nuns whose life stories contained the most words describing positive emotions lived, on average, nine years longer than nuns who reported the fewest positive feelings. These differences in longevity could not have been due to the stress of poverty, raising children, or particular experiences. The women all had the same experiences and standard of living, at least after they entered the convent.

Hostility is hazardous, but humour is healthful!

An emerging area of psychology, referred to as *positive psychology*, seeks to examine the ways in which positive emotions such as happiness and positive personality traits enhance well-being, health, and resilience

👁 **Watch**
Humour and Brains

(Seligman & Csikszentmihalyi, 2000; Hart & Sasso, 2011). Research demonstrates that when experiencing severe stressors, people who adopt a proactive coping style experience less depression and report more positive experiences than those who do not (Greenglass, 2002; Greenglass & Fiksenbaum, 2009). This proactive coping is not naive, "Polyanna"-ish optimism, but rather a realistic assessment of all possible outcomes, both good and bad. Such an evaluation allows people to develop possible responses and to assess how well they are progressing (Churchill & Davis, 2010; Davis & Asliturk, 2011).

Psychologists are trying to find out just what it is about positive personality traits, emotions, and attitudes that protects people from getting sick. Of course, perhaps the cheerfulness of the long-lived nuns simply reflected an easygoing temperament or other genetic influences that promote long life. But positive emotions could also be physically beneficial because they soften or counteract the high arousal caused by negative emotions or chronic stressors. They may dispose people to think more creatively about their opportunities and choices and to take action to achieve their goals (Kok, Catalino, & Frederickson, 2008). People who express positive feelings are also more likely to attract friends and supporters than are people who are always bitter and brooding, and, as we will see, social support contributes to good health (Pressman & Cohen, 2005).

If you don't feel bouncy and happy all the time, don't worry; everyone feels grumpy, irritable, and unhappy on occasion. But according to one study in which university students kept a daily diary of their positive and negative emotions for 28 days, the students who had the greatest emotional well-being had a ratio of positive to negative emotions of at least three to one (Fredrickson & Losada, 2005). You might want to keep track of your own positive-to-negative emotion ratio for the next month to see where yours falls, and whether it seems related to any colds, flu, or other physical symptoms you might be having. Are positive emotions more typical of your emotional life than negative ones, or is it the other way around?

👁 **Watch**
The Study of Happy Brains

Emotional Inhibition and Expression

Well, then, if positive emotions are beneficial and negative emotions are risky, you might assume that the safest thing to do when you feel angry, depressed, or worried is to try to suppress those feelings. But anyone who has tried to banish an unwelcome thought or a bitter memory knows how hard it can be to do this. When you are trying to avoid a thought, you are in fact processing the thought more frequently; you are rehearsing it. That is why, when you are obsessed with something, trying not to think of it actually prolongs your emotional responsiveness (Wegner & Gold, 1995).

The continued inhibition of thoughts and emotions actually requires physical effort that can be stressful to the body. People who are able to express matters of great emotional importance to them show elevated levels of disease-fighting white blood cells, whereas people who suppress such feelings tend to have decreased levels (Petrie, Booth, & Pennebaker, 1998). There is also a social cost to suppressing important feelings. In a longitudinal study that followed first-year university students as they adjusted to being in a new environment, those who expressed their worries and fears openly with other students ended up with better relationships and greater satisfaction compared to those who said they preferred to keep their emotions to themselves (Srivastava et al., 2009).

Everyone has secrets and private moments of sad reflection. But when you feel sad or fearful for too long, keeping your feelings to yourself may increase your stress.

Another familiar, and negative, feeling when someone is in a new environment is loneliness. Ken Cramer and colleagues (Cramer & Neyedley, 1998) from the University of Windsor found that male students, who may feel the need to conceal their feelings to conform to traditional sex roles, are in fact lonelier than female students. It has also been found that lonely students, regardless of sex, are less likely to stay in

TRUE CONFESSIONS

To see whether the research on the benefits of confession will be helpful to you, take a moment to write down your deepest thoughts and feelings about being in university, your past, a secret, your future—anything you have never told anyone. Do this again tomorrow and then again for a few days in a row. Note your feelings after writing, too. Are you upset, troubled, sad, or relieved? Does your account change over time? Research suggests that if you do this exercise now, you may have fewer colds, headaches, and trips to the doctor over the next few months (Pennebaker, Colder, & Sharp, 1990).

school, tend to trust others less, and change their eating patterns more than students who are not lonely (Rotenberg, 1994, 1998; Rotenberg & Flood, 1999; Rotenberg & Kmill, 1992; Rotenberg & Morrison, 1993; Rotenberg et al., 2010). As well, lonely people have been found to be the harshest judges, not only of themselves but of others (Rotenberg & MacKie, 1999). Thus, lonely people may, because of their judgmental attitudes, discourage others from getting close to them—thus keeping the cycle of loneliness going.

THE BENEFITS OF CONFESSION.   Given the findings on the harmful effects of feeling negative emotions and also the difficulty and costs of suppressing them, what is a person supposed to do with them? One way to reduce the wear and tear of negative emotions comes from research on the benefits of confession: divulging (even if only to yourself) private thoughts and feelings that make you ashamed, worried, or sad (Pennebaker, 2002). For example, first-year students who wrote about their "deepest thoughts and feelings" in a private journal reported greater short-term homesickness and anxiety, compared to students who wrote about trivial topics. But by the end of the school year they had had fewer bouts of flu and fewer visits to the infirmary than the control group did (Pennebaker, Colder, & Sharp, 1990).

This method is especially powerful when people write about traumatic experiences. When a group of university students was asked to write about a personal, traumatic experience for 20 minutes a day for four days, many told stories of sexual coercion, physical beatings, humiliation, or parental abandonment. Yet most had never discussed these experiences with anyone. The researchers collected data on the students' physical symptoms, white blood cell counts, emotions, and visits to the health centre. On every measure, the students who wrote about traumatic experiences were better off than those who wrote only about neutral topics (Pennebaker, Kiecolt-Glaser, & Glaser, 1988). Subsequent research has confirmed the benefits of expressing and working through memories of traumatic events head on, rather than trying to suppress intrusive, troubling thoughts (Dalgleish, Hauer, & Kuyken, 2008; see Chapter 16).

The benefits of confession occur primarily when the revelation produces insight and understanding, thereby ending the stressful repetition of obsessive thoughts and unresolved feelings (Kennedy-Moore & Watson, 2001;

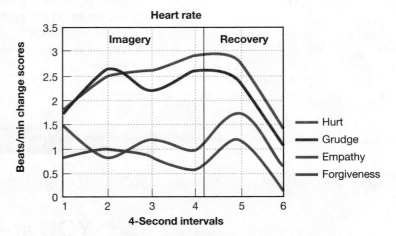

FIGURE 11.5   Heartfelt Forgiveness

Participants in a study were asked to think of someone who they felt had offended or hurt them. Then they were asked to imagine unforgiving reactions (rehearsing the hurt and harbouring a grudge) and forgiving reactions (feeling empathy, forgiving). People's heart rates increased much more sharply, and took longer to return to normal, when their thoughts were unforgiving.

Lepore, Ragan, & Jones, 2000). One young woman, who had been molested at the age of nine by a boy a year older, at first wrote about her feelings of embarrassment and guilt. By the third day, she was writing about how angry she felt at the boy. By the last day, she had begun to see the whole event differently; he was a child too, after all. When the study was over, she said, "Before, when I thought about it, I'd lie to myself. . . . Now, I don't feel like I even have to think about it because I got it off my chest. I finally admitted that it happened."

THE BENEFITS OF LETTING GRIEVANCES GO. Another way of letting go of negative emotions is to give up the thoughts that produce them and adopt a perspective that might lead to forgiveness. When people rehearse their grievances and hold on to their grudges, their blood pressure, heart rate, and skin conductance rise. Forgiving thoughts (as in the preceding example—"He was a child too") reduce these signs of physiological arousal and restore feelings of control (Whited, Wheat, & Larkin, 2010; Witvliet, Ludwig, & Vander Laan, 2001). (See Figure 11.5.) Forgiveness, like confession, can help people see events in a new light. It promotes empathy, the ability to see the situation from another person's perspective. It strengthens and repairs relationships (Karremans et al., 2003).

Forgiveness does *not* mean that the offended person denies, ignores, or excuses the offence, which might be serious. It does mean that the victim is able, finally, to come to terms with the injustice and let go of obsessive feelings of hurt, rage, and vengefulness. As the Chinese proverb says, "He who pursues revenge should dig two graves."

quick**QUIZ**

✔•⬜Quick Review on MyPsychLab

We'll never forgive you if you skip this quiz.

1. Which aspect of Type A behaviour is most hazardous to the heart? (a) working hard, (b) being in a hurry, (c) cynical hostility, (d) irritability in traffic, (e) general grumpiness

2. Amber has many worries about being in university, but she is afraid to tell anyone. What might be the healthiest solution for her? (a) trying not to think about her feelings, (b) writing down her feelings and then rereading and rethinking what she wrote, (c) talking frequently to anyone who will listen, (d) tweeting her friends about her moods

3. We are giving away an answer to #2, but why might answer *d* not be helpful to Amber?

Answers:

1. c 2. b 3. Sending tweets, or posting her feelings on her Facebook page, might make Amber momentarily feel good, but she probably won't retrieve those messages later to reread and rethink about what she wrote, and rethinking her story is the important element.

 YOU are about to learn . . .

- ◆ ways of calming the body when you are feeling stressed.
- ◆ the difference between emotion-focused and problem-focused coping.
- ◆ how to reduce stress by rethinking and reappraising your problems.
- ◆ the importance and limitations of social support.

COPING WITH STRESS

We have noted that most people who are under stress, even those living in difficult situations, do not become ill. In addition to feeling optimistic and in control, and not wallowing around in negative emotions, how do they manage to cope?

The most immediate way to deal with the physiological tension of stress and negative emotions is to take time out and reduce the body's physical arousal. Many people, from infants to the old, respond beneficially to the soothing touch of massage (Moyer, Rounds, & Hannum, 2004). Another successful method is the ancient Buddhist practice of *mindfulness meditation*, which fosters emotional tranquility. The goal is to learn to accept feelings of anger, sadness, or anxiety without judging them or trying to get rid of them (a form of secondary control) (Davidson et al., 2003). A third effective buffer between stressors and illness is exercise. People who are physically fit have fewer health problems than people who are less fit, even when they are under the same pressures. They also show lower physiological arousal to stressors (Vita et al., 1998). These activities, along with any others that calm your body and focus your mind—prayer, music, dancing, baking bread—are all good for health. But if your house has burned down or you need a serious operation, other coping strategies will be necessary.

Solving the Problem

Years ago, at the age of 23, a friend of ours named Simi Linton was struck by tragedy. Linton, her new husband, and her best friend were in a horrific car accident. When she awoke in a hospital room, with only a vague memory of the crash, she learned that her husband and friend had been killed and that she herself had permanent spinal injury and would never walk again.

How in the world does anyone recover from such a devastating event? Some people advise survivors of disaster or tragedy to "get it out of your system" or to "get in touch with your feelings." But survivors know they feel miserable. What should they *do*? This question gets to the heart of the difference between *emotion-focused* and *problem-focused coping* (Lazarus, 2000a; Lazarus & Folkman, 1984). Emotion-focused coping concentrates on the emotions the problem has caused, whether anger, anxiety, or grief. For a period of time after any tragedy or disaster, it is normal to give in to these emotions and feel overwhelmed by them. In this stage, people often need to talk obsessively about the event in order to come to terms with it, make sense of it, and decide what to do about it (Lepore, Ragan, & Jones, 2000).

Eventually, most people become ready to concentrate on solving the problem itself. The specific steps in problem-focused coping depend on the nature of the problem: whether it is a pressing but one-time decision; a continuing difficulty, such as living with a disability; or an anticipated event, such as having an operation. Once the problem is identified, the coper can learn as much as possible about it from professionals, friends, books, and others in the same predicament (Clarke & Evans, 1998). Becoming informed increases the feeling of control and can speed recovery (Doering et al., 2000).

As for Simi Linton, she learned how to do just about everything in her wheelchair (including dancing!), and she went back to school. She got a PhD in psychology, remarried, and became a highly respected teacher, counsellor, writer, and activist committed to improving conditions and opportunities for people with disabilities (Linton, 2006).

This athlete know all about surviving and thriving.

◄◉ **Simulate**
Stress and Health

Rethinking the Problem

Some problems cannot be solved; these are the unavoidable facts of life, such as an inability to have children, losing your job, or developing a chronic illness. Now what? Health psychologists have identified three effective cognitive coping methods:

1 **Reappraising the situation.** Although you may not be able to get rid of a stressor, you can choose to think about it differently, a process called *reappraisal*. Reappraisal can turn anger into sympathy, worry into determination, and feelings of loss into feelings of opportunity. Maybe that job you lost was dismal but you were too afraid to quit and look for another; now you can. Reappraisal improves well-being and reduces negative emotions (Gross & John, 2003; Haga, Kraft, & Corby, 2009; Moskowitz et al., 2009).

2 **Learning from the experience.** Most victims of traumatic events and life-threatening illnesses report that the experience made them stronger, more resilient, and even better human beings because they grew and learned from the event (McFarland & Alvaro, 2000). Those who draw lessons from the inescapable tragedies of life, and find meaning in them, thrive as a result of adversity instead of simply surviving it (Davis, Nolen-Hoeksema, & Larson, 1998; Folkman & Moskowitz, 2000). The ability to find meaning in adversity may even slow the course of serious diseases. In a longitudinal study of men with HIV who had been recently bereaved, those who "tried not to think about it" showed sharper declines in immune function than men who found meaning and purpose in the loss. The latter said they had acquired greater appreciation of the loved one, a perception of life as being fragile and precious, or other benefits. "I would say that his death lit up my faith," said one man (Taylor, Kemeny, et al., 2000).

3 **Making social comparisons.** In a difficult situation, successful copers often compare themselves to others who they feel are less fortunate. Even if they have fatal diseases, they find someone who is worse off (Taylor & Lobel, 1989; Wood, Michela, & Giordano, 2000). One person with AIDS said in an interview, "I made a list of all the other diseases I would rather not have than AIDS. Lou Gehrig's disease; being in a wheelchair; rheumatoid arthritis, when you are in knots and in terrible pain." Sometimes successful copers also compare themselves to those who are doing better than they are (Collins, 1996). They might say, "Look at her—she's had such family troubles and survived that awful bout with cancer, and she's happier than ever with her life. How did she do it?" or "He and I have the same kinds of problems. How come he's doing so much better in school than I am? What does he know that I don't?" Such *social comparisons* are beneficial when they provide a person with information about ways of coping, managing an illness, or improving a stressful situation (Suls, Martin, & Wheeler, 2002).

Watch
Coping Strategies and Their Effects

Drawing on Social Support

A final way to deal with negative emotions and stress is to reach out to others. Your health depends not only on what is going on in your body and mind but also on what is going on in your relationships: what you take from them, and what you give to them. When social groups provide individuals with a sense of meaning, purpose, and belonging, they produce positive psychological benefits for their members' health and well-being (Haslam et al., 2009).

WHEN FRIENDS HELP YOU COPE . . .   Think of all the ways in which family members, friends, neighbours, and co-workers can help you. They can offer concern and affection. They can help you evaluate problems and plan a course of action. They can offer resources and services such as lending you money or a car, or taking notes in class for you when you are sick. Most of all, they are sources of attachment and connection, which everyone needs throughout life. Perhaps this is why old people who have dogs as companions visit medical clinics less often than their peers who have no pets—or who have cats! Dogs provide nonjudgmental companionship and the gift of a truly best friend, and they lower the blood pressure of people in high-stress jobs (Allen, 2003).

Friends can even improve your health. For example, in general, work-related stress and unemployment increase a person's vulnerability to the common cold, but having a lot of friends and social contacts helps to reduce that risk (Cohen et al., 2003). Social support is especially important for people who have stressful jobs that require high cardiovascular responsiveness day after day, such as firefighters. Having social support helps the heart rate and stress hormones return to normal more quickly after a stressful episode (Roy, Steptoe, & Kirschbaum, 1998).

People who live in a network of close connections actually live longer than those who do not. In studies that followed thousands of adults for 10 years, people who had many friends, connections, or memberships in church and other groups lived longer on average than those who had few. The importance of having social networks was unrelated to physical health at the time the studies began, to socioeconomic status, and to risk factors like smoking (House, Landis, & Umberson, 2003).

When social support comes from a loving partner, its benefits on the immune system are especially powerful. In one study of 16 couples, the wives had to lie in an MRI machine, periodically receiving a mild but stressful electric shock on their ankle (Coan, Schaefer, & Davidson, 2006). During the procedure, some women received a touch on the hand from a stranger; others held hands with their husbands. The women's brain images showed activation in the hypothalamus and other regions involved with pain, physical arousal, and negative emotions. Yet, as you can see in Figure 11.6, the moment the women felt a husband's reassuring hand, their brain activation subsided in all the regions that had been revved up to cope with threat and fear. Holding hands with a stranger, while comforting, did not produce as great a decrease in brain activation as did a husband's touch.

When a touch is affectionate and welcome, it can actually elevate some "therapeutic" hormones, especially *oxytocin*, the hormone that induces relaxation and is associated with mothering and attachment. In fact, as health psychologist Shelley Taylor observes, human bodies are designed not only for a "fight or flight" response to stress and challenge, but also a "tend and befriend" response—being friendly and conciliatory, seeking out a friend or loved one, taking care of others (Taylor, 2006; Taylor, Klein, et al., 2000). Animal studies find that early nurturing by parents or other adults who "tend and befriend" the young can affect the sensitivity of the HPA axis, making the infants more resilient to later chronic stressors. Such findings may help explain why, without such nurturing, stressed

Friends don't have to be human. Kirby, dressed here in a sheep costume for Halloween, is a certified therapy dog who delights the hospital patients he visits.

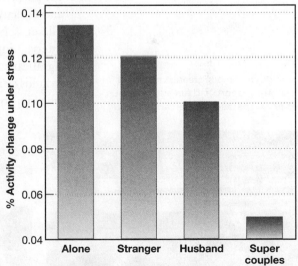

FIGURE 11.6 Hugs and Health
Women had to lie in an MRI machine while receiving mild but stressful shocks on their ankle. Those who showed the highest activation of the hypothalamus and other regions of the brain involved in stress and anxiety went through the test alone. A stranger's calming touch reduced activation somewhat and a husband's touch reduced it even more. The women in "super couples," those who felt the closest to their husbands (right bar), showed the lowest signs of stress (Coan, Schaefer, & Davidson, 2006).

children become physically more vulnerable to illness (Young & Francis, 2008). Oxytocin might even be the key link between hugging and lower blood pressure, in men as well as women (Grewen et al., 2005).

However, once again it is important not to oversimplify, for instance by concluding that if people just have the right amount and kind of social support they can defeat any illness. Some years ago, a psychiatrist claimed, on the basis of a preliminary study, that women with advanced breast cancer lived longer if they joined support groups, but the study has been completely discredited and was never replicated (Coyne et al., 2009). Therapy does not prolong survival, although it is often emotionally and socially beneficial to individual members.

Moreover, not all cultural groups define "social support" the same way or benefit from the same kind. People from Asian backgrounds tend to be more reluctant than other North Americans to ask for help explicitly from friends, colleagues, and family and to disclose feelings of distress. Being particularly attuned to the harmony of their relationships (see Chapter 14), many Asians are concerned about the potentially negative and embarrassing effects of self-disclosure or of seeking help. As a result, they often feel more stressed and have elevated stress hormones when they are required to ask for help or reveal their private feelings (Kim, Sherman, & Taylor, 2008). But Asians do not differ from others in their reliance on, and need for, *implicit* social support—the knowledge that someone will be there to help if they need it.

... AND COPING WITH FRIENDS.

Needless to say, sometimes other people aren't helpful. Sometimes they themselves are the source of unhappiness, stress, and anger.

In close relationships, the same person who is a source of support can also become a source of stress, especially if the two parties are arguing all the time. Being in an unhappy, bitter, uncommunicative relationship can significantly impair health. It makes the partners depressed and angry, affects their health habits, elevates stress hormones, and directly influences their cardiovascular, endocrine, and immune systems (Kiecolt-Glaser & Newton, 2001). Married couples who argue in a hostile fashion—criticizing, interrupting, or insulting the other person, and becoming angry and defensive—show significant elevations of cortisol and poorer immune function afterward. In fact, any wounds or blisters a hostile couple has actually heal more slowly than they do in couples who do not argue in a hostile way (Kiecolt-Glaser et al., 2005). Couples who argue in a positive fashion—trying to find common ground, compromising, listening to each other's concerns, and using humour to defuse tension—do not show these impairments. As one student of ours observed, "This study gives new meaning to the accusation 'You make me sick!'"

In addition to being sources of conflict, friends and relatives may be unsupportive in times of trouble simply out of ignorance or awkwardness. They may abandon you or say something stupid and hurtful. Sometimes they actively block your efforts to change bad health habits, such

Friends can be our greatest source of warmth, support, and fun and also sources of exasperation, anger, and misery.

as binge drinking or smoking, by making fun of you or pressuring you to conform to what "everyone" does. And sometimes, because they have never been in the same situation and do not know what to do to help, they offer the wrong kind of support. For example, they may try to cheer you up, saying, "Everything will be fine," rather than let you talk about your fears or find solutions. Or they may try to press you to join a support group "for your own good" even if you regard disclosing your feelings in groups as culturally or personally inappropriate for you.

Finally, we should not forget the benefits of giving support, rather than always being on the receiving end. Julius Segal (1986), a psychologist who worked with Holocaust survivors, hostages, refugees, and other survivors of catastrophe, wrote that a key element in their recovery was compassion for others: "healing through helping." Why? The ability to look outside yourself is related to all the successful coping mechanisms we have discussed. It encourages you to solve problems instead of blaming others or just venting your emotions, helps you reappraise the situation by seeing it from another person's perspective, fosters forgiveness, and allows you to gain perspective on your own problems (Brown et al., 2003). Healing through helping thus helps everyone to accept difficult situations that are facts of life.

---

quickQUIZ

✓ **Quick Review** on **MyPsychLab**

Can you cope with these questions?

1. You accidentally broke your glasses. Which response is an example of cognitive reappraisal? (a) "I am such a stupid, clumsy idiot!" (b) "I never do anything right." (c) "What a shame, but I've been wanting new frames anyway." (d) "I'll forget about it in aerobics class."

2. Finding out what your legal and financial resources are when you have been victimized by a crime is an example of (a) problem-focused coping, (b) emotion-focused coping, (c) distraction, (d) reappraisal.

3. "This class drives me crazy, but I'm better off than my friends who aren't in university" is an example of (a) distraction, (b) social comparison, (c) denial, (d) empathy.

4. What hormone is elevated when happy couples hug one another?

5. Your roommate has turned your room into a garbage dump, filled with rotten leftover food and unwashed clothes. Assuming that you don't like living with rotting food and dirty clothes, what coping strategies described in this section might help you?

Answers:

1. c 2. a 3. b 4. oxytocin 5. You might solve the problem by finding a compromise (e.g., cleaning the room together). You could reappraise the seriousness of the problem ("I only have to live with this person until the end of the term") or compare your roommate to others who are worse ("At least mine is generous and friendly"). And you might mobilize some social support, perhaps by offering your friends a pizza if they help you clean up.

Simulate
Survey of Happiness

As you can see in Review 11.2, the factors that affect health and illness range from those we can't do anything about to those that we can. Successful coping does not mean eliminating all sources of stress or all difficult emotions. It does not mean constant happiness or a life without anger, grief, and frustration. The healthy person faces problems, deals with them, learns from them, and gets beyond them. To wish for a life without stress, or a life without emotion, would be like wishing for a life without friends. The result might be calm, but it would be joyless. Chronic problems, difficult decisions, and occasional tragedies are inescapable. How we handle them is the test of our humanity.

REVIEW 11.2

Factors That Increase the Risk of Illness

	Factors	Examples
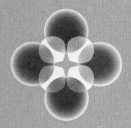	**Environmental**	Poverty, lack of access to health care, exposure to toxins, crime, discrimination
	Experiential	Childhood neglect, traumatic events, chronic job stress, unemployment
	Biological	Viral or bacterial infections, disease, genetic vulnerability, toxins
	Psychological	Hostility, chronic major depression, emotional inhibition, pessimism, external locus of control (fatalism), feeling powerless
	Behavioural	Smoking, poor diet, lack of exercise, abuse of alcohol and other drugs, lack of sleep
	Social	Lack of supportive friends, low involvement in meaningful groups, being in a hostile, bitter relationship

Taking Psychology with YOU

Thinking Critically in Everyday Life

How Much Control Do We Have over Our Emotions and Our Health?

Clara Harris, whose story opened this chapter, killed her husband in "the heat of anger." Could she have controlled herself? When we are feeling extreme emotions or when major stressors require the body to cope with threat, fear, or danger, the body whirls into action to give us the energy to respond. Just about everyone, for example, has had the unpleasant experience of a racing heart, sweaty palms, and other emotional symptoms upon seeing a former lover with a new partner. But does that mean we have no control over our emotions—that if we yell, scream, or become violent when we're angry, it's not our fault?

How about our health? People do have some control over the psychological and social factors involved in the onset and course of many illnesses, such as negative emotions, pessimism, and lack of supportive friends. And we can choose to do the three things that are the strongest behavioural predictors of longevity and health, which are not psychological at all: not smoking (or quitting), eating a healthful diet, and exercising regularly. But does that mean that if we become sick, it's our own fault?

Life is full of stressful experiences, emotional problems, and disastrous bolts out of the blue that we cannot predict or avoid. At such times, critical thinking becomes especially important, because the temptation is great to slide into oversimplified, either–or thinking: For example, if you are angry about some injustice, *either* you try to squelch your feelings *or* you take them out on the nearest innocent target. If you become ill, *either* you accept traditional medical procedures *or* you use alternative psychological ones, such as visual imagery, meditation, and support groups. It seems easier to jump to one explanation or solution and stick with it, without examining the evidence (pro and con) for its effectiveness. In stressful times, everyone is inclined to let emotional reasoning cloud their good judgment.

Usually, though, there are solutions and ways of coping that do not require either–or answers. For example, people can endorse traditional medical treatments while also appreciating the power of optimism and social support in their recovery and well-being. In the case of managing anger, Clara Harris could surely have found a course of action between suppressing her feelings completely and driving her SUV over her husband in a parking lot!

Hostile anger, as we have seen in this chapter, is particularly hazardous to health, but what should people do when they are as enraged as Clara Harris was? When we examine the evidence, we find that the pop-psych advice to "ventilate your anger and get it out of your system" often backfires: Many people feel worse both physically and mentally after an angry confrontation. When people brood and ruminate about their anger,

talk to others incessantly about how angry they are, or ventilate their feelings in hostile acts, their blood pressure shoots up, they often feel angrier, and they behave even *more* aggressively later than if they had just let their feelings of anger subside (Bushman et al., 2005; Tavris, 1989). Conversely, when people learn to control their tempers and express anger constructively, they usually feel better, not worse; calmer, not angrier.

When people are feeling angry, they may not be able to control that racing heart or the emotion itself, but they can control what they do next: They can take five, calm down, and cool off rather than acting impulsively and making matters worse. They can use their critical-thinking skills to avoid emotional reasoning and check their perceptions of the situation for accuracy. People who are quick to feel anger tend to interpret other people's actions as intentional offences. People who are slow to

anger tend to give others the benefit of the doubt, and they are not as focused on their own injured pride.

Critical thinkers might also learn to think carefully about how to express anger, and to make calm decisions about how to proceed so that they will get the results they want. Many people say harsh and hurtful things in anger simply to make the other person feel bad. But shouting "You moron! How could you be so stupid!" is not likely to get the person to apologize, let alone to change his or her behaviour. If the goal is to improve a bad situation or achieve justice, learning how to express anger so that the other person will listen is essential.

In short, we may not be able to control the stressors in our lives or the intensity of some emotions we feel after great loss, injustice, or tragedy, but we human beings have something almost better: The ability to think about our actions and to control what we do next.

SUMMARY

THE NATURE OF EMOTION

◆ Although negative emotions are often painful, emotions evolved to bind people together, motivate them to achieve their goals, and help them make decisions and plans. The experience of *emotion* involves physiological changes in the face, brain, and autonomic nervous system; cognitive processes; and cultural norms and regulations. *Primary emotions* are thought to be universal, whereas *secondary emotions* are specific to cultures.

◆ Some basic facial expressions—anger, fear, sadness, happiness, disgust, surprise, contempt, and possibly pride—are widely recognized across cultures. They foster communication with others, signal our intentions to others, enhance infant survival, and, as studies of *facial feedback* show, help us to identify our own emotional states. But an accurate reading of others' facial expressions increases among members of the same ethnicity, and depends on the social context. Also, because people can and do disguise their emotions, their expressions do not always communicate accurately.

◆ Many aspects of emotion are associated with specific parts of the brain. The amygdala is responsible for initially evaluating the emotional importance of incoming sensory information and is especially involved in fear. The cerebral cortex provides the cognitive ability to override this initial appraisal. Emotions generally involve the motivation to approach or withdraw; regions of the *left* prefrontal cortex appear to be specialized for the motivation to approach others (as with happiness and anger), whereas regions of the *right* prefrontal region are specialized for withdrawal or escape (as with disgust and fear).

◆ *Mirror neurons* throughout the brain are activated when people observe others. These neurons are involved in empathy, imitation, synchrony, understanding another person's intentions, and *mood contagion*.

◆ During the experience of any emotion, *epinephrine* and *norepinephrine* produce a state of physiological arousal to prepare the body for an output of energy. Different emotions are also associated with different patterns of autonomic nervous system activity.

◆ As discussed in "Biology and Deception," the most popular method of lie detection is the *polygraph machine*, but it has low reliability and validity because there are no patterns of autonomic nervous system activity specific to lying; it has a high rate of labelling innocent people as guilty. Other methods have similar drawbacks. The Guilty Knowledge Test has been more successful but also has limitations.

◆ Cognitive approaches to emotion emphasize the perceptions and *attributions* that are involved in different emotions. Thoughts and emotions operate reciprocally, each influencing the other. Some emotions involve simple, nonconscious reactions; others, such as shame and guilt, require complex cognitive capacities.

EMOTION AND CULTURE

◆ Many psychologists believe that all human beings share the ability to experience primary emotions, whereas secondary emotions may be culture-specific—a view supported by research on *emotion prototypes*. But others believe that culture affects every aspect of emotional experience, including which emotions are considered basic and what people feel emotional about.

◆ Culture strongly influences the *display rules*, including those governing nonverbal *body language*, that regulate how and whether people express their emotions. *Emotion work* is the effort a person makes to display an emotion he or she does not feel but feels obliged to convey.

◆ Women and men are equally likely to feel all emotions, although gender rules shape differences in emotional expression. North American women on average are more expressive than men, except for anger at strangers. But both sexes are less expressive toward a person of higher status, both sexes will do the emotion work their job requires, and some situations foster expressiveness in everybody. Gender differences also vary across cultures.

THE NATURE OF STRESS

◆ The relationship between emotions and stress is both physiological and psychological. Chronic negative emotions can become chronically stressful, and chronic stress can create negative emotions.

◆ Hans Selye argued that environmental stressors such as heat, pain, and danger produce a *general adaptation syndrome*, in which the body responds in three stages: *alarm*, *resistance*, and *exhaustion*. If a stressor persists, it may overwhelm the body's ability to cope, and illness may result. Modern research has added to Selye's work. When a person is under stress or in danger, the hypothalamus

sends messages to the endocrine glands along two major pathways. One activates the sympathetic division of the autonomic nervous system, releasing adrenal hormones from the inner part of the adrenal glands. In the other, the hypothalamus initiates activity along the *HPA axis*. Chemical messengers travel from the hypothalamus to the pituitary, and in turn to the outer part (cortex) of the adrenal glands. The adrenal cortex secretes *cortisol* and other hormones that increase energy. Excess levels of cortisol can become harmful in the long run.

◆ When the stressors of poverty and unemployment become chronic, they can increase people's stress levels and increase their chances of illness. But responses to stress differ across individuals, depending on the type of stressor and the individual's own genetic predispositions.

◆ Health psychologists and researchers in the interdisciplinary field of psychoneuroimmunology (PNI) are studying the interaction among psychological factors, the nervous and endocrine systems, and the immune system (particularly the white blood cells that destroy harmful foreign bodies, called *antigens*). Chronic stress can even shorten *telomeres*, proteins that determine cell life.

◆ Psychological factors affect people's responses to stress. Feeling optimistic rather than pessimistic and having an *internal locus of control* improve immune function and also increase a person's ability to tolerate pain, live with ongoing problems, and recover from illness. As discussed in "Culture and Control," cultures differ in the kind of control they emphasize and value: *primary control*, trying to change the stressful situation, or *secondary control*, learning to accept and accommodate to the stressful situation.

STRESS AND EMOTION

◆ Researchers have sought links between emotions, stress, and illness. There is no "cancer-prone personality," but chronic anger, especially in the form of *cynical* or *antagonistic* hostility, is a strong risk factor in heart disease. Major depression also increases the risk of later heart disease. Positive emotions appear related to well-being, better health, and longevity.

◆ People who consciously suppress their emotions are at greater risk of illness than people who acknowledge and cope with negative emotions. The effort to suppress worries, secrets, and memories of upsetting experiences can become stressful to the body. Two ways of letting go of negative emotions include confession and forgiveness. The goal is to achieve insight and understanding, and let go of grudges.

COPING WITH STRESS

◆ The first step in coping with stress and negative emotions is to reduce their physical effects, for example through relaxation, *mindfulness meditation*, and exercise. The second is to focus on solving the problem (*problem-focused coping*) rather than on venting the emotions caused by the problem (*emotion-focused coping*). A third approach is to rethink the problem, which involves *reappraisal*, learning from the experience, and comparing oneself to others.

◆ Social support is essential in maintaining physical health and emotional well-being; it even prolongs life and speeds recovery from illness. A touch or a hug from a supportive partner calms the alarm circuits of the brain and raises levels of *oxytocin*, which may result in reduced heart rate and blood pressure. However, friends and family can also be sources of stress. In close relationships, couples who fight in a hostile and negative way show impaired immune function. Giving support to others is also associated with health and hastens recovery from traumatic experiences.

◆ Coping with stress does not mean trying to live without pain or problems. It means learning how to live with the inevitable troubles that life dishes out.

TAKING PSYCHOLOGY WITH YOU

◆ We may not always be able to control the physiological arousal produced by stress or intense emotions, but we are generally able to decide how to behave. Coping with stress does not mean trying to live without pain or problems. It means learning how to live with them.

MyPsychLab

Visit **www.mypsychlab.com** to help you get the best grade!
Test your knowledge and grasp difficult concepts through

• Custom study plans: See where you are strong and where you go wrong
• Interactive simulations
• Video and audio clips

KEY TERMS

emotion 408
primary emotions 408
secondary emotions 409
facial feedback 410
mirror neurons 413

display rules 423
emotion work 423
general adaptation syndrome 426
HPA axis 427
psychoneuroimmunology (PNI) 429

locus of control (internal and external) 431
primary control 432
secondary control 432

ASK QUESTIONS . . . be willing to WONDER

- What accounts for the worldwide epidemic of obesity?

- Why do we fall in love, and why with that person?

- Why are some people straight and others gay?

- After a setback, why do some people persist in their goals and others give up?

In 1992, Silken Laumann won a bronze medal at the Barcelona Olympics. Most stories of outstanding Olympic achievement are about gold medals. Indeed, just three months before the event, she was favoured to scull her way to the gold. However, in a horrible training accident, Silken severely injured one of her legs. By some accounts, the leg was "half-amputated." Following five hasty reconstructive surgeries and a skin graft, her physicians told her that her Olympic dreams would not become reality. In fact, they even told her that she might never be able to row again, even recreationally. In an incredible demonstration of motivation, Silken chose to endure the pain of catch-up training shortly before the big event. This determination paid off. She earned a place in the final and pushed her ailing body to the limit, earning Canada's most famous Olympic bronze medal.

In 1875, a teenager named Annie Oakley defeated Frank Butler, the star of the Buffalo Bill Wild West Show, in an arranged sharp-shooting competition. "It was her first big match—my first defeat," wrote Butler. "The next day I came back to see the little girl who had beaten me, and it was not long until we married." He became her manager, and for the next 50 years they travelled together across Europe and North America, where her skills with a gun made her the toast of both continents. Throughout his life, Frank published love poems to Annie, and they remained devoted until their deaths, within 18 days of one another, in 1926 (Kreps, 1990).

What motivated Silken Laumann to risk permanent disability and successfully compete for an Olympic medal? What kept Annie Oakley and Frank Butler in love for 50 years, when so many other romantic passions die in five years—or five weeks?

The word motivation, like the word emotion, comes from the Latin root meaning "to move," and the psychology of motivation is indeed the study of what moves us, why we do what we do. To psychologists, **motivation** refers to a process within a person or animal that causes that organism to move toward a goal or away from an unpleasant situation. The motive may be to satisfy a psychological goal, say, by getting married or avoiding marriage; it may be to satisfy a biological need, say, by eating a sandwich to reduce hunger; or it may be to fulfill a psychological ambition, say, by being the first to row across the Atlantic in a dinghy (it's been done).

For many decades, the study of motivation was dominated by a focus on biological drives, such as those to acquire food and water, to have sex, to seek novelty, and to avoid cold and pain. Some psychologists still think that people are motivated by certain drives, especially sex and hunger. But drive theories cannot account for the full complexity of human motivation, because people are conscious creatures who think and plan ahead, set goals for themselves,

motivation An inferred process within a person or animal that causes movement either toward a goal or away from an unpleasant situation.

intrinsic motivation The pursuit of an activity for its own sake.

extrinsic motivation The pursuit of an activity for external rewards, such as money or fame.

set point The genetically influenced weight range for an individual; it is maintained by biological mechanisms that regulate food intake, fat reserves, and metabolism.

⏴⊙ **Simulate**
Psychology Experiments Survey: What Motivates You?

and plot strategies to reach those goals. People are motivated to eat, for instance, but that information doesn't tell us why some individuals with strong political commitments will go on hunger strikes to protest injustice.

In this chapter, we will examine four central areas of human motivation: food, love, sex, and achievement. We will see how happiness and well-being are affected by the kinds of goals we set for ourselves, and by whether we are spurred to reach them because of **intrinsic motivation,** the desire to do something for its own sake and the pleasure it brings, or **extrinsic motivation,** the desire to pursue a goal for external rewards.

 YOU are about to learn . . .

◆ the biological mechanisms that make it difficult for obese people to lose weight and keep it off.

◆ how notions of the ideal male and female body change over time and across cultures.

◆ why people all over the world are getting fatter.

◆ the major forms of eating disorders, and why they are increasing among young men as well as women.

THE HUNGRY ANIMAL: MOTIVES TO EAT

Some people are skinny; others are plump. Some are shaped like string beans; others look more like pears. Some can eat anything they want without gaining an ounce; others struggle unsuccessfully their whole lives to shed pounds. Some hate being fat, and others think that fat is just fine. How much do genes, psychology, and environment affect our motivation to eat or not to eat?

The Biology of Weight

At one time, most psychologists thought that being overweight was a sign of emotional disturbance. If you were fat, it was because you hated your mother, feared intimacy, or were trying to fill an emotional hole in your psyche by loading up on rich desserts. The evidence for psychological theories of overweight, however, came mainly from self-reports and from flawed studies that lacked control groups or objective measures of how much people were actually eating. When researchers did controlled experiments, they learned that fat people, on average, are no more and no less emotionally disturbed than average-weight people. Even more surprising, they found that heaviness is not always caused by overeating (Stunkard, 1980). Many heavy people do eat large quantities of food, but so do some thin people. In one study, in which volunteers gorged themselves for months, it was as hard for slender people to gain weight as it is for most heavy people to lose weight. The minute the study was over, the slender people lost weight as fast as dieters gained it back (Sims, 1974).

GENETIC INFLUENCES ON WEIGHT AND BODY SHAPE. The explanation that emerged from such findings was that a biological mechanism keeps your body weight at a genetically influenced **set point**, the weight you stay at when you are not trying to gain or lose (Lissner et al., 1991). The set point can vary about 10% in either direction. For example,

Thinking ⚙ Critically

Analyze Assumptions and Biases

Obesity is caused mainly by psychological problems and lack of willpower, isn't it? When researchers questioned this common assumption, they were in for a surprise.

Body weight and shape are strongly affected by genetic factors. Set-point theory helps explain why the Pimas of the American Southwest gain weight easily but lose it slowly, whereas the Bororo nomads of Nigeria can eat a lot of food yet remain slender.

a woman with a set point of 150 pounds might weigh anywhere from 135 to 165. But if her weight dips below 135 or goes above 165, her body will produce either an insatiable urge to eat or a loss of appetite to bring its fat levels back into line. Set-point research has focused on how the body regulates appetite, eating, and weight gain and loss. Everyone has a genetically programmed *basal metabolism rate*, the rate at which the body burns calories for energy, and a fixed number of fat cells, which store fat for energy and can change in size. Obese people have about twice the number of fat cells as normal-weight adults do, and their fat cells are bigger (Spalding et al., 2008). When people lose weight, they don't lose the fat cells; the cells just get thinner, and easily plump up again.

A complex interaction of metabolism, fat cells, and hormones keeps people at the weight their bodies are designed to be, much as a thermostat keeps a house at a constant temperature. When a heavy person diets, the body's metabolism slows down to conserve energy and fat reserves (Ravussin et al., 1988). When a thin person overeats, metabolism speeds up, burning energy. In one study, in which 16 slender volunteers ate 1000 extra calories every day for eight weeks, their metabolisms sped up to burn the excess calories. They were like hummingbirds, in constant movement: fidgeting, pacing, changing their positions frequently while seated, and so on (Levine, Eberhardt, & Jensen, 1999).

Set-point theory predicts that the heritability of weight and body fat should be high, and indeed it is: In twin and adoption studies, heritability estimates fall between 0.40 and 0.70 (Comuzzie & Allison, 1998). Pairs of adult identical twins who grew up in different families are just as similar in body weight and shape as twins raised together. And when identical twins gain weight, they gain it in the same place: Some pairs store extra pounds around their waists, others on their hips and thighs (Bouchard et al., 1990). Genes also determine how much "brown fat" a person has in addition to the usual white fat. Brown fat is an energy-burning type of fat that seems important in regulating body weight and blood sugar. It is lacking in obese people, which may be one reason that fat people can't burn all the calories they consume (Cypess et al., 2009).

Genes are also involved in some types of obesity. In a study of 171 Pima Indians in Arizona, two-thirds of the women and half of the men became obese over time, and the slower their metabolisms, the greater the weight gain. After adding anywhere from

Among the Inuit of the Canadian Arctic, obesity and Type II diabetes are largely the result of ingesting too many calories (high-fat foods, sugars, and carbohydrates). Although Inuit cultures ate fatty food traditionally (whale skin, for instance), it was in limited supply—especially the sugar and carbohydrates. In modern Inuit society, the supply of fats, sugars, and carbohydrates is virtually unlimited.

Both of these mice have a mutation in the *ob* gene, which usually makes mice chubby, like the one on the left. But when leptin is injected daily, the mice eat less and burn more calories, causing the chubby one to become slim, like his friendly pal. Unfortunately, leptin injections have not had the same results in most human beings.

◉ **Watch**
Kids and Food

20 to 45 pounds, however, the Pimas stopped gaining weight. Their metabolism rates rose, and their weights stabilized at the new, higher level (Ravussin et al., 1988). Many Pimas apparently have a set point for plumpness. Similarly, the Inuit of the Canadian Arctic (Young, 1996) and other indigenous peoples of Canada have much higher rates of obesity than other Canadians (Harris et al., 1997; Katzmarzyk & Malina, 1998, 1999; Orr et al., 1998). Furthermore, obesity in these groups has serious consequences—including Type II diabetes. Among the indigenous peoples of Canada, the rate of Type II diabetes is higher than among any other group in the world (Harris et al., 1997).

A few years ago, a team of researchers isolated a genetic variation that causes mice to become obese (Zhang et al., 1994). The usual form of the gene, called *obese*, or *ob* for short, causes fat cells to secrete a protein, which researchers have named *leptin* (from the Greek *leptos*, "slender"). Leptin travels through the blood to the brain's hypothalamus, which is involved in the regulation of appetite. When leptin levels are normal, people eat just enough to maintain their weight. When a mutation of the *ob* gene causes leptin levels to be too low, however, the hypothalamus thinks the body lacks fat reserves and signals the individual to overeat (Zhang et al., 1994). Injecting leptin into leptin-deficient mice reduces the animals' appetites, speeds up their metabolisms, and makes them more active; as a result, the animals shed weight (Friedman, 2003). Some extremely obese individuals who lack leptin for genetic reasons likewise benefit from injections of the hormone. A 200-pound nine-year-old girl, whose legs were so large she could hardly walk, dramatically reduced her food intake and weight to normal levels after treatment with leptin (Farooqi et al., 2002, 2007).

Studies of mice suggest that leptin plays its most crucial role early in life, by altering the brain chemistry that influences how much an animal or person later eats. More specifically, leptin helps regulate body weight by strengthening neural circuits in the hypothalamus that reduce appetite and by weakening circuits that stimulate it (Elmquist & Flier, 2004). During a critical period in infancy, leptin influences the formation of those neural connections, and the set point is, well, set (Bouret, Draper, & Simerly, 2004). Some researchers speculate that because of this early neural plasticity, overfeeding infants while the hypothalamus is developing may later produce childhood obesity.

Researchers have identified a number of other genes that are linked to being overweight (Farooqi & O'Rahilly, 2004; Frayling et al., 2007; Friedman, 2003; Herbert et al., 2006; Stice et al., 2008). For example, they have discovered a gene that modulates production of a protein that apparently converts excess calories into heat rather than fat. Possession of this gene may be one reason why slim people stay slim even when they temporarily overeat (Arsenijevic et al., 2000).

Findings such as these often raise the public's hopes for a breakthrough drug that will help people lose weight easily and quickly. One pharmaceutical company thought leptin would be the answer: Take leptin, lose weight! Alas, for most obese people, and for people who are merely overweight, taking leptin does not produce much weight loss (Comuzzie & Allison, 1998). Just to make life more complicated, leptin is only one influence on body weight. Dozens of genes and body chemicals are involved in appetite, metabolism rates, and weight regulation. You have receptors in your nose and mouth that keep urging you to eat more ("The food is right there! It's good! Eat!"), receptors in your gut telling you to quit ("You've had enough already!"), and leptin and other chemicals telling you that you have stored enough fat or not enough. One hormone makes you hungry and eager to eat more, and another turns off your appetite after a meal, making you eat less.

As if all this weren't enough, your brain will get high on sugary foods even if your tongue can't taste them or enjoy their texture. Sweets increase pleasure-inducing dopamine levels in the brain, making you crave more rich food (de Araujo et al., 2008). (Forget about trying to fool your brain with artificial sweeteners; they just make you want the real thing.) Some obese individuals may have underactive reward circuitry, which leads them to overeat to boost their dopamine levels (Stice et al., 2008). When heavy people joke (or lament) that they are "addicted" to rich food, they may literally be right.

The complexity of the mechanisms governing appetite and weight explains why appetite-suppressing drugs inevitably fail in the long run: They target only one of the many factors that conspire to keep you the weight you are.

THE OVERWEIGHT DEBATE. If genes are so strongly implicated in weight and body shape, and if most people have normal set points, why are so many people, all over the world, getting fatter? Increases in obesity rates have occurred in both sexes, all social classes, and all age groups, and in many other countries (Popkin, 2009). More than half of all North American adults, and at least 25% of all children and teenagers, are now overweight or obese. The increase has been greatest among the very fat: The number of North Americans who are at least 100 pounds overweight has quadrupled since the 1980s. Increases in obesity rates have occurred in both sexes, all social classes, and all age groups, and in many countries (Taubes, 1998). The United Nations, so used to dealing with problems of starvation and malnutrition, has announced that "obesity is the dominant unmet global health issue," especially in the United States, Canada, Great Britain, Mexico, Egypt, North Africa, Japan, and Australia, and even in coastal China and Southeast Asia.

The prevalence of obesity in Canada has increased in the past few years (Millar & Stephens, 1993); in 1994, it was estimated that 26% of women and 35% of men in Canada were obese, and that by government standards, half of the adult population was overweight (MacDonald et al., 1997; Trakas, Lawrence, & Shear, 1999). So people are a little plump, what does it matter? For the year 1994, obesity was estimated to directly cost Canadian taxpayers more than $1.8 billion in health care; approximately 2.4% of the health-care budget was spent treating obesity or diseases directly resulting from obesity (Birmingham et al., 1999). This increase in obesity is not restricted to Canadians, as it has also been observed in the United Kingdom, the United States, and other Western cultures (Flegal, 1999).

The reasons have little to do with the prevalence of obesity genes, which cannot have changed much in just a couple of decades. In fact, among recent immigrants to Canada, the longer they have lived in this country, the greater the chance that they will become overweight or obese (Cairney & Ostbye, 1999). These people have not changed their genes—just their addresses and thus their diets.

Many health researchers are worried about this trend because obesity is considered a leading risk factor in diabetes, high blood pressure, heart disease, stroke, cancer, infertility, sleep apnea, and many other disorders. But are there comparable health risks to being overweight by, say, 20 to 30 pounds? What if a person is genetically predisposed to be fat, though not obese? Lately some scientists have been cautioning against the emotional reasoning that so often accompanies discussions of this subject in North America, where "thin is in." They believe that for most people, the real health culprit is not overweight but lack

✱ **Explore**
The Effects of the Hypothalamus on Eating Behaviour

◉ **Watch**
Urban Sprawl and Obesity

of fitness. Fat people who are physically fit are healthier and have lower risk of illness, on average, than thin people who are sedentary (Campos, 2004). Because many overweight people have sedentary habits, few scientists have thought to separate these two factors. In a representative sample of more than 5000 American adults over the age of 20, about 24% of the normal-weight adults were metabolically unhealthy—that is, they had high blood pressure, "bad" cholesterol, elevated triglycerides, and other risk factors for heart disease—whereas 51% of the overweight adults and nearly 32% of the obese adults were metabolically healthy (Wildman et al., 2008).

Scientists are currently debating the extent of the problem and what can be done about it. One scientist, Jeffrey Friedman, the primary discoverer of the gene for leptin, said in an interview that the obesity epidemic is mainly a result of the fact that fat people are getting fatter; thin people have remained pretty much the same (Kolata, 2004). Thin people do not balloon into obesity, he observes—remember those hummingbird metabolisms that so many of them have—nor can fat people lose weight permanently through willpower, because body weight is genetically determined. Other scientists agree that genes play a powerful role, but they observe that changes in the environment and culture are the reason why so many people are putting on the pounds. After all, in between the extremes of thin and fat are the millions of people whose weights have risen 10 to 30 to 50 pounds, and that's not trivial. What has caused that increase?

Whatever the health implications of being overweight, a puzzle remains: If genes and all the chemical factors and fat cells they regulate are so strongly implicated in weight and body shape, why are so many people, all over the world, getting fatter? In Mexico in 1989, for example, fewer than 10% of its citizens were overweight; the country's greatest concern was poverty and hunger. Yet by 2006, 71% of Mexican women and 66% of the men were overweight or obese, with corresponding increases in diabetes and other diseases (Popkin, 2009). What has caused that increase in Mexico and so many other nations in so short a time?

Another major influence on weight is exercise, which boosts the body's metabolic rate, even in people who are genetically susceptible to obesity (Esparza et al., 2000). When obese women are put on severely restricted diets, their metabolic rates drop sharply, as set-point theory would predict. But when they combine the diet with moderate physical activity—daily walking—they lose weight and their metabolic rates rise almost to previous levels (Wadden et al., 1990).

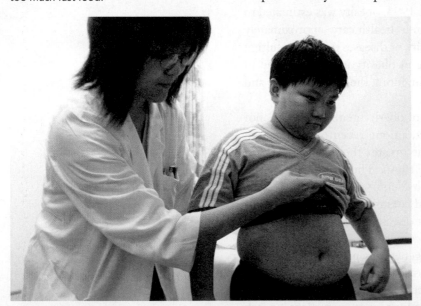

Obesity is a global problem. Children around the world are eating more like North Americans—too much food, and too much fast food.

Environmental Influences on Weight

The leading culprits causing the worldwide rise in weight have to do with five sweeping changes in the environment (Critser, 2002; Popkin, 2009; Taubes, 2008):

1 **The increased abundance of fast food and processed foods** that are inexpensive, readily available, and high in sugar, starch, fat, and carbohydrates (Taubes, 2008). Human beings are genetically predisposed to gain weight when rich food is abundant because, in our species'

evolutionary past, starvation was all too often a real possibility. Therefore, a tendency to store calories in the form of fat provided a definite survival advantage. Unfortunately, evolution did not produce a comparable mechanism to prevent people who do not have hummingbird metabolisms from gaining weight when food is easily available, tasty, rich, varied, and cheap. That, of course, is precisely the situation today, surrounded as we are by three-quarter–pound burgers, fries, chips, tacos, candy bars, pizzas, and sodas.

One research team observed the direct effects of the proximity of fast-food outlets on obesity. They followed thousands of grade 9 schoolchildren, before and after a new fast-food restaurant opened near their schools. Those whose schools were within a block of a burger or pizza outlet were more likely to become obese in the next year than students whose schools were a quarter of a mile or more away (Currie et al., 2009). Proximity to fast food seems to be a major cause of the "freshman 15" as well. In a study at two very different universities, one in the American Midwest and the other in the East, more than 70% of all freshmen gained significant amounts of weight in their first year (Lloyd-Richardson et al., 2009).

2 **The widespread consumption of high-sugar, high-calorie soft drinks.** Throughout most of human history, the proportion of calories consumed in beverages (milk, wine, fruit juice, and the like) was very low, and thus the human body did not evolve a mechanism that would compensate for fluid intake by lowering food intake. Then, fifty years ago, soft drinks, which are loaded with sugar and calories, began spreading across the globe. Putting sweeteners into drinks has led to a weight gain of up to 14 pounds per person in those who drink two to three sodas a day (Popkin, 2009).

3 **The sharp decline in exercise and other expenditures of energy** because of remote controls, a preference for sedentary activities such as watching videos and television, and the speed and convenience of driving rather than walking or biking.

4 **The increased portion sizes of food and drink.** Servings of food and drink have become supersized, double or triple what they were only one generation ago. Even babies and toddlers up to two years of age are being fed as much as 30% more calories than they need (Fox et al., 2004). In France, people eat rich food but much less of it than North Americans do (Rozin et al., 2003). Their notion of what a proper portion is—for yogurt, soda, a salad, a sandwich, anything—is much lower than in Canada.

◉ **Watch**
You Are What You Eat

5 **The abundance of highly varied foods.** When diets are predictable and routine, people habituate to what they are eating and eat less of it. That is why all diets that restrict people to eating only a few kinds of foods (only watermelon, only protein, only whatever) are successful at first. As soon as food becomes more varied, however, people eat more and gain more weight (Remick, Polivy, & Pliner, 2009). In fact, people will even eat more M&Ms when they are available in a bowl containing 10 colours than when the same number of candies are in a bowl containing only seven colours (Wansink, 2006).

Get INVOLVED!

WHAT'S CONTROLLING HOW MUCH YOU EAT?

Many people believe that what they eat and how much they eat is regulated by how hungry they feel. But the motivation to eat is complicated. Here are some invisible external influences on your eating habits (Wansink, 2006):

- **Package size:** People eat more from a large container (say, of popcorn) than a small one.

- **Plate size:** People eat more when they serve themselves on large plates rather than small ones.

- **Cues for how much has been eaten:** People eat more from a buffet when waiters quickly replace their dirty dishes, thereby eliminating tell-tale signs of how much food has already been consumed.

- **Kitchen and table layouts:** People eat more when food and snacks are displayed prominently, are varied, and are easily accessible.

- **Distraction:** People eat more when they are being distracted by friends and the environment.

The next time you are out with friends, take notes on how much everyone is eating (including yourself), and notice whether any of the above influences are at work. If you are trying to lose weight, how can you alter your own "food environment" to correct for these influences?

CULTURE and *the Ideal Body*

Norms, Gender, and Weight

Eating habits and activity levels are shaped by a culture's customs and standards of what the ideal body should look like: fat or thin, muscular or soft? In many places around the world, especially where famine and crop failures are common, fat is taken as a sign of health, of affluence in men, and of sexual desirability in women (Stearns, 1997). Among the Calabari of Nigeria, brides are put in special fattening huts where they do nothing but eat, so as to become fat enough to please their husbands.

Studies of English Canadians suggest that we hold negative attitudes toward obese people (LeBow, 1988; LeBow et al., 1989; Morrison & O'Connor, 1999). Interestingly, when asked what type of body they prefer, most anglophone Canadians indicate that they prefer smaller body shapes than their own, while people of the Ojibway–Cree First Nations indicate that they also prefer smaller body shapes than their own, but not as small as those preferred by the Anglos. This was despite the fact that only 16% of *both* groups indicated they were happy with their current physique (Gittelsohn et al., 1996). Obviously, researchers must conduct more studies of indigenous peoples of Canada before concluding whether all indigenous peoples hold similar body-image values.

Ironically, while people of all ethnicities and social classes have been getting fatter, the cultural ideal for women in the United States, Canada, and Europe has been getting thinner. Why have these changes in cultural norms occurred? One explanation

Should a woman be voluptuous and curvy or slim as a reed? Should a man be thin and smooth or strong and buff? What explains cultural changes in attitudes toward the ideal body? During the 1950s, actresses like Jayne Mansfield embodied the postwar ideal: curvy, buxom, and "womanly." In the 1980s and 1990s, many women struggled to be skinny and boyish; today, they want to be thin but also have prominent breasts. Men, too, have been caught up in body-image changes. The 1960s' ideal was the soft and scrawny hippie; today's ideal man is tough and muscular.

is that white men and women are more likely than blacks or Latinos to associate overweight with softness, laziness, and weakness (Crandall & Martinez, 1996). In particular, the curvy, big-breasted female body is associated in people's minds with femininity, nurturance, and motherhood. Hence, big breasts have been fashionable in eras that celebrate women's role as mothers, such as after World War II, when women were encouraged to give up their wartime jobs and have many children (Stearns, 1997). However, among many whites, femininity has also often been associated, alas, with incompetence. Thus, whenever women have entered traditionally male spheres of education and work, as they did in the 1920s and again beginning in the 1970s, bright, ambitious women have tried to look boyishly thin and muscular in order to avoid being perceived as soft, feminine, and dumb (Silverstein & Perlick, 1995). Today's big-breasted but otherwise skinny female ideal may reflect today's norm: Women are supposed to be both professionally competent *and* maternal.

The cultural ideal for North American men has changed, too. Until relatively recently, most heavily muscled men were labourers and farmers, so being physically strong and muscular was considered unattractive, a sign of being working class. In the past decade, pressures have increased for middle-class men to be buff and strong (Bordo, 2000). Today, having a strong, muscular body is a sign of affluence rather than poverty. It means a man has the money and the time to join a gym and work out. (Some fashion designers, though, are using male models that are as skinny and gaunt as their female counterparts.)

Another factor that must be considered is the difference in weight satisfaction levels between men and women. Although more Canadian men than women are overweight or obese, more Canadian women are currently dieting, even when their weight is in the healthy range (Green et al., 1997). Research studying Canadian teenagers has found that most girls (69%) wanted to lose weight, while most boys (54%) wanted to gain weight (Barr, 1995), regardless of their actual weight. It seems that these cultural norms of what women and men should look like appear by the teen years and persist into adulthood. Programs designed to promote acceptance of healthy weights in men and women must consider these gender differences in attitudes and, potentially, culture; otherwise, they may not succeed.

You can see why many people, especially women, find themselves caught in a battle between their biology and their culture. Evolution has designed women to store fat, which is necessary for the onset of menstruation, for pregnancy and nursing, and, after menopause, for the production of estrogen. In cultures that think women should be very thin, therefore, many women become obsessed with weight and are continually dieting, forever fighting their bodies' need for a little healthy roundness.

The Body as Battleground: Eating Disorders

Because the motivation to eat, or not eat, is so complicated, you can see why many people, especially women, find themselves caught in a battle between their biology and their culture. Evolution has designed women to store fat, which is necessary for the onset of menstruation, healthy childbearing, nursing, and, after menopause, the production and storage of estrogen. In cultures that think women should be very thin, therefore, many women become obsessed with weight and are continually dieting, forever fighting their bodies' need for a little healthy roundness.

Some people lose that battle, developing serious eating disorders that reflect an irrational terror of being fat. In **bulimia**, the person binges (eats vast quantities of rich food) and then purges by inducing vomiting or using laxatives. In **anorexia**, the person eats hardly anything and therefore becomes dangerously thin; anorexics have severely distorted body images, thinking they are fat even when they are emaciated. Although many people with these disorders recover, others damage their health permanently, or, in the case of anorexia, die of heart or kidney failure or complications of osteoporosis. Their weakened bones simply collapse.

Bulimia and anorexia are the most well-known eating disorders, and occur most often among young white women. But more than 40% of all cases of eating disorders occur among men, the elderly, ethnic minority groups, young children, and athletes, and do not fit the diagnostic criteria for bulimia or anorexia (Thomas, Vartanian, & Brownell, 2009). For example, people with binge-eating disorder binge without purging; others chew whatever food they want but spit it out without swallowing; others are normal weight but take no joy in eating because they worry obsessively about gaining a pound; some develop phobias about eating certain kinds of food. All of these disorders involve an unhealthy attitude toward food, weight, and the body.

Genes may play a role in the development of eating disorders, particularly anorexia nervosa, which has been found across cultures and throughout history (Striegel-Moore & Bulik, 2007), but so do psychological factors, including depression and anxiety, low self-esteem, perfectionism, a distorted body image, drug use, and perceived pressure from peers to lose weight (Presnell, Bearman, & Stice, 2004; Ricciardelli & McCabe, 2004; Sherry & Hall, 2009). Cultural factors are also important. For example, bulimia is rare to nonexistent in non-Western cultures and has only become a significant problem in Western cultures with the rise of the thin ideal for women (Keel & Klump, 2003). A meta-analysis of experimental and correlational studies found that women's exposure to the media ideal of impossibly thin women fosters the belief that "thin is beautiful" and increases the risk of disordered eating (Grabe, Ward, & Hyde, 2008). American culture is also rife with "bodysnarking"— the relentlessly critical and snide appraisals of other people's bodies that get posted

👁 **Watch**
Eating Disorders

👁 **Watch**
Natasha: Anorexia Nervosa

Natasha: Living with Anorexia

bulimia An eating disorder characterized by episodes of excessive eating (bingeing) followed by forced vomiting or use of laxatives (purging).

anorexia (anorexia nervosa) An eating disorder characterized by fear of being fat, a distorted body image, radically reduced consumption of food, and emaciation.

 **Thinking Critically** Ask Questions: Define Your Terms

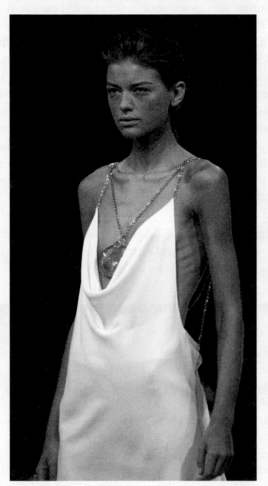 

What is the difference between being slender and being too thin? Does the fashion model on the left look good to you or does she look emaciated? Likewise, what is the difference between being "pleasantly plump" and being too fat? Nikki Blonsky, the exuberant star of the movie *Hairspray*, is overweight but physically fit. Does she look good to you or does she look too fat?

on blogs, YouTube, Facebook, and Twitter, and are constant topics for entertainment magazines and talk shows.

Female ballet dancers and actors, jockeys of both sexes, some other athletes, and of course models are under enormous professional pressure to be thin. (In 2006, many fashion models had become so gaunt and emaciated that the Fashion Week organizers in Madrid, Spain, announced they would ban ultrathin models, women with a body mass index lower than 18.) In the United States, a recent meta-analysis found that women's levels of dissatisfaction with their bodies, once highest for Anglo women, now cross all ethnic lines; Asian-American, black, Hispanic, and Anglo women are virtually alike (Grabe & Hyde, 2006). Unhappiness with one's body, in turn, increases the likelihood of disordered eating. In a study of women students from Hong Kong, Taiwan, and Japan who were studying in the United States, those who had internalized

Western notions of the ultrathin ideal were more likely to develop eating disorders (Stark-Wroblewski, Yanico, & Lupe, 2005).

Eating disorders and body-image distortions among boys and men are increasing too, though they take different forms. Just as anorexic women see their gaunt bodies as being too fat, some men have the delusion that their muscular bodies are too puny. So they abuse steroids and exercise or pump iron compulsively (Pope, Phillips, & Olivardia, 2000; Thompson & Cafri, 2007). Many North American men mistakenly think that most women prefer extremely muscular guys, partly because media images of muscular men in North America often show them with bared pecs or abs. As a result, some men develop a distorted body image in which they think they are not muscular and strong enough. In contrast, Chinese men in Taiwan and pastoral nomads of northern Kenya do not think the heavily muscled male body is especially desirable or attractive, and these cultures do not promote media images of muscular males. Men in these cultures have fewer body-image disorders than North American men do and virtually no interest in muscle-building drugs (Campbell, Pope, & Filiault, 2005; Yang, Gray, & Pope, 2005).

In sum, within a given environment, genetic predispositions for a certain body weight and metabolism interact with psychological needs, cultural norms, and individual habits to shape, in this case quite literally, who we are.

◉**Watch**
Food and the Brain

quick**QUIZ**

✓●—⎡**Quick Review** on **MyPsychLab**

Is all this information about eating making you hungry for knowledge?

1. *True or false:* Most fat people are heavy because their emotional problems cause them to overeat.

2. What theory seems to explain why thin people rarely become fat and fat people have so much trouble losing weight?

3. Which hormone helps regulate appetite by telling the hypothalamus that the body has stored enough fat?

4. Rising rates of overweight and obesity can best be explained by (a) genetic changes over the past few decades, (b) a lack of willpower, (c) an abundance of high-calorie food and sedentary lifestyles, (d) the increase in eating disorders.

5. Bill, who is thin, reads in the newspaper that genes set the range of body weight and shape. "Oh, good," he exclaims, "now I can eat all the junk food I want; I was born to be skinny." What's wrong with Bill's conclusion?

Answers:

1. false **2.** set-point theory **3.** leptin **4.** c **5.** Bill is right to recognize that there may be limits to how heavy he can become. But he is oversimplifying and jumping to conclusions. Many people who have a set point for leanness will gain considerable weight on rich food and excess calories, especially if they don't exercise. Also, junk food is unhealthy for reasons that have nothing to do with becoming overweight.

YOU are about to learn . . .

◆ how biology affects attachment and love.

◆ some key psychological influences on whom and how you love.

◆ the three basic styles of attachment and how they affect relationships.

◆ how economic concerns influence love and marriage.

THE SOCIAL ANIMAL: MOTIVES TO LOVE

Do you have a favourite love story? Is it one where the couple falls madly in love at first sight and, after a couple of silly misunderstandings, lives happily ever after, without a single quarrel or miserable moment? Or is it more like the story of Annie Oakley and Frank Butler, one of lifelong mutual respect and companionship? What *is* love, anyway—the crazy, passionate, heart-palpitating feeling of falling for another person, or the steady, stable feeling of deep and abiding attachment and trust?

The Biology of Love

Psychologists who study love (a tough job, but someone has to do it) distinguish *passionate ("romantic") love*, characterized by a whirlwind of intense emotions and sexual passion, from *companionate love*, characterized by affection and trust. Passionate love is the stuff of crushes, infatuations, "love at first sight," and the early stage of love affairs. It may burn out completely or evolve into companionate love. Passionate love is known in all cultures and has a long history. Wars and duels have been fought because of it, people have committed suicide because of it, great love affairs have begun, and been torn apart, because of it. Yet, although the experience of romantic love is universal, many cultures have not regarded it as the proper basis for anything serious—such as marriage (Hatfield & Rapson, 2008).

In this era of PET scans, fMRIs, and biotechnical advances, it was inevitable that researchers would seek to explain passionate love by rummaging around in the brain. There are olfactory cues in a potential partner's scent that can turn you on (or off). There are physical cues in the potential partner's voice and body shape, and even in how similar his or her face is to yours. There is the dopamine jolt of reward, from the same dopamine that makes anticipation of a fabulous meal or an addictive drug so pleasurable, and there are the arousal and excitement provided by adrenaline (Aron et al., 2005; Cozolino, 2006). And then there are key hormones that turn that first phase of exhilaration into the longer-lasting phase of attachment and bonding. Neuroscientists hope to find answers to the great mysteries of attraction: why people are often hopelessly smitten with someone who is "unsuitable," why the heart seems to overrule the head in matters of love ("He/she is perfectly nice, but I just didn't feel any *chemistry*"), and why many people feel obsessed with a new beloved and can barely sleep or eat when they are apart.

Many biologically oriented researchers believe that the neurological origins of passionate love begin in infancy, in the baby's attachment to the mother. In this view, maternal and romantic love, the deepest of human attachments, share a common evolutionary purpose—preserving the species—and so they share common neural mechanisms, the ones that make attachment and pair-bonding feel good. And, in fact, certain key neurotransmitters and hormones that are involved in pleasure and reward are activated in the mother–baby pair-bond and again later in the pair-bond of adult lovers and even of passionate friends (Bartels & Zeki, 2004; Diamond, 2004).

The hormone *oxytocin* plays a crucial role in the attachment-caregiving system, influencing feelings and expressions of love, caring, and trust not only between mothers and babies but also between friends and between lovers (Walum et al., 2008; Taylor, Klein, et al., 2000). In one extraordinary study, researchers administered oxytocin in a nasal spray to volunteers, who were later more likely than control subjects to trust one

In the musical comedy *Annie Get Your Gun*, Annie Oakley lets Frank Butler beat her in a sharp-shooting competition as she sings, "You can't get a man with a gun." But she did. In real life, she beat him in the contest, they fell in love, married, and worked together.

The biology of the baby–mother bond may be the origin of adult romantic love, with its exchange of loving gazes and depth of attachment.

another in various risky interactions (Kosfeld et al., 2005). In another study, couples given oxytocin increased their nonverbal expressions of love for one another—gazing, smiling, and fondling—in contrast to couples given a placebo (Gonzaga et al., 2006). Conversely, when prairie voles, a monogamous species, are given a drug that blocks oxytocin, they continue to mate, but they don't get attached to their partners (Ross et al., 2009).We can just imagine what the pharmaceutical industry will try to do with this information!

Studies of animals also find that the characteristic feelings and actions that occur during attachment are mediated by reward circuits in the brain and involve the release of **endorphins**, the brain's natural opiates (see Chapter 4). When baby mice and other animals are separated from their mothers, they cry out in distress, and the mother's touch (or lick) releases endorphins that soothe the infant. But when puppies, guinea pigs, and chicks are injected with low doses of either morphine or endorphins, the animals show much less distress than usual when separated from their mothers; the chemicals seem to be a biological replacement for Mom (Panksepp et al., 1980). And when mice are genetically engineered to lack certain opioid receptors, they become less attached to their mothers and do not show signs of distress when separated from them. This is the same kind of social aloofness that autistic children display (Moles, Kieffer, & D'Amato, 2004). These findings suggest that endorphin-stimulated euphoria may be a child's initial motive for seeking affection and cuddling—that, in effect, a child attached to a parent is a child addicted to love. The addictive quality of adult passionate love, including the physical and emotional distress that lovers feel when they are apart, may involve the same biochemistry (Diamond, 2004).

Using functional magnetic resonance imaging (fMRI), neuroscientists have found other neurological similarities between infant–mother love and adult romantic love. Two researchers, for example, have found that certain parts of the brain light up when people look at images of their sweethearts, in contrast to other parts that are activated when they see pictures of friends or furniture. And these are the same areas that are activated when mothers see images of their own children as opposed to pictures of other children (Bartels & Zeki, 2004).

Clearly, then, the bonds of attachment are biologically based. Yet, as always, it is important to avoid biological reductionism and the conclusion that "love is all in our hormones" or "love occurs in this corner of the brain but not that one." Human love affairs involve many other factors that affect whom we choose, how we get along, and whether we stay with a partner over the years.

The Psychology of Love

Many romantics believe there is only one true love awaiting them. Considering that there are seven billion people on the planet, the odds of finding said person are a bit daunting! What if you're in Omaha or Winnipeg and your true love is in Dubrovnik or Kankakee? You could wander for years and never cross paths.

Fortunately, evolution has made it possible to form deep and lasting attachments without travelling the world. In fact, the first major predictor of whom we love is plain proximity. In what is known as the **proximity effect**, the people who are nearest to you are most likely to be dearest to you, too. We choose our friends and lovers from the set of people who live close by, or who study or work near us. Of course, today's love-seekers can use the internet to find remote kindred spirits, but proximity remains a highly desirable attribute; dating sites can filter out anyone who is geographically undesirable. The **similarity effect** holds that likeness—in looks, attitudes, beliefs, values, personality, and interests—is the second key predictor of whom we love (Berscheid & Reis, 1998). Although it is commonly believed that opposites attract, the

⊙ Watch
Love Marriage: Scherazade and Roderick—Late 30s

endorphins [en-DOR-fins] Chemical substances in the nervous system that are similar in structure and action to opiates; they are involved in pain reduction, pleasure, and memory and are known technically as *endogenous opioid peptides*.

proximity effect The people who are nearest to you geographically are most likely to be dearest to you, too.

similarity effect Similarity—in looks, attitudes, beliefs, values, personality, and interests—is attractive to human beings; we tend to choose friends and loved ones who are most like us.

fact is that we tend to choose friends and loved ones who are most like us. Many students use Facebook to find romantic prospects who share their love of poker, the TV show *Smallville*, the hip-hop artist K'naan, or any other passion.

The internet has made similarity-matching possible on all kinds of dimensions. There are thousands of dating websites, matching couples by age, political attitudes, religion or secularism, sexual orientation, and many other criteria. There are sites for people with disabilities, preferences for particular sexual activities, and even beloved pets. Some prominent matchmaking sites administer questionnaires and personality inventories, claiming to use scientific principles to pair up potential soulmates (Sprecher et al., 2008). These efforts vary in effectiveness. Can you think why? One reason is that many people think they know exactly what they "must have" in a partner, and then they meet someone who has few of those qualities but a whole bunch of others that suddenly become essential. (A woman we know thought she must have a man who was taller than she, until she met the love of her life, who is three inches shorter.) Another reason, though, is that the premises of some of these sciency-sounding matchmaking sites may be faulty, especially those based on unvalidated personality types and anecdotal testimonials (King, Austin-Oden, & Lohr, 2009). But one underlying premise of most internet-matching sites is basically right—like attracts like.

Internet services capitalize on the fact that like attracts like. "What type turns you on?," asks this ad. Usually, the type that is similar to you.

THE ATTACHMENT THEORY OF LOVE.   Once you find someone to love, *how* do you love? According to Phillip Shaver and Cindy Hazan (1993), adults, just like babies, can be secure, anxious, or avoidant in their attachments (see Chapter 13). Securely attached lovers are rarely jealous or worried about being abandoned. They are more compassionate and helpful than insecurely attached people and are quicker to understand and forgive their partners if the partner does something thoughtless or annoying (Mikulincer et al., 2005; Mikulincer & Shaver, 2007). Anxious lovers are always agitated about their relationships; they want to be close but worry that their partners will leave them. Other people often describe them as clingy, which may be why they are more likely than secure lovers to suffer from unrequited love (Aron, Aron, & Allen, 1998). Avoidant people distrust and avoid intimate attachments.

Where do these differences come from? According to the **attachment theory of love**, people's attachment styles as adults derive in large part from how their parents cared for them (Dinero et al., 2008; Mikulincer & Shaver, 2007; Fraley & Shaver, 2000; Mikulincer & Goodman, 2006). Children form internal "working models" of relationships: Can I trust others? Am I worthy of being loved? Will my parents leave me? If a child's parents were cold and rejecting and provided little or no emotional and physical comfort, the child learns to expect other relationships to be the same. If children form secure attachments to trusted parents, they become more trusting of others, expecting to form other secure attachments with friends and lovers in adulthood (Feeney & Cassidy, 2003).

The distribution of the three basic styles of attachment among adults is in fact very similar to that found for infants: about 64% are secure, 25% are avoidant, and 11% are anxious. Further, the kinds of relationships people have as adults are strongly related to their reports of how their parents treated them (Mickelson, Kessler, & Shaver, 1997).

"My preference is for someone who's afraid of closeness, like me."

attachment theory of love
People's attachment styles as adults derive in large part from how their parents cared for them.

In one observational study of young adults in family interactions, their ratings of their families' warmth and sensitivity were positively related to how they behaved with their own romantic partners and to their own degree of attachment security (Dinero et al., 2008). Securely attached adults report having had warm, close relationships with their parents. Although they recognize their parents' flaws, they describe their parents as having been more loving and kind than insecurely attached people do. Anxious people feel more ambivalence toward their parents, especially their mothers, and also describe their parents ambivalently, as having been both harsh and kind. And people with an avoidant attachment style describe their parents in almost entirely negative terms. These individuals are most likely to report having had cold, rejecting parents, extended periods of separation from their mothers, or childhood environments that prevented them from forging close ties with others (Hazan & Shaver, 1994; Klohnen & Bera, 1998).

The avoidant style is particularly resistant to change, because people who are busy avoiding one another never learn to trust someone long enough to become securely attached (Klohnen & Bera, 1998). However, even avoidant or anxiously attached people can have successful, stable relationships if they find securely attached partners who will put up with their insecurities (Kirkpatrick & Davis, 1994; Koski & Shaver, 1997). Although those who display an avoidant style are not necessarily pathological, this style is commonly reported by people who also display pathological behaviours. For example, at Queen's University, Jamieson and Marshall (2000) found that nonfamilial child molesters were five times more likely to report an avoidant relationship than those in the community sample.

Keep in mind, though, that a person's own temperament could also account for the consistency of attachment styles from childhood to adulthood, as well as for the working models of relationships that are formed during childhood (Gillath et al., 2008). Certainly some parents are cold, punitive, and rejecting. But a child who is temperamentally fearful or whose reward circuits do not function normally may reject even a kind parent's efforts to console and cuddle. That child may therefore come to believe that all relationships are untrustworthy.

Gender, Culture, and Love

Which sex is more romantic? Which sex truly understands true love? Which sex falls in love but won't commit?

Pop-psych books are full of answers, along with advice for dealing with all those love-challenged heartbreakers who love you and leave you (fools that they are). But all stereotypes oversimplify. Neither sex loves more than the other in terms of love at first sight, passionate love, or companionate love over the long haul (Dion & Dion, 1993; Fehr, 1993; Hatfield & Rapson, 1996/2005). Men and women are equally likely to suffer the heart-crushing torments of unrequited love. They are equally likely to be securely or insecurely attached (Feeney & Cassidy, 2003). Both sexes suffer mightily when a love relationship ends, assuming they did not want it to.

However, women and men do differ, on average, in how they *express* love. Males in many cultures learn early that revelations of emotion can be construed as evidence of vulnerability and weakness, which are considered unmasculine (see Chapter 11). Thus, men in such cultures often develop ways of revealing love that differ from the ways women do. In contemporary Western society, many women express feelings of love

Watch
Early Gender Typing

Arranged Marriage: Rati and Subas—Early 20s

Thinking **Critically**

Define Your Terms

Many people define love as an overwhelming romantic passion. What are the consequences of defining love that way? What other definitions might lead to greater satisfaction in a relationship over time?

in words, whereas many men express these feelings in actions—doing things for the partner, supporting the family financially, or just sharing the same activity, such as watching TV or a football game together (Shields, 2002; Baumeister & Bratslavsky, 1999; Cancian, 1987; Swain, 1989). Similarly, many women tend to define intimacy as shared revelations of feelings, but many men define intimacy as just hanging out together.

These gender differences in ways of expressing the universal motives of love and intimacy do not just pop up out of nowhere; they reflect social, economic, and cultural forces. For example, for many years, Western men were more romantic than women in their choice of partner, and women in turn were far more pragmatic than men. One reason was that a woman did not just marry a man; she married a standard of living. Therefore, she could not afford to marry someone unsuitable or waste her time in a relationship that was not going anywhere, even if she loved the guy. She married, in short, for extrinsic reasons rather than intrinsic ones. In contrast, a man could afford to be sentimental in his choice of partner. In the 1960s, two-thirds of a sample of university men said they would not marry someone they did not love, but only one-fourth of the women ruled out the possibility (Kephart, 1967).

As women entered the workforce and as two incomes became necessary in most families, however, the gender difference in romantic love faded, and so did economic motivations to marry, all over the world. Nowadays, in every developed nation, only tiny numbers of women and men would consider marrying someone they did not love, even if the person had all the right qualities. Pragmatic reasons for marriage, with romantic love being a remote luxury, persist only in countries where the extended family still controls female sexuality and the financial terms of marriage (Hatfield & Rapson, 1996/2005). Yet even in these countries, such as India and Pakistan, the tight rules governing marriage choices are loosening. So are the rules forbidding divorce, even in extremely traditional nations such as Japan and South Korea.

As you can see, our motivations to love may start with biology and the workings of the brain, but they are shaped and directed by our early experiences with parents, the culture we live in, the historical era that shapes us, and something as utterly unromantic as economic dependency or self-sufficiency.

Economic and social changes are transforming gender roles in all developed nations. But marriage for financial security is still the only option for many women from impoverished nations—like this bride, whose husband chose her from a mail-order catalogue.

◉ **Watch**
Flirting

Qualities in a Mate

Marriage and Cheaters

Are you passionately committed to quizzes yet?

1. How are adult passionate love and infant–mother love biologically similar?
2. The two major predictors of whom we love are _____ and _____.
3. Tiffany is wildly in love with Timothy, and he with her, but she can't stop worrying about his fidelity and doubting his love. She wants to be with him constantly, but when she feels jealous she pushes him away and finds it hard to forgive him. According to the attachment theory of love, which style of attachment does Tiffany have?
4. *True or false:* Until recently, men in Western societies were more likely than women to marry for love.

Answers:

1. Both involve the release of neurotransmitters, the hormone oxytocin, and endorphins that make attachment literally feel good, by activating the pleasure–reward circuits in the brain. 2. proximity and similarity. 3. anxious 4. true

quickQUIZ

✓• Quick Review on **MyPsychLab**

YOU are about to learn . . .

◆ which part of the anatomy is the "sexiest sex organ."
◆ why pleasure is only one of many motives for having sex.
◆ how culture affects sexual practices.

THE EROTIC ANIMAL: MOTIVES FOR SEX

⦿ Watch
Human Sexuality

Most people believe that sex is a biological drive, merely a matter of doing what comes naturally. "What's there to discuss about sexual motivation?" they say. "Isn't it all intrinsic, inborn, inevitable, and inherently pleasurable?"

It is certainly true that in most other species, sexual behaviour is genetically programmed. Without instruction, a male stickleback fish knows exactly what to do with a female stickleback, and a whooping crane knows when to whoop. But as sex researcher Leonore Tiefer (2004) has observed, for human beings "sex is not

Desire and sensuality are lifelong pleasures.

a natural act." For one thing, the activities that one culture considers natural—such as mouth-to-mouth kissing or oral sex—are often considered unnatural in another culture or historical time. Second, people have to learn from experience and culture what they are supposed to do with their sexual desires and how they are expected to behave. And third, people's motivations for sexual activity are by no means always and only for intrinsic pleasure. Human sexuality is influenced by a blend of biological, psychological, and cultural factors. As Canadians, we live in a relatively sexually active culture. The average Canadian adult has sex around 150 times a year, which is the fourth-highest frequency among 22 countries surveyed (Durex, 2002). This rate of activity has a downside, though. Canadians tend to start having sex at earlier ages than is evident in other countries, which leads to relatively higher rates of teenage pregnancy.

The Biology of Desire

Biological researchers have contributed to our understanding of sexual motivation by sweeping away the cobwebs of superstition and ignorance about how the body works.

HORMONES AND SEXUAL RESPONSE. One biological factor that seems to promote sexual desire in both sexes is the hormone testosterone, an androgen (masculinizing hormone) that both sexes produce (see Chapter 4). Its role has been documented in studies of men who have been given synthetic hormones that suppress the production of testosterone; of men and women who have abnormally low testosterone levels; and of women who have kept diaries of their sexual activity while also having their hormone levels periodically measured (Bradford & Pawlak, 1993; Dabbs, 2000; Sherwin, 1998b). This fact has created a market for the legal and illegal use of androgens. The assumption is that if the goal is to reduce sexual desire, for example in sex offenders, testosterone should be lowered, say, through chemical castration; if the goal is to increase sexual desire in women and men who complain of low libido, testosterone should be increased—like adding fuel to your gas tank. Yet these efforts often fail to produce the expected results (Berlin, 2003; M. Anderson, 2005). Why?

One reason is that the symptoms of androgen deficiency (low libido, fatigue, lack of well-being) are also those of depression and marital problems. There is also no consensus on how much sexual activity is "not enough" or on the difference between normally low and abnormally deficient levels of testosterone. Measures of testosterone taken at different intervals do not correlate strongly because the hormone fluctuates. Moreover, hormones and behaviour travel a two-way street: Testosterone does contribute to sexual arousal, but sexual activity also produces higher levels of testosterone (Sapolsky, 1997). And, in a significant number of cases, the side effects of androgen range from unpleasant to harmful (International Consensus Conference, 2002), and side effects are unlikely to increase desire.

Another reason is that in primates, unlike other mammals, sexual motivation requires more than hormones; it is also affected by social experience and context (Wallen, 2001). That is why desire can persist in sex offenders who have lost testosterone, and why desire might remain low in people who have been given testosterone. Indeed, artificially administered testosterone does not do much more than a placebo to increase sexual satisfaction in healthy people, nor does a drop in testosterone invariably cause a loss of sexual motivation or enjoyment. For example, in studies of women who had had their uteruses or ovaries surgically removed or who were going through menopause, use of a testosterone patch increased their sexual activity to only one more time a month over the placebo group (Buster et al., 2005).

AROUSAL AND ORGASM. Physiological research has dispelled a lot of nonsense written about female sexuality, such as the once-common notions that "good" women don't have orgasms or that mature women should have the "right kind" of orgasm (Ehrenreich, 1978). The first modern attack on these beliefs came from Alfred Kinsey and his associates (1948, 1953) in their pioneering books on male and female sexuality. Kinsey's team surveyed thousands of people about their sexual attitudes and behaviour, and they also reviewed the existing research on sexual physiology. In *Sexual Behaviour in the Human Female*, they observed that "males would be better prepared to understand females, and females to understand males, if they realized that they are alike in their basic anatomy and physiology." For example, the penis and the clitoris develop from the same embryonic tissues; they differ in size, of course, but not in sensitivity. Kinsey did believe, however, that women overall have a "lesser sexual capacity" than men, reflected in women's lower frequency of masturbation and orgasm. Although he acknowledged that many women are taught to avoid, dislike, or feel ambivalent about sex, he tended to attribute this gender difference to biology.

The idea that men and women are sexually similar in any way was extremely shocking in 1953. At that time many people believed that women were not as sexually motivated as men and that women cared more about affection than sexual satisfaction—notions soundly refuted by Kinsey's interviews. The national hysteria that accompanied the Kinsey Reports seems hard to believe today. Yet it is still difficult for social scientists to conduct serious, methodologically sound research on the development of human sexuality. As John Bancroft, the current head of the Kinsey Institute, has observed, because many American adults need to believe that young children have no sexual feelings, they interpret any evidence of normal sexual expression in childhood (such as masturbation or "playing doctor") as a symptom of sexual abuse. And because many adults are uncomfortable about sexual activity among teenagers, they try to restrict or eliminate it by prohibiting sex education and promoting abstinence; then they reject research showing that such prohibitions actually increase the behaviour they consider taboo (Bancroft, 2006; Levine, 2002).

◆ **Research**
Alfred Kinsey

Thinking ⚙ Critically   Avoid Emotional Reasoning

The "Kinsey Report" on women, officially titled *Sexual Behaviour in the Human Female*, was not exactly greeted with praise and acceptance—or with clear thinking. Many people were so emotionally upset by the findings that many women enjoy sex and have had premarital sex that they chose to attack Kinsey instead of coolly appraising his research.

◈ Research
Masters and Johnson

The next wave of sex research began in the 1960s with the laboratory research of physician William Masters and his associate Virginia Johnson (1966). In studies of physiological changes during sexual arousal and orgasm, Masters and Johnson confirmed that male and female orgasms are indeed remarkably similar and that all orgasms are physiologically the same, regardless of the source of stimulation. But Masters and Johnson disagreed with Kinsey's assertion that women have a lesser sexual capacity than men. On the contrary, they argued, women's capacity for sexual response "infinitely surpasses that of men" because women, unlike most men, are able to have repeated orgasms until exhaustion or a ringing telephone makes them stop.

However, just as Kinsey might have underestimated women's sexual capacity, Masters and Johnson might have overestimated it. Their research was limited by the selection of a sample consisting only of men and women who were easily orgasmic, and they did not investigate how people's physiological responses might vary according to their age, experience, and culture (Tiefer, 2004). Thus, in their eagerness to show that the physiology of arousal and orgasm was the same in both sexes, Masters and Johnson tended to overlook individual differences. Since Masters and Johnson's studies, sex researchers have learned much more about individual variation in sexual physiology and responsiveness (Ellison, 2000; Laumann et al., 1994). For example, people vary not only in their propensity for sexual excitation and responsiveness, but also in their ability to inhibit and control that excitement (Bancroft et al., 2009). That is, some people are all accelerator and no brakes, and others are slow to accelerate but quick to brake.

If you have ever taken a sex-ed class, you may have had to memorize Masters and Johnson's description of the "four stages of the sexual response cycle": desire, arousal (excitement), orgasm, resolution. Unfortunately, the impulse to oversimplify—treating these four stages as if they were akin to the invariable cycles of a washing machine—led to a mistaken inference of universality. It later turned out that not everyone has an orgasm even following great excitement, and that in many women, desire follows arousal (Laan & Both, 2008).

SEX AND THE "SEX DRIVE." The question of whether men and women are alike or different in some underlying, biologically based sex drive continues to provoke lively debate. Although women on average are certainly as capable as men of sexual pleasure, men have higher rates of almost every kind of sexual behaviour, including masturbation, erotic fantasies, and orgasm (Oliver & Hyde, 1993; Peplau, 2003). These sex differences occur even when men are forbidden by cultural or religious rules to engage in sex at all; for example, Catholic priests have more of these sexual experiences than Catholic nuns do (Baumeister, Catanese, & Vohs, 2001). Men are also more likely than women to admit to having sex because "I was slumming" or "The opportunity presented itself" (Meston & Buss, 2007).

Biological psychologists argue that these differences occur universally because the hormones and brain circuits involved in sexual behaviour differ for men and women. They maintain that for men, the wiring for sex overlaps with that for dominance and aggression, which is why sex and aggression are more likely to be linked in men than women. For women, the circuits and hormones governing sexuality and nurturance seem to overlap, which is why sex and love are more likely to be linked in women than in men (Diamond, 2008).

Other psychologists, however, maintain that most gender differences in sexual behaviour reflect women's and men's different roles and experiences in life and have little or nothing to do with biologically based drives or brain circuits (Eagly & Wood, 1999; Tiefer, 2008). Sex surveys generally find that men and women are, overall, more alike than different, for example in preferring sex with love (Laumann et al., 1994). In the sociocultural view, as long as large numbers of women learn to fear, dislike, or avoid sex, whether through cultural and familial messages or through coercive or otherwise unpleasant sexual experiences, it is impossible to know what women's sexual drive might really be like (Kaschak & Tiefer, 2002).

A middle view is that men's sexual behaviour is more biologically influenced than is women's, whereas women's sexual desires and responsiveness are more affected by circumstances, the specific relationship, and cultural norms (Baumeister, 2000; Peplau et al., 2000).

Thinking Critically

Don't Oversimplify

Given that a minimum level of testosterone is important in sexual desire, many people assume that adding testosterone will increase desire and removing it will lower desire. Why does this assumption oversimplify the issue?

"Go ahead. Press one for more options."

The Psychology of Desire

Psychologists are fond of observing that the sexiest sex organ is the brain, where perceptions begin. People's values, fantasies, and beliefs profoundly affect their sexual desire and behaviour. That is why a touch on the knee by an exciting new date feels terrifically sexy, but the same touch by a creepy stranger on a bus feels disgusting. It is why a worried thought can kill sexual arousal in a second, and why a fantasy can be more erotic than reality.

The many motivations for sex range from sex for profit to sex for fun.

THE MANY MOTIVES FOR SEX. To most people, the primary motives for sex are pretty obvious: to enjoy the pleasure of it, to express love and intimacy, or to make babies. But there are other motives too, not all of them so positive: for money or perks, duty or feelings of obligation, rebellion, power over the partner, submission to the partner in order to avoid his or her anger or rejection, and so on.

One survey of nearly 2000 people yielded 237 motives for having sex, and nearly every one of them had been rated as the most important motive for someone. Most men and women listed the same top 10, including attraction to the partner, love, fun, and physical pleasure. But some said, "I wanted to feel closer to God," "I was drunk," "to get rid of a headache" (that was #173), "to help me fall asleep," "to make my partner feel powerful," "to return a favour," "because someone dared me," or to hurt an enemy or a rival ("I wanted to make him pay so I slept with his girlfriend"; "I wanted someone else to suffer from herpes as I do"). In this survey, men were more likely than women to say they use sex to gain status, enhance their reputation (e.g., because the partner was normally "out of my league"), or get things (such as a promotion) (Meston & Buss, 2007).

Across the many studies of motives for sex, there appear to be several major categories (Cooper, Shapiro, & Powers, 1998; Meston & Buss, 2007):

◆ **Pleasure:** the satisfaction and physical pleasure of sex.

◆ **Intimacy:** emotional closeness with the partner; spiritual transcendence.

◆ **Insecurity:** reassurance that you are attractive or desirable.

◆ **Partner approval:** the desire to please or appease the partner; the desire to avoid the partner's anger or rejection.

◆ **Peer approval:** the wish to impress friends, be part of the group, and conform to what everyone else seems to be doing.

◆ **Attaining a goal:** to get status, money, revenge, or to "even the score."

In this research, men and women did not differ in their motives for intimacy, but men more strongly endorsed all the other motives, especially peer approval. The older people were, the more likely they were to have sex for intimacy and for self-enhancement (pleasure), and the less likely they were to have sex for peer or partner approval. White adolescents were more often motivated by a desire for intimacy than black adolescents were, and black teenagers were more often motivated by coping and peer pressure.

Perhaps you can think of other motives for sex, too: spiritual transcendence, money or perks, duty or feelings of obligation, power over the partner, submission to the partner in order to avoid his or her anger or rejection, rebellion. . . . People's motives for having sex affect many aspects of their sexual behaviour, including whether they engage in sex in the first place, whether they enjoy it, whether they have unprotected or otherwise risky sex, and whether they have few or many partners (Browning et al., 2000). Extrinsic motives, such as having sex for purposes of coping and gaining approval, are most strongly associated with risky sexual behaviour, including having many partners, not using birth control, and pressuring a partner into sex (Cooper, Shapiro, & Powers, 1998; Hamby & Koss, 2003; Impett, Peplau, & Gable, 2005).

Unfortunately, significant numbers of women and men are having sex for extrinsic rather than intrinsic motives. In one study, university students in dating relationships kept a daily diary of their sexual experiences; 50% of the women and 26% of the men reported consenting to unwanted sexual activity during that time (O'Sullivan & Allgeier, 1998). Men typically do so because of peer pressure, inexperience, a desire for popularity, or a fear of seeming homosexual or unmasculine. Women typically do so because they do not want to lose the relationship; because they feel obligated, once the partner has spent time and money on them; because the partner makes them feel guilty; or because they want to satisfy the partner and avoid conflict (Impett, Gable, & Peplau, 2005).

People's motives for consenting to unwanted sex depend in part on their own feelings of security in the relationship. In a study of 125 university women, one-half to two-thirds of Asian-American, white, and Latina women had consented to having sex when they didn't really want to, and all of the black women said they had. Do you remember the attachment theory of love discussed earlier? Anxiously attached women were the most willing to consent to unwanted sex, especially if they feared their partners were less committed than they were. They reported that they often had sex out of feelings of obligation and to prevent the partner from leaving. Securely attached women also occasionally had unwanted sex, but their reasons were different: to gain sexual experience, to satisfy their curiosity, or to actively please their partners and further the intimacy between them (Impett, Gable, & Peplau, 2005).

SEXUAL COERCION AND RAPE.   One of the most persistent differences in the sexual experiences of women and men has to do with their perceptions of, and experiences with, sexual coercion. At Carleton University, DeKeseredy and Kelly (1993) tested a large sample of female undergraduate students and found that 29% reported having experienced at least one incident of sexual assault. In a nationally representative survey of more than 3000 Americans aged 18 to 59, nearly 25% of the women said that a man had forced them to do something sexually that they did not want to do, but only about 3% of the men said they had ever forced a woman into a sexual act. While this percentage is low, studies conducted among Canadian and American university students reveal that men are far more likely than women to admit to coercing a partner into sex—using alcohol or other drugs, or threats or actual physical force (O'Sullivan, Byers, & Finkelman, 1998).

The most extreme form of sexual coercion, of course, is rape. College and university women tend to define rape as being forced into intercourse by an acquaintance or stranger, or as having been molested as a child. They are least likely to call their experience rape if they were sexually assaulted by a boyfriend, were drunk or otherwise drugged, or were forced to have oral or digital sex (Kahn, 2004). About half of all women who report a sexual assault that meets the legal definition of rape—being forced to engage in sexual acts against their will—do not label it as rape (McMullin & White, 2006). Furthermore, the vast majority of these crimes go unpunished. Only 6% of all sexual assaults in Canada are reported to the police (Statistics Canada, 1993). This underreporting might be due to the fact that most women know their attackers; 80% of assaulted women know their male attackers in some capacity (Kinnon, 1981). In fact, 31% of the assaults occur within a dating or acquaintance relationship (Kinnon, 1981).

What causes some men to rape? Sociobiologists often answer by analogy with other animals: For example, because male scorpion flies (and males of other species) force themselves on females, human rape must have the same evolutionary origins and reproductive purposes—for the male to fertilize as many females as possible (Thornhill & Palmer, 2000). But among human beings, rape is often committed by high-status men, including sports heroes and other celebrities, who could easily find consenting sexual partners. All too frequently its victims are children or the elderly, who do not reproduce. And sadistic rapists often injure or kill their victims, hardly a way to perpetuate one's genes. The human motives for rape thus appear to be primarily psychological:

◆ **Narcissism and hostility toward women.** Sexually aggressive males are often narcissistic, are unable to empathize with women, and feel entitled to have sexual

◉ **Watch**
Rape Is Not Sex

relations with whatever woman they choose. They misperceive women's behaviour in social situations, equate feelings of power with sexuality, and accuse women of provoking them (Bushman et al., 2003; Malamuth et al., 1995; Zurbriggen, 2000). One interesting study compared men who had forcibly raped a woman with men who used manipulative techniques to have sex and with men who had had consensual sex only. The rapists were more likely to have grown up in violent households, were more accepting of male violence, and were less likely to endorse love as a motive for sex than were men in the manipulation and consent groups (Lyndon, White, & Kadlec, 2007).

◆ **A desire to dominate, humiliate, or punish the victim.** This motive is apparent among soldiers who rape captive women during war and then often kill them (Olujic, 1998). Similarly, reports of the systematic rapes of female cadets at the U.S. Air Force Academy suggest that the rapists' motives were to humiliate the women and get women to leave the Academy. Aggressive motives also occur in the rape of men by other men, usually by anal penetration (King & Woollett, 1997). This form of rape typically occurs in youth gangs, where the intention is to humiliate rival gang members, and in prison, where again the motive is to conquer and degrade the victim.

◆ **Sadism.** A minority of rapists are violent criminals who get pleasure out of inflicting pain on their victims and who often murder them in planned, grotesque ways (Turvey, 2008).

You can see that the answer to the question "Why do people have sex?" is not at all obvious. It is not a simple matter of "doing what's natural." In addition to the intrinsic motives of intimacy, pleasure, procreation, and love, extrinsic motives include intimidation, dominance, insecurity, appeasing the partner, approval from peers, and the wish to prove oneself a real man or a desirable woman.

The Culture of Desire

Think about kissing. Westerners like to think about kissing, and to do it, too. But if you think kissing is natural, try to remember your first serious kiss and all you had to learn about noses, breathing, and the position of teeth and tongue. The sexual kiss is so complicated that some cultures have never gotten around to it. They think that kissing another person's mouth—the very place that food enters!—is disgusting (Tiefer, 2004). Others have elevated the sexual kiss to high art; why do you suppose one version is called French kissing?

As the kiss illustrates, having the physical equipment to perform a sexual act is not all there is to sexual motivation. People have to learn what is supposed to turn them on (or off), which parts of the body and what activities are erotic (or repulsive), and even how to have pleasurable sexual relations (Laumann & Gagnon, 1995).

Thinking Critically

Consider Other Interpretations

Many people think that all sexual behaviour, including kissing, is universal and caused by a simple physiological drive. What other explanations are possible?

Thus, to men in cultures where women are required to cover up completely in public, the sight of a woman's ankle can be arousing; to Western men today, an ankle doesn't do it. In some cultures, oral sex is regarded as a bizarre sexual deviation; in others, it is considered not only normal but also supremely desirable. In many cultures, men believe that women who have experienced the sexual pleasure of kissing or being caressed, or who enjoy orgasms, will become unfaithful, so sexual relations are limited to quick intercourse; in others, men's satisfaction and pride depend on knowing the woman is sexually satisfied too. In some cultures, sex itself is seen as something joyful and beautiful, an art to be cultivated as one might cultivate the skill of gourmet cooking. In others, it is considered ugly and dirty, something to be gotten through as quickly as possible.

How do cultures transmit their rules and requirements about sex to their members? During childhood and adolescence, people learn their culture's *gender roles*, collections of rules that determine the proper attitudes and behaviour for men and women. Just as an actor in the role of Hamlet needs a script to learn his part, a person following a gender role needs a **sexual script** that instructs men and women on how to behave in sexual situations (Gagnon & Simon, 1973; Laumann & Gagnon, 1995). If you are a teenaged girl, are you supposed to be sexually adventurous and assertive or sexually modest and passive? What if you are a teenaged boy? What if you are an older woman or man? The answers differ from culture to culture, as members act in accordance with the sexual scripts for their gender, age, religion, social status, and peer group.

In many parts of the world, boys acquire their attitudes about sex in a competitive atmosphere where the goal is to impress other males, and they talk and joke about masturbation and other sexual experiences with their friends. While their traditional sexual scripts are encouraging them to value physical sex, traditional scripts are teaching girls to value relationships and make themselves attractive. Many girls learn that their role is to be sexually desirable (which is good), but not to indulge in their own sexual pleasures (which would be bad). Modern scripts for women in many places are changing, however, as illustrated by the sexual scripts followed by the characters in *Grey's Anatomy* or *Sex and the City*. But an analysis of 25 prime-time television shows that are most popular with teenagers found that the familiar male and female scripts are alive and well: Male characters frequently act out the traditional male script by actively and aggressively pursuing sex; many female characters still play the part of "sex object" and are judged by their sexual conduct (Kim et al., 2007).

sexual script Set of implicit rules that specify proper sexual behaviour for a person in a given situation, varying with the person's gender, age, religion, social status, and peer group.

These teenagers are following the sexual scripts for their gender and culture—the boys, by ogling and making sexual remarks about girls in order to impress their peers, and the girls, by preening and wearing makeup to look good for boys.

Gay men and lesbians follow sexual scripts, too. But theirs tend to be more flexible than heterosexual scripts in establishing rules for the relationship because most partners are not following a traditional gender role (Kurdek, 2005; Peplau & Spalding, 2000).

Scripts can be powerful determinants of behaviour. Because black women now account for 58% of reported AIDS cases among women in the United States, researchers have sought to understand how sexual scripts might be reducing their likelihood of practising safe sex. In interviews with 14 black women aged 22 to 39, researchers found that the women's behaviour was governed by scripts fostering these beliefs: *Men control relationships; women sustain relationships; male infidelity is normal; men control sexual activity; women want to use condoms, but men control condom use* (Bowleg, Lucas, & Tschann, 2004). As one woman summarized, "The ball was always in his court." These scripts, the researchers noted, are rooted in black North American history and the recurring scarcity of men available for long-term commitments. The scripts originated to preserve the stability of the family, but today they encourage some women to establish and maintain sexual relationships at the expense of their own needs and safety.

Gender, Culture, and Sex

As we discussed in Chapter 3, evolutionary psychologists believe that gender roles and sexual scripts simply reflect hardwired biological sex differences that resulted from natural selection. In contrast, social and cultural psychologists believe that gender roles and sexual scripts reflect a culture's economic, demographic, and social arrangements. As evidence for their point of view, they have found that when those arrangements change, so do women's and men's attitudes and behaviour. A meta-analysis of 530 studies, involving nearly 270 000 individuals, showed that in North America, young people's sexual attitudes and behaviour changed dramatically between 1943 and 1999, with the largest changes occurring among girls and young women (Wells & Twenge, 2005). Approval of premarital sex leapt from 12% to 73% among young women, and from 40% to 79% among young men; feelings of sexual guilt decreased sharply for both sexes; and, for women, average age at first intercourse dropped from 19 to 15 over the five decades, with small fluctuations.

Most people choose sexual partners by using the same criteria they apply in the search for love partners: similarity and proximity (availability). What happens, then, when large-scale demographic changes result in a lopsided ratio of heterosexual men and women? In China and India, countries in which most parents value boys and disparage girls, the ratio of young men to women is now about 120 to 100, a result of decades of abortions of female fetuses. In contrast, among black North Americans there are more women than available men, because so many young black men are unemployed, are in prison, or die young.

More than 20 years ago, an important book assessed the social and sexual consequences of these uneven ratios (Guttentag & Secord, 1983). When men are scarce, the ball is always in their court: Men are more likely to have multiple sexual partners, divorce rates and numbers of single-parent families increase, and women become more independent. When women are scarce, men vie for wives, divorce rates

In the TV series *Sex and the City*, the women shopped for men the way they shopped for shoes. This rewriting of the traditional sexual script for women drew both fans and critics.

IS THE DOUBLE STANDARD STILL ALIVE?

Think of all the words you know to describe a sexually active woman and then think of words for a sexually active man. Is one list longer than the other? Are the two lists equally negative or positive in their connotations? What does this exercise tell you about the survival of the double standard and your culture's sexual scripts?

Get INVOLVED!

Watch
Gender vs. Sex

Straightening Out Homosexuals

Explore
Attractiveness

drop, both sexes have fewer sexual partners, and women become less independent. Societies (like Afghanistan's) that have large numbers of young, unemployed, and unattached men are also more vulnerable to internal disruption, violence, and extremist groups (like the Taliban) (Hudson & den Boer, 2004).

Sexual attitudes and motives likewise change along with women's economic status. Whenever women have needed marriage to ensure their social and financial security, they have regarded sex as a bargaining chip, an asset to be rationed rather than an activity to be enjoyed for its own sake (Hatfield & Rapson, 1996/2005). A woman with no economic resources of her own cannot afford to casually seek sexual pleasure if that means risking an unwanted pregnancy, the security of marriage, her reputation in society, her physical safety, or, in some cultures, her very life. When women become self-supporting and able to control their own fertility, however, they are more likely to want sex for pleasure rather than as a means to another goal.

Lopsided sex ratios and other social factors also help account for the different sexual practices, values, and norms that occur within a nation. One research team, surveying a random sample of more than 2000 people in Chicago, has used the term *sex market* to describe a geographical and cultural boundary within which people seek partners (Laumann et al., 2004). Big cities will have many different sex markets, formed by the ethnicity, age, status, and sexual orientation of their "shoppers." A bisexual black man, an immigrant Latina woman, a single young white woman, and an older gay man will seek out different sex markets that determine where and how they will find sexual partners: through work, church, bars, friends, social institutions, the internet, and so on. Sex markets vary tremendously in the sexual behaviour they consider appropriate, the sexual scripts they endorse for their members, and the meanings they attribute to sex—which is why so many groups in North America are quarrelling about what is right or normal sexual behaviour. Although big cities consist of many different sex markets, people rarely travel across them. They prefer the familiarity and proximity of the market they know best.

BIOLOGY and *Sexual Orientation*

Elusive Causes, Recent Clues

Why is it that most people become heterosexual, some homosexual, and others bisexual? Many psychological explanations for homosexuality have been proposed over the years, but none of them has been supported. Homosexuality is not a result of having a smothering mother, an absent father, or emotional problems. It is not caused by same-sex sexual play in childhood or adolescence, which is actually quite common

Marc Hall (left), with his boyfriend Jean-Paul Doumond. An Ontario court ruled that Hall should be allowed to bring his boyfriend to his Catholic high school prom in Oshawa on May 10, 2002. Why are some people homosexual in spite of enormous social pressures to be heterosexual, including laws and customs that typically deny them the benefits accorded to straights?

⊙**Watch**
Gay in the Military

(Lamb, 2002). It is not caused by seduction by an older adult (Rind, Tromovich, & Bauserman, 1998). It is not caused by parental practices or role models. Most gay men recall that they rejected the typical boy role and boys' toys and games from an early age, in spite of enormous pressures from their parents and peers to conform to the traditional male role (Bailey & Zucker, 1995). Conversely, the overwhelming majority of children of gay parents do not become gay, as a learning model would predict, although they are more likely than the children of straight parents to be open-minded about homosexuality and gender roles (Bailey et al., 1995; Patterson, 1992, 2006).

Many researchers, therefore, have been turning to biological explanations of sexual orientation. One line of supporting evidence is that homosexual behaviour—including courtship displays, sexual activity, and the rearing of young by two males or two females—has been documented in some 450 species, including bottlenose dolphins, penguins, and primates (Bagemihl, 1999). Sexual orientation also seems to be moderately heritable, particularly in men (Bailey, Dunne, & Martin, 2000; Rahman & Wilson, 2003). But the large majority of gay men and lesbians do not have a close gay relative, and their siblings, including twins, are overwhelmingly likely to be heterosexual (Peplau et al., 2000).

In the early 1990s, a few studies of gay men reported associations between sexual orientation and specific areas of the brain (Allen & Gorski, 1992; LeVay, 1991). These studies got lots of press, but they were not replicated (Byne, 1995). Researchers have also examined the role of prenatal exposure to androgens and how this might affect brain organization and partner preference (McFadden, 2008; Rahman & Wilson, 2003). Female babies accidentally exposed in the womb to masculinizing hormones are more likely than other girls to become bisexual or lesbian and to prefer typical boys' toys and activities (Collaer & Hines, 1995; Meyer-Bahlburg et al., 1995). However, most androgenized girls do not become lesbians, and most lesbians were not exposed in the womb to atypical prenatal hormones (Peplau et al., 2000).

One new line of research is investigating the possibility that other prenatal events might predispose a child toward a same-sex orientation. For example, more than a dozen studies have found that the probability of a man's becoming gay rises significantly according to the number of older brothers he has—gay or not—when these brothers are born of the same mother. (Remember, though, that the percentage of males who become homosexual is very small.) A recent study of 944 homosexual and heterosexual men suggests that this "brother effect" has nothing to do with family environment, but rather with conditions within the womb before birth (Bogaert, 2006). In this study, the only factor that predicted sexual orientation was having older biological brothers; growing up with older stepbrothers or adoptive brothers (or sisters) had no influence at all. The increased chance of homosexuality occurred even when men had older brothers born to the same mother but raised in a different home. No one yet has any idea, however, what prenatal influence might account for these results.

Several other intriguing biological findings are also associated with sexual orientation. In two studies, a team of Swedish scientists exposed people to two odours: a testosterone derivative found in men's sweat and an estrogen-like compound found in women's urine. It appears that when a hormone is from the sex you are *not* turned on by, your olfactory system registers it, but not your hypothalamus and through that, your sexual arousal and response system. Thus, the brain activity of homosexual women in response to the odours was similar to that of heterosexual men, and the brain activity of gay men was similar to that of heterosexual women (Berglund, Lindström, & Savic, 2006; Savic, Berglund, & Lindström, 2005). But the researchers wisely noted that their study could not answer questions of cause and effect. "We can't say whether the differences are because of pre-existing differences in their brains, or if past sexual experiences have conditioned their brains to respond differently," said the lead researcher.

Thinking Critically   Examine the Evidence

Many people think that homosexuality is abnormal, unnatural, or a matter of preference, but there is ample evidence of same-sex sexual activity in more than 450 nonhuman species. These young male penguins, Squawk and Milou, entwine their necks, kiss, call to each other, and have sex—and they firmly reject females. Another male pair in the same zoo, Silo and Roy, seemed so desperate to incubate an egg together that they put a rock in their nest and sat on it. Their human keeper was so touched that he gave them a fertile egg to hatch. Silo and Roy sat on it for the necessary 34 days until their chick, Tango, was born, and then they raised Tango beautifully. "They did a great job," said the zookeeper.

The basic problem with trying to find a single origin of sexual orientation is that sexual identity and behaviour take different forms, and they don't correlate strongly (Savin-Williams, 2006). Some people are heterosexual in behaviour but have homosexual fantasies and even define themselves as gay or lesbian. Some men, such as prisoners, are homosexual in behaviour because they lack opportunities for heterosexual sex, but they do not define themselves as gay and prefer women as sexual partners. In some cultures, teenage boys go through a homosexual phase that they do not define as homosexual and that does not affect their future relations with women (Herdt, 1984). Some gay men are feminine in interests and manner, but many are not; some lesbians are "butch" (i.e., masculine in interests and manner) but many other lesbians are not (Singh et al., 1999).

Moreover, although some lesbians have an exclusively same-sex orientation their whole lives, many have more fluid sexual orientations: They have sex with the person they fall in love with, male or female (Peplau et al., 2000). Some women are lesbian for a particular time in their lives, as reflected in the joking term LUG—lesbian until graduation (Diamond, 2003). A researcher interviewed 100 lesbian and bisexual women over a

10-year span, and found that only one-third reported consistent attraction only to other women; two-thirds also felt attracted to men. For most of these women, love was truly blind as far as gender was concerned; their sexual behaviour depended on whether they loved the partner, not what sex he or she was (Diamond, 2008). Similarly, when men and women watch erotic films, men are more influenced than women are by the sex of the people having sex, whereas women are more influenced than men are by the context in which the sex occurs. Thus, most straight men are turned off by watching gay male couples coupling, most gay men are turned off by watching heterosexual couples, and most straight and lesbian women are turned on by watching anyone of either sex, as long as the context is erotic (Rupp & Wallen, 2008). In Lesotho, in South Africa, women have intimate relations with other women, including passionate kissing and oral sex, but they do not define these acts as sexual, as they do when a man is the partner (Kendall, 1999).

Biological factors cannot account for the diversity of such customs or for the diversity of experience among gay men and lesbians. At present, therefore, we must tolerate uncertainty about the origins of sexual orientation. Perhaps the origins will turn out to differ, on average, for males and females, and also differ among individuals, whatever their primary orientation.

Now, how are you reacting to these findings? Your responses are probably affected by your feelings about the subject. Many gay men and lesbians welcome biological research on the grounds that it supports what they have been saying all along: Sexual orientation is not a matter of choice but a fact of nature. Others fear that people who are prejudiced against homosexuals will use this research to argue that gay people have a biological defect that should be eradicated. But people who are hostile to homosexuals can use any theory, biological or psychological, to justify their wish to eliminate homosexuality. They have often used learning theories to argue, mistakenly, that "if it's learned, it can be unlearned," and thus to subject gay men, and even "unboyish" boys as young as three years old, to harsh and punitive forms of behaviour modification (Burke, 1996).

Political storms about sex research are no less heated today than they were in Kinsey's time. Some conservative and evangelical Christians, including the Traditional Values Coalition, are trying to block research on sexual behaviour they say the Bible disapproves of, such as masturbation, homosexuality, and any form of sexual behaviour outside of marriage. Other conservative Christians, however, call on modern research to make the case that homosexuality is not a preference but a natural disposition. In their book *What God Has Joined Together: A Christian Case for Gay Marriage*, David

Gay and lesbian couples have all the joys and problems of straight couples. Phyllis Lyon and Del Martin (left) lived together for 56 years. In 2008, two months after they were finally legally allowed to marry, Del Martin died. On the right, Tom Howard is shown with the three children he is raising with his partner. Howard left his job as a professor in order to be a stay-at-home dad. Why does the issue of legalizing gay and lesbian marriage evoke so much emotion and controversy?

Myers and Letha Scanzoni (2005) argue that the Bible's seven brief comments opposing same-sex behaviour are really condemnations of the exploitation of children, promiscuity, idolatry, and acting against one's nature, and that these verses pale in importance beside the Bible's thousands of verses about love, compassion, and empathy.

As you see, research on sexuality can be used for many purposes and political goals, depending on the values and attitudes of the culture in which such findings emerge and people's own religious passions or personal beliefs. But as long as people are morally opposed to homosexuality, preconceptions and prejudice are likely to cloud their reactions to anything that psychologists learn about it.

quickQUIZ

✓ Quick Review on MyPsychLab

Were you motivated to learn about sexual motivation?

1. Biological research finds that (a) homosexual behaviour is found in hundreds of animal species, (b) male and female sexual responses are physiologically very different, (c) all women can have multiple orgasms, (d) women have a stronger sex drive than men do, contrary to the stereotype.

2. Research on the motives of rapists finds that rape is usually a result of (a) thwarted sexual desire, (b) hostility or a need for peer approval, (c) crossed signals, (d) female provocation.

3. When men are scarce, what are some consequences for the sexual behaviour of both sexes?

4. Under what conditions are women most likely to use sex as a "bargaining chip"? (a) when they are employed and thus have their own money to bargain with, (b) when they don't know how to play poker, (c) when they are using birth control, (d) when they are financially dependent

5. *True or false:* Exclusively psychological theories of the origins of homosexuality have never been supported.

Answers:

1. a 2. b 3. Men are more likely to have multiple sexual partners, divorce rates and single-parent families increase, and women become more independent. 4. d 5. true

◆ YOU are about to learn . . .

◆ the three kinds of goals most likely to boost the motivation to succeed.

◆ the important difference between mastery goals and performance goals.

◆ how the desire to achieve is affected by the opportunity to achieve.

◆ which aspects of a job are more important than money in increasing satisfaction with work.

THE COMPETENT ANIMAL: MOTIVES TO ACHIEVE

Almost every adult works. But work does not only mean paid employment. Students work at studying. Homemakers work, often more hours than salaried employees, at running a household. Artists, poets, and actors work, even if they are paid erratically (or

"Finish it? Why would I want to finish it?"

not at all). Most people are motivated to work in order to meet the basic needs for food and shelter. Yet survival does not explain why some people want to do their work well and others just want to get it done. And it does not explain why some people work to make a basic living and then put their passions for achievement into unpaid activities—learning to become an accomplished trail rider or travelling to Madagascar to catch sight of a rare bird for their bird-watching list. What keeps everybody doing what they do?

Psychologists, particularly those in the field of industrial/ organizational psychology, have measured the psychological qualities that spur achievement and success and also the environmental conditions that influence productivity and satisfaction. Their findings apply not only to understanding why people thrive or wilt at their jobs, but also to understanding people's aspirations and achievements in general.

The Many Motives of Accomplishment

IMMORTALITY

Marshall McLuhan
Media scholar
"Tomorrow is our permanent address."

TRUTH

John Ralston Saul
Writer
"... Socrates was executed not for saying what things were or should be, but for seeking practical indications of where some reasonable approximation of truth might be. He was executed not for his megalomania or grandiose propositions or certitudes, but for stubbornly doubting the absolute truths of others."

JUSTICE

Bruce Cockburn
Singer, poet, civil rights activist
"Everybody wants to see justice done, to somebody else."

AUTONOMY

Farley Mowat
Writer
"After all, we fought the Yanks in 1812 and kicked them the hell out of our country—but not with blanks."

The Effects of Motivation on Work

In the early 1950s, David McClelland and his associates (1953) speculated that some people have a *need for achievement* that motivates them as much as hunger motivates people to eat. To measure the strength of this motive, McClelland used a variation of the **Thematic Apperception Test (TAT)**, which requires the test-taker to make up a story about a set of ambiguous pictures, such as a young man sitting at a desk. (The TAT is one of many *projective tests*, which are based on the assumption that a person will project unconscious motives and feelings onto an ambiguous stimulus; see Chapter 16.) The strength of the achievement motive, said McClelland (1961), is captured in the fantasies the test-taker reveals. High achievers tell stories of challenge and success; lower achievers tell stories of idyllic vacations at the beach.

The TAT is one of the few projective tests that has modest empirical support for the measurement of achievement motivation. But it does not have strong *test–retest reliability*, meaning that people's responses are easily influenced by what is going on

Thematic Apperception Test (TAT)   A projective test that asks respondents to interpret a series of drawings showing scenes of people; usually scored for unconscious motives, such as the need for achievement, power, or affiliation.

◈ Research
David McClelland

✳ Explore
Theories of Motivation and Job Performance

SECURITY

Pierre Trudeau
Former prime minister of Canada
"In a very real sense we are not so much threatened by the ideologies of communism or of fascism or even, I would say, so much threatened by atomic bombs and ICBMs, as we are by the very large sectors of the world—two-thirds of the world's population—that goes to bed hungry every night."

DUTY

General Rick Hillier
Former chief of the defence staff
"I will be the public champion for those brave men and women. They're Canada's sons and daughters, ladies and gentlemen. If we can't market Canada's sons and daughters back to Canada's moms and dads, we need to find somebody to replace us to do the job. Because that's what needs to be done."

EXCELLENCE

Chantal Petitclerc
Athlete
"To me, this is the ultimate proof that if you have a strong commitment to your goals and dreams, if you wake up every day with a passion to do your job or your sport, everything is possible."

GREED

Ivan Boesky
Financier, convicted of insider trading violations
"Greed is all right... I think greed is healthy. You can be greedy and still feel good about yourself."

approach goals Goals framed in terms of desired outcomes or experiences, such as learning to scuba dive.

avoidance goals Goals framed in terms of avoiding unpleasant experiences, such as trying not to look foolish in public.

◉**Watch**
Women Can Do It

at that moment in their lives rather than by some inner drive to succeed (Lilienfeld, Wood, & Garb, 2000). Some people might tell stories of achieving against all odds, not because they are determined to do so, but because they are idly daydreaming about dazzling the world on *Canadian Idol*. But the method launched many investigations into the question of why some people seem to have a drive to make it no matter what, and others drift along.

THE IMPORTANCE OF GOALS. Today the predominant approach to understanding achievement motivation emphasizes goals rather than inner drives: What you accomplish depends on the goals you set for yourself and the reasons you pursue them (Dweck & Grant, 2008). Not just any old goals will promote achievement, though. A goal is most likely to improve your motivation and performance when three conditions are met (Higgins, 1998; Locke & Latham, 2002, 2006):

- ◆ **The goal is specific.** Defining a goal vaguely, such as "doing your best," is as ineffective as having no goal at all. You need to be specific about what you are going to do and when you are going to do it: "I will write four pages of this paper today."

- ◆ **The goal is challenging but achievable.** You are apt to work hardest for tough but realistic goals. The highest, most difficult goals produce the highest levels of motivation and performance, unless, of course, you choose impossible goals that you can never attain.

- ◆ **The goal is framed in terms of getting what you want rather than avoiding what you do not want. Approach goals** are positive experiences that you seek directly, such as getting a better grade or learning to scuba dive. **Avoidance goals** involve the effort to avoid unpleasant experiences, such as trying not to make a fool of yourself at parties or trying to avoid being dependent.

All the motives discussed in this chapter are affected by approach versus avoidance goals. People who frame their goals in specific, achievable approach terms (e.g., "I'm going to lose weight by jogging three times a week") feel better about themselves, are happier, feel more competent, are more optimistic, and are less depressed than people who frame the same goals in avoidance terms (e.g., "I'm going to lose weight by cutting out rich foods") (Coats, Janoff-Bulman, & Alpert, 1996; Updegraff, Gable, & Taylor, 2004). Framing goals in terms of approach or avoidance can even affect the quality of close relationships. For example, people who have sex for *approach* motives—to enjoy their own physical pleasure, to promote a partner's happiness, or to seek enhanced intimacy—tend to have happier and less conflicted relationships than those who have sex to *avoid* a partner's loss of interest or quarrels with the partner (Impett & Tolman, 2006; Impett, Peplau, & Gable, 2005).

Get INVOLVED!

(RE)FRAMING YOUR GOALS

As the text discusses, people sometimes frame their goals in vague, unrealistic, or negative ways. Think of two goals you would like to accomplish. For example, you might consider goals related to studying more efficiently, improving communication with a family member, solving problems in a particular relationship, or becoming more physically fit. Now phrase each of your two goals in a way that makes it (1) specific, (2) challenging but achievable, and (3) something to be approached rather than avoided. How can framing your goals in this way improve your motivation to reach them?

Can you guess why approach goals produce better results than avoidance goals? Approach goals allow you to focus on what you can actively do to accomplish them and on the intrinsic pleasure of the activity. Avoidance goals make you focus on what you have to give up (Elliot & Sheldon, 1998).

In the case of work, defining your goals will move you along the road to success, but what happens when you hit a pothole? Some people give up when a goal becomes difficult or they are faced with a setback, whereas others become even more determined to succeed. The crucial difference between them is why they are working for that goal: to show off in front of others or to learn the task for the satisfaction of it.

People who are motivated by *performance goals* are concerned primarily with being judged favourably and avoiding criticism. Those who are motivated by *mastery (learning) goals* are concerned with increasing their competence and skills and finding intrinsic pleasure in what they are learning (Grant & Dweck, 2003; Senko, Durik, & Harackiewicz, 2008). When people who are motivated by performance goals do poorly, they will often decide the fault is theirs and stop trying to improve. Because their goal is to demonstrate their abilities, they set themselves up for grief when they temporarily fail, as all of us must if we are to learn anything new. In contrast, people who are motivated to master new skills will generally regard failure and criticism as sources of useful information that will help them improve. They know that learning takes time.

Why do some children choose performance goals and others choose mastery goals? In a study of 128 grade 5 students, the children worked independently on sets of puzzle problems (Mueller & Dweck, 1998). The experimenter scored their results, told them all they had done well, and gave them one of two additional types of feedback: She praised some of them for their ability ("You must be smart to do these problems!") and others for their effort ("You must have worked hard at these problems!"). The children then worked on a more difficult set of problems, but this time the experimenter told them they had done a lot worse. Finally, the children described which goals they preferred to work for: performance (e.g., doing "problems that aren't too hard, so I don't get many wrong") or mastery (e.g., doing "problems that I'll learn a lot from, even if I won't look so smart").

The children praised for being smart rather than for working hard tended to lose the pleasure of learning and focused instead on how well they were doing. After these children failed the second set of problems, they tended to give up on subsequent ones, enjoyed them less, and actually performed less well than children who had been praised for their efforts. As you can see in Figure 12.1, nearly 70% of the grade 5 students who were praised for their intelligence later chose performance goals rather than learning goals, compared to fewer than 10% of those who were praised for their efforts. When children realize that all effort is subject to improvement, however, they realize that they can always try again. That is the key to mastery. As one learning-oriented child said to the experimenters, "Mistakes are our friends" (Dweck & Sorich, 1999).

Mastery goals are powerful intrinsic motivators at all levels of education and throughout life. Students who are in college primarily to master new areas of knowledge choose more challenging projects, persist in the face of difficulty, use deeper and more elaborate study strategies, are less likely than other students to cheat, and enjoy learning more than do

Why will some children become engrossed in a project and work on it for hours, whereas others give up in frustration if they can't get it just right?

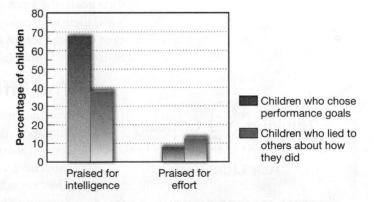

FIGURE 12.1 Mastery and Motivation

Children praised for "being smart" rather than for "working hard" tend to lose the pleasure of learning and focus on how well they are doing. Nearly 70% of grade 5 students who were praised for intelligence later chose performance goals (green bars) rather than learning goals, compared to fewer than 10% of those who were praised for their efforts (Mueller & Dweck, 1998). Notice also that the children praised for intelligence were much more likely to lie to others about how well they had done (purple bars)—since their goal was showing off, not learning.

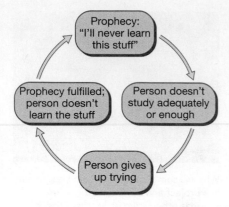

students who are there only to get a degree and a meal ticket (Elliot & McGregor, 2001; Grant & Dweck, 2003). As usual, though, we should avoid oversimplifying: Olympic athletes, world-class musicians, and others who are determined to become the best in their field blend performance and mastery goals.

EXPECTATIONS AND SELF-EFFICACY.   How hard you work for something also depends on your expectations. If you are fairly certain of success, you will work harder to reach your goal than if you are fairly certain of failure.

A classic experiment showed how quickly experience affects these expectations. Young women were asked to solve 15 anagram puzzles. Before working on each one, they had to estimate their chances of solving it. Half of the women started off with very easy anagrams, but half began with insoluble ones. Sure enough, those who started with the easy ones increased their estimates of success on later ones. Those who began with the impossible ones decided they would all be impossible. These expectations, in turn, affected the young women's ability to actually solve the last 10 anagrams, which were the same for everyone. The higher the expectation of success, the more anagrams the women solved (Feather, 1966). Once acquired, therefore, expectations can create a *self-fulfilling prophecy* (Merton, 1948): Your expectations make you behave in ways that make the expectation come true. You expect to succeed, so you work hard—and succeed. Or you expect to fail, so you don't do much work—and do poorly.

Your expectations are further influenced by your level of confidence in yourself and your abilities (Dweck & Grant, 2008; Judge, 2009). No one is born with a feeling of confidence, or *self-efficacy*. You acquire it through experience in mastering new skills, overcoming obstacles, and learning from occasional failures. Self-efficacy also comes from having successful role models who teach you that your ambitions are possible and from having people around to give you constructive feedback and encouragement (Bandura, 2006).

People who have a strong sense of self-efficacy are quick to cope with problems rather than stewing and brooding about them. Studies in North America, Europe, and Russia find that self-efficacy has a positive effect on just about every aspect of people's lives: how well they do on a task, the grades they earn, how persistently they pursue their goals, the kinds of career choices they make, their ability to solve complex problems, their motivation to work for political and social goals, their health habits, and even their chances of recovery from heart attack (Bandura et al., 2001; Maddux, 1995; Stajkovic & Luthans, 1998).

The Effects of Work on Motivation

Imagine that you live in a town that has one famous company, Boopsie's Biscuits & Buns. Everyone in the town is grateful for the 3B company and goes to work there with high hopes. Soon, however, an odd thing starts happening to many employees. They complain of fatigue and irritability. They are taking lots of sick leave. Productivity declines. What's going on at Boopsie's Biscuits & Buns? Is everybody suffering from sheer laziness?

Most observers would answer that something is wrong with those employees. But what if something is wrong with Boopsie's? Some people undoubtedly do lack motivation, but accomplishment does not depend on internal motives alone. Psychologists also want to know how the work we do, as well as the conditions under which we do it, nurtures or crushes our motivation to succeed.

Thinking ⚙️ **Critically**

Ask Questions

If a person isn't doing well at work, North Americans tend to ask, "What's the matter with that person's motivation? How come that person is a lazy slug?" What other questions would lead to different answers about why the employee seems so lazy?

For example, one simple but powerful external factor that affects many people's motivation to work in a particular field is the proportion of men and women in that occupation (Kanter, 2006). When occupations are segregated by gender, many people form gender stereotypes about the requirements of such careers: Female jobs require kindness and nurturance; male jobs require strength and smarts. These stereotypes, in turn, stifle many people's aspirations to enter a nontraditional career and also create prejudices in employers (Agars, 2004; Cejka & Eagly, 1999).

Thus, when law, veterinary medicine, and bartending were almost entirely male professions, and nursing, teaching, and child care were almost entirely female, few women aspired to enter the "male" professions and few men to enter the "female" ones. As job segregation began breaking down, however, people's career motivations changed. Today, it isn't at all unusual to see a female lawyer, vet, or bartender, or a male nurse or even nanny.

And although women are still a minority in engineering, math, and science, their numbers are rising: In 1970–1971, women earned 0.6% of the doctorates in engineering, 7.6% of those in mathematics, and 16.3% of those in biological sciences. By 2001–2002, the percentages had jumped to 17.3%, 29%, and 44.3%, respectively (Cox & Alm, 2005). As these numbers have increased, the view that women are not suited to engineering, math, and science has been fading, though slowly.

WORKING CONDITIONS. Once they are in a job, what motivates people to do well? Why do others lose their motivation altogether? To begin with, achievement depends on having the *opportunity* to achieve. When someone does not do well at work, others are apt to say it is the individual's own fault because he or she lacks the internal drive to make it. But what the person may really lack is a fair chance to make it, and this is especially true for those who have been subjected to systematic discrimination (Sabattini & Crosby, 2009). Once they have entered a career, people may become more motivated to advance up the ladder or less so, depending on how many rungs they are permitted to climb. Women used to be rare in politics, but today it's not news that they are counsellors, mayors, MPs, or prime ministers.

Several aspects of the work environment are likely to increase work motivation and satisfaction and reduce the chances of emotional burnout (Bond et al., 2004; Maslach, Schaufeli, & Leiter, 2001; Rhoades & Eisenberger, 2002):

♦ The work feels meaningful and important to employees.

♦ Employees have control over many aspects of their work, such as setting their own hours and making decisions.

♦ Tasks are varied rather than repetitive.

♦ The company maintains clear and consistent rules.

♦ Employees have supportive relationships with their superiors and co-workers.

♦ Employees receive useful feedback about their work, so they know what they have accomplished and what they need to do to improve.

♦ The company offers opportunities for its employees to learn and advance.

Like employees, students can have poor working conditions that affect their motivation. They may have to study in crowded quarters or may have young siblings who interrupt and distract them.

Did you notice anything missing from that list of beneficial working conditions? Where is money, supposedly the great motivator? Actually, work motivation is related not to the amount of money you get, but to how and when you get it. The strongest motivator is *incentive pay*, bonuses that are given upon completion of a goal rather than as an automatic raise (Locke et al., 1981). Incentive pay increases people's feelings of competence and accomplishment ("I got this raise because I deserved it"). This doesn't mean that people should accept low pay so that they will like their jobs better or that they should never demand cost-of-living raises!

Companies that foster these conditions tend to have more productive and satisfied employees. Workers tend to become more creative in their thinking and feel better about themselves and their work than they do if they feel stuck in routine jobs that give them no control or flexibility over their daily tasks.

Conversely, when people are put in situations that frustrate their desire and ability to succeed, they become dissatisfied and stressed out, and their desire to succeed declines (Jenkins, 1994). For example, while the rising number of women entering the sciences is heartening news, many are not staying. A study of nearly 2500 women and men in science, engineering, and technology found that although women made up 41% of the entry-level jobs, more than half of them had left their jobs by age 35, and a fourth had abandoned science altogether. The women who lost their motivation to work in these fields reported feeling isolated (many said they were the only woman in their work group), and two-thirds said they had been sexually harassed (Hewlitt, Luce, & Servon, 2008). Other reasons included being paid less than men for the same work and having working conditions that did not allow them to handle their family obligations. Mothers are still more likely than fathers to reduce their work hours, modify their work schedules, and report feeling distracted on the job because of child-care concerns (Sabattini & Crosby, 2009).

In sum, work motivation and satisfaction depend on the right fit between qualities of the individual and conditions of the work.

quickQUIZ

✔• Quick Review on MyPsychLab

Work on your understanding of work motivation.

1. Horatio wants to earn a black belt in karate. Which way(s) of thinking about this goal are most likely to help him reach it? (a) "I should do the best I can," (b) "I should make sure not to lose many matches," (c) "I will set specific goals that are tough but attainable," (d) "I will set specific goals that I know I can reach easily," (e) "I will strive to achieve key milestones on the way to my goal."

2. Ramón and Ramona are learning to ski. Every time she falls, Ramona says, "This is the most humiliating experience I've ever had! Everyone is watching me behave like a clumsy dolt!" When Ramón falls, he says, "&*!!@$@! I'll show these dratted skis who's boss!" Why is Ramona more likely than Ramón to give up? (a) she *is* a clumsy dolt, (b) she is less competent at skiing, (c) she is focused on learning, (d) she is focused on performance

3. Which of these factors significantly increases work motivation? (a) specific goals, (b) regular pay, (c) feedback, (d) general goals, (e) being told what to do, (f) being able to make decisions, (g) the chance of promotion, (h) having routine, predictable work

Answers:

1.c,e 2.d 3.a,c,f,g

YOU are about to learn . . .

♦ why people are poor at predicting what will make them happy or miserable.

♦ why money can't buy happiness.

♦ three basic kinds of motivational conflicts.

MOTIVES, VALUES, AND WELL-BEING

When you think about setting goals for yourself, here is a crucial psychological finding to keep in mind: People are really bad at predicting what will make them happy and what will make them miserable, and at estimating how long those feelings will last (Wilson & Gilbert, 2005). In one study, college students were asked how happy or unhappy they imagined they would feel after being randomly assigned to live in a dorm they thought was "desirable" or "undesirable" (Dunn, Wilson, & Gilbert, 2003). The students predicted that their dorm assignments would have a huge impact on their overall level of happiness and that being assigned to an undesirable dorm would essentially wreck their satisfaction for the whole year. In fact, as you can see from Figure 12.2, one year later everyone had nearly identical levels of happiness no matter where they were living.

Perhaps the undesirable dorms turned out to be unexpectedly pleasant, with cool people living in them? No. The students had focused on the wrong factors when imagining their future feelings of happiness in the houses; they had placed far more importance on what the house looked like and on its location than on its inhabitants. But in fact it's people who make a place fun or unpleasant to live in, and all the houses had likable people in them. Because the students could not foresee this, or how much they would like their new roommates, they mispredicted their future happiness.

This result has been replicated in many different contexts: The good is rarely as good as we imagine it will be, and the bad is rarely as terrible. The reason is that people adjust quickly to happy changes—new relationships, a promotion, even winning the lottery—and fail to anticipate that they will cope with bad experiences just as quickly. They will make sense of unexpected events, cope with tragedies, and make excuses for loved ones who hurt them. Yet people make many decisions based on false assumptions about how they will feel in the future. For example, they might spend more money than they can afford on a car or sound system because they think that this is what will make them truly happy.

What, then, does make people happy? In all the domains of human motivation we have examined, a key conclusion emerges: People who are motivated by the intrinsic satisfaction of an activity are happier and more satisfied than those motivated solely by extrinsic rewards (Deci & Ryan, 1985; Kasser & Ryan, 2001). We also saw how intrinsic motivation in any domain will rise or fall depending on the goals we choose and the way we think of them. Goals, in turn, are determined by our values about what is important in life: freedom, religion, equality, wealth, fame, wisdom, serenity, salvation, sexual passion, the desire to improve the world, or anything else. Psychological research cannot tell us which values to choose, but it does help illuminate the consequences of our choices.

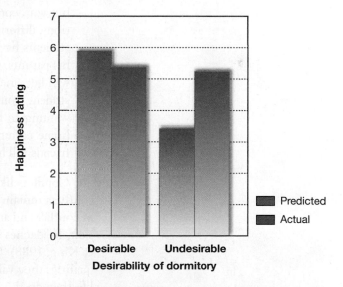

FIGURE 12.2 The Misprediction of Emotion

In a real-life longitudinal study, college students about to be randomly assigned to a dorm had to predict how happy or unhappy they would feel about being assigned to a house they had ranked as "desirable" or "undesirable." Most students thought they would be much less happy in an "undesirable" dorm, but in fact, one year later, there was no difference between the two groups (Dunn, Wilson, & Gilbert, 2003).

→◉ Simulate
Motivation

→◉ Simulate
Survey of Happiness

For example, many North Americans are more motivated to make money than to find activities they enjoy. Psychotherapist Allen Kanner noticed this difference in attitude among the children he saw in his practice: Ten years earlier, the children he treated had told him they wanted to be astronauts, baseball players, ballerinas, and doctors when they grew up, while the children he was currently treating told him they just want to be rich. They didn't want to play with conventional toys, but only with better, newer toys (Kanner & Kasser, 2003). Yet research finds repeatedly that having positive, intrinsically enjoyable *experiences* makes most people happier than having *things*: Doing is more satisfying than buying (Van Boven & Gilovich, 2003). Although people imagine that greater wealth will bring greater happiness, once they are at a level that provides basic comfort and security, more isn't necessarily better. They adjust quickly to the greater wealth and then think they need even more of it to be happier (Gilbert, 2006a).

Whichever values and goals you choose, if they are in conflict, the discrepancy can produce emotional stress and unhappiness. Two motives conflict when the satisfaction of one leads to the inability to act on the other—when, that is, you want to have your cake and eat it, too. Researchers have identified three kinds of motivational conflicts (Lewin, 1948):

1 **Approach–approach conflicts** occur when you are equally attracted to two or more possible activities or goals. For example, you would like to be a veterinarian *and* a rock singer; you would like to go out Tuesday night with friends *and* study like mad for an exam Wednesday.

2 **Avoidance–avoidance conflicts** require you to choose the lesser of two evils because you dislike both alternatives. Novice parachute jumpers, for example, must choose between the fear of jumping and the fear of losing face if they don't jump.

3 **Approach–avoidance conflicts** occur when a single activity or goal has both a positive and a negative aspect. For example, you want to be a powerful executive but you worry about losing your friends if you succeed. In culturally diverse nations, differing cultural values produce many approach–avoidance conflicts, as our students have revealed. A Chicano student said he wants to become a lawyer, but his parents, valuing family closeness, worry that if he goes to graduate school, he will become independent and feel superior to his working-class family. A black student from a poor neighbourhood, in university on scholarship, is torn between wanting to leave his background behind him forever and returning to help his home community. And a white student wants to be a marine biologist, but her friends tell her that only nerdy guys and dweebs go into science.

Conflicts like these are inevitable, part of the price and pleasure of living. But if conflicts remain unresolved, they can take an emotional toll. In students, high levels of conflict and ambivalence about goals and values are associated with anxiety, depression, headaches and other symptoms, and more visits to the health centre (Emmons & King, 1988). In contrast, students who strive for goals that are consistent with the qualities they value are healthier and have a greater sense of meaning and purpose in life than do those who are pursuing goals discrepant with their core values (Sheldon & Houser-Marko, 2001).

Are some psychological goals more important to our well-being than others? The humanist psychologist Abraham Maslow (1970) thought so. Maslow envisioned people's motives as forming a pyramid, a *hierarchy of needs*. At the bottom level of the pyramid were basic survival needs for food, sleep, and water; at the next level were security needs, for shelter and safety; at the third level were social needs, for belonging and affection; at the fourth level were esteem needs, for self-respect and the respect of others; and at the top were needs for self-actualization and self-transcendence. Maslow argued that your needs must be met at each level before you can even think of the matters posed by the level above it. You can't worry about achievement if you are hungry, cold, and poor. You can't become self-actualized if you haven't satisfied your needs for self-esteem and love. Human beings behave badly, he argued, only when their lower needs are frustrated.

This theory, which seemed so logical and optimistic about human progress, became immensely popular. Motivational speakers still often refer to it, using colourful pictures of Maslow's pyramid. But the theory, which was based mostly on Maslow's observations and intuitions, has had little empirical support (Sheldon et al., 2001; Smither, 1998). On the contrary, people may have *simultaneous* needs for comfort and safety and also for attachments, self-esteem, and competence. And individuals who have met their lower needs do not inevitably seek higher ones, nor is it the case that people behave badly only when their lower needs are frustrated. Higher needs may even supersede lower ones. History is full of examples of people who would rather die of torture or starvation than sacrifice their convictions, or who would rather explore, risk, or create new art than be safe and secure at home.

A different way of thinking about universal psychological needs has been developed by researchers who studied large samples of students in the United States and South Korea (Sheldon et al., 2001). Although students are not actually typical of all human beings, and two cultures do not represent all cultures on the planet, the findings are provocative and support many of the points in this chapter. The top four psychological needs turned out to be *autonomy* (feeling that you are making choices based on your "true interests and values"), *competence* (feeling able to master challenges), *relatedness* (feeling close to others who are important to you), and *self-esteem* (having self-respect). Other needs were of lesser importance, including pleasure, self-actualization (which was at the top of Maslow's list), popularity, and, at the bottom, once again . . . money and luxury.

As we have seen in this chapter, there are many motives that spur us to action, but psychological well-being depends on finding activities and choosing goals that are intrinsically satisfying and on developing the self-efficacy to achieve them. The motives and goals that inspire us, and the choices we make in their pursuit, are what give our lives passion, colour, and meaning. Choose them wisely.

✻ Explore
Evolutionary, Drive, Arousal, Cognitive, and Humanistic Theories of Motivation

---

quickQUIZ

✓●Quick Review on MyPsychLab

Do you wish to approach or avoid this quiz?

1. Max has applied for a junior year abroad, but couldn't get into his first choice, a drama school in London. He is feeling so miserable about the rejection that he is thinking of staying home. "Why should I go to a second-rate school somewhere else?," he reasons. What is the matter with his reasoning?

2. A Pakistani student says she desperately wants an education and a career as a pharmacist, but she also does not want to be disobedient to her parents, who have arranged a marriage for her back home. Which kind of conflict does she have?

3. Maslow's popular hierarchy of needs has several flaws. What are they?

Answers:

1. Max assumes that how he feels now is how he will feel in the future. He can't imagine the more likely scenario, that he will find things to like about any program he enters. 2. approach–avoidance 3. It was not based on extensive empirical research; it has not been well supported by research; the needs he proposed can be simultaneous rather than hierarchical; higher needs often supersede lower ones.

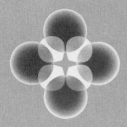

Taking Psychology with YOU

Thinking Critically in Everyday Life

How to Attain Your Goals

What are your values? What would you most like to achieve and accomplish in your life? Love, wealth, security, passion, freedom, fame, the desire to improve the world, being the best in a sport or other skill? Something else? What are your short-term goals: Would you like to improve your love life? Get better grades? Enjoy school more? Lose weight? Become a better tennis player?

There is a whole world of "motivational speakers," books, and tapes that offer inspiration, enthusiasm, and a few magic steps to change your life, but we hope that by now you will apply critical thinking to their promises. Enthusiastic inspiration is fine as far as it goes, but it doesn't usually transfer into helping you make real-life changes. In contrast, think about some of the lessons of motivational research that you have learned in this chapter:

Seek activities that are intrinsically pleasurable, even if they don't pay off. If you really, really want to study Swahili or Swedish even though these languages are not in your pre-law requirements, try to find a way to do it. If you are not enjoying your major or your job, consider finding a career that would be more intrinsically pleasurable, or at least make sure you have other projects and activities that you do enjoy for their own sake.

Focus on learning goals, not only on performance goals. In general, you will be better able to cope with setbacks if your goal is to learn rather than to show how good you are. Regard failure as a chance to learn rather than as a sign of incompetence.

Assess your working conditions. Everyone has working conditions. Whether you are a student, a self-employed writer, or a homemaker, if your motivation and well-being are start-

ing to wilt, check out your environment. Are you getting support from others? Do you have opportunities to develop ideas and vary your routine, or are you expected to do the same thing day after day? Are there barriers that might limit your advancement in your chosen field?

Take steps to resolve motivational conflicts. Are you torn between competing goals? For instance, are you unhappily stuck between the goal of achieving independence and a desire to be cared for by your parents? The reconciliation of conflicts like these is important for your well-being (Emmons & King, 1988).

Most important, think critically about the goals you have chosen for yourself: Are they what you want to do or what someone else wants you to do? Do they reflect your values? If you are not happy with your body, your relationships, or your work, why not? Think about it.

SUMMARY

◆ *Motivation* refers to an inferred process within a person or animal that causes that organism to move toward a goal—to satisfy a biological need or achieve a psychological ambition—or away from an unpleasant situation. A few primary *drives* are based on physiological needs, but all human motives are affected by psychological, social, and cultural factors. Motivation may be *intrinsic,* for the inherent pleasure of an activity, or *extrinsic,* for external rewards.

THE HUNGRY ANIMAL: MOTIVES TO EAT

◆ Overweight and obesity are not simply a result of failed willpower, emotional disturbance, or overeating. Hunger,

weight, and eating are regulated by a set of bodily mechanisms, such as *basal metabolism rate* and number of fat cells, that keep people close to their genetically influenced *set point.* Genes influence body shape, distribution of fat, and whether the body will convert excess calories into fat. Genes may also account for certain types of obesity; for example, the *ob* gene regulates *leptin,* which enables the hypothalamus to regulate appetite and metabolism.

◆ Genetics alone cannot explain why rates of overweight and obesity are rising all over the world among all social classes, ethnicities, and ages. The reasons reflect the interaction of an evolved genetic disposition to gain weight when rich food is plentiful and an environment that provides cheap, varied, high-calorie food and rewards sedentary lifestyles.

Eating habits and activity levels are also affected by cultural standards of what the ideal body should look like—heavy or thin, soft or muscular.

◆ When genetic predispositions clash with culture, physical and mental problems can result. In cultures that foster overeating and regard overweight as a sign of attractiveness and health, obesity is acceptable, but obesity increases the risk of various physical problems. In cultures that foster unrealistically thin bodies, eating disorders increase, especially *bulimia* and *anorexia*. These disorders are far more common in women than in men, but as pressures on men to have muscular bodies have increased, rates of body-image problems and eating disorders among men are increasing too.

THE SOCIAL ANIMAL: MOTIVES TO LOVE

◆ All human beings have a need for connection, attachment, and love. Psychologists who study love distinguish *passionate* ("romantic") *love* from *companionate love*. Biologically oriented researchers believe that the neurological origins of passionate love begin in the baby's attachment to the mother. Attachment stimulates the release of various brain chemicals, including the hormone oxytocin, associated with bonding and trust, and *endorphins*, which create rushes of pleasure and reward.

◆ Two strong predictors of whom people will love are *proximity* and *similarity*. Once in love, people form different kinds of attachments. *Attachment theory* views adult love relationships, like those of infants, as being secure, avoidant, or anxious. People's attachment styles tend to be stable from childhood to adulthood and affect their close relationships.

◆ For most people, love consists of passion, intimacy, and commitment. Men and women are equally likely to feel love and need attachment, but they differ, on average, in how they express feelings of love and how they define intimacy. In Western societies, women often express love in words, whereas men express it in actions. But as women have entered the workforce in large numbers and pragmatic (extrinsic) reasons for marriage have faded, the two sexes have become more alike in endorsing romantic love as a requirement for marriage.

THE EROTIC ANIMAL: MOTIVES FOR SEX

◆ Biological research finds that testosterone influences sexual desire in both sexes, although hormones do not cause sexual behaviour in a simple, direct way. The Kinsey surveys of male and female sexuality and the laboratory research of William Masters and Virginia Johnson showed that physiologically, there is no right kind of orgasm for women to have, and that both sexes are capable of sexual arousal and response.

◆ Some researchers believe that men have a higher frequency of many sexual behaviours, on average, because they have a stronger sex drive than women do. Others believe that gender differences in sexual motivation and behaviour are a result of differences in roles, cultural norms, and opportunity. A compromise view is that men's sexuality is more biologically influenced than is women's, whereas female sexuality is more governed by circumstances, relationships, and cultural norms.

◆ Men and women have sex to satisfy many different psychological motives, including pleasure, intimacy, coping, self-affirmation, the partner's approval, or peer approval. Extrinsic motives for sex, such as the need for approval, are associated with riskier sexual behaviour than intrinsic motives are. Both sexes may agree to intercourse for non-sexual motives: Men sometimes feel obligated to make a move to prove their masculinity, and women sometimes feel obliged to give in to preserve the relationship. People's motives for consenting to unwanted sex vary depending on their feelings of security and commitment in the relationship.

◆ A major gender difference in sexual experience has to do with rape and perceptions of sexual coercion: What many women regard as coercion is not always seen as such by men. Men who rape do so for diverse reasons, including peer pressure; anger, revenge, or a desire to humiliate the victim; narcissism and hostility toward women; and sometimes sadism.

◆ Cultures differ widely in determining what parts of the body people learn are erotic, which sexual acts are considered erotic or repulsive, and whether sex itself is good or bad. Cultures transmit these ideas through *gender roles* and *sexual scripts*, which specify appropriate behaviour during courtship and sex, depending on a person's gender, age, and sexual orientation.

◆ As in the case of love, gender differences (and growing similarities) in sexuality are strongly affected by cultural and economic factors, such as the ratio of women to men and the resulting availability of partners. As gender roles have become more alike, so has the sexual behaviour of men and women, with women wanting sex for pleasure rather than as a bargaining chip. Big cities have many different "sex markets," geographical and cultural areas in which people seek partners, and people tend not to cross them.

◆ As discussed in "Biology and Sexual Orientation," traditional psychological explanations for homosexuality have not been supported. Genetic and hormonal factors seem to be involved, although the evidence is stronger for gay men than for lesbians. The larger the number of older biological brothers a man has, the greater his likelihood of becoming homosexual, suggesting that prenatal events might be involved. In spite of the evidence of a biological contribution to sexual orientation, there is great variation in the expression of homosexuality around the world, and women's sexual orientation seems more fluid than men's. Research on this issue is sensitive because people's reactions to scientific findings on the origins of homosexuality are affected by their emotional and religious feelings about the topic.

THE COMPETENT ANIMAL: MOTIVES TO ACHIEVE

◆ The study of achievement motivation began with research using the *Thematic Apperception Test (TAT)*. People who are motivated by a high *need for achievement* set high but realistic standards for success and excellence. The TAT has empirical problems, but it launched the study of the factors that motivate achievement.

◆ People achieve more when they have specific, focused goals; when they set high but achievable goals for themselves; and when they have *approach goals* (seeking a positive outcome) rather than *avoidance goals* (avoiding an unpleasant outcome). People who focus on approach goals have greater well-being, better health, and even better intimate and sexual relationships than those who focus on avoidance goals.

◆ Work motivation also depends on circumstances of the job itself. Working conditions that promote motivation and satisfaction are those that provide workers with a sense of meaningfulness, control, variation in tasks, clear rules, feedback, and social support. *Incentive pay* is more effective than predictable raises in elevating work motivation. Other conditions that affect people's work motivation are the gender ratio of members in an occupation and whether the job provides opportunities for promotion and success.

MOTIVES, VALUES, AND WELL-BEING

◆ Satisfaction and well-being increase when people enjoy the intrinsic satisfaction of an activity and when their goals and values are in harmony. Having positive, intrinsically enjoyable experiences makes most people happier than having things. In an *approach–approach conflict*, a person is equally attracted to two goals. In an *avoidance–avoidance conflict*, a person is equally repelled by two goals. An *approach–avoidance conflict* is the most difficult to resolve because the person is both attracted to and repelled by the same goal. Prolonged conflict can lead to physical symptoms and reduced well-being.

◆ Abraham Maslow believed that human motives could be ranked in a *hierarchy of needs*, from basic biological needs for survival to higher psychological needs for self-actualization. This popular theory has not been well supported empirically. A more recent approach suggests that people have four major psychological needs, for autonomy, relatedness, competence, and self-esteem.

TAKING PSYCHOLOGY WITH YOU

◆ Motivational research suggests that people are happiest and most fulfilled when they seek intrinsically pleasurable activities, focus on learning, improve their working conditions, resolve competing goals, and choose the goals that reflect their most important values.

MyPsychLab

Visit **www.mypsychlab.com** to help you get the best grade!
Test your knowledge and grasp difficult concepts through

• Custom study plans: See where you are strong and where you go wrong
• Interactive simulations
• Video and audio clips

KEY TERMS

motivation 450

intrinsic motivation 450

extrinsic motivation 450

set point 450

bulimia 458

anorexia 458

endorphins 462

proximity effect 462

similarity effect 462

attachment theory of love 463

sexual script 473

Thematic Apperception Test (TAT) 481

approach goals 482

avoidance goals 482

13 DEVELOPMENT OVER THE LIFE SPAN

ASK QUESTIONS . . . be willing to WONDER

- How does a baby's thinking differ from an adult's?
- What makes the years from 18 to 25 unlike adolescence or adulthood?
- Is mental decline inevitable in old age?
- Do childhood experiences affect us for our entire lives?

In 1999, Arceli Keh, then aged 63, gave birth to a healthy baby girl. The child was conceived through in vitro fertilization, with sperm from Keh's 60-year-old husband and an egg donated by a younger woman. Keh and her family were delighted, but some fertility experts and ethicists had misgivings. Dr. Mark Sauer, who pioneered the use of donor eggs in older women, said, "I lose my comfort level after 55 because I have to believe that there are quality-of-life issues involved in raising a child at [the parent's] age. When [the baby] is five, her mother will be 68. And I have to believe that a 78-year-old dealing with a teenager may have some problems."

How do *you* react to the idea of a 63-year-old woman having a baby? Arceli Keh soon lost her "world's oldest mother" title to Adriana Iliescu, aged 66. She in turn lost the title to Carmela Bousada, who, after being impregnated with an embryo from a donor egg and sperm, delivered twin boys a week before her 67th birthday. (When her mother died at the age of 101, Bousada decided it was "the right time" for her to have children.) As we write this, Arceli Keh is 73 years old, her daughter is 10, and an extended family is involved in her care. Adriana Iliescu is raising her child on her own. But Carmela Bousada, who had no husband or other children, died of stomach cancer when her twins were only three years old.

When, if ever, is a human being "too old" to have a baby, whether by in vitro fertilization or adoption? Would it make any difference if the mother were "only" 55 years old? 50? Is there a "right time" to become a parent? Does age matter as much for fathers? Consider that former prime minister Pierre Trudeau became a father at 71. For that matter, is there a right time to do anything in life—go to school, get married, retire . . . die?

The universal human journey from birth to death was once far more predictable than it is today. Getting an education, choosing a job, starting a family, and retirement were all events that tended to happen in sequence. But because of demographic changes, an unpredictable economy, advances in reproductive technology, and many other forces, millions of people are now doing things out of order, if they do them at all. Today, getting an education, having children, changing careers, or starting a family may occur in almost any decade of adulthood.

Developmental psychologists study physiological and cognitive changes across the life span and how these are affected by a person's genetic predispositions, culture, circumstances, and experiences. Some focus on children's mental and social development, including **socialization**, the process by which children learn the rules and behaviour expected of them by society. Others specialize in the study of adolescents, adults, or the very old. In this chapter, we will explore some of their major findings, starting at the very beginning of human development, with the period before birth, and continuing through adulthood into old age.

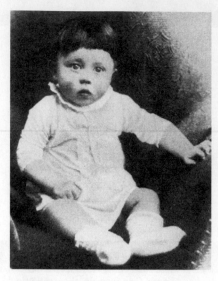

Development depends on the genetic hand you are dealt at birth, the resources and opportunities your parents provide for you, experiences that happen to you, and the unexpected events of history. What futures might you imagine for these three children? At the end of this chapter, you'll see who they are.

 YOU are about to learn . . .

◆ the stages of prenatal development and some factors that can harm an embryo or fetus during pregnancy.

◆ how culture affects a baby's physical maturation.

◆ why contact comfort and attachment are so important for infants (and adults).

◆ the varieties of infant attachment.

FROM CONCEPTION THROUGH THE FIRST YEAR

A baby's development, before and after birth, is a marvel of *maturation*, the sequential unfolding of genetically influenced behaviour and physical characteristics. In only nine months of a mother's pregnancy, a fetus grows from a dot this big (.) to a squalling bundle of energy who looks just like Aunt Sarah. In another 15 months, that bundle of energy grows into a babbling toddler who is curious about everything. No other time in human development brings so many changes so fast.

Prenatal Development

Prenatal development is divided into three stages: the germinal, the embryonic, and the fetal. The *germinal stage* begins at fertilization, when the male sperm unites with the female ovum (egg); the fertilized single-celled egg is called a *zygote*. The zygote soon begins to divide, and in 10 to 14 days it has become a cluster of cells that attaches itself to the wall of the uterus. The outer portion of this cluster will form part of the placenta and umbilical cord, and the inner portion becomes the embryo. The placenta, connected to the embryo by the umbilical cord, serves as the growing embryo's link

◀●Simulate
Psychology Experiments Survey: What Has Your Father Done for You?

👁Watch
Fetal Development

socialization   The process by which children learn the behaviours, attitudes, and expectations required of them by their society or culture.

for food from the mother. It allows nutrients to enter and wastes to exit, and it screens out some, but not all, harmful substances.

Once implantation is completed, about two weeks after fertilization, the *embryonic stage* begins, lasting until the eighth week after conception, at which point the embryo is only four centimetres long. During the fourth to eighth weeks, the hormone testosterone is secreted by the rudimentary testes in embryos that are genetically male; without this hormone, the embryo will develop to be anatomically female. After eight weeks, the *fetal stage* begins. The organism, now called a *fetus*, further develops the organs and systems that existed in rudimentary form in the embryonic stage.

Although the womb is a fairly sturdy protector of the growing embryo or fetus, the prenatal environment—which is influenced by the mother's own health, allergies, and diet—can affect the course of development, for example by predisposing an infant to later obesity or immune problems (Coe & Lubach, 2008). Most people don't realize it, but fathers play an important role in prenatal development, too. Because of genetic mutations, fathers over 50 have three times the risk of conceiving a child who develops schizophrenia as fathers under age 25 do (Malaspina, 2001); teenage fathers have an increased risk that their babies will be born prematurely or have low birth weight; babies of men exposed to solvents and other chemicals in the workplace are more likely to be miscarried or stillborn, or develop cancer later in life; and being an older father increases the probability that a child will be autistic or bipolar (Frans et al., 2008; Reichenberg et al., 2006; Saey, 2008).

During a woman's pregnancy, some harmful influences can cross the placental barrier (O'Rahilly & Müller, 2001). These influences include the following:

✱ Explore
The Embryonic Period

1 **German measles** (rubella), especially early in the pregnancy, can affect the fetus's eyes, ears, and heart. The most common consequence is deafness. Rubella is preventable if the mother has been vaccinated, which can be done up to three months before pregnancy.

⬅⊙ Simulate
Teratogens and Their Effects

2 **X rays or other radiation and toxic substances like lead** can cause fetal deformities and cognitive abnormalities that can last throughout life. Exposure to lead is associated with attention problems and lower IQ scores (see Chapter 3), as is exposure to mercury, found most commonly in contaminated fish (Newland & Rasmussen, 2003).

3 **Sexually transmitted diseases** can cause mental retardation, blindness, and other physical disorders. Genital herpes affects the fetus only if the mother has an outbreak at the time of delivery, which exposes the newborn to the virus as the baby passes through the birth canal. (This risk can be avoided by having a Caesarean section.) HIV, the virus that causes AIDS, can also be transmitted to the fetus, especially if the mother has developed AIDS and has not been treated.

4 **Cigarette smoking** during pregnancy increases the likelihood of miscarriage, premature birth, an abnormal fetal heartbeat, and an underweight baby. The negative effects may last long after birth, showing up in increased rates of infant sickness, sudden infant death syndrome (SIDS), and, in later childhood, hyperactivity, learning difficulties, asthma, and even antisocial behaviour (Button, Thapar, & McGuffin, 2005). Despite these dangers, only 25–40% of smokers quit smoking during pregnancy, and approximately 24% of Canadian women smoke cigarettes at some time during pregnancy (Connor & McIntyre, 1999; Moner, 1994). Moreover, most smokers resume smoking following the birth of their infant (Connor & McIntyre, 1999; Moner, 1994).

⊙ Watch
Effects of Prenatal Smoking on Children's Development

⊙ **Watch**
Fetal Alcohol Damage

5   Regular consumption of alcohol can kill neurons throughout the fetus's developing brain and impair the child's later mental abilities, attention span, and academic achievement (Ikonomidou et al., 2000; Streissguth, 2001). Having more than two drinks a day significantly increases the risk of *fetal alcohol syndrome (FAS)*, which is associated with low birth weight, a smaller brain, facial deformities, lack of coordination, and mental retardation. Because alcohol can affect many different aspects of fetal brain development, most specialists recommend that a pregnant woman abstain from drinking alcohol.

Before you think that FAS is not a problem in Canada—think again. Approximately 25% of Canadian women report consuming some alcohol during their pregnancy, and FAS is thought to affect one to three babies in every 1000 live births, a rate that means one FAS child is born every day in Canada (Health Canada, 1998). Unfortunately, FAS appears to disproportionately affect the impoverished and individuals who are ethnic minorities (Abel, 1995). Still, FAS is one of the most preventable of birth defects. According to Health Canada (2000), the incidence of FAS can be reduced through education. However, knowledge of FAS may not be enough to prevent its occurrence, as several studies have demonstrated. One study of a high-risk group observed that 51% of the women surveyed reported that they consumed alcohol during one or more of their pregnancies, although 80% of these same women indicated that they knew FAS was a possible consequence (Williams & Gloster, 1999). Furthermore, the rate of FAS has not decreased in 20 years—again, despite concentrated efforts to educate women about the causes and consequences of FAS (Habbick et al., 1996).

6   Drugs other than alcohol can be harmful to the fetus, whether they are illicit ones such as cocaine and heroin, or commonly used legal substances such as antibiotics, antihistamines, tranquilizers, acne medication, and diet pills. Cocaine can cause subtle impairments in children's cognitive and language abilities and larger ones in the ability to manage impulses and frustrations (Lester, LaGasse, & Seifer, 1998; Stanwood & Levitt, 2001).

The lesson is clear. A pregnant woman does well to stop smoking and drinking alcohol, and to take no other drugs of any kind unless they are medically necessary.

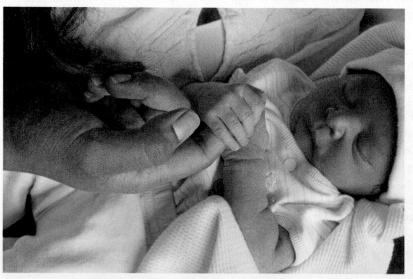

Infants are born with a grasping reflex; they will cling to any offered finger. And they need the comfort of touch, which their adult caregivers love to provide.

The Infant's World

Newborn babies could never survive on their own, but they are far from being passive and inert. Many abilities, tendencies, and characteristics are universal in human beings and are present at birth or develop very early, given certain experiences. Indeed, experience plays a crucial role in shaping the infant's mind, brain, and gene expression right from the get-go. For example, newborn infants who get little touching will grow more slowly and release less growth hormone than their amply cuddled peers, and throughout their lives they have stronger reactions to stress and are more prone to depression and its cognitive deficits (Diamond & Amso, 2008; Field, 2009).

PHYSICAL AND PERCEPTUAL ABILITIES. Newborns begin life with several *motor reflexes*, automatic behaviours that are necessary for survival. They will suck on anything suckable, such as a nipple or finger. They will tightly grasp a finger pressed on their tiny palms. They will turn their heads toward a touch on the cheek or corner of the mouth and search for something to suck on, a handy rooting reflex that allows them to find the breast or bottle. Many of these reflexes eventually disappear, but others—such as the knee-jerk, eye-blink, and sneeze reflexes—remain.

Babies are also equipped with a set of inborn perceptual abilities (see Chapter 6). They can see, hear, touch, smell, and taste (bananas and sugar water are in, rotten eggs are out). A newborn's visual focus range is only about 20 centimetres, the average distance between the baby and the face of the person holding the baby, but visual ability develops rapidly. Newborns can distinguish contrasts, shadows, and edges. And they can discriminate their mother or other primary caregiver on the basis of smell, sight, or sound almost immediately.

CULTURE AND MATURATION. Although infants everywhere develop according to the same maturational sequence, many aspects of their development depend on cultural customs that govern how their parents hold, touch, feed, and talk to them (Rogoff, 2003). For example, in Canada, and most other Western countries, babies are expected to sleep for eight uninterrupted hours by the age of four or five months. This milestone is considered a sign of neurological maturity, although many babies wail when the parent puts them in the crib at night and leaves the room. But among Mayan peoples, rural Italians, African villagers, Indian Rajput villagers, and urban Japanese, this nightly clash of wills rarely occurs because the infant sleeps with the mother for the first few years of life, waking and nursing about every four hours. These differences in babies' sleep arrangements reflect cultural and parental values. Mothers in these cultures believe that sleeping with the baby forges a close bond; in contrast, many urban North American and German parents believe it is important to foster the child's independence as soon as possible (Keller et al., 2005; Morelli et al., 1992).

Developmental milestones can change quickly when there is a cultural change in baby-care practices. For example, the milestone for crawling has traditionally been about six to eight months. Nowadays, however, many babies do not begin crawling at that age, or even at all; they go directly from sitting to toddling. Why? When babies are put to sleep on their stomachs, a little squirming and a push-up leads to crawling. But since the early 1990s, physicians have been advising parents to put babies on their backs to reduce the risk of suffocation. In that position, it is more difficult for a baby to roll over and start crawling, and more and more babies never do; yet they are perfectly normal by every other measure (Davis et al., 1998). And they all eventually get up and walk.

Most Navaho babies calmly accept being strapped to a cradle board (left), whereas non-Navaho babies will often protest vigorously (right). Yet despite cultural differences in such practices, babies everywhere eventually sit up and walk.

Attachment

Emotional attachment is a universal capacity of all primates and is crucial for health and survival all through life. The mother is usually the first and primary object of attachment for an infant, but in many cultures (and other species), babies become just as attached to their fathers, siblings, and grandparents (Hrdy, 1999).

Interest in the importance of early attachment began with the work of British psychiatrist John Bowlby (1969, 1973, 1982), who observed the devastating effects on babies raised in orphanages without touches or cuddles, and on other children raised in conditions of severe deprivation or neglect. The babies were physically healthy but emotionally despairing, remote, and listless. By becoming attached to their caregivers,

◆ **Research**
John Bowlby

FIGURE 13.1 The Comfort of Contact

Infants need cuddling as much as they need food. In Margaret and Harry Harlow's studies, infant rhesus monkeys were reared with a cuddly terry-cloth "mother" and with a bare wire "mother" that provided milk (left). The infants would cling to the terry mother when they were not being fed. And when they were frightened (as the infant on the right was by a toy spider put in his enclosure), it was the terry-cloth mother they ran to.

Bowlby said, children gain a secure base from which they can explore the environment and a haven of safety to return to when they are afraid. Ideally, infants will find a balance between feeling securely attached to the caregiver and feeling free to explore and learn in new environments. Recent research suggests that Bowlby's observations remain valid (Gunnar et al., 2007). Reactive Attachment Disorder, a failure to form normal attachment with primary caregivers, has been documented by following the outcomes of children raised in orphanages under conditions of severe deprivation (O'Connor et al., 2000). Long-term study of these children suggests that there are profound, long-lasting emotional and cognitive consequences of early deprivation (Colvert, Rutter, Beckett, et al., 2008; Colvert, Rutter, Krepner, et al., 2008).

CONTACT COMFORT. Attachment begins with physical touching and cuddling between infant and parent. **Contact comfort**, the pleasure of being touched and held, is not only crucial for newborns; it continues to be important throughout life, releasing a flood of pleasure-producing and stress-reducing endorphins (see Chapter 12). In hospital settings, for example, even the mildest touch by a nurse or physician on the patient's arm or forehead is reassuring psychologically and lowers blood pressure.

Margaret and Harry Harlow first demonstrated the importance of contact comfort by raising infant rhesus monkeys with two kinds of artificial mothers (Harlow, 1958; Harlow & Harlow, 1966). One, which they called the "wire mother," was a forbidding construction of wires and warming lights, with a milk bottle connected to it. The other, the "cloth mother," was constructed of wire but covered in foam rubber and cuddly terry cloth (see Figure 13.1). At the time, many psychologists thought that babies become attached to their mothers simply because mothers provide food (Blum, 2002). But the Harlows' baby monkeys ran to the terry-cloth mother when they were frightened or startled, and snuggling up to it calmed them down. Human children also seek contact comfort when they are in an unfamiliar situation, are scared by a nightmare, or fall and hurt themselves.

SEPARATION AND SECURITY. Once babies are emotionally attached to the mother or other caregiver, separation can be a wrenching experience. Between six and eight months of age, babies become wary or fearful of strangers. They wail if they are put in an unfamiliar setting or are left with an unfamiliar person. And they show

◆❖ **Research**
Harry Harlow

◉ **Watch**
Attachment in Infants

contact comfort In primates, the innate pleasure derived from close physical contact; it is the basis of the infant's first attachment.

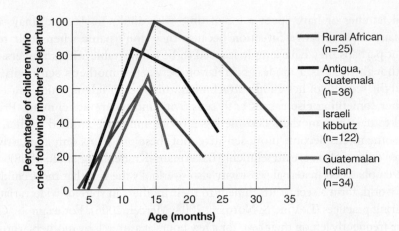

FIGURE 13.2 The Rise and Fall of Separation Anxiety

At around six months of age, many babies begin to show separation anxiety when the person who is their main source of attachment tries handing them over to someone else or leaves the room. This anxiety typically peaks at about one year of age and then steadily declines. But the proportion of children responding this way varies across cultures. It is high among rural African children and low among children raised in a communal Israeli kibbutz, where children become attached to many adults (Kagan, Kearsley, & Zelazo, 1978).

👁 **Watch**
Separation Anxiety

separation anxiety if the primary caregiver temporarily leaves them. This reaction usually continues until the middle of the second year, but many children show signs of distress until they are about three years old (Hrdy, 1999). All children go through this phase, though cultural child-rearing practices influence how strongly the anxiety is felt and how long it lasts (see Figure 13.2). In cultures where babies are raised with lots of adults and other children, separation anxiety is not as intense or as long-lasting as it can be in countries where babies form attachments primarily or exclusively with the mother (Rothbaum et al., 2000).

To study the nature of the attachment between mothers and babies, Mary Ainsworth (1973, 1979) devised an experimental method called the *Strange Situation*. A mother brings her baby into an unfamiliar room containing lots of toys. After a while a stranger comes in and attempts to play with the child. The mother leaves the baby with the stranger. She then returns and plays with the child, and the stranger leaves. Finally, the mother leaves the baby alone for three minutes and returns. In each case, observers carefully note how the baby behaves with the mother, with the stranger, and when the baby is alone.

Ainsworth divided children into three categories on the basis of their reactions to the Strange Situation. Some babies are *securely attached*: They cry or protest if the parent leaves the room; they welcome her back and then play happily again; they are clearly more attached to the mother than to the stranger. Other babies are *insecurely attached*, and this insecurity can take two forms. The child may be *avoidant*, not caring if the mother leaves the room, making little effort to seek contact with her on her return, and treating the stranger about the same as the mother. Or the child may be *anxious* or *ambivalent*, resisting contact with the mother at reunion but protesting loudly if she leaves. Anxious-ambivalent babies may cry to be picked up and then demand to be put down, or they may behave as if they are angry with the mother and resist her efforts to comfort them.

WHAT CAUSES INSECURE ATTACHMENT? Ainsworth believed that the difference between secure and avoidant or anxious-ambivalent attachment lies primarily in the way mothers treat their babies during the first year. Mothers who are sensitive and responsive to their babies' needs, she said, create securely attached infants; mothers who are uncomfortable with or insensitive to their babies create insecurely attached infants. To many, the implication was that babies needed exactly the right kind of mothering from the very start in order to become securely attached, and that putting a child in daycare would retard this important development—notions that have caused considerable insecurity among mothers!

Ainsworth's measure of attachment, however, did not take the baby's experience into account. Babies who become attached to many adults, because they live in large

STYLES OF ATTACHMENT

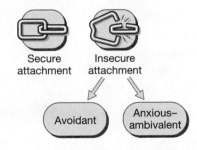

Secure attachment   Insecure attachment

Avoidant   Anxious–ambivalent

separation anxiety The distress that most children develop, at about six to eight months of age, when their primary caregivers temporarily leave them with strangers.

extended families or have spent a lot of time with adults in daycare, may seem to be avoidant in the Strange Situation because they don't panic when their mothers leave. But perhaps they have simply learned to be comfortable with strangers. Moreover, although there is a modest correlation between a mother's sensitivity to her child and the security of her child's attachment, this doesn't tell us which causes what, or whether something else causes both sensitivity and secure attachment. Programs designed to help new mothers become less anxious and more attuned to their babies do help some moms become more sensitive, but these programs only modestly affect the child's degree of secure attachment (Bakermans-Kranenburg et al., 2008).

The emphasis on maternal sensitivity also overlooks the fact that most children, all over the world, form a secure attachment to their mothers in spite of wide variations in child-rearing practices (LeVine & Norman, 2008; Mercer, 2006). For example, German babies are frequently left on their own for a few hours at a stretch by mothers who believe that even babies should become self-reliant. And among the Efe of Africa, babies spend about half their time away from their mothers in the care of older children and other adults (Tronick, Morelli, & Ivey, 1992). Yet German and Efe children are not insecure, and they develop as normally as children who spend more time with their mothers.

Likewise, time spent in daycare has no effect on the security of a child's attachment. In a longitudinal study of more than 1000 children, researchers compared infants who were in child care 30 hours or more a week, from age 3 months to age 15 months, with children who spent fewer than 10 hours a week in child care. The two groups did not differ on any measure of attachment (McKim et al., 1999; NICHD Early Child Care Research Network, 2006) and in fact, the group in daycare did better on some measures of cognition and language skills. Recently, Canadian researchers examined the question again and compared babies whose mothers went back to work before they were a year old with those who stayed home for longer (Baker & Milligan, 2010). They found very few differences between the two groups of children, in terms of motor skill, temperament, or acquisition of developmental milestones.

Longitudinal studies find that good daycare does not affect the security of children's attachments and often produces many social and intellectual benefits.

What factors, then, do promote insecure attachment?

- **Abandonment and deprivation in the first year or two of life.** Institutionalized babies are more likely than adopted children to have later problems with attachment, whereas babies adopted before age 1 or 2 eventually become as securely attached as their non-adopted peers (Rutter et al., 2004; van den Dries et al., 2009).

- **Parenting that is abusive, neglectful, or erratic because the parent is chronically irresponsible or clinically depressed.** A South African research team observed 147 mothers with their two-month-old infants and followed up when the babies were 18 months old. Many of the mothers who had suffered from postpartum depression became either too intrusive with their infants or too remote and insensitive. In turn, their babies were more likely to be insecurely attached at 18 months (Tomlinson, Cooper, & Murray, 2005).

- **The child's own genetically influenced temperament.** Babies who are fearful and prone to crying from birth are more likely to show insecure behaviour in the Strange Situation, suggesting that their later insecure attachment may reflect a temperamental predisposition (Belsky, Hsieh, & Crnic, 1996; Gillath et al., 2008; Seifer et al., 1996).

- **Stressful circumstances in the child's family.** Infants and young children may temporarily shift from secure to insecure attachment, becoming clingy and fearful of being left alone, if their families are undergoing a period of stress, as during parental divorce or a parent's chronic illness (Belsky et al., 1996; Mercer, 2006).

The bottom line, however, is that infants are biologically disposed to become attached to their caregivers. Normal, healthy attachment will occur within a wide range of cultural, family, and individual variations in child-rearing customs. Although, sadly, things can go wrong in prenatal development and in the first year after birth, the plasticity of the brain and human resilience can often overcome early deprivation or even harm. We will revisit the issue of resilience at the end of this chapter, and in "Taking Psychology with You" we will consider other information that might alleviate the anxieties many parents feel about whether they are doing the right thing.

Simulate
Attachment Classifications in the Strange Situation

Are you feeling secure, anxious, or avoidant about quizzes?

1. Name as many potentially harmful influences on fetal development as you can.
2. Melanie is playing happily on a jungle gym at her daycare centre when she falls off and badly scrapes her knee. She runs to her caregiver for a consoling cuddle. Melanie seeks _____.
3. *True or false:* To develop normally, infants must sleep in their own cribs, apart from their mothers.
4. A baby left in the Strange Situation does not protest when his mother leaves the room, and he seems to ignore her when she returns. What style of attachment does this behaviour reflect?
5. In question 4, what else besides the child's style of attachment could account for the child's reaction?

quickQUIZ

✓ **Quick Review** on **MyPsychLab**

Answers:

1. German measles early in pregnancy; exposure to radiation or toxic substances such as lead or mercury; sexually transmitted diseases; the mother's use of cigarettes, alcohol, or other drugs 2. contact comfort 3. false 4. insecure (avoidant) 5. the child's own temperament and familiarity with being temporarily left alone

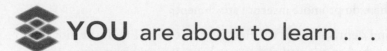

YOU are about to learn . . .

♦ two general ways that people explain their own or other people's behaviour—and why it matters.

♦ the importance of "baby talk" in the development of language.

♦ basic milestones in the development of language.

♦ Piaget's description of the major stages of cognitive development and their hallmarks.

♦ modern approaches to children's mental development.

COGNITIVE DEVELOPMENT

A friend of ours told us about a charming exchange he had with his two-year-old grandson. "You're very old," the little boy said. "Yes, I am," said his grandfather. "I'm very new," said the child. Two years old, and already this little boy's mind is working away, making observations, trying to understand the differences he observes, and using language (creatively!) to describe them. The development of language and thought from infancy throughout childhood is a marvel to anyone who has ever watched a baby grow up.

Language

In Chapter 3, we saw that the ability to use language is an evolutionary adaptation of the human species. In only a few years, children are able to understand thousands of words, use rules of syntax to string them together in meaningful sentences, and produce and understand an endless number of new word combinations.

The acquisition of language begins in the first few months. Infants may only be able to cry and coo, but they are already responsive to the pitch, intensity, and sound of language, and they react to the emotions and rhythms in voices. When most people speak to babies, their pitch is higher and more varied than usual and their intonation and emphasis on vowels are exaggerated. Adult use of baby talk, which researchers call *parentese*, has been documented all over the world. In fact, adult members of the Shuar, a nonliterate hunter-gatherer culture in South America, can accurately distinguish English-speaking mothers' infant-directed speech from their adult-directed speech just by tone (Bryant & Barrett, 2007). Parentese helps babies learn the melody and rhythm of their native language (Burnham, Kitamura, & Vollmer-Conna, 2002; Fernald & Mazzie, 1991).

By four to six months of age, babies can often recognize their own names and other words that are regularly spoken with emotion, such as "mommy" and "daddy." They also know many of the key consonant and vowel sounds of their native language and can distinguish such sounds from those of other languages (Kuhl et al., 1992). Over time, exposure to the baby's native language reduces

Say out loud, "Where is my nose?" Now repeat the question as if you were talking to this baby. Chances are your voice will shift to "parentese," becoming more singsong, rhythmic, and higher in pitch. The melodic rhythms of baby talk help babies learn language.

the child's ability to perceive speech sounds in other languages. Thus Japanese infants can hear the difference between the English sounds *la* and *ra*, but older Japanese children cannot. Because this contrast does not exist in their language, they become insensitive to it.

Between six months and one year, infants become increasingly familiar with the sound structure of their native language. They are able to distinguish words from the flow of speech. They will listen longer to words that violate their expectations of what words should sound like and even to sentences that violate their expectations of how sentences should be structured (Jusczyk, 2002). They start to babble, making many ba-ba and goo-goo sounds, endlessly repeating sounds and syllables. At seven months, they begin to remember words they have heard, but

Symbolic gestures emerge early!

because they are also attending to the speaker's intonation, speaking rate, and volume, they can't always recognize the same word when it is spoken by different people (Houston & Jusczyk, 2003). Then, by 10 months, they can suddenly do it—a remarkable leap forward in only three months. And at about one year of age, though the timing varies considerably, children take another giant step: They start to name things. They already have some concepts in their minds for familiar people and objects, and their first words represent these concepts ("mama," "doggie," "truck").

Also at the end of the first year, babies develop a repertoire of symbolic gestures. They gesture to refer to objects (e.g., sniffing to indicate "flower"), to request something (smacking the lips for "food"), to describe objects (raising the arms for "big"), and to reply to questions (opening the palms or shrugging the shoulders for "I don't know"). They clap in response to pictures of things they like. Children whose parents encourage them to use gestures acquire larger vocabularies, have better comprehension, are better listeners, and are less frustrated in their efforts to communicate than children who are not encouraged to use gestures (Goodwyn & Acredolo, 1998; Rowe & Goldin-Meadow, 2009). When babies begin to speak, they continue to gesture along with their words, just as adults often gesture when talking. These gestures are not a substitute for language but are deeply related to its development, as well as to the development of thinking and problem-solving (Goldin-Meadow, Cook, & Mitchell, 2009).

One surprising discovery is that babies who are given infant "brain stimulation" videos to look at are actually *slower* at acquiring words than babies who do not watch videos (Zimmerman, Christakis, & Meltzoff, 2007). Babies and children whose parents read to them, or even watch videos with them and talk about what they are all seeing, have larger vocabularies.

Between the ages of 18 months and two years, toddlers begin to produce words in two- or three-word combinations ("Mama here," "go 'way bug," "my toy"). The child's first combinations of words have been described as **telegraphic**. When people had to pay for every word in a telegram, they quickly learned to drop unnecessary articles (*a, an,* or *the*) and auxiliary verbs (*is* or *are*). Similarly, the two-word sentences of toddlers omit articles, word endings, auxiliary verbs, and other parts of speech, yet these sentences are remarkably accurate in conveying meaning. Children use two-word sentences to locate things ("there toy"), make demands ("more milk"), negate

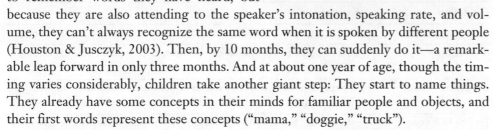

Watch

Language Learning

Child-Directed Speech

Stimulating Language Development

telegraphic speech A child's first word combinations, which omit (as a telegram did) unnecessary words.

actions ("no want," "all gone milk"), describe events ("Bambi go," "hit ball"), describe objects ("pretty dress"), show possession ("Mama dress"), and ask questions ("where Daddy?"). Two-year-olds also use syntax to help them acquire new verbs in context: They understand that "Jane blicked the baby!" involves two people, but the use of the same verb in "Jane blicked!" involves only Jane (Yuan & Fisher, 2009). Pretty good for a little kid, don't you think?

By the age of six, the average child has a vocabulary of between 8000 and 14 000 words, meaning that children acquire between five and eight new words a day between the ages of two and six. (When did you last learn and use five new words in a day?) They absorb new words as they hear them, inferring their meaning from their knowledge of grammatical contexts and from the social contexts in which they hear the words used (Golinkoff & Hirsh-Pasek, 2006; Rice, 1990).

Review 13.1 summarizes the early stages of language development.

REVIEW 13.1

The Early Development of Language

Guideline	Example
First few months	Babies cry and coo; they respond to emotions and rhythms in voices.
4–6 months	Babies begin to recognize key vowel and consonant sounds of their native language.
6 months–1 year	Infants' familiarity with the sound structure of their native language increases and they can distinguish words from the flow of speech.
End of first year	Infants start to name things based on familiar concepts and use symbolic gestures to communicate.
18–24 months	Children begin to speak in two- and three-word phrases (telegraphic speech) and understand verbs from the context in which they occur.
2–6 years	Children rapidly acquire new words, inferring their meaning from the grammatical and social contexts in which they hear them.

Thinking

Children do not think the way adults do. For most of the first year of life, if something is out of sight, it's out of mind: If you cover a baby's favourite rattle with a cloth, the baby thinks the rattle has vanished and stops looking for it. And a four-year-old may protest that a sibling has more fruit juice when it is only the shapes of the glasses that differ, not the amount of juice.

Yet children are smart in their own way. Like good little scientists, children are always testing their child-sized theories about how things work (Gopnik, Meltzoff, & Kuhl, 1999). When your toddler throws her spoon on the floor for the sixth time as you try to feed her, and you say, "That's enough! I will *not* pick up your spoon again!" the child will immediately test your claim. Are you serious? Are you angry? What will happen if she throws the spoon again? She is not doing this to drive you crazy; rather, she is learning that her desires and yours can differ, and that sometimes those differences are important and sometimes they are not.

How and why does children's thinking change? Do their cognitive abilities unfold naturally, like the blooming of a flower, almost independent of what else is happening

Like a good little scientist, this child is trying to figure out cause and effect: "If I throw this dish, what will happen? Will there be a noise? Will Mom come and give it back to me? How many times will she give it back to me?"

in their lives? Or are children little information processors, striving to make sense of things and solve problems, coming up with right and wrong answers depending on the problem at hand and what they have been taught?

In the 1920s, Swiss psychologist Jean Piaget [Zhan Pee-ah-ZHAY] (1896–1980) proposed a "flower-blooming" theory of cognitive development. Piaget was to child development what Freud was to psychoanalysis and Skinner to behaviourism. Although many of his specific conclusions have been rejected or modified over the years, his keen observations of children caused a revolution in thinking about how thinking develops. His ideas inspired thousands of studies by investigators all over the world.

PIAGET'S THEORY OF COGNITIVE STAGES. According to Piaget (1929/1960, 1984), as children develop, their minds constantly adapt to new situations and experiences. Sometimes they *assimilate* new information into their existing mental categories; for example, a Doberman and a terrier both fit the category *dogs*. At other times, however, children must change their mental categories to *accommodate* their new experiences; for example, a cat does not belong to the category *dogs* and a new category is required, one for *cats*. Both processes are constantly interacting, Piaget said, as children go through four stages of cognitive development.

From birth to age 2, said Piaget, babies are in the *sensorimotor stage*. In this stage, the infant learns through concrete actions: looking, touching, putting things in the mouth, sucking, grasping. "Thinking" consists of coordinating sensory information with bodily movements. Gradually these movements become more purposeful as the child explores the environment and learns that specific movements will produce specific results. Pulling a cloth away will reveal a hidden toy; letting go of a fuzzy toy duck will cause it to drop out of reach; banging on the table with a spoon will produce dinner (or Mom, taking the spoon away).

A major accomplishment at this stage, said Piaget, is **object permanence**, the understanding that something continues to exist even when you can't see or touch it. In the first few months, infants will look intently at a little toy, but if you hide it behind a piece of paper they will not look behind the paper or make an effort to get the toy. By about six months of age, however, infants begin to grasp the idea that the toy exists whether or not they can see it. If a baby of this age drops a toy from her playpen, she will look for it; she also will look under a cloth for a toy that is partially hidden. By one year of age, most babies have developed an awareness of the permanence of objects; even if a toy is covered by a cloth, it must be under there. This is when they love to play peekaboo. Object permanence, said Piaget, represents the beginning of the child's capacity to use mental imagery and symbols. The child becomes able to hold a concept in mind, to learn that the word *fly* represents an annoying, buzzing creature and that *Daddy* represents a friendly, playful one.

From about ages 2 to 7, the child's use of symbols and language accelerates. Piaget called this the *preoperational stage*, because he believed that children still lack the cognitive abilities necessary for understanding abstract principles and *mental operations*. An operation is a train of thought that can be run backward or forward. Multiplying 2 times 6 to get 12 is an operation; so is the reverse operation, dividing 12 by 6 to get 2. Thus a preoperational child knows that Jessie is his sister, but he may not get the reverse operation, the idea that he is Jessie's brother. Piaget also believed (mistakenly, as we will see) that preoperational children cannot take another person's point of view because their thinking is *egocentric*: They see the world only from their own frame of reference and cannot imagine that others see things differently.

Further, said Piaget, preoperational children cannot grasp the concept of **conservation**, the notion that physical properties do not change when their form or

◆ **Research**
Jean Piaget

✳ **Explore**
Piaget's Stages of Cognitive Development

object permanence The understanding, which develops throughout the first year, that an object continues to exist even when you cannot see it or touch it.

conservation The understanding that the physical properties of objects, such as the number of items in a cluster or the amount of liquid in a glass, can remain the same even when their form or appearance changes.

FIGURE 13.3 Piaget's Principle of Conservation
In a typical test for conservation of number (left), the number of blocks is the same in two sets, but those in one set are then spread out and the child must say whether one set has more blocks than another. Preoperational children think that the set that takes up more space has more blocks. In a test for conservation of quantity (right), the child is shown two short glasses with equal amounts of liquid. Then the contents of one glass are poured into a tall, narrower glass, and the child is asked whether one container now has more. Most preoperational children do not understand that pouring liquid from a short glass into a taller one leaves the amount of liquid unchanged. They judge only by the height of liquid in the glass.

appearance changes. Children at this age do not understand that an amount of liquid or a number of blocks remains the same even if you pour the liquid from one glass to another of a different size or if you stack the blocks (see Figure 13.3). If you pour liquid from a short, fat glass into a tall, narrow glass, preoperational children will say there is more liquid in the second glass. They attend to the appearance of the liquid (its height in the glass) to judge its quantity, and so they are misled.

From about ages 7 to 12, Piaget said, children become increasingly able to take other people's perspectives and make fewer logical errors. Piaget called this the *concrete operations stage* because he thought children's mental abilities are tied to information that is concrete, that is, to actual experiences that have happened or to concepts that have a tangible meaning for them. Children at this stage make errors of reasoning when they are asked to think about abstract ideas such as "patriotism" or "future education." During these years, nonetheless, children's cognitive abilities expand rapidly. They come to understand the principles of conservation, reversibility, and cause and effect. They learn mental operations, such as addition, subtraction, multiplication, and division. They are able to categorize things (e.g., oaks as trees) and to order things serially from smallest to largest, lightest to darkest, and shortest to tallest.

Get INVOLVED!

A TEST OF CONSERVATION

If you know any young children, try one of Piaget's conservation experiments. A simple one is to make two rows of seven buttons or pennies, aligned identically. Ask the child whether one row has more. Now simply spread out the buttons in one of the rows, and ask the child again whether one row has more. If the child says "Yes," ask which one, and why. Try to do this experiment with a three-year-old and a seven- or eight-year-old. You will probably see a big difference in their answers.

Finally, said Piaget, beginning at about age 12 or 13 and continuing into adulthood, people become capable of abstract reasoning and enter the *formal operations stage*. They are able to reason about situations they have not experienced firsthand, and they can think about future possibilities. They are able to search systematically for answers to problems. They are able to draw logical conclusions from premises common to their culture and experience.

VYGOTSKY'S THEORY OF SOCIOCULTURAL INFLUENCES. North Americans were forever asking Piaget what they could do to speed up their children's mental development. Piaget was amused by what he called "the American question." Forget it, he would tell them. You can't rush the qualitative changes that occur as children go through each cognitive stage.

In contrast, the Russian psychologist Lev Vygotsky (1896–1934) emphasized the *sociocultural* influences on children's cognitive development. Vygotsky (1962, 1978) believed that the child develops mental representations of the world through culture and language, and that adults do play a major role in their children's development by constantly guiding and teaching them. Once children acquire language and internalize the rules of their culture, said Vygotsky, they start using *private speech*, talking to themselves to direct their own behaviour. At first, children's private speech is actually spoken aloud. You can often observe preschoolers talking to themselves when they have done something they know is naughty or when they are faced with a problem. Over time, private speech becomes internalized and silent.

◆ **Research**
Lev Vygotsky

Vygotsky did not share Piaget's view that children go through invariant stages. Once children have language, he said, their cognitive development may proceed in any number of directions, depending on what adults teach them, what their culture makes possible for them, and the particular environment they live in.

CURRENT VIEWS OF COGNITIVE DEVELOPMENT. Piaget was a brilliant observer of children, and his major point has been well supported: New reasoning abilities depend on the emergence of previous ones. You cannot learn algebra before you can count, and you cannot learn philosophy before you understand logic. But since Piaget's original work, the field of developmental psychology has undergone an explosion of imaginative research that has allowed investigators to get into the minds of even the youngest infants. The result has been a modification of Piaget's ideas, and some scientists go so far as to say that his ideas have been overturned. Here's why:

1 **Cognitive abilities develop in continuous, overlapping waves rather than discrete steps or stages.** If you observe children at different ages, as Piaget did, it will seem that they reason differently. But if you study the everyday learning of children at any given age, you will find that a child may use several different strategies to solve a problem, some more complex or accurate than others (Siegler, 2006). Learning occurs gradually, with retreats to former ways of thinking as well as advances to new ones. Children's reasoning ability also depends on the circumstances—who is asking them questions, the specific words used, the materials used, and what they are reasoning about—and not just on the stage they are in. In short, cognitive development is *continuous*; new abilities do not simply pop up when a child turns a certain age (Courage & Howe, 2002).

2 **Preschoolers are not as egocentric as Piaget thought.** Most three- and four-year-olds *can* take another person's perspective (Flavell, 1999). When four-year-olds play with two-year-olds, for example, they modify and simplify their speech so the younger children will understand (Shatz & Gelman, 1973). One preschooler

Possible event

Impossible event

FIGURE 13.4 Testing Infants' Knowledge

In this clever procedure, a baby watches as a box is pushed from left to right along a striped platform. The box is pushed until it reaches the end of the platform (a possible event) or until only a bit of it rests on the platform (an impossible event). Babies look longer at the impossible event, suggesting that it surprises them. Somehow they know that an object needs physical support and can't just float on air (Baillargeon, 1994).

theory of mind A system of beliefs about the way one's own mind and the minds of others work, and of how individuals are affected by their beliefs and feelings.

we know showed her teacher a picture she had drawn of a cat and an unidentifiable blob. "The cat is lovely," said the teacher, "but what is this thing here?" "That has nothing to do with you," said the child. "That's what the *cat* is looking at."

By about ages 3 to 4, children also begin to understand that you cannot predict what a person will do just by observing a situation or knowing the facts. You also have to know what the person is feeling and thinking; the person might even be lying. They start asking why other people behave as they do ("Why is Johnny so mean?"). In short, they are developing a **theory of mind**, a system of beliefs about how their own and other people's minds work and how people are affected by their beliefs and emotions (see Chapter 9). They start using verbs like *think* and *know*, and by age 4 they understand that what another person thinks might not match their own beliefs (Flavell, 1999; Wellman, Cross, & Watson, 2001). The ability to understand that people can have false beliefs is a milestone, because it means the child is beginning to question how we know things—the foundation for later higher-order thinking.

3 **Children, even infants, reveal cognitive abilities much earlier than Piaget believed possible.** Taking advantage of the fact that infants look longer at novel or surprising stimuli than at familiar ones, psychologists have designed delightfully innovative methods of testing what babies know. These methods reveal that babies may be born with mental modules or core knowledge systems for numbers, spatial relations, the properties of objects, and other features of the physical world (Izard et al., 2009; Spelke & Kinzler, 2007; see Chapter 3).

For example, at only four months of age, babies will look longer at a ball if it seems to roll through a solid barrier, leap between two platforms, or hang in midair than they do when the ball obeys the laws of physics. This suggests that the unusual event is surprising to them (see Figure 13.4). Infants as young as two-and-a-half to three-and-a-half months are aware that objects continue to exist even when masked by other objects, a form of object permanence that Piaget never imagined possible in babies so young (Baillargeon, 2004). And, most devastating to Piaget's notion of infant egocentrism, even five-month-old infants are able to perceive other people's actions as being intentional; they detect the difference between a person who is reaching for a toy with her hand rather than accidentally touching it with a stick (Woodward, 2009). Even three-month-old infants can learn this. At that tender age,

Experience and culture influence cognitive development. Children who work with clay, wood, and other materials, such as this young potter in India, tend to understand the concept of conservation sooner than children who have not had this kind of experience.

they are obviously not yet skilled at intentionally reaching for objects. But when experimenters covered their little hands with "sticky mittens"—covered with Velcro—so that soft toys would stick to them, the babies actually learned from that experience to distinguish the intentional versus accidental reaches of others (Sommerville, Woodward, & Needham, 2005).

4 **Cognitive development is influenced by a child's culture.** Vygotsky was correct that culture—the world of tools, language, rituals, beliefs, games, and social institutions—shapes and structures children's cognitive development, fostering some abilities and not others (Tomasello, 2000). For example, nomadic hunters excel in spatial abilities, because spatial orientation is crucial for finding watering holes and successful hunting

routes. In contrast, children who live in settled agricultural communities develop the ability to quantify rapidly but are much slower at developing spatial reasoning.

Despite these modifications, Piaget left an enduring legacy: the insight that children are not passive vessels into which education and experience are poured. Children actively interpret their worlds, using their developing abilities to assimilate new information and figure things out.

Please use language (and thought) to answer these questions.

1. "More cake!" and "Mommy come" are examples of _____ speech.
2. Understanding that two rows of six pennies are equal in number, even if one row is flat and the other is stacked up, is an example of _____.
3. Understanding that a toy exists even after Mom puts it in her purse is an example of _____.
4. Three-year-old Tasha accidentally breaks a glass. "You bad girl!" she exclaims. Reprimanding herself is an example of Vygotsky's notion of _____.
5. A five-year-old boy who tells his dad that "Sally said she saw a bunny but she was lying" has developed a _____.
6. List four findings from contemporary research on children's cognitive development that have modified Piaget's theory.

Answers:

1. telegraphic 2. conservation 3. object permanence 4. private speech 5. theory of mind 6. The changes from one stage to another occur in continuous, overlapping waves rather than distinct stages. Children are less egocentric than Piaget thought. Infants and young children reveal cognitive abilities much earlier than Piaget believed possible. And cognitive development is affected by cultural practices and experiences.

YOU are about to learn . . .

♦ how moral feelings and behaviour develop.

♦ why shouting "Because I say so!" does not get most children to behave well.

♦ the importance of a child's ability to delay gratification.

MORAL DEVELOPMENT

How do children learn to tell right from wrong, resist the temptation to behave selfishly, and obey the rules of social conduct? In the 1960s, Lawrence Kohlberg (1964), inspired by Piaget's work, argued that children's ability to understand right from wrong evolved along with the rest of their cognitive abilities, progressing through three levels. In studies of how children reason about moral dilemmas, he found that very young children obey rules because they fear being punished if they disobey, and later because they think it is in their best interest to obey. At about age 10, their moral judgments shift to ones based on conformity and loyalty to others, and then to an understanding of the rule of law. In adulthood, a few individuals go on to develop a moral standard based on universal human rights. For example, Martin Luther King, Jr. fought against laws supporting segregation, Mohandas

How do children internalize moral rules? How do they learn that cheating, stealing, and grabbing a younger sibling's toy are wrong?

◆ Research
Lawrence Kohlberg

◆○ Simulate
Kohlberg's Stages of Moral
Reasoning

✱ Explore
Ages and Stages of Cognitive and
Moral Development

◉ Watch
Temperament

Gandhi advocated nonviolent solutions to injustice, and Nellie McClung fought for women's rights.

Kohlberg was right that moral reasoning ability increases during the school years. Unfortunately, so do cheating, lying, cruelty, and the cognitive ability to rationalize these actions. As Thomas Lickona (1983) wryly summarized, "We can reach high levels of moral-reasoning, and still behave like scoundrels." Accordingly, developmental psychologists today place greater emphasis on how children learn to regulate their own emotions and behaviour (Mischel & Ayduk, 2004). Most children learn to inhibit their wishes to hit their younger siblings, steal a classmate's toy, or scream at the top of their lungs if they don't get their way. The child's emerging ability to understand right from wrong, and to behave accordingly, depends on the emergence of conscience and moral emotions such as shame, guilt, and empathy (Kochanska et al., 2005).

As we saw in discussing criticisms of Piaget's theory, even very young children are capable of feeling empathy for others and taking another person's point of view. Children do not obey rules only because they are afraid of what will happen to them if they disobey, but also because they understand right and wrong. By age 5, they know it is wrong to hurt someone even if a teacher tells them to (Turiel, 2002). Therefore, many psychologists conclude that the capacity for differentiating right from wrong, like that for language, is inborn. Jerome Kagan (1984) wrote, "Without this fundamental human capacity, which nineteenth-century observers called a *moral sense*, the child could not be socialized." Evolutionary psychologists argue that this moral sense underlies the basic beliefs, judgments, and behaviour that are considered moral almost everywhere, and that it originated in cooperative, altruistic strategies that permitted our forebears to resolve conflicts and get along (Krebs, 2008).

Can the moral sense and a desire to behave well with others be nurtured or extinguished by specific methods of child rearing? For decades, most developmental psychologists assumed that the answer was "Of course!" and they set about trying to pinpoint which parental techniques create well-behaved, kind, unselfish children. Then came a flood of behavioural–genetic studies that led to a very different assumption: The effects of the parents' methods depend—of course!—on the kind of child they have. Is it a child who heeds discipline or one who becomes more resistant and hostile? One who is easygoing or one who is difficult?

Today many researchers are seeking a middle ground by studying gene–environment interactions (Schmidt et al., 2009). For example, as we discuss in Chapter 15, aggressive, antisocial adolescents often have a history of maltreatment and abuse in childhood *and* a gene variant linked to aggressive behaviour. Good parenting, however, can help to override a genetic vulnerability. One controversial hypothesis suggests that infants and toddlers who show high levels of distress and irritability are actually more responsive to, and influenced by, styles of parenting than easygoing babies are. When temperamentally difficult babies have impatient, rejecting, or coercive parents, they later tend to become aggressive and even more difficult and defiant. When they have patient, supportive, firm parents, they become better-natured and happier. In contrast, easygoing babies may not benefit as much from good parenting nor suffer as much from bad parenting because they are, well, easygoing (Belsky, Bakermans-Kranenburg, & van IJzendoorn, 2007; Belsky & Pluess, 2009).

Keeping the complexity of this issue in mind, let's look at how parental discipline methods interact with a child's temperament in the development of conscience and moral behaviour.

Power assertion is the use of physical force, threats, insults, or other kinds of power to get the child to obey ("Do it because I say so!" "Stop that right now!"). The child may obey, but only when the parent is present, and the child often feels resentful.

The parent who uses induction appeals to the child's good nature, empathy, love for the parent, and sense of responsibility toward others and offers explanations of rules ("You're too grown up to behave like that"; "Fighting hurts your little brother"). The child tends to internalize reasons for good behaviour.

GETTING CHILDREN TO BE GOOD. When you did something wrong as a child, did the adults in your family spank you, shout at you, threaten you, or explain the error of your ways? One of the most common methods used by parents to enforce moral standards and good behaviour is **power assertion**, which includes threats, physical punishment, depriving the child of privileges, and generally taking advantage of being bigger, stronger, and more powerful. Of course, a parent may have no alternative other than "Do it because I say so!" if the child is too young to understand a rule or impishly keeps trying to break it. Moreover, the culture and context in which the discipline occurs makes an enormous difference. Is the parent–child relationship fundamentally loving and trusting or is it one full of hostility and fighting? Does the child interpret the parents' actions as being fair and caring, or unfair and cruel?

When power assertion consists of sheer parental bullying, cruel insults ("You are so stupid, I wish you'd never been born"), and frequent physical punishment, it is associated with greater aggressiveness in children and reduced empathy (Alink et al., 2009; Gershoff, 2002; Moore & Pepler, 2006). As we saw in Chapter 7, physical punishment often backfires, especially when it is used inappropriately or harshly; it spirals out of control, causing the child to become angry and resentful. Moreover, harsh but ineffective discipline methods are often transmitted to the next generation: Aggressive parents teach their children that the way to discipline children is by behaving aggressively (Capaldi et al., 2003).

What is the alternative? In contrast to power assertion, a parent can use **induction**, appealing to the child's own abilities, empathy, helpful nature, affection for others, and sense of responsibility ("You made Doug cry; it's not nice to bite"; "You must never poke anyone's eyes because that could seriously hurt them"). Or the parent might appeal to the child's own helpful inclinations ("I know you're a person who likes

←◉ Simulate
Baumrind's Parenting Styles

power assertion A method of child rearing in which the parent uses punishment and authority to correct the child's misbehaviour.

induction A method of child rearing in which the parent appeals to the child's own abilities, sense of responsibility, and feelings for others in correcting the child's misbehaviour.

Children's abilities to regulate their impulses and delay gratification are important milestones in the development of conscience and moral behaviour.

👁 **Watch**
Death of the Family Dinner

to be nice to others") rather than citing external reasons to be good ("You'd better be nice or you won't get dessert").

SELF-CONTROL AND CONSCIENCE. One of the most important social-emotional skills that children need to acquire is *self-regulation*, the ability to suppress their initial wish to do something in favour of doing something else that is not as much fun. This ability predicts a child's ability to delay gratification now for a larger reward later, control negative emotions, pay attention to the task at hand, and do well in school, from kindergarten to university (Eigsti et al., 2006; Ponitz et al., 2009). Children who can self-regulate usually do so across situations—even on holidays!—and this ability becomes a fairly stable aspect of personality (Raffaelli, Crockett, & Shen, 2005).

To explore the links between parental discipline, the child's self-regulation, and the emergence of conscience, Grazyna Kochanska and Amy Knaack (2003) conducted a longitudinal study of 106 children at ages 22, 33, and 45 months. When the children were 56 and 73 months old, the researchers measured the development of conscience by giving the children a series of charming tests disguised as games. Some of the games required the child to whisper instead of shout, walk instead of run, ignore the dominant image in a picture and find a more subtle one, and delay gratification by not reaching immediately for an M&M under a cup or by resisting the urge to open a bag to get out a toy. The researchers also observed what the mothers did when they were asked to get their child to clean up the play area or to prevent the child from playing with some appealing, easily accessible toys. Did the mother explain the reasons for her request to the child (induction) or did she issue strict orders (power assertion)? After interacting with her child, the mother left the room, and the child was free to obey or disobey. The researchers observed what the child did in her absence.

When the children were 56 months old, the researchers assessed the children's conscience in several moral realms, including being willing to apologize, feeling empathy, being concerned about others' wrongdoing, feeling guilty after doing something naughty or wrong, and being concerned about their parents' feelings. The researchers also measured the children's actual behaviour—for example, whether they cheated on the rules in playing a ball-tossing game. Then the researchers devised a composite conscience score for each child. Finally, when the children were 73 months old, their mothers rated them on the frequency of antisocial problems such as being irritable and quick to fly off the handle, destroying their own or others' belongings, and fighting with other children.

The children who were most able to regulate their impulses early in life were the least likely to get in trouble later by fighting or destroying things, and the most likely to have a high conscience score at 56 months of age. Self-regulation was negatively correlated with the mother's use of power assertion, meaning that mothers who ordered their children to "behave" tended to have children who were impulsive and aggressive (see also Alink et al., 2009). But cause and effect worked in both directions: Some mothers relied on power assertion *because* their children were impulsive, defiant, and aggressive and would not listen to them. This pattern of findings teaches us to avoid oversimplification by concluding that "It's all in what the mother does" or that "It's all in the child's personality." Mothers and children, it seems, raise each other.

YOU are about to learn . . .

◆ why some people fail to identify themselves as either male or female.
◆ the biological explanation of why most little boys and girls are "sexist" in their choice of toys, at least for a while.
◆ when and how children learn that they are male or female.
◆ learning explanations of some typical sex differences in childhood behaviour.

GENDER DEVELOPMENT

No parent ever excitedly calls a relative to exclaim, "It's a baby! It's a black-haired baby!" The baby's sex is the first thing everyone notices and announces. How soon do children notice that boys and girls are different sexes and understand which sex they themselves are? How do children learn the rules of masculinity and femininity, the things that boys do that are different from what girls do? Why, as one friend of ours observed, do most preschool children act like the "gender police," insisting, say, that boys can't be nurses and girls can't be doctors? And why do some children come to feel they don't belong to the sex everyone else thinks they do?

Gender Identity

Let's start by clarifying some terms. **Gender identity** refers to a child's sense of being male or female, of belonging to one sex and not the other. **Gender typing** is the process of socializing children into their gender roles, and thus reflects society's ideas about which abilities, interests, traits, and behaviours are appropriately masculine or feminine. A person can have a strong gender identity and not be gender typed: A man may be confident in his maleness and not feel threatened by doing "unmasculine" things such as needlepoint; a woman may be confident in her femaleness and not feel threatened by doing "unfeminine" things such as serving in combat.

In the past, psychologists tried to distinguish the terms *sex* and *gender*, reserving "sex" for the physiological or anatomical attributes of males and females and "gender" for differences that are learned. Thus they might speak of a sex difference in the frequency of baldness but a gender difference in fondness for romance novels. Today, these two terms are often used interchangeably because, as we have noted repeatedly in this book, nature and nurture are inextricably linked (Roughgarden, 2004).

↔⊙ **Simulate**
Psychology Experiments Survey:
How Does Gender Affect You?

gender identity   The fundamental sense of being male or female; it is independent of whether the person conforms to the social and cultural rules of gender.

gender typing   The process by which children learn the abilities, interests, and behaviours associated with being masculine or feminine in their culture.

Ann Bonny *and* Mary Read *convicted of Piracy Nov.* 28th 1720 *at a Court of Vice Admiralty held at* S.t Jago de la Vega *in ye Island of Jamaica.*

Throughout history and across cultures, there have been people who broke out of conventional gender categories. Some women have lived as men, as did the eighteenth-century pirates Ann Bonny and Mary Read (left). Some men have lived as women: The Muxes (pronounced moo-shays) of Oaxaca, Mexico, are men who consider themselves women, live as women, and are a socially accepted category. Carmelo López Bernal, age 13, first appeared publicly as a female at the annual town-wide muxe celebration (centre). Chaz Bono (right), who was born and raised female, has come out as a male, and is an LGBT activist.

The complexity of sex and gender development is especially apparent in the cases of people who do not fit the familiar categories of male and female. Every year, thousands of babies are born with **intersex conditions**, formerly known as *hermaphroditism*. In these conditions, chromosomal or hormonal anomalies cause the child to be born with ambiguous genitals, or genitals that conflict with the infant's chromosomes, and the child becomes "gender variant." A child who is genetically female, for example, might be born with an enlarged clitoris that looks like a penis. A child who is genetically male might be born with androgen insensitivity, a condition that causes the external genitals to appear female.

As adults, many intersexed individuals call themselves *transgender*, a term describing a broad category of people who do not fit comfortably into the usual categories of male and female, masculine and feminine. Some transgender people are comfortable living with the physical attributes of both sexes, considering themselves to be "gender queer" and even refusing to be referred to as *he* or *she*. Some feel uncomfortable in their sex of rearing and wish to be considered a member of the other sex. You have probably also heard the term *transsexual*, describing people who are not intersexed yet who feel that they are male in a female body or vice versa; their gender identity is at odds with their anatomical sex or appearance. Many transsexuals try to make a full transition to the other sex through surgery or hormones. Intersexed people and transsexuals have been found in virtually all cultures throughout history (Denny, 1998; Roughgarden, 2004).

Influences on Gender Development

To understand the typical course of gender development, as well as the variations, developmental psychologists study the interacting influences of biology, cognition, and learning on gender identity and gender typing.

intersex conditions (intersexuality) Conditions in which chromosomal or hormonal anomalies cause a child to be born with ambiguous genitals, or genitals that conflict with the infant's chromosomes.

BIOLOGICAL INFLUENCES. Starting in the preschool years, boys and girls congregate primarily with other children of their sex, and most prefer the toys and games of their own sex. They will play together if required to, but given their druthers, they usually choose to play with same-sex friends. The kind of play that young boys and girls enjoy also differs, on average. Little boys, like young males in all primate species, are more likely than females to go in for physical roughhousing, risk taking, and aggressive displays. These sex differences occur all over the world, almost regardless of how adults treat children—for example, whether they encourage boys and girls to play together or separate them (Lytton & Romney, 1991; Maccoby, 1998, 2002). Many parents lament that although they try to give their children the same toys, it makes no difference; their sons want trucks and guns and their daughters want dolls.

Biological researchers believe that these play and toy preferences have a basis in prenatal hormones, particularly the presence or absence of prenatal androgens (masculinizing hormones). Girls who were exposed to higher-than-normal prenatal androgens in the womb are later more likely than nonexposed girls to prefer "boys' toys" such as cars and fire engines, and they are also more physically aggressive than other girls (Berenbaum & Bailey, 2003). A study of more than 200 healthy children in the general population also found a relation between fetal testosterone and play styles. (Testosterone is produced in fetuses of both sexes, although it is higher on average in males.) The higher the levels of fetal testosterone, as measured in the amniotic fluid of the children's mothers during pregnancy, the higher the children's later scores on a measure of male-typical play (Auyeung et al., 2009). In studies of rhesus monkeys, who of course are not influenced by their parents' possible gender biases, male monkeys, like human boys, consistently and strongly prefer to play with wheeled toys rather than cuddly plush toys, while female monkeys, like human girls, are more varied in their toy preferences (Hassett, Siebert, & Wallen, 2008).

Do these findings have anything to do with gender identity, the core sense of being male or female? In the past, gender identity was believed to be almost entirely learned, a result of the child's socialization and learning. Then, a few years ago, a widely publicized case study appeared to show that gender identity is hardwired in the brain. At the age of seven months, a genetically and hormonally male child had lost his penis in a freak accident during a routine surgical procedure. When he was nearly two years old, his desperate parents, on the advice of a leading scientist in the field of gender identity, agreed to raise him as a girl, renaming him Brenda. But Brenda preferred boys' toys and by the age of 14 refused to keep living as a female. Her father told her the truth and, in relief, Brenda turned to a male identity (Diamond & Sigmundson, 1997). He changed his name to David, had reconstructive surgery to build a penis, and, in his twenties, got married. Tragically, the story did not end happily. After David's twin brother, who had schizophrenia, committed suicide, and after David lost his job and separated from his wife, he became deeply depressed. At the age of 38, David killed himself.

Unfortunately, dramatic case studies such as this one cannot really tell us whether gender identity is fixed in the brain prenatally. Perhaps David's experience was atypical. Perhaps there is a critical period after

Look familiar? In a scene typical of many nursery schools and homes, the boy builds a gun out of anything he can, and the girl dresses up in any pretty thing she can find. Whether or not such behaviour is biologically based, the gender rigidity of the early years does not inevitably continue into adulthood unless cultural rules reinforce it.

Thinking Critically

Tolerate Uncertainty

Most people fall into the categories "male" or "female." This makes it difficult for parents and doctors to be certain about how best to treat infants who are born with intersex conditions. Should such infants be assigned surgically to one sex or the other, or should they be left alone until they are grown? In the absence of clear answers, how would you make this decision?

gender schema A cognitive schema (mental network) of knowledge, beliefs, metaphors, and expectations about what it means to be male or female.

birth during which gender identity develops. (David's parents did not decide to raise him as a girl until he was nearly two.) A psychologist who reviewed hundreds of cases of children whose sex of rearing was discrepant with their anatomical or genetic sex found that the picture is enormously complex: A person's gender identity depends on the interactions of genes, prenatal hormones, anatomical structures, and experiences in life (Zucker, 1999). As a result, the outcome in any particular case is hard to predict. Consider a longitudinal study of 16 genetic males who had a rare condition that caused them to be born without a penis. The babies were otherwise normal males, with testicles and appropriate androgen levels. Two of the boys were raised as male and developed a male gender identity. Fourteen had been socially and surgically assigned to the female sex, according to the custom when they were born. Of those 14, eight have declared themselves male, five are living as females, and one has an unclear gender identity (Reiner & Gearheart, 2004).

COGNITIVE INFLUENCES. Cognitive psychologists explain the mystery of children's gender segregation and toy and play preferences by studying children's changing cognitive abilities. Even before babies can speak, they recognize that there are two sexes. By the age of nine months, most babies can discriminate male from female faces (Fagot & Leinbach, 1993), and they can match female faces with female voices (Poulin-Dubois et al., 1994). By the age of 18 to 20 months, most toddlers have a concept of gender labels; for example, they can accurately identify the gender of people in picture books and begin correctly using the words *boy*, *girl*, and *man* (interestingly, *lady* and *woman* come later) (Zosuls et al., 2009).

Once children can label themselves and others consistently as being a boy or a girl, shortly before age 2, they change their behaviour to conform to the category they belong to. Many begin to prefer same-sex playmates and sex-traditional toys without being explicitly taught to do so (Martin, Ruble, & Szkrybalo, 2002; Zosuls et al., 2009). They become more gender typed in their toy play, games, aggressiveness, and verbal skills than children who still cannot consistently label males and females. Most notably, girls stop behaving aggressively (Fagot, 1993). It is as if they go along behaving like boys until they know they are girls. At that moment, they seem to decide: "Girls don't do this; I'm a girl; I'd better not either."

It's great fun to watch three- to five-year-old children struggle to figure out what makes boys and girls different: "The ones with eyelashes are girls; boys don't have eyelashes," said one four-year-old girl to her aunt in explaining her drawing. After dinner at an Italian restaurant, a four-year-old boy told his parents that he'd got the answer: "Men eat pizza and women don't" (Bjorkland, 2000).

At about age 5, most children develop a stable gender identity, a sense of themselves as being male or female regardless of what they wear or how they behave. Only then do they understand that what boys and girls do does not necessarily indicate what sex they are: A girl remains a girl even if she can climb a tree (or eats a pizza!), and a boy remains a boy even if he has long hair. At this age, children consolidate their knowledge, with all of its mistakes and misconceptions, into a **gender schema**, a mental network of beliefs and expectations about what it means to be male or female and about what each sex is supposed to wear, do, feel, and think (Bem, 1993; Martin & Ruble, 2004). Gender schemas even include metaphors. For example, after age 4, children of both sexes will usually say that rough, spiky, black, or mechanical

"Jason, I'd like to let you play, but soccer is a girls' game."

things are male and that soft, pink, fuzzy, or flowery things are female; that black bears are male and pink poodles are female (Leinbach, Hort, & Fagot, 1997). Gender schemas are most rigid between ages 5 and 7; at this age, it's really hard to dislodge a child's notion of what boys and girls can do (Martin, Ruble, & Szkrybalo, 2002). A little girl at this stage may tell you stoutly that "girls can't be doctors" even if her own mother is a doctor.

Many people retain inflexible gender schemas throughout their lives, feeling uncomfortable or angry with men or women who break out of traditional roles—let alone with transgendered individuals who don't fit either category or want to change the one they grew up with. However, with experience and cognitive sophistication, older children often become more flexible in their gender schemas, especially if they have friends of the other sex and if their families and cultures encourage such flexibility (Martin & Ruble, 2004). Children begin to modify their gender schemas, understanding, for example, that women can be engineers and men can be cooks.

Cultures and religions, too, differ in their schemas for the roles of women and men. In all Western, industrialized nations, it is taken for granted that women and men alike should be educated; indeed, laws mandate a minimum education for both sexes. But in cultures where female education is prohibited in the name of religious law, as in the parts of Afghanistan controlled by the Taliban, many girls who attend school receive death threats and some have had acid thrown on their faces. Gender schemas can be very powerful, and events that challenge their legitimacy can be enormously threatening.

LEARNING INFLUENCES. A third influence on gender development is the environment, which is full of subtle and not-so-subtle messages about what girls and boys are supposed to do. Behavioural and social-cognitive learning theorists study how the process of gender socialization instills these messages in children (Bussey & Bandura, 1999). They find that gender socialization begins at the moment of birth. Parents tend to portray their newborn girls as more feminine and delicate than boys, and boys as stronger and more athletic than girls, although it is hard to know how athletic a newborn boy could be (Karraker, Vogel, & Lake, 1995). Many parents are careful to dress their baby in outfits they consider to be the correct colour and pattern for his or her sex. Clothes don't matter to the infant, of course, but they are signals to adults about how to treat the child. Adults often respond to the same baby differently, depending on whether the child is dressed as a boy or a girl.

Parents, teachers, and other adults convey their beliefs and expectations about gender even when they are entirely unaware that they are doing so. For example, when parents believe that boys are naturally better at math or sports and that girls are naturally better at English, they unwittingly communicate those beliefs by how

Get **INVOLVED!**

GENDER AND GENERATIONS

Gender norms have been changing rapidly, and one way to see this for yourself is to interview older members of your family. Ask at least one man and one woman these questions: (1) When you were growing up, was there anything your parents did not permit you to do because of your sex? (2) Is there any job you think is unsuitable for a man or a woman to do? (3) Did you ever experience discrimination because of your sex? Now consider how *you* would answer those questions. Do your answers agree with theirs? Why or why not?

they respond to a child's success or failure. They may tell a son who did well in math, "You're a natural math whiz, Johnny!" But if a daughter gets good grades, they may say, "Wow, you really worked hard in math, Joanie, and it shows!" The implication is that girls have to try hard but boys have a natural gift. Messages like these are not lost on children. Both sexes tend to lose interest in activities that are supposedly not natural for them, even when they all start out with equal abilities (Dweck, 2006; Frome & Eccles, 1998).

In today's fast-moving world, society's messages to men and women keep shifting. As a result, gender development has become a lifelong process, in which gender schemas, attitudes, and behaviour evolve as people have new experiences and as society itself changes. Five-year-old children may behave like sexist piglets while they are trying to figure out what it means to be male or female. Their behaviour is shaped by a combination of hormones, genetics, cognitive schemas, parental and social lessons, religious and cultural customs, and experiences. But their gender-typed behaviour as five-year-olds often has little to do with how they will behave at 25 or 45. In fact, by early adulthood, men and women show virtually no average differences in cognitive abilities, personality traits, self-esteem, or psychological well-being (Hyde, 2007). Children can grow up in an extremely

Shocking images or nothing new? The idea of women serving in the military would once have startled most people and offended others. As women soldiers, sailors, and airwomen became common, they lost the power to shock, at least if they remained in service jobs. But, in recent years, the gender rules have changed again, creating a generation of female soldiers, sailors, and airwomen who fight on the front lines with their male peers. Master Seaman Eileen Boutilier stands watch on Her Majesty's Canadian Ship (HMCS) Winnipeg (left) and Lieutenant Kathy Hanna unloads a Browning 9mm semi-automatic pistol into a clearing bay at the Canadian International Security Assistance Force (ISAF) camp in Kabul, Afghanistan (right).

gender-typed family and yet, as adults, choose careers or relationships they would never have imagined for themselves. If five-year-olds are the gender police, many adults end up breaking the law.

Quiz-taking is appropriate behaviour for all sexes and genders.

1. Three-year-old Paulo thinks that if he changed from wearing pants to wearing dresses he could become a girl. He still lacks a stable _____.

2. *True or false:* All intersexed people are transsexual.

3. From a biological perspective, a three-year-old boy's love of going "vroom, vroom" with his truck collection is probably a result of _____.

4. Which statement about gender schemas is false? (a) They are present in early form by age 1; (b) they are permanent conceptualizations of what it means to be masculine or feminine; (c) they eventually expand to include many meanings of and associations with being male and female; (d) they reflect the status of women and men in society.

5. Doug hopes his four-year-old daughter will become a doctor like him, but she refuses to play with the toy stethoscope he bought her and insists that she will be a princess when she grows up. What conclusions can Doug draw about his daughter's future career?

Answers:

1. gender identity 2. false 3. prenatal hormones, specifically androgens 4. b 5. Not many. His daughter's rigid gender-typed behaviour is typical when children are acquiring gender schemas, but it does not necessarily predict much of anything about her adult interests or occupation.

⬧ YOU are about to learn . . .

◆ the physiological changes of adolescence.

◆ the psychological issues of adolescence.

◆ findings on brain development in adolescence.

ADOLESCENCE

Adolescence refers to the period of development between **puberty**, the age at which a person becomes capable of sexual reproduction, and adulthood. In some cultures, the time span between puberty and adulthood is only a few months; a sexually mature boy or girl is expected to marry and assume adult tasks. In modern Western societies, however, teenagers are not considered emotionally mature enough to assume the full rights, responsibilities, and roles of adulthood.

The Physiology of Adolescence

Until puberty, boys and girls produce roughly the same levels of male hormones (androgens) and female hormones (estrogens). At puberty, however, the brain's pituitary gland begins to stimulate hormone production in the adrenal and reproductive glands. From then on, boys have a higher level of androgens than girls do, and girls have a higher level of estrogens than boys do.

⦿ **Watch**
Adolescent Behaviour

puberty The age at which a person becomes capable of sexual reproduction.

menarche [men-ARR-kee] The onset of menstruation during puberty.

⊙ Watch
Body Image

To their embarrassment, children typically reach puberty at different times. These boys are the same age, but they differ considerably in physical maturity.

In boys, the reproductive glands are the testes (testicles), which produce sperm; in girls, the reproductive glands are the ovaries, which release eggs. During puberty, these organs mature and the individual becomes capable of reproduction. In girls, signs of sexual maturity are the development of breasts and **menarche**, the onset of menstruation. In boys, the signs are the onset of nocturnal emissions and the growth of the testes, scrotum, and penis. Hormones are also responsible for the emergence of *secondary sex characteristics*, such as a deepened voice and facial and chest hair in boys and pubic hair in both sexes.

The onset of puberty depends on both biological and environmental factors. Menarche, for example, depends on a female's having a critical level of body fat, which is necessary to sustain a pregnancy and which triggers the hormonal changes associated with puberty. An increase in body fat among children in developed countries may help explain why the average age of puberty declined in Europe and North America until the mid-twentieth century. In North America, the average age of menarche is 12.5 years, whereas in many European countries it is 13. In many parts of Africa, menarche is typical of young women between the ages of 14 and 17 (Anderson, Dallal, & Must, 2003; Tanner, 1990; Wheeler, 1991).

Individuals vary enormously in the onset and length of puberty. Some girls go through menarche at 9 or 10 and some boys are still growing in height after age 19. Early-maturing boys generally have a more positive view of their bodies than late-maturing boys do, and their relatively greater size and strength give them a boost in sports and the prestige that being a good athlete brings young men. But they are also more likely to smoke, drink alcohol, use other drugs, and break the law than later-maturing boys (Cota-Robles, Duncan et al., 1985; Neiss, & Rowe, 2002). Some early-maturing girls have the prestige of being socially popular, but, partly because others in their peer group regard them as being sexually precocious, they are also more likely to fight with their parents, drop out of school, have a negative body image, and be angry or depressed. Early menarche itself does not cause these problems; rather, it tends to accentuate existing behavioural problems and family conflicts. Girls who go through puberty relatively late, in contrast, have a more difficult time at first, but by the end of adolescence many are happier with their appearance and are more popular than their early-maturing classmates (Caspi & Moffitt, 1991; Stattin & Magnusson, 1990).

BIOLOGY and *the Teen Brain*

Less Guilty by Reason of Adolescence?

When does a teenager become capable of thinking like an adult? This is not just an academic question; it can be a matter of life or death. In many American states, teenaged criminals are tried and sentenced as adults and, until recently, 21 states allowed the execution of juveniles under the age of 18, or even 16. In 2005, however, the Supreme Court banned the death penalty for juveniles as cruel and unusual punishment. The Court based this decision in part on evidence showing that adolescents often get into trouble not because of their hormones but because of their brains—in particular, because their brains are still neurologically immature (Steinberg, 2007). Indeed, full neurological and cognitive maturity often does not occur until about age 25, much later than commonly believed. For that reason, Laurence Steinberg and Elizabeth Scott (2003) have argued that many teenagers who commit crimes should be considered "less guilty by reason of adolescence." In Canada, there is no death penalty, although the *Youth Criminal Justice Act* suggests that for major offences (e.g., murder), youths who are 14 or older can be transferred to adult court for trial. Since its introduction in 2001, there has been a significant reduction in the incarceration of young offenders in Canada (Statistics Canada, 2007).

When people think of physical changes in adolescence, they usually think of hormones and maturing bodies. But the adolescent brain undergoes significant developmental changes, notably a major pruning of synapses. This pruning occurs primarily in the prefrontal cortex, which is responsible for impulse control and planning, and the limbic system, which is involved in emotional processing (Spear, 2000a, 2000b). In Chapter 15 we will see that errors in the pruning process during adolescence may be involved in the onset of schizophrenia in vulnerable individuals.

Thinking Critically

Analyze Assumptions and Biases

In April 2006, the bodies of Marc, Debra, and Jacob Richardson were found in their house in Medicine Hat. A 12-year-old* from Medicine Hat and her 23-year-old boyfriend, Jeremy Steinke, were convicted of murdering her parents and brother. Was she responsible for these heartless crimes? Many people assume that by late adolescence, individuals are legally, socially, and physically adult, but some researchers in neuroscience and developmental psychology disagree.

Given her age, her name cannot be revealed.

Another change involves myelinization, which provides insulation for the cells and improves the efficiency of neural transmission (see Chapter 4), strengthening the connections between the emotional limbic system and the reasoning prefrontal cortex. This process may continue through the late teens or early twenties, which would help explain why the strong emotions of the adolescent years often overwhelm rational decision making and cause some teenagers to behave more impulsively than adults. It would explain why adolescents are more vulnerable to peer pressure that encourages them to try risky, dumb, or dangerous things—why taunts of "I dare you!" and "You're chicken!" have more power over a 15-year-old than a 25-year-old. Even when teenagers know they are doing the wrong thing, many lack the reasoning ability to foresee the consequences of their actions down the line (Reyna & Farley, 2006).

If adolescence is literally a state of diminished responsibility, how should the courts treat underage offenders? Should 12-year-olds be less accountable than 14-year-olds or 18-year-olds? What do you think?

The Psychology of Adolescence

The media love sensational stories about teenagers who are angry or violent, live in emotional turmoil, feel lonely, hate their parents, and run wild sexually. We often hear warnings about an alleged teenage "sex crisis," in which teens are having sex at ever-younger ages. Parents and prosecutors are alarmed about "sexting," the practice of emailing nude pictures to friends. (Although in the States there have been prosecutions for underage sexting, no such cases have been tried in Canada.) Some observers worry that teenagers have too little self-esteem, which is why they are forever getting in trouble; others worry that, thanks to the "self-esteem movement," teenagers have too much self-esteem. One psychologist argues that today's young people have become so narcissistic that they deserve to be called "Generation Me" (Twenge et al., 2008).

How realistic is this portrait of adolescence? Not very. The rate of violent crimes committed by adolescents has been dropping steadily since 1993. Overall feelings of self-esteem do not suddenly plummet after the age of 13 for either sex (Gentile et al., 2009; Kling et al., 1999). How about overinflated self-esteem? One team of researchers analyzed changes in the narcissism scores of large samples of undergraduates and in a national probability study of grade 12 students that has been conducted every year since 1976. In addition to looking at scores on the Narcissistic Personality Inventory, which measures a grandiose sense of importance and entitlement, they developed another measure of narcissism: unreasonable self-enhancement, the discrepancy between how good you actually are academically and how good you *think* you are. They found very little change in narcissism on either measure over the decades (Trzesniewski, Donnellan, & Robins, 2008).

What about sex? According to Statistics Canada, today's teenagers may actually be more conservative than their parents were at their age. In 1996, 47% of teens aged 15 to 19 had had sex; in 2005, that number dropped to 43% (Rotermann, 2008). The age at which people first had sex had also increased, with less than 8% of teens reporting that they had had sex before the age of 15 (Rotermann, 2008). Only the rate of births to teenage girls has risen in the last few years, a result of declining contraceptive use. As for sexting, an article in *Maclean's* (Kingston, 2009) suggests that it is hardly an epidemic, with less than 25% of Canadian teens reporting that they had ever sent nude or semi-nude pictures of themselves electronically.

Similarly, studies of representative samples of adolescents find that only a small minority are seriously troubled, angry, or unhappy. Most teenagers have supportive families, a sense of purpose and self-confidence, good friends, and the skill to cope with their problems. Nevertheless, three kinds of problems are more common during adolescence than during childhood or adulthood: conflict with parents, mood swings and depression, and, as we saw, higher rates of reckless, rule-breaking, and risky behaviour (Steinberg, 2007). Rule-breaking often occurs because teenagers are developing their own standards and values by trying on the styles, actions, and attitudes of their peers, in contrast to those of their parents.

Peers become especially important to adolescents because they represent the values and style of the generation that teenagers identify with, the generation that they will share experiences with as adults (Bukowski, 2001; Harris, 2009). Many people report that feeling rejected by their peers when they were teenagers was more devastating than punitive treatment by parents. According to a government-sponsored review of whether and how online technologies affect child

"So I blame you for everything—whose fault is that?"

safety, the most frequent dangers teenagers face on the internet are not pornography or even predatory adults, and definitely not sexting. "Bullying and harassment, most often by peers, are the most frequent threats that minors face, both online and offline," the report found (Berkman Center for Internet & Society, 2008).

Adolescents who are lonely, depressed, worried, or angry tend to express these concerns in ways characteristic of their sex. Boys are more likely than girls to externalize their emotional problems in acts of aggression and other antisocial behaviour. Girls are more likely than boys to internalize their feelings and problems, for example by becoming withdrawn or developing eating disorders (Wicks-Nelson & Israel, 2003). Although, as we said, there are no gender differences in overall self-esteem, a gender gap in two specific *areas* of self-esteem emerges in adolescence, reflecting the externalizing/internalizing difference in habits of coping. Girls are more dissatisfied than boys with their bodies and general appearance; boys are more dissatisfied than girls with their social behaviour at school and with friends (Gentile et al., 2009).

---

quick**QUIZ**

✓•Quick Review on **MyPsychLab**

If you are not in the midst of adolescent turmoil, try these questions.

1. What is the difference between *puberty* and *adolescence*?
2. *True or false:* Teenagers today are more likely to be sexually active and commit violent crimes than the teenagers of the previous generation.
3. *True or false:* Teenage boys have much higher self-esteem than teenage girls do.
4. What changes occur in the brain during adolescence?

Answers:

1. Puberty refers to the physiological process of sexual maturation; adolescence is a social category marking the years between puberty and adulthood. 2. false 3. false 4. pruning of synapses, myelinization, and strengthening of connections between the limbic system and the prefrontal cortex

---

 YOU are about to learn . . .

◆ Erik Erikson's theory of the stages of adult development.
◆ the typical attitudes and experiences of "emerging adulthood," the years from 18 to 25.
◆ some common mid-life changes for women and men.
◆ which mental abilities decline in old age and which ones do not.

ADULTHOOD

According to ancient Greek legend, the Sphinx was a monster—half lion, half woman—who terrorized passersby on the road to Thebes. The Sphinx would ask each traveller a question and then murder those who failed to answer correctly. (The Sphinx was a pretty tough grader.) The question was this: What animal walks on four feet in the morning, two feet at noon, and three feet in the evening? Only one traveller, Oedipus, knew the solution to the riddle. The animal, he said, is Man, who crawls on all fours as a baby, walks upright as an adult, and limps in old age with the aid of a staff.

The Sphinx was the first life-span theorist. Since then, many philosophers, writers, and scientists have speculated on the course of adult development. Are the changes of adulthood predictable, like those of childhood? What are the major psychological issues of adult life? Is mental and physical deterioration in old age inevitable?

Stages and Ages

One of the first modern theorists to propose a life-span approach to psychological development was psychoanalyst Erik H. Erikson (1902–1994). Erikson (1950/1963, 1982) wrote that all individuals go through eight stages in their lives. Each stage is characterized by what he called a "crisis," a particular psychological challenge that ideally should be resolved before the individual moves on.

1   **Trust versus mistrust** is the challenge that occurs during the baby's first year, when the baby depends on others to provide food, comfort, cuddling, and warmth. If these needs are not met, the child may never develop the essential trust of others necessary to get along in the world.

2   **Autonomy (independence) versus shame and doubt** is the challenge that occurs when the child is a toddler. The young child is learning to be independent and must do so without feeling too ashamed or uncertain about his or her actions.

3   **Initiative versus guilt** is the challenge that occurs as the preschooler develops. The child is acquiring new physical and mental skills, setting goals, and enjoying newfound talents, but must also learn to control impulses. The danger lies in developing too strong a sense of guilt over his or her wishes and fantasies.

4   **Competence versus inferiority** is the challenge for school-age children, who are learning to make things, use tools, and acquire the skills for adult life. Children who fail these lessons of mastery and competence may come out of this stage feeling inadequate and inferior.

5   **Identity versus role confusion** is the great challenge of adolescence, when teenagers must decide who they are, what they are going to do, and what they hope to make of their lives. Erikson used the term *identity crisis* to describe what he considered to be the primary conflict of this stage. Those who resolve it will emerge with a strong identity, ready to plan for the future. Those who do not will sink into confusion, unable to make decisions.

6   **Intimacy versus isolation** is the challenge of young adulthood. Once you have decided who you are, said Erikson, you must share yourself with another and learn to make commitments. No matter how successful you are at work, you are not complete until you are capable of intimacy.

7   **Generativity versus stagnation** is the challenge of the middle years. Now that you know who you are and have an intimate relationship, will you sink into complacency and selfishness, or will you experience generativity—creativity and renewal? Parenthood is the most common route to generativity, but people can be productive, creative, and nurturing in other ways, in their work or their relationships with the younger generation.

8   **Ego integrity versus despair** is the final challenge of late adulthood and old age. As they age, people strive to reach the ultimate goals of wisdom, spiritual tranquility, and acceptance of their lives. Just as the healthy child will not fear life, said Erikson, the healthy adult will not fear death.

Erikson recognized that cultural and economic factors affect people's progression through these stages. Some societies, for example, make the passages relatively easy. If you know you are going to be a farmer like your parents and you have no alternative, you are unlikely to have an adolescent identity crisis (unless you hate farming). If you have many choices, however, as adolescents in urban societies often do, the transition can become prolonged (Schwartz, 2004). Similarly, cultures that place a high premium on independence and individualism will make it difficult for many of their members to resolve Erikson's sixth crisis, that of intimacy versus isolation.

Erikson was also aware that the psychological themes and crises of life can occur out of order, although that was not his emphasis. As people's lives became less traditional and predictable, researchers discovered just how out of order they can be. For example, although in Western societies adolescence is often a time of confusion about identity and aspirations, an identity crisis is not limited to the teen years. A man who has worked in one job for 20 years, and then is laid off at 45 and must find an entirely new career, may have an identity crisis too. Likewise, competence is not mastered once and for all in childhood. People learn new skills and lose old ones throughout their lives, and their sense of competence rises and falls accordingly. And people who are highly generative, in terms of being committed to helping their communities or the next generation, tend to do volunteer work or choose occupations that allow them to contribute to society throughout their lives (McAdams, 2006). As one psychologist observed many years ago, "There is not one process of aging, but many; there is not one life course followed, but multiple courses. . . . The variety is as rich as the historic conditions people have faced and the current circumstances they experience" (Pearlin, 1982).

Stage theories, therefore, do not adequately describe how adults grow and change, or remain the same, across the life span. Yet Erikson was right to show that development does not stop at adolescence or young adulthood; it is an ongoing process. His ideas were important because he placed adult development in the context of family, work, and society, and he specified many of the essential concerns of adulthood: trust, competence, identity, generativity, and the ability to enjoy life and accept death. Modern psychologists who study life-span development recognize that social and cultural factors affect the way each of these adult concerns is expressed and mastered. Yet collectively they reflect the timeless and universal human concerns of adulthood (Dunkel & Sefcek, 2009).

According to Erik Erikson, children must master the crisis of competence and older adults must resolve the challenge of generativity. This child and her grandmother are certainly helping each other with their life tasks. But are the needs for competence and generativity important at only one stage of life?

✱ Explore

Erikson's First Four Stages of Psychosocial Development

Erikson's Last Four Stages of Psychosocial Development

The Transitions of Life

Certain events tend to occur at particular times in life: going to school, learning to drive a car, having a baby, retiring from work. When nearly everyone your age goes through the same experience or enters a new role at the same time, adjusting to these transitions is relatively easy. Similarly, if you aren't doing these things and hardly anyone you know is doing them either, you will not feel out of step.

In modern societies, however, most people will face unanticipated transitions, events that happen without warning, such as being fired from a job because of downsizing. And many people have to deal with changes they expect to happen but do not: for example, not getting a job right out of school, not getting married at the age they expected, not getting promoted, not being able to afford to retire, or realizing that they cannot have children (Schlossberg & Robinson, 1996). With this in mind, let's consider some of the major transitions of life.

Thinking Critically

Avoid Emotional Reasoning

What is your reaction to these two first-time parents? Adriana Iliescu gave birth at age 66; the young man became a father at 15. Many people react negatively to individuals who they feel are "off time" for the transition to parenthood. How young is too young and how old is too old to become a parent?

EMERGING ADULTHOOD. In industrialized nations, major demographic changes have postponed the timing of career decisions, marriage or cohabitation, and parenthood until a person's late twenties or even thirties, on the average. Many young people between the ages of 18 and 25 (would that include anyone you know?) are in some form of post-secondary education and at least partly dependent financially on their parents. This phenomenon has created a phase of life that some call *emerging adulthood* (Arnett, 2004). When emerging adults are asked whether they feel they have reached adulthood, the majority answer: in some ways yes, in some ways no (see Figure 13.5).

FIGURE 13.5 Are You an Adult Yet?

When people are asked, "Do you feel that you have reached adulthood?" the percentage that answers "yes" steadily increases over time. But as you can see, people between the ages of 18 and 25, emerging adults, are most likely to say "yes *and* no" (Arnett, 2004).

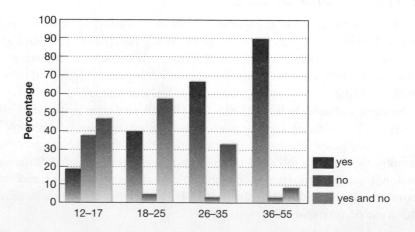

In certain respects, emerging adults have moved beyond adolescence into maturity, becoming more emotionally controlled, more confident, less dependent, and less angry and alienated (Roberts, Caspi, & Moffitt, 2001). But they are also the group most likely to live unstable lives and feel unrooted. Emerging adults move more often than people in other demographic groups do—back to their parents' homes and then out again, from one city to another, from living with roommates to living on their own. And their rates of risky behaviour (such as binge drinking, having unprotected sex, and driving at high speeds or while drunk) are higher than those of any other age group, including adolescents (Arnett, 2004).

Of course, not all young people in this age group are alike. Some groups within the larger society, such as Mormons, promote early marriage and parenthood. And young people who are poor, who have dropped out of school, who had a child at 16, or who have few opportunities to get a good job will not have the income or leisure to explore many options. But the overall shift in all industrialized nations toward a global economy, increased education, and delayed career and family decisions means that emerging adulthood is likely to grow in importance as a distinct phase of prolonged exploration and freedom.

THE MIDDLE YEARS. For most women and men, the mid-life years between 35 and 65 are the prime of life (MacArthur Foundation, 1999; Mroczek & Spiro, 2005). These years are typically a time of the greatest psychological well-being, good health, productivity, and community involvement. They are also often a time of reflection and reassessment. People look back on what they have accomplished, take stock of what they regret not having done, and think about what they want to do with their remaining years. When crises occur, it is for reasons not related to aging but to specific life-changing events, such as illness or the loss of a job or partner (Wethington, 2000).

But doesn't menopause make most mid-life women depressed, irritable, and irrational? **Menopause**, which usually occurs between ages 45 and 55, is the cessation of menstruation after the ovaries stop producing estrogen and progesterone. Menopause does produce physical symptoms in many women, notably hot flashes, as the vascular system adjusts to the decrease in estrogen. But only about 10% of all women have unusually severe physical symptoms.

The negative view of menopause as a syndrome that causes depression and other negative emotional reactions is based on women who have undergone early menopause following a hysterectomy (removal of the uterus) or who have had a lifetime history of depression. But these women are not typical. According to many surveys of thousands of healthy, randomly chosen women in the general population, most women view menopause with relief that they no longer have to worry about pregnancy or menstrual periods. The vast majority have only a few physical symptoms (which can be annoying and bothersome but are temporary) and most do not become depressed; only 3% even report regret at having reached menopause (McKinlay, McKinlay, & Brambilla, 1987). In one study of 1000 postmenopausal women, fewer than half reported physical symptoms and only 5% of those complained of mood symptoms (Ness, Aronow, & Beck, 2006).

Although women lose their fertility after menopause and men theoretically remain fertile throughout their lives, men have a biological clock too. Testosterone diminishes, although it never drops as sharply in men as estrogen does in women. The sperm count may also gradually drop, and the sperm that remain are more susceptible to genetic mutations that can increase the risk of certain diseases in children conceived by older fathers, as we saw earlier (Wyrobek et al., 2006).

⊙ Watch
Menopause

Male Menopause

menopause The cessation of menstruation and of the production of ova; it is usually a gradual process lasting up to several years.

←⊙ **Simulate**
Aging and Changes in Physical
Appearance

Major Changes in Important
Domains of Adult Functioning

✱ **Explore**
Physical Changes in Late Adulthood

The physical changes of mid-life do not by themselves predict how people will feel about aging or how they will respond to it (Schaie & Willis, 2002). People's views of aging are profoundly influenced by the culture they live in and by the promises of technology to prolong life and health—some realistic, some still science fiction. Is aging something natural and inevitable, to be accepted gracefully? Or is it a process to be fought tooth and nail, with every chemical, surgical, and genetic weapon we can lay our hands on? If we can live to 100, why not have a baby at 70? To what extent should society pay for life-extending interventions? These issues will be hotly debated in the years to come.

Old Age

When does old age start? In Canada, the average life expectancy for men is 77 years of age, whereas the average life expectancy for women is 82 years (Statistics Canada, 2010). As our life expectancies increase, many gerontologists are beginning to divide the elderly into the following categories: the young old (ages 60–75); the old old (ages 75–85); and the oldest old (ages 85+). Today, the fastest-growing segment of the population in Canada is the oldest old. For instance, in 1971, 8% of Canadians were over age 65, whereas in 2000, 13% of Canadians were over age 65. From 1952 to 1991, the number of Canadians who were over 100 increased from 175 to 2884 people (most of whom were women; Bourbeau & Lebel, 2000). Some estimates suggest that by 2051, oldest old Canadians will number more than 2 million individuals (Health Canada, 2001). How will these people do? *Gerontologists*, researchers who study aging and the old, have been providing some answers.

The first prediction is that the life phase of retirement will change significantly because of demographic changes affecting older people. When people expected to live only until their early seventies, retirement at 65 was associated with loss—a withdrawal from work and fulfilling activities, with not much to look forward to but illness

The two images of old age: More and more old people are living healthy, active, mentally stimulating lives. But with increasing longevity, many people are also falling victim to degenerative diseases such as Alzheimer's.

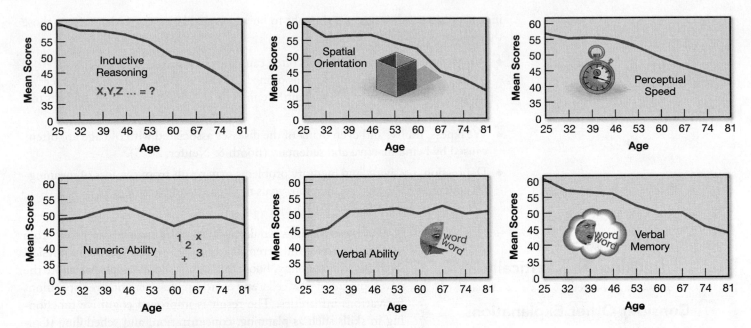

FIGURE 13.6 Changes in Mental Functioning over Time

As these graphs show, some intellectual abilities tend to dwindle with age, but numerical and verbal abilities remain relatively steady over the years.

and old age. Today, thanks to the enormous cohort of healthy baby boomers and a changed economy, retirement might last 20 or 30 years. Thus it is no longer simply a life transition from working to not working. People in the phase of what some psychologists are calling "positive retirement" often find a new career, volunteer work, or new, engrossing activities (Halpern, 2008).

Still, various aspects of intelligence, memory, and other forms of mental functioning do decline significantly with age. Older adults score lower on tests of reasoning, spatial ability, and complex problem solving than do younger adults. The ability to produce and spell familiar words declines, a change that often causes great frustration and annoyance (Burke & Shafto, 2004). It takes older people longer to retrieve names, dates, and other information; in fact, the speed of cognitive processing in general slows down. However, older people vary, with some declining significantly and others remaining sharp (Salthouse, 2006).

Fortunately, not all cognitive abilities worsen with age. **Fluid intelligence** is the capacity for deductive reasoning and the ability to use new information to solve problems. It reflects in part an inherited predisposition, and it parallels other biological capacities in its growth and later decline (Bosworth & Schaie, 1999; Li et al., 2004). **Crystallized intelligence** consists of knowledge and skills built up over a lifetime, the kind of intelligence that gives us the ability to do arithmetic, define words, or take political positions. It depends heavily on education and experience, and it tends to remain stable or even improve over the life span (see Figure 13.6). This is why physicians, lawyers, teachers, farmers, musicians, insurance agents, politicians, psychologists, and people in many other occupations can continue working well into old age (Halpern, 2008).

Many of the physical and mental losses that do occur in old age are genetically based and are seen in all societies, but others have to do with cultural, behavioural, and psychological factors (Park & Gutchess, 2006). Psychologists have made great strides

◉ **Watch**
Centenarian

What Happens with Alzheimer's

Successfully Aging: Thelma

fluid intelligence The capacity for deductive reasoning and the ability to use new information to solve problems; it is relatively independent of education and tends to decline in old age.

crystallized intelligence Cognitive skills and specific knowledge of information acquired over a lifetime; it is heavily dependent on education and tends to remain stable over the lifetime.

in separating conditions once thought to be an inevitable part of old age from those that are preventable or treatable:

◆ Apparent senility in the elderly is often caused by malnutrition, prescription medications, harmful combinations of medications, and even over-the-counter drugs (such as sleeping pills and antihistamines), all of which can be hazardous to old people.

◆ Weakness, frailty, and even many of the diseases associated with old age are often caused by being inactive and sedentary (Booth & Neufer, 2005).

◆ Depression, passivity, and memory problems may result from the loss of meaningful activity, intellectual stimulation, goals to pursue, and control over events (Hess, 2005; Schaie & Zuo, 2001).

Thinking Critically

Consider Other Explanations

People assume that aging inevitably produces senility, depression, weakness, and a decline in mental abilities. What else could be causing these problems?

As these findings would predict, older people can profit from aerobic exercise and strength training, which maintain physical strength and flexibility, boost the brain's blood supply, promote the development of new cells, and even suppress genetic predispositions for various infirmities. The result is improved cognitive functioning in skills such as planning, concentration, and scheduling (Colcombe & Kramer, 2003; Hertzog et al., 2008). Mental stimulation also fosters the growth of neural connections in the brain, even well into old age. Older adults can sometimes do as well on memory tests as people in their twenties, when given instruction and training. In one project, older people who had shown a decline in inductive reasoning and spatial ability over a 14-year span were given five hours of training in these skills. This brief intervention produced significant improvements in two-thirds of the sample, and many people performed at or above the level of skill they had had 14 years earlier. More impressive, the effects were still apparent up to seven years later (Kramer & Willis, 2002). Cognitive enrichment cannot prevent most cases of serious cognitive decline and dementia, which are often strongly influenced or

Remember the cute children pictured at the beginning of this chapter? They are Adolph Hitler, Queen Elizabeth II, and Albert Einstein. Now that you have read this chapter, what kinds of genetic, familial, and historical influences can you think of that might explain what made these three famous people so remarkably different?

even caused directly by genes, but the declines may be delayed (Gatz, 2007; Hertzog et al., 2008).

Perhaps the best news is that as people get older, most become better able to regulate negative feelings and emphasize the positive. The frequency of intense negative emotions is highest among people aged 18 to 34, then drops sharply to age 65. After 65, it levels off, rising only slightly among old people facing crises of illness and bereavement (Charles & Carstensen, 2004; Charles, Reynolds, & Gatz, 2001). Apparently, many people do grow wiser, or at least more tranquil, with age.

Some researchers who study aging are therefore optimistic. In their view, people who have challenging occupations and interests, who remain active mentally, who exercise regularly, and who adapt flexibly to change and loss are likely to maintain their cognitive abilities and well-being. "Use it or lose it," they say. Other researchers, however, are less upbeat. "When you've lost it, you can't use it," they reply. They are worried about the growing numbers of people living into their nineties and beyond, when rates of cognitive impairment and dementia rise dramatically. The challenge for society is to prepare for the many people who will be living into advanced old age, by helping as many as possible to keep using their brains instead of losing them.

quickQUIZ

Quick Review on MyPsychLab

People of any age can answer this quiz.

1. The key psychological issue during adolescence, said Erikson, is a(n) _____ crisis.
2. What new phase of life development has emerged because of demographic changes, and what years does it include?
3. Most women react to menopause by (a) feeling depressed, (b) regretting the loss of femininity, (c) going a little crazy, (d) feeling relieved or neutral.
4. Which of these statements about the decline of mental abilities in old age is false? (a) It can often be lessened with training programs; (b) it inevitably declines sharply; (c) it is sometimes a result of malnutrition, medication, or disease rather than aging; (d) it is slowed when people live in stimulating environments
5. Suddenly, your 80-year-old grandmother has become confused and delusional. Before concluding that old age has made her senile, what other explanations should you rule out?

Answers:

1. identity 2. emerging adulthood, ages 18 to 25 3. d 4. b 5. You should be sure she is not malnourished and you should rule out the possibility that she is taking too many medications, including nonprescription drugs.

YOU are about to learn . . .

◆ why terrible childhood experiences do not inevitably affect a person forever.
◆ what makes most children resilient in the face of adversity.

THE WELLSPRINGS OF RESILIENCE

Most people take it for granted that the path from childhood to adolescence to adulthood is a fairly straight one. We think of the lasting attitudes, habits, and values our parents taught us. We continue to have deep attachments to our families, even

Analyze Assumptions and Biases

Many people are convinced that childhood traumas always cause emotional problems in adulthood. What is wrong with this assumption, and what evidence does it overlook?

when we are fighting with them. And many people carry with them the scars of emotional wounds they suffered as children. Children who have been beaten, neglected, or subjected to verbal or physical abuse by their parents are more likely than other children to have emotional problems, become delinquent and violent, commit crimes, have low IQs, drop out of school, develop mental disorders such as depression, and develop chronic stress-related illnesses (Emery & Laumann-Billings, 1998; Margolin & Gordis, 2004; Repetti, Taylor, & Seeman, 2002).

And yet, when researchers began to question the entrenched assumption that early trauma always has long-lasting negative effects and considered the evidence for alternative views, they got quite a different picture. Most children, they found, are resilient, eventually overcoming even the effects of war, childhood illness, having abusive or alcoholic parents, early deprivation, or being sexually molested (Kaufman & Zigler, 1987; Nelson et al., 2007; Rathbun, DiVirgilio, & Waldfogel, 1958; Rind, Tromovitch, & Bauserman, 1998; Rutter et al., 2004; Werner, 1989; West & Prinz, 1987). Most adults eventually recover after a disaster, too. For example, a study of thousands of Jewish immigrants to Canada and the States who had survived the Holocaust found, in most, resiliency and successful integration into their new lives rather than persisting traumatic distress (Helmreich, 1992).

Psychologist Ann Masten (2001) observed that most people assume there is something special and rare about people who recover from adversity. But "the great surprise" of the research, she concluded, is how ordinary resilience is. Many of the children who outgrow early deprivation and trauma have easygoing temperaments or personality traits, such as self-efficacy and self-control, that help them roll with even severe punches. They have a secure attachment style, which helps them work through traumatic events in a way that heals their wounds and restores hope and emotional balance (Mikulincer, Shaver, & Horesh, 2006). If children lack secure attachments with their own parents, they may be rescued by love and attention from their siblings, peers, extended family members, or other caring adults. And some have experiences outside the family—in schools, places of worship, or other organizations—that give them a sense of competence, moral support, solace, religious faith, and self-esteem (Cowen et al., 1990; Garmezy, 1991).

Perhaps the most powerful reason for the resilience of so many children, and for the changes that all of us make throughout our lives, is that we are all constantly interpreting our experiences. We can decide to repeat the mistakes our parents made or break free of them. We can decide to remain prisoners of childhood or to strike out in new directions at age 20, 50, or 70. In the next decades, as the world changes in unpredictable ways, the territory of adulthood will continue to expand, providing new frontiers as well as fewer signposts and road maps to guide us. Increasingly, age will be what we make of it.

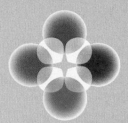
Bringing Up Baby

Every year or so another best-selling book arrives to tell parents they've been doing it all wrong. Countless books have advised parents to treat their children in very specific, if contradictory, ways: Pick them up, don't pick them up; respond when they cry, don't respond when they cry; let them sleep with you, never let them sleep with you; be affectionate, be stern; be highly sensitive to their every need so they will securely attach to you, don't overreact to their every mood or complaint or you will spoil them. A billion-dollar industry has emerged to calm (and inflame) parental worries, offering expensive strollers, toys, and "fetal education" and baby sign-language programs—all to create the perfect child (Paul, 2008).

No need to panic. Critical thinkers can call upon two lines of evidence, described in this chapter, to protect themselves from the guilt-mongers and marketers. One is that babies and young children thrive under a wide variety of child-rearing methods. The second is that babies bring their own temperaments and other genetic predispositions to the matter of how best to raise them. Most respond readily to induction, for example, but others require stricter discipline.

Well, then, how should you treat your children? Should you be strict or lenient, powerful or permissive? Should you require your child to stop having tantrums, to clean up his or her room, to be polite? Should you say, "Oh, nothing I do will matter, anyway" or "If I don't get 100% compliance on every order, this kid is going to boot camp"? Child development research does suggest certain general principles that can help parents find that middle way and foster their children's confidence and helpfulness:

Set high expectations that are appropriate to the child's age and temperament, and teach the child how to meet them. Some parents make few demands on their children, either unintentionally or because they believe a parent should not impose standards. Others make many demands, such as requiring children to be polite, help with chores, control their anger, be thoughtful of others, and do well in school. The children of parents who make few demands tend to be aggressive, impulsive, and immature. The children of parents who have high but realistic expectations tend to be helpful and above average in competence and self-confidence (Damon, 1995).

Explain, explain, explain. Induction, telling a child why you have applied a rule, teaches a child to be responsible. Punitive methods ("Do it or I'll spank you") may result in compliance, but the child will tend to disobey as soon as you are out of sight. Explanations also teach children how to reason and understand. While setting standards for your children, you can also allow them to express disagreements and feelings. This does not mean you have to argue with a four-year-old about the merits of table manners or permit antisocial and destructive behaviour. Once you have explained a rule, you need to enforce it consistently.

Encourage empathy. Call the child's attention to the effects of his or her actions on others and appeal to the child's sense of fair play and desire to be good. As we saw, even very young children are capable of empathy. Vague orders, such as "Don't fight," are less effective than showing the child how fighting disrupts and hurts others.

Notice, approve of, and reward good behaviour. Many parents punish the behaviour they dislike, a form of attention that may be rewarding to the child. It is much more effective to praise the behaviour you do want, which teaches the child what is expected.

Remember the critical-thinking guideline "don't oversimplify." The challenge is to avoid the twin fallacies of "It's all genetic" and "If I just do all the right things, whatever they are, my child will be intelligent, kind, and successful." Even with the best skills and intentions, you cannot control everything that happens to your child or remodel your child's temperamental dispositions. Besides, as children grow up, they are influenced by their peers and generation and by particular experiences that shape their interests and motivation. But you do have the power to make your children's lives miserable or secure. You also have the power to profoundly affect the *quality* of the relationship you will have with your child throughout life: one filled with conflict and resentment, or one that is close and loving.

SUMMARY

◆ *Developmental psychologists* study how people grow and change over the life span. Many study socialization, the process by which children learn the rules and behaviour society expects of them.

FROM CONCEPTION THROUGH THE FIRST YEAR

◆ *Maturation* is the unfolding of genetically influenced behaviour and characteristics. Prenatal development consists of the germinal, embryonic, and fetal stages. Harmful influences that can adversely affect the fetus's development include German measles, toxic substances, some sexually transmitted diseases, cigarettes, alcohol (which can cause fetal alcohol syndrome and cognitive deficits), illegal drugs, and even over-the-counter medications. Fathers affect prenatal development too; the sperm of teenage boys and men over 50 may have mutations that increase the risk of miscarriage, birth defects, and certain diseases in their offspring.

◆ Babies are born with *motor reflexes* and a number of perceptual abilities. Cultural practices affect the timing of physical milestones.

◆ Babies' innate need for *contact comfort* gives rise to emotional attachment to their caregivers, and by the age of six to eight months, infants begin to feel *separation anxiety*. Studies of the *Strange Situation* have distinguished *secure* from *insecure* attachment; insecurity can take one of two forms, *avoidant* or *anxious-ambivalent* attachment.

◆ Styles of attachment are relatively unaffected by the normal range of child-rearing practices, and also by whether or not babies spend time in daycare. Insecure attachment is promoted by parents' rejection, mistreatment, or abandonment of their infants; by a mother's postpartum depression, which can affect her ability to care for the baby; by the child's own fearful, insecure temperament; or by stressful family situations.

COGNITIVE DEVELOPMENT

◆ Infants are responsive to the pitch, intensity, and sound of language, which may be why adults in many cultures speak to babies in *parentese*, using higher-pitched words and exaggerated intonation of vowels. At four to six months of age, babies begin to recognize the sounds of their own language. They go through a babbling phase from age 6 months to 1 year, and at about 1 year, they start saying single words and using symbolic gestures, which continue to be important for language, thinking, and problem solving. At age 2, children speak in two- or three-word *telegraphic* sentences that convey a variety of messages.

◆ Jean Piaget argued that cognitive development depends on an interaction between maturation and a child's experiences in the world. Children's thinking changes and adapts through *assimilation* and *accommodation*. Piaget proposed four stages of cognitive development: *sensorimotor* (birth to age 2), during which the child learns *object permanence*; *preoperational* (ages 2 to 7), during which language and symbolic thought develop, although the child remains *egocentric* in reasoning and has difficulty with some *mental operations*; *concrete operations* (ages 7 to 12), during which the child comes to understand *conservation*, identity, and serial ordering; and *formal operations* (age 12 to adulthood), during which abstract reasoning develops.

◆ Lev Vygotsky, working at about the same time as Piaget, emphasized a sociocultural approach to children's cognitive development. He noted that once children develop language, they begin speaking to themselves, using *private speech* to direct their own behaviour.

◆ Modern researchers have found that the changes from one stage to another are not as clear-cut as Piaget implied; development is more continuous and overlapping. More important, babies and young children have greater cognitive abilities, at earlier ages, than Piaget thought, perhaps because of the "core knowledge" they are born with. Young children are not always egocentric in their thinking. By the age of four or five they have developed a *theory of mind* to account for their own and other people's behaviour. Cultural practices affect the pace and content of cognitive development.

MORAL DEVELOPMENT

◆ Lawrence Kohlberg proposed that as children mature cognitively, they go through three levels of moral reasoning. But people can reason morally without behaving morally. Developmental psychologists study how children learn to internalize standards of right and wrong and to behave accordingly. This ability depends on the emergence of conscience and the moral emotions of guilt, shame, and empathy, and on the ability of children to learn to regulate their impulses, wishes, and feelings.

◆ As a strategy for teaching children to behave, a parent's use of *power assertion* is associated with a child's aggressiveness and lack of empathy. *Induction* is associated with children who develop empathy, internalize moral standards, and can resist temptation. But all methods of discipline interact with the child's own temperament.

◆ The capacity of very young children for *self-regulation* is associated with the development of internalized moral standards and conscience. This ability is enhanced by mothers who use induction as a primary form of discipline. It may also reflect a personality trait, because it tends to emerge very early in life and to be consistent over time and across situations.

GENDER DEVELOPMENT

◆ Gender development includes the emerging awareness of *gender identity*, the understanding that a person is biologically male or female regardless of what he or she does or wears, and *gender typing*, the process by which boys and girls learn what it means to be masculine or feminine in their culture. Some individuals are born with *intersex conditions*, living with the physical attributes of both sexes, and consider themselves to be *transgender*. *Transsexuals* feel that they are male in a female body or vice versa; their gender identity is at odds with their anatomical sex.

◆ Universally, young children tend to prefer same-sex toys and playing with other children of their own sex. Biological psychologists account for this phenomenon in terms of genes and prenatal androgens, which appear to be involved in gender-typed play. Cognitive psychologists study how children develop *gender schemas* for the categories "male" and "female," which in turn shape their gender-typed behaviour. Gender schemas tend to be inflexible at first. Later they become more flexible as the child cognitively matures and assimilates new information, if the child's culture promotes flexible gender schemas. Learning theorists study the direct and subtle reinforcers and social messages that foster gender typing.

◆ Gender development changes over the life span, depending on people's experiences with work and family life and larger events in society and their culture.

ADOLESCENCE

◆ Adolescence begins with the physical changes of puberty. In girls, puberty is signalled by *menarche* and the development of breasts; in boys, it begins with the onset of nocturnal emissions and the development of the testes, scrotum, and penis. Hormones produce secondary sex characteristics, such as pubic hair in both sexes and a deeper voice in males.

◆ As discussed in "Biology and the Teen Brain," the adolescent brain undergoes a major pruning of synapses, primarily in the prefrontal cortex and the limbic system, and myelinization, which improves the efficiency of neural transmission and strengthens the connections between these two brain areas. These neurological changes may not be complete until the early twenties, which would help explain why the strong emotions of the adolescent years sometimes overwhelm rational decision making and why teenagers often behave more impulsively than adults. This evidence may have implications for how teenagers who break the law should be treated.

◆ Most North American adolescents do not go through extreme emotional turmoil, anger, or rebellion, and do not dislike their parents. They do not suffer from unusually low self-esteem or its opposite, extreme narcissism. However, conflict with parents, mood swings and depression, and reckless or rule-breaking behaviour do increase in adolescence. The peer group becomes especially important and peer bullying, online or offline, is often the source of teenagers' greatest unhappiness. Boys tend to externalize their emotional problems in acts of aggression and other antisocial behaviour; girls tend to internalize their problems by becoming depressed or developing eating disorders.

ADULTHOOD

◆ Erik Erikson proposed that life consists of eight stages, each with a unique psychological challenge, or crisis, that must be resolved, such as an *identity crisis* in adolescence. Erikson identified many of the essential concerns of adulthood and showed that development is a lifelong process. However, psychological issues or crises are not confined to particular chronological periods or stages.

◆ When most people in an age group go through the same event at about the same time, transitions are easier than when people feel out of step. In industrialized nations, major demographic changes have caused young adults to postpone the timing of career decisions, marriage or commitment to a partner, and parenthood. Many people between the ages of 18 and 25, especially if they are not financially independent, find themselves in a life phase often called *emerging adulthood*.

◆ The middle years are generally not a time of turmoil or crisis but the prime of most people's lives. In women, *menopause* begins in the late forties or early fifties. Many women have temporary physical symptoms, but most do not regret the end of fertility or become depressed and irritable. In middle-aged men, hormone production slows down and sperm counts decline; fertility continues, but with increased risk of fetal abnormalities.

◆ *Gerontologists* have revised our ideas about old age, now that people are living longer and healthier lives and entering an extended phase of "positive retirement." The speed of cognitive processing slows down, and *fluid intelligence* parallels other biological capacities in its eventual decline. *Crystallized intelligence*, in contrast, depends heavily on culture, education, and experience, and tends to remain stable over the life span.

◆ Many supposedly inevitable results of aging, such as senility, depression, and physical frailty, are often avoidable. They may result from disease, medication, or poor nutrition, and also from lack of stimulation, control of one's environment, and physical strength and fitness. Exercise and mental stimulation promote the growth of synapses in the human brain, even well into old age, although some mental losses are inevitable.

THE WELLSPRINGS OF RESILIENCE

◆ Children who experience violence or neglect are at risk of many problems later in life, but most children are resilient and are able to overcome early adversity. Psychologists now study not only the sad consequences of neglect, poverty, and violence but also the reasons for resilience under adversity.

TAKING PSYCHOLOGY WITH YOU

◆ Many child-rearing experts claim to have "the" way to make children smarter, nicer, and more successful. Research in child development can help people think critically about such claims and also offers some general guidelines: Set high but realistic expectations, explain the reasons for your rules, encourage empathy, and reward good behaviour.

MyPsychLab

Visit **www.mypsychlab.com** to help you get the best grade!
Test your knowledge and grasp difficult concepts through

• Custom study plans: See where you are strong and where you go wrong
• Interactive simulations
• Video and audio clips

KEY TERMS

ASK QUESTIONS . . . be willing to WONDER

- How accurate are those tests that tell you what "personality type" you are?

- When people talk about "repressing" a memory or being "in denial," where does that language come from?

- If you hear that shyness or another personality trait is "inherited," does that mean it can't be changed?

- Why is the same person often so different with family, with friends, and in the classroom?

She was the eldest daughter of eight children in an Italian immigrant family. Only six years old when her mother died, she became the dutiful caretaker of her siblings. She faithfully attended Catholic school, and throughout childhood she was deeply religious. But her earliest passion was to dance, and when her reluctant father finally allowed her to take lessons, her instructors immediately recognized and encouraged her talent. As a young woman, driven to succeed, she dropped out of college and made her way to New York with a one-way ticket and $35 in her purse. She found part-time work, met some musicians, connected with some influential DJs . . . and became the superstar the world knows as Madonna.

Today, Madonna works tirelessly and demands total control over her shows. Her friends and associates have observed that she also obsessively controls her films, public appearances, and even her private life in the service of her public image. And that image is a continual work in progress: good-girl virgin in white, androgynous robot, provocative sex symbol, glamour queen, devoted Catholic, practitioner of the Kabbalah (a mystical wing of Judaism), doting mother. At the 2009 Oscars, the newly divorced Madonna, age 50, turned up with a new facelift and a new, 22-year-old boyfriend. Who is Madonna? The flamboyant performer who loves to shock or a regular mom, sex symbol or spiritual seeker? Was she born to be an exhibitionist, or did she create a persona to make herself famous? Which personality traits best describe her: extroverted, ambitious, outrageous, motherly, obsessive, funny, selfish, rebellious? Who is the "real" Madonna amid the changing public images? *Is* there a real one?

In this chapter, we will see how psychologists answer such questions—how they define and study personality. **Personality** refers to a distinctive pattern of behaviour, mannerisms, thoughts, motives, and emotions that characterizes an individual over time and across different situations. This pattern consists of many distinctive **traits**, habitual ways of behaving, thinking, and feeling: shy, outgoing, friendly, hostile, gloomy, confident, and so on.

We will begin with the oldest theory of personality, the psychodynamic view, so that you will have a sense of how influential it was, why it still appeals to some, and why many of its ideas have become outdated. Next we will consider evidence for the newest theory, the genetic view. Few scientists think anymore that babies are tiny lumps of clay, shaped entirely by their experiences, or that parents alone determine whether their infant becomes an adventurer, a sourpuss, a worrywart . . . or an extrovert like Madonna. On the other hand, even if half of the human variation in personality traits is due to genetics, what is responsible for the other half?

To answer that question, we will then examine leading approaches to personality that are neither psychodynamic nor biological: the environmental approach, which emphasizes the role of social learning, situations, parents, and peers; the cultural approach, which emphasizes cultural influences on traits and behaviour; and the humanist and narrative approaches, which emphasize self-determination and people's own view of themselves.

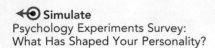
Simulate
Psychology Experiments Survey:
What Has Shaped Your Personality?

◆ YOU are about to learn . . .

◆ Freud's theory of the structure and development of personality.

◆ Carl Jung's theory of the collective unconscious and how it applies to Harry Potter's arch-enemy, Lord Voldemort.

◆ the nature of the "objects" in the object-relations approach to personality.

◆ why many psychologists reject most psychodynamic ideas.

PSYCHODYNAMIC THEORIES OF PERSONALITY

A man apologizes for "displacing" his frustrations at work onto his family. A woman suspects that she is "repressing" a childhood trauma. An alcoholic reveals that he is no longer "in denial" about his drinking. A teacher informs a divorcing couple that their eight-year-old child is "regressing" to immature behaviour. All of this language about displacing, repressing, denying, and regressing can be traced to the first psychodynamic theory of personality, Sigmund Freud's theory of **psychoanalysis**.

Freud's theory is called **psychodynamic** because it emphasizes the movement of psychological energy within the person, in the form of attachments, conflicts, and motivations. (Freud did not use "dynamic" in today's sense, to mean "powerful" or "energetic." *Dynamics* is a term from physics that refers to the motion and balance of systems under the action of external or internal forces.) Today's psychodynamic theories differ from Freudian theory and from one another, but they all share an emphasis on unconscious processes going on within the mind. They also share an assumption that adult personality and ongoing problems are formed primarily by experiences in early childhood. These experiences produce unconscious thoughts and feelings, which later form characteristic habits, conflicts, and often self-defeating behaviour.

Freud and Psychoanalysis

To enter the world of Sigmund Freud is to enter a realm of unconscious motives, passions, guilty secrets, unspeakable yearnings, and conflicts between desire and duty. These unseen forces, Freud believed, have far more power over our personalities than our conscious intentions do. The unconscious reveals itself, said Freud, in art, dreams, jokes, apparent accidents, and slips of the tongue (which have come to be called "Freudian slips"). According to Freud (1920/1960), the British member of Parliament who referred to the "honourable member from Hell" when he meant to say "from Hull" was revealing his actual unconscious appraisal of his colleague.

THE STRUCTURE OF PERSONALITY.   In Freud's theory, personality consists of three major systems: the id, the ego, and the superego. Any action we take or problem we have results from the interaction and degree of balance among these systems (Freud, 1905b, 1920/1960, 1923/1962).

Sigmund Freud (1856–1939).

personality   A distinctive and relatively stable pattern of behaviour, thoughts, motives, and emotions that characterizes an individual.

trait   A characteristic of an individual, describing a habitual way of behaving, thinking, or feeling.

psychoanalysis   A theory of personality and a method of psychotherapy developed by Sigmund Freud; it emphasizes unconscious motives and conflicts.

psychodynamic theories   Theories that explain behaviour and personality in terms of unconscious energy dynamics within the individual.

The **id**, which is present at birth, is the reservoir of unconscious psychological energies and the motives to avoid pain and obtain pleasure. The id contains two competing instincts: the life, or sexual, instinct (fuelled by psychic energy called the **libido**) and the death, or aggressive, instinct. As energy builds up in the id, tension results. The id may discharge this tension in the form of reflex actions, physical symptoms, or uncensored mental images and unbidden thoughts.

The **ego**, the second system to emerge, is a referee between the needs of instinct and the demands of society. It bows to the realities of life, putting a rein on the id's desire for sex and aggression until a suitable, socially appropriate outlet for them can be found. The ego, said Freud, is both conscious and unconscious, and it represents "reason and good sense."

The **superego**, the last system of personality to develop, is the voice of conscience, representing morality and parental authority. The superego judges the activities of the id, handing out good feelings of pride and satisfaction when you do something well and handing out miserable feelings of guilt and shame when you break the rules. The superego is partly conscious but largely unconscious.

According to Freud, the healthy personality must keep all three systems in balance. Someone who is too controlled by the id is governed by impulse and selfish desires. Someone who is too controlled by the superego is rigid, moralistic, and bossy. Someone who has a weak ego is unable to balance personal needs and wishes with social duties and realistic limitations.

If a person feels anxious or threatened when the wishes of the id conflict with social rules, the ego has weapons at its command to relieve the tension. These unconscious strategies, called **defence mechanisms**, deny or distort reality, but they also protect us from conflict and anxiety. They become unhealthy only when they cause self-defeating behaviour and emotional problems. Here are five of the primary defences identified by Freud and later analysts (A. Freud, 1967; Vaillant, 1992):

1 **Repression** occurs when a threatening idea, memory, or emotion is blocked from consciousness. A woman who had a frightening childhood experience that she cannot remember, for example, is said to be repressing her memory of it. Freud used the term *repression* to mean both unconscious expulsion of disturbing material from awareness and conscious suppression of such material. But modern analysts tend to think of it only as an unconscious defence mechanism.

2 **Projection** occurs when a person's own unacceptable or threatening feelings are repressed and then attributed to someone else. A person who is embarrassed about having sexual feelings toward members of a different ethnic group, for example, may project this discomfort onto them, saying, "Those people are dirty-minded and oversexed."

3 **Displacement** occurs when people direct their emotions (especially anger) toward things, animals, or other people that are not the real object of their feelings. A boy who

id In psychoanalysis, the part of personality containing inherited psychic energy, particularly sexual and aggressive instincts.

libido (li-BEE-do) In psychoanalysis, the psychic energy that fuels the life or sexual instincts of the id.

ego In psychoanalysis, the part of personality that represents reason, good sense, and rational self-control.

superego In psychoanalysis, the part of personality that represents conscience, morality, and social standards.

defence mechanisms Methods used by the ego to prevent unconscious anxiety or threatening thoughts from entering consciousness.

"I'm sorry, I'm not speaking to anyone tonight. My defence mechanisms seem to be out of order."

is forbidden to express anger toward his father, for example, may "take it out" on his toys or his younger sister. When displacement serves a higher cultural or socially useful purpose, as in the creation of art or inventions, it is called *sublimation*. Freud argued that society has a duty to help people sublimate their unacceptable impulses for the sake of civilization. Sexual passion, for example, may be sublimated into the creation of art or literature.

4 **Regression** occurs when a person reverts to a previous phase of psychological development. An eight-year-old boy who is anxious about his parents' divorce may regress to earlier habits of thumb sucking or clinging. Adults may regress to immature behaviour when they are under pressure—for example, by having temper tantrums when they don't get their way.

5 **Denial** occurs when people refuse to admit that something unpleasant is happening, such as mistreatment by a partner; that they have a problem, such as drinking too much; or that they are feeling a forbidden emotion, such as anger. Denial protects a person's self-image and preserves the illusion of invulnerability: "It can't happen to me."

THE DEVELOPMENT OF PERSONALITY. Freud argued that personality develops in a series of **psychosexual stages**, in which sexual energy takes different forms as the child matures. Each new stage produces a certain amount of frustration, conflict, and anxiety. If these are not resolved properly, normal development may be interrupted, and the child may remain *fixated*, or stuck, at the current stage.

For example, said Freud, some people remain fixated at the *oral stage*, which occurs during the first year of life, when babies experience the world through their mouths. As adults, they will seek oral gratification in smoking, overeating, nail biting, or chewing on pencils; some may become clinging and dependent, like a nursing child. Others remain fixated at the *anal stage*, at ages 2 to 3, when toilet training and control of bodily wastes are the key issues. They may become "anal retentive," holding everything in, obsessive about neatness and cleanliness. Or they may become just the opposite, "anal expulsive"—messy and disorganized.

For Freud, however, the most crucial stage for the formation of personality was the *phallic (Oedipal) stage*, which lasts roughly from age 3 to age 5 or 6. During this stage, said Freud, the child unconsciously wishes to possess the parent of the other sex and to get rid of the parent of the same sex. Children often proudly announce, "I'm going to marry Daddy (or Mommy) when I grow up," and they reject the same-sex "rival." Freud labelled this phenomenon the **Oedipus complex**, after the Greek legend of King Oedipus, who unwittingly killed his father and married his mother.

Boys and girls, Freud believed, go through the Oedipal stage differently. Boys are discovering the pleasure and pride of having a penis, so when they see a naked girl for the first time, they are horrified. Their unconscious exclaims (in effect), "Her penis has been cut off! Who could have done such a thing to her? Why, it must have been her powerful father. And if he could do it to her, my father could do it to me!" This realization, said Freud, causes the boy to repress his desire for his mother and identify with his father. He accepts his father's authority and the father's standards of conscience and morality; the superego has emerged.

Freud admitted that he did not quite know what to make of girls, who, lacking the penis, could not go through the same steps. He speculated that a girl, upon discovering

A Freudian would say that this woman's nail-biting is a sign of an oral fixation.

psychosexual stages In Freud's theory, the idea that sexual energy takes different forms as the child matures; the stages are oral, anal, phallic (Oedipal), latency, and genital.

Oedipus complex In psychoanalysis, a conflict occurring in the phallic (Oedipal) stage, in which a child desires the parent of the other sex and views the same-sex parent as a rival.

male anatomy, would panic that she had only a puny clitoris instead of a stately penis. She would conclude that she had already lost her penis. As a result, Freud said, girls do not have the powerful motivating fear that boys do to give up their Oedipal feelings and develop a strong superego; they have only a lingering sense of "penis envy."

Freud believed that when the Oedipus complex is resolved, at about age 5 or 6, the child's personality is fundamentally formed. Unconscious conflicts with parents, unresolved fixations and guilts, and attitudes toward the same and the other sex will continue to replay themselves throughout life. The child settles into a supposedly nonsexual *latency* stage, in preparation for the *genital stage*, which begins at puberty and leads to adult sexuality.

In Freud's view, therefore, your adult personality is shaped by how you progressed through the early psychosexual stages, which defence mechanisms you developed to reduce anxiety, and whether your ego is strong enough to balance the conflict between the id (what you would like to do) and the superego (your conscience).

As you might imagine, Freud's ideas were not exactly received with yawns. Sexual feelings in five-year-olds! Repressed longings in respectable adults! Unconscious meanings in dreams! Penis envy! This was strong stuff in the early years of the twentieth century, and before long psychoanalysis had captured the public imagination in Europe and the United States. But it also produced a sharp rift with the emerging schools of empirical psychology.

This rift continues to divide scholars today. Many believe that the overall framework of Freud's theory is timeless and brilliant, even if some specific ideas have proven faulty (Westen, 1998). Others think that psychoanalytic theory is nonsense, with little empirical support, and that Freud was not the theoretical genius, impartial scientist, or even successful clinician that he claimed to be. On the contrary, Freud often bullied his patients into accepting his explanations of their symptoms and ignored all evidence disconfirming his ideas (McNally, 2003; Powell & Boer, 1995; Webster, 1995).

On the positive side, Freud welcomed women into the profession of psychoanalysis, wrote eloquently about the devastating results to women of society's suppression of their sexuality, and argued, ahead of his time, that homosexuality was neither a sin nor a perversion but a "variation of the sexual function" and "nothing to be ashamed of" (Freud, 1961). Freud was thus a mixture of intellectual vision and blindness, sensitivity and arrogance. His provocative ideas left a powerful legacy to psychology, one that others began to tinker with immediately.

✱ Explore
Freud's Five Psychosexual Stages of Personality Development

---

quickQUIZ

✓ Quick Review on **MyPsychLab**

Have Freudian concepts registered in your unconscious?

Which Freudian concepts do the following events suggest?

1. A four-year-old girl wants to snuggle on Daddy's lap but refuses to kiss her mother.
2. A celibate priest writes poetry about sexual passion.
3. A man who is angry with his boss shouts at his kids for making noise.
4. A racist justifies segregation by saying that black men are only interested in sex with white women.
5. A nine-year-old boy who moves to a new city starts having tantrums.

Answers:

1. Oedipus complex 2. sublimation 3. displacement 4. projection 5. regression

Other Psychodynamic Approaches

Some of Freud's followers stayed in the psychoanalytic tradition and modified Freud's theories from within. Women, as you might imagine, were not too pleased about "penis envy." Clara Thompson (1943/1973) and Karen Horney [HORN-eye] (1926/1973) argued that it was insulting and unscientific to claim that half the human race is dissatisfied with its anatomy. When women feel inferior to men, they said, we should look for explanations in the disadvantages that women live with and their second-class status. Other psychoanalysts broke away from Freud, or were actively rejected by him, and went off to start their own schools.

JUNGIAN THEORY. Carl Jung (1875–1961) was originally one of Freud's closest friends and a member of his inner circle, but the friendship ended with a furious quarrel about the nature of the unconscious. In addition to the individual's own unconscious, said Jung (1967), all human beings share a vast **collective unconscious**, containing universal memories, symbols, images, and themes, which he called **archetypes**.

An archetype can be an image, such as the "magic circle," called a mandala in Eastern religions, which Jung thought symbolizes the unity of life and "the totality of the self." Or it can be a figure found in fairy tales, legends, and popular stories, such as the Hero, the nurturing Earth Mother, the Powerful Father, or the Wicked Witch. It can even be an aspect of the self. For example, the *shadow* archetype reflects the prehistoric fear of wild animals and represents the bestial, evil side of human nature. Scholars have found that some basic archetypes, such as the Hero and the Earth Mother, do appear in the stories and images of virtually every society (Campbell, 1949/1968; Neher, 1996). Jungians would recognize dragons, Darth Vader, the Dark Lord Sauron, Dracula, and Harry Potter's tormentor Lord Voldemort as expressions of the shadow archetype. In Canada, we regard Karla Homolka, who aided her husband, Paul Bernardo, in the sexual assault and murder of several teenage girls in Ontario, as an example of the wicked witch or shadow archetype. Few figures in Canadian history elicit as repulsed a reaction among so many people as do these two.

◆ **Research**
Karen Horney

◆ **Research**
Carl Jung

collective unconscious In Jungian theory, the universal memories and experiences of humankind, represented in the symbols, stories, and images (archetypes) that occur across all cultures.

archetypes [AR-ki-tipes] Universal, symbolic images that appear in myths, art, stories, and dreams; to Jungians, they reflect the collective unconscious.

In the Jungian view, the Joker is a modern archetype of evil, along with Darth Vader, Lord Voldemort, Dracula, and the Wicked Witch of the West. Historically, the Hero archetype has always been male, but that's clearly changing, as fans of *Battlestar Galactica* know. Captain Kara Thrace bravely fights the odds to save the world, just as those guys with Bat-, Spider-, and Super- in their names do.

Although Jung shared with Freud a fascination with the darker aspects of the personality, he had more confidence in the positive, forward-moving strengths of the ego. He believed that people are motivated not only by past conflicts but also by their future goals and their desire to fulfill themselves. Jung was also among the first to identify extroversion/introversion as a basic dimension of personality. Nonetheless, many of Jung's ideas were more suited to mysticism and philosophy than to empirical psychology, which may be why so many Jungian ideas became popular with New Age movements.

Jung had a psychotic breakdown after his split with Freud. And he revealed his own "dark side" when he supported the Nazis, writing vicious attacks on Jews and claiming that their collective unconscious differed from that of gentiles (so much for its universality). But he continued to treat patients and attract many worshipful followers by virtue of his charisma (Hayman, 2001). Like Freud, therefore, Jung left a troubling personal legacy along with theories that appealed to legions of believers.

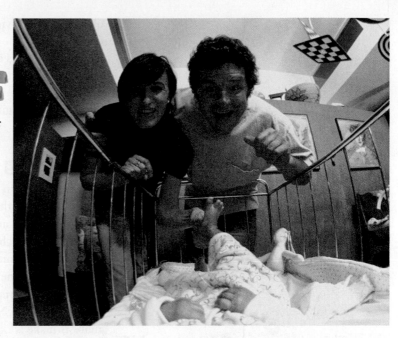

According to object-relations theory, a baby constructs unconscious representations of his or her parents that will influence the child's relations with others throughout life.

THE OBJECT-RELATIONS SCHOOL. Freud essentially regarded the baby as if it were an independent, greedy little organism ruled by its own instinctive desires; other people were relevant only insofar as they gratified the infant's drives or blocked them. But by the 1950s, increased awareness of the importance of human attachments led to a different view of infancy, put forward by the object-relations school, which was developed in Great Britain by Melanie Klein, D. W. Winnicott, and others. To object-relations theorists, the central problem in life is to find a balance between the need for independence and the need for others. This balance requires constant adjustment to separations and losses: small ones such as disagreements during quarrels, moderate ones such as leaving home for the first time, and major ones such as divorce or death. The way we react to these separations, according to object-relations analysts, is largely determined by our experiences in the first year or two of life. In order to get the mother's recognition, the baby will find parts of himself or herself that the mother appreciates and values. If the baby's need for recognition goes unheeded, the baby's personality will be warped. The infant may develop what Winnicott called a "false self," because certain parts of the baby's "true self" remain undeveloped (Orbach, 2009).

The reason for the clunky word "object" in object-relations, instead of the warmer word "human" or "parent," is that the infant's attachment is not only to a real person (usually the mother) but also to the infant's evolving perception of her. The child creates a *mental representation* of the mother—someone who is kind or fierce, protective or rejecting. The child's representations of important adults, whether realistic or distorted, unconsciously affect personality throughout life, influencing whether the person relates to others with trust or suspicion, acceptance or criticism.

Object-relations theorists have applied this approach in many ways: for example, to predict whether a client will benefit from psychotherapy (Mallinckrodt, Porter, & Kivlighan, 2005), to help people deal with disability and other losses in life (Goldstein, 2002), and even to try to explain why some distrustful, cynical people harass others on the internet (Whitty & Carr, 2006).

The object-relations school also departs from Freudian theory regarding the nature of male and female development (Sagan, 1988; Winnicott, 1957/1990). In the

object-relations school A psychodynamic approach that emphasizes the importance of the infant's first two years of life and the baby's formative relationships, especially with the mother.

Analyze Assumptions

Freud and his followers assumed they could derive general principles of personality by studying patients in therapy, that childhood traumas inevitably have life-long emotional consequences, and that memories are reliable guides to the past. What is wrong with these assumptions?

Examine the Evidence

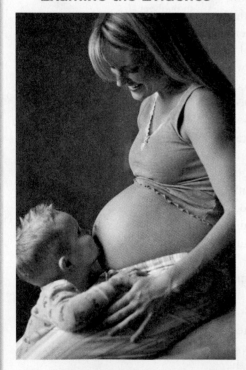

Freud claimed, without much empirical evidence, that all little girls suffer from "penis envy." But studies of preschool girls and boys find that young children of *both* sexes are curious about, and often imagine having, the reproductive abilities of the other sex (Linday, 1994).

object-relations view, children of both sexes identify first with the mother. Girls, who are the same sex as the mother, do not need to separate from her; the mother treats a daughter as an extension of herself. But boys must break away from the mother in order to develop a masculine identity; the mother encourages a son to be independent and separate. Thus men, in this view, develop more rigid boundaries between themselves and other people than women do.

Evaluating Psychodynamic Theories

Although modern psychodynamic theorists differ in many ways, they share a general belief that to understand personality we must explore its unconscious dynamics and origins. Many psychologists in other fields, however, regard most psychodynamic ideas as literary metaphors rather than as scientific explanations (Cioffi, 1998; Crews, 1998). They point out that most of the cornerstone assumptions in psychoanalytic theory, such as the notion that the mind "represses" traumatic experiences, have not been supported scientifically (McNally, 2003; Rofé, 2008; see Chapter 10). Object-relations analysts make all kinds of assumptions about what an infant feels and wants, but how do they know that a "true self" is being suppressed? Moreover, psychological scientists have shown that psychodynamic theories are guilty of three scientific failings:

1 **Violating the principle of falsifiability.** As we saw in Chapter 2, a theory that is impossible to disconfirm in principle is not scientific. Many psychodynamic concepts about unconscious motivations are, in fact, impossible to confirm or disconfirm. Followers often accept an idea because it seems intuitively right or their experience seems to support it. Anyone who doubts the idea or offers disconfirming evidence is then accused of being "defensive" or "in denial."

2 **Drawing universal principles from the experiences of a few atypical patients.** Freud and most of his followers generalized from a few individuals, often patients in therapy, to all human beings. Of course, sometimes case studies can generate valid insights about human behaviour. The problem occurs when the observer fails to confirm his or her observations by studying larger, more representative samples and including appropriate control groups. For example, some psychodynamically oriented therapists, believing in Freud's notion of a childhood "latency" stage, have assumed that if a child masturbates or enjoys sex play, the child has probably been sexually molested. But research finds that masturbation and sexual curiosity are not found just in abused children; these are normal and common childhood behaviours (Bancroft, 2006; Friedrich et al., 1998).

3 **Basing theories of personality development on the retrospective accounts of adults.** Most psychodynamic theorists have not observed random samples of children at different ages, as modern child psychologists do, to construct their theories of development. Instead they have worked backward, creating theories based on themes in adults' recollections of childhood. The analysis of memories can be an illuminating way to achieve insights about our lives; in fact, it is the only way we can

think about our own lives! But memory is often inaccurate, influenced as much by what is going on in our lives now as by what happened in the past. If you are currently not getting along with your mother, you may remember all the times when she was hard on you and forget the counterexamples of her kindness.

Retrospective analysis has another problem: It creates an *illusion of causality* between events. People often assume that if A came before B, then A must have caused B. For example, if your mother spent three months in the hospital when you were five years old and today you feel shy and insecure in college, an object-relations analyst might draw a connection between the two facts. But a lot of other things could be causing your shyness and insecurity, such as being away from home for the first time at a large and impersonal college. When psychologists conduct longitudinal studies, following people from childhood to adulthood, they often get a very different picture of causality from the one that emerges by looking backward (see Chapter 13).

Despite these serious problems, some psychodynamic concepts have been empirically tested and validated. Researchers have identified unconscious processes in thought, memory, and behaviour (Bargh & Morsella, 2008). They have found evidence for the major defence mechanisms, such as projection, denial, and displacement (Baumeister, Dale, & Sommer, 1998; Cramer, 2000; Marcus-Newhall et al., 2000). They have demonstrated the interaction of mind and body in the generation of stress-related physical problems. And they have confirmed the important psychodynamic idea that we are often unaware of the motives behind our own puzzling or self-defeating actions.

---

quickQUIZ

Quick Review on **MyPsychLab**

Are you feeling defensive about answering this quiz?

1. An eight-year-old boy is hitting classmates and disobeying his teacher. Which of the following explanations of his behaviour might come from a Freudian, Jungian, or object-relations analyst? (a) The boy is expressing his shadow archetype. (b) The boy is expressing the aggressive energy of the id and has not developed enough ego control. (c) The boy has had unusual difficulty separating from his mother and is compensating by behaving aggressively.

2. What criticism of all three of the preceding explanations might a psychological scientist make?

3. In the 1950s and 1960s, many psychoanalysts, working with unhappy gay men who had sought therapy, concluded that homosexuality was a mental illness. What violation of the scientific method were they committing?

Answers:

1. a. Jungian b. Freudian c. object-relations analyst 2. All three explanations are nonfalsifiable; that is, there is no way to disconfirm them or confirm them. They are just subjective interpretations. 3. The analysts were drawing conclusions from patients in therapy and failing to test these conclusions with gay men who were not in therapy or with heterosexuals. When such research was done using appropriate control groups, it turned out that gay men were not more mentally disturbed or depressed than heterosexuals (Hooker, 1957).

YOU are about to learn . . .

- whether you can trust tests that tell you what "personality type" you are.
- how psychologists can tell which personality traits are more central or important than others.
- the five dimensions of personality that describe people the world over.

THE MODERN STUDY OF PERSONALITY

People love to fit themselves and their friends into "types"; they have been doing it forever. Early Greek philosophers thought our personalities fell into four fundamental categories depending on mixes of body fluids. For example, if you were an angry, irritable sort of person, you supposedly had an excess of choler, and even now the word *choleric* describes a hothead. And if you were sluggish and unemotional, you supposedly had an excess of phlegm, making you a "phlegmatic" type.

Popular Personality Tests

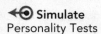
Simulate
Personality Tests

That particular theory is long gone, but other unscientific tests of personality types still exist, aimed at predicting how people will do at work, whether they will get along with others, or whether they will succeed as leaders. One such test, the Myers-Briggs Type Indicator, is hugely popular in business, at motivational seminars, and with matchmaking services; at least 2.5 million Americans a year take it (Gladwell, 2004). The test assigns people to one of 16 different types, depending on how the individual scores on the dimensions of introverted or extroverted, logical or intuitive. Unfortunately, the Myers-Briggs test is not much more reliable than measuring body fluids; one study found that fewer than half of the respondents scored as the same type a mere five weeks later. And there is little evidence that knowledge of a person's type reliably predicts behaviour on the job or in relationships (Barbuto, 1997; Paul, 2004; Pittenger, 1993). Equally useless from a scientific point of view are many of the tests used by business and government to predict which "types" are apt to steal, take drugs, or be disloyal on the job (Ehrenreich, 2001).

In contrast, there are many measures of personality traits that are scientifically valid and useful in research. These **objective tests (inventories)** are standardized questionnaires requiring written responses, typically to multiple-choice or true–false items. They provide information about literally hundreds of different aspects of personality, including needs, values, interests, self-esteem, emotional problems, and typical ways of responding to situations. Using well-constructed inventories, psychologists have identified hundreds of traits, ranging from sensation seeking (the enjoyment of risk) to "erotophobia" (the fear of sex).

Core Personality Traits

objective tests (inventories)
Standardized questionnaires requiring written responses; they typically include scales on which people are asked to rate themselves.

Are some personality traits more important or central than others? Do some of them overlap or cluster together? For Gordon Allport, one of the most influential psychologists in the empirical study of personality, the answer to both questions was yes. Allport (1961) recognized that not all traits have equal weight and significance in people's lives. Most of us, he said, have five to ten *central traits* that reflect a characteristic way of behaving, dealing with others, and reacting to new situations. For instance, some people see the world as a hostile, dangerous place, whereas others see it as a place for fun and frolic. *Secondary traits*, in contrast, are more changeable aspects of personality, such as music preferences, habits, casual opinions, and the like.

Raymond B. Cattell (1973) advanced the study of this issue by applying a statistical method called **factor analysis**. Performing a factor analysis is like adding water to flour: It causes the material to clump up into little balls. When applied to traits, this procedure identifies clusters of correlated items that seem to be measuring some common, underlying factor. Today, hundreds of factor-analytic studies support the existence of a cluster of five central "robust factors," known informally as the *Big Five* (McCrae & Costa, 2008; McCrae et al., 2005; Paunonen, 2003; Roberts & Mroczek, 2008):

◆ **Research**
Gordon Allport

Raymond Cattell

1 **Extroversion versus introversion** describes the extent to which people are outgoing or shy. It includes such traits as being sociable or reclusive, adventurous or cautious, socially dominant or more passive, eager to be in the limelight or inclined to stay in the shadows.

2 **Neuroticism (negative emotionality) versus emotional stability** describes the extent to which a person suffers from such traits as anxiety, an inability to control impulses, and a tendency to feel negative emotions such as anger, guilt, contempt, and resentment. Neurotic individuals are worriers, complainers, and defeatists, even when they have no major problems. They are always ready to see the sour side of life and none of its sweetness.

Where do you think this man would score on extroversion?

3 **Agreeableness versus antagonism** describes the extent to which people are good-natured or irritable, cooperative or abrasive, secure or suspicious and jealous. It reflects the tendency to have friendly relationships or hostile ones.

4 **Conscientiousness versus impulsiveness** describes the degree to which people are responsible or undependable, persevering or quick to give up, steadfast or fickle, tidy or careless, self-disciplined or impulsive.

5 **Openness to experience versus resistance to new experience** describes the extent to which people are curious, imaginative, questioning, and creative or conforming, unimaginative, predictable, and uncomfortable with novelty.

Culture can affect the prominence of these personality factors and how they are reflected in language (Toomela, 2003). Nonetheless, in spite of some semantic and cultural variations, the Big Five have emerged as distinct, central personality dimensions throughout the world, in countries as diverse as Britain, Canada, the Czech Republic, China, Ethiopia, Turkey, the Netherlands, Japan, Spain, the Philippines, Germany, Portugal, Israel, Korea, Russia, and Australia (Digman & Shmelyov, 1996; Katigbak et al., 2002; McCrae et al., 2005; Somer & Goldberg, 1999). One monumental

factor analysis A statistical method for analyzing the intercorrelations among various measures or test scores; clusters of measures or scores that are highly correlated are assumed to measure the same underlying trait or ability (factor).

research venture gathered data from thousands of people across 50 cultures. In this massive project, as in many smaller ones, the five personality factors emerged whether people were asked for self-reports or were assessed by others (McCrae et al., 2005; Terracciano & McCrae, 2006).

✱ Explore
The Five Factor Model

People's personalities are often reflected in how they arrange their work spaces!

Although the Big Five are quite stable over a lifetime, especially once a person hits 30, there are some exceptions. In later adulthood people tend to become less extroverted and less open to new experiences (see Figure 14.1), and, with the right experiences, many young people eventually become more self-confident and emotionally stable (Roberts & Mroczek, 2008). There is also some good news for crabby neurotics, especially young ones. A survey of thousands of people in 10 countries, and a meta-analysis of 92 longitudinal studies, found that young people aged 16 to 21 are the most neurotic (emotionally negative) and the least agreeable and conscientious. But fortunately, people tend to become more agreeable and conscientious and less negative between ages 30 and 40 (Costa et al., 1999; Roberts, Walton, & Viechtbauer, 2006). Because these changes have been found in many different countries, they may reflect the universality of adult experiences—such as work and family responsibilities—or common maturational changes over the life span.

The Big Five do not provide a complete picture of personality, of course. Clinical psychologists note that important traits involved in mental disorders are missing, such as psychopathy (lack of remorse and empathy), self-absorption, and obsessionality (Westen & Shedler, 1999). Personality researchers note that other important traits are missing, such as religiosity, dishonesty, humorousness, independence, and conventionality (Abrahamson, Baker, & Caspi, 2002; Paunonen & Ashton, 2001). But most researchers today agree that the Big Five do lie at the core of key personality variations among individuals, and not only human individuals, either.

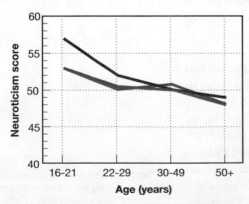

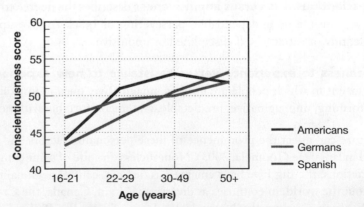

FIGURE 14.1 Consistency and Change in Personality over the Life Span
Although the Big Five traits are fairly stable, changes do occur over the life span. As you can see, neuroticism (negative emotionality) is highest among young adults and then declines, whereas conscientiousness is lowest among young adults and then steadily increases (Costa et al., 1999).

RATE YOUR TRAITS

For each of the 10 items that follow, write a number from 1 to 7 indicating the extent to which you see that trait as being characteristic of you, where 1 = "I *disagree* strongly that this trait describes me" to 7 = "I *agree* strongly that this trait describes me." Use the midpoint, 4, if you neither agree nor disagree that the trait describes you. (This self-test was designed by Samuel D. Gosling.)

1. _____ Extroverted, enthusiastic
2. _____ Critical, quarrelsome
3. _____ Dependable, self-disciplined
4. _____ Anxious, easily upset
5. _____ Open to new experiences, complex
6. _____ Reserved, quiet
7. _____ Sympathetic, warm
8. _____ Disorganized, careless
9. _____ Calm, emotionally stable
10. _____ Conventional, uncreative

To score yourself on the Big Five traits, use this key:

Extroversion:	High on question 1, low on question 6
Neuroticism:	High on question 4, low on question 9
Agreeableness:	High on question 7, low on question 2
Conscientiousness:	High on question 3, low on question 8
Openness:	High on question 5, low on question 10

Now ask a friend or relative to rate you on each of the 10 items. How closely does that rating match your own? If there is a discrepancy, what might be the reason for it?

Show that you have the trait of conscientiousness by taking this quiz.

1. What is the advantage of inventories over projective tests in measuring personality?
2. Raymond Cattell advanced the study of personality by (a) developing case-study analysis, (b) using factor analysis, (c) devising the Myers-Briggs Type Indicator.
3. Which of the following are *not* among the Big Five personality factors? (a) introversion, (b) agreeableness, (c) psychoticism, (d) openness to experience, (e) intelligence, (f) neuroticism, (g) conscientiousness
4. Which one of the Big Five typically decreases by age 40? (a) agreeableness, (b) extroversion, (c) openness to experience, (d) neuroticism

quickQUIZ

✓ **Quick Review** on **MyPsychLab**

Answers:

1. In general, they have better reliability and validity. 2. b 3. c, e 4. d

YOU are about to learn . . .

◆ whether animals have "personalities" just as people do.

◆ the extent to which temperamental and personality differences among people are influenced by genes.

◆ why people who have highly heritable personality traits are not necessarily stuck with them forever.

GENETIC INFLUENCES ON PERSONALITY

A mother we know was describing her two children: "My daughter has always been difficult, intense, and testy," she said, "but my son is the opposite, placid and good-natured. They came out of the womb that way." Was this mother right? Is it possible to be born touchy or good-natured? What aspects of personality might have an inherited component?

Researchers measure genetic contributions to personality in three ways: by studying personality traits in other species, by studying the temperaments of human infants and children, and by doing heritability studies of twins and adopted individuals. These methods, to date, permit us only to *infer* the existence of relevant genes—just as, if you find your toddler covered in chocolate, it's pretty safe to infer that candy is somewhere close by. Scientists hope that the actual genes underlying key traits will one day be discovered, and dozens of possible associations between specific genes and personality traits have already been reported (Fox, Nichols, et al., 2005; Plomin et al., 2001). You will be hearing lots more about genetic discoveries in the coming years, so it is important to understand what they mean and don't mean.

BIOLOGY and *Animal Traits*

Do Puppies Have Personalities?

When we think of an individual who has a personality, we usually think of a human being. But members of many other species, including bears, dogs, hyenas, goats, cats, and of course our fellow primates, also vary in their characteristic ways of responding to the environment and to one another (Weinstein, Capitanio, & Gosling, 2008). Some chimpanzees are warm, friendly, and cooperative; others are conniving and mean. Some are "extroverts," bold and impulsive; others are "introverts," shy and cautious (Fairbanks, 2001). Apparently, then, you don't have to be a person to have a personality.

Recently, researchers have been crossing the border between traditional personality research and physiology, genetics, ecology, and ethology (the study of animals in their natural habitats) to investigate the nature of "personality" in our fellow animals (Fairbanks, 2001). These investigators argue that just as it has been evolutionarily adaptive for human beings to vary in their temperaments and ways of responding to the world and those around them (see Chapter 3), so it has been for animals. It would be beneficial for a species if some, but not all, of its members were bold or impulsive enough to risk life and limb to confront a stranger or experiment with a new food, and if some of its members were appropriately cautious.

In an imaginative set of studies, Samuel D. Gosling and his colleagues (2003) recruited dog owners and their dogs in a local park. All the owners provided personality assessments of their dogs and filled out the same personality inventory for themselves. The owners then designated another person who knew them and their dogs and who could judge the personalities of both. In a second study, the owners brought their dogs to an enclosed section of the park where three independent observers rated the dogs so that the researchers could compare the owners' judgments of their dogs' personalities with the observers' ratings. And in a third study, the investigators took photos of the dogs at play in order to examine the effects of breed and appearance on the animals' personalities.

In their previous work with dogs and 11 other species, the psychologists had found evidence of all the Big Five traits except conscientiousness, which requires considerable cognitive ability and to date has turned up only in humans and chimpanzees (Gosling & John, 1999). In this research too, they found four doggie dimensions of extroversion, agreeableness, emotional reactivity (neuroticism), and openness to experience. The dog owners, their friends, and the neutral observers all agreed quite strongly in their ratings of the dogs' personalities along these four dimensions. So when you hear your dog-crazy friend say, "Barkley is such a shy and nervous little pup, whereas Barker is outgoing and sociable," she is probably right.

Future studies that blur the "border" between humans and other species will help researchers to better understand the complex interaction of genetic, biological, and environmental effects on personality.

Heredity and Temperament

Let's turn now to human personalities. Even in the first weeks after birth, human babies differ in activity level, mood, responsiveness, heart rate, and attention span (Fox, Henderson, et al., 2005). Some are irritable and cranky; others are placid and calm. Some will cuddle up in an adult's arms and snuggle; others squirm and fidget, as if they cannot stand being held. Some smile easily; others fuss and cry. These differences appear even when you control for possible prenatal influences, such as the

Extreme shyness and fear of new situations tend to be biologically based, stable aspects of temperament, both in human beings and in monkeys. On the right, a timid infant rhesus monkey cowers behind a friend in the presence of an outgoing stranger.

temperaments Physiological dispositions to respond to the environment in certain ways; they are present in infancy and in many nonhuman species and are assumed to be innate.

heritability A statistical estimate of the proportion of the total variance in some trait that is attributable to genetic differences among individuals within a group.

Watch
Twins Separated at Birth, Reunited

Thinking Critically

Tolerate Uncertainty

Identical twins Gerald Levey (left) and Mark Newman were separated at birth and raised in different cities. When they were reunited at age 31, they discovered some astounding similarities. Both were volunteer firefighters, wore moustaches, and were unmarried. Both liked to hunt, watch old John Wayne movies, and eat Chinese food. They drank the same brand of beer, held the can with the little finger curled around it, and crushed the can when it was empty. It's tempting to conclude that all of these similarities are due to heredity, but we should also consider other explanations: Some could result from shared environmental factors such as social class and upbringing and some could be due merely to chance. For any given set of twins, we can never know for sure.

mother's nutrition, drug use, or problems with the pregnancy. The reason is that babies are born with genetically determined **temperaments**, dispositions to respond to the environment in certain ways (Clark & Watson, 2008). Temperaments include *reactivity* (how excitable, arousable, or responsive a baby is), *soothability* (how easily the baby is calmed when upset), and positive and negative emotionality. Temperaments are quite stable over time and are the clay out of which later personality traits are moulded (Clark & Watson, 2008; Else-Quest et al., 2006; Rothbart, Ahadi, & Evans, 2000).

Jerome Kagan (1997) has spent years studying the temperament of reactivity, following children from infancy to adolescence. About 20% of all children are either highly reactive or nonreactive; the other 80% fall somewhere in between. Highly reactive infants, even at four months of age, are excitable, nervous, and fearful; they overreact to any little thing, even a colourful picture placed in front of them. As toddlers, they tend to be wary and fearful of new things—toys that make noise, odd-looking robots—even when their moms are right there with them. At five years, many of these children are still timid and uncomfortable in new situations. At seven years, many still have symptoms of anxiety. They are afraid of being kidnapped, they need to sleep with the light on, and they are afraid of sleeping in an unfamiliar house—even if they have never experienced any sort of trauma.

In contrast, nonreactive infants, Kagan (1998) says, are "California, laid-back babies." They lie there without fussing; they rarely cry; they babble happily. As toddlers, they are outgoing and curious about new toys and events. They continue to be easygoing and extroverted throughout childhood.

Children at these two extremes differ physiologically, too (Rothbart, Ahadi, & Evans, 2000). During mildly stressful tasks, reactive children are more likely than nonreactive children to have increased heart rates, heightened brain activity, and high levels of stress hormones. The same physiological attributes appear in shy, anxious infant rhesus monkeys (Suomi, 1991). Starting early in life, these "uptight" monkeys respond with anxiety to novelty and challenge, just as highly reactive children do. They too have high heart rates and elevated stress hormones.

You can see how biologically based temperaments might form the basis of the later personality traits we call extroversion, agreeableness, or neuroticism.

Heredity and Traits

A third way to study genetic contributions to personality is to estimate the **heritability** of specific traits within groups of children or adults. As we discuss in Chapter 3, heritability refers to the proportion of the total variation in a trait that is attributable to genetic variation within a group. Estimates of heritability come from behavioural–genetic studies of adopted children and of identical and fraternal twins reared apart and together. (If you need to review these methods and how they are used to estimate the role of genetics, see pages 93–96.)

Findings from adoption and twin studies have provided compelling support for a genetic contribution to personality. Identical twins reared apart will often have unnerving similarities in gestures, mannerisms, and moods; indeed, their personalities often seem as similar as their physical features. If one twin tends to be optimistic, glum, or excitable, the other will probably be that way too (Braungert et al., 1992; Plomin et al., 2001). Researchers have begun to identify some of the different patterns of brain activity that underlie such traits. For example, just about everyone feels some discomfort when facing the unknown. But people who score high on neuroticism find uncertainty almost intolerable at a neurological level; their brains show high reactivity in certain key areas (Hirsch & Inzlicht, 2008).

Behavioural–genetic findings have produced remarkably consistent results on the heritability of traits. For the Big Five and for many other traits, from aggressiveness to overall happiness, heritability is about 0.50 (Bouchard, 1997a; Jang et al., 1998; Lykken & Tellegen, 1996; Waller et al., 1990; Weiss, Bates, & Luciano, 2008). This means that within a group of people, about 50% of the variation in such traits is attributable to genetic differences among the individuals in the group. These findings have been replicated in many countries.

Evaluating Genetic Theories

We think you will agree that these behavioural–genetic findings are pretty amazing. "It will doubtless seem incredible to many readers that variables such as social class, educational opportunities, religious training, and parental love and discipline have no substantial influence on adult personality," wrote Robert McCrae and Paul Costa in 1988, "but imagine for a moment that it is correct. Psychologists hope that one intelligent use of such findings will be to help people become more accepting of themselves and their children. Although we can all learn to make improvements and modifications to our personalities, most of us probably will never be able to *transform* our personalities completely because of our genetic dispositions and temperaments—a realization that might make people more realistic about what psychotherapy can do for them, and about what they can do for their children" (as cited in Efran, Greene, & Gordon, 1998).

On the other hand, it is important not to oversimplify by assuming that "It's all in our genes!" A genetic *predisposition* does not necessarily imply genetic *inevitability*. A person might have a gene that, for example, predisposes him or her to depression, but without certain environmental stresses or circumstances, the person will probably never become depressed (see Chapter 15). When people oversimplify, they mistakenly assume that personality problems that have a genetic component are permanent—say, that someone is "born to be bad" or to be a miserable grump forever (Dweck, 2008). Oversimplification can also lead people to incorrectly assume that if a problem, such as depression or shyness, has a genetic contribution, it will respond only to medication, so there is no point trying other interventions; we discuss this fallacy further in Chapter 16.

As Robert Plomin (1989), a leading behavioural geneticist, observed, "The wave of acceptance of genetic influence on behaviour is growing into a tidal wave that threatens to engulf the second message of this research: These same data provide the best available evidence for the importance of environmental influences." Let us now see what some of those influences might be.

Thinking Critically

Don't Oversimplify

Some personality traits, such as shyness, are highly heritable. Some people think that means "genes are everything"; a shy person can never learn to be comfortable in new situations, so there's no point trying to change. What is a more accurate way to think about the impact of heredity on personality?

quickQUIZ

✓•⌐Quick Review on MyPsychLab

We hope you have a few quiz-taking genes.

1. What three broad lines of research support the hypothesis that personality differences are due in part to genetic differences?
2. In behavioural–genetic studies, the heritability of personality traits, including the Big Five, is typically about (a) 0.50, (b) 0.90, (c) 0.10 to 0.20, (d) zero.
3. Researchers announce that their study of identical twins has revealed a high heritability for divorce (McGue & Lykken, 1992). Given that our prehistoric ancestors hadn't yet invented marriage, let alone divorce, what on earth could this finding mean?

Answers:

1. Research on animal personalities, human temperaments, and the heritability of traits 2. a 3. There obviously cannot be a "divorce gene," but perhaps personality factors with a heritable component, such as neuroticism and hostility, make it harder for a person to get along with a partner and thereby increase the likelihood of getting divorced (Rogge et al., 2006).

 YOU are about to learn . . .

◆ how social-cognitive theory accounts for Madonna's "personality" changes (and everyone else's).

◆ the extent to which parents can—and can't—influence their children's personalities.

◆ how your peers shape certain of your personality traits, and suppress others.

ENVIRONMENTAL INFLUENCES ON PERSONALITY

The environment may be half of the influence on variations in personality, but what *is* the environment, exactly? In this section, we will consider the relative influence of three aspects of the environment: the particular situations you find yourself in, how your parents treat you, and who your peers are.

Situations and Social Learning

The very definition of a trait is that it is consistent across situations. But people often behave one way with their parents and a different way with their friends, one way at home and a different way in other situations. In learning terms, the reason for people's inconsistency is that different behaviours are rewarded, punished, or ignored in different contexts. For example, you are likely to be more extroverted in an audience of screaming, cheering *American Idol* fans than at home with relatives who would regard such noisy displays with alarm and condemnation. This is why some behaviourists think it does not even make much sense to talk about "personality."

Social-cognitive learning theorists, however, argue that people do acquire central personality traits from their learning history and their resulting expectations and beliefs. (To refresh your memory of learning principles and of how strict behaviourists differ from social-cognitive learning theorists, see Chapter 7.) A child who studies hard

◉**Watch**
Set in Your Ways

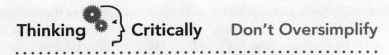

Thinking Critically Don't Oversimplify

Who is the "real" Madonna—doting mother or flamboyant performer? By understanding reciprocal determinism, we can avoid oversimplifying. Our genetic dispositions and personality traits cause us to choose some situations over others, but situations then influence which aspects of our personalities we express.

and gets good grades, attention from teachers, admiration from friends, and praise from parents will come to expect that hard work in other situations will also pay off. That child will become, in terms of personality traits, "ambitious" and "industrious." A child who studies hard and gets poor grades, is ignored by teachers and parents, and is rejected by friends for being a grind will come to expect that working hard isn't worth it. That child will become, in terms of personality traits, "unambitious" or "unmotivated."

Today, most personality researchers recognize that people can have a core set of stable traits *and* that their behaviour can vary across situations (Fleeson, 2004). There is a continual interaction between your particular qualities and the situation you are in. Your temperaments, habits, and beliefs influence how you respond to others, whom you hang out with, and the situations you seek (Bandura, 2001; Cervone & Shoda, 1999; Mischel & Shoda, 1995). In turn, the situation influences your behaviour and beliefs, rewarding some behaviours and extinguishing others. In social-cognitive learning theory, this process is called **reciprocal determinism**.

◆ **Research**
Walter Mishcel

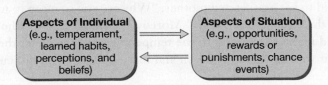

| Aspects of Individual (e.g., temperament, learned habits, perceptions, and beliefs) | Aspects of Situation (e.g., opportunities, rewards or punishments, chance events) |

reciprocal determinism In social-cognitive theories, the two-way interaction between aspects of the environment and aspects of the individual in the shaping of personality traits.

The two-way process of reciprocal determinism (as opposed to the one-way determinism of "genes determine everything" or "everything is learned") helps answer a question asked by everyone who has a sibling: What makes children who grow up in the same family so different, apart from their genes? The answer seems to be: an assortment of experiences that affect each child differently, chance events that cannot be predicted, situations that children find themselves in, and peer groups that the children belong to (Harris, 2006; Plomin, Asbury, & Dunn, 2001; Rutter et al., 2001). Behavioural geneticists refer to these unique and chance experiences that are not shared with other family members as the **nonshared environment**; for example, being in Mrs. Miller's class in grade 4 (which might inspire you to become a scientist), winning the lead in the school play (which might push you toward an acting career), or being bullied at school (which might have caused you to see yourself as weak and powerless). All these experiences work reciprocally with your own interpretation of them, your temperament, and your perceptions (did Mrs. Miller's class excite you or bore you?).

Keeping the concept of reciprocal determinism in mind, let us take a look at two of the most powerful environmental influences in people's lives: their parents and their friends.

Thinking Critically

Examine the Evidence

Most people assume that parents are almost entirely responsible for their children's personality and behaviour. What evidence challenges this popular belief?

Parental Influence—and Its Limits

If you check out parenting books online or in a bookstore, you will find that in spite of the zillion different kinds of advice they offer, they share one entrenched belief: Parental child-rearing practices are the strongest influence, maybe even the *sole* influence, on children's personality development. For many decades, few psychologists thought to question this assumption, and many still accept it. Yet the belief that personality is primarily determined by how parents treat their children has begun to crumble under the weight of three kinds of evidence (Harris, 2006, 2009):

1   The shared environment of the home has little if any influence on most personality traits. In behavioural–genetic research, the "shared environment" includes the family you grew up with and the experiences and background you shared with your siblings and parents. If these had as powerful an influence as commonly assumed, then studies should find a strong correlation between the personality traits of adopted children and those of their adoptive parents. In fact, the correlation is weak to nonexistent, indicating that the influence of child-rearing practices and family life is very small compared to the influence of genetics (Cohen, 1999; Plomin, Asbury, & Dunn, 2001). It is only the nonshared environment that has a strong impact.

2   Few parents have a single child-rearing style that is consistent over time and that they use with all their children. Developmental psychologists have tried for many years to identify the effects of specific child-rearing practices on children's personality traits. The problem is that parents are inconsistent from day to day and over the years. Their child-rearing practices vary, depending on their own stresses, moods, and marital satisfaction (Holden & Miller, 1999). As one child we know said to her exasperated mother, "Why are you so mean to me today, Mommy? I'm this naughty every day." Moreover, parents tend to adjust their methods of child rearing according to the temperament of the child; they are often more lenient with easygoing children and more punitive with difficult ones.

nonshared environment   Unique aspects of a person's environment and experience that are not shared with family members.

3 Even when parents try to be consistent in the way they treat their children, there may be little relation between what they do and how the children turn out. Some children of troubled and abusive parents are resilient and do not suffer lasting emotional damage, and some children of the kindest and most nurturing parents succumb to drugs, mental illness, or gangs.

Of course, parents do influence their children in lots of ways that are unrelated to the child's personality. They contribute to their children's religious beliefs, intellectual and occupational interests, motivation to succeed, skills, values, and adherence to traditional or modern notions of masculinity and femininity (Beer, Arnold, & Loehlin, 1998; Krueger, Hicks, & McGue, 2001). Above all, what parents do profoundly affects the quality of their relationship with their children—whether their children feel loved, secure, and valued or humiliated, frightened, and worthless (Harris, 2009).

Parents also have some influence even on traits in their children that are highly heritable. In one longitudinal study that followed children from age 3 to age 21, those who were impulsive, uncontrollable, and aggressive at age 3 were far more likely than calmer children to grow up to be impulsive, unreliable, and antisocial and more likely to commit crimes (Caspi, 2000). Early temperament was a strong and consistent predictor of these later personality traits. But not *every* child came out the same way. What protected some of those at risk, and helped them move in a healthier direction, was having parents who made sure they stayed in school, supervised them closely, and gave them consistent discipline.

Nevertheless, it is clear that, in general, parents have less influence on a child's personality than many people think. Because of reciprocal determinism, the relationship runs in both directions, with parents and children continually influencing one another. Moreover, as soon as children leave home, starting in preschool, parental influence on children's behaviour *outside* the home begins to wane. The nonshared environment—peers, chance events, and circumstances—takes over.

The Power of Peers

When two psychologists surveyed 275 freshmen at Cornell University, they found that most of them had secret lives and private selves that they never revealed to their parents (Garbarino & Bedard, 2001). On Facebook, too, many teenagers report having committed crimes, drinking, doing drugs, cheating in school, sexting, and having sex, all without their parents having a clue. (They assume, incorrectly, that what they reveal is "private" and read only by their several hundred closest friends.) This phenomenon of showing only one facet of your personality to your parents and an entirely different one to your peers becomes especially apparent in adolescence.

Children, like adults, live in two environments: their homes and their world outside the home. At home, children learn how their parents want them to behave and what they can get away with; as soon as they go to school, however, they conform to the dress, habits, language, and rules of their peers. Most adults can remember how terrible they felt when their classmates laughed at them for pronouncing a word "the wrong way" or doing something "stupid" (i.e., not what the rest of the kids were doing), and many recall the pain of being excluded. To avoid the controlling forces of being laughed at or rejected, most children will do what they can to conform to the norms and rules of their immediate peer group (Harris, 2009). Children who were law-abiding in grade 5 may start breaking the law in high school, if that is what it takes—or what they think it takes—to win the respect of their peers.

SITUATION AND SELF

Are you a different person when you are alone, with your parents, hanging out with friends, in class, or at a party? If so, in what ways? Do you have a secret self that you do not show to your family? Consider the Big Five factors, or any other personality traits that are important to you, as you answer these questions.

It has been difficult to tease apart the effects of parents and peers because parents usually try to arrange things so that their children's environments duplicate their own values and customs. To see which has the stronger influence on personality and behaviour, therefore, we must look at situations in which the peer group's values clash with the parents' values. For example, when parents value academic achievement and their child's peers think that success in school is only for sellouts or geeks, whose view wins? The answer, typically, is peers (Arroyo & Zigler, 1995; Harris, 2009). Conversely, children whose parents gave them no encouragement or motivation to succeed may find themselves with peers who are working like mad to get into college or university, and start studying hard themselves.

Thus, peers play a tremendous role in shaping our personality traits and behaviour, causing us to emphasize some attributes or abilities and downplay others. Of course, as the theory of reciprocal determinism would predict, our temperaments and dispositions also cause us to select particular peer groups (if they are available) instead of others, and our temperaments influence how we behave within the group. But once we are among peers, most of us go along with them, moulding facets of our personalities to the pressures of the group.

In sum, core personality traits may stem from genetic dispositions, but they are profoundly shaped by learning, peers, situations, experience, and, as we will see next, the largest environment of all: the culture.

quickQUIZ

✓◻ **Quick Review** on **MyPsychLab**

Do your peers take these quizzes? Does the answer determine whether you will?

1. What three lines of evidence have challenged the belief that parents are the major influence on their children's personalities?

2. Which contributes most to the variation among siblings in their personality traits? (a) the unique experiences they have that are not shared with their families, (b) the family environment that all of them share, or (c) the way their parents treat them

3. Eight-year-old Dwayne is pretty shy at home, where he is the middle of 12 children, but extroverted at school, where he is the leader of his friends. What might be the reason for his personality change?

Answers:

1. The shared family environment has little if any influence on personality; few parents have a consistent child-rearing style; and even when parents try to be consistent in the way they treat their children, there may be little relation between what they do and how the children turn out. 2. a 3. Peer groups have a powerful influence on which personality traits are encouraged and expressed, and peers can even override the child's situation at home.

YOU are about to learn . . .

◆ how culture influences your personality, and even whether you think you have a stable one.

◆ why men in the American South and West are more likely to get angry when insulted than other American men are.

◆ how to appreciate cultural influences on personality without stereotyping.

CULTURAL INFLUENCES ON PERSONALITY

If you get an invitation to come to a party at seven, at what time do you arrive? Conscientiousness about time is an individual personality trait. However, culture has a profound effect on people's behaviour, attitudes, and the traits they value or disdain. Culture provides rules that govern our behaviour and values that shape our beliefs (see Chapter 8). And it is just as powerful an influence on personality and behaviour as any biological process.

Culture, Values, and Traits

Quick! Answer this question: "Who are you?"

Your answer will be influenced by your cultural background, and particularly by whether your culture emphasizes individualism or community (Hofstede & Bond, 1988; Kanagawa, Cross, & Markus, 2001; Markus & Kitayama, 1991; Triandis, 1996, 2007). In **individualist cultures**, the independence of the individual often takes precedence over the needs of the group, and the self is often defined as a collection of personality traits ("I am outgoing, agreeable, and ambitious") or in occupational terms ("I am a psychologist"). In **collectivist cultures**, group harmony often takes precedence over the wishes of the individual, and the self is defined in the context of relationships and the community ("I am the son of a farmer, descended from three generations of storytellers on my mother's side and five generations of farmers on my father's side . . . "). In one fascinating study that showed how embedded this dimension is in language and how it shapes our thinking, bicultural individuals born in China tended to answer "Who am I?" in terms of their own individual attributes when they were writing in English—but they described themselves in terms of their relations to others when they were writing in Chinese (Ross, Xun, & Wilson, 2002).

culture A program of shared rules that governs the behaviour of members of a community or society and a set of values, beliefs, and attitudes shared by most members of that community.

individualist cultures Cultures in which the self is regarded as autonomous, and individual goals and wishes are prized above duty and relations with others.

collectivist cultures Cultures in which the self is regarded as embedded in relationships, and harmony with one's group is prized above individual goals and wishes.

Individualistic Americans exercise by running, walking, bicycling, and skating, all in different directions and wearing different clothes. Collectivist Japanese employees at their hiring ceremony exercise in identical fashion.

> ### TABLE 14.1 Some Average Differences between Individualist and Collectivist Cultures
>
> | Members of Individualist Cultures | Members of Collectivist Cultures |
> | --- | --- |
> | Define the self as autonomous, independent of groups. | Define the self as an interdependent part of groups. |
> | Give priority to individual, personal goals. | Give priority to the needs and goals of the group. |
> | Value independence, leadership, achievement, self-fulfillment. | Value group harmony, duty, obligation, security. |
> | Give more weight to an individual's attitudes and preferences than to group norms as explanations of behaviour. | Give more weight to group norms than to individual attitudes as explanations of behaviour. |
> | Attend to the benefits and costs of relationships; if costs exceed advantages, a person is likely to drop a relationship. | Attend to the needs of group members; if a relationship is beneficial to the group but costly to the individual, the individual is likely to stay in the relationship. |
>
> *Source*: Triandis, 1996.

As Table 14.1 shows, individualist and collectivist ways of defining the self influence many aspects of life, including which personality traits we value, how and whether we express emotions, how much we value having relationships or maintaining freedom, and how freely we express angry or aggressive feelings (Forbes et al., 2009; Oyserman & Lee, 2008). With its multicultural population, Canada is a unique environment within which to see both perspectives. Romin Tafarodi and colleagues at the University of Toronto examined the interaction between both individualist and collectivist cultural affiliations on self-esteem. Overall, their findings indicate that whether or not we feel good about ourselves stems largely from how our culture defines our specific role in society—as either individuals struggling to compete with others to reach personal goals, or as one of many in the larger community helping each other to reach common goals (Tafarodi, 1998; Tafarodi & Milne, 2002; Tafarodi, Lang, & Smith, 1999; Tafarodi, Tam, & Milne, 2001).

Individualist and collectivist orientations affect us in countless subtle but powerful ways. For example, in one study, Chinese and American pairs had to play a communication game that required each partner to be able to take the other's perspective. Eye-gaze measures showed that the Chinese players were almost always able to look at the target from their partner's perspective, whereas the American players often completely failed at this task (Wu & Keysar, 2007). Of course, members of both cultures understand the difference between their own view of things and another person's, but the collectivist-oriented Chinese pay closer attention to other people's nonverbal expressions, the better to monitor and modify their own responses.

Because people from collectivist cultures are concerned with adjusting their own behaviour depending on the social context, they tend to regard personality and the sense of self as being more flexible than people from individualist cultures do. In a study comparing Japanese and Americans, the Americans reported that their sense of self changes only 5 to 10% in different situations, whereas the Japanese said that 90 to 99% of their sense of self changes (de Rivera, 1989). For the group-oriented Japanese, it is important to enact *tachiba*, to perform your social roles correctly so that there will be harmony with others. Americans, in contrast, tend to value "being true to yourself" and having a "core identity."

In many cultures, children are expected to contribute to the family income and to take care of their younger siblings. These experiences encourage helpfulness over independence.

CULTURE AND TRAITS.   When people fail to understand the influence of culture on behaviour, they often attribute another person's mysterious or annoying actions to individual personality traits when they are really due to cultural norms. Take cleanliness. How often do you bathe? Once a day, once a week? Do you regard baths as healthy and invigorating or as a disgusting wallow in dirty water? How often, and where, do you wash your hands—or feet? A person who would seem obsessively clean in one culture might seem an appalling slob in another (Fernea & Fernea, 1994).

Or consider helpfulness. Many years ago, in a classic cross-cultural study of children in Kenya, India, Mexico, the Philippines, Japan, the United States, and five other countries, researchers measured how often children behaved altruistically (offering help, support, or unselfish suggestions) or egoistically (seeking help and attention or wanting to dominate others) (Whiting & Edwards, 1988; Whiting & Whiting, 1975). American children were the least altruistic on all measures and the most egoistic. The most altruistic children came from societies in which children are assigned many tasks, such as caring for younger children and gathering and preparing food. These children knew that their work made a genuine contribution to the well-being or economic survival of the family. In cultures that value individual achievement and self-advancement, taking care of others has less importance, and altruism as a personality trait is not cultivated to the same extent.

Or consider tardiness. Individuals differ in whether they try to be places "on time" or are always late, but cultural norms affect how individuals regard time in the first place. In northern Europe, Canada, the United States, and most other individualistic cultures, time is organized into linear segments in which people do one thing "at a time" (Hall, 1983; Hall & Hall, 1990; Leonard, 2008). The day is divided into appointments, schedules, and routines, and because time is a precious commodity, people don't like to "waste" time or "spend" too much time on any one activity (hence the popularity of multitasking). In such cultures, being on time is taken as a sign of conscientiousness or thoughtfulness and being late as a sign of indifference or intentional disrespect. Therefore, it is considered the height of rudeness (or high status) to keep someone waiting. But in Mexico, southern Europe, the Middle East, South

America, and Africa, time is organized along parallel lines. People do many things at once, and the needs of friends and family supersede mere appointments; they think nothing of waiting for hours or days to see someone. The idea of having to be somewhere "on time," as if time were more important than a person, is unthinkable.

CULTURE and *Violence*
The Cultivation of Male Aggression

Many people think that men are more violent than women because men have higher levels of testosterone. But if that is so, then why, given that men everywhere have testosterone, do rates of male aggressiveness vary enormously across cultures and throughout history? Why are rates of violence higher in some regions of the United States than others?

To answer these questions, Richard Nisbett (1993) began by examining the historical record. He found that the American South, along with some western regions of the country originally settled by Southerners, have much higher rates of white homicide and other violence than the rest of the country has—but only particular kinds of violence: the use of fists or guns to protect a man's sense of honour, protect his property, or respond to perceived insults. Nisbett considered various explanations, such as poverty or racial tensions. But when he controlled for regional differences in poverty and the percentage of blacks in the population, by county, "Southernness" remained an independent predictor of homicide. Nisbett also ruled out a history of slavery as an explanation: Regions of the South that had the highest concentrations of slaves in the past have the lowest white homicide rates today.

Nisbett hypothesized that the higher rates of violence in the South derive from economic causes: The higher rates occur in cultures that were originally based on herding, in contrast to cultures based on agriculture. Why would this be so? People who depend economically on agriculture tend to develop and promote cooperative strategies for survival. But people who depend on their herds are extremely vulnerable; their livelihoods can be lost in an instant by the theft of their animals. To reduce the likelihood of theft, Nisbett theorized, herders learn to be hyperalert to any threatening act (real or perceived) and respond to it immediately with force. This would explain why cattle rustling and horse thievery were capital crimes in the Old West, and why Mediterranean and Middle Eastern herding cultures even today place a high value on male aggressiveness. And indeed, when Nisbett looked at agricultural practices *within* the South, he found that homicide rates were more than twice as high in the hills and dry plains areas (where herding occurs) as in farming regions.

The emphasis on aggressiveness and vigilance in herding communities, in turn, fosters a *culture of honour*, in which even small disputes and trivial insults (trivial to people from other cultures, that is) put a man's reputation for toughness on the line, requiring him to respond with violence to restore his status (Cohen, 1998). Although the herding economy has become much less important in the South and West, the legacy of its culture of honour remains. These regions have rates of honour-related homicides (such as murder to avenge a perceived insult to one's family) that are *five times higher* than in other regions of the country. Cultures of honour also have higher rates of domestic violence. Both sexes in such cultures believe it is appropriate for a man to physically assault a woman if he believes she is threatening his honour and reputation by being unfaithful or by leaving him (Vandello & Cohen, 2008). Why do

Thinking Critically   Analyze Assumptions and Biases

Many people assume that men can't help being violent because of their biology. Yet, on average, men in agricultural economies are far more cooperative and nonviolent than men in herding economies. Amish farmers have always had very low rates of violence, whereas in the Old West, the cattle-herding cowboy culture was a violent one. (Fortunately, the shootout here is a reenactment.)

these practices continue long after they are functional, considering that most young Southern college men aren't herding cattle on their campuses? In a series of experiments, Southern men were more likely than Northern men to assume that their male peers believe that aggressive action is *required* to restore honour. Thus the cultural practice is perpetuated because "everyone else" seems to demand it (Vandello, Cohen, & Ransom, 2008).

Nisbett and his colleagues also wanted to demonstrate how these external cultural norms literally "get under the skin" to affect physiology and personality. They brought 173 Northern and Southern male students into their lab and conducted three experiments to measure how these students would respond psychologically and physiologically to being insulted (Cohen et al., 1996). They explained that the experiment would assess the students' performance on various tasks and that the experimenter would be taking saliva samples to measure everyone's blood sugar levels throughout the procedure. Actually, the saliva samples were used to measure levels of cortisol, a hormone associated with high levels of stress, and testosterone, which is associated with dominance and aggression. At one point in the experiment, a confederate of the experimenter, who seemed to be another student participant, bumped into each man and called him an insulting name (a seven-letter word beginning with "a," if you want to know).

As you can see in Figure 14.2, Northerners responded calmly to the insult; if anything, they thought it was funny. But many Southerners were

FIGURE 14.2 Aggression and Cultures of Honour

As these two graphs show, when young men from Northern states were insulted in an experiment, they shrugged it off, thinking it was funny or unimportant. But for young Southern men, levels of the stress hormone cortisol and of testosterone shot up—and they were more likely to retaliate aggressively (Cohen et al., 1996).

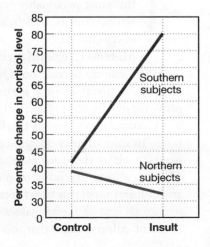 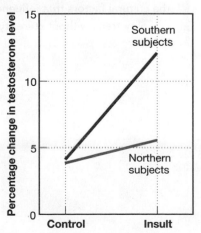

immediately inflamed and their levels of cortisol and testosterone shot up. They were more likely to feel that their masculinity had been threatened, and they were more likely to retaliate aggressively than Northerners were. Southerners and Northerners who were not insulted were alike on most measures, with the exception that the Southerners were actually more polite and deferential. It appears that they have more obliging manners than Northerners—until they are insulted. Then, look out.

Being raised in a culture of honour, however, is only one cause of male aggression. Another cause has to do with the dangers that a culture faces. In cultures in which competition for resources is fierce and survival is difficult, men are "toughened up" and pushed to take risks, even with their lives (Gilmore, 1990). In contrast, among the Ifaluk, the Tahitians, and the people of Sudest Island near New Guinea, where resources are abundant and there are no serious hazards or enemies to worry about, men do not feel they have to prove themselves and they are not raised to be tough and aggressive (Lepowsky, 1994; Levy, 1984). When a society becomes more peaceful, so do its men.

Evaluating Cultural Approaches

A woman we know, originally from England, married a Lebanese man. They were happy together but had the usual number of marital misunderstandings and squabbles. After a few years, they visited his family home in Lebanon, where she had never been before. "I was stunned," she told us. "All the things I thought he did because of his *personality* turned out to be because he's *Lebanese*! Everyone there was just like him!"

Our friend's reaction illustrates both the contributions and the limitations of cultural studies of personality. She was right in recognizing that some of her husband's behaviour was attributable to his culture; for example, his Lebanese notions of time were very different from her English notions. But she was wrong to infer that the Lebanese are all "like him": Individuals are affected by their culture, but they vary within it.

Cultural psychologists face the problem of how to describe cultural influences on personality without oversimplifying or stereotyping (Church & Lonner, 1998). As one student of ours put it, "How come when we students speak of 'the' Japanese or 'the' blacks or 'the' whites or 'the' Latinos, it's called stereotyping, and when you do it, it's called 'cross-cultural psychology'?" This question shows excellent critical thinking! The study of culture does not rest on the assumption that all members of a culture behave the same way or have the same personality traits. As we have seen, people vary according to their temperaments, beliefs, and learning histories, and this variation occurs within every culture.

Moreover, regional variations occur in every society. Canada may be an "individualist" culture overall, but Quebec and the Maritime provinces, with their history of strong regional identity, are more collectivist than the rugged, independent western province of Alberta.

Cultural psychologists also face the risk of exaggerating the contrasts between cultures. In spite of their differences, all cultures reflect adaptations to universal human needs, such as those for love, attachment, family, work, identity, and self-esteem. As one cultural psychologist put it, "Human beings are not blank slates on which any cultural form can be written" (Cohen, 2001). Yet the existence of cross-cultural universals and of individual variations within cultures does not negate the importance of cultural rules that, on average, make Swedes different from Bedouins, or

Thinking Critically

Don't Oversimplify

Many people will collectively characterize the personality of people from Alberta, or from Toronto. How can we think about the cultural factors that influence personality traits without stereotyping?

Cambodians different from Italians. The traits that we value, our sense of self versus community, and our notions of the right way to behave—all key aspects of personality—begin with the culture in which we are raised.

◉ **Watch**
Cognition, Emotion, and Motivation Across Cultures

At the moment, you live in a culture that values the importance of quizzes.

1. Are cultures whose members regard the "self" as a collection of stable personality traits individualist or collectivist?

2. Which cultural practice tends to foster the traits of helpfulness and altruism? (a) every family member "does his or her own thing," (b) parents insist that children obey, (c) children contribute to the family welfare, (d) parents remind children often about the importance of being helpful

3. Why, according to one theory, do men in the American South and West respond more aggressively to perceived insults than other American men do?

Answers:

1. individualist   2. c   3. These men come from regions in which economies based on herding gave rise to "cultures of honour," requiring males to be vigilant and aggressive toward potential threats.

quick**QUIZ**

✓•—Quick Review on **MyPsychLab**

 YOU are about to learn . . .

◆ how humanist approaches to personality differ from psychodynamic and genetic ones.

◆ the contributions of Abraham Maslow, Carl Rogers, and Rollo May to understanding our "inner lives."

◆ how your life story affects your personality—and vice versa.

◆ how psychological scientists evaluate humanist and narrative views of personality.

THE INNER EXPERIENCE

A final way to look at personality starts from each person's own point of view, from the inside out. Biology may hand us temperamental dispositions that benefit or limit us, the environment may deal us some tough or fortunate experiences, our parents may treat us as we would or would not have wished, but the sum total of our personality is how we, individually, weave all of these elements together.

Humanist Approaches

One such approach to personality comes from **humanist psychology**, which was launched as a movement in the early 1960s. The movement's chief leaders—Abraham Maslow (1908–1970), Carl Rogers (1902–1987), and Rollo May (1909–1994)—argued that it was time to replace psychoanalysis and behaviourism with a "third force" in psychology, one that would draw a fuller picture of human potential and personality. Psychologists who take a humanist approach to personality emphasize our uniquely human capacity to determine our own actions and futures.

humanist psychology   A psychological approach that emphasizes personal growth, resilience, and the achievement of human potential.

You are never too old for self-actualization. Hulda Crooks, shown here at age 91 climbing Mt. Fuji, took up mountain climbing at 54. "It's been a great inspiration for me," she said. "When I come down from the mountain I feel like I can battle in the valley again." She died at the age of 101.

◈ Research
Abraham Maslow

unconditional positive regard
To Carl Rogers, love or support given to another person with no conditions attached.

existentialism A philosophical approach that emphasizes the inevitable dilemmas and challenges of human existence.

ABRAHAM MASLOW.   The trouble with psychology, said Maslow (1970, 1971), was that it had ignored many of the positive aspects of life, such as joy, laughter, love, happiness, and *peak experiences*, rare moments of rapture caused by the attainment of excellence or the experience of beauty. The traits that Maslow thought most important to personality were not the Big Five, but rather the qualities of the *self-actualized person*—the person who strives for a life that is meaningful, challenging, and satisfying (see Chapter 12).

For Maslow, personality development could be viewed as a gradual progression toward self-actualization. Most psychologists, he argued, had a lopsided view of human nature, a result of their emphasis on studying emotional problems and negative traits such as neuroticism or insecurity. As Maslow (1971) wrote, "When you select out for careful study very fine and healthy people, strong people, creative people . . . then you get a very different view of mankind. You are asking how tall can people grow, what can a human being become?"

CARL ROGERS.   As a clinician, Carl Rogers (1951, 1961) was interested not only in why some people cannot function well but also in what he called the "fully functioning individual." How you behave, he said, depends on your subjective reality, not on the external reality around you. Fully functioning people experience *congruence*, or harmony, between the image they project to others and their true feelings and wishes. They are trusting, warm, and open, rather than defensive or intolerant. Their beliefs about themselves are realistic.

To become fully functioning people, Rogers maintained, we all need **unconditional positive regard**, love and support for the people we are, without strings (conditions) attached. This doesn't mean that Winifred should be allowed to kick her brother when she is angry with him or that Wilbur may throw his dinner out the window because he doesn't like pot roast. In these cases, a parent can correct the child's behaviour without withdrawing love from the child. The child can learn that the behaviour, not the child, is what is bad. "House rules are 'no violence,' children," is a very different message from "You are horrible children for behaving so badly."

Unfortunately, Rogers observed, many children are raised with *conditional* positive regard: "I will love you if you behave well, and I won't love you if you behave badly." Adults often treat each other this way, too. People treated with conditional regard begin to suppress or deny feelings or actions that they believe are unacceptable to those they love. The result, said Rogers, is incongruence, a sense of being out of touch with your feelings, of not being true to your real self, which in turn produces low self-regard, defensiveness, and unhappiness. A person experiencing incongruence scores high on neuroticism, becoming bitter and negative.

ROLLO MAY.   May shared with the humanists a belief in free will. But he also emphasized some of the inherently difficult and tragic aspects of the human condition, including loneliness, anxiety, and alienation. May brought to American psychology elements of the European philosophy of **existentialism**, which emphasizes such inevitable challenges of human existence as the search for the meaning of life, the need to confront death, and the necessity of taking responsibility for our actions.

Free will, wrote May, carries a price in anxiety and despair, which is why so many people try to escape from freedom into narrow certainties and blame others for their misfortunes. For May, our personalities reflect the ways we cope with the struggles to find meaning in existence, to use our freedom wisely, and to face suffering and death bravely. May popularized the humanist idea that we can choose to make the best of ourselves by drawing on inner resources such as love and courage, but he added that we can never escape the harsh realities of life and loss.

Existential psychologists remind us of the inevitable struggles of human existence, such as the fight against loneliness and alienation.

Narrative Approaches

In the past two decades, another approach to personality has focused on the importance of the *life narrative*, the story that each of us develops over time to explain ourselves and make meaning of everything that has happened to us (Bruner, 1990; McAdams, 2008; McAdams & Pals, 2006; Sarbin, 1997a, 1997b). In the narrative view, your distinctive personality rests on the story you tell to answer the question "Who am I?"

Because the narrative approach emphasizes how the stories we tell give us an identity, shape our behaviour, and motivate us to pursue or abandon our goals, it integrates the many diverse influences on personality that we have discussed in this chapter. Do you believe you are a victim of bad childhood experiences or a survivor of them? Do you believe that your mood swings are caused by a biochemical imbalance or an imbalanced love affair? When you tell about your life to others, do you play the hero or the passive bystander?

The life narrative you create for yourself reflects your needs and justifies the actions you take, or fail to take, to solve your problems. It affects whether you even feel that you can solve your problems and transform your life (McAdams, 2008). For example, therapist David Epston worked with an immigrant woman named Marisa, who had been abused and rejected all her life. "To tell a story about your life turns it into a history," he told her, "one that can be left behind, and makes it easier for you to create a future of your own design" (as cited in O'Hanlon, 1994). Marisa came to see that she could tell a new story about her experiences, one that did not emphasize the tragedies that had befallen her but rather her triumphs in overcoming them. "My life has a future now," she told Epston. "It will never be the same again."

In the narrative view, your stories about how you see and explain yourself are the essence of your personality, capturing everything that has happened to you and all the factors that affect your biology, psychology, and relationships. They are what make you unique in all the world.

Evaluating Humanist and Narrative Approaches

As with psychodynamic theories, the major scientific criticism of humanist psychology is that many of its assumptions are untestable. Freud looked at humanity and saw destructive drives, selfishness, and lust. Maslow and Rogers looked at humanity and saw cooperation, selflessness, and love. May looked at humanity and saw fear of freedom, loneliness, and the struggle for meaning. These differences, say critics, may tell us more about the observers than about the observed.

Many humanist concepts, although intuitively appealing, are hard to define operationally (see Chapter 2). How can we know whether a person is self-fulfilled or self-actualized? How can we tell whether a woman's decision to quit her job and become a professional rodeo rider represents an "escape from freedom" or a freely made choice? And what exactly is unconditional positive regard? If it is defined as unquestioned support of a child's efforts at mastering a new skill, or as assurance that the child is loved in spite of his or her mistakes, then it is clearly a good idea. But in the popular culture, it has often been interpreted as an unwillingness ever to say no to a child or to offer constructive criticism and set limits, which children need.

Despite such concerns, humanist psychologists have added balance to the study of personality. A contemporary specialty known as "positive psychology" (see Chapter 1) follows in the footsteps of humanism by focusing on the qualities that enable people to be optimistic and resilient in times of stress (Gable & Haidt, 2005; Seligman & Csikszentmihaly, 2000). Influenced in part by the humanists, psychologists are studying many positive human traits, such as courage, altruism, the motivation to excel, and self-confidence. Developmental psychologists are studying ways to foster children's empathy and creativity. And some researchers are studying the emotional and existential effects of the fear of death.

As for narrative approaches, research is flourishing, showing how the stories we tell about ourselves play a crucial role in shaping our distinctive personalities (McAdams & Pals, 2006). Cognitive psychologists emphasize how our stories shape and distort our memories. Psychotherapists are exploring the ways in which clients who tell self-defeating life stories might turn them around, creating more hopeful and positive ones. Social and cultural psychologists examine how a culture or society's dominant myths and shared stories influence people's ambitions and expectations, political views, and beliefs that the world can be improved or will never change.

The humanist, existential, and narrative views of personality share one central message: We have the power to choose our own destinies, even when fate delivers us into tragedy. Across psychology, this message has fostered an appreciation of resilience in the face of adversity.

Now that you have read about the major influences on personality (see Review 14.1), how would you explain why Madonna is who she is? Some aspects of her character and temperament, such as extroversion

Thinking Critically

Define Your Terms

Unconditional positive regard sounds like a good thing, but what does it mean, exactly? Does it mean giving loved ones your total support and approval, no matter what they do? Does it permit setting limits and offering constructive criticism?

IF YOU WERE AN ICEBERG...

THE PART EVERYONE GETS TO SEE

ALL THE GREAT ASPECTS OF YOUR PERSONALITY

S. Harris

S. Harris / www.CartoonStock.com

Exercise free will, as a humanist would advise you to, by choosing to take this quiz.

1. According to Carl Rogers, a man who loves his wife only when she is looking her best is giving her _____ positive regard.
2. The humanist who described the importance of having peak experiences was (a) Abraham Maslow, (b) Rollo May, (c) Carl Rogers.
3. A humanist and a Freudian psychoanalyst are arguing about human nature. What underlying assumptions about psychology and human potential are they likely to bring to their discussion? How can they resolve their differences without either–or thinking?

Answers:

1. conditional 2. a 3. The Freudian assumes that human nature is basically selfish and destructive; the humanist assumes that it is basically loving and cooperative. They can resolve this either–or debate by recognizing that human beings have both capacities, and that the situation and culture often determine which capacity is expressed at a given time.

quickQUIZ

✓ Quick Review on MyPsychLab

REview 14.1

The Major Influences on Personality

Psychodynamic 	Unconscious dynamics shape human motives, guilts, conflicts, and defences.
Genetic 	Children are born with particular temperaments, and most traits are highly influenced by genes.
Environmental 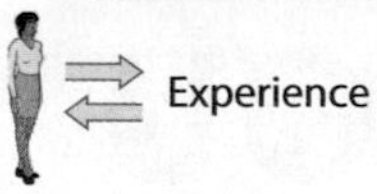 — Experience	Learning, situations, and unique experiences affect which traits are encouraged and which genes are expressed.
Parents	Modify and shape a child's temperament and genetic predispositions; affect gender roles, attitudes, and self-concept; affect the quality of the relationship with the child.
Peer group	Influences an individual's values, behaviour, ambitions, goals, etc.
Situation	Determines which behaviours are rewarded and which are punished or ignored, thereby shaping the expression or suppression of particular traits.
Chance events	May influence a person's experiences and choices in unexpected ways, thus encouraging the development of some traits over others.
Cultural 	Cultural norms specify which traits are valued, affect basic notions of the self and personality, and shape behaviours from aggressiveness to altruism.
Humanist 	Despite genetic, environmental, cultural, and psychodynamic influences, people can exercise free will to become the kind of person they want to be.
Narrative 	Personality rests on the stories people create to explain their lives (e.g., whether they see themselves as victims or survivors); these stories can change.

and conscientiousness, seem likely to have a genetic component. Her personality was perhaps also shaped, however, by unique experiences in her childhood and young adulthood that were not shared with her siblings: having the opportunity to take dance classes, later seizing the chance and running away to New York. Madonna's chameleon-like persona, which changes every couple of years, is further shaped and rewarded by today's culture, which often values image over reality, transience over permanence, style over substance, celebrity over obscurity. Psychodynamic theorists might wonder whether Madonna's unconscious motivations for success and her constant changing of public personalities stem from the shock of losing her mother when she was only six; Madonna was her mother's first name, too. Humanists might remind us that we do not know anything about the real Madonna, because the faces she presents to the public might reveal nothing at all about her inner, private self. And psychologists who study life narratives would have a full-time job keeping up with the stories that Madonna spins about herself!

For Madonna and for all the rest of us, genetic influences, learned habits, cultural norms, unconscious fears and conflicts, and visions of possibility, filtered through our interior sense of self and our life story, give each of us the stamp of our personality, the qualities that make us feel uniquely . . . us.

✳ **Explore**
Approaches to Personality

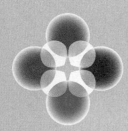

Taking Psychology with YOU

Thinking Critically in Everyday Life

How to Avoid the "Barnum Effect"

How well does the following paragraph describe you?

Some of your aspirations tend to be pretty unrealistic. At times you are extroverted, affable, and sociable, while at other times you are introverted, wary, and reserved. You pride yourself on being an independent thinker and do not accept others' opinions without satisfactory proof. You prefer a certain amount of change and variety, and you become dissatisfied when hemmed in by restrictions and limitations. At times you have serious doubts as to whether you have made the right decision or done the right thing.

When people believe that this description was written just for them, as the result of a personalized horoscope or handwriting analysis, they all say the same thing: "It describes me *exactly!*" Everyone thinks this description is accurate because it is vague enough to apply to almost everyone and it is flattering. Don't we all consider ourselves to be "independent thinkers"?

This is why many psychologists worry about the "Barnum effect" (Snyder & Shenkel, 1975). P. T. Barnum was the great circus showman who said, "There's a sucker born every minute." He knew that the formula for success was to "have a little something for everybody," which is just what unscientific personality profiles, horoscopes, and handwriting analysis (graphology) have in common. They have "a little something for everyone" and are therefore nonfalsifiable.

For example, graphologists claim that they can identify your personality traits from the form and distribution of your handwritten letters. Wide spacing between words means you feel isolated and lonely. If your lines drift upward, you are an "uplifting" optimist, and if your lines droop downward, you are a pessimist who feels you are being "dragged down." If you make large capital *I*'s, you have a large ego.

Graphologists are not the same as handwriting experts, who are trained to determine, say, whether a document is a forgery. Graphologists, like astrologers, usually know little or nothing about the scientific method, how to correct for their biases, or how to empirically test their claims. That is why the many different graphological approaches usually conflict. For example, according to one system, a certain way of crossing *t*'s reveals someone who is vicious and sadistic; according to another, it reveals a practical joker (Beyerstein, 1996).

Whenever graphology *has* been tested empirically, it has failed. A meta-analysis of 200 published studies found no validity or reliability to graphology in predicting work performance, aptitudes, or personality. No school

of graphology fared better than any other, and no graphologist was able to perform better than untrained amateurs making guesses from the same writing samples (Dean, 1992; Klimoski, 1992).

If graphology were just an amusing game, no one would worry about it, but unfortunately it can have harmful consequences. Graphologists have been hired by companies to predict a person's leadership ability, attention to detail, willingness to be a good team player, and more. They pass judgment on people's honesty, generosity, and even supposed criminal tendencies. How would you feel if you were turned down for a job because some graphologist branded you a potential thief on the basis of your alleged "desire-for-possession hooks" on your *S*'s?

If you do not want to be a victim of the Barnum effect, research offers this advice to help you think critically about graphology and its many cousins:

Beware of all-purpose descriptions that could apply to anyone. Sometimes you doubt your decisions; who among

us has not? Sometimes you feel outgoing and sometimes shy; who does not? Do you "have sexual secrets that you are afraid of confessing"? Just about everybody does.

Beware of your own selective perceptions. Most of us are so impressed when an astrologer, psychic, or graphologist gets something right that we overlook all the descriptions that are plain wrong. Be aware of the confirmation bias—the tendency to explain away all the descriptions that don't fit.

Resist flattery and emotional reasoning. This is a hard one! It is easy to reject a profile that describes you as selfish or stupid. Watch out for the ones that make you feel good by telling you how wonderful and smart you are, what a great leader you will be, or how modest you are about your exceptional abilities.

If you keep your ability to think critically with you, you won't end up paying hard cash for soft answers or taking a job you dislike because it fits your "personality type." In other words, you'll have proven Barnum wrong.

SUMMARY

◆ *Personality* refers to an individual's distinctive and relatively stable pattern of behaviour, motives, thoughts, and emotions. Personality is made up of many different *traits*, characteristics that describe a person across situations.

PSYCHODYNAMIC THEORIES OF PERSONALITY

◆ Sigmund Freud was the founder of *psychoanalysis*, which was the first *psychodynamic* theory. Modern psychodynamic theories share an emphasis on unconscious processes and a belief in the formative role of childhood experiences and early unconscious conflicts.

◆ To Freud, the personality consists of the *id* (the source of sexual energy, which he called the *libido*, and the aggressive instinct), the *ego* (the source of reason), and the *superego*

(the source of conscience). *Defence mechanisms* protect the ego from unconscious anxiety. They include, among others, repression, projection, displacement (one form of which is sublimation), regression, and denial.

◆ Freud believed that personality develops in a series of *psychosexual stages*, with the *phallic (Oedipal) stage* most crucial. During this stage, Freud believed, the *Oedipus complex* occurs, in which the child desires the parent of the other sex and feels rivalry with the same-sex parent. When the Oedipus complex is resolved, the child identifies with the same-sex parent, but females retain a lingering sense of inferiority and "penis envy"—a notion later contested by female psychoanalysts like Clara Thompson and Karen Horney.

◆ Carl Jung believed that people share a *collective unconscious* that contains universal memories and images, or *archetypes*, such as the *shadow* (evil) and the Earth Mother.

◆ The *object-relations school* emphasizes the importance of the first two years of life rather than the Oedipal phase; the infant's representations of important figures, especially the mother, rather than sexual needs and drives; and the problem in male development of breaking away from the mother.

◆ Psychodynamic approaches have been criticized for violating the principle of falsifiability; for overgeneralizing from atypical patients to everyone; and for basing theories on the unreliable memories and retrospective accounts of adults, which can create an *illusion of causality*. However, some psychodynamic ideas have received empirical support, including the existence of nonconscious processes and defences.

THE MODERN STUDY OF PERSONALITY

◆ Most popular tests that divide personality into "types" are not valid or reliable. In research, psychologists typically rely on *objective tests (inventories)* to identify and study personality traits and disorders.

◆ Gordon Allport argued that people have a few *central traits* that are key to their personalities and a greater number of *secondary traits* that are less fundamental. Raymond Cattell used *factor analysis* to identify clusters of traits that he considered the basic components of personality. There is strong evidence, from studies around the world, for the *Big Five* dimensions of personality: extroversion versus introversion, neuroticism (negative emotionality) versus emotional stability, agreeableness versus antagonism, conscientiousness versus impulsiveness, and openness to experience versus resistance to new experience. Although these dimensions are quite stable over time and across circumstances, some of them do change over the life span, reflecting maturational development or common adult responsibilities.

GENETIC INFLUENCES ON PERSONALITY

◆ As discussed in "Biology and Animal Traits," members of many other species, including octopuses, pigs, hyenas, bears, horses, dogs, and all primates, vary in the same characteristic traits as humans do—such as shyness, aggressiveness, extroversion, agreeableness, and neuroticism. This evidence suggests that certain key personality traits (and the Big Five factors) have an evolutionary, biological basis.

◆ In human beings, individual differences in *temperaments*, such as reactivity, soothability, and positive or negative emotionality, appear to be inborn, emerging early in life and influencing subsequent personality development. Temperamental differences in extremely reactive and nonreactive children may be due to variations in the responsiveness of the sympathetic nervous system to change and novelty.

◆ Behavioural–genetic data from twin and adoption studies suggest that the *heritability* of many adult personality traits is about 0.50. Genetic influences create dispositions and set limits on the expression of specific traits. But even traits that are highly heritable are often modified throughout life by circumstances, chance, and learning.

ENVIRONMENTAL INFLUENCES ON PERSONALITY

◆ People often behave inconsistently in different circumstances when behaviours that are rewarded in one situation are punished or ignored in another. According to *social-cognitive learning theory*, personality results from the interaction of the environment and aspects of the individual, in a pattern of *reciprocal determinism*.

◆ Behavioural geneticists have found that an important influence on personality is the *nonshared environment*, the unique experiences that each child in a family has.

◆ Three lines of evidence challenge the popular assumption that parents have the greatest impact on their children's personalities and behaviour: (1) Behavioural–genetic studies find that shared family environment has little if any influence on variations in most personality traits; (2) few parents have a consistent child-rearing style over time and with all their children; and (3) even when parents try to be consistent, there may be little relation between what they do and how the children turn out. However, parents can modify their children's temperaments, prevent children at risk of delinquency and crime from choosing a path of antisocial behaviour, influence many of their children's values and attitudes, and teach them to be kind and helpful. And, of course, parents profoundly affect the quality of their relationship with their children.

◆ One major environmental influence on personality comes from a person's peer groups, which can be more powerful than parents. Most children and teenagers behave differently with their parents than with their peers.

CULTURAL INFLUENCES ON PERSONALITY

◆ Many qualities that Western psychologists treat as individual personality traits are heavily influenced by *culture*. People from *individualist cultures* define themselves in different terms than those from *collectivist cultures*, and they perceive their "selves" as more stable across situations. Cultures vary in their norms for many behaviours, such as cleanliness and notions of time. Altruistic children tend to come from cultures in which their families assign them many tasks that contribute to the family's well-being or economic survival.

◆ As discussed in "Culture and Violence," male aggression is not simply a result of male hormones; it is also influenced by the economic requirements of the culture a man grows up in, which in turn shape men's beliefs about when violence is necessary. Herding economies foster male aggressiveness more than agricultural economies do. Men in *cultures of honour*, including certain regions of the American South and West, are more likely to become angry when they feel insulted and to behave aggressively to restore their sense of honour than are men from other cultures; when they are insulted, their levels of cortisol and testosterone rise quickly, whereas men from other cultures generally do not show this reaction.

◆ Cultural theories of personality face the problem of describing broad cultural differences and their influences on personality without promoting stereotypes or overlooking universal human needs.

THE INNER EXPERIENCE

◆ *Humanist psychologists* focus on a person's subjective sense of self and the free will to change. They emphasize human potential and the strengths of human nature, as in Abraham Maslow's concepts of *peak experiences* and *self-actualization*.

Carl Rogers stressed the importance of *unconditional positive regard* in creating a fully functioning person. Rollo May brought *existentialism* into psychology, emphasizing some of the inherent challenges of human existence that result from having free will, such as the search for meaning in life.

◆ As another way of understanding personality from the "inside," some personality psychologists study *life narratives*, the stories people create to explain themselves and make sense of their lives. These stories may serve to suppress changes in our lives or encourage them.

◆ Some ideas from humanist psychology are subjective and difficult to measure, but others have fostered research on positive aspects of personality, such as optimism, hope, and resilience under adversity. Research on the importance of life narratives has influenced the study of personality, memory, health, and psychotherapy.

◆ Genetic influences, life experiences and learned habits, cultural norms, unconscious fears and conflicts, and our private, inner sense of self all combine in complex ways to create our distinctive personalities.

TAKING PSYCHOLOGY WITH YOU

◆ Critical thinkers can learn to avoid the "Barnum effect"— being a sucker for fake inventories, horoscopes, handwriting analysis, and other pseudoscientific "tests" of personality.

MyPsychLab

Visit **www.mypsychlab.com** to help you get the best grade!
Test your knowledge and grasp difficult concepts through

• Custom study plans: See where you are strong and where you go wrong

• Interactive simulations

• Video and audio clips

KEY TERMS

15 PSYCHOLOGICAL DISORDERS

- Are mental disorders the same in every culture?

- Why do some people get over a traumatic experience fairly quickly, yet others develop PTSD?

- Why do some people get depressed for no reason, while others have reason, but don't get depressed?

- What's the matter with psychopaths that makes them capable of such heartless deception and cruelty?

- Can problem drinkers ever learn to drink moderately?

Margaret Mary Ray believed with all her heart that late-night talk-show host David Letterman was in love with her. Caught up in this delusion, she stalked Letterman day and night for a decade, writing him letters and repeatedly breaking into his house. She camped out on his tennis court and once stole his car. The tabloids treated her delusions as a running joke. Finally, she gave up. She wrote to her mother, "I'm all travelled out," and put herself in front of a coal train. She was killed instantly.

You don't have to be a psychologist to know that something was terribly wrong with Margaret Mary Ray. When people think of "mental illness," they usually think of individuals like her—people with delusions or people who behave in bizarre ways, such as walking the streets wearing layers of clothing on a hot summer day.

Most psychological problems are far less dramatic than the public's impression of them and far more common. Some people go through episodes of complete inability to function, yet get along fine between those episodes. Many people function adequately every day, yet suffer constant melancholy, always feeling below par. And some people cannot control their worries or tempers. In this chapter, you will learn about the many psychological problems that cause people unhappiness and anguish. You will learn about the severe disorders that really do make people unable to control their behaviour. But you will also learn why psychologists and psychiatrists often find it difficult to agree on a diagnosis, and why diagnosing mental problems is not the same as diagnosing medical problems such as diabetes or appendicitis.

One of the most common worries that people have is "Am I normal?" It is normal to fear being abnormal—especially when you are reading about psychological problems! But it is also normal to have problems. All of us on occasion have difficulties that seem too much to handle, and it is often unclear precisely when "normal" problems shade into "abnormal" ones.

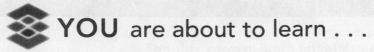

YOU are about to learn . . .

◆ why insanity is not the same thing as having a mental disorder.

◆ how mental disorders differ from normal problems.

◆ why the standard professional guide to the diagnosis of mental disorders is controversial.

◆ why popular "projective" tests like the Rorschach Inkblot Test are not reliable.

DEFINING AND DIAGNOSING DISORDER

➔◉ **Simulate**
Psychology Experiments Survey:
How Do You Take Care of Your
Mental Health?

Many people confuse unusual behaviour—behaviour that deviates from the norm—with mental disorder, but the two are not the same. A person may behave in ways that are statistically rare (collecting ceramic pigs, being a genius at math, committing murder) without having a mental illness. Conversely, some mental disorders, such as depression and anxiety, are extremely common.

People also confuse mental disorder and insanity. In the law, the definition of *insanity* rests primarily on whether a person is aware of the consequences of his or her actions and can control his or her behaviour. But *insanity* is a legal term only; a person may have a mental illness and yet be considered sane by the court.

If frequency of the problem is not a guide, and insanity reflects only one extreme kind of mental illness, how then should we define a "mental disorder"?

Dilemmas of Definition

One problem is that the definition of a disorder depends on whether we are taking society's point of view, the view of people who are affected by the troubled individual, or the perspective of troubled individuals themselves.

1 **Mental disorder as a violation of cultural standards.** One definition emphasizes the roles and rules of the culture. Every society sets up standards for its members to follow, and those who break the most important rules governing appropriate behaviour are usually considered deviant or disturbed. However, many of these rules are specific to a particular time or group. For example, it is not uncommon for bereaved people to have momentary visions of a deceased relative or to "hear" the loved one's voice. But in most of North America, these hallucinations are considered abnormal, and people who have them often fear they might be "crazy." In contrast, the Chinese, the Hopi, and members of many other cultures regard such visions as perfectly normal.

2 **Mental disorder as emotional distress.** A second approach identifies mental disorder in terms of a person's suffering—as from depression, anxiety, incapacitating fears, or problems with drugs. In this definition, a behaviour that is unendurable or upsetting for one person, such as lack of interest in sex, may be acceptable and normal for another. But this definition does not cover the behaviour of people who are clearly disturbed and dangerous to others, yet who are not troubled about their actions.

➔◉ **Simulate**
Psychological Disorders

3 **Mental disorder as behaviour that is self-destructive or harmful to others.** A third approach emphasizes the negative consequences of a person's behaviour. Some behaviour is harmful to the individual sufferer, such as the behaviour of a woman who is so afraid of crowds that she cannot leave her house, a man who

Thinking 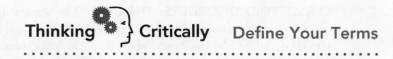 Critically Define Your Terms

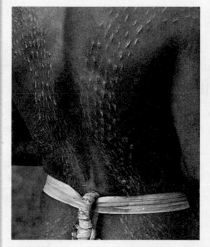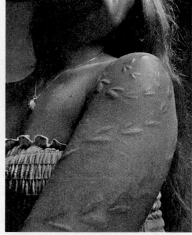

What's normal? In many places around the world, it is normal for women and men to create scars on their bodies for decoration or symbolic meaning. In Papua New Guinea, all young men go through an initiation rite in which small, deep cuts are made on their backs to create permanent scars that signify a crocodile's scales (left). In contrast, in most places it is abnormal to mutilate oneself for the sole purpose of inflicting injury and pain, as the patient on the right has done. But what about the decorative scars on the arm of the 23-year-old woman from upstate New York (middle), who had them made by a "body artist"? She also has scars on her leg and her stomach, along with 29 piercings. Is her behaviour "normal" or "abnormal"?

drinks so much that he cannot keep a job, or a student who is so anxious that she cannot take exams. In other cases, the individual may report feeling fine and deny that anything is wrong, yet will behave in ways that are disruptive, dangerous, or out of touch with reality—as when a child sets fires, a compulsive gambler loses the family savings, or a woman hears voices telling her to stalk a celebrity.

In this chapter, we define **mental disorder** broadly, as any behaviour or emotional state that causes a person to suffer, is self-destructive, seriously impairs the person's ability to work or get along with others, or endangers others or the community. By this definition, many people will have some mental-health problem in the course of their lives, or their loved ones will. A nationwide survey of more than 9000 randomly selected adults in the United States found that only about 7% of the population suffer from mental illnesses that are "seriously debilitating." But nearly half, at some time in their lives, temporarily fall prey to severe anxiety, depression, drug abuse, and other problems that can make their lives miserable (Kessler et al., 2005). In Canada, mental disorders are the leading cause of disability in people aged 15–44 (WHO, 2004).

Dilemmas of Diagnosis

Even armed with a general definition of mental disorder, psychologists have found that classifying mental disorders into distinct categories is not an easy job. In this section we will see why this is so.

⊷⊙Simulate
Psychology Experiments Survey:
How Do You Take Care of Your
Mental Health?

mental disorder Any behaviour or emotional state that causes an individual great suffering, is self-destructive, seriously impairs the person's ability to work or get along with others, or endangers others or the community.

CLASSIFYING DISORDERS: THE DSM. The standard reference manual used to diagnose mental disorders is the *Diagnostic and Statistical Manual of Mental Disorders (DSM)*, published by the American Psychiatric Association (1994, 2000). The DSM's primary aim is *descriptive:* to provide clear diagnostic categories so that clinicians and researchers can agree on which disorders they are talking about and then can study and treat these disorders.

TABLE 15.1 Major Diagnostic Categories in the DSM-IV

Disorders usually first diagnosed in infancy, childhood, or adolescence include mental retardation, attention deficit disorders (such as hyperactivity or an inability to concentrate), and developmental problems.

Delirium, dementia, amnesia, and other cognitive disorders are those resulting from brain damage, degenerative diseases such as syphilis or Alzheimer's, toxic substances, or drugs.

Substance-related disorders are problems associated with excessive use of or withdrawal from alcohol, amphetamines, caffeine, cocaine, hallucinogens, nicotine, opiates, or other drugs.

Schizophrenia and other psychotic disorders are disorders characterized by delusions, hallucinations, and severe disturbances in thinking and emotion.

Mood disorders include major depression, bipolar disorder (manic depression), and dysthymia (chronic depressed mood).

Anxiety disorders include generalized anxiety disorder, phobias, panic attacks with or without agoraphobia, posttraumatic stress disorder, and obsessive thoughts or compulsive rituals.

Eating disorders include anorexia nervosa (self-starvation because of an irrational fear of being or becoming fat) and bulimia nervosa (episodes of binge eating and vomiting).

Dissociative disorders include dissociative amnesia (in which important events cannot be remembered after a traumatic event) and dissociative identity disorder, characterized by the presence of two or more distinct identities or personalities.

Sexual and gender identity disorders include problems of sexual (gender) identity, such as transsexualism (wanting to be the other gender), problems of sexual performance (such as premature ejaculation or lack of orgasm), and paraphilias (needing unusual or bizarre imagery or acts for sexual arousal, as in sadomasochism or exhibitionism).

Impulse control disorders involve an inability to resist an impulse to perform some act that is harmful to the individual or to others, such as pathological gambling, stealing (kleptomania), setting fires (pyromania), or having violent rages.

Personality disorders are inflexible and maladaptive patterns that cause distress to the individual or impair the ability to function; they include paranoid, narcissistic, borderline, and antisocial personality disorders.

Additional conditions that may be a focus of clinical attention include "problems in living" such as bereavement, academic difficulties, spiritual problems, and acculturation problems.

✳ **Explore**
The Axes of the DSM

In addition, clinicians are encouraged to evaluate each client according to five *axes*, or dimensions:

1. The primary clinical problem, such as depression.

2. Ingrained aspects of the client's personality that are likely to affect the person's ability to be treated, such as negative emotionality (neuroticism), a disposition to be pessimistic and bitter (see Chapter 14).

3. Medical conditions or medications that might contribute to the symptoms.

4. Social and environmental stressors that can make the disorder worse, such as job and housing troubles or having recently left a network of close friends.

5. A global assessment of the client's overall level of functioning in work, relationships, and leisure time, including whether the problem is of recent origin or of long duration and how incapacitating it is.

The DSM has had an extraordinary impact worldwide. Virtually all textbooks in psychiatry and psychology base their discussions of mental disorders on the DSM. Lawyers and judges often refer to the manual's list of mental disorders, even though the DSM warns that its categories "may not be wholly relevant to legal judgments." With each new edition of the manual, the number of mental disorders has grown (see Figure 15.1). The first edition, in 1952, was only 86 pages long and contained about 100 diagnoses. The DSM-IV, published in 1994 and slightly revised in 2000, is 900 pages long and contains nearly 400 diagnoses of mental disorder. The DSM-V, due out in 2012, will contain even more diagnoses.

What is the reason for this explosion of mental disorders? Supporters of the new categories answer that it is important to distinguish disorders precisely in order to treat them properly. However, the DSM is an American publication, and health care in the United States is privatized to a much greater extent than is the case in Canada. Critics point to an economic reason: Insurance companies require clinicians to assign their clients an appropriate DSM code number for the diagnosed disorder, which puts pressure on compilers of the manual to add more diagnoses so that physicians and psychologists will be compensated.

PROBLEMS WITH THE DSM. Because of the DSM's powerful influence, critics maintain that it is important to be aware of its limitations and some inherent problems in the very effort to classify and label mental disorders:

1 **The danger of overdiagnosis.** "If you give a small boy a hammer," wrote Abraham Kaplan (1967), "it will turn out that everything he runs into needs pounding." Likewise, say critics, if you give mental-health professionals a diagnostic label, it will turn out that everyone they run into has the symptoms of the new disorder.

Consider "attention deficit/hyperactivity disorder" (ADHD), a diagnostic label given to children and adults who are impulsive, messy, restless, and easily frustrated and who have trouble concentrating. Since ADHD was added to the DSM, it has become the fastest-growing disorder in both Canada and the United States, where it is diagnosed at least 10 times as often as it is in Europe. Critics therefore fear that parents, teachers, and mental-health professionals are overusing this diagnosis, especially on boys, who make up 80–90% of all ADHD cases. The critics argue that normal boyish behaviour—being rambunctious, refusing to nap, being playful, not listening to teachers in school—is being turned into a psychological problem (Panksepp, 1998; Cummings & O'Donohue, 2008). A longitudinal study of more than a hundred four- to six-year-olds found that the number of children who met the criteria for ADHD declined over time (Lahey et al., 2005). Some remained highly impulsive and unable to concentrate, but others, it seems, simply matured!

Likewise, the fastest-growing diagnosis given to young children is bipolar disorder, once thought to occur only in adolescents and adults; the number of diagnoses rose from 20 000 to 800 000 in just one year (Moreno et al., 2007). Many experts think that only about 20% of the children currently diagnosed as bipolar meet the strict criteria for the disorder (Leibenluft & Rich, 2008).

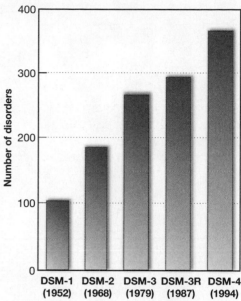

FIGURE 15.1 The Rising Number of Disorders in the DSM
Mental disorders in the DSM have increased nearly fourfold since the first edition (Houts, 2002).

Thinking Critically

Analyze Assumptions and Biases

Many people assume that diagnosing mental disorders is as straightforward and objective as diagnosing appendicitis. Is this assumption correct?

👁 **Watch**
Attention Deficit Disorder

2 The power of diagnostic labels. Being given a diagnosis reassures people who are seeking an explanation for their emotional symptoms or problems ("Whew! So *that's* what I've got!"). But once a person has been given a diagnosis, other people begin to see that person primarily in terms of the label; it sticks like lint. For example, when a rebellious, disobedient teenager is diagnosed as having "oppositional defiant disorder," people tend to see him as a person with a permanent, official condition; something is wrong with his personality. They then overlook other possible explanations of his actions: Maybe he is "defiant" because he has been mistreated or his parents don't listen to him. And once he is labelled, observers tend to ignore changes in his behaviour and the times when he is not being defiant.

3 The confusion of serious mental disorders with normal problems. The DSM is not called "The Diagnostic and Statistical Manual of Mental Disorders and a Whole Bunch of Everyday Problems." Yet each edition of the DSM has added more everyday problems, including "disorder of written expression" (having trouble writing clearly), "mathematics disorder" (not doing well in math), "religious or spiritual problem," and "caffeine-induced sleep disorder" (which at least is easy to cure; just switch to decaf). Some critics fear that by lumping together such normal difficulties with true mental illnesses, such as schizophrenia, the DSM implies that everyday problems are comparable to disorders—and equally likely to require treatment (Houts, 2002). Revisers of the current DSM are debating whether to include "binge eating" and "shopping addiction," behaviours that in their extreme form can certainly be troublesome, but which many (if not most) people experience on occasion.

4 The illusion of objectivity and universality. Finally, some psychologists argue that the whole enterprise of the DSM is a vain attempt to impose a veneer of science on an inherently subjective process (Houts, 2002; Kutchins & Kirk, 1997; Tiefer, 2004). Many decisions about what to include as a disorder, say these critics, are based not on empirical evidence but on group consensus. The problem is that group consensus often reflects prevailing attitudes and prejudices rather than objective evidence.

Harriet Tubman helped others escape from slavery on the "underground railroad." Slaveholders welcomed the idea that Tubman and others who insisted on their freedom had a mental disorder called "drapetomania."

It is easy to identify prejudices in *past* notions of mental problems. In the early years of the nineteenth century, a physician named Samuel Cartwright argued that many slaves were suffering from *drapetomania, an urge to escape from slavery* (Kutchins & Kirk, 1997; Landrine, 1988). (He made up the word from *drapetes*, the Latin word for "runaway slave," and *mania*, meaning "mad" or "crazy.") Thus, doctors could assure slave owners that a mental illness, not the intolerable condition of slavery, made slaves seek freedom. Today, of course, "drapetomania" seems foolish and cruel.

Over the years, psychiatrists have quite properly rejected many other "disorders" that reflected cultural prejudices and lacked empirical validation, such as lack of vaginal orgasm, childhood masturbation disorder, and homosexuality (Wakefield, 1992). But critics argue that many disorders still in the DSM are just as affected by contemporary prejudices and values. Today you don't have a disorder if you want to have sex "too often" (once called, in women, "nymphomania"), but you do if you do not want to have sex often "enough" (hypoactive sexual desire disorder) (Groneman, 2000). Emotional problems allegedly associated with menstruation remain in the DSM, but behavioural problems associated with testosterone have never even been considered for inclusion. In short, critics maintain, many diagnoses still depend on a cultural consensus—not on empirical evidence—about what constitutes normal behaviour, as well as what constitutes a mental disorder.

ADVANTAGES OF THE DSM. Defenders of the DSM agree that the boundaries between "normal problems" and "mental disorders" are fuzzy and often difficult to determine (Kessler et al., 2005). They also recognize that many psychological symptoms fall along a continuum, ranging from mild to severe (Helzer et al., 2008). But they believe that when the manual is used correctly and diagnoses are made with valid objective tests, the DSM improves the reliability of diagnosis (Beutler & Malik, 2002; Widiger & Clark, 2000). This is important, they maintain, because the DSM's categories help clinicians distinguish among disorders that share certain symptoms (such as anxiety, irritability, or delusions) in order to select the most appropriate treatment.

CULTURE and *Mental Illness*

Are Mental Problems the Same Everywhere?

Researchers are making great progress in separating mental disorders that are universal—usually involving genetic vulnerabilities, brain disease, or brain damage—from those that are specific to particular cultural contexts, norms, and traditions. In response to critics who argue that almost all diagnoses of mental disorder are matters of consensus, clinicians point out that certain disorders occur everywhere. From the Inuit to the Pacific Islanders to the Yoruba of Nigeria, some individuals have schizophrenic delusions, are severely depressed, cannot control their aggressive behaviour, or have panic attacks (Butcher, Lim, & Nezami, 1998; Kleinman, 1988).

However, culture does influence and shape the particular symptoms a sufferer of these disorders will have, and how the disorder expresses itself (Barlow, Chorpita, & Turovsky, 1996). In Latin America and southern Europe, a person having a panic attack may report feelings of choking, being smothered, and fear of dying. In America, the fear of "going crazy" is a more common symptom than elsewhere. In Greenland, some fishermen suffer from "kayak-angst": a sudden attack of dizziness and fear that occurs while they are fishing in small, one-person kayaks (Amering & Katschnig, 1990). Likewise, depression occurs all over the world, but members of various ethnic groups differ in what symptoms they reveal (drinking, crying, withdrawing . . .), in their willingness to talk about their feelings and seek help, and in the likelihood of committing suicide. In the United States, the group at highest risk of suicide is Native American men, and the group at lowest risk is African American women (Goldston et al., 2008).

One difficulty in diagnosing mental disorders is raised by **culture-bound syndromes**, sets of symptoms specific to the culture in which they occur (see Table 15.2). The DSM acknowledges that these syndromes rarely overlap with DSM diagnostic categories, yet they can cause great suffering and qualify as true mental disorders in their own context. For example, in Japan, where people are extremely sensitive to matters of social harmony and concerned about not offending other people, *taijin kyofusho* is a disorder in which a person feels intensely frightened and irrationally embarrassed that his or her body parts or functions are disgusting to others. Some culture-bound syndromes might best be understood as culturally permitted expressions of extreme psychological distress: For example, Latinos may experience an *ataque de nervios*, an

culture-bound syndromes Disorders that are specific to particular cultural contexts.

TABLE 15.2 From Amok to Zar: Some Culture-Bound Syndromes

Problem Name	Where Recognized	Description
Amok	Malaysia; similar patterns elsewhere	Brooding followed by a violent outburst; often precipitated by a slight or insult; seems to be prevalent only among men
Ataque de nervios	Latin America and Mediterranean countries	An episode of uncontrollable shouting, crying, trembling, heat in chest rising to the head, verbal or physical aggression
Brain fag	West Africa	"Brain tiredness," a mental and physical reaction to the challenges of schooling
Ghost sickness	Native American tribes	Preoccupation with death and the dead, with bad dreams, fainting, appetite loss, fear, hallucinations, etc.
Pibloktoq	Arctic and subarctic Inuit communities	Episodes of extreme excitement of up to 30 minutes, during which the individual behaves irrationally or violently
Qi-gong psychotic reaction	China	A short episode of mental symptoms after engaging in the Chinese folk practice of qi-gong, or "exercise of vital energy"
Taijin kyofusho	Japan	An intense fear that the body, its parts, or its functions displease, embarrass, or are offensive to others
Zar	North Africa and Middle East	Belief in possession by a spirit, causing shouting, laughing, head banging, weeping, withdrawal, etc.

Source: DSM-IV

episode of uncontrollable screaming, crying, and agitation, and Malaysian men may run *amok* in a violent, even murderous outburst. Students may have special sympathy for sufferers of the West African syndrome of *brain fag*, mental exhaustion due to excessive studying.

By comparing mental and emotional symptoms across different times and places, researchers can distinguish universal disorders from those that are culture-bound. One meta-analysis found that bulimia nervosa, involving cycles of binge eating and vomiting to maintain weight, is a culture-bound syndrome that occurs primarily in the United States and is unknown in most other parts of the world. Yet anorexia, a body-image disorder in which the sufferer usually feels "too fat" even at the point of starving to death, has been found throughout history and across cultures (Keel & Klump, 2003).

Dilemmas of Measurement

Clinical psychologists and psychiatrists usually arrive at a diagnosis by interviewing a patient and observing the person's behaviour when he or she arrives at the office, hospital, or clinic. But many also use psychological tests to help them decide on a diagnosis. Such tests are also commonly used in schools (e.g., to determine whether a child has a learning disorder or emotional problem) and in court settings (e.g., to try to determine which parent should have custody in a divorce case, whether a child has been sexually abused, or whether a defendant is mentally competent).

PROJECTIVE TESTS. Projective tests consist of ambiguous pictures, sentences, or stories that the test taker interprets or completes. A child or adult may be asked to draw a person, a house, or some other object, or to finish a sentence (such as "My father . . ." or "Women are . . ."). The psychodynamic assumption behind all projective tests is that the person's unconscious thoughts and feelings will be "projected" onto the test and revealed in the person's responses. (See Chapter 14 for a discussion of psychodynamic theories and their emphasis on unconscious motives and conflicts.)

projective tests Psychological tests used to infer a person's motives, conflicts, and unconscious dynamics on the basis of the person's interpretations of ambiguous stimuli.

Projective tests can help clinicians establish rapport with their clients and can encourage clients to open up about anxieties and conflicts they might be ashamed to discuss. But the evidence is overwhelming that these tests lack reliability and validity, which makes them inappropriate for their most common uses—assessing personality traits or diagnosing mental disorders (Wood et al., 2003). They lack reliability because different clinicians often interpret the same person's scores differently, perhaps projecting their own beliefs and assumptions when they decide what a specific response means. The tests have low validity because they fail to measure what they are supposed to measure (Hunsley, Lee, & Wood, 2003). One reason is that responses to a projective test are significantly affected by sleepiness, hunger, medication, worry, verbal ability, the clinician's instructions, the clinician's own personality (friendly and warm, or cool and remote), and other events occurring that day.

One of the most popular projectives is the *Rorschach Inkblot Test*, which was devised by the Swiss psychiatrist Hermann Rorschach in 1921. It consists of 10 cards with symmetrical abstract patterns, originally formed by spilling ink on paper and folding the paper in half. The test taker reports what he or she sees in the inkblots, and the clinician interprets the answers according to the symbolic meanings emphasized by psychodynamic theories. One kind of response, for example, might be interpreted as evidence of a person's dependency.

Although the Rorschach is widely used among clinicians, efforts to confirm its reliability and validity have repeatedly failed. The Rorschach does not reliably diagnose depression, posttraumatic stress reactions, personality disorders, or serious mental disorders. In recent years, a scoring method called the Comprehensive System has become popular (Exner, 1993). But this method, too, shows significant reliability and validity problems. Claims of the system's success often come from testimonials at workshops where clinicians are taught how to use the test, which is hardly an impartial way of assessing it (Wood et al., 2003). Furthermore, some investigators, such as the University of Ottawa's John Hunsley and Gina Di Giulio (2001), have questioned whether Exner's large sample of "normal" responses to this test actually represents normal responding.

Many psychotherapists use projective tests with young children to help them express feelings they cannot reveal verbally. But during the 1980s, some therapists began using projective methods for another purpose: to determine whether a child had been sexually abused. They claimed they could identify a child who had been abused by observing how the child played with "anatomically detailed" dolls (dolls with realistic genitals), and that is how many of them testified in hundreds of court cases (Ceci & Bruck, 1995).

Unfortunately, these therapists had not tested their beliefs by using a fundamental scientific procedure: comparison with a control group (see Chapter 2). They had not asked, "How do *nonabused* children play with these dolls?" When psychological scientists conducted controlled research to answer this question, they found that large percentages of nonabused children are also fascinated with the doll's genitals. They will poke at them, grab them, pound sticks into a female doll's vagina, and do other things that alarm adults! The crucial conclusion was that you cannot reliably diagnose sexual abuse on the basis of children's doll play (Bruck et al., 1995; Hunsley, Lee, & Wood, 2003; Koocher et al., 1995; Wood et al., 2003). You can see how someone who

A Rorschach inkblot. What do you see in it?

Thinking Critically

Examine the Evidence

For years, many therapists used anatomically detailed dolls as a projective test to determine whether a child had been sexually abused. But the empirical evidence, including studies of nonabused children in a control group, shows that this practice is simply not valid. It can lead to false allegations because it often misidentifies nonabused children who are merely fascinated with the doll's genitals.

objective tests (inventories)
Standardized objective questionnaires requiring written responses; they typically include scales on which people are asked to rate themselves.

did not understand the problems with projective tests might end up making inferences about a child's behaviour that were dangerously wrong.

Another situation in which projective tests are used widely yet often inappropriately is in child-custody assessments. Understandably, when faced with divorcing partners who are bitterly quarrelling, calling each other names, and accusing each other of being a terrible parent, the courts long for an objective way to determine which one is better suited to have custody. But when a panel of psychological scientists impartially examined the leading psychological assessment measures, most of which are projective tests, they found that "these measures assess ill-defined constructs, and they do so poorly, leaving no scientific justification for their use in child custody evaluations" (Emery, Otto, & O'Donohue, 2005).

OBJECTIVE TESTS. Many clinicians also use **objective tests (inventories)**, standardized questionnaires that ask about the test taker's behaviour and feelings. Some inventories, such as the Beck Depression Inventory, the Spielberger State–Trait Anger Inventory, and the Taylor Manifest Anxiety Scale, assess specific emotional problems. The most widely used test for assessing personality and emotional disorders, the *Minnesota Multiphasic Personality Inventory (MMPI)*, is organized into 10 categories, or *scales*, covering such problems as depression, paranoia, schizophrenia, and introversion. Four additional *validity scales* indicate whether a test taker is likely to be lying, defensive, or evasive while answering the items.

Inventories are generally more reliable and more valid than either projective methods or subjective clinical judgments (Dawes, 1994; Meyer et al., 2001). But inventories also have some limitations; one continuing problem is that they often fail to take into account differences among cultural, regional, and socioeconomic groups. In response to this criticism, the developers of the MMPI released a major revision, the MMPI-2, with norms based on a sample that was more representative in terms of ethnicity, region, age, and gender (Butcher et al., 1989; Lucio et al., 1999). Explicit tests of whether this new structure actually represents personality in current clinical and nonclinical groups of people have been quite encouraging. At the University of Toronto, Michael Bagby and his colleagues gave the MMPI-2 test to more than 600 people (clinical and nonclinical participants) and found that its structure provided an accurate framework for describing personality in both groups of people (Bagby et al., 2002). However, despite these recent revisions of the MMPI the problem persists; for example, Mexican, Puerto Rican, and Argentine respondents score differently from non-Hispanic Americans, on average, on the Masculinity–Femininity Scale. This difference does not reflect emotional problems but rather traditional Latino attitudes toward sex roles (Cabiya et al., 2000). Also, the MMPI and other objective tests have a significant rate of false positives; that is, they sometimes label a person's responses as evidence of mental disorder when no serious problem actually exists (Guthrie & Mobley, 1994; Leib, 2008). And, finally, objective tests such as the MMPI are often inappropriately used in business, industry, legal settings, and schools by persons who are not well trained in testing.

We turn now to a closer examination of some of the disorders described in the DSM. Of course, we cannot cover all of them in one chapter, so we have singled out several that illustrate the range of psychological problems that afflict humanity, from the common to the very rare.

quickQUIZ

✓ Quick Review on MyPsychLab

Your mental health will be enhanced if you can answer these questions.

1. Ruthie is afraid to leave her apartment unless she is with a close friend or relative, yet she says she feels fine and she angrily resists her friends' advice that she get help. What definition of mental disorder does Ruthie's behaviour meet?
2. The primary purpose of the DSM is to (a) provide descriptive criteria for diagnosing mental disorders, (b) help psychologists assess normal as well as abnormal behaviour, (c) describe the causes of common disorders, (d) keep the number of diagnostic categories of mental disorders to a minimum.
3. List four criticisms of the DSM.
4. What is the advantage of inventories, compared with clinical judgments and projective tests, in diagnosing mental disorders?

Answers:

1. Mental disorder as behaviour that is self-destructive 2. a 3. It can foster overdiagnosis; it overlooks the influence of diagnostic labels on the perceptions of clinicians and the behaviour of clients; it confuses serious mental disorders with everyday problems in living; and it falsely implies that its diagnoses apply universally and are always based on objective evidence. 4. Inventories have better reliability and validity.

YOU are about to learn . . .

◆ the difference between ordinary anxiety and an anxiety disorder.
◆ why the most disabling of all phobias is known as the "fear of fear."
◆ why some people recover quickly after a trauma whereas others develop posttraumatic stress disorder.

ANXIETY DISORDERS

Anyone who is waiting for important news or living in an unpredictable situation quite sensibly feels *anxiety, a general state of apprehension or psychological tension*. And anyone who is in a dangerous and unfamiliar situation, such as making a first parachute jump or facing a peevish python, quite sensibly feels flat-out fear. In the short run, these emotions are adaptive because they energize us to cope with danger. They ensure that we don't make that first jump without knowing how to operate the parachute, and that we get away from that snake as fast as we can.

But sometimes fear and anxiety become detached from any actual danger, or these feelings continue even when danger and uncertainty are past. The result may be *chronic anxiety,* marked by long-lasting feelings of apprehension and doom; *panic attacks,* short-lived but intense feelings of anxiety; *phobias,* excessive fears of specific things or situations; or *obsessive-compulsive disorder,* in which repeated thoughts and rituals are used to ward off anxiety.

((•Listen
Anxiety Disorders

Anxiety and Panic

generalized anxiety disorder
A continuous state of anxiety marked by feelings of worry and dread, apprehension, difficulties in concentration, and signs of motor tension.

posttraumatic stress disorder (PTSD) An anxiety disorder in which a person who has experienced a traumatic or life-threatening event has symptoms such as psychic numbing, reliving of the trauma, and increased physiological arousal.

👁 **Watch**
Clinical Anxiety

The chief characteristic of **generalized anxiety disorder** is continuous, uncontrollable anxiety or worry—a feeling of foreboding and dread—that occurs on a majority of days during a six-month period and that is not brought on by physical causes such as disease, drugs, or drinking too much coffee. Symptoms include restlessness or feeling keyed up, difficulty concentrating, irritability, jitteriness, sleep disturbance, and unwanted, intrusive worries.

Some people suffer from generalized anxiety disorder without having lived through any specific anxiety-producing event. They may have a physiological tendency to experience anxiety symptoms—sweaty palms, a racing heart, shortness of breath—when they are in challenging or uncontrollable situations. Genes may also be involved in causing abnormalities in the amygdala, the core structure for the acquisition of fear (see Chapter 11), and in the prefrontal cortex, which is associated with the ability to realize when danger has passed (Lonsdorf et al., 2009). As we saw in Chapter 13, temperamentally shy children are already predisposed to react with anxiety in novel situations. Other chronically anxious people may have a history, starting in childhood, of being unable to control or predict their environments (Barlow, 2000; Mineka & Zinbarg, 2006). Whatever the origin of generalized anxiety disorder, its sufferers have mental biases in the way they attend to and process threatening information. They perceive everything as an opportunity for disaster, a cognitive habit that fuels their worries and keeps their anxiety bubbling along (Mitte, 2008).

Thinking 🧠 Critically

Ask Questions

This grief-stricken soldier has just learned that the body bag on the flight with him contains the remains of a close friend who was killed in action. Understandably, many soldiers suffer posttraumatic stress symptoms. But why do most eventually recover, whereas others have PTSD for many years?

POSTTRAUMATIC STRESS DISORDER. Stress symptoms, including insomnia, agitation, and jumpiness, are entirely normal in the immediate aftermath of any crisis or trauma, such as war, rape, torture, natural disasters, sudden bereavement, or terrorist attacks. But if the symptoms persist for one month or longer and begin to impair a person's functioning, the sufferer may have **posttraumatic stress disorder (PTSD)**. Typical symptoms of PTSD include reliving the trauma in recurrent, intrusive thoughts; a sense of detachment from others and a loss of interest in familiar activities; and increased physiological arousal, reflected in insomnia, irritability, and impaired concentration.

At the University of Western Ontario, Ruth Lanius and her colleagues (2002) used fMRI technology to study the neural circuitry of seven people who suffered from PTSD as the result of sexual abuse. The trouble is, PTSD symptoms can be intermittent rather than continuous, making them very difficult to study. To make sure that the participants were experiencing symptoms of PTSD, researchers read them a story about sexual abuse during the brain scan. Participants who reported a sense of detachment, or a "dissociative response," after they heard the story were exhibiting symptoms of PTSD. The scans showed that this detachment was accompanied by increased activity across all four lobes of the participants' brains, with most activity concentrated in the prefrontal cortex and the cortex in and around the limbic brain structures (such as the cingulated cortex, amygdala, and hippocampus). This result supports the finding that PTSD is associated with changes in activity levels of particular brain structures.

Watch
PTSD 9/11

Interestingly, in PTSD sufferers, the hippocampus is apt to be smaller than average (McNally, 2003). The hippocampus is crucially involved in autobiographical memory. An abnormally small one may figure in the difficulty of some trauma survivors to react to their memories as events from their past, which may be why they keep reliving them in the present. Originally, researchers thought that severe trauma caused neuron damage or loss of cells in the hippocampus, producing PTSD symptoms—impaired memory, recurrent fears, and so forth. But this hypothesis has been refuted. One team used MRIs to measure hippocampal size in identical twins, only one of whom in each pair had been in combat in Vietnam. If trauma shrinks the hippocampus, then the size of the hippocampus should have been different in the veterans who developed PTSD and their identical twins. But this was not what the researchers found. Two things were necessary for a vet to develop chronic PTSD: serving in combat *and* having a smaller hippocampus than normal (Gilbertson et al., 2002). Twins who had smaller hippocampi but no military service did not develop PTSD, and neither did the twins who *did* experience combat but who had normal-sized hippocampi.

Most people who live through a traumatic experience eventually recover without developing PTSD. For example, one major national survey of Americans found that about 60% had experienced a traumatic event, but only 8% of the men and 20% of the women developed PTSD (Kessler et al., 1995). Some experts predicted an epidemic of PTSD after 9/11, but it never materialized (Bonanno et al., 2006). Why, then, if most people recover from a traumatic experience, do some continue to have PTSD symptoms for years, sometimes for decades?

One answer may involve a genetic predisposition. Behavioural–genetic studies of twins in the general population as well as among combat veterans have found that PTSD symptoms have a heritable component (Stein et al., 2002).

Another answer is that people who develop long-lasting PTSD often have a prior history of psychological problems and other traumatic experiences with poor emotional adjustment to them (Ozer et al., 2003). One reason for their poor adjustment is that they are more likely to have self-defeating, anxiety-producing ways of thinking in general—for example, they tend to "catastrophize" about every little thing that goes wrong, to believe they are inadequate, and to feel that no one can be trusted (Bryant & Guthrie, 2005). Many PTSD sufferers also lack the social, psychological, and neurological resources to deal with their difficult experiences. They are more likely than resilient people to have the personality trait of neuroticism and to have lower-than-average intelligence, which may impair their ability to cope cognitively with trauma (McNally, 2003).

In sum, many cases of PTSD seem to be a result of impaired cognitive and neurological functioning that existed *before* the trauma took place, triggered by the eventual traumatic experience.

PANIC DISORDER. Another kind of anxiety disorder is **panic disorder**, in which a person has recurring attacks of intense fear or panic, often with feelings of impending doom or death. These panic attacks may last from a few minutes to (more rarely) several hours. Symptoms include trembling and shaking, dizziness, chest pain or discomfort, rapid heart rate, feelings of unreality, hot and cold flashes, sweating, and—as a result of all these scary physical reactions—a fear of dying, going crazy, or losing control. Many sufferers fear they are having a heart attack.

panic disorder An anxiety disorder in which a person experiences recurring panic attacks, periods of intense fear, and feelings of impending doom or death, accompanied by physiological symptoms such as rapid heart rate and dizziness.

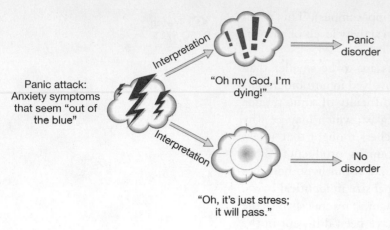

Panic attack: Anxiety symptoms that seem "out of the blue"

Interpretation → "Oh my God, I'm dying!" → Panic disorder

Interpretation → "Oh, it's just stress; it will pass." → No disorder

◉ Watch
Panic Disorder

◉ Watch
Phobias

phobia An exaggerated, unrealistic fear of a specific situation, activity, or object.

agoraphobia A set of phobias, often set off by a panic attack, involving the basic fear of being away from a safe place or person.

Although panic attacks seem to come out of nowhere, they in fact usually occur in the aftermath of stress, prolonged emotion, specific worries, or frightening experiences (McNally, 1998). For example, a friend of the authors was on a plane that was a target of a bomb threat while airborne at 33 000 feet. He coped beautifully at the time, but two weeks later, seemingly out of nowhere, he had a panic attack.

Such delayed attacks after life-threatening scares are common. The essential difference between people who develop panic disorder and those who do not lies in *how they interpret their bodily reactions* (Barlow, 2000). Healthy people who have occasional panic attacks see them correctly as a result of a passing crisis or period of stress, comparable to another person's migraines. But people who develop panic disorder regard the attack as a sign of illness or impending death, and they begin to live their lives in restrictive ways, trying to avoid future attacks.

Fears and Phobias

Are you afraid of bugs, snakes, or dogs? Are you vaguely uncomfortable with them or so afraid that you can't stand to be around one? A **phobia** is an exaggerated fear of a specific situation, activity, or thing. Some common phobias—such as fear of snakes, insects, heights (acrophobia), thunder (brontophobia), or being trapped in enclosed spaces (claustrophobia)—may have evolved to be easily acquired in human beings because these fears reflected real dangers for the species (Öhman & Mineka, 2003). Other phobias, such as a fear of cats (ailurophobia) or the colour purple (porphyrophobia), may be acquired through classical conditioning or even through observation of a frightening event that is happening to someone else (Mineka & Zinbarg, 2006). Still other phobias, such as fear of dirt and germs (mysophobia) or of the number 13 (triskaidekaphobia), may reflect personality differences or cultural traditions. Whatever its source, a phobia is truly frightening and often incapacitating for its sufferer. It is not just a tendency to say "ugh" at tarantulas or skip the snake display at the zoo.

People who have a *social phobia* become extremely anxious in situations in which they will be observed by others—eating in a restaurant, speaking in front of a group or crowd, having to perform for others. They worry that they will do or say something that will be excruciatingly humiliating or embarrassing. These phobias are more severe forms of the occasional shyness and social anxiety that everyone experiences. For people with a social phobia, the mere thought of being in a new situation with unfamiliar people is scary enough to cause sweating, trembling, nausea, and an overwhelming feeling of inadequacy. So they don't go, increasing their isolation and imagined fears.

By far the most disabling fear disorder is agoraphobia. In ancient Greece, the *agora* was the social, political, business, and religious centre of town, the public meeting place away from home. The fundamental fear in agoraphobia is of being trapped in a crowded public place, where escape might be difficult or where help might be unavailable if the person has a panic attack. Individuals with agoraphobia report many specific fears—of being in a crowded movie theatre, driving in traffic or tunnels, or going to parties—but the underlying fear is of being away from a safe place, usually home, or a safe person, usually a parent or partner.

Agoraphobia typically begins with a panic attack that seems to have no cause. The attack is so unexpected and scary that the agoraphobic-to-be begins to avoid situations

WHAT SCARES YOU?

Everyone fears something. Stop for a moment to think about what you fear most. Is it heights? Snakes? Speaking in public? Ask yourself these questions: (1) How long have you feared this thing or situation? (2) How would you respond if you could not avoid this thing or situation? (3) How much would you be willing to rearrange your life to avoid this feared thing or situation? After considering these questions, would you regard your fear as a full-blown phobia or merely a normal source of apprehension?

that he or she thinks may provoke another one. For example, a woman the authors know had a panic attack while driving on a highway. This was a perfectly normal post-traumatic response to the suicide of her husband a few weeks earlier. But thereafter she avoided highways—as if the highway, and not the suicide, had caused the attack. Because so many of the actions associated with agoraphobia arise as a mistaken effort to avoid a panic attack, psychologists regard agoraphobia as a "fear of fear" rather than simply a fear of places.

Obsessions and Compulsions

Obsessive-compulsive disorder (OCD) is characterized by recurrent, persistent, unwished-for thoughts or images (*obsessions*) or by repetitive, ritualized, stereotyped behaviours that the person feels must be carried out to avoid disaster (*compulsions*). Of course, many people have trivial compulsions and practise superstitious rituals; baseball players are famous for them—one won't change his socks and another will eat chicken every day while he is on a hitting streak. Obsessions and compulsions become a disorder when they become uncontrollable and interfere with a person's life.

People who have obsessive thoughts often find them frightening or repugnant: thoughts of killing a child, of becoming contaminated by a handshake, or of having unknowingly hurt someone in a traffic accident. Obsessive thoughts take many forms, but they are alike in reflecting impaired ways of reasoning and processing information.

People who suffer from compulsions likewise feel they have no control over them. The most common compulsions are hand washing, counting, touching, and checking. A woman *must* check the furnace, lights, locks, oven, and fireplace three times before she can sleep; or a man *must* wash his hands and face precisely eight times before he leaves the house. OCD sufferers usually realize that their behaviour is senseless, and they are often tormented by their rituals. But if they try to forgo the ritual, they feel mounting anxiety that is relieved only by giving in to it. For one young man with OCD, stairs became a treadmill he could not get off: "At first I'd walk up and down the stairs only three or four times," he recalled. "Later I had to run up and down 63 times in 45 minutes. If I failed, I had to start all over again from the beginning" (as cited in King, 1989).

In many people with OCD, the prefrontal cortex is depleted of serotonin, which creates a kind of cognitive rigidity—an inability to let go of certain thoughts (Clarke et al., 2004). In addition, several parts of the brain are hyperactive in people with OCD. One area of the frontal lobes sends messages of impending danger to other areas involved in controlling the movement of the limbs and preparing the body to feel fear and respond to external threats. Normally, once danger is past or a person realizes that there is no cause for fear, the brain's alarm signal turns off. In people

▶ **Watch**
John: OCD

obsessive-compulsive disorder (OCD)   An anxiety disorder in which a person feels trapped in repetitive, persistent thoughts (*obsessions*) and repetitive, ritualized behaviours (*compulsions*) designed to reduce anxiety.

Extreme hoarding is a form of obsessive-compulsive disorder. The person who lived here was unable to throw away any papers or magazines without feeling tremendous anxiety.

with OCD, however, false alarms keep clanging and the emotional networks keep sending out mistaken "fear!" messages (Schwartz et al., 1996). The sufferer feels in a constant state of danger and tries repeatedly to reduce the resulting anxiety.

OCD is not a single, unified disorder (Taylor, McKay, & Abramowitz, 2005). One subtype afflicts pathological hoarders who fill their homes with newspapers, bags of old clothing, used tissue boxes—all kinds of junk. They are tormented by fears of throwing out something they will need later. A PET-scan study that compared obsessive hoarders with other people with obsessive symptoms found that hoarders had less activity in parts of the brain involved in decision making, problem solving, spatial orientation, and memory (Saxena et al., 2004). Perhaps these deficits explain why hoarders keep things (their inability to decide what to throw away creates a constant struggle) and why they often keep their papers and junk in the living room, in the kitchen, or even on the bed. They have trouble remembering where things are and thus feel the need to have them in sight.

quick**QUIZ**

✔•─Quick Review on **MyPsychLab**

We hope you don't feel anxious about matching each term on the left with its description on the right.

1. social phobia
2. generalized anxiety disorder
3. posttraumatic stress disorder
4. agoraphobia
5. compulsion
6. obsession

a. need to perform a ritual
b. fear of fear; of being trapped with no way of escape
c. continuing sense of doom
d. repeated, unwanted thoughts
e. fear of meeting new people
f. anxiety following severe shock

Answers:

1.e 2.c 3.f 4.b 5.a 6.d

 YOU are about to learn . . .

◆ the difference between major depression and the blues.
◆ four contributing factors in depression.
◆ how some people can think themselves into depression.

MOOD DISORDERS

In the DSM, *mood disorders* include disturbances in mood ranging from extreme depression to extreme mania. Of course, most people feel sad from time to time, and also joyful. And most people, at some time in their lives, will know the wild grief that accompanies tragedy and bereavement. These feelings, however, are a far cry from the clinical disorders described by the DSM.

Depression

Anxiety, painful though it is, is at least a sign that a person is engaged in the future: It reflects the belief that something bad will happen. But depressed people feel burned out about the future: They are sure that nothing good will ever happen. Some people go through life with constant but low-grade unhappiness; they can do what they need to but nearly always report their mood as sad or "down in the dumps." Others suffer from **major depression**, a serious mood disorder that involves emotional, behavioural, cognitive, and physical changes severe enough to disrupt a person's ordinary functioning. The writer William Styron, who fought and recovered from major depression, used the beginning of Dante's classic poem *The Divine Comedy* to convey his suffering:

> *In the middle of the journey of our life*
> *I found myself in a dark wood,*
> *For I had lost the right path.*

"For those who have dwelt in depression's dark wood," wrote Styron (1990) in *Darkness Visible*, "and known its inexplicable agony, the return from the abyss is not unlike the ascent of the poet, trudging upward and upward out of hell's black depths and at last emerging into what he saw as 'the shining world.'"

People with major depression feel despairing and hopeless. They may think often of death or suicide. They feel unable to get up and do things; it takes an enormous effort even to get dressed. Their thinking patterns feed their bleak moods. They exaggerate minor failings, ignore or discount positive events, and interpret any little thing that goes wrong as evidence that nothing will ever go right. Emotionally healthy people who are sad or grieving do not see themselves as completely worthless and unlovable. Depressed people interpret losses as signs of failure and conclude that they will never be happy again.

Depression is accompanied by physical changes as well. The depressed person may overeat or stop eating, have difficulty falling asleep or sleeping through the night, have trouble concentrating, and feel tired all the time. Some sufferers have other physical reactions, such as headaches or inexplicable pain.

Major depression occurs at least twice as often among women as among men, all over the world. However, because women are more likely than men to talk about their feelings and more likely to seek help, depression in males is probably underdiagnosed. Men who are depressed often try to mask their feelings by withdrawing, abusing drugs, or behaving violently (Canetto, 1992; Kessler et al., 1995). As Susan Nolen-Hoeksema, a leading depression researcher, put it, "Women think and men drink."

Even people who are rich, successful, and adored by millions can suffer from major depression. The suicide of Nirvana's lead singer, Kurt Cobain, shocked and saddened his many fans.

👁 **Watch**
William: Double Depression

Listening to Blues Test

Bipolar Disorder

At the opposite pole from depression is *mania*, an abnormally high state of exhilaration. You might think it's impossible to feel too good, but mania is not the normal joy of being in love or winning the Pulitzer Prize. Instead of feeling fatigued and listless, the manic person is excessively wired and often irritable when thwarted. Instead of feeling hopeless and powerless, the person feels powerful and is full of plans; but these plans are usually based on delusional ideas, such as thinking that he or she has solved

major depression A mood disorder involving disturbances in emotion (excessive sadness), behaviour (loss of interest in one's usual activities), cognition (thoughts of hopelessness), and body function (fatigue and loss of appetite).

✱ Explore
Bipolar Disorder

👁 Watch
Bipolar Disorder

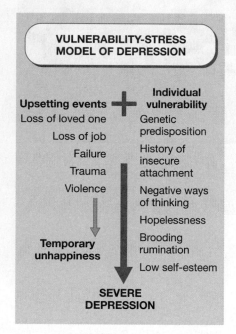

VULNERABILITY-STRESS MODEL OF DEPRESSION

Upsetting events + **Individual vulnerability**

Loss of loved one

Loss of job

Failure

Trauma

Violence

Genetic predisposition

History of insecure attachment

Negative ways of thinking

Hopelessness

Brooding rumination

Low self-esteem

Temporary unhappiness

SEVERE DEPRESSION

bipolar disorder A mood disorder in which episodes of both depression and mania (excessive euphoria) occur.

vulnerability-stress models Approaches that emphasize how individual vulnerabilities interact with external stresses or circumstances to produce mental disorders.

the world's problems. People in a state of mania often get into terrible trouble, going on extravagant spending sprees, making impulsive and bad decisions, or having risky sexual adventures.

When people experience at least one episode of mania alternating with episodes of depression, they are said to have **bipolar disorder** (formerly called *manic-depressive disorder*). This is a rarer problem than depression and distinctly different. Although more women than men suffer from depression, bipolar disorder occurs equally in both sexes. The great humorist Mark Twain had bipolar disorder, which he described as "periodical and sudden changes of mood . . . from deep melancholy to half-insane tempests and cyclones." Other writers, artists, musicians, and scientists have suffered from this disorder (Jamison, 1992). During the highs, many of these artists create their best work, but the price of the lows is disastrous relationships, bankruptcy, and sometimes suicide. As noted earlier, bipolar disorder, once thought to emerge only in adulthood, is now being widely diagnosed among young children and adolescents, although the symptoms and mood swings often look different from those in adults and the diagnosis in children remains controversial (Holden, 2008).

Origins of Depression

Psychologists have investigated many different contributing factors to major depression: genetic factors, life experiences, problems with close attachments, and cognitive habits. Few researchers think that any one of these factors alone produces chronic depression. Most researchers now emphasize **vulnerability-stress models** of mental disorders, in which a person's vulnerabilities (in genetic predispositions, personality traits, or habits of thinking) interact with stressful events (such as sexual victimization, violence, or loss of a close relationship) to produce any given case (Hankin & Abramson, 2001). Let's consider the evidence for each contributing factor in depression:

1   **Genetic factors.** Studies of adopted children and twins support the notion that major depression is a moderately heritable disorder (Bierut et al., 1999). Psychologists are hunting for the genes that might be involved, although it is unlikely that a single gene directly or inevitably "causes" severe depression. As in the case of posttraumatic stress disorder, a genetic predisposition must interact with stressful events to create the disorder.

Psychologists have identified one gene (called 5-HTT) that comes in two forms: a long form that apparently helps protect people from depression, and a short form that makes them more vulnerable to it (Caspi et al., 2003). In a study of 847 New Zealanders who were followed from birth to age 26, the researchers found that 43% of those who possessed two copies of the short form of this gene (one from each parent) became severely depressed in the aftermath of major stress (such as the loss of a job, disabling injuries, a death in the family, or abuse suffered in childhood). Yet only 17% of those with two copies of the long form of this gene became depressed, even when they suffered the same stresses. And people who inherited one long form of the gene from one parent and a short form from the other fell in between in their susceptibility to depression (33%). Genes may exert their effects on depression by affecting levels of serotonin and other neurotransmitters in the brain. Genes may also affect production of the stress hormone cortisol, which, at high levels, can damage cells in the hippocampus and amygdala (Sapolsky, 2000; Sheline, 2000). In depressed patients, the system that regulates reactions to stress is in overdrive; it doesn't shut down when it should, and it keeps overproducing cortisol (Plotsky, Owens, & Nemeroff, 1998). Nonetheless, genes cannot account for all cases of depression; even among the New Zealanders with the greatest genetic vulnerability, more than half did not become depressed. Nor do genes seem to account for the sex difference in depression rates. In the New Zealand study, women were no more likely than men to have the short form of the 5-HTT gene.

Depleting animals of serotonin does not induce depression, nor does increasing brain serotonin necessarily alleviate it. The fact that some antidepressants raise serotonin levels (see Chapter 16) does not mean that low serotonin levels caused the depression—a common but mistaken inference (Lacasse & Leo, 2005).

2 **Life experiences and circumstances.** One powerful experience that often generates depression is violence. Adolescents of both sexes who are exposed to high rates of violence report higher levels of depression and more attempts to commit suicide than those who are not subjected to constant violence in their lives or communities (Mazza & Reynolds, 1999). Domestic violence also contributes to the higher rates of depression among women. One major longitudinal study followed men and women from ages 18 to 26, and compared those in physically abusive relationships with those in nonabusive ones. Although depressed women are more likely to enter abusive relationships to begin with, involvement in a violent relationship independently increased their rates of depression and anxiety— but, interestingly, not men's (Ehrensaft, Moffitt, & Caspi, 2006). Women are also more likely than men to be sexually abused as children and young adults, which creates a higher risk of depression in adulthood (Weiss, Longhurst, & Mazure, 1999).

However, the common belief that the higher rates of depression among adult women is due to their having been sexually molested in childhood has not been supported. This belief originated with retrospective studies, where researchers asked already-depressed adult women about events in their pasts. But prospective studies, which follow children into adulthood, lead to a different conclusion. In one, nearly 700 children with substantiated cases of physical and sexual abuse and neglect before age 11 were matched with a control group of non-abused and non-neglected children. All were followed into their late twenties. Physical beatings and neglect were strongly related to depression and other problems in young adults, but, surprisingly, childhood sexual abuse was not (Widom, DuMont, & Czaja, 2007).

In addition, the conditions of people's lives—the roles they occupy, their status, their satisfaction with work and family—can affect their likelihood of becoming depressed. Men are more likely than women to be both married and working full time, a combination of roles that is strongly associated with mental health and lower rates of depression (Brown, 1993). Women are more likely than men to live in poverty and suffer from discrimination, two additional sources of depression (Belle & Doucet, 2003).

Childhood maltreatment, independent of all other childhood and adult risk factors, is associated with a particularly high risk of adult depressive episodes lasting a year or more (Brown & Harris, 2008). A mechanism that might explain this increased risk is that prolonged stress in childhood puts the body's responses to stress in overdrive, so that it overproduces the stress hormone cortisol (Gotlib et al., 2008; see Chapter 11). Depressed people have high levels of cortisol, which can affect the hippocampus and amygdala, causing mood and memory abnormalities.

3 **Losses of important relationships.** A third line of investigation emphasizes the loss of important relationships in setting off depression in vulnerable individuals. Many depressed people have a history of separations and losses, both past and

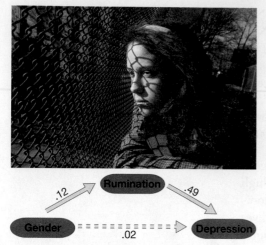

FIGURE 15.2 Gender and Depression

Women are far more likely than men to ruminate and brood when they are sad. This mental habit, however, can easily turn into depression. As the correlations show, the relationship between gender and depression is itself almost insignificant. But women are more likely to ruminate, and rumination, especially when combined with stressful experiences, is very highly correlated with depression (Nolen-Hoeksema, 2004).

present; insecure attachments; and rejection by parents or peers (Nolan, Flynn, & Garber, 2003; Weissman, Markowitz, & Klerman, 2000). As we noted earlier, however, people with a history of happy and secure attachments may also fall into prolonged depression because of the loss of a beloved partner (Wakefield et al., 2007).

4 Cognitive habits. Finally, depression involves specific, negative ways of thinking about one's situation (Beck, 2005). Typically, depressed people believe that their situation is *permanent* ("Nothing good will ever happen to me") and *uncontrollable* ("I'm depressed because I'm ugly and horrible and I can't do anything about it"). Expecting nothing to get better, they do nothing to improve their lives and therefore remain unhappy. They feel hopeless and pessimistic, believing that nothing good will ever happen to them and that they are powerless to change the future (Abramson, Metalsky, & Alloy, 1989; Seligman, 1991). When depressed and nondepressed people are put into a sad mood and given a choice between looking at sad faces or happy faces, depressed people choose the sad faces—a metaphor for how they process the world in general, attending to everything that confirms the gloominess of life rather than any of its joys (Joormann & Gotlib, 2007). And when asked to recall happier times, nondepressed people cheer up. But depressed people feel even worse, as if the happy memory makes them feel that they will never be happy again (Joormann, Siemer, & Gotlib, 2007).

One of the strongest bad cognitive habits associated with depression is *rumination*—brooding about everything that is wrong in your life, sitting alone thinking about how unmotivated you feel, and persuading yourself that no one loves you or ever will. People with ruminating cognitive styles that foster hopelessness are at greater risk of developing full-blown major depression than are people who are able to distract themselves, look outward, and seek solutions (Chorpita & Barlow, 1998). Beginning in adolescence, women are much more likely than men to develop a ruminating, introspective style, rehearsing the reasons for their unhappiness. This tendency contributes both to longer-lasting depressions in women and to the sex difference in reported rates, as you can see in Figure 15.2 (Nolen-Hoeksema, 2004).

The factors we have described, ranging from genetics to jobs, from what happens in people's lives to how they think about it, combine in different ways to produce any given case of depression. That is why the same precipitating event can affect two people entirely differently: why one is able to roll with the punches of life and another is knocked flat.

---

quickQUIZ

✓• **Quick Review** on **MyPsychLab**

Don't let another quiz make you vulnerable to depression!

1. Biological researchers find that depressed people have unusually high levels of the stress hormone _____.
2. Depressed people tend to believe that the reasons for their unhappiness are (a) controllable, (b) temporary, (c) out of their hands, (d) caused by the situation.
3. A news headline announces that a gene has been identified as the cause of depression. Does this mean that everyone with the gene will become depressed? How should critical thinkers interpret this research?

Answers:

1. cortisol 2. c 3. No, it means that people with the gene are more *likely* to become depressed if they also undergo severely stressful experiences. Critical thinkers would also want to make sure the research is replicated, and they would realize that not all kinds of depression might be influenced by genetics.

YOU are about to learn . . .

◆ what a charming but heartless tycoon and a remorseless killer have in common.

◆ why some people are incapable of feeling guilt or pangs of conscience.

PERSONALITY DISORDERS

Personality disorders involve unchanging, maladaptive traits that cause great distress or an inability to get along with others. The DSM-IV describes such a disorder as "an enduring pattern of inner experience and behaviour that deviates markedly from the expectations of the individual's culture [and] is pervasive and inflexible." Personality disorders are not caused by medical conditions, stress, or situations that temporarily induce a person to behave in ways that are out of character.

Problem Personalities

Personality disorders come in many varieties. **Paranoid personality disorder** involves pervasive, unfounded suspiciousness and mistrust of other people, irrational jealousy, secretiveness, and doubt about the loyalty of others. People with paranoid personalities have delusions of being persecuted by everyone from their closest relatives to government agencies, and their beliefs are immune to disconfirming evidence.

Narcissistic personality disorder involves an exaggerated sense of self-importance and self-absorption. The word *narcissism* gets its name from the Greek myth of Narcissus, a beautiful young man who fell in love with his own image. Narcissistic individuals are preoccupied with fantasies of their own importance, power, and brilliance. They demand constant attention and admiration and feel entitled to special favours, without, however, being willing to reciprocate.

Borderline personality disorder characterizes people who have a history of intense but unstable relationships in which they alternate between idealizing the partner and then devaluing the partner. They frantically try to avoid real or imagined abandonment by others, even if the "abandonment" is only a friend's brief vacation. They have profoundly unrealistic self-images. They are self-destructive and impulsive, often spending too much, abusing drugs, cutting themselves, and threatening to commit suicide. And they are emotionally volatile, careening from anger to euphoria to anxiety.

Notice that although these descriptions evoke flashes of recognition ("I know that type!"), it is hard to know where value judgments end (say, that someone is self-absorbed or suspicious) and a clear disorder begins (Maddux & Mundell, 1997). Cultures differ, too, in how they draw the line. For example, Western society often encourages people to pursue dreams of unlimited success, physical beauty, and ideal love, but such dreams might be considered signs of serious disturbance in a more group-oriented society. How would you distinguish between having a narcissistic personality disorder and being a normal member of a group or culture that encourages putting your own needs ahead of those of your family and friends and puts a premium on youth and beauty?

Narcissus fell in love with his own image, and now he has a personality disorder named after him—just what a narcissist would expect!

paranoid personality disorder
A disorder characterized by unreasonable, excessive suspiciousness and mistrust, and irrational feelings of being persecuted by others.

narcissistic personality disorder
A disorder characterized by an exaggerated sense of self-importance and self-absorption.

borderline personality disorder
A disorder characterized by intense but unstable relationships, a fear of abandonment by others, an unrealistic self-image, and emotional volatility.

Criminals and Psychopaths

Throughout history, people have been fascinated and horrified by the "bad seeds" among them—people who, even as children, are ready to break the rules and seem unable to be socialized. Societies have also recognized and feared the few members in their midst who lack all human connection to anyone else, people who can cheat, con, and kill without flinching. (In the 1800s these individuals were said to be afflicted with "moral insanity.")

Simulate
Psychological Disorders

In 1976, in his influential book *The Mask of Sanity*, Hervey Cleckley popularized and standardized the term *psychopath* to describe a person who lacks all conscience. A key characteristic of **psychopathy**, said Cleckley, is an inability to feel normal emotions. Psychopaths are incapable not only of remorse but also of fear of punishment and of shame, guilt, and empathy for the misery they cause others. Because they lack emotional connections to others, they often behave cruelly and irresponsibly—usually more for the thrill than for personal gain.

If caught in a lie or a crime, psychopaths may seem sincerely sorry and promise to make amends, but it is all an act. They can be utterly charming, but they use their charm to manipulate and deceive others (Cleckley, 1976; Hare, Hart, & Harpur, 1991). Some psychopaths are violent and sadistic, able to kill a pet, a child, or a random adult without a twinge of regret, but others direct their energies into con games or career advancement, abusing other people emotionally or economically rather than physically (Robins, Tipp, & Przybeck, 1991). A leading researcher in this field, Robert Hare, calls corporate psychopaths "snakes in suits."

Psychopaths are believed to exist in all cultures and throughout history, although they are more prevalent in individualistic Western societies. Even a close-knit culture such as the Yupik in Canada has a word for them—*kunlangeta* (Seabrook, 2008). An anthropologist once asked a member of the tribe what the group would do with a *kunlangeta*, and he said, "Somebody would have pushed him off the ice when nobody else was looking." Psychopaths are feared and detested everywhere.

In the 1990s, the clinicians who were revising the DSM decided to replace the term *psychopathy* with **antisocial personality disorder (APD)**, which applies to people who show "a pervasive pattern of disregard for, and violation of, the rights of others." People with APD repeatedly break the law; they are impulsive and seek quick thrills; they show reckless disregard for their own safety or that of others; they often get into physical fights or assault others; and they are irresponsible, failing to hold jobs or meet obligations (Widiger et al., 1996). Crucially for the diagnosis, they have had a history of these behavioural problems since childhood; they aren't just teenage delinquents who have been hanging out with a bad peer group. In people with APD, as one researcher found, rule breaking and irresponsibility start in early childhood and then take different forms at different ages: "biting and hitting at age 4, shoplifting and truancy at age 10, selling drugs and stealing cars at age 16, robbery and rape at age 22, and fraud and child abuse at age 30" (Moffitt, 1993). The DSM criteria for diagnosing APD also include "lack of remorse," the prime feature of psychopathy, but this entry is far down on the list and is not essential for the diagnosis.

The DSM made the change in labelling to emphasize the *behavioural* signs of antisocial personality disorder. But to many clinicians, the defining essence of psychopaths is their heartlessness and conniving charm. People who commit violent crimes may be antisocial, reckless, and irresponsible, these clinicians point out, yet differ greatly in their motivations for behaving this way. People with APD also vary widely in their capacity for empathy, remorse, guilt, anxiety, or loyalty (Hare, Hart, & Harpur, 1991). Thus, not all people with APD are psychopaths. Conversely, as we just noted, not all

psychopathy A personality disorder characterized by a lack of remorse, empathy, anxiety, and other social emotions; the use of deceit and manipulation; and impulsive thrill seeking.

antisocial personality disorder (APD) A personality disorder characterized by a lifelong pattern of irresponsible, antisocial behaviour such as lawbreaking, violence, and other impulsive, reckless acts.

Some psychopaths are sadistic and violent. Gary L. Ridgway (left), the deadliest convicted serial killer in U.S. history, strangled 48 women, placing their bodies in "clusters" around the country. He did this because, he said coolly, he wanted to keep track of them. "I killed so many women, I have a hard time keeping them straight," he told the court. But others are confident men who use charm and elaborate scams to deceive and defraud. Christopher Rocancourt (right, with model Naomi Campbell) conned celebrities and others out of millions of dollars by adopting false identities, including movie producer, Brazilian race driver, Russian prince, son of Sophia Loren, and financier. He was caught in Canada and spent a year in a correctional centre—hosting media interviews and writing his autobiography.

psychopaths are "antisocial" and aggressive in the typical ways that people with APD are. However, sometimes the two disorders converge, as in the case of sadistic, "cold-blooded" killers.

While at the University of British Columbia, Robert Hare developed a widely used, 20-item checklist for assessing psychopathy: the Psychopathy Checklist, Revised (PCL-R) (Hare, 1990). It is clear that APD and psychopathy are similar conditions with similar diagnostic criteria. In fact, some have questioned whether the two can be dissociated (Zagon, 1995). However, Hare argues that the two conditions are readily dissociable, and the accurate diagnosis of APD is useful in psychiatric settings when one wants to predict a variety of antisocial behaviours, such as substance abuse. Further, he points out that most psychopaths meet the criteria for APD, but most people with APD are not psychopaths (Hare, 1996). Accurately differentiating between the conditions is perhaps most important in legal settings. A convicted killer who meets the diagnostic criteria for APD but not psychopathy is not nearly as likely to reoffend as a psychopath (Hare & Neumann, 2008).

Researchers have identified a number of factors involved in these disorders:

1 **Abnormalities in the central nervous system.** Something certainly seems to be amiss in the emotional wiring of psychopaths, the wiring that allows all primates, not just human beings, to feel connected to others of their kind. When that wiring goes awry, even some chimpanzees will behave in ways that are comparable to the actions of human psychopaths. They, too, deceive and manipulate others to get their way and they are unmoved by the suffering of others of their kind (Lilienfeld, Gershon, et al., 1999).

The psychopath's inability to feel emotional arousal—empathy, guilt, fear of punishment, and anxiety under stress—suggests some aberration in the central nervous system (Hare, 1965, 1996; Lykken, 1995; Raine et al., 2000). Indeed, psychopaths do not respond physiologically to the threat of punishment the way other people do; this may be why they can behave fearlessly in situations that would scare others to death. Normally, when a person is anticipating danger, pain, or punishment, the electrical conductance of the skin changes, a classically

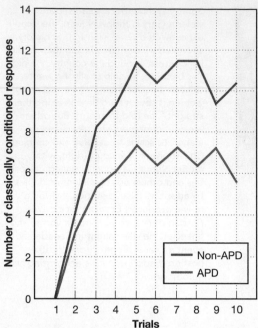

FIGURE 15.3 Emotions and Antisocial Personality Disorder

In several experiments, people with antisocial personality disorder (APD) were slow to develop classically conditioned responses to anticipated danger, pain, or shock—responses that indicate normal anxiety. This deficit may be related to the ability of psychopaths to behave in destructive ways without remorse or regard for the consequences (Hare, 1965, 1993).

conditioned response that indicates anxiety or fear. But psychopaths are slow to develop such responses, which suggests that they are unable to feel the anxiety necessary for learning that their actions will have unpleasant consequences (see Figure 15.3). Their lack of empathy for others who are suffering also seems to have a physiological basis. When psychopaths are shown pictures of people crying and in distress, their skin conductance barely shifts, in contrast to nonpsychopaths, whose skin conductance shoots up (Blair et al., 1997).

This emotional flatness may help distinguish psychopaths from other aggressive people with antisocial personality disorder (Lorber, 2004). For example, antisocial, violent adolescents who have normal levels of physiological arousal in response to danger and threat, and whose responses can be classically conditioned, do not usually get involved in a life of crime as adults, suggesting that they "outgrow" the disorder with maturity (Raine & Liu, 1998). But those who are likely to become career criminals have the same unusually low levels of physiological arousal that psychopaths do.

2 **Impaired frontal-lobe functioning.** One trait shared by psychopaths and people with APD is impulsivity, an inability to control responses to frustration and provocation (Luengo et al., 1994; van Goozen et al., 2007; Raine, 1996). Such an inability, which often leads to breaking rules and laws, may have a biological basis. Many psychopaths have abnormalities in the prefrontal cortex, which, as we saw in Chapter 4, is responsible for planning and impulse control. They don't do as well as other individuals on neuropsychological tests of frontal-lobe functioning, and they have less grey matter in the frontal lobes than other people do (Dinn & Harris, 2000; Raine, 2008). One PET-scan study found that cold-blooded "predatory" murderers had less brain activity in the frontal lobe than did men who murdered in the heat of passion or controls who had not murdered anybody (Raine et al., 1998).

One reason for these frontal-lobe abnormalities may be brain damage resulting from physical neglect, accidents, battering, or injury. Men convicted of violent crimes are more likely than nonviolent criminals and noncriminals to have been severely battered as children (Lewis, 1992; Milner & McCanne, 1991; Raine et al., 2001). And an in-depth analysis of two young adults whose prefrontal cortex was damaged in infancy—one was run over by a car when she was 15 months old and the other had a brain tumour removed—showed that both grew up to be compulsive liars, thieves, and heartless rule breakers. They could not hold jobs or plan for the future, could not distinguish right from wrong, and lacked empathy (Anderson et al., 1999).

3 **Genetic influences.** Several genes seem to be involved in a range of disorders that involve frontal-lobe causes of impulsivity—not only APD but also alcoholism, drug dependence, and childhood conduct disorder (Dick, 2007; Fowles & Dindo, 2009). More than 100 studies have investigated the role of genetic influences, and meta-analyses find that genes account for 40–50% of the variation in antisocial behaviour (Moffitt, 2005). In a longitudinal study of boys who had been physically abused in childhood, those who had a deficiency in a crucial gene later had far more arrests for violent crimes than did abused boys who had a normal gene (Caspi et al., 2002). Although only 12% of the abused boys had this genetic deficiency, they accounted for nearly half of all later convictions for violent crimes. However, boys who had the deficient gene but who were not maltreated did not grow up to be violent.

4 **Environmental events.** Genes, however, are not destiny. In the study we just described, boys who had the genetic variant but whose parents treated them lovingly did not grow up to be violent. Genes may affect the brain, in turn predisposing a child to heartlessness or violent behaviour, but there are many environmental influences that can disrupt that pathway and alter the ways that genes express themselves. For example, poor nutrition in the first three years of life has been linked with antisocial behaviour up through adolescence; so has early separation from the mother; and so has brain damage caused by parental cruelty (Raine, 2008).

Keep in mind that some children may have no genetic predisposition to psychopathy or APD, but years of living in violent worlds may blunt their ability to empathize with the suffering of others and may teach them that violence is a survival strategy. A culture that rewards ruthless behaviour in work and politics will generate many "snakes in suits," and a culture that rewards the slaughter of innocents for purposes of political or religious genocide will generate many cases of "antisocial personality disorder." And genetics will not be the reason.

In short, as with depression and other disorders, the causes of psychopathy and APD reflect an interaction between an individual's own genetic or biological vulnerabilities and experiences or stressors, in this case physical abuse, parental neglect or rejection, or living in a subculture that rewards ruthlessness and hard-heartedness.

There is no such thing as Test-Avoidance Personality Disorder, so take this quiz.

1. Can you diagnose each of the following disorders? (a) Ann can barely get out of bed in the morning. She feels that life is hopeless and despairs of ever feeling good about herself. (b) Connie constantly feels a sense of impending doom; for days her heart has been beating rapidly, and she can't relax. (c) Damon is totally absorbed in his own feelings and wishes. (d) Edna has a long history of unstable relationships, emotional ups and downs, and an intense fear of being abandoned. (e) Finn is the most charming of con artists; he can rob a widow of her life's savings without flinching.

2. What is the central difference in the diagnosis of psychopathy and antisocial personality disorder?

3. Suppose you read about a brutal assault committed by a gang member during a robbery. Should you assume that he has antisocial personality disorder? Why or why not?

Answers:

1. **a.** major depression **b.** generalized anxiety disorder **c.** narcissistic personality disorder **d.** borderline personality disorder **e.** psychopathy   2. Psychopathy is characterized by lack of remorse, guilt, shame, and empathy, whereas antisocial personality disorder is characterized by a lifelong history of reckless rule breaking, aggression, and irresponsibility.   3. Committing a violent act does not necessarily mean a person has antisocial personality disorder. This gang member may have acted violently as a way of conforming to the norms of his fellow gang members or because he felt afraid of getting caught during the robbery.

quickQUIZ

✓●—[Quick Review on **MyPsychLab**

YOU are about to learn . . .

◆ how genes might contribute to alcoholism.

◆ why alcoholism is more common in some cultures than others.

◆ why policies of abstinence from alcohol do not reduce problem drinking.

◆ why narcotics are not usually addictive when people take them for pain.

DRUG ABUSE AND ADDICTION

Robert Downey, Jr., shown here in a police mug shot at his arrest in 1991, went to prison numerous times for abusing cocaine, heroin, and valium. He told a judge: "It's like I have a loaded gun in my mouth and my finger's on the trigger, and I like the taste of the gunmetal." Downey's addictions nearly destroyed his acting career.

Most people who use drugs (legal, illegal, or prescription) use them in moderation, but some people depend too much on them, and others abuse drugs even at the cost of their own health. The DSM-IV defines *substance abuse* as "a maladaptive pattern of substance use leading to clinically significant impairment or distress." Symptoms of such impairment include failure to hold a job, care for children, or complete schoolwork; use of the drug in hazardous situations (e.g., while driving a car or operating machinery); and frequent conflicts with others about use of the drug or as a result of using the drug.

In Chapter 5, we described the major psychoactive drugs and their effects. In this section, focusing on the example of alcoholism, we will consider the two dominant approaches to understanding addiction and drug abuse—the biological model and the learning model—and then see how they might be reconciled.

Biology and Addiction

The *biological model of addiction* holds that addiction, whether to alcohol or any other drug, is due primarily to a person's biochemistry, metabolism, and genetic predisposition. Most of the genetic evidence comes from twin and family studies of alcoholism. These studies show that although genes are involved, it is too simple to say, as some people do, that "genes cause alcoholism." Evidence of an inherited vulnerability to alcohol is stronger for men than for women, but even this link depends on the *kind* of alcoholism (Cloninger, 1990; Goodwin et al., 1994; McGue, 1999; Schuckit & Smith, 1996). There is a heritable component in the kind of alcoholism that begins in adolescence and is linked to impulsivity, antisocial behaviour, and criminality (Bohman et al., 1987; McGue, 1999). But for male alcoholics who begin drinking heavily in adulthood, genetic factors are involved only weakly, if at all.

For a while researchers thought they had found an "alcoholism gene" that affected brain receptors for dopamine, a neurotransmitter involved in the sensation of pleasure. This hypothesis has not been well supported (Plomin & McGuffin, 2003). Actually, the strongest evidence to date is not that genes are involved with alcoholism but with protection *against* alcoholism. There is a genetic factor that causes low activity of an enzyme that is important in the metabolism of alcohol. People who lack this enzyme respond to alcohol with unpleasant symptoms, such as flushing and nausea. This genetic protection is common among Asians but rare among Europeans, which may be one reason why rates of alcoholism are much lower in Asian than in Caucasian populations—the Asian sensitivity to alcohol discourages them from drinking a lot (Heath et al., 2003). Not all Asians are the same in this regard, however. Korean-American college students have higher rates of alcohol-use disorders and family histories of alcoholism than do Chinese-American students (Duranceaux et al., 2008). And Native Americans have the same genetic protection that Asians do, yet they have much higher rates of alcoholism.

Within populations, genes might contribute to traits or temperaments (such as impulsivity) that predispose a person to become alcoholic. Genes may also affect how much a person needs to drink before feeling high. For alcoholism, the picture is more complicated. Genes are involved in some kinds of alcoholism but not all. There is a heritable component in the kind of alcoholism that begins in early adolescence and is linked to impulsivity, antisocial behaviour, and criminality (Dick, 2007; Dick et al., 2008; Schuckit et al., 2007), but not in the kind of alcoholism that begins in adulthood and is unrelated to other disorders. (Robert Downey, Jr., shown in the margin,

◉ **Watch**
Smoking Damage

Alcoholism

Alcohol Withdrawal

said he had been addicted to drugs since the age of seven.) Genes also affect alcohol "sensitivity"—how quickly people respond to alcohol, whether they tolerate it, and how much they need to drink before feeling high (Hu et al., 2008). In an ongoing longitudinal study of 450 young men, those who at age 20 had to drink more than others to feel any reaction were at increased risk of becoming alcoholic within the decade. This was true regardless of their initial drinking habits or family history of alcoholism (Schuckit, 1998; Schuckit & Smith, 1996).

Some people may inherit not only a general susceptibility to substance abuse but also a vulnerability to specific drugs—such as nicotine (Tsuang et al., 2001). Although smoking rates have declined over the past 50 years, nicotine addiction remains one of the most serious health problems in the United States and worldwide. Unlike other addictions, it can begin quickly, within a month after the first cigarette—and for some teenagers, after only one cigarette—because nicotine almost immediately changes neuron receptors in the brain that react chemically to the drug (DiFranza, 2008). Genes produce variation in these nicotine receptors, which is one reason that some people are especially vulnerable to becoming addicted to cigarettes and have tremendous withdrawal symptoms when they try to give them up, whereas other people, even if they have been heavy smokers, can quit cold turkey (Bierut et al., 2008). As with so many other disorders, however, tracking down the genes involved has been difficult.

The usual way of looking at the relationship between biological factors and addiction is to assume that the biological factors cause the addiction. However, there is strong evidence that the relationship also works the other way: *Addictions can result from the abuse of drugs* (Crombag & Robinson, 2004). Drugs change the brain. Heavy drinking alters brain function, reduces the level of painkilling endorphins, produces nerve damage, shrinks the cerebral cortex, and damages the liver. As you can see in Figure 15.4, heavy use of alcohol, cocaine, heroin, methamphetamine, or other drugs also reduces the number of receptors for dopamine (Volkow et al., 2001). These changes can then create addiction, a craving for more of the drug.

Thus, drug abuse, which begins as a voluntary action, can turn into drug addiction, a compulsive behaviour that the addict finds almost impossible to control.

Learning, Culture, and Addiction

The *learning model of addiction* examines the role of the environment, learning, and culture in encouraging or discouraging drug abuse and addiction. Four major findings underscore the importance of understanding these factors:

1 **Addiction patterns vary according to cultural practices and the social environment.** Alcoholism is much more likely to occur in societies that forbid children to drink but condone drunkenness in adults (as in Ireland) than in societies that teach children how to drink responsibly and moderately but condemn adult drunkenness (as in Italy, Greece, and France). In cultures with low rates of alcoholism (except for those committed to a religious rule that forbids use of all psychoactive drugs), adults demonstrate correct drinking habits to their children, gradually introducing them to alcohol in safe family settings. Alcohol is not used as a rite of passage into adulthood, nor is it associated with masculinity and power (Peele & Brodsky, 1991; Vaillant, 1983). Abstainers are not sneered at, and drunkenness is not considered charming, comical, or manly; it is considered stupid or obnoxious.

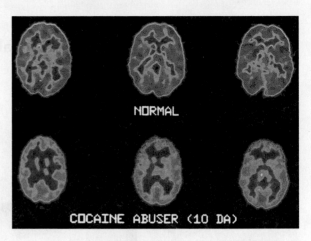

FIGURE 15.4 The Addicted Brain

PET studies show that the brains of cocaine addicts have fewer receptors for dopamine, a neurotransmitter involved in pleasurable sensations. (The more yellow and red in the brain image, the more receptors.) The brains of people addicted to methamphetamine, alcohol, and even food show a similar dopamine deficiency (Volkow et al., 2001).

Thinking Critically   Analyze Assumptions and Biases

The disease model assumes that because the consequences of drug use are automatic, if children are given any taste of a drink or a drug they are more likely to become addicted. The learning model assumes that the cultural context is crucial in determining whether people will become addicted or learn to use drugs moderately. In fact, when children learn the rules of social drinking with their families, as at this Jewish family's seder (left), alcoholism rates are much lower than in cultures in which drinking occurs mainly in bars or in privacy. Likewise, when marijuana is used as part of a religious tradition, as it is by members of the Rastafarian church in Jamaica (right), use of the "wisdom weed" does not lead to addiction or harder drugs.

The cultural environment may be especially crucial for the development of alcoholism among young people with a genetic vulnerability to alcohol (Schuckit et al., 2008). In one such group of 401 Native American youths, those who later developed drinking problems lived in a community in which heavy drinking was encouraged and modelled by their parents and peers. But those who felt a cultural and spiritual pride in being Native American, and who were strongly attached to their religious traditions, were less likely to develop drinking problems, even when their parents and peers were encouraging them to drink (Yu & Stiffman, 2007).

Within a particular country, addiction rates can rise or fall rapidly in response to cultural changes. During the colonial period in the United States, the average American actually drank two to three times the amount of liquor consumed today, yet alcoholism was not a serious problem. Drinking was a universally accepted social activity; families drank and ate together. Alcohol was believed to produce pleasant feelings and relaxation, and Puritan ministers endorsed its use (Critchlow, 1986). Then, between 1790 and 1830, when the American frontier was expanding, drinking came to symbolize masculine independence and toughness. The saloon became the place for drinking away from home. As people stopped drinking in moderation, with their families, alcoholism rates shot up—as the learning model would predict.

2 **Policies of total abstinence tend to increase rates of addiction rather than reduce them.** The temperance movement of the early twentieth century held that drinking inevitably leads to drunkenness, and drunkenness to crime. The solution for the Prohibition years (1920 to 1933) was relative abstinence in the United States (alcohol was legal in Canada throughout most of the U.S. period of prohibition). But this victory backfired: Again in accordance with the learning model, Prohibition reduced rates of drinking overall, but it *increased* rates of alcoholism among those who did drink. Because people were denied the opportunity to learn to drink moderately, they drank excessively when given the chance (McCord, 1989). And, of course, when a substance is forbidden, it becomes more attractive to some people. Most schools in North America have zero-tolerance policies regarding marijuana and alcohol, but large numbers of students have tried them or use them regularly. These issues are currently fuelling the debate over the decriminalization of marijuana in Canada. After allowing medicinal use of the drug, Canada became the first country in the world to regulate and sell marijuana to patients. Our government has also taken steps to decriminalize possession of marijuana (which is *not* the same thing as making possession *legal*), but this process is ongoing, and it currently faces vehement opposition.

3 **Not all addicts have withdrawal symptoms when they stop taking a drug.** When heavy users of a drug stop taking it, they often suffer such unpleasant symptoms as nausea, abdominal cramps, depression, and sleep problems, depending on the drug. But these symptoms are far from universal. During the Vietnam War, nearly 30% of American soldiers were taking heroin in doses far stronger than those available on the streets of U.S. cities. These men believed themselves to be addicted, and experts predicted a drug-withdrawal disaster among the returning veterans. It never materialized; over 90% of the men simply gave up the drug,

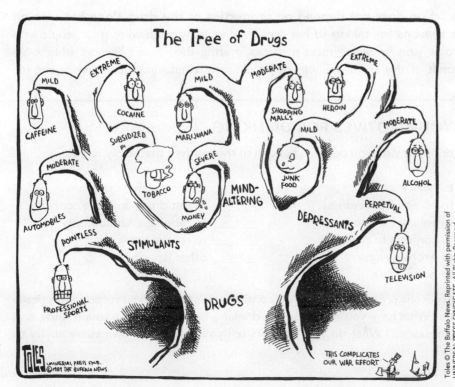

This cartoon, by poking fun at the things people do to make themselves feel better, reminds us that a person can become dependent on many things besides alcohol or other drugs.

without significant withdrawal pain, when they came home to new circumstances (Robins, Davis, & Goodwin, 1974). Researchers have largely interpreted the fact that soldiers gave up heroin after the Vietnam War as evidence that abusers of opiate drugs are attempting to reduce stress. When soldiers returned home and the stress was no longer present, neither was the need to abuse the drug. However, as Simon Fraser University's Bruce Alexander and Patricia Hardaway point out, the evidence for this position is almost entirely retrospective, not experimental (Alexander & Hardaway, 1982).

The majority of people who are addicted to cigarettes, tranquilizers, or pain-killers are able to stop taking these drugs without outside help and without severe withdrawal symptoms (Prochaska, Norcross, & DiClemente, 1994). Many people find this information startling, even unbelievable. That is because people who can quit without help aren't entering programs to help them quit, so they are invisible to the general public and to the medical and therapeutic world! But they have been identified in random-sample community surveys.

One reason why many people are able, on their own, to quit abusing drugs is that the environment in which a drug is used (the setting) and a person's expectations (mental set) have a powerful influence on the drug's *physiological* effects as well as its psychological ones (see Chapter 5).

For example, you might think a lethal dose of, say, amphetamines would be the same wherever the drug was taken. But studies of mice have found that the lethal dose varies depending on the mice's environment—whether they are in a large or small test cage, or whether they are alone or with other mice. Similarly, the physiological response of human addicts to certain drugs also changes, depending on whether the addicts are in a "druggie" environment, such as a crack house, or an unfamiliar one (Crombag & Robinson, 2004; Siegel, 2005). This is the primary reason why addicts need to change environments if they are going to kick their habits. It's not just to get away from a peer group that might be encouraging them, but also to literally change and "rewire" their brain's response to the drug.

4   **Addiction does not depend on properties of the drug alone but also on the reasons for taking it.** For decades, doctors were afraid to treat people with chronic pain by giving them narcotics, fearing they would become addicts. As a result of this belief, millions of people were condemned to live with chronic

Get INVOLVED!   TEST YOUR MOTIVES FOR DRINKING

If you drink, why do you do so? Check all of the motives that apply to you:

_____ to relax   _____ to cope with depression
_____ to escape from worries   _____ to get drunk and lose control
_____ to enhance a good meal   _____ to rebel against authority
_____ to conform to peers   _____ to relieve boredom
_____ to express anger   _____ other (specify)
_____ to be sociable

Do your reasons promote abuse or responsible use? How do you respond physically to alcohol? What have you learned about drinking from your family, your friends, and cultural messages? What do your answers tell you about your own vulnerability to addiction?

suffering from back pain, arthritis, nerve disorders, and other conditions. Then researchers found that the vast majority of pain sufferers—who use morphine and other opiates not to escape from the world, as addicts do, but to function in the world—do not become addicted (Portenoy, 1994; Raja, 2008). This was such good news that many researchers then went to the opposite extreme, optimistically believing that no one would become addicted to slow-release narcotic painkillers such as OxyContin. But again they underestimated the importance of the motives for taking the drugs. People who are searching for escape and euphoria will find a way to abuse *any* mood-altering drug, or, as many teenagers are now doing, to create drug "cocktails" to give them a high. That is why the abuse of narcotic painkillers and even the stimulants in flu medication has become a significant social problem.

In the case of alcohol, most people drink simply to be sociable, to conform to the group they are with, or to relax when they are stressed, and these people are unlikely to become addicted. *Problem* drinking occurs when people drink in order to disguise or suppress their anxiety or depression, or when they drink alone to drown their sorrows and forget their worries (Cooper et al., 1995; Mohr et al., 2001). College and university students who feel alienated and uninvolved with their studies are more likely than their happier peers to go binge drinking, with the conscious intention of getting drunk (Flacks & Thomas, 1998). In many cases, then, the decision to start abusing drugs depends more on your motives, and on the norms of your peer group, than on the chemical properties of the drug itself.

Thinking Critically

Avoid Emotional Reasoning

People disagree passionately about whether alcoholics can learn to drink moderately. How can we move beyond emotional reasoning on this contentious issue?

Debating the Causes of Addiction

The biological and learning models both contribute to our understanding of drug use and addiction. Yet, among many researchers and public-health professionals, these views are quite polarized, especially when it comes to thinking about treatment (see Review 15.1). The result is either–or thinking on a national scale: Either complete abstinence is the solution, or it is the problem. Those who advocate the disease model say that alcoholics and problem drinkers must abstain completely. Those who champion the learning model argue that most problem drinkers can learn to drink moderately if they learn safe-drinking skills, acquire better ways of coping with stress, avoid situations that evoke conditioned responses to using drugs, and avoid friends who pressure them to drink excessively (Denning, Little, & Glickman, 2004; Marlatt et al., 1998; Sobell & Sobell, 1993).

How can we assess these two positions critically? Because alcoholism and problem drinking occur for many reasons, neither model offers the only solution. Many alcoholics cannot learn to drink moderately, especially if they have been drinking heavily for many years, by which time, as we saw earlier, physiological changes in their brains and bodies may have turned them from drug abusers into drug addicts. On the other hand, total-abstinence groups like Alcoholics Anonymous (AA) are ineffective for many people. According to its own surveys and those done independently, one-third to one-half of all people who join AA drop out. Many of these dropouts benefit from programs such as Harm Reduction, Rational Recovery, Moderation Management, and DrinkWise, which teach people how to drink moderately and keep their drinking under control (Denning, Little, & Glickman, 2004; Fletcher, 2001; Marlatt, 1996; Peele & Brodsky, 1991; Rosenberg, 1993; Witkiewitz & Marlatt, 2006).

So instead of asking, "Can addicts and problem drinkers learn to drink moderately?" perhaps we should ask, "What are the factors that make it more or less likely that someone can learn to control problem drinking?" Problem drinkers who are most

After five years in and out of rehab and facing more prison time, Robert Downey, Jr., got serious about getting help and was able to overcome his addictions. He is shown here at the 2009 premiere of his film *The Soloist*.

REVIEW 15.1

Biological and Learning Models of Addiction Contrasted

The biological and learning models of addiction differ in how they explain drug abuse and the solutions they propose:

The Biological Model	The Learning Model
Addiction is genetic, biological.	Addiction is a way of coping.
Once an addict, always an addict.	A person can grow beyond the need for alcohol or other drugs.
An addict must abstain from the drug forever.	Most problem drinkers can learn to drink in moderation.
A person is either addicted or not.	The degree of addiction will vary depending on the situation.
The solution is medical treatment and membership in groups that reinforce one's permanent identity as a recovering addict.	The solution involves learning new coping skills and changing one's environment.
An addict needs the same treatment and group support forever.	Treatment lasts only until the person no longer abuses the drug.

Source: Adapted from Peele & Brodsky, 1991.

likely to become moderate drinkers have a history of less severe dependence on the drug. They lead more stable lives and have jobs and families. In contrast, those who are at greater risk of drug abuse or alcoholism have these risk factors: (1) They have a physiological vulnerability to a drug or have been using a drug long enough for it to damage or change their brain; (2) they believe that they have no control over the drug; (3) they live in a culture or a peer group that promotes and rewards binge drinking and discourages moderate drug use; and (4) they have come to rely on the drug as a way of avoiding problems, suppressing anger or fear, or coping with stress.

quickQUIZ

✓ Quick Review on MyPsychLab

If you are addicted to passing exams, answer these questions.

1. What is the most reasonable conclusion about the role of genes in alcoholism? (a) Without a key gene, a person cannot become alcoholic; (b) the presence of a key gene will almost always cause a person to become alcoholic; (c) genes may increase a person's vulnerability to some kinds of alcoholism

2. Which cultural practice is associated with *low* rates of alcoholism? (a) gradual introduction to drinking in family settings, (b) infrequent binge drinking, (c) drinking as a rite of passage into adulthood, (d) policies of prohibition

3. Many college and university students drink to get drunk, and this is often accomplished by binge drinking. To reduce this problem, some schools and fraternities have instituted "zero-tolerance" programs. According to the research described in this section, are these programs likely to work? Why or why not?

Answers:

1. c   2. a   3. They are not likely to be successful because zero-tolerance programs do not address the reasons students binge, do not affect the student culture that fosters binge drinking, and do not teach students how to drink moderately.

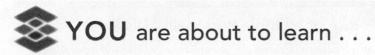

YOU are about to learn . . .

◆ why most clinicians and researchers are skeptical about multiple personality disorder.

◆ why the number of "multiple personality" cases jumped from a handful to many thousands in only a decade.

DISSOCIATIVE IDENTITY DISORDER

In this section we will examine one of the most controversial diagnoses ever to arise in psychiatry and psychology: **dissociative identity disorder,** formerly and still popularly called *multiple personality disorder (MPD).* This label describes the apparent emergence, within one person, of two or more distinct identities, each with its own name, memories, and personality traits.

THE MPD CONTROVERSY. Cases of multiple personality portrayed on TV, in popular books, and in films such as *The Three Faces of Eve* and *Sybil* have captivated the public for years, and they keep appearing. In 2005, Robert Oxnam published the book *A Fractured Mind,* which claimed that his alcoholism, bulimia, and rages were a result of having 11 competing "personalities," some old, some young, some male, some female. In 2009, Showtime came up with *United States of Tara,* in which a woman with a very tolerant husband and two teenagers keeps breaking into one of her three identities—a sex-and-shopping-mad teenage girl, a gun-loving redneck male, and a 1950s-style homemaker. However, the diagnostic label of MPD is an extremely controversial one. A survey of 180 Canadian psychiatrists revealed that almost 30% doubted the existence of the disorder (Mai, 1995).

Among mental-health professionals, two competing views of MPD exist. On one side are those who think that MPD is common but often unrecognized or misdiagnosed. They believe the disorder originates in childhood as a means of coping with trauma, such as abuse (Gleaves, 1996). In this view, the trauma produces a mental "splitting" (dissociation): One personality emerges to handle everyday experiences, another personality (called an "alter") emerges to cope with the bad ones. MPD patients are frequently described as having lived for years with several alters of which they were unaware until therapy.

On the other side are those who believe that most cases of MPD are unwittingly generated by clinicians themselves, during their interactions with vulnerable clients who have other psychological problems (Lilienfeld & Lohr, 2003). Researchers have shown that "dissociative amnesia," the mechanism that supposedly causes traumatized children to repress their ordeal and develop several identities as a result, lacks historical and empirical support (see Chapter 10). Truly traumatic experiences are remembered all too long and all too well (McNally, 2003; Pope et al., 2007). These researchers point out that before 1980, only a handful of MPD cases had ever been diagnosed anywhere in the world; yet by the mid-1990s, tens of thousands of cases had been reported. (See Table 15.3.) MPD became a lucrative business, benefiting hospitals that opened MPD clinics, therapists who had a new disorder to treat, and psychiatrists and patients who wrote best-selling books. Skeptics think the sudden increase in cases was a sign that the disorder was being wildly overdiagnosed by its proponents.

dissociative identity disorder
A controversial disorder marked by the apparent appearance within one person of two or more distinct personalities, each with its own name and traits; formerly known as multiple personality disorder (MPD).

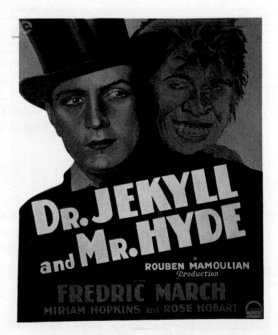

Why did the number of "alters" reported by people with MPD increase over the years? In the earliest cases, multiple personalities came only in pairs. In the 1886 story of Dr. Jekyll and Mr. Hyde, the kindly Dr. Jekyll turned into the murderous Mr. Hyde. At the height of the MPD epidemic in North America in the 1990s, people were claiming to have several dozen, even hundreds, of alters, including demons, children, extraterrestrials, and animals.

TABLE 15.3 The Rise of Multiple Personality Disorder

1789	An early case is reported of a young German woman with several "personalities," including a French woman and a little boy.
1816	The first recorded case of "multiple personality" appears in the United States (Mary Reynolds).
1875	The condition is renamed "multiple personality" in France.
1886	Robert Louis Stevenson's *Strange Case of Dr. Jekyll and Mr. Hyde* popularizes the notion of two personalities in one body.
1957	*The Three Faces of Eve* is published and the film is released.
1960	Eight cases have been reported.
1976	The movie *Sybil* is released.
1980	The DSM includes the MPD diagnosis for the first time.
1980	The book *Michelle Remembers* claims that "Satanic ritual abuse" is a leading cause of MPD.
1980–1991	Media coverage escalates in popular books and on talk shows that feature MPD "victims."
1985	Psychiatrist Richard Kluft claims to have treated 250 MPD patients.
1986	6000 cases have been reported in North America.
1987	The first MPD inpatient treatment unit is established at Rush Presbyterian Hospital in Chicago; others follow across the country.
1995	More than 40 000 cases have been reported in North America.
1995	Diane Humenansky becomes the first psychiatrist found guilty of malpractice for inducing multiple personalities in a vulnerable patient.
1996–present	Other successful lawsuits are filed against major proponents of the MPD diagnosis and against treatment units in hospitals. Hospitals begin closing these units. Epidemic of cases subsides.

Sources: Acocella, 1999; Kenny, 1986; Loftus, 1996; Nathan, 1994; Pendergrast, 1995.

Clinicians who deeply believed in the prevalence of MPD may have even been creating the disorder in their clients through the power of suggestion, sometimes bordering on coercion, and through techniques like hypnosis (McHugh, 2008; Merskey, 1995; Rieber, 2006; Spanos, 1996).

You can see this pressure at work in the comments of psychiatrist Richard Kluft (1987), who wrote that efforts to determine the presence of MPD—that is, to get the person to reveal a "dissociated" personality—may require "between two-and-a-half and four hours of continuous interviewing. Interviewees must be prevented from taking breaks to regain composure. . . . In one recent case of singular difficulty, the first sign of dissociation was noted in the sixth hour, and a definitive spontaneous switching of personalities occurred in the eighth hour." Mercy! After eight hours of "continuous interviewing" without a single break, how many of us wouldn't do what the interviewer wanted?

Clinicians who conducted such interrogations argued that they were merely *permitting* other personalities to reveal themselves. However, in numerous malpractice cases across the country, courts have ruled, on the

Thinking Critically

Consider Other Interpretations

A man appeared on *60 Minutes* to talk about his new book, in which he described his 11 personalities—male and female, old and young. These emerged, he said, because he was sexually abused as a child. What else might explain how and why he developed "MPD"?

basis of the testimony of scientific experts in psychiatry and psychology, that it was more likely that these clinicians were actively *creating* personalities through suggestion and sometimes outright intimidation (Loftus, 1996). The MPD clinics in hospitals closed, psychiatrists became more wary, and the number of cases dropped sharply almost overnight.

THE SOCIOCOGNITIVE EXPLANATION. No one disputes that some troubled, highly imaginative individuals can produce many different "personalities" when asked. But the *sociocognitive explanation* of MPD holds that this phenomenon is simply an extreme form of the ability we all have to present different aspects of our personalities to others (Lilienfeld, Lynn, et al., 1999). In this view, the diagnosis of MPD provides a culturally acceptable way for some troubled people to make sense of their problems (Hacking, 1995; Showalter, 1997). It allows them to account for sexual or criminal behaviour that they now regret or find intolerably embarrassing; they can claim their "other personality did it." In turn, therapists who are looking for MPD reward such patients with attention and praise for revealing more and more personalities (Piper & Merskey, 2004).

The story of the rise and fall of MPD offers an important lesson in critical thinking, because unskeptical media coverage of sensational MPD cases played a major role in fostering the rise of MPD diagnoses. When Canadian psychiatrist Harold Merskey (1992) reviewed the published cases of MPD, he was unable to find a single one in which a patient developed MPD without being influenced by the therapist's suggestions or reports about the disorder in books and the media. Even the famous case of "Sybil," a huge hit as a book, film, and television special, was a hoax. Sybil never had a traumatic childhood of sexual abuse, she did not have multiple personality disorder, and her "symptoms" were largely generated by her psychiatrist (Borch-Jacobson, 1997, 2009; Rieber, 2006).

The story of MPD teaches us to think critically about disorders that become trendy: to consider other explanations, to examine assumptions and biases, and to demand good evidence.

* Explore
Dissociative Identity Disorder

Any one of your personalities may answer this question.

In August 2003, Donna Walker was arrested for trying to convince an Indiana couple that she was their long-missing daughter. She claimed that her "bad girl" personality (Allison) was responsible for this deception and also for her long history of perpetrating hoaxes on police, friends, and the media. Her "good girl" personality (Donna), she said, was a victim of childhood sexual abuse who spent years working as an FBI informant. The FBI verified that Walker had worked for them, although some of her reports were fabricated. One agent said that Walker has as many as seven personalities who come and go. As a critical thinker, what questions would you want to ask about Walker and her multiple-personality defence?

quickQUIZ

✔ Quick Review on **MyPsychLab**

Answers:

Some possible questions to ask: Is there corroborating evidence for Walker's claims? (She said she was sexually abused from ages four to 13 by a family member and then by the minister of her church, and that she was sent to a psychiatric hospital at age 13.) How much of the rest of her life story can be independently corroborated? Did Walker claim to have "other personalities" only when she was in a jam with the law or was there evidence of MPD throughout her life? Could she have another mental disorder, such as schizophrenia or antisocial personality disorder?

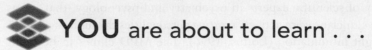

YOU are about to learn . . .

◆ the difference between schizophrenia and a "split personality."
◆ the five key signs of schizophrenia.
◆ whether schizophrenia is partly heritable.
◆ why schizophrenia might begin in the womb yet not emerge until adolescence.

SCHIZOPHRENIA

To be schizophrenic is best summed up in a repeating dream that I have had since childhood. In this dream I am lying on a beautiful sunlit beach but my body is in pieces. . . . I realize that the tide is coming in and that I am unable to gather the parts of my dismembered body together to run away. . . . This to me is what schizophrenia feels like; being fragmented in one's personality and constantly afraid that the tide of illness will completely cover me. (As cited in Rollin, 1980)

In 1911, Swiss psychiatrist Eugen Bleuler coined the term **schizophrenia** to describe cases in which the personality loses its unity. Contrary to popular belief, people with schizophrenia do not have a "split" or "multiple" personality. As this haunting quotation illustrates, schizophrenia is a fragmented condition in which words are split from meaning, actions from motives, perceptions from reality. It is an example of a **psychosis**, a mental condition that involves distorted perceptions of reality and an inability to function in most aspects of life.

Symptoms of Schizophrenia

Schizophrenia is the cancer of mental illness: elusive, complex, and varying in form. The disorder involves the following symptoms:

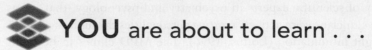

✱ **Explore**
Types and Symptoms of Schizophrenia

schizophrenia A psychotic disorder marked by delusions, hallucinations, disorganized and incoherent speech, inappropriate behaviour, and cognitive impairments.

psychosis An extreme mental disturbance involving distorted perceptions and irrational behaviour; it may have psychological or organic causes. (Plural: *psychoses*.)

1   **Bizarre delusions.** A schizophrenic may believe, for example, that dogs are extraterrestrials disguised as pets. Some people with schizophrenia have delusions of identity, believing that they are Moses, Jesus, or another famous person. Some have paranoid delusions, taking innocent events—a stranger's cough, a helicopter overhead—as evidence that everyone is plotting against them. They often report that their thoughts have been inserted into their heads by someone controlling them or are being broadcast on television. Some, like Margaret Mary Ray, whose story opened this chapter, have delusions that a celebrity loves them.

2   **Hallucinations, false sensory experiences that feel intensely real.** By far the most common hallucination among people with schizophrenia is hearing voices; it is virtually a hallmark of the disease. Some sufferers of schizophrenia are so tormented by these voices that they commit suicide to escape them. One man described how he heard as many as 50 voices cursing him, urging him to steal other people's brain cells, or ordering him to kill himself. Once he picked up a ringing telephone and heard them screaming, "You're guilty!" over and over. They yelled "as loud as humans with megaphones," he told a reporter. "It was utter despair. I felt scared. They were always around" (Goode, 2003).

3   **Disorganized, incoherent speech.** Schizophrenics may give voice to an illogical jumble of ideas and symbols, linked by meaningless rhyming words or by

remote associations, called *word salads*. A patient of Bleuler's wrote, "Olive oil is an Arabian liquor-sauce which the Afghans, Moors and Moslems use in ostrich farming. The Indian plantain tree is the whiskey of the Parsees and Arabs. Barley, rice and sugar cane called artichoke, grow remarkably well in India. The Brahmins live as castes in Baluchistan. The Circassians occupy Manchuria and China. China is the Eldorado of the Pawnees" (Bleuler, 1911/1950).

4 **Grossly disorganized and inappropriate behaviour.** A schizophrenic's behaviour may range from childlike silliness to unpredictable and violent agitation. The person may wear three overcoats and gloves on a hot day, start collecting garbage, or hoard scraps of food.

5 **Impaired cognitive abilities.** People with schizophrenia do much worse than healthy people in almost every cognitive domain, especially verbal learning and recall of words and stories, language, perception, working memory, selective attention, and problem solving (Barch, 2003; Dominguez et al., 2009; Uhlhaas & Silverstein, 2005). Their speech is often impoverished; they make only brief, empty replies in conversation, because of diminished thought rather than an unwillingness to speak. Many of these cognitive impairments emerge in vulnerable children long before an actual schizophrenic breakdown occurs, and they last after the patient's psychotic symptoms subside as a result of medication (Heinrichs, 2005).

Other symptoms may appear months before hallucinations or delusions do, and they often persist even when more dramatic symptoms are in remission. For example, many people with schizophrenia lose the motivation to take care of themselves and interact with others; they may stop working or bathing, and become isolated and withdrawn. They seem emotionally "flat"; their facial expressions are unresponsive and they make poor eye contact. Some completely withdraw into a private world, sitting for hours without moving, a condition called *catatonic stupor*. (Catatonic states can also produce frenzied, purposeless behaviour that goes on for hours.)

Bryan Charnley painted 17 self-portraits, with comments, reflecting his battle with schizophrenia. He painted the one above in March 1991, when his mind was clear. In June, he committed suicide.

👁 **Watch**
The Three Faces of Eve

April 20: "[I am feeling] paranoid. The person upstairs was reading my mind and speaking back to me to keep me in a sort of ego crucifixion. . . . I felt this was because I was discharging very strong vibrations."

May 6: "I had no tongue, no real tongue, and could only flatter. . . . The nail in the mouth expresses this. The people around me cannot understand how I was so stupid and cannot forgive me . . . thus I am a target. The nails in my eyes express that I cannot see whereas other people seem to have extrasensory perception and I am blind in this respect."

May 18: "My mind seemed to be thought broadcasting [and] it was beyond my will to do anything about it. I summed this up by painting my brain as an enormous mouth. . . . The trouble seemed to stem from a broken heart so I painted a great mass of gore there. . . . I feel I am giving off strong personality vibrations, hence the wavy lines emanating from my head."

The cognitive and social deficits in schizophrenia may emerge early, in late childhood or early adolescence (Tarbox & Pogue-Geile, 2008), but the first full-blown psychotic episode typically occurs in late adolescence or early adulthood. In some individuals, the breakdown occurs suddenly; in others, it is more gradual, a slow change in personality. The more breakdowns and relapses the individual has had, the poorer the chances for complete recovery. Yet, contrary to stereotype, many people with schizophrenia do recover from this illness and go on to hold good jobs and have successful relationships, especially if they have strong family support and access to community programs (Harding, 2005; Hopper et al., 2007).

The mystery of this disease is that some people with schizophrenia are almost completely impaired in all spheres; others do well in certain areas. Still others have normal moments of lucidity in otherwise withdrawn lives. One adolescent crouched in a rigid catatonic posture in front of a television for the month of October; later, he was able to report on all the highlights of the World Series he had seen. A middle-aged man, hospitalized for 20 years, believing he was a prophet of God and that monsters were coming out of the walls, was able to interrupt his ranting to play a good game of chess (Wender & Klein, 1981).

Simulate
Schizophrenia Overview

Origins of Schizophrenia

Any disorder that has so many variations and symptoms will pose many problems for those trying to find its origins. Early psychodynamic and learning theories, which held that schizophrenia results from being raised by an erratic, cold, rejecting mother or from living in an unpredictable environment, have not been supported. Most researchers now believe that schizophrenia is caused by genetic problems that produce subtle abnormalities in the brain. As usual, however, genes must interact with certain stressors in the environment during prenatal development, birth, or adolescence. Here is some evidence on the contributing factors:

Watch
Genetic Schizophrenia

1 **Genetic predispositions.** A person has a much greater risk of developing schizophrenia if an identical twin develops the disorder, even if the twins are reared apart (Gottesman, 1991; Heinrichs, 2005). Children with one schizophrenic parent have a lifetime risk of 12%, and children with two schizophrenic parents have a lifetime risk of 35–46%, compared to a risk in the general population of only 1–2% (see Figure 15.5). In a Finnish study of identical twins, fully 83% of the variation in the risk of becoming schizophrenic was due to combined genetic factors and only 17% to unique environmental factors (Cannon et al., 1998). Researchers all over the world are trying to track down the genes that might be involved in specific symptoms, such as hallucinations, sensitivity to sounds, and cognitive impairments (Desbonnet, Waddington, & O'Tuathaigh, 2009; Tomppo et al., 2009). One team has identified one such gene, called DISC1 or "disrupted-in-schizophrenia." Chromosomal aberrations on this gene are involved in schizophrenia and bipolar disorder, which share severe disturbances of emotion and cognition (Millar et al., 2005; Walker & Tessner, 2008).

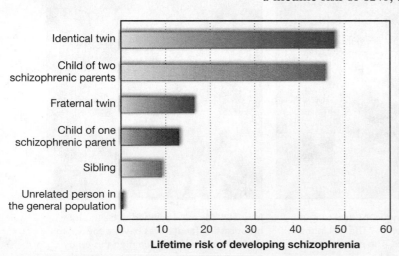

FIGURE 15.5 Genetic Vulnerability to Schizophrenia

This graph, based on combined data from 40 European twin and adoption studies conducted over seven decades, shows that the closer the genetic relationship to a person with schizophrenia, the higher the risk of developing the disorder. (Based on Gottesman, 1991.)

2 **Structural brain abnormalities.** Most individuals with schizophrenia have abnormalities in the brain,

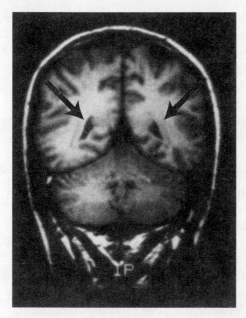

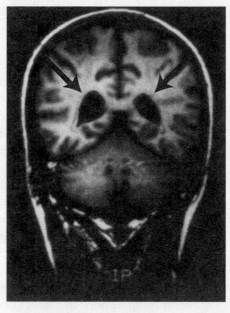

Healthy   Schizophrenic

FIGURE 15.6 Schizophrenia and the Brain

People with schizophrenia are more likely to have enlarged ventricles (spaces) in the brain than healthy people are. These MRI scans of 28-year-old male identical twins show the difference in the size of ventricles between the healthy twin (left) and the one with schizophrenia (right).

including a decrease in the volume of the temporal lobe or hippocampus, reduced neuronal connections in the prefrontal cortex, or enlargement of the *ventricles*, spaces in the brain that are filled with cerebrospinal fluid (see Figure 15.6) (Black et al., 2004; Heinrichs, 2005; Zorrilla et al., 1997). Schizophrenics are also more likely than healthy individuals to have abnormalities in the thalamus, the traffic-control centre that filters sensations and focuses attention (Andreasen et al., 1994; Gur et al., 1998). Schizophrenics also may have abnormalities in the auditory cortex and Broca's and Wernicke's areas, all involved in speech perception and processing. Such abnormalities might explain the nightmare of voice hallucinations.

3   **Neurotransmitter abnormalities.** Schizophrenia has been associated with abnormalities in several neurotransmitters, including serotonin, glutamate, and dopamine (Sawa & Snyder, 2002). However, similar neurotransmitter abnormalities are also found in many other mental disorders, such as depression, OCD, and alcoholism, making it difficult to know whether these abnormalities play a specific role in schizophrenia.

4   **Prenatal problems or birth complications.** Damage to the fetal brain significantly increases the likelihood of schizophrenia later in life. Such damage may occur if the mother suffers from malnutrition; schizophrenia rates rise during times of famine, as happened in China and elsewhere (St. Clair et al., 2005). Damage may also occur if the mother gets the flu virus during the first four months of prenatal development, which triples the risk of schizophrenia (Brown et al., 2004; Mednick, Huttunen, & Machón, 1994). And it may occur if there are complications during birth that injure the baby's brain or deprive it of oxygen (Cannon et al., 2000). However, prenatal stress—on the mother or the fetus—is a risk factor for the development of other psychological disorders later in life, too, not only schizophrenia (Huizink, Mulder, & Buitelaar, 2004).

5   **Adolescent abnormalities in brain development.** The last factor contributing to schizophrenia occurs in adolescence, when the brain undergoes a natural

👁 **Watch**
Rodney: Schizophrenia

((•●Listen
Schizophrenia and Smoking

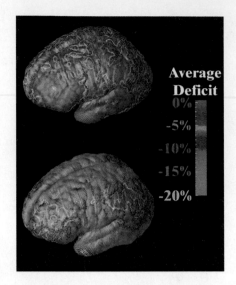

FIGURE 15.7 The Adolescent Brain and Schizophrenia

These dramatic images highlight areas of brain-tissue loss in adolescents with schizophrenia. Using a new method that detects fine changes, neuroscientists tracked the loss of grey matter over five years. The areas of greatest tissue loss (regions that control memory, hearing, motor functions, and attention) are shown in red and magenta; a healthy brain (top) looks almost entirely blue (Thompson et al., 2001).

pruning away of synapses. Normally, this pruning helps make the brain more efficient in handling the new challenges of adulthood. But it appears that schizophrenic brains aggressively prune away too many synapses, which may explain why the first full-blown schizophrenic episode typically occurs in adolescence or early adulthood. Healthy teenagers lose about 1% of the brain's grey matter between ages 13 and 18. But as you can see in Figure 15.7, adolescents with schizophrenia show much more extensive and rapid tissue loss, primarily in the sensory and motor regions (Thompson et al., 2001). "We were stunned to see a spreading wave of tissue loss that began in a small region of the brain," said Paul Thompson, who headed the study that tracked the loss of grey matter in the brain over five years. "It moved across the brain like a forest fire, destroying more tissue as the disease progressed." The reason for the excessive pruning is not yet known, but it may involve genetic dispositions, fetal brain damage, or stressful life experiences (McGlashan & Hoffman, 2000).

Thus, the developmental pathway of schizophrenia is something of a relay. It starts with a genetic predisposition, which must combine with prenatal risk factors or birth complications that affect brain development. The resulting vulnerability then awaits events in adolescence—synaptic pruning within the brain (Walker & Tessner, 2008) or external stressors—that serve as a trigger for the disease (Conklin & Iacono, 2002). This model explains why one identical twin may develop schizophrenia but not the other: Both may have the genetic susceptibility, but only one may have been exposed to other risk factors in the womb, birth complications, or stressful life events. These factors may combine in different ways as well, explaining why some schizophrenics recover and others do not. The riddle of schizophrenia is likely to be several riddles, waiting to be solved.

quickQUIZ

✔•⃞ **Quick Review** on **MyPsychLab**

The following quiz is not a hallucination.

1. What are the five major kinds of symptoms in schizophrenia?

2. What are the three likely stages in the "relay" that produces schizophrenia?

Answers:

1. delusions, hallucinations, disorganized speech, inappropriate behaviour, and impaired cognitive abilities 2. genetic predispositions; prenatal risk factors or birth complications; events during adolescence, such as excessive pruning of synapses in the brain or external stressors

MENTAL DISORDER AND PERSONAL RESPONSIBILITY

We have come to the end of a long walk along the spectrum of psychological problems—from those that are normal conditions of life, such as occasional anxiety or "caffeine-induced sleep disorder," to mental disorders that can be severely disabling, such as major depression or schizophrenia.

One of the great debates generated by all diagnoses of mental disorder concerns the question of personal responsibility. In law and in everyday life, many people reach for a psychological reason to exonerate themselves of responsibility for their actions.

Romance writer Janet Dailey, who, when caught, admitted she had plagiarized whole passages from another writer's work, said she was suffering from "a psychological problem that I never even suspected I had." Many people—as an excuse for some habit that is immoral, illegal, or fattening—claim they are "addicted" to the behaviour, whether it is sex, shopping, eating chocolate, jogging, or spending hours on the internet. These activities may be highly pleasurable, to be sure, but are they "addictions" in the customary meaning of the word?

Some psychologists think these activities are indeed comparable to drug addiction or to any other compulsive behaviour: They can be maladaptive, disrupting the lives of those who spend thousands of hours shopping or having adventures in cyberspace instead of the real world; they can cause emotional distress to the individual or to his or her friends and family. Other psychologists, however, think that students who spend too much time online are no different from previous generations who also found plenty of ways to distract themselves and avoid the common problems facing students everywhere—insecurity, worry about grades, a disappointing social life. This is not a "mental disorder," they say, it's a normal problem, called "Learning to Pass Courses and Figure Out Life." Certainly, some students who use internet addiction as an excuse for not studying are making an obvious effort to avoid responsibility for a bad grade. Others may be spending too much time on the internet as a way of coping with depression, anxiety, or another emotional problem.

The difficulty of knowing where to draw the line of responsibility is apparent in the tragic story of Andrea Yates, a Texas woman who killed her five young children in a state of extreme despair. She had suffered from clinical depression and psychotic episodes for years and in her blackest depressions became mute and catatonic. She tried to kill herself twice. Her father, two brothers, and a sister had suffered varying degrees of mental illness, including depression. Yates was overwhelmed by raising and home schooling all her children by herself, with no help from her reportedly domineering husband, who permitted her two hours a week of personal time. Although she suffered a postpartum psychotic episode after the birth of their fourth child and a clinical psychologist warned against her having another baby, her husband refused to consider birth control, although not for religious reasons. "We want as many as nature will allow," he said (Yardley, 2001). In 2002, Yates was convicted of murder and sentenced to life in prison after a jury rejected her claim that she was so psychotic that she thought she was saving the souls of her children by killing them. That conviction was overturned on appeal. In 2006, another jury found her not guilty by reason of insanity and she was sent to a mental institution. The defence saw this verdict as a triumph for the understanding of mental illness; the prosecution saw it as a failure of justice.

Does Andrea Yates deserve our condemnation for her horrible acts of murder or our pity? Was her punishment appropriate? We noted at the beginning of this chapter that "insanity" refers only to the defendant's ability to know right from wrong at the time the crime was committed. It is used in only a tiny percentage of all criminal cases. But in some jurisdictions, a defendant may claim to have "diminished responsibility" for a crime. This claim does not exonerate the defendant, but it may result in reduced charges, for example from

Thinking Critically

Ask Questions

The legal system is based on the assumption of personal responsibility, but it also recognizes that some people cannot control their behaviour. When does a mental disorder become an excuse to "get away with murder," and when does it truly diminish a person's legal and moral responsibility?

Andrea Yates was convicted of the murder of her children and sent to a mental institution. Do you agree that this was the appropriate punishment? Why or why not?

premeditated first-degree murder to manslaughter. A diminished-capacity defence holds that the defendant lacked the mental capacity to form a calculated and malicious plan but instead was impaired by mental illness or the great provocation of the situation. In some jurisdictions, diminished capacity and other mitigating factors are considered only at the sentencing phase, once the defendant has been found guilty.

When thinking about the relationship of mental disorder to personal responsibility, we face a dilemma. The law recognizes, rightly, that people who are mentally incompetent, delusional, or disturbed should not be judged by the same standards as mentally healthy individuals. At the same time, society has an obligation to protect its citizens from harm and to reject easy excuses for violations of the law. To balance these two positions, we need to find ways to ensure that people who commit crimes or behave reprehensibly face the consequences of their behaviour. We must also ensure that people who are suffering from psychological problems have the compassionate support of society in their search for help. After all, psychological problems of one kind or another are challenges that all of us will face at some time in our lives.

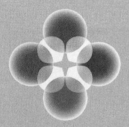

Taking Psychology with YOU

Thinking Critically in Everyday Life

When a Friend Is Suicidal

Suicide can be frightening to those who find themselves fantasizing about it, and it is devastating to the family and friends of those who go through with it. In Canada, it is the ninth leading cause of death, far surpassing homicide (Statistics Canada, 1997). The suicide rate is highest among white men over the age of 65, but suicide rates have nearly tripled in the past 40 years among adolescents and young adults, especially among college and university students and black teenagers. In the United States, about 1300 college or university students commit suicide every year, and nearly 32 000 more make an unsuccessful attempt (Farrell, 2005).

Women are more likely than men to attempt suicide, primarily as a cry for help, whereas men are four times more likely than women to succeed.

But this gender difference depends on culture and circumstances. In Finland, for example, more males than females attempt suicide; and in Canada and the United States, men in prison have high rates of attempted suicide (Canetto & Sakinofsky, 1998). Moreover, men's efforts to commit suicide are not always obvious: Some men provoke confrontations with the police, hoping to be shot; some intentionally kill themselves in car accidents; and men are more likely than women to destroy themselves with drugs.

Because of the many widespread myths about suicide, it is important to become informed and know what to do in a crisis:

♦ *Take all suicide threats seriously.* Some people assume they can't do anything when a friend talks about

committing suicide. "He'll just do it at another place, another time," they think. In fact, most suicides occur during an acute crisis. Once the person gets through the crisis, the desire to die fades.

Others believe that if a friend is *talking* about committing suicide, he or she won't really *do* it. This belief is also false. Few people commit suicide without signalling their intentions. Most are ambivalent: "I want to kill myself, but I don't want to be dead—at least not forever." Most suicidal people want relief from the terrible pain of feeling that nobody cares and that life is not worth living. Getting these thoughts and fears out in the open is an important first step.

♦ *Know the danger signs.* A person is at risk of trying to commit suicide if he or she has tried to do it before;

has become withdrawn and listless; has a history of depression; reveals specific plans for carrying out the suicide or gives away cherished possessions; expresses no concern about religious prohibitions or the impact on family members; and has access to a lethal method, such as a gun.

◆ *Get involved: Ask questions and get help.* If you believe a friend is suicidal, do not be afraid to ask, "Are you thinking of suicide?" This question does not "put the idea" in anyone's mind. If your friend is contemplating the action, he or she will probably be relieved to talk about it, which in turn will reduce feelings of isolation and despair. Don't try to talk your friend out of it by debating whether suicide is right or wrong, and don't put on phony cheerfulness. If your friend's words

scare you, say so. By allowing your friend to unburden his or her grief, you help the person get through the immediate crisis.

◆ *Do not leave your friend alone.* If necessary, get the person to a clinic or a hospital emergency room, or call a local suicide hotline or the Canadian nationwide referral hotline, 1-(800)-449-3000. Don't worry about doing the wrong thing. In an emergency, the worst thing you can do is nothing at all.

◆ If you are the one who is contemplating suicide, remember that you are not alone and that help is a phone call or an email away. You can call the national hotline number (mentioned above) or your school's counselling services. For more information, the Centers for Disease Control and Prevention has a website

that provides facts about suicide (www.cdc.gov/safeusa/suicide.htm). Many students fear getting help because they think no one will understand, or they fear they will be made fun of by their friends, or they believe they cannot be helped. Wrong, wrong, wrong.

In her book *Night Falls Fast: Understanding Suicide*, Kay Jamison (1999), a psychologist who suffers from bipolar disorder, explored this difficult subject from the standpoint of both a mental-health professional and a person who has "been there." In describing the aftermath of her own suicide attempt, she wrote: "I do know . . . that I should have been dead but was not—and that I was fortunate enough to be given another chance at life, which many others were not."

SUMMARY

DEFINING AND DIAGNOSING DISORDER

◆ When defining *mental disorder*, mental-health professionals emphasize the violation of cultural standards, the emotional suffering caused by the behaviour, and whether the behaviour is harmful to others or society.

◆ The *Diagnostic and Statistical Manual of Mental Disorders (DSM)*, which is used throughout the world, is designed to provide objective criteria and categories for diagnosing mental disorder. Critics argue that the diagnosis of mental disorders, unlike those of medical diseases, is inherently a subjective process that can never be entirely objective. They believe the DSM fosters overdiagnosis, overlooks the influence of diagnostic labels on clients and therapists, confuses serious mental disorders with everyday problems in living, and creates an illusion of objectivity and universality.

◆ Supporters of the DSM believe that when the DSM criteria are used correctly and when empirically validated objective tests are used, reliability in diagnosis improves. The DSM now lists many *culture-bound syndromes* in addition to disorders (such as depression and schizophrenia) that are found all over the world.

◆ In diagnosing psychological disorders, clinicians often use *projective tests* such as the *Rorschach Inkblot Test* or, with children, anatomically detailed dolls. These methods have low reliability and validity, creating problems when they are used in the legal arena, as in custody disputes, or in diagnosing disorders. In general, *objective tests (inventories)*, such as the *MMPI*, are more reliable and valid than projective ones.

ANXIETY DISORDERS

◆ *Generalized anxiety disorder* involves continuous, chronic *anxiety*, with signs of nervousness, worry, and irritability. When anxiety results from exposure to uncontrollable or unpredictable danger, it can lead to *posttraumatic stress disorder (PTSD)*, which involves mentally reliving the trauma, emotional detachment, and increased physiological arousal.

◆ Most people who live through a traumatic experience eventually recover without developing PTSD. But a minority do. The reasons for their increased vulnerability to posttraumatic symptoms include having a history of psychological problems and other traumatic experiences; lacking social support and psychological resources; having lower-than-average intelligence; having a relatively smaller hippocampus than normal; and having a genetic vulnerability.

◆ *Panic disorder* involves sudden, intense attacks of profound fear. Panic attacks are common in the aftermath of stress or frightening experiences; those who go on to develop a disorder tend to interpret the attacks as a sign of impending disaster.

◆ *Phobias* are unrealistic fears of specific situations, activities, or things. Common *social phobias* include fears of speaking in public, going on a date, or being observed by others. *Agoraphobia*, the fear of being away from a safe place or person, is the most disabling phobia—a "fear of fear." It often begins with a panic attack, which the person tries to avoid in the future by staying close to "safe" places or people.

◆ *Obsessive-compulsive disorder (OCD)* involves recurrent, unwished-for thoughts or images (obsessions) and repetitive, ritualized behaviours (compulsions) that a person feels unable to control. Some people with OCD have depleted levels of serotonin in their prefrontal cortex, which may contribute to their cognitive rigidity. Parts of the brain involved in fear and responses to threat are also more active than normal in people with OCD; the "alarm mechanism," once activated, does not turn off when danger is past. One kind of OCD creates pathological hoarding and may involve deficiencies in other parts of the brain.

MOOD DISORDERS

◆ Symptoms of *major depression* include distorted thinking patterns, low self-esteem, physical ailments such as fatigue and loss of appetite, and prolonged grief and despair. Women are twice as likely as men to suffer from major depression, but depression in men may be underdiagnosed. In *bipolar disorder*, a person experiences episodes of both depression and *mania* (excessive euphoria). It is equally common in both sexes.

◆ *Vulnerability-stress models* of depression (or any other disorder) look at interactions between individual vulnerabilities and stressful experiences. Some people have a genetic predisposition to become depressed when they undergo severe stress, and others may be genetically protected. Genes may affect levels of serotonin and the stress hormone cortisol. For some vulnerable individuals, repeated losses of important people can set off episodes of major depression. Life experiences that increase the risk of depression include violence, problems with work and family, poverty, discrimination, and sexual abuse. Cognitive habits also play an important role: believing that the origin of one's unhappiness is permanent and uncontrollable; feeling hopeless and pessimistic; and brooding or ruminating about one's problems.

PERSONALITY DISORDERS

◆ *Personality disorders* are characterized by rigid, self-destructive traits that cause distress or an inability to get along with others. They include, among others, *paranoid*, *narcissistic*, *borderline*, and *antisocial personality disorders*.

◆ The term *psychopath* describes people who lack conscience and emotional connection to others; they don't feel remorse, shame, guilt, or anxiety over wrongdoing; and they can charm and con others with ease. *Antisocial personality disorder (APD)* applies to people with a lifelong pattern of aggressive, reckless, impulsive, and criminal behaviour. Not all psychopaths have APD, and not all people with APD are psychopaths, but in some individuals the two disorders converge. Researchers have identified abnormalities in the central nervous system and prefrontal cortex that are associated with lack of emotional responsiveness and with impulsivity. APD has a genetic component, but biological vulnerabilities must interact with stressful or violent environments to produce the disorder.

DRUG ABUSE AND ADDICTION

◆ The effects of drugs depend on whether they are used moderately or are abused. Signs of *substance abuse* include impaired ability to work or get along with others, use of the drug in hazardous situations, recurrent arrests for drug use, and conflicts with others caused by drug use.

◆ According to the *biological model of addiction*, some people have a biological vulnerability to alcoholism and other addictions due to genetic factors that affect their metabolism, biochemistry, or personality traits. But heavy drug abuse also changes the brain in ways that make addiction more likely.

◆ Advocates of the *learning model of addiction* point out that addiction patterns vary according to culture, learning, and accepted practice; that many people can stop taking drugs without experiencing withdrawal symptoms; that drug abuse depends on the reasons for taking a drug; and that abuse increases when people are not taught moderate use.

◆ Although the biological and learning models are polarized on many issues, the evidence suggests that addiction and abuse result from an interaction between biological and psychological vulnerability and a person's culture, learning history, motives for taking a drug, and situation.

DISSOCIATIVE IDENTITY DISORDER

◆ In *dissociative identity disorder* (formerly called multiple personality disorder, or MPD), two or more distinct personalities and identities appear to split off (dissociate) within one person. Considerable controversy surrounds the validity and nature of MPD. Some clinicians think it is common, often goes undiagnosed, and originates in childhood trauma. Others offer a *sociocognitive* explanation. They argue that most cases result from pressure and suggestion by clinicians who believe in the disorder, interacting with vulnerable patients who find MPD a plausible explanation for their problems. Media coverage of sensational alleged cases of MPD greatly contributed to the rise in the number of cases after 1980.

SCHIZOPHRENIA

◆ *Schizophrenia* is a psychotic disorder involving delusions, hallucinations, disorganized speech (called *word salads*), inappropriate behaviour, and severe cognitive impairments. Other symptoms, such as loss of motivation to take care of oneself and emotional flatness, may appear before a psychotic episode and persist even when the more dramatic symptoms are in remission. Some people with schizophrenia fall into a *catatonic stupor*. Cases of schizophrenia vary in their specific symptoms, severity, duration, and prognosis.

◆ Schizophrenia appears to involve genetic predispositions that lead to structural brain abnormalities, such as enlarged ventricles and neurotransmitter abnormalities. However, in the "relay" that produces the disorder, genetic predispositions must interact with certain stressors in the environment during prenatal development (such as the mother's malnutrition or a prenatal viral infection), birth complications, and excessive pruning of synapses during adolescence.

MENTAL DISORDER AND PERSONAL RESPONSIBILITY

◆ The diagnosis of mental disorder raises important questions for issues of personal responsibility in the law and in everyday life. When people claim to have a mental disorder, psychologists and others struggle to decide whether the claim is being used as an excuse for illegal or destructive behaviour, or whether these individuals truly have a disorder that reduces their ability to control their behaviour.

TAKING PSYCHOLOGY WITH YOU

◆ The diagnosis of mental disorder raises important questions about the degree to which mentally ill people are responsible for illegal or destructive behaviour and how the criminal justice system should treat them.

MyPsychLab

Visit **www.mypsychlab.com** to help you get the best grade!
Test your knowledge and grasp difficult concepts through

• Custom study plans: See where you are strong and where you go wrong

• Interactive simulations

• Video and audio clips

KEY TERMS

16 APPROACHES TO TREATMENT AND THERAPY

ASK QUESTIONS . . . be willing to WONDER

- Why are there so many kinds of therapies, and how do they differ?
- Should a client see a therapist of the same ethnicity?
- What kind of therapy works best, and for which problems?
- Can therapy ever be harmful?

The vast majority of people who experience a traumatic event—including combat during war, the sudden death of a loved one, or a natural disaster such as an earthquake or hurricane—recover from their immediate post-shock symptoms and go on to lead normal lives. The two greatest allies in helping them do this are time, which does heal, and the support of friends. For some people, however, time and friends are not enough, and they develop one or more of the disorders described in the previous chapter: depression, generalized anxiety disorder, specific phobias, or posttraumatic stress disorder. What kind of therapy might help them? People have many other problems too, ranging from normal life difficulties (such as marital conflict or fear of public speaking) to the delusions of schizophrenia. What kind of therapy might help them?

As we saw in Chapter 1, to become a licensed clinical psychologist, a person must have an advanced degree and a period of supervised training. However, the title *psychotherapist* is unregulated; anyone can set up any kind of program and call it "therapy"— and, by the thousands, they do! Increasingly in Canada and the United States, people can get credentialed as "experts" in various techniques and therapies—doing hypnotherapy, diagnosing child sexual abuse, becoming a practitioner of some pop-psych method— simply by attending a weekend seminar or a training program lasting a week or two. To protect themselves as well as to get the best possible help when it is necessary, consumers need to be informed and know how to choose that help wisely.

In this chapter, we will evaluate two major approaches to treatment. Biological treatments, primarily provided by psychiatrists or other physicians, include drugs or direct intervention in brain function. Psychotherapy covers an array of psychological interventions, including psychodynamic therapies, cognitive and behaviour therapies, humanist therapies, and family or couples therapy. In addition to these major schools of psychotherapy, there are literally hundreds of offshoots and specialties. We will assess which kinds of therapy work best for which problems, which kinds of therapy are ineffective, and which ones carry a significant risk of harm to the client.

YOU are about to learn . . .

◆ the types of medications used to treat psychological disorders.

◆ six important cautions about medications for emotional problems.

◆ ways of electrically stimulating the brain—and whether they work.

BIOLOGICAL TREATMENTS FOR MENTAL DISORDERS

For hundreds of years, people have tried to identify the origins of mental illness, attributing the causes at various times to evil spirits, pressure in the skull, disease, or bad environments. The contemporary mental-health world continues to alternate between viewing mental disorders as diseases that can be treated medically and as emotional problems that must be treated psychologically (Luhrmann, 2000). Today, biological explanations and treatments are in the ascendance. This is partly because of evidence that some disorders have a genetic component or involve a biochemical or neurological abnormality (see Chapter 15), and partly, as we will see, because physicians and pharmaceutical companies are promoting biomedical solutions (Angell, 2004; Healy, 2002).

The Question of Drugs

The most commonly used biological treatment is medication that alters the production of or response to neurotransmitters in the brain (see Chapter 4). Because drugs are so widely prescribed these days, both for severe disorders such as schizophrenia and for more common problems such as anxiety and depression, consumers need to understand what these drugs are, how they can best be used, and their limitations.

DRUGS COMMONLY PRESCRIBED FOR MENTAL DISORDERS. The main classes of drugs used in the treatment of mental and emotional disorders are the following:

1 **Antipsychotic drugs,** also called *neuroleptics*—older ones such as chlorpromazine (trade name Largactil in Canada and Thorazine in the U.S.) and haloperidol (Haldol) and second-generation ones such as clozapine (Clozaril and the two market leaders Risperdal and Zyprexa)—are used primarily in the treatment of schizophrenia and other psychoses. Although the newer drugs have been promoted as being safer and more effective, a large federally funded study found that the older medications often alleviate schizophrenia symptoms about as well as the newer, far more expensive ones do (Lieberman et al., 2005). And although antipsychotics are increasingly being prescribed to treat the symptoms of nonpsychotic disorders such as severe depression, bipolar disorder, attention deficit disorder, dementia, and mental retardation, they are ineffective for these disorders. One study followed 86 people, aged 18 to 65, who were given Risperdal, Haldol, or a placebo to treat their aggressive outbursts (Tyrer et al., 2008). The placebo group improved the most.

Because many psychoses are thought to be caused by an excess of the neurotransmitter dopamine, many antipsychotic drugs are designed to block or reduce the sensitivity of brain receptors that respond to dopamine. Some also increase levels of serotonin, a neurotransmitter that inhibits dopamine activity. Antipsychotic drugs can reduce agitation, delusions, and hallucinations, and they can shorten schizophrenic episodes. However, they offer little relief from other symptoms, such as jumbled thoughts, difficulty concentrating, apathy, emotional

In the years before the advent of antipsychotic medication, patients with severe mental disorders were often put in straitjackets or chained to their beds to avoid harming themselves or others. Notice that this young woman in a restraining jacket, sitting alone and weeping in an Ohio mental institution in 1946, has open, untreated sores on her leg.

◉ **Watch**
Asylum: A History of the Medical Institution in America

antipsychotic drugs (neuroleptics)
Drugs used primarily in the treatment of schizophrenia and other psychotic disorders; they are often used off label and inappropriately for other disorders such as dementia and impulsive aggressiveness.

These photos show the effects of antipsychotic drugs on the symptoms of a young man with schizophrenia. In the photo on the left, he was unmedicated; in the photo on the right, he had taken medication. However, these drugs do not help all people with psychotic disorders.

flatness, or inability to interact with others. While antipsychotic medication allows many people to be released from hospitals, these individuals cannot always care for themselves, and they often fail to keep taking their medication because of the unpleasant and sometimes dangerous side effects. These side effects can include muscle rigidity, hand tremors, and other involuntary muscle movements that can develop into a neurological disorder called *tardive dyskinesia* (*tardive* means "late-appearing"). About one-fourth of all adults who take these drugs, and fully one-third of elderly patients who do so, develop this disorder (Saltz et al., 1991).

In addition, Zyprexa, Risperdal, and other antipsychotics, which manufacturers have been marketing for children and the elderly, often carry unacceptable risks for these very groups. The immediate side effect is extreme weight gain—anywhere from 24 to 100 extra pounds a year—which has led to the development of thousands of cases of diabetes; other risks include strokes and death from sudden heart failure (Masand, 2000; Ray et al., 2009; Wallace-Wells, 2009). In 2003, the makers of Risperdal cautioned physicians to stop prescribing the drug to elderly patients with dementia, because it can cause strokes and is ineffective for this population.

2 **Antidepressant drugs** are used primarily in the treatment of depression, anxiety, phobias, and obsessive-compulsive disorder. *Monoamine oxidase inhibitors* *(MAOIs)*, such as Nardil, elevate the levels of norepinephrine and serotonin in the brain by blocking or inhibiting an enzyme that deactivates these neurotransmitters. *Tricyclic* antidepressants, such as Elavil and Tofranil, boost norepinephrine and serotonin levels by preventing the normal reabsorption, or "reuptake," of these substances by the cells that have released them. Selective serotonin reuptake inhibitors (SSRIs), such as Prozac and Zoloft, Lexapro, Paxil, and Celexa, work on the same principle as the tricyclics but specifically target serotonin. Cymbalta and Remeron target both serotonin and norepinephrine. Another drug, Wellbutrin, is chemically unrelated to the other antidepressants but is often prescribed for depression and, under the trade name Zyban, as an aid to quitting smoking.

All three classes of antidepressants are nonaddictive and about equally effective, but they all tend to produce some unpleasant physical reactions, including dry mouth, headaches, constipation, nausea, restlessness, gastrointestinal problems,

◉ **Watch**
Alternative Approaches
to Treating ADHD

antidepressant drugs Drugs
used primarily in the treatment of mood
disorders, especially depression and
anxiety.

tranquilizers Drugs commonly but often inappropriately prescribed for patients who complain of unhappiness, anxiety, or worry.

lithium carbonate A drug frequently given to people suffering from bipolar disorder.

weight gain, and, in as many as one-third of all patients, decreased sexual desire and blocked or delayed orgasm (Hollon, Thase, & Markowitz, 2002). The specific side effects may vary with the particular drug. MAOIs interact with certain foods (such as cheese) and have the most risks, such as dangerously high blood pressure in some individuals, so they are prescribed least often nowadays.

Some investigators are studying herbs like St. John's wort. A meta-analysis of clinical studies found that St. John's wort was more effective than a placebo for milder forms of depression (Kim, Streltzer, & Goebert, 1999), but the efficacy of this herb remains in dispute. Also, the herb is now known to affect metabolism and to interact with about half of all prescription medications, including birth-control pills, blood thinners, and some AIDS drugs (Markowitz et al., 2003). Anyone taking St. John's wort along with a prescription drug should inform his or her physician.

3 **Anti-anxiety drugs (tranquilizers),** such as Valium and Xanax, increase the activity of the neurotransmitter gamma-aminobutyric acid (GABA). Although they were developed to treat people with mild anxiety, they are often overprescribed by general physicians for patients who complain of more serious mood disorders. Tranquilizers may help people with panic disorder and individuals who are having an acute anxiety attack, but they are not considered the treatment of choice over a long period of time. Symptoms almost always return if the medication is stopped, and a significant percentage of people who take tranquilizers overuse them and develop problems with withdrawal and tolerance (i.e., they need larger and larger doses). Beta blockers, a class of drugs primarily used to manage heart irregularities and hypertension, are sometimes prescribed to relieve acute anxiety—for example, caused by stage fright or athletic competition—which they do by slowing the heart rate and lowering blood pressure. But beta blockers are not approved for anxiety disorders.

✳ Explore
Drugs Commonly Used to Treat
Psychiatric Disorders

4 **A special category of drug, a salt called lithium carbonate,** often helps people who suffer from bipolar disorder (depression alternating with euphoria). It may produce its effects by moderating levels of norepinephrine or by protecting brain cells from being overstimulated by another neurotransmitter, glutamate (Nonaka, Hough, & Chuang, 1998). Lithium must be given in exactly the right dose, and bloodstream levels of the drug must be carefully monitored, because too little will not help and too much is toxic—sometimes even fatal. Unfortunately, in some people, lithium produces short-term side effects (tremors) and long-term problems (kidney damage). Other drugs for people with bipolar disorder include Tegretol, Depakote, and some of the newer antipsychotics (McElroy & Keck, 2000).

For a review of these drugs and their uses, see Review 16.1.

SOME CAUTIONS ABOUT DRUG TREATMENTS. Without question, drugs have rescued some people from emotional despair, suicide, obsessive-compulsive disorder, and panic attacks. They have enabled severely depressed or mentally disturbed people to function and respond to psychotherapy. Yet many psychiatrists and drug companies are trumpeting the benefits of medication without informing the public of its limitations, so some words of caution are in order.

Most people are unaware of how a publication bias—the tendency for journals to publish positive findings but not negative or ambiguous ones—affects what we know. Independent researchers reviewed unpublished data

Thinking ⚙ Critically
· · · · · · · · · · · · · · · · · ·
Avoid Emotional Reasoning

You hear a researcher claiming that a new drug is "a breakthrough drug for depression," or for anxiety, or for some other problem. Such announcements always generate a lot of excitement. Why should people be cautious before concluding that a new drug is the miracle they are longing for it to be? What information is the public often not getting from the company making the drug?

REView 16.1

Drugs Commonly Used in the Treatment of Psychological Disorders

	Antipsychotics (Neuroleptics)	Antidepressants	Anti-Anxiety Drugs	Lithium Carbonate
Examples	Thorazine Haldol Clozaril Risperdal Seroquel	Prozac (SSRI) Nardil (MAOI) Elavil (tricyclic) Paxil (SSRI) Wellbutrin (other) Cymbalta (other) Remeron (other)	Valium Xanax Klonapin Beta blockers	
Primarily used for	Schizophrenia Other psychoses Impulsive anger Bipolar disorder	Depression Anxiety disorders Panic disorder Obsessive-compulsive disorder	Mood disorders Panic disorder Acute anxiety (e.g., stage fright)	Bipolar disorder

submitted to the U.S. Food and Drug Administration (FDA) on 12 popular antidepressants. Of the 74 studies they examined, 38 reported positive results, and all but one of those was later published. Of the remaining studies with negative or mixed results, only 14 were published—and most of them were given a positive spin (Turner et al., 2008). In 2003, British drug authorities reported that nine unpublished studies of Paxil found that it tripled the risk of suicidal thoughts and suicide attempts in young people who were taking the drug compared to those given a placebo (Harris, 2003). Paxil and other SSRIs can cause a severe form of restlessness and agitation in the first few weeks they are taken, and this reaction might push vulnerable young people to a precipice. Today, the U.S. Food and Drug Administration (FDA) has cautioned against prescribing SSRIs to anyone under 18.

Most worrisome for the future of impartial research is that most researchers who are studying the effectiveness of medication have strong financial ties to the pharmaceutical industry, in the form of lucrative consulting fees, funding for studies, stock investments, and patents. Indeed, funding for some research is available only from pharmaceutical companies, which may require investigators to sign contracts allowing the companies to determine whether, where, and when the research findings will be published. (For example, Pfizer delayed publication of research it had sponsored in the United States showing that Viagra was ineffective for women; eventually, an independent Canadian study reported the same results [Basson et al., 2002].) Studies that are independently funded often do not get the strong positive results that industry-funded drug trials do (Angell, 2004; Healy, 2002; Krimsky, 2003). In this section, therefore, we want to give you an idea of what you are not hearing from the drug companies.

1 **The placebo effect.** New drugs, like new psychotherapies, often promise quick and effective cures. But the placebo effect ensures that many people will respond positively to a new drug just because of the enthusiasm surrounding it and because of their own expectations that the drug will make them feel better. After a while, when placebo effects decline, many drugs turn out to be neither as effective as promised nor as widely applicable. This has happened repeatedly with each new generation of tranquilizer and each new "miracle" antipsychotic drug and

placebo effect The apparent success of a medication or treatment due to the patient's expectations or hopes rather than to the drug or treatment itself.

antidepressant, including Clozaril and Prozac (Healy, 2004; Moncrieff, 2001). In fact, some investigators maintain that much of the effectiveness of antidepressants is due to a placebo effect (Khan et al., 2003; Kirsch & Sapirstein, 1998). Even researchers who quarrel with that strong conclusion acknowledge that the drugs are less effective than commonly believed. Overall, only about half of all depressed patients respond positively to any given antidepressant medication, and of those, only about 40% are actually responding to the specific biological effects of the drugs (Hollon, Thase, & Markowitz, 2002). In a meta-analysis of more than 5000 patients in 47 clinical trials, investigators found that the placebo effect was "exceptionally large," accounting for more than 80% of the alleviation of symptoms. The drugs were most effective for patients with severe depression (Kirsch et al., 2008). New research in neuroscience is illuminating the reason why placebos work for some people: The psychological expectation of improvement actually produces some of the same brain changes that medication does (Benedetti et al., 2005; see Chapter 6).

2 **High relapse and dropout rates.** A person may have short-term success with antipsychotic or antidepressant drugs. However, in part because of these drugs' unpleasant side effects, one-half to two-thirds of people stop taking them. When they do, they are quite likely to relapse, especially if they have not learned how to cope with their problems (Hollon, Thase, & Markowitz, 2002).

3 **Dosage problems.** The challenge with drugs is to find the **therapeutic window,** the amount that is enough but not too much. This problem is compounded by the fact that the same dose of a drug may be metabolized differently in men and women, old people and young people, and different ethnic groups. When psychiatrist Keh-Ming Lin moved from Taiwan to the United States, he was amazed to learn that the dosage of antipsychotic drugs given to American patients with schizophrenia was often 10 times higher than the dose for Chinese patients. In subsequent studies, Lin and his colleagues confirmed that Asian patients require significantly lower doses of the medication for optimal treatment (Lin, Poland, & Chien, 1990). Similarly, black people suffering from depression or bipolar disorder seem to need lower dosages of tricyclic antidepressants and lithium than other ethnic groups do (Strickland et al., 1991, 1995). Groups may differ in the dosages they can tolerate because of variations in metabolic rates, amount of body fat, the number or type of drug receptors in the brain, or cultural practices such as smoking and eating certain foods.

4 **Disregard for effective, possibly better, nonmedical treatments.** Because ads promise such wonderful results, medication often seems the best way to deal with an emotional or behavioural problem, yet nonmedical treatments may work just as well or better. For example, two psychologists examined data on more than 168 000 children with attention deficit disorder who had been referred for treatment to a behavioural-care facility. More than 60% of the boys and 23% of the girls were on Ritalin or another drug. But after six sessions of behaviour therapy for the children and 10 sessions for the parent, only 11% of the boys and 2% of the girls remained on medication (Cummings & Wiggins, 2001).

The popularity of drugs has also been fuelled by pressure from managed-care organizations, which prefer to pay for one patient visit for a prescription rather than 10 visits for psychotherapy, and by drug company advertising. In 1997 the

"I think the dosage needs adjusting. I'm not nearly as happy as the people in the ads."

therapeutic window The amount of a drug that is enough but not too much, taking into account the fact that the same dose of a drug may be metabolized differently in men and women, old people and young people, and different ethnic groups.

FDA permitted pharmaceutical companies to advertise directly to consumers, a practice still forbidden in Canada and Europe; sales of new drugs skyrocketed because of consumer demand.

5 **Unknown long-term risks.** We saw that antipsychotic drugs can have danger-ous and even fatal consequences if taken for many years. Antidepressants have been assumed to be quite safe, but the effects of taking them indefinitely are still unknown. The general public and even many physicians do not realize that new drugs are often tested on only a few hundred people for only a few weeks or months, even when the drug is one that patients might take for years (Angell, 2004). (The cost of bringing most new drugs to market is very high, and manu-facturers feel they cannot afford to wait years to determine whether there might be long-term hazards.) Many physicians and laypeople, feeling reassured if a drug is effective in the short run, overlook the possibility of long-term dangers, as well as the potential risks of drug interactions. Yet psychiatrists, understandably frus-trated by the failure of existing antipsychotics and antidepressants to help all of their clients, are increasingly prescribing "cocktails" of medications—this one for anxiety, plus this one for depression, plus another to manage the side effects. They report anecdotal success in some cases, but as yet there has been virtually no research on the benefits and risks of these combination approaches.

6 **Untested off-label uses.** Most consumers do not realize that once a drug is approved by Health Canada, doctors are then permitted to prescribe it for other conditions and to populations other than those on which it was originally tested. That is why antidepressants are now being marketed for "social phobias"; why Prozac, when its patent expired, was renamed Sarafem and marketed to women for "premenstrual dysphoric disorder"; why Ritalin, widely given to school-aged children, is now being prescribed for two- and three-year-olds; why the number of antidepressants given to preschoolers has doubled; and why antipsychotics such as Risperdal are being used for nonpsychotic disorders such as impulsive aggression.

Medications have saved lives and improved the lives of thousands of people suf-fering from severe mental illness as well as those suffering from milder forms of depression, anxiety, and other emotional problems. Yet the cautions we have listed are the reason why it is important to think critically about this issue. In coming years, you will be hearing about many "promising medications" for such common psychological problems as memory loss, eating disorders, smoking, and alcoholism (Miller, 2008). Every major pharmaceutical company is working on one or more of these, and you are likely to hear enthusiastic researchers promising "We'll have it within five years!" But we hope you will resist the impulse to jump on any new-drug bandwagon. Drugs for mental disorders are neither totally miraculous, as some of their promoters say, nor totally worthless, as some of their critics maintain. Critical thinkers must weigh the benefits and limitations of medication for psychological problems; wait for the data on safety and effectiveness; and resist the temptation to oversimplify.

Direct Brain Intervention

For most of human history, a person suffering from mental illness often got a rather extreme form of "help." A well-meaning tribal healer or, in later centuries, a doctor would try to release the "psychic pressures" believed to be causing the symptoms by drilling holes in the victim's skull. It didn't work! However, the basic impulse—to try to cure mental illness by intervening directly in the brain—has continued.

Thinking Critically

Tolerate Uncertainty

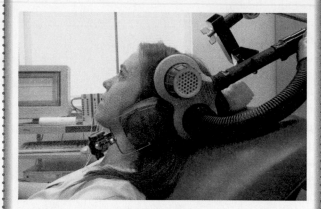

A researcher demonstrates transcranial magnetic stimulation (TMS). One neurosurgeon who uses this technology with depressed patients told a reporter why he thinks the results have been unpredictable so far. "The effect is very dependent on who is delivering the TMS," he said. "The way you hold the coil, where you put it, the rotation, the angle" affect what happens in the brain. As a critical thinker, what warning lights should go off in your own brain when you read a statement like that? One answer: If a method depends more on who is doing it than on what is being done, the placebo effect is likely to be the reason for any benefits, rather than the technology itself. Until controlled studies are done, we need to tolerate some uncertainty about whether TMS will prove to be effective.

psychosurgery Any surgical procedure that destroys selected areas of the brain believed to be involved in emotional disorders or violent, impulsive behaviour.

electroconvulsive therapy (ECT) A procedure used in cases of prolonged and severe major depression, in which a brief brain seizure is induced.

One approach, **psychosurgery**, is designed to surgically destroy selected areas of the brain thought to be responsible for emotional disorders or disturbed behaviour. The most famous form of modern psychosurgery was invented in 1935, when a Portuguese neurologist, Antonio Egas Moniz, drilled two holes into the skull of a mental patient and used a specially designed instrument to cut or crush nerve fibres running from the prefrontal lobes to other areas. Moniz called this operation a "leukotomy," which means "white matter cutting." Moniz developed this procedure before the invention of psychoactive medications for the treatment of mental illness, and argued that his surgical procedure should be used extremely conservatively. His wishes were not granted. In 1945, American physician Walter Freeman adapted the "leukotomy" procedure (now called a prefrontal lobotomy), aggressively promoted it, and eventually performed more than 3500 operations himself, including one on John F. Kennedy's sister Rosemary. Similarly, thousands of lobotomies were performed in Canada during the same time period (Simmons, 1987). The procedure, which had been intended to reduce a patient's emotional symptoms without impairing intellectual ability, tragically left many patients apathetic, withdrawn, and unable to care for themselves (Valenstein, 1986). Despite Freeman's reckless adaptation and administration of the original leukotomy procedure, Moniz won a Nobel Prize for his work.

Today, psychosurgery is rare, but some neurosurgeons have not given up on the effort to cure mental illness by operating on the brain. Some are burning holes in the frontal lobes of the brain (cingulotomies) as a last resort on people with intractable cases of obsessive-compulsive disorder and severe depression, people who have not responded to drugs or psychotherapy (Cosgrove & Rauch, 2003). Unfortunately, reports of success are largely anecdotal and no controlled studies have been conducted on any of the new forms of psychosurgery (Lopes et al., 2004).

Instead of operating on the brain, therefore, other psychiatrists and neurologists prefer to stimulate it electrically. The oldest method is **electroconvulsive therapy (ECT)**, or "shock therapy," which is used for the treatment of severe depression, although no one knows how or why it works. An electrode is placed on one side of the head (rarely on both), and a brief current is turned on. The current triggers a seizure that typically lasts one minute, causing the body to convulse. Today, unlike in the past, patients are given muscle relaxants and anesthesia, so they sleep through the procedure and their convulsions are minimized. ECT has helped some people who are suicidal and who have not responded to medication or any other treatments. The World Psychiatric Association has endorsed ECT as safe and effective, especially for people with crippling depression and suicidal impulses and for those who have not responded to other treatments (Shorter & Healy, 2008). However, the mood-improving effect of ECT is usually short-lived, and the depression almost always returns within a few weeks or months (Hollon, Thase, & Markowitz, 2002). And ECT is ineffective with other disorders, such as schizophrenia or alcoholism, though it is occasionally misused for these conditions. Critics of ECT have long argued that the method is often used improperly and that it can in fact damage the brain and impair memory. However, it is largely accepted that ECT works, even if its mechanism of action is poorly understood, and its practice is still accepted by the Canadian Psychiatric Association (Flint & Gagnon, 2002).

While this debate continues, researchers are looking for milder ways to electrically stimulate the brains of severely depressed individuals. One method, transcranial magnetic stimulation (TMS), involves the use of a pulsing magnetic coil held to a person's skull over the left prefrontal cortex. This area of the brain is less active in people with depression, and repeated TMS seems to give it a boost. The patient stays awake, and the procedure does not cause memory loss or other side effects (Wasserman & Lisanby, 2001). In one well-controlled study of depressed patients who had not improved on medication, those who were given TMS treatments every day for four weeks were more likely to improve than those given a "sham" treatment with no stimulation (Fitzgerald et al., 2003). Nonetheless, as yet, no one knows why magnetic stimulation might ease a patient's emotional suffering. It is still experimental, and since claims of its success are based only on patients' self-reports, the powerful placebo effect of surgery cannot be ruled out (Lozano et al., 2008). The company that developed this $25,000-per-patient device has hired psychiatrists to lobby for it, mounted a vigorous marketing campaign to get it approved, and funded virtually all of the so-far unsuccessful efforts to show that it works (Barglow, 2008).

---

quickQUIZ

✔ Quick Review on **MyPsychLab**

No amount of electric shock will stimulate test-taking ability.

1. Match these treatments with the problems for which they are typically used.
   i. antipsychotic drugs
   ii. antidepressant drugs
   iii. lithium carbonate
   iv. electroconvulsive therapy
   a. suicidal depression
   b. bipolar disorder
   c. schizophrenia
   d. depression and anxiety
   e. obsessive-compulsive disorder

2. Give four reasons to be cautious about claims that drugs for psychological disorders are miracle cures.

3. Tanya has had occasional episodes of depression that seem to be getting worse. Her physician prescribes an antidepressant. Before taking it, what questions should Tanya ask herself and the doctor?

Answers:

1. i. c ii. d, e iii. b iv. a 2. Placebo effects are common; dropout and relapse rates are high; appropriate dosages can be difficult to determine and can vary by sex, age, and ethnicity; and some drugs have unknown or long-term risks. 3. Has the physician prescribed the drug without taking her full medical and psychological history? Has the physician considered other possible reasons for her depression? Would psychotherapy be appropriate, either with or without medication? Does the medication have any unpleasant side effects or long-term risks? Will the doctor continue to monitor her reactions to the drug on a regular basis?

◆ YOU are about to learn . . .

- the major approaches to psychotherapy.
- how behaviour therapists can help you change bad habits and cognitive therapists can help you get rid of self-defeating thoughts.
- why humanist and existential therapists focus on the "here and now" instead of the "why and how."
- the benefits of treating a whole family instead of only one of its members.

KINDS OF PSYCHOTHERAPY

All good psychotherapists want to help clients think about their lives in new ways and find solutions to the problems that plague them. In this section we will consider the major schools of psychotherapy. To illustrate the philosophy and methods of each one, we will focus on a fictional fellow named Murray. Murray is a smart guy whose problem is all too familiar to many students: He procrastinates. He just can't seem to settle down and write his term papers. He keeps getting incompletes, and before long the incompletes turn to F's. Why does Murray procrastinate, manufacturing his own misery? What kind of therapy might help him?

Psychodynamic Therapy

psychoanalysis A theory of personality and a method of psychotherapy, originally formulated by Sigmund Freud, that emphasizes unconscious motives and conflicts.

transference In psychodynamic therapies, a critical process in which the client transfers unconscious emotions or reactions, such as emotional feelings about his or her parents, onto the therapist.

Sigmund Freud was the father of the "talking cure," as one of his patients called it. In his method of **psychoanalysis**, patients talk not about their immediate problems but about their dreams and their memories of childhood. Freud believed that intensive analysis of these dreams and memories would give patients insight into the unconscious reasons for their symptoms. With insight and emotional release, the person's symptoms would disappear.

In orthodox psychoanalysis, which is rarely practised today, the client meets with the therapist as often as several times a week for a period of years. The client lies on a sofa, with the analyst sitting out of view, and says whatever comes to mind without censoring, a technique called *free association.* The analyst listens to the client's free associations and dreams, but rarely comments. There is no rush to solve the problem that brought the client into therapy. In fact, a person may come in complaining of a symptom, such as anxiety or headaches, and the therapist may not get around to that symptom for months or even years. The analyst views the symptom as only the tip of the mental iceberg.

Freud's psychoanalytic method has evolved into many different *psychodynamic therapies,* which share the goal of exploring the unconscious dynamics of personality, such as defences and conflicts (see Chapter 13). Proponents of these therapies often refer to them as *"depth" therapies* because the goal is to delve into the deep, unconscious processes believed to be the source of the patient's problems, rather than to concentrate on "superficial" symptoms and conscious beliefs. As we saw in Chapter 13, one modern psychodynamic approach is based on object-relations theory, which emphasizes the unconscious influence of people's earliest mental representations of their parents and how these affect reactions to separations and losses throughout life.

Psychodynamic therapists emphasize the clinical importance of transference, the process by which the client transfers emotional feelings toward other important people in his or her life (usually the parents) onto the therapist. Therapists know that "love's arrow" isn't really intended for them!

A major element of most psychodynamic therapies, from Freudian to present forms, is transference, the client's transfer (displacement) of emotional elements of his or her inner life—usually feelings about the client's parents—outward onto the analyst. Have you ever found yourself responding to a new acquaintance with unusually quick affection or dislike, and later realized it was because the person reminded you of a relative whom you loved or loathed? That experience is similar to transference. In therapy, a woman who has failed to resolve her Oedipal love for her father might believe she has fallen in love with the analyst. A man who is unconsciously angry at his mother for rejecting him might become furious with his analyst for going on vacation. Through analysis of transference in the therapy setting, psychodynamic therapists believe, clients can see their emotional conflicts in action and work through them (Schafer, 1992; Westen, 1998). Experimental studies have found that transference is not limited to psychotherapy; mental representations of significant others are stored in memory and are often activated in new encounters (Andersen & Berk, 1998; Andersen & Chen, 2002).

Today, most psychodynamic therapists reject the orthodox psychoanalytic approach of having the silent analyst listen to a client free associating. They face the client, they are more goal directed, and they limit therapy to a specific number of sessions, say, 10 or 20. Perhaps they might help our friend Murray gain the insight that he procrastinates as a way of expressing anger toward his parents. He might realize that he is angry because they insist that he study for a career he dislikes. Ideally, Murray will come to this insight by himself. If the analyst suggests it, Murray might feel too defensive to accept it.

Behaviour and Cognitive Therapy

Unlike psychodynamic therapists, psychologists who practise behaviour therapy or cognitive therapy would not worry much about Murray's past, his parents, or his unconscious anxieties. Psychologists who practise behaviour therapy would get right to the problem: What are the reinforcers in Murray's environment that are maintaining his behaviour? "Mur," they would say, "forget about insight. You have lousy study habits." Psychologists who practise cognitive therapy would focus on helping Murray understand how his beliefs about studying, writing papers, and success are woefully unrealistic. Often these two approaches are combined.

BEHAVIOURAL TECHNIQUES. Behaviour therapy is based on applied behavioural analysis, the application of techniques derived from the behavioural principles of classical and operant conditioning that we discussed in Chapter 7. (You may want to review those principles before going on.) Here are some of these methods (Kazdin, 2001; Martin & Pear, 2007):

1 **Exposure.** The most widely used behavioural approach for treating fears and panic is graduated exposure. When people are afraid of some situation, object, or upsetting memory, they usually do everything they can to avoid confronting or thinking of it. Naturally, this only makes the fear worse. Exposure treatments, either in the client's imagination or in actual situations, are aimed at reversing this tendency. In graduated exposure, the client controls the degree of confrontation with the source of the fear. For example, someone who is trying to avoid thinking of a traumatic event might be asked to imagine the event over and over, until it no longer evokes the same degree of panic. A more dramatic form of exposure is flooding, in which the therapist takes the client directly into the feared situation and remains there until the client's panic and anxiety decline. Thus a person suffering from agoraphobia might be taken into a department store or a subway, an action that would normally be terrifying to contemplate. Notice how different this approach is from the psychodynamic one, in which the goal is to uncover the presumably unconscious reason that the agoraphobic feels afraid of going out.

2 **Systematic desensitization.** Systematic desensitization is an older behavioural method, a step-by-step process of breaking down a client's conditioned associations with a feared object or experience (Wolpe, 1958). It is based on the classical-conditioning procedure of *counterconditioning*, in which a stimulus (such as a dog) for an unwanted response (such as fear) is paired with some other stimulus or situation that elicits a response incompatible with the undesirable one (see Chapter 7). In this case, the incompatible response is usually relaxation. The client learns to relax

behaviour therapy A form of therapy that applies principles of classical and operant conditioning to help people change self-defeating or problematic behaviours.

graduated exposure In behaviour therapy, a method in which a person suffering from a phobia or panic attacks is gradually taken into the feared situation or exposed to a traumatic memory until the anxiety subsides.

flooding In behaviour therapy, a form of exposure treatment in which the client is taken directly into the feared situation and remains there until his or her panic subsides.

systematic desensitization In behaviour therapy, a step-by-step process of desensitizing a client to a feared object or experience; it is based on the classical-conditioning procedure of counterconditioning.

In this virtual reality version of systematic desensitization, people with spider phobias are gradually exposed to computerized but extremely lifelike images of spiders in a realistic, three-dimensional environment (Wiederhold & Wiederhold, 2000).

deeply while imagining or looking at a sequence of feared stimuli, arranged in a hierarchy from the least frightening to the most frightening. The hierarchy itself is provided by the client. The sequence for a person who is terrified of spiders might be to read the classic children's story *Charlotte's Web*, then look at pictures of small, cute spiders, then look at pictures of tarantulas, then move on to observing a real spider, and so on. At each step the person must become relaxed before going on. Eventually, the fear responses are extinguished.

Some behaviour therapists have developed virtual-reality (VR) programs to desensitize clients to various phobias, notably of flying, heights, spiders, and public speaking, and to help clients reduce anxiety (Gregg & Tarrier, 2007). Others are experimenting with VR to treat combat veterans who are suffering from intractable posttraumatic stress symptoms. In a program called Virtual Iraq, vets get a combination of exposure and desensitization. They wear a helmet with video goggles and earphones to hear the sounds of war, and then play a modified version of the VR game Full Spectrum Warrior adapted to the Iraq experience (Halpern, 2008).

3   Behavioural self-monitoring. Before people can change their behaviour, they have to identify the reinforcers that are supporting their unwanted habits: attention from others, temporary relief from tension or unhappiness, or tangible rewards such as money or a good meal. One way to do this is through **behavioural self-monitoring**, in which the client keeps a record of the behaviour that he or she wishes to change. A man who wants to curb his overeating may not be aware of how much he eats throughout the day to relieve tension; a behavioural record might show that he eats more junk food than he realized in the late afternoon. A mother might complain that her child "always" has temper tantrums; a behavioural record will show when, where, and with whom they occur. Once the unwanted behaviour is identified, along with the reinforcers that have been maintaining it, a treatment program can be designed to change it. For instance, the man might find other ways to reduce stress and make sure that he is nowhere near junk food in the late afternoon. The mother can learn to respond to her child's tantrum not with her attention (or a cookie to buy silence) but with a time-out: banishing the child to a corner where no positive reinforcers are available.

4   Skills training. It is not enough to tell someone "Don't be shy" if the person does not know how to make small talk with others, or "Don't yell!" if the person does not know how to express feelings calmly. Therefore, some behaviour therapists use operant-conditioning techniques, modelling, and role-playing to teach the skills a client might lack. For example, a shy person might learn how to converse in social settings by focusing on other people rather than on his or her own insecurity. **Skills-training** programs have been designed for all kinds of behavioural problems, such as teaching parents how to discipline their children, impulsive adults how to manage anger, and people with schizophrenia how to get along in the world. These skills are also being taught in virtual worlds, such as Second Life. After face-to-face sessions with a therapist, the client creates an avatar to explore a virtual environment and experiment with new behaviours; the therapist can be monitoring the client's psychological and even physiological reactions at the same time. One widely used

behavioural self-monitoring In behaviour therapy, a method of keeping careful data on the frequency and consequences of the behaviour to be changed.

skills training In behaviour therapy, an effort to teach the client skills that he or she may lack, as well as new constructive behaviours to replace self-defeating ones.

CURE YOUR FEARS

In Chapter 15, a Get Involved exercise asked you to identify your greatest fear. Now see whether systematic desensitization procedures will help you conquer it. Write down a list of situations that evoke your fear, starting with one that produces little anxiety (e.g., seeing a photo of a tiny spider) and ending with the most frightening one possible (e.g., looking at live tarantulas at the pet store). Then find a quiet room where you will have no distractions or interruptions, sit in a comfortable reclining chair, and relax all the muscles of your body. Breathe slowly and deeply. Imagine the first, easiest scene, remaining as relaxed as possible. Do this until you can confront the image without becoming the least bit anxious. When that happens, go on to the next scene in your hierarchy. Do not try this all at once; space out your sessions over time. Does it work?

therapy for autistic children applies principles of operant conditioning to reduce the child's inappropriate or self-destructive behaviour and help the child acquire specific social and linguistic skills (Green, 1996a, 1996b).

A behaviourist would treat Murray's procrastination in several ways. Murray might not know how he actually spends his time when he is avoiding his studies. Afraid that he hasn't time to do everything, he does nothing. Monitoring his own behaviour with a diary would let Murray know exactly how he spends his time, and how much time he should realistically allot to a project. Instead of having a vague, impossibly huge goal, such as "I'm going to reorganize my life," Murray would establish specific small goals, such as reading the two books necessary for an English paper and writing one page of an assignment. If Murray does not know how to write clearly, however, even writing one page might feel overwhelming; he might also need some skills training, such as a basic composition class. Most important, the therapist would change the reinforcers that are maintaining Murray's "procrastination behaviour"—perhaps the immediate gratification of partying with friends—and replace them with reinforcers for getting the work done.

COGNITIVE TECHNIQUES. As we saw in Chapter 11, gloomy thoughts can generate an array of negative emotions and self-defeating behaviours. The underlying premise of cognitive therapy is that constructive thinking can do the opposite, reducing or dispelling anger, fear, and depression. This is not a new idea. It originated 2000 years ago, with the Stoic philosophers, and was popularized in North America in the "mind cure" movement of the nineteenth century (Caplan, 1998). Cognitive therapists help clients identify the beliefs and expectations that might be unnecessarily prolonging their unhappiness, conflicts, and other problems (Persons, Davidson, & Tompkins, 2001). Clients examine the evidence for their beliefs—say, that everyone is mean and selfish, that ambition is hopeless, or that love is doomed. They learn to consider other explanations for the behaviour of people who annoy them: for example, perhaps their father's strict discipline was intended not to control but to protect them. By requiring people to identify their assumptions and biases,

cognitive therapy A form of therapy designed to identify and change irrational, unproductive ways of thinking and, hence, to reduce negative emotions

Cognitive therapists encourage clients to emphasize the positive (the early sunny signs of spring) rather than always focusing on the negative (the lingering icy clutch of winter). Poet Michael Casey described the first daffodil that bravely rises through the snow as "a gleam of laughter in a sullen face."

◆ **Research**
Albert Ellis

examine the evidence, and consider other interpretations, cognitive therapy, as you can see, teaches critical thinking.

One of the best-known contemporary schools of cognitive therapy is Albert Ellis's rational emotive behaviour therapy (REBT) (Ellis, 1993; Ellis & Blau, 1998). In this approach, which reflects Ellis's own no-nonsense, get-on-with-it attitude, the therapist uses rational arguments to directly challenge a client's unrealistic beliefs or expectations. Ellis has pointed out that people who are emotionally upset often *over-generalize*: They decide that one annoying act by someone means that person is totally bad in every way, or that a normal mistake they made is evidence that they are rotten to the core. Many people also *catastrophize*, transforming a small problem into disaster: "I failed this test, and now I'll flunk out of school, and no one will ever like me, and even my cat will hate me, and I'll never get a job." Ellis also observed that many people drive themselves crazy with notions of what they "must" do. The therapist challenges these thoughts directly, showing the client why they are irrational and misguided.

◆ **Research**
Aaron Beck

Another leading form of cognitive therapy, devised by Aaron Beck (1976, 2005), avoids direct challenges to the client's beliefs. Beck pioneered the application of cognitive therapy for depression. As we saw in Chapter 16, depression often arises from specific pessimistic thoughts—for example, that the sources of your misery are permanent and that nothing good will ever happen to you again. For Beck, these beliefs are not "irrational"; rather, they are unproductive or based on misinformation. A therapist using Beck's approach would ask you to test your beliefs against the evidence. If you say, "But I *know* no one likes me," the therapist might say, "Oh, yes? How do you know? Do you really not have a single friend? Has anyone in the past year been nice to you?"

Similarly, the University of Waterloo's Donald Meichenbaum developed a form of cognitive-behaviour therapy called "stress inoculation" to treat anxiety (Meichenbaum & Deffenbacher, 1988). Some degree of anxiety is normal—and sometimes even helpful. When imagining ourselves dealing with a difficult task, most of us will feel some anxiety. This anxiety can help motivate us, and perhaps even help us perform better than we would have had we been more relaxed. However, excessive anxiety can be crippling, keeping us from working efficiently and finishing our projects. Stress inoculation training was designed to reduce anxiety in both academic settings, especially in taking tests, and nonacademic settings. It consists of three stages. During the *education phase*, the individual is taught about the nature of anxiety, and

rational emotive behaviour therapy (REBT) A form of cognitive therapy devised by Albert Ellis, designed to challenge the client's unrealistic thoughts.

Get INVOLVED!

MIND OVER MOOD

◉ **Watch**
Cognitive Behavioural Therapy

See whether cognitive-therapy techniques can help you control your moods. Think of a time recently when you felt a particularly strong emotion, such as depression, anger, or anxiety. On a piece of paper, record (1) the situation—who was there, what happened, and when; (2) the intensity of your feeling at the time, from weak to strong; and (3) the thoughts that were going through your mind (e.g., "She never cares about what I want to do"; "He's going to leave me").

Now examine your thoughts. What is the worst thing that could happen if those thoughts are true? Are your thoughts accurate or are you "mind-reading" another person's intentions and motives? Is there another way to think about this situation or the other person's behaviour? If you practise this exercise repeatedly, you may learn how your thoughts affect your moods—and find out that you have more control over your feelings than you realized (Greenberger & Padesky, 1995).

the client and therapist work together to identify the situations that generate anxiety for the client. In the *rehearsal phase*, the person is taught how to better manage anxiety, and he or she practises being exposed to threatening situations in safe surroundings. During the *implementation phase*, the client deals with anxiety-provoking stimuli in real-world situations. Stress inoculation has become a widely accepted technique for controlling anxiety.

A cognitive therapist might treat Murray's procrastination by having Murray write down his thoughts about work, read the thoughts as if someone else had said them, and then write a rational response to each one. This technique would encourage Murray to examine the validity of his assumptions and beliefs. Many procrastinators are perfectionists; if they cannot do something perfectly, they will not do it at all. Unable to accept their limitations, they set impossible standards and catastrophize:

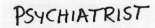

Negative Thought	Rational Response
If I don't get an A+ on this paper, my life will be ruined.	My life will be a lot worse if I keep getting incompletes. It's better to get a B or even a C than to do nothing.
My professor is going to think I'm an idiot when he reads this. I'll feel humiliated by his criticism.	He hasn't accused me of being an idiot yet. If he makes some criticisms, I can learn from them and do better next time.

Strict behaviourists consider thoughts to be "behaviours" that are modifiable by learning principles; they do not regard thoughts themselves as causes of behaviour. But most psychologists believe that thoughts and behaviour influence each other, which is why cognitive-behaviour therapy (CBT) is more common than either cognitive or behaviour therapy alone. In recent years, some CBT practitioners, inspired by Eastern philosophies such as Buddhism, have begun to question the goal of changing a client's self-defeating thoughts. They argue that it is difficult if not impossible to get rid of unwanted thoughts and feelings, especially when people have been rehearsing them for years. They therefore propose a form of CBT based on "mindfulness" and "acceptance": Clients learn to explicitly identify and accept whatever negative thoughts and feelings arise, without trying to eradicate them or letting them derail healthy behaviour (Hayes, Follette, & Linehan, 2004). For example, instead of trying to persuade a client who is afraid of making public speeches that her fear is irrational, therapists who adopt this approach would encourage her to accept the anxious thoughts and feelings without judging them—or herself—harshly. Then she can focus on coping techniques and ways of giving speeches despite her anxiety.

Humanist and Existential Therapy

Humanist therapy, like its parent philosophy humanism, starts from the assumption that human nature is basically good and that people behave badly or develop problems when

humanist therapy A form of psychotherapy based on the philosophy of humanism, which emphasizes the client's free will to change rather than past conflicts.

Humanist therapists emphasize the importance of warmth, concern, and empathic listening to the client.

they are warped by self-imposed limits. Humanist therapists, therefore, want to know how clients subjectively see their own situations and how they construe the world around them. These therapists generally do not dig into the client's past but instead focus on helping the person develop the will and confidence to change and achieve his or her goals. That is why these therapists explore what is going on "here and now," not past issues of "why and how."

In **client-centred (nondirective) therapy,** developed by Carl Rogers, the therapist's role is to listen to the client's needs in an accepting, nonjudgmental way and offer what Rogers called *unconditional positive regard* (see Chapter 13). Whatever the client's specific complaint is, the goal is to build the client's self-esteem and self-acceptance and help the client find a more productive way of seeing his or her problems. Thus a Rogerian might assume that Murray's procrastination masks his low self-regard and that Murray is out of touch with his real feelings and wishes. Perhaps he is not passing his courses because he is trying to please his parents by majoring in pre-law, when secretly he would rather become an artist.

Rogers (1951, 1961) believed that effective therapists must be warm and genuine. For Rogerians, *empathy*, the therapist's ability to understand and accept what the client says, is the crucial ingredient of successful therapy. The therapist shows a basic level of empathy by listening carefully and being able to restate the client's remarks accurately: "You tell me that you feel frustrated, Murray, because no matter how hard you try, you don't succeed." And the therapist shows advanced empathy by understanding the *meaning* of the client's remarks: "Working that hard without results must really make you unhappy and maybe make you feel a bit sorry for yourself." The client, according to humanist therapists, will eventually internalize the therapist's support and become more self-accepting.

Existential therapy helps clients explore the meaning of existence and face with courage the great questions of life, such as death, freedom, alienation from oneself and others, loneliness, and meaninglessness. Existential therapists, like humanist therapists, believe that our lives are not inevitably determined by our pasts or our circumstances; we have the power and free will to choose our own destinies. As Irvin Yalom (1989) explained, "The crucial first step in therapy is the patient's assumption of responsibility for his or her life predicament. As long as one believes that one's problems are caused by some force or agency outside oneself, there is no leverage in therapy."

Yalom argues that the goal of therapy is to help clients cope with the inescapable realities of life and death and the struggle for meaning. However grim our experiences may be, he believes, "they contain the seeds of wisdom and redemption." Perhaps the most remarkable example of a man able to find seeds of wisdom in a barren landscape was Victor Frankl (1905–1997), who developed a form of existential therapy after surviving a Nazi concentration camp. In that pit of horror, Frankl (1955) observed, some people maintained their sanity because they were able to find meaning in the experience, shattering though it was.

Some observers believe that, ultimately, all therapies are existential. In different ways, therapy helps people determine what is important to them, what values guide them, and what changes they will have the courage to make. An existential therapist might help Murray think about the significance of his procrastination, what his ultimate goals in life are, and how he might find the strength to carry out his ambitions.

Family and Couples Therapy

Murray's situation is getting worse. His father has begun to call him Tomorrow Man, which upsets his mother, and his younger brother, the math major, has been calculating how much tuition money Murray's incompletes are costing. His older sister, Isabel, the biochemist who's never had an incomplete in her life, now proposes that they all go to a family therapist. "Murray's not the only one in this family with complaints," she says.

client-centred (nondirective) therapy A humanist approach, devised by Carl Rogers, which emphasizes the therapist's empathy with the client and the use of unconditional positive regard.

existential therapy A form of therapy designed to help clients explore the meaning of existence and face the great questions of life, such as death, freedom, alienation, and loneliness.

A practitioner of *family therapy* would maintain that Murray's problem developed in the context of his family, that it is sustained by the dynamics of his family, and that any change he makes will affect all members of his family (McDaniel, Lusterman, & Philpot, 2001; Nichols & Schwartz, 2008). One of the most famous early family therapists, Salvador Minuchin (1984), compared the family to a kaleidoscope, a changing pattern of mosaics in which the pattern is larger than any one piece. In this view, efforts to isolate and treat one member of the family without the others are doomed. Only if all family members reveal their differing perceptions of each other can mistakes and misperceptions be identified. A teenager, for instance, may see his mother as crabby and nagging when actually she is tired and worried. A parent may see a child as rebellious when in fact the child is lonely and desperate for attention.

Family members are usually unaware of how they influence one another. By observing the entire family, the family therapist hopes to discover tensions and imbalances in power and communication. For example, in some families a child may have a chronic illness or a psychological problem, such as anorexia, that affects the workings of the whole family. One parent may become overinvolved with the sick child while the other parent retreats, and each may start blaming the other. The child, in turn, may cling to the illness or disorder as a way of expressing anger, keeping the parents together, getting the parents' attention, or asserting control.

Some family therapists look for patterns of behaviour across generations. The therapist and client may create a family tree showing psychologically significant events across as many generations as possible (McGoldrick, Gerson, & Shellenberger, 1999). This method may reveal historical patterns, as you can see in Figure 16.1.

Some family therapists use photographs to help people identify themes and problems in their family histories. Does this picture convey a happy and cohesive family to you or a divided one? Shortly after it was taken, the couple divorced; the father took custody of the children . . . and the mother kept the dog (Entin, 1992).

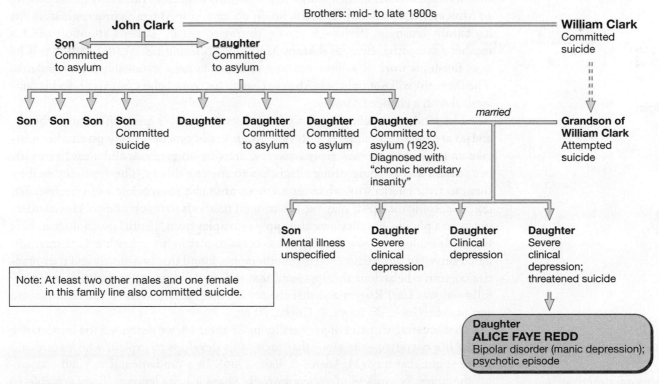

FIGURE 16.1 One Family's History of Mental Illness

Family trees of mental disorders can reveal patterns across generations. Alice Faye Redd was convicted of defrauding elderly investors of $10 million, money she then lost in lavish spending and extravagant investment schemes. Prosecution and defence psychiatrists agreed that she suffered from bipolar disorder. Alice Redd's daughter constructed this multigenerational family record of depression and suicide in an effort to have her mother committed for treatment, but the court sentenced Redd to 15 years in prison.

Even when it is not possible to treat the whole family, some therapists will treat individuals in a **family-systems perspective**, which recognizes that people's behaviour in a family is as interconnected as that of two dancers (Bowen, 1978; Cox & Paley, 2003). Clients learn that if they change in any way, even for the better, their families may protest noisily or may send subtle messages that read, "Change back!" Why? Because when one family member changes, each of the others must change too. As the saying goes, it takes two to tango, and if one dancer stops, so must the other. But most people do not like change. They are comfortable with old patterns and habits, even those that cause them trouble. They want to keep dancing the same old dance, even if their feet hurt.

When members of a couple argue frequently about issues that never seem to get resolved, they may be best helped by going together to *couples therapy*, which is designed to help couples manage the inevitable conflicts that occur in all relationships (Christensen & Jacobson, 2000). Couples therapists generally insist on seeing both partners so that they will hear both sides of the story. They cut through the blaming and attacking ("She never listens to me!" "He never does anything!") and instead focus on helping the couple resolve their differences, get over hurt and blame, and make specific behavioural changes to reduce anger and conflict. Recently, however, many couples therapists have been moving away from the "fix all the differences" approach and are instead helping couples learn to accept and live with qualities in both partners that aren't going to change much (Hayes, 2004). For example, a wife can stop trying to turn her calm, steady husband into a spontaneous adventurer ("After all, that's what I originally loved about him—he's as steady as a rock") and a husband can stop trying to make his shy wife more assertive ("I have always loved her remarkable serenity").

Family and couples therapists may use psychodynamic, behavioural, cognitive, or humanist approaches in their work; they share only a focus on the family or the couple. In Murray's case, a family therapist would observe how Murray's procrastination fits his family dynamics. Perhaps it allows Murray to get his father's attention and his mother's sympathy. Perhaps it keeps Murray from facing his greatest fear: that if he does finish his work, it will not measure up to his father's impossibly high standards. The therapist will not only help Murray change his work habits, but also help his family deal with a changed Murray.

The kinds of psychotherapy we have discussed are all quite different in theory, and so are their techniques (see Review 16.2). Yet in practice, many psychotherapists take an *integrative approach to psychotherapy*, drawing on methods and ideas from various schools and avoiding strong allegiances to any one theory. This flexibility enables them to treat clients with whatever methods are most appropriate and effective. For example, some therapists may use behavioural methods to quickly help a client suffering from a phobia, but they may also apply principles from "depth" psychology to help the client explore the role the phobia has come to play in his or her life. One internet-based survey of more than 2400 psychotherapists found that two-thirds said they practise cognitive-behaviour therapy—and that the single most influential therapist they followed was Carl Rogers and that they often incorporate ideas of mindfulness and acceptance (Cook, Biyanova, & Coyne, 2009).

In discussing theories of personality in Chapter 14, we described the importance of the life narrative—the story that each of us develops to explain who we are and how we got that way (McAdams & Pals, 2006). In a fundamental way, all successful therapies, regardless of their approach, share a key element: They are able to motivate the client into wanting to change, and they replace a client's pessimistic or unrealistic life narrative with one that is more hopeful or attainable (Howard, 1991; Schafer, 1992).

◉ **Watch**
Family Therapist

family-systems perspective An approach to doing therapy with individuals or families by identifying how each family member forms part of a larger interacting system.

REVieW 16.2

The Major Schools of Therapy Compared

	Primary Goal	Methods
Psychodynamic	Insight into unconscious motives and feelings that prolong symptoms	Probing unconscious motives, examining the process of transference, exploring childhood experiences
Cognitive-Behavioural		
Behavioural	Modification of self-defeating behaviours	Graduated exposure (flooding), systematic desensitization, behavioural records, skills training
Cognitive	Modification of irrational or unvalidated beliefs	Prompting the client to test beliefs against evidence; exposing the faulty reasoning in catastrophizing and mind-reading; sometimes helping the client accept unpleasant thoughts and feelings and live with them
Humanist and Existential		
Humanist	Insight; self-acceptance and self-fulfillment; new, optimistic perceptions of oneself and the world	Providing a nonjudgmental setting in which to discuss issues; use of empathy and unconditional positive regard by the therapist
Existential	Finding meaning in life and accepting inevitable losses	Varies with the therapist; philosophic discussions about the meaning of life, the client's goals, finding the courage to survive loss and suffering
Family and Couples		
Family	Modification of family patterns	May use any of the preceding methods to change family patterns that perpetuate problems and conflicts
Couples	Resolution of conflicts, breaking out of destructive habits	May use any of the preceding methods to help the couple communicate better, resolve conflicts, or accept what cannot be changed

✴ Explore
Key Components of Therapies

Don't be a procrastinator like our friend Murray; take this quiz now.

Match each method or concept with the therapy associated with it.

1. transference
2. systematic desensitization
3. facing the fear of death
4. reappraisal of thoughts
5. unconditional positive regard
6. exposure to feared situation
7. avoidance of "catastrophizing"
8. analysis of generational patterns

a. cognitive therapy
b. psychodynamic therapy
c. humanist therapy
d. behaviour therapy
e. family therapy
f. existential therapy

quickQUIZ

✔•⟦Quick Review on **MyPsychLab**

Answers:

1.b 2.d 3.f 4.a 5.c 6.d 7.a 8.e

YOU are about to learn . . .

- the meaning of "scientist–practitioner gap" and why it has been widening.
- which form of psychotherapy is most likely to help if you are anxious or depressed.
- why psychotherapy can sometimes be harmful.

EVALUATING PSYCHOTHERAPY

Poor Murray! He is getting a little baffled by all these therapies. He wants to make a choice soon; there's no sense in procrastinating about that, too! Is there any scientific evidence, he wonders, that might help him decide which therapy—or therapist—will be best for him?

Psychotherapy is, first and foremost, a relationship. Its success depends on the bond the therapist and client establish between them, called the **therapeutic alliance**. When both parties respect and understand each other and agree on the goals of treatment, the client is more likely to improve, regardless of the specific techniques the therapist uses (Klein et al., 2003).

 # CULTURE and *Psychotherapy*

Does a Therapist–Client "Match" Matter?

Many therapists and clients establish successful therapeutic alliances in spite of coming from different backgrounds. But sometimes cultural differences cause misunderstandings that result from ignorance or prejudice (Comas-Dìaz, 2006; Sue et al., 2007). A lifetime of experience with racism and a general "cultural distrust" may keep some indigenous peoples of Canada from revealing feelings that they believe a white therapist would not understand or accept (Whaley & Davis, 2007). Similarly, indigenous Canadian therapists frequently have to deal with clients who are uncomfortable with them. Misunderstandings and prejudice may be one reason why clients are more likely to stay in therapy when their therapists' ethnicity matches their own. If such clients stay in therapy and do not drop out early, however, most are as likely to do as well with an "unmatched" therapist as with a matched one. But a cultural "match" is also important because it often makes it more likely that clients and therapists share perceptions of what the client's problem is, agree on the best way of coping, and have the same expectations about what therapy can accomplish (Zone et al., 2005).

In establishing a bond with clients, therapists must distinguish normal cultural patterns from individual psychological problems. An Irish-American family therapist, Monica McGoldrick (2005), described some problems that are typical of Irish-American families. These problems arise from Irish history and religious beliefs, and they are deeply ingrained. "In general, the therapist cannot expect the family to turn into a physically affectionate, emotionally intimate group, or to enjoy being in therapy very much," she observed. "The notion of Original Sin—that you are guilty before you are born—leaves them with a heavy sense of burden. Someone not sensitized to these issues may see this as pathological. It is not. But it is also not likely to change and the therapist should help the family tolerate this inner guilt rather than try to get rid of it."

However, therapy is not always a one-on-one interaction. Group therapies are often employed, particularly with some cultural groups. In Canada, group therapy has been a particularly popular approach with indigenous Canadian clients, in part

therapeutic alliance The bond of confidence and mutual understanding established between therapist and client, which allows them to work together to solve the client's problems.

because the practice bears more similarity to traditional healing practices in these groups. However, the composition of a group structured in a manner that mirrors the social, racial, cultural, and class structure of Euro-Canadian society is problematic for treating relatively traditional indigenous Canadians (Waldram & Wong, 1995).

More and more psychotherapists are becoming "sensitized to the issues" caused by cultural differences (Arredondo et al., 2005; Sue et al., 2007). For example, many Latino and Asian clients are likely to react to a formal interview with a therapist with relative passivity and deference, leading some therapists to misdiagnose this cultural norm as a problem with shyness. In Latin American cultures, *susto*, or "loss of the soul," is a common response to extreme grief or fright; the person believes that his or her soul has departed along with that of the deceased relative. A psychotherapist unfamiliar with this culturally determined response might conclude that the sufferer was delusional or psychotic. Latino clients are also more likely than Anglos to value harmony in their relationships, which often translates into an unwillingness to express negative emotions or confront family members or friends directly, so therapists need to help such clients find ways to communicate better within that cultural context (Arredondo & Perez, 2003).

Being aware of cultural differences, however, does not mean that the therapist should stereotype clients. Some Asians, after all, do have problems with excessive shyness, some Latinos do have emotional disorders, and some Irish do not carry burdens of guilt! It does mean that therapists must ensure that their clients find them to be trustworthy and effective; and it means that clients must be aware of their own prejudices, too.

Some psychotherapists fit their approach to the client's cultural background. "Cuento" (story) therapy is a popular form of therapy among Latino psychotherapists, building as it does on a cultural tradition of storytelling and folk heroes (Comas-Díaz, 2006). For example, most Puerto Rican children know the tales of Juan Bobo (left), a foolish child who is always getting into trouble. The therapists on the right have adapted these stories for Puerto Rican children who are coping with new problems and temptations in North America. The children and their mothers watch a videotape of the folktale, discuss it together, and role-play its major themes, such as controlling aggression and understanding right and wrong. This method has been more successful than traditional therapies in reducing the children's transitional anxieties and improving their attention spans and achievement motivation (Costantino & Malgady, 1996).

The Scientist–Practitioner Gap

Now suppose that Murray has found a nice psychotherapist who seems pretty smart and friendly. Is a good alliance enough? How important is the *kind* of therapy that an individual practises? Have some methods of psychotherapy been scientifically shown to be more effective than others, are some totally useless, and are some potentially harmful?

These questions have generated a huge debate among clinical practitioners and psychological scientists. Many psychotherapists believe that trying to evaluate psychotherapy using standard empirical methods is an exercise in futility: Numbers and graphs, they say, cannot possibly capture the complex exchange that takes place between a therapist and a client. What "works" in psychotherapy is usually not a good technique but a good *relationship*. Psychotherapy, they maintain, is an art that you acquire from clinical experience; it is not a science. You can't measure its effectiveness the way you can measure, say, the effectiveness of a new drug, because so many diverse ingredients go into a good psychotherapeutic experience (Wampold, 2001). Other clinicians fear that efforts to measure the effectiveness of psychotherapy oversimplify the process, because, among other reasons, many patients have an assortment of emotional problems and need therapy for a longer time than research can reasonably allow (Westen, Novotny, & Thompson-Brenner, 2004).

For their part, psychological scientists agree that therapy is often a complex process. But that is no reason it cannot be scientifically investigated, they argue, just like any other complex psychological process such as the development of language or personality (Crits-Christoph, Wilson, & Hollon, 2005; Kazdin, 2008). Moreover, they are concerned that when therapists fail to keep up with empirical findings in the field, their clients may suffer. It is crucial, scientists say, for therapists to be aware of research findings on the most beneficial methods for particular problems, on ineffective or potentially harmful techniques, and on topics relevant to their practice, such as memory, hypnosis, and child development (Lilienfeld, Lynn, & Lohr, 2003).

Over the years, the breach between scientists and therapists has widened, creating what is commonly called the *scientist–practitioner gap*. As we saw in Chapter 1, one reason for the growing split has been the rise of professional schools that are not connected to academic psychology departments and that train students solely to do therapy. Similarly, the popularity of PsyD programs (which de-emphasize the research component of clinical training) is on the rise in the United States, and the Canadian Psychological Association supports the development of similar programs in Canada (Robinson, 1988). Graduates of these schools sometimes know little about research methods or even about research assessing different therapy techniques.

The scientist–practitioner gap has also widened because of the proliferation of new therapies trying to gain a foothold in a crowded market. According to Simon Fraser University's Barry Beyerstein (1999), some of these therapies are packaged and promoted without any scientific support at all. One such therapy, Neurolinguistic Programming (NLP), claims to match people's learning styles with their "brain types" and thereby enhance their communication skills. The U.S. National Research Council concluded that there is no credible evidence for NLP's claims or methods (Druckman & Swets, 1988).

Other therapies repackage established techniques, using a new name and terminology. For example, Eye Movement Desensitization and Reprocessing (EMDR) is built on the tried-and-true behavioural techniques of desensitization and exposure for treating anxiety (Lohr, Tolin, & Lilienfeld, 1998). EMDR's founder, Francine Shapiro (1995), added eye-movement exercises: Clients move their eyes from side to side, following the therapist's moving finger, while concentrating on the memory to be desensitized. Shapiro's (1994) explanation for why such eye movements work is that "the system may become unbalanced due to a trauma or through stress engendered during a developmental window, but once appropriately catalyzed and maintained in a dynamic state by EMDR, it transmutes information to a state of therapeutically appropriate resolution." (If you do not understand that, don't worry; we don't either.)

Thousands of therapists have been trained to do EMDR, and they have claimed success in treating everything from posttraumatic stress disorder and panic attacks to eating disorders and sexual dysfunction. EMDR has even won endorsements from some prominent psychologists. Yet there is no evidence from controlled studies that it is any better than standard exposure treatments (Goldstein et al., 2000; Lohr et al., 1999; Taylor, Thordarson, et al., 2003). One clinical researcher who reviewed the evidence concluded that the eye movements that are supposedly essential to this technique do not constitute "anything more than pseudoscientific window dressing" (Lilienfeld, 1996).

Thinking Critically

Analyze Assumptions and Biases

Many psychotherapists assume that therapy is an art, an exchange between therapist and client whose essence cannot be captured by research. How valid is this assumption? Should consumers assume they can rely on the testimonials of satisfied clients?

Recently, a blue-ribbon panel of clinical scientists, convened to assess the problem of the scientist–practitioner gap for the journal *Psychological Science in the Public Interest*, reported that the current state of clinical psychology is comparable to that of medicine in the early 1900s, when physicians typically valued personal experience over scientific research. The authors wrote, "A promising strategy for improving the quality and clinical and public health impact of clinical psychology is through a new accreditation system that demands high quality science training as a central feature of doctoral training in clinical psychology" (Baker, McFall, & Shoham, 2008). The Academy of Psychological Clinical Science, an alliance of 49 clinical science graduate programs and nine clinical science internships, has begun a concerted effort to institute just such a system (Bootzin, 2009).

PROBLEMS IN ASSESSING THERAPY. Because of the proliferation of therapies, including many that are questionable at best, and because of economic pressures on insurers and rising health costs, clinical psychologists are increasingly being called on to provide empirical assessments of therapy. But you can't just ask people if the therapy helped them, because no matter what kind of therapy is involved, clients are motivated to tell you it worked. "Dr. Blitznik is a genius!" they will exclaim. "I would *never* have taken that job (or moved to Saskatoon, or found my true love) if it hadn't been for Dr. Blitznik!" Every kind of therapy ever devised produces enthusiastic testimonials from people who feel it saved their lives.

The problem with testimonials is that none of us can be our own control group. How do people know they wouldn't have taken the job, moved to Saskatoon, or found true love anyway—maybe even sooner, if Dr. Blitznik had not kept them in treatment? Second, Dr. Blitznik's success could be due to the placebo effect: The client's anticipation of success and the buzz about Dr. B.'s fabulous new method might be the active ingredients, rather than Dr. B.'s therapy itself. And third, notice that you never hear testimonials from the people who dropped out, who weren't helped, or who actually got worse. So researchers cannot be satisfied with testimonials, no matter how glowing. They know that thanks to the *justification of effort* effect (see Chapter 9), people who have put time, money, and effort into something will tell you it was worth it. No one wants to say, "Yeah, I saw Dr. Blitznik for five years, and boy, was it ever a waste of time." To guard against these problems, some clinical researchers conduct **randomized controlled trials**, in which people with a given problem or disorder are randomly assigned to one or more treatment groups or to a control group.

Sometimes the results of randomized controlled trials have been surprising, even shocking. For example, in the aftermath of natural and human-made disasters, such as earthquakes or terrorist attacks, disaster therapists often arrive on the scene to treat survivors for symptoms of trauma, hoping to prevent survivors from later developing posttraumatic stress disorder (PTSD). In one of the most popular interventions, called Critical Incident Stress Debriefing (CISD), survivors gather in a group for "debriefing," which generally lasts from one to three hours. Participants are expected to disclose their thoughts and emotions about the traumatic experience, and the group leader warns members about possible trauma symptoms that might develop.

Several independent investigators have *analyzed the assumptions* that underlie CISD: that a traumatic experience almost invariably causes long-lasting posttraumatic stress disorder (as we saw in Chapter 15, it does not); that venting negative emotions is "cathartic" and helps you "get rid" of them (as we saw in Chapter 11, it often does just the opposite); and that early intervention—getting to survivors in the immediate aftermath of a disaster—is necessary to head off the development of serious PTSD. All of these assumptions seem to be perfectly reasonable, but when psychological

randomized controlled trials Research designed to determine the effectiveness of a new medication or form of therapy, in which people with a given problem or disorder are randomly assigned to one or more treatment groups or to a control group.

FIGURE 16.2 Do Posttraumatic Interventions Help—or Harm?

In this study, victims of serious car accidents were assessed at the time of the event, four months later, and three years later. Half received a form of posttraumatic intervention called Critical Incident Stress Debriefing (CISD); half received no treatment. As you can see, almost everyone had recovered within four months, but one group had higher stress symptoms than everyone else even after three years: the people who were the most emotionally distressed right after the accident *and* who received CISD. The therapy actually impeded their recovery (Mayou, Ehlers, & Hobbs, 2000).

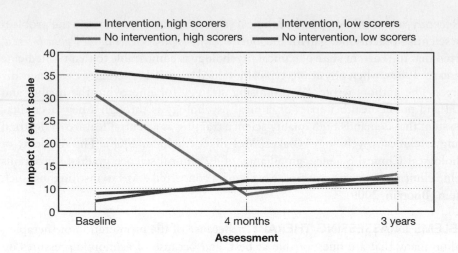

scientists *avoided emotional reasoning* ("It feels reasonable, so it must be true") and *examined the evidence* for the assumptions, they were in for a surprise.

Richard Gist, a community psychologist who works with firefighters and has witnessed many tragedies and disasters in that capacity, investigated the efficacy of debriefing following a plane crash in Sioux City, Iowa, in which 112 of 296 passengers died. Rescue teams faced with the grisly job of recovering bodies were randomly assigned to either CISD or no treatment and were followed up two years later (Gist, Lubin, & Redburn, 1998). The researchers found no evidence that "debriefed" firefighters were doing any better than those who had not had the intervention; in fact, there was a slight but statistically significant trend toward the *worsening* of anxiety symptoms in those who had been in CISD. The rescuers who were doing the best had relied on informal sources of support and help—friends and co-workers who had shared the experience.

Researchers have *considered other explanations* for these findings. Perhaps the results were unique to the kind of disaster or specific to the kinds of survivors, in this case professional firefighters who are used to dealing with traumatic events. But many other studies have replicated and extended these findings with a wide assortment of human tragedies and with all sorts of people, including victims of burns, accidents, miscarriages, violent crimes, and combat (Van Emmerik et al., 2002; McNally, Bryant, & Ehlers, 2003).

For example, in one randomized controlled trial, people who were victims of serious car accidents were followed for three years; some had received the CISD intervention and some had not. As you can see in Figure 16.2, almost everyone had recovered in only four months and remained fine after three years; those who received the intervention actually fared worse on several measures. The researchers, however, *did not oversimplify* their results. They divided the survivors into two groups: those who had had a highly emotional reaction to the accident at the outset ("high scorers"), and those who had not. For the latter group, the intervention made no difference; they improved quickly. But look at what happened to the people who really were quite traumatized by the accident: If they did *not* get CISD, they were fine in four months, too, like everyone else. But for those who *did* get the intervention, CISD actually blocked their improvement, and they had higher stress symptoms than all the others in the study even after three years. The researchers concluded that "psychological debriefing is ineffective and has adverse long-term effects. It is not an appropriate treatment for trauma victims" (Mayou, Ehlers, & Hobbs, 2000). In 2005, the World Health Organization, which deals with survivors of trauma around the world, agreed with this assessment (Van Ommeren, Saxena, & Saraceno, 2005).

◀ⒸSimulate
Ineffective Therapy

You can see, then, why the scientific assessment of psychotherapeutic claims and methods is so important.

When Therapy Helps

We turn now to the evidence showing the benefits of psychotherapy and which therapies work best. There have been a number of important efforts to review the overall effectiveness of different therapeutic approaches for different disorders (e.g., Chambless et al., 1998; Chambless & Ollendick, 2001; Hollon, Thase, & Markowitz, 2002). For many problems and most emotional disorders, cognitive and behaviour therapies have emerged as the method of choice.

♦ *Depression.* Cognitive therapy's greatest success has been in the treatment of mood disorders, especially depression (Beck, 2005). As we saw earlier in this chapter, it is often as effective as antidepressants, and people in cognitive therapy are less likely than those on drugs to relapse when the treatment is over. The reason may be that the lessons learned in cognitive therapy last a long time after treatment, according to follow-ups done from 15 months to many years later (Antonuccio et al., 1999; Hayes et al., 2004; Hollon, Thase, & Markowitz, 2002; McNally, 1994; Seligman et al., 1999).

♦ *Prevention of suicide.* In a randomized controlled study of 120 adults who had attempted suicide and had been sent to a hospital emergency room, those who were given 10 sessions of cognitive therapy, in comparison to those who were simply given the usual follow-up care (being tracked and given referrals for help), were only about half as likely to attempt suicide again in the next 18 months. They also scored significantly lower on tests of depressive mood and hopelessness (Brown et al., 2005).

♦ *Anxiety disorders.* Exposure techniques are more effective than any other treatment for posttraumatic stress disorder, agoraphobia, and specific phobias such as fear of dogs or flying. Cognitive-behaviour therapy is often more effective than medication for panic disorder, generalized anxiety disorder, and obsessive-compulsive disorder (Barlow, 2004; Dalgleish, 2004; Mitte, 2005).

♦ *Anger and impulsive violence.* Cognitive therapy is often successful in reducing chronic anger, abusiveness, and hostility, and it also teaches people how to express anger more calmly and constructively (Deffenbacher et al., 2003; Kassinove, 1995).

♦ *Health problems.* Cognitive and behaviour therapies are highly successful in helping people cope with pain, chronic fatigue syndrome, headaches, and irritable bowel syndrome; quit smoking or overcome other addictions; recover from eating disorders such as bulimia and binge eating; overcome insomnia and improve their sleeping patterns; and manage other health problems (Butler et al., 1991; Crits-Christoph, Wilson, & Hollon, 2005; Skinner et al., 1990; Stepanski & Perlis, 2000; Wilson & Fairburn, 1993).

♦ *Childhood and adolescent behaviour problems.* Behaviour therapy is the most effective treatment for behaviour problems that range from bed-wetting to impulsive anger, and even for problems that have biological origins, such as autism, as we noted earlier. A meta-analysis of more than 100 studies of children and adolescents found that behavioural treatments worked better than others regardless of the child's age, the therapist's experience, or the specific problem (Weisz et al., 1995).

Cognitive-behaviour therapy can help people who are grumpy, bashful, and maybe even dopey—as well as people who have far more serious problems.

THE SEVEN DWARFS AFTER THERAPY

◆ *Relapse prevention.* Cognitive-behaviour approaches have also been highly effective in reducing the rate of relapse among people with problems such as substance abuse, depression, sexual offending, and even schizophrenia (Hayes et al., 2004; Witkiewitz & Marlatt, 2004).

However, no single type of therapy can help everyone. Cognitive-behaviour therapies are designed for specific, identifiable problems, but sometimes people seek therapy for less clearly defined reasons, such as wishing to be introspective about their feelings or explore moral issues. Moreover, in spite of their many successes, behaviour and cognitive therapies have had failures, especially with people who are unmotivated to carry out a behavioural or cognitive program or who have ingrained personality disorders and psychoses.

Sometimes a single session of encouragement and practical advice is enough to bring improvement. A therapy for treating alcohol abuse, *motivational interviewing*, which focuses specifically on increasing a client's motivation to change problem drinking, has been shown to be effective in as few as one or two sessions (Burke, Arkowitz, & Menchola, 2003; Cassin et al., 2008; Miller & Rollnick, 2002). The therapist, essentially, puts the client into a state of cognitive dissonance (see Chapter 9)—"I want to be healthy and I see myself as a smart, competent person, but here I am doing something stupid and self-defeating. Do I want to feel better or not?"—and then offers the client a cognitive and behavioural strategy of improvement (Wagner & Ingersoll, 2008).

Some problems, however, are chronic or particularly difficult to treat and respond better to longer therapy. According to one meta-analysis that included eight randomized controlled studies, long-term psychodynamic therapy (lasting a year or more) can be more effective than short-term approaches for complex mental problems and chronic personality disorders (Leichsenring & Rabung, 2008). And some problems respond better to combined approaches rather than a single one. Young adults with schizophrenia are greatly helped by family intervention therapies that teach parents behavioural skills for dealing with their troubled children, and that educate the family about how to cope with the illness constructively (Chambless et al., 1998; Goldstein & Miklowitz, 1995). In studies over a two-year period, only

30% of the schizophrenic patients in such family interventions relapsed, compared to 65% of those whose families were not involved. The same combined approach—medication and family-focused therapy—also reduces the severity of symptoms in adolescents with bipolar disorder and delays relapses (Miklowitz, 2007). In the treatment of sex offenders, combined methods are essential because of the complex causes of pedophilia, rape, and other sex crimes. One leading approach combines cognitive therapy, behavioural techniques, group therapy, and social-skills training (Abel et al., 1988; Kaplan, Morales, & Becker, 1993). Thus far, then, we can see that the factors contributing to successful therapy are qualities of the participants, the therapeutic alliance, and the specific methods of the therapy.

SPECIAL PROBLEMS AND POPULATIONS.   Some therapies are targeted for the problems of particular populations. For example, rehabilitation psychologists are concerned with the assessment and treatment of people who are physically disabled, temporarily or permanently, because of chronic pain, physical injuries, epilepsy, addictions, or other conditions. They conduct research to find the best ways to teach disabled people to live independently, improve their motivation, enjoy their sex lives, and follow healthy regimens. Because more people are surviving traumatic injuries and living long enough to develop chronic medical conditions, rehabilitation psychology is one of the fastest-growing areas of health care.

Other problems require more than one-on-one help from a psychotherapist. Community psychologists set up programs at a community level, often coordinating outpatient services at local clinics with support from family and friends. Some community programs help people who have severe mental disorders, such as schizophrenia, by setting up group homes where the mentally ill get counselling, job and skills training, and a support network. Without such community support, many mentally ill people are treated at hospitals, released to the streets, and stop taking their medications. Their psychotic symptoms return, they are rehospitalized, and a revolving-door cycle is established (Luhrmann, 2000).

Community psychologists can prevent problems, too. In the Pacific Northwest, where substance abuse among indigenous peoples has widespread and devastating effects, successful prevention and intervention programs combine bicultural life-skills training and community involvement (Hawkins, Cummins, & Marlatt, 2004).

An important community intervention called *multisystemic therapy (MST)* has been highly successful in reducing teenage violence, criminal activity, drug abuse, and

Indigenous peoples from British Columbia and the American Northwest have been renewing their ancient cultural tradition of building ocean-going canoes and using them to visit other tribes. In Seattle, a community program designed to prevent drug abuse and other problems among urban indigenous adolescents uses these canoe journeys as a metaphor for the journey of life. The youths learn the psychological and practical skills, along with the cultural values, that they would need to undertake a canoe journey—skills they will also need to navigate throughout life (Hawkins, Cummins, & Marlatt, 2004).

school problems in troubled inner-city communities. Its practitioners combine family-systems techniques with behavioural methods, but apply them in the context of forming "neighbourhood partnerships" with local leaders, residents, parents, and teachers to help prevent or reduce teenagers' problems (Henggeler et al., 1998; Swenson et al., 2005). The premise of multisystemic therapy is that because aggressiveness and drug abuse are often reinforced or caused by the adolescent's family, classroom, peers, and local culture, you can't successfully treat the adolescent without also "treating" his or her environment. Indeed, MST has been shown to be more effective than other methods on their own (Schaeffer & Borduin, 2005).

When Therapy Harms

In May 2000, police arrested four people on charges of recklessly causing the death of 10-year-old Candace Newmaker during a session of "rebirthing" therapy. The procedure, which its proponents claim helps adopted children form attachments to their adoptive parents by "reliving" birth, was captured on closed-circuit television as the girl's mother watched in a nearby room.

The child was completely wrapped in a blanket that supposedly simulated the womb and was surrounded by large pillows. The therapists then pressed in on the pillows to simulate contractions and told the girl to push her way out of the blanket over her head. Candace repeatedly said that she could not breathe and felt she was going to die. But instead of unwrapping her, the therapists said, "You've got to push hard if you want to be born—or do you want to stay in there and die?"

Candace lost consciousness and was rushed to a local hospital, where she died the next day. Connell Watkins and Julie Ponder, unlicensed social workers who operated the counselling centre, were sentenced to 16 years in prison for reckless child abuse resulting in death. Their two assistants, Brita St. Clair and Jack McDaniels, who used the age-old "we were only following orders" defence, were sentenced to 10 years' probation for sitting on the struggling child as she smothered to death. To date, eight other children have died during this kind of therapy; five others were rescued in the nick of time; and one child committed suicide.

Every treatment and intervention, including Aspirin, carries risks, and so does psychotherapy. In a small percentage of cases, a person's symptoms may actually worsen as a result of the therapy, the client may become too dependent on the therapist, or the client's outside relationships may deteriorate (Lilienfeld, 2007). But the risks to clients increase when any of the following occurs:

1   **The use of empirically unsupported, potentially dangerous techniques.** The techniques used in "rebirthing" therapy are unsupported by scientific research. This therapy was born in the 1970s, when its founder claimed he had re-experienced his own birth while taking a bath. (Many psychological problems, he somehow decided, can be traced to a traumatic experience in the womb or during birth.) But the basic assumptions of this method—that people can recover from trauma, insecure attachment, or other psychological problems by "reliving" their births—are completely contradicted by the vast research on infancy, attachment, memory, and posttraumatic stress disorder and its treatment. For that matter, why should anyone assume that the experience of being born is traumatic? Isn't it pretty nice to be let out of cramped quarters and see daylight and beaming parental faces?

Rebirthing is one of a variety of practices, collectively referred to as "attachment therapy," that are based on the use of harsh tactics that will allegedly help children "bond" with their parents. These techniques include withholding food,

Candace Newmaker, aged 10 (left), was smothered to death during a session of "rebirthing" therapy. The therapists, Julie Ponder and Connell Watkins (right), were convicted of reckless child abuse resulting in death and were sentenced to 16 years in prison.

isolating the children for extended periods, humiliating them, wrapping them in sheets or blankets, pressing great weights upon them, and requiring them to exercise to exhaustion or, conversely, to spend hours sitting motionless. As we saw in Chapter 7, however, severe, abusive punishments are ineffective in treating behaviour problems and often backfire, making the child angry, resentful, and withdrawn. They are hardly a way to help an adopted or emotionally troubled child feel more attached to his or her parents. The American Psychiatric Association officially opposes attachment therapies, noting that "there is *no* scientific evidence to support the effectiveness of such interventions." Other kinds of unsupported and potentially harmful therapy are aimed at helping clients retrieve painful memories. In Chapter 10 we saw that memory does not work like a video camera or tape recorder; memories are not "buried" in the brain, awaiting methods that will magically root them out. Yet many therapists still use unreliable methods such as hypnosis, sodium amytal (a barbiturate misleadingly called "truth serum"), guided imagery, and dream analysis—all of which are known to enhance a client's suggestibility (Mazzoni, Loftus, & Kirsch, 2001). When a therapist tells clients that their dreams are memories of something that really happened, many clients begin to confuse their dreams with reality (Mazzoni et al., 1999).

Many research psychologists are greatly concerned that a significant minority of registered, licensed psychotherapists—between one-fourth and one-third of them—have used one or more of these inappropriate techniques specifically to help clients "retrieve" memories of sexual abuse, as you can see in Figure 16.3 (Poole et al., 1995). Research in Canada and the United States finds that the percentages have not declined appreciably in recent years (Katz, 2001; Nunez, Poole, & Memon, 2002; Polusny & Follette, 1996).

Table 16.1 lists a number of therapies that have been shown, through randomized controlled trials or meta-analysis, to have a significant risk of harming their clients.

2   Inappropriate or coercive influence, which can create new problems for the client. In a healthy therapeutic alliance, therapist and client come to agree on an explanation for the client's problems. Of course, the therapist will influence this explanation, according to his or her training and philosophy. Some therapists,

Thinking Critically

Examine the Evidence

New therapies are often established on the basis of notions that someone thought sounded plausible—for example, that accurate memories can be "uprooted" through hypnosis or that emotional problems stem from the "trauma" of childbirth. What is wrong with basing a new form of therapy on an untested hunch instead of on evidence that it works?

TABLE 16.1 Potentially Harmful Therapies

Intervention	Potential Harm
Critical Incident Stress Debriefing (CISD)	Heightened risk of PTSD
Scared Straight interventions	Worsening of conduct problems
Facilitated communication	False allegations of sexual and child abuse
Attachment therapies	Death and serious injury to children
Recovered-memory techniques (e.g., dream analysis)	Induction of false memories of trauma, family breakups
"Multiple personality disorder"-oriented therapy	Induction of "multiple" personalities
Grief counseling for people with normal bereavement reactions	Increased depressive symptoms
Expressive-experiential therapies	Worsening and prolonging painful emotions
Boot-camp interventions for conduct disorder	Worsening of aggression and conduct problems
DARE (Drug Abuse and Resistance Education)	Increased use of alcohol and other drugs

Source: Lilienfeld (2007)

however, cross the line. They so zealously believe in the prevalence of certain problems or disorders that they actually induce the client to produce the symptoms they are looking for (Mazzoni, Loftus, & Kirsch, 2001; McHugh, 2008; McNally, 2003; Watters & Ofshe, 1999). Therapist influence, and sometimes downright coercion, is a likely reason for the huge numbers of people who were diagnosed with multiple personality disorder in the 1980s and 1990s (see Chapter 15) and for an epidemic of recovered memories of sexual abuse during this period (see Chapter 10).

3 **Prejudice or cultural ignorance on the part of the therapist.** Some therapists may be prejudiced against some clients because of the client's gender, culture, religion, or sexual orientation. They may be unaware of their prejudices, yet express them in nonverbal ways that make the client feel ignored, disrespected, and devalued (Sue et al., 2007). A therapist may try to induce a client to conform to the therapist's standards and values, even if they are not appropriate for the client or in the client's best interests. For example, for many years gay men and

FIGURE 16.3 Psychologists' Attitudes toward the Use of Suggestive Techniques for Recovering Memories of Sexual Abuse

Between one-fourth and one-third of licensed clinical psychologists have used suggestive methods regularly "to help clients recall memories of sexual abuse," although these techniques can produce confabulation and false memories. The percentages are from two combined samples of American clinical psychologists with PhDs, randomly drawn from names listed in the National Register of Health Service Providers in Psychology (Poole et al., 1995). The numbers have not changed appreciably in recent years.

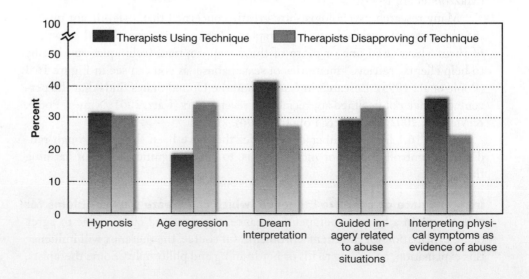

lesbians who entered therapy were told that homosexuality was a mental illness that could be cured. Some of the so-called treatments were harsh, such as electric shock for "inappropriate" arousal. Although these methods were discredited many years ago (Davison, 1976), other "reparative" therapies that supposedly turn gay men and lesbians into heterosexuals still surface from time to time. They are often promoted in campaigns by conservative Christians who believe that homosexuality is a sin, with testimonials from alleged converts. But there is no reliable empirical evidence from scientifically designed studies supporting these claims, and both the American Psychological Association and the American Psychiatric Association have gone on record opposing reparative therapies on ethical and scientific grounds.

4 **Sexual intimacies or other unethical behaviour on the part of the therapist.** The Canadian Psychological Association's ethical guidelines prohibit therapists from having any sexual intimacies with their clients or violating other professional boundaries. Occasionally, some therapists behave like cult leaders, persuading their clients that their mental health depends on staying in therapy and severing their connections to their "toxic" families (Singer, 2003; Watters & Ofshe, 1999). Such "psychotherapy cults" are created by the therapist's use of techniques that foster the client's isolation, prevent the client from terminating therapy, and reduce the client's ability to think critically (see Chapter 8).

To avoid these risks and benefit from what good, effective psychotherapy has to offer, people looking for the right therapy must become educated consumers—able and willing to use the critical-thinking skills we have emphasized throughout this book.

Find out whether you are an educated consumer of quizzes.

quickQUIZ

✓•⌐Quick Review on **MyPsychLab**

1. Which of the following is the most important predictor of successful therapy? (a) how long it lasts, (b) the insight it provides the client, (c) the bond between therapist and client, (d) whether the therapist and client are matched according to gender

2. In general, which type of psychotherapy is most effective for anxiety and depression?

3. What kind of psychologist is trained to help people cope with chronic illness or disability or recover from injury?

4. What are four possible sources of harm in psychotherapy?

5. Ferdie is spending too much time playing softball and not enough time studying, so he signs up for "sportaholic therapy (ST)." The therapist tells him the cure for his "addiction" is to quit softball cold turkey and tap his temples three times whenever he feels the urge to play. After a few months, Ferdie announces that ST isn't helping and he's going to stop coming. The therapist gives him testimonials of other clients who swear by ST, explaining that Ferdie's doubts are actually a sign that the therapy is working. What are some problems with this argument? (*Bonus:* What kind of therapy might help Ferdie manage his time better?)

Answers:

1. c 2. cognitive-behaviour therapy 3. rehabilitation psychologist 4. the use of empirically unsupported techniques, prejudice or biased treatment, inappropriate or coercive influence, and unethical behaviour 5. The therapist has violated the principle of falsifiability (see Chapter 2). If Ferdie is helped by the treatment, that shows it he is not helped, that still shows it works but Ferdie is "denying" its benefits. Also, Ferdie is not hearing testimonials from people who have dropped out of ST and were not helped by it. (*Bonus:* A good behavioural time-management program might help, so Ferdie can play softball *and* get other things done, too.)

THE VALUE AND VALUES OF PSYCHOTHERAPY

Modern psychotherapy has been of enormous value to many people. But psychotherapists themselves have raised some important questions about the values inherent in what they do (Cushman, 1995; Hillman & Ventura, 1992). How much personal change is possible, and do some therapists promise their clients too much? Does psychotherapy, by encouraging people to look inward to their feelings and woes, foster a preoccupation with the self over relationships and the importance of contributing to the larger world? Does it promise unrealistic notions of endless happiness and complete self-fulfillment?

Many people in North America have an optimistic, can-do, let's-fix-this-fast attitude toward all problems, whether mental, physical, or social. In contrast, as discussed in Chapter 15, Eastern cultures have a less optimistic view of change, and they tend to be more tolerant of events they regard as being outside of human control. In the Japanese practice of Morita therapy, therefore, clients are taught to accept and live with their most troubling emotions, instead of trying to eradicate these psychological weeds from the lawn of life (Reynolds, 1987). Some Western psychotherapists also now teach techniques of mindful meditation and greater self-acceptance instead of constant self-improvement, and they have been successful with problems ranging from depression to borderline personality disorder (Hayes, 2004; Kabat-Zinn, 1994; Linehan, 1993; Segal, Williams, & Teasdale, 2001). Most people get all the help they need from talking things over with good friends or with others who are in the same situation they are. But if you have a persistent problem that you do not know how to solve, one that causes you considerable unhappiness and that has lasted six months or more, it may be time to look for help. As the research in this chapter suggests, consumers who are thinking about psychotherapy should consider these important matters:

- *Choosing a therapist.* Make sure you are dealing with a reputable individual with appropriate credentials and training. Your school counselling centre is a good place to start. You might also seek out a university psychology clinic, where you can get therapy with a graduate student in training; these students are closely supervised and the fees will be lower. If you know the kind of therapy you want, check your phone book; many therapists are listed according to the kind of therapy they do.

- *Choosing a therapy.* As we have seen, not all therapies are equally effective for all problems. You should not spend four years in psychodynamic therapy for panic attacks, which can generally be helped in a few sessions of cognitive-behaviour therapy. Likewise, if you have a specific emotional problem, such as depression, anger, or anxiety, or if you are coping with chronic health problems, look for a cognitive or behaviour therapist. However, if you just want to discuss your life with a wise and empathic counsellor, the kind of therapy may not matter so much. If a physician or psychiatrist prescribes drugs, it is best to talk to a competent psychotherapist or counsellor about your problems and what intervention might help you before you begin medication.

- *Deciding when to leave.* For the common emotional problems of life, short-term treatment is usually sufficient. Some people are helped in only one or two sessions; about half improve within eight to 11 sessions, and three-fourths improve within six months to a year. After a year, further change is usually minimal (Kopta et al., 1994). However, people with more severe mental disorders do often require and benefit from continued therapeutic care (Shadish et al., 2000).

Thinking Critically

Ask Questions

The benefits of psychotherapy are well documented, but we can ask questions about its implicit message. Does psychotherapy foster unrealistic expectations of personal change? When should clients think about living with problems or situations they cannot change?

◄◉Simulate
Person-Centred Therapy

If you begin a time-limited treatment, such as a seven-session airplane-phobia program, you ought to stick with it to the end. In unlimited therapy, however, you have the right to determine when enough is enough, especially if the therapist has been unable to help you with your problem after a considerable length of time.

If you have made a real effort to work with a therapist and there has been no result after ample time and effort, the reason could have as much to do with the treatment or the therapist as with you.

In the hands of an empathic and knowledgeable practitioner, psychotherapy can help you make decisions and clarify your values and goals. It can teach you new skills and new ways of thinking. It can help you get along better with your family and break out of destructive family patterns. It can get you through bad times when no one seems to care or to understand what you are feeling. It can teach you how to manage depression, anxiety, and anger.

However, despite its many benefits, psychotherapy cannot transform you into someone you're not. It cannot turn an introvert into an extrovert. It cannot cure an emotional disorder overnight. It cannot provide a life without problems. And it is not intended to substitute for experience—for work that is satisfying, relationships that are sustaining, activities that are enjoyable. As Socrates knew, the unexamined life is not worth living. Yet, as we would add, the unlived life is not worth examining.

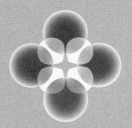

Taking Psychology with YOU

Thinking Critically in Everyday Life

How to Evaluate Self-Help Groups and Books

Not all psychological problems require the aid of a professional. Nowadays, thousands of programs and books are designed to help people help themselves. More than 2000 self-help books are published every year, and an estimated 7 million to 15 million adults belong to self-help groups. Do these books and groups help?

Self-help groups are available (online and in person) for alcoholics and relatives of alcoholics; people suffering from depression, anorexia, or schizophrenia; women with breast cancer; parents of murdered children; diabetics; rape victims; step-parents; relatives of people with Alzheimer's; and people with just about any other concern you can think of (Davison, Pennebaker, & Dickerson, 2000). Members say that the primary benefits are the awareness that they are not alone, encouragement when they are feeling down, and help in feeling better about themselves.

Self-help groups offer understanding, empathy, and solutions to shared problems. Such groups can be reassuring and supportive in ways that family, friends, and psychotherapists sometimes may not be. For example, people with disabilities face unique challenges that involve coping not only with physical problems but also with the condescension, hostility, and prejudice of many nondisabled people (Linton, 1998). Other disabled people, who share these challenges, can offer the right kind of empathy and useful advice.

Self-help groups do not provide psychotherapy, and they are not designed to help people with serious psychological difficulties. They are not regulated by law or by professional standards, and they vary widely in their philosophies and methods. Some are accepting and tolerant, offering support and spiritual guidance. Others are confrontational and coercive, and members who disagree with the premises of the group may be made to feel deviant, crazy, or "in denial." If you choose to become part of a support group, make sure it falls into the first category.

As for self-help books, there is one for every problem, from how to toilet train your children to how to find happiness. When self-help books propose a specific, well-supported program for the reader to follow, they can actually be as effective as treatment administered by a therapist—*if* the reader follows through with the program (Rosen, Glasgow, & Moore, 2003). Unfortunately, most books do not do this. After serving as chair of the APA's Task Force on Self-Help Therapies, Gerald Rosen (1981) concluded, "Psychologists have published untested materials, advanced exaggerated claims, and accepted the use

of misleading titles that encourage unrealistic expectations regarding outcome." That was many years ago, and the situation is worse today. The information in this chapter suggests some guidelines for evaluating a self-help book:

- The book's advice should be based on sound scientific theory and should propose a program that has been empirically supported. It should not be based on the author's pseudoscientific theories, armchair observations, or political views. This criterion rules out, among other kinds of books, most of the love manuals in which the author's own tales of woe become the basis of an entire philosophy of love, marriage, and happiness. Personal accounts by people who have survived difficulties can be helpful and inspirational, of course, but an author's own experience is not grounds for generalizing to everyone.

- The book should not promise the impossible. This rules out books that promise perfect sex, total love, or high self-esteem in 30 days. It also rules out books or tapes that promote techniques whose effectiveness has been disconfirmed by research, such as dream analysis or "subliminal" messages.
- The advice should be organized in a systematic program. It should be given step by step, not as a vague pep talk to "take charge of your life" or "find love in your heart," and the reader should be told how to evaluate his or her progress.

Some books do meet these criteria. One is *Changing for Good* (Prochaska, Norcross, & DiClemente, 1994), which describes the ingredients of effective change that apply to people in and out of therapy. But as long as people yearn for a magic bullet to cure their problems, quick-fix solutions will find a ready audience.

SUMMARY

BIOLOGICAL TREATMENTS FOR MENTAL DISORDERS

- Over the centuries, people trying to understand and treat psychological disorders have alternated between biological and psychological explanations. Today, biological treatments are in the ascendance because of research findings on the genetic and biological causes of some disorders and because of economic and social factors.

- The medications most commonly prescribed for mental disorders include *antipsychotic drugs*, used in treating schizophrenia and other psychotic disorders; *antidepressant drugs*, used in treating depression, anxiety disorders, and obsessive-compulsive disorder; *tranquilizers*, often prescribed for emotional problems; and *lithium carbonate*, a salt used to treat bipolar disorder.

- Drawbacks of drug treatment include the *placebo effect*; high dropout and relapse rates among people who take medica-

tions without also learning how to cope with their problems; the difficulty of finding the correct dose (the *therapeutic window*) for each individual, compounded by the fact that a person's ethnicity, sex, and age can influence a drug's effectiveness; the long-term risks of medication, known and unknown; and the risk of possible drug interactions when several are being taken. Medication can be helpful and can even save lives, but in an age in which commercial interests are heavily invested in promoting drugs for psychological problems, the public is largely unaware of drugs' limitations and potential risks. Medication should not be prescribed uncritically and routinely, especially when non-drug therapies can work as well as drugs for many mood and behavioural problems.

- When drugs and psychotherapy have failed to help seriously disturbed people, some psychiatrists have intervened directly in the brain. *Psychosurgery*, which destroys selected areas of the brain thought to be responsible for a psychological problem, is rarely done today. *Electroconvulsive therapy (ECT)*, in which a brief current is sent through the brain, has been used successfully to treat suicidal depression. However, controversy exists about its effects on the brain and the appropriateness of its use. A newer method, transcranial magnetic stimulation (TMS), in which a magnetic coil is applied over the left prefrontal cortex, is being studied as a way of treating severe depression.

KINDS OF PSYCHOTHERAPY

◆ *Psychodynamic ("depth") therapies* include Freudian *psychoanalysis* and its modern variations, such as approaches based on object-relations theory. These therapies explore unconscious dynamics by using *free association* and by focusing on the process of *transference* to break through the patient's defences.

◆ Practitioners of *behaviour therapy* draw on classical and operant principles of learning, called applied behavioural analysis. Behaviour therapists use such methods as *graduated exposure*, and sometimes immediate exposure, called *flooding*; *systematic desensitization*, based on *counterconditioning*; *behavioural self-monitoring*; and *skill straining*.

◆ Practitioners of *cognitive therapy* aim to change the irrational thoughts involved in negative emotions and self-defeating actions. Albert Ellis's *rational emotive behaviour therapy (REBT)* and Aaron Beck's form of cognitive therapy are two leading cognitive approaches.

◆ *Humanist therapy* holds that human nature is essentially good and attempts to help people feel better about themselves by focusing on here-and-now issues and on their capacity for change. Carl Rogers's *client-centred (nondirective) therapy* emphasizes the importance of the therapist's empathy and ability to provide *unconditional positive regard*. *Existential therapy* helps people cope with the dilemmas of existence, such as the meaning of life and the fear of death.

◆ *Family therapy* holds the view that individual problems develop in the context of the whole family network. It has a *family-systems perspective*, understanding that any one person's behaviour in the family affects everyone else, sometimes across generations. In *couples therapy*, the therapist usually sees both partners in a relationship to help them resolve ongoing quarrels and disputes or to help them accept and live with qualities of both partners that are unlikely to change.

◆ In practice, most therapists take an *integrative approach to psychotherapy*, drawing on many methods and ideas. Whatever their approach, successful therapies help people form more adaptive "life stories."

EVALUATING PSYCHOTHERAPY

◆ Successful therapy requires a *therapeutic alliance* between the therapist and the client, so that they understand each other and can work together. The clients who benefit most from psychotherapy are motivated to solve their problems; hostile, negative individuals are more resistant to treatment. For their part, good therapists are empathic and constructive. When therapist and client are of different ethnicities, the therapist must be able to distinguish normal cultural patterns from signs of mental illness, and both parties must be aware of potential prejudice and misunderstandings.

◆ A *scientist–practitioner gap* has developed because of the different assumptions held by researchers and many clinicians regarding the value of empirical research for doing psychotherapy and for assessing its effectiveness. The gap has led to a proliferation of scientifically unsupported psychotherapies.

◆ In assessing the effectiveness of psychotherapy, researchers need to control for the placebo effect and the *justification of effort* effect. They rely on *randomized controlled trials* to determine which therapies are empirically supported. For example, randomized controlled trials have shown that postcrisis debriefing programs are usually ineffective at best and can even slow recovery for some survivors.

◆ Some psychotherapies are better than others for specific problems. Behaviour therapy and cognitive-behaviour therapy are the most effective for depression, anxiety disorders, anger problems, certain health problems (such as pain, insomnia, and eating disorders), and childhood and adolescent behaviour problems. Family-systems therapies, especially when combined with behavioural techniques as in *multisystemic therapy*, are helpful for children and young adults with schizophrenia and for aggressive adolescents. Some problems and target populations, such as sex offenders, respond best to combined therapeutic approaches. Some methods, such as *motivational interviewing*, have been able to change a client's willingness to begin a program of change in only a session or two.

TAKING PSYCHOLOGY WITH YOU

◆ Because of the growing number of therapy providers and therapies that lack empirical validation, people seeking mental health services need to choose a therapist very carefully. Further, some therapeutic approaches are better suited to specific problems, and one should be quite selective when choosing self-help groups or books.

MyPsychLab

Visit **www.mypsychlab.com** to help you get the best grade!
Test your knowledge and grasp difficult concepts through

- **Custom study plans:** See where you are strong and where you go wrong
- **Interactive simulations**
- **Video and audio clips**

KEY TERMS

antipsychotic drugs (neuroleptics) *626*
antidepressant drugs *627*
tranquilizers *628*
lithium carbonate *628*
placebo effect *629*
therapeutic window *630*
psychosurgery *632*
electroconvulsive therapy (ECT) *632*

psychoanalysis *634*
transference *634*
behaviour therapy *635*
graduated exposure *635*
flooding *635*
systematic desensitization *635*
behavioural self-monitoring *636*
skills training *636*
cognitive therapy *637*

rational emotive behaviour therapy
  (REBT) *638*
humanist therapy *639*
client-centred (nondirective)
  therapy *640*
existential therapy *640*
family-systems perspective *642*
therapeutic alliance *644*
randomized controlled trials *647*

Appendix

STATISTICAL METHODS

Nineteenth-century English statesman Benjamin Disraeli reportedly once named three forms of dishonesty: "lies, damned lies, and statistics." It is certainly true that people can lie with the help of statistics. It happens all the time: Advertisers, politicians, and others with some claim to make either use numbers inappropriately or ignore certain critical ones. People also use numbers to convey a false impression of certainty and objectivity when the true state of affairs is uncertainty or ignorance. But it is people, not statistics, that lie. When statistics are used correctly, they neither confuse nor mislead. On the contrary, they expose unwarranted conclusions, promote clarity and precision, and protect us from our own biases and blind spots.

If statistics are useful anywhere, it is in the study of human behaviour. If human beings were all alike, and psychologists could specify all the influences on behaviour, there would be no need for statistics. But any time we measure human behaviour, we are going to wind up with different observations or scores for different individuals. Statistics can help us spot trends amid the diversity.

This appendix will introduce you to some basic statistical calculations used in psychology. Reading the appendix will not make you a statistician, but it will acquaint you with some ways of organizing and assessing research data. If you suffer from a "number phobia," relax: You do not need to know much math to understand this material. However, you should have read Chapter 2, which discussed the rationale for using statistics and described various research methods. You may want to review the basic terms and concepts covered in that chapter. Make sure that you can define *hypothesis, sample, independent variable, dependent variable, random assignment, experimental group, control group, descriptive statistics, inferential statistics, test of statistical significance,* and *effect size.* (Correlation coefficients, which are described in some detail in Chapter 2, will not be covered here.)

To read the tables in this appendix, you will also need to know the following symbols:

N = the total number of observations or scores in a set

X = an observation or score

Σ = the Greek capital letter sigma, read as "the sum of"

$\sqrt{}$ = the square root of

(*Note:* Boldfaced terms in this appendix are defined in the glossary at the end of the book.)

Organizing Data

Before we can discuss statistics, we need some numbers. Imagine that you are a psychologist and that you are interested in that most pleasing of human qualities, a sense of humour. You suspect that a well-developed funny bone can protect people from the negative emotional effects of stress. You already know that in the months following a stressful event, people who score high on sense-of-humour tests tend to feel less tense and moody than more sobersided individuals do. You realize, though, that this correlational evidence does not prove cause and effect. Perhaps people with a healthy sense of humour have other traits, such as flexibility or creativity, that act as the true stress buffers. To find out whether humour itself really softens the impact of stress, you do an experiment.

First, you randomly assign subjects to two groups, an experimental group and a control group. To keep our calculations simple, let's assume there are only 15 people per group. Each person individually views a silent film that most North Americans find fairly stressful, one showing Australian aboriginal boys undergoing a puberty rite involving genital mutilation. Subjects in the experimental group are instructed to make up a humorous monologue while watching the film. Those in the control group are told to make up a straightforward narrative. After the film, each person answers a mood questionnaire that measures current feelings of tension, depression, aggressiveness, and anxiety. A person's overall score on the questionnaire can range from 1 (no mood disturbance) to 7 (strong mood disturbance). This procedure provides you with 15 "mood disturbance" scores for each group. Have people who tried to be humorous reported less disturbance than those who did not?

Constructing a Frequency Distribution

Your first step might be to organize and condense the "raw data" (the obtained scores) by constructing a frequency distribution for each group. A **frequency distribution** shows how often each possible score actually occurred. To construct one, you first order all the possible scores from highest to lowest. (Our mood disturbance scores will be ordered from 7 to 1.) Then you tally how often each score was actually obtained. Table A.1 gives some hypothetical raw data for the two groups, and Table A.2 shows the two frequency distributions based on these data. From these distributions you can see that the two groups differed. In the experimental group, the extreme scores of 7 and 1 did not occur

TABLE A.1

Some Hypothetical Raw Data

These scores are for the hypothetical humour-and-stress study described in the text.

Experimental group	4,5,4,4,3,6,5,2,4,3,5,4,4,3,4
Control group	6,4,7,6,6,4,6,7,7,5,5,5,7,6,6

at all, and the most common score was the middle one, 4. In the control group, a score of 7 occurred four times, the most common score was 6, and no one obtained a score lower than 4.

Because our mood scores have only seven possible values, our frequency distributions are quite manageable. Suppose, though, that your questionnaire had yielded scores that could range from 1 to 50. A frequency distribution with 50 entries would be cumbersome and might not reveal trends in the data clearly. A solution would be to construct a *grouped frequency distribution* by grouping adjacent scores into equal-sized *classes* or *intervals*. Each interval could cover, say, five scores (1–5, 6–10, 11–15, and so forth). Then you could tally the frequencies within each *interval*. This procedure would reduce the number of entries in each distribution from 50 to only 10, making the overall results much easier to grasp. However, information would be lost. For example, there would be no way of knowing how many people had a score of 43 versus 44.

Graphing the Data

As everyone knows, a picture is worth a thousand words. The most common statistical picture is a **graph**, a drawing that depicts numerical relationships. Graphs appear at several points in this book, and are routinely used by psychologists to convey their findings to others. From graphs, we can get a general impression of what the data are like, note the relative frequencies of different scores, and see which score was most frequent.

TABLE A.2

Two Frequency Distributions

The scores are from Table A.1.

Experimental Group			Control Group		
Mood Disturbance Score	Tally	Frequency	Mood Disturbance Score	Tally	Frequency
7		0	7	////	4
6	/	1	6	7HL /	6
5	///	3	5	///	3
4	7HL //	7	4	//	2
3	///	3	3		0
2	/	1	2		0
1		0	1		0
		N = 15			N = 15

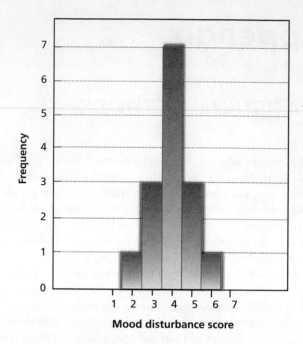

FIGURE A.1   A Histogram

This graph depicts the distribution of mood disturbance scores shown on the left side of Table A.2.

In a graph constructed from a frequency distribution, the possible score values are shown along a horizontal line (the *x-axis* of the graph) and frequencies along a vertical line (the *y-axis*), or vice versa. To construct a **histogram,** or **bar graph,** from our mood scores, we draw rectangles (bars) above each score, indicating the number of times it occurred by the rectangle's height (Figure A.1).

A slightly different kind of "picture" is provided by a **frequency polygon,** or **line graph.** In a frequency polygon, the frequency of each score is indicated by a dot placed directly over the score on the horizontal axis, at the appropriate height on the vertical axis. The dots for the various scores are then joined together by straight lines, as in Figure A.2. When necessary, an "extra" score, with a frequency of zero, can be added at each end of the horizontal axis so that the polygon will rest on this axis instead of floating above it.

A word of caution about graphs: They may either exaggerate or mask differences in the data, depending on which units are used on the vertical axis. The two graphs in Figure A.3, although they look quite different, actually depict the same data. Always read the units on the axes of a graph; otherwise, the shape of a histogram or frequency polygon may be misleading.

Describing Data

Having organized your data, you are now ready to summarize and describe them. As you will recall from Chapter 2, procedures for doing so are known as **descriptive statistics**. In the following discussion, the word *score* will stand for any numerical observation.

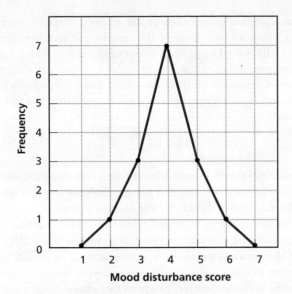

FIGURE A.2   Frequency Polygon
This graph depicts the same data as Figure A.1.

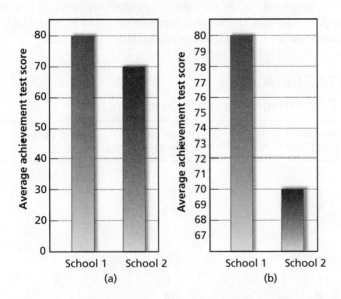

FIGURE A.3   Same Data, Different Impressions
These two graphs depict the same data, but have different units on the vertical axis.

Measuring Central Tendency

Your first step in describing your data might be to compute a **measure of central tendency** for each group. Measures of central tendency characterize an entire set of data in terms of a single representative number.

The Mean.   The most popular measure of central tendency is the arithmetic mean, usually called simply the **mean**. It is often expressed by the symbol *M*. Most people are thinking of the mean when they say "average." We run across means all the time: in grade-point averages, temperature averages, and batting averages. The mean is valuable to the psychologist because it takes all the data into account and can be used in further statistical analyses. To compute the mean, you simply add up a set of scores and divide the total by the number of scores in the set. Recall that in mathematical notation, Σ means "the sum of," X stands for the individual scores, and N represents the total number of scores in a set. Thus the formula for calculating the mean is:

$$M = \frac{\Sigma X}{N}$$

Table A.3 on the next page shows how to compute the mean for our experimental group. Test your ability to perform this calculation by computing the mean for the control group yourself. (You can find the answer, along with other control group statistics, on page A-7.) Later, we will describe how a psychologist would compare the two means statistically to see if there is a significant difference between them.

The Median.   Despite its usefulness, sometimes the mean can be misleading, as we noted in Chapter 2. Suppose you piled some children on a seesaw in such a way that it was perfectly balanced, and then a 200-pound adult came and sat on one end. The centre of gravity would quickly shift toward the adult. In the same way, one extremely high score can dramatically raise the mean (and one extremely low score can dramatically lower it). In real life, this can be a serious problem. For example, in the calculation of a town's mean income, one millionaire would offset hundreds of poor people. The mean income would be a misleading indication of the town's actual wealth.

When extreme scores occur, a more representative measure of central tendency is the **median**, or midpoint in a set of scores or observations ordered from highest to lowest. In any set of scores, the same *number* of scores falls above the median as below it. The median is not affected by extreme scores. If you were calculating the median income of that same town, the one millionaire would offset only one poor person.

TABLE A.3

Calculating a Mean and a Median

The scores are from the left side of Table A.1.

Median (M)

$$M = \frac{4 + 5 + 4 + 4 + 3 + 6 + 5 + 2 + 4 + 3 + 5 + 4 + 4 + 3 + 4}{15}$$

$$= \frac{60}{15}$$

$$= 4$$

Median

Scores, in order: 2, 3, 3, 3, 4, 4, 4, $\boxed{4}$, 4, 4, 4, 5, 5, 5, 6

↑
Median

When the number of scores in the set is odd, calculating the median is a simple matter of counting in from the ends to the middle. However, if the number of scores is even, there will be two middle scores. The simplest solution is to find the mean of those two scores and use that number as the median. (When the data are from a grouped frequency distribution, a more complicated procedure is required, one beyond the scope of this appendix.) In our experimental group, the median score is 4 (see Table A.3 again). What is it for the control group?

The Mode.   A third measure of central tendency is the **mode**, the score that occurs most often. In our experimental group, the modal score is 4. In our control group, it is 6. In some distributions, all scores occur with equal frequency, and there is no mode. In others, two or more scores "tie" for the distinction of being most frequent. Modes are used less often than other measures of central tendency. They do not tell us anything about the other scores in the distribution; they are often not very "central"; and they tend to fluctuate from one random sample of a population to another more than either the median or the mean.

Measuring Variability

A measure of central tendency may or may not be highly representative of other scores in a distribution. To understand our results, we also need a **measure of variability** that will tell us whether our scores are clustered closely around the mean or widely scattered.

The Range.   The simplest measure of variability is the **range,** which is found by subtracting the lowest score from the highest one. For our hypothetical set of mood disturbance scores, the range in the experimental group is 4 and in the control group it is 3. Unfortunately, simplicity is not always a virtue. The range gives us some information about variability but ignores all scores other than the highest and lowest ones.

The Standard Deviation.   A more sophisticated measure of variability is the **standard deviation (SD)**. This statistic takes every score in the distribution into account. Loosely speaking, it gives us an idea of how much, on the average, scores in a distribution differ from the mean. If the scores were all the same, the standard deviation would be zero. The higher the standard deviation, the more variability there is among scores.

To compute the standard deviation, we must find out how much each individual score deviates from the mean. To do so we simply subtract the mean from each score. This gives us a set of *deviation scores*. Deviation scores for numbers above the mean will be positive, those for numbers below the mean will be negative, and the positive scores will exactly balance the negative ones. In other words, the sum of the deviation scores will be zero. That is a problem, since the next step in our calculation is to add. The solution is to *square* all the deviation scores (that is, to multiply each score by itself). This step gets rid of negative values. Then

we can compute the average of the squared deviation scores by adding them up and dividing the sum by the number of scores (*N*). Finally, we take the square root of the result, which takes us from squared units of measurement back to the same units that were used originally (in this case, mood disturbance levels).

The calculations just described are expressed by the following formula:

$$SD = \sqrt{\frac{\Sigma(X - M)^2}{N}}$$

Table A.4 shows the calculations for computing the standard deviation for our experimental group. Try your hand at computing the standard deviation for the control group.

Remember, a large standard deviation signifies that scores are widely scattered, and that therefore the mean is not terribly typical of the entire population. A small standard deviation tells us that most scores are clustered near the mean, and that therefore the mean is representative. Suppose two classes took a psychology exam, and both classes had the same mean score, 75 out of a possible 100. From the means alone, you might conclude that the classes were similar in performance. But if Class A had a standard deviation of 3 and Class B had a standard deviation of 9, you would know that there was much more variability in performance in Class B. This information could be useful to an instructor in planning lectures and making assignments.

TABLE A.4

Calculating a Standard Deviation

Scores (X)	Deviation scores (X − M)	Squared deviation scores (X − M)²
6	2	4
5	1	1
5	1	1
5	1	1
4	0	0
4	0	0
4	0	0
4	0	0
4	0	0
4	0	0
4	0	0
3	−1	1
3	−1	1
3	−1	1
2	−2	4
	0	14

$$SD = \sqrt{\frac{\Sigma(X - M)^2}{N}} = \sqrt{\frac{14}{15}} = \sqrt{.93} = .97$$

Note: When data from a sample are used to estimate the standard deviation of the population from which the sample was drawn, division is by *N* − 1 instead of *N*, for reasons that will not concern us here.

Transforming Scores

Sometimes researchers do not wish to work directly with raw scores. They may prefer numbers that are more manageable, such as when the raw scores are tiny fractions. Or they may want to work with scores that reveal where a person stands relative to others. In such cases, raw scores can be transformed into other kinds of scores.

Percentile Scores. One common transformation converts each raw score to a **percentile score** (also called a *centile rank*). A percentile score gives the percentage of people who scored at or below a given raw score. Suppose you learn that you have scored 37 on a psychology exam. In the absence of any other information, you may not know whether to celebrate or cry. But if you are told that 37 is equivalent to a percentile score of 90, you know that you can be pretty proud of yourself; you have scored as well as, or higher than, 90 percent of those who have taken the test. On the other hand, if you are told that 37 is equivalent to a percentile score of 50, you have scored only at the median—only as well as, or higher than, half of the other students. The highest possible percentile rank is 99, or more precisely, 99.99, because you can never do better than 100 percent of a group when you are a member of the group. (Can you say what the lowest possible percentile score is? The answer is on page A-7.) Standardized tests such as those described in previous chapters often come with tables that allow for the easy conversion of any raw score to the appropriate percentile score, based on data from a larger number of people who have already taken the test.

Percentile scores are easy to understand and easy to calculate. However, they also have a drawback: They merely rank people and do not tell us how far apart people are in terms of raw scores. Suppose you scored in the 50th percentile on an exam, June scored in the 45th, Tricia scored in the 20th, and Sean scored in the 15th. The difference between you and June may seem identical to that between Tricia and Sean (five percentiles). But in terms of raw scores you and June are probably more alike than Tricia and Sean, because exam scores usually cluster closely together around the midpoint of the distribution and are farther apart at the extremes. Because percentile scores do not preserve the spatial relationships in the original distribution of scores, they are inappropriate for computing many kinds of statistics. For example, they cannot be used to calculate means.

Z-scores. Another common transformation of raw scores is to **z-scores**, or **standard scores**. A **z-score** tells you how far a given raw score is above or below the mean, using the standard deviation as the unit of measurement. To compute a z-score, you subtract the mean of the distribution from the raw score and divide by the standard deviation:

$$z = \frac{X - M}{SD}$$

Unlike percentile scores, z-scores preserve the relative spacing of the original raw scores. The mean itself always corresponds to a z-score of zero, since it cannot deviate from itself. All scores above the mean have positive z-scores and all scores below the mean have negative ones. When the raw scores form a certain pattern called a *normal distribution* (to be described shortly), a z-score tells you how high or low the corresponding raw score was, relative to the other scores. If your exam score of 37 is equivalent to a z-score of +1.0, you have scored 1 standard deviation above the mean. Assuming a roughly normal distribution, that's pretty good, because in a normal distribution only about 16 percent of all scores fall at or above 1 standard deviation above the mean. But if your 37 is equivalent to a z-score of −1.0, you have scored 1 standard deviation below the mean—a poor score.

Z-scores are sometimes used to compare people's performance on different tests or measures. Say that Elsa earns a score of 64 on her first psychology test and Manuel, who is taking psychology from a different instructor, earns a 62 on his first test. In Elsa's class, the mean score is 50 and the standard deviation is 7, so Elsa's z-score is (64 − 50)/7 = 2.0. In Manuel's class, the mean is also 50, but the standard deviation is 6. Therefore, his z-score is also 2.0 [(62 − 50)/6]. Compared to their respective classmates, Elsa and Manuel did equally well. But be careful: This does not imply that they are equally able students. Perhaps Elsa's instructor has a reputation for giving easy tests and Manuel's for giving hard ones, so Manuel's instructor has attracted a more industrious group of students. In that case, Manuel faces stiffer competition than Elsa does, and even though he and Elsa have the same z-score, Manuel's performance may be more impressive.

You can see that comparing z-scores from different people or different tests must be done with caution. Standardized tests, such as IQ tests and various personality tests, use z-scores derived from a large sample of people assumed to be representative of the general population taking the tests. When two tests are standardized for similar populations, it is safe to compare z-scores on them. But z-scores derived from special samples, such as students in different psychology classes, may not be comparable.

Curves

In addition to knowing how spread out our scores are, we need to know the pattern of their distribution. At this point we come to a rather curious phenomenon. When researchers make a very large number of observations, many of the physical and psychological variables they study have a distribution that approximates a pattern called a **normal distribution**. (We say "approximates" because a perfect normal distribution is a theoretical construct and is not actually found in nature.) Plotted in a frequency polygon, a normal distribution has a symmetrical, bell-shaped form known as a **normal curve** (see Figure A.4).

A normal curve has several interesting and convenient properties. The right side is the exact mirror image of the left. The mean, median, and mode all have the same value and are at the exact centre of the curve, at the top of the "bell." Most observations or scores cluster around the centre of the curve, with far fewer out at the ends, or "tails," of the curve. Most important, as Figure A.4

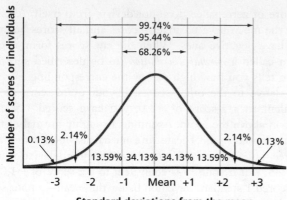

FIGURE A.4   A Normal Curve

When standard deviations (or z-scores) are used along the horizontal axis of a normal curve, certain fixed percentages of scores fall between the mean and any given point. As you can see, most scores fall in the middle range (between +1 and −1 standard deviations from the mean).

shows, when standard deviations (or z-scores) are used on the horizontal axis of the curve, the percentage of scores falling between the mean and any given point on the horizontal axis is always the same. For example, 68.26 percent of the scores will fall between plus and minus 1 standard deviation from the mean; 95.44 percent of the scores will fall between plus and minus 2 standard deviations from the mean; and 99.74 percent of the scores will fall between plus and minus 3 standard deviations from the mean. These percentages hold for any normal curve, no matter what the size of the standard deviation. Tables are available showing the percentages of scores in a normal distribution that lie between the mean and various points (as expressed by z-scores).

The normal curve makes life easier for psychologists when they want to compare individuals on some trait or performance. For example, because IQ scores from a population form a roughly normal curve, the mean and standard deviation of a test are all the information you need if you want to know how many people score above or below a particular score. On a test with a mean of 100 and a standard deviation of 15, about 68.26 percent of the population scores between 85 and 115—1 standard deviation below and 1 standard deviation above the mean (see Chapter 9).

Not all types of observations, however, are distributed normally. Some curves are lopsided, or *skewed*, with scores clustering at one end or the other of the horizontal axis (see Figure A.5). When the tail of the curve is longer on the right than on the left, the curve is said to be positively, or right, skewed. When the opposite is true, the curve is said to be negatively, or left, skewed. In experiments, reaction times typically form a right-skewed distribution. For example, if people must press a button whenever they hear some signal, most will react quite quickly; but a few will take an unusually long time, causing the right tail of the curve to be stretched out.

Knowing the shape of a distribution can be extremely valuable. Paleontologist Stephen Jay Gould (1985) once told how such

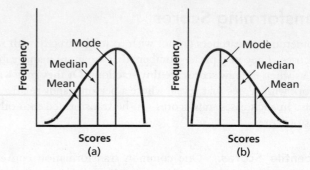

FIGURE A.5   Skewed Curves

Curve (a) is skewed negatively, to the left. Curve (b) is skewed positively, to the right. The direction of a curve's skewness is determined by the position of the long tail, not by the position of the bulge. In a skewed curve, the mean, median, and mode fall at different points.

information helped him cope with the news that he had a rare and serious form of cancer. Being a researcher, he immediately headed for the library to learn all he could about the disease. The first thing he found was that it was incurable, with a median mortality of only eight months after discovery. Most people might have assumed that a "median mortality of eight months" means "I will probably be dead in eight months." But Gould realized that although half of all patients died within eight months, the other half survived longer than that. Since his disease had been diagnosed in its early stages, he was getting top-notch medical treatment, and he had a strong will to live, Gould figured he could reasonably expect to be in the half of the distribution that survived beyond eight months. Even more cheering, the distribution of deaths from the disease was right-skewed: The cases to the left of the median of eight months could only extend to zero months, but those to the right could stretch out for years. Gould saw no reason why he should not expect to be in the tip of that right-hand tail.

ANSWERS TO QUESTIONS IN THIS CHAPTER:

Control group statistics:

$$\text{Mean} = \frac{\Sigma X}{N} = \frac{87}{15} = 5.8$$

$$\text{Medain} = 6$$

$$\text{Standard Deviation} = \sqrt{\frac{\Sigma (X - M)^2}{N}} = \sqrt{\frac{14.4}{15}}$$

$$= \sqrt{.96} = .98$$

Lowest possible percentile score: 1
(or, more precisely, .01).

For Stephen Jay Gould, statistics, properly interpreted, were "profoundly nurturant and life-giving." They offered him hope and inspired him to fight his disease. The initial diagnosis was made in 1982. Gould remained professionally active for 20 more years. When he died in 2002, it was from an unrelated type of cancer.

Drawing Inferences

Once data are organized and summarized, the next step is to ask whether they differ from what might have been expected purely by chance (see Chapter 2). A researcher needs to know whether it is safe to infer that the results from a particular sample of people are valid for the entire population from which the sample was drawn. **Inferential statistics** provide this information. They are used in both experimental and correlational studies.

The Null versus the Alternative Hypothesis

In an experiment, the scientist must assess the possibility that his or her experimental manipulations will have no effect on the subjects' behaviour. The statement expressing this possibility is called the **null hypothesis**. In our stress-and-humour study, the null hypothesis states that making up a funny commentary will not relieve stress any more than making up a straightforward narrative will. In other words, it predicts that the difference between the means of the two groups will not deviate significantly from zero. Any obtained difference will be due solely to chance fluctuations. In contrast, the **alternative hypothesis** (also called the *experimental* or *research hypothesis*) states that on average, the experimental group will have lower mood disturbance scores than the control group.

The null hypothesis and the alternative hypothesis cannot both be true. Our goal is to reject the null hypothesis. If our results turn out to be consistent with the null hypothesis, we will not be able to do so. If the data are inconsistent with the null hypothesis, we will be able to reject it with some degree of confidence. Unless we study the entire population, though, we will never be able to say that the alternative hypothesis has been proven. No matter how impressive our results are, there will always be some degree of uncertainty about the inferences we draw from them. Since we cannot prove the alternative hypothesis, we must be satisfied with showing that the null hypothesis is unreasonable.

Students are often surprised to learn that in traditional hypothesis testing it is the null hypothesis, not the alternative hypothesis, that is tested. After all, it is the alternative hypothesis that is actually of interest. But this procedure does make sense. The null hypothesis can be stated precisely and tested directly. In the case of our fictitious study, the null hypothesis predicts that the difference between the two means will be zero. The alternative hypothesis does not permit a precise prediction because we don't know how much the two means might differ (if, in fact, they do differ). Therefore, it cannot be tested directly.

Testing Hypotheses

Many computations are available for testing the null hypothesis. The choice depends on the design of the study, the size of the sample, and other factors. We will not cover any specific tests here. Our purpose is simply to introduce you to the kind of reasoning that underlies hypothesis testing. With that in mind, let us return once again to our data. For each of our two groups we have calculated a mean and a standard deviation. Now we want to compare the two sets of data to see if they differ enough for us to reject the null hypothesis. We wish to be reasonably certain that our observed differences did not occur entirely by chance.

What does it mean to be "reasonably certain"? How different from zero must our result be to be taken seriously? Imagine, for a moment, that we had infinite resources and could somehow repeat our experiment, each time using a new pair of groups, until we had run the entire population through the study. It can be shown mathematically that if only chance were operating, our various experimental results would form a normal distribution. This theoretical distribution is called "the sampling distribution of the difference between means," but since that is quite a mouthful, we will simply call it the *sampling distribution* for short. If the null hypothesis were true, the mean of the sampling distribution would be zero. That is, on average, we would find no difference between the two groups. Often, however, because of chance influences or *random error*, we would get a result that deviated to one degree or another from zero. On rare occasions, the result would deviate a great deal from zero.

We cannot test the entire population, though. All we have are data from a single sample. We would like to know whether the difference between means that we actually obtained would be close to the mean of the theoretical sampling distribution (if we could test the entire population) or far away from it, out in one of the tails of the curve. Was our result highly likely to occur on the basis of chance alone or highly unlikely?

Before we can answer that question, we must have some precise way to measure distance from the mean of the sampling distribution. We must know exactly how far from the mean our obtained result must be to be considered "far away." If only we knew the standard deviation of the sampling distribution, we could use it as our unit of measurement. We don't know it, but fortunately, we can use the standard deviation of our *sample* to estimate it. (We will not go into the reasons that this is so.)

Now we are in business. We can look at the mean difference between our two groups and figure out how far it is (in terms of standard deviations) from the mean of the sampling distribution. As mentioned earlier, one of the convenient things about a normal distribution is that a certain fixed percentage of all observations falls between the mean of the distribution and any given point above or below the mean. These percentages are available from tables. Therefore, if we know the distance of our obtained result from the mean of the theoretical sampling distribution, we automatically know how likely our result is to have occurred strictly by chance.

To give a specific example, if it turns out that our obtained result is 2 standard deviations above the mean of the theoretical sampling distribution, we know that the probability of its having occurred by chance is less than 2.3 percent. If our result is 3 standard deviations above the mean of the sampling distribution, the probability of its having occurred by chance is less than .13 percent—less than 1 in 800. In either case, we might well suspect that our result did not occur entirely by chance after all. We would call the result **statistically significant**. (Psychologists usually consider any highly unlikely result to be of interest, no matter which direction it takes. In other words, the result may be in either tail of the sampling distribution.)

To summarize: Statistical significance means that if only chance were operating, our result would be highly improbable, so we are fairly safe in concluding that more than chance was operating—namely, the influence of our independent variable. We can reject the null hypothesis and open the champagne. As we noted in Chapter 2, psychologists usually accept a finding as statistically significant if the likelihood of its occurring by chance is 5 percent or less (see Figure A.6). This cutoff point gives the researcher a reasonable chance of confirming reliable results as well as reasonable protection against accepting unreliable ones.

Some cautions are in order, however. As noted in Chapter 2, conventional tests of statistical significance have drawn serious criticisms in recent years. Statistically significant results are not always psychologically interesting or important. Further, statistical significance is related to the size of the sample. A large sample increases the likelihood of reliable results. But there is a tradeoff: The larger the sample, the more probable it is that a small result

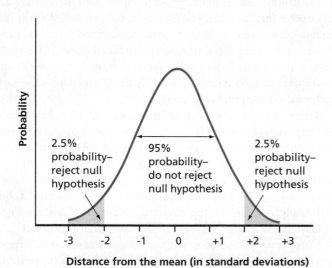

FIGURE A.6   Statistical Significance
This curve represents the theoretical sampling distribution discussed in the text. The curve is what we would expect by chance if we did our hypothetical stress-and-humour study many times, testing the entire population. If we used the conventional significance level of .05, we would regard our obtained result as significant only if the probability of getting a result that far from zero by chance (in either direction) totalled 5 percent or less. As shown, the result must fall far out in one of the tails of the sampling distribution. Otherwise, we cannot reject the null hypothesis.

having no practical importance will reach statistical significance. On the other hand, with the sample sizes typically used in psychological research, there is a good chance of falsely concluding that an experimental effect has not occurred when one actually has. For these reasons, it is always useful to know how much of the total variability in scores was accounted for by the independent variable (the **effect size**). (The computations are not discussed here.) If only 3 percent of the variance was accounted for, then 97 percent was due either to chance factors or to systematic influences of which the researcher was unaware. Because human behaviour is affected by so many factors, the amount of variability accounted for by a single psychological variable is often modest. But sometimes the effect size is considerable even when the results don't quite reach significance.

Oh, by the way, the study of humour's effect on stress and health turns out to be pretty complicated. The results depend on how you define "sense of humour," how you do the study, and what aspects of humour you are investigating. Researchers have learned that humour probably doesn't help people live longer or hasten recovery from injury or illness. But it is certainly more emotionally beneficial than moping around. So, when gravity gets you down, try a little levity.

Summary

1. When used correctly, statistics expose unwarranted conclusions, promote precision, and help researchers spot trends amid diversity.

2. Often, the first step in data analysis is to organize and condense data in a *frequency distribution*, a tally showing how often each possible score (or interval of scores) occurred. Such information can also be depicted in a *histogram* (bar graph) or a *frequency polygon* (line graph).

3. Descriptive statistics summarize and describe the data. *Central tendency* is measured by the *mean*, *median*, or, less frequently, the *mode*. Since a measure of central tendency may or may not be highly representative of other scores in a distribution, it is also important to analyze variability. A large *standard deviation* means that scores are widely scattered about the mean; a small one means that most scores are clustered near the mean.

4. Raw scores can be transformed into other kinds of scores. *Percentile scores* indicate the percentage of people who scored at or below a given raw score. *Z-scores* (*standard scores*) indicate how far a given raw score is above or below the mean of the distribution.

5. Many variables have a distribution approximating a *normal distribution*, depicted as a *normal curve*. The normal curve has a convenient property: When standard deviations are used as the units on the horizontal axis, the percentage of scores falling between any two points on the horizontal axis is always the same. Not all types of observations are distributed normally, however. Some distributions are *skewed* to the left or right.

6. Inferential statistics can be used to test the *null hypothesis* and to tell a researcher whether a result differed significantly from what might have been expected purely by chance. Basically, hypothesis testing involves estimating where the obtained result would have fallen in a theoretical *sampling distribution* based on studies of the entire population in question. If the result would have been far out in one of the tails of the distribution, it is considered statistically significant. A statistically significant result may or may not be psychologically interesting or important, so many researchers prefer to compute the *effect size*.

Key Terms

frequency distribution   A-1
graph   A-2
histogram/bar graph   A-2
frequency polygon/line graph   A-2

descriptive statistics   A-2
measure of central tendency   A-3
mean   A-3
median   A-3
mode   A-4
measure of variability   A-4
range   A-4
standard deviation   A-4
percentile score (centile rank)   A-5
z-score (standard score)   A-5
normal distribution   A-5
normal curve   A-5
inferential statistics   A-7
null hypothesis   A-7
alternative hypothesis   A-7
statistically significant   A-8
effect size   A-8

Glossary

absolute threshold The smallest quantity of physical energy that can be reliably detected by an observer.

accommodation In Piaget's theory, the process of modifying existing cognitive structures in response to experience and new information.

acculturation The process by which members of minority groups come to identify with and feel part of the mainstream culture.

action potential A brief change in electrical voltage that occurs between the inside and the outside of an axon when a neuron is stimulated; it serves to produce an electrical impulse.

activation–synthesis theory The theory that dreaming results from the cortical synthesis and interpretation of neural signals triggered by activity in the lower part of the brain.

adrenal hormones Hormones that are produced by the adrenal glands and that are involved in emotion and stress.

affect heuristic The tendency to consult one's emotions instead of estimating probabilities objectively.

agoraphobia A set of phobias, often set off by a panic attack, involving the basic fear of being away from a safe place or person.

algorithm A problem-solving strategy guaranteed to produce a solution even if the user does not know how it works.

Gordon Allport One of the most influential psychologists in the empirical study of personality.

alpha waves On an EEG recording, alpha waves have a regular, slow rhythm and a high amplitude (height).

alternate-forms reliability The ability of a test to return similar individual scores from one session to the next when different versions of the same test are given to the same group on two separate occasions.

altruism The willingness to take selfless or dangerous action on behalf of others.

amnesia The partial or complete loss of memory for important personal information.

amygdala [uh-MIG-dul-uh] A brain structure involved in the arousal and regulation of emotion and the initial emotional response to sensory information.

anabolic steroids Synthetic derivatives of testosterone that are taken in pill form or by injection, to increase muscle mass and strength.

anorexia (anorexia nervosa) An eating disorder characterized by fear of being fat, a distorted body image, radically reduced consumption of food, and emaciation.

anthropodenial The tendency to think, mistakenly, that human beings have nothing in common with other animals.

anthropomorphism The tendency to falsely attribute human qualities to nonhuman beings.

antidepressant drugs Drugs used primarily in the treatment of mood disorders, especially depression and anxiety.

antipsychotic drugs (neuroleptics) Drugs used primarily in the treatment of schizophrenia and other psychotic disorders.

antisocial personality disorder (APD) A personality disorder characterized by a lifelong pattern of irresponsible, antisocial behaviour such as lawbreaking, violence, and other impulsive, reckless acts.

anxiety A general state of apprehension or psychological tension.

applied behaviour analysis *See* behaviour modification.

applied psychology The study of psychological issues that have direct practical significance; also, the application of psychological findings.

approach–approach conflicts Conflicts that occur when you are equally attracted to two or more possible activities or goals.

approach–avoidance conflicts Conflicts that occur when a single activity or goal has both a positive and a negative aspect.

approach goals Goals framed in terms of desired outcomes or experiences, such as learning to scuba dive.

archetypes [AR-ki-tipes] Universal, symbolic images that appear in myths, art, stories, and dreams; to Jungians, they reflect the collective unconscious.

arithmetic mean An average that is calculated by adding up a set of quantities and dividing the sum by the total number of quantities in the set.

assimilation In Piaget's theory, the process of absorbing new information into existing cognitive structures.

association cortex Part of the brain that is involved in higher mental processes.

attachment theory Describes the relatively stable pattern of relationships that one forms from birth to death.

attachment theory of love People's attachment styles as adults derive in large part from how their parents cared for them.

attitude A belief about people, groups, ideas, or activities.

attributions The explanations that people make of their own and other people's behaviour.

attribution theory The theory that people are motivated to explain their own and other people's behaviour by attributing causes of that behaviour to a situation or a disposition.

audition The sense of hearing.

auditory cortex The part of the brain that processes sounds.

automatic encoding Mental processing and storage of information that takes place automatically, without deliberate effort.

autonomic nervous system The subdivision of the peripheral nervous system that regulates the internal organs and glands.

availability heuristic The tendency to judge the probability of a type of event by how easy it is to think of examples or instances.

avoidance–avoidance conflicts Conflicts that require you to choose the lesser of two evils because you dislike both alternatives.

avoidance goals Goals framed in terms of avoiding unpleasant experiences, such as trying not to look foolish in public.

axon A neuron's extending fibre that conducts impulses away from the cell body and transmits them to other neurons.

axon terminals Branches into which axons commonly divide at their ends.

basal metabolism rate The rate at which the body burns calories for energy.

basic concepts Concepts that have a moderate number of instances and that are easier to acquire than those having few or many instances.

basic psychology The study of psychological issues in order to seek knowledge for its own sake rather than for its practical application.

basilar membrane The rubbery membrane that stretches across the interior of the cochlea, in which the hair cells of the cochlea are embedded.

behavioural "ABCs" Antecedents (events preceding behaviours), behaviours, and consequences.

behavioural genetics An interdisciplinary field of study concerned with the genetic bases of individual differences in behaviour and personality.

behavioural self-monitoring In behaviour therapy, a method of keeping careful data on the frequency and consequences of the behaviour to be changed.

behaviourism An approach to psychology that emphasizes the study of observable behaviour and the role of the environment as a determinant of behaviour.

behaviour modification The application of operant conditioning techniques to teach new responses or to reduce or eliminate maladaptive or problematic behaviour; also called *applied behaviour analysis*.

behaviour therapy A form of therapy that applies principles of classical and operant conditioning to help people change self-defeating or problematic behaviours.

benevolent sexism Sexism in which superficially positive attitudes put women on a pedestal but nonetheless reinforce women's subordination.

Big Five personality factors A cluster of five "robust" central personality traits: extroversion/introversion, neuroticism/emotional stability, agreeableness/antagonism, conscientiousness/impulsiveness, openness/resistance to experience.

binocular cues Visual cues to depth or distance requiring two eyes.

biological model of addiction Addiction, whether to alcohol or any other drug, is due primarily to a person's biochemistry, metabolism, and genetic predisposition.

biological perspective A psychological approach that emphasizes bodily events and changes associated with actions, feelings, and thoughts.

biological rhythm A periodic, more or less regular fluctuation in a biological system; it may or may not have psychological implications.

bipolar disorder A mood disorder in which episodes of both depression and mania (excessive euphoria) occur.

blaming the victim Thinking that the victim of an action must have done something to deserve what happened or to provoke it.

body language Nonverbal signals of body movement, posture, gesture, and gaze.

borderline personality disorder A disorder characterized by intense but unstable relationships, a fear of abandonment by others, an unrealistic self-image, and emotional volatility.

brain stem The part of the brain at the top of the spinal cord, consisting of the medulla and the pons.

brightness Lightness or luminance; the dimension of visual experience related to the amount (intensity) of light emitted from or reflected by an object.

Broca's area The part of the brain that handles speech production.

bulimia An eating disorder characterized by episodes of excessive eating (bingeing) followed by forced vomiting or use of laxatives (purging).

bystander apathy In crowds, individuals' failure to take action or call for help because they assume that someone else will do so.

case study A detailed description of a particular individual being studied or treated.

catatonic stupor A condition in which a person has withdrawn into a private world, and sits for hours without moving.

Raymond Cattell Devised the factor analysis statistical method for analyzing personality traits.

cell body The part of the neuron that keeps it alive and determines whether it will fire.

central nervous system (CNS) The portion of the nervous system consisting of the brain and spinal cord.

central traits Aspects of personality that reflect a characteristic way of behaving, dealing with others, and reacting to new situations.

cerebellum A brain structure that regulates movement and balance and is involved in the learning of certain kinds of simple responses.

cerebral cortex A collection of several thin layers of cells covering the cerebrum; it is largely responsible for higher mental functions. *Cortex* is Latin for "bark" or "rind."

cerebral hemispheres The two halves of the cerebrum.

cerebrum [suh-REE-brum] The largest brain structure, consisting of the upper part of the brain; divided into two hemispheres, it is in charge of most sensory, motor, and cognitive processes. From the Latin for "brain."

childhood (infantile) amnesia The inability to remember events and experiences that occurred during the first two or three years of life.

chromosomes Within every cell, rod-shaped structures that carry the genes.

chunk A meaningful unit of information; it may be composed of smaller units.

circadian [sur-CAY-dee-un] rhythm A biological rhythm with a period (from peak to peak or trough to trough) of about 24 hours; from the Latin *circa*, "about," and *dies*, "a day."

classical conditioning The process by which a previously neutral stimulus acquires the capacity to elicit a response through association with a stimulus that already elicits a similar or related response.

client-centred (nondirective) therapy A humanist approach, devised by Carl Rogers, which emphasizes the therapist's empathy with the client and the use of unconditional positive regard.

clinical psychologist Practitioner who diagnoses, treats, and studies mental or emotional problems.

cochlea [KOCK-lee-uh] A snail-shaped, fluid-filled organ in the inner ear, containing the organ of Corti, where the receptors for hearing are located.

coefficient of correlation A measure of correlation that ranges in value from −1.00 to +1.00.

coercive persuasion Persuasive techniques designed to suppress an individual's ability to reason, think critically, and make choices in his or her own best interests.

cognitive approach to intelligence Assumes there are many kinds of intelligence and emphasizes the strategies people use when thinking about a problem and arriving at a solution.

cognitive dissonance A state of tension that occurs when a person simultaneously holds two cognitions that are psychologically inconsistent or when a person's belief is incongruent with his or her behaviour.

cognitive ethology The study of cognitive processes in nonhuman animals.

cognitive perspective A psychological approach that emphasizes mental processes in perception, memory, language, problem solving, and other areas of behaviour.

cognitive schema An integrated mental network of knowledge, beliefs, and expectations concerning a particular topic or aspect of the world.

cognitive therapy A form of therapy designed to identify and change irrational, unproductive ways of thinking and, hence, to reduce negative emotions.

collective unconscious In Jungian theory, the universal memories and experiences of humankind, represented in the symbols, stories, and images (archetypes) that occur across all cultures.

collectivist cultures Cultures in which the self is regarded as embedded in relationships, and harmony with one's group is prized above individual goals and wishes.

companionate love Love characterized by affection and trust.

componential intelligence The information-processing strategies you draw on when you are thinking intelligently about a problem.

computer neural networks Mathematical models of the brain that "learn" by adjusting the connections among hypothetical neurons in response to incoming data.

concept A mental category that groups objects, relations, activities, abstractions, or qualities having common properties.

conditioned response (CR) The classical-conditioning term for a response that is elicited by a conditioned stimulus; it occurs after the conditioned stimulus is associated with an unconditioned stimulus.

conditioned stimulus (CS) The classical-conditioning term for an initially neutral stimulus that comes to elicit a conditioned response after being associated with an unconditioned stimulus.

conditioning A basic kind of learning that involves associations between environmental stimuli and the organism's responses.

cones Visual receptors involved in colour vision.

confabulation Confusion of an event that happened to someone else with one that happened to you, or a belief that you remember something when it never actually happened.

confirmation bias The tendency to look for or pay attention to only information that confirms one's own belief.

congruence Harmony between the image people project to others and their true feelings and wishes.

consciousness Awareness of oneself and the environment.

conservation The understanding that the physical properties of objects—such as the number of items in a cluster or the amount of liquid in a glass—can remain the same even when their form or appearance changes.

consolidation A process by which the synaptic changes associated with recently stored memories become durable and stable, causing memory to become more reliable.

contact comfort In primates, the innate pleasure derived from close physical contact; it is the basis of the infant's first attachment.

contact hypothesis Prejudice declines when people have the chance to get used to one another's rules, food, music, customs, and attitudes, thereby discovering their shared interests and shared humanity.

content validity The ability of a test to assess the trait in question.

contextual (practical) intelligence The practical application of intelligence, which requires you to take into account the different contexts in which you find yourself.

continuous reinforcement A reinforcement schedule in which a particular response is always reinforced.

control condition In an experiment, a comparison condition in which subjects are not exposed to the same treatment as in the experimental condition.

control group Participants in an experiment who are not exposed to the manipulation of the independent variable.

convergence The turning inward of the eyes, which occurs when they focus on a nearby object.

convergent thinking Thinking typical of uncreative people, who follow a particular set of steps that they think will converge on one correct solution; once they have solved a problem, they tend to develop a mental set and approach future problems the same way.

conversational distance How close people normally stand to one another when they are speaking.

coping Actively trying to manage demands that feel stressful.

corpus callosum [CORE-puhs cah-LOW-suhm] The bundle of nerve fibres connecting the two cerebral hemispheres.

correlation A measure of how strongly two variables are related to one another.

correlational study A descriptive study that looks for a consistent relationship between two phenomena.

counselling psychologist Practitioner who generally helps people deal with problems of everyday life, such as test anxiety, family conflicts, or low job motivation.

counterconditioning In classical conditioning, the process of pairing a conditioned stimulus with a stimulus that elicits a response that is incompatible with an unwanted conditioned response.

couples therapy An approach to doing therapy with couples, in which the therapist sees both partners and helps them manage the inevitable conflicts that occur in all relationships.

criterion validity The ability of a test to predict independent measures, or criteria, of the trait in question.

critical period A crucial window of time during which certain experiences must be had or perception will be impaired.

critical thinking The ability and willingness to assess claims and make objective judgments on the basis of well-supported reasons and evidence rather than emotion or anecdote.

cross-sectional study A study in which subjects of different ages are compared at a given time.

crystallized intelligence Cognitive skills and specific knowledge of information acquired over a lifetime; it is heavily dependent on education and tends to remain stable over the lifetime.

cue-dependent forgetting The inability to retrieve information stored in memory because of insufficient cues for recall.

cultural psychologists Practitioners who examine how cultural rules and values—both explicit and unspoken—affect people's development, behaviour, and feelings.

culture A program of shared rules that govern the behaviour of people in a community or society, and a set of values, beliefs, and customs shared by most members of that community.

culture-bound syndromes Disorders that are specific to particular cultural contexts.

culture of honour Culture in which even apparently small disputes and trivial insults threaten the reputation of an individual, family, or group, requiring a violent response to restore its status.

dark adaptation A process by which visual receptors become maximally sensitive to dim light.

Charles Darwin (1809–1882) British naturalist who pioneered the theory of evolution of species.

decay theory The theory that information in memory eventually disappears if it is not accessed; this theory applies better to short-term than to long-term memory.

declarative memories Memories of facts, rules, concepts, and events ("knowing that"); they include semantic and episodic memories.

deductive reasoning A form of reasoning in which a conclusion follows necessarily from certain premises; if the premises are true, the conclusion must be true.

deep processing In the encoding of information, the processing of meaning rather than simply the physical or sensory features of a stimulus.

deep structure How a sentence is to be understood.

defence mechanisms Methods used by the ego to prevent unconscious anxiety or threatening thoughts from entering consciousness.

deindividuation In groups or crowds, the loss of awareness of one's own individuality.

delta waves Very slow brain waves with very high peaks.

dendrites A neuron's branches that receive information from other neurons and transmit it toward the cell body.

denial In psychoanalytic theory, when people refuse to admit that something unpleasant is happening, that they have a problem, or that they are feeling a forbidden emotion; denial protects the self-image and preserves the illusion of invulnerability.

dependent variable A variable that an experimenter predicts will be affected by manipulations of the independent variable.

depressants Drugs that slow activity in the central nervous system.

descriptive methods Methods that yield descriptions of behaviour but not necessarily causal explanations.

descriptive statistics Statistical procedures that organize and summarize research data.

developmental psychologist Practitioner who studies how people change and grow over time—physically, mentally, and socially.

***Diagnostic and Statistical Manual of Mental Disorders* (DSM)** The standard reference manual used to diagnose mental disorders, published by the American Psychiatric Association.

dialectical reasoning A process in which opposing facts or ideas are weighed and compared, with a view to determining the best solution or resolving differences.

difference threshold The smallest difference in stimulation that can be reliably detected by an observer when two stimuli are compared; also called *just noticeable difference (jnd)*.

diffusion of responsibility In groups, the tendency of members to avoid taking action because they assume that others will.

discriminative stimulus A stimulus that signals when a particular response is likely to be followed by a certain type of consequence.

displacement In psychoanalytic theory, when people direct their emotions (especially anger) toward things, animals, or other people that are not the real object of their feelings.

display rules Social and cultural rules that regulate when, how, and where a person may express (or must suppress) emotions.

dispositional attribution Identifying the cause of an action as something in the person, such as a trait or a motive.

dissociation A split in consciousness in which one part of the mind operates independently of other parts.

dissociative identity disorder A controversial disorder marked by the apparent appearance within one person of two or more distinct personalities, each with its own name and traits; formerly known as *multiple personality disorder (MPD)*.

divergent thinking Thinking typical of creative people, who, instead of stubbornly sticking to one tried-and-true path, explore side alleys and generate several possible solutions; they come up with new hypotheses, imagine other interpretations, and look for connections that are not immediately obvious.

DNA (deoxyribonucleic acid) The chromosomal molecule that transfers genetic characteristics by way of coded instructions for the structure of proteins.

doctrine of specific nerve energies The principle that different sensory modalities exist because signals received by the sense organs stimulate different nerve pathways leading to different areas of the brain.

dominance (hemispheric) The left hemisphere of the brain usually exerts control over the right hemisphere.

double-blind study An experiment in which neither the subjects nor the individuals running the study know which subjects are in the control group and which are in the experimental group until after the results are tallied.

drives Biological urges, such as those to acquire food and water, to have sex, to seek novelty, and to avoid cold and pain.

educational psychologist Practitioner who studies psychological principles that explain learning and searches for ways to improve educational systems.

effect size The amount of variance, a statistical measure of the variability among scores in a study accounted for by the independent variable.

effortful encoding Deliberate efforts to retain complex information, which may include selecting the main points, labelling concepts, or actively associating the information with personal experiences or with already familiar material.

ego In psychoanalysis, the part of personality that represents reason, good sense, and rational self-control.

egocentric thinking Seeing the world from only your own point of view; the inability to take another person's perspective.

elaborative rehearsal Association of new information with already stored knowledge and analysis of the new information to make it memorable.

electroconvulsive therapy (ECT) A procedure used in cases of prolonged and severe major depression, in which a brief brain seizure is induced.

electroencephalogram (EEG) A recording of neural activity detected by electrodes.

embryo In prenatal development, the organism between the time of implantation and the eighth week of pregnancy.

embryonic stage Stage of prenatal development that begins once implantation is completed, about two weeks after fertilization, and lasts until the eighth week after conception.

emerging adulthood Phase of life of many young people aged 18–25 who are in college or university and at least partly dependent financially on their parents; in some ways, they consider themselves to have reached adulthood, and in other ways, they feel they have not.

emotion A state of arousal involving facial and bodily changes, brain activation, cognitive appraisals, subjective feelings, and tendencies toward action, all shaped by cultural rules.

emotional intelligence The ability to identify your own and other people's emotions accurately, express your emotions clearly, and regulate emotions in yourself and others.

emotion-focused coping Dealing with a problem by concentrating on the emotions the problem has caused, whether anger, anxiety, or grief.

emotion regulation Modifying and controlling what we feel.

emotion work Expression of an emotion that the person does not really feel, often because of a role requirement.

empirical Relying on or derived from observation, experimentation, or measurement.

empiricists Psychologists who focused on learning and experience, or nurture, as accounting for the similarities and differences among people.

endocrine glands Internal organs that produce hormones and release them into the bloodstream.

endogenous Generated from within rather than by external cues.

endorphins [en-DOR-fins] Chemical substances in the nervous system that are similar in structure and action to opiates; they are involved in pain reduction, pleasure, and memory and are known technically as *endogenous opioid peptides*.

entrainment The synchronization of biological rhythms with external cues, such as fluctuations in daylight.

entrapment A gradual process in which individuals escalate their commitment to a course of action to justify their investment of time, money, or effort.

episodic memories Memories of personally experienced events and the contexts in which they occurred.

equilibrium The sense of balance.

Erik Erikson (1902–1994) One of the first modern theorists to propose a lifespan approach to psychological development. Erikson proposed that all individuals go through eight stages in their lives, each characterized by a particular "crisis" that ideally should be resolved before the individual moves on.

ethnic identity A person's identification with a racial or ethnic group.

ethnocentrism The belief that one's own ethnic group, nation, or religion is superior to all others.

eugenics A discredited social movement that aimed to "improve" the species through forced sterilization of low-IQ people.

evolution A change in gene frequencies within a population over many generations; a mechanism by which genetically influenced characteristics of a population may change.

evolutionary psychology A field of psychology emphasizing evolutionary mechanisms that may help explain human commonalities in cognition, development, emotion, social practices, and other areas of behaviour.

existentialism A philosophical approach that emphasizes the inevitable dilemmas and challenges of human existence.

existential therapy A form of therapy designed to help clients explore the meaning of existence and face the great questions of life, such as death, freedom, alienation, and loneliness.

experiential (creative) intelligence Your creativity in transferring skills to new situations.

experiment A controlled test of a hypothesis in which the researcher manipulates one variable to discover its effect on another.

experimental group Participants in an experiment who are exposed to the manipulation of the independent variable.

experimental psychologist Practitioner who conducts laboratory studies of learning, motivation, emotion, sensation and perception, physiology, and cognition.

experimenter effects Unintended changes in subjects' behaviour due to cues inadvertently given by the experimenter.

explicit attitude An attitude that we are aware of, that shapes our conscious decisions and actions, and that can be measured on self-report questionnaires.

explicit memory Conscious, intentional recollection of an event or of an item of information.

extinction The weakening and eventual disappearance of a learned response. In classical conditioning, it occurs when the conditioned stimulus is no longer paired with the unconditioned stimulus; in operant conditioning, it occurs when a response is no longer followed by a reinforcer.

extrinsic motivation The pursuit of an activity for external rewards, such as money or fame.

extrinsic reinforcers Reinforcers that are not inherently related to the activity being reinforced.

facial feedback The process by which the facial muscles send messages to the brain about the basic emotion being expressed.

factor analysis A statistical method for analyzing the intercorrelations among various measures or test scores; clusters of measures or scores that are highly correlated are assumed to measure the same underlying trait, ability, or aptitude (factor).

fairness bias A sense of fairness often takes precedence over rational self-interest when people make economic choices.

familiarity effect The tendency of people to feel more positively toward a person, item, product, or other stimulus the more familiar they are with it.

family-systems perspective An approach to doing therapy with individuals or families by identifying how each family member forms part of a larger interacting system.

family therapy An approach to doing therapy with individuals or families holding that an individual's problem develops in the context of the family, that it is sustained by the dynamics of the family, and that any change the individual makes will affect all members of the family.

feature detector cells Cells in the visual cortex that are sensitive to specific features of the environment.

feminist psychology A psychological approach that analyzes the influence of social inequities on gender relations and on the behaviour of the two sexes.

fetal alcohol syndrome (FAS) Birth defect caused by maternal alcohol consumption during pregnancy, associated with low birth weight, a smaller brain, facial deformities, lack of coordination, and mental retardation.

fetal stage Stage of prenatal development from eight weeks after conception until birth, during which the fetus further develops the organs and systems that existed in rudimentary form in the embryonic stage.

fetus In prenatal development, the organism between the eighth week of pregnancy and the time of birth.

field research Descriptive or experimental research conducted in a natural setting outside the laboratory.

figure The item of interest that stands out from the rest of the environment.

flashbulb memories Memories characterized by surprise, illumination, and seemingly photographic detail about some unusual, shocking, or tragic events, such as earthquakes or accidents, especially when we have experienced them personally; such events seem frozen in time, with all the details intact.

flooding In behaviour therapy, a form of exposure treatment in which the client is taken directly into the feared situation and remains there until his or her panic subsides.

fluid intelligence The capacity for deductive reasoning and the ability to use new information to solve problems; it is relatively independent of education and tends to decline in old age.

formal reasoning problems Problems that can be solved using established methods and clearly specified information; you usually know when it has been solved, and there is a single right (or best) answer.

framing effect The tendency for people's choices to be affected by how a choice is presented, or framed; for example, whether it is worded in terms of potential losses or gains.

fraternal (dizygotic) twins Twins that develop from two separate eggs fertilized by different sperm; they are no more alike genetically than are any other pair of siblings.

free association In psychodynamic therapies, the process of saying freely whatever comes to mind in connection with dreams, memories, fantasies, or conflicts.

frequency (sound wave) How rapidly the air (or other medium) vibrates—that is, the number of times per second the wave cycles through a peak and a low point.

Sigmund Freud (1856–1939) Austrian neurologist who pioneered the field of psychoanalysis.

frontal lobes Lobes at the front of the brain's cerebral cortex; they contain areas involved in short-term memory, higher-order thinking, initiative, social judgment, and (in the left lobe, typically) speech production.

functionalism An early psychological approach that emphasized the function or purpose of behaviour and consciousness.

fundamental attribution error The tendency, in explaining other people's behaviour, to overestimate personality factors and underestimate the influence of the situation.

g factor A general intellectual ability assumed by many theorists to underlie specific mental abilities and talents.

ganglion cells Neurons in the retina of the eye that gather information from receptor cells (by way of intermediate bipolar cells); their axons make up the optic nerve.

gate-control theory of pain The theory that the experience of pain depends in part on whether pain impulses get past a neurological "gate" in the spinal cord and thus reach the brain.

gender identity The fundamental sense of being male or female; it is independent of whether the person conforms to the social and cultural rules of gender.

gender roles Collections of rules that determine the proper attitudes and behaviour for men and women.

gender schema A cognitive schema (mental network) of knowledge, beliefs, metaphors, and expectations about what it means to be male or female.

gender typing The process by which children learn the abilities, interests, and behaviours associated with being masculine or feminine in their culture.

general adaptation syndrome According to Hans Selye, a series of physiological responses to stressors that occur in three phases: alarm, resistance, and exhaustion.

generalized anxiety disorder A continuous state of anxiety marked by feelings of worry and dread, apprehension, difficulties in concentration, and signs of motor tension.

genes The functional units of heredity; they are composed of DNA and specify the structure of proteins.

genetic marker A segment of DNA that varies among individuals, has a known location on a chromosome, and can function as a genetic landmark for a gene involved in a physical or mental condition.

genome The full set of genes in each cell of an organism (with the exception of sperm and egg cells).

germinal stage Stage of prenatal development that begins at conception, when the male's sperm unites with the female's ovum (egg).

gerontologist Researcher who studies aging and the old.

Gestalt principles Principles that describe the brain's organization of sensory information into meaningful units and patterns.

glia [GLY-uh or GLEE-uh] Cells that support, nurture, and insulate neurons, remove debris when neurons die, enhance the formation and maintenance of neural connections, and modify neuronal functioning.

graduated exposure In behaviour therapy, a method in which a person suffering from a phobia or panic attacks is gradually taken into the feared situation or exposed to a traumatic memory until the anxiety subsides.

ground The environment or background.

group-serving bias The tendency to explain favourably the behaviours of members of groups to which we belong.

groupthink The tendency for all members of a group to think alike for the sake of harmony and to suppress disagreement.

Guilty Knowledge Test A test for lying that uses a series of multiple-choice questions, each offering one relevant answer about the crime under investigation and several neutral answers, chosen so that an innocent suspect will not be able to discriminate them from the relevant one.

gustation The sense of taste.

health psychology Studying the biological, psychological, social, and cultural factors that influence health and illness.

heritability A statistical estimate of the proportion of the total variance in some trait that is attributable to genetic differences among individuals within a group.

heuristic A rule of thumb that suggests a course of action or guides problem solving but does not guarantee an optimal solution.

hidden observer According to Ernest Hilgard, in many hypnotized persons, one part of the mind that is watching but not participating while most of the mind is subject to hypnotic suggestion.

higher-order conditioning In classical conditioning, a procedure in which a neutral stimulus becomes a conditioned stimulus through association with an already established conditioned stimulus.

hindsight bias The tendency to overestimate one's ability to have predicted an event once the outcome is known; the "I knew it all along" phenomenon.

hippocampus A brain structure involved in the storage of new information in memory.

hormones Chemical substances, secreted by organs called *glands*, that affect the functioning of other organs.

hostile sexism Sexism that reflects active dislike of women.

HPA (hypothalamus–pituitary–adrenal cortex) axis A system activated to energize the body to respond to stressors. The hypothalamus sends chemical messengers to the pituitary, which in turn prompts the adrenal cortex to produce cortisol and other hormones.

hue The dimension of visual experience specified by colour names and related to the wavelength of light.

humanist psychology A psychological approach that emphasizes personal growth and the achievement of human potential rather than the scientific understanding and assessment of behaviour.

humanist therapy A form of psychotherapy based on the philosophy of humanism, which emphasizes the client's free will to change rather than past conflicts.

hypnosis A procedure in which the practitioner suggests changes in the sensations, perceptions, thoughts, feelings, or behaviour of the participant.

hypothalamus A brain structure involved in emotions and drives vital to survival, such as fear, hunger, thirst, and reproduction; it regulates the autonomic nervous system.

hypothesis A statement that attempts to predict or to account for a set of phenomena; scientific hypotheses specify relationships among events or variables and are empirically tested.

id In psychoanalysis, the part of personality containing inherited psychic energy, particularly sexual and aggressive instincts.

identical (monozygotic) twins Twins that develop when a fertilized egg divides into two parts that develop into separate embryos.

identity crisis A person's internal struggle to decide what to be and what to make of this life; those who resolve it will have a strong identity and be ready to plan for the future; those who do not will sink into confusion, unable to make decisions.

illusion of causality Assuming that if A came before B, then A must have caused B.

imagination inflation The more people think about an imagined event, the more their active imaginations inflate their belief that the event really occurred.

implicit attitude An attitude that we are unaware of, that may influence our behaviour in ways we do not recognize, and that is measured in various indirect ways.

implicit learning Learning that occurs when you acquire knowledge about something without being aware of how you did so and without being able to state exactly what it is you have learned.

implicit memory Unconscious retention in memory, as evidenced by the effect of a previous experience or previously encountered information on current thoughts or actions.

inattentional blindness Failure to consciously perceive something you are looking at because you are not attending to it.

incentive pay Bonuses that are given upon completion of a goal rather than as an automatic raise.

independent variable A variable that an experimenter manipulates.

individualist cultures Cultures in which the self is regarded as autonomous, and individual goals and wishes are prized above duty and relations with others.

induction A method of child rearing in which the parent appeals to the child's own abilities, sense of responsibility, and feelings for others in correcting the child's misbehaviour.

inductive reasoning A form of reasoning in which the premises provide support for a conclusion, but it is still possible for the conclusion to be false.

industrial/organizational psychologist Practitioner who studies behaviour in the workplace.

inferential statistics Statistical procedures that allow researchers to draw inferences about how statistically meaningful a study's results are.

informal reasoning problems Problems with no clearly correct solution in which many approaches, viewpoints, or possible solutions may compete; information may be incomplete, or people may disagree on what the premises should be.

information-processing models of memory Models that liken human cognitive processes to the workings of a computer, in which we encode information (convert it to a form that the brain can process and use), store the information (retain it over time), and retrieve the information (recover it for use). In storage, the information may be represented as concepts, propositions, images, or cognitive schemas.

informed consent The doctrine that human research subjects must participate voluntarily and must know enough about the study to make an intelligent decision about whether to participate.

instinctive drift During operant learning, the tendency for an organism to revert to instinctive behaviour.

integrative approach to psychotherapy Drawing on methods and ideas from various schools and avoiding strong allegiances to any one theory enables therapists to treat clients with whatever methods are most appropriate and effective.

intelligence An inferred characteristic of an individual, usually defined as the ability to profit from experience, acquire knowledge, think abstractly, act purposefully, or adapt to changes in the environment.

intelligence quotient (IQ) A measure of intelligence originally computed by dividing a person's mental age by his or her chronological age and multiplying the result by 100; it is now derived from norms provided for standardized intelligence tests.

intermittent (partial) schedule of reinforcement A reinforcement schedule in which a particular response is sometimes but not always reinforced.

internal desynchronization A state in which biological rhythms are not in phase (synchronized) with one another.

intersex conditions Conditions, occurring in about one of every 2000 births, in which chromosomal or hormonal anomalies cause a child to be born with ambiguous genitals, or genitals that conflict with the infant's chromosomes (formerly called *hermaphroditism*).

intrinsic motivation The pursuit of an activity for its own sake.

intrinsic reinforcers Reinforcers that are inherently related to the activity being reinforced.

William James (1842–1910) American philosopher, physician, and psychologist and a leader of functionalism.

Carl Jung (1875–1961) Originally one of Freud's collaborators; Jung proposed the idea of the collective unconscious and pioneered the school of Jungian analysis.

justification of effort The tendency of individuals to increase their liking for something that they have worked hard or suffered to attain; a common form of dissonance reduction.

just-world hypothesis The notion that many people need to believe that the world is fair and that justice is served, that bad people are punished and good people rewarded.

kinesthesis [KIN-es-THEE-sís] The sense of body position and movement of body parts; also called *kinesthesia*.

laboratory observation Observing how people or animals act in a laboratory setting.

language A system that combines meaningless elements such as sounds or gestures to form structured utterances that convey meaning.

language acquisition device According to many psycholinguists, an innate mental module that allows young children to develop language if they are exposed to an adequate sampling of conversation.

latent content The aspects of a dream that are unconscious wishes and thoughts being expressed symbolically.

latent learning A form of learning that is not immediately expressed in an overt response; it occurs without obvious reinforcement.

lateralization Specialization of the two cerebral hemispheres for particular operations.

leading questions Questions asked using words chosen to lead the witness to answer as the questioner wishes.

learning A relatively permanent change in behaviour (or behavioural potential) due to experience.

learning model of addiction Examines the role of the environment, learning, and culture in encouraging or discouraging drug abuse and addiction.

learning perspective A psychological approach that emphasizes how the environment and experience affect a person's or animal's actions; it includes behaviourism and social-cognitive learning theories.

leptin A protein secreted by fat cells that acts upon the brain's hypothalamus, which is involved in the regulation of appetite.

lesion method An approach to studying the brain that involves damaging or removing sections of brain in animals and then observing the effects.

libido [li-BEE-do] In psychoanalysis, the psychic energy that fuels the life or sexual instincts of the id.

life narratives The stories that each of us develops over time to explain ourselves and make meaning of everything that has happened to us.

limbic system A group of brain areas involved in emotional reactions and motivated behaviour.

linkage studies Studies that look for patterns of inheritance of genetic markers in large families in which a particular condition is common.

lithium carbonate A drug frequently given to people suffering from bipolar disorder.

localization of function Specialization of particular brain areas for particular functions.

locus of control A general expectation about whether the results of your actions are under your own control (internal locus) or beyond your control (external locus).

longitudinal study A study in which subjects are followed and periodically reassessed over a period of time.

long-term memory (LTM) In the three-box model of memory, the memory system involved in the long-term storage of information.

long-term potentiation A long-lasting increase in the strength of synaptic responsiveness, thought to be a biological mechanism of long-term memory.

loudness The dimension of auditory experience related to the intensity of a pressure wave.

lucid dream A dream in which the dreamer is aware of dreaming.

maintenance rehearsal Rote repetition of material in order to maintain its availability in memory.

major depression A mood disorder involving disturbances in emotion (excessive sadness), behaviour (loss of interest in one's usual activities), cognition (thoughts of hopelessness), and body function (fatigue and loss of appetite).

mania An abnormally high state of exhilaration.

manifest content The aspects of a dream that we consciously experience during sleep and may remember upon wakening.

Abraham Maslow (1908–1970) One of three chief leaders of the humanist psychology movement; Maslow believed in the importance of peak experiences and self-actualization.

Maslow's hierarchy of needs A pyramid expressing the relative importance of different motives for people: at the bottom level of the pyramid are basic survival needs, for food, sleep, and water; at the next level are security needs, for shelter and safety; at the third level are social needs, for belonging and affection; at the fourth level are esteem needs, for self-respect and the respect of others; and at the top are needs for self-actualization and self-transcendence.

maturation The sequential unfolding of genetically influenced physical and behavioural characteristics.

Rollo May (1909–1994) One of three chief leaders of the humanist psychology movement; an existentialist who believed in free will but also emphasized some of the inherently difficult and tragic aspects of the human condition, including loneliness, anxiety, and alienation.

mean *See* arithmetic mean.

medulla [muh-DUL-uh] A structure in the brain stem responsible for certain automatic functions, such as breathing and heart rate.

melatonin A hormone, secreted by the pineal gland, that is involved in the regulation of daily biological (circadian) rhythms.

memory The capacity to retain and retrieve information, and the changes in the structures that account for this capacity.

menarche [men-ARR-kee] The onset of menstruation.

menopause The cessation of menstruation and of the production of ova; it is usually a gradual process lasting up to several years.

mental age (MA) A measure of mental development expressed in terms of the average mental ability at a given age.

mental disorder Any behaviour or emotional state that causes an individual great suffering, is self-destructive, seriously impairs the person's ability to work or get along with others, or endangers others or the community.

mental image A mental representation that mirrors or resembles the thing it represents; mental images occur in many and perhaps all sensory modalities.

mental modules A collection of specialized and independent sections of the brain, developed to handle specific survival problems, such as the need to locate food or find a mate.

mental set A tendency to solve problems using procedures that worked before on similar problems.

meta-analysis A procedure for combining and analyzing data from many studies; it determines how much of the variance in scores across all studies can be explained by a particular variable.

metacognition The knowledge or awareness of one's own cognitive processes.

mindlessness Mental inflexibility, inertia, and obliviousness to the present context.

Minnesota Multiphasic Personality Inventory (MMPI) A widely used objective personality test.

mirror neurons A class of cells, distributed throughout various parts of the brain, that fire when an animal sees or hears an action and carries out the same action on its own; these cells are far more evolved and varied in human beings than in other animals.

mnemonics [neh-MON-iks] Strategies and tricks for improving memory, such as the use of a verse or a formula.

monocular cues Visual cues to depth or distance that can be used by one eye alone.

mood-congruent memory The tendency to remember experiences that are consistent with one's current mood and overlook or forget experiences that are not.

mood contagion A mood spreading from one person to another, as facial expressions of emotion in the first person generate emotions in the other.

mood disorders Disturbances in mood ranging from extreme depression to extreme mania.

motivation An inferred process within a person or animal that causes movement either toward a goal or away from an unpleasant situation.

motivational interviewing A therapy for treating alcohol abuse that focuses specifically on increasing a client's motivation to change problem drinking.

motor cortex The part of the brain that issues orders to the 600 muscles of the body that produce voluntary movement.

motor nerves Nerves in the peripheral nervous system that carry orders from the central nervous system to muscles, glands, and internal organs; they enable us to move, and they cause glands to contract and to secrete substances, including hormones.

motor reflexes Automatic behaviours that are necessary for survival.

MRI (magnetic resonance imaging) A method for studying body and brain tissue, using magnetic fields and special radio receivers.

multisystemic therapy (MST) An important community intervention whose practitioners combine family systems techniques with behavioural methods, but apply them in the context of forming "neighbourhood partnerships" with local leaders, residents, parents, and teachers to help prevent or reduce teenagers' problems.

mutation Changes in genes, sometimes due to an error in the copying of the original DNA sequence during the division of the cells that produce sperm and eggs.

myelin sheath A fatty insulation that may surround the axon of a neuron.

narcissistic personality disorder A disorder characterized by an exaggerated sense of self-importance and self-absorption.

narcolepsy A sleep disorder involving sudden and unpredictable daytime attacks of sleepiness or lapses into REM sleep.

narratives Stories that human beings tell.

nativists Psychologists who emphasized genes and inborn characteristics, or nature, as accounting for the similarities and differences among people.

naturalistic observation Observing how people or animals act in their normal social environments.

natural selection The evolutionary process in which individuals with genetically influenced traits that are adaptive in a particular environment tend to survive and to reproduce in greater numbers than do other individuals; as a result, their traits become more common in the population.

need for achievement A learned motive to meet personal standards of success and excellence in a chosen area.

negative afterimage Seeing, for instance, red after staring at green; the cells that switch on or off to signal the presence of "green" send the opposite signal ("red") when the green is removed—and vice versa.

negative correlation An association between increases in one variable and decreases in another.

negative reinforcement A reinforcement procedure in which a response is followed by the removal, delay, or decrease in intensity of an unpleasant stimulus; as a result, the response becomes stronger or more likely to occur.

nerve A bundle of nerve fibres (axons and sometimes dendrites) in the peripheral nervous system.

neuroethics A new interdisciplinary specialty addressing the legal, ethical, and scientific implications of brain research.

neurogenesis The production of new neurons from immature stem cells.

neuron A cell that conducts electrochemical signals; the basic unit of the nervous system; also called a *nerve cell*.

neurotransmitter A chemical substance that is released by a transmitting neuron at the synapse and that alters the activity of a receiving neuron.

nodes Constrictions in the myelin sheath.

nonconscious processes Mental processes occurring outside of and not available to conscious awareness.

non-REM (NREM) sleep Sleep periods characterized by fewer eye movements than in REM sleep.

nonshared environment Unique aspects of a person's environment and experience that are not shared with family members.

norms In test construction, established standards of performance.

norms (social) Rules that regulate social life, including explicit laws and implicit cultural conventions.

objective tests (inventories) Standardized questionnaires requiring written responses; they typically include scales on which people are asked to rate themselves.

object permanence The understanding, which develops throughout the first year, that an object continues to exist even when you cannot see it or touch it.

object-relations school A psychodynamic approach that emphasizes the importance of the infant's first two years of life and the baby's formative relationships, especially with the mother.

observational learning A process in which an individual learns new responses by observing the behaviour of another (a model) rather than through direct experience; sometimes called *vicarious conditioning*.

observational studies Studies in which the researcher carefully and systematically observes and records behaviour without interfering with the behaviour; it may involve either naturalistic or laboratory observation.

obsessive-compulsive disorder (OCD) An anxiety disorder in which a person feels trapped in repetitive, persistent thoughts (obsessions) and repetitive, ritualized behaviours (compulsions) designed to reduce anxiety.

Occam's Razor The principle of choosing the solution that accounts for the most evidence while making the fewest unverified assumptions.

occipital [ahk-SIP-uh-tuhl] lobes Lobes at the lower back part of the brain's cerebral cortex; they contain areas that receive visual information.

Oedipus complex In psychoanalysis, a conflict occurring in the phallic (Oedipal) stage, in which a child desires the parent of the other sex and views the same-sex parent as a rival.

olfaction The sense of smell.

operant conditioning The process by which a response becomes more likely to occur or less so, depending on its consequences.

operational definition A precise definition of a term in a hypothesis, which specifies the operations for observing and measuring the process or phenomenon being defined.

operations In Piaget's theory, mental actions that are cognitively reversible.

opiates Drugs, derived from the opium poppy, that relieve pain and commonly produce euphoria.

opponent-process theory A theory of colour perception that assumes that the visual system treats pairs of colours as opposing or antagonistic.

organ of Corti [core-tee] A structure in the cochlea containing hair cells that serve as the receptors for hearing.

overregularizations Non-random errors in grammar that show a child has grasped a grammatical rule.

oxytocin A hormone, secreted by the pituitary gland, that stimulates uterine contractions during childbirth, facilitates the ejection of milk during nursing, and seems to promote, in both sexes, attachment and trust in relationships.

panic disorder An anxiety disorder in which a person experiences recurring panic attacks, periods of intense fear, and feelings of impending doom or death, accompanied by physiological symptoms such as rapid heart rate and dizziness.

papillae [pa-PILL-ee] Knoblike elevations on the tongue, containing the taste buds. (Singular: papilla.)

parallel distributed processing (PDP) model A model of memory in which knowledge is represented as connections among thousands of interacting processing units, distributed in a vast network, and all operating in parallel.

paranoid personality disorder A disorder characterized by unreasonable, excessive suspiciousness and mistrust, and irrational feelings of being persecuted by others.

parapsychology The study of purported psychic phenomena such as ESP and mental telepathy.

parasympathetic nervous system The subdivision of the autonomic nervous system that operates during relaxed states and that conserves energy.

"parentese" Adult use of baby talk, using pitch that is higher and more varied than usual and exaggerating intonation and emphasis on vowels.

parietal [puh-RYE-uh-tuhl] lobes Lobes at the top of the brain's cerebral cortex; they contain areas that receive information on pressure, pain, touch, and temperature.

passionate ("romantic") love Love characterized by a whirlwind of intense emotions and sexual passion; it is the stuff of crushes, infatuations, "love at first sight," and the early stage of love affairs.

peak experiences Rare moments of rapture caused by the attainment of excellence or the experience of beauty.

peer review The process by which scientists submit their results to professional journals, which send the findings to experts in the field for evaluation and suggest revisions before publishing them.

perception The process by which the brain organizes and interprets sensory information.

perceptual constancy The accurate perception of objects as stable or unchanged despite changes in the sensory patterns they produce.

perceptual set A habitual way of perceiving, based on expectations.

peripheral nervous system (PNS) All portions of the nervous system outside the brain and spinal cord; includes sensory and motor nerves.

personality A distinctive and relatively stable pattern of behaviour, thoughts, motives, and emotions that characterizes an individual.

personality disorder A pattern in the personality that involves unchanging, maladaptive traits that cause great distress or an inability to get along with others.

PET scan (positron-emission tomography) A method for analyzing biochemical activity in the brain, using injections of a glucose-like substance containing a radioactive element.

phantom pain The experience of pain in a missing limb or other body part.

phobia An exaggerated, unrealistic fear of a specific situation, activity, or object.

phrenology The now discredited theory that different brain areas account for specific character and personality traits, which can be "read" from bumps on the skull.

Jean Piaget (1896–1980) Swiss psychologist who studied child development, created the "flower-blooming" school of cognitive development, and proposed the theory of cognitive stages.

pitch The dimension of auditory experience related to the frequency of a pressure wave; the height or depth of a tone.

pituitary gland A small endocrine gland at the base of the brain, which releases many hormones and regulates other endocrine glands.

placebo An inactive substance or fake treatment used as a control in an experiment or given by a medical practitioner to a patient.

placebo effect The apparent success of a medication or treatment due to the patient's expectations or hopes rather than to the drug or treatment itself.

plasticity The brain's ability to change and adapt in response to experience—for example, by reorganizing or growing new neural connections.

polygraph machine ("lie detector") A machine to measure increased activity in a person's autonomic nervous system—a faster heart rate, increased respiration rate, and increased electrical conductance of the skin—when the person responds to incriminating questions. In theory, the emotional arousal of a person responding to incriminating questions suggests that the person is guilty and fearful of being found out.

pons A structure in the brain stem involved in, among other things, sleeping, waking, and dreaming.

positive correlation An association between increases in one variable and increases in another—or between decreases in one and in another.

positive reinforcement A reinforcement procedure in which a response is followed by the presentation of, or increase in intensity of, a reinforcing stimulus; as a result, the response becomes stronger or more likely to occur.

postdecision dissonance In the theory of cognitive dissonance, tension that occurs when you believe you may have made a bad decision.

posttraumatic stress disorder (PTSD) An anxiety disorder in which a person who has experienced a traumatic or life-threatening event has symptoms such as psychic numbing, reliving of the trauma, and increased physiological arousal.

power assertion A method of child rearing in which the parent uses punishment and authority to correct the child's misbehaviour.

prefrontal cortex The most forward part of the frontal lobes of the brain.

prejudice A strong, unreasonable dislike or hatred of a group, based on a negative stereotype.

"premenstrual syndrome" ("PMS") A vague cluster of physical and emotional symptoms—including fatigue, headache, irritability, and depression—associated with the days preceding menstruation that came to be thought of as an illness and was given a label.

premises A set of observations or propositions.

primacy effect Recall of items in a list will be best for items at the beginning of the list.

primary control An effort to modify reality by changing other people, the situation, or events; a "fighting back" philosophy.

primary emotions Emotions considered to be universal and biologically based; they generally include fear, anger, sadness, joy, surprise, disgust, and contempt.

primary punisher A stimulus that is inherently punishing; an example is electric shock.

primary reinforcer A stimulus that is inherently reinforcing, typically satisfying a physiological need; an example is food.

priming A method used to measure unconscious cognitive processes, in which a person is exposed to information and is later tested to see whether the information affects behaviour or performance on another task or in another situation.

principle of falsifiability The principle that a scientific theory must make predictions that are specific enough to expose the theory to the possibility of disconfirmation; that is, the theory must predict not only what will happen but also what will not happen.

private speech According to Vygotsky, how children talk to themselves to direct their own behaviour; over time, private speech becomes internalized and silent.

proactive interference Forgetting that occurs when previously stored material interferes with the ability to remember similar, more recently learned material.

problem-focused approach to dreams An explanation in which the symbols and metaphors in a dream do not disguise its true meaning; they convey it.

problem-focused coping Dealing with a problem by solving the problem itself.

procedural memories Memories for the performance of actions or skills ("knowing how").

projection In psychoanalytic theory, a person's own unacceptable or threatening feelings being repressed and then attributed to someone else.

projective tests Psychological tests used to infer a person's motives, conflicts, and unconscious dynamics on the basis of the person's interpretations of ambiguous stimuli.

proposition A unit of meaning that is made up of concepts and expresses a single idea.

prototype An especially representative example of a concept.

proximity effect The people who are nearest to you geographically are most likely to be dearest to you, too.

psychedelic drugs Consciousness-altering drugs that produce hallucinations, change thought processes, or disrupt the normal perception of time and space.

psychiatrist A medical doctor (MD) who has completed a three-year residency in psychiatry to learn how to diagnose and treat mental disorders under the supervision of more experienced physicians.

psychoactive drug A drug capable of influencing perception, mood, cognition, or behaviour.

psychoanalysis A theory of personality and a method of psychotherapy, originally formulated by Sigmund Freud, that emphasizes unconscious motives and conflicts.

psychoanalyst A person who practises psychoanalysis, has obtained specialized training at a psychoanalytic institute, and has undergone extensive psychoanalysis personally.

psychobabble Pseudoscience and quackery covered by a veneer of psychological and scientific-sounding language.

psychodynamic theories Theories that explain behaviour and personality in terms of unconscious energy dynamics within the individual, such as inner forces, conflicts, or the movement of instinctual energy.

psychodynamic ("depth") therapies Psychotherapies that share the psychoanalytic goal of exploring the unconscious dynamics of personality, although they differ from Freudian analysis in various ways.

psychogenic amnesia Massive memory loss including loss of personal identity, with psychological causes, such as a need to escape feelings of embarrassment, guilt, shame, disappointment, or emotional shock.

psycholinguists Researchers who study the psychology of language.

psychological tests Procedures used to measure and evaluate personality traits, emotional states, aptitudes, interests, abilities, and values.

psychology The discipline concerned with behaviour and mental processes and how they are affected by an organism's physical state, mental state, and external environment; the term is often represented by ψ, the Greek letter *psi* (usually pronounced "sigh").

psychometric approach to intelligence The measurement of mental abilities, traits, and processes.

psychometric psychologist Practitioner who designs and evaluates tests of mental abilities, aptitudes, interests, and personality.

psychoneuroimmunology (PNI) The study of the relationships among psychology, the nervous and endocrine systems, and the immune system.

psychopathy A personality disorder characterized by a lack of remorse, empathy, anxiety, and other social emotions; the use of deceit and manipulation; and impulsive thrill seeking.

psychophysics The field concerned with how the physical properties of stimuli are related to our psychological experience of them.

psychosexual stages In psychoanalytic theory, a series of different forms of sexual energy into which personality develops as the child matures; they are the oral, anal, phallic, latency, and genital stages.

psychosis An extreme mental disturbance involving distorted perceptions and irrational behaviour; it may have psychological or organic causes. (Plural: psychoses.)

psychosurgery Any surgical procedure that destroys selected areas of the brain believed to be involved in emotional disorders or violent, impulsive behaviour.

psychotherapist Unregulated person who does any kind of psychotherapy.

puberty The age at which a person becomes capable of sexual reproduction.

punishment The process by which a stimulus or event weakens or reduces the probability of the response that it follows.

random assignment A procedure for assigning people to experimental and control groups in which each individual has the same probability as any other of being assigned to a given group.

randomized controlled trials Research designed to determine the effectiveness of a new medication or form of therapy, in which people with a given problem or disorder are randomly assigned to one or more treatment groups or to a control group.

rapid eye movement (REM) sleep Sleep periods characterized by eye movement, loss of muscle tone, and dreaming.

rational emotive behaviour therapy (REBT) A form of cognitive therapy devised by Albert Ellis, designed to challenge the client's unrealistic thoughts.

reappraisal Choosing to think about a problem differently.

reasoning The drawing of conclusions or inferences from observations, facts, or assumptions.

recall The ability to retrieve and reproduce from memory previously encountered material.

recency effect Recall of items in a list will be best for items at the end of the list.

reciprocal determinism In social-cognitive theories, the two-way interaction between aspects of the environment and aspects of the individual in the shaping of personality traits.

recognition The ability to identify previously encountered material.

reconstructive memory We may reproduce some kinds of simple information by rote, but when we remember complex information, we typically alter it in ways that help us make sense of the material, based on what we already know or think we know.

regression In psychoanalytic theory, when a person reverts to a previous phase of psychological development.

reinforcement The process by which a stimulus or event strengthens or increases the probability of the response that it follows.

relearning method A method for measuring retention that compares the time required to relearn material with the time used in the initial learning of the material.

reliability In test construction, the consistency of scores derived from a test, from one time and place to another.

representative sample A group of participants, selected from a population for study, which matches the population on important characteristics such as age and sex.

repression In psychoanalytic theory, the selective, involuntary pushing of threatening or upsetting information into the unconscious.

reticular activating system (RAS) A dense network of neurons found in the core of the brain stem; it arouses the cortex and screens incoming information.

retina Neural tissue lining the back of the eyeball's interior, which contains the receptors for vision.

retinal disparity The slight difference in lateral separation between two objects as seen by the left eye and the right eye.

retrieval cues Items of information that can help us find the specific information we're looking for.

retroactive interference Forgetting that occurs when recently learned material interferes with the ability to remember similar material stored previously.

rods Visual receptors that respond to dim light.

Carl Rogers (1902–1987) One of three chief leaders of the humanist psychology movement; he posited the importance of the fully functioning individual and unconditional positive regard.

role A given social position that is governed by a set of norms for proper behaviour.

Rorschach Inkblot Test A projective personality test that requires respondents to interpret abstract, symmetrical inkblots.

saturation Vividness or purity of colour; the dimension of visual experience related to the complexity of light waves.

schizophrenia A psychotic disorder marked by delusions, hallucinations, disorganized and incoherent speech, inappropriate behaviour, and cognitive impairments.

school psychologist Practitioner who works with parents, teachers, and students to enhance students' performance and resolve emotional difficulties.

scientist–practitioner gap The breach between scientists and therapists over different assumptions regarding the value of empirical research for doing psychotherapy and for assessing its effectiveness.

seasonal affective disorder (SAD) A controversial disorder in which a person experiences depression during the winter and an improvement of mood in the spring.

secondary control An effort to accept reality by changing your own attitudes, goals, or emotions; a "learn to live with it" philosophy.

secondary emotions Emotions that develop with cognitive maturity and vary across individuals and cultures.

secondary punisher A stimulus that has acquired punishing properties through association with other punishers.

secondary reinforcer A stimulus that has acquired reinforcing properties through association with other reinforcers.

secondary sex characteristics Secondary signs of physical maturity at puberty, such as a deepened voice and facial and chest hair in boys and pubic hair in both sexes.

secondary traits Changeable aspects of personality.

selective attention The focusing of attention on selected aspects of the environment and the blocking out of others.

self-actualized person A person who strives for a life that is meaningful, challenging, and satisfying.

self-serving bias The tendency, in explaining one's own behaviour, to take credit for one's good actions and rationalize one's mistakes.

semantic category A larger grouping into which items similar in some characteristic can be placed; *chair*, for example, belongs to the category *furniture*.

semantic memories Memories of general knowledge, including facts, rules, concepts, and propositions.

semicircular canals Sense organs in the inner ear that contribute to equilibrium by responding to rotation of the head.

sensation The detection of physical energy emitted or reflected by physical objects; it occurs when energy in the external environment or the body stimulates receptors in the sense organs.

sense receptors Specialized cells that convert physical energy in the environment or the body to electrical energy that can be transmitted as nerve impulses to the brain.

sensory adaptation The reduction or disappearance of sensory responsiveness when stimulation is unchanging or repetitious.

sensory deprivation The absence of normal levels of sensory stimulation.

sensory nerves Nerves in the peripheral nervous system that carry messages from special receptors in the skin, muscles, and other internal and external sense organs to the spinal cord, which sends them along to the brain.

sensory register A memory system that momentarily preserves extremely accurate images of sensory information.

separation anxiety The distress that most children develop, at about six to eight months of age, when their primary caregivers temporarily leave them with strangers.

serial-position effect The tendency for recall of the first and last items on a list to surpass recall of items in the middle of the list.

set point The genetically influenced weight range for an individual; it is maintained by biological mechanisms that regulate food intake, fat reserves, and metabolism.

sex hormones Hormones that regulate the development and functioning of reproductive organs and that stimulate the development of male and female sexual characteristics; they include androgens, estrogens, and progesterone.

sexual script Set of implicit rules that specify proper sexual behaviour for a person in a given situation, varying with the person's gender, age, religion, social status, and peer group.

shadow In Jungian thought, archetype that reflects the prehistoric fear of wild animals and represents the bestial, evil side of human nature.

shallow processing In the encoding of information, the processing of the physical or sensory features of a stimulus.

shaping An operant-conditioning procedure in which successive approximations of a desired response are reinforced.

short-term memory (STM) In the three-box model of memory, a limited-capacity memory system involved in the retention of information for brief periods; it is also used to hold information retrieved from long-term memory for temporary use.

signal-detection theory A psychophysical theory that divides the detection of a sensory signal into a sensory process and a decision process.

significance tests Statistical tests that show how likely it is that a study's results occurred merely by chance.

similarity effect Similarity—in looks, attitudes, beliefs, values, personality, and interests—is attractive to human beings; we tend to choose friends and loved ones who are most like us.

single-blind study An experiment in which subjects do not know whether they are in an experimental or a control group, but the researchers do.

situational attribution Identifying the cause of an action as something in the situation or environment.

skills training In behaviour therapy, an effort to teach the client skills that he or she may lack, as well as new constructive behaviours to replace self-defeating ones.

Skinner box A cage equipped with a device that delivers food into a dish when an animal makes a desired response.

sleep apnea A disorder in which breathing briefly stops during sleep, causing the person to choke and gasp and momentarily awaken.

sleep spindles Short bursts of rapid, high-peaking brain waves.

social cognition An area in social psychology concerned with social influences on thought, memory, perception, and beliefs.

social-cognitive learning theorists Practitioners who combine elements of behaviourism with research on thoughts, values, expectations, and intentions.

social-cognitive theories Theories that emphasize how behaviour is learned and maintained through observation and imitation of others, positive consequences, and cognitive processes such as plans, expectations, and beliefs.

social comparison A coping strategy in which people compare themselves to others who are (they feel) less fortunate.

social Darwinism The notion that the wealthy and successful are more reproductively fit than other people.

social identity The part of a person's self-concept that is based on his or her identification with a nation, religious or political group, occupation, or other social affiliation.

socialization The process by which children learn the behaviours, attitudes, and expectations required of them by their society or culture.

social phobia An irrational fear, the sufferers of which become extremely anxious in situations in which they will be observed by others, worrying that they will do or say something that will be excruciatingly humiliating or embarrassing.

social psychologist Practitioner who focuses on social rules and roles, how groups affect attitudes and behaviour, why people obey authority, and how each of us is affected by other people—spouses, lovers, friends, bosses, parents, and strangers.

sociobiology An interdisciplinary field that emphasizes evolutionary explanations of social behaviour in animals, including human beings.

sociocognitive explanation of hypnosis The effects of hypnosis result from an interaction between the social influence of the hypnotist (the "socio" part) and the abilities, beliefs, and expectations of the subject (the "cognitive" part).

sociocognitive explanation of MPD The ability of some troubled, highly imaginative individuals to produce many different "personalities" when asked is simply an extreme form of the ability we all have to present different aspects of our personalities to others.

sociocultural perspective A psychological approach that emphasizes social and cultural influences on behaviour.

somatic nervous system The subdivision of the peripheral nervous system that connects to sensory receptors and to skeletal muscles; sometimes called the *skeletal nervous system*.

somatosensory cortex The part of the brain that receives information about pressure, pain, touch, and temperature from all over the body.

source misattribution The inability to distinguish an actual memory of an event from information you learned about the event elsewhere.

spinal cord A collection of neurons and supportive tissue running from the base of the brain down the centre of the back, protected by a column of bones (the spinal column).

spinal reflexes Automatic behaviours produced by the spinal cord without help from the brain.

split-brain surgery Surgery in which the corpus callosum is severed, stopping the spread of electrical activity from one side of the brain to the other.

spontaneous recovery The reappearance of a learned response after its apparent extinction.

standard deviation A commonly used measure of variability that indicates the average difference between scores in a distribution and their mean; more precisely, the square root of the average squared deviation from the mean.

standardize In test construction, to develop uniform procedures for giving and scoring a test.

Stanford–Binet Intelligence Scale Intelligence test first published in 1916 by Stanford's Lewis Terman, who had revised Binet's test and established norms for North American children.

state-dependent memory The tendency to remember something when the rememberer is in the same physical or mental state as during the original learning or experience.

statistical significance An attribute of a result whose likelihood of occurring by chance is extremely low.

stem cells Immature cells that renew themselves and have the potential to develop into mature cells; given encouraging environments, stem cells from early embryos can develop into any cell type.

stereotype A summary impression of a group, in which a person believes that all members of the group share a common trait or traits (positive, negative, or neutral).

stereotype threat A burden of doubt a person feels about his or her performance, due to negative stereotypes about his or her group's abilities.

stimulants Drugs that speed up activity in the central nervous system.

stimulus discrimination The tendency to respond differently to two or more similar stimuli. In classical conditioning, it occurs when a stimulus similar to the conditioned stimulus fails to evoke the conditioned response; in operant conditioning, it occurs when an organism learns to make a response in the presence of other, similar stimuli that differ from it on some dimension.

stimulus generalization After conditioning, the tendency to respond to a stimulus that resembles one involved in the original conditioning. In classical conditioning, it occurs when a stimulus that resembles the conditioned stimulus elicits the conditioned response; in operant conditioning, it occurs when a response that has been reinforced (or punished) in the presence of one stimulus occurs (or is suppressed) in the presence of other, similar stimuli.

Strange Situation Experimental method devised by Mary Ainsworth to study the nature of the attachment between mothers and babies.

structuralism An early psychological approach that emphasized the analysis of immediate experience into basic elements.

subconscious processes Mental processes occurring outside of conscious awareness but accessible to consciousness when necessary.

sublimation In psychoanalytic theory, when displacement serves a higher cultural or socially useful purpose, as in the creation of art or inventions.

substance abuse A maladaptive pattern of substance use leading to clinically significant impairment or distress.

successive approximations In the operant-conditioning procedure of shaping, behaviours that are ordered in terms of increasing similarity or closeness to the desired response.

superego In psychoanalysis, the part of personality that represents conscience, morality, and social standards.

suprachiasmatic [soo-pruh-kye-az-MAT-ick] nucleus (SCN) An area of the brain containing a biological clock that governs circadian rhythms.

surface structure The way a sentence is actually spoken or signed.

surveys Questionnaires and interviews that ask people directly about their experiences, attitudes, or opinions.

sympathetic nervous system The subdivision of the autonomic nervous system that mobilizes bodily resources and increases the output of energy during emotion and stress.

synapse The site where transmission of a nerve impulse from one nerve cell to another occurs; includes the axon terminal, the synaptic cleft, and receptor sites in the membrane of the receiving cell.

synaptic cleft A minuscule space between neurons where the axon terminal of one neuron nearly touches a dendrite or the cell body of another.

synaptic vesicles Tiny sacs in the tip of an axon terminal.

synesthesia A condition in which stimulation of one sense also evokes another.

syntax Grammatical rules governing word order and other linguistic features that determine the role a word plays in a sentence.

systematic desensitization In behaviour therapy, a step-by-step process of desensitizing a client to a feared object or experience; based on the classical-conditioning procedure of *counterconditioning*.

tacit knowledge Strategies for success that are not explicitly taught but that instead must be inferred.

tardive dyskinesia A neurological disorder involving muscle rigidity, hand tremors, and other involuntary muscle movements, commonly experienced by people taking antipsychotic medications.

taste buds Nests of taste-receptor cells.

telegraphic speech A child's first word combinations, which omit (as a telegram did) unnecessary words.

telomere A protein complex that tells the cell how long it has to live.

temperaments Physiological dispositions to respond to the environment in certain ways; they are present in infancy and in many nonhuman species and are assumed to be innate.

temporal lobes Lobes at the sides of the brain's cerebral cortex; they contain areas involved in hearing, memory, perception, emotion, and (in the left lobe, typically) language comprehension.

test–retest reliability The ability of a test to return similar individual scores from one session to the next when the test is given twice to the same group of people and the two sets of scores are compared statistically.

thalamus A brain structure that relays sensory messages to the cerebral cortex.

Thematic Apperception Test (TAT) A projective test that asks respondents to interpret a series of drawings showing scenes of people; usually scored for unconscious motives, such as the need for achievement, power, or affiliation.

theory An organized system of assumptions and principles that purports to explain a specified set of phenomena and their interrelationships.

theory of mind A system of beliefs about the way one's own mind and the minds of others work, and of how individuals are affected by their beliefs and feelings.

therapeutic alliance The bond of confidence and mutual understanding established between therapist and client, which allows them to work together to solve the client's problems.

therapeutic window The amount of a drug that is enough but not too much, taking into account the fact that the same dose of a drug may be metabolized differently in men and women, old people and young people, and different ethnic groups.

three-box model of memory Model that proposes three "boxes"—the sensory register, short-term memory, and long-term memory—into which information is placed as it is processed by the brain; information can pass from the sensory register to short-term memory and in either direction between short-term and long-term memory.

timbre The distinguishing quality of a sound; the dimension of auditory experience related to the complexity of the pressure wave.

tip-of-the-tongue (TOT) state Knowing that the word you are trying to retrieve is just out of your reach, experienced especially when trying to recall the names of acquaintances or famous people, the names of objects and places, or the titles of movies or books.

tolerance Increased resistance to a drug's effects accompanying continued use.

trait A characteristic of an individual, describing a habitual way of behaving, thinking, or feeling.

tranquilizers Drugs commonly but often inappropriately prescribed for patients who complain of unhappiness, anxiety, or worry.

transcranial magnetic stimulation (TMS) A method of stimulating brain cells, using a powerful magnetic field produced by a wire coil placed on a person's head; it can be used by researchers to temporarily inactivate neural circuits and is also being used therapeutically.

transference In psychodynamic therapies, a critical process in which the client transfers unconscious emotions or reactions, such as emotional feelings about his or her parents, onto the therapist.

transgender A term describing a broad category of people who do not fit comfortably into the usual categories of male and female, masculine and feminine.

traumatic amnesia Temporary memory loss that allegedly involves the burying of specific traumatic events for a long period of time, often for many years; when the memory returns, it is supposedly immune to the usual processes of distortion and confabulation, and is recalled with perfect accuracy.

triarchic [try-ARE-kick] theory of intelligence A theory of intelligence that emphasizes information-processing strategies, the ability to creatively transfer skills to new situations, and the practical application of intelligence.

trichromatic theory A theory of colour perception that proposes three mechanisms in the visual system, each sensitive to a certain range of wavelengths; their interaction is assumed to produce all the different experiences of hue.

unconditional positive regard To Carl Rogers, love or support given to another person with no conditions attached.

unconditioned response (UR) The classical-conditioning term for a reflexive response elicited by a stimulus in the absence of learning.

unconditioned stimulus (US) The classical-conditioning term for a stimulus that elicits a reflexive response in the absence of learning.

universal grammar The core features common to all languages, such as nouns and verbs, subjects and objects, and negatives.

validity The ability of a test to measure what it was designed to measure.

validity effect The tendency of people to believe that a statement is true or valid simply because it has been repeated many times.

variables Characteristics of behaviour or experience that can be measured or described by a numeric scale.

visual cortex The part of the brain where visual signals are processed.

volunteer bias A shortcoming of findings derived from a sample of volunteers instead of a representative sample; the volunteers may differ from those who did not volunteer.

vulnerability-stress models Approaches that emphasize how individual vulnerabilities interact with external stresses or circumstances to produce mental disorders.

Lev Vygotsky (1896–1934) Psychologist who emphasized the sociocultural influences of language and culture on children's cognitive development.

Wechsler Adult Intelligence Scale (WAIS) Intelligence test for adults devised by David Wechsler that produces a general IQ score and also provides specific scores for different kinds of ability.

Wechsler Intelligence Scale for Children (WISC) Intelligence test for children devised by David Wechsler that produces a general IQ score and also provides specific scores for different kinds of ability.

Wernicke's area The part of the brain that is involved in language comprehension.

Benjamin Lee Whorf A linguist and anthropologist who proposed that language moulds cognition and perception.

withdrawal Physical and psychological symptoms that occur when someone addicted to a drug stops taking it.

word salad An illogical jumble of ideas and symbols, linked by meaningless rhyming words or by remote associations.

working memory In many models of memory, a memory system comprising short-term memory plus the mental processes that control retrieval of information from long-term memory and interpret that information appropriately for a given task.

Wilhelm Wundt (1832–1920) German trained in medicine and philosophy, who wrote many volumes on psychology, physiology, natural history, ethics, and logic, and was the first person to announce (in 1873) that he intended to make psychology a science; his laboratory was the first to have its results published in a scholarly journal.

zygote In prenatal development, the fertilized single-celled egg.

References

Note: Coloured type indicates a Canadian researcher or a researcher associated with a Canadian university.

Abel, G. G., Mittelman, M., Becker, J. V., et al. (1988). Predicting child molesters' response to treatment. *Annals of the New York Academy of Sciences, 528,* 223–234.

Abel, E. L. (1995). An update of incidence of FAS: FAS is not an equal opportunity birth defect. *Neurotoxicology and Teratology, 17*(4), 437–443.

Abrahamson, A. C., Baker, L. A., & Caspi, A. (2002). Rebellious teens? Genetic and environmental influences on the social attitudes of adolescents. *Journal of Personality and Social Psychology, 83,* 1392–1408.

Abrams, D. B., & Wilson, G. T. (1983). Alcohol, sexual arousal, and self-control. *Journal of Personality and Social Psychology, 45,* 188–198.

Abrams, R. (1997). *Electroconvulsive therapy* (3rd ed.). Oxford, England: Oxford University Press.

Abramson, L. Y., Metalsky, G. I., & Alloy, L. B. (1989). Hopelessness depression: A theory-based subtype of depression. *Psychological Review, 96,* 358–372.

Acocella, J. (1999). *Creating hysteria: Women and multiple personality disorder.* San Francisco: Jossey-Bass.

Adair, J. G., & Vohra, N. (2003). The explosion of knowledge, references, and citations: Psychology's unique response to a crisis. *American Psychologist, 58,* 15–23.

Adams, J. L. (1986). *Conceptual blockbusting: A guide to better ideas* (3rd ed.). Boston, MA: Addison-Wesley.

Ader, R. (2000). True or false: The placebo effect as seen in drug studies is definitive proof that the mind can bring about clinically relevant changes in the body: The placebo effect: If it's all in your head, does that mean you only think you feel better? *Advances in Mind-Body Medicine, 16,* 7–11.

Adler, N. E., & Snibbe, A. C. (2003). The role of psychosocial processes in explaining the gradient between socioeconomic status and health. *Current Directions in Psychological Science, 12,* 119–123.

Adolphs, R. (2001). Emotion, social cognition, and the human brain. Invited address presented at the annual meeting of the American Psychological Society, Toronto, Canada.

Affleck, G., Tennen, H., Croog, S., & Levine, S. (1987). Causal attribution, perceived control, and recovery from a heart attack. *Journal of Social and Clinical Psychology, 5,* 339–355.

Agars, M. D. (2004). Reconsidering the impact of gender stereotypes on the advancement of women in organizations. *Psychology of Women Quarterly, 28,* 103–111.

Agrawal, Y., Platz, E. A., & Niparko, J. K. (2008). Prevalence of hearing loss and differences by demographic characteristics among US adults. *Archives of Internal Medicine, 168,* 1522–1530.

Aguiar, P., Vala, J., Correia, I., & Pereira, C. (2008). Justice in our world and in that of others: Belief in a just world and reactions to victims. *Social Justice Research, 21,* 50–68.

Ainsworth, M. D. S. (1973). The development of infant–mother attachment. In B. M. Caldwell & H. N. Ricciuti (Eds.), *Review of child development research* (Vol. 3). Chicago, IL: University of Chicago Press.

Ainsworth, M. D. S. (1979). Infant–mother attachment. *American Psychologist, 34,* 932–937.

Alexander, B. K., & Hardaway, P. F. (1982). Opiate addiction: The case for an adaptive orientation. *Psychological Bulletin, 92*(2), 367–381.

Alford, C. Fred. (2001). *Whistleblowers: Broken lives and organizations.* Ithaca, NY: Cornell University Press.

Alford, J. R., Funk, C. L., & Hibbing, J. R. (2005). Are political orientations genetically transmitted? *American Political Science Review, 99,* 153–167.

Alink, L. R. A., Mesman, J., van Zeijl, J., et al. (2009). Maternal sensitivity moderates the relation between negative discipline and aggression in early childhood. *Social Development, 18,* 99–120.

Allen, K. (2003). Are pets a healthy pleasure? The influence of pets on blood pressure. *Current Directions in Psychological Science, 12,* 236–239.

Allen, L. S., & Gorski, R. A. (1992). Sexual orientation and the size of the anterior commissure in the human brain. *Proceedings of the National Academy of Sciences, 89,* 7199–7202.

Allport, G. W. (1954/1979). *The nature of prejudice.* Reading, MA: Addison-Wesley.

Allport, G. W. (1961). *Pattern and growth in personality.* New York, NY: Holt, Rinehart and Winston.

Amabile, T. M. (1983). *The social psychology of creativity.* New York, NY: Springer-Verlag.

Amabile, T. M., & Khaire, M. (2008). Creativity and the role of the leader. *Harvard Business Review, 86.* Retrieved from http://hbr. harvardbusiness.org/2008/10/creativity-and-the-role-of-the-leader/ar/1

Amedi, A., Merabet, L., Bermpohl, F., & Pascual-Leone, A. (2005). The occipital cortex in the blind: Lessons about plasticity and vision. *Current Directions in Psychological Science, 14,* 306–311.

American Enterprise Institute. (2004, July 6). *Attitudes about homosexuality and gay marriage.* Compiled by Karlyn Bowman and Bryan O'Keefe. Retrieved from http://www.aei.org/paper/14882

American Psychiatric Association. (1994). *The diagnostic and statistical manual of mental disorders* (4th ed.). Washington, DC: American Psychiatric Association.

American Psychiatric Association. (2000). *The diagnostic and statistical manual of mental disorders, IV-TR.* Washington, DC: American Psychiatric Association.

Amering, M., & Katschnig, H. (1990). Panic attacks and panic disorder in cross-cultural perspective. *Psychiatric Annals, 20,* 511–516.

Anand, S. S., Yusuf, S., Jacobs, R., et al. (2001). Risk factors, atherosclerosis, and cardiovascular disease among Aboriginal people in Canada: The study of health assessment and risk evaluation in Aboriginal peoples (SHARE-AP). *Lancet, 358*(9288), 1147–1153.

Anastasi, A., & Urbina, S. (1997). *Psychological testing* (7th ed.). Upper Saddle River, NJ: Prentice-Hall.

Andersen, S. M., & Berk, M. S. (1998). Transference in everyday experience: Implications of experimental research for relevant clinical phenomena. *Review of General Psychology, 2,* 81–120.

Andersen, S. M., & Chen, S. (2002). The relational self: An interpersonal social-cognitive theory. *Psychological Review, 109,* 619–645.

Anderson, A. (2005). *The way we argue now: A study in the cultures of theory.* Princeton, NJ: Princeton University Press.

Anderson, C. A., Berkowitz, L., Donnerstein, E., et al. (2003). The influence of media violence on youth. *Psychological Science in the Public Interest, 4*(3), [whole issue].

Anderson, C. A., & Bushman, B. J. (2001). Effects of violent video games on aggressive behavior, aggressive cognition, aggressive affect, physiological arousal, and prosocial behavior: A meta-analytic review of the scientific literature. *Psychological Science, 12,* 353–359.

Anderson, J. R. (1990). *The adaptive nature of thought.* Hillsdale, NJ: Erlbaum.

Anderson, M. (2005). Is lack of sexual desire a disease? Is testosterone the cure? *Medscape Ob/Gyn & Women's Health.* Retrieved from http://www.medscape.com/viewarticle/512218

Anderson, S. E., Dallal, G. E., & Must, A. (2003). Relative weight and race influence average age at menarche: Results from two nationally representative surveys of US girls studied 25 years apart. *Pediatrics, 111,* 844–850.

Anderson, S. W., Bechara, A., Damasio, H., et al. (1999). Impairment of social and moral behavior related to early damage in human prefrontal cortex. *Nature Neuroscience, 2,* 1032–1037.

Anderson-Barnes, V. C., McAuliffe, C., Swanberg, K. M., & Tsao, J. W. (2009, October). Phantom limb pain: A phenomenon of proprioceptive memory? *Medical Hypotheses, 73,* 555–558.

Andreano, J. M., & Cahill, L. (2006). Glucocorticoid release and memory consolidation in men and women. *Psychological Science, 17,* 466–470.

Andreasen, N. C., Arndt, S., Swayze, V., II, et al. (1994). Thalamic abnormalities in schizophrenia visualized through magnetic resonance image averaging. *Science, 266,* 294–298.

Angell, M. (2004). *The truth about the drug companies: How they deceive us and what to do about it.* New York, NY: Random House.

Antonuccio, D. O., Danton, W. G., DeNelsky, G. Y., et al. (1999). Raising questions about antidepressants. *Psychotherapy and Psychosomatics, 68,* 3–14.

Antrobus, J. (1991). Dreaming: Cognitive processes during cortical activation and high afferent thresholds. *Psychological Review, 98,* 96–121.

Antrobus, J. (2000). How does the dreaming brain explain the dreaming mind? *Behavioral and Brain Sciences, 23,* 904–907.

Archer, J. (2004). Sex differences in aggression in real-world settings: A meta-analytic review. *Review of General Psychology, 8,* 291–322.

Archer, S. N., Robilliard, D. L., Skene, D. J., et al. (2003). A length polymorphism in the circadian clock gene Per3 is linked to delayed sleep phase syndrome and extreme diurnal preference. *Sleep, 26,* 413–415.

Arendt, H. (1963). *Eichmann in Jerusalem: A report on the banality of evil.* New York, NY: Viking.

Arkes, H. R. (1993). Some practical judgment and decision-making research. In N. J. Castellan, Jr., et al. (Eds.), *Individual and group decision making: Current issues.* Hillsdale, NJ: Erlbaum.

Arkes, H. R., Boehm, L. E., & Xu, G. (1991). The determinants of judged validity. *Journal of Experimental Social Psychology, 27,* 576–605.

Arnett, J. J. (2004). Emerging adulthood: The winding road from the late teens through the twenties. New York, NY: Oxford University Press.

Aron, A., Aron, E. N., & Allen, J. (1998). Motivations for unreciprocated love. *Personality and Social Psychology Bulletin, 24,* 787–796.

Aron, A., Fisher, H., Mashek, D. J., et al. (2005). Reward, motivation, and emotion systems associated with early-stage intense romantic love. *Journal of Neurophysiology, 94,* 327–337.

Aronson, E. (2000). *Nobody left to hate.* New York, NY: Freeman.

Aronson, E. (2008). *The social animal* (10th ed.). New York, NY: Worth.

Aronson, E., & Mills, J. (1959). The effect of severity of initiation on liking for a group. *Journal of Abnormal and Social Psychology, 59,* 177–181.

Aronson, J. (2010). Jigsaw and the nurture of human intelligence. In M. H. Gonzales, C. Tavris, & J. Aronson (Eds.), *The scientist and the humanist: A festschrift in honor of Elliot Aronson.* New York, NY: Psychology Press.

Arredondo, P., & Perez, P. (2003). Counseling paradigms and Latina/o Americans. In F. Harper & J. McFadden (Eds.), *Culture and counseling: New approaches.* Boston, MA: Allyn & Bacon.

Arredondo, P., Rosen, D. C., Rice, T., et al. (2005). Multicultural counseling: A 10-year content analysis of the *Journal of Counseling & Development. Journal of Counseling and Development, 83,* 155–161.

Arroyo, C. G., & Zigler, E. (1995). Racial identity, academic achievement, and the psychological well-being of economically disadvantaged adolescents. *Journal of Personality and Social Psychology, 69,* 903–914.

Arsenijevic, D., Onuma, H., Pecqueur, C., et al. (2000, December 26). Disruption of the uncoupling protein-2 gene in mice reveals a role in immunity and reactive oxygen species production. *Nature Genetics, 4,* 387–388.

Asch, S. E. (1952). *Social psychology.* Englewood Cliffs, NJ: Prentice-Hall.

Asch, S. E. (1965). Effects of group pressure upon the modification and distortion of judgments. In H. Proshansky & B. Seidenberg (Eds.), *Basic studies in social psychology.* New York, NY: Holt, Rinehart and Winston.

Aserinsky, E., & Kleitman, N. (1955). Two types of ocular motility occurring in sleep. *Journal of Applied Physiology, 8,* 1–10.

Atkinson, R. C., & Shiffrin, R. M. (1968). Human memory: A proposed system and its control processes. In K. W. Spence & J. T. Spence (Eds.), *The psychology of learning and motivation: Vol. 2. Advances in research and theory.* New York, NY: Academic Press.

Atkinson, R. C., & Shiffrin, R. M. (1971). The control of short-term memory. *Scientific American, 225*(2), 82–90.

Atran, S. (2003). Genesis of suicide terrorism. *Science, 299,* 1534–1539.

Auyeung, B., Baron-Cohen, S., Ashwin, E., et al. (2009). Fetal testosterone predicts sexually differentiated childhood behavior in girls and in boys. *Psychological Science, 20,* 144–148.

Aviezer, H., Hassin, R. R., Ryan, J., et al. (2008). Angry, disgusted, or afraid? Studies on the malleability of emotion perception. *Psychological Science, 19,* 724–732.

Axel, R. (1995). The molecular logic of smell. *Scientific American, 273,* 154–159.

Azuma, H. (1984). Secondary control as a heterogeneous category. *American Psychologist, 39,* 970–971.

Baas, M., De Dreu, C. K. W., & Nijstad, B. A. (2008). A meta-analysis of 25 years of mood-creativity research: Hedonic tone, activation, or regulatory focus? *Psychological Bulletin, 134,* 779–806.

Baddeley, A. D. (1992). Working memory. *Science, 255,* 556–559.

Baddeley, A. D. (2007). *Working memory, thought, and action.* New York, NY: Oxford.

Bagby, R. M., Ryder, A. G., Ben-Dat, D., et al. (2002). Validation of the dimensional factor structure of the Personality Psychopathology Five in clinical and nonclinical samples. *Journal of Personality Disorders, 16* (4), 304–316.

Bagemihl, B. (1999). *Biological exuberance: Animal homosexuality and natural diversity.* New York, NY: St. Martin's Press.

Bahill, A. T., & Karnavas, W. J. (1993). The perceptual illusion of baseball's rising fastball and breaking curveball. *Journal of Experimental Psychology: Human Perception & Performance, 19,* 3–14.

Bahrick, H. P. (1984). Semantic memory content in permastore: Fifty years of memory for Spanish learned in school. *Journal of Experimental Psychology: General, 113,* 1–29.

Bahrick, H. P., Bahrick, P. O., & Wittlinger, R. P. (1975). Fifty years of memory for names and faces: A cross-sectional approach. *Journal of Experimental Psychology: General, 104,* 54–75.

Bailey, J. M., Bobrow, D., Wolfe, M., & Mikach, S. (1995). Sexual orientation of adult sons of gay fathers. *Developmental Psychology, 31,* 124–129.

Bailey, J. M., Dunne, M. P., & Martin, N. G. (2000). Genetic and environmental influences on sexual orientation and its correlates in an Australian twin sample. *Journal of Personality and Social Psychology, 78,* 524–536.

Bailey, J. M., Gaulin, S., Agyei, Y., & Gladue, B. A. (1994). Effects of gender and sexual orientation on evolutionarily relevant aspects of human mating psychology. *Journal of Personality and Social Psychology, 66,* 1081–1093.

Bailey, J. M., & Zucker, K. J. (1995). Childhood sex-typed behavior and sexual orientation: A conceptual analysis and quantitative review. *Developmental Psychology, 31,* 43–55.

Baillargeon, R. (1994). How do infants learn about the physical world? *Current Directions in Psychological Science, 5,* 133–140.

Baillargeon, R. (2004). Infants' physical world. *Current Directions in Psychological Science, 13,* 89–94.

Baker, M., & Milligan, K. (2010). Evidence from maternity leave expansions of the impact of maternal care on early child development. *The Journal of Human Resources, 45,* 1–32.

Baker, M. C. (2001). *The atoms of language: The mind's hidden rules of grammar.* New York, NY: Basic Books.

Baker, T. B., McFall, R. M., & Shoham, V. (2008). Current status and future prospects of clinical psychology: Toward a scientifically principled approach to mental and behavioral health care. *Psychological Science in the Public Interest, 9,* entire issue.

Bakermans-Kranenburg, M. J., Breddels-van Baardewijk, P., Juffer, F., et al. (2008). Insecure mothers with temperamentally reactive infants: A chance for intervention. In F. Juffer, M. J. Bakermans-Kranenburg, & M. H. van IJzendoorn (Eds.), *Promoting positive parenting: An attachment-based intervention.* New York, NY: Taylor & Francis.

Balcetis, E., Dunning, D., & Miller, R. L. (2008). Do collectivists know themselves better than individualists? Cross-cultural studies of the holier than thou phenomenon. *Journal of Personality and Social Psychology, 95,* 1252–1267.

Bancroft, J. (2006). Normal sexual development. In H. E. Barbaree & W. L. Marshall (Eds.), *The juvenile sex offender* (2nd ed.). New York, NY: Guilford.

Bancroft, J., Graham, C. A., Janssen, E., Sanders, S. A. (2009). The dual control model: Current status and future directions. *Journal of Sex Research, 46,* 121–142.

Bandura, A. (1977). *Social learning theory.* Englewood Cliffs, NJ: Prentice-Hall.

Bandura, A. (1986). *Social foundations of thought and action: A social cognitive theory.* Englewood Cliffs, NJ: Prentice-Hall.

Bandura, A. (1999). Moral disengagement in the perpetration of inhumanities. *Personality and Social Psychology Review, 3,* 193–209.

Bandura, A. (2001). Social cognitive theory: An agentic perspective. *Annual Review of Psychology, 52,* 1–26. Palo Alto, CA: Annual Reviews.

Bandura, A. (2004). Health promotion by social cognitive means. *Health Education and Behavior, 31,* 143–164.

Bandura, A. (2006). Toward a psychology of human agency. *Perspectives on Psychological Science, 1,* 164–180.

Bandura, A., Caprara, G. V, Barbaranelli, C., Pastorelli, C., & Regalia, C. (2001). Sociocognitive self-regulatory mechanisms governing transgressive behavior. *Journal of Personality and Social Psychology, 80,* 125–135.

Bandura, A., Ross, D., & Ross, S. A. (1963). Vicarious reinforcement and imitative learning. *Journal of Abnormal and Social Psychology, 67,* 601–607.

Banks, M. S. (with P. Salapatek). (1984). Infant visual perception. In P. Mussen. (Series Ed.), M. M. Haith & J. J. Campos. (Vol. Eds.), *Handbook of child psychology: Vol. II. Infancy and developmental psychobiology* (4th ed.). New York, NY: Wiley.

Bannerman, D. M. (2009). Fractionating spatial memory with glutamate receptor subunit-knockout mice. *Biochemical Society Transactions, 37,* 1323–1327.

Barash, D. P. (2001, April 20). Deflating the myth of monogamy. *The Chronicle of Higher Education,* B16–B17.

Barash, D. P., & Lipton, J. E. (2001). *The myth of monogamy: Fidelity and infidelity in animals and people.* New York, NY: W. H. Freeman.

Barbuto, J. E. (1997). A critique of the Myers-Briggs Type Indicator and its operationalization of Carl Jung's psychological types. *Psychological Reports, 80,* 611–625.

Barch, D. M. (2003). Cognition in schizophrenia: Does working memory work? *Current Directions in Psychological Science, 12,* 146–150.

Bargary, G., & Mitchell, K. J. (2008). Synaesthesia and cortical connectivity. *Trends in Neurosciences, 31,* 335–342.

Bargh, J. A. (1999, January 29). The most powerful manipulative messages are hiding in plain sight. *The Chronicle of Higher Education,* B6.

Bargh, J. A., & Morsella, E. (2008). The unconscious mind. *Perspectives on Psychological Science, 3,* 73–79.

Barglow, P. (2008). Corporate self interest and vagus nerve stimulation for depression. *Skeptical Inquirer, 32.5,* 35–40.

Barlow, D. H. (2000). Unraveling the mysteries of anxiety and its disorders from the perspective of emotion theory. *American Psychologist, 55,* 1247–1263.

Barlow, D. H. (2004). Psychological treatments. *American Psychologist, 59,* 869–878.

Barlow, D. H., Chorpita, B. F., & Turovsky, J. (1996). Fear, panic, anxiety, and disorders of emotion. In D. A. Hope et al. (Eds.), *Nebraska Symposium on Motivation, 1995: Perspectives on anxiety, panic, and fear.* Lincoln: University of Nebraska Press.

Baron-Cohen, S., & Harrison, J. E. (Eds.). (1997). *Synaesthesia: Classic and contemporary readings.* Cambridge, MA: Blackwell.

Barr, S. I. (1995). Dieting attitudes and behavior in urban high school students: Implications for calcium intake. *Journal of Adolescent Health, 16,* 458–464.

Barrett, D. (2001). *The committee of sleep.* New York, NY: Crown/Random House.

Barrett, L. F. (2006). Are emotions natural kinds? *Perspectives on Psychological Science, 1,* 28–58.

Barry, P. (2007). Genome 2.0: Mountains of new data are challenging old views. *Science News, 172,* 154–156.

Barsky, S. H., Roth, M. D., Kleerup, E. C., et al. (1998). Histopathologic and molecular alterations in bronchial epithelium in habitual smokers of marijuana, cocaine, and/or tobacco. *Journal of the National Cancer Institute, 90,* 1198–1205.

Bartels, A., & Zeki, S. (2004). The neural correlates of material and romantic love. *NeuroImage, 21,* 1155–1166.

Bartlett, F. C. (1932). *Remembering.* Cambridge, England: Cambridge University Press.

Bartoshuk, L. M. (1998). *Born to burn: Genetic variation in taste.* Paper presented at the annual meeting of the American Psychological Association, San Francisco, CA.

Bartoshuk, L. M., Duffy, V. B., Lucchina, L. A., et al. (1998). PROP (6-n-propylthiouracil) supertasters and the saltiness of NaCl. *Annals of the New York Academy of Sciences, 855,* 793–796.

Bassetti, C., Vella, S., Donati, F., et al. (2000). SPECT during sleepwalking. *Lancet, 356,* 484–485.

Basson, R., McInnis, R., Smith, M. D., Hodgson, G., & Koppiker, N. (2002). Efficacy and safety of sidenafil citrate in women with sexual dysfunction associated with female sexual arousal disorder. *Journal of Women's Health and Gender-Based Medicine, 11,* 367–377.

Bauer, P. (2002). Long-term recall memory: Behavioral and neurodevelopmental changes in the first 2 years of life. *Current Directions in Psychological Science, 11,* 137–141.

Baumeister, R. F. (2000). Gender differences in erotic plasticity: The female sex drive as socially flexible and responsive. *Psychological Bulletin, 126,* 347–374.

Baumeister, R. F., & Bratslavsky, E. (1999). Passion, intimacy, and time: Passionate love as a function of change in intimacy. *Personality and Social Psychology Review, 3,* 49–67.

Baumeister, R. F., Brewer, L. E., Tice, D. M., & Twenge, J. M. (2007). The need to belong: Understanding the interpersonal and inner effects of social exclusion. *Social and Personality Psychology Compass, 1,* 506–520.

Baumeister, R. F., Campbell, J. D., Krueger, J. I., & Vohs, K. D. (2003). Does high self-esteem cause better performance, interpersonal success, happiness, or healthier lifestyles? *Psychological Science in the Public Interest, 4*(1), [whole issue].

Baumeister, R. F., Catanese, K. R., & Vohs, K. D. (2001). Is there a gender difference in strength of sex drive? Theoretical views, conceptual distinctions, and a review of relevant evidence. *Personality and Social Psychology Review, 5,* 242–273.

Baumeister, R. F., Dale, K., & Sommer, K. L. (1998). Freudian defense mechanisms and empirical findings in modern social psychology: Reaction formation, projection, displacement, undoing, isolation, sublimation, and denial. *Journal of Personality, 66,* 1081–1124.

Baumeister, R. F., Stillwell, A. M., & Heatherton, T. F. (1994). Guilt: An interpersonal approach. *Psychological Bulletin, 115,* 243–267.

Baumrind, D., Larzelere, R. E., & Cowan, P. (2002). Ordinary physical punishment—Is it harmful? Commentary on Gershoff's Review. *Psychological Bulletin, 128,* 580–589.

Bechara, A., Dermas, H., Tranel, D., & Damasio, A. R. (1997). Deciding advantageously before knowing the advantageous strategy. *Science, 275,* 1293–1294.

Beck, A. T. (1976). *Cognitive therapy and the emotional disorders.* New York, NY: International Universities Press.

Beck, A. T. (2005). The current state of cognitive therapy: A 40-year retrospective. *Archives of General Psychiatry, 62,* 953–959.

Becker, D. V., Kenrick, D. T., Neuberg, S. L., et al. (2007). The confounded nature of angry men and happy women. *Journal of Personality and Social Psychology, 92,* 179–190.

Becker, J. B., Berkley, K. J., Geary, N., et al. (Eds.). (2008). *Sex differences in the brain: From genes to behavior.* New York, NY: Oxford University Press.

Becker, S. W., & Eagly, A. H. (2004). The heroism of women and men. *American Psychologist, 59,* 163–178.

Beer, J. M., Arnold, R. D., & Loehlin, J. C. (1998). Genetic and environmental influences on MMPI factor scales: Joint model fitting to twin and adoption data. *Journal of Personality and Social Psychology, 74,* 818–827.

Belle, D., & Doucet, J. (2003). Poverty, inequality, and discrimination as sources of depression among U.S. women. *Psychology of Women Quarterly, 27,* 101–113.

Belsky, J., Bakermans-Kranenburg, M. J., & van IJzendoorn, M. H. (2007). For better *and* for worse: Differential susceptibility to environmental influences. *Current Directions in Psychological Science, 16,* 300–304.

Belsky, J., Hsieh, K.-H., & Crnic, K. (1996). Infant positive and negative emotionality: One dimension or two? *Developmental Psychology, 32,* 289–298.

Belsky, J., & Pluess, M. (2009). The nature (and nurture?) of plasticity in early human development. *Perspectives on Psychological Science, 4,* 345–351.

Bem, D. J., & Honorton, C. (1994). Does psi exist? Replicable evidence for an anomalous process of information transfer. *Psychological Bulletin, 115,* 4–18.

Bem, S. L. (1993). *The lenses of gender.* New Haven, CT: Yale University Press.

Benedetti, F., & Levi-Montalcini, R. (2001). *Opioid and non-opioid mechanisms of placebo analgesia.* Paper presented at the annual meeting of the American Psychological Society, Toronto, Canada.

Benedetti, F., Mayberg, H. S., Wager, T. D., et al. (2005). Neurobiological mechanisms of the placebo effect. *The Journal of Neuroscience, 45,* 10390–10402.

Benjamin, L. T., Jr. (1998). Why Gorgeous George, and not Wilhelm Wundt, was the founder of psychology: A history of popular psychology in America. Invited address presented at the National Institute on the Teaching of Psychology, St. Petersburg Beach, FL.

Benjamin, L. T., Jr. (2003). Why can't psychology get a stamp? *Journal of Applied Psychoanalytic Studies, 5*, 443–454.

Ben-Shakhar, G., & Elaad, E. (2003). The validity of psychophysiological detection of information with the Guilty Knowledge Test: A meta-analytic review. *Journal of Applied Psychology, 88*, 131–151.

Beran, M. J., & Beran, M. M. (2004). Chimpanzees remember the results of one-by-one addition of food items to sets over extended time periods. *Psychological Science, 15*, 94–99.

Berenbaum, S. A., & Bailey, J. M. (2003). Effects on gender identity of prenatal androgens and genital appearance: Evidence from girls with congenital adrenal hyperplasia. *Journal of Clinical Endocrinology and Metabolism, 88*, 1102–1106.

Berger, F., Gage, F. H., & Vijayaraghavan, S. (1998). Nicotinic receptor-induced apoptotic cell death of hippocampal progenitor cells. *Journal of Neuroscience, 18*, 6871–6881.

Berglund, H., Lindström, P., & Savic, I. (2006). Brain response to putative pheromones in lesbian women. *Proceedings of the National Academy of Sciences, 103*, 8269–8274.

Berkman Center for Internet & Society. (2008, December 31). Enhancing child safety and online technologies: Final report of the Internet Safety Task Force. Retrieved from http://cyber.law.harvard.edu/sites/cyber.law.harvard.edu/files/ISTTF_Final_Report.pdf

Berkowitz, S. R., Nelson, K. J., Newman, E. J., et al. (2008, May). Attitudes toward cosmetic neurology: An international perspective. Poster presented at the meeting of the Association for Psychological Science, Chicago, IL.

Berlin, F. S. (2003). Sex offender treatment and legislation. *Journal of the American Academy of Psychiatry and the Law, 31*, 510–513.

Bernstein, D. M., & Loftus, E. F. (2009). How to tell if a particular memory is true or false. *Perspectives on Psychological Science, 4*, 370–374.

Berntsen, D., & Thomsen, D. K. (2005). Personal memories for remote historical events: Accuracy and clarity of flashbulb memories related to World War II. *Journal of Experimental Psychology: General, 134*, 242–257.

Berscheid, E., & Reis, H. T. (1998). Attraction and close relationships. In D. T. Gilbert, S. T. Fiske, & G. Lindzey (Eds.), *The handbook of social psychology, Vol. 2* (4th ed.). New York, NY: McGraw-Hill.

Best, J. (2001). *Damned lies and statistics.* Berkeley: University of California Press.

Beutler, L. E. (2000). David and Goliath: When empirical and clinical standards of practice meet. *American Psychologist, 55*, 997–1007.

Beutler, L. E., & Malik, M. L. (Eds.). (2002). *Rethinking the DSM: A psychological perspective.* Washington, DC: American Psychological Association.

Beydoun, M. A., Kaufman, J. S., Satia, J. A., et al. (2007). Plasma n-3 fatty acids and the risk of cognitive decline in older adults: The Atherosclerosis Risk in Communities Study. *American Journal of Clinical Nutrition, 85*, 1103–1111.

Beyerstein, B. L. (1996). Graphology. In G. Stein (Ed.), *The encyclopedia of the paranormal.* Amherst, NY: Prometheus Books.

Beyerstein, B. L. (1999). Fringe psychotherapies: The public at risk. In W. Sampson (Ed.), *A guide to alternative medicine.* London, England: Gordon and Breach.

Bhatarah, P., Ward, G., & Tan, L. (2008). Examining the relationship between free recall and immediate serial recall: The serial nature of recall and the effect of test expectancy. *Memory & Cognition, 36*, 20–34.

Bianchi, S. M., Robinson, J. P., & Milkie, M. A. (2006). *Changing rhythms of American family life.* New York, NY: Russell Sage Foundation.

Bierut, L. J., Heath, A. C., Bucholz, K. K., et al. (1999). Major depressive disorder in a community-based twin sample: Are there different genetic contributions for men and women? *Archives of General Psychiatry, 56*, 557–563.

Bierut, L. J., Stitzel, J. A., Wang, J. C., et al. (2008). Variants in nicotinic receptors and risk for nicotine dependence. *American Journal of Psychiatry, 165*, 1163–1171.

Binder, J., Zagefka, H., Brown, R., et al. (2009). Does contact reduce prejudice or does prejudice reduce contact? A longitudinal test of the contact hypothesis among majority and minority groups in three European countries. *Journal of Personality and Social Psychology, 96*, 843–856.

Birdwhistell, R. L. (1970). *Kinesics and context: Essays on body motion communication.* Philadelphia: University of Pennsylvania Press.

Birkhead, T. (2001). *Promiscuity: An evolutionary history of sperm competition.* Cambridge, MA: Harvard University Press.

Birmingham, C. L., Muller, J. L., Palepu, A., et al. (1999). The cost of obesity in Canada. *Canadian Medical Association Journal, 160*, 483–488.

Bischof, M., & Bassetti, C. L. (2004). Total dream loss: A distinct neuropsychological dysfunction after bilateral PCA stroke. *Annals of Neurology.* doi:10.1002/ana.20246

Bjork, R. A. (2000). Human factors 101: How about just trying things out? *APS Observer, 13*(3), 30.

Bjorkland, D. F. (2000). *Children's thinking: Developmental function and individual differences.* Belmont, CA: Wadsworth.

Black, J. E., Kodish, I. M., Grossman, A. W., et al. (2004). Pathology of layer V pyramidal neurons in the prefrontal cortex of patients with schizophrenia. *American Journal of Psychiatry, 161*, 742–744.

Blackmore, S. (2001). Giving up the ghosts: End of a personal quest. *Skeptical Inquirer, 25*(2), 25.

Blagrove, M. (1996). Problems with the cognitive psychological modeling of dreaming. *Journal of Mind and Behavior, 17*, 99–134.

Blair, R. D. J., Jones, L., Clark, F., & Smith, M. (1997). The psychopathic individual: A lack of responsiveness to distress cues? *Psychophysiology, 45*, 192–198.

Blakemore, C., & Cooper, G. F. (1970). Development of the brain depends on the visual environment. *Nature, 228*, 477–478.

Blanchette, I., & Richards, A. (2004). Reasoning about emotional and neutral materials. *Psychological Science, 15*, 745–752.

Blass, T. (Ed.). (2000). *Obedience to authority: Current perspectives on the Milgram paradigm.* Mahwah, NJ: Erlbaum.

Blazer, D. G., Kessler, R. C., & Swartz, M. S. (1998). Epidemiology of recurrent major and minor depression with a seasonal pattern: The National Comorbidity Survey. *British Journal of Psychiatry, 172*, 164–167.

Bleuler, E. (1911/1950). *Dementia praecox or the group of schizophrenias.* New York, NY: International Universities Press.

Bliss, T. V., & Collingridge, G. L. (1993). A synaptic model of memory: Long-term potentiation in the hippocampus. *Nature, 361*(6407), 31–39.

Bliss, T. V., & Lomo, T. (1973). Long-lasting potentiation of synaptic transmission in the dentate area of the anaesthetized rabbit following stimulation of the perforant path. *Journal of Physiology (London), 232*(2), 331–356.

Bloom, M. (2005). *Dying to kill: The allure of suicide terror.* New York, NY: Columbia University Press.

Blum, D. (2002). *Love at Goon Park: Harry Harlow and the science of affection.* Cambridge, MA: Perseus Books.

Bluming, A., & Tavris, C. (2009). Hormone replacement therapy: Real concerns and false alarms. *The Cancer Journal, 15*, 93–104.

Boesch, C. (1991). Teaching among wild chimpanzees. *Animal Behavior, 41*, 530–532.

Bogaert, A. F. (2006, June 28). Biological versus nonbiological older brothers and men's sexual orientation. *Proceedings of the National Academy of Sciences.* doi:10.1073/pnas.0511152103

Bohannon, J. N., & Stanowicz, L. (1988). The issue of negative evidence: Adult responses to children's language errors. *Developmental Psychology, 24*, 684–689.

Bohannon, J. N., & Symons, V. (1988). *Conversational conditions of children's imitation.* Paper presented at the biennial Conference on Human Development, Charleston, SC.

Bohman, M., Cloninger, R., Sigvardsson, S., & von Knorring, A.-L. (1987). The genetics of alcoholism and related disorders. *Journal of Psychiatric Research, 21*, 447–452.

Bolshakov, V. Y., & Siegelbaum, S. A. (1994). Postsynaptic induction and presynaptic expression of hippocampal long-term depression. *Science, 264*, 1148–1152.

Bonanno, G. A. (2004). Loss, trauma, and human resilience. *American Psychologist, 59*, 20–28.

Bonanno, G. A., Galea, S., Bucciarelli, A., & Vlahov, D. (2006). Psychological resilience after disaster. *Psychological Science, 17*, 181–186.

Bond, C. F., & DePaulo, B. M. (2008). Individual differences in judging deception: Accuracy and bias. *Psychological Bulletin, 134*, 477–492.

Bond, M. A., Punnett, L., Pyle, J. L., et al. (2004). Gendered work conditions, health, and work outcomes. *Journal of Occupational Health Psychology, 91*, 28–45.

Bond, R., & Smith, P. B. (1996). Culture and conformity: A meta-analysis of studies using Asch's (1952b, 1956) line judgment task. *Psychological Bulletin, 119*, 111–137.

Booth, F. W., & Neufer, P. D. (2005). Exercise controls gene expression. *American Scientist, 93*, 28–35.

Bootzin, R. R. (2009, March). Update on the psychological science accreditation system. Association for Psychological Science, *Observer*, 20–21.

Borch-Jacobsen, M. (1997, April 24). Sybil—The making of a disease: An interview with Dr. Herbert Spiegel. *The New York Review of Books*, 60–64.

Borch-Jacobsen, M. (2009). *Making minds and madness: From hysteria to depression.* Cambridge, MA: Cambridge University Press.

Bordo, S. (2000). *The male body.* New York, NY: Farrar, Straus and Giroux.

Boring, E. G. (1953). A history of introspection. *Psychological Bulletin, 50*, 169–187.

Bornstein, R. F., Leone, D. R., & Galley, D. J. (1987). The generalizability of subliminal mere exposure effects: Influence of stimuli perceived without awareness on social behavior. *Journal of Personality and Social Psychology, 53*, 1070–1079.

Boroditsky, L. (2003). Linguistic relativity. In L. Nadel (Ed.), *Encyclopedia of cognitive science.* London, England: Nature Publishing Group.

Boroditsky, L., Schmidt, L., & Phillips, W. (2003). Sex, syntax, and semantics. In D. Gentner & S. Goldin-Meadow (Eds.), *Language in mind: Advances in the study of language and thought.* Cambridge, MA: MIT Press.

Bosworth, H. B., & Schaie, K. W. (1999). Survival effects in cognitive function, cognitive style, and sociodemographic variables in the Seattle Longitudinal Study. *Experimental Aging Research, 25*, 121–139.

Bouchard, C., Tremblay, A., Despres, J. P., et al. (1990). The response to long-term overfeeding in identical twins. *New England Journal of Medicine, 322*, 1477–1482.

Bouchard, T. J., Jr. (1995). *Nature's twice-told tale: Identical twins reared apart—what they tell us about human individuality.* Paper presented at the annual meeting of the Western Psychological Association, Los Angeles, CA.

Bouchard, T. J., Jr. (1997a). The genetics of personality. In K. Blum & E. P. Noble (Eds.), *Handbook of psychiatric genetics.* Boca Raton, FL: CRC Press.

Bouchard, T. J., Jr. (1997b). IQ similarity in twins reared apart: Findings and responses to critics. In R. J. Sternberg & E. Grigorenko (Eds.), *Intelligence: Heredity and environment.* New York, NY: Cambridge University Press.

Bouchard, T. J., Jr. (2004). Genetic influence on human psychological traits: A survey. *Current Directions in Psychological Science, 13*, 148–151.

Bouchard, T. J., Jr., & McGue, M. (1981). Familial studies of intelligence: A review. *Science, 212*, 1055–1058.

Bourbeau, R., & Lebel, A. (2000). Mortality statistics for the oldest-old: An evaluation of Canadian data. *Demographic Research, 2*(2). doi:10.4054/DemRes.2000.2.2

Bouret, S. G., Draper, S. J., & Simerly, R. B. (2004). Trophic action of leptin on hypothalamic neurons that regulate feeding. *Science, 304*, 108–110.

Bousfield, W. A. (1953). The occurrence of clustering in the recall of randomly arranged associates. *Journal of General Psychology, 49*, 229–240.

Bowen, M. (1978). *Family therapy in clinical practice.* New York, NY: Jason Aronson.

Bower, B. (1998). All fired up: Perception may dance to the beat of collective neuronal rhythms. *Science News, 153*, 120–121.

Bower, B. (2008). Road to Eureka! Insight may lie at the end of a chain of neural reactions. *Science News, 173*, 184–185.

Bower, G. H., & Forgas, J. P. (2000). Affect, memory, and social cognition. In E. Eich et al. (Eds.), *Cognition and emotion.* New York, NY: Oxford University Press.

Bowers, K. S., Regehr, G., Balthazard, C., & Parker, K. (1990). Intuition in the context of discovery. *Cognitive Psychology, 22*, 72–110.

Bowlby, J. (1969). *Attachment and loss. Vol. 1. Attachment.* New York, NY: Basic Books.

Bowlby, J. (1973). *Attachment and loss: Vol. 2. Separation.* New York, NY: Basic Books.

Bowlby, J. (1982). *Attachment and loss. Vol. 1. Attachment.* (Rev. ed.). New York, NY: Basic Books.

Bowleg, L., Lucas, K. J., & Tschann, J. M. (2004). "The ball was always in his court": An exploratory analysis of relationship scripts, sexual scripts, and condom use among African American women. *Psychology of Women Quarterly, 28,* 70–82.

Bowles, S. (2008). Policies designed for self-interested citizens may undermine "the moral sentiments": Evidence from economic experiments. *Science, 320,* 1605–1609.

Bradford, J. M., & Pawlak, A. (1993). Effects of cyproterone acetate on sexual arousal patterns of pedophiles. *Archives of Sexual Behavior, 22,* 629–641.

Braun, K. A., Ellis, R., & Loftus, E. F. (2002). Make my memory: How advertising can change our memories of the past. *Psychology & Marketing, 19,* 1–23.

Braungert, J. M., Plomin, R., DeFries, J. C., & Fulker, D. W. (1992). Genetic influence on tester-rated infant temperament as assessed by Bayley's Infant Behavior Record: Nonadoptive and adoptive siblings and twins. *Developmental Psychology, 28,* 40–47.

Bregman, A. S. (1990). *Auditory scene analysis: The perceptual organization of sound.* Cambridge, MA: MIT Press.

Breland, K., & Breland, M. (1961). The misbehavior of organisms. *American Psychologist, 16,* 681–684.

Brennan, P. A., & Mednick, S. A. (1994). Learning theory approach to the deterrence of criminal recidivism. *Journal of Abnormal Psychology, 103,* 430–440.

Brescoll, V. L., & Uhlmann, E. L. (2008). Can an angry woman get ahead? Status conferral, gender, and expression of emotion in the workplace. *Psychological Science, 19,* 268–275.

Brewer, M. B., & Gardner, W. (1996). Who is this "we"? Levels of collective identity and self representations. *Journal of Personality and Social Psychology, 71,* 83–93.

Brissette, I., Scheier, M. F., & Carver, C. S. (2002). The role of optimism in social network development, coping, and psychological adjustment during a life transition. *Journal of Personality and Social Psychology, 82,* 102–111.

Brockner, J., & Rubin, J. Z. (1985). *Entrapment in escalating conflicts: A social psychological analysis.* New York, NY: Springer-Verlag.

Bröder, A. (1998). Deception can be acceptable. *American Psychologist, 53,* 805–806.

Broks, P. (2004). *Into the silent land: Travels in neuropsychology.* New York, NY: Grove Press.

Brooks-Gunn, J. (1986). Differentiating premenstrual symptoms and syndromes. *Psychosomatic Medicine, 48,* 385–387.

Brosnan, S. F., & de Waal, F. B. M. (2003). Monkeys reject unequal pay. *Nature, 425,* 297–299.

Brosnan, S. F. (2011). An evolutionary perspective on morality. *Journal of Economic Behavior & Organization, 77,* 23–30.

Brown, A. S. (2004). *The déjà vu experience: Essays in cognitive psychology.* New York, NY: Psychology Press.

Brown, A. S., Begg, M. D., Gravenstein, S., et al. (2004). Serologic evidence of prenatal influenza in the etiology of schizophrenia. *Archives of General Psychiatry, 61,* 774–780.

Brown, D., Scheflin, A. W., & Whitfield, C. L. (1999). Recovered memories: The current weight of the evidence in science and in the courts. *Journal of Psychiatry and Law, 27,* 5–156.

Brown, G. W., & Harris, T. O. (2008). Depression and the serotonin transporter 5-HTTLPR polymorphism: A review and a hypothesis concerning gene-environment interaction. *Journal of Affective Disorders, 111,* 1–12.

Brown, G. W. (1993). Life events and affective disorder: Replications and limitations. *Psychosomatic Medicine, 55,* 248–259.

Brown, G. R., Laland, K. N., & Mulder, M. B. (2009). Bateman's principles and human sex roles. *Trends in Ecology & Evolution, 24,* 297–304.

Brown, G. K., Ten Have, T., Henriques, G. R., et al. (2005, August 3). Cognitive therapy for the prevention of suicide attempts. *Journal of the American Medical Association, 294,* 563–570.

Brown, R., & Middlefell, R. (1989). Fifty-five years of cocaine dependence [letter]. *British Journal of Addiction, 84,* 946.

Brown, R. (1986). *Social psychology* (2nd ed.). New York, NY: Free Press.

Brown, R., Cazden, C., & Bellugi, U. (1969). The child's grammar from I to III. In J. P. Hill (Ed.), *Minnesota Symposium on Child Psychology* (Vol. 2). Minneapolis: University of Minnesota Press.

Brown, R., & Kulik, J. (1977). Flashbulb memories. *Cognition, 5,* 73–99.

Brown, R., & McNeill, D. (1966). The "tip of the tongue" phenomenon. *Journal of Verbal Learning and Verbal Behavior, 5,* 325–337.

Brown, R. P., & Josephs, R. A. (1999). A burden of proof: Stereotype relevance and gender differences in math performance. *Journal of Personality and Social Psychology, 76,* 246–257.

Brown, S. L., Nesse, R. M., Vinokur, A. D., & Smith, D. M. (2003). Providing social support may be more beneficial than receiving it: Results from a prospective study of mortality. *Psychological Science, 14,* 320–327.

Bruck, M. (2003). Effects of suggestion on the reliability and credibility of children's reports. Invited address at the annual meeting of the American Psychological Society, Atlanta, GA.

Bruck, M., Ceci, S. J., Francoeur, E., & Renick, A. (1995). Anatomically detailed dolls do not facilitate preschoolers' reports of a pediatric examination involving genital touching. *Journal of Experimental Psychology: Applied, 1,* 95–109.

Bruder, C. E. G. E., Piotrowski, A., Gijsbers, A. A., et al. (2008). Phenotypically concordant and discordant monozygotic twins display different DNA copy-number-variation profiles. *American Journal of Human Genetics, 82,* 763–771.

Bruinius, H. (2006). *Better for all the world: The secret history of forced sterilization and America's quest for racial purity.* New York, NY: Alfred A. Knopf.

Bruner, J. S. (1990). *Acts of meaning.* Cambridge, MA: Harvard University Press.

Bryant, G. A., & Barrett, H. C. (2007). Recognizing intentions in infant-directed speech. *Psychological Science, 18,* 746–751.

Bryant, R. A., & Guthrie, R. M. (2005). Maladaptive appraisals as a risk factor for posttraumatic stress. *Psychological Science, 16,* 749–752.

Buchanan, T. W. (2007). Retrieval of emotional memories. *Psychological Bulletin, 133,* 761–779.

Buchert, R., Thomasius, R., Nebeling, B., et al. (2003). Long-term effects of "ecstasy" use on serotonin transporters of the brain investigated by PET. *Journal of Nuclear Medicine, 44,* 375–384.

Buck, L., & Axel, R. (1991). A novel multigene family may encode odorant receptors: A molecular basis for odor recognition. *Cell, 65,* 175–187.

Bukowski, W. M. (2001). Friendship and the worlds of childhood. In D. W. Nangle & C. A. Erdley (Eds.), *The role of friendship in psychological adjustment.New directions for child and adolescent development, No. 91.* San Francisco, CA: Jossey-Bass.

Buller, D. J. (2005). *Adapting minds: Evolutionary psychology and the persistent quest for human nature.* Cambridge MA: MIT Press.

Burger, J. M. (2009). Replicating Milgram: Would people still obey today? *American Psychologist, 64,* 1–11.

Burke, B. L., Arkowitz, H., & Menchola, M. (2003). The efficacy of motivational interviewing: A meta-analysis of controlled clinical trials. *Journal of Consulting and Clinical Psychology, 71,* 843–861.

Burke, D. M., MacKay, D. G., Worthley, J. S., & Wade, E. (1991). On the tip of the tongue: What causes word finding failures in young and older adults? *Journal of Memory and Language, 30,* 237–246.

Burke, D. M., & Shafto, M. A. (2004). Aging and language production. *Current Directions in Psychological Science, 13,* 21–24.

Burke, P. (1996). *Gender shock.* New York, NY: Basic Books.

Burnham, D., Kitamura, C., & Vollmer-Conna, U. (2002, May 24). What's new, pussycat? On talking to babies and animals. *Science, 296,* 1435.

Bushman, B. J., & Anderson, C. A. (2001). Media violence and the American public: Scientific facts versus media misinformation. *American Psychologist, 56,* 477–489.

Bushman, B. J., & Anderson, C. A. (2009). Comfortably numb: Desensitizing effects of violent media on helping others. *Psychological Science, 20,* 273–277.

Bushman, B. J., Bonacci, A. M., Pedersen W. C., et al. (2005). Chewing on it can chew you up: Effects of rumination on triggered displaced aggression. *Journal of Personality and Social Psychology, 88,* 969–983.

Bushman, B., Bonacci, A. M., van Dijk, M., & Baumeister, R. F. (2003). Narcissism, sexual refusal, and aggression: Testing a narcissistic reactance model of sexual coercion. *Journal of Personality and Social Psychology, 84,* 1027–1040.

Bushman, B. J., Ridge, R. D., Das, E., et al. (2007). When God sanctions killing. *Psychological Science, 18,* 204–207.

Buss, D. M. (1994). *The evolution of desire: Strategies of human mating.* New York, NY: Basic Books.

Buss, D. M. (1995). Evolutionary psychology: A new paradigm for psychological science. *Psychological Inquiry, 6,* 1–30.

Buss, D. M. (1996). Sexual conflict: Can evolutionary and feminist perspectives converge? In D. M. Buss & N. Malamuth (Eds.), *Sex, power, conflict: Evolutionary and feminist perspectives.* New York, NY: Oxford University Press.

Buss, D. M. (1999). *Evolutionary psychology: The new science of the mind.* Boston, MA: Allyn & Bacon.

Buss, D. M. (2000). *The dangerous passion: Why jealousy is as necessary as love or sex.* New York, NY: The Free Press.

Buss, D. M., & Barnes, M. L. (1986). Preferences in human mate selection. *Journal of Personality and Social Psychology, 50,* 559–570.

Bussey, K., & Bandura, A. (1999). Social-cognitive theory of gender development and differentiation. *Psychological Review, 106,* 676–713.

Buster, J. E., Kingsberg, S. A., Aguirre, O., et al. (2005). Testosterone patch for low sexual desire in surgically menopausal women: A randomized trial. *Obstetrics and Gynecology, 105*(Pt 1), 944–952.

Butcher, J. N., Dahlstrom, W. G., Graham, J. R., et al. (1989). *Minnesota Multiphasic Personality Inventory-II: Manual for administration and scoring.* Minneapolis: University of Minnesota Press.

Butcher, J. N., Lim, J., & Nezami, E. (1998). Objective study of abnormal personality in cross-cultural settings: The MMPI-2. *Journal of Cross-Cultural Psychology, 29,* 189–211.

Butler, S., Chalder, T., Ron, M., et al. (1991). Cognitive behaviour therapy in chronic fatigue syndrome. *Journal of Neurology, Neurosurgery & Psychiatry, 54,* 153–158.

Button, T. M. M., Thapar, A., & McGuffin, P. (2005). Relationship between antisocial behaviour, attention-deficit hyperactivity disorder and maternal prenatal smoking. *British Journal of Psychiatry, 187,* 155–160.

Buunk, B., Angleitner, A., Oubaid, V., & Buss, D. M. (1996). Sex differences in jealousy in evolutionary and cultural perspective: Tests from the Netherlands, Germany, and the United States. *Psychological Science, 7,* 359–363.

Byne, W. (1995). Science and belief: Psychobiological research on sexual orientation. *Journal of Homosexuality, 28,* 303–344.

Cabiya, J. J., Lucio, E., Chavira, D. A., et al. (2000). MMPI-2 scores of Puerto Rican, Mexican, and U.S. Latino college students: A research note. *Psychological Reports, 87,* 266–268.

Cacioppo, J. T., Berntson, G. G., Lorig, T. S., et al. (2003). Just because you're imaging the brain doesn't mean you can stop using your head: A primer and set of first principles. *Journal of Personality and Social Psychology, 85,* 650–661.

Cadinu, M., Maass, A., Rosabianca, A., & Kiesner, J. (2005). Why do women underperform under stereotype threat? Evidence for the role of negative thinking. *Psychological Science, 16,* 472–578.

Cahill, L. (2005, May). His brain, her brain. *Scientific American, 292,* 40–47.

Cahill, L., Prins, B., Weber, M., & McGaugh, J. L. (1994). ß-adrenergic activation and memory for emotional events. *Nature, 371,* 702–704.

Cai, D. J., Mednick, S. A., Harrison, E. M., et al. (2009). REM, not incubation, improves creativity by priming associative networks. *Proceedings of the National Academy of Sciences, 106,* 10130–10134.

Cain, D. P., Saucier, D. M., & Boon, F. (1997). Testing hypotheses of spatial learning: The role of NMDA receptors and NMDA-mediated long-term potentiation. *Behavioural Brain Research, 84,* 179–193.

Cain, D. P., Saucier, D. M., Hall, J. A., et al. (1996). Detailed behavioural analysis of water maze acquisition under APV or CNQX: Contribution of sensorimotor disturbances to drug-induced acquisition deficits. *Behavioral Neuroscience, 110,* 86–102.

Cairney, J., & Ostbye, T. (1999). Time since immigration and excess body weight. *Canadian Journal of Public Health–Revue Canadienne de Santé Publique, 90,* 120–124.

Calder, A. J., Keane, J., Manes, F., Antoun, N., & Young, A. W. (2000). Impaired recognition and experience of disgust following brain injury. *Nature Neuroscience, 3,* 1077–1078.

Camerer, Colin F. (2003). Strategizing in the brain. *Science, 300,* 1673–1675.

Cameron, J., Banko, K. M., & Pierce, W. D. (2001). Pervasive negative effects of rewards on intrinsic motivation: The myth continues. *Behavior Analyst, 24,* 1–44.

Campbell, B. C., Pope, H. G., & Filiault, S. (2005). Body image among Ariaal men from Northern Kenya. *Journal of Cross-Cultural Psychology, 36,* 371–379.

Campbell, F. A., & Ramey, C. T. (1995). Cognitive and school outcomes for high risk students at middle adolescence: Positive effects of early intervention. *American Educational Research Journal, 32,* 743–772.

Campbell, J. (1949/1968). *The hero with 1,000 faces* (2nd ed.). Princeton, NJ: Princeton University Press.

Campos, P. (2004). *The obesity myth: Why America's obsession with weight is hazardous to your health.* New York, NY: Gotham Books.

Cancian, F. M. (1987). *Love in America: Gender and self-development.* Cambridge, England: Cambridge University Press.

Canetto, S. S. (1992). Suicide attempts and substance abuse: Similarities and differences. *Journal of Psychology, 125,* 605–620.

Canetto, S. S., & Sakinofsky, I. (1998). The gender paradox in suicide. *Suicide and Life-Threatening Behavior, 28,* 1–23.

Cannon, T. D., Huttunen, M. O., Loennqvist, J., et al. (2000). The inheritance of neuropsychological dysfunction in twins discordant for schizophrenia. *American Journal of Human Genetics, 67,* 369–382.

Cannon, T. D., Kaprio, J., Loennqvist, J., et al. (1998). The genetic epidemiology of schizophrenia in a Finnish twin cohort: A population-based modeling study. *Archives of General Psychiatry, 55,* 67–74.

Cannon, W. B. (1929). *Bodily changes in pain, hunger, fear and rage* (2nd ed.). New York, NY: Appleton.

Cao, X., Wang, H., Mei, B., et al. (2008). Inducible and selective erasure of memories in the mouse brain via chemical-genetic manipulation. *Neuron, 60,* 353–366.

Capaldi, D. M., Pears, K. C., Patterson, G. R., & Owen, L. D. (2003). Continuity of parenting practices across generations in an at-risk sample: A prospective comparison of direct and mediated associations. *Journal of Abnormal Child Psychology, 31,* 127–142.

Caplan, E. (1998). *Mind games: American culture and the birth of psychotherapy.*(See Chapter 4: Inventing psychotherapy: The American Mind Cure movement, 1830–1900.) Berkeley: University of California Press.

Carnagey, N. L., & Anderson, C. A. (2005). The effects of reward and punishment in violent video games on aggressive affect, cognition, and behavior. *Psychological Science, 16,* 882–889.

Cartwright, R. (1977). *Night life: Explorations in dreaming.* Englewood Cliffs, NJ: Prentice-Hall.

Cartwright, R. D. (1996). Dreams and adaptations to divorce. In D. Barrett (Ed.), *Trauma and dreams.* Cambridge, MA: Harvard University Press.

Cartwright, R. D., Young, M. A., Mercer, P., & Bears, M. (1998). Role of REM sleep and dream variables in the prediction of remission from depression. *Psychiatry Research, 80,* 249–255.

Carver, C. S., & Harmon-Jones, E. (2009). Anger is an approach-related affect: Evidence and implications. *Psychological Bulletin, 135,* 183–204.

Carver, C. S., & Scheier, M. F. (2002). Optimism. In C. R. Snyder & S. J. Lopes (Eds.), *The handbook of positive psychology.* New York, NY: Oxford University Press.

Caspi, A. (2000). The child is father of the man: Personality continuities from childhood to adulthood. *Journal of Personality and Social Psychology, 78,* 158–172.

Caspi, A., McClay, J., Moffitt, T. E., et al. (2002, August 2). Role of genotype in the cycle of violence in maltreated children. *Science, 297,* 851–857.

Caspi, A., & Moffitt, T. E. (1991). Individual differences are accentuated during periods of social change: The sample case of girls at puberty. *Journal of Personality and Social Psychology, 61,* 157–168.

Caspi, A., Sugden, K., Moffitt, T. E., et al. (2003). Influence of life stress on depression: Moderation by a polymorphism in the 5-HTT gene. *Science, 301,* 386–389.

Cassin, S. E., von Ranson, K. M., Heng, K., et al. (2008). Adapted motivational interviewing for women with binge eating disorder: A randomized controlled trial. *Psychology of Addictive Behaviors, 22,* 417–425.

Cattell, R. B. (1973). *Personality and mood by questionnaire.* San Francisco, CA: Jossey-Bass.

Ceci, S. J., & Bruck, M. (1995). *Jeopardy in the courtroom: A scientific analysis of children's testimony.* Washington, DC: American Psychological Association.

Cejka, M. A., & Eagly, A. H. (1999). Gender-stereotypic images of occupations correspond to the sex segregation of employment. *Personality and Social Psychology Bulletin, 25,* 413–423.

Cermak, L. S., & Craik, F. I. M. (Eds.). (1979). *Levels of processing in human memory.* Hillsdale, NJ: Erlbaum.

Cervone, D., & Shoda, Y. (1999). Beyond traits in the study of personality coherence. *Current Directions in Psychological Science, 8,* 27–32.

Chabat, D.-R., Rainville, C., Kupers, R., & Ptito, M. (2007). Tactile-'visual' acuity of the tongue in early blind individuals. *Neuroreport, 18,* 1901–1904.

Chambless, D. L., & Ollendick, T. H. (2001). Empirically supported psychological interventions: Controversies and evidence. *Annual Review of Psychology, 52,* 685–716.

Chambless, D. L., & the Task Force on Psychological Interventions. (1998). Update on empirically validated therapies II. *The Clinical Psychologist, 51,* 3–16.

Champagne, F. A. (2009). Nurturing nature: Epigenetics and the transmission of behavior across generations. Invited address at the annual meeting of the Association for Psychological Science, San Francisco, CA.

Chan, B. L., Witt, R., Charrow, A. P., et al. (2007). Mirror therapy for phantom limb pain [correspondence]. *New England Journal of Medicine, 357,* 2206–2207.

Chandrashekar, J., Hoon, M. A., Ryba, N. J. P., & Zuker, C. S. (2006). The receptors and cells for mammalian taste. *Nature, 444,* 288–294.

Chang, E. C. (1998). Dispositional optimism and primary and secondary appraisal of a stressor. *Journal of Personality and Social Psychology, 74,* 1109–1120.

Chapin, H., Jantzen, K., Kelso, J. A. S., et al. (2010). Dynamic emotional and neural responses to music depend on performance expression and listener experience. *PLoS ONE, 5:* e13812. doi:10.1371/journal.pone.0013812

Charles, S. T., & Carstensen, L. L. (2004). A life-span view of emotional functioning in adulthood and old age. In P. Costa (Ed.), *Recent advances in psychology and aging* (Vol. 15). Amsterdam, the Netherlands: Elsevier.

Charles, S. T., Reynolds, C. A., & Gatz, M. (2001). Age-related differences and change in positive and negative affect over 23 years. *Journal of Personality and Social Psychology, 80,* 136–151.

Chaudhari, N., Landin, A. M., & Roper, S. D. (2000). A metabotropic glutamate receptor variant functions as a taste receptor. *Nature Neuroscience, 3,* 113–119.

Chaves, J. F. (1989). Hypnotic control of clinical pain. In N. P. Spanos & J. F. Chaves (Eds.), *Hypnosis: The cognitive-behavioral perspective.* Buffalo, NY: Prometheus Books.

Cheesman, J., & Merikle, P. M. (1986). Distinguishing conscious from unconscious perceptual processes. *Canadian Journal of Psychology, 40*(4), 343–367.

Chen, G., Meckle, W., & Wilson, J. (2002). Speed and safety effect of photo radar enforcement on a highway corridor in British Columbia. *Accident Analysis and Prevention, 34*(2), 129–138.

Chen, Z., Williams, K. D., Fitness, J., & Newton, N. C. (2008). When hurt will not heal. *Psychological Science, 19,* 789–795.

Cheney, D. L., & Seyfarth, R. M. (1985). Vervet monkey alarm calls: Manipulation through shared information? *Behavior, 94,* 150–166.

Chida, Y., & Hamer, M. (2008). Chronic psychosocial factors and acute physiological responses to laboratory-induced stress in healthy populations: A quantitative review of 30 years of investigations. *Psychological Bulletin, 134,* 829–885.

Chipuer, H. M., Rovine, M. J., & Plomin, R. (1990). LISREL modeling: Genetic and environmental influences on IQ revisited. *Intelligence, 14,* 11–29.

Choi, I., Dalal, R., Kim-Prieto, C., & Park, H. (2003). Culture and judgment of causal relevance. *Journal of Personality and Social Psychology, 84,* 46–59.

Chomsky, N. (1957). *Syntactic structures.* The Hague, the Netherlands: Mouton.

Chomsky, N. (1980). Initial states and steady states. In M. Piatelli-Palmerini (Ed.), *Language and learning: The debate between Jean Piaget and Noam Chomsky.* Cambridge, MA: Harvard University Press.

Chorpita, B. F., & Barlow, D. H. (1998). The development of anxiety: The role of control in the early environment. *Psychological Bulletin, 124,* 3–21.

Christakis, D. A., Zimmerman, F. J., DiGiuseppe, D. L., & McCarty, C. A. (2004). Early television exposure and subsequent attentional problems in children. *Pediatrics, 113,* 708–713.

Christensen, A., & Jacobson, N. S. (2000). *Reconcilable differences.* New York, NY: Guilford.

Christensen, H., Leach, L. S., & Mackinnon, A. (2010). Cognition in pregnancy and motherhood: Prospective cohort study. *British Journal of Psychiatry, 196,* 126–132.

Christopher, A. N., & Wojda, M. R. (2008). Social dominance orientation, right-wing authoritarianism, sexism, and prejudice toward women in the workforce. *Psychology of Women Quarterly, 32,* 65–73.

Church, A. T., & Lonner, W. J. (1998). The cross-cultural perspective in the study of personality: Rationale and current research. *Journal of Cross-Cultural Psychology, 29,* 32–62.

Churchill, A. C., & Davis, C. G. (2010). Realistic orientation and the transition to motherhood. *Journal of Social and Clinical Psychology, 22,* 97–114.

Cialdini, R. B. (2009). We have to break up. *Perspectives on Psychological Science, 4,* 5–6.

Cinque, G. (1999). *Adverbs and functional heads: A cross-linguistic approach.* New York, NY: Oxford University Press.

Cioffi, F. (1998). *Freud and the question of pseudoscience.* Chicago, IL: Open Court.

Clancy, S. A. (2005). *Abducted: How people come to believe they were kidnapped by aliens.* Cambridge, MA: Harvard University Press.

Clark, L. A., & Watson, D. (2008). Temperament: An organizing paradigm for trait psychology. In O. P. John, R. W. Robbins, & L. A. Pervin (Eds.), *Handbook of personality: Theory and research* (3rd ed.). New York, NY: Guilford.

Clarke, H. F., Dalley, J. W., Crofts, H. S., et al. (2004, May 7). Cognitive inflexibility after prefrontal serotonin depletion. *Science, 304,* 878–880.

Clarke, P., & Evans, S. H. (1998). *Surviving modern medicine.* Rutgers, NJ: Rutgers University Press.

Cleary, A. M. (2008). Recognition memory, familiarity, and déjà vu experiences. *Current Directions in Psychological Science, 17,* 353–357.

Cleckley, H. (1976). *The mask of sanity* (5th ed.). St. Louis, MO: Mosby.

Cloninger, C. R. (1990). *The genetics and biology of alcoholism.* Cold Springs Harbor, ME: Cold Springs Harbor Press.

Coan, J. A., Schaefer, H., & Davidson, R. J. (2006). Lending a hand: Social regulation of the neural response to threat. *Psychological Science, 17*(12), 1032–1039.

Coats, E. J., Janoff-Bulman, R., & Alpert, N. (1996). Approach versus avoidance goals: Differences in self-evaluation and well-being. *Personality and Social Psychology Bulletin, 22,* 1057–1067.

Coe, C. L., & Lubach, G. R. (2008). Fetal programming: Prenatal origins of health and illness. *Current Directions in Psychological Science, 17,* 36–41.

Cohen, D. B. (1999). Stranger in the nest: Do parents really shape their child's personality, intelligence, or character? New York, NY: Wiley.

Cohen, D. (1998). Culture, social organization, and patterns of violence. *Journal of Personality and Social Psychology, 75,* 408–419.

Cohen, D. (2001). Cultural variation: Considerations and implications. *Psychological Bulletin, 127*(4), 451–471.

Cohen, D., Nisbett, R. E., Bowdle, B. F., & Schwarz, N. (1996). Insult, aggression, and the Southern culture of honor: An "experimental ethnography." *Journal of Personality and Social Psychology, 70,* 945–960.

Cohen Kadosh, R., Henik, A., Catena, A., et al. (2009). Induced cross-modal synaesthetic experience without abnormal neuronal connections. *Psychological Science, 20,* 258–265.

Cohen, S., Doyle, W. J., Turner, R., et al. (2003). Sociability and susceptibility to the common cold. *Psychological Science, 14,* 389–395.

Cohen, S., Frank, E., Doyle, W. J., et al. (1998). Types of stressors that increase susceptibility to the common cold in healthy adults. *Health Psychology, 17,* 214–223.

Cohen, S., Tyrrell, D. A., & Smith, A. P. (1993). Negative life events, perceived stress, negative affect, and susceptibility to the common cold. *Journal of Personality and Social Psychology, 64,* 131–140.

Colcombe, S., & Kramer, A. F. (2003). Fitness effects on the cognitive function of older adults: A meta-analytic study. *Psychological Science, 14,* 125–130.

Cole, M., & Scribner, S. (1974). *Culture and thought.* New York, NY: Wiley.

Collaer, M. L., & Hines, M. (1995). Human behavioral sex differences: A role for gonadal hormones during early development? *Psychological Bulletin, 118,* 55–107.

Collins, A. M., & Loftus, E. F. (1975). A spreading-activation theory of semantic processing. *Psychological Review, 82,* 407–428.

Collins, B. E., & Brief, D. E. (1995). Using person-perception vignette methodologies to uncover the symbolic meanings of teacher behaviors in the Milgram paradigm. *Journal of Social Issues, 51,* 89–106.

Collins, R. L. (1996). For better or worse: The impact of upward social comparison on self-evaluations. *Psychological Bulletin, 119,* 51–69.

Colman, A. (1991). Crowd psychology in South African murder trials. *American Psychologist, 46,* 1071–1079.

Coltman, D. W., O'Donoghue, P., Jorgenson, J. T., et al. (2003). Undesirable evolutionary consequences of trophy hunting. *Nature, 426,* 655–658.

Colvert, E., Rutter, M., Beckett, C., et al. (2008). Emotional difficulties in early adolescence following severe early deprivation: Findings from the English and Romanian adoptees study. *Development and Psychopathology, 20,* 547–567.

Colvert, E., Rutter, M., Kreppner, J., et al. (2008). Do theory of mind and executive function deficits underlie the adverse outcomes associated with profound early deprivation? Findings from the English and Romanian adoptees study. *Journal of Abnormal Child Psychology, 36,* 1057–1068.

Comas-Díaz, L. (2006). Latino healing: The integration of ethnic psychology into psychotherapy. *Psychotherapy: Theory, Research, Practice, Training, 43,* 436–453.

Comuzzie, A. G., & Allison, D. B. (1998). The search for human obesity genes. *Science, 280,* 1374–1377.

Conklin, H. M., & Iacono, W. G. (2002). Schizophrenia: A neurodevelopmental perspective. *Current Directions in Psychological Science, 11,* 33–37.

Connor, S. K., & McIntyre, L. (1999). The sociodemographic predictors of smoking cessation among pregnant women in Canada. *Canadian Journal of Public Health, 90*(5), 352–355.

Conroy, J. (2000). *Unspeakable acts, ordinary people: The dynamics of torture.* New York, NY: Knopf.

Corriveau, K. H., Fusaro, M., & Harris, P. L. (2009). Going with the flow: Preschoolers prefer nondissenters as informants. *Psychological Science, 20,* 372–377.

Cook, J. M., Biyanova, T., & Coyne, J. C. (2009). Influential psychotherapy figures, authors, and books: An Internet survey of over 2,000 psychotherapists. *Psychotherapy: Theory, Research, Practice, Training, 46,* 42–51.

Cooper, M. L., Frone, M. R., Russell, M., & Mudar, P. (1995). Drinking to regulate positive and negative emotions: A motivational model of alcohol use. *Journal of Personality and Social Psychology, 69,* 990–1005.

Cooper, M. L., Shapiro, C. M., & Powers, A. M. (1998). Motivations for sex and risky sexual behavior among adolescents and young adults: A functional perspective. *Journal of Personality and Social Psychology, 75,* 1528–1558.

Copi, I. M., & Burgess-Jackson, K. (1992). *Informal logic* (2nd ed.). New York, NY: Macmillan.

Corcoran, M. E., Saucier, D. M., Zhang, X., et al. (2005). Cannabinoids and kindling. In M. E. Corcoran & S. L. Moshe (Eds.), *Kindling 6.* New York, NY: Springer-Kluwer.

Coren, S. (1996). Accidental death and the shift to daylight savings time. *Perceptual and Motor Skills, 83,* (3, Pt 1), 921–922.

Corkin, S. (1984). Lasting consequences of bilateral medial temporal lobectomy: Clinical course and experimental findings in H. M. *Seminars in Neurology, 4,* 249–259.

Corkin, S. (2002). What's new with the amnesic patient HM? *Nature Reviews Neuroscience, 3,* 153–160.

Corkin, S., Amaral, D. G., Gonzalez, R. G., et al. (1997). H. M.'s medial temporal lobe lesion: Findings from magnetic resonance imaging. *Journal of Neuroscience, 17,* 3964–3979.

Cosgrove, G. R., & Rauch, S. L. (2003). Stereotactic cingulotomy. *Neurosurgery Clinics of North America, 14,* 225–235.

Cosmides, L., Tooby, J., & Barkow, J. H. (1992). Introduction: Evolutionary psychology and conceptual integration. In J. H. Barkow, L. Cosmides, & J. Tooby (Eds.), *The adapted mind: Evolutionary psychology and the generation of culture.* New York, NY: Oxford University Press.

Costa, P. T., Jr., McCrae, R. R., Martin, T. A., et al. (1999). Personality development from adolescence through adulthood: Further cross-cultural comparisons of age differences. In V. J. Molfese & D. Molfese (Eds.), *Temperament and personality development across the life span.* Hillsdale, NJ: Erlbaum.

Costantino, G., & Malgady, R. G. (1996). Culturally sensitive treatment: Cuento and hero/heroine modeling therapies for Hispanic children and adolescents. In E. D. Hibbs & P. S. Jensen (Eds.), *Psychosocial treatments for child and adolescent disorders: Empirically based strategies for clinical practice.* Washington, DC: American Psychological Association.

Cota-Robles, S., Neiss, M., & Rowe, D. C. (2002). The role of puberty in violent and nonviolent delinquency among Anglo American, Mexican American, and African American boys. *Journal of Adolescent Research, 17,* 364–376.

Council, J. R., Kirsch, I., & Grant, D. L. (1996). Imagination, expectancy and hypnotic responding. In R. G. Kunzendorf, N. K. Spanos, & B. J. Wallace (Eds.), *Hypnosis and imagination.* Amityville, NY: Baywood.

Courage, M. L., & Howe, M. L. (2002). From infant to child: The dynamics of cognitive change in the second year of life. *Psychological Bulletin, 128,* 250–277.

Cowan, N. (2001). The magical number 4 in short-term memory: A reconsideration of mental storage capacity. *Behavioral and Brain Sciences, 24,* 87–185.

Cowan, N., & Chen, Z. (2009). How chunks form in long-term memory and affect short-term memory limits. In A. S. Thorn & M. P. Page (Eds.), *Interactions between short-term and long-term memory in the verbal domain.* New York, NY: Psychology Press.

Cowan, N., Morey, C. C., Chen, Z., et al. (2008). Theory and measurement of working memory capacity limits. In B. H. Ross (Ed.), *The psychology of learning and motivation.* San Diego, CA: Elsevier.

Cowan, R. S. (2008). *Heredity and hope: The case for genetic screening.* Cambridge, MA: Harvard University Press.

Cowen, E. L., Wyman, P. A., Work, W. C., & Parker, G. R. (1990). The Rochester Child Resilience Project (RCRP): Overview and summary of first year findings. *Development and Psychopathology, 2,* 193–212.

Cox, M. J., & Paley, B. (2003). Understanding families as systems. *Current Directions in Psychological Science, 12,* 193–196.

Cox, W. M., & Alm, R. (2005, February 28). Scientists are made, not born. *The New York Times* op-ed page. Retrieved from http://www.nytimes.com/2005/02/28/opinion/28cox.html

Coyne, J. C., Thombs, B. D., Stefanek, M., & Palmer, S. C. (2009). Time to let go of the illusion that psychotherapy extends the survival of cancer patients. *Psychological Bulletin, 135,* 179–182.

Coyne, J. A. (2009). *Why evolution is true.* New York, NY: Viking.

Cozolino, L. (2006). *The neuroscience of human relationships: Attachment and the developing social brain.* New York, NY: Norton.

Craik, F. I. M., & Lockhart, R. (1972). Levels of processing: A framework for memory research. *Journal of Verbal Learning and Verbal Behavior, 11,* 671–684.

Craik, F. I. M., & Tulving, E. (1975). Depth of processing and the retention of words in episodic memory. *Journal of Experimental Psychology: General, 104,* 268–294.

Crair, M. C., Gillespie, D. C., & Stryker, M. P. (1998). The role of visual experience in the development of columns in cat visual cortex. *Science, 279,* 566–570.

Cramer, K. M., & Neyedley, K. A. (1998). Mediating the sex difference in loneliness: The role of masculinity and femininity. *Sex Roles, 38,* 645–653.

Cramer, P. (2000). Defense mechanisms in psychology today: Further processes for adaptation. *American Psychologist, 55,* 637–646.

Crandall, C. S., & Martinez, R. (1996). Culture, ideology, and antifat attitudes. *Personality and Social Psychology Bulletin, 22,* 1165–1176.

Crawford, M., & Marecek, J. (1989). Psychology constructs the female: 1968–1988. *Psychology of Women Quarterly, 13,* 147–165.

Crawley, R., Grant, S., & Hinshaw, K. (2008). Cognitive changes in pregnancy: Mild decline or society stereotype? *Applied Cognitive Psychology, 22,* 1142–1162.

Crews, F. (Ed.). (1998). *Unauthorized Freud: Doubters confront a legend.* New York, NY: Viking.

Critchlow, B. (1986). The powers of John Barleycorn: Beliefs about the effects of alcohol on social behavior. *American Psychologist, 41,* 751–764.

Crits-Christoph, P., Wilson, G. T., & Hollon, S. D. (2005). Empirically supported psychotherapies: Comment on Westen, Novotny, and Thompson-Brenner (2004). *Psychological Bulletin, 131,* 412–417.

Critser, G. (2002). *Supersize.* New York, NY: Houghton-Mifflin.

Crombag, H. S., & Robinson, T. E. (2004). Drugs, environment, brain, and behavior. *Current Directions in Psychological Science, 13,* 107–111.

Cronbach, L. (1990). *Essentials of psychological testing* (5th ed.). New York, NY: Harper & Row.

Cruz, V. T., Nunes, B., Reis, A. M., & Pereira, J. R. (2005). Cortical remapping in amputees and dysmelic patients: A functional MRI study. *NeuroRehabilitation, 18,* 299–305.

Cumming, G. (2008). Replication and p intervals. *Perspectives on Psychological Science, 3,* 286–300.

Cumming, G., Fidler, F., Leonard, M., et al. (2007). Statistical reform in psychology: Is anything changing? *Psychological Science, 18,* 230–232.

Cummings, B. J., Uchida, N., Tamaki, S. J., et al. (2005). Human neural stem cells differentiate and promote locomotor recovery in spinal cord–injured mice. *Proceedings of the National Academy of Science, 102,* 14069–14074.

Cummings, N. A., & O'Donohue, W. T. (2008). *Eleven blunders that cripple psychotherapy in America.* New York, NY: Routledge/Taylor & Francis.

Cummings, N. A., & Wiggins, J. G. (2001). A collaborative primary care/behavioral health model for the use of psychotropic medication with children and adolescents. *Issues in Interdisciplinary Care, 3,* 121–128.

Currie, J., DellaVigna, S., Moretti, E., & Pathania, V. (2009, April). The effect of fast food restaurants on obesity. Unpublished paper. Retrieved from http://www.econ.berkeley.edu/~moretti/obesity.pdf

Curtiss, S. (1977). *Genie: A psycholinguistic study of a modern-day "wild child."* New York, NY: Academic Press.

Curtiss, S. (1982). Developmental dissociations of language and cognition. In L. Obler & D. Fein (Eds.), *Exceptional language and linguistics.* New York, NY: Academic Press.

Cushman, P. (1995). *Constructing the self, constructing America: A cultural history of psychotherapy.* New York, NY: Addison-Wesley.

Cypess, A. M., Lehman, S., Williams, G., et al. (2009, April 9). Identification and importance of brown adipose tissue in adult humans. *New England Journal of Medicine, 360,* 1509–1517.

Czeisler, C. A., Duffy, J. F., Shanahan, T. L., et al. (1999). Stability, precision, and near-24-hour period of the human circadian pacemaker. *Science, 284,* 2177–2181.

Dabbs, J. M., Jr. (2000). *Heroes, rogues, and lovers: Testosterone and behavior.* New York, NY: McGraw-Hill.

Dadds, M. R., Bovbjerg, D. H., Redd, W. H., & Cutmore, T. R. H. (1997). Imagery in human classical conditioning. *Psychological Bulletin, 122,* 89–103.

Daley, T. C., Whaley, S. E., Sigman, M. D., et al. (2003). IQ on the rise: The Flynn Effect in rural Kenyan children. *Psychological Science, 14,* 215–219.

Dalgleish, T. (2004). Cognitive approaches to posttraumatic stress disorder: The evolution of multirepresentational theorizing. *Psychological Bulletin, 130,* 228–260.

Dalgliesh, T., Hauer, B., & Kuyken, W. (2008). The mental regulation of autobiographical recollection in the aftermath of trauma. *Current Directions in Psychological Science, 17,* 259–263.

Dalton, K. S., Morris, D. L., Delanoy, D. I., et al. (1996). Security measures in an automated ganzfeld system. *Journal of Parapsychology, 60,* 129–147.

Daly, M., & Wilson, M. (1983). *Sex, evolution, and behavior* (2nd ed.). Belmont, CA: Wadsworth.

Damak, S., Rong, M., Yasumatsu, K., et al. (2003). Detection of sweet and umami taste in the absence of taste receptor T1r3. *Science, 301,* 850–853.

Damasio, A. R. (1994). *Descartes' error: Emotion, reason, and the human brain.* New York, NY: Grosset/Putnam.

Damasio, A. R. (2003). *Looking for Spinoza: Joy, sorrow, and the feeling brain.* San Diego, CA: Harcourt.

Damasio, A. R., Grabowski, T. J., Bechara, A., et al. (2000). Subcortical and cortical brain activity during the feeling of self-generated emotions. *Nature Neuroscience, 3,* 1049–1056.

Damasio, H., Grabowski, T. J., Frank, R., et al. (1994). The return of Phineas Gage: Clues about the brain from the skull of a famous patient. *Science, 264*, 1102–1105.

Damon, W. (1995). *Greater expectations.* New York, NY: Free Press.

Danner, D. D., Snowdon, D. A., & Friesen, W. V. (2001). Positive emotions in early life and longevity: Findings from the nun study. *Journal of Personality and Social Psychology, 80*, 804–813.

D'Antonio, M. (2004, May 2). How we think. *Los Angeles Times Magazine*, 18–20, 30–32.

Darley, J. M. (1995). Constructive and destructive obedience: A taxonomy of principal agent relationships. *Journal of Social Issues, 51*(3), 125–154.

Darley, J. M., & Latané, B. (1968). Bystander intervention in emergencies: Diffusion of responsibility. *Journal of Personality and Social Psychology, 8*, 377–383.

Darnaudery, M., Perez-Martin, M., Del Favero, F., et al. (2007). Early motherhood in rats is associated with a modification of hippocampal function. *Psychoneuroendocrinology, 32*, 803–812.

Darou, W. G. (1992). Native Canadians and intelligence testing. *Canadian Journal of Counselling, 26*(2), 96–99.

Darwin, C. (1859). *On the origin of species.* [A facsimile of the first edition, edited by Ernst Mayer, 1964.] Cambridge, MA: Harvard University Press.

Darwin, C. (1872/1965). *The expression of the emotions in man and animals.* Chicago, IL: The University of Chicago Press.

Darwin, C. (1874). *The descent of man, and selection in relation to sex* (2nd ed.). New York, NY: Hurst.

Daum, I., & Schugens, M. M. (1996). On the cerebellum and classical conditioning. *Psychological Science, 5*, 58–61.

Davelaar, E. J., Goshen-Gottstein, Y., Ashkenazi, A., et al. (2004). The demise of short-term memory revisited: Empirical and computational investigations of recency effects. *Psychological Review, 112*, 3–42.

Davidson, R. J., Abercrombie, H., Nitschke, J. B., & Putnam, K. (1999). Regional brain function, emotion, and disorders of emotion. *Current Opinion in Neurobiology, 9*, 228–234.

Davidson, R. J., Kabat-Zinn, J., Schumacher, J., et al. (2003). Alterations in brain and immune function produced by mindfulness meditation. *Psychosomatic Medicine, 65*, 564–570.

Davies, M. J., Baer, D. J., Judd, J. T., et al. (2002). Effects of moderate alcohol intake on fasting insulin and glucose concentrations and insulin sensitivity in postmenopausal women: A randomized controlled trial. *Journal of the American Medical Association, 287*, 2559–2562.

Davis, B. E., Moon, R. Y., Sachs, H. C., & Ottolini, M. C. (1998). Effects of sleep position on infant motor development. *Pediatrics, 102*, 1135–1140.

Davis, C. G., & Asliturk, E. (2011). Toward a positive psychology of coping with anticipated events. *Canadian Psychology, 52*, 101–110.

Davis, C. G., Nolen-Hoeksema, S., & Larson, J. (1998). Making sense of loss and benefiting from the experience: Two construals of meaning. *Journal of Personality and Social Psychology, 75*, 561–574.

Davis, D. (2010). Lies, *damned* lies, and the path from police interrogation to wrongful conviction. In M. H. Gonzales, C. Tavris, & J. Aronson (Eds.), *The scientist and the humanist: A festschrift in honor of Elliot Aronson.* New York, NY: Psychology Press.

Davis, K. D., Kiss, Z. H., Luo, L., et al. (1998). Phantom sensations generated by thalamic microstimulation. *Nature, 391*, 385–387.

Davis, M., Myers, K. M., Ressler, K. J., & Rothbaum, B. O. (2005). Facilitation of extinction of conditioning fear by D-cycloserine. *Current Directions in Psychological Science, 14*, 214–219.

Davison, G. C. (1976). Homosexuality: The ethical challenge. *Journal of Consulting and Clinical Psychology, 44*, 157–162.

Davison, K. P., Pennebaker, J. W., & Dickerson, S. S. (2000). Who talks? The social psychology of illness support groups. *American Psychologist, 55*, 205–217.

Dawes, R. M. (1994). *House of cards: Psychology and psychotherapy built on myth.* New York, NY: Free Press.

Dawson, N. V., Arkes, H. R., Siciliano, C., et al. (1988). Hindsight bias: An impediment to accurate probability estimation in clinicopathologic conferences. *Medical Decision Making, 8*(4), 259–264.

Dean, G. (1992). The bottom line: Effect size. In B. Beyerstein & D. Beyerstein (Eds.), *The write stuff: Evaluations of graphology—The study of handwriting analysis.* Buffalo, NY: Prometheus Books.

de Araujo, I. E., Oliveira-Maia, A. J., Sotnikova, T. D., et al. (2008, March 27). Food reward in the absence of taste receptor signaling. *Neuron, 57*, 930–941.

de Bono, E. (1985). *De Bono's thinking course.* New York, NY: Facts on File.

Deci, E. L., Koestner, R., & Ryan, R. M. (1999). A meta-analytic review of experiments examining the effects of extrinsic rewards on intrinsic motivation. *Psychological Bulletin, 125*, 627–668.

Deci, E. L., & Ryan, R. M. (1985). *Intrinsic motivation and self-determination of human behavior.* New York, NY: Plenum.

Deffenbacher, J. L., Deffenbacher, D. M., Lynch, R. S., & Richards, T. L. (2003). Anger, aggression, and risky behavior: A comparison of high and low anger drives. *Behaviour Research and Therapy, 41*, 701–718.

de Groot, R. H., Hornstra, G., Roozendaal, N., Jolles, J. (2003). Memory performance, but not information processing speed, may be reduced during early pregnancy. *Journal of Clinical and Experimental Neuropsychology, 25*, 482–488.

Dehaene, S., Spelke, E., Pinel, P., et al. (1999). Sources of mathematical thinking: Behavioral and brain-imaging evidence. *Science, 284*, 970–974.

De Houwer, J., Teige-Mocigemba, S., Spruyt, A., & Moors, A. (2009). Implicit measures: A normative analysis and review. *Psychological Bulletin, 135*, 347–368.

DeKeseredy, W., & Kelly, K. (1993). *The incidence and prevalence of woman abuse in Canadian university and college dating relationships: Results from a national survey.* Ottawa: Health Canada.

Dement, W. (1978). *Some must watch while some must sleep.* New York, NY: Norton.

Dement, W. (1992). *The sleepwatchers.* Stanford, CA: Stanford Alumni Association.

Dennett, D. C. (1991). *Consciousness explained.* Boston, MA: Little, Brown.

Denning, P., Little, J., & Glickman, A. (2004). *Over the influence: The harm reduction guide for managing drugs and alcohol.* New York, NY: Guilford.

Denny, D. (Ed.). (1998). *Current concepts in transgender identity.* New York, NY: Garland Press.

DePaulo, B. M. (1992). Nonverbal behavior and self-presentation. *Psychological Bulletin, 111*, 203–243.

DePaulo, B. M., Lindsay, J. J., Malone, B. E., et al. (2003). Cues to deception. *Psychological Bulletin, 129*, 74–118.

de Rivera, J. (1989). Comparing experiences across cultures: Shame and guilt in America and Japan. *Hiroshima Forum for Psychology, 14*, 13–20.

De Robertis, M. M., & Delaney, P. A. (2000). A second survey of the attitudes of university students to astrology and astronomy. *Journal of the Royal Astronomical Society of Canada, 94*, 112–122.

Desbonnet, L., Waddington, J. L., & O'Tuathaigh, C. M. (2009). Mutant models for genes associated with schizophrenia. *Biochemical Society Transactions, 37*(Pt 1), 308–312.

Desmarais, S., & Curtis, J. (1997). Gender differences in pay histories and views on pay entitlement among university students. *Sex Roles, 37*, 623–642.

Desmarais, S., & Curtis, J. (2001). Gender and perceived income entitlement among full-time workers: Analyses for Canadian national samples, 1984 and 1994. *Basic and Applied Social Psychology, 23*, 157–168.

DeValois, R. L., & DeValois, K. K. (1975). Neural coding of color. In E. C. Carterette & M. P. Friedman (Eds.), *Handbook of perception* (Vol. 5). New York, NY: Academic Press.

Devlin, B., Daniels, M., & Roeder, K. (1997). The heritability of IQ. *Nature, 388*, 468–471.

de Waal, F. (2001). *The ape and the sushi master: Cultural reflections by a primatologist.* New York, NY: Basic Books.

de Waal, F. B. M. (2002). Evolutionary psychology: The wheat and the chaff. *Current Directions in Psychological Science, 11*, 187–191.

Diamond, A., & Amso, D. (2008). Contributions of neuroscience to our understanding of cognitive development. *Current Directions in Psychological Science, 17*, 136–141.

Diamond, L. M. (2003). Was it a phase? Young women's relinquishment of lesbian/bisexual identities over a 5-year period. *Journal of Personality and Social Psychology, 84*, 352–364.

Diamond, L. M. (2004). Emerging perspectives on distinctions between romantic love and sexual desire. *Current Directions in Psychological Science, 13*, 116–119.

Diamond, L. (2008). *Sexual fluidity: Understanding women's love and desire.* Cambridge, MA: Harvard University Press.

Diamond, M., & Sigmundson, H. K. (1997). Sex reassignment at birth: Long-term review and clinical implications. *Archives of Pediatrics and Adolescent Medicine, 151*, 298–304.

Diamond, M. C. (1993). An optimistic view of the aging brain. *Generations, 17*, 31–33.

Dick, D. M. (2007). Identification of genes influencing a spectrum of externalizing psychopathology. *Current Directions in Psychological Science, 16*, 331–335.

Dick, D. M., Aliev, F., Wang, J. C., et al. (2008). A systematic single nucleotide polymorphism screen to fine-map alcohol dependence genes on chromosome 7 identifies association with a novel susceptibility gene ACN9. *Biological Psychiatry, 63*, 1047–1053.

Dickerson, S. S., & Kemeny, M. E. (2004). Acute stressors and cortisol responses: A theoretical integration and synthesis of laboratory research. *Psychological Bulletin, 130*, 355–391.

DiFranza, J. R. (2008, May). Hooked from the first cigarette. *Scientific American*, 82–87.

Digman, J. M., & Shmelyov, A. G. (1996). The structure of temperament and personality in Russian children. *Journal of Personality and Social Psychology, 71*, 341–351.

Dijk, C., de Jong, P. J., & Peters, M. L. (2009). The remedial value of blushing in the context of transgressions and mishaps. *Emotion, 9*, 287–291.

Dijksterhuis, A., Bos, M. W., Nordgren, L. F., & van Baaren, R. B. (2006). On making the right choice: The deliberation-without-attention effect. *Science, 311*, 1005–1007.

Dimberg, U., Thunberg, M., & Elmehed, K. (2000). Unconscious facial reactions to emotional facial expressions. *Psychological Science, 11*, 86–89.

Dinero, R. E., Conger, R. D., Shaver, P. R., et al. (2008). Influence of family of origin and adult romantic partners on romantic attachment security. *Journal of Family Psychology, 22*, 622–632.

Dinges, D. F., Whitehouse, W. G., Orne, E. C., et al. (1992). Evaluating hypnotic memory enhancement. (hypermnesia and reminiscence) using multitrial forced recall. *Journal of Experimental Psychology: Learning, Memory, and Cognition, 18*, 1139–1147.

Dinn, W. M., & Harris, C. L. (2000). Neurocognitive function in antisocial personality disorder. *Psychiatry Research, 97*, 173–190.

Dion, K. L., & Dion, K. K. (1993). Gender and ethnocultural comparisons in styles of love. *Psychology of Women Quarterly, 17*, 463–474.

Dixon, M. J., Smilek, D., Cudahy, C., & Merikle, P. M. (2000). Five plus two equals yellow: Mental arithmetic in people with synaesthesia is not coloured by visual experience. *Nature, 406*(6794), 365.

Doering, S., Katzlberger, F., Rumpold, G., et al. (2000). Videotape preparation of patients before hip replacement surgery reduces stress. *Psychosomatic Medicine, 62*, 365–373.

Dolnick, E. (1990, July). What dreams are (really) made of. *The Atlantic Monthly, 226*, 41–45, 48–53, 56–58, 60–61.

Domhoff, G. W. (1996). *Finding meaning in dreams: A quantitative approach.* New York, NY: Plenum.

Domhoff, G. W. (2003). *The scientific study of dreams: Neural networks, cognitive development, and content analysis.* Washington, DC: American Psychological Association.

Dominguez, M. de G., Viechtbauer, W., Simons, C. J. P., et al. (2009). Are psychotic psychopathology and neurocognition orthogonal? A systematic review of their associations. *Psychological Bulletin, 135*, 157–171.

Donlea, J. M., Ramanan, N., & Shaw, P. J. (2009). Use-dependent plasticity in clock neurons regulates sleep need in *Drosophila. Science, 324*, 105–108.

Dovidio, J. F. (2001). On the nature of contemporary prejudice: The third wave. *Journal of Social Issues, 57* (Winter), 829–849.

Dovidio, J. F., & Gaertner, S. L. (2008). New directions in aversive racism research: Persistence and pervasiveness. In C. Willis-Esqueda (Ed.), *Motivational aspects of prejudice and racism.* Nebraska Symposium on Motivation. New York, NY: Springer Science + Business Media.

Dovidio, J. F., Gaertner, S. L., & Validzic, A. (1998). Intergroup bias: Status, differentiation, and a common in-group identity. *Journal of Personality and Social Psychology, 75*, 109–120.

Drayna, D., Manichaikul, A., de Lange, M., et al. (2001). Genetic correlates of musical pitch recognition in humans. *Science, 291,* 1969–1972.

Drevets, W. C. (2000). Neuroimaging studies of mood disorders. *Biological Psychiatry, 48,* 813–829.

Druckman, D., & Swets, J. A. (Eds.). (1988). *Enhancing human performance: Issues, theories, and techniques.* Washington, DC: National Academy Press.

Duckworth, A. L., & Seligman, M. E. P. (2005). Self-discipline outdoes IQ in predicting academic performance of adolescents. *Psychological Science, 16*(12), 939–944.

Dumit, J. (2004). *Picturing personhood: Brain scans and biomedical identity.* Princeton, NJ: Princeton University Press.

Dunbar, R. I. M. (2004). Gossip in evolutionary perspective. *Review of General Psychology, 8,* 100–110.

Duncan, P. D., Ritter, P. L., Dornbusch, S. M., et al. (1985). The effects of pubertal timing on body image, school behavior, and deviance. *Journal of Youth and Adolescence, 14,* 227–235.

Dunkel, C. S., & Sefcek, J. A. (2009). Eriksonian lifespan theory and life history theory: An integration using the example of identity formation. *Review of General Psychology, 13,* 13–23.

Dunlosky, J., & Lipko, A. R. (2007). Metacomprehension: A brief history and how to improve its accuracy. *Current Directions in Psychological Science, 16,* 228–232.

Dunn, E. W., Wilson, T. D., & Gilbert, D. T. (2003). Location, location, location: The misprediction of satisfaction in housing lotteries. *Personality and Social Psychology Bulletin, 29,* 1421–1432.

Dunning, D. (2005). *Self-insight: Roadblocks and detours on the path to knowing thyself.* New York, NY: Psychology Press.

Dunning, D., Johnson, K., Ehrlinger, J., & Kruger, J. (2003). Why people fail to recognize their own incompetence. *Current Directions in Psychological Science, 12,* 83–87.

Duranceaux, N. C. E., Schuckit, M. A., Luczak, S. E., et al. (2008). Ethnic differences in level of response to alcohol between Chinese Americans and Korean Americans. *Journal of Studies on Alcohol and Drugs, 69,* 227–234.

Durex. (2002). *Global sex survey, 2002.* Retrieved May 3, 2005, from http://www.durex.com

Dutton, D. G., & Aron, A. P. (1974). Some evidence for heightened sexual attraction under conditions of high anxiety. *Journal of Personality and Social Psychology, 30*(4), 510–517.

Dweck, C. S. (2006). *Mindset: The new psychology of success.* New York, NY: Random House.

Dweck, C. S. (2008). Can personality be changed? *Current Directions in Psychological Science, 17,* 391–394.

Dweck, C. S., & Grant, H. (2008). Self-theories, goals, and meaning. In J. Y. Shah & W. L. Gardner (Eds.), *Handbook of motivation science.* New York, NY: Guilford.

Dweck, C. S., & Sorich, L. A. (1999). Mastery-oriented thinking. In C. R. Snyder (Ed.), *Coping: The psychology of what works.* New York, NY: Oxford University Press.

Eagly, A. H., & Wood, W. (1999). The origins of sex differences in human behavior: Evolved dispositions versus social roles. *American Psychologist, 54,* 408–423.

Ebbinghaus, H. M. (1885/1913). *Memory: A contribution to experimental psychology.* (H. A. Ruger & C. E. Bussenius, trans.). New York, NY: Teachers College Press, Columbia University.

Edwards, K., & Smith, E. E. (1996). A disconfirmation bias in the evaluation of arguments. *Journal of Personality and Social Psychology, 71,* 5–24.

Efran, J. S., Greene, M. A., & Gordon, D. E. (1998, March/April). Lessons of the new genetics: Finding the right fit for our clients. *Family Therapy Networker, 22,* 26–41.

Ehrenreich, B. (1978). *For her own good: 150 years of the experts' advice to women.* New York, NY: Doubleday.

Ehrenreich, B. (2001, June 4). What are they probing for? [essay.] *Time,* 86.

Ehrensaft, M. K., Moffitt, T. E., & Caspi, A. (2006). Is domestic violence followed by an increased risk of psychiatric disorders among women but not among men? A longitudinal cohort study. *American Journal of Psychiatry, 163,* 885–892.

Eich, E., & Hyman, R. (1992). Subliminal self-help. In D. Druckman & R. A. Bjork (Eds.), *In the mind's eye: Enhancing human performance.* Washington, DC: National Academy Press.

Eigsti, I.-M., Zayas, V., Mischel, W., et al. (2006). Predicting cognitive control from preschool to late adolescence and young adulthood. *Psychological Science, 17,* 478–484.

Ekman, P. (2003). *Emotions revealed.* New York, NY: Times Books.

Ekman, P., Friesen, W. V., & O'Sullivan, M. (1988). Smiles when lying. *Journal of Personality and Social Psychology, 54,* 414–420.

Ekman, P., Friesen, W. V., O'Sullivan, M., et al. (1987). Universals and cultural differences in the judgments of facial expression of emotion. *Journal of Personality and Social Psychology, 53,* 712–717.

Elfenbein, H. A., & Ambady, N. (2003). When familiarity breeds accuracy: Cultural exposure and facial emotion recognition. *Journal of Personality and Social Psychology, 85,* 276–290.

Elias, L. J., Saucier, D. M., Hardie, C., & Sarty, G. E. (2002). Dissociating semantic and perceptual components of synaesthesia: Behavioural and functional neuroanatomical investigations. *Cognitive Brain Research, 16*(2), 232–237.

Elliot, A. J., & McGregor, H. A. (2001). A 2x2 achievement goal framework. *Journal of Personality and Social Psychology, 80,* 501–519.

Elliot, A. J., & Sheldon, K. M. (1998). Avoidance personal goals and the personality-illness relationship. *Journal of Personality and Social Psychology, 75,* 1282–1299.

Ellis, A. (1993). Changing rational-emotive therapy (RET) to rational emotive behavior therapy (REBT). *Behavior Therapist, 16,* 257–258.

Ellis, A., & Blau, S. (1998). Rational emotive behavior therapy. *Directions in Clinical and Counseling Psychology, 8,* 41–56.

Ellison, C. R. (2000). *Women's sexualities.* Oakland, CA: New Harbinger.

Elmquist, J. K., & Flier, J. S. (2004, April 2). The fat–brain axis enters a new dimension. *Science, 304,* 63–64.

Else-Quest, N. M., Hyde, J. S., Goldsmith, H. H., & Can Hulle, C. A. (2006). Gender differences in temperament: A meta-analysis. *Psychological Bulletin, 132,* 33–72.

Emery, R. E., & Laumann-Billings, L. (1998). An overview of the nature, causes, and consequences of abusive family relationships. *American Psychologist, 53,* 121–135.

Emery, R. E., Otto, R. K., & O'Donohue, W. T. (2005). A critical assessment of child custody evaluations: Limited science and a flawed system. *Psychological Science in the Public Interest, 6,* 1–29.

Emmons, R. A., & King, L. A. (1988). Conflict among personal strivings: Immediate and long-term implications for psychological and physical well-being. *Journal of Personality and Social Psychology, 54,* 1040–1048.

Emmons, R. A., & McCullough, M. E. (2003). Counting blessings versus burdens: An experimental investigation of gratitude and subjective well-being in daily life. *Journal of Personality and Social Psychology, 84,* 377–389.

Engle, R. W. (2002). Working memory capacity as executive attention. *Current Directions in Psychological Science, 11,* 19–23.

Epel, E. S. (2009). Telomeres in a life-span perspective: A new "psychobiomarker"? *Current Directions in Psychological Science, 18,* 6–10.

Epel, E. S., Blackburn, E. H., Lin, J., et al. (2004, December 7). Accelerated telomere shortening in response to life stress. *Proceedings of the National Academy of Science, 101,* 17312–17315.

Epel, E. S., Daubenmier, J., Moskowitz, J. T., et al., 2009. Can meditation slow rate of cellular aging? Cognitive stress, mindfulness, and telomeres. *Annals of the New York Academy of Sciences, 1172,* 34–53.

Erceg-Hurn, D. M., & Mirosevich, V. M. (2008). Modern robust statistical methods. *American Psychologist, 63,* 591–601.

Erikson, E. H. (1950/1963). *Childhood and society* (2nd ed.). New York, NY: Norton.

Erikson, E. H. (1982). *The life cycle completed.* New York, NY: Norton.

Ervin-Tripp, S. (1964). Imitation and structural change in children's language. In E. H. Lenneberg (Ed.), *New directions in the study of language.* Cambridge, MA: MIT Press.

Escera, C., Cilveti, R., & Grau, C. (1992). Ultradian rhythms in cognitive operations: Evidence from the P300 component of the event-related potentials. *Medical Science Research, 20,* 137–138.

Esparza, J., Fox, C., Harper, I. T., et al. (2000, January 24). Daily energy expenditure in Mexican and USA Pima Indians: Low physical activity as a possible cause of obesity. *International Journal of Obesity and Related Metabolic Disorders, 1,* 55–59.

Euston, D. R., Tatsuno, M., & McNaughton, B. L. (2007). Fast-forward playback of recent memory sequences in prefrontal cortex during sleep. *Science, 318,* 1147–1150.

Evans, C. (1984). *Landscapes of the night* [edited and completed by P. Evans]. New York, NY: Viking.

Evans, G. W., & Kim, P. (2007). Childhood poverty and health. *Psychological Science, 18,* 953–957.

Evans, G. W., Lepore, S. J., & Allen, K. M. (2000). Cross-cultural differences in tolerance for crowding: Fact or fiction? *Journal of Personality and Social Psychology, 79,* 204–210.

Evans, G. W., & Schamberg, M. A. (2009, March 30). Childhood poverty, chronic stress, and adult working memory. *Proceedings of the National Academy of Sciences, 106.*

Ewart, C. K. (1995). Self-efficacy and recovery from heart attack. In J. E. Maddux (Ed.), *Self-efficacy, adaptation, and adjustment: Theory, research, and application.* New York, NY: Plenum.

Ewart, C. K., & Kolodner, K. B. (1994). Negative affect, gender, and expressive style predict elevated ambulatory blood pressure in adolescents. *Journal of Personality and Social Psychology, 66,* 596–605.

Exner, J. E. (1993). *The Rorschach: A comprehensive system: Vol. 1. Basic foundations* (3rd ed.). New York, NY: Wiley.

Eyferth, K. (1961). [The performance of different groups of the children of occupation forces on the Hamburg-Wechsler Intelligence Test for Children.] *Archiv für die Gesamte Psychologie, 113,* 222–241.

Fagan, J. F., III. (1992). Intelligence: A theoretical viewpoint. *Current Directions in Psychological Science, 1,* 82–86.

Fagot, B. I. (1993, June). *Gender role development in early childhood: Environmental input, internal construction.* Invited address presented at the annual meeting of the International Academy of Sex Research, Monterey, CA.

Fagot, B. I., & Leinbach, M. D. (1993). Gender-role development in young children: From discrimination to labeling. *Developmental Review, 13,* 205–224.

Fairbanks, L. A. (2001). Individual differences in response to a stranger: Social impulsivity as a dimension of temperament in vervet monkeys (*Cercopithecus aethiops sabaeus*). *Journal of Comparative Psychology, 115,* 22–28.

Fairholme, C. P., Boisseau, C. L., Ellard, K. K., et al. (2009). Emotions, emotion regulation, and psychological treatment: A unified perspective. In A. M. Kring & D. M. Sloan (Eds.), *Emotion regulation and psychopathology.* New York, NY: Guilford.

Fallon, J. H., Keator, D. B., Mbogori, J., et al. (2004). Hostility differentiates the brain metabolic effects of nicotine. *Cognitive Brain Research, 18,* 142–148.

Fallone, G., Acebo, C., Seifer, R., & Carskadon, M. A. (2005). Experimental restriction of sleep opportunity in children: Effects on teacher ratings. *Sleep, 28,* 1280–1286.

Farooqi, S., Bullmore, E., Keogh, J., et al. (2007, Sept. 7). Leptin regulates striatal regions and human eating behavior. *Science, 317,* 1355–1355.

Farooqi, I. S., Matarese, G., Lord, G. M., et al. (2002). Beneficial effects of leptin on obesity, T cell hyporesponsiveness, and neuroendocrine/metabolic dysfunction of human congenital leptin deficiency. *Journal of Clinical Investigation, 110,* 1093–1103.

Farooqi, I. S., & O'Rahilly, S. (2004). Monogenic human obesity syndromes. *Recent Progress in Hormone Research, 59,* 409–424.

Farrell, E. F. (2005, December 16). Need therapy? Check your in box. *Chronicle of Higher Education,* A35.

Fausto-Sterling, A. (1997). Beyond difference: A biologist's perspective. *Journal of Social Issues, 53,* 233–258.

Feather, N. T. (1966). Effects of prior success and failure on expectations of success and subsequent performance. *Journal of Personality and Social Psychology, 3,* 287–298.

Feeney, B. C., & Cassidy, J. (2003). Reconstructive memory related to adolescent–parent conflict interactions. *Journal of Personality and Social Psychology, 85,* 945–955.

Fehr, B. (1993). How do I love thee... Let me consult my prototype. In S. Duck (Ed.), *Individuals in relationships* (Vol. 1). Newbury Park, CA: Sage.

Fehr, B., Baldwin, M., Collins, L., et al. (1999). Anger in close relationships: An interpersonal script analysis. *Personality and Social Psychology Bulletin, 25,* 299–312.

Fehr, E., & Fischbacher, U. (2003). The nature of human altruism. *Nature, 425,* 785–791.

Fein, S., & Spencer, S. J. (1997). Prejudice as self-image maintenance: Affirming the self through derogating others. *Journal of Personality and Social Psychology, 73*, 31–44.

Feinberg, A. P. (2008). Epigenetics at the epicenter of modern medicine. *Journal of the American Medical Association, 299*, 1345–1350.

Ferguson, C. J. (2007). The good, the bad and the ugly: A meta-analytic review of positive and negative effects of violent video games. *Psychiatric Quarterly, 78*, 309–316.

Ferguson, C. (2009). Media violence effects: Confirmed truth or just another X-file? *Journal of Forensic Psychology Practice, 9*, 103–126.

Fernald, A., & Mazzie, C. (1991). Prosody and focus in speech to infants and adults. *Developmental Psychology, 27*, 209–221.

Fernandez, E., & Turk, D. C. (1992). Sensory and affective components of pain: Separation and synthesis. *Psychological Bulletin, 112*, 205–217.

Fernea, E., & Fernea, R. (1994). Cleanliness and culture. In W. J. Lonner & Malpass (Eds.), *Psychology and culture*. Boston, MA: Allyn & Bacon.

Ferrari, P. F., Rozzi, S., & Fogassi, L. (2005). Mirror neurons responding to observation of actions made with tools in monkey ventral premotor cortex. *Journal of Cognitive Neuroscience, 17*, 212–226.

Feshbach, S., & Tangney, J. (2008). Television viewing and aggression: Some alternative perspectives. *Perspectives on Psychological Science, 3*, 387–389.

Festinger, L. (1957). *A theory of cognitive dissonance*. Evanston, IL: Row, Peterson.

Festinger, L., & Carlsmith, J. M. (1959). Cognitive consequences of forced compliance. *Journal of Abnormal and Social Psychology, 58*, 203–210.

Festinger, L., Pepitone, A., & Newcomb, T. (1952). Some consequences of deindividuation in a group. *Journal of Abnormal and Social Psychology, 47*, 382–389.

Festinger, L., Riecken, H. W., & Schachter, S. (1956). *When prophecy fails*. Minneapolis: University of Minnesota Press.

Fiedler, K., Nickel, S., Muehlfriedel, T., & Unkelbach, C. (2001). Is mood congruency an effect of genuine memory or response bias? *Journal of Experimental Social Psychology, 37*, 201–214.

Field, T. (2009). The effects of newborn massage: United States. In T. Field et al. (Eds.), *The newborn as a person: Enabling healthy infant development worldwide*. Hoboken, NJ: John Wiley & Sons.

Fields, H. (1991). Depression and pain: A neurobiological model. *Neuropsychiatry, Neuropsychology, and Behavioral Neurology, 4*, 83–92.

Fields, R. D. (2004, April). The other half of the brain. *Scientific American*, 54–61.

Fiez, J. A. (1996). Cerebellar contributions to cognition. *Neuron, 16*, 13–15.

Fine, I., Wade, A. R., Brewer, A. A., et al. (2003). Long-term deprivation affects visual perception and cortex. *Nature Neuroscience, 6*, 915–916.

Fischer, P. C., Smith, R. J., Leonard, E., et al. (1993). Sex differences on affective dimensions: Continuing examination. *Journal of Counseling and Development, 71*, 440–443.

Fischhoff, B. (1975). Hindsight is not equal to foresight: The effect of outcome knowledge on judgment under uncertainty. *Journal of Experimental Psychology: Human Perception and Performance, 1*, 288–299.

Fitzgerald, P. B., Brown, T. L., Marston, N. A., et al. (2003). Transcranial magnetic stimulation in the treatment of depression: A double-blind, placebo-controlled trial. *Archives of General Psychiatry, 60*, 1002–1008.

Fivush, R., & Hamond, N. R. (1991). Autobiographical memory across the school years: Toward reconceptualizing childhood amnesia. In R. Fivush and J. A. Hudson (Eds.), *Knowing and remembering in young children*. New York, NY: Cambridge University Press.

Fivush, R., & Nelson, K. (2004). Culture and language in the emergence of autobiographical memory. *Psychological Science, 15*, 573–582.

Flacks, R., & Thomas, S. L. (1998, November 27). Among affluent students, a culture of disengagement. *Chronicle of Higher Education*, A48.

Flavell, J. H. (1999). Cognitive development: Children's knowledge about the mind. *Annual Review of Psychology, 50*, 21–45.

Flegal, K. M. (1999). The obesity epidemic in children and adults: Current evidence and research issues. *Medicine and Science in Sports and Exercise, 31*(Supplement 11), S509–S514.

Fleeson, W. (2004). Moving personality beyond the person-situation debate. *Current Directions in Psychological Science, 13*, 83–87.

Fletcher, A. M. (2001). *Sober for good*. New York, NY: Houghton-Mifflin.

Flint, A. J., & Gagnon, N. (2002). Effective use of electroconvulsive therapy in late-life depression. *Canadian Journal of Psychiatry, 47*, 734–741.

Flynn, J. R. (1987). Massive IQ gains in 14 nations: What IQ tests really measure. *Psychological Bulletin, 95*, 29–51.

Flynn, J. R. (1999). Searching for justice: the discovery of IQ gains over time. *American Psychologist, 54*, 5–20.

Fogassi, L., & Ferrari, P. F. (2007). Mirror neurons and the evolution of embodied language. *Current Directions in Psychological Science, 16*, 136–141.

Folkman, S., & Moskowitz, J. T. (2000). Positive affect and the other side of coping. *American Psychologist, 55*, 647–654.

Forbes, G., Zhang, X., Doroszewicz, K., & Haas, K. (2009). Relationships between individualism-collectivism, gender, and direct or indirect aggression: A study in China, Poland, and the US. *Aggressive Behavior, 35*, 24–30.

Forgas, J. P. (1998). On being happy and mistaken: Mood effects on the fundamental attribution error. *Journal of Personality and Social Psychology, 75*, 318–331.

Forgas, J. P., & Bond, M. H. (1985). Cultural influences on the perception of interaction episodes. *Personality and Social Psychology Bulletin, 11*, 75–88.

Foulkes, D. (1962). Dream reports from different states of sleep. *Journal of Abnormal and Social Psychology, 65*, 14–25.

Foulkes, D. (1999). *Children's dreaming and the development of consciousness*. Cambridge, MA: Harvard University Press.

Fouts, R. S. (with Stephen T. Mills). (1997). *Next of kin: What chimpanzees have taught me about who we are*. New York, NY: Morrow.

Fouts, R. S., & Rigby, R. L. (1977). Man–chimpanzee communication. In T. A. Seboek (Ed.), *How animals communicate*. Bloomington: University of Indiana Press.

Fowler, J. H., & Christakis, N. A. (2008, December 4). Dynamic spread of happiness in a large social network: Longitudinal analysis over 20 years in the Framingham Heart Study. *British Medical Journal, 337*, a2338.

Fowles, D. C., & Dindo, L. (2009). Temperament and psychopathy: A dual-pathway model. *Current Directions in Psychological Science, 18,* 179–183.

Fox, M. K., Pac, S., Devaney, B., & Jankowski, L. (2004). Feeding Infants and Toddlers Study: What foods are infants and toddlers eating? *Journal of the American Dietetic Association, 104,* 22–30.

Fox, N. A., Henderson, H. A., Marshall, P. J., et al. (2005). Behavioral inhibition: Linking biology and behavior within a developmental framework. *Annual Review of Psychology, 56,* 235–262.

Fox, N. A., Nichols, K. E., Henderson, H. A., et al. (2005). Evidence for a gene-environment interaction in predicting behavioral inhibition in middle childhood. *Psychological Science, 16,* 921–926.

Fraga, M. F., Ballestar, E., Paz, M. F., et al. (2005). Epigenetic differences arise during the lifetime of monozygotic twins. *Proceedings of the National Academy of Sciences, 102,* 10604–10609.

Fraley, R. C., & Shaver, P. R. (2000). Adult romantic attachment: Theoretical developments, emerging controversies, and unanswered questions. *Review of General Psychology, 4,* 132–154.

Frankl, V. E. (1955). *The doctor and the soul: An introduction to logotherapy.* New York, NY: Knopf.

Frans, E. M., Sandin, S., Reichenberg, A., et al. (2008). Advancing paternal age and bipolar disorder. *Archives of General Psychiatry, 65,* 1034–1040.

Frasure-Smith, N., & Lespérance, F. (2005). Depression and coronary heart disease: Complex synergism of mind, body, and environment. *Current Directions in Psychological Science, 14,* 39–43.

Frasure-Smith, N., Lespérance, F., Juneau, M., et al. (1999). Gender, depression, and one-year prognosis after myocardial infarction. *Psychosomatic Medicine, 61,* 26–37.

Frayling, T. M., Timpson, N. J., Weedon, M. N., et al. (2007, May 11). A common variant in the *FTO* gene is associated with body mass index and predisposes to childhood and adult obesity. *Science, 316,* 889–894.

Frazier, P. A. (2003). Perceived control and distress following sexual assault: A longitudinal test of a new model. *Journal of Personality and Social Psychology, 84,* 1257–1269.

Fredrickson, B. L., & Losada, M. F. (2005). Positive affect and the complex dynamics of human flourishing. *American Psychologist, 60,* 678–686.

Freedman, J. (2002). *Media violence and its effect on aggression.* Toronto, Canada: University of Toronto Press.

Frensch, P. A., & Rünger, D. (2003). Implicit learning. *Current Directions in Psychological Science, 12,* 13–18.

Freud, A. (1967). *Ego and the mechanisms of defense (The writings of Anna Freud, Vol. 2)* (Rev. ed.). New York, NY: International Universities Press.

Freud, S. (1900/1953). The interpretation of dreams. In J. Strachey (Ed.), *The standard edition of the complete psychological works of Sigmund Freud* (Vols. 4 and 5). London, England: Hogarth Press.

Freud, S. (1905a). Fragment of an analysis of a case of hysteria. In J. Strachey (Ed. and Trans.), *The standard edition of the complete psychological works of Sigmund Freud* (Vol. 7). London, England: Hogarth Press.

Freud, S. (1905b). Three essays on the theory of sexuality. In J. Strachey (Ed.), *Standard edition* (Vol. 7).

Freud, S. (1920/1960). *A general introduction to psychoanalysis* (J. Riviere, Trans.). New York, NY: Washington Square Press.

Freud, S. (1923/1962). *The ego and the id* (J. Riviere, Trans.). New York, NY: Norton.

Freud, S. (1961). *Letters of Sigmund Freud, 1873–1939.* (E. L. Freud, Ed.). London, England: Hogarth Press.

Fridlund, A. J. (1994). *Human facial expression: An evolutionary view.* San Diego, CA: Academic Press.

Friedman, J. M. (2003). A war on obesity, not the obese. *Science, 299,* 856–858.

Friedrich, W., Fisher, J., Broughton, D., et al. (1998). Normative sexual behavior in children: A contemporary sample. *Pediatrics, 101,* 1–8. Retrieved from http://www.pediatrics.org/cgi/content/full/101/4/e9

Frome, P. M., & Eccles, J. S. (1998). Parents' influence on children's achievement-related perceptions. *Journal of Personality and Social Psychology, 74,* 435–452.

Frye, R. E., Schwartz, B. S., & Doty, R. L. (1990). Dose-related effects of cigarette smoking on olfactory function. *Journal of the American Medical Association, 263,* 1233–1236.

Fuchs, C. S., Stampfer, M. J., Colditz, G. A., et al. (1995, May 11). Alcohol consumption and mortality among women. *New England Journal of Medicine, 332,* 1245–1250.

Gable, S. L., & Haidt, J. (2005). What (and why) is positive psychology? *Review of General Psychology, 9,* 103–110.

Gaertner, S. L., Mann, J. A., Dovidio, J. F., et al. (1990). How does cooperation reduce intergroup bias? *Journal of Personality and Social Psychology, 59,* 692–704.

Gagnon, J., & Simon, W. (1973). *Sexual conduct: The social sources of human sexuality.* Chicago, IL: Aldine.

Galanter, E. (1962). Contemporary psychophysics. In R. Brown, E. Galanter, H. Hess, & G. Mandler (Eds.), *New directions in psychology.* New York, NY: Holt, Rinehart and Winston.

Galea, L. A., Ormerod, B. K., Sampath, S., et al. (2000). Spatial working memory and hippocampal size across pregnancy in rats. *Hormones and Behavior, 37,* 86–95.

Galotti, K. (1989). Approaches to studying formal and everyday reasoning. *Psychological Bulletin, 105,* 331–351.

Gao, J.-H., Parsons, L. M., Bower, J. M., et al. (1996). Cerebellum implicated in sensory acquisition and discrimination rather than motor control. *Science, 272,* 545–547.

Garbarino, J., & Bedard, C. (2001). *Parents under siege.* New York, NY: The Free Press.

Garcia, J., & Gustavson, C. R. (1997, January). Carl R. Gustavson (1946–1996): Pioneering wildlife psychologist. *APS Observer,* 34–35.

Garcia, J., & Koelling, R. A. (1966). Relation of cue to consequence in avoidance learning. *Psychonomic Science, 4,* 23–124.

Gardner, H. (1983). *Frames of mind: The theory of multiple intelligences.* New York, NY: Basic Books.

Gardner, H. (1995). Perennial antinomies and perpetual redrawings: Is there progress in the study of mind? In R. L. Solso & D. W. Massar (Eds.), *The science of the mind: 2001 and beyond.* New York, NY: Oxford University Press.

Gardner, R. A., & Gardner, B. T. (1969). Teaching sign language to a chimpanzee. *Science, 165,* 664–672.

Garmezy, N. (1991). Resilience and vulnerability to adverse developmental outcomes associated with poverty. *American Behavioral Scientist, 34,* 416–430.

Garry, M., Manning, C. G., Loftus, E. F., & Sherman, S. J. (1996). Imagination inflation: Imagining a childhood event inflates confidence that it occurred. *Psychonomic Bulletin & Review, 3,* 208–214.

Garry, M., & Polaschek, D. L. L. (2000). Imagination and memory. *Current Directions in Psychological Science, 9,* 6–10.

Garven, S., Wood, J. M., Malpass, R. S., & Shaw, J. S., III. (1998). More than suggestion: The effect of interviewing techniques from the McMartin Preschool case. *Journal of Applied Psychology, 83,* 347–359.

Gatz, M. (2007). Genetics, dementia, and the elderly. *Current Directions in Psychological Science, 16,* 123–127.

Gauthier, I., Skudlarksi, P., Gore, J. C., & Anderson, A. W. (2000). Expertise for cars and birds recruits brain areas involved in face recognition. *Nature Neuroscience, 3,* 191–197.

Gauthier, I., Tarr, M. J., Anderson, A. W., et al. (1999). Activation of the middle fusiform "face area" increases with expertise in recognizing novel objects. *Nature Neuroscience, 2,* 568–573.

Gawande, A. (2009, March 30). Hellhole. *The New Yorker,* 36–45.

Gazzaniga, M. S. (1967). The split brain in man. *Scientific American, 217*(2), 24–29.

Gazzaniga, M. S. (1983). Right hemisphere language following brain bisection: A 20-year perspective. *American Psychologist, 38,* 525–537.

Gazzaniga, M. S. (1988). *Mind matters.* Boston, MA: Houghton-Mifflin.

Gazzaniga, M. S. (1998). *The mind's past.* Berkeley: University of California Press.

Gazzaniga, M. S. (2005). *The ethical brain.* Washington, DC: Dana Press.

Gazzaniga, M. S. (2008). *Human: The science behind what makes us unique.* New York, NY: Ecco/Harper Collins.

Geary, D. C., & Huffman, K. J. (2002). Brain and cognitive evolution: Forms of modularity and the functions of mind. *Psychological Bulletin, 128,* 667–698.

Geers, A. L., Wellman, J. A., & Lassiter, G. D. (2009). Dispositional optimism and engagement: The moderating influence of goal prioritization. *Journal of Personality and Social Psychology, 96,* 913–932.

Gelbard-Sagiv, H., Mukamel, R., Harel, M., et al. (2008, October 3). Internally generated reactivation of single neurons in human hippocampus during free recall. *Science, 322,* 96–101.

Gentile, B., Grabe, S., Dolan-Pascoe, B., et al. (2009). Gender differences in domain-specific self-esteem: A meta-analysis. *Review of General Psychology, 13,* 34–45.

Gentner, D., & Goldin-Meadow, S. (Eds.). (2003). *Language in mind: Advances in the study of language and thought.* Cambridge, MA: MIT Press.

Gerken, L. A., Wilson, R., & Lewis, W. (2005). Infants can use distributional cues to form syntactic categories. *Journal of Child Language, 32,* 249–268.

Gershoff, E. T. (2002). Parental corporal punishment and associated child behaviors and experiences: A meta-analytic and theoretical review. *Psychological Bulletin, 128,* 539–579.

Gibson, E., & Walk, R. (1960). The "visual cliff." *Scientific American, 202,* 80–92.

Giesbrecht, T., Lynn, S. J., Lilienfeld, S. O., & Merckelbach, H. (2008). Cognitive processes in dissociation: An analysis of core theoretical assumptions. *Psychological Bulletin, 134,* 617–647.

Gigerenzer, G., Gaissmaier, W., Kurz-Milcke, E., et al. (2008). Helping doctors and patients make sense of health statistics. *Psychological Science in the Public Interest, 8,* 53–96.

Gilbert, D. (2006a). *Stumbling on happiness.* New York, NY: Knopf.

Gilbert, D. (2006b, July 2). If only gay sex caused global warming. *Los Angeles Times,* Comment section, M1, M6.

Gilbertson, M. W., Shenton, M. E., Ciszewski, A., et al. (2002). Hippocampal volume predicts pathologic vulnerability to psychological trauma. *Nature Neuroscience, 5,* 1242–1247.

Gilestro, G. F., Tononi, G., & Cirelli, C. (2009). Widespread changes in synaptic markers as a function of sleep and wakefulness in *Drosophila. Science, 324,* 109–112.

Gillath, O., Shaver, P. R., Baek, J.-M., & Chun, D. S. (2008). Genetic correlates of adult attachment style. *Personality and Social Psychology Bulletin, 34,* 1396–1405.

Gilmore, D. D. (1990). *Manhood in the making: Cultural concepts of masculinity.* New Haven, CT: Yale University Press.

Gist, R., Lubin, B., & Redburn, B. G. (1998). Psychosocial, ecological, and community perspectives on disaster response. *Journal of Personal and Interpersonal Loss, 3,* 25–51.

Gittelsohn, J., Harris, S. B., Thorne-Lyman, A. L., et al. (1996). Body image concepts differ by age and sex in an Ojibway–Cree community in Canada. *Journal of Nutrition, 126,* 2990–3000.

Gladwell, M. (2004, September 20). Personality plus. *The New Yorker,* 42–48.

Gleaves, D. H. (1996). The sociocognitive model of dissociative identity disorder: A reexamination of the evidence. *Psychological Bulletin, 120,* 42–59.

Glick, P. (2006). Ambivalent sexism, power distance, and gender inequality across cultures. In S. Guimond (Ed.), *Social comparison and social psychology: Understanding cognition, intergroup relations, and culture.* New York, NY: Cambridge University Press.

Glick, P., Fiske, S. T., Mladinic, A., et al. (2000). Beyond prejudice as simple antipathy: Hostile and benevolent sexism across cultures. *Journal of Personality and Social Psychology, 79,* 763–775.

Glick, P., Lameiras, M., Fiske, S. T., et al. (2004). Bad but bold: Ambivalent attitudes toward men predict gender inequality in 16 nations. *Journal of Personality and Social Psychology, 86,* 713–728.

Glynn, L. M. (2010). Giving birth to a new brain: Hormone exposures of pregnancy influence human memory. *Psychoneuroendocrinology, 35,* 1148–1155.

Gobodo-Madikizela, P. (1994). *The notion of the "collective" in South African "political" murder cases: The "deindividuation" argument revisited.* Paper presented to the biennial conference of the American Psychology and Law Society, Santa Fe, NM.

Golden, R. M., Gaynes, B. N., Ekstrom, R. D., et al. (2005). The efficacy of light therapy in the treatment of mood disorders: A review and meta-analysis of the evidence. *American Journal of Psychiatry, 162,* 656–662.

Goldin-Meadow, S. (2003). *The resilience of language.* New York, NY: Psychology Press.

Goldin-Meadow, S., Cook, S. W., & Mitchell, Z. A. (2009). Gesturing gives children new ideas about math. *Psychological Science, 20*, 267–272.

Goldman-Rakic, P. S. (1996). *Opening the mind through neurobiology.* Invited address at the annual meeting of the American Psychological Association, Toronto, Canada.

Goldstein, A. J., de Beurs, E., Chambless, D. L., & Wilson, K. A. (2000). EMDR for panic disorder with agoraphobia: Comparison with waiting list and credible attention-placebo control conditions. *Journal of Consulting and Clinical Psychology, 68*, 947–956.

Goldstein, E. G. (2002). *Object relations theory and self psychology in social work practice.* New York, NY: Free Press.

Goldstein, J. M., Seidman, L. J., Horton, N. J., et al. (2001). Normal sexual dimorphism of the adult human brain assessed by in vivo magnetic resonance imaging. *Cerebral Cortex, 11*, 490–497.

Goldstein, M., & Miklowitz, D. (1995). The effectiveness of psycho-educational family therapy in the treatment of schizophrenic disorders. *Journal of Marital and Family Therapy, 21*, 361–376.

Goldstein, N. J., Cialdini, R. B., & Griskevicius, V. (2008). A room with a viewpoint: Using social norms to motivate environmental conservation in hotels. *Journal of Consumer Research, 35*, 472–482.

Goldston, D. B., Molock, S. D., Whitbeck, L. B., et al. (2008). Cultural considerations in adolescent suicide prevention and psychosocial treatment. *American Psychologist, 63*, 14–31.

Goldstone, R. L., Roberts, M. E., & Gureckis, T. M. (2008). Emergent processes in group behavior. *Current Directions in Psychological Science, 17*, 10–15.

Golinkoff, R. M., & Hirsh-Pasek, K. (2006). Baby wordsmith: From associationist to social sophisticate. *Current Directions in Psychological Science, 15*, 30–33.

Gonzaga, G. C., Turner, R. A., Keltner, D., et al. (2006). Romantic love and sexual desire in close relationships. *Emotion, 6*, 163–179.

Goode, E. (2003, May 6). Experts see mind's voices in new light. *The New York Times*, Science Times, D1, D4.

Goodwin, D. W., Knop, J., Jensen, P., et al. (1994). Thirty-year follow-up of men at high risk for alcoholism. In T. F. Babor & V. M. Hesselbrock (Eds.), *Types of alcoholics: Evidence from clinical, experimental, and genetic research.* New York, NY: New York Academy of Sciences.

Goodwyn, S., & Acredolo, L. (1998). Encouraging symbolic gestures: A new perspective on the relationship between gesture and speech. In J. Iverson & S. Goldin-Meadow (Eds.), *The nature and functions of gesture in children's communication.* San Francisco, CA: Jossey-Bass.

Gopnik, A. (2009). *The philosophical baby.* New York, NY: Farrar, Straus and Giroux.

Gopnik, A., Meltzoff, A. N., & Kuhl, P. K. (1999). *The scientist in the crib.* New York, NY: Morrow.

Gopnik, M., Choi, S., & Baumberger, T. (1996). Cross-linguistic differences in early semantic and cognitive development. *Cognitive Development, 11*, 197–227.

Gorn, G. J. (1982). The effects of music in advertising on choice behavior: A classical conditioning approach. *Journal of Marketing, 46*, 94–101.

Gosling, S. D., & John, O. P. (1999). Personality dimensions in nonhuman animals: A cross-species review. *Current Directions in Psychological Science, 8*, 69–75.

Gosling, S. D., Kwan, V. S. Y., & John, O. P. (2003). A dog's got personality: A cross-species comparative approach to personality judgments in dogs and humans. *Journal of Personality and Social Psychology, 85*, 1161–1169.

Gosling, S. D., Vazire, S., Srivatava, S., & John, O. P. (2004). Should we trust web-based studies? A comparative analysis of six preconceptions about Internet questionnaires. *American Psychologist, 59*, 93–104.

Gotlib, I. H., Joormann, J., Minor, K. L., & Hallmayer, J. (2008). HPA axis reactivity: A mechanism underlying the associations among 5-HTTLPR, stress, and depression. *Biological Psychiatry, 63*, 847–851.

Gottesman, I. I. (1991). *Schizophrenia genesis: The origins of madness.* New York, NY: Freeman.

Gottfredson, L. S. (2002). g: Highly general and highly practical. In R. J. Sternberg & E. L. Grigorenko (Eds.), *The general intelligence factor: How general is it?* Mahwah, NJ: Erlbaum.

Gottfried, J. A., O'Doherty, J., & Dolan, R. J. (2003). Encoding predictive reward value in human amygdala and orbitofrontal cortex. *Science, 301*, 1104–1107.

Gougoux, F., Zatorre, R. J., Lassonde, M., et al. (2005). A functional neuroimaging study of sound localization: Visual cortex activity predicts performance in early-blind individuals. *PloS Biology, 3*, 324–333.

Gouin, J.-P., Kiecolt-Glaser, J. K., Malarkey, W. B., & Glaser, R. (2008). The influence of anger expression on wound healing. *Brain, Behavior, and Immunity, 22*, 699–708.

Gould, S. J. (1994, November 28). Curveball. [Review of *The Bell Curve*, by Richard J. Herrnstein and Charles Murray.] *The New Yorker*, 139–149.

Gould, S. J. (1996). *The mismeasure of man* (Rev. ed.). New York, NY: Norton.

Gourevitch, P. (2009, May 4). The life after. *The New Yorker*, 36–49.

Grabe, S., & Hyde, J. S. (2006). Ethnicity and body dissatisfaction among women in the United States: A meta-analysis. *Psychological Bulletin, 132*, 622–640.

Grabe, S., Ward, L. M., & Hyde, J. S. (2008). The role of the media in body image concerns among women: A meta-analysis of experimental and correlational studies. *Psychological Bulletin, 134*, 460–476.

Graham, J., Haidt, J., & Nosek, B. A. (2009). Liberals and conservatives rely on different sets of moral foundations. *Journal of Personality and Social Psychology, 96*, 1029–1046.

Graham, J. W. (1986). Principled organizational dissent: A theoretical essay. *Research in Organizational Behavior, 8*, 1–52.

Grahe, J. E., & Bernieri, F. J. (1999). The importance of nonverbal cues in judging rapport. *Journal of Nonverbal Behavior, 23*, 253–269.

Grant, H., & Dweck, C. S. (2003). Clarifying achievement goals and their impact. *Journal of Personality and Social Psychology, 85*, 541–553.

Gray, K., & Wegner, D. M. (2008). The sting of intentional pain. *Psychological Science, 19*, 1260–1261.

Greely, H. T., & Illes, J. (2007). Neuroscience-based lie detection: The urgent need for regulation. *American Journal of Law & Medicine, 35*.

Greely, H., Sahakian, B., Harris, J., et al. (2008). Towards responsible use of cognitive-enhancing drugs by the healthy. *Nature, 455*, 702–705. doi:10.1038/456702a

Green, G. (1996a). Behavioral treatment of autistic persons: A review of research from 1980 to the present. *Research in Developmental Disabilities, 17*, 433–465.

Green, G. (1996b). Early behavioral intervention for autism: What does research tell us? In C. Maurice, G. Green, & S. C. Luce (Eds.), *Behavioral intervention for young children with autism.*Austin, TX: PRO-ED.

Green, K. L., Cameron, R., Polivy, J., et al. (1997). Weight dissatisfaction and weight loss attempts among Canadian adults. Canadian Heart Health Survey Research Group. *Canadian Medical Association Journal, 157*(Suppl. 1), S17–S25.

Greenberg, J., Solomon, S., & Arndt, J. (2008). A basic but uniquely human motivation: Terror management. In J. Shah & W. Gardner (Eds.), *Handbook of motivation science*. New York, NY: Guilford Press.

Greenberger, E., Lessard, J., Chen, C., & Farruggia, S. P. (2008). Self-entitled college students: Contributions of personality, parenting, and motivational factors. *Journal of Youth & Adolescence, 37*, 1193–1204.

Greenberger, D., & Padesky, C. A. (1995). *Mind over mood: A cognitive therapy treatment manual for clients*. New York, NY: Guilford.

Greenfield, S. A., & Collins, T. F. T. (2005). A neuroscientfic approach to consciousness. *Progress in Brain Research, 150*, 11–23.

Greenglass, E. R. (2002). Proactive coping and quality of life management. In E. Frydenberg (Ed.), *Beyond coping: Meeting goals, visions, and challenges*. London: Oxford University Press.

Greenglass, E. R., & Fiksenbaum, L. (2009). Proactive coping, positive affect, and well-being: Testing for mediation using path analysis. *European Psychologist, 14*, 29–39.

Greenough, W. T. (1984). Structural correlates of information storage in the mammalian brain: A review and hypothesis. *Trends in Neurosciences, 7*, 229–233.

Greenough, W. T., & Anderson, B. J. (1991). Cerebellar synaptic plasticity: Relation to learning vs. neural activity. *Annals of the New York Academy of Sciences, 627*, 231–247.

Greenough, W. T., & Black, J. E. (1992). Induction of brain structure by experience: Substrates for cognitive development. In M. Gunnar & C. A. Nelson (Eds.), *Behavioral developmental neuroscience: Vol. 24. Minnesota Symposia on Child Psychology*. Hillsdale, NJ: Erlbaum.

Greenwald, A. G., McGhee, D. E., & Schwartz, J. L. K. (1998). Measuring individual differences in implicit cognition: The Implicit Association Test. *Journal of Personality and Social Psychology, 74*, 1464–1480.

Greenwald, A. G., Poehlman, T. A., Uhlmann, E. L., & Banaji, M. R. (2009). Understanding and using the Implicit Association Test: III. Meta-analysis of predictive validity. *Journal of Personality and Social Psychology, 97*, 17–41.

Greenwald, A. G., Spangenberg, E. R., Pratkanis, A. R., & Eskenazi, J. (1991). Double-blind tests of subliminal self-help audiotapes. *Psychological Science, 2*, 119–122.

Gregg, L., & Tarrier, N. (2007). Virtual reality in mental health: A review of the literature. *Social Psychiatry and Psychiatric Epidemiology, 42*, 343–54.

Gregory, R. L. (1963). Distortion of visual space as inappropriate constancy scaling. *Nature, 199*, 678–679.

Grewen, K. M., Girdler, S. S., Amico, J., & Light, K. C. (2005). Effects of partner support on resting oxytocin, cortisol, norepinephrine, and blood pressure before and after warm partner contact. *Psychosomatic Medicine, 67*, 531–538.

Griffin, D. R. (2001). *Animal minds: Beyond cognition to consciousness*. Chicago, IL: University of Chicago Press.

Grinspoon, L., & Bakalar, J. B. (1993). *Marihuana, the forbidden medicine*. New Haven, CT: Yale University Press.

Groneman, C. (2000). *Nymphomania: A history*. New York, NY: Norton.

Gross, J. J. (1998). The emerging field of emotion regulation: An integrative review. *Review of General Psychology, 2*, 271–299.

Gross, J. J., & John, O. P. (2003). Individual differences in two emotion regulation processes: Implications for affect, relationships, and well-being. *Journal of Personality and Social Psychology, 85*, 348–362.

Grossman, M., & Wood, W. (1993). Sex differences in intensity of emotional experience: A social role interpretation. *Journal of Personality and Social Psychology, 65*, 1010–1022.

Guilford, J. P. (1988). Some changes in the structure-of-intellect model. *Educational and Psychological Measurement, 48*, 1–4.

Gunnar, M. R., van Dulmen, M. H., & International Adoption Project Team. (2007). Behaviour problems in postinstitutionalized internationally adopted children. *Developmental Psychopathology, 19*, 129–148.

Gur, R. E., Maany, V., Mozley, P. D., et al. (1998). Subcortical MRI volumes in neuroleptic-naive and treated patients with schizophrenia. *American Journal of Psychiatry, 155*, 1711–1717.

Gur, R. C., Gunning-Dixon, F., Bilker, W. B., & Gur, R. E. (2002). Sex differences in temporo-limbic and frontal brain volumes of healthy adults. *Cerebral Cortex, 12*, 998–1003.

Guralnick, M. J (Ed.). (1997). *The effectiveness of early intervention*. Baltimore, MD: Brookes.

Guse, B., Falkai, P., & Wobrock, T. (2010). Cognitive effects of high-frequency repetitive transcranial magnetic stimulation: A systematic review. *Journal of Neural Transmission, 117*(1), 105–122. doi:10.1007/s00702-009-0333-7

Gustavson, C. R., Garcia, J., Hankins, W. G., & Rusiniak, K. W. (1974). Coyote predation control by aversive conditioning. *Science, 184*, 581–583.

Guthrie, P. C., & Mobley, B. D. (1994). A comparison of the differential diagnostic efficiency of three personality disorder inventories. *Journal of Clinical Psychology, 50*, 656–665.

Guthrie, R. (1976). *Even the rat was white: A historical view of psychology*. New York, NY: Harper & Row.

Guttentag, M., & Secord, P. (1983). *Too many women?* Beverly Hills, CA: Sage.

Guzman-Marin, R., Suntsova, N., Methippara, M., et al. (2005). Sleep deprivation suppresses neurogenesis in the adult hippocampus of rats. *European Journal of Neuroscience, 22*, 2111–2116.

Habbick, B. F., Nanson, J. L., Snyder, R. E., et al. (1996). Foetal alcohol syndrome in Saskatchewan: Unchanged incidence in a 20-year period. *Canadian Journal of Public Health, 87*(3), 204–207.

Haber, R. N. (1970, May). How we remember what we see. *Scientific American, 222*, 104–112.

Hacking, I. (1995). *Rewriting the soul: Multiple personality and the sciences of memory*. Princeton, NJ: Princeton University Press.

Hafer, C. L. (2000a). Do innocent victims threaten the belief in a just world? Evidence from a modified Stroop task. *Journal of Personality and Social Psychology, 79*(2), 165–173.

Hafer, C. L. (2000b). Investment in long-term goals and commitment to just means drive the need to believe in a just world. *Personality and Social Psychology Bulletin, 26*, 1059–1073.

Hafer, C. L., & Begue, L. (2005). Experimental research on just-world theory: Problems, developments and future challenges. *Psychological Bulletin, 131*(1), 128–167.

Haga, S. M., Kraft, P., & Corby, E. K. (2009). Emotion regulation: Antecedents and well-being outcomes of cognitive reappraisal and expressive suppression in cross-cultural samples. *Journal of Happiness Studies, 10*, 271–291.

Hahn, R., Fuqua-Whitley, D., Wethington, H., et al. (2008). Effectiveness of universal school-based programs to prevent violent and aggressive behaviour: A systematic review. *Child: Care, Health, & Development, 34*, 139.

Haier, R. J., Jung, R. E., Yeo, R. A., et al. (2005). The neuroanatomy of general intelligence: Sex matters. *NeuroImage, 25*, 320–327.

Haimov, I., & Lavie, P. (1996). Melatonin—A soporific hormone. *Current Directions in Psychological Science, 5*, 106–111.

Hall, C. (1953a). A cognitive theory of dreams. *Journal of General Psychology, 49*, 273–282.

Hall, C. (1953b). *The meaning of dreams.* New York, NY: McGraw-Hill.

Hall, E. T. (1959). *The silent language.* Garden City, NY: Doubleday.

Hall, E. T. (1976). *Beyond culture.* New York, NY: Anchor.

Hall, E. T. (1983). *The dance of life: The other dimension of time.* Garden City, NY: Anchor Press/Doubleday.

Hall, E. T., & Hall, M. R. (1987). *Hidden differences: Doing business with the Japanese.* Garden City, NY: Anchor Press/Doubleday.

Hall, E. T., & Hall, M. R. (1990). *Understanding cultural differences.* Yarmouth, ME: Intercultural Press.

Hall, G. S. (1899). A study of anger. *American Journal of Psychology, 10*, 516–591.

Hall, N. C., Perry, R. P., Ruthig, J. C., et al. (2006). Primary and secondary control in achievement settings: A longitudinal field study of academic motivation, emotions, and performance. *Journal of Applied Social Psychology, 36*, 1430–1470.

Halliday, G. (1993). Examination dreams. *Perceptual and Motor Skills, 77*, 489–490.

Halpern, D. (2002). *Thought and knowledge: An introduction to critical thinking* (4th ed.). Hillsdale, NJ: Erlbaum.

Halpern, D. F. (2008). Psychologists are redefining retirement as a new phase of life. *The General Psychologist, 43*, 22–29.

Hamby, S. L., & Koss, M. P. (2003). Shades of gray: A qualitative study of terms used in the measurement of sexual victimization. *Psychology of Women Quarterly, 27*, 243–255.

Han, J.-H., Kushner, S. A., Yiu, A. P., et al. (2009). Selective erasure of a fear memory. *Science, 323*, 1492–1496.

Haney, C., Banks, C., & Zimbardo, P. (1973). Interpersonal dynamics in a simulated prison. *International Journal of Criminology and Penology, 1*, 69–97.

Haney, C., & Zimbardo, P. (1998). The past and future of U.S. prison policy: Twenty-five years after the Stanford Prison Experiment. *American Psychologist, 53*, 709–727.

Hankin, B. L., & Abramson, L. Y. (2001). Development of gender differences in depression: An elaborated cognitive vulnerability-transactional stress theory. *Psychological Bulletin, 127*, 773–796.

Harding, C. M. (2005). Changes in schizophrenia across time: Paradoxes, patterns, and predictors. In L. Davidson, C. Harding, & L. Spaniol (Eds.), *Recovery from severe mental illnesses: Research evidence and implications for practice* (Vol. 1). Boston, MA: Center for Psychiatric Rehabilitation/ Boston U.

Harding, C. M., Zubin, J., & Strauss, J. S. (1992). Chronicity in schizophrenia: Revisited. *British Journal of Psychiatry, 161*(Suppl. 18), 27–37.

Hare, R. D., & Neumann, C. S. (2008). Psychopathy as a clinical and empirical construct. *Annual Review of Clinical Psychology, 4*, 217–246.

Hare, R. D. (1965). Temporal gradient of fear arousal in psychopaths. *Journal of Abnormal Psychology, 70*, 442–445.

Hare, R. D. (1990). *The Hare psychopathy checklist revised manual.* Toronto, Canada: Multi-Health Systems.

Hare, R. D. (1996). Psychopathy: A clinical construct whose time has come. *Criminal Justice and Behavior, 23*, 24–54.

Hare, R. D., Hart, S. D., & Harpur, T. J. (1991). Psychopathy and the DSM-IV criteria for antisocial personality disorder. *Journal of Abnormal Psychology, 100*, 391–398.

Hare, W. (2009, March/April). What open-mindeness requires. *Skeptical Inquirer, 33*, 36–39.

Hare-Mustin, R. T. (1991). Sex, lies, and headaches: The problem is power. In T. J. Goodrich (Ed.), *Women and power: Perspectives for therapy.* New York, NY: Norton.

Hare-Mustin, R. T., & Marecek, J. (1990). Gender and the meaning of difference: Postmodernism and psychology. In R. Hare-Mustin & J. Maracek (Eds.), *Psychology and the construction of gender.* New Haven, CT: Yale University Press.

Haritos-Fatouros, M. (1988). The official torturer: A learning model for obedience to the authority of violence. *Journal of Applied Social Psychology, 18*, 1107–1120.

Harlow, H. F. (1958). The nature of love. *American Psychologist, 13*, 673–685.

Harlow, H. F., & Harlow, M. K. (1966). Learning to love. *American Scientist, 54*, 244–272.

Harlow, H. F., Harlow, M. K., & Meyer, D. R. (1950). Learning motivated by a manipulation drive. *Journal of Experimental Psychology, 40*, 228–234.

Harmon-Jones, E., Peterson, C. K., & Harris, C. R. (2009). Jealousy: Novel methods and neural correlates. *Emotion, 9*, 113–117.

Harris, C. (2003). Factors associated with jealousy over real and imagined infidelity: An examination of the social-cognitive and evolutionary psychology perspectives. *Psychology of Women Quarterly, 27*, 319–329.

Harris, G. (2003, August 7). Debate resumes on the safety of depression's wonder drugs. *The New York Times*, A1, C4.

Harris, J. R. (1998). *The nurture assumption.* New York, NY: The Free Press.

Harris, J. R. (2006). *No two alike: Human nature and human individuality.* New York, NY: Norton.

Harris, J. R. (2009). *The nurture assumption* (2nd ed.). New York, NY: Free Press.

Harris, L. T., & Fiske, S. T. (2006). Dehumanizing the lowest of the low: Neuro-imaging responses to extreme outgroups. *Psychological Science, 17*(10), 847–853.

Harris, S. B., Gittelson, J., Hanley, A., et al. (1997). The prevalence of NDDM and associated risk factors in native Canadians. *Diabetes Care, 20*, 185–187.

Hart, A. J., Whalen, P. J., Shin, L. M., et al. (2000). Differential response in the human amygdala to racial outgroup vs. ingroup face stimuli. *NeuroReport, 11*, 2351–2355.

Hart, J., Jr., Berndt, R. S., & Caramazza, A. (1985, August 1). Category-specific naming deficit following cerebral infarction. *Nature, 316*, 339–340.

Hart, K. E., & Sasso, T. (2011). Mapping the contours of contemporary positive psychology. *Canadian Psychology, 52*, 82–92.

Haslam, S. A., Jetten, J., Postmes, T., & Haslam, C. (2009). Social identity, health and well-being: An emerging agenda for applied psychology. *Applied Psychology: An International Review, 58*, 1–23.

Haslam, S. A., & Reicher, S. (2003, Spring). Beyond Stanford: Questioning a role-based explanation of tyranny. *Society for Experimental Social Psychology Dialogue, 18*, 22–25.

Hassett, J. M., Siebert, E. R., Wallen, K. (2008). Sex differences in rhesus monkey toy preferences parallel those of children. *Hormones and Behavior, 54*, 359–364.

Hatfield, E., & Rapson, R. L. (1996/2005). *Love and sex: Cross-cultural perspectives.* Boston, MA: University Press of America.

Hatfield, E., & Rapson, R. L. (2008). Passionate love and sexual desire: Multidisciplinary perspectives. In J. P. Forgas & J. Fitness (Eds.), *Social relationships: Cognitive, affective, and motivational processes.* New York, NY: Psychology Press.

Haut, J. S., Beckwith, B. E., Petros, T. V., & Russell, S. (1989). Gender differences in retrieval from long-term memory following acute intoxication with ethanol. *Physiology and Behavior, 45*, 1161–1165.

Hawkins, E. H., Cummins, L. H., & Marlatt, G. A. (2004). Preventing substance abuse in American Indian and Alaska Native Youth: Promising strategies for healthier communities. *Psychological Bulletin, 130*, 304–323.

Hawkins, S. A., & Hastie, R. (1990). Hindsight: Biased judgments of past events after the outcomes are known. *Psychological Bulletin, 107*, 311–327.

Hayes, S. C. (2004). Acceptance and commitment therapy and the new behavior therapies: Mindfulness, acceptance, and relationship. In S. C. Hayes, V. M. Follette, & M. M. Linehan (Eds.), *Mindfulness and acceptance: Expanding the cognitive-behavioral tradition.* New York, NY: Guilford.

Hayes, S. C., Follette, V. M., & Linehan, M. M. (Eds.). (2004). *Mindfulness and acceptance: Expanding the cognitive-behavioral tradition.* New York, NY: The Guilford Press.

Hayman, R. (2001). *A life of Jung.* New York, NY: W. W. Norton.

Hazan, C., & Diamond, L. M. (2000). The place of attachment in human mating. *Review of General Psychology, 4*, 186–204.

Hazan, C., & Shaver, P. R. (1994). Attachment as an organizational framework for research on close relationships. *Psychological Inquiry, 5*, 1–22.

Health Canada. (1998, November). *Canadian perinatal surveillance system: Alcohol and pregnancy.* Retrieved June 4, 2003, from http://www.hc-sc.gc.ca/pphb-dgspsp/rhs-ssg/factshts/alcprg_e.html

Health Canada. (1999). *Canadian injury data. Mortality 1997 and hospitalizations 1996–97.* Ottawa: Bureau of Reproductive and Child Health, Laboratory for Disease Control, Health Protection Branch, Department of National Health and Welfare.

Health Canada. (2000). *How much is too much when you're pregnant?* Retrieved June 4, 2003, from http://www.hc-sc.gc.ca/english/feature/magazine/2000_08/fas.htm

Health Canada. (2001). *No. 2—Canada's oldest seniors.* Ottawa: Author.

Health Canada. (2008). *Reach for the top: A report by the advisor on healthy children & youth.* Retrieved April 1, 2008, from http://www.hc-sc.gc.ca/hl-vs/pubs/child-enfant/advisor-conseillere/appendices_e.html

Healy, D. (2002). *The creation of psychopharmacology.* Cambridge, MA: Harvard University Press.

Healy, D. (2004). *Let them eat Prozac.* New York, NY: New York University Press.

Heath, A. C., Madden, P. A. F., Bucholz, K. K., et al. (2003). Genetic and genotype x environment interaction effects on risk of dependence on alcohol, tobacco, and other drugs: New research. In R. Plomin et al. (Eds.), *Behavioral genetics in the postgenomic era.* Washington, DC: APA Books.

Hebb, D. O. (1949). *The organization of behavior.* New York, NY: Wiley-Interscience.

Hedden, T., Ketay, S., Aron, A., et al. (2008). Cultural influences on neural substrates of attentional control. *Psychological Science, 19*, 12–17.

Hein, G., Silani, G., Preuschoff, K., et al. (2010). Neural responses to ingroup and outgroup members' suffering predict individual differences in costly helping. *Neuron, 68*, 149–160.

Heine, S. J., & Lehman, D. R. (1997). The cultural construction of self-enhancement: An examination of group-serving biases. *Journal of Personality and Social Psychology, 72*(6), 1268–1283.

Heine, S. J., & Norenzayan, A. (2006). Toward a psychological science for a cultural species. *Perspectives on Psychological Science, 1*, 251–269.

Heinrichs, R. W. (2005). The primacy of cognition in schizophrenia. *American Psychologist, 60*, 229–242.

Helmreich, W. (1992). *Against all odds: Holocaust survivors and the successful lives they led.* New York, NY: Simon & Schuster.

Helson, R., Roberts, B., & Agronick, G. (1995). Enduringness and change in creative personality and the prediction of occupational creativity. *Journal of Personality and Social Psychology, 6*, 1173–1183.

Helzer, J. E., Wittchen, H.-U., Krueger, R. F., & Kraemer, H. C. (2008). Dimensional options for DSM-V: The way forward. In J. E. Helzer, H. C. Kramer, & R. F. Krueger (Eds.), *Dimensional approaches in diagnostic classification: Refining the research agenda for DSM-V.* Washington, DC: American Psychiatric Association.

Henderlong, J., & Lepper, M. (2002). The effects of praise on children's intrinsic motivation: A review and synthesis. *Psychological Bulletin, 128*, 774–795.

Henggeler, S. W., Schoenwald, S. K., Borduin, C. M., et al. (1998). *Multisystemic treatment of antisocial behavior in children and adolescents*. New York, NY: Guilford Press.

Henrich, J., Boyd, R., Bowles, S., et al. (2001). In search of *Homo economicus*: Behavioral experiments in 15 small scale societies. *American Economics Review, 91*, 73–78.

Henry, J. D., & Rendell, P. G. (2007). A review of the impact of pregnancy on memory function. *Journal of Clinical and Experimental Neuropsychology, 29*, 793–803.

Herbert, A., Gerry, N. P., McQueen, M. B., et al. (2006, April 14). A common genetic variant is associated with adult and childhood obesity. *Science, 312*, 279–283.

Herdt, G. (1984). *Ritualized homosexuality in Melanesia*. Berkeley: University of California Press.

Herek, G. M., & Capitanio, J. P. (1996). "Some of my best friends": Intergroup contact, concealable stigma, and heterosexuals' attitudes toward gay men and lesbians. *Personality and Social Psychology Bulletin, 22*, 412–424.

Herman, J. H. (1992). Transmutative and reproductive properties of dreams: Evidence for cortical modulation of brainstem generators. In J. Antrobus & M. Bertini (Eds.), *The neuropsychology of dreaming*. Hillsdale, NJ: Erlbaum.

Herman, J. (1992). *Trauma and recovery*. New York, NY: Basic Books.

Herman, L. M., Kuczaj, S. A., & Holder, M. D. (1993). Responses to anomalous gestural sequences by a language-trained dolphin: Evidence for processing of semantic relations and syntactic information. *Journal of Experimental Psychology: General, 122*, 184–194.

Herman, L. M., & Morrel-Samuels, P. (1996). Knowledge acquisition and asymmetry between language comprehension and production: Dolphins and apes as general models for animals. In M. Bekoff & D. Jamieson et al. (Eds.), *Readings in animal cognition*. Cambridge, MA: MIT Press.

Heron, W. (1957). The pathology of boredom. *Scientific American, 196*(1), 52–56.

Herrnstein, R. J., & Murray, C. (1994). *The bell curve: Intelligence and class structure in American life*. New York, NY: Free Press.

Hertzog, C., Kramer, A. F., Wilson, R. S., & Lindenberger, U. (2008). Enrichment effects on adult cognitive development: Can the functional capacity of older adults be preserved and enhanced? *Psychological Science in the Public Interest, 9*, 1–65.

Herz, R. S., & Cupchik, G. C. (1995). The emotional distinctiveness of odor-evoked memories. *Chemical Senses, 20*, 517–528.

Hess, T. M. (2005). Memory and aging in context. *Psychological Bulletin, 131*, 383–406.

Hess, U., Adams, R. B., Jr., & Kleck, R. (2005). Who may frown and who should smile? Dominance, affiliation, and the display of happiness and anger. *Cognition and Emotion, 19*, 515–536.

Hess, U., & Thibault, P. (2009). Darwin and emotional expression. *American Psychologist, 64*, 120–128.

Hewlitt, S. A., Luce, C. B., & Servon, L. J. (2008, June). Stopping the exodus of women in science. *Harvard Business Review, 86*(6), 22–24, 139. Retrieved from http://hbr.org/2008/06/stopping-the-exodus-of-women-in-science/ar/1

Higgins, E. T. (1998). Promotion and prevention: Regulatory focus as a motivational principle. *Advances in Experimental Social Psychology, 30*, 1–46.

Hilgard, E. R. (1977). *Divided consciousness: Multiple controls in human thought and action*. New York, NY: Wiley-Interscience.

Hilgard, E. R. (1986). *Divided consciousness: Multiple controls in human thought and action* (2nd ed.). New York, NY: Wiley.

Hillman, J., & Ventura, M. (1992). *We've had a hundred years of psychotherapy—and the world's getting worse*. San Francisco, CA: HarperCollins.

Hilts, P. J. (1995). *Memory's ghost: The strange tale of Mr. M. and the nature of memory*. New York, NY: Simon & Schuster.

Hines, T. M. (1998). Comprehensive review of biorhythm theory. *Psychological Reports, 83*, 19–64.

Hirsch, H. V. B., & Spinelli, D. N. (1970). Visual experience modifies distribution of horizontally and vertically oriented receptive fields in cats. *Science, 168*, 869–871.

Hirsch, J. B., & Inzlicht, M. (2008). The devil you know: Neuroticism predicts neural response to uncertainty. *Psychological Science, 19*, 962–967.

Hobson, J. A. (1988). *The dreaming brain*. New York, NY: Basic Books.

Hobson, J. A. (1990). Activation, input source, and modulation: A neurocognitive model of the state of the brain mind. In R. R. Bootzin, J. F. Kihlstrom, & D. L. Schacter (Eds.), *Sleep and cognition*. Washington, DC: American Psychological Association.

Hobson, J. A. (2002). *Dreaming: An introduction to the science of sleep*. New York, NY: Oxford University Press.

Hobson, J. A., Pace-Schott, E. F., & Stickgold, R. (2000). Dreaming and the brain: Toward a cognitive neuroscience of consicous states. *Behavioral and Brain Sciences, 23*, 793–842, 904–1018, 1083–1121.

Hochschild, A. R. (2003). *The managed heart: Commercialization of human feeling* (2nd ed.). Berkeley, CA: University of California Press.

Hoffmann, D. E., & Rothenberg, K. H. (2005). When should judges admit or compel genetic tests? *Science, 310*, 241–242.

Hoffrage, U., Hertwig, R., & Gigerenzer, G. (2000). Hindsight bias: A by-product of knowledge updating? *Journal of Experimental Psychology: Learning, Memory, & Cognition, 26*, 566–581.

Hofstede, G., & Bond, M. H. (1988). The Confucius connection: From cultural roots to economic growth. *Organizational Dynamics*, 5–21.

Holden, C. (2008, July 11). Poles apart. *Science, 321*, 193–195.

Holden, G. W., & Miller, P. C. (1999). Enduring and different: A meta-analysis of the similarity in parents' child rearing. *Psychological Bulletin, 125*, 223–254.

Holland, R. W., Hendriks, M., & Aarts, H. (2005). Smells like clean spirit: Nonconscious effects of scent on cognition and behavior. *Psychological Science, 16*, 689–693.

Hollon, S. D., Thase, M. E., & Markowitz, J. C. (2002). Treatment and prevention of depression. *Psychological Science in the Public Interest, 3*, 39–77.

Hood, B. (2009). *SuperSense: Why we believe in the unbelievable*. San Francisco, CA: HarperOne.

Hooker, E. (1957). The adjustment of the male overt homosexual. *Journal of Projective Techniques, 21*, 18–31.

Hopper, K., Harrison, G., Janca, A., & Sartorius, N.(Eds.). (2007). *Recovery from schizophrenia: An international investigation.* New York, NY: Oxford University Press.

Horgan, J. (1995, November). Get smart, take a test: A long-term rise in IQ scores baffles intelligence experts. *Scientific American, 273,* 12, 14.

Horney, K. (1926/1973). The flight from womanhood. *The International Journal of Psycho-Analysis, 7,* 324–339. Reprinted in J. B. Miller (Ed.), *Psychoanalysis and women.* New York, NY: Brunner/Mazel, 1973.

Hornung, R. W., Lanphear, B. P., & Dietrich, K. N. (2009). Age of greatest susceptibility to childhood lead exposure: A new statistical approach. *Environmental Health Perspectives, 117,* 1309–1312.

Hotz, R. L. (2000, November 29). Women use more of brain when listening, study says. *Los Angeles Times,* A1, A18–19.

House, J. S., Landis, K. R., & Umberson, D. (1988, July 19). Social relationships and health. *Science, 241,* 540–545.

Houston, D. M., & Jusczyk, P. W. (2003). Infants' long-term memory for the sound patterns of words and voices. *Journal of Experimental Psychology: Human Perception & Performance, 29,* 1143–1154.

Houts, A. C. (2002). Discovery, invention, and the expansion of the modern Diagnostic and Statistical Manuals of Mental Disorders. In L. E. Beutler & M. L. Malik (Eds.), *Rethinking the DSM: A psychological perspective.* Washington, DC: American Psychological Association.

Howard, G. S. (1991). Culture tales: A narrative approach to thinking, cross-cultural psychology, and psychotherapy. *American Psychologist, 46,* 187–197.

Howe, M. L. (2000). *The fate of early memories: Developmental science and the retention of childhood experiences.* Washington, DC: American Psychological Association.

Howe, M. L., Courage, M. L., & Peterson, C. (1994). How can I remember when "I" wasn't there? Long-term retention of traumatic experiences and emergence of the cognitive self. *Consciousness and Cognition, 3,* 327–355.

Hrdy, S. B. (1988). Empathy, polyandry, and the myth of the coy female. In R. Bleier (Ed.), *Feminist approaches to science.* New York, NY: Pergamon.

Hrdy, S. B. (1994). What do women want? In T. A. Bass (Ed.), *Reinventing the future: Conversations with the world's leading scientists.* Reading, MA: Addison-Wesley.

Hrdy, S. B. (1999). *Mother nature.* New York, NY: Pantheon.

Hu, H., Real, E., Takamiya, K., et al. (2007). Emotion enhances learning via norepinephrine regulation of AMPA-receptor trafficking. *Cell, 131,* 160–173.

Hu, P., Stylos-Allan, M., & Walker, M. (2006). Sleep facilitates consolidation of emotional declarative memory. *Psychological Science, 17,* 891–898.

Hu, W., Saba, L., Kechris, K., et al. (2008). Genomic insights into acute alcohol tolerance. *Journal of Pharmacology and Experimental Therapeutics, 326,* 792–800.

Huang, L., Shanker, Y. G., Dubauskaite, J., et al. (1999). Ggamma13 colocalizes with gustducin in taste receptor cells and mediates IP3 responses to bitter denatonium. *Nature Neuroscience, 2,* 1055–1062.

Hubel, D. H., & Wiesel, T. N. (1962). Receptive fields, binocular interaction and functional architecture in the cat's visual cortex. *Journal of Physiology (London), 160,* 106–154.

Hubel, D. H., & Wiesel, T. N. (1968). Receptive fields and functional architecture of monkey striate cortex. *Journal of Physiology (London), 195,* 215–243.

Hudson, V. M., & den Boer, A. M. (2004). *Bare branches: The security implications of Asia's surplus male population.* Cambridge, MA: MIT Press.

Huggins, M. K., Haritos-Fatouros, M., & Zimbardo, P. G. (2003). *Violence workers: Police torturers and murderers reconstruct Brazilian atrocities.* Berkeley, CA: University of California Press.

Huizink, A. C., Mulder, E. J. H., & Buitelaar, J. K. (2004). Prenatal stress and risk for psychopathology: Specific effects or induction of general susceptibility. *Psychological Bulletin, 130,* 115–142.

Hunsley, J., & Di Giulio, G. (2001). Norms, norming, and clinical assessment. *Clinical Psychology: Science and Practice, 8*(3), 378–382.

Hunsley, J., Lee, C. M., & Wood, J. (2003). Controversial and questionable assessment techniques. In S. O. Lilienfeld, S. J. Lynn, & J. M. Lohr (Eds.), *Science and pseudoscience in clinical psychology.* New York, NY: Guilford.

Huntington's Disease Collaborative Research Group. (1993). A novel gene containing a trinucleotide repeat that is expanded and unstable on Huntington's disease chromosomes. *Cell, 72,* 971–983.

Hupka, R. B. (1981). Cultural determinants of jealousy. *Alternative Lifestyles, 4,* 310–356.

Hupka, R. B. (1991). The motive for the arousal of romantic jealousy. In P. Salovey (Ed.), *The psychology of jealousy and envy.* New York, NY: Guilford Press.

Hupka, R. B., Lenton, A. P., & Hutchison, K. A. (1999). Universal development of emotion categories in natural language. *Journal of Personality and Social Psychology, 77,* 247–278.

Hur, Y.-M., Bouchard, T. J., Jr., & Lykken, D. T. (1998). Genetic and environmental influence on morningness-eveningness. *Personality and Individual Differences, 25,* 917–925.

Huron, D. (1991). Review of *Auditory scene analysis: The perceptual organization of sound* by Albert S. Bregman. *Psychology of Music, 19*(1), 77–82.

Hyde, J. S. (2005). The gender similarities hypothesis. *American Psychologist, 60,* 581–592.

Hyde, J. S. (2007). New directions in the study of gender similarities and differences. *Current Directions in Psychological Science, 16,* 259–263.

Hyde, J. S., & Linn, M. C. (2006). Gender similarities in mathematics and science. *Science, 314,* 599–600.

Hyman, I. E., Jr., & Pentland, J. (1996). The role of mental imagery in the creation of false childhood memories. *Journal of Memory and Language, 35,* 101–117.

Iacoboni, M. (2008). *Mirroring people: The new science of how we connect with others.* New York, NY: Farrar, Straus and Giroux.

Iacoboni, M., Molnar-Szakacs, I., Gallese, V., et al. (2005). Grasping the intentions of others with one's own mirror neuron system. *Public Library of Science: Biology 3*(3): e79. doi:10.1371/journal.pbio.003079

Ikonomidou, C., Bittigau, P., Ishimaru, M. J., et al. (2000, February 11). Ethanol-induced apoptotic neurodegeneration and fetal alcohol syndrome. *Science, 287,* 1056–1060.

Impett, E. A., Gable, S., & Peplau, L. A. (2005). Giving up and giving in: The costs and benefits of daily sacrifice in intimate relationships. *Journal of Personality and Social Psychology, 89,* 327–344.

Impett, E. A., Peplau, L. A., & Gable, S. (2005). Approach and avoidance sexual motives: Implications for personal and interpersonal well-being. *Personal Relationships, 12,* 465–482.

Impett, E. A., & Tolman, D. L. (2006). Late adolescent girls' sexual experiences and sexual satisfaction. *Journal of Adolescent Research, 21,* 628–646.

International Consensus Conference. (2002, June). *Female androgen deficiency syndrome: Definition, diagnosis, and classification.* International Consensus Conference, Princeton, NY. Retrieved from http://www.medscape.com/viewprogram/302

Inzlicht, M., & Ben-Zeev, T. (2000). A threatening intellectual environment: Why females are susceptible to experiencing problem-solving deficits in the presence of males. *Psychological Science, 11,* 365–371.

Islam, M. R., & Hewstone, M. (1993). Intergroup attributions and affective consequences in majority and minority groups. *Journal of Personality and Social Psychology, 64,* 936–950.

Ito, T. A., & Urland, G. R. (2003). Race and gender on the brain: Electrocortical measures of attention to the race and gender of multiply categorizable individuals. *Journal of Personality and Social Psychology, 85,* 616–626.

Izard, C. E. (1990). Facial expressions and the regulation of emotions. *Journal of Personality and Social Psychology, 58,* 487–498.

Izard, C. E. (1994a). Four systems for emotion activation: Cognitive and noncognitive processes. *Psychological Review, 100,* 68–90.

Izard, C. E. (1994b). Innate and universal facial expressions: Evidence from developmental and cross-cultural research. *Psychological Bulletin, 115,* 288–299.

Izard, C. E. (2007). Basic emotions, natural kinds, emotion schemas, and a new paradigm. *Perspectives on Psychological Science, 2,* 260–280.

Izard, V., Sann, C., Spelke, E. S., & Streri, A. (2009). Newborn infants perceive abstract numbers. *Proceedings of the National Academy of Sciences, 106,* 10382–10385.

Izumikawa, M., Minoda, R., Kawamoto, K. A., et al. (2005). Auditory hair cell replacement and hearing improvement by *Atoh1* gene therapy in deaf mammals. *Nature Medicine, 11,* 271–276.

Jackson, D. C., Mueller, C. J., Dolski, I., et al. (2003). Now you feel it, now you don't: Frontal brain electrical asymmetry and individual differences in emotion regulation. *Psychological Science, 14,* 612–617.

Jacobs, T. L., Epel, E. S., Lin, J., et al. (2010). Intensive meditation training, immune cell telomerase activity, and psychological mediators. *Psychoneuroendocrinology, 36,* 664–681.

Jacobsen, P. B, Bovbjerg, D. H., Schwartz, M. D., et al. (1995). Conditioned emotional distress in women receiving chemotherapy for breast cancer. *Journal of Consulting & Clinical Psychology, 63,* 108–114.

Jaffe, E. (2005). How random is that? Students are convenient research subjects but they're not a simple sample. *APS Observer, 18,* 19–30.

James, W. (1890/1950). *Principles of psychology* (Vol. 1). New York, NY: Dover.

James, W. (1902/1936). *The varieties of religious experience.* New York, NY: Modern Library.

Jamieson, S., & Marshall, W. L. (2000). Attachment styles and violence in child molesters. *Journal of Sexual Aggression, 5*(2): 88–98.

Jamison, K. (1992). *Touched with fire: Manic depressive illness and the artistic temperament.* New York, NY: Free Press.

Jamison, K. (1999). *Night falls fast: Understanding suicide.* New York, NY: Knopf.

Jancke, L., Schlaug, G., & Steinmetz, H. (1997). Hand skill asymmetry in professional musicians. *Brain and Cognition, 34,* 424–432.

Jang, K. L., McCrae, R. R., Angleitner, A., et al. (1998). Heritability of facet-level traits in a cross-cultural twin sample: Support for a hierarchical model of personality. *Journal of Personality and Social Psychology, 74,* 1556–1565.

Janis, I. L. (1982). *Groupthink: Psychological studies of policy decisions and fiascos* (2nd ed.). Boston, MA: Houghton-Mifflin.

Janis, I. L. (1989). *Crucial decisions: Leadership in policymaking and crisis management.* New York, NY: Free Press.

Jenkins, J. G., & Dallenbach, K. M. (1924). Obliviscence during sleep and waking. *American Journal of Psychology, 35,* 605–612.

Jenkins, S. R. (1994). Need for power and women's careers over 14 years: Structural power, job satisfaction, and motive change. *Journal of Personality and Social Psychology, 66,* 155–165.

Jensen, A. R. (1969). How much can we boost IQ and scholastic achievement? *Harvard Educational Review, 39,* 1–123.

Jensen, A. R. (1981). *Straight talk about mental tests.* New York, NY: Free Press.

Jensen, A. R. (1998). *The g factor: The science of mental ability.* Westport, CT: Praeger/Greenwood.

Jiang, Y., Saxe, R., & Kanwisher, N. (2004). Functional magnetic resonance imaging provides new constraints on theories of the psychological refractory period. *Psychological Science, 15,* 390–396.

Johanek, L. M., Meyer, R. A., Friedman, R. M., et al. (2008). A role for polymodal C-fiber afferents in nonhistaminergic itch. *The Journal of Neuroscience, 28,* 7659–7669.

Johns, M., Schmader, T., & Martens, A. (2005). Knowing is half the battle: Teaching stereotype threat as a means of improving women's math performance. *Psychological Science, 16,* 175–179.

Johnson, A. J., & Miles, C. (2009). Serial position effects in 2-alternative forced choice recognition: functional equivalence across visual and auditory modalities. *Memory, 17,* 84–91.

Johnson, M. K., Hashtroudi, S., & Lindsay, D. S. (1993). Source monitoring. *Psychological Bulletin, 114,* 3–28.

Johnson-Down, L., O'Loughlin, J., Koski, K. G., & Gray-Donald, K. (1997). High prevalence of obesity in low income and multiethnic schoolchildren: A diet and physical activity assessment. *Journal of Nutrition, 127*(12), 2310–2315.

Jones, E. E. (1990). *Interpersonal perception.* New York, NY: Macmillan.

Jones, M. C. (1924). A laboratory study of fear: The case of Peter. *Pedagogical Seminary, 31,* 308–315.

Jones, S. (1994). *The language of genes.* New York, NY: Anchor/Doubleday.

Joormann, J., & Gotlib, I. H. (2007). Selective attention to emotional faces following recovery from depression. *Journal of Abnormal Psychology, 116,* 80–85.

Joormann, J., Siemer, M., & Gotlib, I. H. (2007). Mood regulation in depression: Differential effects of distraction and recall of happy memories on sad mood. *Journal of Abnormal Psychology, 116,* 484–490.

Jordan, K. E., & Brannon, E. M. (2006). The multisensory representation of number in infancy. *Proceedings of the National Academy of Sciences, 103*, 3486–3489.

Jost, J. T. (2006). The end of the end of ideology. *American Psychologist, 61*, 651–670.

Jost, J. T., Glaser, J., Kruglanski, A. W., & Sulloway, F. J. (2003). Political conservatism as motivated social cognition. *Psychological Bulletin, 129*, 339–375.

Jost, J. T., Nosek, B. A., & Gosling, S. D. (2008). Ideology: Its resurgence in social, personality, and political psychology. *Perspectives on Psychological Science, 3*, 126–136.

Judd, C. M., Park, B., Ryan, C. S., et al. (1995). Stereotypes and ethnocentrism: Diverging interethnic perceptions of African American and white American youth. *Journal of Personality and Social Psychology, 69*, 460–481.

Judge, T. A. (2009). Core self-evaluations and work success. *Current Directions, 18*, 18–22.

Jung, C. (1967). *Collected works*. Princeton, NJ: Princeton University Press.

Jusczyk, P. W. (2002). How infants adapt speech-processing capacities to native-language structure. *Current Directions in Psychological Science, 11*, 15–18.

Jussim, L., Cain, T. R., Crawford, J. T., et al. (2009). The unbearable accuracy of stereotypes. In T. Nelson (Ed.), *The handbook of prejudice, sterotyping, and discrimination*. New York, NY: Psychology Press.

Just, M. A., Carpenter, P. A., Keller, T. A., et al. (2001). Interdependence of nonoverlapping cortical systems in dual cognitive tasks. *NeuroImage, 14*, 417–426.

Kabat-Zinn, J. (1994). *Wherever you go, there you are: Mindfulness meditation in everyday life*. New York, NY: Hyperion.

Kagan, J. (1998). *Three seductive ideas*. Cambridge, MA: Harvard University Press.

Kagan, J. (1984). *The nature of the child*. New York, NY: Basic Books.

Kagan, J. (1989). *Unstable ideas: Temperament, cognition, and self*. Cambridge, MA: Harvard University Press.

Kagan, J. (1997). Temperament and the reactions to unfamiliarity. *Child Development, 68*, 139–143.

Kagan, J., Kearsley, R. B., & Zelazo, P. R. (1978). *Infancy: Its place in human development*. Cambridge, MA: Harvard University Press.

Kahn, A. S. (2004). 2003 Carolyn Sherif Award Address: What college women do and do not experience as rape. *Psychology of Women Quarterly, 28*, 9–15.

Kahneman, D. (2002). Maps of bounded rationality: A perspective on intuitive judgment and choice. Nobel Prize lecture. Retrieved February 11, 2008, from http://nobelprize.org/nobel_prizes/economics/laureates/2002/kahnemann-lecture.pdf

Kahneman, D. (2003). A perspective on judgment and choice: Mapping bounded rationality. *American Psychologist, 58*, 697–720.

Kaminski, J., Call, J., & Fisher, J. (2004). Word learning in a domestic dog: Evidence for "fast mapping." *Science, 304*, 1682–1683.

Kanagawa, C., Cross, S. E., & Markus, H. R. (2001). "Who am I?" The cultural psychology of the conceptual self. *Personality and Social Psychology Bulletin, 27*, 90–103.

Kandel, E. R. (2001). The molecular biology of memory storage: A dialogue between genes and synapses. *Science, 294*, 1030–1038.

Kandel, E. R., & Schwartz, J. H. (1982). Molecular biology of learning: Modulation of transmitter release. *Science, 218*, 433–443.

Kane, M. J., Brown, L. H., McVay, J. C., et al. (2007). For whom the mind wanders, and when: An experience-sampling study of working memory and executive control in daily life. *Psychological Science, 18*, 614–621.

Kanner, A., & Kasser, T. (2003). *Psychology and consumer culture: The struggle for a good life in a materialistic society*. Washington, DC: American Psychological Association.

Kanter, R. M. (2006). Some effects of proportions on group life: Skewed sex ratios and responses to token women. In J. N. Levine & R. L. Moreland (Eds.), *Small groups. Key Readings in Social Psychology*. New York, NY: Psychology Press.

Kanwisher, N. (2000). Domain specificity in face perception. *Nature Neuroscience, 3*, 759.

Kaplan, A. (1967). A philosophical discussion of normality. *Archives of General Psychiatry, 17*, 325–330.

Kaplan, M. S., Morales, M., & Becker, J. V. (1993). The impact of verbal satiation of adolescent sex offenders: A preliminary report. *Journal of Child Sexual Abuse, 2*, 81–88.

Karasek, R., & Theorell, T. (1990). *Healthy work: Stress, productivity, and the reconstruction of working life*. New York, NY: Basic Books.

Karney, B., & Bradbury, T. N. (2000). Attributions in marriage: State or trait? A growth curve analysis. *Journal of Personality and Social Psychology, 78*, 295–309.

Karni, A., Tanne, D., Rubenstein, B. S., et al. (1994). Dependence on REM sleep of overnight improvement of a perceptual skill. *Science, 265*, 679–682.

Karpicke, J. D., & Roediger, H. L., III. (2008, February 15). The critical importance of retrieval for learning. *Science, 319*, 966–968.

Karraker, K. H., Vogel, D. A., & Lake, M. A. (1995). Parents' gender-stereotyped perceptions of newborns: The eye of the beholder revisited. *Sex Roles, 33*, 687–701.

Karremans, J. C., Van Lange, P. A. M., Ouwerkerk, J. W., & Kluwer, E. S. (2003). When forgiving enhances psychological well-being: The role of interpersonal commitment. *Journal of Personality and Social Psychology, 84*, 1011–1026.

Kaschak, E., & Tiefer, L. (Eds.). (2002). *A new view of women's sexual problems*. Binghamton, NY: Haworth Press.

Kasser, T., & Ryan, R. M. (2001). Be careful what you wish for: Optimal functioning and the relative attainment of intrinsic and extrinsic goals. In P. Schmuck & K. M. Sheldon (Eds.), *Life goals and well-being*. Lengerich, Germany: Pabst Science Publishers.

Kassinove, H. (Ed.). (1995). *Anger disorders: Definition, diagnosis, treatment*. Washington, DC: Taylor & Francis.

Katigbak, M. S., Church, A. T., Guanzon-Lapeña, Ma. A., et al. (2002). Are indigenous personality dimensions culture specific? Philippine inventories and the Five-Factor model. *Journal of Personality and Social Psychology, 82*, 89–101.

Katz, Z. (2001). Canadian psychologists' education, trauma history, and the recovery of memories of childhood sexual abuse [doctoral dissertation]. Simon Fraser University. *Dissertations Abstracts International, 61*, 3848.

Katzmarzyk, P. T., & Malina, R. M. (1998). Obesity and relative subcutaneous fat distribution among Canadians of First Nation and European ancestry. *International Journal of Obesity and Related Metabolic Disorders, 22*, 1127–1131.

Katzmarzyk, P. T., & Malina, R. M. (1999). Body size and physique among Canadians of First Nation and European ancestry. *American Journal of Physical Anthropology, 108*, 161–172.

Kaufman, J., & Zigler, E. (1987). Do abused children become abusive parents? *American Journal of Orthopsychiatry, 57*, 186–192.

Kay, K. N., Naselaris, T., Prenger, R, J., & Gallant, J. L. (2008). Identifying natural images from human brain activity [letter]. *Nature, 452*, 352–355.

Kazdin, A. E. (2001). *Behavior modification in applied settings* (6th ed.). Belmont, CA: Wadsworth.

Kazdin, A. E. (2008). Evidence-based treatment and practice: New opportunities to bridge clinical research and practice, enhance the knowledge base, and improve patient care. *American Psychologist, 63*, 146–150.

Keating, C. F. (1994). World without words: Messages from face and body. In W. J. Lonner & R. Malpass (Eds.), *Psychology and culture*. Needham Heights, MA: Allyn & Bacon.

Keel, P. K., & Klump, K. L. (2003). Are eating disorders culture-bound syndromes? Implications for conceptualizing their etiology. *Psychological Bulletin, 129*, 747–769.

Keen, S. (1986). *Faces of the enemy: Reflections of the hostile imagination*. San Francisco, CA: Harper & Row.

Keizer, K., Lindenberg, S., & Steg, L. (2008, December 12). The spreading of disorder. *Science, 322*, 1681–1685.

Keller, H., Abels, M., Lamm, B., et al. (2005). Ecocultural effects on early infant care: A study in Cameroon, India, and Germany. *Ethos, 33*, 512–541.

Kelman, H. C., & Hamilton, V. L. (1989). *Crimes of obedience: Toward a social psychology of authority and responsibility*. New Haven, CT: Yale University Press.

Keltner, D., & Anderson, C. (2000). Saving face for Darwin: The functions and uses of embarrassment. *Current Directions in Psychological Science, 9*, 187–192.

Kemeny, M. E. (2003). The psychobiology of stress. *Current Directions in Psychological Science, 12*, 124–129.

Kempermann, G. (2006). Adult neurogenesis: Stem cells and neuronal development in the adult brain. New York, NY: Oxford University Press.

Kendall (1999). Women in Lesotho and the (Western) construction of homophobia. In E. Blackwood & S. E. Wieringa (Eds.), *Female desires: Same-sex relations and transgender practices across cultures*. New York, NY: Columbia University Press.

Kennedy, D., & Norman, C. (2005). Introduction to special issue: What don't we know? *Science, 309*, 75.

Kennedy-Moore, E., & Watson, J. C. (2001). How and when does emotional expression help? *Review of General Psychology, 5*, 187–212.

Kenny, M. G. (1986). *The passion of Ansel Bourne: Multiple personality in American culture*. Washington, DC: Smithsonian Press.

Kenrick, D. T., Sundie, J. M., Nicastle, L. D., & Stone, G. O. (2001). Can one ever be too wealthy or too chaste? Searching for nonlinearities in mate judgment. *Journal of Personality and Social Psychology, 80*, 462–471.

Kephart, W. M. (1967). Some correlates of romantic love. *Journal of Marriage and the Family, 29*, 470–474.

Kessler, R. C., Chiu, W. T., Demler, O., Merikangas, K. R., & Walters, E. E. (2005). Prevalence, severity, and comorbidity of 12-month DSM-IV disorders in the National Comorbidity Survey Replication. *Archives of General Psychiatry, 62*, 590–592.

Kessler, R. C., Sonnega, A., Bromet, E., et al. (1995). Posttraumatic stress disorder in the National Comorbidity Survey. *Archives of General Psychiatry, 52*, 1048–1060.

Khan, A., Detke, M., Khan, S. R., & Mallinckrodt, C. (2003). Placebo response and antidepressant clinical trial outcome. *Journal of Nervous and Mental Diseases, 191*, 211–218.

Kida, T. (2006). *Don't believe everything you think: The 6 basic mistakes we make in thinking*. Amherst, NY: Prometheus Books.

Kiecolt-Glaser, J. K., Loving, T. J., Stowell, J. R., et al. (2005). Hostile marital interactions, proinflammatory cytokine production, and wound healing. *Archives of General Psychiatry, 62*, 1377–1384.

Kiecolt-Glaser, J. K., & Newton, T. L. (2001). Marriage and health: His and hers. *Psychological Bulletin, 127*, 472–503.

Kiecolt-Glaser, J. K., Page, G. G., Marucha, P. T., et al. (1998). Psychological influences on surgical recovery: Perspectives from psychoneuroimmunology. *American Psychologist, 53*, 1209–1218.

Kihlstrom, J. F. (1994). Hypnosis, delayed recall, and the principles of memory. *International Journal of Clinical and Experimental Hypnosis, 40*, 337–345.

Kihlstrom, J. F. (1995). *From a subject's point of view: The experiment as conversation and collaboration between investigator and subject*. Invited address presented at the annual meeting of the American Psychological Society, New York, NY.

Kim, H. L., Streltzer, J., & Goebert, D. (1999). St. John's wort for depression: A meta-analysis of well-defined clinical trials. *Journal of Nervous and Mental Diseases, 187*, 532–538.

Kim, H. S., Sherman, D. K., & Taylor, S. E. (2008). Culture and social support. *American Psychologist, 63*, 518–526.

Kim, J. L., Sorsoli, C. L., Collins, K., et al. (2007). From sex to sexuality: Exposing the heterosexual script on primetime network television. *Journal of Sex Research, 44*, 145–157.

King, A. E., Austin-Oden, D., & Lohr, J. M. (2009, January). Browsing for love in all the wrong places. *Skeptic, 15*, 48–55.

King, M., & Woollett, E. (1997). Sexually assaulted males: 115 men consulting a counseling service. *Archives of Sexual Behavior, 26*, 579–588.

King, P. (1989, October). The chemistry of doubt. *Psychology Today, 58*, 60.

King, P. M., & Kitchener, K. S. (1994). Developing reflective judgment: Understanding and promoting intellectual growth and critical thinking in adolescents and adults. San Francisco, CA: Jossey Bass.

King, P. M., & Kitchener, K. S. (2002). The reflective judgment model: Twenty years of research on epistemic cognition. In B. K. Hofer & P. R. Pintrich (Eds.), *Personal epistemology: The psychology of beliefs about knowledge and knowing*. Mahway, NJ: Erlbaum.

King, P. M., & Kitchener, K. S. (2004). Reflective judgment: Theory and research on the development of epistemic assumptions through adulthood. *Educational Psychologist, 39,* 5–18.

Kingston, A. (2009, March 12). The sexting scare. Though no 'epidemic,' it raises big issues for parents and the law. *Macleans.* Retrieved from http://www2.macleans.ca/2009/03/12/the-sexting-scare

Kinnon, D. (1981). *Report on sexual assault in Canada.* **Ottawa: Canadian Advisory Council on the Status of Women.**

Kinoshita, S., & Peek-O'Leary, M. (2005). Does the compatibility effect in the race Implicit Association Test reflect familiarity or affect? *Psychonomic Bulletin & Review, 12,* 442–452.

Kinsey, A. C., Pomeroy, W. B., & Martin, C. E. (1948). *Sexual behavior in the human male.* Philadelphia, PA: Saunders.

Kinsey, A. C., Pomeroy, W. B., Martin, C. E., & Gebhard, P. H. (1953). *Sexual behavior in the human female.* Philadelphia, PA: Saunders.

Kirkpatrick, L. A., & Davis, K. A. (1994). Attachment style, gender, and relationship stability: A longitudinal analysis. *Journal of Personality and Social Psychology, 66,* 502–512.

Kirsch, I. (1997). Response expectancy theory and application: A decennial review. *Applied and Preventive Psychology, 6,* 69–70.

Kirsch, I. (2004). Conditioning, expectancy, and the placebo effect: Comment on Stewart-Williams and Podd (2004). *Psychological Bulletin, 130,* 341–343.

Kirsch, I., Deacon, B. J., Huedo-Medina, T. B., et al. (2008). Initial severity and antidepressant benefits: A meta-analysis of data submitted to the Food and Drug Administration. *PLoS Medicine, 5,* e45.

Kirsch, I., & Lynn, S. J. (1995). The altered state of hypnosis: Changes in the theoretical landscape. *American Psychologist, 50,* 846–858.

Kirsch, I., & Lynn, S. J. (1998). Dissociation theories of hypnosis. *Psychological Bulletin, 123,* 100–113.

Kirsch, I., & Sapirstein, G. (1998). Listening to Prozac but hearing placebo: A meta-analysis of antidepressant medication. *Prevention & Treatment, 1,* Article 0002a, posted electronically June 26, 1998, on the website of the American Psychological Association. Retrieved August 21, 2011, from http://psychrights.org/Research/Digest/CriticalThinkRxCites/KirschandSapirstein1998.pdf

Kirsch, I., Silva, C. E., Carone, J. E., Johnston, J. D., & Simon, B. (1989). The surreptitious observation design: An experimental paradigm for distinguishing artifact from essence in hypnosis. *Journal of Abnormal Psychology, 98,* 132–136.

Kish, S. J. (2003). What is the evidence that Ecstasy (MDMA) can cause Parkinson's disease? *Movement Disorders, 18,* 1219–1223.

Kitayama, S., & Markus, H. R. (1994). Introduction to cultural psychology and emotion research. In S. Kitayama & H. R. Markus (Eds.), *Emotion and culture: Empirical studies of mutual influence.* Washington, DC: American Psychological Association.

Kitchener, K. S., Lynch, C. L., Fischer, K. W., & Wood, P. K. (1993). Developmental range of reflective judgment: The effect of contextual support and practice on developmental stage. *Developmental Psychology, 29,* 893–906.

Klauer, S. G., Dingus, T. A., Neale, V. L., et al. (2006). *The impact of driver inattention on near-crash/crash risk: An analysis using the 100-car naturalistic driving study data.* Performed by Virginia Tech Transportation Institute, Blacksburg, VA, sponsored by National Highway Traffic Safety Administration, Washington, DC. DOT HS 810 594. Retrieved from http://www.nhtsa.gov/DOT/NHTSA/NRD/Multimedia/PDFs/Crash%20Avoidance/2006/DriverInattention.pdf

Klein, D. N., Schwartz, J. E., Santiago, N. J., et al. (2003). Therapeutic alliance in depression treatment: Controlling for prior change and patient characteristics. *Journal of Consulting & Clinical Psychology, 71,* 997–1006.

Klein, R., & Armitage, R. (1979). Rhythms in human performance: 1 1/2-hour oscillations in cognitive style. *Science, 204,* 1326–1328.

Kleinke, C. L., Peterson, T. R., & Rutledge, T. R. (1998). Effects of self-generated facial expressions on mood. *Journal of Personality and Social Psychology, 74,* 272–279.

Kleinman, A. (1988). *Rethinking psychiatry: From cultural category to personal experience.* New York, NY: Free Press.

Klima, E. S., & Bellugi, U. (1966). Syntactic regularities in the speech of children. In J. Lyons & R. J. Wales (Eds.), *Psycholinguistics papers.* Edinburgh, Scotland: Edinburgh University Press.

Klimoski, R. (1992). Graphology and personnel selection. In B. Beyerstein & D. Beyerstein (Eds.), *The write stuff: Evaluations of graphology—The study of handwriting analysis.* Buffalo, NY: Prometheus Books.

Kling, K. C., Hyde, J. S., Showers, C. J., & Buswell, B. N. (1999). Gender differences in self-esteem: A meta-analysis. *Psychological Bulletin, 125,* 470–500.

Klohnen, E. C., & Bera, S. (1998). Behavioral and experiential patterns of avoidantly and securely attached women across adulthood: A 31-year longitudinal perspective. *Journal of Personality and Social Psychology, 74,* 211–223.

Kluft, R. P. (1987). The simulation and dissimulation of multiple personality disorder. *American Journal of Clinical Hypnosis, 30,* 104–118.

Koch, C. (2004). *The quest for consciousness: A neurobiological approach.* Greenwood Village, CO: Roberts & Company Publishers.

Kochanska, G., Forman, D. R., Aksan, N., & Dunbar, S. B. (2005). Pathways to conscience: Early mother–child mutually responsive orientation and children's moral emotion, conduct, and cognition. *Journal of Child Psychology and Psychiatry, 46,* 19–34.

Kochanska, G., & Knaack, A. (2003). Effortful control as a personality characteristic of young children: Antecedents, correlates, and consequences. *Journal of Personality, 71,* 1087–1112.

Kohlberg, L. (1964). Development of moral character and moral ideology. In M. Hoffman & L. W. Hoffman (Eds.), *Review of child development research.* New York, NY: Russell Sage Foundation.

Köhler, W. (1925). *The mentality of apes.* New York, NY: Harcourt, Brace.

Köhler, W. (1929). *Gestalt psychology.* New York, NY: Horace Liveright.

Köhler, W. (1959). *Gestalt psychology today.* Presidential address to the American Psychological Association, Cincinnati, OH. [Reprinted in E. R. Hilgard (Ed.), *American psychology in historical perspective: Addresses of the presidents of the American Psychological Association, 1892–1977.* Washington, DC: American Psychological Association, 1978.]

Kohsaka, A., Laposky, A. D., Ramsey, K. M., et al. (2007). High-fat diet disrupts behavioral and molecular circadian rhythms in mice. *Cell Metabolism, 6,* 414–421.

Kok, B. E., Catalino, L. I., & Fredrickson, B. L. (2008). The broadening, building, buffering effects of positive emotions. In S. J. Lopez (Ed.),

Positive psychology: Exploring the best in people (Vol 2). Westport, CT: Praeger Publishers/Greenwood.

Kolata, G. (2004, June 8). The fat epidemic: He says it's an illusion. *The New York Times*, Science section, D5.

Kolb, B., Gibb, R., & Robinson, T. E. (2003). Brain plasticity and behavior. *Current Directions in Psychological Science, 12*, 1–5.

Koocher, G. P., Goodman, G. S., White, C. S., et al. (1995). Psychological science and the use of anatomically detailed dolls in child sexual-abuse assessments. *Psychological Bulletin, 118*, 199–222.

Kopta, S. M., Howard, K. I., Lowry, J. L., & Beutler, L. E. (1994). Patterns of symptomatic recovery in psychotherapy. *Journal of Consulting and Clinical Psychology, 62*, 1009–1016.

Kornell, N. (2009). Metacognition in humans and animals. *Current Directions in Psychological Science, 18*, 11–15.

Kosfeld, M., Heinrichs, M., Zak, P. J., et al. (2005). Oxytocin increases trust in humans. *Nature, 435*, 673–676.

Koski, L. R., & Shaver, P. R. (1997). Attachment and relationship satisfaction across the lifespan. In R. J. Sternberg & M. Hojjatt (Eds.), *Satisfaction in close relationships.* New York, NY: Guilford.

Kosslyn, S. M. (1980). *Image and mind.* Cambridge, MA: Harvard University Press.

Kosslyn, S. M., Pascual-Leone, A., Felician, O., et al. (1999). The role of area 17 in visual imagery: Convergent evidence from PET and rTMS. *Science, 284*, 167–170.

Kosslyn, S. M., Thompson, W. L., Costantini-Ferrando, M. F., et al. (2000). Hypnotic visual illusion alters color processing in the brain. *American Journal of Psychiatry, 157*, 1279–1284.

Kramer, A. F., & Willis, S. L. (2002). Enhancing the cognitive vitality of older adults. *Current Directions in Psychological Science, 11*, 173–177.

Krantz, D. S., Olson, M. B., Francis, J. L., et al. (2006). Anger, hostility, and cardiac symptoms in women with suspected coronary artery disease: The women's ischemia syndrome evaluation (WISE) study. *Journal of Women's Health, 15*, 1214–1223.

Krebs, D. L. (2008). Morality: An evolutionary account. *Perspectives on Psychological Science, 3*, 149–172.

Kreps, B. (1990). *Subversive thoughts, authentic passions.* San Francisco, CA: Harper & Row.

Krieger, N., & Sidney, S. (1996). Racial discrimination and blood pressure: The CARDIA study of young black and white adults. *American Journal of Public Health, 86*, 1370–1378.

Krimsky, S. (2003). *Science in the private interest.* Lanham, MD: Rowman & Littlefield.

Kring, A. M., & Gordon, A. H. (1998). Sex differences in emotion: Expression, experience, and physiology. *Journal of Personality and Social Psychology, 74*, 686–703.

Kripke, D. F. (1974). Ultradian rhythms in sleep and wakefulness. In E. D. Weitzman (Ed.), *Advances in sleep research* (Vol. 1). Flushing, NY: Spectrum.

Kroll, B. M. (1992). *Teaching hearts and minds: College students reflect on the Vietnam War in literature.* Carbondale: Southern Illinois University Press.

Krueger, R. F., Hicks, B. M., & McGue, M. (2001). Altruism and antisocial behavior: Independent tendencies, unique personality correlates, distinct etiologies. *Psychological Science, 12*, 397–402.

Krupa, D. J., Thompson, J. K., & Thompson, R. F. (1993). Localization of a memory trace in the mammalian brain. *Science, 260*, 989–991.

Krützen, M., Mann, J., Heithaus, M. R., et al. (2005). Cultural transmission of tool use in bottlenose dolphins. *Proceedings of the National Academy of Sciences, 102*: 8939–8943. doi:10.1073/pnas.0500232102

Kuhl, P. K., Williams, K. A., Lacerda, F., et al. (1992, January 31). Linguistic experience alters phonetic perception in infants by 6 months of age. *Science, 255*, 606–608.

Kuhn, D., Weinstock, M., & Flaton, R. (1994). How well do jurors reason? Competence dimensions of individual variation in a juror reasoning task. *Psychological Science, 5*, 289–296.

Kuncel, N. R., Hezlett, S. A., & Ones, D. S. (2004). Academic performance, career potential, creativity, and job performance: Can one construct predict them all? *Journal of Personality and Social Psychology, 86*, 148–161.

Kunda, Z. (1990). The case for motivated reasoning. *Psychological Bulletin, 108*, 480–498.

Kupersmidt, J. B., Griesler, P. C., DeRosier, M. E., et al. (1995). Childhood aggression and peer relations in the context of family and neighborhood factors. *Child Development, 66*(2), 360–375.

Kurdek, L. A. (2005). What do we know about gay and lesbian couples? *Current Directions in Psychological Science, 14*, 251–254.

Kutchins, H., & Kirk, S. A. (1997). *Making us crazy: DSM. The psychiatric bible and the creation of mental disorders.* New York, NY: Free Press.

Laan, E., & Both, S. (2008). What makes women experience desire? In L. Tiefer (Ed.), The New View campaign against the medicalization of sex (Special Issue). *Feminism and Psychology, 18*, 505–514.

LaBerge, S., & Levitan, L. (1995). Validity established of DreamLight cues for eliciting lucid dreaming. *Dreaming: Journal of the Association for the Study of Dreams, 5*, 159–168.

Lacasse, J. R., & Leo, J. (2005, December). Serotonin and depression: A disconnect between the advertisements and the scientific literature. *PloS Medicine, 2*(12): e392. doi:10.1371/journal.pmed.0020392

Lachman, M. E., & Weaver, S. L. (1998). The sense of control as a moderator of social class differences in health and well-being. *Journal of Personality and Social Psychology, 74*, 763–773.

Lachman, S. J. (1996). Processes in perception: Psychological transformations of highly structured stimulus material. *Perceptual and Motor Skills, 83*, 411–418.

LaFrance, M., Hecht, M. A., & Paluck, E. L. (2003). The contingent smile: A meta-analysis of sex differences in smiling. *Psychological Bulletin, 129*, 305–334.

Lahey, B. B., Pelham, W. E., Loney, J., et al. (2005). Instability of the DSM-IV subtypes of ADHD from preschool through elementary school. *Archives of General Psychiatry, 62*, 896–902.

Lam, R. W., & Levitt, A. J. (1999). *Canadian consensus guidelines for the treatment of seasonal affective disorder.* Vancouver, Canada: Clinical & Academic Publishing.

Lamb, S. (2002). *The secret lives of girls.* New York, NY: The Free Press.

Landrigan, C. P., Fahrenkopf, A. M., Lewin, D., et al. (2008). Effects of the Accreditation Council for Graduate Medical Education duty hour limits on sleep, work hours, and safety. *Pediatrics, 122*, 250–258.

Landrine, H. (1988). Revising the framework of abnormal psychology. In P. Bronstein & K. Quina (Eds.), *Teaching a psychology of people.* Washington, DC: American Psychological Association.

Lang, A. J., Craske, M. G., Brown, M., & Ghaneian, A. (2001). Fear-related state dependent memory. *Cognition & Emotion, 15*, 695–703.

Lang, F. R., & Heckhausen, J. (2001). Perceived control over development and subjective well-being: Differential benefits across adulthood. *Journal of Personality and Social Psychology, 81*, 509–523.

Langer, E. J. (1997). *The power of mindful learning.* Reading, MA: Addison-Wesley.

Langer, E. J., Blank, A., & Chanowitz, B. (1978). The mindlessness of ostensibly thoughtful action: The role of placebic information in interpersonal interaction. *Journal of Personality and Social Psychology, 36*, 635–642.

Lanius, R. A., Williamson, P. C., Boksman, K., et al. (2002). Brain activation during script-driven imagery induced dissociative responses in PTSD: A functional magnetic resonance imaging investigation. *Biological Psychiatry, 52*(4), 305–311.

Lanphear, B. P., Hornung, R., Ho, M., et al. (2002). Environmental lead exposure during early childhood. *Journal of Pediatrics, 140*, 49–47.

Lanphear, B. P., Hornung, R., Khoury, J., et al. (2005). Low-level environmental lead exposure and children's intellectual function: An international pooled analysis. *Environmental Health Perspectives, 113*, 894–899.

Lany, J., & Gómez, R. L. (2008). Twelve-month-old infants benefit from prior experience in statistical learning. *Psychological Science, 19*, 1247–1252.

Lau, H., Alger, S., & Fishbein, W. (2008, November). *Naps and relational memory—a daytime nap facilitates extraction of general concepts.* Paper presented at the annual meeting of the Society for Neuroscience, Washington, DC.

Laumann, E. O., Ellingson, S., Mahay, J., Paik, A., & Youm, Y. (Eds.). (2004). *The sexual organization of the city.* Chicago, IL: University of Chicago Press.

Laumann, E. O., & Gagnon, J. H. (1995). A sociological perspective on sexual action. In R. G. Parker & J. H. Gagnon (Eds.), *Conceiving sexuality: Approaches to sex research in a postmodern world.* New York, NY: Routledge.

Laumann, E. O., Gagnon, J. H., Michael, R. T., & Michaels, S. (1994). *The social organization of sexuality.* Chicago, IL: University of Chicago Press.

Laurence, J. R., & Perry, C. (1988). *Hypnosis, will, and memory: A psycho-legal history.* New York, NY: Guilford Press.

Lavie, P. (1976). Ultradian rhythms in the perception of two apparent motions. *Chronobiologia, 3*, 21–218.

Lavie, P. (2001). Sleep-wake as a biological rhythm. *Annual Review of Psychology, 52*, 277–303.

Lazarus, R. S. (2000a, Spring). Reason and our emotions: A hard sell. *The General Psychologist, 35*, 16–20.

Lazarus, R. S. (2000b). Toward better research on stress and coping. *American Psychologist, 55*, 665–673.

Lazarus, R. S., & Folkman, S. (1984). *Stress, appraisal, and coping.* New York, NY: Springer.

LeBow, M. D. (1988). Attitudes, perceptions, and practices of Canadian school children towards obesity. *Journal of Obesity and Weight Regulation, 7*(1), 43–55.

LeBow, M. D., Ness, D., Makarenko, P., & Lam, T. (1999). Attitudes, perceptions, and practices of Canadian teenagers towards obesity. *Journal of Obesity and Weight Regulation, 8*, 53–65.

LeDoux, J. E. (1996). *The emotional brain.* New York, NY: Simon & Schuster.

Lee, S. J., & McEwen, B. S. (2001). Neurotrophic and neuroprotective actions of estrogens and their therapeutic implications. *Annual Review of Pharmacology & Pharmacological Toxicology, 41*, 569–591.

Lefton, L. A., Boyes, M., & Ogden, N. (2000). *Psychology* (Canadian ed.). Needham Heights, MA: Allyn & Bacon, Inc.

Leib, R. (2008). MMPI-2 family problems scales in child-custody litigants. *Dissertation Abstracts International,* Section B: The Sciences and Engineering, 68(7-B), 4879.

Leibenluft, E., & Rich, B. A. (2008). Pediatric bipolar disorder. *Annual Review of Clinical Psychology, 4*, 163–187.

Leichsenring, F., & Rabung, S. (2008, October 1). Effectiveness of long-term psychodynamic therapy: A meta-analysis. *Journal of the American Medical Association, 300*, 1551–1565.

Leinbach, M. D., Hort, B. E., & Fagot, B. I. (1997). Bears are for boys: Metaphorical associations in young children's gender stereotypes. *Cognitive Development, 12*, 107–130.

Leo, R. A. (2008). *Police interrogation and American justice.* Cambridge, MA: Harvard University Press.

Leonard, K. M. (2008). A cross-cultural investigation of temporal orientation in work organizations: A differentiation matching approach. *International Journal of Intercultural Relations, 32*, 479–492.

Lepore, S. J., Ragan, J. D., & Jones, S. (2000). Talking facilitates cognitive-emotional processes of adaptation to an acute stressor. *Journal of Personality and Social Psychology, 78*, 499–508.

Lepowsky, M. (1994). *Fruit of the motherland: Gender in an egalitarian society.* New York, NY: Columbia University Press.

Lepper, M. R., Greene, D., & Nisbett, R. E. (1973). Undermining children's intrinsic interest with extrinsic rewards. *Journal of Personality and Social Psychology, 28*, 129–137.

Leproult, R., Copinschi, G., Buxton, O., & Van Cauter, E. (1997). Sleep loss results in an elevation of cortisol levels the next evening. *Sleep, 20*, 865–870.

Leproult, R., Van Reeth, O., Byrne, M. M., et al. (1997). Sleepiness, performance, and neuroendocrine function during sleep deprivation: Effects of exposure to bright light or exercise. *Journal of Biological Rhythms, 12*, 245–258.

Lerner, M. J. (1980). *The belief in a just world: A fundamental delusion.* New York, NY: Plenum.

Lester, B. M., LaGasse, L. L., & Seifer, R. (1998, October 23). Cocaine exposure and children: The meaning of subtle effects. *Science, 282*, 633–634.

LeVay, S. (1991). A difference in hypothalamic structure between heterosexual and homosexual men. *Science, 253*, 1034–1037.

Levenson, R. W. (1992). Autonomic nervous system differences among emotions. *Psychological Science, 3*, 23–27.

Levenson, R. W., Ekman, P., & Friesen, W. V. (1990). Voluntary facial action generates emotion-specific autonomic nervous system activity. *Psychophysiology, 27*, 363–384.

Levenson, R. W., & Miller, B. L. (2007). Loss of cells—loss of self. *Current Directions in Psychological Science, 16*, 289–294.

Levin, D. T. (2000). Race as a visual feature: Using visual search and perceptual discrimination tasks to understand face categories and the cross-race recognition deficit. *Journal of Experimental Psychology: General, 129,* 559–574.

Levine, J. A., Eberhardt, N. L., & Jensen, M. D. (1999, January 8). Role of nonexercise activity thermogenesis in resistance to fat gain in humans. *Science, 283,* 212–214.

Levine, J., & Suzuki, D. (1993). *The secret of life: Redesigning the living world.* Boston, MA: WGBH Educational Foundation.

Levine, J. (2002). *Harmful to minors.* Minneapolis: University of Minnesota Press.

LeVine, R. A., & Norman, K. (2008). Attachment in anthropological perspective. In R. A. LeVine & R. S. New (Eds.), *Anthropology and child development: A cross-cultural reader.* Malden, MA: Blackwell.

Levine, R. V. (2003, May–June). The kindness of strangers. *American Scientist, 91,* 227–233.

Levine, R. V., Norenzayan, A., & Philbrick, K. (2001). Cross-cultural differences in helping strangers. *Journal of Cross-Cultural Psychology, 32,* 543–560.

Levy, B. (1996). Improving memory in old age through implicit self-stereotyping. *Journal of Personality and Social Psychology, 71,* 1092–1107.

Levy, D. A. (1997). *Tools of critical thinking: Metathoughts for psychology.* Boston, MA: Allyn & Bacon.

Levy, J., Trevarthen, C., & Sperry, R. W. (1972). Perception of bilateral chimeric figures following hemispheric deconnection. *Brain, 95,* 61–78.

Levy, R. I. (1984). The emotions in comparative perspective. In K. R. Scherer & P. Ekman (Eds.), *Approaches to emotion.* Hillsdale, NJ: Erlbaum.

Lewin, K. (1948). *Resolving social conflicts.* New York, NY: Harper.

Lewis, D. O. (1992). From abuse to violence: Psychophysiological consequences of maltreatment. *Journal of the American Academy of Child and Adolescent Psychiatry, 31,* 383–391.

Lewontin, R. C. (1970). Race and intelligence. *Bulletin of the Atomic Scientists, 26*(3), 2–8.

Lewontin, R. C. (2001, March 5). *Genomania: A disorder of modern biology and medicine.* Invited address at the University of California, Los Angeles, CA.

Lewontin, R. C., Rose, S., & Kamin, L. J. (1984). *Not in our genes: Biology, ideology, and human nature.* New York, NY: Pantheon.

Lewy, A. J., Ahmed, S., Jackson, J. L., & Sack, R. L. (1992). Melatonin shifts human circadian rhythms according to a phase response curve. *Chronobiology International, 9,* 380–392.

Lewy, A. J., Lefler, B. J., Emens, J. S., & Bauer, V. K. (2006). The circadian basis of winter depression. *Proceedings of the National Academy of Sciences, 103,* 7414–7419.

Li, S.-C., Lindenberger, U., Hommel, B., et al. (2004). Transformations in the couplings among intellectual abilities and constituent cognitive processes across the life span. *Psychological Science, 15,* 155–163.

Lickona, T. (1983). *Raising good children.* New York, NY: Bantam.

Lieberman, J. A., Stroup, T. S., McEvoy, J. P., et al. (2005, September 22). Effectiveness of antipsychotic drugs in patients with chronic schizophrenia. *New England Journal of Medicine, 353,* 1209–1223.

Lieberman, M. (2000). Intuition: A social cognitive neuroscience approach. *Psychological Bulletin, 126,* 109–137.

Lien, M.-C., Ruthruff, E., & Johnston, J. C. (2006). Attentional limitations in doing two tasks at once: The search for exceptions. *Current Directions in Psychological Science, 16,* 89–93.

Liepert, J., Bauder, H., Miltner, W. H., et al. (2000). Treatment-induced cortical reorganization after stroke in humans. *Stroke, 31,* 1210–1216.

Lilienfeld, S. O., Wood, J. M., & Garb, H. N. (2000). The scientific status of projective techniques. *Psychological Science in the Public Interest, 1,* 27–66.

Lilienfeld, S. O. (1996, January/February). EMDR treatment: Less than meets the eye? *Skeptical Inquirer,* 25–31.

Lilienfeld, S. O. (2007). Psychological treatments that cause harm. *Perspectives on Psychological Science, 2,* 53–70.

Lilienfeld, S. O., Gershon, J., Duke, M., Marino, L., & De Waal, F. B. M. (1999). A preliminary investigation of the construct of psychopathic personality (psychopathy) in chimpanzees (*Pan troglodytes*). *Journal of Comparative Psychology, 113,* 365–375.

Lilienfeld, S. O., & Lohr, J. (2003). Dissociative identity disorder: Multiple personalities, multiple controversies. In S. O. Lilienfeld, S. J. Lynn, & J. M. Lohr (Eds.), *Science and pseudoscience in clinical psychology.* New York, NY: Guilford.

Lilienfeld, S. O., Lynn, S. J., Kirsch, I., et al. (1999). Dissociative identity disorder and the sociocognitive model: Recalling the lessons of the past. *Psychological Bulletin, 125,* 507–523.

Lilienfeld, S. O., Lynn, S. J., & Lohr, J. M. (Eds.). (2003). *Science and pseudoscience in clinical psychology.* New York, NY: Guilford.

Lin, J., Epel, E. S., & Blackburn, E. H. (2009). Telomeres, telomerase stress and aging. In G. G. Bernston & J. T. Cacioppo (Eds.), *Handbook of Neuroscience for the Behavioral Sciences.* New York, NY: Wiley.

Lin, K.-M., Poland, R. E., & Chien, C. P. (1990). Ethnicity and psychopharmacology: Recent findings and future research directions. In E. Sorel (Ed.), *Family, culture, and psychobiology.* New York, NY: Legas.

Lin, L., Hungs, M., & Mignot, E. (2001). Narcolepsy and the HLA region. *Journal of Neuroimmunology, 117,* 9–20.

Linday, L. A. (1994). Maternal reports of pregnancy, genital, and related fantasies in preschool and kindergarten children. *Journal of the American Academy of Child and Adolescent Psychiatry, 33,* 416–423.

Lindsay, D. S., Hagen, L., Read, J. D., et al. (2004). True photographs and false memories. *Psychological Science, 15,* 149–154.

Lindsay, D. S., & Read, J. D. (1994). Psychotherapy and memories of childhood sexual abuse: A cognitive perspective. *Applied Cognitive Psychology, 8,* 281–338.

Lindquist, K. A., & Barrett, L. F. (2008). Constructing emotion. *Psychological Science, 19,* 898–903.

Linehan, M., M. (1993). *Cognitive-behavioral treatment of borderline personality disorder.* New York, NY: Guilford Press.

Linton, M. (1978). Real-world memory after six years: An in vivo study of very long-term memory. In M. M. Gruneberg, P. E. Morris, & R. N. Sykes (Eds.), *Practical aspects of memory.* London, England: Academic Press.

Linton, S. (1998). *Claiming disability: Knowledge and identity.* New York, NY: New York University Press.

Linton, S. (2006). *My body politic.* Ann Arbor: University of Michigan Press.

Linville, P. W., Fischer, G. W., & Fischhoff, B. (1992). AIDS risk perceptions and decision biases. In J. B. Pryor & G. D. Reeder (Eds.), *The social psychology of HIV infection*. Hillsdale, NJ: Erlbaum.

Lipps, J. H. (2004, January/February). Judging authority. *Skeptical Inquirer*, 35–37.

Lissner, L., Odell, P. M., D'Agostino, R. B., et al. (1991, June 27). Variability of body weight and health outcomes in the Framingham population. *New England Journal of Medicine, 324*, 1839–1844.

Lloyd-Richardson, E. E., Bailey, S., Fava, J. L., Wing, R., Tobacco Etiology Research Network. (TERN). (2009). A prospective study of weight gain during the college freshman and sophomore years. *Preventive Medicine, 48*, 256–261.

LoBue, V., & DeLoache, J. S. (2008). Detecting the snake in the grass. *Psychological Science, 19*, 284–289.

Locke, E. A., & Latham, G. P. (2002). Building a practically useful theory of goal setting and task motivation. *American Psychologist, 57*, 705–717.

Locke, E. A., & Latham, G. P. (2006). New directions in goal-setting theory. *Current Directions in Psychological Science, 15*, 265–268.

Locke, E. A., Shaw, K., Saari, L., & Latham, G. (1981). Goal-setting and task performance: 1969–1980. *Psychological Bulletin, 90*, 125–152.

Loehlin, J. C., Horn, J. M., & Willerman, L. (1996). Heredity, environment, and IQ in the Texas adoption study. In R. J. Sternberg & E. Grigorenko (Eds.), *Intelligence: Heredity and environment*. New York, NY: Cambridge University Press.

Loftus, E. F. (1996). Memory distortion and false memory creation. *Bulletin of the American Academy of Psychiatry and the Law, 24*, 281–295.

Loftus, E. F., & Greene, E. (1980). Warning: Even memory for faces may be contagious. *Law and Human Behavior, 4*, 323–334.

Loftus, E. F., Miller, D. G., & Burns, H. J. (1978). Semantic integration of verbal information into a visual memory. *Journal of Experimental Psychology: Human Learning and Memory, 4*, 19–31.

Loftus, E. F., & Palmer, J. C. (1974). Reconstruction of automobile destruction: An example of the interaction between language and memory. *Journal of Verbal Learning and Verbal Behavior, 13*, 585–589.

Loftus, E. F., & Pickrell, J. E. (1995). The formation of false memories. *Psychiatric Annals, 25*, 720–725.

Loftus, E. F., & Zanni, G. (1975). Eyewitness testimony: The influence of the wording of a question. *Bulletin of the Psychonomic Society, 5*, 86–88.

Lohr, J. M., Montgomery, R. W., Lilienfeld, S. O., & Tolin, D. F. (1999). Pseudoscience and the commercial promotion of trauma treatments. In R. Gist & B. Lubin (Eds.), *Response to disaster: Psychosocial, community, and ecological approaches*. Philadelphia, PA: Brunner/Mazel (Taylor & Francis).

Lohr, J. M., Tolin, D. F., & Lilienfeld, S. O. (1998). Efficacy of eye movement desensitization and reprocessing: Implications for behavior therapy. *Behavior Therapy, 29*, 123–156.

Lonner, W. J. (1995). Culture and human diversity. In E. Trickett, R. Watts, & D. Birman (Eds.), *Human diversity: Perspectives on people in context*. San Francisco, CA: Jossey-Bass.

Lonner, W. J., Malpass, R. S. (Eds.). (1994). *Psychology and culture*. Needham Heights, MA: Allyn & Bacon.

Lonsdorf, T. B., Weike, A. I., Nikamo, P., et al. (2009). Genetic gating of human fear learning and extinction: Possible implications for gene-environment interaction in anxiety disorder. *Psychological Science, 20*, 198–206.

Lopes, A. C., de Mathis, M. E., Canteras, M. M., et al. (2004). Update on neurosurgical treatment for obsessive compulsive disorder [original article in Portuguese]. *Rev bras Psiquiatr, 26*, 62–66.

López, S. R. (1995). Testing ethnic minority children. In B. B. Wolman (Ed.), *The encyclopedia of psychology, psychiatry, and psychoanalysis*. New York, NY: Holt.

Lorber, M. F. (2004). Psychophysiology of aggression, psychopathy, and conduct problems: A meta-analysis. *Psychological Bulletin, 130*, 531–552.

Löw, A., Lang, P. J., Smith, J. C., & Bradley, M. M. (2008). Both predator and prey: Emotional arousal in threat and reward. *Psychological Science, 19*, 865–873.

Lozano, A. M., Mayberg, H. S., Giacobbe, P., et al. (2008). Subcallosal cingulate gyrus deep brain stimulation for treatment-resistant depression. *Biological Psychiatry, 64*, 461–467.

Lubinski, D. (2004). Introduction to the special section on cognitive abilities: 100 years after Spearman's (1904) "'General intelligence,' objectively determined and measured." *Journal of Personality and Social Psychology, 86*, 96–111.

Lucas, T. H., McKhann, G. M., & Ojemann, G. (2004). Functional separation of languages in the bilingual brain: A comparison of electrical stimulation language mapping in 25 bilingual patients and 177 monolingual control patients. *Journal of Neurosurgery, 101*, 449–457.

Lucchina, L. A., Curtis, O. F., Putnam, P., et al. (1998). Psychophysical measurement of 6-n-propylthiouracil (PROP) taste perception. *Annals of the New York Academy of Sciences, 855*, 816–819.

Lucio, G. M. E., Palacios, H., Duran, C., Butcher, J. N. (1999). MMPI-2 with Mexican psychiatric inpatients: Basic and content scales. *Journal of Clinical Psychology, 55*, 1541–1552.

Luders, E., Narr, K. L., Thompson, P. M., et al. (2004). Gender differences in cortical complexity. *Nature Neuroscience, 7*, 799–800.

Luengo, M. A., Carrillo-de-la-Peña, M. T., Otero, J. M., & Romero, E. (1994). A short-term longitudinal study of impulsivity and antisocial behavior. *Journal of Personality and Social Psychology, 66*, 542–548.

Lugaresi, E., Medori, R., Montagna, P., et al. (1986, October 16). Fatal familial insomnia and dysautonomia with selective degeneration of thalamic nuclei. *New England Journal of Medicine, 315*, 997–1003.

Luhrmann, T. M. (2000). *Of two minds: The growing disorder in American psychiatry*. New York, NY: Knopf.

Luria, A. R. (1968). *The mind of a mnemonist* (L. Soltaroff, Trans.). New York, NY: Basic Books.

Luria, A. R. (1980). *Higher cortical functions in man* (2nd Rev. ed.). New York, NY: Basic Books.

Lutz, C. (1988). *Unnatural emotions*. Chicago, IL: University of Chicago Press.

Lykken, D. T. (1995). *The antisocial personalities*. Hillsdale, NJ: Erlbaum.

Lykken, D. T. (1998). *A tremor in the blood: Uses and abuses of the lie detector.* New York, NY: Plenum Press.

Lykken, D. T., & Tellegen, A. (1996). Happiness is a stochastic phenomenon. *Psychological Science, 7*, 186–189.

Lyndon, A. E., White, J. W., Kadlec, K. M. (2007). Manipulation and force as sexual coercion tactics: Conceptual and empirical differences. *Aggressive Behavior, 33*, 291–303.

Lynn, S. J., Rhue, J. W., & Weekes, J. R. (1990). Hypnotic involuntariness: A social cognitive analysis. *Psychological Review, 97*, 69–184.

Lytton, H., & Romney, D. M. (1991). Parents' differential socialization of boys and girls: A meta-analysis. *Psychological Bulletin, 109*, 267–296.

Maas, J. B. (1998). *Power sleep.* New York, NY: Villard.

Maass, A., Cadinu, M., Guarnieri, G., & Grasselli, A. (2003). Sexual harassment under social identity threat: The computer harassment paradigm. *Journal of Personality and Social Psychology, 85*, 853–870.

MacArthur Foundation Research Network on Successful Midlife Development. (1999). Report of latest findings. (Orville G. Brim, director, 2145 14th Avenue, Vero Beach, FL 32960.)

Maccoby, E. E. (1998). *The two sexes: Growing up apart, coming together.* Cambridge, MA: Belknap Press/Harvard University Press.

Maccoby, E. E. (2002). Gender and group process: A developmental perspective. *Current Directions in Psychological Science, 11*, 54–58.

MacDonald, S. M., Reeder, B. A., Chen, Y., Despres, J. P., & the Canadian Heart Health Surveys Research Group. (1997). Obesity in Canada: A descriptive analysis. *Canadian Medical Association Journal, 157*(Supplement 1), S3–S9.

Mack, A. (2003). Inattentional blindness: Looking without seeing. *Current Directions in Psychological Science, 12*, 180–184.

MacLean, P. (1993). Cerebral evolution of emotion. In M. Lewis & J. M. Haviland (Eds.), *Handbook of emotions.* New York, NY: Guilford Press.

Macleod, J., Oakes, R., Copello, A., et al. (2004). Psychological and social sequelae of cannabis and other illicit drug use by young people: A systematic review of longitudinal, general population studies. *The Lancet, 363*, 1568–1569.

Macrae, C. N., & Bodenhausen, G. V. (2000). Social cognition: Thinking categorically about others. *Annual Review of Psychology, 51*, 93–120.

Maddux, J. E. (Ed.). (1995). *Self-efficacy, adaptation, and adjustment: Theory, research, and application.* New York, NY: Plenum.

Maddux, J. E., & Mundell, C. E. (1997). Disorders of personality. In V. Derlega, B. Winstead, & W. Jones (Eds.), *Personality: Contemporary theory and research* (2nd ed.). Chicago, IL: Nelson-Hall.

Madsen, K. M., Hviid, A., Vestergaard, M., et al. (2002). A population-based study of measles, mumps, and rubella vaccination and autism. *New England Journal of Medicine, 347*, 1477–1482.

Maguire, E. A., Gadian, D. G., Johnsrude, I. S., et al. (2000). Navigation-related structural change in the hippocampi of taxi drivers. *Proceedings of the National Academy of Sciences, 97*, 4398–4403.

Mai, F. M. (1995). Psychiatrists' attitudes to multiple personality disorder: A questionnaire study. *Canadian Journal of Psychiatry, 40*(3), 154–157.

Maki, P. M., & Resnick, S. M. (2000). Longitudinal effects of estrogen replacement therapy on PET cerebral blood flow and cognition. *Neurobiology of Aging, 21*, 373–383.

Malamuth, N. M., Linz, D., Heavey, C. L., et al. (1995). Using the confluence model of sexual aggression to predict men's conflict with women: A 10-year follow-up study. *Journal of Personality and Social Psychology, 69*, 353–369.

Malaspina, D. (2001). Paternal factors and schizophrenia risk: De novo mutations and imprinting. *Schizophrenia Bulletin, 27*, 379–393.

Mallinckrodt, B., Porter, M. J., & Kivlighan, D. M. (2005). Client attachment to therapist, depth of in-session exploration, and object relations in brief psychotherapy. *Psychotherapy: Theory, Research, Practice, Training, 42*, 85–100.

Manning, C. A., Hall, J. L., & Gold, P. E. (1990). Glucose effects on memory and other neuropsychological tests in elderly humans. *Psychological Science, 1*, 307–311.

Maquet, P., Laereys, S., Peigneux, P., et al. (2000). Experience-dependent changes in cerebral activation during human REM sleep. *Nature Neuroscience, 8*, 831–836.

Marcus, G. (2004). *The birth of the mind: How a tiny number of genes creates the complexities of human thought.* New York, NY: Basic Books.

Marcus, G. F., Pinker, S., Ullman, M., et al. (1992). Overregularization in language acquisition. *Monographs of the Society for Research in Child Development, 57*(Serial No. 228), 1–182.

Marcus, G. F., Vijayan, S., Rao, S. B., & Vishton, P. M. (1999). Rule learning by seven-month-old infants. *Science, 283*, 77–80.

Marcus-Newhall, A., Pedersen, W. C., Carlson, M., & Miller, N. (2000). Displaced aggression is alive and well: A meta-analytic review. *Journal of Personality and Social Psychology, 78*, 670–689.

Margolin, G., & Gordis, E. B. (2004). Children's exposure to violence in the family and community. *Current Directions in Psychological Science, 13*, 152–155.

Markowitz, J. S., Donovan, J. L., DeVane, C. L., et al. (2003, September 17). Effect of St John's wort on drug metabolism by induction of cytochrome P450 3A4 enzyme. *Journal of the American Medical Association, 290*, 1519–1520.

Markus, H. R., & Kitayama, S. (1991). Culture and the self: Implications for cognition, emotion, and motivation. *Psychological Review, 98*, 224–253.

Marlatt, G. A. (1996). Models of relapse and relapse prevention: A commentary. *Experimental and Clinical Psychopharmacology, 4*, 55–60.

Marlatt, G. A., Baer, J. S., Kivlahan, D. R., et al. (1998). Screening and brief intervention for high-risk college student drinkers. *Journal of Consulting and Clinical Psychology, 66*, 604–615.

Marlatt, G. A., & Rohsenow, D. J. (1980). Cognitive processes in alcohol use: Expectancy and the balanced placebo design. In N. K. Mello (Ed.), *Advances in substance abuse* (Vol. 1). Greenwich, CT: JAI Press.

Marsh, E. J., & Tversky, B. (2004). Spinning the stories of our lives. *Applied Cognitive Psychology, 18*, 491–503.

Martin, C. L., & Ruble, D. (2004). Children's search for gender cues. *Current Directions in Psychological Science, 13*, 67–70.

Martin, C. L., Ruble, D. N., & Szkrybalo, J. (2002). Cognitive theories of early gender development. *Psychological Bulletin, 128*, 903–933.

Martin, G., & Pear, J. (2007). *Behavior modification: What it is and how to do it* (8th ed.). New York, NY: Prentice Hall.

Martinez, G. M., Chandra, A., Abma, J. C., et al. (2006). *Fertility, contraception, and fatherhood: Data on men and women from Cycle 6 of the 2002 National Survey of Family Growth.* DHHS Publication No. (PHS) 2006-1978. Washington, DC: Centers for Disease Control.

Martino, G., & Marks, L. E. (2001). Synesthesia: Strong and weak. *Current Directions in Psychological Science, 10*, 61–69.

Maruta, T., Colligan R. C., Malinchoc, M., & Offord, K. P. (2000). Optimists vs. pessimists: Survival rate among medical patients over a 30-year period. *Mayo Clinic Proceedings, 75*, 140–143.

Masand, P. S. (2000). Side effects of antipsychotics in the elderly. *Journal of Clinical Psychiatry, 61*(Suppl. 8), 43–49.

Maslach, C., Schaufeli, W. B., & Leiter, M. P. (2001). Job burnout. *Annual Review of Psychology, 52*, 397–422.

Maslow, A. H. (1970). *Motivation and personality* (2nd ed.). New York, NY: Harper & Row.

Maslow, A. H. (1971). *The farther reaches of human nature.* New York, NY: Viking.

Mason, M. P. (2008). *Head cases: Stories of brain injury and its aftermath.* New York, NY: Farrar, Straus & Giroux.

Masten, A. S. (2001). Ordinary magic: Resilience processes in development. *American Psychologist, 56*, 227–238.

Masters, W. H., & Johnson, V. E. (1966). *Human sexual response.* Boston, MA: Little, Brown.

Masuda, T., & Nisbett, R. E. (2001). Attending holistically versus analytically: Comparing the context sensitivity of Japanese and Americans. *Journal of Personality and Social Psychology, 81*, 922–934.

Mather, M., Shafir, E., & Johnson, M. K. (2000). Misremembrance of options past: Source monitoring and choice. *Psychological Science, 11*, 132–138.

Matsumoto, D. (1996). *Culture and psychology.* Pacific Grove, CA: Brooks-Cole.

Matsumoto, D., & Yoo, S. H. (2006). Toward a new generation of cross-cultural research. *Perspectives on Psychological Science, 1*, 234–250.

Matthews, G., Zeidner, M., & Roberts, R. D. (2003). *Emotional intelligence: Science and myth.* Cambridge, MA: MIT Press/Bradford Books.

Maurer, D., Lewis, T. L., Brent, H. P., & Levin, A. V. (1999). Rapid improvement in the acuity of infants after visual input. *Science, 286*, 108–110.

Mauser, G. (1995). Do Canadians use firearms in self-protection? *Canadian Journal of Criminology, 37*(4), 556–561.

Mauser, G. A., & Buckner, H. T. (1997). Canadian attitudes toward gun control: The real story. A Mackenzie Institute Occasional Paper, The Mackenzie Institute, Toronto, Canada.

Maviel, T., Durkin, T. P., Menzaghi, F., & Bontempi, B. (2004). Sites of neocortical reorganization critical for remote spatial memory. *Science, 305*, 96–99.

Max, M., Shanker, Y. G., Huang, L., et al. (2001). Tas1r3, encoding a new candidate taste receptor, is allelic to the sweet responsiveness locus Sac. *Nature Genetics, 28*, 58–63.

Mayer, J. (2009). *The dark side: The inside story of how the war on terror turned into a war on American ideals* (reprint edition). New York, NY: Anchor.

Mayer, J. D., & Salovey, P. (1997). What is emotional intelligence? In P. Salovey & D. Sluyter (Eds.), *Emotional development and emotional intelligence: Implications for educators.* New York, NY: Basic Books.

Mayou, R. A., Ehlers, A., & Hobbs, M. (2000). Psychological debriefing for road traffic accident victims. *British Journal of Psychiatry, 176*, 589–593.

Mazza, J. J., & Reynolds, W. M. (1999). Exposure to violence in young inner-city adolescents: Relationships with suicidal ideation, depression, and PTSD symptomatology. *Journal of Abnormal Child Psychology, 27*, 203–213.

Mazzoni, G. A., Loftus, E. F., & Kirsch, I. (2001). Changing beliefs about implausible autobiographical events: A little plausibility goes a long way. *Journal of Experimental Psychology: Applied, 7*, 51–59.

Mazzoni, G. A., Loftus, E. F., Seitz, A., & Lynn, S. J. (1999). Changing beliefs and memories through dream interpretation. *Applied Cognitive Psychology, 13*, 125–144.

McAdams, D. P. (2006). *The redemptive self: Stories Americans live by.* New York, NY: Oxford University Press.

McAdams, D. P. (2008). Personal narratives and the life story. In O. P. John, R. W. Robbins, & L. A. Pervin (Eds.), *Handbook of personality: Theory and research* (3rd ed.). New York, NY: Guilford.

McAdams, D. P., & Pals, J. L. (2006). A new Big Five: Fundamental principles for an integrative science of personality. *American Psychologist, 61*, 204–217.

McClearn, G. E., Johanson, B., Berg, S., et al. (1997). Substantial genetic influence on cognitive abilities in twins 80 or more years old. *Science, 176*, 1560–1563.

McClelland, D. C. (1961). *The achieving society.* New York, NY: Free Press.

McClelland, D. C., Atkinson, J. W., Clark, R. A., & Lowell, E. L. (1953). *The achievement motive.* New York, NY: Appleton-Century-Crofts.

McClelland, J. L. (1994). The organization of memory: A parallel distributed processing perspective. *Revue Neurologique, 150*, 570–579.

McCord, J. (1989). *Another time, another drug.* Paper presented at conference on Vulnerability to the Transition from Drug Use to Abuse and Dependence, Rockville, MD.

McCrae, R. R. (1987). Creativity, divergent thinking, and openness to experience. *Journal of Personality and Social Psychology, 52*, 1258–1265.

McCrae, R. R., & Costa P. T. (1988). Do parental influences matter? A reply to Halverson. *Journal of Personality, 56*, 445–449.

McCrae, R. R., & Costa, P. T. (2008). The five-factor theory of personality. In O. P. John, R. W. Robbins, & L. A. Pervin (Eds.), *Handbook of personality: Theory and research* (3rd ed.). New York, NY: Guilford.

McCrae, R. R., Terracciano, A., & members of the Personality Profiles of Cultures Project. (2005). Universal features of personality traits from the observer's perspective: Data from 50 cultures. *Journal of Personality and Social Psychology, 88*, 547–561.

McDaniel, M. A., Howard, D. C., & Einstein, G. O. (2009). The Read-Recite-Review study strategy: Effective and portable. *Psychological Science, 20*, 516–522.

McDaniel, S. H., Lusterman, D.-D., & Philpot, C. L. (Eds.). (2001). *Casebook for integrating family therapy: An ecosystemic approach.* Washington, DC: American Psychological Association.

McDonough, L., & Mandler, J. M. (1994). Very long-term recall in infancy. *Memory, 2*, 339–352.

McElroy, S. L., & Keck, P. E., Jr. (2000). Pharmacologic agents for the treatment of acute bipolar mania. *Biological Psychiatry, 48*, 539–557.

McEwen, B. S. (1998). Protective and damaging effects of stress mediators. *New England Journal of Medicine, 338*, 171–179.

McEwen, B. S. (2000). Allostasis and allostatic load: Implications for neuropsychopharmacology. *Neuropsychopharmacology, 22*, 108–124.

McEwen, B. S. (2007). Physiology and neurobiology of stress and adaptation: Central role of the brain. *Physiological Review, 87*, 873–904.

McFadden, D. (2008). What do sex, twins, spotted hyenas, ADHD, and sexual orientation have in common? *Perspectives on Psychological Science, 3*, 309–322.

McFarland, C., & Alvaro, C. (2000). The impact of motivation on temporal comparisons: Coping with traumatic events by perceiving personal growth. *Journal of Personality and Social Psychology, 79*, 327–343.

McGaugh, J. L. (1990). Significance and remembrance: The role of neuromodulatory systems. *Psychological Science, 1*, 15–25.

McGlashan, T. H., & Hoffman, R. E. (2000). Schizophrenia as a disorder of developmentally reduced synaptic connectivity. *Archives of General Psychiatry, 57*, 637–648.

McGoldrick, M. (2005). Irish families. In M. McGoldrick, J. Giordano, & N. Garcia-Preto (Eds.), *Ethnicity and family therapy* (3rd ed.). New York, NY: Guilford.

McGoldrick, M., Gerson, R., & Shellenberger, S. (1999). *Genograms: Assessment and intervention* (2nd ed.). New York, NY: W. W. Norton.

McGregor, I., & Holmes, J. G. (1999). How storytelling shapes memory and impressions of relationship events over time. *Journal of Personality and Social Psychology, 76*, 403–419.

McGue, M. (1999). The behavioral genetics of alcoholism. *Current Directions in Psychological Science, 8*, 109–115.

McGue, M., & Lykken, D. T. (1992). Genetic influence on risk of divorce. *Psychological Science, 3*, 368–373.

McHugh, P. R. (2008). *Try to remember: Psychiatry's clash over meaning, memory, and mind*. New York, NY: Dana Press.

McHugh, P. R., Lief, H. I., Freyd, P. P., & Fetkewicz, J. M. (2004). From refusal to reconciliation: Family relationships after an accusation based on recovered memories. *Journal of Nervous and Mental Disease, 192*, 525–531.

McIntyre, L., Connor, S. K., & Warren, J. (2000). Child hunger in Canada: Results of the 1994 National Longitudinal Survey of Children and Youth. *Canadian Medical Association Journal, 163*(8), 961–965.

McKee, R. D., & Squire, L. R. (1992). Equivalent forgetting rates in long-term memory for diencephalic and medial temporal lobe amnesia. *Journal of Neuroscience, 12*, 3765–3772.

McKee, R. D., & Squire, L. R. (1993). On the development of declarative memory. *Journal of Experimental Psychology: Learning, Memory, and Cognition, 19*, 397–404.

McKemy, D. D., Neuhausser, W. M., & Julius, D. (2002). Identification of a cold receptor reveals a general role for TRP channels in thermosensation. *Nature, 416*, 52–58.

McKim, M. K., Cramer, K. M., Stuart, B., & O'Connor, D. L. (1999). Infant care decisions and attachment security: The Canadian Transition to Child Care Study. *Canadian Journal of Behavioural Science, 31*, 92–106.

McKinlay, J. B., McKinlay, S. M., & Brambilla, D. (1987). The relative contributions of endocrine changes and social circumstances to depression in mid-aged women. *Journal of Health and Social Behavior, 28*, 345–363.

McLoyd, V. C. (1998). Socioeconomic disadvantage and child development. *American Psychologist, 53*(2), 185–204.

McMullin, D., & White, J. W. (2006). Long-term effects of labeling a rape experience. *Psychology of Women Quarterly, 30*, 96–105.

McNally, R. J. (1994). *Panic disorder: A critical analysis*. New York, NY: Guilford.

McNally, R. J. (1998). Panic attacks. In *Encyclopedia of mental health* (Vol. 3). New York, NY: Academic Press.

McNally, R. J. (2003). *Remembering trauma*. Cambridge, MA: Harvard University Press.

McNally, R. J., Bryant, R. A., & Ehlers, A. (2003). Does early psychological intervention promote recovery from posttraumatic stress? *Psychological Science in the Public Interest, 4*, 45–79.

McNeill, D. (1966). Developmental psycholinguistics. In F. L. Smith & G. A. Miller (Eds.), *The genesis of language: A psycholinguistic approach*. Cambridge, MA: MIT Press.

Mealey, L. (1996). Evolutionary psychology: The search for evolved mental mechanisms underlying complex human behavior. In J. P. Hurd (Ed.), *Investigating the biological foundations of human morality* (Vol. 37). Lewiston, NY: Edwin Mellen Press.

Mealey, L. (2000). *Sex differences: Developmental and evolutionary strategies*. San Diego, CA: Academic Press.

Medawar, P. B. (1979). *Advice to a young scientist*. New York, NY: Harper & Row.

Mednick, S. C., Nakayama, K., Cantero, J. L., et al. (2002). The restorative effect of naps on perceptual deterioration. *Nature Neuroscience, 5*, 677–681.

Mednick, S. A. (1962). The associative basis of the creative process. *Psychological Review, 69*, 220–232.

Mednick, S. A., Huttunen, M. O., & Machón, R. (1994). Prenatal influenza infections and adult schizophrenia. *Schizophrenia Bulletin, 20*, 263–267.

Medvec, V. H., Madey, S. F., & Gilovich, T. (1995). When less is more: Counterfactual thinking and satisfaction among Olympic medalists. *Journal of Personality and Social Psychology, 69*, 603–610.

Meeus, W. H. J., & Raaijmakers, Q. A. W. (1995). Obedience in modern society: The Utrecht studies. In A. G. Miller, B. E. Collins, & D. E. Brief (Eds.), Perspectives on obedience to authority: The legacy of the Milgram experiments. *Journal of Social Issues, 51*(3), 155–175.

Mehl, M. R., Vazire, S., Ramírez-Esparza, N., & Pennebacker, J. W. (2007). Are women really more talkative than men? *Science, 317*, 82.

Meichenbaum, D. H., & Deffenbacher, J. L. (1988). Stress inoculation training. *Counselling Psychologist, 16*(1), 69–90.

Meindl, J. R., & Lerner, M. J. (1985). Exacerbation of extreme responses to an out-group. *Journal of Personality and Social Psychology, 47*, 71–84.

Meissner, C. A., & Brigham, J. C. (2001). Thirty years of investigating the own-race bias in memory for faces: A meta-analytic review. *Psychology, Public Policy, & Law, 7*, 3–35.

Meltzoff, A. N., & Gopnik, A. (1993). The role of imitation in understanding persons and developing a theory of mind. In S. Baron-Cohen, H. Tager-Flusberg, & D. Cohen (Eds.), *Understanding other minds*. New York, NY: Oxford University Press.

Melzack, R. (1992, April). Phantom limbs. *Scientific American, 266*, 120–126. [Reprinted in the special issue Mysteries of the Mind, 1997.]

Melzack, R. (1993). Pain: Past, present and future. *Canadian Journal of Experimental Psychology, 47*, 615–629.

Melzack, R., & Wall, P. D. (1965). Pain mechanisms: A new theory. *Science, 13*, 971–979.

Mendoza-Denton, R., & Page-Gould, E. (2008). Can cross-group friendships influence minority students' well-being at historically white universities? *Psychological Science, 19,* 933–939.

Mennella, J. A., Jagnow, C. P., & Beauchamp, G. K. (2001). Prenatal and postnatal flavor learning by human infants. *Pediatrics, 107,* E88.

Mercer, J. (2006). *Understanding attachment.* Westport, CT: Praeger.

Merikle, P. M., & Skanes, H. E. (1992). Subliminal self-help audiotapes: A search for placebo effects. *Journal of Applied Psychology, 77,* 772–776.

Merskey, H. (1992). The manufacture of personalities: The production of MPD. *British Journal of Psychiatry, 160,* 327–340.

Merskey, H. (1995). The manufacture of personalities: The production of multiple personality disorder. In L. M. Cohen, J. N. Berzoff, & M. R. Elin (Eds.), *Dissociative identity disorder: Theoretical and treatment controversies.* Northvale, NJ: Aronson.

Merton, R. K. (1948). The self-fulfilling prophecy. *Antioch Review, 8,* 193–210.

Mesquita, Batja, & Frijda, Nico H. (1992). Cultural variations in emotions: A review. *Psychological Bulletin, 112,* 179–204.

Meston, C. M., & Buss, D. M. (2007). Why humans have sex. *Archives of Sexual Behavior, 36,* 477–507.

Metcalfe, J. (2009). Metacognitive judgments and control of study. *Current Directions in Psychological Science, 18,* 159–163.

Meyer, G. J., Finn, S. E., Eyde, L. D., et al. (2001). Psychological testing and psychological assessment. *American Psychologist, 56,* 128–165.

Meyer-Bahlburg, H. F. L., Ehrhardt, A. A., Rosen, L. R., et al. (1995). Prenatal estrogens and the development of homosexual orientation. *Developmental Psychology, 31,* 12–21.

Mezulis, A. H., Abramson, L. Y., Hyde, J. S., & Hankin, B. L. (2004). Is there a positivity bias in attributions? *Psychological Bulletin, 130,* 711–747.

Mickelson, K. D., Kessler, R. C., & Shaver, P. R. (1997). Adult attachment in a nationally representative sample. *Journal of Personality and Social Psychology, 73,* 1092–1106.

Mieda, M., Willie, J. T., Hara, J., et al. (2004). Orexin peptides prevent cataplexy and improve wakefulness in an orexin neuron-ablated model of narcolepsy in mice. *Proceedings of the National Academy of Science, 101,* 4649–4654.

Miklowitz, D. J. (2007). The role of the family in the course and treatment of bipolar disorder. *Current Directions in Psychological Science, 16,* 192–196.

Mikulincer, M., & Goodman, G. (Eds.). (2006). *Dynamics of romantic love: Attachment, caregiving, and sex.* New York, NY: Guilford.

Mikulincer, M., & Shaver, P. R. (2007). *Attachment in adulthood: Structure, dynamics, and change.* New York, NY: Guilford Press.

Mikulincer, M., Shaver, P. R., Gillath, O., & Nitzberg, R. E. (2005). Attachment, caregiving, and altruism: Boosting attachment security increases compassion and helping. *Journal of Personality and Social Psychology, 89,* 817–839.

Mikulincer, M., Shaver, P. R., & Horesh, N. (2006). Attachment bases of emotion regulation and posttraumatic adjustment. In D. K. Snyder, J. A. Simpson, & J. N. Hughes (Eds.), *Emotion regulation in couples and families: Pathways to dysfunction and health.* Washington, DC: American Psychological Association.

Milgram, S. (1963). Behavioral study of obedience. *Journal of Abnormal and Social Psychology, 67,* 371–378.

Milgram, S. (1974). *Obedience to authority: An experimental view.* New York, NY: Harper & Row.

Millar, J. K., Pickard, B. S., Mackie, S., et al. (2005, November 18). DISC1 and PDE4B are interacting genetic factors in schizophrenia that regulate cAMP signaling. *Science, 310,* 1187–1191.

Millar, W. J., & Stephens, T. (1993). Social status and health risks in Canadian adults: 1985 and 1991. *Health Report, 5,* 143–156.

Miller, G. (2000). *The mating mind: How sexual choice shaped the evolution of human nature.* New York, NY: Doubleday.

Miller, G. A. (1956). The magical number seven, plus or minus two: Some limits on our capacity for processing information. *Psychological Review, 63,* 81–97.

Miller, G. (2008, April 11). Tackling alcoholism with drugs. *Science, 320,* 168–170.

Miller, G. E., Chen, E., & Zhou, E. S. (2007). If it goes up, must it come down? Chronic stress and the hypothalamic-pituitary-adrenocortical axis in humans. *Psychological Bulletin, 133,* 25–45.

Miller, G. E., & Cohen, S. (2001). Psychological interventions and the immune system: A meta-analytic review and critique. *Health Psychology, 20,* 47–63.

Miller, I. J., & Reedy, F. E. (1990). Variations in human taste bud density and taste intensity perception. *Physiology and Behavior, 47,* 1213–1219.

Miller, J. G., Bersoff, D. M., & Harwood, R. L. (1990). Perceptions of social responsibilities in India and in the United States: Moral imperatives or personal decisions? *Journal of Personality and Social Psychology, 58,* 33–47.

Miller, W. R., & Rollnick, S. (2002). *Motivational interviewing: Preparing people for change* (2nd ed.). New York, NY: Guilford Press.

Miller-Jones, D. (1989). Culture and testing. *American Psychologist, 44,* 360–366.

Milner, B. (1970). Memory and the temporal regions of the brain. In K. H. Pribram & D. E. Broadbent (Eds.), *Biology of memory.* New York, NY: Academic Press.

Milner, J. S., & McCanne, T. R. (1991). Neuropsychological correlates of physical child abuse. In J. S. Milner (Ed.), *Neuropsychology of aggression.* Norwell, MA: Kluwer Academic.

Milton, J., & Wiseman, R. (1999). Does psi exist? Lack of replication of an anomalous process of information transfer. *Psychological Bulletin, 125,* 387–391.

Milton, J., & Wiseman, R. (2001). Does psi exist? Reply to Storm and Ertel (2001). *Psychological Bulletin, 127,* 434–438.

Mineka, S., & Zinbarg, R. (2006). A contemporary learning theory perspective on the etiology of anxiety disorders: It's not what you thought it was. *American Psychologist, 61,* 10–26.

Minuchin, S. (1984). *Family kaleidoscope.* Cambridge, MA: Harvard University Press.

Minzenberg, M. J., & Carter, C. S. (2008). Modafinil: A review of neurochemical actions and effects on cognition. *Neuropsychopharmacology, 33,* 1477–1502.

Mischel, W. (1973). Toward a cognitive social learning reconceptualization of personality. *Psychological Review, 80,* 252–253.

Mischel, W. (2009, May 24). *The new genetics and what it means for psychological science.* Introduction to the presidential symposium at the annual meeting of the Association for Psychological Science, San Francisco, CA.

Mischel, W., & Ayduk, O. (2004). Willpower in a cognitive-affective processing system: The dynamics of delay of gratification. In R. F. Baumeister & K. D. Vohs (Eds.), *Handbook of self-regulation: Research, theory, and applications.* New York, NY: Guilford Press.

Mischel, W., & Shoda, Y. (1995). A cognitive affective system theory of personality: Reconceptualizing situations, dispositions, dynamics, and invariance in personality structures. *Psychological Review, 102,* 246–268.

Mistry, J., & Rogoff, B. (1994). Remembering in cultural context. In W. J. Lonner & R. Malpass (Eds.), *Psychology and culture.* Needham Heights, MA: Allyn & Bacon.

Mitchell, D. B. (2006). Nonconscious priming after 17 years: Invulnerable implicit memory? *Psychological Science, 17,* 925–929.

Mitchell, K. J., & Johnson, M. K. (2009). Source monitoring 15 years later: What have we learned from fMRI about the neural mechanisms of source memory? *Psychological Bulletin, 135,* 638–677.

Mitte, K. (2005). Meta-analysis of cognitive-behavioral treatments for generalized anxiety disorder: A comparison with pharmacotherapy. *Psychological Bulletin, 131,* 785–795.

Mitte, K. (2008). Memory bias for threatening information in anxiety and anxiety disorders: A meta-analytic review. *Psychological Bulletin, 134,* 886–911.

Mitterer, H., & de Ruiter, J. P. (2008). Recalibrating color categories using world knowledge. *Psychological Science, 19,* 629–634.

Miyamoto, Y., Nisbett, R. E., & Masuda, T. (2006). Culture and the physical environment: Holistic versus analytic perceptual affordances. *Psychological Science, 17,* 113–119.

Modigliani, A., & Rochat, F. (1995). The role of interaction sequences and the timing of resistance in shaping obedience and defiance to authority. In A. G. Miller, B. E. Collins, & D. E. Brief (Eds.), Perspectives on obedience to authority: The legacy of the Milgram experiments. *Journal of Social Issues, 51*(3), 107–125.

Moffitt, Terrie E. (1993). Adolescence-limited and life-course-persistent antisocial behavior: A developmental taxonomy. *Psychological Review, 100,* 674–701.

Moffitt, T. E. (2005). The new look of behavioral genetics in developmental psychopathology: Gene–environment interplay in antisocial behaviors. *Psychological Bulletin, 131,* 533–554.

Moghaddam, F. M. (2005). The staircase to terrorism: A psychological exploration. *American Psychologist, 60,* 161–169.

Mohr, C., Armeli, S., Tennen, H., et al. (2001). Daily interpersonal experiences, context, and alcohol consumption: Crying in your beer and toasting good times. *Journal of Personality and Social Psychology, 80,* 489–500.

Moles, A., Kieffer, B., & D'Amato, F. (2004). Deficit in attachment behavior in mice lacking the μ-opioid receptor gene. *Science, 304,* 1983–1986.

Molnar-Szakacs, I., Iacoboni, M., Koski, L., & Mazziotta, J. C. (2005). Functional segregation with pars opercularis of the inferior frontal gyrus: Evidence from fMRI studies of imitation and action observation. *Cerebral Cortex, 15,* 986–994.

Monahan, J. L., Murphy, S. T., & Zajonc, R. B. (2000). Subliminal mere exposure: Specific, general, and diffuse effects. *Psychological Science, 11,* 462–466.

Moncrieff, J. (2001). Are antidepressants overrated? A review of methodological problems in antidepressant trials. *Journal of Nervous and Mental Disease, 189,* 288–295.

Moner, S. (1994). Smoking and pregnancy. In Health Canada, *The Canadian guide to clinical preventative health care.* Cat. no. H21-117-1994E. Ottawa: Ministry of Supply and Services Canada.

Montmayeur, J. P., Liberies, S. D., Matsunami, H., & Buck, L. B. (2001). A candidate taste receptor gene near a sweet taste locus. *Nature Neuroscience, 4,* 492–498.

Moore, R. Y. (1997). Circadian rhythms: Basic neurobiology and clinical applications. *Annual Review of Medicine, 48,* 253–266.

Moore, T. E. (1992, Spring). Subliminal perception: Facts and fallacies. *Skeptical Inquirer, 16,* 273–281.

Moore, T. E. (1995). Subliminal self-help auditory tapes: An empirical test of perceptual consequences. *Canadian Journal of Behavioural Science, 27,* 9–20.

Moore, T. E., & Pepler, D. J. (2006). Wounding words: Maternal verbal aggression and children's adjustment. *Journal of Family Violence, 21,* 89–93.

Morell, V. (2008, March). Minds of their own. *National Geographic, 213,* 36–61.

Morelli, G. A., Rogoff, B., Oppenheim, D., & Goldsmith, D. (1992). Cultural variation in infants' sleeping arrangements: Questions of independence. *Developmental Psychology, 28,* 604–613.

Moreno, C., Laje, G., Blanco, C., et al. (2007). National trends in the outpatient diagnosis and treatment of bipolar disorder in youth. *Archives of General Psychiatry, 64,* 1032–1039.

Morgan, C. A., Hazlett, G., Baranoski, M., et al. (2007). Accuracy of eyewitness identification is significantly associated with performance on a standardized test of face recognition. *International Journal of Law and Psychiatry, 30,* 213–223.

Morin, C. M., Vallières, A., Guay, B., et al. (2009). Cognitive behavioral therapy, singly and combined with medication, for persistent insomnia. *Journal of the American Medical Association, 301,* 2005–2015.

Morris, R. G., Garrud, P., Rawlins, J. N., & O'Keefe, J. (1982). Place navigation impaired in rats with hippocampal lesions. *Nature, 297* (5868), 681–683.

Morrison, T. G., & O'Connor, W. E. (1999). Psychometric properties of a scale measuring negative attitudes toward overweight individuals. *Journal of Social Psychology, 139,* 436–445.

Morton, L. L., Allen, J. D., & Williams, N. (1994). Hemisphericity and information processing North American native (Objiwa) and non-native adolescents. *International Journal of Neuroscience, 75*(3–4), 189–202.

Morton, T. A., Postmes, T., Haslam, S. A., & Hornsey, M. J. (2009). Theorizing gender in the face of social change: Is there anything essential about essentialism? *Journal of Personality and Social Psychology, 96,* 653–664.

Moscovitch, M., Winocur, G., & Behrmann, M. (1997). What is special about face recognition? Nineteen experiments on a person with visual object agnosia and dyslexia but normal face recognition. *Journal of Cognitive Neuroscience, 9,* 555–604.

Moskowitz, E. (2001). *In therapy we trust*. Baltimore, MD: Johns Hopkins University Press.

Moskowitz, J. T., Hult, J. R., Bussolari, C., & Acree, M. (2009). What works in coping with HIV? A meta-analysis with implications for coping with serious illness. *Psychological Bulletin, 135*, 121–141.

Mostert, M. P. (2001). Facilitated communication since 1995: A review of published studies. *Journal of Autism and Developmental Disorders, 31*, 287–313.

Moyer, C. A., Rounds, J., & Hannum, J. W. (2004). A meta-analysis of massage therapy research. *Psychological Bulletin, 130*, 3–18.

Mozell, M. M., Smith, B. P., Smith, P. E., et al. (1969). Nasal chemoreception in flavor identification. *Archives of Otolaryngology, 90*, 367–373.

Mroczek, D. K., & Spiro, A., III. (2005). Changes in life satisfaction during adulthood: Findings from the veterans affairs normative aging study. *Journal of Personality and Social Psychology, 88*, 189–202.

Mueller, C. M., & Dweck, C. S. (1998). Praise for intelligence can undermine children's motivation and performance. *Journal of Personality and Social Psychology, 75*, 33–52.

Mukamal, K. J., Conigrove, K. M, Mittleman, M. A., et al. (2003). Roles of drinking pattern and type of alcohol consumed in coronary heart disease in men. *New England Journal of Medicine, 348*, 109–118.

Müller, R.-A., Courchesne, E., & Allen, G. (1998). The cerebellum: So much more [letter.] *Science, 282*, 879–880.

Murphy, S. T., Monahan, J. L., & Zajonc, R. B. (1995). Additivity of nonconscious affect: Combined effects of priming and exposure. *Journal of Personality and Social Psychology, 69*, 589–602.

Murray, C. (2008). Real education: Four simple truths for bringing America's schools back to reality. New York, NY: Crown Forum.

Myers, D. G., & Scanzoni, L. D. (2005). *What God has joined together: The Christian case for gay marriage*. San Francisco, CA: HarperSanFrancisco.

Myrtek, M. (2007). Type A behavior and hostility as independent risk factors for coronary heart disease. In J. Jordan et al. (Eds.), *Contributions toward evidence-based psychocardiology: A systematic review of the literature*. Washington, DC: American Psychological Association.

Nachman, M. W., Hoekstra, H. E., & D'Agostino, S. L. (2003). The genetic basis of adaptive melanism in pocket mice. *Proceedings of the National Academy of Science, 100*, 5268–5273.

Nakaya, N., Tsubono, Y., Hosokawa, T., et al. (2003). Personality and the risk of cancer. *Journal of the National Cancer Institute, 95*, 799–805.

Nash, M. R. (1987). What, if anything, is regressed about hypnotic age regression? A review of the empirical literature. *Psychological Bulletin, 102*, 42–52.

Nash, M. R. (2001, July). The truth and the hype of hypnosis. *Scientific American, 285*, 46–49, 52–55.

Nash, M. R., & Barnier, A. J. (2007). *The Oxford handbook of hypnosis*. Oxford, England: Oxford University Press.

Nash, M. R., & Nadon, R. (1997). Hypnosis. In D. L. Faigman, D. Kaye, M. J. Saks, & J. Sanders (Eds.), *Modern scientific evidence: The law and science of expert testimony*. St. Paul, MN: West.

Nathan, D. (1994, Fall). Dividing to conquer? Women, men, and the making of multiple personality disorder. *Social Text, 40*, 77–114.

National Science Board. (2000). *Science & engineering indicators 2000*. Chapter 8: Science and technology: Attitudes and public understanding. Arlington, VA: National Science Foundation. [A reprint of the relevant section of this chapter can be found in the January/February 2001 issue of *Skeptical Inquirer*, pp. 12–15.]

Navarrete, C. D., Olsson, A., Ho, A. K., et al. (2009). Fear extinction to an out-group face: The role of target gender. *Psychological Science, 20*, 155–158.

Needleman, H. L., Riess, J. A., Tobin, M. J., et al. (1996). Bone lead levels and delinquent behavior. *Journal of the American Medical Association, 275*, 363–369.

Neher, A. (1996). Jung's theory of archetypes: A critique. *Journal of Humanistic Psychology, 36*, 61–91.

Neisser, U. (Ed.). (1998). *The rising curve: Long-term gains in IQ and related measures*. Washington, DC: American Psychological Association.

Neisser, U., & Harsch, N. (1992). Phantom flashbulbs: False recollections of hearing the news about *Challenger*. In E. Winograd & U. Neisser (Eds.), *Affect and accuracy in recall: Studies of "flashbulb memories."* New York, NY: Cambridge University Press.

Nelson, C. A., III, Zeanah, C. H., Fox, N. A., et al. (2007). Cognitive recovery in socially deprived young children: The Bucharest early intervention project. *Science, 318*, 1937–1940.

Nelson, G., Westhues, A., & MacLeod, J. (2003). A meta-analysis of longitudinal research on preschool prevention programs for children. *Prevention & Treatment, 6*(1), article 31. Retrieved from http://webarchive.nationalarchives.gov.uk/+/http://www.hm-treasury.gov.uk/d/cypreview2006_cphva7.pdf

Ness, J., Aronow, W. S., & Beck, G. (2006). Menopausal symptoms after cessation of hormone replacement therapy. *Maturitas, 53*, 356–361.

Nesse, R. M., & Ellsworth, P. C. (2009). Evolution, emotion, and emotional disorders. *American Psychologist, 64*, 129–139.

Newcombe, N. S., Drummey, A. B., Fox, N. A., et al. (2000). Remembering early childhood: How much, how, and why (or why not). *Current Directions in Psychological Science, 9*, 55–58.

Newland, M. C., & Rasmussen, E. B. (2003). Behavior in adulthood and during aging is affected by contaminant exposure in utero. *Current Directions in Psychological Science, 12*, 212–217.

Newman, L. S., & Baumeister, R. F. (1996). Toward an explanation of the UFO abduction phenomenon: Hypnotic elaboration, extraterrestrial sadomasochism, and spurious memories. *Psychological Inquiry, 7*, 99–126.

NICHD Early Child Care Research Network. (2006). Infant-mother attachment classification: Risk and protection in relation to changing maternal caregiving quality. *Developmental Psychology, 42*, 38–58.

Nichols, M. P., & Schwartz, R. C. (2008). *Family therapy: Concepts and methods* (8th ed.). Boston, MA: Allyn & Bacon.

Nickerson, R. S. (1998). Confirmation bias: A ubiquitous phenomenon in many guises. *Review of General Psychology, 2*, 175–220.

Nickerson, R. A., & Adams, M. J. (1979). Long-term memory for a common object. *Cognitive Psychology, 11*, 287–307.

Nisbett, R. E. (1993). Violence and U.S. regional culture. *American Psychologist, 48*, 441–449.

Nisbett, R. E. (2009). *Intelligence and how to get it: Why schools and culture count*. New York, NY: W. W. Norton.

Nisbett, R. E., & Ross, L. (1980). *Human inference: Strategies and shortcomings of social judgment*. Englewood Cliffs, NJ: Prentice-Hall.

Nolan, S. A., Flynn, C., & Garber, J. (2003). Prospective relations between rejection and depression in young adolescents. *Journal of Personality and Social Psychology, 85,* 745–755.

Nolen-Hoeksema, S. (2004). *Lost in thought: Rumination and depression.* Paper presented at the National Institute on the Teaching of Psychology, St. Petersburg, FL.

Nonaka, S., Hough, C. J., & Chuang, D.-M. (1998, March 3). Chronic lithium treatment robustly protects neurons in the central nervous system against excitotoxicity by inhibiting N-methyl-D-aspartate receptor-mediated calcium influx. *Proceedings of the National Academy of Sciences, 95,* 2642–2647.

Norcross, J. C., Kohout, J. L., & Wicherski, M. (2005). Graduate study in psychology: 1971 to 2004. *American Psychologist, 60,* 959–975.

Norman, D. A. (1988). *The psychology of everyday things.* New York, NY: Basic Books.

Nosek, B. A., Greenwald, A. G., & Banaji, M. R. (2007). The Implicit Association Test at 7: A methodological and conceptual review. In J. A. Bargh (Ed.), *Social psychology and the unconscious.* New York, NY: Psychology Press.

Nunez, N., Poole, D. A., & Memon, A. (2002). Psychology's two cultures revisited: Implications for the integration of science with practice. *Scientific Review of Mental Health Practice, 1.*

Nunn, J. A., Gregory, L. J., Brammer, M., et al. (2002). Functional magnetic resonance imaging of synesthesia: Activation of V4/V8 by spoken words. *Nature neuroscience, 5,* 371–375.

Nyberg, L., Habib, R., McIntosh, A. R., & Tulving, E. (2000). Reactivation of encoding-related brain activity during memory retrieval. *Proceedings of the National Academy of Sciences, 97,* 11120–11124.

Oaten, M., Stevenson, R. J., & Case, T. I. (2009). Disgust as a disease-avoidance mechanism. *Psychological Bulletin, 125,* 303–321.

Oatley, K., & Jenkins, J. M. (1996). *Understanding emotions.* Cambridge, MA: Blackwell.

Oatridge, A., Holdcroft, A., Saeed, N., et al. (2002). Change in brain size during and after pregnancy: Study in healthy women and women with preeclampsia. *American Journal of Neuroradiology, 23,* 19–26.

O'Connor, T. G., Rutter, M., Beckett, C., et al. (2000). English and Romanian Adoptees Study Team. The effects of global severe privation on cognitive competence: Extension and longitudinal follow-up. *Child Development, 71*(2), 376–390.

Offit, P. A. (2008). Autism's false prophets: Bad science, risky medicine, and the search for a cure. New York, NY: Columbia University Press.

Ofshe, R. J., & Watters, E. (1994). *Making monsters: False memory, psychotherapy, and sexual hysteria.* New York, NY: Scribners.

Ogden, J. A., & Corkin, S. (1991). Memories of H. M. In W. C. Abraham, M. C. Corballis, & K. G. White (Eds.), *Memory mechanisms: A tribute to G. V. Goddard.* Hillsdale, NJ: Erlbaum.

O'Hanlon, B. (1994, November/December). The third wave. *Family Therapy Networker,* 18–29.

Öhman, A., & Mineka, S. (2001). Fears, phobias, and preparedness: Toward an evolved module of fear and fear learning. *Psychological Review, 108,* 483–522.

Öhman, A., & Mineka, S. (2003). The malicious serpent: Snakes as a prototypical stimulus for an evolved module of fear. *Current Directions in Psychological Science, 12,* 5–9.

Olds, J. (1975). Mapping the mind onto the brain. In F. G. Worden, J. P. Swazy, & G. Adelman (Eds.), *The neurosciences: Paths of discovery.* Cambridge, MA: Colonial Press.

Olds, J., & Milner, P. (1954). Positive reinforcement produced by electrical stimulation of septal area and other regions of the rat brain. *Journal of Comparative and Physiological Psychology, 47,* 419–429.

Oliver, M. B., & Hyde, J. S. (1993). Gender differences in sexuality: A meta-analysis. *Psychological Bulletin, 114,* 29–51.

Olson, J. M., Vernon, P. A., Harris, J. A., & Jang, K. L. (2001). The heritability of attitudes: A study of twins. *Journal of Personality and Social Psychology, 80,* 845–850.

Olson, M. A. (2009). Measures of prejudice. In T. Nelson (Ed.), *The handbook of prejudice, sterotyping, and discrimination.* New York, NY: Psychology Press.

Olsson, A., & Phelps, E. (2004). Learned fear of "unseen" faces after Pavlovian, observational, and instructed fear. *Psychological Science, 15,* 822–828.

Olsson, A., Ebert, J., Banaji, M., & Phelps, E. A. (2005). The role of social groups in the persistence of learned fear. *Science, 309,* 785–787.

Olujic, M. B. (1998). Embodiment of terror: Gendered violence in peacetime and wartime in Croatia and Bosnia-Herzegovina. *Medical Anthropology Quarterly, 12,* 31–50.

Ophir, E., Nass, C., & Wagner, A. D. (2009). Cognitive control in media multitaskers. *Proceedings of the National Academy of Sciences.* doi:10.1073/pnas.0903620106

O'Rahilly, R., & Müller, F. (2001). *Human embryology and teratology.* New York, NY: Wiley.

Orbach, S. (2009). *Bodies.* London, England: Profile Books.

Orians, G. H., & Heerwagen, J. H. (1992). Evolved responses to landscapes. In J. Barkow, L. Cosmides, & J. Tooby (Eds.), *The adapted mind* (pp. 555–579). New York, NY: Oxford University Press.

Orr, P. H., Martin, B. D., Patterson, K., & Moffat, M. E. (1998). Prevalence of diabetes mellitus and obesity in the Keewatin District of the Canadian Arctic. *International Journal of Circumpolar Health, 57*(Supplement 1), 340–347.

Ó Scalaidhe, S. P., Wilson, F. A. W., & Goldman-Rakic, P. S. (1997). A real segregation of face-processing neurons in prefrontal cortex. *Science, 278,* 1135–1138.

O'Sullivan, L. F., & Allgeier, Elizabeth R. (1998). Feigning sexual desire: Consenting to unwanted sexual activity in heterosexual dating relationships. *Journal of Sex Research, 35,* 234–243.

O'Sullivan, L. F., Byers, E. S., & Finkelman, L. (1998). A comparison of male and female college students' experiences of sexual coercion. *Psychology of Women Quarterly, 22,* 177–195.

Oyserman, D., & Lee, S. W. S. (2008). Does culture influence what and how we think? Effects of priming individualism and collectivism. *Psychological Bulletin, 134,* 311–342.

Ozer, E. J., Best, S. R., Lipsey, T. L., & Weiss, D. S. (2003). Predictors of posttraumatic stress disorder and symptoms in adults: A meta-analysis. *Psychological Bulletin, 129,* 52–73.

Özgen, E. (2004). Language, learning, and color perception. *Current Directions in Psychological Science, 13,* 95–98.

Packer, D. J. (2009). Avoiding groupthink: Whereas weakly identified members remain silent, strongly identified members dissent about collective problems. *Psychological Science, 20,* 619–626.

Pagel, J. F. (2003). Non-dreamers. *Sleep Medicine, 4*, 235–241.

Panksepp, J. (1998). Attention deficit hyperactivity disorders, psycho-stimulants, and intolerance of childhood playfulness: A tragedy in the making? *Current Directions in Psychological Science, 7*, 91–98.

Panksepp, J., Herman, B. H., Vilberg, T., et al. (1980). Endogenous opioids and social behavior. *Neuroscience and Biobehavioral Reviews, 4*, 473–487.

Park, D., & Gutchess, A. (2006). The cognitive neuroscience of aging and culture. *Current Directions in Psychological Science, 15*, 105–108.

Park, R. L. (2000). *Voodoo science: The road from foolishness to fraud.* New York, NY: Oxford University Press.

Parker, E. S., Birnbaum, I. M., & Noble, E. P. (1976). Alcohol and memory: Storage and state dependency. *Journal of Verbal Learning and Verbal Behavior, 15*, 691–702.

Parker, E. S., Cahill, L., & McGaugh, J. L. (2006). A case of unusual autobiographical remembering. *Neurocase, 12*, 35–49.

Parlee, M. B. (1994). The social construction of premenstrual syndrome: A case study of scientific discourse as cultural contestation. In M. G. Winkler & L. B. Cole (Eds.), *The good body: Asceticism in contemporary culture.* New Haven, CT: Yale University Press.

Pascual-Leone, A., Amedi, A., Fregni, F., & Merabet, L. B. (2005). The plastic human brain cortex. *Annual Review of Neuroscience, 28*, 377–401.

Pastalkova, E., Itskov, V., Amarasingham, A., & Buzsáki, G. (2008, September 5). Internally generated cell assembly sequences in the rat hippocampus. *Science, 321*, 1322–1327.

Patterson, C. J. (1992). Children of lesbian and gay parents. *Child Development, 63*, 1025–1042.

Patterson, C. J. (2006). Children of lesbian and gay parents. *Current Directions in Psychological Science, 15*, 241–244.

Patterson, D. R., & Jensen, M. P. (2003). Hypnosis and clinical pain. *Psychological Bulletin, 129*, 495–521.

Patterson, F., & Linden, E. (1981). *The education of Koko.* New York, NY: Holt, Rinehart and Winston.

Paul, A. M. (2004). *The cult of personality.* New York, NY: The Free Press.

Paul, P. (2008). *Parenting, Inc.: How the billion-dollar baby business has changed the way we raise our children.* New York, NY: Henry Holt.

Paul, R. W. (1984, September). Critical thinking: Fundamental to education for a free society. *Educational Leadership*, 4–14.

Paulhus, D. L., & Landholt, M. A. (2000). Paragons of intelligence: Who gets nominated and why. *Canadian Journal of Behavioural Science, 32*, 168–177.

Paulhus, D. L., Wehr, P., Harms, P. D., & Strasser, D. I. (2002). Use of exemplar surveys to reveal implicit types of intelligence. *Personality and Social Psychology Bulletin, 28*, 1051–1062.

Paunonen, S. V. (2003). Big Five factors or personality and replicated predictions of behavior. *Journal of Personality & Social Psychology, 84*, 411–422.

Paunonen, S. V., & Ashton, M. C. (2001). Big Five factors and facets and the prediction of behavior. *Journal of Personality and Social Psychology, 81*, 524–539.

Pavlov, I. P. (1927). *Conditioned reflexes* (G. V. Anrep, Trans.). London, England: Oxford University Press.

Pawluski, J. L., & Galea, L. A. (2006). Hippocampal morphology is differentially affected by reproductive experience in the mother. *Journal of Neurobiology, 66*, 71–81.

Pawluski, J. L., Walker, S. K., & Galea L. A. (2006). Reproductive experience differentially affects spatial reference and working memory performance in the mother. *Hormones and Behavior, 49*(2), 143–149. doi:10.1016/j.yhbeh.2005.05.016

Payne, J. D., Stickgold, R., Swanberg, K., & Kensinger, E. A. (2008). Sleep preferentially enhances memory for emotional components of scenes. *Psychological Science, 19*, 781–788.

Pearlin, L. (1982). Discontinuities in the study of aging. In T. K. Hareven & K. J. Adams (Eds.), *Aging and life course transitions: An interdisciplinary perspective.* New York, NY: Guilford.

Peele, S., & Brodsky, A. (with Mary Arnold). (1991). *The truth about addiction and recovery.* New York, NY: Simon & Schuster.

Peier, A. M., Moqrich, A., Hergarden, A. C., et al. (2002). A TRP channel that senses cold stimuli and menthol. *Cell, 108*, 705–715.

Pellegrini, A. D., & Galda, L. (1993). Ten years after: A reexamination of symbolic play and literacy research. *Reading Research Quarterly, 28*, 163–175.

Pendergrast, M. (1995). *Victims of memory* (2nd ed.). Hinesburg, VT: Upper Access Press.

Peng, Y., McCann-Hiltz, D., & Goddard, E. (2004). Consumer demand for meat in Alberta, Canada: Impact of BSE. Retrieved February 11, 2008, from http://ageconsearch.umn.edu/bitstream/123456789/15505/1/sp04pe07.pdf

Pennebaker, J. W. (2002). Writing, social processes, and psychotherapy: From past to future. In S. J. Lepore & J. M. Smyth (Eds.), *The writing cure: How expressive writing promotes health and emotional well-being.* Washington, DC: American Psychological Association.

Pennebaker, J. W., Colder, M., & Sharp, L. K. (1990). Accelerating the coping process. *Journal of Personality and Social Psychology, 58*, 528–527.

Pennebaker, J. W., Kiecolt-Glaser, J., & Glaser, R. (1988). Disclosure of traumas and immune function: Health implications for psychotherapy. *Journal of Consulting and Clinical Psychology, 56*, 239–245.

Pennisi, E. (2005). Why do humans have so few genes? *Science, 309*, 80.

Peplau, L. A. (2003). Human sexuality: How do men and women differ? *Current Directions in Psychological Science, 12*, 37–40.

Peplau, L. A., & Spalding, L. R. (2000). The close relationships of lesbians, gay men and bisexuals. In C. Hendrick & S. Hendrick (Eds.), *Close relationships: A sourcebook.* Thousand Oaks, CA: Sage.

Peplau, L. A., Spalding, L. R., Conley, T. D., & Veniegas, R. C. (2000). The development of sexual orientation in women. *Annual Review of Sex Research, 10*, 70–99.

Pepperberg, I. (2000). *The Alex studies: Cognitive and communicative abilities of grey parrots.* Cambridge, MA: Harvard University Press.

Pepperberg, I. M. (2002). Cognitive and communicative abilities of grey parrots. *Current Directions in Psychological Science, 11*, 83–87.

Pepperberg, I. M. (2006). Grey parrot (*Psittacus erithacus*) numerical abilities: Addition and further experiments on a zero-like concept. *Journal of Comparative Psychology, 120*, 1–11.

Perera, F. P., Rauh, V., Whyatt, R. M., et al. (2006). Effect of prenatal exposure to airborne polycyclic aromatic hydrocarbons on neurodevelopment in the first three years of life among inner-city children. *Environmental Health Perspectives.*doi:10.1289/ehp.9084

Persinger, M. A., & Makarec, K. (1987). Temporal lobe epileptic signs and correlative behaviors displayed by normal populations. *Journal of General Psychology, 114*(2), 179–195.

Persons, J., Davidson, J., & Tompkins, M. A. (2001). *Essential components of cognitive-behavior therapy for depression.* Washington, DC: American Psychological Association.

Pesetsky, D. (1999). *Introduction to symposium: "Grammar: What's innate?"* Paper presented at the annual meeting of the American Association for the Advancement of Science, Anaheim, CA.

Peterson, C., Seligman, M. E. P., Yurko, K. H., et al. (1998). Catastrophizing and untimely death. *Psychological Science, 9*, 127–130.

Peterson, D. R. (2003). Unintended consequences: Ventures and misadventures in the education of professional psychologists. *American Psychologist, 58*, 791–800.

Peterson, L. R., & Peterson, M. J. (1959). Short-term retention of individual verbal items. *Journal of Experimental Psychology, 58*, 193–198.

Peterson, R. A. (2001). On the use of college students in social science research: Insights from a second-order meta-analysis. *Journal of Consumer Research, 28*, 450–461.

Petersson, K. M., Silva, C., Castro-Caldas, A., et al. (2007). Literacy: a cultural influence on functional left-right differences in the inferior parietal cortex. *European Journal of Neuroscience, 26*, 791–799.

Petkova, V. I., & Ehrsson, H. H. (2008). If I were you: Perceptual illusion of body swapping. *PLoS ONE, 3*: e3832. doi:10.1371/journal.pone.0003832

Petrie, K. J., Booth, R. J., & Pennebaker, J. W. (1998). The immunological effects of thought suppression. *Journal of Personality and Social Psychology, 75*, 1264–1272.

Pettigrew, T. T., & Tropp, L. R. (2006). A meta-analytic test of intergroup contact theory. *Journal of Personality and Social Psychology, 90*, 751–783.

Pfungst, O. (1911/1965). *Clever Hans (The horse of Mr. von Osten): A contribution to experimental animal and human psychology.* New York, NY: Holt, Rinehart and Winston.

Phillips, M. D., Lowe, M. J., Lurito, J. T., et al. (2001). Temporal lobe activation demonstrates sex-based differences during passive listening. *Radiology, 220*, 202–207.

Phinney, J. S. (1996). When we talk about American ethnic groups, what do we mean? *American Psychologist, 51*, 918–927.

Piaget, J. (1929/1960). *The child's conception of the world.* Paterson, NJ: Littlefield, Adams.

Piaget, J. (1952). *Play, dreams, and imitation in childhood.* New York, NY: W. W. Norton.

Pierce, W. D., Cameron, J., Banko, K. M., & So, S. (2003). Positive effects of rewards and performance standards on intrinsic motivation. *Psychological Record, 53*, 561–579.

Pika, S., & Mitani, J. (2006). Referential gesture communication in wild chimpanzees (*Pan troglodytes*). *Current Biology, 16*, 191–192.

Pinker, S. (1994). *The language instinct: How the mind creates language.* New York, NY: Morrow.

Pinker, S. (1997). *How the mind works.* New York, NY: Norton.

Pinker, S. (2002). *The blank slate: The modern denial of human nature.* New York, NY: Viking.

Piper, A., & Merskey, H. (2004). The persistence of folly: A critical examination of dissociative identity disorder. Part I: The excesses of an improbable concept. *Canadian Journal of Psychiatry, 49*, 592–600. [Note: Part II. (The defence and decline of multiple personality or dissociative identity disorder) appeared in the subsequent issue of the *Canadian Journal of Psychiatry, 49*, 678–683.]

Pittenger, D. J. (1993). The utility of the Myers-Briggs Type Indicator. *Review of Educational Research, 63*, 467–488.

Plant, E. A., & Devine, P. G. (1998). Internal and external motivation to respond without prejudice. *Journal of Personality and Social Psychology, 75*, 811–832.

Plomin, R. (1989). Environment and genes: Determinants of behavior. *American Psychologist, 44*, 105–111.

Plomin, R., Asbury, K., & Dunn, J. F. (2001). Why are children in the same family so different? Nonshared environment a decade later. *Canadian Journal of Psychiatry, 46*, 225–233.

Plomin, R., & Crabbe, J. (2000). DNA. *Psychological Bulletin, 126*, 806–828.

Plomin, R., & DeFries, J. C. (1985). *Origins of individual differences in infancy: The Colorado Adoption Project.* New York, NY: Academic Press.

Plomin, R., DeFries, J. C., Craig, I. W., & McGuffin, P. (2003). *Behavioral genetics in the postgenomic era.* Washington, DC: American Psychological Association.

Plomin, R., DeFries, J. C., McClearn, G. E., & McGuffin, P. (2001). *Behavioral genetics* (4th ed.). New York, NY: Worth.

Plomin, R., & McGuffin, P. (2003). Psychopathology in the postgenomic era. *Annual Review of Psychology, 54*, 205–228.

Plotnik, J. M., de Waal, F. B. M., & Reiss, D. (2006). Self-recognition in an Asian elephant. *Proceedings of the National Academy of Sciences, 103*(45), 17053–17057.

Plotsky, P. M., Owens, M. J., & Nemeroff, C. B. (1998). Psychoneuroendocrinology of depression: Hypothalamic–pituitary–adrenal axis. *Psychoneuroendocrinology, 21*, 293–307.

Polusny, M. A., & Follette, V. M. (1996). Remembering childhood sexual abuse: A national survey of psychologists' clinical practices, beliefs, and personal experiences. *Professional Psychology: Research and Practice, 27*, 41–52.

Ponitz, C. C., McClelland, M. M., Matthews, J. S., & Morrison, F. J. (2009). A structured observation of behavioral self-regulation and its contribution to kindergarten outcomes. *Developmental Psychology, 45*, 605–619.

Poole, D. A., Lindsay, D. S., Memon, A., & Bull, R. (1995). Psychotherapy and the recovery of memories of childhood sexual abuse: U.S. and British practitioners' opinions, practices, and experiences. *Journal of Consulting and Clinical Psychology, 63*, 426–437.

Poole, D. A., & Lamb, M. E. (1998). *Investigative interviews of children.* Washington, DC: American Psychological Association.

Pope, H. G., & Katz, D. L. (1992). Psychiatric effects of anabolic steroids. *Psychiatric Annals, 22*, 24–29.

Pope, H. G., Jr., Phillips, K. A., & Olivardia, R. (2000). *The Adonis complex: The secret crisis of male body obsession.* New York, NY: Free Press.

Pope, H. G., Jr., Poliakoff, M. B., Parker, M. P., et al. (2007). Is dissociative amnesia a culture-bound syndrome? Findings from a survey of historical literature. *Psychological Medicine, 37,* 225–233.

Popkin, B. M. (2009). *The world is fat: The fads, trends, policies, and products that are fattening the human race.* New York, NY: Avery.

Portenoy, R. K. (1994). Opioid therapy for chronic nonmalignant pain: Current status. In H. L. Fields & J. C. Liebeskind (Eds.), *Progress in pain research and management. Pharmacological approaches to the treatment of chronic pain: Vol. 1.*Seattle, WA: International Association for the Study of Pain.

Postmes, T., & Spears, R. (1998). Deindividuation and antinormative behavior: A meta-analysis. *Psychological Bulletin, 123,* 238–259.

Potter, W. J. (1987). Does television viewing hinder academic achievement among adolescents? *Human Communication Research, 14,* 27–46.

Poulin-Dubois, D., Serbin, L. A., Kenyon, B., & Derbyshire, A. (1994). Infants' intermodal knowledge about gender. *Developmental Psychology, 30,* 436–442.

Powell, R. A., & Boer, D. P. (1995). Did Freud misinterpret reported memories of sexual abuse as fantasies? *Psychological Reports, 77,* 563–570.

Premack, D., & Premack, A. J. (1983). *The mind of an ape.* New York, NY: Norton.

Presnell, K., Bearman, S. K., & Stice, E. (2004). Risk factors for body dissatisfaction in adolescent boys and girls: A prospective study. *International Journal of Eating Disorders, 36,* 389–401.

Pressman, S. D., & Cohen, S. (2005). Does positive affect influence health? *Psychological Bulletin, 131,* 925–971.

Preston, J., & Epley, N. (2005). Explanations versus applications: The explanatory power of valuable beliefs. *Psychological Science, 16,* 826–832.

Principe, G., Kanaya, T., Ceci, S. J., & Singh, M. (2006). Believing is seeing: How rumors can engender false memories in preschoolers. *American Psychologist, 17,* 243–248.

Probst, P. (2005). "Communication unbound—or unfound"?—Ein integratives Literatur-Review zur Wirksamkeit der "Gestützten Kommunikation" ("Facilitated Communication/FC") bei nichtsprechenden autistischen und intelligenzgeminderten Personen. *Zeitschrift für Klinische Psychologie, Psychiatrie und Psychotherapie, 53,* 93–128.

Prochaska, J. O., Norcross, J. C., & DiClemente, C. C. (1994). *Changing for good.* New York, NY: Morrow.

Proffitt, D. R. (2006). Distance perception. *Current Directions in Psychological Science, 3,* 131–135.

Pronin, E. (2008, May 30). How we see ourselves and how we see others. *Science, 320,* 1177–1180.

Pronin, E., Gilovich, T., & Ross, L. (2004). Objectivity in the eye of the beholder: Divergent perceptions of bias in self versus others. *Psychological Review, 111,* 781–799.

Pryor, K. (1999). *Don't shoot the dog: The new art of teaching and training.* New York, NY: Bantam Books.

Ptito, M., Moesgaard, S. M., Gjedde, A., & Kupers, R. (2005). Crossmodal plasticity revealed by electrotactile stimulation of the tongue in the congenitally blind. *Brain, 128,* 606–614.

Punamaeki, R.-L., & Joustie, M. (1998). The role of culture, violence, and personal factors affecting dream content. *Journal of Cross-Cultural Psychology, 29,* 320–342.

Pynoos, R. S., & Nader, K. (1989). Children's memory and proximity to violence. *Journal of the American Academy of Child and Adolescent Psychiatry, 28,* 236–241.

Pyszczynski, T., Rothschild, Z., & Abdollahi, A. (2008). Terrorism, violence, and hope for peace: A terror management perspective. *Current Directions in Psychological Science, 17,* 318–322.

Pyter, L. M., Pineros, V., Galang, J. A., et al. (2009, June 2). Peripheral tumors induce depressive-like behaviors and cytokine production and alter hypothalamic-pituitary-adrenal axis regulation. *Proceedings of the National Academy of Sciences, 106,* 9069–9074.

Quinn, D. M., & Spencer, S. J. (2001). The interference of stereotype threat with women's generation of mathematical problem-solving strategies. *Journal of Social Issues, 57,* 55–71.

Quinn, P., & Bhatt, R. (2005). Learning perceptual organization in infancy. *Psychological Science, 16,* 511–515.

Radford, B. (2005, June). Psychic predictions (and rationalizations) fail again. *Skeptical Briefs, 15,* 529.

Raffaelli, M., Crockett, L. J., & Shen, Y.-L. (2005). Developmental stability and change in self-regulation from childhood to adolescence. *The Journal of Genetic Psychology, 166,*54–75.

Rahman, Q., & Wilson, G. D. (2003). Born gay? The psychobiology of human sexual orientation. *Personality and Individual Differences, 34,* 1337–1382.

Räikkönen, K., Matthews, K. A., Flory, J. D., et al. (1999). Effects of optimism, pessimism, and trait anxiety on ambulatory blood pressure and mood during everyday life. *Journal of Personality and Social Psychology, 76,* 104–113.

Raine, A. (1996). Autonomic nervous system factors underlying disinhibited, antisocial, and violent behavior. Biosocial perspectives and treatment implications. *Annals of the New York Academy of Sciences, 794,* 46–59.

Raine, A. (2008). From genes to brain to antisocial behavior. *Current Directions in Psychological Science, 17,* 323–328.

Raine, A., Lencz, T., Bihrle, S., et al. (2000). Reduced prefrontal gray matter volume and reduced autonomic activity in antisocial personality disorder. *Archives of General Psychiatry, 57,* 119–127.

Raine, A., & Liu, J.-H. (1998). Biological predispositions to violence and their implications for biosocial treatment and prevention. *Psychology, Crime & Law, 4,* 107–125.

Raine, A., Meloy, J. R., Bihrle, S., et al. (1998). Reduced prefrontal and increased subcortical brain functioning assessed using positron emission tomography in predatory and affective murderers. *Behavioral Science and Law, 16,* 319–332.

Raine, A., Park, S., Lencz, T., et al. (2001). Reduced right hemisphere activation in severely abused violent offenders during a working memory task: An fMRI study. *Aggressive Behavior, 27,* 111–129.

Raja, S. (2008, May 8). *From poppies to pill-popping: Is there a "middle way"?* Paper presented at the annual meeting of the American Pain Society, Tampa, FL.

Ramachandran, V. S., & Altschuler, E. L. (2009). The use of visual feedback, in particular mirror visual feedback, in restoring brain function. *Brain, 132,* 1693–1710.

Ramachandran, V. S., & Blakeslee, S. (1998). *Phantoms in the brain.* New York, NY: William Morrow.

Ramey, C. T., & Ramey, S. L. (1998). Early intervention and early experience. *American Psychologist, 53,* 109–120.

Rankin, L. E., & Eagly, A. H. (2008). Is his heroism hailed and hers hidden? Women, men, and the social construction of heroism. *Psychology of Women Quarterly, 32,* 414–422.

Rasch, B., & Born, J. (2008). Reactivation and consolidation of memory during sleep. *Current Directions in Psychological Science,17,* 188–192.

Rasch, B., Büchel, C., Gais, S., & Born, J. (2007). Odor cues during slow-wave sleep prompt declarative memory consolidation. *Science,315,* 1426–1429.

Rasch, B., Pommer, J., Diekelmann, S., & Born, J. (2009). Pharmacological REM sleep suppression paradoxically improves rather than impairs skill memory. *Nature Neuroscience,12,* 396–397. doi:10.1038/nn.2206

Raser, J. M., & O'Shea, E. K. (2005). Noise in gene expression: Origins, consequences, and control. *Science, 309,* 2010–2013.

Rathbun, C., DiVirgilio, L., & Waldfogel, S. (1958). A restitutive process in children following radical separation from family and culture. *American Journal of Orthopsychiatry, 28,* 408–415.

Rauschecker, J. P. (1999). Making brain circuits listen. *Science, 285,* 1686–1687.

Ravussin, E., Lillioja, S., Knowler, W., et al. (1988). Reduced rate of energy expenditure as a risk factor for body-weight gain. *New England Journal of Medicine, 318,* 467–472.

Ray, W. A., Chung, C. P., Murray, K. T., et al. (2009). Atypical antipsychotic drugs and the risk of sudden cardiac death. *New England Journal of Medicine, 360,* 225–235.

Raz, A., Fan, J., & Posner, M. I. (2005). Hypnotic suggestion reduces conflict in the human brain. *Proceedings of the National Academy of Science, 102,* 9978–9983.

Raz, A., Kirsch, I., Pollard, J., & Nitkin-Kamer, Y. (2006). Suggestion reduces the Stroop effect. *Psychological Science, 17,* 91–95.

Reber, P. J., Stark, C. E. L., & Squire, L. R. (1998). Contrasting cortical activity associated with category memory and recognition memory. *Learning & Memory, 5,* 420–428.

Redd, W. H., Dadds, M. R., Futterman, A. D., et al. (1993). Nausea induced by mental images of chemotherapy. *Cancer, 72,* 629–636.

Redelmeier, D. A., & Tversky, A. (1996). On the belief that arthritis pain is related to the weather. *Proceedings of the National Academy of Sciences, 93,* 2895–2896.

Reedy, F. E., Bartoshuk, L. M., Miller, I. J., et al. (1993). Relationships among papillae, taste pores, and 6-n-propylthiouracil (PROP) suprathreshold taste sensitivity. *Chemical Senses, 18,* 618–619.

Regard, M., & Landis, T. (1997). "Gourmand syndrome": Eating passion associated with right anterior lesions. *Neurology, 48,* 1185–1190.

Reichenberg, A., Gross, R., Weiser, M., Bresnahan, M., et al. (2006). Advancing paternal age and autism. *Archives of General Psychiatry, 63,* 1026–1032.

Reid, R. L. (1991). Premenstrual syndrome. *New England Journal of Medicine, 324,* 1208–1210.

Reiner, W. G., & Gearhart, J. P. (2004, January 22). Discordant sexual identity in some genetic males with cloacal exstrophy assigned to female sex at birth. *New England Journal of Medicine, 350,* 333–341.

Remick, A. K., Polivy, J., & Pliner, P. (2009). Internal and external moderators of the effect of variety on food intake. *Psychological Bulletin, 135,* 434–451.

Rendell, P. G., & Henry, J. D. (2008). Prospective-memory functioning is affected during pregnancy and postpartum. *Journal of Clinical and Experimental Neuropsychology, 30*(8), 913–919.

Rensink, R. (2004). Visual sensing without seeing. *Psychological Science, 15,* 27–32.

Repetti, R. L., Taylor, S. E., & Seeman, T. E. (2002). Risky families: Family social environments and the mental and physical health of offspring. *Psychological Bulletin, 128,* 330–366.

Rescorla, R. A. (1988). Pavlovian conditioning: It's not what you think it is. *American Psychologist, 43,* 151–160.

Restak, R. M. (1994). *The modular brain.* New York, NY: Macmillan.

Revell, V. L., & Eastman, C. I. (2005). How to fool Mother Nature into letting you fly around or stay up all night. *Journal of Biological Rhythms, 20,* 353–365.

Reyna, V., & Farley, F. (2006). Risk and rationality in adolescent decision making. *Psychological Science in the Public Interest, 7,* 1–44.

Reynolds, B. A., & Weiss, S. (1992). Generation of neurons and astrocytes from isolated cells of the adult mammalian central nervous system. *Science, 255,* 1707–1710.

Reynolds, D. K. (1987). *Water bears no scars: Japanese lifeways for personal growth.* New York, NY: Morrow.

Reynolds, K., Lewis, L. B., Nolen, J. D. L., et al. (2003). Alcohol consumption and risk of stroke: A meta-analysis. *Journal of the American Medical Association, 289,* 579–588.

Reza, H. G., Williams, C. J., & Dahlburg, J.-T. (2001, Sept 27). Mainly they just waited. *Los Angeles Times.* Retrieved from http://space.crono911.net/EBook/063_LAT_27092001.pdf

Rhoades, L., & Eisenberger, R. (2002). Perceived organizational support: A review of the literature. *Journal of Applied Psychology, 87,* 698–714.

Ricciardelli, L. A., & McCabe, M. P. (2004). A biopsychosocial model of disordered eating and the pursuit of muscularity in adolescent boys. *Psychological Bulletin, 130,* 179–205.

Rice, M. L. (1990). Preschoolers' QUIL: Quick incidental learning of words. In G. Conti-Ramsden & C. E. Snow (Eds.), *Children's language* (Vol. 7). Hillsdale, NJ: Erlbaum.

Richardson-Klavehn, A., & Bjork, R. A. (1988). Measures of memory. *Annual Review of Psychology, 39,* 475–543.

Ridley, M. (2000). *Genome. The autobiography of a species in 23 chapters.* New York, NY: HarperCollins.

Ridley-Johnson, R., Cooper, H., & Chance, J. (1983). The relation of children's television viewing to school achievement and I.Q. *Journal of Educational Research, 76,* 294–297.

Rieber, R. W. (2006). *The bifurcation of the self.* New York, NY: Springer.

Rind, B., Tromovitch, P., & Bauserman, R. (1998). A meta-analytic examination of assumed properties of child sexual abuse using college samples. *Psychological Bulletin, 124,* 22–53.

Ro, T., Farnè, A., Johnson, R., et al. (2007). Feeling sounds after a thalamic lesion. *Annals of Neurology,62,* 433–441.

Roberson, D., Davies, I., & Davidoff, J. (2000). Color categories are not universal: Replications and new evidence in favor of linguistic relativity. *Journal of Experimental Psychology: General, 129*, 369–398.

Roberts, B. W., Caspi, A., & Moffitt, T. E. (2001). The kids are alright: Growth and stability in personality development from adolescence to adulthood. *Journal of Personality and Social Psychology, 81*, 670–683.

Roberts, B. W., & Mroczek, D. (2008). Personality trait change in adulthood. *Current Directions in Psychological Science, 17*, 31–35.

Roberts, B. W., Walton, K. E., & Viechtbauer, W. (2006). Patterns of mean-level change in personality traits across the life course: A meta-analysis of longitudinal studies. *Psychological Bulletin, 132*, 1–25.

Robins, L. N., Davis, D. H., & Goodwin, D. W. (1974). Drug use by U.S. Army enlisted men in Vietnam: A follow-up on their return home. *American Journal of Epidemiology, 99*, 235–249.

Robins, L. N., Tipp, J., & Przybeck, T. R. (1991). Antisocial personality. In L. N. Robins & D. A. Regier (Eds.), *Psychiatric disorders in America.* New York, NY: Free Press.

Robins, R. W., Gosling, S. D., & Craik, K. H. (1999). An empirical analysis of trends in psychology. *American Psychologist, 54*, 117–128.

Robinson, B. (1988). Final report to the Canadian Psychological Association Board of Directors. Psy.D. Task Force.

Robinson, T., Wilde, M. L., Navracruz, L. C., et al. (2001). Effects of reducing children's television and video game use on aggressive behavior: A randomized controlled trial. *Archives of Pediatric and Adolescent Medicine, 155*, 13–14.

Rocha, B. A., Scearce-Levie, K., Lucas, J. J., et al. (1998). Increased vulnerability to cocaine in mice lacking the serotonin-1B receptor. *Nature, 393*, 175–178.

Rodriguez, P., Wiles, J., & Elman, J. L. (1999). A recurrent neural network that learns to count. *Connection Science, 11*, 5–40.

Roediger, H. L. (1990). Implicit memory: Retention without remembering. *American Psychologist, 45*, 1043–1056.

Roediger, H. L., & McDermott, K. B. (1995). Creating false memories: Remembering words not presented in lists. *Journal of Experimental Psychology, Learning, Memory, & Cognition, 21*, 803–814.

Rofé, Y. (2008). Does repression exist? Memory, pathogenic, unconscious and clinical evidence. *Review of General Psychology, 12*, 63–85.

Rogers, C. (1951). *Client-centered therapy: Its current practice, implications, and theory.* Boston, MA: Houghton-Mifflin.

Rogers, C. (1961). *On becoming a person.* Boston, MA: Houghton-Mifflin.

Rogers, R. W., & Prentice-Dunn, S. (1981). Deindividuation and anger-mediated interracial aggression: Unmasking regressive racism. *Journal of Personality and Social Psychology, 41*, 63–73.

Rogge, R. D., Bradbury, T. N., Hahlweg, K., et al. (2006). Predicting marital distress and dissolution: Refining the two-factor hypothesis. *Journal of Family Psychology, 20*, 156–159.

Rogoff, B. (2003). *The cultural nature of human development.* New York, NY: Oxford University Press.

Rollin, H. (Ed.). (1980). *Coping with schizophrenia.* London, England: Burnett.

Romanczyk, R. G., Arnstein, L., Soorya, L. V., & Gillis, J. (2003). The myriad of controversial treatments for autism: A critical evaluation of efficacy. In S. O. Lilienfeld, S. J. Lynn, & J. M. Lohr (Eds.), *Science and pseudoscience in clinical psychology.* New York, NY: Guilford.

Rosch, E. H. (1973). Natural categories. *Cognitive Psychology, 4*, 328–350.

Rosen, G. M. (1981). Guidelines for the review of do-it-yourself treatment books. *Contemporary Psychology, 26*, 189–191.

Rosen, G. M., Glasgow, R. E., & Moore, T. E. (2003). Self-help therapy: The science and business of giving psychology away. In S. O. Lilienfeld, S. J. Lynn, & J. M. Lohr (Eds.), *Science and pseudoscience in clinical psychology.* New York, NY: Guilford.

Rosenberg, H. (1993). Prediction of controlled drinking by alcoholics and problem drinkers. *Psychological Bulletin, 113*, 129–139.

Rosenthal, N. E. (2006). *Winter blues: Everything you need to know to beat seasonal affective disorder* (Rev. ed.). New York, NY: Guilford Press.

Rosenthal, R. (1966). *Experimenter effects in behavioral research.* New York, NY: Appleton-Century-Crofts.

Rosenthal, R. (1994). Interpersonal expectancy effects: A 30-year perspective. *Current Directions in Psychological Science, 3*, 176–179.

Rosenzweig, M. R. (1984). Experience, memory, and the brain. *American Psychologist, 39*, 365–376.

Roser, M. E., & Gazzaniga, M. S. (2004). Automatic brains: Interpretive minds. *Current Directions in Psychological Science, 13*, 56–59.

Ross, H. E., Freeman, S. M., Spiegel, L. L., et al. (2009). Variation in oxytocin receptor density in the nucleus accumbens has differential effects on affiliative behaviors in monogamous and polygamous voles. *Journal of Neuroscience, 29*, 1312–1318.

Ross, L. (2010). Dealing with conflict: Experiences and experiments. In M. H. Gonzales, C. Tavris, & J. Aronson (Eds.), *The scientist and the humanist: A festschrift in honor of Elliot Aronson.* New York, NY: Psychology Press.

Ross, M., Xun, W. Q. E., & Wilson, A. E. (2002). Language and the bicultural self. *Personality and Social Psychology Bulletin, 28*, 1040–1050.

Rotenberg, K. J. (1994). Loneliness and interpersonal trust. *Journal of Social and Clinical Psychology, 13*, 152–173.

Rotenberg, K. J. (1998). Stigmatization of transitions in loneliness. *Journal of Social and Personal Relationships, 15*, 565–576.

Rotenberg, K. J., Addis, N., Betts, L. R., et al. (2010). The relation between trust beliefs and loneliness during early childhood, middle childhood, and adulthood. *Personality and Social Psychology Bulletin, 36*, 1086–1100.

Rotenberg, K. J., & Flood, D. (1999). Loneliness, dysphoria, dietary restraint, and eating behaviour. *International Journal of Eating Disorders, 25*, 55–64.

Rotenberg, K. J., & Kmill, J. (1992). Perception of lonely and nonlonely persons as a function of individual differences in loneliness. *Journal of Social and Personal Relationships, 9*, 325–330.

Rotenberg, K. J., & MacKie, J. (1999). Stigmatization of social and intimacy loneliness. *Psychological Reports, 84*, 147–148.

Rotenberg, K. J., & Morrison, J. (1993). Loneliness and college achievement: Do loneliness scale scores predict college drop-out? *Psychological Reports, 73*, 1283–1288.

Rotermann, M. (2008). Trends in teen sexual behaviour and condom use. Component of Statistics Canada Catalogue no. 82-003-X. Retrieved from http://www.statcan.gc.ca/pub/82-003-x/2008003/article/10664-eng.pdf

Rothbart, M. K., Ahadi, S. A., & Evans, D. E. (2000). Temperament and personality: Origins and outcomes. *Journal of Personality and Social Psychology, 78*, 122–135.

Rothbaum, F., Weisz, J., Pott, M., et al. (2000). Attachment and culture: Security in the United States and Japan. *American Psychologist, 55*, 1093–1104.

Rothbaum, F. M., Weisz, J. R., & Snyder, S. S. (1982). Changing the world and changing the self: A two-process model of perceived control. *Journal of Personality and Social Psychology, 42*, 5–37.

Rothermund, K., & Wentura, D. (2004). Underlying processes in the Implicit Association Test: Dissociating salience from associations. *Journal of Experimental Psychology: General, 133*, 139–165.

Rotter, J. B. (1990). Internal versus external control of reinforcement: A case history of a variable. *American Psychologist, 45*, 489–493.

Roughgarden, J. (2004). *Evolution's rainbow: Diversity, gender, and sexuality in nature and people.* Berkeley: University of California Press.

Rouw, R., & Scholte, S. S. (2007). Increased structural connectivity in grapheme-color synesthesia. *Nature Neuroscience,10*, 792–797.

Roy, M. P., Steptoe, A., & Kirschbaum, C. (1998). Life events and social support as moderators of individual differences in cardiovascular and cortisol reactivity. *Journal of Personality and Social Psychology, 75*, 1273–1281.

Rowe, M. L., & Goldin-Meadow, S. (2009, February 13). Differences in early gesture explain SES disparities in child vocabulary size at school entry. *Science, 323*, 951–953.

Røysamb, E., Tambs, K., Reichborn-Kjennerud, T., et al. (2003). Happiness and health: Environmental and genetic contributions to the relationship between subjective well-being, perceived health, and somatic illness. *Journal of Personality and Social Psychology, 85*, 1136–1146.

Rozin, P., Kabnick, K., Pete, E., et al. (2003). The ecology of eating: Smaller portion sizes in France than in the United States help explain the French paradox. *Psychological Science, 14*, 450–454.

Rozin, P., Lowery, L., & Ebert, R. (1994). Varieties of disgust faces and the structure of disgust. *Journal of Personality and Social Psychology, 66*, 870–881.

Ruggiero, V. R. (1988). *Teaching thinking across the curriculum.* New York, NY: Harper & Row.

Ruggiero, V. R. (2004). *The art of thinking: A guide to critical and creative thought* (7th ed.). Pearson/Longman.

Rumbaugh, D. M. (1977). *Language learning by a chimpanzee: The Lana project.* New York, NY: Academic Press.

Rumbaugh, D. M., Savage-Rumbaugh, E. S., & Pate, J. L. (1988). Addendum to "Summation in the chimpanzee (*Pan troglodytes*)." *Journal of Experimental Psychology: Animal Behavior Processes, 14*, 118–120.

Rumelhart, D. E., & McClelland, J. L. (1987). Learning the past tenses of English verbs: Implicit rules or parallel distributed processing. In B. MacWhinney (Ed.), *Mechanisms of language acquisition.* Hillsdale, NJ: Erlbaum.

Rumelhart, D. E., McClelland, J. L., & the PDP Research Group. (1986). *Parallel distributed processing: Explorations in the microstructure of cognition* (Vols. 1 and 2). Cambridge, MA: MIT Press.

Rupp, H. A., & Wallen, K. (2008). Sex differences in response to visual sexual stimuli: A review. *Archives of Sexual Behavior, 37*, 206–218.

Rushton, J. P. (1988). Race differences in behavior: A review and evolutionary analysis. *Personality and Individual Differences, 9*, 1009–1024.

Rushton, J. P., & Jensen, A. R. (2005). Thirty years of research on race differences in cognitive ability. *Psychology, Public Policy, and Law, 11*, 235–294.

Russell, J. A., & Fehr, B. (1994). Fuzzy concepts in a fuzzy hierarchy: Varieties of anger. *Journal of Personality and Social Psychology, 67*, 186–205.

Rutter, M., O'Connor, T. G., & the English and Romanian Adoptees (ERA) Study Team. (2004). Are there biological programming effects for psychological development? Findings from a study of Romanian adoptees. *Developmental Psychology, 40*, 81–94.

Rutter, M., Pickles, A., Murray, R., & Eaves, L. (2001). Testing hypotheses on specific environmental causal effects on behavior. *Psychological Bulletin, 127*, 291–324.

Ruys, K. I., & Stapel, D. A. (2008). The secret life of emotions. *Psychological Science, 19*, 385–391.

Rymer, R. (1993). *Genie: An abused child's flight from silence.* New York, NY: HarperCollins.

Sabattini, L., & Crosby, F. (2009). Work ceilings and walls: Work-life and "family-friendly" policies. In M. Barreto, M. Ryan, & M. Schmitt (Eds.), *The glass ceiling in the 21st century: Understanding barriers to gender equality.* Washington, DC: American Psychological Association.

Sack, R. L., & Lewy, A. J. (1997). Melatonin as a chronobiotic: Treatment of circadian desynchrony in night workers and the blind. *Journal of Biological Rhythms, 12*, 595–603.

Sackett, P. R., Hardison, C. M., & Cullen, M. J. (2004). On interpreting stereotype threat as accounting for African American–white differences on cognitive tests. *American Psychologist, 59*, 7–13.

Sacks, O. (1985). *The man who mistook his wife for a hat and other clinical tales.* New York, NY: Simon & Schuster.

Saffran, J. R., Aslin, R. N., & Newport, E. L. (1996). Statistical learning by 8-month-old infants. *Science, 274*, 1926–1928.

Sagan, E. (1988). *Freud, women, and morality: The psychology of good and evil.* New York, NY: Basic Books.

Sage, C., Huang, M., Karimi, K., et al. (2005). Proliferation of functional hair cells in vivo in the absence of the retinoblastoma protein. *Science, 307*, 114–118.

Sahley, C. L., Rudy, J. W., & Gelperin, A. (1981). An analysis of associative learning in a terrestrial mollusk: 1. Higher-order conditioning, blocking, and a transient US preexposure effect. *Journal of Comparative Physiology, 144*, 1–8.

Salovey, P., & Grewal, D. (2005). The science of emotional intelligence. *Current Directions in Psychological Science, 14*, 281–285.

Salthouse, T. A. (2006). Mental exercise and mental aging: Evaluating the validity of the "use it or lose it" hypothesis. *Perspectives on Psychological Science, 1*, 68–87.

Saltz, B. L., Woerner, M. G., Kane, J. M., et al. (1991). Prospective study of tardive dyskinesia incidence in the elderly. *Journal of the American Medical Association, 266*(17), 2402–2406.

Sameroff, A. J., Seifer, R., Barocas, R., et al. (1987). Intelligence quotient scores of 4-year-old children: Social-environmental risk factors. *Pediatrics, 79*, 343–350.

Sampson, R. J, Sharkey, P., & Raudenbush, S. W. (2008). Durable effects of concentrated disadvantage among verbal ability of African-American children. *Proceedings of the National Academy of Sciences, 105*, 845–853.

Sandel, M. (2007). *The case against perfection: Ethics in the age of genetic engineering*. Cambridge, MA: Belknap/Harvard University Press.

Sanfey, A. G., Rilling, J. K., & Aronson, J. K. (2003). The neural basis of economic decision-making in the Ultimatum Game. *Science, 300,* 1755–1758.

Sapolsky, R. M. (1997). *The trouble with testosterone*. New York, NY: Touchstone.

Sapolsky, R. M. (2000). The possibility of neurotoxicity in the hippocampus in major depression: A primer on neuron death. *Biological Psychiatry, 48,* 755–765.

Sarbin, T. R. (1991). Hypnosis: A fifty year perspective. *Contemporary Hypnosis, 8,* 1–15.

Sarbin, T. R. (1997a). The poetics of identity. *Theory & Psychology, 7,* 67–82.

Sarbin, T. R. (1997b). The power of believed-in imaginings. *Psychological Inquiry, 8,* 322–325.

Saucier, D. M., & Cain, D. P. (1995). NMDA-dependent long-term potentiation is not required for spatial learning in the water maze. *Nature, 378,* 186–189.

Saucier, D. M., Hargreaves, E. L., Boon, F., & Cain, D. P. (1996). Detailed behavioural analysis of water maze acquisition under systemic NMDA or muscarinic blockade: Nonspatial pretraining eliminates spatial learning deficits. *Behavioral Neuroscience, 110,* 103–116.

Saucier, G. (2000). Isms and the structure of social attitudes. *Journal of Personality and Social Psychology, 78,* 366–385.

Savage-Rumbaugh, S., & Lewin, R. (1994). *Kanzi: The ape at the brink of the human mind*. New York, NY: Wiley.

Savage-Rumbaugh, S., Shanker, S., & Taylor, T. (1998). *Apes, language and the human mind*. New York, NY: Oxford University Press.

Savic, I., Berglund, H., & Lindström, P. (2005, May 17). Brain response to putative pheromones in homosexual men. *Proceedings of the National Academy of Sciences, 102,* 7356–7361.

Savin-Williams, R. C. (2006). Who's gay? Does it matter? *Current Directions in Psychological Science, 15,* 40–44.

Sawa, A., & Snyder, S. H. (2002, April 26). Schizophrenia: Diverse approaches to a complex disease. *Science, 296,* 692–694.

Saxe, L. (1994). Detection of deception: Polygraph and integrity tests. *Current Directions in Psychological Science, 3,* 69–73.

Saxena, S., Brody, A. L., Maidment, K. M., et al. (2004). Cerebral glucose metabolism in obsessive-compulsive hoarding. *American Journal of Psychiatry, 161,* 1038–1048.

Scarr, S. (1993). Biological and cultural diversity: The legacy of Darwin for development. *Child Development, 64,* 1333–1353.

Scarr, S., Pakstis, A. J., Katz, S. H., & Barker, W. B. (1977). Absence of a relationship between degree of white ancestry and intellectual skill in a black population. *Human Genetics, 39,* 69–86.

Scarr, S., & Weinberg, R. A. (1994). Educational and occupational achievement of brothers and sisters in adoptive and biologically related families. *Behavioral Genetics, 24,* 301–325.

Schachter, S., & Singer, J. E. (1962). Cognitive, social, and physiological determinants of emotional state. *Psychological Review, 69,* 379–399.

Schacter, D. L. (2001). *The seven sins of memory: How the mind forgets and remembers*. Boston, MA: Houghton-Mifflin.

Schacter, D. L., Chiu, C.-Y., & Ochsner, K. N. (1993). Implicit memory: A selective review. *Annual Review of Neuroscience, 16,* 159–182.

Schaeffer, C. M., & Borduin, C. M. (2005). Long-term follow-up to a randomized clinical trial of multisystemic therapy with serious and violent juvenile offenders. *Journal of Consulting and Clinical Psychology, 73,* 445–453.

Schafer, R. (1992). *Retelling a life: Narration and dialogue in psychoanalysis*. New York, NY: Basic Books.

Schaie, K. W., & Willis, S. L. (2002). *Adult development and aging* (5th ed.). Upper Saddle River, NJ: Prentice Hall.

Schaie, K. W., & Zuo, Y.-L. (2001). Family environments and cognitive functioning. In R. J. Sternberg & E. Grigorenko (Eds.), *Cognitive development in context*. Hillsdale, NJ: Erlbaum.

Schank, R. (with Peter Childers). (1988). *The creative attitude*. New York, NY: Macmillan.

Scharfman, H. E., & Hen, R. (2007). Is more neurogenesis always better? *Science, 315,* 336–338.

Schellenberg, E. G. (2004). Music lessons enhance IQ. *Psychological Science, 15,* 511–514.

Scherer, K. R. (1997). The role of culture in emotion-antecedent appraisal. *Journal of Personality and Social Psychology, 73,* 902–922.

Schiff, N. D., Giacino, J. T., Kalmar, K., et al. (2007). Behavioural improvements with thalamic stimulation after severe traumatic brain injury [letter]. *Nature, 448,* 600–603.

Schlossberg, N. K., & Robinson, S. P. (1996). *Going to plan B*. New York, NY: Simon & Schuster/Fireside.

Schmelz, M., Schmidt, R., Bickel, A., et al. (1997). Specific C-receptors for itch in human skin. *Journal of Neuroscience, 17,* 8003–8008.

Schmidt, F. L., & Hunter, J. (2004). General mental ability in the world of work: Occupational attainment and job performance. *Journal of Personality and Social Psychology, 86,* 162–173.

Schmidt, L. A., Fox, N. A., Perez-Edgar, K., & Hamer, D. H. (2009). Linking gene, brain, and behavior: DRD4, frontal asymmetry, and temperament. *Psychological Science, 20,* 831–837.

Schmitt, D. P. (2003). Universal sex differences in the desire for sexual variety: Tests from 52 nations, 6 continents, and 13 islands. *Journal of Personality and Social Psychology, 85,* 85–104.

Schnell, L., & Schwab, M. E. (1990, January 18). Axonal regeneration in the rat spinal cord produced by an antibody against myelin-associated neurite growth inhibitors. *Nature, 343,* 269–272.

Schofield, P., Ball, D., Smith, J. G., et al. (2004). Optimism and survival in lung carcinoma patients. *Cancer, 100,* 1276–1282.

Schuckit, M. A. (1998). *Relationship among genetic, environmental, and psychological variables in predicting alcoholism*. Invited address presented at the annual meeting of the American Psychological Association, San Francisco, CA.

Schuckit, M. A., & Smith, T. L. (1996). An 8-year follow-up of 450 sons of alcoholic and control subjects. *Archives of General Psychiatry, 53,* 202–210.

Schuckit, M. A., Smith, T. L., Pierson, J., et al. (2007). Patterns and correlates of drinking in offspring from the San Diego Prospective Study. *Alcoholism: Clinical and Experimental Research, 31,* 1681–1691.

Schuckit, M. A., Smith, T. L., Trim, R., et al. (2008). The performance of elements of a "level of response to alcohol"-based model of drinking behaviors in 13-year-olds. *Addiction, 103,* 1786–1792.

Schulz, R., Beach, S. R., Ives, D. G., et al. (2000). Association between depression and mortality in older adults: The Cardiovascular Health Study. *Archives of Internal Medicine, 160,* 1761–1768.

Schwartz, B. (2004). *The paradox of choice: Why more is less.* New York, NY: Ecco Press.

Schwartz Bennett, L. (2010). The effects of emotion on tip-of-the-tongue states. *Psychonomic Bulletin & Review, 17*(1), 82–87.

Schwartz, J., Stoessel, P. W., Baxter, L. R., et al. (1996). Systematic changes in cerebral glucose metabolic rate after successful behavior modification treatment of obsessive–compulsive disorder. *Archives of General Psychiatry, 53,* 109–113.

Seabrook, J. (2008, November 10). Suffering souls: The search for the roots of psychopathy. *The New Yorker,* 64–73.

Sears, P., & Barbee, A. H. (1977). Career and life satisfactions among Terman's gifted women. In J. C. Stanley, W. C. George, & C. H. Solano (Eds.), *The gifted and the creative: A fifty-year perspective.* Baltimore, MD: Johns Hopkins University Press.

Segal, J. (1986). *Winning life's toughest battles.* New York, NY: McGraw-Hill.

Segal, Z. V., Williams, J. Mark G., & Teasdale, J. D. (2001). *Mindfulness-based cognitive therapy for depression: A new approach to preventing relapse.* New York, NY: Guilford Press.

Segall, M. H., Dasen, P. P., Berry, J. W., & Poortinga, Y. H. (1999). *Human behavior in global perspective* (2nd ed.). Boston, MA: Allyn & Bacon.

Segall, M. H., Campbell, D. T., & Herskovits, M. J. (1966). *The influence of culture on visual perception.* Indianapolis, IN: Bobbs-Merrill.

Segerstrom, S. C. (2007). Optimism and resources: Effects on each other and on health over 10 years. *Journal of Research in Personality, 41,* 772–786.

Segerstrom, S. C., & Miller, G. E. (2004). Psychological stress and the human immune system: A meta-analytic study of 30 years of inquiry. *Psychological Bulletin, 130,* 601–630.

Seidenberg, M. S. (1997). Language acquisition and use: Learning and applying probabilistic constraints. *Science, 275,* 1599–1603.

Seidenberg, M. S., MacDonald, M. C., & Saffran, J. R. (2002). Does grammar start where statistics stop? *Science, 298,* 553–554.

Seifer, R., Schiller, M., Sameroff, A., et al. (1996). Attachment, maternal sensitivity, and infant temperament during the first year of life. *Developmental Psychology, 32,* 12–25.

Sekuler, R., & Blake, R. (1994). *Perception* (3rd ed.). New York, NY: Knopf.

Seligman, M. E. P. (1991). *Learned optimism.* New York, NY: Knopf.

Seligman, M. E. P., & Csikszentmihaly, M. (2000). Positive psychology: An introduction. *American Psychologist, 55,* 5–14.

Seligman, M. E. P., & Hager, J. L. (1972, August). Biological boundaries of learning: The sauce-béarnaise syndrome. *Psychology Today,* 59–61, 84–87.

Seligman, M. E. P., Schulman, P., DeRubeis, R. J., & Hollon, S. D. (1999). The prevention of depression and anxiety. *Prevention & Treatment, 2,* Retrieved from http://www.ppc.sas.upenn.edu/depprevseligman1999.pdf

Selye, H. (1956). *The stress of life.* New York, NY: McGraw-Hill.

Senghas, A., & Coppola, M. (2001). Children creating language: How Nicaraguan Sign Language acquired a spatial grammar. *Psychological Science, 12,* 323–328.

Senghas, A., Kita, S., & Özyürek, A. (2004). Children creating core properties of language: Evidence from an emerging sign language in Nicaragua. *Science, 305,* 1779–1782.

Senko, C., Durik, A. M., & Harackiewicz, J. M. (2008). Historical perspectives and new directions in achievement goal theory: Understanding the effects of mastery and performance-approach goals. In J. Y. Shah & W. L. Gardner (Eds.), *Handbook of motivation science.* New York, NY: Guilford.

Serpell, R. (1994). The cultural construction of intelligence. In W. J. Lonner & R. S. Malpass (Eds.), *Psychology and culture.* Needham Heights, MA: Allyn & Bacon.

Serrano, P., Friedman, E. L., Kenney, J., et al. (2008). PKMz maintains spatial, instrumental, and classically conditioned long-term memories. *PLoS Biology, 6:* e318. doi:10.1371/journal/pbio.0060318

Shadish, W. R., Matt, G. E., Navarro, A. M., & Phillips, G. (2000). The effects of psychological therapies under clinically representative conditions: A meta-analysis. *Psychological Bulletin, 126,* 512–529.

Shafto, M. A., Burke, D. M., Stamatakis, E. A., et al. (2007). On the tip-of-the-tongue: Neural correlates of increased word-finding failures in normal aging. *Journal of Cognitive Neuroscience, 19,* 2060–2070.

Shapiro, F. (1994). EMDR: In the eye of a paradigm shift. *Behavior Therapist, 17,* 153–156.

Shapiro, F. (1995). *Eye movement desensitization and reprocessing: Basic principles, protocols, and procedures.* New York, NY: Guilford.

Shariff, A. F., & Tracy, J. L. (2009). Knowing who's boss: Implicit perceptions of status from the nonverbal expression of pride source. *Emotion, 9,* 631–639.

Sharman, S. J., Manning, C. G., & Garry, M. (2005). Explain this: Explaining childhood events inflates confidence for those events. *Applied Cognitive Psychology, 19,* 16–74.

Sharot, T., Martorella, E. A., Delgado, M. R., & Phelps, E. A. (2007). How personal experience modulates the neural circuitry of memories of September 11. *Proceedings of the National Academy of Science, 104,* 389–394.

Shatz, M., & Gelman, R. (1973). The development of communication skills: Modifications in the speech of young children as a function of the listener. *Monographs of the Society for Research in Child Development, 38.*

Shaver, P. R., & Hazan, C. (1993). Adult romantic attachment: Theory and evidence. In D. Perlman & W. H. Jones (Eds.), *Advances in personal relationships* (Vol. 4). London, England: Kingsley.

Shaver, P. R., Wu, S., & Schwartz, J. C. (1992). Cross-cultural similarities and differences in emotion and its representation: A prototype approach. In M. S. Clark (Ed.), *Review of Personality and Social Psychology* (Vol. 13). Newbury Park, CA: Sage.

Shaywitz, B. A., Shaywitz, S. E., Pugh, K. R., et al. (1995). Sex differences in the functional organization of the brain for language. *Nature, 373,* 607–609.

Shea, C. (2001, September). White man can't contextualize. *Lingua Franca,* 44–47, 49–51.

Sheldon, K. M., Elliot, A. J., Kim, Y., & Kasser, T. (2001). What is satisfying about satisfying events? Testing 10 candidate psychological needs. *Journal of Personality and Social Psychology, 80,* 325–339.

Sheldon, K. M., & Houser-Marko, L. (2001). Self-concordance, goal attainment, and the pursuit of happiness: Can there be an upward spiral? *Journal of Personality and Social Psychology, 80*, 152–165.

Sheline, Y. I. (2000). 3D MRI studies of neuroanatomic changes in unipolar major depression: The role of stress and medical comorbidity. *Biological Psychiatry, 48*, 791–800.

Shepard, R. N., & Metzler, J. (1971). Mental rotation of three-dimensional objects. *Science, 171*, 701–703.

Sherif, M. (1958). Superordinate goals in the reduction of intergroup conflicts. *American Journal of Sociology, 63*, 349–356.

Sherif, M., Harvey, O. J., White, B. J., Hood, W., & Sherif, C. (1961). *Intergroup conflict and cooperation: The Robbers Cave experiment.* Norman: University of Oklahoma Institute of Intergroup Relations.

Sherry, J. L. (2001). The effects of violent video games on aggression: A meta-analysis. *Human Communication Research, 27*, 409–431.

Sherry, S. B., & Hall, P. A. (2009). The perfectionism model of binge eating: Tests of an integrative model. *Journal of Personality and Social Psychology, 96*, 690–709.

Shermer, M. (1997). *Why people believe weird things: Pseudoscience, superstition, and other confusions of our time.* New York, NY: Freeman.

Sherwin, B. B. (1998a). Estrogen and cognitive functioning in women. *Proceedings of the Society for Experimental Biological Medicine, 217*, 17–22.

Sherwin, B. B. (1998b). Use of combined estrogen-androgen preparations in the postmenopause: Evidence from clinical studies. *International Journal of Fertility & Women's Medicine, 43*, 98–103.

Sheth, B. R., Sandkühler, S., & Bhattacharya, J. (2009). Posterior beta and anterior gamma oscillations predict cognitive insight. *Journal of Cognitive Neuroscience, 21*, 1269–1279.

Shields, S. A. (2002). *Speaking from the heart: Gender and the social meaning of emotion.* New York, NY: Cambridge University Press.

Shields, S. A. (2005). The politics of emotion in everyday life: "Appropriate" emotion and claims on identity. *Review of General Psychology, 9*, 3–15.

Shors, T. J. (2009, March). Saving new brain cells. *Scientific American*, 46–54.

Shorter, E., & Healy, D. (2008). *Shock therapy: A history of electroconvulsive treatment in mental illness.* New Brunswick, NJ: Rutgers University Press.

Showalter, E. (1997). *Hystories: Hysterical epidemics and modern culture.* New York, NY: Columbia University Press.

Sidanius, J., Pratto, F., & Bobo, L. (1996). Racism, conservatism, affirmative action, and intellectual sophistication: A matter of principled conservatism or group dominance? *Journal of Personality and Social Psychology, 70*, 476–490.

Sidanius, J., Van Laar, C., Levin, S., & Sinclair, S. (2004). Ethnic enclaves and the dynamics of social identity on the college campus: The good, the bad, and the ugly. *Journal of Personality and Social Psychology, 87*, 96–110.

Siegel, R. K. (1989). *Intoxication: Life in pursuit of artificial paradise.* New York, NY: Dutton.

Siegel, S. (2005). Drug tolerance, drug addiction, and drug anticipation. *Current Directions in Psychological Science, 14*, 296–300.

Siegler, R. S. (2006). Microgenetic analyses of learning. In D. Kuhn & R. S. Siegler (Eds.), *Handbook of child psychology: Vol. 2. Cognition, perception, and language* (6th ed.). New York, NY: Wiley.

Silverstein, B., & Perlick, D. (1995). *The cost of competence: Why inequality causes depression, eating disorders, and illness in women.* New York, NY: Oxford University Press.

Simcock, G., & Hayne, H. (2002). Breaking the barrier: Children fail to translate their preverbal memories into language. *Psychological Science, 13*, 225–231.

Simmons, H. G. (1987). Psychosurgery and the abuse of psychiatric authority in Ontario. *Journal of Health Politics, Policy, and Law, 12*, 537–550.

Simon, H. A. (1955). A behavioral model of rational choice. *Quarterly Journal of Economics, 69*, 99–118.

Simons, D. J., & Chabris, C. F. (1999). Gorillas in our midst: Sustained inattentional blindness for dynamic events. *Perception, 28*, 1059–1974.

Simons, D. J., & Chabris, C. F. (2011). What people believe about how memory works: A representative survey of the U.S. population. *PLoS One, 6*: e22757.

Simonton, D. K., & Song, A. (2009). Eminence, IQ, physical and mental health, and achievement domain. *Psychological Science, 20*, 429–434.

Sims, E. A. (1974). Studies in human hyperphagia. In G. Bray & J. Bethune (Eds.), *Treatment and management of obesity.* New York, NY: Harper & Row.

Sinaceur, M., Heath, C., & Cole, S. (2005). Emotional and deliberative reactions to a public crisis: Mad cow disease in France. *Psychological Science, 16*, 247–254.

Singer, M. T. (2003). *Cults in our midst* (Rev. ed.). New York, NY: Wiley.

Singh, D., Vidaurri, M., Zambarano, R. J., & Dabbs, J. M., Jr. (1999). Lesbian erotic role identification: Behavioral, morphological, and hormonal correlates. *Journal of Personality and Social Psychology, 76*, 1035–1049.

Skinner, B. F. (1938). *The behavior of organisms: An experimental analysis.* New York, NY: Appleton-Century-Crofts.

Skinner, B. F. (1948/1976). *Walden two.* New York, NY: Macmillan.

Skinner, B. F. (1956). A case history in the scientific method. *American Psychologist, 11*, 221–233.

Skinner, B. F. (1972). The operational analysis of psychological terms. In *B. F. Skinner, cumulative record* (3rd ed.). New York, NY: Appleton-Century-Crofts.

Skinner, B. F. (1990). Can psychology be a science of mind? *American Psychologist, 45*, 1206–1210.

Skinner, E. A. (1996). A guide to constructs of control. *Journal of Personality and Social Psychology, 71*, 549–570.

Skinner, E. A. (2007). Secondary control critiqued: Is it secondary? Is it control? *Psychological Bulletin, 133*, 911–916.

Skinner, J. B., Erskine, A., Pearce, S. A., et al. (1990). The evaluation of a cognitive behavioural treatment programme in outpatients with chronic pain. *Journal of Psychosomatic Research, 34*, 13–19.

Slackman, M. (2006, August 6). Iranian 101: A lesson for Americans. The fine art of hiding what you mean to say. *New York Times.* Retrieved from http://www.nytimes.com/2006/08/06/weekinreview/06slackman.html?scp=1&sq=tajbakhsh&st=nyt

Slavin, R. E., & Cooper, R. (1999). Improving intergroup relations: Lessons learned from cooperative learning programs. *Journal of Social Issues, 55*, 647–663.

Slobin, D. I. (Ed.). (1985). *The cross-linguistic study of language acquisition* (Vols. 1 and 2). Hillsdale, NJ: Erlbaum.

Slobin, D. I. (Ed.). (1991). *The cross-linguistic study of language acquisition* (Vol. 3). Hillsdale, NJ: Erlbaum.

Slovic, P., Finucane, M. L., Peters, E., & MacGregor, D. G. (2002). The affect heuristic. In T. Gilovich, D. Griffin, & D. Kahneman (Eds.), *Heuristics and biases: The psychology of intuitive judgment*. New York, NY: Cambridge University Press.

Slovic, P., & Peters, E. (2006). Risk perception and affect. *Current Directions in Psychological Science, 15*, 322–325.

Small, G. (2008). *iBrain: Surviving the technological alteration of the modern mind*. New York, NY: Collins Living.

Smilek, D., Dixon, M. J., Cudahy, C., & Merikle, P. (2002). Synesthetic color experiences influence memory. *Psychological Science, 13*, 548–552.

Smith, D. N. (1998). The psychocultural roots of genocide: Legitimacy and crisis in Rwanda. *American Psychologist, 53*, 743–753.

Smith, J. F., & Kida, T. (1991). Heuristics and biases: Expertise and task realism in auditing. *Psychological Bulletin, 109*, 472–489.

Smith, P. B., & Bond, M. H. (1994). *Social psychology across cultures: Analysis and perspectives*. Boston, MA: Allyn & Bacon.

Smither, R. D. (1998). *The psychology of work and human performance* (3rd ed.). New York, NY: Longman.

Snodgrass, S. E. (1992). Further effects of role versus gender on interpersonal sensitivity. *Journal of Personality and Social Psychology, 62*, 154–158.

Snowdon, C. T. (1997). The "nature" of sex differences: Myths of male and female. In P. A. Gowaty (Ed.), *Feminism and evolutionary biology*. New York, NY: Chapman and Hall.

Snyder, C. R., & Shenkel, R. J. (1975, March). The P. T. Barnum effect. *Psychology Today*, 52–54.

Sobell, M. B., & Sobell, L. C. (1993). *Problem drinkers: Guided self-change treatment*. New York, NY: Guilford.

Somer, O., & Goldberg, L. R. (1999). The structure of Turkish trait-descriptive adjectives. *Journal of Personality and Social Psychology, 76*, 431–450.

Sommer, R. (1969). *Personal space: The behavioral basis of design*. Englewood Cliffs, NJ: Prentice-Hall.

Sommer, R. (1977, January). Toward a psychology of natural behavior. *APA Monitor*. (Reprinted in *Readings in psychology 78/79*. Guilford, CT: Dushkin, 1978.)

Sommerville, J. A., Woodward, A. L., & Needham, A. (2005). Action experience alters 3-month-old infants' perception of others' actions. *Cognition, 96*, B1–B11.

Sorce, J. F., Emde, R. N., Campos, J., & Klinnert, M. D. (1985). Maternal emotional signaling: Its effect on the visual cliff behavior of 1-year-olds. *Developmental Psychology, 21*, 195–200.

Spalding, K. L., Arner, E., Westermark, P. O., et al. (2008, June 5). Dynamics of fat cell turnover in humans. *Nature, 453*, 783–787.

Spanos, N. P. (1991). A sociocognitive approach to hypnosis. In S. J. Lynn & J. W. Rhue (Eds.), *Theories of hypnosis: Current models and perspectives*. New York, NY: Guilford Press.

Spanos, N. P. (1996). *Multiple identities and false memories: A sociocognitive perspective*. Washington, DC: American Psychological Association.

Spanos, N. P., Burgess, C. A., Roncon, V., et al. (1993). Surreptitiously observed hypnotic responding in simulators and in skill-trained and untrained high hypnotizables. *Journal of Personality and Social Psychology, 65*, 391–398.

Spanos, N. P., Flynn, D. M., & Gabora, N. J. (1989). Suggested negative visual hallucinations in hypnotic subjects: When no means yes. *British Journal of Experimental and Clinical Hypnosis, 6*(2), 63–67.

Spanos, N. P., James, B., & de Groot, H. P. (1990). Detection of simulated hypnotic amnesia. *Journal of Abnormal Psychology, 99*(2), 179–182.

Spanos, N. P., Menary, E., Gabora, N. J., et al. (1991). Secondary identity enactments during hypnotic past-life regression: A sociocognitive perspective. *Journal of Personality and Social Psychology, 61*, 308–320.

Spanos, N. P., Stenstrom, R. J., & Johnson, J. C. (1988). Hypnosis, placebo, and suggestion in the treatment of warts. *Psychosomatic Medicine, 50*, 245–260.

Spanswick, S., Lehmann, H., & Sutherland, R. J. (2011). A novel model of hippocampal cognitive deficits, slow neurodegeneration, and neuro-regeneration. *Journal of Biomedicine and Biotechnology*, Article ID 527201. doi:10.1155/2011/527201

Spear, L. P. (2000a). Neurobiological changes in adolescence. *Current Directions in Psychological Science, 9*, 111–114.

Spear, L. P. (2000b). The adolescent brain and age-related behavioral manifestations. *Neuroscience and Biobehavioral Review, 24*, 417–463.

Spearman, C. (1927). *The abilities of man*. London, England: Macmillan.

Spelke, E. S. (2005). Sex differences in intrinsic aptitude for mathematics and science? A critical review. *American Psychologist, 60*, 950–958.

Spelke, E. S., & Kinzler, K. D. (2007). Core knowledge. *Developmental Science, 10*, 89–96.

Sperling, G. (1960). The information available in brief visual presentations. *Psychological Monographs, 74*(498).

Sperry, R. W. (1964). The great cerebral commissure. *Scientific American, 210*(1), 42–52.

Sperry, R. W. (1982). Some effects of disconnecting the cerebral hemispheres. *Science, 217*, 1223–1226.

Spitz, H. H. (1997). *Nonconscious movements: From mystical messages to facilitated communication*. Mahwah, NJ: Erlbaum.

Sprecher, S., Schwartz, P., Harvey, J., & Hatfield, E. (2008). The businessoflove.com: Relationship initiation at Internet matchmaking services. In S. Sprecher, A. Wenzel, & J. Harvey (Eds.), *The handbook of relationship initiation*. New York, NY: Psychology Press.

Sprecher, S., Sullivan, Q., & Hatfield, E. (1994). Mate selection preferences: Gender differences examined in a national sample. *Journal of Personality and Social Psychology, 66*, 1074–1080.

Spring, B., Chiodo, J., & Bowen, D. J. (1987). Carbohydrates, tryptophan, and behavior: A methodological review. *Psychological Bulletin, 102*, 234–256.

Springer, S. P., & Deutsch, G. (1998). *Left brain, right brain: Perspectives from cognitive neuroscience*. New York, NY: Freeman.

Squier, L. H., & Domhoff, G. W. (1998). The presentation of dreaming and dreams in introductory psychology textbooks: A critical examination with suggestions for textbook authors and course instructors. *Dreaming, 8*, 149–168.

Squire, L. R. (2007, April 6). Rapid consolidation. *Science, 316*, 57–58.

Squire, L. R., Ojemann, J. G., Miezin, F. M., et al. (1992). Activation of the hippocampus in normal humans: A functional anatomical study of memory. *Proceedings of the National Academy of Science, 89*, 1837–1841.

Squire, L. R., & Zola-Morgan, S. (1991). The medial temporal lobe memory system. *Science, 253*, 1380–1386.

Srivastava, S., Tamir, M., McGonigal, K. M., et al. (2009). The social costs of emotional suppression: A prospective study of the transition to college. *Journal of Personality and Social Psychology, 96*, 883–897.

Staats, C. K., & Staats, A. W. (1957). Meaning established by classical conditioning. *Journal of Experimental Psychology, 54*, 74–80.

Stajkovic, A. D., & Luthans, F. (1998). Self-efficacy and work-related performance: A meta-analysis. *Psychological Bulletin, 124*, 240–261.

Stanley, D., Phelps, E., & Banaji, M. (2008). The neural basis of implicit attitudes. *Current Directions in Psychological Science, 17*, 164–170.

Stanovich, K. (2006). *How to think straight about psychology* (7th ed.). Boston, MA: Allyn & Bacon.

Stanwood, G. D., & Levitt, P. (2001). *The effects of cocaine on the developing nervous system.* In C. A. Nelson & M. Luciana (Eds.), *Handbook of developmental cognitive neuroscience.* Cambridge, MA: The MIT Press.

Stark-Wroblewski, K., Yanico, B. J., & Lupe, S. (2005). Acculturation, internalization of Western appearance norms, and eating pathology among Japanese and Chinese international student women. *Psychology of Women Quarterly, 29*, 38–46.

Statistics Canada. (1993). The Violence against Women Survey. *The Daily*, November 18, 1993.

Statistics Canada. (1997). *Canadian injury data: Mortality, 1997 and hospitalizations, 1996–97.* Catalogue 93-356-XPB. Ottawa.

Statistics Canada. (2005). *Insomnia.* Health Report 17(1), Catalogue 82-003-XPE2005001. Ottawa.

Statistics Canada. (2007, March 14). Youth custody and community services. *The Daily.* Retrieved June 20, 2007, from http://www.statcan.ca/Daily/English/070314/d070314d.htm

Statistics Canada. (2008, April 2). 2006 Census: Ethnic origin, visible minorities, place of work and mode of transportation. *The Daily.* Retrieved from http://www.statcan.ca/Daily/English/080402/d080402a.htm

Statistics Canada. (2010). *Life expectancy at birth, by sex, by province.* Retrieved from http://www40.statcan.ca/l01/cst01/health26-eng.htm

Stattin, H., & Magnusson, D. (1990). *Pubertal maturation in female development.* Hillsdale, NJ: Erlbaum.

Staub, E. (1999). The roots of evil: Social conditions, culture, personality, and basic human needs. *Personality and Social Psychology Review, 3*, 179–192.

St. Clair, D., Xu, M., Wang, P., et al. (2005, August 3). Rates of adult schizophrenia following prenatal exposure to the Chinese famine of 1959–1961. *Journal of the American Medical Association, 294*, 557–562.

Stearns, P. N. (1997). *Fat history: Bodies and beauty in the modern West.* New York, NY: New York University Press.

Steele, C. M. (1992, April). Race and the schooling of black Americans. *Atlantic Monthly*, 68–78.

Steele, C. M. (1997). A threat in the air: How stereotypes shape intellectual identity and performance. *American Psychologist, 52*, 613–629.

Steele, C. M., & Aronson, J. (1995). Stereotype threat and the intellectual test performance of African-Americans. *Journal of Personality and Social Psychology, 69*, 797–811.

Stein, M. B., Jang, K. L., Taylor, S., et al. (2002). Genetic and environmental influences on trauma exposure and posttraumatic stress disorder symptoms: A general population twin study. *American Journal of Psychiatry, 159*, 1675–1681.

Steinberg, L. (2007). Risk taking in adolescence. *Current Directions in Psychological Science, 16*, 55–59.

Steinberg, L., & Scott, E. S. (2003). Less guilty by reason of adolescence. *American Psychologist, 58*, 1009–1018.

Steiner, R. A. (1989). *Don't get taken!* El Cerrito, CA: Wide-Awake Books.

Steinvorth, S., Levine, B., & Corkin, S. (2005). Medial temporal lobe structures are needed to re-experience remote autobiographical memories: Evidence from H. M. and W. R. *Neuropsychologia, 43*, 479–496.

Stenberg, C. R., & Campos, J. (1990). The development of anger expressions in infancy. In N. Stein, B. Leventhal, & T. Trabasso (Eds.), *Psychological and biological approaches to emotion.* Hillsdale, NJ: Erlbaum.

Stepanski, E., & Perlis, M. (2000). Behavioral sleep medicine: An emerging subspecialty in health psychology. *Journal of Psychosomatic Research, 49*, 343–347.

Stephan, W. G., Ageyev, V., Coates-Shrider, L., et al. (1994). On the relationship between stereotypes and prejudice: An international study. *Personality and Social Psychology Bulletin, 20*, 277–284.

Sternberg, R. J. (1988). *The triarchic mind: A new theory of human intelligence.* New York, NY: Viking.

Sternberg, R. J. (2004). Culture and intelligence. *American Psychologist, 59*, 325–338.

Sternberg, R. J., Forsythe, G. B., Hedlund, J., et al. (2000). *Practical intelligence in everyday life.* New York, NY: Cambridge University Press.

Sternberg, R. J., Wagner, R. K., Williams, W. M., & Horvath, Joseph A. (1995). Testing common sense. *American Psychologist, 50*, 912–927.

Stevenson, H. W., Chen, C., & Lee, S.-Y. (1993, January 1). Mathematics achievement of Chinese, Japanese, and American children: Ten years later. *Science, 259*, 53–58.

Stevenson, H. W., & Stigler, J. W. (1992). *The learning gap.* New York, NY: Summit.

Stewart-Williams, S., & Podd, J. (2004). The placebo effect: Dissolving the expectancy versus conditioning debate. *Psychological Bulletin, 130*, 324–340.

Stice, E., Spoor, S., Bohon, C., & Small, D. M. (2008, October 17). Relation between obesity and blunted striatal response to food is moderated by *Taq*IA A1 allele. *Science, 322*, 449–452.

Stickgold, R. (2005). Sleep-dependent memory consolidation. *Nature, 437*, 1272–1278.

Stix, G. (2008, August). Lighting up the lies. *Scientific American*, 18–19.

Stoch, M. B., & Smythe, P. M. (1963). Does undernutrition during infancy inhibit brain growth and subsequent intellectual development? *Archives of Diseases in Childhood, 38*, 546–552.

Strahan, E. J., Spencer, S. J., & Zanna, M. P. (2002). Subliminal priming and persuasion: Striking while the iron is hot. *Journal of Experimental Social Psychology, 38*(6), 556–568.

Strauss, E., Wada, J., & Hunter, M. (1994). Callosal morphology and performance on intelligence tests. *Journal of Clinical and Experimental Neuropsychology, 16*(1), 79–83.

Strayer, D. L., & Drews, F. A. (2007). Cell-phone-induced driver distraction. *Current Directions in Psychology, 16,* 128–131.

Streissguth, A. P. (2001). Recent advances in fetal alcohol syndrome and alcohol use in pregnancy. In D. P. Agarwal & H. K. Seitz (Eds.), *Alcohol in health and disease.* New York, NY: Marcel Dekker.

Streyffeler, L. L., & McNally, R. J. (1998). Fundamentalists and liberals: Personality characteristics of Protestant Christians. *Personality and Individual Differences, 24,* 579–580.

Strickland, B. R. (1989). Internal–external control expectancies: From contingency to creativity. *American Psychologist, 44,* 1–12.

Strickland, T. L., Lin, K.-M., Fu, P., et al. (1995). Comparison of lithium ratio between African-American and Caucasian bipolar patients. *Biological Psychiatry, 37,* 325–330.

Strickland, T. L., Ranganath, V., Lin, K.-M., et al. (1991). Psychopharmacological considerations in the treatment of black American populations. *Psychopharmacology Bulletin, 27,* 441–448.

Striegel-Moore, R. H., & Bulik, C. M. (2007). Risk factors for eating disorders. *American Psychologist, 62,* 181–198.

Stunkard, A. J. (Ed.). (1980). *Obesity.* Philadelphia, PA: Saunders.

Styron, W. (1990). Darkness visible: A memoir of madness. New York, NY: Random House.

Suddendorf, T., & Whiten, A. (2001). Mental evolution and development: Evidence for secondary representation in children, great apes, and other animals. *Psychological Bulletin, 127,* 629–650.

Sue, D. W., Capodilupo, C. M., Torino, G. C., et al. (2007). Racial microaggressions in everyday life: Implications for clinical practice. *American Psychologist, 62,* 271–286.

Suedfeld, P. (1975). The benefits of boredom: Sensory deprivation reconsidered. *American Scientist, 63*(1), 60–69.

Suinn, R. M. (2001). The terrible twos—Anger and anxiety. *American Psychologist, 56,* 27–36.

Sullivan, M. J. L., Tripp, D. A., & Santor, D. (1998). *Gender differences in pain and pain behaviour: The role of catastrophizing.* Paper presented at the annual meeting of the American Psychological Association, San Francisco, CA.

Suls, J., Martin, R., & Wheeler, L. (2002). Social comparison: Why, with whom, and with what effect? *Current Directions in Psychological Science, 11,* 159–163.

Suomi, S. J. (1991). Uptight and laid-back monkeys: Individual differences in the response to social challenges. In S. Branch, W. Hall, & J. E. Dooling (Eds.), *Plasticity of development.* Cambridge, MA: MIT Press.

Surowiecki, J. (2004). *The wisdom of crowds.* New York, NY: Doubleday.

Sutherland, R. J., Sparks, F. T., & Lehmann, H. (2010). Hippocampus and retrograde amnesia in the rat model: A modest proposal for the situation of systems consolidation. *Neuropsychologia, 48,* 2357–2369.

Sutherland, R. J., Whishaw, I. Q., & Regehr, J. C. (1982). Cholinergic receptor blockade impairs spatial localization by use of distal cues in the rat. *Journal of Comparative and Physiological Psychology, 96*(4), 563–573.

Svoboda, E., & Richards, B. (2009). Compensating for anterograde amnesia: A new training method that capitalizes on emerging smart-phone technologies. *Journal of the International Neuropsychological Society, 15,* 629–638.

Svoboda, E., Richards, B., Polsinelli, A., & Guger, S. (2010). A theory-driven training programme in the use of emerging commercial technology: Application to an adolescent with severe memory impairment. *Neuropsychological Rehabilitation, 20*(4), 562–586. doi:10.1080/09602011003669918

Swain, S. (1989). Covert intimacy: Closeness in men's friendships. In B. J. Risman & P. Schwartz (Eds.), *Gender in intimate relationships.* Belmont, CA: Wadsworth.

Swartz, M. S., Perkins, D. O., Stroup, T. S., et al., & CATIE Investigators. (2007). Effects of antipsychotic medications on psychosocial functioning in patients with chronic schizophrenia: Findings from the NIMH CATIE study. *American Journal of Psychiatry, 164,* 428–36.

Swenson, C. C., Henggeler, S. W., Taylor, I. S., & Addison, O. W. (2005). *Multisystemic therapy and neighborhood partnerships: Reducing adolescent violence and substance abuse.* New York, NY: Guilford Press.

Symons, D. (1979). *The evolution of human sexuality.* New York, NY: Oxford University Press.

Tafarodi, R. W. (1998). Paradoxical self-esteem and selectivity in the processing of social information. *Journal of Personality and Social Psychology, 74,* 1118–1196.

Tafarodi, R. W., Lang, J. M., & Smith, A. J. (1999). Self-esteem and the cultural trade-off: Evidence for the role of individualism-collectivism. *Journal of Cross-Cultural Psychology, 30,* 620–640.

Tafarodi, R. W., & Milne, A. B. (2002). Decomposing global self-esteem. *Journal of Personality, 70,* 443–483.

Tafarodi, R. W., Tam, J., & Milne, A. B. (2001). Selective memory and the persistence of paradoxical self-esteem. *Personality and Social Psychology Bulletin, 27,* 1179–1189.

Tajfel, H., Billig, M. G., Bundy, R. P., & Flament, C. (1971). Social categorization and intergroup behavior. *European Journal of Social Psychology, 1,* 149–178.

Tajfel, H., & Turner, J. C. (1986). The social identity theory of intergroup behavior. In S. Worchel & W. G. Austin (Eds.), *Psychology of intergroup relations.* Chicago, IL: Nelson-Hall.

Takahashi, K., Tanabe, K., Ohnuki, M., et al. (2007). Induction of pluripotent stem cells from adult human fibroblasts by defined factors. *Cell, 131,* 861–872.

Talarico, J. M., & Rubin, D. C. (2003). Confidence, not consistency, characterizes flashbulb memories. *Psychological Science, 14,* 455–461.

Talbot, M. (2008, May 12). Birdbrain: The woman behind the world's chattiest parrots. *The New Yorker.* Retrieved from http://www.newyorker.com/reporting/2008/05/12/080512fa_fact_talbot

Talbot, M. (2009, April 27). Brain gain: The underground world of neuroenhancing drugs. *The New Yorker,* 32–43.

Talmi, D., Grady, C. L., Goshen-Gottstein, Y., & Moscovitch, M. (2005). Neuroimaging the serial position curve: A test of single-store versus dual-store models. *Psychological Science, 16,* 716–723.

Tang, Y., Zhang, W., Chen, K., et al. (2006). Arithmetic processing in the brain shaped by cultures. *Proceedings of the National Academy of Sciences, 103,* 10775–10780.

Tangney, J. P., Wagner, P. E., Hill-Barlow, D., et al. (1996). Relation of shame and guilt to constructive versus destructive responses to anger across the lifespan. *Journal of Personality and Social Psychology, 70*, 797–809.

Tanner, J. (1990). *Fetus into man: Physical growth from conception to maturity.* Cambridge, MA: Harvard University Press.

Tarbox, S. I., & Pogue-Geile, M. F. (2008). Development of social functioning in preschizophrenia children and adolescents: A systematic review. *Psychological Bulletin, 34*, 561–583.

Taubes, G. (1998). As obesity rates rise, experts struggle to explain why. *Science, 280*, 1367–1368.

Taubes, G. (2008). *Good calories, bad calories: Fats, carbs, and the controversial science of diet and health.* New York, NY: Anchor.

Tavris, C. (1989). *Anger: The misunderstood emotion* (Rev. ed.). New York, NY: Simon & Schuster/Touchstone.

Tavris, C, & Aronson, E. (2007). *Mistakes were made (but not by me).* Orlando, FL: Houghton Mifflin Harcourt.

Taylor, A. K., & Kowalski, P. (2004). Naïve psychological science: The prevalence, strength, and sources of misconceptions. *Psychological Record, 54*, 15–25.

Taylor, S. E., Lichtman, R. R., & Wood, J. V. (1984). Attributions, beliefs about control, and adjustment to breast cancer. *Journal of Personality and Social Psychology, 46*, 489–502.

Taylor, S. E. (2006). Tend and befriend: Biobehavioral bases of affiliation under stress. *Current Directions in Psychological Science, 15*, 273–277.

Taylor, S. E., Kemeny, M. E., Reed, G. M., et al. (2000). Psychological resources, positive illusions, and health. *American Psychologist, 55*, 99–109.

Taylor, S. E., Klein, L. C., Lewis, B. P., et al. (2000). Biobehavioral responses to stress in females: Tend-and-befriend, not fight-or-flight. *Psychological Review, 107*, 411–429.

Taylor, S. E., Lerner, J. S., Sherman, D. K., et al. (2003). Are self-enhancing cognitions associated with healthy or unhealthy biological profiles? *Journal of Personality and Social Psychology, 85*, 605–615.

Taylor, S. E., & Lobel, M. (1989). Social comparison activity under threat: Downward evaluation and upward contacts. *Psychological Review, 96*, 569–575.

Taylor, S. E., Repetti, R., & Seeman, T. (1997). Health psychology: What is an unhealthy environment and how does it get under the skin? *Annual Review of Psychology, 48*, 411–447.

Taylor, S., McKay, D., & Abramowitz, J. S. (2005). Is obsessive-compulsive disorder a disturbance of security motivation? *Psychological Review, 112*, 650–657.

Taylor, S., Thordarson, D. S., Maxfield, L., et al. (2003). Comparative efficacy, speed, and adverse effects of three PTSD treatments: Exposure therapy, EMDR, and relaxation training. *Journal of Consulting and Clinical Psychology, 71*, 330–338.

Terman, L. M., & Oden, M. H. (1959). *Genetic studies of genius: Vol. 5. The gifted group at mid-life.* Stanford, CA: Stanford University Press.

Terracciano, A., & McCrae, R. R. (2006, February). National character does not reflect mean personality traits levels in 49 cultures: Reply. *Science, 311*, 777–779.

The Vanier Institute (2010). *Families count. Profiling Canada's families.* Ottawa: Vanier Institute of the Family.

Thomas, J. J., Vartanian, L. R., & Brownell, K. D. (2009). The relationship between eating disorder not otherwise specified (EDNOS) and officially recognized eating disorders: Meta-analysis and implications for DSM. *Psychological Bulletin, 135*, 407–433.

Thomas, Michael S. C., & Johnson, Mark H. (2008). New advances in understanding sensitive periods in brain development. *Current Directions in Psychological Science, 17*, 1–5.

Thompson, C. (1943/1973). Penis envy in women. *Psychiatry, 6*, 123–125. (Reprinted in J. B. Miller (Ed.), *Psychoanalysis and women.* New York, NY: Brunner/Mazel, 1973.)

Thompson, J. K., & Cafri, G. (Eds.). (2007). *The muscular ideal: Psychological, social, and medical perspectives.* Washington, DC: American Psychological Association.

Thompson, P. M., Vidal, C. N., Giedd, J. N., et al. (2001). Mapping adolescent brain change reveals dynamic wave of accelerated gray matter loss in very early-onset schizophrenia. *Proceedings of the National Academy of Sciences, 98*, 11650–11655.

Thompson, R. F. (1983). Neuronal substrates of simple associative learning: Classical conditioning. *Trends in Neurosciences, 6*, 270–275.

Thompson, R. F. (1986). The neurobiology of learning and memory. *Science, 233*, 941–947.

Thompson, R. F., & Kosslyn, S. M. (2000). Neural systems activated during visual mental imagery: A review and meta-analyses. In A. W. Toga & J. C. Mazziotta (Eds.), *Brain mapping: The systems.* San Diego, CA: Academic Press.

Thompson, R., Emmorey, K., & Gollan, T. H. (2005). "Tip of the fingers" experiences by deaf signers. *Psychological Science, 16*, 856–860.

Thorndike, E. L. (1898). Animal intelligence: An experimental study of the associative processes in animals. *Psychological Review Monograph Supplement, 2* (Whole No. 8).

Thorndike, E. L. (1903). *Educational psychology.* New York, NY: Columbia University Teachers College.

Thornhill, R., & Palmer, C. T. (2000). *A natural history of rape: Biological bases of sexual coercion.* Cambridge, MA: MIT Press.

Tiefer, L. (2004). *Sex is not a natural act, and other essays* (Rev. ed.). Boulder, CO: Westview.

Tiefer, L. (2008). Sexual problems. In Clouse, A. (Ed.), *Women's health in clinical practice: A handbook for primary care.* Totowa, NJ: Humana Press.

Timmann, D., Drepper, J., Frings, M., et al. (2010). The human cerebellum contributes to motor, emotional and cognitive associative learning. A review. *Cortex, 46*(7), 845–857.

Timmers, M., Fischer, A. H., & Manstead, A. S. R. (1998). Gender differences in motives for regulating emotions. *Personality and Social Psychology Bulletin, 24*, 974–985.

Tolman, E. C. (1938). The determiners of behavior at a choice point. *Psychological Review, 45*, 1–35.

Tolman, E. C., & Honzik, C. H. (1930). Introduction and removal of reward and maze performance in rats. *University of California Publications in Psychology, 4*, 257–275.

Tomasello, M. (2000). Culture and cognitive development. *Current Directions in Psychological Science, 9*, 37–40.

Tomasello, M. (2008). *Origins of human communication.* Cambridge, MA: MIT Press.

Tomlinson, M., Cooper, P., & Murray, L. (2005). The mother–infant relationship and infant attachment in a South African peri-urban settlement. *Child Development, 76*, 1044–1054.

Tomppo, L., Hennah, W., Miettunen, J., et al. (2009). Association of variants in DISC1 with psychosis-related traits in a large population cohort. *Archives of General Psychiatry, 66,* 134–141.

Toomela, A. (2003). Relationships between personality structure, structure of word meaning, and cognitive ability: A study of cultural mechanisms of personality. *Journal of Personality and Social Psychology, 85,* 723–735.

Tormala, Z. L., & Petty, R. E. (2002). What doesn't kill me makes me stronger: The effects of resisting persuasion on attitude certainty. *Journal of Personality and Social Psychology, 83,* 1298–1313.

Tourangeau, R., & Yan, T. (2007). Sensitive questions in surveys. *Psychological Bulletin, 133,* 859–883.

Tracy, J. L., & Robins, R. W. (2007). Emerging insights into the nature and function of pride. *Current Directions in Psychological Science, 16,* 147–151.

Tracy, J. L., & Robins, R. W. (2008). The nonverbal expression of pride: Evidence for cross-cultural recognition. *Journal of Personality and Social Psychology, 94,* 516–530.

Trakas, K., Lawrence, K., & Shear, N. H. (1999). Utilization of health care resources by obese Canadians. *Canadian Medical Association Journal, 160,* 1457–1462.

Transport Canada. (1998). *Seat belt use in Canada: 1998 survey results.* Retrieved from http://www.tc.gc.ca/roadsafety/stats/sbuse98/English/sb98sume.htm

Triandis, H. C. (1996). The psychological measurement of cultural syndromes. *American Psychologist, 51,* 407–415.

Triandis, H. C. (2007). Culture and psychology: A history of the study of their relationship. In S. Kitayama & D. Cohen (Eds.), *Handbook of cultural psychology.* New York, NY: Guilford Press.

Trivers, R. (1972). Parental investment and sexual selection. In B. Campbell (Ed.), *Sexual selection and the descent of man.* New York, NY: Aldine de Gruyter.

Trivers, R. (2004). Mutual benefits at all levels of life [book review.] *Science, 304,* 965.

Tronick, E. Z., Morelli, G. A., & Ivey, P. K. (1992). The Efe forager infant and toddler's pattern of social relationships: Multiple and simultaneous. *Developmental Psychology, 28,* 568–577.

Trzesniewski, K. H., Donnellan, M. B., & Robins, R. W. (2008). Do today's young people really think they are so extraordinary? An examination of secular changes in narcissism and self-enhancement. *Psychological Science, 19,* 181–188.

Tsuang, M. T., Bar, J. L., Harley, R. M., & Lyons, M. J. (2001). The Harvard Twin Study of Substance Abuse: What we have learned. *Harvard Review of Psychiatry, 9,* 267–279.

Tulving, E. (1985). How many memory systems are there? *American Psychologist, 40,* 385–398.

Turati, C. (2004). Why faces are not special to newborns: An alternative account of the face preference. *Current Directions in Psychological Science, 13,* 5–8.

Turiel, E. (2002). *The culture of morality.* Cambridge, England: Cambridge University Press.

Turkheimer, E., Haley, A., Waldron, M., D'Onofrio, B., & Gottesman, I. I. (2003). Socioeconomic status modifies heritability of IQ in young children. *Psychological Science, 14,* 623–628.

Turner, C. F., Ku, L., Rogers, S. M., et al. (1998). Adolescent sexual behavior, drug use, and violence: Increased reporting with computer survey technology. *Science, 280,* 867–873.

Turner, E. H., Matthews, A. M., Linardatos, E., et al. (2008). Selective publication of antidepressant trials and its influence on apparent efficacy. *New England Journal of Medicine, 358,* 252–60.

Turner, M. E., Pratkanis, A. R., & Samuels, T. (2003). Identity metamorphosis and groupthink prevention: Examining Intel's departure from the DRAM industry. In A. Haslam, D. van Knippenberg, M. Platow, & N. Ellemers (Eds.), *Social identity at work: Developing theory for organizational practice.* Philadelphia, PA: Psychology Press.

Turvey, B. E. (2008). Serial crime. In B. E. Turvey (Ed.), *Criminal profiling: An introduction to behavioral evidence analysis* (3rd ed.). San Diego, CA: Elsevier Academic Press.

Tustin, K., & Hayne, H. (2006). *A new method to measure childhood amnesia in children, adolescents, and adults.* Poster presented at the annual meeting of the International Society for the Study of Behavioural Development, Melbourne, Australia.

Tversky, A., & Kahneman, D. (1973). Availability: A heuristic for judging frequency and probability. *Cognitive Psychology, 5,* 207–232.

Tversky, A., & Kahneman, D. (1981). The framing of decisions and the psychology of choice. *Science, 211,* 453–458.

Twenge, J. (2009). Change over time in obedience: The jury's still out, but it might be decreasing. *American Psychologist, 64,* 28–31.

Twenge, J. M., Konrath, S., Foster, J. D., et al. (2008). Egos inflating over time: A cross-temporal meta-analysis of the Narcissistic Personality Inventory. *Journal of Personality, 76,* 875–901.

Tyrer, P., Oliver-Africano, P. C., Ahmed, Z., et al. (2008, January 5). Risperidone, haloperidol, and placebo in the treatment of aggressive challenging behaviour in patients with intellectual disability: A randomised controlled trial. *Lancet, 371,* 57–63.

Uhlhaas, P. J., & Silverstein, S. M. (2005). Perceptual organization in schizophrenia spectrum disorders: Empirical research and theoretical implications. *Psychological Bulletin, 131,* 618–632.

Ullian, E. M., Chrisopherson, K. S., & Barres, B. A. (2004). Role for glia in synaptogenesis. *Glia, 47,* 209–216.

Unsworth, N., & Engle, R. W. (2007). On the division of short-term and working memory: An examination of simple and complex span and their relation to higher order abilities. *Psychological Bulletin, 133,* 1038–1066.

Updegraff, J. A., Gable, S. L., & Taylor, S. E. (2004). What makes experiences satisfying? The interaction of approach-avoidance motivations and emotions in well-being. *Journal of Personality and Social Psychology, 86,* 496–504.

Urry, H. L., Nitschke, J. B., Dolski, I., et al. (2004). Making a life worth living: Neural correlates of well-being. *Psychological Science, 15,* 367–372.

Usher, J. A., & Neisser, U. (1993). Childhood amnesia and the beginnings of memory for four early life events. *Journal of Experimental Psychology: General, 122,* 155–165.

Uttal, W. R. (2001). *The new phrenology: The limits of localizing cognitive processes in the brain.* Cambridge, MA: MIT Press/Bradford Books.

Vaillant, G. E. (1983). *The natural history of alcoholism: Causes, patterns, and paths to recovery.* Cambridge, MA: Harvard University Press.

Vaillant, G. E. (Ed.). (1992). *Ego mechanisms of defense.* Washington, DC: American Psychiatric Press.

Valenstein, E. (1986). *Great and desperate cures: The rise and decline of psychosurgery and other radical treatments for mental illness.* New York, NY: Basic Books.

Valentine, T., & Mesout, J. (2009). Eyewitness identification under stress in the London dungeon. *Applied Cognitive Psychology,23,* 151–161.

Van Boven, L., & Gilovich, T. (2003). To do or to have? That is the question. *Journal of Personality and Social Psychology, 85,* 1193–1202.

Van Cantfort, T. E., & Rimpau, J. B. (1982). Sign language studies with children and chimpanzees. *Sign Language Studies, 34,* 15–72.

Van de Castle, R. (1994). *Our dreaming mind.* New York, NY: Ballantine Books.

van den Dries, L., Juffer, F., van IJzendoorn, M. H., & Bakermans-Kranenburg, M. J. (2009). Fostering security? A meta-analysis of attachment in adopted children. *Children and Youth Services Review, 31,* 410–421.

Vandello, J. A., & Cohen, D. (2008). U.S. Southern and Northern differences in perceptions of norms about aggression: Mechanisms for the perpetuation of a culture of honor. *Social and Personality Psychology Compass, 2,* 652–667.

Vandello, J. A., Cohen, D., Ransom, S. (2008). U.S. Southern and Northern differences in perceptions of norms about aggression: Mechanisms for the perpetuation of a culture of honor. *Journal of Cross-Cultural Psychology, 39,* 162–177.

Vandenberg, B. (1985). Beyond the ethology of play. In A. Gottfried & C. C. Brown (Eds.), *Play interactions.* Lexington, MA: Lexington Books.

Van Emmerik, A. A., Kamphuis, J. H., Hulsbosch, A. M., & Emmelkamp, P. M. G. (2002, September 7). Single session debriefing after psychological trauma: A meta-analysis. *The Lancet, 360,* 766–771.

van Gelder, B. M., Tijhuis, M., Kalmijn, S., & Kromhout, D. (2007). Fish consumption, n-3 fatty acids, and subsequent 5-y cognitive decline in elderly men: The Zutphen Elderly Study. *American Journal of Clinical Nutrition, 85,* 1142–1147.

van Goozen, S. H. M., Fairchild, G., Snoek, H., & Harold, G. T. (2007). The evidence for a neurobiological model of childhood antisocial behavior. *Psychological Bulletin, 133,* 149–182.

van Laar, C., Levin, S., & Sidanius, J. (2008). Ingroup and outgroup contact: A longitudinal study of the effects of cross-ethnic friendships, dates, roommate relationships and participation in segregated organizations. In U. Wagner, L. R. Tropp, G. Finchilescu, & C. Tredoux (Eds.), *Improving intergroup relations: Building on the legacy of Thomas F. Pettigrew.* Malden, MA: Blackwell.

Van Ommeren, M., Saxena, S., & Saraceno, B. (2005, January). Mental and social health during and after acute emergencies: Emerging consensus? *Bulletin of the World Health Organization, 83,* 71–76.

van Schaik, C. (2006, April). Why are some animals so smart? *Scientific American,* 64–71.

Vecera, S. P., Vogel, E., K., & Woodman, G. F. (2002). Lower region: A new cue for figure-ground assignment. *Journal of Experimental Psychology: General, 131,* 194–205.

Vertes, R. P., & Siegel, J. M. (2005). Time for the sleep community to take a critical look at the purported role of sleep in memory processing. *Sleep, 28,* 1228–1229.

Vita, A. J., Terry, R. B., Hubert, H. B., & Fries, J. F. (1998). Aging, health risks, and cumulative disability. *New England Journal of Medicine, 338,* 1035–1041.

Vogelzangs, N., Kritchevsky, S. B., Beekman, A. T., et al. (2008). Depressive symptoms and change in abdominal obesity in older persons. *Archives of General Psychiatry, 65,* 1386–1393.

Voigt, B. F., Kudaravalli, S., Wen, X., & Pritchard, J. K. (2006). A map of recent positive selection in the human genome. *PLoS Biology, 4,* e72.

Volkow, N. D., Chang, L, Wang, G.-J., et al. (2001). Association of dopamine transporter reduction with psychomotor impairment in methamphetamine abusers. *American Journal of Psychiatry, 158,* 377–382.

Voyer, D., Voyer, S., & Bryden, M. P. (1995). Magnitude of sex differences in spatial abilities: A meta-analysis and consideration of critical variables. *Psychological Bulletin, 117,* 250–270.

Vroon, P. (1997). *Smell: The secret seducer* [P. Vincent, Trans.] New York, NY: Farrar, Straus & Giroux.

Vul, E., Harris, C., Winkielman, P., & Pashler, Harold. (2009). Puzzlingly high correlations in fMRI studies of emotion, personality, and social cognition. *Perspectives on Psychological Science, 4,* 274–290.

Vul, E., & Pashler, H. (2008). Measuring the crowd within. *Psychological Science, 19,* 645–647.

Vygotsky, L. (1962). *Thought and language.* Cambridge, MA: MIT Press.

Vygotsky, L. (1978). *Mind in society: The development of higher psychological processes.*Cambridge, MA: Harvard University Press. (Originals published in 1930, 1933, and 1935.)

Wadden, T. A., Foster, G. D., Letizia, K. A., & Mullen, J. L. (1990, August 8). Long-term effects of dieting on resting metabolic rate in obese outpatients. *Journal of the American Medical Association, 264,* 707–711.

Wade, C. (2006). Some cautions about jumping on the brain-scan bandwagon. *APS Observer, 19,* 23–24.

Wagenaar, W. A. (1986). My memory: A study of autobiographical memory over six years. *Cognitive Psychology, 18,* 225–252.

Wagner, C. C., & Ingersoll, K. S. (2008). Beyond cognition: Broadening the emotional base of motivational interviewing. *Journal of Psychotherapy Integration, 18,* 191–206.

Wagner, U., Gais, S., Haider, H., et al. (2004). Sleep inspires insight. *Nature, 427,* 352–355.

Wakefield, J. C. (1992). Disorder as harmful dysfunction: A conceptual critique of DSM-III-R's definition of mental disorder. *Psychological Review, 99,* 232–247.

Wakefield, J. C., Schmitz, M. F., First, M. B., & Horwitz, A. V. (2007). Extending the bereavement exclusion for major depression to other losses: Evidence from the National Comorbidity Survey. *Archives of General Psychiatry, 64,* 433–440.

Waldram, J. B., & Wong, S. (1995). Group therapy of Aboriginal offenders in a Canadian forensic psychiatric facility. *American Indian and Alaska Native Mental Health Research, 6(2),* 34–56.

Wahlheim, C. N., & Dunlosky, J., & Jacoby, L. L. (in press). Spacing enhances the learning of natural concepts: An investigation of mechanisms, metacognition, and aging. *Memory and Cognition.*

Walker, A. (1994). Mood and well-being in consecutive menstrual cycles: Methodological and theoretical implications. *Psychology of Women Quarterly, 18,* 271–290.

Walker, D. L., Ressler, K. J., Lu, K.-T., & Davis, M. (2002). Facilitation of conditioned fear extinction by systemic administration or intra-amygdala infusions of D-cycloserine as assessed with fear-potentiated startle in rats. *The Journal of Neuroscience, 22,* 2343–2351.

Walker, E., & Tessner, K. (2008). Schizophrenia. *Perspectives on Psychological Science, 3,* 30–37.

Walker-Andrews, A. S. (1997). Infants' perception of expressive behaviors: Differentiation of multimodal information. *Psychological Bulletin, 121,* 437–456.

Wallace-Wells, B. (2009, February 5). Bitter pill. *Rolling Stone,* 56–63, 74–76.

Wallbott, H. G., Ricci-Bitti, P., & Bänninger-Huber, E. (1986). Non-verbal reactions to emotional experiences. In K. R. Scherer, H. G. Wallbott, & A. B. Summerfield (Eds.), *Experiencing emotion: A cross-cultural study.* Cambridge, England: Cambridge University Press.

Wallen, K. (2001). Sex and context: Hormones and primate sexual motivation. *Hormones and Behavior, 40,* 339–357.

Waller, N. G., Kojetin, B. A., Bouchard, T. J., Jr., et al. (1990). Genetic and environmental influences on religious interests, attitudes, and values: A study of twins reared apart and together. *Psychological Science, 1,* 138–142.

Walum, H., Westberg, L., Henningsson, S., et al. (2008). Genetic variation in the vasopressin receptor 1a gene (AVPR1A) associates with pair-bonding behavior in humans. *Proceedings of the National Academy of Sciences, 105,* 14153–14156.

Wampold, B. (2001). *The great psychotherapy debate: Models, methods, and findings.* Mahwah, NJ: Erlbaum.

Wandersman, A., & Nation, M. (1998). Urban neighborhoods and mental health: Psychological contributions to understanding toxicity, resilience, and interventions. *American Psychologist, 53,* 647–656.

Wang, Q. (2008). Being American, being Asian: The bicultural self and autobiographical memory in Asian Americans. *Cognition, 107,* 743–751.

Wang, R., & Bianchi, S. (2009). ATUS fathers' involvement in childcare. *Social Indicator Research, 93,* 141–145.

Wansink, B. (2006). *Mindless eating.* New York, NY: Bantam.

Warren, G. H., & Raynes, A. E. (1972). Mood changes during three conditions of alcohol intake. *Quarterly Journal of Studies on Alcohol, 33,* 979–989.

Wasserman, E. W., & Lisanby, S. H. (2001). Therapeutic application of repetitive transcranial magnetic stimulation: A review. *Clinical Neurophysiology, 112,* 1367–1377.

Watanabe, S. (2001). Van Gogh, Chagall and pigeons: Picture discrimination in pigeons and humans. *Animal Cognition, 4,* 1435–9448.

Watkins, L. R., & Maier, S. F. (2003). When good pain turns bad. *Current Directions in Psychological Science, 12,* 232–236.

Watson, J. B. (1925). *Behaviorism.* New York, NY: Norton.

Watson, J. B., & Rayner, R. (1920). Conditioned emotional reactions. *Journal of Experimental Psychology, 3,* 1–14. (Reprinted May 2000 in *American Psychologist, 55,* 313–317.)

Watters, E., & Ofshe, R. (1999). *Therapy's delusions.* New York, NY: Scribner.

Weaver, C. N. (2008). Social distance as a measure of prejudice among ethnic groups in the United States. *Journal of Applied Social Psychology, 38,* 778–795.

Webster, R. (1995). *Why Freud was wrong.* New York, NY: Basic Books.

Wechsler, D. (1955). *Manual for the Wechsler Adult Intelligence Scale.* New York, NY: Psychological Corporation.

Wegner, D. M., Fuller, V. A., & Sparrlow, B. (2003). Clever hands: Uncontrolled intelligence in facilitated communication. *Journal of Personality and Social Psychology, 85,* 5–19.

Wegner, D. M., & Gold, D. B. (1995). Fanning old flames: Emotional and cognitive effects of suppressing thoughts of a past relationship. *Journal of Personality and Social Psychology, 68,* 782–792.

Wehr, T. A., Duncan, W. C., Sher, L., et al. (2001). A circadian signal of change of season in patients with seasonal affective disorder. *Archives of General Psychiatry, 58,* 1108–1114.

Weil, A. T. (1972/1986). *The natural mind: A new way of looking at drugs and the higher consciousness.* Boston, MA: Houghton-Mifflin.

Weil, A. T. (1974a, June). Parapsychology: Andrew Weil's search for the true Geller. *Psychology Today,* 45–50.

Weil, A. T. (1974b, July). Parapsychology: Andrew Weil's search for the true Geller: Part II. The letdown. *Psychology Today,* 74–78, 82.

Weiner, B. (1986). *An attributional theory of motivation and emotion.* New York, NY: Springer-Verlag.

Weinstein, T. A., Capitanio, J. P., & Gosling, S. D. (2008). Personality in animals. In O. P. John, R. W. Robbins, & L. A. Pervin (Eds.), *Handbook of personality: Theory and research.* New York, NY: Guilford.

Weiss, A., Bates, T. C., & Luciano, M. (2008). Happiness is a personal(ity) thing. *Psychological Science, 19,* 205–210.

Weiss, E., Longhurst, J. G., & Mazure, C. M. (1999). Childhood sexual abuse as a risk factor for depression in women: Psychological and neurological correlates. *American Journal of Psychiatry, 156,* 816–828.

Weissman, M. M., Markowitz, J. C., & Klerman, G. L. (2000). *Comprehensive guide to interpersonal psychotherapy.* New York, NY: Basic Books.

Weisz, J. R., Weiss, B., Han, S. S., et al. (1995). Effects of psychotherapy with children and adolescents revisited: A meta-analysis of treatment outcome studies. *Psychological Bulletin, 117,* 450–468.

Wellman, H. M., Cross, D., & Watson, J. (2001). Meta-analysis of theory-of-mind development: The truth about false belief. *Child Development, 72,* 655–684.

Wells, B. E., & Twenge, J. (2005). Changes in young people's sexual behavior and attitudes, 1943–1999: A cross-temporal meta-analysis. *Review of General Psychology, 9,* 249–261.

Wells, G. L., & Olson, E. A. (2003). Eyewitness testimony. *Annual Review of Psychology, 54,* 277–295.

Wells, G. L., Small, M., Penrod, S., et al. (1998). Eyewitness identification procedures: Recommendations for lineups and photospreads. *Law and Human Behavior, 22,* 602–647.

Wender, P. H., & Klein, D. F. (1981). *Mind, mood, and medicine: A guide to the new biopsychiatry.* New York, NY: Farrar, Straus and Giroux.

Wenzel, A. (2005). Autobiographical memory tasks in clinical research. In A. Wenzel & D. C. Rubin (Eds.), *Cognitive methods and their application to clinical research.* Washington, DC: American Psychological Association.

Werner, E. E. (1989). High-risk children in young adulthood: A longitudinal study from birth to 32 years. *American Journal of Orthopsychiatry, 59,* 72–81.

Wertheimer, M. (1958). Principles of perceptual organization. In D. C. Beardslee & M. Wertheimer (Eds.), *Readings in perception.* Princeton, NJ: Van Nostrand. [Original work published 1923.]

West, M. O., & Prinz, R. J. (1987). Parental alcoholism and childhood psychopathology. *Psychological Bulletin, 102,* 204–218.

Westen, D. (1998). The scientific legacy of Sigmund Freud: Toward a psychodynamically informed psychological science. *Psychological Bulletin, 124,* 333–371.

Westen, D., Novotny, C. M., & Thompson-Brenner, H. (2004). The empirical status of empirically supported psychotherapies: Assumptions, findings, and reporting in controlled clinical trials. *Psychological Bulletin, 130,* 631–663.

Westen, D., & Shedler, J. (1999). Revising and assessing axis II, Part II: Toward an empirically based and clinically useful classification of personality disorders. *American Journal of Psychiatry, 156,* 273–285.

Wethington, E. (2000). Expecting stress: Americans and the "midlife crisis." *Motivation & Emotion, 24,* 85–103.

Whaley, A. L., & Davis, K. E. (2007). Cultural competence and evidence-based practice in mental health services. *American Psychologist, 62,* 563–574.

Wheeler, D. L. (1998, September 11). Neuroscientists take stock of brain-imaging studies. *Chronicle of Higher Education,* A20–A21.

Wheeler, M. D. (1991). Physical changes of puberty. *Endocrinology and Metabolism Clinics of North America,20*(1), 1–14.

Wheeler, M. E., & Fiske, S. T. (2005). Controlling racial prejudice: Social-cognitive goals affect amygdala and stereotype activation. *Psychological Science, 16,* 56–63.

Whiting, B., & Whiting, J. (1975). *Children of six cultures.* Cambridge, MA: Harvard University Press.

Whiting, B. B., & Edwards, C. P. (1988). *Children of different worlds: The formation of social behavior.* Cambridge, MA: Harvard University Press.

Whitlock, J. R., Heynen, A. J., Shuler, M. G., & Bear, M. F. (2006, August 25). Learning induces long-term potentiation in the hippocampus. *Science, 313,* 1093–1098.

Whitty, M. T., & Carr, A. N. (2006). New rules in the workplace: Applying object-relations theory to explain problem Internet and email behaviour in the workplace. *Computers in Human Behavior, 22,* 235–250.

Whooley, M. A., de Jonge, P., Vittinghoff, E., et al. (2008). Depressive symptoms, health behaviors, and risk of cardiovascular events in patients with coronary heart disease. *Journal of the American Medical Association, 300,* 2379–2388.

Whorf, B. L. (1956). *Language, thought and reality.* Cambridge, MA: MIT Press. [Original work published 1940.]

Wickett, J. C., Vernon, P. A., & Lee, D. H. (2000). Relationships between factors of intelligence and brain volume. *Personality and Individual Differences, 29*(6), 1095–1122.

Wicks-Nelson, R., & Israel, A. C. (2003). *Behavior disorders of childhood* (5th ed.). Upper Saddle River, NJ: Prentice Hall.

Widiger, T. A., Cadoret, R., Hare, R., et al. (1996). DSM-IV antisocial personality disorder field trial. *Journal of Abnormal Psychology, 105,* 3–16.

Widiger, T., & Clark, L. A. (2000). Toward DSM-V and the classification of psychopathology. *Psychological Bulletin, 126,* 946–963.

Widom, C. S., DuMont, K., & Czaja, S. J. (2007). A prospective investigation of major depressive disorder and comorbidity in abused and neglected children grown up. *Archives of General Psychiatry, 64,* 49–56.

Wildman, R. P., Muntner, P., Reynolds, K., et al. (2008, August 11). The obese without cardiometabolic risk factor clustering and the normal weight with cardiometabolic risk factor clustering: Prevalence and correlates of 2 phenotypes among the US population. *Archives of Internal Medicine, 168,* 1617–1624.

Williams, J. E., Paton, C. C., Siegler, I. C., et al. (2000). Anger proneness predicts coronary heart disease risk. *Circulation, 101,* 2034–2039.

Williams, K. D. (2009). Ostracism: Effects of being excluded and ignored. *Advances in Experimental Social Psychology, 41,* 279–314.

Williams, L. A., & DeSteno, D. (2009). Pride: Adaptive social emotion or seventh sin? *Psychological Science, 20,* 284–288.

Williams, R. J., & Gloster, S. P. (1999). Knowledge of fetal alcohol syndrome (FAS) among natives in Northern Manitoba. *Journal of Studies on Alcohol, 60*(6), 833–836.

Williams, R. B., Jr., Barefoot, J. C., & Shekelle, R. B. (1985). The health consequences of hostility. In M. A. Chesney & R. H. Rosenman (Eds.), *Anger and hostility in cardiovascular and behavioral disorders.* New York, NY: Hemisphere.

Williamson, D. L., & Fast, J. E. (1998). Poverty and medical treatment: When public policy compromises accessibility. *Canadian Journal of Public Health, 89*(2), 120–124.

Wilner, D., Walkley, R., & Cook, S. (1955). *Human relations in interracial housing.* Minneapolis: University of Minnesota Press.

Wiltermuth, S. S., & Heath, C. (2009). Synchrony and cooperation. *Psychological Science, 20,* 1–5.

Wilson, E. O. (1975). *Sociobiology: The new synthesis.* Cambridge, MA: Belknap/Harvard University Press.

Wilson, G. T., & Fairburn, C. G. (1993). Cognitive treatments for eating disorders. *Journal of Consulting and Clinical Psychology, 61,* 261–269.

Wilson, S. J., & Lipsey, M. W. (2007). School-based interventions for aggressive and disruptive behavior: Update of a meta-analysis. *American Journal of Preventive Medicine, 33,* S130–S143.

Wilson, T. D., & Gilbert, D. T. (2005). Affective forecasting: Knowing what to want. *Current Directions in Psychological Science, 14,* 131–134.

Winick, M., Meyer, K. K., & Harris, R. C. (1975). Malnutrition and environmental enrichment by early adoption. *Science, 190,* 1173–1175.

Winnicott, D. W. (1957/1990). *Home is where we start from.* New York, NY: Norton.

Wirth, J. H., & Bodenhausen, G. V. (2009). The role of gender in mental-illness stigma: A national experiment. *Psychological Science, 20,* 169–173.

Wirz-Justice, A., Benedetti, F., Berger, M., et al. (2005). Chronotherapeutics (light and wake therapy) in affective disorders. *Psychological Medicine, 35,* 939–944.

Wispé, L. G., & Drambarean, N. C. (1953). Physiological need, word frequency, and visual duration thresholds. *Journal of Experimental Psychology, 46,* 25–31.

Witelson, S. F., Glazer, I. I., & Kigar, D. L. (1994). Sex differences in numerical density of neurons in human auditory association cortex. *Society for Neuroscience Abstracts, 30.* (Abstr. No. 582.12).

Witkiewitz, K., & Marlatt, G. A. (2004). Relapse prevention for alcohol and drug problems: That was Zen, this is Tao. *American Psychologist, 59,* 224–235.

Witkiewitz, K., & Marlatt, G. A. (2006). Overview of harm reduction treatments for alcohol problems. *International Journal of Drug Policy, 17,* 285–294.

Witvliet, C. vanOyen, Ludwig, T. E., & Vander Laan, K. L. (2001). Granting forgiveness or harboring grudges: Implications for emotion, physiology, and health. *Psychological Science, 12,* 117–123.

Wolfson, A. R., and Carskadon, M. A. (1998). Sleep schedules and daytime functioning in adolescents. *Child Development, 69,* 875–887.

Wolpe, J. (1958). *Psychotherapy by reciprocal inhibition.* Palo Alto, CA: Stanford University Press.

Wood, E., Tyndall, M. W., Kerr, T., et al. (2002). Safer injection facilitates for injection drug users: The debate continues. *Canadian Medical Association Journal, 166*(4), 422.

Wood, J. M., Nezworski, M. T., Lilienfeld, S. O., & Garb, H. N. (2003). *What's wrong with the Rorschach?* San Francisco, CA: Jossey-Bass.

Wood, J. V., Michela, J. L., & Giordano, C. (2000). Downward comparison in everyday life: Reconciling self-enhancement models with the mood-cognition priming model. *Journal of Personality and Social Psychology, 79,* 563–579.

Wood, W., Lundgren, S., Ouellette, J. A., et al. (1994). Minority influence: A meta-analytic review of social influence processes. *Psychological Bulletin, 115,* 323–345.

Woodward, A. L. (2009). Infants' grasp of others' intentions. *Current Directions in Psychological Science, 18,* 53–57.

Woody, E. Z., & Bowers, K. S. (1994). A frontal assault on dissociated control. In S. J. Lynn & J. W. Rhue (Eds.), *Dissociation: Clinical, theoretical and research perspectives.* New York, NY: Guilford.

World Health Organization (WHO) (2004). Annex Table 3: Burden of disease in DALYs by cause, sex, and mortality stratum in WHO regions, estimates for 2002. *The World Health Report 2004: Changing History.* Geneva, Switzerland: WHO.

Wright, S. C., Taylor, D. M., & Ruggiero, K. M. (1996). Examining the potential for academic achievement among Inuit children: Comparisons on the Raven Coloured Progressive Matrices. *Journal of Cross Cultural Psychology, 27*(6), 733–753.

Wu, S., & Keysar, B. (2007). The effect of culture on perspective taking. *Psychological Science, 18,* 600–606.

Wynne, C. D. L. (2004). *Do animals think?* Princeton, NJ: Princeton University Press.

Wyrobek, A. J., Eskenazi, B., Young, S., et al. (2006, June 9). Advancing age has differential effects on DNA damage, chromatin integrity, gene mutations, and aneuploidies in sperm. *Proceedings of the National Academy of Sciences, 103,* 9601–9606.

Xiu, L. J., Lin, H. M., & Wei, P. K. (2010). The effect of chronic mild stress on tumor-bearing rats' behavior and its mechanism. *Neuroscience Letters, 473,* 1–4.

Yalom, I. D. (1989). *Love's executioner and other tales of psychotherapy.* New York, NY: Basic Books.

Yang, C.-F. J., Gray, P., & Pope, H. G., Jr. (2005). Male body image in Taiwan versus the West: Yanggang Zhiqi meets the Adonis Complex. *American Journal of Psychiatry, 162,* 263–269.

Yapko, M. (1994). *Suggestions of abuse: True and false memories of childhood sexual trauma.* New York, NY: Simon & Schuster.

Yardley, J. (2001, September 8). Despair plagued mother held in children's deaths. *The New York Times,* A16.

Yee, N., Bailenson, J. N., Urbanek, M., et al. (2007). The unbearable likeness of being digital: The persistence of nonverbal social norms in online virtual environments. *CyberPsychology & Behavior, 10,* 115–121.

Young, L. J., & Francis, D. D. (2008). The biochemistry of family commitment and youth competence: Lessons from animal models. In K. Kline (Ed.), *Authoritative communities: The scientific case for nurturing the whole child.* New York, NY: Springer Science + Business Media.

Young, M. P., & Yamane, S. (1992). Sparse population coding of faces in the inferotemporal cortex. *Science, 256,* 1327–1331.

Young, T. K. (1996). Obesity, central fat patterning, and their metabolic correlated among Inuit of the central Canadian Arctic. *Human Biology, 68,* 245–263.

Young, T., Finne, L., Peppard, P. E., et al. (2008). Sleep-disordered breathing and mortality: Eighteen-year follow-up of the Wisconsin Sleep Cohort. *Sleep, 31,* 1071–1078.

Yu, J., Vodyanik, M. A., Smuga-Otto, K., et al. (2007). Induced pluripotent stem cell lines derived from human somatic cells. *Science, 318,* 1917–1920.

Yu, M., & Stiffman, A. R. (2007). Culture and environment as predictors of alcohol abuse/dependence symptoms in American Indian youths. *Addictive Behaviors, 32,* 2253–2259.

Yzerbyt, V. Y., Corneille, O., Dumont, M., & Hahn, K. (2001). The dispositional inference strikes back: Situational focus and dispositional suppression in causal attribution. *Journal of Personality and Social Psychology, 81,* 365–376.

Zagon, I. K. (1995). Psychopathy: A viable alternative to antisocial personality disorder? *Australian Psychologist, 30*(1), 11–16.

Zajonc, R. B. (1968). Attitudinal effects of mere exposure. *Journal of Personality and Social Psychology, 9,* Monograph Supplement 2, 1–27.

Zhang, Y., Hoon, M. A., Chandrashekar, J., et al. (2003). Coding of sweet, bitter, and umami tastes: Different receptor cells sharing similar signaling pathways. *Cell, 112,* 293–301.

Zhang, Y., Proenca, R., Maffei, M., et al. (1994). Positional cloning of the mouse obese gene and its human homologue. *Nature, 372*(6505), 425–432.

Zhu, L. X., Sharma, S., Stolina, M., et al. (2000). Delta-9-tetrahydrocannabinol inhibits antitumor immunity by a CB2 receptor-mediated, cytokine-dependent pathway. *Journal of Immunology, 165,* 373–380.

Zimbardo, P. G., & Leippe, M. R. (1991). *The psychology of attitude change and social influence.* New York, NY: McGraw-Hill.

Zimmer, L., & Morgan, J. P. (1997). *Marijuana myths, marijuana fact: A review of the scientific evidence.* New York, NY: Lindesmith Center.

Zimmerman, F. J., Christakis, D. A., & Meltzoff, A. N. (2007). Associations between media viewing and language development in children under age 2 years. *Journal of Pediatrics, 151,* 364–368.

Zone, N., Sue, S., Chang, J., et al. (2005). Beyond ethnic match: Effects of client–therapist cognitive match in problem perception, coping orientation, and therapy goals on treatment outcomes. *Journal of Community Psychology, 33,* 569–585.

Zorrilla, L. T., Cannon, T. D., Kronenberg, S., et al. (1997, December 15). Structural brain abnormalities in schizophrenia: A family study. *Biological Psychiatry, 42,* 1080–1086.

Zosuls, K. M., Ruble, D. N., Tamis-LeMonda, C. S., et al. (2009). The acquisition of gender labels in infancy: Implications for gender-typed play. *Developmental Psychology, 45,* 688–701.

Zou, Z., & Buck, L. (2006). Combinatorial effects of odorant mixes in olfactory cortex. *Science, 311,* 1477–1481.

Zucker, K. J. (1999). Intersexuality and gender identity differentiation. *Annual Review of Sex Research, 10,* 1–69.

Zurbriggen, E. L. (2000). Social motives and cognitive power-sex associations: Predictors of aggressive sexual behavior. *Journal of Personality and Social Psychology, 78,* 559–581.

Credits

Text, Table, and Figure Credits

Chapter 2 *Page 50:* Figure 2.2(a and c) From WRIGHT. Understanding Statistics, 1E. © 1976 Wadsworth, a part of Cengage Learning, Inc. Reproduced by permission. www.cengage.com/permissions; *page 50:* Figure 2.2(b) From *INTRODUCTION TO THE PRACTICE OF STATISTICS*, 3e by D. S. Moore and G. P. McCabe. Copyright © 1999 by W.H. Freeman and Company. Used with permission.

Chapter 3 *Page 88:* Figure 3.2 Adapted from "Evolutionary Psychology: A New Paradigm for Psychological Science" by David M. Buss, *Psychological Inquiry, 6,* (1995). Copyright © 1995 by Lawrence Erlbaum Associates, Inc. Reprinted by permission.; *page 90:* Figure 3.3 Adapted from "Evolutionary Psychology: A New Paradigm for Psychological Science" by David M. Buss, *Psychological Inquiry, 6,* (1995). Copyright © 1995 by Lawrence Erlbaum Associates, Inc. Reprinted by permission.; *page 98:* Figure 3.4 Based on Bouchard & McGue, 1981.; *page 101:* Figure 3.6 Adapted from p. 14 in "Get Smart: Take a Test. A Long-Term Rise in IQ Scores Baffles Intelligence Experts" by J. Horgan, *Scientific American,* November 1995. Copyright © 1995. Reprinted by permission of Dimitry Schildlovsky.

Chapter 4 *Page 119:* Figure 4.7 Adapted from Gougoux, Zatorre, Lassonde, Maryse et al. (2005).

Chapter 5 *Page 158:* Figure 5.2 From "Physiology of Sleeping and Dreaming" in PRINCIPLES OF NEURAL SCIENCE by Dennis Kelly. Copyright © 1981. Reprinted by permission of The McGraw-Hill Companies.; *page 161:* Figure 5.3 From Figure 3, a&b, "Sleep Preferentially Enhances Memory for Emotional Components of Scenes" by J.D. Payne, R. Stickgold, K. Swanberg, and E. A. Kensinger, (2008), *Psychological Science, (19)*8 , 781-788. Copyright © 2008 by Association for Psychological Science. Reprinted by permission of Sage Publications.

Chapter 6 *Page 212:* Figure 6.10 Reprinted with permission of the Canadian Centre for Occupational Health and Safety (CCOHS). http://www.ccohs.ca; *page 217:* Figure 6.13 From "Taste Test" by Mozell, et al., *Archives of Otolaryngology, 90,* (1969). Copyright © 1969 by American Medical Association. Reprinted by permission.; *page 223:* Figure 6.16 Based on Blakemore & Cooper, 1970.

Chapter 7 *Page 238:* Figure 7.2 From "Acquisition and Extinction of a Salivary Response" by Ivan P. Pavlov in CONDITIONED RESPONSES translated by G. V. Anrep. Copyright 1927. Reprinted by permission of Oxford University Press, UK.; *page 246:* Figure 7.4 Based on Davis et al., 2005.; *page 252:* Figure 7.5 From p. 96 in "Teaching Machines" by B. F. Skinner, *Scientific American,* November 1961. Copyright © 1961. Reprinted by permission.; *page 262:* Figure 7.6 From "Undermining Children's Intrinsic Interest with Extrinsic Rewards" by M. R. Lepper, D. Greene, & R. E. Nisbett (1973), *Journal of Personality & Social Psychology, 28,* 129-137. Copyright © 1973 by American Psychological Association.; *page 265:* Figure 7.7 From "Introduction and Removal of Reward and Maze Performance in Rate" by E. C. Tolman and C. H. Honzik, *Psychology, 4* (1930). Reprinted by permission.

Chapter 8 *Page 286:* Figure 8.2 Abridged Table 1, p. 159 from "Are Political Orientations Genetically Transmitted?" by Alford, Funk & Hibbing, *American Political Science Review, 99,* (2), May 2005. Copyright © 2005. Reprinted with the permission of Cambridge University Press.; *page 298:* Figure 8.3 From "The Robber's Cave Experiment" by Muzafer Sharif. Copyright © 1988 University Press of New England. Reprinted by permission.; *page 309:* Figure 8.4 Graph, p. 935 from "Can Cross-Group Friendships Influence Minority Students' Well-Being at Historically White Universities?" by R. Mendoza-Denton & E. Page-Gould (2008), *Psychological Science, 19,* 933-939. Copyright © 2008 by Association for Psychological Science. Reprinted by permission of SAGE Publications.

Chapter 9 *Page 329:* Figure 9.1 From ESSENTIALS OF PSYCHOLOGICAL TESTING 4th edition by Lee J. Cronbach, p. 208. Copyright © 1984 by HarperCollins Publishers. Reprinted by permission; *page 335:* Figure 9.2 From "The Effect of Severity of Initiation on Liking for a Group" by E. Aronson & J. Mills, (1959), *Journal of Abnormal & Social Psychology, 59,* 177-181. Copyright © 1959 by American Psychological Association; *page 343:* Figure 9.5 From "Why People Fail to Recognize Their Own Incompetence" by D. Dunning, K. Johnson, J. Ehrlinger, & J. Kruger, (2003), *Current Directions in Psychological Science,* June 2003 (12), 83-87. Copyright © 2003 by Sage Publications. Reprinted by permission of the publisher. doi: 10.1111/1467-8721.01235; *page 347:* Figure 9.6 From "Self-Discipline Outdoes IQ in Predicting Academic Performance of Adolescents" by Duckworth and Seligman, *Psychological Science* 16 (12) p. 943. Copyright © 2005 by Sage Publications. Reprinted by permission of the publisher. doi: 10.1111/j.1467-9280.2005.01641.x.

Chapter 10 *Page 370:* Figure 10.2 From "More than Suggestion: The Effect of Interviewing Techniques from the McMartin Preschool Case" by S. Garven, J. M. Wood, R. S. Malpass, & J. S. Shaw, (1998), *Journal of Applied Psychology, 83,* 347-359. Copyright © 1998 by American Psychological Association; *page 381:* Figure 10.6 Based on Glanzer & Cunitz, 1966; *page 389:* From "Long-Term Memory for a Common Object" by R. S. Nickerson & M. J. Adams, (1979), *Cognitive Psychology,* 11 (3), 287-307. Copyright © 1979 by Elsevier. Reprinted with permission of Elsevier. doi:10.1016/0010-0285(79)90013-6; *page 392:* Figure 10.8 (left) Ebbinghaus (1885/1913); *page 392:* Figure 10.8 (right) Graph,

© Picture Partners / Alamy; *p. 16:* © North Wind Picture Archives / Alamy; *p. 17:* Getty Images; *p. 18:* Library of Congress; *p. 19:* Getty Images; *p. 20:* The Canadian Press Images/Montreal Gazette; *p. 21:* Comstock/ Thinkstock; *p. 27* (tl): George Ruhe/ENELYSION®; *p. 27* (bl): © Alina Solovyova-Vincent /istockphoto; *p. 29* (tl): Sean McCann/United States Olympic Committee; *p. 29* (tr): Ed Kashi / Getty Images; *p. 31:* Feng Yu / Shutterstock.

Chapter 2 *Page 36:* Helder Almeida/ Shutterstock; *p. 38* (tl): Taskeng | Dreamstime.com; *p. 38* (tr): Rosca Gabriel | Dreamstime.com; *p. 40* (tl): © Jodi Jacobson / istockphoto; *p. 40* (bl): © Peter Titmuss / Alamy; *p. 43:* This article was published in Genie: A Psycholinguistic Study of a Modern Day "Wild Child" by Susan Curtiss, © 1977, Elsevier Science (USA); *p. 44* (bl): Richard Damoret/The New York Times; *p. 44* (br): © Grant V. Faint/Image Bank/Getty Images, Inc.; *p. 51* (tl): greenland/ Shutterstock; *p. 51* (tr): Jose Azel, Aurora Photos, Inc.; *p. 61:* © Vladimir Mucibabic /istockphoto; *p. 66* (tl): ©James Marshall / The Image Works; *p. 66* (tl): Ann Borden / Newscom.

Chapter 3 *Page 72:* © Blend Images / Alamy; *p. 74:* Richard Hutchings / Photo Researchers, Inc.; *p. 76* (tl): Biophoto Associates / Photo Researchers, Inc.; *p. 76* (tr): Macmillan Publishers; *p. 77* (tr): © DLILLC / CORBIS All Rights Reserved; *p. 77* (br): © Martin Shields / Alamy; *p. 78:* Copyright 2003 National Academy of Sciences, U.S.A.; *p. 80:* Barbara Mather/Associated Press; *p. 81* (tl): © Johner Images / Alamy; *p. 81* (tr): istockphoto; *p. 83:* © Bill Bachmann / Alamy; *p. 85:* Ann Senghas; *p. 86:* wavebreakmedia ltd / shutterstock; *p. 88:* Canadian Press/Ryan Remiorz; *p. 89:* Gentoo Mutimedia Ltd / Shutterstock; *p. 91:* © Bureau L.A. Collection/ CORBIS; *p. 100:* Marc Asnin/Queen Esther Production; *p.101* (tl): China Photos/Stringer/Getty Images; *p.101* (tr): Kali Nine LLC / istockphoto; *p. 103:* Photo used with permission from Texas A&M College of Veterinary Medicine & Biomedical Sciences.

Chapter 4 *Page 108:* istockphoto; *p. 110:* © Maartje van Caspel / istockphoto; *p. 113:* CNRI / Photo Researchers, Inc.; *p. 115:* Marc Lieberman/Salk Institute; *p. 116:* © Henrik Jonsson / istockphoto; *p. 120:* © Ron Sachs/CNP/Corbis; *p. 123:* Keith Brofsky/Getty Images; *p. 125* (tl): Michael E. Phelps/Mazziotta UCLA School of Medicine; *p. 125* (tr): Needell MD / Custom Medical Stock Photo; *p. 126:* Custom Medical Stock Photo; *p. 133* (tl): © Collection of Jack and Beverly Wilgus; *p. 133* (tr): Patrick Landmann / Scienc Photo Library; *p. 135:* Garry Watson/Science Photo Library, Photo Researchers, Inc.; *p. 141:* Phillips M D, Lowe M J, Lurito J T, et al. Temporal lobe activation demonstrates sex-based differences during passive listening. Radiological Society of North America. Radiology 2001; 220: 202-207. Figure 3.

Chapter 5 *Page 148:* © Matthias Clamer/Getty Images, Inc.; *p. 151:* Thomas H. Ives; *p. 152:* © webphotographeer /istockphoto; *p. 154:* Pascal Goetgheluck / Science Photo Library; *p. 157:* Patti Altridge; *p. 159* (tl): Jessica T. Offir; *p. 159* (tr): © Mary Hope / istockphoto; *p. 160:* © Carmen Sorvillo / istockphoto; *p. 161:* Digital Vision / Thinkstock; *p. 165:* J. Allan Hobson / Photo Researchers,

Inc.; *p. 170:* Bookstaver/ Associated Press; *p. 171:* Ernest R. Hilgard; *p. 176* (tl): mehmetcan / Shutterstock; *p. 176* (c): Cyril Hou / Shutterstock; *p. 176* (tr): © Hemis / Alamy; *p. 179* (top): Triangle, "The Sandoz Journal of Medical Science," 1955-56, Vol. 2, pp.117-124. (c) Novartis Pharma AG, Basel, Switzerland. ; *p. 179* (br): CP PHOTO/ COC/ Cromby McNeil; *p. 181* (bl): © Forest Woodward / istockphoto; *p. 181* (br): © Image Source / Alamy; *p. 182* (bl): George Marks/Retrofile/Getty Images; *p. 182* (br) The Granger Collection.

Chapter 6 *Page 188:* © FocusCulture / Alamy; *p. 191:* © Rex Features [2005] all rights reserved"/ Canadian Press; *p. 193:* Cordelia Molloy / Science Photo Library; *p. 195* (top): National Library of Medicine; *p. 195* (br): Yellow / Shutterstock; *p. 196* (tl): Picture Desk, Inc./Kobal Collection; *p. 196* (bl): ©Lisa Maree Williams/ Stringer/Getty Images, Inc.; *p. 201:* Giuseppe Arcimboldo (1527-93), "Vertumnus (Emperor Rudolf II)," 1590. Oil on wood, 70.5 x 57.5 cm. Stocklosters Slott, Sweden. Erich Lessing/Art Resource, NY; *p. 202:* Greebles created by Isabel Gauthier (Vanderbilt University), Scott Yu and Michael J. Tarr.; *p. 204:* M.C. Escher's "Symmetry Drawing E69" © 2006 The M.C. Escher Company-Holland. All rights reserved.; *p. 206* (bl): © Robyn Mackenzie | Dreamstime.com; *p. 206* (tr): © James Randklev/Stone/Getty Images, Inc.; *p. 206* (br): Richard Susanto / Shutterstock.com; *p. 207* (tl): © oleg filipchuk /istockphoto; *p. 207* (tr): istockphoto / Thinkstock; *p. 207* (bl): mikeledray/Shutterstock; *p. 207* (br): Getty Images / Thinkstock; *p. 209:* Josef Albers, "Plate VI-3 from 'Interaction of Color' ". © Josef Albers Foundation/Yale University Press. © 2000 The Josef and Anni Albers Foundation/Artists Rights Society (ARS), New York.; *p. 210:* © Niklas Larsson/AP Wide World; *p. 214* (tl): © PhotoStock-Israel / Alamy; *p. 214* (c): © SPL / Photo Researchers, Inc.; *p. 214* (bl): Eric Lam / Shutterstock; *p. 218:* © Christophe Boisvieux/Corbis; *p.219:* Stephen Morton/Associated Press; *p. 221* (tr): © Donna Miles/US Army; *p. 221* (br): ©Rex Features(2005) All rights reserved/Canadian Press; *p. 223:* Professor Joseph Campos, University of California, Berkeley; *p. 224:* © J. Pat Carter/AP Wide World; *p. 226* (l): © Steve Skjold / Alamy; *p. 226* (r): HIROSHI WATANABE/a.collectionRF/Getty Images.

Chapter 7 *Page 234:* © Don Mason/Corbis; *p. 236:* The Granger Collection; *p. 241:* © Hulton Archive /Getty Images, Inc.; *p. 242:* © Nico Smit/istockphoto; *p. 244:* B&C Alexander / Arctic Photo; *p. 245:* © Regien Paassen/Shutterstock; *p. 246:* Olivier Voisin / Photo Researchers, Inc.; *p. 252:* Time & Life Pictures/Getty Images; *p. 254* (bl): Rita Nannini / Photo Researchers, Inc; *p. 254* (br): Lars Christensen / Shutterstock; *p. 256:* Courtesy of The Dominion Post; *p. 257* (l): City of Calgary Emergency Medical Services; *p. 257* (r): Chris Maynard/The New York Times/Redux Pictures; *p. 259:* Dennis MacDonald, PhotoEdit Inc.; *p. 260:* © bildagentur-online/ begsteiger / Alamy; *p. 264:* Losevsky Pavel / Shutterstock; *p. 266:* © South West Images Scotland/Alamy; *p. 267:* Courtesy of Albert Bandura.

Chapter 8 *Page 272:* © Jacob Wackerhausen/istockphoto; *p. 274* (tl): Associated Press; *p. 274* (c): © Reuters/CORBIS; *p. 274* (tr): Getty Images; *p. 275:* © nobleIMAGES / Alamy; *p. 276* (tl):

Name Index

A

Aarts, H., 219
Abdollahi, A., 302
Abel, E.L., 498
Abel, G.G., 651
Abrahamson, A.C., 552
Abramowitz, J.S., 594
Abrams, D.B., 182
Abramson, L.Y., 596, 598
Acocella, J., 612n
Acredolo, L., 505
Adair, J.G., 30
Adams, M.J., 389
Adams, R.B.Jr., 424
Ader, R., 245
Adler, N.E., 427
Adolphs, R., 412
Affleck, G., 431
Agars, M.D., 485
Agrawal, Y., 213
Agronick, G., 355
Aguiar, P., 283
Ahadi, S.A., 556
Ainsworth, M.D.S., 501
Alexander, B.K., 608
Alford, C.F., 294
Alford, J.R., 286, 287
Alger, S., 162
Alink, L.R.A., 513, 514
Allen, G., 128
Allen, J., 463
Allen, J.D., 341
Allen, K., 441
Allen, K.M., 431
Allen, L.S., 476
Allgeier, E.R., 470
Allison, D.B., 451, 452
Alloy, L.B., 598
Allport, G.W., 301, 306, 550
Alm, R., 485
Alpert, N., 482
Altschuler, E.L., 221
Alvaro, C., 440
Amabile, T.M., 355
Ambady, 341
Ambady, N., 411, 421
Amedi, A., 119
Amering, M., 585
Amso, D., 498
Anand, S.S., 428
Anastasi, A., 341
Andersen, S.M., 635
Anderson, A., 8
Anderson, B.J., 118

Anderson, C., 408
Anderson, C.A., 268, 269
Anderson, J.R., 379
Anderson, M., 466
Anderson, S.E., 522
Anderson, S.W., 602
Anderson-Barnes, V.C., 221
Andreano, J.M., 387
Andreasen, N.C., 617
Angell, M., 626, 629, 631
Antonuccio, D.O., 649
Antrobus, J., 165
Archer, J., 423
Archer, S.N., 153
Arendt, H., 312
Arkes, H.R., 284–285
Arkowitz, H., 650
Armitage, R., 150
Arndt, J., 303
Arnett, J.J., 528, 529
Arnold, R.D., 561
Aron, A., 461, 463
Aron, A.P., 417
Aron, E.N., 463
Aronow, W.S., 529
Aronson, E., 41, 279, 280, 284, 304,
    310, 334, 335, 336
Aronson, J., 341
Aronson, J.K., 331
Arredondo, P., 645
Arroyo, C.G., 562
Arsenijevic, D., 452
Asbury, K., 560
Asch, S.E., 290
Aserinsky, E., 156
Ashton, M.C., 552
Aslin, R.N., 86
Asliturk, E., 436
Atkinson, R.C., 374
Atran, S., 288
Austin-Oden, D., 463
Auyeung, A., 517
Aviezer, H., 411
Axel, R., 218
Ayduk, O., 512
Azuma, H., 432

B

Baas, M., 408
Baddeley, A.D., 378
Bagby, R.M., 588
Bagemihl, B., 476
Bahill, A.T., 210
Bahrick, H.P., 372, 393

Bahrick, P.O., 372
Bailey, J.M., 89, 476, 517
Baillargeon, R., 510
Bains, 113
Bakalar, J.B., 184
Baker, L.A., 552
Baker, M., 502
Baker, M.C., 84
Baker, T.B., 647
Bakermans-Kranenburg, M.J., 502, 512
Balcetis, E., 282
Banaji, M., 284, 307, 308
Bancroft, J., 467, 468, 548
Bandura, A., 265, 266, 267, 283, 484,
    519, 559
Banko, K.M., 262
Banks, C., 278
Banks, M.S., 223
Bannerman, D.M., 383
Bänninger-Huber, E., 425
Barash, D.P., 89, 104
Barbee, A.H., 346
Barbuto, J.E., 550
Barch, D.M., 615
Barefoot, J.C., 434
Bargary, G., 192
Bargh, J.A., 228, 549
Barglow, P., 633
Barkow, J.H., 79
Barlow, D.H., 585, 590, 592, 598, 649
Barnes, M.L., 78
Barnier, A.J., 170
Baron-Cohen, S., 192
Barr, S.I., 457
Barres, B.A., 113
Barrett, D., 164
Barrett, H.C., 504
Barrett, L.F., 417, 421
Barry, P., 102
Barsky, S.H., 179
Bartels, A., 461, 462
Bartlett, F.C., 363
Bartoshuk, L.M., 217
Bassetti, C., 157
Bassetti, C.L., 158
Basson, R., 68, 629
Bates, T.C., 557
Bauer, P., 399
Baumberger, T., 86
Baumeister, R.F., 172, 261, 289, 419,
    465, 469, 549
Baumrind, D., 258
Bauserman, R., 476, 534
Bearman, S.K., 458
Beauchamp, G.K., 217

Subject Index

Note: Entries for tables and figures are followed by "*t*" and "*f*," respectively.